THE CONCISE
SPANISH
DICTIONARY

THE CONCISE SPANISH DICTIONARY

Spanish-English, English-Spanish

Wordsworth Editions

This edition published 1991 by Wordsworth Editions Ltd,
8b East Street, Ware, Hertfordshire, under licence
from the proprietor.

ISBN 1-85326-959-X

Printed and bound in Great Britain by Mackays of Chatham.

INTRODUCCIÓN

INTRODUCTION

Quien desee leer y entender el inglés encontrará en este diccionario un extenso léxico moderno que abarca una amplia gama de locuciones de uso corriente. Igualmente encontrará, en su debido orden alfabético, las abreviaturas, las siglas, los nombres geográficos más conocidos y, además, las principales formas de verbo irregulares, donde se le referirá a las respectivas formas de base, hallándose allí la traducción.

Quien aspire comunicarse y expresarse en lengua extranjera, hallará aquí una clara y detallada explicación de las palabras básicas, empleándose un sistema de indicadores que le remitirán a la traducción más apta y le señalarán su correcto uso.

The user whose aim is to read and understand Spanish will find a comprehensive and up-to-date wordlist including numerous phrases in current use. He will also find listed alphabetically the main irregular forms with a cross-reference to the basic form where a translation is given, as well as some of the most common abbreviations, acronyms and geographical names.

The user who wishes to communicate and to express himself in the foreign language will find clear and detailed treatment of all the basic words, with numerous indicators pointing to the appropriate translation, and helping him to use it correctly.

ABREVIATURAS

ABBREVIATIONS

adjetivo, locución adjetivo	**a**	adjective, adjectival phrase
abreviatura	**ab(b)r**	abbreviation
adverbio, locución adverbial	**ad**	adverb, adverbial phrase
administración, lengua administrativa	**ADMIN**	administration
agricultura	**AGR**	agriculture
América Latina	**AM**	Latin America
anatomía	**ANAT**	anatomy
arquitectura	**ARQ, ARCH**	architecture
astrología, astronomía	**ASTRO**	astrology, astronomy
el automóvil	**AUT(O)**	the motor car and motoring
aviación, viajes aéreos	**AVIAT**	flying, air travel
biología	**BIO(L)**	biology
botánica, flores	**BOT**	botany
inglés británico	**Brit**	British English
química	**CHEM**	chemistry
conjunción	**conj**	conjunction
lengua familiar	**col**	colloquial usage
comercio, finanzas, banca	**COM(M)**	commerce, finance, banking
construcción	**CONSTR**	building
compuesto	**cpd**	compound element
cocina	**CULIN**	cookery
determinante, artículo	**det**	determiner, article
economía	**ECON**	economics
electricidad, electrónica	**ELEC**	electricity, electronics
enseñanza, sistema escolar y universitario	**ESCOL**	schooling, schools and universities
especialmente	**esp**	especially
exclamación, interjección	**excl**	exclamation, interjection
feminino	**f**	feminine
lengua familiar	**fam**	colloquial usage
ferrocarril	**FERRO**	railways
uso figurado	**fig**	figurative use
fotografía	**FOTO**	photography
(verbo inglés) del cual la partícula es inseparable	**fus**	(phrasal verb) where the particle is inseparable
generalmente	**gen**	generally
geografía, geología	**GEO**	geography, geology
geometría	**GEOM**	geometry
invariable	**inv**	invariable
irregular	**irg**	irregular
lo jurídico	**JUR**	law
gramática, lingüística	**LING**	grammar, linguistics
masculino	**m**	masculine

iv

matemáticas	**MAT(H)**	mathematics
medicina	**MED**	medical term, medicine
masculino/feminino	**m/f**	masculine/feminine
lo militar, ejército	**MIL**	military matters
música	**MUS**	music
sustantivo, nombre	**n**	noun
navegación, náutica	**NAUT**	sailing, navigation
sustantivo numérico	**num**	numeral noun
complemento	**obj**	(grammatical) object
	o.s.	oneself
peyorativo	**pey, pej**	derogatory, pejorative
fotografia	**PHOT**	photography
fisiología	**PHYSIOL**	physiology
plural	**pl**	plural
política	**POL**	politics
participio de pasado	**pp**	past participle
prefijo	**pref**	prefix
preposición	**prep**	preposition
pronombre	**pron**	pronoun
psicología, psiquiatría	**PSICO, PSYCH**	psychology, psychiatry
tiempo pasado	**pt**	past tense
sustantivo no empleado en el plural	**q**	collective (uncountable) noun, not used in plural
ferrocarril	**RAIL**	railways
religión, lo eclesiástico	**REL**	religion, church service
	sb	somebody
escolar, universitario	**SCOL**	schools, universities
singular	**sg**	singular
	sth	something
sujeto	**su(b)j**	(grammatical) subject
sufijo	**suff**	suffix
tauromaquia	**TAUR**	bullfighting
técnica, tecnología	**TEC(H)**	technical term, technology
telecomunicaciones	**TELEC, TEL**	telecommunications
televisión	**TV**	television
imprenta, tipografia	**TYP**	typography, printing
inglés norteamericano	**US**	American English
verbo	**vb**	verb
verbo intransitivo	**vi**	intransitive verb
verbo pronominal	**vr**	reflexive verb
verbo transitivo	**vt**	transitive verb
zoologia, animales	**ZOOL**	zoology
marca registrada	**®**	registered trademark
indica un equivalente cultural	**≈**	introduces a cultural equivalent

SPANISH PRONUNCIATION

Consonants

c	[k]	caja	c before a, o or u is pronounced as in cat
ce, ci	[θe, θi]	cero cielo	c before e or i is pronounced as in thin
ch	[tʃ]	chiste	ch is pronounced as ch in chair
d	[d, ð]	danés ciudad	at the beginning of a phrase or after l or n, d is pronounced as in English. In any other position it is pronounced like th in the
g	[g, ɤ]	gafas paga	g before a, o or u is pronounced as in gap, if at the beginning of a phrase or after n. In other positions the sound is softened
ge, gi	[xe, xi]	gente girar	g before e or i is pronounced similar to ch in Scottish loch
h		haber	h is always silent in Spanish
j	[x]	jugar	j is pronounced similar to ch in Scottish loch
ll	[ʎ]	talle	ll is pronounced like the lli in million
ñ	[ɲ]	niño	ñ is pronounced like the ni in onion
q	[k]	que	q is pronounced as k in king
r, rr	[r, rr]	quitar garra	r is always pronounced in Spanish, unlike the silent r in dancer. rr is trilled, like a Scottish r
s	[s]	quizás isla	s is usually pronounced as in pass, but before b, d, g, l, m or n it is pronounced as in rose
v	[b, ß]	vía dividir	v is pronounced something like b. At the beginning of a phrase or after m or n it is pronounced as b in boy. In any other position the sound is softened
z	[θ]	tenaz	z is pronounced as th in thin

b, f, k, l, m, n, p, t and x are pronounced as in English.

Vowels

[a]	p*a*ta	not as long as *a* in f*a*r. When followed by a consonant in the same syllable (i.e. in a closed syllable), as in am*a*nte, the *a* is short, as in b*a*t
[e]	m*e*	like *e* in th*e*y. In a closed syllable, as in g*e*nte, the *e* is short as in p*e*t
[i:]	p*i*no	as in m*e*an or mach*i*ne
[o]	l*o*	as in l*o*cal. In a closed syllable, as in c*o*ntrol, the *o* is short as in c*o*t
[u:]	l*u*nes	as in r*u*le. It is silent after *q*, and in *gue*, *gui*, unless marked *güe*, *güi* e.g. ant*i güe*dad

Diphthongs

ai, ay	ba*i*le	as *i* in r*i*de
au	a*u*to	as *ou* in sh*ou*t
ei, ey	bu*ey*	as *ey* in gr*ey*
eu	de*u*da	both elements pronounced independently [e] + [u:]
oi, oy	h*oy*	as *oy* in t*oy*

Stress

The rules of stress in Spanish are as follows:
(a) when a word ends in a vowel or in *n* or *s*, the second last syllable is stressed: pat*a*ta, pat*a*tas, c*o*me, c*o*men
(b) when a word ends in a consonant other than *n* or *s*, the stress falls on the last syllable: par*e*d, habl*a*r
(c) when the rules set out in a and b are not applied, an acute accent appears over the stressed vowel: com*ú*n, geograf*í*a, ingl*é*s

In the phonetic transcription, the symbol [´] precedes the syllable on which the stress falls.

PRONUNCIACIÓN INGLESA

Vocales y diptongos

	Ejemplo inglés	Ejemplo español/explicación
ɑ:	father	Entre *a* de *padre* y *o* de *noche*
ʌ	but, come	*a* muy breve
æ	man, cat	Se mantienen los labios en la posición de *e* en *pena* y luego se pronuncia el sonido *a*
ə	father, ago	Sonido indistinto parecido a una *e* u *o* casi mudas
ə:	bird, heard	Entre *e* abierta, y *o* cerrada, sonido alargado
ɛ	get, bed	como en *perro*
ɪ	it, big	Más breve que en *si*
i:	tea, see	Como en *fino*
ɔ	hot, wash	Como en *torre*
ɔ:	saw, all	Como en *por*
u	put, book	Sonido breve, más cerrado que *burro*
u:	too, you	Sonido largo, como en *uno*
aɪ	fly, high	Como en *fraile*
au	how, house	Como en *pausa*
ɛə	there, bear	Casi como en *vea*, pero el sonido *a* se mezcla con el indistinto [ə]
eɪ	day, obey	*e* cerrada seguida por una *i* débil
ɪə	here, hear	Como en *manía*, mezclándose el sonido *a* con el indistinto [ə]
əu	go, note	[ə] seguido por una breve *u*
ɔɪ	boy, oil	Como en *voy*
uə	poor, sure	*u* bastante larga más el sonido indistinto [ə]

Consonantes

	Ejemplo inglés	*Ejemplo español/explicación*
d	men*d*ed	Como en con*d*e, an*d*ar
g	*g*o, *g*et, bi*g*	Como en *g*rande, *g*ol
dʒ	*g*in, ju*dge*	Como en la *ll* andaluza y en *G*eneralitat (catalán)
ŋ	si*ng*	Como en ví*n*culo
h	*h*ouse, *h*e	Como la jota hispanoamericana
j	*y*oung, *y*es	Como en *y*a
k	*c*ome, mo*ck*	Como en *c*aña, Es*c*ocia
r	*r*ed, t*r*ead	Se pronuncia con la punta de la lengua hacia atrás y sin hacerla vibrar
s	*s*and, ye*s*	Como en ca*s*a, *s*esión
z	ro*s*e, *z*ebra	Como en de*s*de, mi*s*mo
ʃ	*sh*e, ma*ch*ine	Como en *ch*ambre (francés), ro*x*o (portugués)
tʃ	*ch*in, ri*ch*	Como en *ch*ocolate
v	*v*alley	Como en f, pero se retiran los dientes superiores vibrándolos contra el labio inferior
w	*w*ater, *wh*ich	Como en la *u* de h*u*evo, p*u*ede
ʒ	vi*si*on	Como en *j*ournal (francés)
θ	*th*ink, my*th*	Como en re*c*eta, *z*apato
ð	*th*is, *th*e	Como en la *d* de habla*d*o, verda*d*

b, p, f, m, n, l, t iguales que en español
El signo * indica que la r final escrita apenas se pronuncia en inglés británico cuando la palabra siguiente empieza con vocal. El signo ['] indica la sílaba acentuada.

ESPAÑOL - INGLÉS
SPANISH - ENGLISH

A

a [a] *prep* (*a* + *el* = *al*) (*lugar*) at, in, on; (*dirección*) to; (*destino*) to, towards; (*tiempo*) at; ~ **la derecha/ izquierda** on the right/left; **al lado de** beside, at the side of; **subir** ~ **un avión/tren** to get on *or* board a plane/train; **hablar** ~ **larga distancia** to speak long distance; ~ **las cuatro** at four o'clock; ¿~ **qué hora?** at what time?; ~ **los 30 años** at 30 years of age; **al día siguiente** the next day; ~ **eso de las cuatro** at about four o'clock; **al poco tiempo** a short time later; **al verlo yo** when I saw it; (*manera*): **hacerlo** ~ **la fuerza** to do it by force; **ir** ~ **caballo/pie** to go on horseback/foot; (*evaluación*): **poco** ~ **poco** little by little; **de dos** ~ **tres** from two to three; **ocho horas al día** eight hours a *or* per day; ~ **50 ptas el kilo** 50 pesetas a kilo; (*con verbo*): **empezó** ~ **llover** it started raining; **enseñar** ~ **leer** to teach to read; **voy** ~ **llevarlo** I am going to carry it; (*complemento de objeto*): **quiero** ~ **mis padres** (*not translated*) I love my parents; (*complemento circunstancial*): **cercano** ~ near (to); **por miedo** ~ out of fear of; (*frases elípticas*): ¡~ **comer!** let's eat!; ¿~ **qué viene eso?** what's the meaning of this?; ~ **ver** let's see.

abacero, a [aβa'θero, a] *nm/f* grocer.

abad, esa [a'βað, 'ðesa] *nm/f* abbot/abbess; ~ **ia** *nf* abbey.

abajo [a'βaxo] *ad* (*situación*) down, below, underneath; (*en casa*) downstairs; (*dirección*) down, downwards; ~ **de** *prep* below, under; **el piso de** ~ the downstairs flat; **la parte de** ~ the lower part; ¡~ **el gobierno!** down with the government!; **cuesta/río** ~ downhill/downstream; **de arriba** ~ from top to bottom; **el** ~ **firmante** the undersigned; **más** ~ lower *or* further down; **echar** ~ to bring down.

abalanzar [aβalan'θar] *vt* to weigh; (*equilibrar*) to balance; (*arrojar*) to hurl; ~**se** *vr*: ~**se sobre** *o* **contra** to throw o.s. at.

abandonado, a [aβando'naðo, a] *a* derelict; (*desatendido*) abandoned; (*desierto*) deserted; (*descuidado*) neglected.

abandonar [aβando'nar] *vt* (*dejar*) to leave, abandon, desert; (*descuidar*) to neglect; (*ceder, dejar de*) to give up; ~**se** *vr*: ~**se a** to abandon o.s. to.

abandono [aβan'dono] *nm* (*acto*) desertion, abandonment; (*estado*) abandon, neglect; (*renuncia*) withdrawal, retirement; **perdió por** ~ he lost by default.

abanicar [aβani'kar] *vt* to fan; **abanico** *nm* fan; (*NAUT*) derrick.

abaratar [aβara'tar] *vt* to lower (the price of) // *vi*, ~**se** *vr* to go *or* come down in price.

abarcar [aβar'kar] *vt* to include, embrace; (*AM*) to monopolize.

abarrotar [aβarro'tar] *vt/v* to bar; (*NAUT*) to stow; (*fig*) to overstock.

abarrote [aβa'rrote] *nm* packing; ~**s** *nmpl* (*AM*) groceries, provisions; ~**ro, a** *nm/f* (*AM*) grocer.

abastecer [aβaste'θer] *vt* to supply; **abastecimiento** *nm* supply; (*suministrar*) supplying.

abasto [a'βasto] *nm* supply; (*abundancia*) abundance; **dar** ~ **con** to manage to finish.

abatido, a [aβa'tiðo, a] *a* dejected, downcast.

abatimiento [aβati'mjento] *nm* (*acto*) demolition; (*moral*) dejection, depression.

abatir [aβa'tir] *vt* (*muro*) to demolish; (*pájaro*) to shoot, bring down; (*fig*) to depress; (*humillar*) to humiliate // *vi* to go off course; ~**se** *vr* to be depressed; ~**se sobre** to swoop *or* pounce on.

abdicación [aβðika'θjon] *nf* abdication; **abdicar** *vi* to abdicate.

abdomen [aβ'ðomen] *nm* abdomen.

abecedario [aβeθe'ðarjo] *nm* alphabet; (*libro*) spelling book.

abedul [aβe'ðul] *nm* birch.

abeja [a'βexa] *nf* bee.

aberración [aβerra'θjon] *nf* aberration.

abertura [aβer'tura] *nf* opening, gap; (*fig*) openness.

abeto [a'βeto] *nm* fir.

abierto, a [a'βjerto, a] *pp de* **abrir** // *a* open; (*AM*) generous.

abigarrado, a [aβiɤa'rraðo, a] *a* multi-coloured.

abismar [aβis'mar] *vt* to humble, cast down; ~**se** *vr* to sink; ~**se en** (*fig*) to be plunged into.

abismo [a'βismo] *nm* abyss.

abjurar [aβxu'rar] *vt*, *vi* to abjure, forswear.

ablandar [aβlan'dar] *vt* to soften up; (*AUTO*) to run in // *vi*, ~**se** *vr* to grow softer.

ablución [aβlu'θjon] *nf* ablution.

abnegación [aβneɤa'θjon] *nf* self-denial; **abnegarse** *vr* to act unselfishly.

abobado, a [aβo'βaðo, a] a silly.
abobar [aβo'βar] vt to daze.
abocar [aβo'kar] vt to seize in one's mouth; ~**se** vr to approach.
abochornar [aβotʃor'nar] vt to embarrass; ~**se** vr to get flustered; (BOT) to wilt.
abofetear [aβofete'ar] vt to slap (in the face).
abogacía [aβoχa'θia] nf legal profession; (ejercicio) practice of the law; **abogado** nm lawyer.
abogar [aβo'χar] vi: ~ **por** to plead for; (fig) to advocate.
abolengo [aβo'lengo] nm ancestry, lineage.
abolición [aβoli'θjon] nf abolition.
abolir [aβo'lir] vt to abolish; (cancelar) to cancel.
abolladura [aβoʎa'ðura] nf dent; (chichón, choque) bump; **abollar** vt to dent; to raise a bump on.
abominación [aβomina'θjon] nf abomination.
abonado, a [aβo'naðo, a] a (deuda) paid // nm/f subscriber.
abonar [aβo'nar] vt (deuda) to settle; (terreno) to fertilize; (idea) to endorse; ~**se** vr to subscribe; **abono** nm payment; fertilizer; subscription.
abordar [aβor'ðar] vt to board; (fig) to broach.
aborigen [aβo'rixen] nm aborigine.
aborrecer [aβorre'θer] vt to hate, loathe; **aborrecible** a hateful, loathsome.
abortar [aβor'tar] vi (malparir) to have a miscarriage; (deliberadamente) to have an abortion; **hacerse** ~ to have an abortion; **aborto** nm miscarriage; abortion.
abotonar [aβoto'nar] vt to button (up), do up // vi to bud.
abovedado, a [aβoβe'ðaðo, a] a vaulted, domed.
abrasar [aβra'sar] vt to burn (up); (AGR) to dry up, parch.
abrazar [aβra'θar] vt to embrace.
abrazo [a'βraθo] nm embrace, hug; **un** ~ (en carta) with best wishes.
abrelatas [aβre'latas] nm inv tin opener.
abreviar [aβre'βjar] vt to abbreviate; (texto) to abridge; (plazo) to reduce; **abreviatura** nf abbreviation.
abrigar [aβri'χar] vt (proteger) to shelter; (suj: ropa) to keep warm; (fig) to cherish; **abrigo** nm shelter; (apoyo) support; (prenda) coat, overcoat.
abril [a'βril] nm April.
abrir [a'βrir] vt to open (up) // vi to open; ~**se** vr to open (up); (extenderse) to open out; (cielo) to clear; ~**se paso** to find or force a way through.
abrochar [aβro'tʃar] vt (vestido) to button (up); (AM) to staple; (zapato) to buckle; (atar) to lace up.
abrumar [aβru'mar] vt to overwhelm; (sobrecargar) to weigh down; (agotar) to wear out; ~**se** vr to become foggy.

abrupto, a [a'βrupto, a] a abrupt; (empinado) steep.
absceso [aβs'θeso] nm abscess.
absolución [aβsolu'θjon] nf (REL) absolution; (JUR) pardon; (: de acusado) acquittal.
absoluto, a [aβso'luto, a] a absolute; **en** ~ ad in no way, not at all.
absolver [aβsol'βer] vt to absolve; (JUR) to pardon; (: acusado) to acquit.
absorber [aβsor'βer] vt to absorb; (embeber) to soak up.
absorción [aβsor'θjon] nf absorption.
absorto, a [aβ'sorto, a] pp de **absorber** // a absorbed, engrossed.
abstemio, a [aβs'temjo, a] a teetotal.
abstención [aβsten'θjon] nf abstention; **abstenerse** vr: **abstenerse de** to abstain or refrain from.
abstinencia [aβsti'nenθja] nf abstinence; (ayuno) fasting.
abstracción [aβstrak'θjon] nf abstraction; (despiste) absent-mindedness; ~ **hecha de** leaving aside.
abstraer [aβstra'er] vt to abstract // vi: ~ **de** to leave aside; ~**se** vr to be/become absorbed.
abstraído, a [aβstra'iðo, a] a preoccupied; (despistado) absent-minded.
absuelto [aβ'swelto] pp de **absolver.**
absurdo, a [aβ'surðo, a] a absurd.
abuelo, a [a'βwelo, a] nm/f grandfather/mother.
abulia [a'βulja] nf spinelessness, weakness.
abultado, a [aβul'taðo, a] a bulky.
abultar [aβul'tar] vt to enlarge; (aumentar) to increase; (fig) to exaggerate // vi to be bulky.
abundancia [aβun'danθja] nf abundance, plenty; **abundante** a abundant, plentiful; **abundar** vi to abound, be plentiful.
aburrido, a [aβu'rriðo, a] a (hastiado) bored; (que aburre) boring; **aburrimiento** nm boredom, tedium; **aburrir** vt to bore; **aburrirse** vr to be bored, get bored.
abusar [aβu'sar] vi to go too far; ~ **de** to abuse; **abuso** nm imposition; abuse.
abyecto, a [aβ'jekto, a] a wretched, abject.
A.C. abr de **Año de Cristo** A.D. (Anno Domini).
a/c abr de **al cuidado de** c/o (care of).
acá [a'ka] ad (lugar) here; (tiempo) now.
acabado, a [aka'βaðo, a] a finished, complete; (perfecto) perfect; (agotado) worn out; (fig) masterly // nm finish.
acabar [aka'βar] vt (llevar a su fin) to finish, complete; (llegar al final de) to finish, conclude; (perfeccionar) to complete; (consumir) to use up; (rematar) to finish off // vi to finish, end, come to an end; ~ **con** to put an end to; ~ **de llegar** to have just arrived; ~ **por** to end (up) by; ~**se** vr to finish, stop; (terminarse) to be over; (agotarse) to run out; **¡se acabó!** that's enough!; it's all over!

academia [aka'ðemja] *nf* academy; **académico, a** *a* academic.

acaecer [akae'θer] *vi* to happen, occur; **acaecimiento** *nm* occurrence, happening.

acalorar [akalo'rar] *vt* to heat; (*fig*) to inflame; ~**se** *vr* (*fig*) to get heated.

acampar [akam'par] *vi* to camp.

acanalar [akana'lar] *vt* to groove; (*ondular*) to corrugate.

acantilado, a [akanti'laðo, a] *a* steep, sheer // *nm* cliff.

acaparar [akapa'rar] *vt* to monopolize; (*acumular*) to hoard.

acariciar [akari'θjar] *vt* to caress; (*fig*) to cherish.

acarrear [akarre'ar] *vt* to transport; (*fig*) to cause, result in; **acarreo** *nm* transport, haulage; (*precio*) carriage.

acaso [a'kaso] *ad* perhaps, maybe // *nm* chance; **por si** ~ just in case; **si** ~ in case; **al** ~ at random.

acatamiento [akata'mjento] *nm* respect; (*reverencia*) reverence; (*deferencia*) deference; **acatar** *vt* to respect; to revere; (*obedecer*) to obey.

acatarrarse [akata'rrarse] *vr* to catch a cold.

acaudalado, a [akauða'laðo, a] *a* well-off; **acaudalar** *vt* to accumulate.

acaudillar [akauði'ʎar] *vt* to lead, command.

acceder [akθe'ðer] *vi* to accede, agree.

accesible [akθe'siβle] *a* accessible.

acceso [ak'θeso] *nm* access, entry; (*camino*) access road; (*MED*) attack, fit.

accesorio, a [akθe'sorjo, a] *a, nm* accessory.

accidentado, a [akθiðen'taðo, a] *a* uneven; (*áspero*) rough; (*montañoso*) hilly; (*azaroso*) eventful // *nm/f* injured person.

accidental [akθiðen'tal] *a* accidental; **accidentarse** *vr* to have an accident.

accidente [akθi'ðente] *nm* accident; (*MED*) faint; ~**s** *nmpl* unevenness *sg*, roughness *sg*.

acción [ak'θjon] *nf* action; (*acto*) action, act, deed; (*COM*) share; (*JUR*) action, lawsuit; ~ **ordinaria/preferente** ordinary/preference share; **accionar** *vt* to work, operate // *vi* to gesticulate.

accionista [akθjo'nista] *nm/f* shareholder.

acebo [a'θeβo] *nm* holly; (*árbol*) holly tree.

acechanza [aθe'tʃanθa] *nf* = **acecho.**

acechar [aθe'tʃar] *vt* to spy on; (*aguardar*) to lie in wait for; **acecho** *nm* spying, watching; ambush.

acedía [aθe'ðia] *nf* acidity; (*MED*) heartburn; (*fig*) sourness.

aceitar [aθei'tar] *vt* to oil, lubricate; **aceite** *nm* oil; (*de oliva*) olive oil; **aceitera** *nf* oilcan; **aceitoso, a** *a* oily.

aceituna [aθei'tuna] *nf* olive.

acelerar [aθele'rar] *vt* to accelerate.

acento [a'θento] *nm* accent; (*acentuación*) stress; **acentuar** *vt* to accent; to stress; (*fig*) to accentuate.

acepción [aθep'θjon] *nf* meaning; (*preferencia*) preference.

acepillar [aθepi'ʎar] *vt* to brush; (*alisar*) to plane.

aceptación [aθepta'θjon] *nf* acceptance; (*aprobación*) approval; **aceptar** *vt* to accept; to approve.

acequia [a'θekja] *nf* irrigation ditch.

acera [a'θera] *nf* pavement.

acerado, a [aθe'raðo, a] *a* steel; (*afilado*) sharp; (*fig: duro*) steely; (: *mordaz*) biting.

acerbo, a [a'θerβo, a] *a* bitter; (*fig*) harsh.

acerca [a'θerka]: ~ **de** *ad* about, concerning.

acercar [aθer'kar] *vt* to bring *or* move nearer; ~**se** *vr* to approach, come near.

acero [a'θero] *nm* steel.

acérrimo, a [a'θerrimo, a] *a* out-and-out, staunch.

acertado, a [aθer'taðo, a] *a* correct; (*apropiado*) apt; (*sensato*) sensible.

acertar [aθer'tar] *vt* (*dar en: el blanco*) to hit; (*llegar a encontrar*) to get right; (*adivinar*) to guess; (*alcanzar*) to achieve // *vi* to get it right, be right; ~ **a** to manage to; ~ **con** to happen on.

acertijo [aθer'tixo] *nm* riddle, puzzle.

acervo [a'θerβo] *nm* heap; ~ **común** undivided estate.

acicalar [aθika'lar] *vt* to polish; (*adornar*) to bedeck; ~**se** *vr* to smarten o.s. up.

acicate [aθi'kate] *nm* spur.

acidez [aθi'ðeθ] *nf* acidity.

ácido, a ['aθiðo, a] *a* sour, acid // *nm* acid.

acierto [a'θjerto] *nm* success; (*buen paso*) wise move; (*solución*) solution; (*habilidad*) skill, ability.

aclamación [aklama'θjon] *nf* acclamation; (*aplausos*) applause; **aclamar** *vt* to acclaim; to applaud.

aclaración [aklara'θjon] *nf* rinsing, rinse; (*clasificación*) classification.

aclarar [akla'rar] *vt* to clarify, explain; (*ropa*) to rinse // *vi* to clear up; ~**se** *vr*: ~ **se la garganta** to clear one's throat.

aclimatación [aklimata'θjon] *nf* acclimatization; **aclimatar** *vt* to acclimatize; **aclimatarse** *vr* to become acclimatized.

acobardar [akoβar'ðar] *vt* to daunt, intimidate.

acodarse [ako'ðarse] *vr*: ~ **en** to lean on.

acogedor, a [akoxe'ðor, a] *a* welcoming; (*hospitalario*) hospitable; **acoger** *vt* to welcome; (*abrigar*) to shelter; **acogerse** *vr* to take refuge; **acogida** *nf* reception; refuge.

acolchar [akol'tʃar] *vt* to pad; (*tapizar*) to upholster; (*fig*) to cushion.

acometer [akome'ter] *vt* to attack; (*emprender*) to undertake; **acometida** *nf* attack, assault.

acomodadizo, a [akomoða'ðiθo, a] *a* obliging, acquiescent.

acomodado, a [akomo'ðaðo, a] a suitable; (*precio*) moderate; (*persona*) well-to-do.

acomodador, a [akomoða'ðor, a] *nm/f* usher/ette.

acomodar [akomo'ðar] *vt* to adjust; (*alojar*) to accommodate; (*convenir*) to suit; (*reparar*) to repair; (*reconciliar*) to reconcile // *vi* to suit, be suitable; ~**se** *vr* to conform; (*instalarse*) to install o.s.; (*adaptarse*) to adapt o.s.

acomodo [ako'moðo] *nm* arrangement; (*puesto*) post.

acompañar [akompa'ɲar] *vt* to accompany; (*documentos*) to enclose.

acondicionar [akondiθjo'nar] *vt* to arrange, prepare; (*determinar*) to condition.

acongojar [akongo'xar] *vt* to distress, grieve.

aconsejar [akonse'xar] *vt* to advise, counsel; ~**se** *vr*: ~**se con** to consult.

acontecer [akonte'θer] *vi* to happen, occur; **acontecimiento** *nm* event.

acopio [a'kopjo] *nm* store, stock; (*asamblea*) gathering.

acoplamiento [akopla'mjento] *nm* coupling, joint; **acoplar** *vt* to fit, couple; (*unir*) to connect.

acorazado, a [akora'θaðo, a] a armour-plated, armoured // *nm* battleship.

acordar [akor'ðar] *vt* (*resolver*) to agree, resolve; (*recordar*) to remind; (*MUS*) to tune; ~**se** *vr* to agree; ~**se (de)** to remember; **acorde** a in agreement; (*MUS*) harmonious // *nm* chord.

acordeón [akorðe'on] *nm* accordion.

acordonado, a [akorðo'naðo, a] a cordoned-off.

acorralar [akorra'lar] *vt* to round up, corral.

acortar [akor'tar] *vt* to shorten; (*duración*) to cut short; (*cantidad*) to reduce; ~**se** *vr* to become shorter.

acosar [ako'sar] *vt* to pursue relentlessly; (*fig*) to hound, pester.

acostar [akos'tar] *vt* (*en cama*) to put to bed; (*en suelo*) to lay down; (*barco*) to bring alongside; ~**se** *vr* to go to bed; to lie down.

acostumbrar [akostum'brar] *vt*: ~ **a uno a** to accustom sb to // *vi*: ~ **a** to be used to; ~**se** *vr*: ~**se a** to get used to.

acotación [akota'θjon] *nf* marginal note; (*GEO*) elevation mark; (*de límite*) boundary mark; (*TEATRO*) stage direction.

acre ['akre] a sharp, bitter; (*fig*) biting // *nm* acre.

acrecentar [akreθen'tar] *vt* to increase, augment.

acreditar [akreði'tar] *vt* (*garantizar*) to vouch for, guarantee; (*autorizar*) to authorize; (*dar prueba de*) to prove; (*COM: abonar*) to credit; (*embajador*) to accredit; ~**se** *vr* to become famous.

acreedor, a [akree'ðor, a] a: ~ **a** worthy of // *nm/f* creditor.

acribillar [akriβi'ʎar] *vt*: ~ **a balazos** to riddle with bullets.

acrimonia [akri'monja], **acritud** [akri-'tuð] *nf* acrimony.

acta ['akta] *nf* certificate; (*de comisión*) minutes *pl*, record; ~ **de nacimiento/matrimonial** birth/marriage certificate; ~ **notarial** affidavit.

actitud [akti'tuð] *nf* attitude; (*postura*) posture.

activar [akti'βar] *vt* to activate; (*acelerar*) to expedite.

actividad [aktiβi'ðað] *nf* activity.

activo, a [ak'tiβo, a] a active; (*vivo*) lively // *nm* assets *pl*.

acto ['akto] *nm* act, action; (*ceremonia*) ceremony; (*TEATRO*) act; **en el** ~ immediately.

actor [ak'tor] *nm* actor; (*JUR*) plaintiff.

actora [ak'tora] a: **parte** ~ prosecution; (*demandante*) plaintiff.

actriz [ak'triθ] *nf* actress.

actuación [aktwa'θjon] *nf* action; (*comportamiento*) conduct, behaviour; (*JUR*) proceedings *pl*; (*desempeño*) performance.

actual [ak'twal] a present(-day), current; ~**idad** *nf* present, present time; ~**idades** *nfpl* news *sg*; (*película, nodo*) newsreel *sg*; **en la** ~**idad** nowadays, at the present time.

actualizar [aktwali'θar] *vt* to update, modernize.

actualmente [aktwal'mente] *ad* now, nowadays, at present.

actuar [ak'twar] *vi* (*obrar*) to work, operate; (*actor*) to act, perform // *vt* to work, operate; ~ **de** to act as.

actuario [ak'twarjo] *nm* clerk; (*COM*) actuary.

acuarela [akwa'rela] *nf* watercolour.

acuario [a'kwarjo] *nm* aquarium; **A**~ (*ASTRO*) Aquarius.

acuático, a [a'kwatiko, a] a aquatic.

acuciar [aku'θjar] *vt* to urge on.

acuclillarse [akukli'ʎarse] *vr* to crouch down.

acudir [aku'ðir] *vi* to come along, turn up; ~ **a** to turn to; ~ **en ayuda de** to go to the aid of.

acuerdo *etc vb ver* **acordar** // [a'kwerðo] *nm* agreement; **¡de** ~**!** agreed!; **de** ~ **con** (*persona*) in agreement with; (*acción, documento*) in accordance with.

acumulador [akumula'ðor] *nm* storage battery; **acumular** *vt* to accumulate, collect.

acuñar [aku'ɲar] *vt* (*moneda*) to coin, mint; (*poner cuñas*) to wedge.

acuoso, a [a'kwoso, a] a watery.

acurrucarse [akurru'karse] *vr* to crouch; (*ovillarse*) to curl up.

acusación [akusa'θjon] *nf* accusation; **acusar** *vt* to accuse; (*revelar*) to reveal; (*denunciar*) to denounce.

acuse [a'kuse] *nm*: ~ **de recibo**

acknowledgement of receipt.
acústico, a [a'kustiko, a] *a* acoustic // *nm* hearing aid.
achacar [atʃa'kar] *vt* to attribute.
achacoso, a [atʃa'koso, a] *a* sickly.
achaque [a'tʃake] *nm* ailment.
achicar [atʃi'kar] *vt* to reduce; (*humillar*) to humiliate; (*NAUT*) to bale out.
achicoria [atʃi'korja] *nf* chicory.
achicharrar [atʃitʃa'rrar] *vt* to scorch, burn.
adagio [a'ðaxjo] *nm* adage; (*MUS*) adagio.
adaptación [aðapta'θjon] *nf* adaptation; **adaptar** *vt* to adapt; (*acomodar*) to fit.
a. de C. *abr* = **a. de J.C.**
A. de C. *abr* = **A.C.**
adecuado, a [aðe'kwaðo, a] *a* adequate; (*apto*) suitable; (*oportuno*) appropriate; **adecuar** *vt* to adapt; to make suitable.
a. de J.C. *abr de* **antes de Jesucristo** B.C. (before Christ).
adelantado, a [aðelan'taðo, a] *a* advanced; (*reloj*) fast; **pagar por** ~ to pay in advance; **adelantamiento** *nm* advance, advancement; (*AUTO*) overtaking; (*progreso*) progress.
adelantar [aðelan'tar] *vt* to move forward; (*avanzar*) to advance; (*acelerar*) to speed up // *vi*, ~**se** *vr* to go forward, advance; (*AUTO*) to overtake.
adelante [aðe'lante] *ad* forward(s), onward(s), ahead // *excl* come in!; **de hoy en** ~ from now on; **más** ~ later on; (*más allá*) further on.
adelanto [aðe'lanto] *nm* advance; (*mejora*) improvement; (*progreso*) progress.
adelgazar [aðelxa'θar] *vt* to thin (down); (*afilar*) to taper // *vi*, ~ **se** *vr* to grow thin.
ademán [aðe'man] *nm* gesture; **ademanes** *nmpl* manners; **en** ~ **de** as if to.
además [aðe'mas] *ad* besides; (*por otra parte*) moreover; (*también*) also; ~ **de** besides, in addition to.
adentro [a'ðentro] *ad* inside, in; **mar** ~ out at sea; **tierra** ~ inland.
adepto, a [a'ðepto, a] *nm/f* supporter.
aderezar [aðere'θar] *vt* to prepare; (*persona, ensalada*) to dress; (*comida*) to season; ~ **se** *vr* to dress up; **aderezo** *nm* preparation; dressing; seasoning.
adeudar [aðeu'ðar] *vt* to owe // *vi* to become related by marriage; ~ **se** *vr* to run into debt.
adherirse [aðe'rirse] *vr*: ~ **a** to adhere to.
adhesión [aðe'sjon] *nf* adhesion; (*fig*) adherence.
adición [aði'θjon] *nf* addition.
adicionar [aðiθjo'nar] *vt* to add.
adicto, a [a'ðikto, a] *a*: ~ **a** given to; (*dedicado*) devoted to // *nm/f* supporter, follower.
adiestrar [aðjes'trar] *vt* to train, teach; (*conducir*) to guide, lead; ~ **se** *vr* to train o.s.; (*enseñarse*) to train o.s.

adinerado, a [aðine'raðo, a] *a* wealthy.
adiós [a'ðjos] *excl* (*para despedirse*) goodbye!, cheerio!; (*para saludar*) hello!
aditivo [aði'tiβo] *nm* additive.
adivinanza [aðiβi'nanθa] *nf* riddle; **adivinar** *vt* to prophesy; (*conjeturar*) to guess; **adivino, a** *nm/f* fortune-teller.
adj *a abr de* **adjunto** encl. (enclosed).
adjetivo [aðxe'tiβo] *nm* adjective.
adjudicación [aðxuðika'θjon] *nf* award; **adjudicar** *vt* to award; **adjudicarse** *vr*: **adjudicarse algo** to appropriate sth.
adjuntar [aðxun'tar] *vt* to attach, enclose; **adjunto, a** *a* attached, enclosed // *nm/f* assistant.
administración [aðministra'θjon] *nf* administration; (*dirección*) management; **administrador, a** *nm/f* administrator; manager/ess.
administrar [aðminis'trar] *vt* to administer; **administrativo, a** *a* administrative.
admirable [aðmi'raβle] *a* admirable; **admiración** *nf* admiration; (*asombro*) wonder; (*LING*) exclamation mark; **admirar** *vt* to admire; (*extrañar*) to surprise; **admirarse** *vr* to be surprised.
admisible [aðmi'siβle] *a* admissible.
admitir [aðmi'tir] *vt* to admit; (*aceptar*) to accept.
admonición [aðmoni'θjon] *nf* warning.
adobe [a'ðoβe] *nm* adobe, sun-dried brick.
adolecer [aðole'θer] *vi* to be ill, fall ill; ~ **de** to suffer from.
adolescente [aðoles'θente] *nm/f* adolescent.
adonde [a'ðonde] *conj* (to) where.
adónde [a'ðonde] *ad* = **dónde**.
adopción [aðop'θjon] *nf* adoption.
adoptar [aðop'tar] *vt* to adopt.
adoquín [aðo'kin] *nm* paving stone.
adorar [aðo'rar] *vt* to adore.
adormecer [aðorme'θer] *vt* to put to sleep; ~ **se** *vr* to become sleepy, fall asleep.
adornar [aðor'nar] *vt* to adorn.
adorno [a'ðorno] *nm* adornment; (*decoración*) decoration.
adquiero *etc vb ver* **adquirir**.
adquirir [aðki'rir] *vt* to acquire, obtain.
adquisición [aðkisi'θjon] *nf* acquisition.
adrede [a'ðreðe] *ad* on purpose.
adscribir [aðskri'βir] *vt* to appoint.
aduana [a'ðwana] *nf* customs *pl*.
aduanero, a [aðwa'nero, a] *a* customs *cpd* // *nm/f* customs officer.
aducir [aðu'θir] *vt* to adduce; (*dar como prueba*) to offer as proof.
adueñarse [aðwe'ɲarse] *vr*: ~ **de** to take possession of.
adulación [aðula'θjon] *nf* flattery.
adular [aðu'lar] *vt* to flatter.
adulterar [aðulte'rar] *vt* to adulterate // *vi* to commit adultery.
adulterio [aðul'terjo] *nm* adultery.
adulto, a [a'ðulto, a] *a*, *nm/f* adult.

adusto, a [a'ðusto, a] *a* stern; (*austero*) austere.

advenedizo, a [aðßene'ðiθo, a] *nm/f* upstart.

advenimiento [aðßeni'mjento] *nm* arrival; (*al trono*) accession.

adverbio [að'ßerßjo] *nm* adverb.

adversario, a [aðßer'sarjo, a] *nm/f* adversary.

adversidad [aðßersi'ðað] *nf* adversity; (*contratiempo*) setback.

adverso, a [að'ßerso, a] *a* adverse; (*opuesto*) opposite.

advertencia [aðßer'tenθja] *nf* warning; (*prefacio*) preface, foreword.

advertir [aðßer'tir] *vt* to notice; (*avisar*) to warn // *vi*: ~ **en** to notice.

Adviento [að'ßjento] *nm* Advent.

adyacente [aðja'θente] *a* adjacent.

aéreo, a [a'ereo, a] *a* aerial.

aerodeslizador [aeroðesliθa'ðor], **aerodeslizante** [aeroðesli'θante] *nm* hovercraft.

aeronáutica [aero'nautika] *nf* aeronautics *sg*.

aeropuerto [aero'pwerto] *nm* airport.

afabilidad [afaßili'ðað] *nf* friendliness; **afable** *a* affable.

afán [a'fan] *nm* hard work; (*deseo*) desire.

afanar [afa'nar] *vt* to harass; ~**se** *vr*: ~**se por** to strive to; **afanoso, a** *a* hard; (*trabajador*) industrious.

afear [afe'ar] *vt* to make ugly; (*mutilar*) to deface.

afección [afek'θjon] *nf* affection; (*MED*) disease.

afectación [afekta'θjon] *nf* affectation; **afectado, a** *a* affected; **afectar** *vt* to affect.

afectísimo, a [afek'tisimo, a] *a* affectionate; ~ **suyo** yours truly.

afecto, a [a'fekto, a] *a* affectionate // *nm* affection; ~ **a** fond of.

afectuoso, a [afek'twoso, a] *a* affectionate.

afeitar [afei'tar] *vt* to shave; ~**se** *vr* to shave.

afeminado, a [afemi'naðo, a] *a* effeminate.

aferrado, a [afe'rraðo, a] *a* stubborn.

aferrar [afe'rrar] *vt* to moor; (*fig*) to grasp // *vi* to moor.

afianzamiento [afjanθa'mjento] *nm* strengthening; (*garantía*) guarantee; (*COM*) security; **afianzar** *vt* to strengthen; to guarantee; to secure; **afianzarse** *vr* to become established.

afición [afi'θjon] *nf* fondness, liking; **la** ~ the fans *pl*; **pinto por** ~ I paint as a hobby; **aficionado, a** *a* keen, enthusiastic; amateur // *nm/f* enthusiast, fan; amateur.

aficionar [afiθjo'nar] *vt*: ~ **a uno a algo** to make sb like sth; ~**se** *vr*: ~**se a algo** to grow fond of sth.

afilado, a [afi'laðo, a] *a* sharp.

afilar [afi'lar] *vt* to sharpen.

afiliarse [afi'ljarse] *vr* to become affiliated to.

afín [a'fin] *a* bordering, adjacent; (*parecido*) similar; (*conexo*) related.

afinar [afi'nar] *vt* (*TEC*) to refine; (*MUS*) to tune // *vi* to play/sing in tune.

afinidad [afini'ðað] *nf* affinity; (*parentesco*) relationship; **por** ~ by marriage.

afirmación [afirma'θjon] *nf* affirmation; **afirmar** *vt* to affirm, state; (*sostener*) to strengthen; **afirmativo, a** *a* affirmative.

aflicción [aflik'θjon] *nf* affliction; (*dolor*) grief.

afligir [afli'xir] *vt* to afflict; (*apenar*) to distress; ~**se** *vr* to grieve.

aflojar [aflo'xar] *vt* to slacken; (*desatar*) to loosen, undo; (*relajar*) to relax // *vi* to drop; (*bajar*) to go down; ~**se** *vr* to relax.

afluente [aflu'ente] *a* flowing; (*elocuente*) eloquent // *nm* tributary.

afluir [aflu'ir] *vi* to flow.

afmo, a *abr de* **afectísimo(a) suyo(a)**.

afónico, a [a'foniko, a] *a* (*ronco*) hoarse; (*sin voz*) voiceless.

afortunado, a [afortu'naðo, a] *a* fortunate, lucky.

afrancesado, a [afranθe'saðo, a] *a* francophile; (*pey*) frenchified.

afrenta [a'frenta] *nf* affront, insult; (*deshonra*) dishonour, shame; **afrentar** *vt* to affront; to dishonour; **afrentarse** *vr* to be ashamed; **afrentoso, a** *a* insulting.

África ['afrika] *nf* Africa; ~ **del Sur** South Africa; **africano, a** *a*, *nm/f* African.

afrontar [afron'tar] *vt* to confront; (*poner cara a cara*) to bring face to face.

afuera [a'fwera] *ad* out, outside; ~**s** *nfpl* outskirts, suburbs.

agachar [aɣa'tʃar] *vt* to bend, bow; ~**se** *vr* to stoop, bend.

agalla [a'ɣaʎa] *nf* (*ZOOL*) gill; ~**s** *nfpl* (*MED*) tonsillitis *sg*; (*ANAT*) tonsils.

agarradera [aɣarra'ðera] *nf* (*AM*), **agarradero** [aɣarra'ðero] *nm* handle; ~**s** *npl* pull *sg*, influence *sg*.

agarrado, a [aɣa'rraðo, a] *a* mean, stingy.

agarrar [aɣa'rrar] *vt* to grasp, grab; (*AM*) to take, catch // *vi* (*planta*) to take root; ~**se** *vr* to hold on (tightly).

agarrotar [aɣarro'tar] *vt* (*lío*) to tie tightly; (*persona*) to squeeze tightly; (*reo*) to garrotte; ~**se** *vr* (*motor*) to seize up; (*MED*) to stiffen.

agasajar [aɣasa'xar] *vt* to treat well, fête; **agasajo** *nm* lavish hospitality.

agencia [a'xenθja] *nf* agency; ~ **de viajes/inmobiliaria** travel/estate agency.

agenda [a'xenda] *nf* diary.

agente [a'xente] *nm* agent; (*de policía*) policeman; ~ **femenino** policewoman.

ágil ['axil] *a* agile, nimble; **agilidad** *nf* agility, nimbleness.

agio ['axjo] *nm* speculation.

agiotista [axjo'tista] *nm* (stock)jobber; (*especulador*) speculator.

agitación [axita'θjon] *nf* shaking, waving, stirring; (*del mar*) roughness; (*fig*) agitation.

agitar [axi'tar] *vt* to wave, shake, stir; (*fig*) to stir up, excite; ~**se** *vr* to get excited.

aglomerar [axlome'rar] *vt*, ~**se** *vr* to agglomerate, crowd together.

agnóstico, a [ax'nostiko, a] *a*, *nm/f* agnostic.

agobiar [axo'βjar] *vt* to weigh down; (*oprimir*) to oppress; (*cargar*) to burden.

agolparse [axol'parse] *vr* to crowd together.

agonía [axo'nia] *nf* agony, anguish.

agonizante [axoni'θante] *a* dying.

agonizar [axoni'θar] *vi* (*también* **estar agonizando**) to be dying.

agosto [a'xosto] *nm* August.

agotado, a [axo'taðo, a] *a* exhausted; (*libros*) out of print; (*acabado*) finished; (*mercancías*) sold out; **agotamiento** *nm* exhaustion.

agotar [axo'tar] *vt* to exhaust; (*consumir*) to drain; (*recursos*) to use up, deplete; ~**se** *vr* to be exhausted; (*acabarse*) to run out; (*libro*) to go out of print.

agraciar [axra'θjar] *vt* (*JUR*) to pardon; (*con premio*) to reward.

agradable [axra'ðaβle] *a* pleasing, pleasant, nice.

agradar [axra'ðar] *vt*, *vi* to please.

agradecer [axraðe'θer] *vt* to thank; (*favor etc*) to be grateful for; **agradecimiento** *nm* thanks *pl*; gratitude.

agrado [a'xraðo] *nm* affability; (*gusto*) liking.

agrandar [axran'dar] *vt* to enlarge; (*fig*) to exaggerate; ~**se** *vr* to get bigger.

agrario, a [a'xrarjo, a] *a* agrarian.

agravar [axra'βar] *vt* to make heavier; (*irritar*) to aggravate; (*oprimir*) to oppress; ~**se** *vr* to worsen, get worse.

agraviar [axra'βjar] *vt* to offend; (*ser injusto con*) to wrong; ~**se** *vr* to take offence; **agravio** *nm* offence; wrong; (*ofensa*) grievance.

agregado [axre'xaðo] *nm* aggregate; (*persona*) attaché.

agregar [axre'xar] *vt* to gather; (*añadir*) to add; (*persona*) to appoint.

agresión [axre'sjon] *nf* aggression; **agresivo, a** *a* aggressive.

agriar [a'xrjar] *vt* to (turn) sour; ~**se** *vr* to turn sour.

agricultor, a [axrikul'tor, a] *nm/f* farmer; **agricultura** *nf* agriculture, farming.

agridulce [axri'ðulθe] *a* bittersweet.

agrietarse [axrje'tarse] *vr* to crack; (*la piel*) to chap.

agrio, a ['axrjo, a] *a* bitter.

agronomía [axrono'mia] *nf* agronomy, agriculture.

agrupación [axrupa'θjon] *nf* group; (*acto*) grouping.

agrupar [axru'par] *vt* to group.

agua ['axwa] *nf* water; (*lluvia*) rain; (*NAUT*) wake; (*ARQ*) slope of a roof; ~**s** *nfpl* (*de piedra*) water *sg*, sparkle *sg*; (*MED*) water *sg*, urine *sg*; (*NAUT*) waters; ~**s abajo/arriba** downstream/upstream; ~ **bendita/destilada/potable** holy/distilled/drinking water; ~ **corriente** running water; ~ **de colonia** eau de cologne; ~**s jurisdiccionales** territorial waters; ~**s mayores** excrement *sg*.

aguacate [axwa'kate] *nm* avocado pear.

aguacero [axwa'θero] *nm* (heavy) shower.

aguado, a [a'xwaðo, a] *a* watery, watered down // *nf* (*AGR*) watering place; (*NAUT*) water supply; (*ARTE*) water-colour.

aguafiestas [axwa'fjestas] *nm/f inv* spoilsport.

aguafuerte [axwa'fwerte] *nf* etching.

aguamar [axwa'mar] *nm* jellyfish.

aguantable [axwan'taβle] *a* bearable; **aguantar** *vt* to bear, put up with; (*contener*) to hold; (*sostener*) to hold up // *vi* to last; **aguantarse** *vr* to restrain o.s.

aguar [a'xwar] *vt* to water down.

aguardar [axwar'ðar] *vt* to wait for.

aguardiente [axwar'ðjente] *nm* brandy.

aguarrás [axwa'rras] *nm* turpentine.

agudeza [axu'ðeθa] *nf* sharpness; (*ingenio*) wit; **agudo, a** *a* sharp; (*voz*) high-pitched, piercing; (*dolor, enfermedad*) acute.

agüero [a'xwero] *nm* omen; (*pronóstico*) prediction.

aguijar [axi'xar] *vt* to goad; (*incitar*) to urge on // *vi* to hurry along.

aguijón [axi'xon] *nm* sting; (*BOT*) spine; (*estímulo, fig*) spur; **aguijonear** *vt* = **aguijar**.

águila ['axila] *nf* eagle; (*fig*) genius.

aguileño, a [axi'leɲo, a] *a* aquiline; (*facciones*) sharp-featured.

aguinaldo [axi'naldo] *nm* Christmas box.

aguja [a'xuxa] *nf* needle; (*de reloj*) hand; (*ARQ*) spire; (*TEC*) firing-pin; ~**s** *nfpl* (*ZOOL*) ribs; (*FERRO*) points.

agujerear [axuxere'ar] *vt* to make holes in; **agujero** *nm* hole.

agujetas [axu'xetas] *nfpl* stitch *sg*; (*rigidez*) stiffness *sg*.

aguzar [axu'θar] *vt* to sharpen; (*fig*) to incite.

ahí [a'i] *ad* there; **de** ~ **que** so that, with the result that; ~ **llega** here he comes; **por** ~ that way; (*allá*) over there.

ahijado, a [ai'xaðo, a] *nm/f* godson/daughter.

ahínco [a'inko] *nm* earnestness.

ahitar [ai'tar] *vt* to surfeit; ~**se** *vr* to stuff o.s.

ahíto, a [a'ito, a] *a*: **estoy** ~ I have indigestion // *nm* indigestion.

ahogar [ao'xar] *vt* to drown; (*asfixiar*) to suffocate, smother; (*fuego*) to put out; ~**se** *vr* (*en el agua*) to drown; (*suicidio*) to drown o.s.; (*por asfixia*) to suffocate.

ahogo [a'oxo] *nm* shortness of breath; (*fig*) financial difficulty.

ahondar [aon'dar] *vt* to deepen, make

deeper; (*fig*) to go deeply into // *vi:* ~ **en** to go deeply into.

ahora [a'ora] *ad* now; (*poco tiempo ha*) a moment ago, just now; (*dentro de poco*) in a moment // *conj* now; ~ **voy** I'm coming; ~ **mismo** right now; ~ **bien** now then; **por** ~ for the present.

ahorcar [aor'kar] *vt* to hang; ~**se** *vr* to hang o.s.

ahorita [ao'rita] *ad* (*fam*) right now.

ahorrar [ao'rrar] *vt* (*dinero*) to save; (*esfuerzos*) to save, avoid; **ahorro** *nm* economy, saving; (*frugalidad*) thrift; **ahorros** *nmpl* savings.

ahuecar [awe'kar] *vt* to hollow (out); (*voz*) to deepen; ~**se** *vr* to give o.s. airs.

ahumar [au'mar] *vt* to smoke, cure; (*llenar de humo*) to fill with smoke // *vi* to smoke; ~**se** *vr* to fill with smoke.

ahuyentar [aujen'tar] *vt* to drive off, frighten off; (*fig*) to dispel; ~**se** *vr* to run away.

airado, a [ai'raðo, a] *a* angry; **airar** *vt* to anger; **airarse** *vr* to get angry.

aire ['aire] *nm* air; (*viento*) wind; (*corriente*) draught; (*MUS*) tune; ~**s** *nmpl:* **darse** ~**s** to give o.s. airs; **al** ~ **libre** in the open air; ~ **acondicionado** air conditioning; **airoso, a** *a* windy; draughty; (*fig*) graceful.

aislador [aisla'ðor] *nm* insulator; **aislar** *vt* to isolate; (*ELEC*) to insulate.

ajar [a'xar] *vt* to spoil; (*fig*) to abuse.

ajedrez [axe'ðreθ] *nm* chess.

ajeno, a [a'xeno, a] *a* (*que pertenece a otro*) somebody else's; (*impropio*) inappropriate; (*extraño*) alien, foreign; ~ **a** a foreign to; ~ **de** free from, devoid of.

ajetreo [axe'treo] *nm* bustle.

ají [a'xi] *nm* chili, red pepper; (*salsa*) chili sauce.

ajo ['axo] *nm* garlic; ~ **porro** *o* **puerro** leek.

ajorca [a'xorka] *nf* bracelet.

ajuar [a'xwar] *nm* household furnishings *pl*; (*de novia*) trousseau; (*de niño*) layette.

ajustado, a [axus'taðo, a] *a* (*tornillo*) tight; (*cálculo*) right; (*ropa*) tight-fitting; (*DEPORTE: resultado*) close.

ajustar [axus'tar] *vt* (*adaptar*) to adjust; (*encajar*) to fit; (*TEC*) to engage; (*contratar*) to hire; (*IMPRENTA*) to make up; (*apretar*) to tighten; (*concertar*) to agree (on); (*reconciliar*) to reconcile; (*cuenta*) to settle // *vi* to fit; ~**se** *vr* to come to an agreement.

ajuste [a'xuste] *nm* adjustment; (*TEC costura*) fitting; (*acuerdo*) compromise; (*de cuenta*) settlement.

al [al] = **a** + **el**, *ver* **a.**

ala ['ala] *nf* wing; (*de sombrero*) brim; (*futbolista*) winger.

alabanza [ala'βanθa] *nf* praise.

alabar [ala'βar] *vt* to praise; ~**se** *vr:* ~**se de** to boast of (being).

alabear [alaβe'ar] *vt*, ~**se** *vr* to warp.

alacena [ala'θena] *nf* cupboard.

alacrán [ala'kran] *nm* scorpion.

alambicado, a [alambi'kaðo, a] *a* distilled; (*fig*) affected.

alambicar [alambi'kar] *vt* to distil.

alambique [alam'bike] *nm* still.

alambrado [alam'braðo] *nm* wire fence; (*red*) wire netting; **alambre** *nm* wire; **alambre de púas** barbed wire; **alambrista** *nm/f* tightrope walker.

alameda [ala'meða] *nf* (*plantío*) poplar grove; (*lugar de paseo*) avenue, tree-lined walk.

álamo ['alamo] *nm* poplar; ~ **temblón** aspen.

alano [a'lano] *nm* mastiff.

alar [a'lar] *nm* eaves *pl.*

alarde [a'larðe] *nm* (*MIL*) review; (*ostentación*) show, display; **hacer** ~ **de** to boast of.

alargar [alar'xar] *vt* to lengthen, extend; (*paso*) to hasten; (*brazo*) to stretch out; (*cuerda*) to pay out; (*conversación*) to spin out; ~**se** *vr* to get longer; ~**se en** to enlarge upon; (*pey*) to drag out.

alarido [ala'riðo] *nm* shriek.

alarma [a'larma] *nf* alarm.

alazán [ala'θan] *nm* sorrel.

alba ['alβa] *nf* dawn.

albacea [alβa'θea] *nm/f* executor/trix.

Albania [al'βanja] *nf* Albania.

albañal [alβa'ɲal] *nm* drain, sewer.

albañil [alβa'ɲil] *nm* bricklayer; (*cantero*) mason.

albaricoque [alβari'koke] *nm* apricot.

albedrío [alβe'ðrio] *nm:* **libre** ~ free will.

alberca [al'βerka] *nf* reservoir.

albergar [alβer'xar] *vt*, ~**se** *vr* to shelter.

albergue [al'βerxe] *nm* shelter, refuge; ~ **de juventud** youth hostel.

albóndiga [al'βondixa] *nf* meatball.

albor [al'βor] *nm* whiteness; (*amanecer*) dawn; ~**ada** *nf* dawn; (*diana*) reveille; ~**ear** *vi* to dawn.

albornoz [alβor'noθ] *nm* (*de los árabes*) burnous; (*para el baño*) bathrobe.

alborotar [alβoro'tar] *vi* to make a row // *vt* to agitate, stir up; ~**se** *vr* to get excited; (*mar*) to get rough; **alboroto** *nm* row, uproar.

alborozar [alβoro'θar] *vt* to gladden; ~**se** *vr* to rejoice.

alborozo [alβo'roθo] *nm* joy.

albricias [al'βriθjas] *nfpl* reward *sg* // *excl* good news!

álbum ['alβum] *nm* album.

albumen [al'βumen] *nm* egg white.

alcachofa [alka'tʃofa] *nf* artichoke.

alcalde [al'kalde] *nm* mayor.

alcaldía [alkal'dia] *nf* mayoralty; (*lugar*) mayor's office.

alcance [al'kanθe] *nm* reach; (*COM*) adverse balance; (*de periódico*) stop-press (news); **de pocos** ~**s** not very clever; ~ **de última hora** late postal collection.

alcancía [alkan'θia] *nf* money box.

alcantarilla [alkanta'riʎa] *nf* (*de aguas*

cloacales) sewer; (*en la calle*) gutter.

alcanzar [alkan'θar] *vt* (*algo: con la mano, el pie*) to reach; (*alguien en el camino*) to catch up with; (*autobús*) to catch; (*suj: bala*) to hit, strike // *vi*: ~ **a hacer** to manage to do.

alcatraz [alka'traθ] *nm* gannet.

alcázar [al'kaθar] *nm* fortress; (*palacio*) royal palace; (*NAUT*) quarter-deck.

alcoba [al'koßa] *nf* bedroom.

alcohol [al'kol] *nm* alcohol; **alcohólico, a** *a* alcoholic; ~ **ismo** *nm* alcoholism.

alcornoque [alkor'noke] *nm* cork tree.

aldaba [al'daßa] *nf* (door) knocker.

aldea [al'dea] *nf* village; ~ **no, a** *a* village *cpd* // *nm/f* villager.

aleación [alea'θjon] *nf* alloy.

aleccionar [alekθjo'nar] *vt* to instruct; (*adiestrar*) to train.

alegación [aleɣa'θjon] *nf* allegation; **alegar** *vt* to allege; (*JUR*) to plead; (*AM*) to dispute, argue.

alegato [ale'ɣato] *nm* (*JUR*) allegation; (*AM*) argument.

alegoría [aleɣo'ria] *nf* allegory.

alegrar [ale'ɣrar] *vt* (*causar alegría*) to cheer (up); (*fuego*) to poke; (*fiesta*) to liven up; ~ **se** *vr* to get merry *or* tight; ~ **se de** to be glad about.

alegre [a'leɣre] *a* happy, cheerful; (*fam*) merry, tight; (*licencioso*) risqué, blue; **alegría** *nf* happiness; merriment.

alejamiento [alexa'mjento] *nm* removal; (*distancia*) remoteness.

alejar [ale'xar] *vt* to remove; (*fig*) to estrange; ~ **se** *vr* to move away.

aleluya [ale'luja] *nm* (*canto*) hallelujah; (*Pascuas*) Easter time // *nf* Easter print.

alemán, ana [ale'man, ana] *a, nm/f* German // *nm* (*lengua*) German.

Alemania [ale'manja] *nf*: ~ **Federal/Oriental** West/East Germany.

alentado, a [alen'taðo, a] *pp de* **alentar** // *a* brave; (*orgulloso*) proud; (*fuerte*) strong.

alentador, a [alenta'ðor, a] *a* encouraging.

alentar [alen'tar] *vt* to encourage; ~ **se** *vr* to cheer up.

alerce [a'lerθe] *nm* larch.

alergia [a'lerxja] *nf* allergy.

alero [a'lero] *nm* (*de tejado*) eaves *pl*; (*de carruaje*) mudguard.

alerta [a'lerta] *a, nm* alert.

aleta [a'leta] *nf* (*de pez*) fin; (*de ave*) wing; (*de coche*) mudguard.

aletargar [aletar'ɣar] *vt* to make drowsy; (*entumecer*) to make numb; ~ **se** *vr* to grow drowsy; to become numb.

aletazo [ale'taθo] *nm* wingbeat, flap of the wing.

aletear [alete'ar] *vi* to flutter.

aleve [a'leße] *a* treacherous.

alevosía [aleßo'sia] *nf* treachery.

alfabeto [alfa'ßeto] *nm* alphabet.

alfarería [alfare'ria] *nf* pottery; (*tienda*) pottery shop; **alfarero** *nm* potter.

alférez [al'fereθ] *nm* (*MIL*) second lieutenant; (*NAUT*) ensign.

alfiler [alfi'ler] *nm* pin; (*broche*) clip; ~ **de seguridad** safety pin.

alfombra [al'fombra] *nf* carpet; (*más pequeña*) rug; **alfombrar** *vt* to carpet; **alfombrilla** *nf* rug, mat; (*MED*) German measles.

alforja [al'forxa] *nf* saddlebag.

alforza [al'forθa] *nf* pleat.

alga ['alɣa] *nf* seaweed, alga.

algarabía [alɣara'ßia] *nf* (*fam*) gibberish; (*BOT*) cornflower.

algarrobo [alɣa'rroßo] *nm* carob tree.

algazara [alɣa'θara] *nf* din, uproar.

álgebra ['alxeßra] *nf* algebra.

algo ['alɣo] *pron* something; anything // *ad* somewhat, rather; **por** ~ **será** there must be some reason for it.

algodón [alɣo'ðon] *nm* cotton; (*planta*) cotton plant; (*dulce*) candy floss; ~ **hidrófilo** cotton wool.

algodonero, a [alɣoðo'nero, a] *a* cotton *cpd* // *nm/f* cotton grower // *nm* cotton plant.

alguacil [alɣwa'θil] *nm* bailiff; (*TAUR*) mounted official.

alguien ['alɣjen] *pron* someone, somebody, anybody.

alguno, a [al'ɣuno, a], **algún** [al'ɣun] *a* some, any // *pron* some; one; someone, somebody; ~ **que otro libro** some book or other; **algún día iré** I'll go one *or* some day; **sin interés** ~ without the slightest interest; ~ **que otro** an occasional one; ~ **s piensan** some (people) think.

alhaja [a'laxa] *nf* jewel; (*tesoro*) precious object, treasure; (*pey*) rogue.

aliado, a [a'ljaðo, a] *a* allied.

alianza [a'ljanθa] *nf* alliance.

aliar [a'ljar] *vt* to ally; ~ **se** *vr* to form an alliance.

alias ['aljas] *ad* alias.

alicantino, a [alikan'tino, a] *a* of *or* from Alicante.

alicates [ali'kates] *nmpl*: ~ **de uñas** nail clippers.

aliciente [ali'θjente] *nm* incentive; (*atracción*) attraction.

alienación [aljena'θjon] *nf* alienation.

aliento [a'ljento] *nm* breath; (*respiración*) breathing; **sin** ~ breathless.

aligerar [alixe'rar] *vt* to lighten; (*reducir*) to shorten; (*aliviar*) to alleviate; (*mitigar*) to ease.

alimaña [ali'maɲa] *nf* pest.

alimentación [alimenta'θjon] *nf* (*comida*) food; (*acción*) feeding; (*tienda*) grocer's (shop); **alimentar** *vt* to feed; (*nutrir*) to nourish; **alimentarse** *vr* to feed.

alimenticio, a [alimen'tiθjo, a] *a* nourishing.

alimento [ali'mento] *nm* food; (*nutrición*) nourishment; ~ **s** *nmpl* (*JUR*) alimony *sg*.

alinear [aline'ar] *vt* to align; ~ **se** *vr*: ~ **se en** to fall in with.

aliñar [ali'ɲar] vt to adorn; (*preparar*) to prepare; (*CULIN*) to season; **aliño** nm decoration; (*esmero*) neatness; (*CULIN*) dressing.

alisar [ali'sar] vt to smooth; (*pulir*) to polish.

aliso [a'liso] nm alder.

alistamiento [alista'mjento] nm recruitment; **alistar** vt to recruit; (*inscribir*) to enrol; **alistarse** vr to enlist; to enrol.

aliviar [ali'ßjar] vt (*carga*) to lighten; (*persona*) to relieve; (*dolor*) to alleviate; ~ **se** vr. ~**se de** to unburden o.s. of.

alivio [a'lißjo] nm alleviation, relief.

aljibe [al'xiße] nm cistern; (*AUTO*) oil tanker.

aljofaina [alxo'faina] nf = **jofaina.**

alma ['alma] nf soul; (*persona*) person; (*que anima*) life and soul; (*TEC*) core.

almacén [alma'θen] nm (*depósito*) warehouse, store; (*MIL*) magazine; (*AM*) shop; **almacenes** nmpl department store sg; **almacenaje** nm storage.

almacenar [almaθe'nar] vt to store, put in storage; (*proveerse*) to stock up (with); **almacenero** nm warehouseman.

almanaque [alma'nake] nm almanac.

almeja [al'mexa] nf shellfish, clam.

almendra [al'mendra] nf almond; **almendro** nm almond tree.

almiar [al'mjar] nm hayrick.

almíbar [al'mißar] nm syrup; **almibarado, a** a syrupy.

almidón [almi'ðon] nm starch; **almidonar** vt to starch.

almirantazgo [almiran'taɣxo] nm admiralty; **almirante** nm admiral.

almohada [almo'aða] nf pillow; (*funda*) pillowcase; **almohadilla** nf cushion; (*TEC*) pad; (*AM*) pincushion.

almoneda [almo'neða] nf auction; (*liquidación*) clearance sale.

almorranas [almo'rranas] nfpl piles, haemorrhoids.

almorzar [almor'θar] vt: ~ **una tortilla** to have an omelette for lunch // vi to (have) lunch.

almuerzo [al'mwerθo] nm lunch.

alnado, a [al'naðo, a] nm/f stepson/daughter.

alocado, a [alo'kaðo, a] a crazy.

alojamiento [aloxa'mjento] nf lodging(s) (*pl*); (*viviendas*) housing.

alojar [alo'xar] vt to lodge; ~**se** vr to lodge, stay.

alondra [a'londra] nf lark, skylark.

alpargata [alpar'ɣata] nf rope-soled sandal; (*de lona*) canvass shoe.

Alpes ['alpes] nmpl: **los** ~ the Alps.

alpinismo [alpi'nismo] nm mountaineering, climbing; **alpinista** nm/f mountaineer, climber.

alquería [alke'ria] nf farmhouse.

alquilar [alki'lar] vt to rent (out), let, hire (out); (*de inquilino*) to rent, hire; **se**

alquilan casas houses to let.

alquiler [alki'ler] nm renting, letting, hiring; (*arriendo*) rent, hire charge; **de** ~ for hire.

alquimia [al'kimja] nf alchemy.

alquitrán [alki'tran] nm tar.

alrededor [alreðe'ðor] ad around, about; ~**es** nmpl surroundings; ~ **de** prep around, about; **mirar a su** ~ to look (round) about one.

alta ['alta] nf ver **alto.**

altanería [altane'ria] nf haughtiness, arrogance; **altanero, a** a arrogant, haughty.

altar [al'tar] nm altar.

altavoz [alta'ßoθ] nm loudspeaker; (*amplificador*) amplifier.

alteración [altera'θjon] nf alteration; (*alboroto*) disturbance; (*discusión*) quarrel; **alterar** vt to alter; to disturb; **alterarse** vr (*alimento etc*) to go bad or off; (*voz*) to falter; (*persona*) to get upset.

altercado [alter'kaðo] nm argument.

alternar [alter'nar] vt to alternate // vi, ~**se** vr to alternate; (*turnar*) to take turns; ~ **con** to mix with; **alternativo, a** a alternative; (*alterno*) alternating // nf alternative; (*elección*) choice; **alternativas** nfpl ups and downs.

alteza [al'teθa] nf (*tratamiento*) highness; (*altura*) height.

altibajos [alti'ßaxos] nmpl ups and downs.

altiplanicie [altipla'niθje] nf, **altiplano** [alti'plano] nm high plateau.

altisonante [altiso'nante] a high-flown.

altitud [alti'tuð] nf altitude.

altivez [alti'ßeθ] nf haughtiness, arrogance; **altivo, a** a haughty, arrogant.

alto, a ['alto, a] a high; (*de tamaño*) tall; (*precio, importante*) high; (*sonido*) high, sharp; (*noble*) high, lofty // nm halt; (*MUS*) alto; (*GEO*) hill; (*AM*) pile // ad (*de sitio*) high; (*de sonido*) loud, loudly // nf (*certificate of*) discharge // excl halt!; **tiene 2 metros de** ~ he is 2 metres tall; **en** ~**a mar** on the high seas; **en voz** ~**a** in a loud voice; **las** ~**as horas de la noche** the small hours; **en lo** ~ **de** at the top of; **pasar por** ~ to overlook; **dar de** ~**a** to discharge.

altoparlante [altopar'lante] nm (*AM*) loudspeaker.

altura [al'tura] nf height; (*NAUT*) depth; (*GEO*) latitude; **tiene 1.80 de** ~ he is 1 metre 80cm tall; **a esta** ~ **del año** at this time of the year.

alubia [a'lußja] nf French bean, kidney bean.

alucinación [aluθina'θjon] nf hallucination; **alucinar** vi to hallucinate // vt to deceive; (*fascinar*) to fascinate.

alud [a'luð] nm avalanche.

aludir [alu'ðir] vi: ~ **a** to allude to; **darse por** ~ to take the hint.

alumbrado [alum'braðo] nm lighting; **alumbramiento** nm lighting; (*MED*) childbirth, delivery.

alumbrar [alum'brar] *vt* to light (up); (*ciego*) to restore the sight of // *vi* to give birth.

aluminio [alu'minjo] *nm* aluminium.

alumno, a [a'lumno, a] *nm/f* pupil, student.

alunizar [aluni'θar] *vi* to land on the moon.

alusión [alu'sjon] *nf* allusion.

alusivo, a [alu'siβo, a] *a* allusive.

aluvión [alu'βjon] *nm* alluvium; (*fig*) flood.

alza ['alθa] *nf* rise; ~s *nfpl* sights.

alzada [al'θaða] *nf* (*de caballos*) height; (*JUR*) appeal.

alzamiento [alθa'mjento] *nm* (*aumento*) rise, increase; (*acción*) lifting, raising; (*mejor postura*) higher bid; (*rebelión*) rising; (*COM*) fraudulent bankruptcy.

alzar [al'θar] *vt* to lift (up); (*precio, muro*) to raise; (*cuello de abrigo*) to turn up; (*AGR*) to gather in; (*IMPRENTA*) to gather; ~**se** *vr* to get up, rise; (*rebelarse*) to revolt; (*COM*) to go fraudulently bankrupt; (*JUR*) to appeal.

allá [a'ʎa] *ad* (*lugar*) there; (*por ahí*) over there; (*tiempo*) then; ~ **abajo** down there; **más** ~ further on; **más** ~ **de** beyond; ¡ ~ **tu!** that's your problem!

allanar [aʎa'nar] *vt* to flatten, level (out); (*igualar*) to smooth (out); (*fig*) to subdue; (*JUR*) to burgle, break into; ~**se** *vr* to fall down; ~**se a** to submit to, accept.

allegado, a [aʎe'xaðo, a] *a* near, close // *nm/f* relation.

allegar [aʎe'xar] *vt* to gather (together); (*añadir*) to add; ~**se** *vr* to approach.

allí [a'ʎi] *ad* there; ~ **mismo** right there; **por** ~ over there; (*por ese camino*) that way.

ama ['ama] *nf* lady of the house; (*dueña*) owner; (*institutriz*) governess; (*madre adoptiva*) foster mother; ~ **de cría** *o* **de leche** wet-nurse; ~ **de llaves** housekeeper.

amabilidad [amaβili'ðað] *nf* kindness; (*simpatía*) niceness; **amable** *a* kind; nice.

amado, a [a'maðo, a] *nm/f* beloved, sweetheart.

amaestrar [amaes'trar] *vt* to train; (*preparar*) to coach.

amagar [ama'xar] *vt, vi* to threaten; **amago** *nm* threat; (*gesto*) threatening gesture; (*MED*) symptom.

amalgama [amal'xama] *nf* amalgam; **amalgamar** *vt* to amalgamate; (*combinar*) to combine, mix.

amamantar [amaman'tar] *vt* to suckle, nurse.

amanecer [amane'θer] *vi* to dawn // *nm* dawn; **el niño amaneció afiebrado** the child woke up with a fever.

amanerado, a [amane'raðo, a] *a* affected.

amansar [aman'sar] *vt* to tame; (*templar*) to subdue.

amante [a'mante] *a*: ~ **de** fond of // *nm/f* lover.

amapola [ama'pola] *nf* poppy.

amar [a'mar] *vt* to love.

amargado, a [amar'xaðo, a] *a* bitter; **amargar** *vt* to make bitter; (*fig*) to embitter; **amargarse** *vr* to get bitter.

amargo, a [a'marxo, a] *a* bitter; **amargura** *nf* bitterness.

amarillento, a [amari'ʎento, a] *a* yellowish; (*tez*) sallow; **amarillo, a** *a, nm* yellow.

amarrar [ama'rrar] *vt* to moor; (*sujetar*) to tie up.

amartelar [amarte'lar] *vt* to make jealous; (*enamorar*) to win the heart of; ~**se** *vr*: ~**se de** to fall in love with.

amartillar [amarti'ʎar] *vt* = **martillar**.

amasar [ama'sar] *vt* to knead; (*mezclar*) to mix, prepare; (*MED*) to massage; (*confeccionar*) to concoct; **amasijo** *nm* kneading; mixing; (*masa*) dough; (*pasta*) paste; (*fig*) hotchpotch.

amateur ['amatur] *nm/f* amateur.

amatista [ama'tista] *nf* amethyst.

amazona [ama'θona] *nf* horsewoman; **A**~**s** *nm*: **el A**~**s** the Amazon.

ambages [am'baxes] *nmpl*: **sin** ~ in plain language.

ámbar ['ambar] *nm* amber.

ambición [ambi'θjon] *nf* ambition; **ambicionar** *vt* to aspire to; **ambicioso, a** *a* ambitious.

ambidextro, a [ambi'ðekstro, a] *a* ambidextrous.

ambiente [am'bjente] *nm* atmosphere; (*medio*) environment.

ambigüedad [ambixwe'ðað] *nf* ambiguity; **ambiguo, a** *a* ambiguous.

ámbito ['ambito] *nm* compass; (*campo*) field; (*límite*) boundary; (*fig*) scope.

ambos, as ['ambos, as] *apl, pron pl* both.

ambulancia [ambu'lanθja] *nf* ambulance.

ambulante [ambu'lante] *a* walking *cpd,* itinerant.

ambulatorio [ambula'torio] *nm* national health clinic.

amedrentar [ameðren'tar] *vt* to scare.

amén [a'men] *excl* amen; ~ **de** except for.

amenaza [ame'naθa] *nf* threat; **amenazar** *vt, vi* to threaten.

amenguar [amen'xwar] *vt* to diminish; (*fig*) to dishonour.

amenidad [ameni'ðað] *nf* pleasantness.

ameno, a [a'meno, a] *a* pleasant.

América [a'merika] *nf* America; ~ **del Norte/del Sur** North/South America; ~ **Central/Latina** Central/Latin America; **americano, a** *a, nm/f* American // *nf* coat, jacket.

ametralladora [ametraʎa'ðora] *nf* machine gun.

amigable [ami'xaβle] *a* friendly.

amígdala [a'mixðala] *nf* tonsil; **amigdalitis** *nf* tonsillitis.

amigo, a [a'mixo, a] *a* friendly // *nm/f* friend.

amilanar [amila'nar] *vt* to scare.

aminorar [amino'rar] *vt* to diminish; (*reducir*) to reduce.
amistad [amis'taδ] *nf* friendship; ~**es** *nfpl* friends; **amistoso, a** *a* friendly.
amnesia [am'nesja] *nf* amnesia.
amnistía [amnis'tia] *nf* amnesty.
amo ['amo] *nm* owner; (*dueño*) boss; ~ **de casa** householder.
amodorrarse [amoδo'rrarse] *vr* to get sleepy.
amolar [amo'lar] *vt* to sharpen; (*fig*) to bore.
amoldar [amol'dar] *vt* to mould; (*adaptar*) to adapt.
amonestación [amonesta'θjon] *nf* warning; **amonestaciones** *nfpl* marriage banns; **amonestar** *vt* to warn; to publish the banns of.
amontonar [amonto'nar] *vt* to collect, pile up; ~**se** *vr* to crowd together; (*acumularse*) to pile up.
amor [a'mor] *nm* love; (*amante*) lover; **hacer el** ~ to make love; (*cortejar*) to court.
amoratado, a [amora'taδo, a] *a* purple, blue with cold.
amordazar [amorδa'θar] *vt* to muzzle; (*fig*) to gag.
amorío [amo'rio] *nm* (*fam*) love affair.
amoroso, a [amo'roso, a] *a* affectionate, loving.
amortajar [amorta'xar] *vt* to shroud.
amortiguador [amortigwa'δor] *nm* shock absorber; (*parachoques*) bumper; (*silenciador*) silencer; **amortiguar** *vt* to deaden; (*ruido*) to muffle; (*color*) to soften.
amortización [amortiθa'θjon] *nf* redemption, repayment.
amotinar [amoti'nar] *vt* to stir up, incite (to riot); ~**se** *vr* to mutiny.
amparar [ampa'rar] *vt* to protect; ~**se** *vr* to seek protection; (*abrigar*) to shelter; **amparo** *nm* help, protection.
ampliación [amplja'θjon] *nf* enlargement; (*extensión*) extension; **ampliar** *vt* to enlarge; to extend.
amplificación [amplifika'θjon] *nf* enlargement; **amplificador** *nm* amplifier; **amplificar** *vt* to amplify.
amplio, a ['ampljo, a] *a* spacious; (*de falda etc*) full; (*extenso*) extensive; (*ancho*) wide; **amplitud** *nf* spaciousness; extent; (*fig*) amplitude.
ampolla [am'poλa] *nf* blister; (*MED*) ampoule.
amputar [ampu'tar] *vt* to cut off, amputate.
amueblar [amwe'βlar] *vt* to furnish.
amurallar [amura'λar] *vt* to wall up/in.
anacronismo [anakro'nismo] *nm* anachronism.
ánade ['anaδe] *nm* duck.
anadear [anaδe'ar] *vi* to waddle.
anales [a'nales] *nmpl* annals.
analfabetismo [analfaβe'tismo] *nm* illiteracy; **analfabeto, a** *a* illiterate.

análisis [a'nalisis] *nm* analysis.
analizar [anali'θar] *vt* to analyse.
analogía [analo'xia] *nf* analogy.
ananá(s) [ana'na(s)] *nm* pineapple.
anaquel [ana'kel] *nm* shelf.
anarquía [anar'kia] *nf* anarchy; **anarquismo** *nm* anarchism; **anarquista** *nm/f* anarchist.
anatomía [anato'mia] *nf* anatomy.
anciano, a [an'θjano, a] *a* old, aged // *nm/f* old man/woman // *nm* elder.
ancla ['ankla] *nf* anchor; ~**dero** *nm* anchorage; **anclar** *vi* to (drop) anchor.
ancho, a ['antʃo, a] *a* wide; (*falda*) full; (*fig*) liberal // *nm* width; (*FERRO*) gauge; **ponerse** ~ to get conceited; **estar a sus** ~**as** to be at one's ease.
anchoa [an'tʃoa] *nf* anchovy.
anchura [an'tʃura] *nf* width; (*extensión*) wideness; (*fig*) freedom.
andaderas [anda'δeras] *nfpl* baby walker *sg*.
andadura [anda'δura] *nf* gait, pace.
Andalucía [andalu'θia] *nf* Andalusia; **andaluz, a** *a*, *nm/f* Andalusian.
andamio [an'damjo], **andamiaje** [anda-'mjaxe] *nm* scaffold.
andar [an'dar] *vt* to go, cover, travel // *vi* to go, walk, travel; (*funcionar*) to go, work; (*estar*) to be // *nm* walk, gait, pace; ~**se** *vr* to go away; ~ **a pie/a caballo/en bicicleta** to go on foot/on horseback/by bicycle; ¡**anda!**, ¡**andando!** go on!; (*vamos*) come on!; (*bien*) well!; **anda en los 40** he's about 40.
andariego, a [anda'rjexo, a] *a* fond of travelling.
andén [an'den] *nm* (*FERRO*) platform; (*NAUT*) quayside; (*AUTO*) hard shoulder.
Andes ['andes] *nmpl*: **los** ~ the Andes.
Andorra [an'dorra] *nf* Andorra.
andrajo [an'draxo] *nm* rag; ~**so, a** *a* ragged.
andurriales [andu'rrjales] *nmpl* out-of-the-way place *sg*.
anduve *etc vb ver* **andar**.
anécdota [a'nekδota] *nf* anecdote, story.
anegar [ane'xar] *vt* to flood; (*ahogar*) to drown; ~**se** *vr* to drown; (*hundirse*) to sink.
anemia [a'nemja] *nf* anaemia.
anestésico [anes'tesiko] *nm* anaesthetic.
anexar [anek'sar] *vt* to annex; (*documento*) to attach; **anexo, a** *a* attached // *nm* annexe.
anfibio, a [an'fiβjo, a] *a* amphibious // *nm* amphibian.
anfiteatro [anfite'atro] *nm* amphitheatre; (*TEATRO*) dress circle.
anfitrión, ona [anfi'trjon, ona] *nm/f* host.
ángel ['anxel] *nm* angel; **angélico, a**, **angelical** *a* angelic(al).
angina [an'xina] *nf* (*MED*) inflammation of the throat; ~ **de pecho** angina (pectoris).
anglicano, a [angli'kano, a] *a*, *nm/f* Anglican.

angosto, a [an'gosto, a] *a* narrow.
angostura [angos'tura] *nf* narrowness; (*paso*) narrow passage.
anguila [an'gila] *nf* eel; ~**s** *nfpl* slipway *sg*.
ángulo ['angulo] *nm* angle; (*esquina*) corner; (*curva*) bend.
angustia [an'gustja] *nf* anguish; **angustiar** *vt* to distress, grieve.
anhelante [ane'lante] *a* eager; (*deseoso*) longing; **anhelar** *vt* to be eager for; to long for, desire // *vi* to pant, gasp; **anhelo** *nm* eagerness; desire.
anidar [ani'ðar] *vi* to nest.
anillo [a'niʎo] *nm* ring; ~ **de boda** wedding ring.
ánima ['anima] *nf* soul; **las** ~**s** the Angelus (bell) *sg*.
animación [anima'θjon] *nf* liveliness; (*vitalidad*) life; (*actividad*) bustle; **animado, a** *a* lively; (*vivaz*) animated.
animadversión [animaðßer'sjon] *nf* ill-will, antagonism.
animal [ani'mal] *a* animal; (*fig*) stupid // *nm* animal; (*fig*) fool; (*bestia*) brute.
animar [ani'mar] *vt* (*BIO*) to animate, give life to; (*fig*) to liven up, brighten up, cheer up; (*estimular*) to stimulate; ~**se** *vr* to cheer up, feel encouraged; (*decidirse*) to make up one's mind.
ánimo ['animo] *nm* soul, mind; (*valentía*) courage // *excl* cheer up!
animosidad [animosi'ðað] *nf* animosity.
animoso, a [ani'moso, a] *a* brave; (*vivo*) lively.
aniquilar [aniki'lar] *vt* to annihilate, destroy; ~**se** *vr* to be wiped out, disappear; (*empeorarse*) to deteriorate.
anís [a'nis] *nm* aniseed.
aniversario [aniß̩er'sarjo] *nm* anniversary.
anoche [a'notʃe] *ad* last night; **antes de** ~ the night before last.
anochecer [anotʃe'θer] *vi* to get dark // *nm* nightfall, dark.
anomalía [anoma'lia] *nf* anomaly.
anonadamiento [anonaða'mjento] *nm* annihilation; (*desaliento*) discouragement; **anonadar** *vt* to annihilate; to discourage; **anonadarse** *vr* to get discouraged.
anónimo, a [a'nonimo, a] *a* anonymous; (*COM*) limited // *nm* anonymity.
anormal [anor'mal] *a* abnormal.
anotación [anota'θjon] *nf* note.
anotar [ano'tar] *vt* to note down; (*comentar*) to annotate.
ansia ['ansja] *nf* anxiety; (*añoranza*) yearning; **ansiar** *vt* to long for.
ansiedad [ansje'ðað] *nf* anxiety.
ansioso, a [an'sjoso, a] *a* anxious; (*anhelante*) eager.
antagónico, a [anta'ɣoniko, a] *a* antagonistic; (*opuesto*) contrasting; **antagonista** *nm/f* antagonist.
antaño [an'taɲo] *ad* long ago.

Antártico [an'tartiko] *nm*: **el** ~ the Antarctic.
ante ['ante] *prep* before, in the presence of; (*encarado con*) faced with // *nm* suede, buckskin; ~ **todo** above all.
anteanoche [antea'notʃe] *ad* the night before last.
anteayer [antea'jer] *ad* the day before yesterday.
antebrazo [ante'ßraθo] *nm* forearm.
antecedente [anteθe'ðente] *a* previous // *nm* antecedent; ~**s** *nmpl* record *sg*, background *sg*.
anteceder [anteθe'ðer] *vt* to precede, go before.
antecesor, a [anteθe'sor, a] *nm/f* predecessor; (*antepasado*) ancestor.
antedicho, a [ante'ðitʃo, a] *a* aforementioned.
antelación [antela'θjon] *nf*: **con** ~ in advance.
antemano [ante'mano]: **de** ~ *ad* beforehand, in advance.
antena [an'tena] *nf* antenna; (*de televisión etc*) aerial.
anteojo [ante'oxo] *nm* eyeglass; ~**s** *nmpl* spectacles, glasses.
antepasados [antepa'saðos] *nmpl* ancestors.
antepecho [ante'petʃo] *nm* guardrail, parapet; (*repisa*) ledge, sill.
anteponer [antepo'ner] *vt* to place in front; (*fig*) to prefer; ~**se** *vr*: ~**se a** to overcome.
anteproyecto [antepro'jekto] *nm* preliminary sketch; (*fig*) blueprint.
anterior [ante'rjor] *a* preceding, previous; ~**idad** *nf*: **con** ~**idad a** a prior to, before.
antes ['antes] *ad* sooner; (*primero*) first; (*con prioridad*) before; (*hace tiempo*) previously, once; (*más bien*) rather // *prep*: ~ **de** before // *conj*: ~ **(de) que** before; ~ **bien** (but) rather; **dos días** ~ two days before or previously; ~ **muerto que esclavo** better dead than enslaved; **tomo el avión** ~ **que el barco** I take the plane rather than the boat; **cuanto** ~, **lo** ~ **posible** as soon as possible.
antesala [ante'sala] *nf* anteroom.
antibiótico [anti'ßjotiko] *nm* antibiotic.
anticipación [antiθipa'θjon] *nf* anticipation; (*COM*) advance; **con 10 minutos de** ~ 10 minutes early; **anticipado, a** *a* (in) advance.
anticipar [antiθi'par] *vt* to anticipate; (*adelantar*) to bring forward; (*COM*) to advance; ~**se** *vr*: ~**se a su época** to be ahead of one's time.
anticipo [anti'θipo] *nm* = **anticipación**.
anticonceptivo, a [antikonθep'tißo, a] *a*, *nm* contraceptive.
anticongelante [antikonxe'lante] *nm* antifreeze.
anticuado, a [anti'kwaðo, a] *a* out-of-date, old-fashioned; (*desusado*) obsolete.
anticuario [anti'kwarjo] *nm* antique dealer.

antídoto [an'tiðoto] *nm* antidote.
antifaz [anti'faθ] *nm* mask; (*velo*) veil.
antigualla [anti'ɣwaʎa] *nf* antique; (*reliquia*) relic.
antiguamente [antiɣwa'mente] *ad* formerly; (*hace mucho tiempo*) long ago.
antigüedad [antiɣwe'ðað] *nf* antiquity; (*artículo*) antique; (*rango*) seniority; **antiguo, a** *a* old, ancient; (*que fue*) former.
antílope [an'tilope] *nm* antelope.
antillano, a [anti'ʎano. a] *a, nm/f* West Indian.
Antillas [an'tiʎas] *nfpl*: **las** ~ the West Indies.
antipara [anti'para] *nf* screen.
antipatía [antipa'tia] *nf* antipathy, dislike; **antipático, a** *a* disagreeable, unpleasant.
antisemita [antise'mita] *nm/f* antisemite.
antítesis [an'titesis] *nf* antithesis.
antojadizo, a [antoxa'ðiθo, a] *a* capricious.
antojarse [anto'xarse] *vr* (*desear*): **se me antoja comprarlo** I have a mind to buy it; (*pensar*): **se me antoja que** I have a feeling that.
antojo [an'toxo] *nm* caprice, whim; (*rosa*) birthmark; (*lunar*) mole.
antología [antolo'xia] *nf* anthology.
antorcha [an'tortʃa] *nf* torch.
antro ['antro] *nm* cavern.
antropófago, a [antro'pofaɣo, a] *a, nm/f* cannibal.
antropología [antropolo'xia] *nf* anthropology.
anual [a'nwal] *a* annual.
anualidad [anwali'ðað] *nf* annuity.
anuario [a'nwarjo] *nm* yearbook.
anublar [anu'ßlar] *vt* to cloud; (*oscurecer*) to darken; ~**se** *vr* to become cloudy, cloud over; (*BOT*) to wither.
anudar [anu'ðar] *vt* to knot, tie; (*unir*) to join; ~**se** *vr* to get tied up.
anulación [anula'θjon] *nf* annulment; (*cancelación*) cancellation; **anular** *vt* to annul; to cancel; (*revocar*) to revoke, repeal // *nm* ring finger.
anunciación [anunθja'θjon] *nf* announcement; **anunciar** *vt* to announce; (*proclamar*) to proclaim; (*COM*) to advertise.
anuncio [a'nunθjo] *nm* announcement; (*señal*) sign; (*COM*) advertisement; (*cartel*) poster.
anzuelo [an'θwelo] *nm* hook; (*para pescar*) fish hook.
añadidura [aɲaði'ðura] *nf* addition, extra; **por** ~ besides, in addition.
añadir [aɲa'ðir] *vt* to add.
añejo, a [a'ɲexo, a] *a* old.
añicos [a'ɲikos] *nmpl*: **hacer** ~ to smash, shatter.
año ['aɲo] *nm* year; **¡Feliz A~ Nuevo!** Happy New Year!; **tener 15** ~**s** to be 15 (years old); **los** ~**s 60** the sixties; ~ **bisiesto/escolar** leap/school year.

añoranza [aɲo'ranθa] *nf* nostalgia; (*anhelo*) longing.
apacentar [apaθen'tar] *vt* to pasture, graze.
apacible [apa'θißle] *a* gentle, mild.
apaciguar [apaθi'ɣwar] *vt* to pacify, calm (down).
apadrinar [apaðri'nar] *vt* to sponsor, support; (*REL*) to act as godfather to.
apagado, a [apa'ɣaðo, a] *a* out; (*volcán*) extinct; (*cal*) slaked; (*color*) dull; (*voz*) quiet, timid; (*sonido*) muted, muffled; (*apático*) listless.
apagar [apa'ɣar] *vt* to put out; (*sonido*) to silence, muffle; (*sed*) to quench; (*fig*) to kill.
apagón [apa'ɣon] *nm* blackout, power cut.
apalabrar [apala'ßrar] *vt* to agree to; (*obrero*) to engage.
apalear [apale'ar] *vt* to beat, thrash; (*AGR*) to winnow.
apañar [apa'ɲar] *vt* to pick up; (*asir*) to take hold of, grasp; (*vestir*) to dress up; (*reparar*) to mend, patch up; ~**se** *vr* to manage, get along.
aparador [apara'ðor] *nm* sideboard; (*escaparate*) shop window.
aparato [apa'rato] *nm* apparatus; (*máquina*) machine; (*doméstico*) appliance; (*boato*) ostentation; ~**so, a** *a* showy, ostentatious.
aparcamiento [aparka'mjento] *nm* car park.
aparcar [apar'kar] *vt, vi* to park.
aparecer [apare'θer] *vi*, ~**se** *vr* to appear.
aparejado, a [apare'xaðo, a] *a* fit, suitable.
aparejar [apare'xar] *vt* to prepare; (*caballo*) to saddle, harness; (*NAUT*) to fit out, rig out; **aparejo** *nm* preparation; harness; rigging; (*de poleas*) block and tackle.
aparentar [aparen'tar] *vt* to feign; (*parecer*) to look, seem (to be).
aparente [apa'rente] *a* apparent; (*adecuado*) suitable.
aparición [apari'θjon] *nf* appearance; (*de libro*) publication.
apariencia [apa'rjenθja] *nf* (outward) appearance; **en** ~ outwardly, seemingly.
apartado, a [apar'taðo, a] *a* separate; (*lejano*) remote // *nm* post office box; (*tipográfico*) paragraph.
apartamento [aparta'mento] *nm* apartment, flat.
apartamiento [aparta'mjento] *nm* separation; (*aislamiento*) remoteness; (*AM*) apartment, flat.
apartar [apar'tar] *vt* to separate; (*quitar*) to remove; (*MINEROLOGÍA*) to extract; ~**se** *vr* to separate, part; (*irse*) to move away, keep away; **aparte** *ad* (*separadamente*) separately; (*además*) besides // *nm* aside; (*tipográfico*) new paragraph.
apasionado, a [apasjo'naðo, a] *a* passionate; biassed, prejudiced.

apasionar [apasjo'nar] vt to arouse passion in; ~se vr to get excited.
apatía [apa'tia] nf apathy.
apático, a [a'patiko, a] a apathetic.
apdo nm abr de **apartado (de correos)**.
apeadero [apea'ðero] nm halt, wayside station.
apearse [ape'arse] vr to dismount; (bajarse) to get down/out.
apedrear [apeðre'ar] vt to stone.
apegarse [ape'ɣarse] vr: ~se a to become attached to; **apego** nm attachment, fondness.
apelación [apela'θjon] nf appeal.
apelante [ape'lante] nm/f appellant.
apelar [ape'lar] vi to appeal; ~ a to resort to.
apellidar [apeʎi'ðar] vt to call, name; ~se vr to be called; **apellido** nm surname, name.
apenar [ape'nar] vt to grieve, trouble; ~se vr to grieve.
apenas [a'penas] ad scarcely, hardly // conj as soon as, no sooner.
apéndice [a'pendiθe] nm appendix; **apendicitis** nf appendicitis.
apercibir [aperθi'ßir] vt to prepare; (avisar) to warn; (JUR) to summon; (AM) to notice, see; ~se vr to get ready.
aperitivo [aperi'tißo] nm aperitif.
apertura [aper'tura] nf opening.
apesadumbrar [apesaðum'brar] vt to grieve, sadden; ~se vr to distress o.s.
apestar [apes'tar] vt to infect // vi to stink.
apetecer [apete'θer] vt: ¿te apetece una tortilla? do you fancy an omelette?; **apetecible** a desirable; (llamativo) attractive.
apetito [ape'tito] nm appetite; ~so, a a appetizing; (fig) tempting.
apiadarse [apja'ðarse] vr: ~ de to take pity on.
ápice ['apiθe] nm apex; (fig) whit, iota.
apio ['apjo] nm celery.
aplacar [apla'kar] vt to placate; ~se vr to calm down.
aplanamiento [aplana'mjento] nm smoothing, levelling.
aplanar [apla'nar] vt to smooth, level; (allanar) to roll flat, flatten.
aplastar [aplas'tar] vt to squash (flat); (fig) to crush.
aplaudir [aplau'ðir] vt to applaud.
aplauso [a'plauso] nm applause; (fig) approval, acclaim.
aplazamiento [aplaθa'mjento] nm postponement, adjournment; **aplazar** vt to postpone, defer.
aplicación [aplika'θjon] nf application; (esfuerzo) effort.
aplicado, a [apli'kaðo, a] a diligent, hard-working.
aplicar [apli'kar] vt (ejecutar) to apply; ~se vr to apply o.s.

aplomo [a'plomo] nm aplomb, self-assurance.
apocado, a [apo'kaðo, a] a timid.
apocamiento [apoka'mjento] nm timidity; (depresión) depression.
apocar [apo'kar] vt to reduce; ~se vr to feel small, feel humiliated.
apodar [apo'ðar] vt to nickname.
apoderado [apoðe'raðo] nm agent, representative; **apoderar** vt to authorize, empower; (JUR) to grant (a) power of attorney to; **apoderarse** vr: **apoderarse de** to take possession of.
apodo [a'poðo] nm nickname.
apogeo [apo'xeo] nm peak, summit.
apología [apolo'xia] nf eulogy; (defensa) defence.
apoplejía [aple'xia] nf apoplexy, stroke.
aporrear [aporre'ar] vt to beat (up); **aporreo** nm beating.
aportar [apor'tar] vt to contribute // vi to reach port; ~se vr (AM) to arrive, come.
aposentar [aposen'tar] vt to lodge, put up; **aposento** nm lodging; (habitación) room.
apostar [apos'tar] vt to bet, stake; (destinar) to station, post // vi to bet.
apostilla [apos'tiʎa] nf note, comment.
apóstol [a'postol] nm apostle.
apóstrofe [a'postrofe] nm insult; (reprimenda) reprimand.
apóstrofo [a'postrofo] nm apostrophe.
apostura [apos'tura] nf neatness, elegance.
apoyar [apo'jar] vt to lean, rest; (fig) to support, back; ~se vr: ~se en to lean on; **apoyo** nm support, backing; (sostén) prop.
apreciable [apre'θjaßle] a considerable; (fig) esteemed.
apreciación [apreθja'θjon] nf appreciation; (COM) valuation; **apreciar** vt to evaluate, assess; (COM) to appreciate, value.
aprecio [a'preθjo] nm valuation, estimate; (fig) appreciation.
aprehender [apreen'der] vt to apprehend, seize; **aprehensión** nf detention, capture.
apremiante [apre'mjante] a urgent, pressing; **apremiar** vt to compel, force // vi to be urgent, press; **apremio** nm compulsion; urgency.
aprender [apren'der] vt, vi to learn.
aprendiz, a [apren'diθ, a] nm/f apprentice; (principiante) learner; ~aje nm apprenticeship.
aprensión [apren'sjon] nm apprehension, fear; (delicadeza) squeamishness; **aprensivo, a** a apprehensive; (nervioso) nervous, timid.
apresar [apre'sar] vt to seize; (capturar) to capture.
aprestar [apres'tar] vt to prepare, get ready; (TEC) to prime, size; ~se vr to get ready.
apresurado, a [apresu'raðo, a] a hurried,

hasty; **apresuramiento** *nm* hurry, haste.
apresurar [apresu'rar] *vt* to hurry, accelerate; ~**se** *vr* to hurry, make haste.
apretado, a [apre'taðo, a] *a* tight; (*escritura*) cramped; (*difícil*) difficult; (*fam*) stingy.
apretar [apre'tar] *vt* to squeeze, press; (*TEC*) to tighten; (*presionar*) to press together, pack // *vi* to be too tight; (*insistir*) to insist.
apretón [apre'ton] *nm* squeeze; (*abrazo*) hug; (*aglomeración*) crush; (*dificultad*) difficulty, jam; (*carrera*) dash, sprint; ~ **de manos** handshake; **apretura** *nf* squeeze; hug; crush; difficulty, jam; (*escasez*) scarcity.
aprieto [a'prjeto] *nm* squeeze, press; (*dificultad*) difficulty, jam.
aprisionar [aprisjo'nar] *vt* to imprison.
aprobación [aproβa'θjon] *nf* approval; (*de examen*) pass; (*nota*) pass mark; **aprobar** *vt* to approve (of); to pass // *vi* to pass.
apropiación [apropja'θjon] *nf* appropriation.
apropiado, a [apro'pjaðo, a] *a* appropriate.
apropiar [apro'pjar] *vt* to adapt, make fit; ~**se** *vr*: ~**se de** to appropriate.
aprovechado, a [aproβe'tʃaðo, a] *a* diligent, hardworking; (*económico*) thrifty; (*pey*) unscrupulous, grasping; **aprovechamiento** *nm* use, exploitation.
aprovechar [aproβe'tʃar] *vt* to use, exploit, profit from; (*sacar partido de*) to take advantage of // *vi* to progress, improve; ~**se** *vr*: ~**se de** to make use of, take advantage of; ¡**que aproveche!** enjoy your meal!
aproximación [aproksima'θjon] *nf* approximation; (*cercanía*) nearness; (*lotería*) consolation prize; **aproximado, a** *a* approximate; **aproximar** *vt* to bring nearer; **aproximarse** *vr* to come near, approach.
aptitud [apti'tuð] *nf* aptitude; (*idoneidad*) suitability.
apto, a ['apto, a] *a* suitable.
apuesto, a [a'pwesto, a] *a* neat, elegant // *nf* bet, wager.
apuntador [apunta'ðor] *nm* prompter.
apuntalar [apunta'lar] *vt* to prop up.
apuntar [apun'tar] *vt* (*con arma*) to aim at; (*con dedo*) to point at *or* to; (*anotar*) to note (down); (*TEATRO*) to prompt; (*dinero*) to stake; ~**se** *vr* to score a point.
apunte [a'punte] *nm* note.
apuñalar [apuɲa'lar] *vt* to stab.
apurado, a [apu'raðo, a] *a* needy; (*difícil*) difficult, dangerous; (*agotado*) exhausted; (*AM*) hurried, rushed.
apurar [apu'rar] *vt* (*purificar*) to purify; (*agotar*) to drain; (*recursos*) to use up; (*molestar*) to annoy; ~**se** *vr* to worry; (*AM*) to hurry.
apuro [a'puro] *nm* (*aprieto*) fix, jam; (*escasez*) want, hardship; (*aflicción*) distress; (*AM*) haste, urgency.

aquejar [ake'xar] *vt* to distress, grieve; (*MED*) to afflict.
aquel, aquella, aquellos, as [a'kel, a'keʎa, a'keʎos, as] *det* that; (*pl*) those.
aquél, aquélla, aquéllos, as [a'kel, a'keʎa, a'keʎos, as] *pron* that (one); (*pl*) those (ones).
aquello [a'keʎo] *pron* that, that business.
aquí [a'ki] *ad* (*lugar*) here; (*tiempo*) now; ~ **arriba** up here; ~ **mismo** right here; ~ **yace** here lies; **de** ~ **a siete días** a week from now.
aquietar [akje'tar] *vt* to quieten (down), calm (down).
árabe ['araβe] *a* Arab, Arabian, Arabic // *nm/f* Arab // *nm* (*lengua*) Arabic.
Arabia Saudita [araβjasau'ðita] *nf* Saudi Arabia.
arado [a'raðo] *nm* plough.
aragonés, esa [arayo'nes, esa] *a, nm/f* Aragonese.
arancel [aran'θel] *nm* tariff, duty; ~ **de aduanas** customs duty.
araña [a'raɲa] *nf* (*ZOOL*) spider; (*de luces*) chandelier.
arañar [ara'ɲar] *vt* to scratch.
arañazo [ara'ɲaθo] *nm* scratch.
arar [a'rar] *vt* to plough, till.
arbitrador, a [arβitra'ðor, a] *nm/f* arbiter.
arbitraje [arβi'traxe] *nm* arbitration.
arbitrar [arβi'trar] *vt* to arbitrate in; (*DEPORTE*) to referee // *vi* to arbitrate.
arbitrariedad [arβitrarje'ðað] *nf* arbitrariness; (*acto*) arbitrary act; **arbitrario, a** *a* arbitrary.
arbitrio [ar'βitrjo] *nm* free will; (*JUR*) adjudication, decision.
árbitro ['arβitro] *nm* arbitrator; (*DEPORTE*) referee; (*TENIS*) umpire.
árbol ['arβol] *nm* (*BOT*) tree; (*NAUT*) mast; (*TEC*) axle, shaft; **arbolado, a** *a* wooded, tree-lined // *nm* woodland.
arboladura [arβola'ðura] *nf* rigging; **arbolar** *vt* to hoist, raise; **arbolarse** *vr* to rear up.
arboleda [arβo'leða] *nf* grove, plantation.
arbusto [ar'βusto] *nm* bush, shrub.
arca ['arka] *nf* chest, box; (*caja fuerte*) strongbox.
arcada [ar'kaða] *nf* arcade; (*de puente*) arch, span; ~**s** *nfpl* retching *sg*.
arcaduz [arka'ðuθ] *nm* pipe, conduit.
arcaico, a [ar'kaiko, a] *a* archaic.
arce ['arθe] *nm* maple tree.
arcediano [arθe'ðjano] *nm* archdeacon.
arcilla [ar'θiʎa] *nf* clay.
arco ['arko] *nm* arch; (*MAT*) arc; (*MIL, MUS*) bow; ~ **iris** rainbow.
archipiélago [artʃi'pjelayo] *nm* archipelago.
archivar [artʃi'βar] *vt* to file (away); **archivo** *nm* archive(s) (*pl*).
arder [ar'ðer] *vi, vt* to burn.
ardid [ar'ðið] *nm* ruse.

ardiente [ar'ðjente] a burning; (apasionado) ardent.

ardilla [ar'ðiʎa] nf squirrel.

ardor [ar'ðor] nm (calor) heat, warmth; (fig) ardour; ~ **de estómago** heartburn; ~**oso, a** a = **ardiente**.

arduo, a ['arðwo, a] a arduous.

área ['area] nf area; (DEPORTE) penalty area.

arena [a'rena] nf sand; (de una lucha) arena; (MED) stone.

arenal [are'nal] nm sandy ground; (arena movediza) quicksand.

arengar [aren'gar] vt to harangue.

arenisco, a [are'nisko, a] a sandy // nf sandstone; (cascajo) grit.

arenoso, a [are'noso, a] a sandy.

arenque [a'renke] nm herring.

arete [a'rete] nm earring.

argamasa [arɣa'masa] nf mortar, plaster; **argamasar** vt to mortar, plaster.

Argel [ar'xel] n Algiers; ~**ia** nf Algeria; **argelino, a** a, nm/f Algerian.

argentino, a [arxen'tino, a] a Argentinian; (de plata) silvery // nm/f Argentinian // nf: **A**~**a** Argentina.

argolla [ar'ɣoʎa] nf (large) ring; (juego) croquet.

argot [ar'ɣo] nm slang.

argucia [ar'ɣuθja] nf subtlety, sophistry.

argüir [ar'ɣwir] vt to deduce; (discutir) to argue; (indicar) to indicate, imply; (censurar) to reproach // vi to argue.

argumentación [arɣumenta'θjon] nf (line of) argument; **argumentar** vt, vi to argue.

argumento [arɣu'mento] nm argument; (de obra) plot.

aria ['arja] nf aria.

aridez [ari'ðeθ] nf aridity, dryness.

árido, a ['ariðo, a] a arid, dry; ~**s** nmpl dry goods.

Aries ['arjes] nm Aries.

ariete [a'rjete] nm battering ram.

ario, a ['arjo, a] a Aryan.

arisco, a [a'risko, a] a surly; (insociable) unsociable.

aristócrata [aris'tokrata] nm/f aristocrat.

aritmética [arit'metika] nf arithmetic.

arma ['arma] nf arm; ~**s** nfpl arms; ~ **blanca** blade, knife; (espada) sword; ~ **de fuego** firearm; ~**s cortas** small arms.

armadillo [arma'ðiʎo] nm armadillo.

armado, a [ar'maðo, a] a armed; (TEC) reinforced // nf armada; (flota) fleet.

armadura [arma'ðura] nf (MIL) armour; (TEC) framework; (ZOOL) skeleton; (FÍSICA) armature.

armamento [arma'mento] nm armament; (NAUT) fitting-out.

armar [ar'mar] vt (soldado) to arm; (máquina) to assemble; (navío) to fit out; ~ **la**, ~ **un lío** to start a row.

armario [ar'marjo] nm wardrobe.

armatoste [arma'toste] nm large useless object, contraption.

armazón [arma'θon] nf body, chassis; (de mueble etc) frame; (ARQ) skeleton.

armería [arme'ria] nf (museo) military museum; (tienda) gunsmith's.

armiño [ar'miɲo] nm stoat; (piel) ermine.

armisticio [armis'tiθjo] nm armistice.

armonía [armo'nia] nf harmony.

armónica [ar'monika] nf harmonica.

armonioso, a [armo'njoso, a] a harmonious.

arnés [ar'nes] nm armour; **arneses** nmpl harness sg.

aro ['aro] nm ring; (tejo) quoit; (pendiente) earring.

aroma [a'roma] nm aroma.

aromático, a [aro'matiko, a] a aromatic.

arpa ['arpa] nf harp.

arpía [ar'pia] nf shrew.

arpista [ar'pista] nm/f harpist.

arpón [ar'pon] nm harpoon.

arquear [arke'ar] vt to arch, bend; ~**se** vr to arch, bend; **arqueo** nm (gen) arching, curve; (de navío) tonnage.

arqueología [arkeolo'xia] nf archaeology; **arqueólogo, a** nm/f archaeologist.

arquero [ar'kero] nm archer, bowman.

arquetipo [arke'tipo] nm archetype.

arquitecto [arki'tekto] nm architect; **arquitectura** nf architecture.

arrabal [arra'ßal] nm suburb; (AM) slum.

arraigado, a [arrai'ɣaðo, a] a deep-rooted; (fig) established.

arraigar [arrai'ɣar] vt to establish // vi, ~**se** vr to take root.

arrancar [arran'kar] vt (sacar) to pull up, extract, pull out; (separar) to snatch (away), wrest; (fig) to extract // vi to start, pull out.

arranque [a'rranke] nm sudden start; (AUTO) start; (fig) fit, outburst.

arras ['arras] nfpl pledge sg, security sg.

arrasar [arra'sar] vt (aplanar) to level, flatten; (destruir) to demolish; (llenar) to fill up // vi to clear.

arrastrado, a [arras'traðo, a] a poor, wretched; (AM) servile.

arrastrar [arras'trar] vt to drag (along); (fig) to drag down, degrade; (suj: agua, viento) to carry away // vi to drag, trail on the ground; ~**se** vr to crawl; (fig) to grovel; **llevar algo arrastrado** to drag sth along.

arrastre [a'rrastre] nm drag, dragging; (DEPORTE) crawl.

arrayán [arra'jan] nm myrtle.

arrear [arre'ar] vt to drive, urge on; (enganchar) to harness // vi to hurry along; ¡**arre(a)!** get up!, gee up!

arrebatado, a [arreßa'taðo, a] a rash, impetuous; (repentino) sudden, hasty.

arrebatar [arreßa'tar] vt to snatch (away), seize; (fig) to captivate; ~**se** vr to get carried away, get excited.

arrebato [arre'ßato] nm fit of rage, fury; (éxtasis) rapture.

arreglado, a [arre'ɣlaðo, a] a (ordenado)

neat, orderly; (*moderado*) moderate, reasonable.

arreglar [arre'ɣlar] *vt* (*poner orden*) to tidy up; (*algo roto*) to fix, repair; (*problema*) to solve; (*MUS*) to arrange; ~**se** *vr* to reach an understanding; **arreglárselas** (*fam*) to get by, manage.

arreglo [a'rreɣlo] *nm* settlement; (*orden*) order; (*acuerdo*) agreement; (*MUS*) arrangement, setting.

arremangar [arreman'gar] *vt* to roll up, turn up; ~**se** *vr* to roll up one's sleeves.

arremeter [arreme'ter] *vt* to attack, assault.

arrendador, a [arrenda'ðor, a] *nm/f* landlord/lady; (*inquilino*) tenant.

arrendamiento [arrenda'mjento] *nm* letting; (*alquilar*) hiring; (*contrato*) lease; (*alquiler*) rent; **arrendar** *vt* to let, lease; to rent; **arrendatario, a** *nm/f* tenant.

arreo [a'rreo] *nm* adornment; ~**s** *nmpl* harness *sg*, trappings.

arrepentimiento [arrepenti'mjento] *nm* regret, repentance.

arrepentirse [arrepen'tirse] *vr*: ~ **de** to regret, repent of.

arrestar [arres'tar] *vt* to arrest; (*encarcelar*) to imprison; **arresto** *nm* arrest; (*MIL*) detention; (*audacia*) boldness, daring; **arresto domiciliario** house arrest.

arriar [a'rrjar] *vt* (*velas, bandera*) to lower, strike; (*un cable*) to pay out; ~**se** *vr* to flood.

arriba [a'rriβa] *ad* (*posición*) above, overhead, on top; (*en casa*) upstairs; (*dirección*) up, upwards; ~ **de** above, higher (up) than; ~ **del todo** at the very top; **el piso de** ~ the flat upstairs; **de** ~ **abajo** from top to bottom; **calle** ~ up the street; **lo** ~ **mencionado** the aforementioned; ~ **de 20 pesetas** more than 20 pesetas; ¡~ **las manos!** hands up!

arribar [arri'βar] *vi* to put into port; (*llegar*) to arrive.

arribista [arri'βista] *nm/f* parvenu/e, upstart.

arriendo [a'rrjendo] *nm* = **arrendamiento**.

arriero [a'rrjero] *nm* muleteer.

arriesgado, a [arrjes'ɣaðo, a] *a* (*peligroso*) risky; (*audaz*) bold, daring; **arriesgar** *vt* to risk; (*poner en peligro*) to endanger; **arriesgarse** *vr* to take a risk.

arrimar [arri'mar] *vt* (*acercar*) to bring close; (*poner de lado*) to set aside; ~**se** *vr* to come close *or* closer; ~**se a** to lean on; **arrimo** *nm* approach; (*fig*) support.

arrinconado, a [arrinko'naðo, a] *a* forgotten, neglected; **arrinconar** *vt* to put in a corner; (*fig*) to put on one side; (*abandonar*) to push aside; **arrinconarse** *vr* to withdraw from the world.

arrodillarse [arroði'ʎarse] *vr* to kneel, kneel down.

arrogancia [arro'ɣanθja] *nf* arrogance; **arrogante** *a* arrogant.

arrojar [arro'xar] *vt* to throw, hurl; (*humo*) to emit, give out; (*COM*) to yield, produce; ~**se** *vr* to throw *or* hurl o.s.

arrojo [a'rroxo] *nm* daring.

arrollador, a [arro/a'ðor, a] *a* crushing, overwhelming.

arropar [arro'par] *vt* to cover, wrap up; ~**se** *vr* to wrap o.s. up.

arrope [a'rrope] *nm* syrup.

arrostrar [arros'trar] *vt* to face (up to); ~**se** *vr* to rush into the fight.

arroyo [a'rrojo] *nm* stream; (*de la calle*) gutter.

arroz [a'rroθ] *nm* rice; ~ **con leche** rice pudding.

arruga [a'rruɣa] *nf* fold; (*de cara*) wrinkle; (*de vestido*) crease; **arrugar** *vt* to fold; to wrinkle; to crease; **arrugarse** *vr* to get creased.

arruinar [arrwi'nar] *vt* to ruin, wreck; ~**se** *vr* to be ruined.

arrullar [arru'ʎar] *vi* to coo // *vt* to lull to sleep.

arsenal [arse'nal] *nm* naval dockyard; (*MIL*) arsenal.

arsénico [ar'seniko] *nm* arsenic.

arte ['arte] *nm* (*gen m en sg y siempre f en pl*) art; (*maña*) skill, guile; ~**s** *nfpl* arts.

artefacto [arte'fakto] *nm* appliance; (*ARQUEOLOGÍA*) artefact.

artejo [ar'texo] *nm* knuckle.

arteria [ar'terja] *nf* artery.

artesanía [artesa'nia] *nf* craftsmanship; (*artículos*) handicrafts *pl*; **artesano** *nm* artisan, craftsman.

ártico, a ['artiko, a] *a* Arctic // *nm*: **el A**~ the Arctic.

articulación [artikula'θjon] *nf* articulation; (*MED, TEC*) joint; **articulado, a** *a* articulated; jointed; **articular** *vt* to articulate; to join together.

artículo [ar'tikulo] *nm* article; (*cosa*) thing, article; ~**s** *nmpl* goods.

artífice [ar'tifiθe] *nm* artist, craftsman; (*fig*) architect.

artificial [artifi'θjal] *a* artificial.

artificio [arti'fiθjo] *nm* art, skill; (*artesanía*) craftsmanship; (*astucia*) cunning; ~**so, a** *a* skilful, clever; cunning.

artillería [artiʎe'ria] *nf* artillery.

artillero [arti'ʎero] *nm* artilleryman, gunner.

artimaña [arti'maɲa] *nf* trap, snare; (*astucia*) cunning.

artista [ar'tista] *nm/f* (*pintor*) artist, painter; (*TEATRO*) artist, artiste; **artístico, a** *a* artistic.

artritis [ar'tritis] *nf* arthritis.

arzobispo [arθo'βispo] *nm* archbishop.

as [as] *nm* ace.

asa ['asa] *nf* handle; (*fig*) lever.

asado [a'saðo] *nm* roast (meat).

asador [asa'ðor] *nm* spit.

asalariado, a [asala'rjaðo, a] *a* paid, wage-earning // *nm/f* wage earner.

asaltabancos [asalta'bankos] *nm inv* bank robber.

asaltador, a [asalta'ðor, a], **asaltante** [asal'tante] *nm/f* assailant; **asaltar** *vt* to attack, assault; (*fig*) to assail; **asalto** *nm* attack, assault; (*DEPORTE*) round.

asamblea [asam'blea] *nf* assembly; (*reunión*) meeting.

asar [a'sar] *vt* to roast.

asbesto [as'ßesto] *nm* asbestos.

ascendencia [asθen'denθja] *nf* ancestry; (*AM*) ascendancy.

ascender [asθen'der] *vi* (*subir*) to ascend, rise; (*ser promovido*) to gain promotion // *vt* to promote; ~ **a** to amount to; **ascendiente** *nm* ascendency, influence // *nm/f* ancestor.

ascensión [asθen'sjon] *nf* ascent; **la A**~ the Ascension.

ascensionista [asθensjo'nista] *nm/f* balloonist.

ascenso [as'θenso] *nm* ascent; (*promoción*) promotion.

ascensor [asθen'sor] *nm* lift, elevator.

ascético, a [as'θetiko, a] *a* ascetic.

asco ['asko] *nm* loathing, disgust; (*cosa*) loathsome thing; **el ajo me da** ~ I hate *or* loathe garlic.

ascua ['askwa] *nf* ember.

aseado, a [ase'aðo, a] *a* clean; (*arreglado*) tidy; (*pulcro*) smart; **asear** *vt* to clean, wash; to tidy (up); (*adornar*) to adorn.

asediar [ase'ðjar] *vt* to besiege, lay siege to; (*fig*) to chase, pester; **asedio** *nm* siege; (*COM*) run.

asegurado, a [aseχu'raðo, a] *a* insured; **asegurador, a** *nm/f* insurer; underwriter.

asegurar [aseχu'rar] *vt* (*consolidar*) to secure, fasten; (*dar garantía de*) to guarantee; (*preservar*) to safeguard; (*afirmar, dar por cierto*) to assure, affirm; (*tranquilizar*) to reassure; (*tomar un seguro*) to insure; ~**se** *vr* to assure o.s., make sure.

asemejarse [aseme'xarse] *vr* to be alike; ~ **a** to be like, resemble.

asentado, a [asen'taðo, a] *a* established, settled.

asentar [asen'tar] *vt* (*sentar*) to seat, sit down; (*poner*) to place, establish; (*alisar*) to level, smooth down *or* out; (*anotar*) to note down; (*afirmar*) to affirm, assert; (*afinar*) to sharpen, hone // *vi* to be suitable, suit.

asentir [asen'tir] *vi* to assent, agree.

aseo [a'seo] *nm* cleanliness; ~**s** *nmpl* toilet *sg*, cloakroom *sg*.

asequible [ase'kißle] *a* attainable, available.

aserradero [aserra'ðero] *nm* sawmill; **aserrar** *vt* to saw.

aserrín [ase'rrin] *nm* sawdust.

asesinar [asesi'nar] *vt* to murder; (*POL*) to assassinate; (*fig*) to pester; **asesinato** *nm* murder; assassination.

asesino, a [ase'sino, a] *nm/f* murderer, killer; (*POL*) assassin.

asesor, a [ase'sor, a] *nm/f* adviser, consultant.

asfalto [as'falto] *nm* asphalt.

asfixia [as'fiksja] *nf* suffocation.

asfixiar [asfik'sjar] *vt*, ~**se** *vr* to asphyxiate, suffocate.

asgo *etc vb ver* **asir**.

así [a'si] *ad* (*de esta manera*) so, in this way, like this, thus; (*aunque*) although; (*tan luego como*) as soon as; ~ **que** so, therefore; ~ **como** as well as; ~ **y todo** even so; ¿**no es** ~**?** isn't it?, didn't you? *etc*.

Asia ['asja] *nf* Asia; **asiático, a** *a* Asiatic, Asian.

asidero [asi'ðero] *nm* handle.

asiduidad [asiðwi'ðað] *nf* assiduousness; **asiduo, a** *a* assiduous; (*frecuente*) frequent // *nm/f* regular (customer).

asiento [a'sjento] *nm* (*mueble*) seat, chair; (*de coche, en tribunal etc*) seat; (*localidad*) seat, place; (*fundamento*) site; (*colocación*) establishment; (*depósito*) sediment; (*cordura*) good sense; ~ **delantero/trasero** front/back seat.

asignación [asiχna'θjon] *nf* (*atribución*) assignment; (*reparto*) allocation; (*cita*) appointment; (*sueldo*) salary; **asignar** *vt* to assign, allocate.

asignatura [asiχna'tura] *nf* subject.

asilo [a'silo] *nm* (*refugio*) asylum, refuge; (*establecimiento*) home, institution.

asimilación [asimila'θjon] *nf* assimilation.

asimilar [asimi'lar] *vt* to assimilate; ~**se** *vr*: ~**se a** to resemble; (*incorporarse*) to become assimilated to.

asimismo [asi'mismo] *ad* in the same way, likewise.

asir [a'sir] *vt* to seize, grasp.

asistencia [asis'tenθja] *nf* audience; (*MED*) attendance; (*ayuda*) assistance; **asistir** *vt* to assist // *vi* to attend, be present.

asma ['asma] *nf* asthma.

asno ['asno] *nm* donkey; (*fig*) ass.

asociación [asoθja'θjon] *nf* association; (*COM*) partnership; ~ **aduanera** customs union; **asociado, a** *a* associate // *nm/f* associate; partner.

asociar [aso'θjar] *vt* to combine.

asolear [asole'ar] *vt* to put in the sun; ~**se** *vr* to sunbathe.

asomar [aso'mar] *vt* to show, stick out // *vi* to appear; ~**se** *vr* to appear, show up; ~ **la cabeza por la ventana** to put one's head out of the window.

asombrar [asom'brar] *vt* (*causar admiración, sorpresa*) to amaze, astonish; (*asustar*) to frighten; (*dar sombra a*) to shade; ~**se** *vr* to be amazed; to be frightened; **asombro** *nm* amazement, astonishment; fright; **asombroso, a** *a* astonishing, amazing.

asomo [a'somo] *nm* hint, sign; (*apariencia*) appearance.

aspa ['aspa] *nf* (*cruz*) cross; (*de molino*) sail.

aspar [as'par] vt to reel, wind; (fig) to vex, annoy.

aspaviento [aspa'ßjento] nm exaggerated display of feeling; (fam) fuss.

aspecto [as'pekto] nm (apariencia) look, appearance; (fig) aspect.

aspereza [aspe'reθa] nf roughness; (agrura) sourness; (severidad) harshness, surliness; **áspero, a** a rough; bitter, sour; harsh.

aspersión [asper'sjon] nf sprinkling.

áspid ['aspið] nm asp.

aspiración [aspira'θjon] nf breath, inhalation; (MUS) short pause; **aspiraciones** nfpl (AM) aspirations.

aspiradora [aspira'ðora] nf vacuum cleaner.

aspirar [aspi'rar] vt to breathe in // vi: ~ a to aspire to.

aspirina [aspi'rina] nf aspirin.

asquear [aske'ar] vt to sicken // vi to be sickening; ~se vr to feel disgusted; **asqueroso, a** a disgusting, sickening.

asta ['asta] nf lance; (arpón) spear; (mango) shaft, handle; (ZOOL) horn; **a media** ~ at half mast.

astilla [as'tiʎa] nf splinter; (pedacito) chip; ~s nfpl firewood sg.

astillero [asti'ʎero] nm shipyard.

astringente [astrin'xente] a, nm astringent.

astringir [astrin'xir] vt to bind.

astro ['astro] nm star.

astrología [astrolo'xia] nf astrology; **astrólogo, a** nm/f astrologer.

astronauta [astro'nauta] nm/f astronaut.

astronomía [astrono'mia] nf astronomy; **astrónomo** nm astronomer.

astucia [as'tuθja] nf astuteness; (destreza) clever trick; **astuto, a** a astute; (taimado) cunning.

asueto [a'sweto] nm holiday; (tiempo libre) time off q.

asumir [asu'mir] vt to assume.

asunción [asun'θjon] nf assumption.

asunto [a'sunto] nm (tema) matter, subject; (negocio) business.

asustar [asus'tar] vt to frighten; ~se vr to be/become frightened.

atacar [ata'kar] vt to attack.

atadura [ata'ðura] nf bond, tie.

atajo [a'taxo] nm short cut; (DEPORTE) tackle.

ataque [a'take] nm attack; ~ cardíaco heart attack.

atar [a'tar] vt to tie, tie up; ~se vr (fig) to be or get embarrassed.

atardecer [atarðe'θer] vi to get dark // nm evening; (crepúsculo) dusk.

atareado, a [atare'aðo, a] a busy.

atarear [atare'ar] vt to give a job to; ~se vr to be busy, keep busy.

atascamiento [ataska'mjento] nm = **atasco.**

atascar [atas'kar] vt to clog up; (obstruir) to jam; (fig) to hinder; ~se vr to stall;

(cañería) to get clogged up; **atasco** nm obstruction; (AUTO) traffic jam.

ataúd [ata'uð] nm coffin.

ataviar [ata'ßjar] vt to deck, array; ~se vr to dress up.

atavío [ata'ßio] nm attire, dress; ~s nmpl finery sg.

atemorizar [atemori'θar] vt to frighten, scare; ~se vr to get scared.

Atenas [a'tenas] n Athens.

atención [aten'θjon] nf attention; (bondad) kindness; (cortesía) civility // excl (be) careful!, look out!

atender [aten'der] vt to attend to, look after // vi to pay attention.

atenerse [ate'nerse] vr: ~ a to abide by, adhere to.

atentado [aten'taðo] nm crime, illegal act; (asalto) assault; (contra la vida de uno) attempt on sb's life.

atentar [aten'tar] vi: ~ a o contra to commit an outrage against.

atento, a [a'tento, a] a attentive, observant; (cortés) polite, thoughtful.

atenuación [atenwa'θjon] nf attenuation, lessening; **atenuante** a attenuating, extenuating; **atenuar** vt to attenuate; (disminuir) to lessen, minimize.

ateo, a [a'teo, a] a atheistic // nm/f atheist.

aterrador, a [aterra'ðor, a] a frightening.

aterrar [ate'rrar] vt to pull down, demolish; (AGR) to cover with earth; (espantar) to frighten; ~se vr to be frightened.

aterrizar [aterri'θar] vi to land.

aterrorizar [aterrori'θar] vt to terrify; (MIL, POL) to terrorize.

atesorar [ateso'rar] vt to hoard, store up.

atestar [ates'tar] vt to pack, stuff; (JUR) to attest, testify to.

atestiguar [atesti'xwar] vt to testify to, bear witness to.

atiborrar [atißo'rrar] vt to fill, stuff; ~se vr to stuff o.s.

ático ['atiko] nm attic.

atildar [atil'dar] vt to criticize; ~se vr to spruce o.s. up.

atisbar [atis'ßar] vt to spy on; (echar ojeada) to peep at.

atizar [ati'θar] vt to poke; (horno etc) to stoke; (fig) to stir up, rouse.

atlántico, a [at'lantiko, a] a Atlantic // nm: **el (océano) A~** the Atlantic (Ocean).

atlas ['atlas] nm atlas.

atleta [at'leta] nm athlete; **atlético, a** a athletic; **atletismo** nm athletics sg.

atmósfera [at'mosfera] nf atmosphere.

atolondramiento [atolondra'mjento] nm bewilderment; (insensatez) silliness.

atollar [ato'ʎar] vi, ~se vr to get stuck; (fig) to get into a jam.

atómico, a [a'tomiko, a] a atomic.

atomizador [atomiθa'ðor] nm atomizer.

átomo ['atomo] nm atom.

atónito, a [a'tonito, a] *a* astonished, amazed.

atontado, a [aton'taðo, a] *a* stunned; (*bobo*) silly, daft.

atontar [aton'tar] *vt* to stun; ~se *vr* to become bewildered.

atormentar [atormen'tar] *vt* to torture; (*molestar*) to torment; (*acosar*) to plague, harass.

atornillar [atorni'ʎar] *vt* to screw on *or* down.

atracar [atra'kar] *vt* (NAUT) to moor; (*robar*) to hold up, rob; (*fam*) to stuff (with food) // *vi* to moor.

atracción [atrak'θjon] *nf* attraction.

atraco [a'trako] *nm* holdup, robbery.

atractivo, a [atrak'tiβo, a] *a* attractive // *nm* attraction; (*belleza*) attractiveness.

atraer [atra'er] *vt* to attract.

atrancar [atran'kar] *vt* (*con tranca, barra*) to bar, bolt.

atrapar [atra'par] *vt* to trap; (*fig*) to take in, deceive.

atrás [a'tras] *ad* (*movimiento*) back, backwards; (*lugar*) behind; (*tiempo*) previously; **ir hacia** ~ to go back *or* backwards; to go to the rear; **estar** ~ to be behind *or* at the back.

atrasado, a [atra'saðo, a] *a* slow; (*pago*) overdue, late; (*país*) backward.

atrasar [atra'sar] *vi* to be slow; ~se *vr* to remain behind; (*llegar tarde*) to arrive late; **atraso** *nm* slowness; lateness, delay; (*de país*) backwardness; **atrasos** *nmpl* arrears.

atravesar [atraβe'sar] *vt* (*cruzar*) to cross (over); (*traspasar*) to pierce, go through; (*poner al través*) to lay *or* put across; ~se *vr* to come in between; (*intervenir*) to interfere.

atrayente [atra'jente] *a* attractive.

atreverse [atre'βerse] *vr* to dare; (*insolentarse*) to be insolent; **atrevido, a** *a* daring; insolent; **atrevimiento** *nm* daring; insolence.

atribuir [atriβu'ir] *vt* to attribute; (*funciones*) to confer.

atribular [atriβu'lar] *vt* to afflict, distress; ~se *vr* to grieve, be distressed.

atributo [atri'βuto] *nm* attribute.

atrocidad [atroθi'ðað] *nf* atrocity, outrage.

atropellar [atrope'ʎar] *vt* (*derribar*) to knock over, knock down; (*empujar*) to push (aside); (*pasar por encima de*) to run over, run down; (*agraviar*) to insult; ~se *vr* to act hastily; **atropello** *nm* accident; push; insult; (*agravio*) wrong; (*atrocidad*) outrage.

atroz [a'troθ] *a* atrocious, awful.

atto, a *abr de* **atento**.

atuendo [a'twendo] *nm* dress.

atún [a'tun] *nm* tuna, tunny.

aturdir [atur'ðir] *vt* to stun; (*de ruido*) to deafen; (*fig*) to dumbfound, bewilder.

audacia [au'ðaθja] *nf* boldness, audacity; **audaz** *a* bold, audacious; (*descarado*) cheeky, impudent.

audible [au'ðiβle] *a* audible.

audición [auði'θjon] *nf* hearing; (TEATRO) audition.

audiencia [au'ðjenθja] *nf* audience; (JUR) high court.

auditor [auði'tor] *nm* (JUR) judge-advocate; (COM) auditor.

auditorio [auði'torjo] *nm* audience; (*sala*) auditorium.

auge ['auxe] *nm* boom; (*clímax*) climax.

augurar [auxu'rar] *vt* to predict; (*presagiar*) to portend; **augurio** *nm* omen; **augurios** *nmpl* good wishes.

aula ['aula] *nf* classroom.

aullar [au'ʎar] *vi* to howl, yell.

aullido [au'ʎiðo] *nm* howl, yell.

aumentar [aumen'tar] *vt* (*precios, sueldo*) to raise; (*producción*) to increase; (*con microscopio, anteojos*) to magnify // *vi*, ~se *vr* to increase; (*subirse*) to rise; (*multiplicarse*) to multiply; **aumento** *nm* increase; rise.

aun [a'un] *ad* even.

aún [a'un] *ad* still, yet.

aunque [a'unke] *conj* though, although, even though, even if.

aura ['aura] *nf* gentle breeze; (*fig*) popularity.

aureola [aure'ola] *nf* halo.

auricular [auriku'lar] *nm* (*dedo*) little finger; (*del teléfono*) earpiece, receiver; ~es *nmpl* headphones.

ausencia [au'senθja] *nf* absence.

ausentarse [ausen'tarse] *vr* to go/stay away, absent o.s.

ausente [au'sente] *a* absent.

auspicios [aus'piθjos] *nmpl* auspices; (*protección*) protection *sg*.

austeridad [austeri'ðað] *nf* austerity; **austero, a** *a* austere.

austral [aus'tral] *a* southern.

Australia [aus'tralja] *nf* Australia; **australiano, a** *a, nm/f* Australian.

Austria ['austrja] *nf* Austria; **austríaco, a** *a, nm/f* Austrian.

autenticar [autenti'kar] *vt* to authenticate; **auténtico, a** *a* authentic.

auto ['auto] *nm* (JUR) edict, decree; (: *orden*) writ; (*fam*) car; ~s *nmpl* (JUR) proceedings; (: *acta*) court record *sg*.

autobiografía [autoβjoɣra'fia] *nf* autobiography.

autobús [auto'βus] *nm* bus.

autocar [auto'kar] *nm* coach.

autócrata [au'tokrata] *nm/f* autocrat.

autóctono, a [au'toktono, a] *a* native, indigenous.

autodefensa [autoðe'fensa] *nf* self-defence.

autodeterminación [autoðetermina-'θjon] *nf* self-determination.

autoescuela [autoes'kwela] *nf* driving school.

autógrafo [au'toɣrafo] *nm* autograph.

autómata [au'tomata] *nm* automaton.

automático, a [auto'matiko, a] a automatic.

automotor, triz [automo'tor, 'triz] a self-propelled // nm Diesel train.

automóvil [auto'moßil] nm (motor) car, automobile; automovilístico, a a driving cpd, motoring cpd.

autonomía [autono'mia] nf autonomy; autónomo, a a autonomous.

autopista [auto'pista] nf motorway.

autopsia [au'topsja] nf autopsy.

autor, a [au'tor, a] nm/f author.

autoridad [autori'ðað] nf authority; autoritario, a a authoritarian.

autorización [autoriθa'θjon] nf authorization; autorizado, a a authorized; (aprobado) approved; autorizar vt to authorize; to approve.

autorretrato [autorre'trato] nm self-portrait.

autoservicio [autoser'ßiθjo] nm self-service restaurant.

autostop [auto'stop] nm hitch-hiking; hacer el ~ to hitch-hike; ~ista nm/f hitch-hiker.

autosuficiencia [autosufi'θjenθja] nf self-sufficiency.

auxiliar [auksi'ljar] vt to help // nm/f assistant; auxilio nm assistance, help; primeros auxilios first aid sg.

Av abr de Avenida.

aval [a'ßal] nm guarantee; (persona) guarantor.

avalancha [aßa'lantʃa] nf avalanche.

avaluar [aßa'lwar] vt to value, appraise.

avance [a'ßanθe] nm advance; (pago) advance payment.

avanzar [aßan'θar] vt, vi, ~se vr to advance.

avaricia [aßa'riθja] nf avarice, greed; avariento, a a avaricious, greedy.

avaro, a [a'ßaro, a] a miserly, mean // nm/f miser.

avasallar [aßasa'ʎar] vt to subdue, subjugate; ~se vr to submit.

Avda abr de Avenida.

ave ['aße] nf bird; ~ de rapiña bird of prey.

avellana [aße'ʎana] nf hazelnut; avellano nm hazel tree.

avemaría [aßema'ria] nf Hail Mary, Ave Maria.

avena [a'ßena] nf oats pl.

avenencia [aße'nenθja] nf agreement; (COM) bargain.

avenida [aße'niða] nf (calle) avenue; (de río) flood, spate.

avenir [aße'nir] vt to reconcile; ~se vr to come to an agreement, reach a compromise.

aventajado, a [aßenta'xaðo, a] a outstanding; aventajar vt (sobrepasar) to surpass, outstrip; (preferir) to prefer; aventajarse vr to surpass or excel o.s.

aventar [aßen'tar] vt to fan, blow; (esparcir) to scatter; (grano) to winnow; ~se vr to fill with air.

aventura [aßen'tura] nf adventure; (casualidad) chance; aventurado, a a risky; aventurero, a a adventurous.

avergonzar [aßerɣon'θar] vt to shame; (desconcertar) to embarrass; ~se vr to be ashamed; to be embarrassed.

avería [aße'ria] nf damage; (TEC) breakdown, fault.

averiguación [aßeriɣwa'θjon] nf investigation; (determinación) ascertainment; averiguar vt to investigate; to find out, ascertain.

aversión [aßer'sjon] nf aversion, dislike.

avestruz [aßes'truθ] nm ostrich.

avezarse [aße'θarse] vr: ~se a algo to grow used to sth.

aviación [aßja'θjon] nf aviation q; (fuerzas aéreas) air force.

aviador, a [aßja'ðor, a] nm/f aviator, airman/woman.

avicultura [aßikul'tura] nf poultry farming.

avidez [aßi'ðeθ] nf avidity, eagerness; ávido, a a avid, eager.

avinagrado, a [aßina'ɣraðo, a] a sour, acid; avinagrarse vr to turn sour.

avío [a'ßio] nm preparation; ~s nmpl gear sg, kit sg.

avión [a'ßjon] nm aeroplane; (ave) martin; ~ de reacción jet plane.

avisar [aßi'sar] vt (advertir) to warn, notify; (informar) to tell; (aconsejar) to advise, counsel; aviso nm warning; (noticia) notice; (prudencia) caution, discretion.

avispa [a'ßispa] nf wasp.

avispado, a [aßis'paðo, a] a sharp, clever.

avispar [aßis'par] vt to spur (on); ~se vr to fret, worry.

avispero [aßis'pero] nm wasp's nest.

avispón [aßis'pon] nm hornet.

avistar [aßis'tar] vt to sight, spot; ~se vr to have an interview.

avituallar [aßitwa'ʎar] vt to supply with food.

avivar [aßi'ßar] vt to strengthen, intensify; ~se vr to revive, acquire new life.

avizorar [aßiθo'rar] vt to spy on.

axila [ak'sila] nf armpit.

axioma [ak'sjoma] nm axiom.

ay [ai] excl (dolor) ow!, ouch!; (aflicción) oh!, oh dear!; ¡~ de mi! poor me!; ¡~ del que! pity help or woe betide whoever!

aya ['aja] nf governess; (niñera) children's nurse.

ayer [a'jer] ad, nm yesterday; antes de ~ the day before yesterday.

ayo ['ajo] nm tutor.

ayuda [a'juða] nf help, assistance; (MED) enema; (AM) laxative // nm page; ayudante, a nm/f assistant, helper; (ESCOL) assistant; (MIL) adjutant; ayudar vt to help, assist.

ayunar [aju'nar] *vi* to fast; **ayunas** *nfpl*: **estar en ayunas** (*no haber comido*) to be fasting; (*ignorante*) to be in the dark; **ayuno** *nm* fasting; ignorance.

ayuntamiento [ajunta'mjento] *nm* (*consejo*) council; (*edificio*) town hall; (*cópula*) sexual intercourse.

azabache [aθa'ßatʃe] *nm* jet.

azada [a'θaða] *nf* hoe.

azafata [aθa'fata] *nf* air hostess.

azafrán [aθa'fran] *nm* saffron.

azahar [aθa'ar] *nm* orange/lemon blossom.

azar [a'θar] *nm* (*casualidad*) chance, fate; (*desgracia*) misfortune, accident; **por** ~ by chance; **al** ~ at random.

azarearse [aθare'arse] *vr* = **azorarse**.

azogue [a'θoxe] *nm* mercury.

azoramiento [aθora'mjento] *nm* alarm; (*confusión*) confusion.

azorar [aθo'rar] *vt* to alarm; ~**se** *vr* to get alarmed.

Azores [a'θores] *nmpl*: **los** ~ the Azores.

azotar [aθo'tar] *vt* to whip, beat; (*pegar*) to spank; **azote** *nm* (*látigo*) whip; (*latigazo*) lash, stroke; (*en las nalgas*) spank; (*calamidad*) calamity.

azotea [aθo'tea] *nf* terrace roof.

azteca [aθ'teka] *a, nm/f* Aztec.

azúcar [a'θukar] *nm* sugar; **azucarado, a** *a* sugary, sweet.

azucarero, a [aθuka'rero, a] *a* sugar *cpd* // *nm* sugar bowl.

azucena [aθu'θena] *nf* white lily.

azufre [a'θufre] *nm* sulphur.

azul [a'θul] *a, nm* blue.

azulejo [aθu'lexo] *nm* glazed tile.

azuzar [aθu'θar] *vt* to incite, egg on.

B

B.A. *abr de* **Buenos Aires.**

baba ['baßa] *nf* spittle, saliva; **babear** *vi* to drool, slaver.

babel [ba'ßel] *nm o f* bedlam.

babero [ba'ßero] *nm* bib.

babor [ba'ßor] *nm* port (side).

babucha [ba'ßutʃa] *nf* slipper.

bacalao [baka'lao] *nm* cod(fish).

bacía [ba'θia] *nf* basin, bowl.

bacín [ba'θin] *nm* chamber pot.

bacteria [bak'terja] *nf* bacterium, germ.

báculo ['bakulo] *nm* stick, staff.

bache ['batʃe] *nm* pothole, rut; (*fig*) bad patch.

bachillerato [batʃiʎe'rato] *nm* (*ESCOL*) school-leaving examination.

bagaje [ba'ɤaxe] *nm* baggage.

bagatela [baɤa'tela] *nf* trinket, trifle.

bahía [ba'ia] *nf* bay.

bailar [bai'lar] *vt, vi* to dance; ~**ín, ina** *nm/f* (*ballet*) dancer; **baile** *nm* dance; (*formal*) ball.

baja ['baxa] *nf ver* **bajo.**

bajada [ba'xaða] *nf* descent; (*camino*) slope; (*de aguas*) ebb.

bajamar [baxa'mar] *nf* low tide.

bajar [ba'xar] *vi* to go/come down; (*temperatura, precios*) to drop, fall; (*de coche*) to get out; (*de autobús*) to get off // *vt* (*cabeza*) to bow, bend; (*escalera*) to go/come down; (*precio, voz*) to lower; (*llevar abajo*) to take down; ~**se** *vr* to bend down; to get out of; to get off; (*fig*) to humble o.s.

bajeza [ba'xeθa] *nf* baseness *q*; (*una* ~) vile deed.

bajío [ba'xio] *nm* shoal, sandbank; (*AM*) lowlands *pl.*

bajo, a ['baxo, a] *a* (*terreno*) low(-lying); (*mueble, número, precio*) low; (*piso*) ground; (*de estatura*) small, short; (*color*) pale; (*sonido*) faint, soft, low; (*voz: en tono*) deep; (*metal*) base; (*humilde*) low, humble // *ad* (*hablar*) low, quietly; (*volar*) low // *prep* under, below, underneath // *nm* (*MUS*) bass // *nf* drop, fall; (*MIL*) casualty; ~ **la lluvia** in the rain; **dar de** ~**a** (*soldado*) to discharge; (*empleado*) to dismiss, sack.

bajón [ba'xon] *nm* (*MUS*) bassoon; (*baja*) decline, fall, drop.

bajorrelieve [baxorre'ljeße] *nm* bas-relief.

bala ['bala] *nf* bullet.

baladí [bala'ði] *a* trivial.

baladrón, ona [bala'ðron, ona] *a* boastful.

bálago ['balaxo] *nm* thatch.

balance [ba'lanθe] *nm* (*balanceo*) oscillation, rocking; (*NAUT*) roll; (*COM*) balance; (: *libro*) balance sheet; (: *cuenta general*) stocktaking; ~**ar** *vt* to balance // *vi*, ~**arse** *vr* to swing (to and fro); (*vacilar*) to hesitate; **balanceo** *nm* swinging.

balanza [ba'lanθa] *nf* balance, scales *pl*; ~ **comercial** balance of trade; ~ **de pagos** balance of payments; (*ASTRO*): **B** ~ = **Libra.**

balar [ba'lar] *vi* to bleat.

balazo [ba'laθo] *nm* (*golpe*) shot; (*herida*) bullet wound.

balbucear [balßuθe'ar] *vi, vt* to stammer, stutter; **balbuceo** *nm* stammering, stuttering.

balbucir [balßu'θir] *vi, vt* to stammer, stutter.

balcón [bal'kon] *nm* balcony.

baldaquín [balda'kin], **baldaquino** [balda'kino] *nm* canopy.

baldar [bal'dar] *vt* to cripple.

balde ['balde] *nm* bucket, pail; **de** ~ *ad* (for) free, for nothing; **en** ~ *ad* in vain.

baldío, a [bal'dio, a] *a* uncultivated // *nm* waste land.

baldón [bal'don] *nm* (*injuria*) insult.

baldosa [bal'dosa] *nf* paving stone.

Baleares [bale'ares] *nfpl*: **las (Islas)** ~ the Balearic Islands.

balido [ba'liðo] *nm* bleat, bleating.

balística [ba'listika] *nf* ballistics *pl.*

baliza [ba'liθa] *nf* (*AVIAT*) beacon; (*NAUT*) buoy.

balneario, a [balne'arjo, a] a: **estación** ~a bathing resort // nm spa, health resort.
balón [ba'lon] nm ball.
baloncesto [balon'θesto] nm basketball.
balsa ['balsa] nf raft; (BOT) balsa wood.
bálsamo ['balsamo] nm balsam, balm.
baluarte [ba'lwarte] nm bastion, bulwark.
ballena [ba'ʎena] nf whale.
ballesta [ba'ʎesta] nf crossbow; (AUTO) spring.
ballet [ba'le] nm ballet.
bambolear [bambole'ar] vi, ~se vr to swing, sway; (silla) to wobble; **bamboleo** nm swinging, swaying; wobbling.
bambú [bam'bu] nm bamboo.
banca ['banka] nf (asiento) bench; (COM) banking; ~da nf (banco) stone bench; (TEC) bench.
bancario, a [ban'karjo, a] a banking cpd, bank cpd.
bancarrota [banka'rrota] nf (esp fraudulent) bankruptcy.
banco ['banko] nm bench; (ESCOL) desk; (COM) bank; (GEO) stratum; ~ **de crédito/de ahorros** credit/ savings bank; ~ **de arena** sandbank; ~ **de hielo** iceberg.
banda ['banda] nf band; (pandilla) gang; (NAUT) side, edge; **la B~ Oriental** Uruguay; ~ **sonora** soundtrack.
bandada [ban'daða] nf (de pájaros) flock; (de peces) shoal.
bandeja [ban'dexa] nf tray.
bandera [ban'dera] nf (de tela) flag; (estandarte) banner.
banderilla [bande'riʎa] nf banderilla.
banderola [bande'rola] nf banderole, pennant.
bandidaje [bandi'ðaxe] nm banditry; **bandido** nm bandit.
bando ['bando] nm (edicto) edict, proclamation; (facción) faction; **los ~s** the banns.
bandolero [bando'lero] nm bandit, brigand.
banquero [ban'kero] nm banker.
banqueta [ban'keta] nf (asiento) bench; (escabel) stool.
banquete [ban'kete] nm banquet; (para convidados) formal dinner.
banquillo [ban'kiʎo] nm (JUR) dock, prisoner's bench; (banco) bench; (para los pies) footstool.
bañador [baɲa'ðor] nm swimming costume.
bañar [ba'ɲar] vt (niño) to bath, bathe; (objeto) to dip; (de barniz) to coat; ~se vr (en el mar) to bathe, swim; (en la bañera) to bath, have a bath.
bañera [ba'ɲera] nf bath(tub).
bañero [ba'ɲero] nm lifeguard.
bañista [ba'ɲista] nm/f bather.
baño ['baɲo] nm (en bañera) bath; (en río) dip, swim; (cuarto) bathroom; (bañera) bath(tub); (capa) coating.

baptista [bap'tista] nm/f baptist.
baqueta [ba'keta] nf (MUS) drumstick.
bar [bar] nm bar.
barahúnda [bara'unda] nf uproar, hubbub.
baraja [ba'raxa] nf pack (of cards); **barajar** vt (naipes) to shuffle; (fig) to jumble up.
baranda [ba'randa] nf rail, railing.
barandilla [baran'diʎa] nf rail, railing.
baratija [bara'tixa] nf trinket.
baratillo [bara'tiʎo] nm (tienda) junkshop; (subasta) bargain sale; (conjunto de cosas) secondhand goods pl.
barato, a [ba'rato, a] a cheap // nm bargain sale // ad cheap, cheaply; **baratura** nf cheapness.
baraúnda [bara'unda] nf = **barahúnda.**
barba ['barßa] nf (ANAT) chin; (pelo) beard, whiskers pl.
barbacoa [barßa'koa] nf (parrilla) barbecue; (carne) barbecued meat.
barbado, a [bar'ßaðo, a] a bearded // nm seedling.
barbaridad [barßari'ðað] nf barbarity; (acto) barbarism; (atrocidad) outrage; **una** ~ (fam) a huge amount; ¡qué ~! (fam) how awful!
barbarie [bar'ßarje] nf, **barbarismo** [barßa'rismo] nm barbarism; (crueldad) barbarity.
bárbaro, a ['barßaro, a] a barbarous, cruel; (grosero) rough, uncouth // nm/f barbarian // ad: **lo pasamos** ~ (fam) we had a tremendous time; ¡qué ~! (fam) how marvellous!; **un éxito** ~ (fam) a terrific success; **es un tipo** ~ (fam) he's a splendid chap.
barbear [barße'ar] vt (AM) to shave.
barbecho [bar'ßetʃo] nm fallow land.
barbero [bar'ßero] nm barber, hairdresser.
barbilampiño [barßilam'piɲo] a smooth-faced; (fig) inexperienced.
barbilla [bar'ßiʎa] nf chin, tip of the chin.
barbotar [barßo'tar], **barbotear** [barßote'ar] vt, vi to mutter, mumble.
barbudo, a [bar'ßuðo, a] a bearded.
barca ['barka] nf (small) boat; ~ **de pesca** fishing boat; ~ **de pasaje** ferry; ~za nf barge; ~za **de desembarco** landing craft.
barcelonés, esa [barθelo'nes, esa] a of or from Barcelona.
barco ['barko] nm boat; (buque) ship; ~ **de carga** cargo boat.
bardar [bar'ðar] vt to thatch.
barítono [ba'ritono] nm baritone.
barman ['barman] nm barman.
Barna abr de **Barcelona.**
barniz [bar'niθ] nm varnish; (en la loza) glaze; (fig) veneer; ~ **para las uñas** nail varnish; ~ar vt to varnish; (loza) to glaze.
barómetro [ba'rometro] nm barometer.
barquero [bar'kero] nm boatman.
barquillo [bar'kiʎo] nm cone, cornet.

barra ['barra] *nf* bar, rod; (*de un bar, café*) bar; (*de pan*) small loaf; (*palanca*) lever; ~ **de carmín** *o* **de labios** lipstick.
barraca [ba'rraka] *nf* hut, cabin.
barranca [ba'rranka] *nf* ravine, gully; **barranco** *nm* ravine; (*fig*) difficulty.
barrena [ba'rrena] *nf* drill; **barrenar** *vt* to drill (through), bore; **barreno** *nm* large drill, borer.
barrer [ba'rrer] *vt* to sweep; (*quitar*) to sweep away.
barrera [ba'rrera] *nf* barrier.
barriada [ba'rrjaða] *nf* quarter, district.
barricada [barri'kaða] *nf* barricade.
barrido [ba'rriðo] *nm,* **barrida** [ba'rriða] *nf* sweep, sweeping.
barriga [ba'rriɣa] *nf* belly; (*panza*) paunch; **barrigón, ona, barrigudo, a** *a* fat, potbellied.
barril [ba'rril] *nm* barrel, cask.
barrio ['barrjo] *nm* (*en el pueblo*) district, quarter; (*fuera del pueblo*) suburb.
barro ['barro] *nm* (*lodo*) mud; (*objetos*) earthenware; (*MED*) pimple.
barroco, a [ba'rroko, a] *a, nm* baroque.
barroso, a [ba'rroso, a] *a* (*lodoso*) muddy; (*MED*) pimply.
barruntar [barrun'tar] *vt* (*conjeturar*) to guess; (*presentir*) to suspect; **barrunto** *nm* guess; suspicion.
bartola [bar'tola]: **a la** ~ *ad*: **tirarse a la** ~ to take it easy, do nothing.
bártulos ['bartulos] *nmpl* things, belongings.
barullo [ba'ruʎo] *nm* row, uproar.
basa ['basa] *nf* base; (*fig*) basis; ~**mento** *nm* base, plinth.
basar [ba'sar] *vt* to base; ~**se** *vr*: ~**se en** to be based on.
basca ['baska] *nf* nausea.
báscula ['baskula] *nf* (platform) scales *pl.*
base ['base] *nf* base; **a** ~ **de** on the basis of.
básico, a ['basiko, a] *a* basic.
basílica [ba'silika] *nf* basilica.
bastante [bas'tante] *a* (*suficiente*) enough, sufficient; (*no poco(s)*) quite a lot of // *ad* (*suficientemente*) enough, sufficiently; (*muy*) quite, rather.
bastar [bas'tar] *vi* to be enough *or* sufficient; ~**se** *vr* to be self-sufficient; ~ **para** to be enough to; **¡basta!** (that's) enough!
bastardilla [bastar'ðiʎa] *nf* italics *pl.*
bastardo, a [bas'tarðo, a] *a, nm/f* bastard.
bastidor [basti'ðor] *nm* frame; (*de coche*) chassis.
basto, a ['basto, a] *a* coarse, rough; ~**s** *nmpl* (*NAIPES*) clubs.
bastón [bas'ton] *nm* (*gen*) stick, staff; (*para el paseo*) walking stick.
basura [ba'sura] *nf* rubbish, refuse.
basurero [basu'rero] *nm* (*hombre*) dustman; (*lugar*) rubbish dump; (*cubo*) (rubbish) bin.
bata ['bata] *nf* (*salto de cama*) dressing gown, housecoat; (*de alumno etc*) smock, overall.
batalla [ba'taʎa] *nf* battle; **de** ~ everyday, for everyday use.
batallar [bata'ʎar] *vi* to fight.
batallón [bata'ʎon] *nm* battalion.
bate ['bate] *nm* bat; ~**ador** *nm* batter, batsman.
batería [bate'ria] *nf* battery; (*MUS*) drums *pl;* ~ **de cocina** kitchen utensils *pl.*
batido, a [ba'tiðo, a] *a* (*camino*) beaten, well-trodden // *nm* (*CULIN*) batter; ~ **de leche** milk shake.
batidora [bati'ðora] *nf* beater, mixer.
batir [ba'tir] *vt* to beat, strike; (*vencer*) to beat, defeat; (*revolver*) to beat, mix; (*acuñar*) to strike, mint; (*pelo*) to comb; ~**se** *vr* to fight; ~ **palmas** to clap, applaud.
batuta [ba'tuta] *nf* baton.
baúl [ba'ul] *nm* trunk; (*AUTO*) boot.
bautismo [bau'tismo] *nm* baptism, christening.
bautizar [bauti'θar] *vt* to baptize, christen; (*fam*) to water down; **bautizo** *nm* baptism, christening.
bayo, a ['bajo, a] *a* bay // *nf* berry.
bayoneta [bajo'neta] *nf* bayonet.
baza ['baθa] *nf* trick.
bazar [ba'θar] *nm* bazaar.
bazofia [ba'θofja] *nf* left-overs *pl.*
beato, a [be'ato, a] *a* blessed; (*piadoso*) pious // *nm/f* lay brother/sister.
bebé [be'ße] *nm* baby.
bebedero, a [beße'ðero, a] *a* drinkable // *nm* (*para animales*) drinking trough; (*de vasija*) spout.
bebedizo, a [beße'ðiθo, a] *a* drinkable // *nm* potion.
bebedor, a [beße'ðor, a] *a* hard-drinking.
beber [be'ßer] *vt, vi* to drink.
bebida [be'ßiða] *nf* drink.
beca ['beka] *nf* grant, scholarship.
befa ['befa] *nf ver* **befo.**
befar [be'far] *vt* to scoff at.
befo, a [be'fo, a] *a* thick-lipped // *nm* lip // *nf*: **hacer** ~**a de** to jeer, mock.
beldad [bel'dað] *nf* beauty.
belfo, a ['belfo, a] = **befo.**
belga ['belɣa] *a, nm/f* Belgian.
Bélgica ['belxika] *nf* Belgium.
bélico, a ['beliko, a] *a* warlike, martial; **belicoso, a** *a* (*guerrero*) warlike; (*agresivo*) aggressive, bellicose.
beligerante [belixe'rante] *a* belligerent.
bellaco, a [be'ʎako, a] *a* sly, cunning // *nm* villain, rogue; **bellaquería** *nf* (*acción*) dirty trick; (*calidad*) wickedness.
belleza [be'ʎeθa] *nf* beauty.
bello, a ['beʎo, a] *a* beautiful, lovely; ~**as artes** fine arts.
bellota [be'ʎota] *nf* acorn.
bemol [be'mol] *nm* (*MUS*) flat; **esto tiene** ~**es** (*fam*) this is a real problem.
bendecir [bende'θir] *vt* to bless.
bendición [bendi'θjon] *nf* blessing.

bendito, a [ben'dito, a] *pp de* **bendecir** // *a* holy; (*afortunado*) lucky; (*feliz*) happy; (*sencillo*) simple // nm/f simple soul.

benedictino, a [beneðik'tino, a] *a, nm* Benedictine.

beneficencia [benefi'θenθja] nf charity.

beneficiar [benefi'θjar] *vt* (*hacer bien a*) to benefit, be of benefit to; (*tierra*) to cultivate; (*mina*) to exploit; (*mineral*) to process, treat; **~se** *vr* to benefit, profit; **~io, a** *nm/f* beneficiary.

beneficio [bene'fiθjo] *nm* (*bien*) benefit, advantage; (*ganancia*) profit, gain; (*AGR*) cultivation; **~so, a** *a* beneficial.

benéfico, a [be'nefiko, a] *a* beneficent, charitable.

beneplácito [bene'plaθito] *nm* approval, consent.

benevolencia [beneßo'lenθja] nf benevolence, kindness; **benévolo, a** *a* benevolent, kind.

benignidad [beniɤni'ðað] nf (*afabilidad*) kindness; (*suavidad*) mildness; **benigno, a** *a* kind; mild.

beodo, a [be'oðo, a] *a* drunk.

berenjena [beren'xena] nf aubergine, eggplant.

Berlín [ber'lin] *n* Berlin; **berlinés, esa** *a* of *or* from Berlin // nm/f Berliner.

bermejo, a [ber'mexo, a] *a* red.

Berna ['berna] *n* Berne.

berrear [berre'ar] *vi* to bellow, low.

berrido [be'rriðo] *nm* bellow, bellowing.

berrinche [be'rrintʃe] *nm* (*fam*) temper, tantrum.

berro ['berro] *nm* watercress.

berza ['berθa] nf cabbage.

besar [be'sar] *vt* to kiss; (*fig*) to graze; **~se** *vr* to kiss (one another); **beso** *nm* kiss.

bestia ['bestja] nf beast, animal; (*fig*) idiot; **~ de carga** beast of burden.

bestial [bes'tjal] *a* bestial; (*fam*) terrific; **~idad** nf bestiality; (*fam*) stupidity.

besuquear [besuke'ar] *vt* to cover with kisses; **~se** *vr* to kiss and cuddle.

betún [be'tun] *nm* bitumen, asphalt; (*para calzado*) shoe polish.

biberón [biße'ron] *nm* feeding bottle.

Biblia ['bißlja] nf Bible.

bíblico, a ['bißliko, a] *a* biblical.

bibliografía [bißljoɤra'fia] nf bibliography.

biblioteca [bißljo'teka] nf library; (*mueble*) bookshelves *pl*; **~ de consulta** reference library; **~rio, a** nm/f librarian.

B.I.C. nf abr de **Brigada de Investigación Criminal** CID (Criminal Investigation Department); FBI (Federal Bureau of Investigation) (*US*).

bicarbonato [bikarßo'nato] *nm* bicarbonate.

bicicleta [biθi'kleta] nf bicycle, bike.

bicho ['bitʃo] *nm* (*animal*) small animal; (*sabandija*) bug, insect; (*TAUR*) bull.

bidé [bi'ðe] *nm* bidet.

bien [bjen] *nm* good; (*interés*) advantage, benefit // *ad* well; (*correctamente*) properly, right; (*oler*) nice; (*muy*) very; **más ~** rather // *excl*: ¡(muy) ~! well done! // *conj*: **no ~ llovió, bajó la temperatura** no sooner had it rained than the temperature dropped; **~ que** although; **~es inmuebles/muebles** real estate *sg*/personal property *sg*; **~es de consumo** consumer goods; **~es raíces** real estate *sg*.

bienal [bje'nal] *a* biennial.

bienandanza [bjenan'danθa] nf happiness.

bienaventurado, a [bjenaßentu'raðo, a] *a* (*feliz*) happy, fortunate; (*sencillo*) simple, naïve.

bienestar [bjenes'tar] *nm* well-being.

bienhechor, a [bjene'tʃor, a] *a* beneficent.

bienvenida [bjenße'niða] nf welcome; **bienvenido** *excl* welcome!

biftec [bif'tek] *nm* (beef)steak.

bifurcación [bifurka'θjon] nf fork.

bigamia [bi'ɤamja] nf bigamy; **bígamo, a** *a* bigamous // nm/f bigamist.

bigote [bi'ɤote] *nm* moustache; **bigotudo, a** *a* moustached.

bilbaíno, a [bilßa'ino, a] *a* of *or* from Bilbao.

bilingüe [bi'lingwe] *a* bilingual.

billar [bi'ʎar] *nm* billiards *sg*; (*lugar*) billiard hall.

billete [bi'ʎete] *nm* ticket; (*de banco*) banknote; (*carta*) note; **~ simple** single (ticket); **~ de ida y vuelta** return (ticket); **~ kilométrico** runabout ticket.

billetera [biʎe'tera] nf, **billetero** [biʎe'tero] *nm* wallet.

billón [bi'ʎon] *nm* billion.

bimensual [bimen'swal] *a* twice monthly.

bimotor [bimo'tor] *a* twin-engined // *nm* twin-engined plane.

binóculo [bi'nokulo] *nm* pince-nez.

biografía [bjoɤra'fia] nf biography; **biógrafo, a** nm/f biographer.

biología [bjolo'xia] nf biology; **biológico, a** *a* biological; **biólogo, a** nm/f biologist.

biombo ['bjombo] *nm* (folding) screen.

biopsia [bi'opsja] nf biopsy.

biplano [bi'plano] *nm* biplane.

birlar [bir'lar] *vt* (*derribar*) to knock down; (*matar*) to kill; (*fam*) to pinch.

bis [bis] *excl* encore! // *ad*: **viven en el 27 ~** they live at 27a.

bisabuelo, a [bisa'ßwelo, a] nm/f great-grandfather/mother.

bisagra [bi'saɤra] nf hinge.

bisbisar [bisßi'sar], **bisbisear** [bisßise-'ar] *vt* to mutter, mumble.

bisexual [bisek'swal] *a* bisexual.

bisiesto [bi'sjesto] *a*: **año ~** leap year.

bisnieto, a [bis'njeto, a] nm/f great-grandson/daughter.

bisonte [bi'sonte] *nm* bison.

bisoño, a [bi'soɲo, a] *a* green, inexperienced.

bistec [bis'tek], **bisté** [bis'te] nm steak.
bisturí [bistu'ri] nm scalpel.
bisutería [bisute'ria] nf imitation or costume jewellery.
bizarría [biθa'rria] nf (valor) bravery; (generosidad) generosity; **bizarro, a** a brave; generous.
bizcar [biθ'kar] vi to squint; **bizco, a** a cross-eyed.
bizcocho [biθ'kotʃo] nm (CULIN) sponge cake.
bizquear [biθke'ar] vi to squint.
blanco, a ['blanko, a] a white // nm/f white man/woman, white // nm (color) white; (intervalo) space, interval; (en texto) blank; (MIL, fig) target // nf (MUS) minim; **en** ~ blank; **noche en** ~ sleepless night; **estar sin** ~ to be broke.
blancura [blan'kura] nf whiteness.
blandir [blan'dir] vt to brandish.
blando, a ['blando, a] a soft; (tierno) tender, gentle; (carácter) mild; (fam) cowardly; **blandura** nf softness; tenderness; mildness.
blanquear [blanke'ar] vt to whiten; (fachada) to whitewash; (paño) to bleach // vi to turn white; **blanquecino, a** a whitish; **blanqueo** nm whitewashing; bleaching.
blanquillo, a [blan'kiʎo, a] a white.
blasfemar [blasfe'mar] vi to blaspheme, curse; **blasfemia** nf blasphemy.
blasón [bla'son] nm coat of arms; (fig) honour; **blasonar** vt to emblazon // vi to boast, brag.
bledo ['bleðo] nm: **(no) me importa un** ~ I don't care two hoots.
blindaje [blin'daxe] nm armour, armour-plating; **blindar** vt to armour, armour-plate.
bloc [blok] nm writing pad.
bloque ['bloke] nm block; (POL) bloc; ~ **de cilindros** cylinder block.
bloquear [bloke'ar] vt to blockade; **bloqueo** nm blockade; (COM) freezing, blocking.
bluejean ['bludʒin] nm inv jeans pl.
blusa ['blusa] nf (de alumno) smock; (de mujer) blouse.
boardilla [boar'ðiʎa] nf = **buhardilla.**
boato [bo'ato] nm show, ostentation.
bobada [bo'ßaða], **bobería** [boße'ria] nf foolish action/ statement.
bobina [bo'ßina] nf (TEC) bobbin; (FOTO) spool; (ELEC) coil; **bobinar** vt to wind.
bobo, a ['boßo, a] a (tonto) daft, silly; (cándido) naïve // nm (TEATRO) clown, funny man, fool.
boca ['boka] nf mouth; (de crustáceo) pincer; (de cañón) muzzle; (de vino) flavour, taste; (entrada) mouth, entrance; ~**s** nfpl (de río) mouth sg; ~ **abajo/arriba** face down/up; a ~ **de jarro** point-blank; **se me hace la** ~ **agua** my mouth is watering.
bocacalle [boka'kaʎe] nf entrance to a street.

bocadillo [boka'ðiʎo] nm (emparedado) sandwich; (comida ligera) snack.
bocado [bo'kaðo] nm mouthful, bite; (de caballo) bridle; ~ **de Adán** Adam's apple.
bocanada [boka'naða] nf (de vino) mouthful, swallow; (de aire) gust, puff.
boceto [bo'θeto] nm sketch, outline.
bocina [bo'θina] nf (MUS) trumpet; (AUTO) horn; (para hablar) megaphone; (para sordos) ear trumpet.
bocha ['botʃa] nf bowl; ~**s** nfpl bowls.
bochinche [bo'tʃintʃe] nm (fam) uproar.
bochorno [bo'tʃorno] nm (calor) sultry weather; (vergüenza) embarrassment; ~**so, a** a sultry; embarrassing; (sofocante) stuffy.
boda ['boða] nf (también ~**s** nfpl) wedding, marriage; (fiesta) wedding reception; ~**s de plata/de oro** silver/golden wedding.
bodega [bo'ðexa] nf (de vino) (wine) cellar; (depósito) storeroom; (de barco) hold.
bodegón [boðe'ɣon] nm cheap restaurant; (ARTE) still life.
bofe ['bofe] nm (también ~**s** nmpl) lung.
bofetada [bofe'taða] nf slap (in the face).
bofetón [bofe'ton] nm punch (in the face).
boga ['boɣa] nf (NAUT) rowing; (fig) vogue, fashion // nm/f rower; **en** ~ in vogue; **bogar** vi (remar) to row; (navegar) to sail.
Bogotá [boɣo'ta] n Bogota; **bogotano, a** a of or from Bogota.
bohardilla [boar'ðiʎa] nf = **buhardilla.**
bohemio, a [bo'emjo, a] a, nm/f Bohemian.
boicot [boi'kot] nm boycott; ~**ear** vt to boycott; ~**eo** nm boycott.
boina ['boina] nf beret.
bola ['bola] nf (gen) ball; (canica) marble; (NAIPES) (grand) slam; (betún) shoe polish; ~ **de billar** billiard ball; ~ **de nieve** snowball.
bolchevique [boltʃe'ßike] nm/f Bolshevik.
boleadoras [bolea'ðoras] nfpl (AM) bolas.
bolera [bo'lera] nf skittle alley.
boleta [bo'leta] nf (billete) ticket; (permiso) pass, permit.
boletín [bole'tin] nm bulletin; (periódico) journal, review; (billete) ticket; ~ **escolar** school report; ~ **de noticias** news bulletin; ~ **de pedido** application form; ~ **de precios** price list; ~ **de prensa** press release.
boleto [bo'leto] nm ticket.
boliche [bo'litʃe] nm (bola) jack; (juego) bowls sg; (lugar) bowling alley.
bolígrafo [bo'liɣrafo] nm ball-point pen.
bolívar [bo'lißar] nm monetary unit of Venezuela.
Bolivia [bo'lißja] nf Bolivia; **boliviano, a** a, nm/f Bolivian.
bolo ['bolo] nm skittle; (píldora) (large) pill; (juego de) ~**s** skittles sg.
bolsa ['bolsa] nf (cartera) purse; (saco) bag; (ANAT) cavity, sac; (COM) stock exchange; (MINERÍA) pocket; ~ **de agua**

caliente hot water bottle; ~ **de aire** air pocket; ~ **de papel** paper bag.

bolsillo [bol'siʎo] *nm* pocket; (*cartera*) purse; **de** ~ pocket(-size).

bolsista [bol'sista] *nm/f* stockbroker.

bolso ['bolso] *nm* (*bolsa*) bag; (*de mujer*) handbag.

bollo ['boʎo] *nm* (*pan*) roll; (*bulto*) bump, lump; (*abolladura*) dent.

bomba ['bomba] *nf* (*MIL*) bomb; (*TEC*) pump // *a* (*fam*): **noticia** ~ shattering piece of news // *ad* (*fam*): **pasarlo** ~ to have a great time; ~ **atómica/de humo/de retardo** atomic/smoke/ time bomb; ~ **de gasolina** petrol pump; ~ **de mano** grenade; ~ **lacrimógena** tear gas bomb.

bombardear [bombarðe'ar] *vt* to bombard; (*MIL*) to bomb; **bombardeo** *nm* bombardment; bombing.

bombardero [bombar'ðero] *nm* bomber.

bombear [bombe'ar] *vt* (*agua*) to pump (out *or* up); (*MIL*) to bomb; ~**se** *vr* to warp.

bombero [bom'bero] *nm* fireman.

bombilla [bom'biʎa] *nf* bulb.

bombín [bom'bin] *nm* bowler hat.

bombo ['bombo] *nm* (*MUS*) bass drum; (*TEC*) drum.

bombón [bom'bon] *nm* chocolate.

bonachón, ona [bona'tʃon, ona] *a* good-natured, easy-going.

bonaerense [bonae'rense] *a* of *or* from Buenos Aires.

bonancible [bonan'θiβle] *a* (*tiempo*) fair, calm.

bonanza [bo'nanθa] *nf* (*NAUT*) fair weather; (*fig*) bonanza; (*MINERÍA*) rich pocket *or* vein.

bondad [bon'dað] *nf* goodness, kindness; **tenga la** ~ **de** (please) be good enough to; ~**oso, a** *a* good, kind.

bonito, a [bo'nito, a] *a* (*lindo*) pretty; (*agradable*) nice.

bono ['bono] *nm* voucher; (*FIN*) bond.

boquear [boke'ar] *vi* to gasp.

boquerón [boke'ron] *nm* (*anchoa*) anchovy; (*agujero*) large hole.

boquete [bo'kete] *nm* gap, hole.

boquiabierto, a [bokia'βjerto, a] *a* open-mouthed (in astonishment).

boquilla [bo'kiʎa] *nf* (*para riego*) nozzle; (*para cigarro*) cigarette holder; (*MUS*) mouthpiece.

borbollar [borβo'ʎar], **borbollear** [borβoʎe'ar], **borbotar** [borβo'tar] *vi* to bubble.

borbotón [borβo'ton] *nm* bubbling.

bordado [bor'ðaðo] *nm* embroidery.

bordar [bor'ðar] *vt* to embroider.

borde ['borðe] *nm* edge, border; (*de camino etc*) side; (*en la costura*) hem; **al** ~ **de** (*fig*) on the verge *or* brink of; ~**ar** *vt* to border.

bordo ['borðo] *nm* (*NAUT*) side; **a** ~ on board.

Borinquén [borin'ken] *nm* Puerto Rico;

borinqueño, a *a*, *nm/f* Puerto Rican.

borra ['borra] *nf* (*pelusa*) fluff; (*sedimento*) sediment.

borrachera [borra'tʃera] *nf* (*ebriedad*) drunkenness; (*orgía*) spree, binge.

borracho, a [bo'rratʃo, a] *a* drunk // *nm/f* (*que bebe mucho*) drunkard, drunk; (*temporalmente*) drunk, drunk man/woman.

borrador [borra'ðor] *nm* (*escritura*) first draft, rough sketch; (*cuaderno*) scribbling pad; (*goma*) rubber, eraser.

borrajear [borraxe'ar] *vt*, *vi* to scribble.

borrar [bo'rrar] *vt* to erase, rub out.

borrascoso, a [borras'koso, a] *a* stormy.

borrica [bo'rrika] *nf* she-donkey; (*fig*) stupid woman; ~**da** *nf* foolish action/statement.

borrico [bo'rriko] *nm* donkey; (*fig*) stupid man.

borrón [bo'rron] *nm* (*mancha*) stain; (*proyecto*) rough draft; (*de cuadro*) sketch.

borroso, a [bo'rroso, a] *a* a vague, unclear; (*escritura*) illegible.

bosque ['boske] *nm* wood, forest.

bosquejar [boske'xar] *vt* to sketch; **bosquejo** *nm* sketch.

bosta ['bosta] *nf* dung, manure.

bostezar [boste'θar] *vi* to yawn; **bostezo** *nm* yawn.

bota ['bota] *nf* (*saco*) leather wine bottle; (*calzado*) boot.

botadura [bota'ðura] *nf* launching.

botánico, a [bo'taniko, a] *nm/f* botanist // *nf* botany.

botar [bo'tar] *vt* to throw, hurl; (*NAUT*) to launch; (*fam*) to throw out // *vi* to bounce.

bote ['bote] *nm* (*salto*) bounce; (*golpe*) thrust; (*vasija*) tin, can; (*embarcación*) boat; **de** ~ **en** ~ packed, jammed full; ~ **salvavidas** lifeboat.

botella [bo'teʎa] *nf* bottle.

botica [bo'tika] *nf* chemist's (shop), pharmacy; ~**rio, a** *nm/f* chemist, pharmacist.

botija [bo'tixa] *nf* (*earthenware*) jug; **botijo** *nm* (*earthenware*) jug; (*tren*) excursion train.

botín [bo'tin] *nm* (*calzado*) half boot; (*polaina*) spat; (*MIL*) booty.

botiquín [boti'kin] *nm* (*armario*) medicine cabinet; (*portátil*) first-aid kit.

botón [bo'ton] *nm* button; (*BOT*) bud; (*de florete*) tip; ~ **de oro** buttercup.

botones [bo'tones] *nm* buttons *sg*, bellboy.

bóveda ['boβeða] *nf* (*ARQ*) vault.

boxeador [boksea'ðor] *nm* boxer.

boxeo [bok'seo] *nm* boxing.

boya ['boja] *nf* (*NAUT*) buoy; (*flotador*) float.

bozal [bo'θal] *a* (*novato*) raw, green; (*tonto*) stupid; (*salvaje*) wild // *nm* (*de caballo*) halter; (*de perro*) muzzle.

bracear [braθe'ar] *vi* (*agitar los brazos*) to wave one's arms; (*nadar*) to swim (the crawl).

bracero [bra'θero] *nm* labourer; (*en el campo*) farmhand.

bracete [bra'θete]: **de** ~ *ad* arm in arm.
braga ['braxa] *nf* (*cuerda*) sling, rope; (*de bebé*) nappy; ~**s** *nfpl* (*de mujer*) panties.
bragueta [bra'xeta] *nf* fly, flies *pl*.
braille [breil] *nm* braille.
bramar [bra'mar] *vi* to bellow, roar; **bramido** *nm* bellow, roar.
brasa ['brasa] *nf* live coal.
brasero [bra'sero] *nm* brazier.
Brasil [bra'sil] *nm*: **el** ~ Brazil; **brasileño, a** *a, nm/f* Brazilian.
bravata [bra'ßata] *nf* boast.
braveza [bra'ßeθa] *nf* (*valor*) bravery; (*ferocidad*) ferocity.
bravío, a [bra'ßio, a] *a* wild; (*feroz*) fierce.
bravo, a ['braßo, a] *a* (*valiente*) brave; (*bueno*) fine, splendid; (*feroz*) ferocious; (*salvaje*) wild // *excl* bravo!; **bravura** *nf* bravery; ferocity; (*pey*) boast.
braza ['braθa] *nf* fathom; **nadar a la** ~ to swim the breast-stroke.
brazada [bra'θaða] *nf* stroke.
brazado [bra'θaðo] *nm* armful.
brazalete [braθa'lete] *nm* (*pulsera*) bracelet; (*banda*) armband.
brazo ['braθo] *nm* arm; (*zool*) foreleg; (*bot*) limb, branch; **a** ~ **partido** hand-to-hand; **del** ~ arm in arm.
brea ['brea] *nf* pitch, tar.
brebaje [bre'ßaxe] *nm* potion.
brecha ['bretʃa] *nf* breach, gap, opening.
brega ['brexa] *nf* (*lucha*) struggle; (*trabajo*) hard work.
breve ['breße] *a* short, brief // *nf* breve; ~**dad** *nf* brevity, shortness.
brezal [bre'θal] *nm* moor(land), heath; **brezo** *nm* heather.
bribón, ona [bri'ßon, ona] *a* idle, lazy // *nm/f* (*vagabundo*) vagabond; (*pícaro*) rascal, rogue.
bricolaje [briko'laxe] *nm* do-it-yourself, DIY.
brida ['briða] *nf* bridle, rein; (*tec*) clamp; **a toda** ~ at top speed.
bridge [britʃ] *nm* bridge.
brigada [bri'xaða] *nf* (*unidad*) brigade; (*trabajadores*) squad, gang // *nm* ≈ staff-sergeant, sergeant-major.
brillante [bri'ʎante] *a* brilliant // *nm* diamond; **brillar** *vi* to shine.
brillo ['briʎo] *nm* shine; (*brillantez*) brilliance; (*fig*) splendour; **sacar** ~ **a** to polish.
brincar [brin'kar] *vi* to skip about, hop about, jump about; **está que brinca** he's hopping mad.
brinco ['brinko] *nm* hop, skip, jump.
brindar [brin'dar] *vi*: ~ **a** *o* **por** to drink (a toast) to // *vt* to offer, present.
brindis ['brindis] *nm* toast; (*taur*) (ceremony of) dedicating the bull.
brío ['brio] *nm* spirit, dash; **brioso, a** *a* spirited, dashing.
brisa ['brisa] *nf* breeze.
británico, a [bri'taniko, a] *a* British // *nm/f* Briton, British person.

brocal [bro'kal] *nm* rim.
brocha ['brotʃa] *nf* brush.
broche ['brotʃe] *nm* brooch; ~ **para papeles** (*am*) paper clip.
broma ['broma] *nf* (*bulla*) fun; (*chanza*) joke; **en** ~ in fun, as a joke; **bromear** *vi* to joke.
bromista [bro'mista] *a* fond of joking // *nm/f* joker, wag.
bronca ['bronka] *nf* row.
bronce ['bronθe] *nm* bronze; ~**ado, a** *a* bronze; (*por el sol*) tanned // *nm* (sun)tan; (*tec*) bronzing.
broncearse [bronθe'arse] *vr* to get a suntan.
bronco, a ['bronko, a] *a* (*superficie*) rough; (*manera*) rude, surly; (*voz*) harsh.
bronquitis [bron'kitis] *nf* bronchitis.
brotar [bro'tar] *vi* (*bot*) to sprout; (*aguas*) to gush (forth), flow; (*med*) to break out; **brote** *nm* (*bot*) shoot; (*med, fig*) outbreak.
bruces ['bruθes]: **de** ~ *ad*: **caer** *o* **dar de** ~ to fall headlong, fall flat; **estar de** ~ to lie face downwards.
bruja ['bruxa] *nf* witch; (*lechuza*) owl; **brujería** *nf* witchcraft.
brujo ['bruxo] *nm* wizard, magician.
brújula ['bruxula] *nf* compass.
bruma ['bruma] *nf* mist; **brumoso, a** *a* misty.
bruñido [bru'ɲiðo] *nm* polish; **bruñir** *vt* to polish.
brusco, a ['brusko, a] *a* (*súbito*) sudden; (*áspero*) brusque.
Bruselas [bru'selas] *n* Brussels.
brutal [bru'tal] *a* brutal; (*fig*) sudden; ~**idad** *nf* brutality.
bruto, a ['bruto, a] *a* (*idiota*) stupid; (*bestial*) brutish; (*peso*) gross; (*diamante etc*) raw, uncut; **en** ~ raw, unworked.
Bs.As. *abr de* **Buenos Aires.**
buba ['bußa] *nf* tumour.
bucal [bu'kal] *a*: **por vía** ~ by *or* through the mouth, orally.
bucear [buθe'ar] *vi* to dive // *vt* to explore; **buceo** *nm* diving; (*fig*) investigation.
bucle ['bukle] *nm* curl.
budismo [bu'ðismo] *nm* Buddhism.
buenamente [bwena'mente] *ad* (*fácilmente*) easily; (*voluntariamente*) willingly.
buenaventura [bwenaßen'tura] *nf* (*suerte*) good luck; (*adivinación*) fortune.
bueno, a ['bweno, a], **buen** [bwen] *a* (*amable*) kind; (*med*) well; (*guapo*) attractive; ¡~**as!** hello!; **buen día**, ~**os días** good morning!; good afternoon!; hello!; ~**as tardes** good afternoon!; good evening!; ~ **as noches** good night!; ¡**buen sinvergüenza resultó!** a fine rascal he turned out to be // *excl* right!, all right!; ~, **¿y qué?** well, so what?
buey [bwei] *nm* ox.
búfalo ['bufalo] *nm* buffalo.
bufanda [bu'fanda] *nf* scarf, muffler.
bufar [bu'far] *vi* to snort.

bufete [bu'fete] *nm* (*mesa*) desk; (*de abogado*) lawyer's office.

bufo, a ['bufo, a] *a* comic.

bufón, ona [bu'fon, ona] *a* funny // *nm* clown.

buhardilla [buar'ðiʎa] *nf* (*ventana*) skylight; (*desván*) attic.

búho ['buo] *nm* owl; (*fig*) hermit, recluse.

buhonero [buo'nero] *nm* pedlar.

buitre ['bwitre] *nm* vulture.

bujía [bu'xia] *nf* (*vela*) candle; (ELEC) candle (power); (AUTO) spark plug.

bula ['bula] *nf* (papal) bull.

bulbo ['bulßo] *nm* bulb.

búlgaro, a ['bulɤaro, a] *a*, *nm/f* Bulgarian.

bulto ['bulto] *nm* (*paquete*) package; (*fardo*) bundle; (*tamaño*) size, bulkiness; (MED) swelling, lump; (*silueta*) vague shape; (*estatua*) bust, statue; **de mucho/poco** ~ important/unimportant.

bulla ['buʎa] *nf* (*ruido*) uproar; (*de gente*) crowd.

bullicio [bu'ʎiθjo] *nm* (*ruido*) uproar; (*movimiento*) bustle.

bullir [bu'ʎir] *vi* (*hervir*) to boil; (*burbujear*) to bubble; (*mover*) to move, stir.

buñuelo [bu'ɲwelo] *nm* fritter.

buque ['buke] *nm* ship, vessel.

burbuja [bur'ßuxa] *nf* bubble; **burbujear** *vi* to bubble.

burdel [bur'ðel] *nm* brothel.

burdo, a ['burðo, a] *a* coarse, rough.

burgués, esa [bur'ɤes, esa] *a* middle-class, bourgeois; **burguesía** *nf* middle class, bourgeoisie.

burla ['burla] *nf* (*mofa*) gibe; (*broma*) joke; (*engaño*) trick.

burladero [burla'ðero] *nm* (bullfighter's) refuge.

burlador, a [burla'ðor, a] *a* mocking // *nm* (*bromista*) joker; (*libertino*) seducer.

burlar [bur'lar] *vt* (*engañar*) to deceive; (*seducir*) to seduce // *vi*, ~**se** *vr* to joke; ~**se de** to make fun of.

burlesco, a [bur'lesko, a] *a* burlesque.

burlón, ona [bur'lon, ona] *a* mocking.

burocracia [buro'kraθja] *nf* civil service; (*pey*) bureaucracy.

burócrata [bu'rokrata] *nm/f* civil servant; (*pey*) bureaucrat.

burra ['burra] *nf* (she-)donkey; (*fig*) stupid woman.

burro ['burro] *nm* donkey; (*fig*) ass, idiot.

bursátil [bur'satil] *a* stock-exchange *cpd*.

busca ['buska] *nf* search, hunt; **en** ~ **de** in search of.

buscapleitos [buska'pleitos] *nm/f inv* troublemaker.

buscar [bus'kar] *vt* to look for, search for, seek // *vi* to look, search, seek; **se busca empleado** employee wanted.

buscón, ona [bus'kon, ona] *a* thieving // *nm* petty thief // *nf* whore.

busilis [bu'silis] *nm* (*fam*) snag.

busque *etc vb ver* **buscar.**

búsqueda ['buskeða] *nf* = **busca.**

busto ['busto] *nm* bust.

butaca [bu'taka] *nf* armchair; (*de cine, teatro*) stall, seat.

butano [bu'tano] *nm* butane.

buzo ['buθo] *nm* diver.

buzón [bu'θon] *nm* letter box; (*en la calle*) pillar box.

C

c. *abr de* **capítulo.**

C. *abr de* **centígrado; compañía.**

C/ *abr de* **calle.**

c.a. *abr de* **corriente alterna.**

cabal [ka'ßal] *a* (*exacto*) exact; (*correcto*) right, proper; (*acabado*) finished, complete; ~**es** *nmpl*: **estar en sus** ~**es** to be in one's right mind.

cabalgadura [kaßal'ɤaˈðura] *nf* mount, horse.

cabalgar [kaßal'ɤar] *vt*, *vi* to ride.

caballa [ka'ßaʎa] *nf* mackerel.

caballeresco, a [kaßaʎe'resko, a] *a* noble, chivalrous.

caballería [kaßaʎe'ria] *nf* mount; (MIL) cavalry.

caballeriza [kaßaʎe'riθa] *nf* stable; **caballerizo** *nm* groom, stableman.

caballero [kaßa'ʎero] *nm* rider, horseman; (*hombre galante*) gentleman; (*de la orden de caballería*) knight; (*hidalgo*) noble(man); (*señor, término de cortesía*) sir.

caballerosidad [kaßaʎerosi'ðað] *nf* chivalry.

caballo [ka'ßaʎo] *nm* horse; (AJEDREZ) knight; (NAIPES) queen; ~ **de vapor** *o* **de fuerza** horsepower.

cabaña [ka'ßaɲa] *nf* (*casita*) hut, cabin; (*rebaño*) flock.

cabaré, cabaret (*pl* **cabarets**) [kaßa're] *nm* cabaret.

cabás [ka'ßas] *nm* satchel.

cabecear [kaßeθe'ar] *vt* to head // *vi* to nod; (*negar*) to shake one's head.

cabecera [kaße'θera] *nf* (*gen*) head; (*de distrito*) chief town; (IMPRENTA) headline.

cabecilla [kaße'θiʎa] *nm/f* ringleader; (*fig: fam*) hothead.

cabellera [kaße'ʎera] *nf* hair; (*de cometa*) tail.

cabello [ka'ßeʎo] *nm* (*también* ~**s** *nmpl*) hair *sg*; **cabelludo, a** *a* hairy.

caber [ka'ßer] *vi* (*entrar*) to fit, go; (*tener lugar*) to have enough room; **caben 3 más** there's room for 3 more.

cabestrillo [kaßes'triʎo] *nm* sling.

cabestro [ka'ßestro] *nm* halter.

cabeza [ka'ßeθa] *nf* head; (POL) chief, leader; ~**da** *nf* (*golpe*) butt; (*al dormirse*) nod.

cabezudo, a [kaße'θuðo, a] *a* bigheaded; (*fig*) pigheaded.

cabida [ka'ßiða] *nf* space.

cabildo [ka'ßildo] *nm* (*de iglesia*) chapter; (POL) town council.

cabina [ka'βina] nf booth; (de camión) cabin.

cabizbajo, a [kaβiθ'βaxo, a] a crestfallen, dejected.

cable ['kaβle] nm cable; ~**grama** nm cablegram.

cabo ['kaβo] nm (de objeto) end, extremity; (de tiempo, proceso) end; (persona) head, chief; (MIL) corporal; (NAUT) rope, cable; (GEO) cape; **al** ~ **de 3 días** after 3 days; **al fin y al** ~ in the end.

cabra ['kaβra] nf (she-)goat, nanny goat.

cabré etc vb ver **caber.**

cabria ['kaβrja] nf hoist, derrick.

cabrío, a [ka'βrio, a] a goatish; **macho** ~ (he-)goat, billy goat.

cabriola [ka'βrjola] nf caper.

cabritilla [kaβri'tiʎa] nf kid, kidskin.

cabrito [ka'βrito] nm kid.

cabrón [ka'βron] nm cuckold; (fig: fam) bastard (fam!).

cacahuete [kaka'wete] nm peanut, monkey nut.

cacao [ka'kao] nm cocoa; (BOT) cacao.

cacarear [kakare'ar] vi (persona) to boast; (gallo) to cackle.

cacería [kaθe'ria] nf hunting, shooting.

cacerola [kaθe'rola] nf pan, saucepan.

cacique [ka'θike] nm chief, local ruler; (POL) local boss; **caciquismo** nm (system of) dominance by the local boss.

caco ['kako] nm pickpocket.

cacto ['kakto], **cactus** ['kaktus] nm cactus.

cacumen [ka'kumen] nm (fig: fam) acumen.

cachar [ka'tʃar] vt to smash, break.

cacharro [ka'tʃarro] nm earthenware pot.

cachear [katʃe'ar] vt to search, frisk.

cachemira [katʃe'mira] nf cashmere.

cacheo [ka'tʃeo] nm searching, frisking.

cachimba [ka'tʃimba] nf, **cachimbo** [ka'tʃimbo] nm pipe.

cachiporra [katʃi'porra] nf truncheon.

cachivache [katʃi'βatʃe] nm pot; (utensilio) utensil; (persona) good-for-nothing.

cacho, a ['katʃo, a] a bent, crooked // nm (small) bit.

cachondeo [katʃon'ðeo] nm (fam) farce, joke.

cachondo, a [ka'tʃondo, a] a (ZOOL) on heat; (vulg) randy, sexy; (gracioso) funny.

cachorro, a [ka'tʃorro, a] nm/f (perro) pup, puppy; (león) cub.

cada ['kaða] a inv each; (antes de número) every; ~ **día** each day, every day; ~ **uno/a** each one, every one; ~ **vez más** more and more; **uno de** ~ **diez** one out of every ten.

cadalso [ka'ðalso] nm scaffold.

cadáver [ka'ðaβer] nm (dead) body, corpse.

cadena [ka'ðena] nf chain; (TV) channel; **trabajo en** ~ assembly line work.

cadencia [ka'ðenθja] nf cadence, rhythm.

cadera [ka'ðera] nf hip.

cadete [ka'ðete] nm cadet.

caducar [kaðu'kar] vi (permiso, ley) to lapse, expire; (persona) to become senile; **caduco, a** a expired; (persona) very old.

C.A.E. abr de **cóbrese al entregar** COD (cash on delivery).

caer [ka'er] vi, ~**se** vr to fall (down); ~ **bien/mal** to make a good/bad impression; **el pago cae mañana** the payment is due tomorrow; ~ **en la cuenta** to catch on.

café [ka'fe] (pl ~s) nm (bebida, planta) coffee; (lugar) café // a (color) brown; **cafetal** nm coffee plantation.

cafetero, a [kafe'tero, a] a coffee cpd // nf coffee pot.

cáfila ['kafila] nf (de personas) group; (de ovejas) flock.

caída [ka'iða] nf (gen) fall; (declive) slope; (disminución) fall, drop.

caigo etc vb ver **caer.**

caimán [kai'man] nm alligator.

caimiento [kai'mjento] nm fall, falling.

caja ['kaxa] nf box; (para reloj) case; (de ascensor) shaft; (COM) cashbox; (donde se hacen los pagos) cashdesk; ~ **de ahorros** savings bank; ~ **de cambios** gearbox; ~ **fuerte**, ~ **de caudales** safe, strongbox.

cajero, a [ka'xero, a] nm/f cashier.

cajetilla [kaxe'tiʎa] nf small box; (de cigarrillos) packet.

cajón [ka'xon] nm big box; (de mueble) drawer.

cal [kal] nf lime.

cala ['kala] nf (GEO) cove, inlet; (de barco) hold; (MED) suppository.

calabaza [kala'βaθa] nf (BOT) pumpkin.

calabozo [kala'βoθo] nm prison (cell).

calamar [kala'mar] nm squid.

calambre [ka'lambre] nm cramp.

calamidad [kalami'ðað] nf calamity, disaster.

calamina [kala'mina] nf calamine.

calaña [ka'laɲa] nf model, pattern.

calar [ka'lar] vt to soak, drench; (penetrar) to pierce, penetrate; (comprender) to see through; (vela, red) to lower; ~**se las gafas** to stick one's glasses on.

calavera [kala'βera] nf skull.

calcañar [kalka'ɲar], **calcañal** [kalka-'ɲal], **calcaño** [kal'kaɲo] nm heel.

calcar [kal'kar] vt (reproducir) to trace; (imitar) to copy.

calceta [kal'θeta] nf (knee-length) stocking; **hacer** ~ to knit; **calcetín** nm sock.

calcina [kal'θina] nf concrete.

calcinar [kalθi'nar] vt to burn, blacken.

calcio ['kalθjo] nm calcium.

calco ['kalko] nm tracing.

calcomanía [kalkoma'nia] nm transfer.

calculadora [kalkula'ðora] nf calculator; ~ **de bolsillo** pocket calculator.

calcular [kalku'lar] vt (MAT) to calculate, compute; (suponer, creer) to reckon,

expect; **cálculo** *nm* calculation; reckoning.
caldear [kalde'ar] *vt* to warm (up), heat (up); (*los metales*) to weld.
caldera [kal'dera] *nf* boiler.
calderilla [kalde'riʎa] *nf* (*REL*) vessel for holy water; (*moneda*) small change.
caldero [kal'dero] *nm* small boiler.
calderón [kalde'ron] *nm* cauldron.
caldo ['kaldo] *nm* stock; (*consomé*) consommé; (*para la ensalada*) dressing.
calefacción [kalefak'θjon] *nf* heating.
calendario [kalen'darjo] *nm* calendar.
calentador [kalenta'ðor] *nm* heater.
calentar [kalen'tar] *vt* to heat (up); ~**se** *vr* to heat up, warm up; (*fig*) to get heated.
calentura [kalen'tura] *nf* (*MED*) fever, (high) temperature; **calenturiento, a** *a* feverish.
calero, a [ka'lero, a] *a* lime *cpd*.
calibrar [kali'ßrar] *vt* to gauge, measure; **calibre** *nm* (*de cañón*) calibre, bore; (*diámetro*) diameter; (*fig*) calibre.
calidad [kali'ðað] *nf* quality; **en ~ de** in the capacity of.
cálido, a ['kaliðo, a] *a* hot; (*fig*) warm.
caliente [ka'ljente] *a* hot; (*sin exceso*) warm; (*fig*) fiery; (*disputa*) heated.
calificación [kalifika'θjon] *nf* qualification; (*de alumno*) grade, mark.
calificado, a [kalifi'kaðo, a] *a* qualified, competent; (*trabajador*) skilled.
calificar [kalifi'kar] *vt* to qualify; (*enaltecer*) to distinguish; (*alumno*) to grade, mark; (*determinar*) to describe.
calma ['kalma] *nf* calm; (*pachorra*) slowness.
calmante [kal'mante] *nm* sedative, tranquillizer.
calmar [kal'mar] *vt* to calm, calm down // *vi* (*tempestad*) to abate; (*mente etc*) to become calm.
calmoso, a [kal'moso, a], **calmudo, a** [kal'muðo, a] *a* calm, quiet.
calofrío [kalo'frio] *nm* = **escalofrío.**
calor [ka'lor] *nm* heat; (~ *agradable*) warmth.
caloría [kalo'ria] *nf* calorie.
calorífero, a [kalo'rifero, a] *a* heat-producing, heat-giving // *nm* heating system.
calumnia [ka'lumnja] *nf* calumny, slander; **calumnioso, a** *a* slanderous.
caluroso, a [kalu'roso, a] *a* hot; (*sin exceso*) warm; (*fig*) enthusiastic.
calva ['kalßa] *nf* bald patch; (*en bosque*) clearing.
calvario [kal'ßarjo] *nm* stations *pl* of the cross.
calvicie [kal'ßiθje] *nf* baldness.
calvo, a ['kalßo, a] *a* bald; (*terreno*) bare, barren; (*tejido*) threadbare.
calza ['kalθa] *nf* wedge, chock.
calzado, a [kal'θaðo, a] *a* shod // *nm* footwear // *nf* roadway, highway.
calzador [kalθa'ðor] *nm* shoehorn.

calzar [kal'θar] *vt* to put on; (*un mueble*) to put a wedge under; ~**se** *vr*: ~**se los zapatos** to put on one's shoes; ¿**qué (número) calza?** what size do you wear or take?
calzón [kal'θon] *nm* (*también* **calzones** *nmpl*) shorts *pl*.
calzoncillos [kalθon'θiʎos] *nmpl* underpants.
callado, a [ka'ʎaðo, a] *a* quiet.
callar [ka'ʎar] *vt* to keep quiet about, say nothing about // *vi*, ~**se** *vr* to keep quiet, be silent.
calle ['kaʎe] *nf* street; (*DEPORTE*) lane; ~ **arriba/abajo** up/down the street; ~ **de un solo sentido** one-way street.
calleja [ka'ʎexa] *nf* alley, narrow street; **callejear** *vi* to wander about the streets; **callejero, a** *a* street *cpd*.
callejón [kaʎe'xon] *nm* alley, passage; ~ **sin salida** one-way street.
callejuela [kaʎe'xwela] *nf* side-street, alley.
callista [ka'ʎista] *nm/f* chiropodist.
callo ['kaʎo] *nm* callus; (*en el pie*) corn; ~**s** *nmpl* tripe *sg*; ~**so, a** a horny, rough.
cama ['kama] *nf* bed; (*GEO*) stratum; ~ **de matrimonio** double bed.
camada [ka'maða] *nf* litter; (*de personas*) gang, band.
camafeo [kama'feo] *nm* cameo.
camandulear [kamandule'ar] *vi* to be a hypocrite.
cámara ['kamara] *nf* (*gen*) chamber; (*habitación*) room; (*sala*) hall; (*CINE*) cine camera; (*fotográfica*) camera; ~ **de aire** inner tube.
camarada [kama'raða] *nm* comrade, companion.
camarera [kama'rera] *nf* (*en restaurante*) waitress; (*en casa, hotel*) maid.
camarero [kama'rero] *nm* waiter.
camarilla [kama'riʎa] *nf* (*clan*) clique; (*POL*) lobby.
camarín [kama'rin] *nm* dressing room.
camarón [kama'ron] *nm* shrimp.
camarote [kama'rote] *nm* cabin.
cambiable [kam'bjaßle] *a* (*variable*) changeable, variable; (*intercambiable*) interchangeable.
cambiante [kam'bjante] *a* variable // *nm* moneychanger.
cambiar [kam'bjar] *vt* (*gen*) to change; (*de moneda*) to change; (*dinero*) to exchange // *vi* (*gen*) to change; ~**se** *vr* (*mudarse*) to move; (*de ropa*) to change; ~**(se) de...** to change one's ... .
cambio ['kambjo] *nm* change; (*trueque*) exchange; (*COM*) rate of exchange; (*oficina*) (foreign) exchange office; (*dinero menudo*) small change; **en ~** on the other hand; (*en lugar de eso*) instead; ~ **de velocidades** gear lever; ~ **de vía** points *pl*.
cambista [kam'bista] *nm* (*COM*) exchange broker; (*FERRO*) switchman.

camelar [kame'lar] *vt* (*galantear*) to flirt with; (*engañar*) to cajole.

camello [ka'meʎo] *nm* camel.

camilla [ka'miʎa] *nf* (*cama*) cot; (*MED*) stretcher.

caminante [kami'nante] *nm/f* traveller.

caminar [kami'nar] *vi* (*marchar*) to walk, go; (*viajar*) to travel, journey // *vt* (*recorrer*) to cover, travel.

caminata [kami'nata] *nf* long walk.

camino [ka'mino] *nm* (*gen*) way, road; (*senda*) track; **a medio** ~ halfway (there); **en el** ~ on the way, en route.

camión [ka'mjon] *nm* lorry, truck.

camisa [ka'misa] *nf* shirt; (*BOT*) skin; ~ **de dormir** nightdress; ~ **de fuerza** straitjacket; **camisería** *nf* outfitter's (shop).

camiseta [kami'seta] *nf* (*prenda*) vest; (*de deportista*) singlet.

camisón [kami'son] *nm* nightdress, nightgown.

campamento [kampa'mento] *nm* camp.

campana [kam'pana] *nf* bell; ~**da** *nf* peal; ~**rio** *nm* belfry.

campanilla [kampa'niʎa] *nf* (*campana*) small bell; (*burbuja*) bubble.

campaña [kam'paɲa] *nf* (*MIL*, *POL*) campaign; (*campo*) countryside.

campar [kam'par] *vi* to camp; (*sobresalir*) to excel, stand out.

campeón, ona [kampe'on, ona] *nm/f* champion; **campeonato** *nm* championship.

campesino, a [kampe'sino, a] *a* country *cpd*, rural // *nm/f* countryman/woman; (*agricultor*) farmer.

campestre [kam'pestre] *a* country *cpd*, rural.

camping ['kampin] *nm* camping; (*lugar*) campsite; **hacer** ~ to go camping.

campiña [kam'piɲa] *nf* countryside.

campo ['kampo] *nm* (*fuera de la ciudad*) country, countryside; (*AGR*, *ELEC*) field; (*de fútbol*) ground, pitch; (*de golf*) course; (*de tenis*) court; (*MIL*) camp.

camposanto [kampo'santo] *nm* cemetery.

camuflaje [kamu'flaxe] *nm* camouflage.

Canadá [kana'ða] *nm* Canada; **canadiense** *a*, *nm/f* Canadian // *nf* fur-lined jacket.

canal [ka'nal] *nm* canal; (*GEO*) channel, strait; (*de televisión*) channel; (*de tejado*) gutter; ~**izar** *vt* to channel.

canalón [kana'lon] *nm* (*conducto vertical*) drainpipe; (*del tejado*) gutter.

canalla [ka'naʎa] *nf* rabble, mob // *nm* swine, rotter.

canapé [kana'pe] (*pl* ~**s**) *nm* sofa, settee; (*CULIN*) canapé.

canario, a [ka'narjo, a] *a*, *nm/f* (native) of the Canary Isles // *nm* canary.

canasta [ka'nasta] *nf* (round) basket; **canasto** *nm* large basket.

cancelación [kanθela'θjon] *nf* cancellation.

cancelar [kanθe'lar] *vt* to cancel; (*una deuda*) to write off.

cáncer ['kanθer] *nm* (*MED*) cancer; **C** ~ (*ASTRO*) Cancer.

canciller [kanθi'ʎer] *nm* chancellor.

canción [kan'θjon] *nf* song; ~ **de cuna** lullaby; **cancionero** *nm* song book.

candado [kan'daðo] *nm* padlock.

candela [kan'dela] *nf* candle.

candelero [kande'lero] *nm* (*para vela*) candlestick; (*de aceite*) oil lamp.

candente [kan'dente] *a* red-hot; (*fig*) burning.

candidato [kandi'ðato] *nm/f* candidate.

candidez [kandi'ðeθ] *nf* (*sencillez*) simplicity; (*simpleza*) naiveté; **cándido, a** *a* simple; naive.

candil [kan'dil] *nm* oil lamp; ~**eja** *nf* small oil lamp.

candor [kan'dor] *nm* (*sinceridad*) frankness; (*inocencia*) innocence.

canela [ka'nela] *nf* cinnamon.

canelón [kane'lon] *nm* (*canal*) drainpipe; (*carámbano*) icicle.

cangrejo [kan'grexo] *nm* crab.

canguro [kan'guro] *nm* kangaroo.

caníbal [ka'niβal] *a*, *nm/f* cannibal.

canica [ka'nika] *nf* marble.

canijo, a [ka'nixo, a] *a* frail, sickly.

canino, a [ka'nino, a] *a* canine // *nm* canine (tooth).

canjear [kanxe'ar] *vt* to exchange.

cano, a ['kano, a] *a* grey-haired, white-haired.

canoa [ka'noa] *nf* canoe.

canon ['kanon] *nm* canon; (*pensión*) rent; (*COM*) tax.

canónigo [ka'nonixo] *nm* canon.

canonizar [kanoni'θar] *vt* to canonize.

canoro, a [ka'noro, a] *a* melodious.

cansado, a [kan'saðo, a] *a* tired, weary; (*tedioso*) tedious, boring.

cansancio [kan'sanθjo] *nm* tiredness, fatigue.

cansar [kan'sar] *vt* (*fatigar*) to tire, tire out, weary; (*aburrir*) to bore; (*fastidiar*) to bother; ~**se** *vr* to tire, get tired; (*aburrirse*) to get bored.

cantante [kan'tante] *a* singing // *nm/f* singer.

cantar [kan'tar] *vt* to sing // *vi* (*gen*) to sing; (*insecto*) to chirp; (*rechinar*) to squeak // *nm* (*acción*) singing; (*canción*) song; (*poema*) poem.

cántara ['kantara] *nf* large pitcher.

cántaro ['kantaro] *nm* pitcher, jug.

cantatriz [kanta'triθ] *nf* singer.

cante ['kante] *nm*: ~ **jondo** flamenco singing.

cantera [kan'tera] *nf* quarry.

cantidad [kanti'ðað] *nf* quantity, amount.

cantilena [kanti'lena] *nf* = **cantinela**.

cantimplora [kantim'plora] *nf* (*frasco*) water bottle, canteen; (*sifón*) syphon.

cantina [kan'tina] *nf* canteen; (*de estación*) buffet; (*sótano*) wine cellar.

cantinela [kanti'nela] *nf* ballad, song.
canto ['kanto] *nm* (*gen*) singing; (*canción*) song; (*borde*) edge, rim; (*de un cuchillo*) back; ~ **rodado** boulder.
cantor, a [kan'tor, a] *nm/f* singer.
canturrear [kanturre'ar], **canturriar** [kantu'rrjar] *vi* to sing softly.
caña ['kaɲa] *nf* (*BOT: tallo*) stem, stalk; (*carrizo*) reed; (*de cerveza*) glass; (*ANAT: del brazo*) long bone; (: *de la pierna*) shinbone; (*MINERÍA*) gallery; ~ **de azúcar** sugar cane.
cañada [ka'ɲaða] *nf* (*entre dos montañas*) gully, ravine; (*camino*) cattle track.
caño ['kaɲo] *nm* (*tubo*) tube; (*de aguas servidas*) sewer; (*MUS*) pipe; (*NAUT*) navigation channel; (*de fuente*) jet.
cañón [ka'ɲon] *nm* tube, pipe; (*MIL*) cannon; (*de fusil*) barrel; (*GEO*) canyon, gorge.
cañonero [kaɲo'nero] *nm* gunboat.
caoba [ka'oßa] *nf* mahogany.
caos ['kaos] *nm* chaos.
cap. *abr de* **capítulo.**
capa ['kapa] *nf* cloak, cape; (*GEO*) layer, stratum; (*pretexto*) pretence.
capacidad [kapaθi'ðað] *nf* (*medida*) capacity; (*aptitud*) capacity, ability.
capacitación [kapaθita'θjon] *nf* training.
capar [ka'par] *vt* to castrate, geld.
caparazón [kapara'θon] *nm* shell.
capataz [kapa'taθ] *nm* foreman.
capaz [ka'paθ] *a* able, capable; (*amplio*) capacious, roomy.
capcioso, a [kap'θjoso, a] *a* wily, deceitful.
capellán [kape'ʎan] *nm* chaplain; (*sacerdote*) priest.
caperuza [kape'ruθa] *nf* hood; **caperucita** *nf*: **Caperucita Roja** Little Red Riding Hood.
capilla [ka'piʎa] *nf* chapel; (*capucha*) hood, cowl.
capital [kapi'tal] *a* capital // *nm* (*COM*) capital // *nf* capital; ~ **social** share capital.
capitalismo [kapita'lismo] *nm* capitalism; **capitalista** *a, nm/f* capitalist.
capitalizar [kapitali'θar] *vt* to capitalize.
capitán [kapi'tan] *nm* captain.
capitana [kapi'tana] *nf* flagship.
capitanear [kapitane'ar] *vt* to captain.
capitolio [kapi'toljo] *nm* capitol.
capitoné [kapito'ne] *nm* removal van.
capitulación [kapitula'θjon] *nf* (*rendición*) capitulation; surrender; (*acuerdo*) agreement, pact.
capitular [kapitu'lar] *vi* to come to terms, make an agreement // *a* chapter *cpd*.
capítulo [ka'pitulo] *nm* chapter; ~s *nmpl*: ~s **matrimoniales** marriage contract *sg*.
capó [ka'po] *nm* bonnet.
caporal [kapo'ral] *nm* chief, leader.
capota [ka'pota] *nf* (*de mujer*) bonnet; (*de coche*) hood, roof.
capote [ka'pote] *nm* (*abrigo, de militar*)

greatcoat; (*de torero*) cloak; (*NAIPES*) slam.
Capricornio [kapri'kornjo] *nm* Capricorn.
capricho [ka'pritʃo] *nm* whim, caprice; ~**so, a** *a* capricious.
cápsula ['kapsula] *nf* capsule; (*de botella*) cap.
captar [kap'tar] *vt* to win (over).
captura [kap'tura] *nf* capture; (*JUR*) arrest; **capturar** *vt* to capture; to arrest.
capucha [ka'putʃa] *nf* hood, cowl.
cara ['kara] *nf* (*ANAT*) face; (*aspecto*) appearance; (*de moneda*) face; (*de disco*) side; (*fig*) boldness; ~ **a** *ad* facing; **de** ~ **opposite**, facing; **dar la** ~ to face the consequences; ¿~ **o cruz?** heads or tails?
carabina [kara'ßina] *nf* carbine, rifle.
caracol [kara'kol] *nm* (*ZOOL*) snail; (*concha*) shell.
caracolear [karakole'ar] *vi* to prance about.
carácter [ka'rakter] (*pl* **caracteres**) *nm* character.
característico, a [karakte'ristiko, a] *a* characteristic // *nf* characteristic.
caracterizar [karakteri'θar] *vt* (*distinguir*) to characterize, typify; (*honrar*) to confer (a) distinction on.
caramba [ka'ramba] *excl* well!, good gracious!
carámbano [ka'rambano] *nm* icicle.
caramelo [kara'melo] *nm* (*dulce*) sweet; (*dulce de* ~) toffee; (*azúcar fundida*) caramel.
caramillo [kara'miʎo] *nm* (*flauta*) recorder; (*montón*) untidy heap; (*chisme, enredo*) bit of gossip.
carapacho [kara'patʃo] *nm* shell, carapace.
caraqueño, a [kara'keɲo, a] *a, nm/f* (native) of Caracas.
carátula [ka'ratula] *nf* (*careta, máscara*) mask; (*TEATRO*): **la** ~ the stage.
caravana [kara'ßana] *nf* caravan; (*fig*) group; (*sucesión de autos*) stream; (*embotellamiento*) traffic jam.
carbón [kar'ßon] *nm* coal; **papel** ~ carbon paper; **carbonero** *nm/f* coal merchant; **carbonilla** *nf* coal dust.
carbonizar [karßoni'θar] *vt* to carbonize; (*quemar*) to char.
carbono [kar'ßono] *nm* carbon.
carburador [karßura'ðor] *nm* carburettor.
carcajada [karka'xaða] *nf* (loud) laugh, guffaw.
cárcel ['karθel] *nf* prison, jail; (*TEC*) clamp; **carcelero, a** *a* prison *cpd* // *nm/f* warder.
carcomer [karko'mer] *vt* to bore into, eat into; (*fig*) to undermine; ~**se** *vr* to become worm-eaten; (*fig*) to decay.
carcomido, a [karko'miðo, a] *a* worm-eaten; (*fig*) rotten.
cardenal [karðe'nal] *nm* (*REL*) cardinal; (*equimosis*) bruise.
cárdeno, a ['karðeno, a] *a* purple; (*lívido*) livid.

cardíaco, a [kar'ðiako, a] *a* cardiac, heart *cpd.*

cardinal [karði'nal] *a* cardinal.

cardo ['karðo] *nm* thistle.

cardumen [kar'ðumen] *nm* shoal.

carear [kare'ar] *vt* to bring face to face; *(comparar)* to compare; ~**se** *vr* to come face to face, meet.

carecer [kare'θer] *vi*: ~ **de** to lack, be in need of.

carencia [ka'renθja] *nf* lack; *(escasez)* shortage; *(MED)* deficiency.

carente [ka'rente] *a*: ~ **de** lacking, devoid of.

carestía [kares'tia] *nf* *(escasez)* scarcity, shortage; *(COM)* high cost.

careta [ka'reta] *nf* mask.

carga ['karɤa] *nf* *(peso, ELEC)* load; *(de barco)* cargo, freight; *(MIL)* charge; *(obligación, responsabilidad)* duty, obligation.

cargadero [karɤa'ðero] *nm* goods platform, loading bay.

cargado, a [kar'ɤaðo, a] *a* loaded; *(ELEC)* live; *(café, te)* strong; *(el cielo)* overcast.

cargamento [karɤa'mento] *nm* *(acción)* loading; *(mercancías)* load, cargo.

cargar [kar'ɤar] *vt* *(barco, arma)* to load; *(ELEC)* to charge; *(COM: algo en cuenta)* to charge, debit; *(MIL: enemigo)* to charge // *vi* to load (up); *(inclinarse)* to lean; ~ **con** to pick up, carry away.

cargo ['karɤo] *nm* *(puesto)* post, office; *(responsabilidad)* duty, obligation; *(fig)* weight, burden; *(JUR)* charge; **hacerse ~ del gobierno** to take charge of the government.

carguero [kar'ɤero] *nm* freighter, cargo boat; *(avión)* freight plane.

caribe [ka'riβe] *a, nm/f* (native) of the Caribbean.

Caribe [ka'riβe] *nm*: **el** ~ the Caribbean.

caricatura [karika'tura] *nf* caricature.

caricia [ka'riθja] *nf* caress.

caridad [kari'ðað] *nf* charity.

cariño [ka'riɲo] *nm* affection, love; *(caricia)* caress; *(en carta)* love...; ~ **so, a** *a* affectionate.

caritativo, a [karita'tiβo, a] *a* charitable.

carmesí [karme'si] *a, nm* crimson.

carnal [kar'nal] *a* carnal; **primo** ~ first cousin.

carnaval [karna'βal] *nm* carnival.

carne ['karne] *nf* flesh; *(CULIN)* meat; **echar** ~**s** to put on weight.

carnero [kar'nero] *nm* sheep, ram; *(carne)* mutton.

carnet [kar'ne] *nm*: ~ **de conducir** driving licence.

carnicería [karniθe'ria] *nf* butcher's (shop); *(mercado)* meat market.

carnicero, a [karni'θero, a] *a* carnivorous // *nm/f* butcher // *nm* carnivore.

carnívoro, a [kar'niβoro, a] *a* carnivorous.

carnoso, a [kar'noso, a] *a* beefy, fat.

caro, a ['karo, a] *a* dear; *(COM)* dear, expensive // *ad* dear, dearly.

carpeta [kar'peta] *nf* table cover; *(para documentos)* folder, file.

carpintería [karpinte'ria] *nf* carpentry, joinery; **carpintero** *nm* carpenter.

carraspera [karras'pera] *nf* hoarseness.

carrera [ka'rrera] *nf* *(DEPORTE)* running; *(espacio recorrido)* run; *(certamen)* race; *(trayecto)* course; *(profesión)* career; *(ESCOL)* course.

carreta [ka'rreta] *nf* wagon, cart.

carrete [ka'rrete] *nm* reel, spool; *(TEC)* coil.

carretel [karre'tel] *nm* reel, spool.

carretera [karre'tera] *nf* (main) road, highway.

carretilla [karre'tiʎa] *nf* trolley; *(AGR)* (wheel)barrow.

carril [ka'rril] *nm* furrow; *(de autopista)* lane; *(FERRO)* rail.

carrillo [ka'rriʎo] *nm* *(ANAT)* cheek; *(TEC)* pulley.

carrizo [ka'rriθo] *nm* reed.

carro ['karro] *nm* cart, wagon; *(MIL)* tank; *(AM: coche)* car.

carrocería [karroθe'ria] *nf* bodywork, coachwork.

carta ['karta] *nf* letter; *(CULIN)* menu; *(naipe)* card; *(mapa)* map; *(JUR)* document; ~ **de crédito** credit card; ~ **certificada** registered letter.

cartel [kar'tel] *nm* *(anuncio)* poster, placard; *(alfabeto)* wall chart; *(COM)* cartel.

cartera [kar'tera] *nf* *(de bolsillo)* wallet; *(de colegial, cobrador)* satchel; *(de señora)* handbag; *(para documentos)* briefcase; *(COM, POL)* portfolio.

cartero [kar'tero] *nm* postman.

cartón [kar'ton] *nm* cardboard; *(ARTE)* cartoon.

cartucho [kar'tutʃo] *nm* *(MIL)* cartridge.

casa ['kasa] *nf* house; *(hogar)* home; *(edificio)* building; *(COM)* firm, company; *(de tablero de ajedrez)* square; ~ **consistorial** town hall; ~ **de huéspedes** boarding house; ~ **de socorro** first aid post; ~ **editorial** publishing house.

casamiento [kasa'mjento] *nm* marriage, wedding.

casar [ka'sar] *vt* to marry; *(JUR)* to quash, annul // *nm* hamlet; ~**se** *vr* to marry, get married.

cascada [kas'kaða] *nf* waterfall.

cascar [kas'kar] *vt*, ~**se** *vr* to crack, split, break (open).

cáscara ['kaskara] *nf* *(de huevo, fruta seca)* shell; *(de fruta)* skin; *(de limón)* peel.

casco ['kasko] *nm* *(de bombero, soldado)* helmet; *(cráneo)* skull; *(de botella, obús)* fragment; *(BOT. de cebolla)* skin; *(tonel)* cask, barrel; *(NAUT. de barco)* hull; *(ZOOL: de caballo)* hoof; *(botella)* empty bottle.

caserío [kase'rio] *nm* hamlet; *(casa)* country house.

casero, a [ka'sero, a] *a* domestic, household *cpd* // *nm/f* *(propietario)*

landlord/lady; (*portero*) caretaker; (*COM*) house agent.
caseta [ka'seta] *nf* hut; (*para bañista*) cubicle; (*de feriantes*) stall.
casi ['kasi] *ad* almost; ~ **te caes** you almost fell.
casilla [ka'siʎa] *nf* (*casita*) hut, cabin; (*TEATRO*) box office; (*de ajedrez*) square.
casino [ka'sino] *nm* club.
caso ['kaso] *nm* case; **en ~ de...** in case of...; **el ~ es que** the fact is that; **hacer ~ a** to pay attention to; **hacer o venir al ~** to be relevant.
caspa ['kaspa] *nf* dandruff.
cassette [ka'set] *nf* cassette.
casta ['kasta] *nf* caste; (*raza*) breed; (*linaje*) lineage.
castaña [kas'taɲa] *nf* chestnut.
castaño, a [kas'taɲo, a] *a* chestnut-brown // *nm* chestnut tree.
castañuela [kasta'ɲwela] *nf* castanet.
castellano, a [kaste'ʎano, a] *a* Castilian // *nm* (*lengua*) Castilian, Spanish.
castidad [kasti'ðað] *nf* chastity, purity.
castigar [kasti'ɣar] *vt* to punish; (*DEPORTE*) to penalize; (*afligir*) to afflict; **castigo** *nm* punishment; (*DEPORTE*) penalty.
castillo [kas'tiʎo] *nm* castle.
castizo, a [kas'tiθo, a] *a* (*LING*) pure; (*de buena casta*) purebred, pedigree.
casto, a ['kasto, a] *a* chaste, pure.
castor [kas'tor] *nm* beaver.
castrar [kas'trar] *vt* to castrate.
casual [ka'swal] *a* fortuitous, accidental; ~**idad** *nf* chance, accident; (*combinación de circunstancias*) coincidence.
cataclismo [kata'klismo] *nm* cataclysm.
catalán, ana [kata'lan, ana] *a, nm/f* Catalan, Catalonian.
catalizador [kataliθa'ðor] *nm* catalyst.
catálogo [ka'taloɣo] *nm* catalogue.
Cataluña [kata'luɲa] *nf* Catalonia.
cataplasma [kata'plasma] *nf* poultice.
catar [ka'tar] *vt* to taste, sample.
catarata [kata'rata] *nf* (*GEO*) waterfall, falls *pl*; (*MED*) cataract.
· **catarro** [ka'tarro] *nm* catarrh; (*constipado*) cold.
catástrofe [ka'tastrofe] *nf* catastrophe.
catedral [kate'ðral] *nf* cathedral.
catedrático, a [kate'ðratiko, a] *nm/f* professor.
categoría [kateɣo'ria] *nf* category; (*rango*) rank, standing; (*calidad*) quality.
categórico, a [kate'ɣoriko, a] *a* categorical.
catolicismo [katoli'θismo] *nm* Catholicism.
católico, a [ka'toliko, a] *a, nm/f* Catholic.
catorce [ka'torθe] *num* fourteen.
caución [kau'θjon] *nf* bail; **caucionar** *vt* to prevent, guard against; (*JUR*) to bail, go bail for.
caucho ['kautʃo] *nm* rubber.
caudal [kau'ðal] *nm* (*de río*) volume, flow;

(*fortuna*) wealth; (*abundancia*) abundance; ~**oso, a** *a* (*río*) large; (*aguas*) copious; (*persona*) wealthy, rich.
caudillo [kau'ðiʎo] *nm* leader, chief.
causa ['kausa] *nf* cause; (*razón*) reason; (*JUR*) lawsuit, case; **causar** *vt* to cause.
cáustico, a ['kaustiko, a] *a* caustic.
cautela [kau'tela] *nf* caution, cautiousness; **cauteloso, a** *a* cautious, wary, careful.
cautivar [kauti'ßar] *vt* to capture; (*fig*) to captivate.
cautiverio [kauti'ßerjo] *nm,* **cautividad** [kautißi'ðað] *nf* captivity.
cautivo, a [kau'tißo, a] *a, nm/f* captive.
cauto, a ['kauto, a] *a* cautious, careful.
cavar [ka'ßar] *vt* to dig.
caverna [ka'ßerna] *nf* cave, cavern.
cavidad [kaßi'ðað] *nf* cavity.
cavilar [kaßi'lar] *vt* to ponder.
cayado [ka'jaðo] *nm* (*de pastor*) staff, crook; (*de obispo*) crozier.
cayó *etc vb ver* **caer.**
caza ['kaθa] *nf* (*gen*) hunting, shooting; (*una ~*) hunt, chase; (*animales*) game // *nm* (*AVIAT*) fighter.
cazador [kaθa'ðor] *nm* hunter.
cazar [ka'θar] *vt* to hunt; (*perseguir*) to chase; (*coger*) to catch.
cazo ['kaθo] *nm* saucepan.
cazuela [ka'θwela] *nf* pan; (*guisado*) casserole.
cebada [θe'ßaða] *nf* barley.
cebar [θe'ßar] *vt* (*animal*) to fatten (up); (*anzuelo*) to bait; (*MIL, TEC*) to prime; (*pasión*) to nourish; (*ira*) to inflame.
cebo ['θeßo] *nm* (*para animales*) feed, food; (*para peces, fig*) bait; (*de arma*) charge.
cebolla [θe'ßoʎa] *nf* onion.
cebra ['θeßra] *nf* zebra.
cecear [θeθe'ar] *vi* to lisp; **ceceo** *nm* lisp.
cedazo [θe'ðaθo] *nm* sieve.
ceder [θe'ðer] *vt* to hand over, give up, part with // *vi* (*renunciar*) to give in, yield; (*disminuir*) to diminish, decline; (*romperse*) to give way.
cedro ['θeðro] *nm* cedar.
cédula ['θeðula] *nf* certificate, document; ~ **de aduana** customs permit.
C.E.E. *nf abr de* **Comunidad Económica Europea** E.E.C. (European Economic Community).
cegar [θe'ɣar] *vt* to blind; (*fig: pozo*) to block up, fill up // *vi* to go blind; ~**se** *vr* to be blinded (*de* by).
ceguedad [θeɣe'ðað], **ceguera** [θe'ɣera] *nf* blindness.
ceja ['θeɣa] *nf* eyebrow.
cejar [θe'xar] *vi* to move back, go back; (*fig*) to back down.
cejijunto, a [θexi'xunto, a] *a* with bushy eyebrows; (*fig*) scowling.
celada [θe'laða] *nf* ambush, trap.
celador, a [θela'ðor, a] *nm/f* (*de edificio*) watchman; (*de museo etc*) attendant.
celar [θe'lar] *vt* (*vigilar*) to watch over; (*encubrir*) to conceal, hide.

celda ['θelda] *nf* cell.
celebración [θeleßra'θjon] *nf* celebration.
celebrar [θele'ßrar] *vt* to celebrate; (*alabar*) to praise // *vi* to be glad; ~**se** *vr* to occur, take place.
célebre ['θelebre] *a* famous; (*chistoso*) witty, funny.
celebridad [θeleßri'ðað] *nf* (*gen*) fame; (*persona*) celebrity; (*festividad*) celebration(s) (*pl*).
celeste [θe'leste] *a* celestial, heavenly.
celestial [θeles'tjal] *a* celestial, heavenly.
celibato [θeli'ßato] *nm* celibacy.
célibe ['θeliße] *a* celibate // *nm/f* unmarried person.
celo ['θelo] *nm* zeal; (*REL*) fervour; (*pey*) envy; (*de animales*) rut, heat; ~**s** *nmpl* jealousy *sg*.
celofán [θelo'fan] *nm* cellophane.
celoso, a [θe'loso, a] *a* (*envidioso*) jealous; (*trabajo*) zealous; (*desconfiado*) suspicious.
celta ['θelta] *nm/f* Celt.
célula ['θelula] *nf* cell.
cementar [θemen'tar] *vt* to cement.
cementerio [θemen'terjo] *nm* cemetery, graveyard.
cemento [θe'mento] *nm* cement; (*hormigón*) concrete.
cena ['θena] *nf* evening meal.
cenagal [θena'xal] *nm* bog, quagmire.
cenar [θe'nar] *vt* to have for supper // *vi* to dine.
cenicero [θeni'θero] *nm* ashtray.
cenit [θe'nit] *nm* zenith.
ceniza [θe'niθa] *nf* ash, ashes *pl*.
censo ['θenso] *nm* (*empadronamiento*) census; (*JUR*) tax; (*renta*) rent; (*carga sobre una casa*) mortgage.
censor [θen'sor] *nm* censor.
censura [θen'sura] *nf* (*POL*) censorship; (*moral*) censure, criticism.
censurar [θensu'rar] *vt* (*idea*) to censure; (*cortar: película*) to censor.
centella [θen'teʎa] *nf* spark.
centellar [θente'ʎar], **centellear** [θenteʎe'ar] *vi* (*metal*) to gleam; (*estrella*) to twinkle; (*fig*) to sparkle; **centelleo** *nm* gleam(ing); twinkling; sparkling.
centenar [θente'nar] *nm* hundred.
centenario, a [θente'narjo, a] *a* centenary.
centésimo, a [θen'tesimo, a] *a* hundredth.
centígrado, a [θen'tixraðo, a] *a* centigrade.
centímetro [θen'timetro] *nm* centimetre.
céntimo, a ['θentimo, a] *a* hundredth // *nm* cent.
centinela [θenti'nela] *nm* sentry, guard.
central [θen'tral] *a* central // *nf* head office; (*TEC*) plant; (*TELEC*) exchange.
centralización [θentraliθa'θjon] *nf* centralization.
centralizar [θentrali'θar] *vt* to centralize.
centrar [θen'trar] *vt* to centre.
céntrico, a ['θentriko, a] *a* centre.
centro ['θentro] *nm* centre.

centroamericano, a [θentroameri'kano, a] *a, nm/f* Central American.
ceñidor [θeɲi'ðor] *nm* sash.
ceñir [θe'ɲir] *vt* (*rodear*) to encircle, surround; (*ajustar*) to fit (tightly); (*apretar*) to tighten.
ceño ['θeɲo] *nm* frown, scowl; **fruncir el** ~ to frown, knit one's brow.
cepillar [θepi'ʎar] *vt* to brush; (*madera*) to plane (down); **cepillo** *nm* (*gen*) brush; (*TEC*) plane.
cera ['θera] *nf* wax.
cerámico, a [θe'ramiko, a] *a* ceramic // *nf* ceramics *sg*.
cerca ['θerka] *nf* fence // *ad* near, nearby, close; ~**s** *nmpl* foreground *sg*; ~ **de** *prep* near, close to.
cercanía [θerka'nia] *nf* nearness, closeness; ~**s** *nfpl* outskirts.
cercano, a [θer'kano, a] *a* close, near.
cercar [θer'kar] *vt* to fence in; (*rodear*) to surround.
cerciorar [θerθjo'rar] *vt* (*informar*) to inform; (*asegurar*) to assure; ~**se** *vr* (*descubrir*) to find out; (*asegurarse*) to make sure.
cerco ['θerko] *nm* (*AGR*) enclosure; (*AM*) fence; (*MIL*) siege.
cerdo ['θerðo] *nm* pig.
cereal [θere'al] *nm* cereal.
cerebro [θe'reßro] *nm* brain; (*fig*) brains *pl*.
ceremonia [θere'monja] *nf* ceremony; **ceremonial** *a, nm* ceremonial; **ceremonioso, a** *a* ceremonious; (*cumplido*) formal.
cereza [θe'reθa] *nf* cherry.
cerilla [θe'riʎa] *nf* (*fósforo*) match.
cerner [θer'ner] *vt* to sift, sieve; (*fig*) to scan, watch // *vi* to blossom; (*lloviznar*) to drizzle; ~**se** *vr* to hover.
cernidor [θerni'ðor] *nm* sieve.
cero ['θero] *nm* nothing, zero.
cerrado, a [θe'rraðo, a] *a* closed, shut; (*con llave*) locked; (*tiempo*) cloudy, overcast; (*curva*) sharp; (*acento*) thick, broad.
cerradura [θerra'ðura] *nf* (*acción*) closing; (*mecanismo*) lock.
cerraja [θe'rraxa] *nf* lock.
cerrar [θe'rrar] *vt* to close, shut; (*paso, carretera*) to close; (*grifo*) to turn off; (*trato, cuenta, negocio*) to close; ~ **con llave** to lock // *vi* to close, shut; (*la noche*) to come down; ~**se** *vr* to close, shut.
cerro ['θerro] *nm* hill.
cerrojo [θe'rroxo] *nm* (*herramienta*) bolt; (*de puerta*) latch.
certamen [θer'tamen] *nm* competition, contest.
certero, a [θer'tero, a] *a* accurate; (*cierto*) sure, certain.
certeza [θer'teθa], **certidumbre** [θerti'ðumbre] *nf* certainty.
certificado [θertifi'kaðo] *nm* certificate.
certificar [θertifi'kar] *vt* (*asegurar*,

atestar) to certify; (*carta*) to register.
cervato [θer'ßato] *nm* fawn.
cervecería [θerßeθe'ria] *nf* (*fábrica*) brewery; (*tienda*) public house.
cerveza [θer'ßeθa] *nf* beer.
cesación [θesa'θjon] *nf* cessation; (*suspensión*) suspension.
cesante [θe'sante] *a* out of a job.
cesar [θe'sar] *vi* to cease, stop.
cese ['θese] *nm* (*de trabajo*) dismissal; (*de pago*) suspension.
césped ['θespeð] *nm* grass, lawn.
cesta ['θesta] *nf* basket; **cesto** *nm* (large) basket, hamper.
ch... *ver bajo la letra* CH, *después de* C.
Cía *abr de* **compañía.**
cianuro [θja'nuro] *nm* cyanide.
ciar [θjar] *vi* to go backwards.
cicatriz [θika'triθ] *nf* scar.
ciclismo [θi'klismo] *nm* cycling.
ciclo ['θiklo] *nm* cycle.
ciclón [θi'klon] *nm* cyclone.
ciego, a ['θjexo, a] *a* blind // *nm/f* blind man/woman.
cielo ['θjelo] *nm* sky; (REL) heaven; ¡~s! good heavens!
ciempiés [θjem'pjes] *nm* centipede.
cien [θjen] *num ver* **ciento.**
ciénaga ['θjenaxa] *nf* marsh, swamp.
ciencia ['θjenθja] *nf* science; ~**-ficción** *nf* science fiction.
cieno ['θjeno] *nm* mud, mire.
científico, a [θjen'tifiko, a] *a* scientific // *nm/f* scientist.
ciento ['θjento], **cien** *num* hundred; **pagar al 10 por** ~ to pay at 10 per cent.
cierne ['θjerne] *nm*: **en** ~ in blossom.
cierre ['θjerre] *nm* closing, shutting; (*con llave*) locking; ~ **a cremallera** zip fastener.
cierro *etc vb ver* **cerrar.**
cierto, a ['θjerto, a] *a* sure, certain; (*un tal*) a certain; (*correcto*) right, correct; ~ **hombre** a certain man; **sí, es** ~ yes, that's correct.
ciervo ['θjerßo] *nm* (*especie*) deer; (*macho*) stag.
cierzo ['θjerθo] *nm* north wind.
cifra ['θifra] *nf* number, numeral; (*cantidad*) number, quantity; (*secreta*) code; (*siglas*) abbreviation.
cifrar [θi'frar] *vt* to code, write in code; (*resumir*) to abridge.
cigarra [θi'xarra] *nf* cicada.
cigarrera [θixa'rrera] *nf* cigar case.
cigarrillo [θixa'rriʎo] *nm* cigarette.
cigarro [θi'xarro] *nm* cigarette; (*puro*) cigar.
cigüeña [θi'xweɲa] *nf* stork.
cilíndrico, a [θi'lindriko, a] *a* cylindrical.
cilindro [θi'lindro] *nm* cylinder; (*rodillo*) roller.
cima ['θima] *nf* (*de montaña*) top, peak; (*de árbol*) top; (*fig*) summit, height.
címbalo ['θimbalo] *nm* cymbal.
cimbrar [θim'brar], **cimbrear** [θimbre-**

'ar] *vt* to brandish; ~**se** *vr* (*al viento*) to sway.
cimentar [θimen'tar] *vt* to lay the foundations of.
cimiento [θi'mjento] *nm* foundation.
cinc [θink] *nm* zinc.
cincel [θin'θel] *nm* chisel; ~**ar** *vt* to chisel.
cinco [θinko] *num* five.
cincuenta [θin'kwenta] *num* fifty.
cincho ['θintʃo] *nm* sash, belt.
cine ['θine] *nm* cinema.
cinematográfico, a [θinemato'xrafiko, a] *a* cine-, film *cpd*.
cínico, a ['θiniko, a] *a* cynical // *nm/f* cynic.
cinismo [θi'nismo] *nm* cynicism.
cinta ['θinta] *nf* band, strip; (*de seda, lana, algodón*) ribbon, tape; (*película*) reel; (*de máquina de escribir*) ribbon; (*métrica*) tape measure; (*magnetofónica*) tape; (*adhesiva*) adhesive tape.
cinto ['θinto] *nm* belt, girdle.
cintura [θin'tura] *nf* waist.
cinturón [θintu'ron] *nm* belt; ~ **de seguridad** safety belt.
ciprés [θi'pres] *nm* cypress (tree).
circo ['θirko] *nm* circus.
circuito [θir'kwito] *nm* circuit.
circulación [θirkula'θjon] *nf* circulation; (AUTO) traffic.
circular [θirku'lar] *a, nf* circular // *vi, vt* to circulate.
círculo ['θirkulo] *nm* circle.
circuncidar [θirkunθi'dar] *vt* to circumcise; **circuncisión** *nf* circumcision; **circunciso, a** *pp de* **circuncidar** // *a* circumcised.
circundar [θirkun'dar] *vt* to surround.
circunferencia [θirkunfe'renθja] *nf* circumference.
circunlocución [θirkunloku'θjon] *nf,* **circunloquio** [θirkun'lokjo] *nm* circumlocution.
circunscribir [θirkunskri'ßir] *vt* to circumscribe; ~**se** *vr* to be limited.
circunscripción [θirkunskrip'θjon] *nf* division; (POL) constituency.
circunspección [θirkunspek'θjon] *nf* circumspection.
circunspecto, a [θirkuns'pekto, a] *a* circumspect, cautious.
circunstancia [θirkuns'tanθja] *nf* circumstance.
circunstante [θirkuns'tante] *nm/f* onlooker, bystander.
cirio ['θirjo] *nm* (wax) candle.
ciruela [θi'rwela] *nf* plum; ~ **pasa** prune.
cirugía [θiru'xia] *nf* surgery; ~ **estética** plastic surgery.
cirujano [θiru'xano] *nm* surgeon.
cisne ['θisne] *nm* swan.
cisterna [θis'terna] *nf* cistern.
cita ['θita] *nf* appointment, engagement; (*de novios*) date; (*referencia*) quotation.
citación [θita'θjon] *nf* (JUR) summons *sg*; (*referencia*) quotation.

citar [θi'tar] vt (gen) to make an appointment with; (JUR) to summons; (un autor, texto) to quote.
citrón [θi'tron] nm lemon.
ciudad [θju'ðað] nf town; (capital de país etc) city; ~ano, a nm/f citizen; ~ela nf citadel, fortress.
cívico, a ['θiβiko, a] a civic.
civil [θi'βil] a civil // nm (guardia) policeman; ~idad nf civility, courtesy.
civilización [θiβiliθa'θjon] nf civilization.
civilizar [θiβili'θar] vt to civilize.
civismo [θi'βismo] nm public spirit.
cizaña [θi'θaɲa] nf discord.
clamar [kla'mar] vt to clamour for // vi to cry out, clamour.
clamor [kla'mor] nm (grito) cry, shout; (gemido) whine; (de campana) knell; (fig) clamour, protest.
clamorear [klamore'ar] vt to clamour for // vi (campana) to toll; **clamoreo** nm clamour(ing).
clandestino, a [klandes'tino, a] a clandestine; (POL) underground.
clara ['klara] nf (de huevo) white of an egg; (del día) bright interval.
claraboya [klara'βoja] nf skylight.
clarear [klare'ar] vi (el día) to dawn; (el cielo) to clear up, brighten up; ~se vr to be transparent.
claridad [klari'ðað] nf (del día) brightness; (de estilo) clarity.
clarificar [klarifi'kar] vt to clarify.
clarín [kla'rin] nm bugle.
clarinete [klari'nete] nm clarinet.
clarividencia [klariβi'ðenθja] nf clairvoyance; (fig) far-sightedness.
claro, a ['klaro, a] a (gen) clear; (luminoso) bright; (poco subido) light; (evidente) clear, evident; (ralo) sparse; (poco espeso) thin // nm (en escritura) space; (en bosque) clearing // ad clearly // excl of course!
clase ['klase] nf class; ~ alta/media/obrera upper/middle/ working class.
clásico, a ['klasiko, a] a classical; (fig) classic.
clasificación [klasifika'θjon] nf classification; (DEPORTE) league.
clasificar [klasifi'kar] vt to classify.
claudicar [klauði'kar] vi to limp; (fig) to back down.
claustro ['klaustro] nm cloister.
cláusula ['klausula] nf clause.
clausura [klau'sura] nf closing, closure.
clavar [kla'βar] vt (clavo) to knock in, drive in; (cuchillo, tenedor) to stick, thrust; (mirada) to fix.
clave ['klaβe] nf key; (MUS) clef.
clavel [kla'βel] nm carnation.
clavícula [kla'βikula] nf collar bone.
clavija [kla'βixa] nf peg, dowel, pin; (ELEC) plug.
clavo ['klaβo] nm (de metal) nail; (BOT) clove; (callo) corn.

claxon ['klakson] nm horn.
clemencia [kle'menθja] nf mercy, clemency; **clemente** a merciful, clement.
cleptómano, a [klep'tomano, a] nm/f kleptomaniac.
clerical [kleri'kal] a clerical // nm clergyman.
clérigo ['klerixo] nm clergyman.
clero ['klero] nm clergy.
cliente ['kljente] nm/f client, customer.
clientela [kljen'tela] nf clientele, customers pl.
clima ['klima] nm climate.
clínica ['klinika] nf clinic; (particular) private hospital.
clip [klip] nm paper clip.
clorhídrico, a [klo'ridriko, a] a hydrochloric.
cloroformo [kloro'formo] nm chloroform.
club [klub] (pl ~s o ~es) nm club.
C.N.T. abr de **Confederación Nacional de Trabajo.**
coacción [koak'θjon] nf coercion, compulsion.
coalición [koali'θjon] nf coalition.
coartar [koar'tar] vt to limit, restrict.
cobarde [ko'βarðe] a cowardly // nm coward; **cobardía** nf cowardice.
cobertizo [koβer'tiθo] nm shelter.
cobertor [koβer'tor] nm bedspread.
cobertura [koβer'tura] nf cover.
cobija [ko'βixa] nf roof; **cobijar** vt (cubrir) to cover; (abrigar) to shelter.
cobra ['koβra] nf cobra.
cobrador [koβra'ðor] nm (de autobús) conductor; (de impuestos, gas) collector.
cobrar [ko'βrar] vt (cheque) to cash; (sueldo) to collect, draw; (objeto) to recover; (precio) to charge; (deuda) to collect // vi to draw one's pay; ~se vr to recover, get well; **cóbrese al entregar** cash on delivery (COD).
cobre ['koβre] nm copper; ~s nmpl brass instruments.
cobro ['koβro] nm recovery; (paga) payment.
cocaína [koka'ina] nf cocaine.
cocción [kok'θjon] nf cooking.
cocear [koθe'ar] vi to kick.
cocer [ko'θer] vt, vi to cook; (en agua) to boil; (en horno) to bake; ~se vr to suffer intensely.
cocido [ko'θiðo] nm stew.
cocina [ko'θina] nf kitchen; (aparato) cooker, stove; (acto) cookery; **cocinar** vt, vi to cook.
cocinero, a [koθi'nero, a] nm/f cook.
coco ['koko] nm (árbol) coconut palm; (fruto) coconut.
cocodrilo [koko'ðrilo] nm crocodile.
coche ['kotʃe] nm car, motorcar; (de tren, de caballos) coach, carriage; (fúnebre) hearse; (para niños) pram; ~ celular Black Maria, prison van.
coche-cama [kotʃekama] (pl coches-camas) nm sleeping car, sleeper.

↘ coch?

cochera [ko'tʃera] nf garage.
cochero [ko'tʃero] nm coachman.
cochino, a [ko'tʃino, a] a filthy, dirty // nm pig.
codazo [ko'ðaθo] nm jab, poke (with the elbow).
codear [koðe'ar] vi to elbow, jostle; ~**se** vr: ~**se con** to rub shoulders with.
códice ['koðiθe] nm manuscript, codex.
codicia [ko'ðiθja] nf greed; (fig) lust; **codiciar** vt to covet; **codicioso, a** a covetous.
código ['koðixo] nm code; ~ **civil** common law.
codillo [ko'ðiʎo] nm (ZOOL) knee; (TEC) elbow (joint).
codo ['koðo] nm (ANAT, de tubo) elbow; (ZOOL) knee.
codorniz [koðor'niθ] nf quail.
coerción [koer'θjon] nf coercion.
coetáneo, a [koe'taneo, a] a contemporary.
coexistencia [koeksis'tenθja] nf coexistence; **coexistir** vi to coexist.
cofradía [kofra'ðia] nf brotherhood, fraternity.
cofre ['kofre] nm chest.
coger [ko'xer] vt (gen) to take (hold of); (objeto caído) to pick up; (frutas) to pick, harvest; (resfriado, ladrón, pelota) to catch // vi: ~ **por el buen camino** to take the right road; ~**se** vr to catch; (robar) to steal.
cogida [ko'xiða] nf gathering, harvesting; (de peces) catch.
cogote [ko'ɣote] nm back or nape of the neck.
cohabitar [koaßi'tar] vi to live together, cohabit.
cohechar [koe'tʃar] vt to bribe; **cohecho** nm (acción) bribery; (soborno) bribe.
coherente [koe'rente] a coherent.
cohesión [koe'sjon] nm cohesion.
cohete [ko'ete] nm rocket.
cohibición [koißi'θjon] nf restraint, restriction.
cohibir [koi'ßir] vt to restrain, restrict.
coincidencia [koinθi'ðenθja] nf coincidence; (acuerdo) agreement.
coincidir [koinθi'ðir] vi (en idea) to coincide, agree; (en lugar) to coincide.
coito ['koito] nm intercourse, coitus.
cojear [koxe'ar] vi (persona) to limp, hobble; (mueble) to wobble, rock.
cojera [ko'xera] nf lameness; (andar cojo) limp.
cojín [ko'xin] nm cushion; **cojinete** nm small cushion, pad; (TEC) ball bearing.
cojo, a ['koxo, a] a (que no puede andar) lame; (manco) crippled; (mueble) shaky // nm/f lame person; cripple.
col [kol] nf cabbage; ~ **de Bruselas** Brussels sprouts.
cola ['kola] nf (gen) tail; (de gente) queue; (lugar) end, last place; (para pegar) glue, gum; **hacer la** ~ to queue (up).

colaborador, a [kolaßora'ðor, a] nm/f collaborator.
colaborar [kolaßo'rar] vi to collaborate.
coladera [kola'ðera] nf strainer.
coladura [kola'ðura] nf (filtración) straining; (residuo) grounds pl, dregs pl.
colapso [ko'lapso] nm collapse; ~ **nervioso** nervous breakdown.
colar [ko'lar] vt (líquido) to strain off; (ropa) to bleach; (metal) to cast // vi to ooze, seep (through); ~**se** vr to slip in or past.
colateral [kolate'ral] nm collateral.
colcha ['koltʃa] nf bedspread.
colchón [kol'tʃon] nm mattress.
colear [kole'ar] vi to wag its tail.
colección [kolek'θjon] nf collection; **coleccionista** nm/f collector.
colecta [ko'lekta] nf collection.
colectar [kolek'tar] vt to collect.
colectivo, a [kolek'tißo, a] a collective, joint.
colector [kolek'tor] nm collector; (sumidero) sewer.
colega [ko'leɣa] nm/f colleague.
colegio [ko'lexjo] nm (gen) college; (escuela) (private) school; (de abogados etc) association.
colegir [kole'xir] vt (juntar, reunir) to collect, gather; (deducir) to infer, conclude.
cólera ['kolera] nf (ira) anger; (MED) cholera.
colérico, a [ko'leriko, a] a angry, furious.
coleta [ko'leta] nf pigtail.
colgadero [kolɣa'ðero] nm (gancho) hook; (percha) hanger.
colgadura [kolɣa'ðura] nf hangings pl, drapery.
colgante [kol'ɣante] a hanging // nm drop earring.
colgar [kol'ɣar] vt to hang (up); (ropa) to hang (out); (teléfono) to hang up // vi to hang.
coliflor [koli'flor] nf cauliflower.
colilla [ko'liʎa] nf fag end, butt.
colina [ko'lina] nf hill.
colindante [kolin'dante] a adjacent, neighbouring.
colindar [kolin'dar] vi to adjoin, be adjacent.
colisión [koli'sjon] nf collision; (choque) crash.
colmado, a [kol'maðo, a] a abundant, copious; (cuchara etc) heaped.
colmar [kol'mar] vt to fill to the brim; (fig) to fulfil, realize.
colmena [kol'mena] nf beehive.
colmillo [kol'miʎo] nm (diente) eye tooth; (de elefante) tusk; (de perro) fang.
colmo ['kolmo] nm height, summit.
colocación [koloka'θjon] nf placing; (empleo) job, position; (de mueble) place, position.
colocar [kolo'kar] vt to place, put,

position; (*poner en empleo*) to find a job for.

Colombia [ko'lombja] *nf* Colombia; **colombiano, a** *a*, *nm/f* Colombian.

colon ['kolon] *nm* colon.

colonia [ko'lonja] *nf* colony; (*de casas*) housing estate; (*agua de ~*) cologne.

colonización [koloniθa'θjon] *nf* colonization.

colonizador, a [koloniθa'θor, a] *a* colonizing // *nm/f* colonist, settler.

colonizar [koloni'θar] *vt* to colonize.

coloquio [ko'lokjo] *nm* conversation; (*congreso*) conference.

color [ko'lor] *nm* colour.

colorado, a [kolo'raðo, a] *a* (*que tiene color*) coloured; (*rojo*) red.

colorar [kolo'rar] *vt* to colour; (*teñir*) to dye.

colorear [kolore'ar] *vt* to colour // *vi* to redden.

colorido [kolo'riðo] *nm* colouring.

colosal [kolo'sal] *a* colossal.

columbrar [kolum'brar] *vt* to glimpse, spy.

columna [ko'lumna] *nf* column; (*pilar*) pillar; (*apoyo*) support.

columpiar [kolum'pjar] *vt*, ~**se** *vr* to swing; **columpio** *nm* swing.

collar [ko'ʎar] *nm* necklace; (*de perro*) collar.

coma ['koma] *nf* comma // *nm* coma.

comadre [ko'maðre] *nf* (*partera*) midwife; (*madrina*) godmother; (*vecina*) neighbour; ~**ar** *vi* to gossip.

comandancia [koman'danθja] *nf* command.

comandante [koman'dante] *nm* commandant.

comandar [koman'dar] *vt* to command.

comarca [ko'marka] *nf* region.

comarcar [komar'kar] *vi*: ~ **con** to border on, be adjacent to.

combar [kom'bar] *vt* to bend, curve.

combate [kom'bate] *nm* fight; (*fig*) battle; **combatiente** *nm* combatant.

combatir [komba'tir] *vt* to fight, combat.

combinación [kombina'θjon] *nf* combination; (*QUÍMICA*) compound; (*bebida*) cocktail; (*plan*) scheme, setup.

combinar [kombi'nar] *vt* to combine.

combustible [kombus'tiβle] *nm* fuel.

combustión [kombus'tjon] *nf* combustion.

comedia [ko'meðja] *nf* comedy; (*TEATRO*) play, drama.

comediante [kome'ðjante] *nm/f* (comic) actor/actress.

comedido, a [kome'ðiðo, a] *a* moderate; (*cortés*) courteous.

comedirse [kome'ðirse] *vr* to behave moderately; (*ser cortés*) to be courteous.

comedor, a [kome'ðor, a] *nm/f* (*persona*) glutton // *nm* (*habitación*) dining room; (*restaurante*) restaurant; (*cantina*) canteen.

comentador, a [komenta'ðor, a] *nm/f* = **comentarista.**

comentar [komen'tar] *vt* to comment on; (*fam*) to discuss.

comentario [komen'tarjo] *nm* comment, remark; (*literario*) commentary; ~**s** *nmpl* gossip *sg*.

comentarista [komenta'rista] *nm/f* commentator.

comento [ko'mento] *nm* = **comentario.**

comenzar [komen'θar] *vt*, *vi* to begin, start, commence.

comer [ko'mer] *vt* (*gen*) to eat; (*DAMAS, AJEDREZ*) to take, capture // *vi* to eat; (*almorzar*) to have lunch; ~**se** *vr* to eat up.

comercial [komer'θjal] *a* commercial; (*relativo al negocio*) business *cpd.*

comerciante [komer'θjante] *nm/f* trader, merchant.

comerciar [komer'θjar] *vi* to trade, do business.

comercio [ko'merθjo] *nm* commerce; (*tráfico*) trade; (*negocio*) business; (*fig*) dealings *pl.*

comestible [komes'tiβle] *a* eatable, edible // *nm* foodstuff.

cometa [ko'meta] *nm* comet // *nf* kite.

cometer [kome'ter] *vt* to commit.

cometido [kome'tiðo] *nm* (*misión*) task, assignment; (*deber*) commitment.

comezón [kome'θon] *nf* itch, itching.

cómico, a ['komiko, a] *a* comic(al) // *nm/f* comedian; (*de teatro*) (comic) actor/actress.

comida [ko'miða] *nf* (*alimento*) food; (*almuerzo, cena*) meal; (*de mediodía*) lunch.

comienzo [ko'mjenθo] *nm* beginning, start.

comillas [ko'miʎas] *nfpl* inverted commas.

comisario [komi'sarjo] *nm* commissary; (*POL*) commissar.

comisión [komi'sjon] *nf* commission.

comité [komi'te] *nm* committee.

como ['komo] *ad* as; (*tal ~*) like; (*aproximadamente*) about, approximately // *conj* (*ya que, puesto que*) as, since; (*en seguida que*) as soon as; ¡~ **no!** of course!; ~ **no lo haga hoy** unless he does it today; ~ **si** as if; **es tan alto** ~ **ancho** it is as high as it is wide.

cómo ['komo] *ad* how?, why? // *excl* what?, I beg your pardon? // *nm*: **el** ~ **y el porqué** the whys and wherefores.

comodidad [komoði'ðað] *nf* comfort; **venga a su** ~ come at your convenience.

comodín [komo'ðin] *nm* joker.

cómodo, a ['komoðo, a] *a* comfortable; (*práctico, de fácil uso*) convenient.

compacto, a [kom'pakto, a] *a* compact.

compadecer [kompaðe'θer] *vt* to pity, be sorry for; ~**se** *vr*: ~**se de** to pity, be sorry for.

compadre [kom'paðre] *nm* (*padrino*) godfather; (*amigo*) friend, pal.

compañero, a [kompa'ɲero, a] *nm/f* companion; ~ **de clase** classmate.

compañía [kompa'ɲia] *nf* company.

comparación [kompara'θjon] *nf* comparison; **en** ~ **con** in comparison with.

comparar [kompa'rar] *vt* to compare.

comparativo, a [kompara'tißo, a] *a* comparative.

comparecer [kompare'θer] *vi* to appear (in court).

compartimiento [komparti'mjento] *nm* division; (*distribución*) distribution; (*FERRO*) compartment.

compartir [kompar'tir] *vt* to divide (up), share (out).

compás [kom'pas] *nm* (*MUS*) beat, rhythm; (*MAT*) compasses *pl*; (*NAUT*) compass.

compasión [kompa'sjon] *nf* compassion, pity.

compasivo, a [kompa'sißo, a] *a* compassionate.

compatibilidad [kompatißili'ðað] *nf* compatibility.

compatible [kompa'tißle] *a* compatible.

compatriota [kompa'trjota] *nm/f* compatriot.

compeler [kompe'ler] *vt* to compel.

compendiar [kompen'djar] *vt* to summarize; (*libro*) to abridge; **compendio** *nm* summary; abridgement.

compensación [kompensa'θjon] *nf* compensation.

compensar [kompen'sar] *vt* to compensate.

competencia [kompe'tenθja] *nf* (*incumbencia*) domain, field; (*aptitud, idoneidad*) competence; (*rivalidad*) competition.

competente [kompe'tente] *a* (*persona, jurado, tribunal*) competent; (*conveniente*) fit, suitable.

competición [kompeti'θjon] *nf* competition.

competir [kompe'tir] *vi* to compete.

compilar [kompi'lar] *vt* to compile.

complacencia [kompla'θenθja] *nf* (*placer*) pleasure; (*satisfacción*) satisfaction; (*buena voluntad*) willingness.

complacer [kompla'θer] *vt* to please; ~**se** *vr* to be pleased.

complaciente [kompla'θjente] *a* kind, obliging, helpful.

complejo, a [kom'plexo, a] *a, nm* complex.

complementario, a [komplemen'tarjo, a] *a* complementary.

completar [komple'tar] *vt* to complete.

completo, a [kom'pleto, a] *a* complete; (*perfecto*) perfect; (*lleno*) full // *nm* full complement.

complicar [kompli'kar] *vt* to complicate.

cómplice ['kompliθe] *nm/f* accomplice.

complot [kom'plot] *nm* plot; (*conspiración*) conspiracy.

componenda [kompo'nenda] *nf*

compromise; (*pey*) shady deal.

componer [kompo'ner] *vt* to make up, put together; (*MUS, LITERATURA, IMPRENTA*) to compose; (*algo roto*) to mend, repair; (*adornar*) to adorn; (*arreglar*) to arrange; (*reconciliar*) to reconcile; ~**se** *vr*: ~**se de** to consist of.

comportamiento [komporta'mjento] *nm* behaviour, conduct.

comportarse [kompor'tarse] *vr* to behave.

composición [komposi'θjon] *nf* composition.

compositor, a [komposi'tor, a] *nm/f* composer.

compostura [kompos'tura] *nf* (*reparación*) mending, repair; (*arreglo*) arrangement; (*acuerdo*) agreement; (*actitud*) composure.

compra ['kompra] *nf* purchase; ~**s** *nfpl* purchases, shopping *sg*.

comprador, a [kompra'ðor, a] *nm/f* buyer, purchaser.

comprar [kom'prar] *vt* to buy, purchase.

comprender [kompren'der] *vt* to understand; (*incluir*) to comprise, include.

comprensión [kompren'sjon] *nf* understanding; (*totalidad*) comprehensiveness.

comprensivo, a [kompren'sißo, a] *a* comprehensive; (*actitud*) understanding.

compresión [kompre'sjon] *nf* compression.

comprimir [kompri'mir] *vt* to compress; (*fig*) to control.

comprobante [kompro'ßante] *a* verifying, supporting // *nm* proof.

comprobar [kompro'ßar] *vt* to check; (*probar*) to prove; (*TEC*) to check, test.

comprometer [komprome'ter] *vt* to compromise; (*exponer*) to endanger; ~**se** *vr* to compromise o.s.; (*involucrarse*) to get involved.

compromiso [kompro'miso] *nm* (*obligación*) obligation; (*cometido*) commitment; (*convenio*) agreement; (*dificultad*) awkward situation.

compuesto, a [kom'pwesto, a] *a*: ~ **de** composed of, made up of // *nm* compound.

compulsión [kompul'sjon] *nf* compulsion.

compunción [kompun'θjon] *nf* compunction, regret.

computador [komputa'ðor] *nm,* **computadora** [komputa'ðora] *nf* computer.

comulgar [komul'ɣar] *vi* to receive communion.

común [ko'mun] *a* common // *nm*: **el** ~ the community.

comunicación [komunika'θjon] *nf* communication; (*ponencia*) report.

comunicar [komuni'kar] *vt, vi*, ~**se** *vr* to communicate; **comunicativo, a** *a* communicative.

comunidad [komuni'ðað] *nf* community.

comunión [komu'njon] *nf* communion.

comunismo [komu'nismo] *nm*

communism; **comunista** a, nm/f communist.

con [kon] prep with; (a pesar de) in spite of; ~ **que** so, and so; ~ **apretar el botón** by pressing the button.

concebir [konθe'ßir] vt, vi to conceive.

conceder [konθe'ðer] vt to concede.

concejo [kon'θexo] nm council.

concentración [konθentra'θjon] nf concentration.

concentrar [konθen'trar] vt, ~**se** vr to concentrate.

concepción [konθep'θjon] nf conception.

concepto [kon'θepto] nm concept.

concertar [konθer'tar] vt (MUS) to harmonize; (acordar: precio) to agree; (: tratado) to conclude; (trato) to arrange, fix up; (combinar: esfuerzos) to coordinate; (reconciliar: personas) to reconcile // vi to harmonize, be in tune.

concesión [konθe'sjon] nf concession.

conciencia [kon'θjenθja] nf conscience.

concienzudo, a [konθjen'θuðo, a] a conscientious.

concierto [kon'θjerto] nm concert; (obra) concerto.

conciliar [konθi'ljar] vt to reconcile.

concilio [kon'θiljo] nm council.

conciso, a [kon'θiso, a] a concise.

concluir [konklu'ir] vt, vi, ~**se** vr to conclude.

conclusión [konklu'sjon] nf conclusion.

concordar [konkor'ðar] vt to reconcile // vi to agree, tally; **concordia** nf concord, harmony.

concretar [konkre'tar] vt to make concrete, make more specific; ~**se** vr to become more definite.

concreto, a [kon'kreto, a] a, nm (AM) concrete; **en** ~ (en resumen) to sum up; (específicamente) specifically; **no hay nada en** ~ there's nothing definite.

concurrir [konku'rrir] vi (juntarse: ríos) to meet, come together; (: personas) to gather, meet; (ponerse de acuerdo, coincidir) to concur; (competir) to compete; (contribuir) to contribute.

concurso [kon'kurso] nm (de público) crowd; (ESCOL, DEPORTE, competencia) competition; (coincidencia) coincidence; (ayuda) help, cooperation.

concusión [konku'sjon] nf concussion.

concha ['kontʃa] nf shell.

conde ['konde] nm count.

condecorar [kondeko'rar] vt to decorate.

condena [kon'dena] nf sentence.

condenación [kondena'θjon] nf (gen) condemnation; (condena) sentence; (REL) damnation.

condenar [konde'nar] vt to condemn; (JUR) to convict; ~**se** vr (JUR) to confess (one's guilt); (REL) to be damned.

condensar [konden'sar] vt to condense.

condescender [kondesθen'der] vi to acquiesce, comply.

condición [kondi'θjon] nf condition;

condicionado, a a conditioned.

condicional [kondiθjo'nal] a conditional.

condimento [kondi'mento] nm seasoning.

condolerse [kondo'lerse] vr to sympathize.

conducir [kondu'θir] vt to take, convey; (AUTO) to drive // vi to drive; (fig) to lead; ~**se** vr to behave.

conducta [kon'dukta] nf conduct, behaviour.

conducto [kon'dukto] nm pipe, tube; (fig) channel.

conductor, a [konduk'tor, a] a leading, guiding // nm (FÍSICA) conductor; (de vehículo) driver.

conduje etc vb ver **conducir**.

conduzco etc vb ver **conducir**.

conectar [konek'tar] vt to connect (up), plug in.

conejo [ko'nexo] nm rabbit.

conexión [konek'sjon] nf connection.

confeccionar [konfekθjo'nar] vt to make (up).

confederación [konfeðera'θjon] nf confederation.

conferencia [konfe'renθja] nf conference; (lección) lecture; (TELEC) call.

conferir [konfe'rir] vt to award.

confesar [konfe'sar] vt to confess, admit.

confesión [konfe'sjon] nf confession.

confesionario [konfesjo'narjo] nm confessional.

confiado, a [kon'fjaðo, a] a (crédulo) trusting; (presumido) confident; (pey) conceited, vain.

confianza [kon'fjanθa] nf trust; (aliento, confidencia) confidence; (familiaridad) intimacy, familiarity; (pey) vanity, conceit.

confiar [kon'fjar] vt to entrust // vi to trust.

confidencia [konfi'ðenθja] nf confidence.

confidencial [konfiðen'θjal] a confidential.

confidente [konfi'ðente] nm/f confidant/e; (policial) informer.

configurar [konfiɣu'rar] vt to shape, form.

confín [kon'fin] nm limit; ~**es** nmpl edges.

confinar [konfi'nar] vi to confine; (desterrar) to banish.

confirmar [konfir'mar] vt to confirm.

confiscar [konfis'kar] vt to confiscate.

confitería [konfite'ria] nf confectionery; (tienda) confectioner's (shop).

confitura [konfi'tura] nf jam.

conflicto [kon'flikto] nm conflict; (fig) clash.

conformar [konfor'mar] vt to shape, fashion // vi to agree; ~**se** vr to conform; (resignarse) to resign o.s.

conforme [kon'forme] a (gen) alike, similar; (de acuerdo) agreed, in agreement; (resignado) resigned // ad as // excl agreed! // nm agreement // prep: ~ **a** in accordance with.

conformidad [konformi'ðað] *nf* (*semejanza*) similarity; (*acuerdo*) agreement; (*resignación*) resignation.
confortable [konfor'taßle] *a* comfortable.
confortar [konfor'tar] *vt* to comfort.
confrontar [konfron'tar] *vt* to confront; (*dos personas*) to bring face to face; (*cotejar*) to compare // *vi* to border.
confundir [konfun'dir] *vt* to blur; (*equivocar*) to mistake, confuse; (*mezclar*) to mix; (*turbar*) to confuse; ~**se** *vr* to become blurred; (*turbarse*) to get confused; (*equivocarse*) to make a mistake; (*mezclarse*) to mix.
confusión [konfu'sjon] *nf* confusion.
confuso, a [kon'fuso, a] *a* confused.
congelar [konxe'lar] *vt* to freeze; ~**se** *vr* (*sangre, grasa*) to congeal.
congeniar [konxe'njar] *vi* to get on (well).
conglomeración [konglomera'θjon] *nf* conglomeration.
congoja [kon'goxa] *nf* distress, grief.
congratular [kongratu'lar] *vt* to congratulate.
congregación [kongreɣa'θjon] *nf* congregation.
congresista [kongre'sista] *nm/f* delegate, congressman/woman.
congreso [kon'greso] *nm* congress.
conjetura [konxe'tura] *nf* guess; **conjeturar** *vt* to guess.
conjugar [konxu'ɣar] *vt* to combine, fit together; (*un verbo*) to conjugate.
conjunción [konxun'θjon] *nf* conjunction.
conjunto, a [kon'xunto, a] *a* joint, united // *nm* whole; (*MUS*) group; **en** ~ as a whole.
conmemoración [konmemora'θjon] *nf* commemoration.
conmemorar [konmemo'rar] *vt* to commemorate.
conmigo [kon'miɣo] *pron* with me; with myself.
conminar [konmi'nar] *vt* to threaten.
conmiseración [konmisera'θjon] *nf* pity, commiseration.
conmoción [konmo'θjon] *nf* shock; (*MED*) concussion; (*fig*) upheaval.
conmovedor, a [konmoße'ðor, a] *a* touching, moving; (*impresionante*) exciting.
conmover [konmo'ßer] *vt* to shake, disturb; (*fig*) to move.
conmutador [konmuta'ðor] *nm* switch.
conocedor, a [konoθe'ðor, a] *a* expert, knowledgeable // *nm/f* expert.
conocer [kono'θer] *vt* (*gen*) to know; (*por primera vez*) to meet, get to know; (*entender*) to know about; (*reconocer*) to know, recognize; ~**se** *vr* (*una persona*) to know o.s.; (*dos personas*) to (get to) know each other.
conocido, a [kono'θiðo, a] *a* (well-)known // *nm/f* acquaintance.
conocimiento [konoθi'mjento] *nm* knowledge; (*MED*) consciousness; ~**s** *nmpl* (*personas*) acquaintances; (*ciencia*) knowledge *sg*.
conozco *etc vb ver* **conocer.**
conque ['konke] *conj* and so, so then.
conquista [kon'kista] *nf* conquest.
conquistador, a [konkista'ðor, a] *a* conquering // *nm* conqueror.
conquistar [konkis'tar] *vt* to conquer.
consagrar [konsa'ɣrar] *vt* (*REL*) to consecrate; (*fig*) to devote.
consciente [kons'θjente] *a* conscious.
consecución [konseku'θjon] *nf* acquisition; (*de fin*) attainment.
consecuencia [konse'kwenθja] *nf* consequence, outcome; (*firmeza*) consistency.
consecuente [konse'kwente] *a* consistent.
consecutivo, a [konseku'tißo, a] *a* consecutive.
conseguir [konse'ɣir] *vt* to get, obtain; (*sus fines*) to attain.
consejero, a [konse'xero, a] *nm/f* adviser, consultant; (*POL*) councillor.
consejo [kon'sexo] *nm* advice; (*POL*) council.
consenso [kon'senso] *nm* consensus.
consentimiento [konsenti'mjento] *nm* consent.
consentir [konsen'tir] *vt* (*permitir, tolerar*) to consent to; (*mimar*) to pamper, spoil; (*admitir*) to admit // *vi* to agree, consent.
conserje [kon'serxe] *nm* caretaker; (*portero*) porter.
conserva [kon'serßa] *nf* (*acción*) preserving; (*alimento*) preserved food.
conservación [konserßa'θjon] *nf* conservation; (*de alimentos, vida*) preservation.
conservador, a [konserßa'ðor, a] *a* preservative; (*POL*) conservative // *nm/f* conservative; (*de museo*) keeper.
conservar [konser'ßar] *vt* to conserve, keep; (*alimentos, vida*) to preserve; ~**se** *vr* to survive.
considerable [konsiðe'raßle] *a* considerable.
consideración [konsiðera'θjon] *nf* consideration; (*estimación*) respect.
considerado, a [konsiðe'raðo, a] *a* (*prudente, reflexivo*) considerate; (*respetado*) respected.
considerar [konsiðe'rar] *vt* to consider.
consigna [kon'siɣna] *nf* (*orden*) order, instruction; (*para equipajes*) left-luggage office.
consigo [kon'siɣo] *pron* (*m*) with him; (*f*) with her; (*Vd.*) with you; (*reflexivo*) with o.s.
consiguiente [konsi'ɣjente] *a* consequent; **por** ~ and so, therefore, consequently.
consistente [konsis'tente] *a* consistent; (*sólido*) solid, firm; (*válido*) sound.
consistir [konsis'tir] *vi*: ~ **en** (*componerse de*) to consist of; (*ser resultado de*) to be due to.
consolación [konsola'θjon] *nf* consolation.

consolar [konso'lar] *vt* to console.
consolidar [konsoli'ðar] *vt* to consolidate.
consomé [konso'me] *nm* consommé, clear soup.
consonante [konso'nante] *a* consonant, harmonious // *nf* consonant.
conspicuo, a [kons'pikwo, a] *a* conspicuous.
conspiración [konspira'θjon] *nf* conspiracy.
conspirador, a [konspira'ðor, a] *nm/f* conspirator.
conspirar [konspi'rar] *vi* to conspire.
constante [kons'tante] *a* constant.
constar [kons'tar] *vi* (*evidenciarse*) to be clear *or* evident; ~ **de** to consist of.
consternación [konsterna'θjon] *nf* consternation.
constipación [konstipa'θjon] *nf* = **constipado**.
constipado, a [konsti'paðo, a] *a*: **estar** ~ to have a cold // *nm* cold.
constitución [konstitu'θjon] *nf* constitution; **constitucional** *a* constitutional.
constituir [konstitu'ir] *vt* (*formar, componer*) to constitute, make up; (*fundar, erigir, ordenar*) to constitute, establish.
constitutivo, a [konstitu'tißo, a] *a* constitutive, constituent.
constituyente [konstitu'jente] *a* constituent.
constreñir [konstre'ɲir] *vt* (*obligar*) to compel, oblige; (*restringir*) to restrict.
construcción [konstruk'θjon] *nf* construction, building.
constructor, a [konstruk'tor, a] *nm/f* builder.
construir [konstru'ir] *vt* to build, construct.
consuelo [kon'swelo] *nm* consolation, solace.
cónsul ['konsul] *nm* consul; **consulado** *nm* consulate.
consulta [kon'sulta] *nf* consultation.
consultar [konsul'tar] *vt* to consult.
consultorio [konsul'torjo] *nm* information bureau; (*MED*) surgery.
consumar [konsu'mar] *vt* to complete, carry out; (*crimen*) to commit; (*matrimonio*) to consummate.
consumición [konsumi'θjon] *nf* consumption; (*bebida*) drink; (*en restaurante*) meal.
consumidor, a [konsumi'ðor, a] *nm/f* consumer.
consumir [konsu'mir] *vt* to consume; ~**se** *vr* to be consumed; (*persona*) to waste away.
consumo [kon'sumo] *nm*, **consunción** [konsun'θjon] *nf* consumption.
contabilidad [kontaßili'ðað] *nf* accounting, book-keeping; (*profesión*) accountancy.
contacto [kon'takto] *nm* contact.
contado, a [kon'taðo, a] *a*: ~**s** (*escasos*) numbered, scarce, few // *nm*: **al** ~ for cash.
contador [konta'ðor] *nm* (*aparato*) meter; (*COM*) accountant; (*de café*) counter.
contagiar [konta'xjar] *vt* (*enfermedad*) to pass on, transmit; (*persona*) to infect; ~**se** *vr* to become infected.
contagio [kon'taxjo] *nm* infection.
contagioso, a [konta'xjoso, a] *a* infectious; (*fig*) catching.
contaminación [kontamina'θjon] *nf* contamination.
contaminar [kontami'nar] *vt* to contaminate.
contar [kon'tar] *vt* (*páginas, dinero*) to count; (*anécdota*) to tell // *vi* to count; ~ **con** to rely on, count on.
contemplación [kontempla'θjon] *nf* contemplation.
contemplar [kontem'plar] *vt* to contemplate; (*mirar*) to look at.
contemporáneo, a [kontempo'raneo, a] *a, nm/f* contemporary.
contender [konten'der] *vi* (*gen*) to contend; (*en un concurso*) to compete.
contener [konte'ner] *vt* to contain, hold; (*retener*) to hold back, contain.
contenido, a [konte'niðo, a] *a* (*moderado*) restrained; (*reprimido*) suppressed // *nm* contents *pl*, content.
contentar [konten'tar] *vt* (*satisfacer*) to satisfy; (*complacer*) to please; ~**se** *vr* to be satisfied.
contento, a [kon'tento, a] *a* contented, content; (*alegre*) pleased; (*feliz*) happy // *nm* contentment; (*felicidad*) happiness.
contestación [kontesta'θjon] *nf* answer, reply.
contestar [kontes'tar] *vt* to answer, reply; (*JUR*) to corroborate, confirm.
contigo [kon'tixo] *pron* with you.
contiguo, a [kon'tixwo, a] *a* (*de al lado*) next; (*vecino*) adjacent, adjoining.
continental [kontinen'tal] *a* continental.
continente [konti'nente] *a, nm* continent.
contingencia [kontin'xenθja] *nf* contingency; (*riesgo*) risk; **contingente** *a, nm* contingent.
continuación [kontinwa'θjon] *nf* continuation; **a** ~ then, next.
continuar [konti'nwar] *vt* to continue, go on with // *vi* to continue, go on.
continuidad [kontinwi'ðað] *nf* continuity.
continuo, a [kon'tinwo, a] *a* (*sin interrupción*) continuous; (*acción perseverante*) continual.
contorno [kon'torno] *nm* outline; (*GEO*) contour; ~**s** *nmpl* neighbourhood *sg*, environs.
contorsión [kontor'sjon] *nf* contortion.
contra ['kontra] *prep, ad* against // *nm* con.
contraataque [kontraa'take] *nm* counter-attack.
contrabajo [kontra'ßaxo] *nm* double bass.

contrabandista [kontraßan'dista] *nm/f* smuggler.

contrabando [kontra'ßando] *nm* (*acción*) smuggling; (*mercancías*) contraband.

contracción [kontrak'θjon] *nf* contraction; (*encogimiento*) shrinkage.

contracepción [kontraθep'θjon] *nf* contraception.

contraceptivo [kontraθep'tißo] *nm* contraceptive.

contradecir [kontraðe'θir] *vt* to contradict.

contradicción [kontraðik'θjon] *nf* contradiction.

contradictorio, a [kontraðik'torjo, a] *a* contradictory.

contraer [kontra'er] *vt* to contract; (*encoger*) to shrink; (*limitar*) to restrict; ~**se** *vr* to contract; to shrink; (*limitarse*) to limit o.s.

contragolpe [kontra'ɣolpe] *nm* backlash.

contrahacer [kontraa'θer] *vt* to copy, imitate; (*falsificar*) to forge.

contramaestre [kontrama'estre] *nm* foreman.

contrapelo [kontra'pelo]: **a** ~ *ad* the wrong way.

contrapesar [kontrape'sar] *vt* to counterbalance; (*fig*) to offset.

contrariar [kontra'rjar] *vt* (*oponerse*) to oppose; (*poner obstáculo*) to impede; (*enfadar*) to vex.

contrariedad [kontrarje'ðað] *nf* (*oposición*) opposition; (*obstáculo*) obstacle, setback; (*disgusto*) vexation, annoyance.

contrario, a [kon'trarjo, a] *a* contrary; (*de persona*) opposed; (*sentido, lado*) opposite // *nm/f* enemy, adversary; (*DEPORTE*) opponent; **de lo** ~ otherwise.

contrarrestar [kontrarres'tar] *vt* to counteract; (*pelota*) to return.

contrastar [kontras'tar] *vt* to resist // *vi* to contrast.

contraste [kon'traste] *nm* contrast.

contratante [kontra'tante] *nm/f* contractor.

contratar [kontra'tar] *vt* (*firmar un acuerdo para*) to contract for; (*empleados, obreros*) to hire, engage; ~**se** *vr* to sign on.

contratiempo [kontra'tjempo] *nm* setback.

contratista [kontra'tista] *nm/f* contractor.

contrato [kon'trato] *nm* contract.

contravención [kontraßen'θjon] *nf* contravention, violation.

contravenir [kontraße'nir] *vi*: ~ **a** to contravene, violate.

contraventana [kontraßen'tana] *nf* shutter.

contribución [kontrißu'θjon] *nf* (*municipal etc*) tax; (*ayuda*) contribution.

contribuir [kontrißu'ir] *vt, vi* to contribute; (*COM*) to pay (in taxes).

contribuyente [kontrißu'jente] *nm/f* (*COM*) taxpayer; (*que ayuda*) contributor.

control [kon'trol] *nm* control; (*inspección*) inspection, check; ~**ar** *vt* to control; to inspect, check.

controversia [kontro'ßersja] *nf* controversy.

convalecencia [konßale'θenθja] *nf* convalescence.

convalecer [konßale'θer] *vi* to convalesce, get better.

convaleciente [konßale'θjente] *a, nm/f* convalescent.

convencer [konßen'θer] *vt* to convince; (*persuadir*) to persuade.

convencimiento [konßenθi'mjento] *nm* convincing; (*persuasión*) persuasion; (*certidumbre*) conviction.

convención [konßen'θjon] *nf* convention.

convencional [konßenθjo'nal] *a* conventional.

convenido, a [konße'niðo, a] *a* agreed.

conveniencia [konße'njenθja] *nf* suitability; (*conformidad*) agreement; (*utilidad, provecho*) usefulness; ~**s** *nfpl* conventions; (*COM*) property *sg*.

conveniente [konße'njente] *a* suitable; (*útil*) useful.

convenio [kon'ßenjo] *nm* agreement, treaty.

convenir [konße'nir] *vi* (*estar de acuerdo*) to agree; (*ser conveniente*) to suit, be suitable; ~**se** *vr* to agree.

convento [kon'ßento] *nm* monastery; (*de monjas*) convent.

converger [konßer'xer], **convergir** [konßer'xir] *vi* to converge.

conversación [konßersa'θjon] *nf* conversation.

conversar [konßer'sar] *vi* to talk, converse.

conversión [konßer'sjon] *nf* conversion.

convertir [konßer'tir] *vt* to convert.

convicción [konßik'θjon] *nf* conviction.

convicto, a [kon'ßikto, a] *a* convicted, found guilty; (*condenado*) condemned.

convidado, a [konßi'ðaðo, a] *nm/f* guest.

convidar [konßi'ðar] *vt* to invite.

convincente [konßin'θente] *a* convincing.

convite [kon'ßite] *nm* invitation; (*banquete*) banquet.

convivencia [konßi'ßenθja] *nf* coexistence, living together.

convocar [konßo'kar] *vt* to summon, call (together).

convulsión [konßul'sjon] *nf* convulsion.

conyugal [konju'ɣal] *a* conjugal.

coñac [ko'ɲak] *nm* cognac, brandy.

cooperación [koopera'θjon] *nf* cooperation.

cooperar [koope'rar] *vi* to cooperate.

cooperativo, a [koopera'tißo, a] *a* cooperative // *nf* cooperative.

coordinación [koorðina'θjon] *nf* coordination.

coordinar [koorði'nar] *vt* to coordinate.

copa ['kopa] *nf* cup; (*vaso*) glass; (*de árbol*) top; (*de sombrero*) crown; ~**s** *nfpl* (*NAIPES*) ≈ hearts.

copia ['kopja] *nf* copy; **copiar** *vt* to copy.

copioso, a [ko'pjoso, a] *a* copious, plentiful.

copita [ko'pita] *nf* (small) glass; (*GOLF*) tee.

copla ['kopla] *nf* verse; (*canción*) (popular) song.

coqueta [ko'keta] *a* flirtatious, coquettish; **coquetear** *vi* to flirt.

coraje [ko'raxe] *nm* courage; (*ánimo*) spirit; (*ira*) anger.

coral [ko'ral] *a* choral // *nf* choir.

corazón [kora'θon] *nm* heart.

corazonada [koraθo'naða] *nf* impulse; (*presentimiento*) presentiment, hunch.

corbata [kor'ßata] *nf* tie.

corcovado, a [korko'ßaðo, a] *a* hunchbacked.

corchete [kor'tʃete] *nm* catch, clasp.

corcho ['kortʃo] *nm* cork; (*PESCA*) float.

cordel [kor'ðel] *nm* cord, line.

cordero [kor'ðero] *nm* lamb.

cordial [kor'ðjal] *a* cordial; ~**idad** *nf* warmth, cordiality.

cordillera [korði'ʌera] *nf* range, chain (of mountains).

Córdoba ['korðoßa] *n* Cordoba; **cordobés, esa** *a* of or from Cordoba.

cordón [kor'ðon] *nm* (*cuerda*) cord, string; (*de zapatos*) lace; (*policía*) cordon.

corneta [kor'neta] *nf* bugle.

coro ['koro] *nm* chorus; (*conjunto de cantores*) choir.

corolario [koro'larjo] *nm* corollary.

corona [ko'rona] *nf* crown; (*de flores*) garland; ~**ción** *nf* coronation; **coronar** *vt* to crown.

coronel [koro'nel] *nm* colonel.

coronilla [koro'niʌa] *nf* crown (of the head).

corporación [korpora'θjon] *nf* corporation.

corporal [korpo'ral] *a* corporal.

corpulento, a [korpu'lento a] *a* (*árbol*) stout; (*persona*) well-built.

corral [ko'rral] *nm* farmyard; ~**illo** *nm* playpen.

correa [ko'rrea] *nf* strap; (*cinturón*) belt.

corrección [korrek'θjon] *nf* correction; (*reprensión*) rebuke; **correccional** *nm* reformatory.

correcto, a [ko'rrekto, a] *a* correct; (*persona*) well-mannered.

corredor, a [korre'ðor, a] *a* running; (*rápido*) fast // *nm* (*COM*) agent, broker; (*pasillo*) corridor, passage; (*DEPORTE*) runner.

corregir [korre'xir] *vt* (*error*) to correct; (*amonestar, reprender*) to rebuke, reprimand; ~**se** *vr* to reform.

correo [ko'rreo] *nm* post, mail; (*persona*) courier; (*cartero*) postman; **C~** Post Office; ~ **aéreo** airmail.

correr [ko'rrer] *vt* to run; (*viajar*) to cover, travel; (*cortinas*) to draw; (*cerrojo*) to shoot // *vi* to run; (*líquido*) to run, flow; (*moneda*) to pass, be valid; ~**se** *vr* to slide, move; (*colores*) to run.

correspondencia [korrespon'denθja] *nf* correspondence; (*FERRO*) connection.

corresponder [korrespon'der] *vi* to correspond; (*convenir*) to be suitable; (*pertenecer*) to belong; (*tocar*) to concern; ~**se** *vr* (*por escrito*) to correspond; (*amarse*) to have mutual affection.

correspondiente [korrespon'djente] *a* corresponding // *nm* correspondent.

corrido, a [ko'rriðo, a] *a* (*avergonzado*) abashed; (*fluido*) fluent // *nf* run, dash; (*de toros*) bullfight; **3 noches** ~**as** 3 nights running; **un kilo** ~ a good kilo.

corriente [ko'rrjente] *a* (*agua*) running; (*fig*) flowing; (*dinero etc*) current; (*común*) ordinary, normal // *nf* current // *nm* current month.

corrillo [ko'rriʌo] *nm* huddle; (*fig*) clique.

corro ['korro] *nm* ring, circle (of people).

corroborar [korroßo'rar] *vt* to corroborate.

corroer [korro'er] *vt* to corrode; (*GEO*) to erode.

corromper [korrom'per] *vt* (*madera*) to rot; (*alimento*) to turn bad; (*fig*) to corrupt.

corrosivo, a [korro'sißo, a] *a* corrosive.

corrupción [korrup'θjon] *nf* rot, decay; (*fig*) corruption.

corsé [kor'se] *nm* corset.

cortado, a [kor'taðo, a] *a* (*con cuchillo*) cut; (*leche*) sour; (*confuso*) confused; (*disconcertado*) embarrassed; (*estilo*) abrupt // *nm* white coffee (with just a little milk).

cortador, a [korta'ðor, a] *a* cutting // *nf* cutter, slicer.

cortadura [korta'ðura] *nf* cut.

cortar [kor'tar] *vt* to cut; (*el agua*) to cut off; (*un pasaje*) to cut out // *vi* to cut; ~**se** *vr* (*turbarse*) to become embarrassed; (*leche*) to turn, curdle; ~**se el pelo** to have one's hair cut.

corte ['korte] *nm* cut, cutting; (*filo*) edge; (*de tela*) piece, length; **las C~s** the Spanish Parliament.

cortedad [korte'ðað] *nf* shortness; (*fig*) bashfulness, timidity.

cortejar [korte'xar] *vt* to court.

cortejo [kor'texo] *nm* entourage; ~ **fúnebre** funeral procession.

cortés [kor'tes] *a* courteous, polite.

cortesía [korte'sia] *nf* courtesy.

corteza [kor'teθa] *nf* (*de árbol*) bark; (*de pan*) crust.

cortina [kor'tina] *nf* curtain.

corto, a ['korto, a] *a* (*breve*) short; (*tímido*) bashful; (*poco inteligente*) not very clever; ~ **de vista** short-sighted; **estar** ~ **de fondos** to be short of funds.

corvo, a ['korßo, a] *a* curved.

cosa ['kosa] *nf* thing; (*asunto*) affair; ~ **de** about; **eso es** ~ **mía** that's my affair.

cosecha [ko'setʃa] *nf* (*AGR*) harvest; (*de vino*) vintage.
cosechar [kose'tʃar] *vt* to harvest, gather (in).
coser [ko'ser] *vt* to sew.
cosmético, a [kos'metiko, a] *a, nm* cosmetic.
cosquillas [kos'kiʎas] *nfpl*: **hacer** ~ to tickle; **tener** ~ to be ticklish.
cosquilloso, a [koski'ʎoso, a] *a* ticklish; (*fig*) touchy.
costa ['kosta] *nf* (*gasto*) cost; (*GEO*) coast.
costado [kos'taðo] *nm* side.
costal [kos'tal] *nm* sack.
costar [kos'tar] *vt* (*valer*) to cost; (*necesitar*) to require, need; **me cuesta hacer** I find it hard to do.
Costa Rica [kosta'rika] *nf* Costa Rica; **costarricense, costarriqueño, a** *a, nm/f* Costa Rican.
coste ['koste] *nm* = **costo**.
costilla [kos'tiʎa] *nf* rib; (*CULIN*) chop.
costo ['kosto] *nm* cost, price; ~ **de la vida** cost of living; ~**so, a** *a* costly, expensive.
costra ['kostra] *nf* crust; (*MED*) scab.
costumbre [kos'tumbre] *nf* custom, habit.
costura [kos'tura] *nf* sewing, needlework; (*de medias*) seam.
costurera [kostu'rera] *nf* dressmaker.
costurero [kostu'rero] *nm* sewing box *or* case.
cotejar [kote'xar] *vt* to compare.
cotejo [ko'texo] *nm* comparison.
cotidiano, a [koti'ðjano, a] *a* daily, day to day.
cotización [kotiθa'θjon] *nf* (*COM*) quotation, price; (*cuota*) dues *pl.*
cotizar [koti'θar] *vt* (*COM*) to quote, price; ~**se** *vr*: ~**se a** to sell at, fetch.
coto ['koto] *nm* (*terreno cercado*) enclosure; (*de caza*) reserve.
coyote [ko'jote] *nm* coyote, prairie wolf.
coyuntura [kojun'tura] *nf* (*ANAT*) joint; (*oportunidad*) opportunity.
cráneo ['kraneo] *nm* skull, cranium.
cráter ['krater] *nm* crater.
creación [krea'θjon] *nf* creation.
creador, a [krea'ðor, a] *a* creative // *nm/f* creator.
crear [kre'ar] *vt* to create, make.
crecer [kre'θer] *vi* (*niño*) to grow; (*precio*) to rise; (*días*) to get longer; (*mar*) to swell.
crecido, a [kre'θiðo, a] *a* (*persona, planta*) full-grown; (*cantidad*) large; (*fig*) conceited.
creciente [kre'θjente] *a* (*persona*) growing; (*cantidad*) increasing; (*luna*) crescent // *nm* crescent // *nf* flood.
crecimiento [kreθi'mjento] *nm* growth; (*aumento*) increase.
credenciales [kreðen'θjales] *nfpl* credentials.
crédito ['kreðito] *nm* credit.
credo ['kreðo] *nm* creed.
crédulo, a ['kreðulo, a] *a* credulous.
creencia [kre'enθja] *nf* belief.

creer [kre'er] *vt, vi* to think, believe; ~**se** *vr* to believe o.s. (to be); ¡**ya lo creo!** I should think so!
creíble [kre'iβle] *a* credible, believable.
crema ['krema] *nf* cream; (*de huevo*) custard.
cremallera [krema'ʎera] *nf* zip (fastener).
crepúsculo [kre'puskulo] *nm* twilight, dusk.
crespón [kres'pon] *nm* crêpe.
creta ['kreta] *nf* chalk.
creyente [kre'jente] *nm/f* believer.
creyó *etc vb ver* **creer.**
cría ['kria] *nf* (*de animales*) rearing, breeding; (*animal*) baby animal; (*niño*) child.
criadero [kria'ðero] *nm* nursery; (*ZOOL*) breeding place.
criado, a [kri'aðo, a] *a* bred, reared // *nm* servant // *nf* servant, maid; **mal/bien** ~ badly/well brought up.
criador [kria'ðor] *nm* breeder.
crianza [kri'anθa] *nf* rearing, breeding; (*fig*) breeding.
criar [kri'ar] *vt* to suckle, feed; (*educar*) to bring up; (*producir*) to grow, produce; (*animales*) to breed.
criatura [kria'tura] *nf* creature; (*niño*) baby, (small) child.
criba ['kriβa] *nf* sieve; **cribar** *vt* to sieve.
crimen ['krimen] *nm* crime.
criminal [krimi'nal] *a, nm/f* criminal.
crin [krin] *nf* (*también* ~**es** *nfpl*) mane.
crisis ['krisis] *nf inv* crisis.
crispar [kris'par] *vt* (*músculo*) to make contract; (*nervios*) to set on edge.
cristal [kris'tal] *nm* crystal; (*de ventana*) glass, pane; (*lente*) lens; ~**ino, a** *a* crystalline; (*fig*) clear // *nm* lens of the eye; ~**izar** *vt, vi* to crystallize.
cristiandad [kristjan'dað] *nf* Christianity.
cristianismo [kristja'nismo] *nm* Christianity.
cristiano, a [kris'tjano, a] *a, nm/f* Christian.
Cristo ['kristo] *nm* (*dios*) Christ; (*crucifijo*) crucifix.
criterio [kri'terjo] *nm* criterion; (*juicio*) judgement.
criticar [kriti'kar] *vt* to criticize.
crítico, a ['kritiko, a] *a* critical // *nm* critic // *nf* criticism.
cromo ['kromo] *nm* chrome.
crónico, a ['kroniko, a] *a* chronic // *nf* chronicle, account.
cronista [kro'nista] *nm/f* chronicler.
cruce ['kruθe] *nm* crossing; (*de carreteras*) crossroads.
crucificar [kruθifi'kar] *vt* to crucify.
crucifijo [kruθi'fixo] *nm* crucifix.
crucigrama [kruθi'ɣrama] *nm* crossword (puzzle).
crudo, a ['kruðo, a] *a* raw; (*no maduro*) unripe; (*petróleo*) crude; (*rudo, cruel*) cruel.

cruel [krwel] *a* cruel.
crueldad [krwel'ðað] *nf* cruelty.
crujido [kru'xiðo] *nm* creak.
crujir [kru'xir] *vi* (*madera*) to creak; (*dedos*) to crack; (*dientes*) to grind; (*nieve, arena*) to crunch.
cruz [kruθ] *nf* cross; (*de moneda*) tails *sg*.
cruzado, a [kru'θaðo, a] *a* crossed // *nm* crusader // *nf* crusade.
cruzar [kru'θar] *vt* to cross; ~**se** *vr* to cross; (*personas*) to pass each other.
cuaderno [kwa'ðerno] *nm* notebook; (*de escuela*) exercise book; (*NAUT*) logbook.
cuadra ['kwaðra] *nf* (*caballeriza*) stable; (*gran sala*) hall.
cuadrado, a [kwa'ðraðo, a] *a* square // *nm* (*MAT*) square; (*regla*) ruler.
cuadrar [kwa'ðrar] *vt* to square // *vi*: ~**con** to square with, tally with; ~**se** *vr* (*soldado*) to stand to attention.
cuadrilla [kwa'ðriλa] *nf* party, group.
cuadro ['kwaðro] *nm* square; (*de vidrio*) frame; (*PINTURA*) painting; (*TEATRO*) scene.
cuádruplo, a ['kwaðruplo, a], **cuádruple** ['kwaðruple] *a* quadruple.
cuajar [kwa'xar] *vt* to thicken; (*leche*) to curdle; (*sangre*) to congeal; (*adornar*) to adorn; ~**se** *vr* to curdle; to congeal; (*llenarse*) to fill up.
cual [kwal] *ad* like, as // *pron*: **el** ~ *etc* which; (*persona: sujeto*) who; (: *objeto*) whom // *a* such as; **cada** ~ each one; ~ **más,** ~ **menos** some more, some less; **tal** ~ just as it is.
cuál [kwal] *pron interr* which (one).
cualesquier(a) [kwales'kjer(a)] *pl de* **cualquier(a).**
cualidad [kwali'ðað] *nf* quality.
cualquiera [kwal'kjera], **cualquier** [kwal'kjer] *a any* // *pron* anybody, anyone; (*quienquiera*) whoever; **en cualquier parte** anywhere; ~ **que sea** whichever it is; (*persona*) whoever it is.
cuando ['kwando] *ad* when; (*aún si*) if, even if // *conj* (*puesto que*) since // *prep*: **yo,** ~ **niño...** when I was a child...; ~ **no sea así** even if it is not so; ~ **más** the more; ~ **menos** the less; ~ **no** if not, otherwise; **de** ~ **en** ~ from time to time.
cuándo ['kwando] *ad* when; ¿**desde** ~?, ¿**de** ~ **acá?** since when?
cuanto, a ['kwanto, a] *a* all that, as much as // *pron* all that (which), as much as; **llévate todo** ~ **quieras** take as much as you like; **en** ~ (*en seguida que*) as soon as; (*ya que*) since, inasmuch as; **en** ~ **profesor** as a teacher; **en** ~ **a** as for; ~ **más difícil sea** the more difficult it is; ~ **más hace (tanto) menos avanza** the more he does, the less he progresses. ~ **antes** as soon as possible; **unos** ~**s libros** a few books.
cuánto, a ['kwanto, a] *a* what a lot of; (*interr: sg*) how much?; (: *pl*) how many? // *pron, ad* how; (*interr: sg*) how much?; (: *pl*) how many?; ¡~**a gente!** what a lot of people!; ¿~ **cuesta?** how much does it

cost?; ¿**a** ~**s estamos?** what's the date?; **Señor no sé** ~**s** Mr. So-and-So.
cuarenta [kwa'renta] *num* forty.
cuarentena [kwaren'tena] *nf* quarantine.
cuartear [kwarte'ar] *vt* to quarter; (*dividir*) to divide up; ~**se** *vr* to crack, split.
cuartel [kwar'tel] *nm* (*de ciudad*) quarter, district; (*MIL*) barracks *pl*; ~ **general** headquarters *pl*.
cuarteto [kwar'teto] *nm* quartet.
cuarto, a ['kwarto, a] *a* fourth // *nm* (*MAT*) quarter, fourth; (*habitación*) room // *nf* (*MAT*) quarter, fourth; (*palmo*) span; ~ **de baño** bathroom; ~ **de hora** quarter (of an) hour.
cuatro ['kwatro] *num* four.
cuba ['kuβa] *nf* cask, barrel; (*fig*) drunkard.
Cuba ['kuβa] *nf* Cuba; **cubano, a** *a, nm/f* Cuban.
cúbico, a ['kuβiko, a] *a* cubic.
cubierto, a [ku'βjerto, a] *pp de* **cubrir** // *a* covered // *nm* cover; (*en la mesa*) place; ~**s** *nmpl* cutlery *sg* // *nf* cover, covering; (*neumático*) tyre; (*NAUT*) deck; **a** ~ **de** covered with *or* in.
cubo ['kuβo] *nm* cube; (*de madera*) bucket, tub; (*TEC*) drum.
cubrir [ku'βrir] *vt* to cover; ~**se** *vr* (*cielo*) to become overcast.
cucaracha [kuka'ratʃa] *nf* cockroach.
cuchara [ku'tʃara] *nf* spoon; (*TEC*) scoop; ~**da** *nf* spoonful; ~**dita** *nf* teaspoonful.
cucharita [kutʃa'rita] *nf* teaspoon.
cucharón [kutʃa'ron] *nm* ladle.
cuchichear [kutʃitʃe'ar] *vi* to whisper.
cuchilla [ku'tʃiλa] *nf* (large) knife; (*de arma blanca*) blade.
cuchillo [ku'tʃiλo] *nm* knife.
cuello ['kweλo] *nm* (*ANAT*) neck; (*de vestido, camisa*) collar.
cuenca ['kwenka] *nf* (*escudilla*) hollow; (*ANAT*) eye socket; (*GEO*) bowl, deep valley.
cuenta ['kwenta] *nf* (*cálculo*) count, counting; (*en café, restaurante*) bill; (*COM*) account; (*de collar*) bead; (*fig*) account; **a fin de** ~**s** in the end; **caer en la** ~ to catch on; **darse** ~ **de** to realize; **tener en** ~ to bear in mind; **echar** ~**s** to take stock; ~ **corriente/de ahorros** current/savings account.
cuento *etc vb ver* **contar** // ['kwento] *nm* story.
cuerdo, a ['kwerðo, a] *a* sane; (*prudente*) wise, sensible // *nf* rope; (*hilo*) string; (*de reloj*) spring; **dar** ~**a a un reloj** to wind up a clock.
cuerno ['kwerno] *nm* horn.
cuero ['kwero] *nm* (*ZOOL*) skin, hide; (*TEC*) leather; **en** ~**s** stark naked; ~ **cabelludo** scalp.
cuerpo ['kwerpo] *nm* body.
cuesta ['kwesta] *nf* slope; (*en camino etc*) hill; ~ **arriba/abajo** uphill/downhill; **a** ~**s** on one's back.
cuestión [kwes'tjon] *nf* matter, question,

issue; (*riña*) quarrel, dispute.
cuesto *etc vb ver* **costar.**
cueva ['kweßa] *nf* cave; (*bodega*) cellar.
cuidado [kwi'ðaðo] *nm* care, carefulness; (*preocupación*) care, worry; *excl* careful!, look out!
cuidadoso, a [kwiða'ðoso, a] *a* careful; (*preocupado*) anxious.
cuidar [kwi'ðar] *vt* (MED) to care for; (*ocuparse de*) to take care of, look after // *vi*: ~ **de** to take care of, look after; ~**se** *vr* to look after o.s.; ~**se de hacer algo** to take care not to do something.
culebra [ku'leßra] *nf* snake.
culebrear [kuleßre'ar] *vi* to wriggle along; (*río*) to meander.
culinario, a [kuli'narjo, a] *a* culinary, cooking *cpd*.
culminación [kulmina'θjon] *nf* culmination.
culo ['kulo] *nm* bottom, backside.
culpa ['kulpa] *nf* fault; (JUR) guilt; **tener la** ~ **(de)** to be to blame (for).
culpabilidad [kulpaßili'ðað] *nf* guilt.
culpable [kul'paßle] *a* guilty // *nm/f* culprit.
culpar [kul'par] *vt* to blame; (*acusar*) to accuse.
cultivador, a [kultißa'ðor, a] *nm/f* farmer // *nf* cultivator.
cultivar [kulti'ßar] *vt* to cultivate.
cultivo [kul'tißo] *nm* cultivation; (*plantas*) crop.
culto, a ['kulto, a] *a* (*cultivado*) cultivated; (*que tiene cultura*) cultured // *nm* (*homenaje*) worship; (*religión*) cult.
cultura [kul'tura] *nf* culture.
cumbre ['kumbre] *nf* summit, top.
cumpleaños [kumple'aɲos] *nm* birthday.
cumplido, a [kum'pliðo, a] *a* complete, perfect; (*abundante*) plentiful; (*cortés*) courteous // *nm* compliment; (*cortesía*) courtesy.
cumplimentar [kumplimen'tar] *vt* to congratulate.
cumplimiento [kumpli'mjento] *nm* (*de un deber*) fulfilment; (*acabamiento*) completion; (*cumplido*) compliment.
cumplir [kum'plir] *vt* (*orden*) to carry out, obey; (*promesa*) to carry out, fulfil; (*condena*) to serve; (*años*) to reach, attain // *vi*: ~ **con** (*deberes*) to carry out, fulfil; ~**se** *vr* (*plazo*) to expire.
cuna ['kuna] *nf* cradle, cot.
cuñado, a [ku'ɲaðo, a] *nm/f* brother/sister-in-law.
cuota ['kwota] *nf* (*parte proporcional*) share; (*cotización*) fee, dues *pl*.
cupe *etc vb ver* **caber.**
cura ['kura] *nf* (*curación*) cure; (*método curativo*) treatment // *nm* priest.
curación [kura'θjon] *nf* cure; (*acción*) curing.
curar [ku'rar] *vt* (*herida*) to treat, dress; (*enfermo*) to cure; (*carne, pescado*) to cure,

salt; (*cuero*) to tan // *vi*, ~**se** *vr* to get well, recover.
curiosear [kurjose'ar] *vt* to glance at, look over // *vi* to look round, wander round.
curiosidad [kurjosi'ðað] *nf* curiosity.
curioso, a [ku'rjoso, a] *a* curious // *nm/f* bystander, onlooker.
cursi ['kursi] *a* (*fam*) in bad taste, vulgar.
cursivo, a [kur'sißo, a] *a* italic // *nf* italics *pl*.
curso ['kurso] *nm* course; **en** ~ (*año*) current; (*proceso*) going on, under way.
curvo, a ['kurßo, a] *a* (*gen*) curved; (*torcido*) bent // *nf* (*gen*) curve, bend.
custodia [kus'toðja] *nf* care, safekeeping, custody.
custodiar [kusto'ðjar] *vt* (*guardar*) to keep, take care of; (*vigilar*) to guard, watch over.
custodio [kus'toðjo] *nm* guardian, keeper.
cutis ['kutis] *nm* skin, complexion.
cuyo, a ['kujo, a] *pron* (*de quien*) whose, of whom; (*de que*) of which.

CH

chabacano, a [tʃaßa'kano, a] *a* vulgar, coarse.
chacal [tʃa'kal] *nm* jackal.
chacota [tʃa'kota] *nf* fun (and games).
chal [tʃal] *nm* shawl.
chalán [tʃa'lan] *nm* (*pey*) shady dealer.
chaleco [tʃa'leko] *nm* waistcoat, vest (US); ~ **salvavidas** life jacket.
chalupa [tʃa'lupa] *nf* launch, boat.
champán [tʃam'pan] *nm*, **champaña** [tʃam'paɲa] *nm* champagne.
champiñón [tʃampi'ɲon] *nm* mushroom.
champú [tʃam'pu] *nm* shampoo.
chamuscar [tʃamus'kar] *vt* to scorch, sear, singe.
chantaje [tʃan'taxe] *nm* blackmail.
chapa ['tʃapa] *nf* (*de metal*) plate, sheet; (*de madera*) board, panel.
chaparrón [tʃapa'rron] *nm* downpour, cloudburst.
chapotear [tʃapote'ar] *vt* to sponge down // *vi* (*fam*) to splash about.
chapucero, a [tʃapu'θero, a] *a* rough, crude // *nm/f* bungler.
chapurrar [tʃapu'rrar], **chapurrear** [tʃapurre'ar] *vt* (*idioma*) to speak badly; (*bebidas*) to mix.
chapuzar [tʃapu'θar] *vi* to duck.
chaqueta [tʃa'keta] *nf* jacket.
charca ['tʃarka] *nf* pond, pool.
charco ['tʃarko] *nm* pool, puddle.
charla ['tʃarla] *nf* talk, chat; (*conferencia*) lecture.
charlar [tʃar'lar] *vi* to talk, chat.
charlatán, ana [tʃarla'tan, ana] *nm/f* chatterbox; (*embaidor*) trickster; (*curandero*) charlatan.
charol [tʃa'rol] *nm* varnish; (*cuero*) patent leather.

chascarrillo [tʃaska'rriʎo] *nm* (*fam*) funny story.

chasco ['tʃasko] *nm* (*broma*) trick, joke; (*desengaño*) disappointment.

chasquear [tʃaske'ar] *vt* (*engañar*) to disappoint; (*bromear*) to play a trick on; (*látigo*) to crack; (*lengua*) to click.

chasquido [tʃas'kiðo] *nm* (*de lengua*) click; (*de látigo*) crack.

chato, a ['tʃato, a] *a* flat // *excl* hey handsome/beautiful!

chaval, a [tʃa'ßal, a] *nm/f* lad/girl.

checo(e)slovaco, a [tʃeko(e)slo'ßako, a] *a*, *nm/f* Czech, Czechoslovak.

Checo(e)slovaquia [tʃeko(e)slo'ßakja] *nf* Czechoslovakia.

cheque ['tʃeke] *nm* cheque.

chequeo [tʃe'keo] *nm* (*MED*) check-up; (*AUTO*) service.

chequera [tʃe'kera] *nf* cheque-book.

chico, a ['tʃiko, a] *a* small, little // *nm/f* (*niño, niña*) child; (*muchacho, muchacha*) boy/girl.

chicharrón [tʃitʃa'rron] *nm* crackling.

chichón [tʃi'tʃon] *nm* bump, hump.

chiflado, a [tʃi'flaðo, a] *a* daft, barmy.

chiflar [tʃi'flar] *vt* to hiss, boo; ~**se** *vr*: ~**se por** to be/go crazy about.

chile ['tʃile] *nm* chilli, red pepper.

Chile ['tʃile] *nm* Chile; **chileno, a** *a*, *nm/f* Chilean.

chillar [tʃi'ʎar] *vi* (*persona*) to yell, scream; (*animal salvaje*) to howl; (*cerdo*) to squeal; (*puerta*) to creak.

chillido [tʃi'ʎiðo] *nm* (*de persona*) yell, scream; (*de animal*) howl; (*de frenos*) screech(ing).

chillón, ona [tʃi'ʎon, ona] *a* (*niño*) noisy; (*color*) loud, gaudy.

chimenea [tʃime'nea] *nf* chimney; (*hogar*) fireplace.

China ['tʃina] *nf*: **la** ~ China.

chinche ['tʃintʃe] *nf* bug; (*TEC*) drawing pin // *nm/f* nuisance, pest.

chino, a ['tʃino, a] *a*, *nm/f* Chinese // *nm* (*lengua*) Chinese.

Chipre ['tʃipre] *nf* Cyprus; **chipriota, chipriote** *a*, *nm/f* Cypriot.

chiquito, a [tʃi'kito, a] *a* very small, tiny // *nm/f* kid.

chirle ['tʃirle] *a* watery, wishy-washy.

chirriar [tʃi'rrjar] *vi* (*goznes*) to creak, squeak; (*pájaros*) to chirp, sing.

chirrido [tʃi'rriðo] *nm* creak(ing), squeak(ing); (*de pájaro*) chirp(ing).

chis [tʃis] *excl* sh!

chisme ['tʃisme] *nm* (*habladurías*) piece of gossip; (*fam: objeto*) thing, thingummyjig.

chismoso, a [tʃis'moso, a] *a* gossiping // *nm/f* gossip.

chispa ['tʃispa] *nf* spark; (*fig*) sparkle; (*ingenio*) wit; (*fam*) drunkenness.

chispeante [tʃispe'ante] *a* sparkling, scintillating.

chispear [tʃispe'ar] *vi* to spark; (*lloviznar*) to drizzle.

chisporrotear [tʃisporrote'ar] *vi* (*fuego*) to throw out sparks; (*leña*) to crackle; (*aceite*) to hiss, splutter.

chiste ['tʃiste] *nm* joke, funny story.

chistoso, a [tʃis'toso, a] *a* (*gracioso*) funny, amusing; (*bromista*) witty.

chivo, a ['tʃißo, a] *nm/f* (billy-) nanny-)goat.

chocante [tʃo'kante] *a* startling; (*extraño*) odd; (*ofensivo*) shocking; (*antipático*) annoying.

chocar [tʃo'kar] *vi* (*coches, trenes*) to collide, crash // *vt* to shock; (*sorprender*) to startle; ~ **con** to collide with; (*fig*) to run into *or* up against; ¡**chócala!** put it there!

chocolate [tʃoko'late] *a*, *nm* chocolate.

chochear [tʃotʃe'ar] *vi* to dodder, be senile.

chocho, a ['tʃotʃo, a] *a* doddering, senile; (*fig*) soft, doting.

chollo ['tʃoʎo] *nm* (*fam*) bargain, snip.

choque ['tʃoke] *nm* (*impacto*) impact; (*golpe*) jolt; (*AUTO*) crash; (*ELEC, MED*) shock; (*MIL*) clash; (*fig*) conflict.

chorizo [tʃo'riθo] *nm* hard pork sausage, salami.

chorrear [tʃorre'ar] *vi* to gush, spout (out); (*gotear*) to drip, trickle.

chorro ['tʃorro] *nm* jet; (*fig*) stream.

choza ['tʃoθa] *nf* hut, shack.

chuleta [tʃu'leta] *nf* chop, cutlet.

chulo ['tʃulo] *nm* (*pícaro*) rascal; (*fam: joven lindo*) dandy.

chupado, a [tʃu'paðo, a] *a* (*delgado*) skinny, gaunt; (*ajustado*) tight.

chupar [tʃu'par] *vt* to suck; (*absorber*) to absorb; ~**se** *vr* to grow thin.

churro ['tʃurro, a] *a* coarse // *nm* fritter.

chuscada [tʃus'kaða] *nf* funny remark, joke.

chusco, a ['tʃusko, a] *a* funny; (*persona*) coarse but amusing.

chusma ['tʃusma] *nf* rabble, mob.

D

D. *abr de* **Don.**

Da. *abr de* **Doña.**

dactilógrafo, a [dakti'loɣrafo, a] *nm/f* typist.

dádiva ['daðißa] *nf* (*donación*) donation; (*regalo*) gift.

dado, a ['daðo, a] *pp de* **dar** // *nm* die; ~**s** *nmpl* dice; ~ **que** *conj* given that.

dador, a [da'ðor, a] *nm/f* (*gen*) giver.

dama ['dama] *nf* (*gen*) lady; (*AJEDREZ*) queen; ~**s** *nfpl* draughts.

damasco [da'masko] *nm* (*tela*) damask.

damnificar [damnifi'kar] *vt* (*gen*) to harm; (*persona*) to injure.

danés, esa [da'nes, esa] *a* Danish // *nm/f* Dane.

danzar [dan'θar] *vt*, *vi* to dance.

dañar [da'ɲar] *vt* (*objeto*) to damage;

(*persona*) to hurt; ~**se** *vr* to get hurt.
dañino, a [da'ɲino, a] *a* harmful.
daño ['daɲo] *nm* (*a un objeto*) damage; (*a una persona*) harm, injury; ~**s y perjuicios** (*JUR*) damages; **hacer** ~ **a** to damage; to harm, injure.
dar [dar] *vt* (*gen*) to give; (*TEATRO*) to perform, put on; (*película*) to show; (*intereses*) to yield; (*naipes*) to deal; (*la hora*): ~ **las 3** to strike 3 // *vi*: ~ **a** to look out on(to), overlook; ~ **con** (*persona etc*) to meet, run into; (*idea*) to hit on; ~ **contra** to knock against, bang into; ~ **de cabeza** to fall on one's head; ~ **en** (*objeto*) to strike, hit; (*broma*) to catch on to; ~ **de sí** to give, stretch; ~**se** *vr* (*pasar*) to happen; (*presentarse*) to occur; ~**se a** to be given to; ~**se por** to consider o.s.; **dárselas de** to pose as; ~ **de comer/beber a uno** to give sb sth to eat/drink; **da lo mismo** o **qué más da** it's all the same; ~ **en el blanco** to hit the mark; **me da pena** it saddens me; ~**se prisa** to hurry (up).
dardo ['darðo] *nm* dart.
dársena ['darsena] *nf* dock.
datar [da'tar] *vi*: ~ **de** to date from.
dátil ['datil] *nm* date.
dato ['dato] *nm* fact, piece of information.
d. de J. C. *abr de* **después de Jesucristo** A.D. (Anno Domini).
de [de] *prep* of; from; **libro** ~ **cocina** cookery book; **el hombre** ~ **largos cabellos** the man with long hair; **guantes** ~ **cuero** leather gloves; **fue a Londres** ~ **profesor** he went to London as a teacher; **una** ~ **dos** one or the other; ~ **mañana** in the morning; **vestido** ~ **negro** dressed in black; **más/menos** ~ more/less than; ~ **cabeza** on one's head; ~ **cara** a facing.
deambular [deambu'lar] *vi* to stroll, wander.
debajo [de'βaxo] *ad* underneath; ~ **de** below, under; **por** ~ **de** beneath.
debate [de'βate] *nm* debate; **debatir** *vt* to debate.
deber [de'βer] *nm* duty // *vt* to owe // *vi*: **debe (de)** it must, it should; **debo hacerlo** I must do it; **debe de ir** he should go; ~**se** *vr*: ~**se a** to be owing or due to.
debido, a [de'βiðo, a] *a* proper, just; ~ **a** due to, because of.
débil ['deβil] *a* (*persona, carácter*) weak; (*luz*) dim; **debilidad** *nf* weakness; dimness; **debilidad senil** senility.
debilitar [deβili'tar] *vt* to weaken; ~**se** *vr* to grow weak.
débito ['deβito] *nm* debit.
década ['dekaða] *nf* decade.
decadencia [deka'ðenθja] *nf* decadence.
decaer [deka'er] *vi* (*declinar*) to decline; (*debilitarse*) to weaken.
decaimiento [dekai'mjento] *nm* (*declinación*) decline; (*desaliento*) discouragement; (*MED: empeoramiento*) weakening; (: *estado débil*) weakness.

decano, a [de'kano, a] *nm/f* dean.
decapitar [dekapi'tar] *vt* to behead.
decena [de'θena] *nf*: **una** ~ ten (or so).
decencia [de'θenθja] *nf* (*modestia*) modesty; (*honestidad*) respectability.
decente [de'θente] *a* (*correcto*) seemly, proper; (*honesto*) respectable.
decepción [deθep'θjon] *nf* disappointment; **decepcionar** *vt* to disappoint.
decidir [deθi'ðir] *vt* (*persuadir*) to convince, persuade; (*resolver*) to decide // *vi* to decide; ~**se** *vr*: ~**se a** to make up one's mind to.
décimo, a ['deθimo, a] *a* tenth // *nm* tenth.
decir [de'θir] *vt* (*expresar*) to say; (*contar*) to tell; (*hablar*) to speak // *nm* saying; ~**se** *vr*: **se dice que** it is said that; ~ **para/entre sí** to say to o.s.; **querer** ~ to mean.
decisión [deθi'sjon] *nf* (*resolución*) decision; (*firmeza*) decisiveness.
decisivo, a [deθi'siβo, a] *a* decisive.
declamar [dekla'mar] *vt, vi* to declaim.
declaración [deklara'θjon] *nf* (*manifestación*) statement; (*explicación*) explanation; **declarar** *vt* to declare, state; to explain // *vi* to declare; (*JUR*) to testify; **declararse** *vr* to propose.
declinar [dekli'nar] *vt* (*gen*) to decline; (*JUR*) to reject // *vi* (*el día*) to draw to a close; (*salud*) to deteriorate.
declive [de'kliβe] *nm* (*cuesta*) slope; (*inclinación*) incline.
decolorarse [dekolo'rarse] *vr* to become discoloured.
decoración [dekora'θjon] *nf* decoration.
decorado [deko'raðo] *nm* scenery, set.
decorar [deko'rar] *vt* to decorate; **decorativo, a** *a* ornamental, decorative.
decoro [de'koro] *nm* (*respeto*) respect; (*dignidad*) decency; (*recato*) decorum, propriety; ~**so, a** *a* (*decente*) decent; (*modesto*) modest; (*digno*) proper.
decrecer [dekre'θer] *vi* to decrease, diminish.
decrépito, a [de'krepito, a] *a* decrepit.
decretar [dekre'tar] *vt* to decree; **decreto** *nm* decree.
dedal [de'ðal] *nm* thimble.
dedicación [deðika'θjon] *nf* dedication; **dedicar** *vt* (*libro*) to dedicate; (*tiempo, dinero*) to devote; (*palabras: decir, consagrar*) to dedicate, devote; **dedicatoria** *nf* (*de libro*) dedication.
dedo ['deðo] *nm* finger; ~ (**del pie**) toe; ~ **pulgar** thumb; ~ **índice** index finger; ~ **mayor** *o* **cordial** middle finger; ~ **anular** ring finger; ~ **meñique** little finger.
deducción [deðuk'θjon] *nf* deduction.
deducir [deðu'θir] *vt* (*concluir*) to deduce, infer; (*COM*) to deduct.
defecto [de'fekto] *nm* defect, flaw; (*ELEC*) fault; **defectuoso, a** *a* defective, faulty.
defender [defen'der] *vt* to defend.
defensa [de'fensa] *nf* defence; (*DEPORTE*)

back; **defensivo, a** a defensive // nf: **a la
defensiva** on the defensive.
defensor, a [defen'sor, a] a defending //
nm/f (abogado) defending counsel;
(protector) protector.
deficiencia [defi'θjenθja] nf deficiency;
deficiente a (defectuoso) defective;
(imperfecto) deficient, wanting.
déficit ['defiθit] nm deficit.
definición [defini'θjon] nf definition.
definir [defi'nir] vt (determinar) to
determine, establish; (decidir) to define;
(aclarar) to clarify; **definitivo, a** a
definitive; **en definitiva** definitively.
deformación [deforma'θjon] nf
(alteración) deformation; (distorsión)
distortion.
deformar [defor'mar] vt (gen) to deform;
~se vr to become deformed; **deforme** a
(informe) deformed; (feo) ugly; (mal
hecho) misshapen.
defraudar [defrau'ðar] vt (decepcionar) to
disappoint; (estafar) to cheat, defraud;
(engañar) to deceive.
defunción [defun'θjon] nf decease,
demise.
degeneración [dexenera'θjon] nf (de las
células) degeneration; (moral)
degeneracy; **degenerar** vi to degenerate.
degollar [dexo'ʎar] vt (animal) to
slaughter; (decapitar) to behead,
decapitate.
degradar [dexra'ðar] vt to debase,
degrade; ~se vr to demean o.s.
degüello [de'xweʎo] nm: **entrar a** ~ to
slaughter, put to the sword.
degustación [dexusta'θjon] nf sampling,
tasting.
deidad [dei'ðað] nf deity, divinity.
deificar [deifi'kar] vt (persona) to deify.
dejación [dexa'θjon] nf (abandono)
abandonment.
dejadez [dexa'ðeθ] nf (negligencia)
neglect; (descuido) untidiness, carelessness; **dejado, a** a (negligente) careless;
(indolente) lazy.
dejar [de'xar] vt (gen) to leave; (permitir)
to allow, let; (abandonar) to abandon,
forsake; (beneficios) to produce, yield //
vi: ~ **de** (parar) to stop; (no hacer) to fail
to; ~ **a un lado** to leave or set aside.
dejo ['dexo] nm (LING) accent; (sabor
fuerte) tang; (sabor que queda) aftertaste.
del [del] = **de** + **el**, ver **de.**
delantal [delan'tal] nm apron.
delante [de'lante] ad in front; (enfrente)
opposite; (adelante) ahead; ~ **de** in front
of, before.
delantero, a [delan'tero, a] a front // nm
(DEPORTE) forward // nf (de vestido, casa)
front part; (DEPORTE) forward line; **llevar
la ~ a a uno** to be ahead of sb.
delatar [dela'tar] vt to inform on or
against, betray; **delator, a** nm/f informer.
delegación [delexa'θjon] nf delegation;
(COM) office, branch; ~ **de policía** police
station; ~ **municipal** local government

office; **delegado, a** nm/f delegate; (COM)
agent; **delegar** vt to delegate.
deleitar [delei'tar] vt to delight; ~se vr:
~se con o en to delight in, take pleasure
in; **deleite** nm delight, pleasure.
deletrear [deletre'ar] vi to spell (out);
(fig) to interpret, decipher; **deletreo** nm
spelling; interpretation, decipherment.
deleznable [deleθ'naßle] a inv (frágil)
fragile; (resbaloso) slippery; (fugaz)
fleeting.
delfín [del'fin] nm dolphin.
delgadez [delxa'ðeθ] nf thinness, slimness;
delgado, a a (gen) thin; (persona) slim,
thin; (tierra) poor; (tela etc) light, delicate.
deliberación [delißera'θjon] nf
deliberation; **deliberar** vt to debate,
discuss.
delicadeza [delika'ðeθa] nf (gen)
delicacy; (refinamiento, sutileza)
refinement.
delicado, a [deli'kaðo, a] a (gen) delicate;
(sensible) sensitive; (quisquilloso) touchy.
delicia [de'liθja] nf delight.
delicioso, a [deli'θjoso, a] a (gracioso)
delightful, agreeable; (placentero)
pleasant; (exquisito) delicious.
delincuencia [delin'kwenθja] nf
delinquency; **delincuente** nm/f
delinquent, criminal.
delinquir [delin'kir] vi to commit an
offence.
delirante [deli'rante] a delirious; **delirar**
vi to be delirious, rave.
delirio [de'lirjo] nm (MED) delirium;
(palabras insensatas) wanderings pl,
ravings pl.
delito [de'lito] nm (infracción) offence;
(crimen) crime; ~ **político/común**
political/common crime.
demagogo [dema'xoxo] nm demagogue.
demanda [de'manda] nf (pedido, COM)
demand; (petición) request; (JUR) action,
lawsuit; **demandante** nm/f claimant.
demandar [deman'dar] vt (gen) to
demand; (JUR) to sue.
demarcación [demarka'θjon] nf (de
terreno) demarcation; **demarcar** vt to
demarcate.
demás [de'mas] a: **los** ~ **niños** the other
children, the remaining children // pron:
los/las ~ the others, the rest (of them);
lo ~ the rest (of it) // ad besides.
demasía [dema'sia] nf (exceso) excess,
surplus; (atrevimiento) boldness; (insolencia) outrage; **comer en** ~ to eat to
excess.
demasiado, a [dema'sjaðo, a] a too, too
much; ~**s** too many // ad too, too much;
¡es ~**!** it's too much!
demencia [de'menθja] nf (locura)
madness; **demente** nm/f lunatic // a mad,
insane.
democracia [demo'kraθja] nf democracy.
demócrata [de'mokrata] nm/f democrat;
democrático, a a democratic.

demoler [demo'ler] *vt* to demolish; **demolición** *nf* demolition.

demonio [de'monjo] *nm* devil, demon; ¡~s! hell!, confound it!; ¿cómo ~s? how the hell?

demora [de'mora] *nf* delay; **demorar** *vt* (*retardar*) to delay, hold back; (*dilatar*) to hold up // *vi* to linger, stay on.

demostración [demostra'θjon] *nf* (*de teorema*) demonstration; (*de afecto*) show, display.

demostrar [demos'trar] *vt* (*probar*) to prove; (*mostrar*) to show; (*manifestar*) to demonstrate; **demostrativo, a** *a* demonstrative.

denegar [dene'ɣar] *vt* (*rechazar*) to refuse; (*JUR*) to reject.

denigrar [deni'ɣrar] *vt* (*desacreditar, infamar*) to denigrate; (*injuriar*) to insult.

denominación [denomina'θjon] *nf* (*nombramiento*) designation; (*clase*) denomination.

denotar [deno'tar] *vt* (*indicar*) to indicate; (*significar*) to denote.

densidad [densi'ðað] *nf* (*FÍSICA*) density; (*fig*) thickness.

denso, a ['denso, a] *a* (*apretado*) solid; (*espeso, pastoso*) thick; (*fig*) heavy.

dentadura [denta'ðura] *nf* (set of) teeth *pl*; ~ **postiza** false teeth *pl*.

dentera [den'tera] *nf* (*sensación desagradable*) the shivers *pl*, the shudders *pl*; (*envidia*) envy, jealousy; (*deseo*) desire.

dentista [den'tista] *nm/f* dentist.

dentro ['dentro] *ad* inside // *prep*: ~ **de** in, inside, within; **vayamos a** ~ let's go inside; **mirar por** ~ to look inside; ~ **de tres meses** within three months.

denuedo [de'nweðo] *nm* boldness, daring.

denuncia [de'nunθja] *nf* (*delación*) denunciation; (*acusación*) accusation; (*de accidente*) report; **denunciar** *vt* to report; (*delatar*) to inform on *or* against.

departamento [departa'mento] *nm* (*sección administrativa*) department, section; (*de caja, tren*) compartment; (*AM: piso*) apartment, flat.

dependencia [depen'denθja] *nf* dependence; (*POL*) dependency; (*COM*) office, section.

depender [depen'der] *vi*: ~ **de** to depend on.

dependienta [depen'djenta] *nf* saleswoman, shop assistant; **dependiente** *a* dependent // *nm* salesman.

deplorable [deplo'raßle] *a* deplorable; **deplorar** *vt* to deplore.

deponer [depo'ner] *vt* to lay down // *vi* (*JUR*) to give evidence; (*declarar*) to testify.

deportar [depor'tar] *vt* to deport.

deporte [de'porte] *nm* sport; **deportista** *a* sports *cpd* // *nm/f* sportsman/woman.

depositante [deposi'tante], **depositador, a** [deposita'ðor, a] *nm/f* depositor.

depositar [deposi'tar] *vt* (*dinero*) to deposit; (*mercaderías*) to put away, store;

(*AM: persona*) to confide; ~**se** *vr* to settle; ~**io, a** *nm/f* trustee.

depósito [de'posito] *nm* (*gen*) deposit; (*de mercaderías*) warehouse, store; (*de agua, gasolina etc*) tank; ~ **de equipajes** cloakroom.

depravar [depra'ßar] *vt* to deprave; ~**se** *vr* to become depraved.

depreciar [depre'θjar] *vt* to depreciate, reduce the value of; ~**se** *vr* to depreciate, lose value.

depredación [depreða'θjon] *nf* (*saqueo, pillaje*) pillage; (*malversación*) depredation.

depresión [depre'sjon] *nf* depression.

deprimido, a [depri'miðo, a] *a* depressed.

deprimir [depri'mir] *vt* to depress; ~**se** *vr* (*persona*) to become depressed.

depuración [depura'θjon] *nf* purification; (*POL*) purge; **depurar** *vt* to purify; (*purgar*) to purge.

derecha [de'retʃa] *nf* right(-hand) side; (*POL*) right.

derechamente [deretʃa'mente] *ad* (*dirección*) straight.

derecho, a [de'retʃo, a] *a* right, right-hand // *nm* (*privilegio*) right; (*lado*) right(-hand) side; (*leyes*) law // *ad* straight, directly; ~**s** *nmpl* (*de aduana*) duty *sg*; (*de autor*) royalties; **tener** ~ **a** to have a right to.

deriva [de'rißa] *nf*: **ir** *o* **estar a la** ~ to drift, be adrift.

derivación [derißa'θjon] *nf* derivation.

derivar [deri'ßar] *vt* (*gen*) to derive; (*desviar*) to drift; ~**se** *vr* to derive, be derived; to drift.

derramamiento [derrama'mjento] *nm* (*de sangre*) shedding; (*dispersión*) spilling.

derramar [derra'mar] *vt* to spill; (*echar*) to pour out; (*dispersar*) to scatter; ~**se** *vr* to pour out; ~ **lágrimas** to weep.

derrame [de'rrame] *nm* (*de líquido*) spilling; (*de sangre*) shedding; (*de tubo etc*) overflow; (*perdida*) loss, leakage; (*MED*) discharge; (*declive*) slope.

derredor [derre'ðor] *ad*: **al** *o* **en** ~ **de** around, about.

derretido, a [derre'tiðo, a] *a* melted, molten.

derretir [derre'tir] *vt* (*gen*) to melt; (*nieve*) to thaw; (*fig*) to squander; ~**se** *vr* to melt.

derribar [derri'ßar] *vt* to knock down; (*construcción*) to demolish; (*persona, gobierno, político*) to bring down; ~**se** *vr* to fall down.

derrocar [derro'kar] *vt* (*despeñar*) to demolish, knock down; (*gobierno*) to bring down, overthrow.

derrochar [derro'tʃar] *vt* to squander; **derroche** *nm* (*despilfarro*) waste, squandering.

derrota [de'rrota] *nf* (*camino, vereda*) road, route; (*NAUT*) course; (*MIL*) defea rout; (*fig*) disaster; **derrotar** *vt* (*gen*) † defeat; (*destruir*) to ruin; **derrotero** *n* (*rumbo*) course.

derrumbar [derrum'bar] *vt* to throw down; ~**se** *vr* (*despeñarse*) to collapse; (*precipitarse*) to throw o.s. down.

desabotonar [desaβoto'nar] *vt* to unbutton, undo // *vi* to open out; ~**se** *vr* to come undone.

desabrido, a [desa'βriðo, a] *a* (*insípido, soso*) insipid, tasteless; (*persona*) rude, surly; (*respuesta*) sharp.

desabrochar [desaβro'tʃar] *vt* (*botones, broches*) to undo, unfasten; (*fig*) to expose; ~**se** *vr* to confide, unburden o.s.

desacato [desa'kato] *nm* (*falta de respeto*) disrespect; (*irreverencia*) insulting behaviour; (*JUR*) contempt.

desacertado, a [desaθer'taðo, a] *a* (*equivocado*) mistaken; (*inoportuno*) unwise.

desacertar [desaθer'tar] *vi* (*errar*) to be mistaken; (*desatinar*) to act unwisely.

desacierto [desa'θjerto] *nm* mistake, error.

desacomodar [desakomo'ðar] *vt* (*molestar*) to put out, inconvenience; **desacomodo** *nm* (*incomodidad*) inconvenience; (*molestia*) trouble.

desaconsejado, a [desakonse'xaðo, a] *a* ill-advised; **desaconsejar** *vt* to dissuade, advise against.

desacordarse [desakor'ðarse] *vr* (*MUS*) to get out of tune; **desacorde** *a inv* discordant.

desacreditar [desakreði'tar] *vt* (*desprestigiar*) to discredit, bring into disrepute; (*denigrar*) to run down.

desacuerdo [desa'kwerðo] *nm* (*conflicto*) discord, disagreement; (*error*) error, blunder.

desafecto, a [desa'fekto, a] *a* (*opuesto*) disaffected // *nm* (*hostilidad*) disaffection.

desafiar [desa'fjar] *vt* (*retar*) to challenge; (*enfrentarse a*) to defy.

desafilar [desafi'lar] *vt* to blunt; ~**se** *vr* to become blunt.

desafinado, a [desafi'naðo] *a*: **estar** ~ to be out of tune; **desafinarse** *vr* (*MUS*) to go out of tune.

desafío [desa'fio] *nm* (*reto*) challenge; (*combate*) duel; (*resistencia*) defiance; (*competencia*) competition.

desafortunado, a [desafortu'naðo, a] *a* (*desgraciado*) unfortunate, unlucky.

desagradable [desaxra'ðaβle] *a* (*fastidioso, enojoso*) unpleasant; (*irritante*) disagreeable.

desagradar [desaxra'ðar] *vi* (*disgustar*) to displease; (*molestar*) to bother; **desagradecido, a** *a* ungrateful.

desagrado [desa'xraðo] *nm* (*disgusto*) displeasure; (*contrariedad*) dissatisfaction.

desagraviar [desaxra'βjar] *vt* to make amends to; **desagravio** *nm* (*recompensa*) amends; (: *en efectivo*) compensation.

desaguadero [desaxwa'ðero] *nm* drain.

desagüe [des'axwe] *nm* (*de un líquido*) drainage; (*cañería*) drainpipe.

desaguisado, a [desaxi'saðo, a] *a* illegal // *nm* outrage.

desahogado, a [desao'xaðo, a] *a* (*descarado*) brazen, impudent; (*holgado*) comfortable; (*espacioso*) roomy.

desahogar [desao'xar] *vt* (*consolar*) to console; (*aliviar*) to ease, relieve; (*ira*) to vent; ~**se** *vr* (*distenderse*) to take it easy; (*desfogarse*) to let off steam.

desahogo [desa'oxo] *nm* (*alivio*) relief; (*comodidad*) comfort, ease; (*descaro*) impudence.

desahuciar [desau'θjar] *vt* (*enfermo*) to give up hope for; (*inquilino*) to evict; **desahucio** *nm* eviction.

desairado, a [desai'raðo, a] *a* (*menospreciado*) disregarded; (*desgarbado*) shabby.

desairar [desai'rar] *vt* (*menospreciar*) to slight, snub; (*ultrajar*) to dishonour.

desaire [des'aire] *nm* (*afrenta*) rebuff; (*menosprecio*) slight; (*falta de garbo*) unattractiveness, lack of charm.

desajustar [desaxus'tar] *vt* (*desarreglar*) to disarrange; (*desconcertar*) to throw off balance; ~**se** *vr* to get out of order; (*cintura*) to loosen.

desajuste [desa'xuste] *nm* (*de máquina*) disorder; (*situación*) imbalance.

desalentador, a [desalenta'ðor, a] *a* disheartening; **desalentar** *vt* (*desanimar*) to discourage; **desalentar a uno** to make sb breathless.

desaliento [desa'ljento] *nm* discouragement.

desalinear [desaline'ar] *vt* to throw out of the straight; ~**se** *vr* to go off the straight.

desaliño [desa'liɲo] *nm* (*negligencia*) slovenliness.

desalmado, a [desal'maðo, a] *a* (*cruel*) cruel, heartless.

desalojamiento [desaloxa'mjento] *nm* ousting; (*cambio de residencia*) removal; (: *forzado*) eviction.

desalojar [desalo'xar] *vt* (*expulsar, echar*) to eject; (*abandonar*) to abandon, evacuate // *vi* to move out.

desamarrar [desama'rrar] *vt* to untie; (*NAUT*) to cast off.

desamor [desa'mor] *nm* (*frialdad*) indifference; (*odio*) dislike; (*enemistad*) enmity.

desamparado, a [desampa'raðo, a] *a* (*persona*) helpless; (*lugar: expuesto*) exposed; (*desierto*) deserted.

desamparar [desampa'rar] *vt* (*abandonar*) to desert, abandon; (*JUR*) to leave defenceless; (*barco*) to abandon.

desandar [desan'dar] *vt*: ~ **lo andado** *o* **el camino** to retrace one's steps.

desanimado, a [desani'maðo, a] *a* (*persona*) downhearted; (*espectáculo, fiesta*) dull; **desanimar** *vt* (*desalentar*) to discourage; (*deprimir*) to depress.

desapacible [desapa'θiβle] *a* (*gen*) unpleasant; (*carácter*) disagreeable; (*voz*) harsh.

desaparecer [desapareˈθer] *vt* (*gen*) to hide // *vi* (*gen*) to disappear; (*el sol, la luz*) to vanish; **desaparición** *nf* disappearance.

desapego [desaˈpeɤo] *nm* (*frialdad*) coolness; (*distancia*) detachment.

desapercibido, a [desaperθiˈβiðo, a] *a* (*desprevenido*) unprepared; **pasar** ~ to go unnoticed.

desaplicación [desaplikaˈθjon] *nf* (*negligencia*) slackness; (*ocio*) laziness; **desaplicado, a** *a* slack; lazy.

desaprensivo, a [desaprenˈsiβo, a] *a* unscrupulous.

desaprobar [desaproˈβar] *vt* (*reprobar*) to disapprove of; (*condenar*) to condemn; (*no consentir*) to reject.

desaprovechado, a [desaproβeˈtʃaðo, a] *a* (*improductivo*) unproductive; (*atrasado*) backward; **desaprovechar** *vt* to waste.

desarmar [desarˈmar] *vt* (*MIL, fig*) to disarm; (*TEC*) to take apart, dismantle; **desarme** *nm* disarmament.

desarraigar [desarraiˈɤar] *vt* to uproot; **desarraigo** *nm* uprooting.

desarreglado, a [desarreˈɤlaðo, a] *a* (*TEC*) out of order; (*desordenado*) disorderly, untidy.

desarreglar [desarreˈɤlar] *vt* (*desordenar*) to disarrange; (*mecánica*) to put out of order; (*trastocar*) to upset, disturb.

desarreglo [desaˈrreɤlo] *nm* (*de casa, persona*) untidiness; (*desorden*) disorder.

desarrollar [desarroˈʎar] *vt* (*gen*) to develop; (*extender*) to unfold; ~**se** *vr* to develop; (*extenderse*) to open (out); (*film*) to develop; **desarrollo** *nm* development.

desarticular [desartikuˈlar] *vt* (*hueso*) to put out; (*objeto*) to take apart; (*fig*) to break up.

desaseo [desaˈseo] *nm* (*suciedad*) slovenliness; (*desarreglo*) untidiness.

desasir [desaˈsir] *vt* to loosen; ~**se** *vr* to extricate o.s.; ~**se de** to let go, give up.

desasosegar [desasoseˈɤar] *vt* (*inquietar*) to disturb; (*afligir*) to make uneasy; ~**se** *vr* to become uneasy.

desasosiego [desasoˈsjeɤo] *nm* (*intranquilidad*) uneasiness; (*aflicción*) restlessness; (*ansiedad*) anxiety.

desastrado, a [desasˈtraðo, a] *a* (*desaliñado*) shabby; (*sucio*) dirty; (*desgraciado, adverso*) wretched.

desastre [deˈsastre] *nm* disaster; **desastroso, a** *a* disastrous.

desatado, a [desaˈtaðo, a] *a* (*desligado*) untied; (*violento*) violent, wild.

desatar [desaˈtar] *vt* (*nudo*) to untie; (*paquete*) to undo; (*separar*) to detach; ~**se** *vr* (*zapatos*) to come untied; (*tormenta*) to break.

desatender [desatenˈder] *vt* (*no prestar atención a*) to disregard; (*abandonar*) to neglect; (*invitado*) to slight.

desatento, a [desaˈtento, a] *a* (*distraído*) inattentive; (*descortés*) discourteous.

desatinado, a [desatiˈnaðo, a] *a* (*disparatado*) wild, reckless; (*absurdo*) foolish, silly; **desatinar** *vi* (*desvariar*) to behave foolishly; **desatino** *nm* (*idiotez*) foolishness, folly; (*error*) blunder.

desautorizado, a [desautoriˈθaðo, a] *a* unauthorized; **desautorizar** *vt* (*oficial*) to deprive of authority; (*informe*) to deny.

desavenencia [desaβeˈnenθja] *nf* (*desacuerdo*) disagreement; (*discrepancia*) rift, quarrel.

desaventajado, a [desaβentaˈxaðo, a] *a* (*inferior*) inferior; (*poco ventajoso*) disadvantageous.

desayunar [desajuˈnar] *vi* to have breakfast // *vt* to have for breakfast; **desayuno** *nm* breakfast.

desazón [desaˈθon] *nf* (*insipidez*) tastelessness; (*angustia*) anxiety; (*fig*) annoyance.

desazonar [desaθoˈnar] *vt* to make tasteless; (*fig*) to annoy, upset; ~**se** *vr* (*enojarse*) to be annoyed; (*preocuparse*) to worry, be anxious; (*MED*) to be off colour.

desbandarse [desβanˈdarse] *vr* (*MIL*) to disband; (*fig*) to flee in disorder.

desbarajuste [desβaraˈxuste] *nm* confusion, disorder.

desbaratar [desβaraˈtar] *vt* (*deshacer, destruir*) to ruin; (*malgastar*) to squander; (*mecánica*) to take apart.

desbordar [desβorˈðar] *vt* (*sobrepasar*) to go beyond; (*exceder*) to exceed // *vi*, ~**se** *vr* (*río*) to overflow; (*entusiasmo*) to erupt; (*persona*) to express one's feelings freely.

descabalgar [deskaβalˈɤar] *vi* to dismount.

descabellado, a [deskaβeˈʎaðo, a] *a* (*disparatado*) wild, crazy; (*insensato*) ridiculous.

descabellar [deskaβeˈʎar] *vt* to ruffle; (*TAUR: toro*) to give the coup de grace to.

descabezar [deskaβeˈθar] *vt* (*persona*) to behead; (*árbol*) to lop; ~**se** *vr* (*AGR*) to shed the grain; (*fig*) to rack one's brains.

descafeinado [deskafeiˈnaðo] *nm* decaffeinated coffee.

descalabro [deskaˈlaβro] *nm* blow; (*desgracia*) misfortune.

descalzar [deskalˈθar] *vt* (*zapato*) to take off; **descalzo, a** *a* barefoot(ed); (*fig*) destitute.

descaminado, a [deskamiˈnaðo, a] *a* (*equivocado*) on the wrong road; (*fig*) misguided.

descaminar [deskamiˈnar] *vt* (*alguien*) to misdirect; (: *fig*) to lead astray; ~**se** *vr* (*en la ruta*) to go the wrong way; (*fig*) to go astray.

descansado, a [deskanˈsaðo, a] *a* (*gen*) rested; (*que tranquiliza*) restful; **descansar** *vt* (*gen*) to rest // *vi* to rest, have a rest; (*echarse*) to lie down.

descanso [desˈkanso] *nm* (*reposo*) rest; (*alivio*) relief; (*pausa*) break; (*DEPORTE*) interval, half time.

descarado, a [deskaˈraðo, a] *a* (*sin*

vergüenza) shameless; (*insolente*) cheeky;
descararse *vr* to be insolent *or* cheeky.
descarga [des'karɣa] *nf* (*ARQ. ELEC. MIL*)
discharge; (*NAUT*) unloading.
descargadero [deskarɣa'ðero] *nm* wharf.
descargar [deskar'ɣar] *vt* to unload;
(*golpe*) to let fly; ~**se** *vr* to unburden o.s.;
descargo *nm* unloading; (*COM*) receipt;
(*JUR*) evidence.
descarnado, a [deskar'naðo, a] *a*
scrawny; (*fig*) bare.
descaro [des'karo] *nm* (*atrevimiento*)
shamelessness, nerve; (*insolencia*) cheek.
descarriar [deska'rrjar] *vt* (*descaminar*)
to misdirect; (*fig*) to lead astray; ~**se** *vr*
(*perderse*) to lose one's way; (*separarse*) to
stray; (*pervertirse*) to err, go astray.
descarrilamiento [deskarrila'mjento]
nm (*de tren*) derailment.
descartar [deskar'tar] *vt* (*rechazar*) to
reject; (*poner a un lado*) to set aside;
(*eliminar*) to rule out; ~**se** *vr* (*NAIPES*) to
discard; ~**se de** to shirk; **descartado, a** *a*
rejected; set aside, eliminated.
descendencia [desθen'denθja] *nf* (*origen*)
origin, descent; (*hijos*) offspring.
descender [desθen'der] *vt* (*bajar:
escalera*) to go down; (*: equipajes*) to take
down // *vi* to descend; (*temperatura, nivel*)
to fall, drop; ~ **de** to be descended from.
descendiente [desθen'djente] *nm/f*
descendant.
descenso [des'θenso] *nm* descent; (*de
temperatura*) drop.
descifrar [desθi'frar] *vt* to decipher.
descolgar [deskol'ɣar] *vt* (*bajar*) to take
down; (*teléfono*) to pick up; ~**se** *vr* to let
o.s. down.
descolorir [deskolo'rir], **descolorar**
[deskolo'rar] *vt* = **decolorar.**
descomedido, a [deskome'ðiðo, a] *a*
(*descortés*) rude; (*excesivo*) excessive.
descompaginar [deskompaxi'nar] *vt*
(*desordenar*) to disarrange, mess up.
descompasado, a [deskompa'saðo, a] *a*
(*sin proporción*) out of all proportion; (*excesivo*) excessive.
descomponer [deskompo'ner] *vt*
(*desordenar*) to disarrange, disturb; (*TEC*)
to put out of order; (*dividir*) to break down
(into parts); (*fig*) to provoke; ~**se** *vr*
(*corromperse*) to rot, decompose; (*el
tiempo*) to change (for the worse); (*TEC*) to
break down; (*irritarse*) to lose one's
temper.
descomposición [deskomposi'θjon] *nf*
(*gen*) breakdown; (*de fruta etc*)
decomposition.
descompostura [deskompos'tura] *nf*
(*TEC*) breakdown; (*desorganización*)
disorganization; (*desorden*) untidiness.
descompuesto, a [deskom'pwesto, a] *a*
(*corrompido*) decomposed; (*roto*) broken;
(*descarado*) brazen; (*furioso*) angry.
desconcertado, a [deskonθer'taðo, a] *a*
disconcerted, bewildered.
desconcertar [deskonθer'tar] *vt*

(*confundir*) to baffle; (*incomodar*) to upset,
put out; (*TEC*) to put out of order; (*ANAT*) to
dislocate; ~**se** *vr* (*turbarse*) to be upset.
desconcierto [deskon'θjerto] *nm* (*gen*)
disorder; (*daño*) damage; (*desorientación*)
uncertainty; (*inquietud*) uneasiness.
desconectar [deskonek'tar] *vt* to
disconnect.
desconfianza [deskon'fjanθa] *nf* distrust;
desconfiar *vi* to be distrustful;
desconfiar de to distrust, suspect.
desconocer [deskono'θer] *vt* (*alguien*) to
ignore; (*ignorar*) not to know, be ignorant
of; (*no recordar*) to fail to remember; (*no
aceptar*) to deny; (*repudiar*) to disown.
desconocimiento [deskonoθi'mjento] *nm*
(*falta de conocimientos*) ignorance;
(*repudio*) disregard; (*ingratitud*)
ingratitude.
desconsiderado, a [deskonsiðe'raðo, a] *a*
(*descuidado*) inconsiderate; (*insensible*)
thoughtless.
desconsolar [deskonso'lar] *vt* to distress;
~**se** *vr* to despair.
desconsuelo [deskon'swelo] *nm* (*tristeza*)
distress; (*desesperación*) despair.
descontar [deskon'tar] *vt* (*deducir*) to
take away, deduct; (*rebajar*) to discount;
(*predecir, dar por cierto*) to take for
granted.
descontento, a [deskon'tento, a] *a*
dissatisfied // *nm* dissatisfaction,
discontent.
descorazonar [deskoraθo'nar] *vt* to
discourage, dishearten.
descorchar [deskor'tʃar] *vt* to uncork.
descortés [deskor'tes] *a* (*mal educado*)
discourteous; (*grosero*) rude.
descoser [desko'ser] *vt* to unstitch; ~**se**
vr to come apart (at the seams).
descosido, a [desko'siðo, a] *a* (*costura*)
unstitched; (*indiscreto*) indiscreet; (*desordenado*) disjointed.
descoyuntar [deskojun'tar] *vt* (*ANAT*) to
dislocate.
descrédito [des'kreðito] *nm* discredit.
descreído, a [deskre'iðo, a] *a* (*incrédulo*)
incredulous; (*falto de fe*) unbelieving.
describir [deskri'ßir] *vt* to describe.
descripción [deskrip'θjon] *nf* description.
descrito [des'krito] *pp de* **describir.**
descuajar [deskwa'xar] *vt* (*disolver*) to
melt; (*planta*) to pull out by the roots.
descubierto, a [desku'ßjerto, a] *pp de*
descubrir // *a* uncovered, bare; (*persona*)
bareheaded; **al** ~ in the open.
descubrimiento [deskußri'mjento] *nm*
(*hallazgo*) discovery; (*revelación*)
revelation.
descubrir [desku'ßrir] *vt* to discover, find;
(*inaugurar*) to unveil; (*vislumbrar*) to
detect; (*revelar*) to reveal, show; (*quitar la
tapa*) to uncover; ~**se** *vr* to reveal o.s.;
(*quitarse sombrero*) to take off one's hat;
(*confesar*) to confess.
descuento [des'kwento] *nm* discount; ~
jubilatorio retirement pension.

descuidado, a [deskwi'ðaðo, a] *a* (*sin cuidado*) careless; (*desordenado*) untidy; (*olvidadizo*) forgetful; (*dejado*) neglected; (*desprevenido*) unprepared.

descuidar [deskwi'ðar] *vt* (*dejar*) to neglect; (*olvidar*) to overlook // *vi*, ~ **se** *vr* (*distraerse*) to be careless; (*estar desaliñado*) to let o.s. go; (*desprevenirse*) to drop one's guard; ¡**descuida!** don't worry!; **descuido** *nm* (*dejadez*) carelessness; (*olvido*) negligence.

desde ['desðe] *ad* from; ~ **que** *conj* since; ~ **lejos** from afar; ~ **ahora en adelante** from now onwards; ~ **hace 3 días** for 3 days now; ~ **luego** of course.

desdecirse [desðe'θirse] *vr* (*de promesa*) to go back on one's word.

desdén [des'ðen] *nm* scorn.

desdeñar [desðe'ɲar] *vt* (*despreciar*) to scorn.

desdicha [des'ðitʃa] *nf* (*desgracia*) misfortune; (*infelicidad*) unhappiness; **desdichado, a** *a* (*sin suerte*) unlucky; (*infeliz*) unhappy.

desdoblar [desðo'ßlar] *vt* (*extender*) to spread out; (*desplegar*) to unfold; (*separar en dos*) to split.

desear [dese'ar] *vt* to want, desire, wish for.

desecar [dese'kar] *vt*, ~ **se** *vr* to dry up.

desechar [dese'tʃar] *vt* (*basura*) to throw out *or* away; (*ideas*) to reject, discard; **desechos** *nmpl* rubbish *sg*, waste *sg*.

desembalar [desemba'lar] *vt* to unpack.

desembarazado, a [desembara'θaðo, a] *a* (*libre*) clear, free; (*desenvuelto*) free and easy.

desembarazar [desembara'θar] *vt* (*desocupar*) to clear; (*desenredar*) to free; ~ **se** *vr*: ~ **se de** to free o.s. of, get rid of.

desembarcar [desembar'kar] *vt*, *vi*, ~ **se** *vr* to land.

desembocadura [desemboka'ðura] *nf* (*de río*) mouth; (*de calle*) opening.

desembocar [desembo'kar] *vi* to flow into; (*fig*) to result in.

desembolso [desem'bolso] *nm* payment; ~ **s** *nmpl* expenses; ~ **inicial** deposit, down payment.

desemejante [deseme'xante] *a* dissimilar, unlike; **desemejanza** *nf* dissimilarity.

desempeñar [desempe'ɲar] *vt* (*cargo*) to hold; (*papel*) to perform; (*lo empeñado*) to redeem; ~ **se** *vr* to get out of debt; ~ **un papel** (*fig*) to play (a role).

desempeño [desem'peɲo] *nm* redeeming; (*de cargo*) occupation; (*TEATRO, fig*) performance.

desempleado, a [desemple'aðo, a] *nm/f* unemployed person; **desempleo** *nm* unemployment.

desencadenar [desenkaðe'nar] *vt* to unchain; (*ira*) to unleash; ~ **se** *vr* to break loose; (*tormenta*) to burst.

desencajar [desenka'xar] *vt* (*hueso*) to put out of joint; (*mandíbula*) to dislocate;

(*mecanismo, pieza*) to disconnect, disengage.

desencanto [desen'kanto] *nm* disillusionment.

desenfadado, a [desenfa'ðaðo, a] *a* (*desenvuelto*) uninhibited; (*descarado*) forward; **desenfado** *nm* (*libertad*) freedom; (*comportamiento*) free and easy manner; (*descaro*) forwardness.

desenfrenado, a [desenfre'naðo, a] *a* (*descontrolado*) uncontrolled; (*inmoderado*) unbridled; **desenfreno** *nm* (*vicio*) wildness; (*de las pasiones*) lack of self-control.

desengañar [desenga'ɲar] *vt* to disillusion; ~ **se** *vr* to become disillusioned; **desengaño** *nm* disillusionment; (*decepción*) disappointment.

desenlace [desen'laθe] *nm* outcome.

desenmarañar [desenmara'ɲar] *vt* (*desenredar*) to disentangle; (*fig*) to unravel.

desenredar [desenre'ðar] *vt* to resolve; (*intriga*) to unravel; ~ **se** *vr* to extricate o.s.

desentenderse [desenten'derse] *vr*: ~ **de** to pretend to be ignorant about; (*apartarse*) to have nothing to do with.

desenterrar [desente'rrar] *vt* to exhume; (*tesoro, fig*) to unearth, dig up.

desentrañar [desentra'ɲar] *vt* to disembowel; (*misterio*) to unravel.

desentumecer [desentume'θer] *vt* (*pierna etc*) to stretch; (*DEPORTE*) to loosen up.

desenvoltura [desenßol'tura] *nf* (*libertad, gracia*) ease; (*descaro*) free and easy manner; (*desvergüenza*) forwardness.

desenvolver [desenßol'ßer] *vt* (*paquete*) to unwrap; (*madeja*) to disentangle; (*fig*) to develop; ~ **se** *vr* (*desarrollarse*) to unfold, develop; (*arreglárselas*) to extricate o.s.

deseo [de'seo] *nm* desire, wish; ~ **so, a** *a*: **estar** ~ **so de** to be anxious to.

desequilibrado, a [desekili'ßraðo, a] *a* unbalanced.

desertar [deser'tar] *vi* to desert.

desesperación [desespera'θjon] *nf* (*impaciencia*) desperation, despair; (*irritación*) fury.

desesperar [desespe'rar] *vt* to drive to despair; (*exasperar*) to drive to distraction // *vi*: ~ **de** to despair of; ~ **se** *vr* to despair, lose hope.

desestimar [desesti'mar] *vt* (*menospreciar*) to have a low opinion of; (*rechazar*) to reject.

desfachatez [desfatʃa'teθ] *nf* (*insolencia*) impudence; (*descaro*) cheek.

desfalco [des'falko] *nm* embezzlement.

desfallecer [desfaʎe'θer] *vi* (*perder las fuerzas*) to become weak; (*desvanecerse*) to faint.

desfavorable [desfaßo'raßle] *a* unfavourable.

desfigurar [desfiɣu'rar] vt (cara) to disfigure; (cuerpo) to deform.

desfilar [desfi'lar] vi to parade; **desfile** nm procession.

desgaire [des'ɣaire] nm (desaliño, desgano) slovenliness; (menosprecio) disdain.

desgajar [desɣa'xar] vt (arrancar) to tear off; (romper) to break off; ~**se** vr to come off.

desgana [des'ɣana] nf (falta de apetito) loss of appetite; (renuencia) unwillingness; **desganarse** vr to lose one's appetite; (cansarse) to become bored.

desgarrar [desɣa'rrar] vt to tear (up); (fig) to shatter; **desgarro** nm (muscular) tear; (aflicción) grief; (descaro) impudence.

desgastar [desɣas'tar] vt (deteriorar) to wear away or down; (estropear) to spoil; ~**se** vr to get worn out; **desgaste** nm wear (and tear); (MED) weakening, decline.

desgracia [des'ɣraθja] nf misfortune; (accidente) accident; (vergüenza) disgrace; (contratiempo) setback; **por** ~ unfortunately.

desgraciado, a [desɣra'θjaðo, a] a (infortunado) unlucky, unfortunate; (miserable) wretched; (infeliz) miserable; (feo) ugly; (desagradable) unpleasant.

desgreñado, a [desɣre'ɲaðo, a] a dishevelled.

deshacer [desa'θer] vt (casa) to break up; (dañar) to damage; (TEC) to take apart; (enemigo) to defeat; (diluir) to melt; (contrato) to break; (intriga) to solve; ~**se** vr (disolverse) to melt; (despedazarse) to come apart or undone; ~**se de** to get rid of; ~**se en lágrimas** to burst into tears.

deshecho, a [des'etʃo, a] a undone.

deshelar [dese'lar] vt (cañería) to thaw; (heladera) to defrost.

desheredar [desere'ðar] vt to disinherit.

deshielo [des'jelo] nm (de cañería) thaw; (de heladera) defrosting.

deshilar [desi'lar] vt (tela) to unravel.

deshonesto, a [deso'nesto, a] a indecent.

deshonra [des'onra] nf (deshonor) dishonour; (vergüenza) shame; **deshonrar** vt to dishonour; (insultar) to insult.

deshora [des'ora]: **a** ~ ad at the wrong time.

desierto, a [de'sjerto, a] a (casa, calle, negocio) deserted // nm desert.

designar [desiɣ'nar] vt (nombrar) to designate; (indicar) to fix.

designio [de'siɣnjo] nm (proyecto) plan; (destino) fate.

desigual [desi'ɣwal] a (terreno) uneven; (lucha etc) unequal.

desilusión [desilu'sjon] nf disappointment, disillusionment; **desilusionar** vt to disappoint; **desilusionarse** vr to become disillusioned.

desinfectar [desinfek'tar] vt to disinfect.

desinflar [desin'flar] vt to deflate.

desintegración [desinteɣra'θjon] nf disintegration.

desinterés [desinte'res] nm (objetividad) disinterestedness; (altruismo) unselfishness.

desistir [desis'tir] vi (renunciar) to stop, desist.

desleal [desle'al] a (infiel) disloyal; ~**tad** nf disloyalty.

deslenguado, a [deslen'gwaðo, a] a (grosero) foul-mouthed.

desligar [desli'ɣar] vt (desatar) to untie, undo; (separar) to separate; ~**se** vr (dos personas) to break up, separate; (de un compromiso) to extricate o.s.

desliz [des'liθ] nm (de coche) skid; (de persona) slip, slide; (fig) lapse; ~**ar** vt to slip, slide; ~**arse** vr (escurrirse: persona) to slip, slide; (coche) to skid; (aguas mansas) to flow gently; (error) to slip in.

deslucido, a [deslu'θiðo, a] a (gen) dull; (torpe) awkward, graceless; (marchitado) tarnished.

deslumbrar [deslum'brar] vt to dazzle.

desmán [des'man] nm (exceso) outrage; (abuso de poder) abuse.

desmandarse [desman'darse] vr (abusarse) to behave badly; (excederse) to get out of hand; (caballo) to bolt.

desmantelar [desmante'lar] vt (deshacer) to dismantle; (casa) to strip.

desmayado, a [desma'jaðo, a] a (sin sentido) unconscious; (carácter) dull; (débil) faint, weak.

desmayar [desma'jar] vi to lose heart; ~**se** vr (MED) to faint; **desmayo** nm (desvanecimiento) faint; (sin conciencia) unconsciousness; (depresión) dejection.

desmedido, a [desme'ðiðo, a] a excessive; **desmedirse** vr to go too far, forget o.s.

desmejorar [desmexo'rar] vt (dañar) to impair, spoil; (MED) to weaken.

desmembrar [desmem'brar] vt (MED) to dismember; (fig) to separate.

desmentir [desmen'tir] vt (contradecir) to contradict; (refutar) to deny // vi: ~ **de** to refute; ~**se** vr to contradict o.s.

desmenuzar [desmenu'θar] vt (deshacer) to crumble; (examinar) to examine closely.

desmerecer [desmere'θer] vt to be unworthy of // vi (deteriorarse) to deteriorate.

desmesurado, a [desmesu'raðo, a] a disproportionate.

desmontar [desmon'tar] vt (deshacer) to dismantle; (tierra) to level // vi to dismount.

desmoralizar [desmorali'θar] vt to demoralize.

desmoronar [desmoro'nar] vt to wear away, erode; ~**se** vr (edificio, dique) to fall into disrepair; (sociedad) to decay; (economía) to decline.

desnivel [desni'ßel] nm (de terreno) unevenness; **paso a** ~ (AUTO) flyover.

desnudar [desnu'ðar] vt (desvestir) to

undress; (*despojar*) to strip; ~**se** *vr* (*des-vestirse*) to get undressed; **desnudo, a** *a* naked // *nm/f* nude; **desnudo de** devoid or bereft of.

desobedecer [desoβeðe'θer] *vt, vi* to disobey; **desobediencia** *nf* disobedience.

desocupación [desokupa'θjon] *nf* (*ocio*) leisure; (*desempleo*) unemployment; **desocupado, a** *a* at leisure; unemployed; (*deshabitado*) empty, vacant; **desocupar** *vt* to vacate.

desodorante [desoðo'rante] *nm* deodorant.

desolación [desola'θjon] *nf* (*lugar*) desolation; (*fig*) grief; **desolar** *vt* to ruin, lay waste; **desolarse** *vr* to grieve.

desorden [des'orðen] *nm* confusion; (*político*) disorder.

desorganizar [desorɣani'θar] *vt* (*desordenar*) to disorganize; (*deshacer*) to disrupt.

desorientar [desorjen'tar] *vt* (*extraviar*) to mislead; (*confundir, desconcertar*) to confuse; ~**se** *vr* (*perderse*) to lose one's way.

despabilado, a [despaβi'laðo, a] *a* (*despierto*) wide-awake; (*fig*) alert, sharp.

despabilar [despaβi'lar] *vt* (*vela*) to snuff; (*el ingenio*) to sharpen; (*fortuna, negocio*) to squander // *vi*, ~**se** *vr* to wake up.

despacio [des'paθjo] *ad* slowly.

despachar [despa'tʃar] *vt* (*negocio*) to do, complete; (*enviar*) to send, dispatch; (*vender*) to sell, deal in; (*billete*) to issue; (*mandar ir*) to send away.

despacho [des'patʃo] *nm* (*oficina*) office; (*de paquetes*) dispatch; (*venta*) sale; (*comunicación*) message; (*eficacia*) efficiency; (*rapidez*) promptness.

desparramar [desparra'mar] *vt* (*esparcir*) to scatter; (*noticia*) to spread; (*dinero, fortuna*) to squander; (*líquido*) to spill.

despavorido, a [despaβo'riðo, a] *a* terrified.

despectivo, a [despek'tiβo, a] *a* (*despreciativo*) derogatory; (*LING*) pejorative.

despecho [des'petʃo] *nm* spite; **a ~ de** in spite of.

despedazar [despeða'θar] *vt* to tear to pieces.

despedida [despe'ðiða] *nf* (*adios*) farewell; (*de obrero*) sacking.

despedir [despe'ðir] *vt* (*visita*) to see off, show out; (*licenciar: empleado*) to discharge; (*inquilino*) to evict; (*objeto*) to hurl; (*flecha*) to fire; (*olor etc*) to give out or off; ~**se** *vr*: ~**se de** to say goodbye to.

despegar [despe'ɣar] *vt* to unstick // *vi* to take off; ~**se** *vr* to come loose, come unstuck; **despego** *nm* detachment.

despegue [des'peɣe] *nm* takeoff.

despeinado, a [despei'naðo, a] *a* dishevelled, unkempt.

despejado, a [despe'xaðo, a] *a* (*lugar*) clear, free; (*cielo*) cloudless, clear; (*persona*) wide-awake.

despejar [despe'xar] *vt* (*gen*) to clear; (*misterio*) to clarify, clear up // *vi* (*el tiempo*) to clear; ~**se** *vr* (*tiempo, cielo*) to clear (up); (*misterio*) to become clearer; (*persona*) to relax.

despejo [des'pexo] *nm* (*de casa, calle etc*) brightness; (*desenvoltura*) self-confidence; (*talento, ingenio*) alertness.

despensa [des'pensa] *nf* larder.

despeñadero [despeɲa'ðero] *nm* (*GEO*) cliff, precipice.

desperdicio [desper'ðiθjo] *nm* (*despilfarro*) squandering; (*residuo*) waste.

desperezarse [despere'θarse] *vr* to stretch (o.s.).

desperfecto [desper'fekto] *nm* (*deterioro*) slight damage; (*defecto*) flaw, imperfection.

despertador [desperta'ðor] *nm* alarm clock.

despertar [desper'tar] *vt* (*persona*) to wake up; (*vocación*) to awaken; (*recuerdos*) to revive; (*apetito*) to arouse // *vi*, ~**se** *vr* to awaken, wake up // *nm* awakening.

despido [des'piðo] *nm* dismissal, sacking.

despierto *etc vb ver* **despertar.**

despierto, a [des'pjerto, a] *a* awake; (*fig*) sharp, alert.

despilfarro [despil'farro] *nm* (*derroche*) squandering; (*lujo desmedido*) extravagance.

despistar [despis'tar] *vt* to throw off the track or scent; (*fig*) to mislead, confuse; ~**se** *vr* to take the wrong road; (*fig*) to become confused.

desplazamiento [desplaθa'mjento] *nm* displacement; ~ **de tierras** landslip.

desplegar [desple'xar] *vt* (*tela, papel*) to unfold, open out; (*bandera*) to unfurl.

despoblar [despo'βlar] *vt* (*de gente*) to depopulate.

despojar [despo'xar] *vt* (*alguien: de sus bienes*) to divest of, deprive of; (*casa*) to strip, leave bare; (*alguien: de su cargo*) to strip of; **despojo** *nm* (*acto*) plundering; (*objetos*) plunder, loot; **despojos** *nmpl* waste *sg*; (*rocas, ladrillos*) debris *sg*.

desposado, a [despo'saðo, a] *a*, *nm/f* newly-wed.

desposeer [despose'er] *vt* (*despojar*) to dispossess.

déspota ['despota] *nm* despot.

despreciar [despre'θjar] *vt* (*desdeñar*) to despise, scorn; (*afrentar*) to slight; **desprecio** *nm* scorn, contempt; slight.

desprender [despren'der] *vt* (*separar*) to separate; (*desatar*) to unfasten; (*olor*) to give off; ~**se** *vr* (*botón: caerse*) to fall off; (*: abrirse*) to unfasten; (*olor, perfume*) to be given off; ~**se de** to follow from; **se desprende que** it transpires that.

desprendimiento [desprendi'mjento] *nm* (*gen*) loosening; (*de botón que se cae*) detachment; (*de botón que se abre*) unfastening; (*generosidad*) disinterestedness; (*indiferencia*) detachment; (*de gas*) release; (*de tierra, rocas*) landslide.

despreocupado, a [despreoku'paðo, a] *a* (*sin preocupación*) unworried, nonchalant; (*desprejuiciado*) impartial; (*negligente*) careless; **despreocuparse** *vr* to be carefree; **despreocuparse de** to have no interest in.

desprevenido, a [despreße'niðo, a] *a* (*no preparado*) unprepared, unready.

desproporción [despropor'θjon] *nf* disproportion, lack of proportion.

después [des'pwes] *ad* afterwards, later; (*próximo paso*) next; ~ **de comer** after lunch; **un año** ~ a year later; ~ **se debatió el tema** next the matter was discussed; ~ **de corregido el texto** after the text had been corrected; ~ **de todo** after all.

desquite [des'kite] *nm* (*satisfacción*) satisfaction; (*venganza*) revenge.

destacar [desta'kar] *vt* to emphasize, point up; (*MIL*) to detach, detail // *vi*, ~**se** *vr* (*resaltarse*) to stand out; (*persona*) to be outstanding *or* exceptional.

destajo [des'taxo] *nm*: **trabajar a** ~ to do piecework.

destapar [desta'par] *vt* (*gen*) to open; (*cacerola*) to take the lid off, uncover; ~**se** *vr* (*revelarse*) to reveal one's true character.

destartalado, a [destarta'laðo, a] *a* (*desordenado*) untidy; (*ruinoso*) tumbledown.

destello [des'teʎo] *nm* (*de estrella*) twinkle; (*de faro*) signal light.

destemplado, a [destem'plaðo, a] *a* (*MUS*) out of tune; (*voz*) harsh; (*MED*) out of sorts, indisposed.

desteñir [deste'ɲir] *vt* to fade // *vi*, ~**se** *vr* (*color*) to fade; **esta tela no destiñe** this fabric will not run.

desterrar [deste'rrar] *vt* (*exilar*) to exile; (*fig*) to banish, dismiss.

destierro [des'tjerro] *nm* exile.

destilación [destila'θjon] *nf* distillation; **destilar** *vt* to distil; **destilería** *nf* distillery.

destinar [desti'nar] *vt* to destine; (*funcionario*) to appoint, assign; (*fondos*) to set aside (a for); ~**se** *vr* to be destined.

destinatario, a [destina'tarjo, a] *nm/f* addressee.

destino [des'tino] *nm* (*suerte*) destiny; (*de viajero*) destination; (*función*) use.

destituir [destitu'ir] *vt* to dismiss.

destornillador [destorniʎa'ðor] *nm* screwdriver; **destornillar** *vt*, **destornillarse** *vr* (*tornillo*) to unscrew.

destreza [des'treθa] *nf* (*habilidad*) skill; (*maña*) dexterity; (*facilidad*) handiness.

destrozar [destro'θar] *vt* (*romper*) to smash, break (up); (*estropear*) to ruin; (*deshacer*) to shatter; (*el corazón*) to break.

destrozo [des'troθo] *nm* (*acción*) destruction; (*desastre*) smashing; ~**s** *nmpl* (*pedazos*) pieces; (*daños*) havoc *sg*.

destrucción [destruk'θjon] *nf* destruction.

destruir [destru'ir] *vt* to destroy.

desunir [desu'nir] *vt* to separate; (*TEC*) to disconnect; (*fig*) to cause a quarrel *or* rift between.

desusado, a [desu'saðo, a] *a* (*anticuado*) obsolete.

desvalido, a [desßa'liðo, a] *a* (*desprotegido*) destitute; (*POL*) underprivileged; (*sin fuerzas*) helpless.

desván [des'ßan] *nm* attic.

desvanecer [desßane'θer] *vt* (*disipar*) to dispel; (*borrar*) to blur; ~**se** *vr* (*humo*) to vanish, disappear; (*color*) to fade; (*recuerdo*) to fade away.

desvanecimiento [desßaneθi'mjento] *nm* (*desaparición*) disappearance; (*de colores*) fading; (*evaporación*) evaporation; (*MED*) fainting fit.

desvariar [desßa'rjar] *vi* (*enfermo*) to be delirious; **desvarío** *nm* delirium.

desvelar [desße'lar] *vt* to keep awake; ~**se** *vr* to stay awake; (*fig*) to be vigilant *or* watchful; **desvelo** *nm* lack of sleep; (*insomnio*) sleeplessness; (*fig*) vigilance.

desventaja [desßen'taxa] *nf* disadvantage.

desventura [desßen'tura] *nf* misfortune.

desvergonzado, a [desßerxon'θaðo, a] *a* shameless.

desvergüenza [desßer'ɣwenθa] *nf* (*descaro*) shamelessness; (*insolencia*) impudence; (*mala conducta*) effrontery.

desviación [desßja'θjon] *nf* deviation.

desviar [des'ßjar] *vt* to turn aside; (*río*) to alter the course of; (*navío*) to divert, re-route; (*conversación*) to sidetrack; ~**se** *vr* (*apartarse del camino*) to turn aside, deviate; (: *barco*) to go off course.

desvío [des'ßio] *nm* (*desviación*) detour, diversion; (*fig*) indifference.

desvirtuar [desßir'twar] *vt*, ~**se** *vr* to spoil.

desvivirse [desßi'ßirse] *vr*: ~ **por** to long for, crave for.

detallar [deta'ʎar] *vt* to detail; (*COM*) to sell retail.

detalle [de'taʎe] *nm* detail; (*fig*) gesture, token; al ~ in detail.

detallista [deta'ʎista] *nm/f* retailer.

detener [dete'ner] *vt* (*tren, persona*) to stop; (*JUR*) to arrest; (*objeto*) to keep; ~**se** *vr* to stop; (*demorarse*): ~**se en** to delay over, linger over.

detenido, a [dete'niðo, a] *a* (*preso*) arrested, under arrest; (*minucioso*) detailed; (*tímido*) timid // *nm/f* person under arrest, prisoner.

detergente [deter'xente] *nm* detergent.

deteriorar [deterjo'rar] *vt* to spoil, damage; ~**se** *vr* to deteriorate; (*relaciones*) to become damaged; **deterioro** *nm* deterioration.

determinación [determina'θjon] *nf* (*empeño*) determination; (*decisión*)

decision; **determinar** vt (plazo) to fix; (precio) to settle; **determinarse** vr to decide.

detestar [detes'tar] vt to detest.

detonar [deto'nar] vi to detonate.

detrás [de'tras] ad behind; (atrás) at the back; ~ **de** behind.

detrimento [detri'mento] nm harm, damage; **en** ~ **de** to the detriment of.

deuda ['deuða] nf (condición) indebtedness, debt; (cantidad) debt.

deudor, a [deu'ðor, a] a: **saldo** ~ debit balance // nm/f debtor.

devaluación [deβalwa'θjon] nf devaluation.

devastar [deβas'tar] vt (destruir) to devastate.

devoción [deβo'θjon] nf devotion.

devolución [deβolu'θjon] nf devolution; (reenvío) return, sending back; (reembolso) repayment.

devolver [deβol'βer] vt (gen) to return; (carta al correo) to send back; (COM) to repay, refund; (visita, la palabra) to return.

devorar [deβo'rar] vt to devour.

devoto, a [de'βoto, a] a devout // nm/f admirer.

di vb ver **dar; decir.**

día ['dia] nm day; **¿qué** ~ **es?** what's the date?; **estar/poner al** ~ to be/keep up to date; **el** ~ **de hoy/de mañana** today/tomorrow; **al** ~ **siguiente** on the following day; **vivir al** ~ to live from hand to mouth; **de** ~ by day, in daylight; **en pleno** ~ in full daylight.

diablo ['djaβlo] nm devil; **diablura** nf prank; **diabluras** nfpl mischief sg.

diabólico, a [dja'βoliko, a] a diabolical.

diafragma [dja'fraxma] nm diaphragm.

diagnosis [djax'nosis] nf, **diagnóstico** [djax'nostiko] nm diagnosis.

dialecto [dja'lekto] nm dialect.

diálogo ['djaloxo] nm dialogue.

diamante [dja'mante] nm diamond.

diapositiva [djaposi'tiβa] nf (FOTO) slide, transparency.

diario, a ['djarjo, a] a daily // nm newspaper.

diarrea [dja'rrea] nf diarrhoea.

dibujar [diβu'xar] vt to draw, sketch; **dibujo** nm drawing; **dibujos animados** cartoons.

diccionario [dikθjo'narjo] nm dictionary.

dice etc vb ver **decir.**

diciembre [di'θjembre] nm December.

dictado [dik'taðo] nm dictation.

dictador [dikta'ðor] nm dictator; **dictadura** nf dictatorship.

dictamen [dik'tamen] nm (opinión) opinion; (juicio) judgment.

dicho, a ['ditʃo, a] pp de **decir** // a: **en** ~**s países** in the aforementioned countries // nm saying // nf happiness.

diente ['djente] nm (ANAT, TEC) tooth; (ZOOL) fang; (: de elefante) tusk; (de ajo) clove; **da** ~ **con** ~ his teeth are

chattering; **hablar entre** ~**s** to mutter, mumble.

dieron vb ver **dar.**

diesel ['disel] a: **motor** ~ diesel engine.

dieta ['djeta] nf diet.

diez [djeθ] num ten.

diferencia [dife'renθja] nf difference; **diferenciar** vt to differentiate between // vi to differ; **diferenciarse** vr to differ, be different; (distinguirse) to distinguish o.s.

diferente [dife'rente] a different.

difícil [di'fiθil] a difficult.

dificultad [difikul'taŏ] nf difficulty; (problema) trouble.

dificultar [difikul'tar] vt (complicar) to complicate, make difficult; (estorbar) to obstruct.

difundir [difun'dir] vt (esparcir) to spread, diffuse; (divulgar) to divulge; ~**se** vr to spread (out).

difunto, a [di'funto, a] a dead, deceased // nm/f deceased (person).

digerir [dixe'rir] vt to digest; (fig) to absorb.

digital [dixi'tal] a digital.

dignarse [dix'narse] vr to deign to.

dignidad [dixni'ðaŏ] nf dignity; (honra) honour.

digno, a ['dixno, a] a worthy.

digo etc vb ver **decir.**

dije etc vb ver **decir.**

dilatación [dilata'θjon] nf (expansión) dilation.

dilatado, a [dila'taŏo, a] a dilated; (ancho) widened; (largo) long drawn-out; (extenso) extensive.

dilatar [dila'tar] vt (cuerpo) to dilate; (prolongar) to stretch; (en el tiempo) to prolong.

dilema [di'lema] nm dilemma.

diligencia [dili'xenθja] nf diligence; (ocupación) errand, job; ~**s** nfpl (JUR) formalities; **diligente** a diligent.

diluir [dilu'ir] vt to dilute.

diluvio [di'luβjo] nm deluge, flood.

dimensión [dimen'sjon] nf dimension.

diminuto, a [dimi'nuto, a] a tiny.

dimitir [dimi'tir] vi to resign.

dimos vb ver **dar.**

Dinamarca [dina'marka] nf Denmark; **dinamarqués, esa** a Danish // nm/f Dane.

dinámico, a [di'namiko, a] a dynamic.

dinamita [dina'mita] nf dynamite.

dínamo ['dinamo] nf dynamo.

dineral [dine'ral] nm large sum of money, fortune.

dinero [di'nero] nm money; ~ **efectivo** cash, ready cash.

dio vb ver **dar.**

dios [djos] nm god.

diosa ['djosa] nf goddess.

diplomacia [diplo'maθja] nf diplomacy; (fig) tact; **diplomático, a** a diplomatic // nm/f diplomat.

diputado, a [dipu'taðo, a] *nm/f* delegate; (*Cortes*) deputy.
diré *etc vb ver* **decir.**
dirección [direk'θjon] *nf* direction; (*señas*) address; (*AUTO*) steering; (*gerencia*) management; (*POL*) leadership; ~ **única** *o* **obligatoria** *o* **prohibida** one-way.
directo, a [di'rekto, a] *a* direct; **transmitir en** ~ to broadcast live.
director, a [direk'tor, a] *a* leading // *nm/f* director; ~ **de cine/de escena** producer/stage manager.
dirigir [diri'xir] *vt* to direct; (*carta*) to address; (*obra de teatro, film*) to produce, direct; (*coche, barco*) to steer; (*avión*) to fly; (*MUS*) to conduct; (*comercio*) to manage; ~**se** *vr*: ~**se a** to go towards, make one's way towards; (*fig*) to speak to.
discernir [disθer'nir] *vt* (*distinguir, discriminar*) to discern.
disciplina [disθi'plina] *nf* discipline; **disciplinar** *vt* to discipline.
discípulo, a [dis'θipulo, a] *nm/f* disciple.
disco ['disko] *nm* disc; (*DEPORTE*) discus; (*TELEC*) dial; (*AUTO*) signal; (*fam*) boring affair; ~ **de larga duración/de duración extendida** long-playing record (L.P.)/extended play record (E.P.); ~ **de freno** brake disc.
discordia [dis'korða] *nf* discord.
discoteca [disko'teka] *nf* discotheque.
discreción [diskre'θjon] *nf* discretion; (*reserva*) prudence; (*secreto*) secrecy; **comer a** ~ to eat as much as one wishes; **discrecional** *a* (*facultativo*) discretionary.
discrepancia [diskre'panθja] *nf* (*diferencia*) discrepancy; (*desacuerdo*) disagreement.
discreto, a [dis'kreto, a] *a* (*diplomático*) discreet; (*sensato*) sensible; (*listo*) shrewd; (*reservado*) quiet; (*sobrio*) sober; (*retraído*) unobtrusive; (*razonable*) reasonable.
discriminación [diskrimina'θjon] *nf* discrimination.
disculpa [dis'kulpa] *nf* excuse; (*pedir perdón*) apology; **disculpar** *vt* to excuse, pardon; **disculparse** *vr* to excuse o.s.; to apologize.
discurrir [disku'rrir] *vt* to invent // *vi* (*pensar, reflexionar*) to think, meditate; (*recorrer*) to roam, wander; (*el tiempo*) to pass, flow by.
discurso [dis'kurso] *nm* speech; (*razonamiento*) reasoning power.
discutir [disku'tir] *vt* (*debatir*) to discuss; (*pelear*) to argue about; (*contradecir*) to contradict.
diseminar [disemi'nar] *vt* to disseminate, spread.
diseño [di'seɲo] *nm* (*dibujo*) design.
disfraz [dis'fraθ] *nm* (*máscara*) disguise; (*excusa*) pretext; ~**ar** *vt* to disguise; ~**arse** *vr*: ~**arse de** to disguise o.s. as.
disfrutar [disfru'tar] *vt* to enjoy // *vi* to enjoy o.s.; ~ **de** to enjoy, possess.
disgustar [disɣus'tar] *vt* (*no gustar*) to displease; (*contrariar, enojar*) to annoy,

upset; ~**se** *vr* to be annoyed; (*dos personas*) to fall out.
disgusto [dis'ɣusto] *nm* (*repugnancia*) disgust; (*contrariedad*) annoyance; (*tristeza*) grief; (*riña*) quarrel; (*avería*) misfortune.
disidente [disi'ðente] *nm* dissident.
disimular [disimu'lar] *vt* (*ocultar*) to hide, conceal; (*perdonar*) to excuse // *vi* to dissemble.
disipar [disi'par] *vt* to dispel; (*fortuna*) to squander; ~**se** *vr* (*nubes*) to vanish; (*indisciplinarse*) to dissipate.
disminución [disminu'θjon] *nf* diminution.
disminuir [disminu'ir] *vt* (*acortar*) to decrease; (*achicar*) to diminish; (*estrechar*) to lessen.
disoluto, a [diso'luto, a] *a* dissolute.
disolver [disol'ßer] *vt* (*gen*) to dissolve; ~**se** *vr* to be dissolved.
disparar [dispa'rar] *vt, vi* to shoot, fire.
disparate [dispa'rate] *nm* (*tontería*) foolish remark; (*error*) blunder.
disparo [dis'paro] *nm* shot.
dispensar [dispen'sar] *vt* to dispense; (*disculpar*) to excuse.
dispersar [disper'sar] *vt* to disperse; ~**se** *vr* to scatter.
disponer [dispo'ner] *vt* (*arreglar*) to arrange; (*ordenar*) to put in order; (*preparar*) to prepare, get ready // *vi*: ~ **de** to have, own; ~**se** *vr*: ~**se para** to prepare to, prepare for.
disponible [dispo'nißle] *a* available.
disposición [disposi'θjon] *nf* arrangement, disposition; (*aptitud*) aptitude; **a la** ~ **de** at the disposal of.
dispuesto, a [dis'pwesto, a] *pp de* **disponer** // *a* (*arreglado*) arranged; (*preparado*) disposed.
disputar [dispu'tar] *vt* (*discutir*) to dispute, question; (*contender*) to contend for // *vi* to argue.
distanciar [distan'θjar] *vt* to space out; ~**se** *vr* to become estranged.
distante [dis'tante] *a* distant.
diste, disteis *vb ver* **dar.**
distinción [distin'θjon] *nf* (*gen*) distinction; (*claridad*) clarity; (*elegancia*) elegance; (*honor*) honour.
distinguir [distin'gir] *vt* to distinguish; (*escoger*) to single out; ~**se** *vr* to be distinguished.
distinto, a [dis'tinto, a] *a* different; (*claro*) clear.
distracción [distrak'θjon] *nf* (*pasatiempo*) hobby, pastime; (*olvido*) absent-mindedness, distraction.
distraer [distra'er] *vt* (*entretener*) to entertain; (*divertir*) to amuse; (*fondos*) to embezzle; ~**se** *vr* (*entretenerse*) to amuse o.s.; (*perder la concentración*) to allow one's attention to wander.
distraído, a [distra'iðo, a] *a* (*gen*) absent-minded; (*entretenido*) amusing.
distribuir [distrißu'ir] *vt* to distribute.

distrito [dis'trito] *nm* (*sector, territorio*) region; (*barrio*) district.
disturbio [dis'turβjo] *nm* disturbance.
disuadir [diswa'ðir] *vt* to dissuade.
disuelto [di'swelto] *pp de* **disolver**.
divagar [diβa'xar] *vi* (*desviarse*) to digress; (*errar*) to wander.
diván [di'βan] *nm* divan.
divergencia [diβer'xenθja] *nf* divergence.
diversidad [diβersi'ðað] *nf* diversity, variety.
diversificar [diβersifi'kar] *vt* to diversify.
diversión [diβer'sjon] *nf* (*gen*) entertainment; (*actividad*) hobby, pastime.
diverso, a [di'βerso, a] *a* diverse; ~ **s** sundry.
divertir [diβer'tir] *vt* (*entretener, recrear*) to amuse, entertain; (*apartar, distraer*) to divert; ~ **se** *vr* (*pasarlo bien*) to have a good time; (*distraerse*) to amuse o.s.
dividir [diβi'ðir] *vt* (*gen*) to divide; (*separar*) to separate; (*distribuir*) to distribute, share out.
divino, a [di'βino, a] *a* divine.
divisa [di'βisa] *nf* (*emblema, moneda*) emblem, badge; ~ **s** *nfpl* currency *sg*.
división [diβi'sjon] *nf* (*gen*) division; (*de partido*) split; (*de país*) partition; (*LING*) hyphen; (*divergencia*) divergence.
divorciar [diβor'θjar] *vt* to divorce; ~ **se** *vr* to get divorced; **divorcio** *nm* divorce.
divulgar [diβul'xar] *vt* (*desparramar*) to spread; (*hacer circular*) to divulge, circulate; ~ **se** *vr* to leak out.
doblar [do'βlar] *vt* (*gen*) to double; (*papel*) to fold; (*caño*) to bend; (*la esquina*) to turn, go round; (*film*) to dub // *vi* to turn; (*campana*) to toll; ~ **se** *vr* (*plegarse*) to fold (up), crease; (*encorvarse*) to bend; ~ **se de risa/dolor** to be doubled up with laughter/pain.
doble ['doβle] *a* (*gen*) double; (*de dos aspectos*) dual; (*fig*) two-faced // *nm* double; (*campana*) toll(ing); ~ **s** *nmpl* (*DEPORTE*) doubles *sg* // *nm/f* (*TEATRO*) double, stand-in; **con** ~ **sentido** with a double meaning.
doblegar [doβle'xar] *vt* to fold, crease; ~ **se** *vr* to yield.
doce ['doθe] *num* twelve.
docena [do'θena] *nf* dozen.
dócil ['doθil] *a* (*pasivo*) docile; (*obediente*) obedient.
doctor, a [dok'tor, a] *nm/f* doctor.
doctrina [dok'trina] *nf* doctrine, teaching.
documentación [dokumenta'θjon] *nf* documentation, papers *pl*.
documento [doku'mento] *nm* (*certificado*) document.
dólar ['dolar] *nm* dollar.
doler [do'ler] *vt, vi* to hurt; (*fig*) to grieve; ~ **se** *vr* (*de su situación*) to grieve, feel sorry; (*de las desgracias ajenas*) to sympathize; **me duele el brazo** my arm hurts.
dolor [do'lor] *nm* pain; (*fig*) grief, sorrow.

domar [do'mar], **domesticar** [domesti'kar] *vt* to tame.
domicilio [domi'θiljo] *nm* home; ~ **particular** private residence; ~ **social** head office.
dominante [domi'nante] *a* dominant; (*person*) domineering.
dominar [domi'nar] *vt* (*gen*) to dominate; (*idiomas etc*) to have a command of // *vi* to dominate, prevail; ~ **se** *vr* to control o.s.
domingo [do'mingo] *nm* Sunday.
dominio [do'minjo] *nm* (*tierras*) domain; (*autoridad*) power, authority; (*de las pasiones*) grip, hold; (*de varios idiomas*) command.
don [don] *nm* (*talento*) gift; ~ **Juan Gómez** Mr Juan Gomez *or* Juan Gomez Esq.
donaire [do'naire] *nm* charm.
doncella [don'θeʎa] *nf* (*criada*) maid; (*muchacha*) girl.
donde ['donde] *ad* where // *prep*: **el coche está allí** ~ **el farol** the car is over there by the lamppost *or* where the lamppost is; **por** ~ through which; **en** ~ where, in which.
dónde ['donde] *ad interr* where?; ¿**a** ~ **vas?** where are you going (to)?; ¿**de** ~ **vienes?** where have you come from?; ¿**por** ~? where?, whereabouts?
dondequiera [donde'kjera] *ad* anywhere; **por** ~ everywhere, all over the place // *conj*: ~ **que** wherever.
doña ['dopa] *nf título de mujer que no se traduce.*
dorado, a [do'raðo, a] *a* (*color*) golden; (*TEC*) gilt.
dormir [dor'mir] *vt*: ~ **la siesta por la tarde** to have an afternoon nap // *vi* to sleep; ~ **se** *vr* to go to sleep.
dormitar [dormi'tar] *vi* to doze.
dormitorio [dormi'torjo] *nm* bedroom; ~ **común** dormitory.
dos [dos] *num* two.
dosis ['dosis] *nf inv* dose, dosage.
dotado, a [do'taðo, a] *a* gifted; ~ **de** endowed with.
dotar [do'tar] *vt* to endow; **dote** *nf* dowry; **dotes** *nfpl* gifts.
doy *vb ver* **dar**.
drama ['drama] *nm* drama.
dramaturgo [drama'turxo] *nm* dramatist, playwright.
droga ['droxa] *nf* drug.
drogadicto, a [droxa'ðikto, a] *nm/f* drug addict.
ducha ['dutʃa] *nf* (*baño*) shower; (*MED*) douche; **ducharse** *vr* to take a shower.
duda ['duða] *nf* doubt.
dudoso, a [du'ðoso, a] *a* (*incierto*) hesitant; (*sospechoso*) doubtful.
duelo ['dwelo] *nm* (*combate*) duel; (*luto*) mourning.
duende ['dwende] *nm* imp, goblin.
dueño, a ['dweɲo, a] *nm/f* (*propietario*)

owner; (*de casa*) landlord/lady; (*empresario*) employer.
duermo *etc vb ver* **dormir.**
dulce ['dulθe] *a* sweet // *ad* gently, softly // *nm* sweet.
dulzura [dul'θura] *nf* sweetness; (*ternura*) gentleness.
duplicar [dupli'kar] *vt* (*hacer el doble de*) to duplicate; ~**se** *vr* to double.
duque ['duke] *nm* duke.
duquesa [du'kesa] *nf* duchess.
duración [dura'θjon] *nf* duration.
duradero, a [dura'ðero, a] *a* lasting.
durante [du'rante] *ad* during.
durar [du'rar] *vi* (*permanecer*) to last; (*recuerdo*) to remain.
dureza [du'reθa] *nf* (*calidad*) hardness.
durmí *etc vb ver* **dormir.**
durmiente [dur'mjente] *nm/f* sleeper.
duro, a ['duro, a] *a* (*gen*) hard; (*carácter*) tough // *ad* hard // *nm* (*moneda*) five peseta coin/note.

E

e [e] *conj* and.
E *abr de* **este.**
ebanista [eβa'nista] *nm* cabinetmaker.
ébano ['eβano] *nm* ebony.
ebrio, a ['eβrjo, a] *a* drunk.
ebullición [eβuʎi'θjon] *nf* boiling; (*fig*) ferment.
eclesiástico, a [ekle'sjastiko, a] *a* ecclesiastical.
eclipse [e'klipse] *nm* eclipse.
eco ['eko] *nm* echo; **tener** ~ to catch on.
ecología [ekolo'xia] *nf* ecology.
economato [ekono'mato] *nm* cooperative store.
economía [ekono'mia] *nf* (*sistema*) economy; (*cualidad*) thrift.
económico, a [eko'nomiko, a] *a* (*barato*) cheap, economical; (*persona*) thrifty; (*COM: plan*) financial; (*: situación*) economic.
economista [ekono'mista] *nm/f* economist.
ecuador [ekwa'ðor] *nm* equator; **el E**~ Ecuador.
ecuánime [e'kwanime] *a* (*carácter*) level-headed; (*estado*) calm.
ecuestre [e'kwestre] *a* equestrian.
echar [e'tʃar] *vt* to throw; (*agua, vino*) to pour (out); (*empleado: despedir*) to fire, sack; (*bigotes*) to grow; (*hojas*) to sprout; (*cartas*) to post; (*humo*) to emit, give out // *vi*: ~ **a correr/llorar** to break into a run/burst into tears; ~**se** *vr* to lie down; ~ **llave a** to lock (up); ~ **abajo** (*gobierno*) to overthrow; (*edificio*) to demolish; ~ **mano a** to lay hands on.
edad [e'ðað] *nf* age; ¿**qué** ~ **tienes?** how old are you?; **tiene ocho años de** ~ he is eight (years old); **de** ~ **mediana/avanzada** middle-aged/ advanced in years; **la E**~ **Media** the Middle Ages.

edición [eði'θjon] *nf* (*acto*) publication; (*ejemplar*) edition.
edicto [e'ðikto] *nm* edict, proclamation.
edificio [eði'fiθjo] *nm* building; (*fig*) edifice, structure.
editar [eði'tar] *vt* (*publicar*) to publish; (*preparar textos*) to edit.
editor, a [eði'tor, a] *nm/f* (*que publica*) publisher; (*de periódico etc*) editor // *a*: **casa** ~**a** publishing house; ~**ial** *a* editorial // *nm* leading article, editorial; **casa** ~**ial** publishing house.
educación [eðuka'θjon] *nf* education; (*crianza*) upbringing; (*modales*) (good) manners *pl.*
educar [eðu'kar] *vt* to educate; (*criar*) to bring up; (*voz*) to train.
EE. UU. *nmpl abr de* **Estados Unidos** USA (United States of America).
efectivo, a [efek'tiβo, a] *a* effective; (*real*) actual, real // *nm*: **pagar en** ~ to pay (in) cash; **hacer** ~ **un cheque** to cash a cheque.
efecto [e'fekto] *nm* effect, result; ~**s** *nmpl* goods; (*COM*) assets; **en** ~ in fact; (*respuesta*) exactly, indeed.
efectuar [efek'twar] *vt* to carry out; (*viaje*) to make.
eficacia [efi'kaθja] *nf* (*de persona*) efficiency; (*de medicamento*) effectiveness.
eficaz [efi'kaθ] *a* (*persona*) efficient; (*acción*) effective.
egipcio, a [e'xipθjo, a] *a, nm/f* Egyptian.
Egipto [e'xipto] *nm* Egypt.
egoísmo [exo'ismo] *nm* egoism.
egoísta [exo'ista] *a* egoistical, selfish // *nm/f* egoist.
egregio, a [e'srexjo, a] *a* eminent, distinguished.
Eire ['eire] *nm* Eire.
ej. *abr de* **ejemplo.**
eje ['exe] *nm* (*GEO, MAT*) axis; (*de rueda*) axle; (*de máquina*) shaft, spindle; **la idea** ~ the central idea.
ejecución [exeku'θjon] *nf* (*gen*) execution; (*cumplimiento*) fulfilment; (*actuación*) performance; (*JUR: embargo de deudor*) attachment, distraint.
ejecutar [exeku'tar] *vt* (*gen*) to execute, carry out; (*matar*) to execute; (*cumplir*) to fulfil; (*MUS*) to perform; (*JUR: embargar*) to attach, distrain (on).
ejecutivo, a [exeku'tiβo, a] *a* executive; **el poder** ~ the Executive (Power).
ejemplar [exem'plar] *a* exemplary // *nm* example; (*ZOOL*) specimen; (*de libro*) copy; (*de periódico*) number, issue.
ejemplo [e'xemplo] *nm* example; **por** ~ for example.
ejercer [exer'θer] *vt* to exercise; (*influencia*) to exert; (*un oficio*) to practise // *vi* (*practicar*) to practise (*de* as); (*tener oficio*) to hold office.
ejercicio [exer'θiθjo] *nm* exercise; (*período*) tenure; ~ **comercial** financial year.
ejército [e'xerθito] *nm* army; **entrar en**

el ~ to join the army, join up.
el [el] *det* the.
él [el] *pron* (*persona*) he; (*cosa*) it; (*después de prep: persona*) him; (: *cosa*) it.
elaborar [elaßo'rar] *vt* to elaborate; (*hacer*) to make; (*preparar*) to prepare; (*trabajar*) to work; (*calcular*) to work out.
elasticidad [elastiθi'ðað] *nf* elasticity; **elástico, a** *a* elastic; (*flexible*) flexible // *nm* elastic.
elección [elek'θjon] *nf* election; (*selección*) choice, selection.
electorado [elekto'raðo] *nm* electorate, voters *pl.*
electricidad [elektriθi'ðað] *nf* electricity.
electricista [elektri'θista] *nm/f* electrician.
eléctrico, a [e'lektriko, a] *a* electric // *nm* electric train.
electrizar [elektri'θar] *vt* to electrify.
electro... [elektro] *pref* electro...; **~cardiógrafo** *nm* electrocardiograph; **~cución** *nf* electrocution; **~cutar** *vt* to electrocute; **~chapado, a** *a* electroplated; **electrodo** *nm* electrode; **~domésticos** *nmpl* (electrical) household appliances; **~imán** *nm* electromagnet; **~magnético, a** *a* electromagnetic; **~motor** *nm* electric motor.
electrónico, a [elek'troniko, a] *a* electronic // *nf* electronics *sg.*
electrotecnia [elektro'teknja] *nf* electrical engineering; **electrotécnico, a** *nm/f* electrical engineer.
electrotermo [elektro'termo] *nm* immersion heater.
elefante [ele'fante] *nm* elephant; **~ marino** elephant seal.
elegancia [ele'xanθja] *nf* (*gracia*) elegance, grace; (*estilo*) stylishness; **elegante** *a* elegant, graceful; stylish, fashionable.
elegía [ele'xia] *nf* elegy.
elegir [ele'xir] *vt* (*escoger*) to choose, select; (*optar*) to opt for; (*presidente*) to elect.
elemental [elemen'tal] *a* (*claro, obvio*) elementary; (*fundamental*) elemental, fundamental.
elemento [ele'mento] *nm* element; (*fig*) ingredient; **~s** *nmpl* elements, rudiments.
elevación [eleßa'θjon] *nf* elevation; (*acto*) raising, lifting; (*de precios*) rise; (*GEO etc*) height, altitude; (*de persona*) loftiness; (*pey*) conceit, pride.
elevar [ele'ßar] *vt* to raise, lift (up); (*precio*) to put up; **~se** *vr* (*edificio*) to rise; (*precios*) to go up; (*transportarse, enajenarse*) to get carried away; (*engreírse*) to become conceited.
eliminar [elimi'nar] *vt* to eliminate, remove.
eliminatoria [elimina'torja] *nf* heat, preliminary (round).
elite [e'lite] *nf* elite.
elocuencia [elo'kwenθja] *nf* eloquence.
elogiar [elo'xjar] *vt* to praise, eulogize;

elogio *nm* praise; (*tributo*) tribute.
eludir [elu'ðir] *vt* (*evitar*) to avoid, evade; (*escapar*) to escape, elude.
ella ['eʎa] *pron* (*persona*) she; (*cosa*) it; (*después de prep: persona*) her; (: *cosa*) it.
ellas ['eʎas] *pron* (*personas y cosas*) they; (*después de prep*) them.
ello ['eʎo] *pron* it.
ellos ['eʎos] *pron* they; (*después de prep*) them.
emanar [ema'nar] *vi*: ~ **de** to emanate from, come from; (*derivar de*) to originate in.
emancipar [emanθi'par] *vt* to emancipate; **~se** *vr* to become emancipated, free o.s.
embadurnar [embaður'nar] *vt* to smear.
embajada [emba'xaða] *nf* embassy; (*mensaje*) message, errand.
embajador, a [embaxa'ðor, a] *nm/f* ambassador/ambassadress.
embalar [emba'lar] *vt* (*envolver*) to parcel, wrap (up); (*envasar*) to package // *vi* to sprint.
embarazada [embara'θaða] *a* pregnant // *nf* pregnant woman.
embarazar [embara'θar] *vt* to obstruct, hamper; (*a una mujer*) to make pregnant; **~se** *vr* (*aturdirse*) to become embarrassed; (*confundirse*) to get into a muddle; (*mujer*) to become pregnant.
embarazo [emba'raθo] *nm* (*de mujer*) pregnancy; (*impedimento*) obstacle, obstruction; (*timidez*) embarrassment.
embarcación [embarka'θjon] *nf* (*barco*) boat, craft; (*acto*) embarkation.
embarcadero [embarka'ðero] *nm* pier, landing stage.
embarcar [embar'kar] *vt* (*cargamento*) to ship, stow; (*persona*) to embark, put on board; **~se** *vr* to embark, go on board.
embargar [embar'xar] *vt* (*impedir*) to impede, hinder; (*JUR*) to seize, impound.
embarque [em'barke] *nm* shipment, loading.
embaular [embau'lar] *vt* to pack (into a trunk); (*fig*) to stuff o.s. with.
embebecerse [embeße'θerse] *vr* (*extasiarse*) to be lost in wonder, be amazed.
embeber [embe'ßer] *vt* (*absorber*) to absorb, soak up; (*empapar*) to saturate // *vi* to shrink; **~se** *vr*: **~se en la lectura** to be engrossed *or* absorbed in a book.
embellecer [embeʎe'θer] *vt* to embellish, beautify.
embestida [embes'tiða] *nf* attack, onslaught; (*carga*) charge; **embestir** *vt* to attack, assault; to charge, attack // *vi* to attack.
emblema [em'blema] *nm* emblem.
embobado, a [embo'ßaðo, a] *a* (*atontado*) stunned, bewildered.
embocadura [emboka'ðura] *nf* narrow entrance; (*de río*) mouth; (*MUS*) mouthpiece.
émbolo ['embolo] *nm* (*AUTO*) piston.

embolsar [embol'sar] *vt* to pocket, put in one's pocket.

emborrachar [emborra'tʃar] *vt* to intoxicate, make drunk; ~**se** *vr* to get drunk.

emboscada [embos'kaða] *nf* (*celada*) ambush.

embotar [embo'tar] *vt* to blunt, dull; ~**se** *vr* (*adormecerse*) to go numb.

embotellar [embote'ʎar] *vt* to bottle; ~**se** *vr* (*circulación*) to get into a jam.

embozar [embo'θar] *vt* to muffle (up).

embragar [embra'xar] *vi* to let in the clutch.

embrague [em'braxe] *nm* (*también* **pedal de** ~) clutch.

embravecer [embraβe'θer] *vt* to enrage, infuriate; ~**se** *vr* to become furious; (*el mar*) to get rough; (*tormenta*) to rage.

embriagado, a [embrja'xaðo, a] *a* (*emborrachado*) intoxicated, drunk.

embriagar [embrja'xar] *vt* (*emborrachar*) to intoxicate, make drunk; (*alegrar*) to delight; ~**se** *vr* (*emborracharse*) to get drunk.

embriaguez [embrja'xeθ] *nf* (*borrachera*) drunkenness; (*fig*) rapture, delight.

embrollar [embro'ʎar] *vt* (*el asunto*) to confuse, complicate; (*persona*) to involve, embroil; ~**se** *vr* (*confundirse*) to get into a muddle *or* mess; ~**se con uno** to get into an argument with sb.

embrollo [em'broʎo] *nm* (*enredo*) muddle, confusion; (*aprieto*) fix, jam; (*pey: engaño*) fraud; (: *trampa*) trick.

embromar [embro'mar] *vt* (*burlarse de*) to tease, make fun of.

embrutecer [embrute'θer] *vt* (*brutalizar*) to brutalize; (*depravar*) to deprave; (*atontar*) to stupefy; ~**se** *vr* to become brutal; to become depraved.

embudo [em'buðo] *nm* funnel; (*fig: engaño*) fraud; (: *trampa*) trick.

embuste [em'buste] *nm* trick; (*impostura*) imposture; (*mentira*) lie; (*hum*) fib; ~**ro, a** *a* lying, deceitful // *nm/f* (*tramposo*) cheat; (*impostor*) impostor; (*mentiroso*) liar; (*hum*) fibber.

embutido [embu'tiðo] *nm* (*CULIN*) sausage; (*TEC*) inlay.

embutir [embu'tir] *vt* (*TEC*) to inlay; (*llenar*) to pack tight, cram, stuff.

emergencia [emer'xenθja] *nf* emergency; (*surgimiento*) emergence.

emerger [emer'xer] *vi* to emerge, appear.

emigración [emixra'θjon] *nf* (*éxodo*) migration; (*destierro*) emigration.

emigrar [emi'xrar] *vi* (*pájaros*) to migrate; (*personas*) to emigrate.

eminencia [emi'nenθja] *nf* eminence; **eminente** *a* eminent, distinguished; (*GEO*) high.

emisario [emi'sarjo] *nm* emissary.

emisión [emi'sjon] *nf* (*acto*) emission; (*COM etc*) issue; (*RADIO, TV: acto*) broadcasting; (: *programa*) broadcast, programme.

emisora [emi'sora] *nf* (*de onda corta*) shortwave radio station; (*aparato*) broadcasting station.

emitir [emi'tir] *vt* (*olor etc*) to emit, give off; (*moneda etc*) to issue; (*opinión*) to express; (*RADIO*) to broadcast.

emoción [emo'θjon] *nf* emotion; (*excitación*) excitement; (*turbación*) worry, anxiety.

emocionante [emoθjo'nante] *a* (*excitante*) exciting, thrilling; (*conmovedor*) moving, touching; (*impresionante*) striking, impressive.

emocionar [emoθjo'nar] *vt* (*excitar*) to excite, thrill; (*conmover*) to move, touch; (*impresionar*) to impress.

empacho [em'patʃo] *nm* (*MED*) indigestion; (*fig*) embarrassment.

empalagoso, a [empala'xoso, a] *a* cloying; (*fig*) tiresome.

empalmar [empal'mar] *vt* to join, connect // *vi* (*dos caminos*) to meet, join; **empalme** *nm* joint, connection; junction; (*de trenes*) connection.

empanada [empa'naða] *nf* pie, patty.

empantanarse [empanta'narse] *vr* to get swamped; (*fig*) to get bogged down.

empañar [empa'ɲar] *vt* (*niño*) to swaddle, wrap up; ~**se** *vr* (*nublarse*) to get misty, steam up.

empapar [empa'par] *vt* (*mojar*) to soak, saturate; (*absorber*) to soak up, absorb; ~**se** *vr*: ~**se de** to soak up.

empapelar [empape'lar] *vt* (*paredes*) to paper; (*envolver con papel*) to wrap (up) in paper.

empaquetar [empake'tar] *vt* to pack, parcel up.

empastar [empas'tar] *vt* (*embadurnar*) to paste; (*diente*) to fill.

empatar [empa'tar] *vi* to draw, tie; **empate** *nm* draw, tie.

empedernido, a [empeðer'niðo, a] *a* hard, heartless; (*fijado*) hardened, inveterate.

empedernir [empeðer'nir] *vt* to harden.

empedrado, a [empe'ðraðo, a] *a* paved // *nm* paving; **empedrar** *vt* to pave.

empeñado, a [empe'ɲaðo, a] *a* (*objeto*) pawned; (*persona*) determined.

empeñar [empe'ɲar] *vt* (*objeto*) to pawn, pledge; (*persona*) to compel; ~**se** *vr* (*obligarse*) to bind o.s., pledge o.s.; (*endeudarse*) to get into debt; ~**se en** to be set on, be determined to.

empeño [em'peɲo] *nm* (*cosa prendada*) pledge; (*determinación, insistencia*) determination, insistence; **banco de** ~**s** pawnshop.

empeorar [empeo'rar] *vt* to make worse, worsen // *vi* to get worse, deteriorate.

empequeñecer [empekeɲe'θer] *vt* to dwarf; (*fig*) to belittle.

emperador [empera'ðor] *nm* emperor.

emperatriz [empera'triθ] *nf* empress.

empezar [empe'θar] *vt*, *vi* to begin, start.

empiezo *etc vb ver* **empezar**.

empinar [empi'nar] vt to raise (up) // vi (fam) to drink, booze (fam); ~se vr (persona) to stand on tiptoe; (animal) to rear up; (camino) to climb steeply; (edificio) to tower.

empírico, a [em'piriko, a] a empirical.

emplasto [em'plasto], **emplaste** [em-'plaste] nm (MED) plaster; (: cataplasma) poultice; (componenda) compromise.

emplazamiento [emplaθa'mjento] nm site, location; (JUR) summons sg.

emplazar [empla'θar] vt (ubicar) to site, place, locate; (JUR) to summons; (convocar) to summon.

empleado, a [emple'aðo, a] nm/f (gen) employee; (de banco etc) clerk.

emplear [emple'ar] vt (usar) to use, employ; (dar trabajo a) to employ; ~se vr (conseguir trabajo) to be employed; (ocuparse) to occupy o.s.

empleo [em'pleo] nm (puesto) job; (puestos: colectivamente) employment; (uso) use, employment.

empobrecer [empoβre'θer] vt to impoverish; ~se vr to become poor or impoverished; **empobrecimiento** nm impoverishment.

emporio [em'porjo] nm emporium, trading centre; (gran almacén) department store.

emprender [empren'der] vt (empezar) to begin, embark on; (acometer) to tackle, take on.

empreñar [empre'ɲar] vt to make pregnant; ~se vr to become pregnant.

empresa [em'presa] nf enterprise.

empréstito [em'prestito] nm (public) loan.

empujar [empu'xar] vt to push, shove; **empuje** nm thrust; (presión) pressure; (fig) vigour, drive.

empujón [empu'xon] nm push, shove.

empuñar [empu'ɲar] vt (asir) to grasp, take (firm) hold of.

emular [emu'lar] vt to emulate; (rivalizar) to rival.

émulo, a ['emulo, a] nm/f rival, competitor.

en [en] prep (gen) in; (sobre) on, upon; **meter** ~ **el bolsillo** to put in or into one's pocket; (lugar): **vivir** ~ **Toledo** to live in Toledo; ~ **casa** at home; (tiempo): **lo terminó** ~ **6 días** he finished it in 6 days; ~ **el mes de enero** in the month of January; ~ **aquel momento/aquella época** at that moment/that time; ~ **aquel día/aquella ocasión** on that day/that occasion; ~ **serio** seriously; ~ **fin** well, well then; **ir** ~ **de puerta** ~ **puerta** to go from door to door; ~ **tren** by train.

enajenación [enaxena'θjon] nf, **enajenamiento** [enaxena'mjento] nm alienation; (fig: distracción) absent-mindedness; (: embelesamiento) rapture, trance; (extrañamiento) estrangement.

enajenar [enaxe'nar] vt to alienate; (fig)

to carry away; ~se vr (de un bien) to deprive o.s.; (amigos) to become estranged, fall out.

enamorado, a [enamo'raðo, a] a in love; **enamorar** vt to inspire love; **enamorarse** vr to fall in love.

enano, a [e'nano, a] a tiny // nm/f dwarf.

enardecer [enarðe'θer] vt (pasiones) to fire, inflame; (persona) to fill with enthusiasm; (: llenar de ira) to fill with anger; ~se vr to get excited; (entusiasmarse) to get enthusiastic (por about); (de cólera) to blaze.

encabezamiento [enkaβeθa'mjento] nm (de carta) heading; (de periódico) headline; (preámbulo) foreword, preface; (registro) roll, register.

encabezar [enkaβe'θar] vt (manifestación) to lead, head; (lista) to be at the top of; (carta) to put a heading to; (libro) to entitle; (empadronar) to register.

encadenar [enkaðe'nar] vt to chain (together); (poner grilletes a) to shackle.

encajar [enka'xar] vt (ajustar) to fit (into); (golpe) to give, deal; (entrometer) to insert // vi to fit (well); (fig: corresponder a) to match; ~se vr to intrude; ~se en un sillón to squeeze into a chair.

encaje [en'kaxe] nm (labor) lace; (inserción) insertion; (ajuste) fitting.

encajonar [enkaxo'nar] vt to box (up), put in a box.

encaminar [enkami'nar] vt to direct, send; ~se vr: ~se a to set out for.

encandilar [enkandi'lar] vt to dazzle; (fuego) to poke.

encantador, a [enkanta'ðor, a] a charming, lovely // nm/f magician, enchanter/tress.

encantar [enkan'tar] vt to charm, delight; (hechizar) to bewitch, cast a spell on; **encanto** nm (magia) spell, charm; (fig) charm, delight.

encarcelar [enkarθe'lar] vt to imprison, jail.

encarecer [enkare'θer] vt to put up the price of; (pedir) tc recommend, urge // vi, ~se vr to get dearer.

encarecimiento [enkareθi'mjento] nm price increase; (pedido insistente) urging.

encargado, a [enkar'ɤaðo, a] a in charge // nm/f agent, representative; (responsable) person in charge; ~ **de negocios** chargé d'affaires.

encargar [enkar'ɤar] vt to entrust; (recomendar) to urge, recommend; ~se vr: ~se de to look after, take charge of.

encargo [en'karɤo] nm (pedido) assignment; job; (responsabilidad) responsibility; (recomendación) recommendation; (COM) order.

encarnación [enkarna'θjon] nf incarnation, embodiment.

encarrilar [enkarri'lar] vt to correct, put on the right track; (tren) to put back on the rails.

encausar [enkau'sar] vt to prosecute, sue.

encauzar [enkau'θar] vt to channel.

enceguecer [enθeϫe'θer] vt to blind // vi, ~**se** vr to go blind.

encendedor [enθende'dor] nm lighter.

encender [enθen'der] vt (con fuego) to light; (incendiar) to set fire to; (luz, radio) to put on, switch on; (inflarse) to inflame; ~**se** vr to catch fire; (excitarse) to get excited; (de cólera) to flare up; (el rostro) to blush.

encendido [enθen'diðo] nm ignition.

encerrar [enθe'rrar] vt (confinar) to shut in, shut up; (comprender, incluir) to include, contain.

encía [en'θia] nf gum.

encierro [en'θjerro] nm shutting in, shutting up; (calabozo) prison.

encima [en'θima] ad (sobre) above, over; (además) besides; ~ **de** (en) on, on top of; (sobre) above, over; (además de) besides, on top of; **por** ~ **de** over; **¿llevas dinero** ~**?** have you any money on you?; **se me vino** ~ it got on top of me.

encinta [en'θinta] a pregnant.

enclavar [enkla'ßar] vt (clavar) to nail; (atravesar) to pierce; (sitio) to set; (fig: fam) to swindle.

encoger [enko'xer] vt (gen) to shrink, contract; (fig: asustar) to scare; (: desanimar) to discourage; ~**se** vr to shrink, contract; (fig) to cringe; ~**se de hombros** to shrug one's shoulders.

encojar [enko'xar] vt to lame; (tullir) to cripple; ~**se** vr to go lame; to become crippled.

encolar [enko'lar] vt (engomar) to glue, paste; (pegar) to stick down.

encolerizar [enkoleri'θar] vt to anger, provoke; ~**se** vr to get angry.

encomendar [enkomen'dar] vt to entrust, commend; ~**se** vr: ~**se a** to put one's trust in.

encomiar [enko'mjar] vt to praise, pay tribute to.

encomienda [enko'mjenda] nf (encargo) charge, commission; (precio) price; (elogio) tribute; ~ **postal** (AM) parcel post.

encomio [en'komjo] nm praise, tribute.

enconado, a [enko'naðo, a] a (MED) inflamed; (: dolorido) sore; (fig) angry.

enconar [enko'nar] vt (MED) to inflame; (fig) to anger, irritate; ~**se** vr (MED) to become inflamed; (fig) to get angry or irritated.

encono [en'kono] nm (rencor) rancour, spite; (odio) ill-feeling.

encontrado, a [enkon'traðo, a] a (contrario) contrary, conflicting; (hostil) hostile.

encontrar [enkon'trar] vt (hallar) to find; (inesperadamente) to meet, run into; ~**se** vr to meet (each other); (situarse) to be (situated); (entrar en conflicto) to crash, collide; ~**se con** to meet (with); ~**se bien de salud** to feel well.

encorvar [enkor'ßar] vt to curve;

(inclinar) to bend (down); ~**se** vr to bend down, bend over, stoop.

encrespar [enkres'par] vt (cabellos) to curl; (agua) to ripple; (fig) to anger, irritate; ~**se** vr (el mar) to get rough; (fig) to get annoyed, irritated.

encrucijada [enkruθi'xaða] nf crossroads sg; (empalme) junction.

encuadernación [enkwaðerna'θjon] nf binding.

encuadernador, a [enkwaðerna'ðor, a] nm/f bookbinder.

encuadrar [enkwa'ðrar] vt (retrato) to frame; (ajustar) to fit, insert; (encerrar) to contain.

encubrir [enku'ßrir] vt (ocultar) to hide, conceal; (criminal) to harbour, shelter.

encuentro etc vb ver **encontrar** // [en-'kwentro] nm (de personas) meeting; (de trenes) collision, crash; (DEPORTE) match, game; (MIL) encounter.

encuesta [en'kwesta] nf inquiry, investigation; ~ **judicial** post mortem.

encumbrado, a [enkum'braðo, a] a (edificio) lofty, towering; (persona) eminent, distinguished.

encumbrar [enkum'brar] vt (edificio) to raise; (elevar) to elevate; (persona) to exalt; ~**se** vr to rise, tower; (fig) to become conceited.

encharcado, a [entʃar'kaðo, a] a still; (estancado) stagnant.

enchufar [entʃu'far] vt (ELEC) to plug in; (TEC) to connect, fit together; **enchufe** nm (ELEC: clavija) plug; (: toma) plug, socket; (de dos tubos) joint, connection; (fam: influencia) contact, connection; (: puesto) cushy job.

endemoniado, a [endemo'njaðo, a] a possessed (of the devil); (endiabolado) devilish; (furioso) furious, wild.

endentar [enden'tar] vt, vi to engage, mesh.

enderezar [endere'θar] vt (poner derecho) to straighten (out); (: verticalmente) to set upright; (carta) to address; (fig) to straighten or sort out; (dirigir) to direct; ~**se** vr (persona sentado) to stand up; (fig) to correct one's ways.

endeudarse [endeu'ðarse] vr to get into debt.

endiablado, a [endja'ßlaðo, a] a devilish, diabolical; (hum) mischievous; (fig) furious, angry.

endomingarse [endomin'garse] vr to dress up, put on one's best clothes.

endosar [endo'sar] vt (cheque etc) to endorse.

endulzar [endul'θar] vt to sweeten; (fig) to soften.

endurecer [endure'θer] vt to harden; (fig) to harden, toughen; ~**se** vr to harden, grow hard.

endurecido, a [endure'θiðo, a] a (duro) hard; (fig) hardy, tough; **estar** ~ **a algo** to be hardened or used to sth.

endurecimiento [endureθi'mjento] nm

(*acto*) hardening; (*tenacidad*) toughness; (*crueldad*) cruelty; (*insensibilidad*) callousness.

enemigo, a [ene'mixo, a] *a* enemy, hostile // *nm/f* enemy // *nf* enmity, hostility.

enemistad [enemis'taδ] *nf* enmity.

enemistar [enemis'tar] *vt* to make enemies of, cause a rift between; ~se *vr* to become enemies; (*amigos*) to fall out.

energía [ener'xia] *nf* (*vigor*) energy, drive; (*TEC, ELEC*) energy, power.

enérgico, a [e'nerxiko, a] *a* (*gen*) energetic; (*voz, modales*) forceful.

enero [e'nero] *nm* January.

enfadar [enfa'δar] *vt* to anger, annoy; ~se *vr* to get angry *or* annoyed.

enfado [en'faδo] *nm* (*enojo*) anger, annoyance; (*disgusto*) trouble, bother; ~so, a *a* annoying; (*aburrido*) tedious.

énfasis ['enfasis] *nm* emphasis, stress.

enfático, a [en'fatiko, a] *a* emphatic; (*afectado*) pompous.

enfermar [enfer'mar] *vt* to make ill // *vi* to fall ill, be taken ill.

enfermedad [enferme'δaδ] *nf* illness; ~ venérea venereal disease.

enfermería [enferme'ria] *nf* infirmary; (*de colegio etc*) sick bay.

enfermero, a [enfer'mero, a] *nm/f* male nurse/nurse.

enfermizo, a [enfer'miθo, a] *a* (*persona*) sickly, unhealthy; (*lugar*) unhealthy.

enfermo, a [en'fermo, a] *a* ill, sick // *nm/f* invalid, sick person; (*en hospital*) patient.

enflaquecer [enflake'θer] *vt* (*adelgazar*) to make thin; (*debilitar*) to weaken; ~se *vr* (*adelgazarse*) to become thin, lose weight; (*debilitarse*) to grow weak; (*fig*) to lose heart.

enfocar [enfo'kar] *vt* (*foto etc*) to focus; (*problema etc*) to approach, look at.

enfoque [en'foke] *nm* focus.

enfrentar [enfren'tar] *vt* (*peligro*) to face (up to), confront; (*oponer, carear*) to put face to face; ~se *vr* (*dos personas*) to face *or* confront each other; (*dos equipos*) to meet; ~se a *o* con to face up to, confront.

enfrente [en'frente] *ad* opposite; ~ de *prep* opposite, facing; la casa de ~ the house opposite, the house across the street.

enfriamiento [enfria'mjento] *nm* chilling, refrigeration; (*MED*) cold, chill.

enfriar [enfri'ar] *vt* (*alimentos*) to cool, chill; (*algo caliente*) to cool down; (*habitación*) to air, freshen; ~se *vr* to cool down; (*MED*) to catch a chill; (*amistad*) to cool.

enfurecer [enfure'θer] *vt* to enrage, madden; ~se *vr* to become furious, fly into a rage; (*mar*) to get rough.

engalanar [engala'nar] *vt* (*adornar*) to adorn; (*ciudad*) to decorate; ~se *vr* to get dressed up.

enganchar [engan'tʃar] *vt* (*gen*) to hook; (*ropa*) to hang up; (*dos vagones*) to hitch up; (*TEC*) to couple, connect; (*MIL*) to

recruit; (*fig: fam: persona*) to rope into; ~se *vr* (*MIL*) to enlist, join up.

enganche [en'gantʃe] *nm* hook; (*TEC*) coupling, connection; (*acto*) hooking (up); (: *ropa*) hanging up; (*MIL*) recruitment, enlistment.

engañar [enga'ɲar] *vt* to deceive; (*trampear*) to cheat, swindle; ~se *vr* (*equivocarse*) to be wrong; (*disimular la verdad*) to deceive *or* kid o.s.

engaño [en'gaɲo] *nm* deceit; (*trampa*) trick, swindle; (*error*) mistake, misunderstanding; (*ilusión*) delusion; ~so, a *a* (*tramposo*) crooked; (*mentiroso*) dishonest, deceitful; (*aspecto*) deceptive; (*consejo*) misleading, wrong.

engarzar [engar'θar] *vt* (*joya*) to set, mount; (*fig*) to link, connect.

engatusar [engatu'sar] *vt* (*fam*) to coax.

engendrar [enxen'drar] *vt* to breed; (*procrear*) to beget; (*fig*) to cause, produce; **engendro** *nm* (*BIO*) foetus; (*fig*) monstrosity; (*idea*) brainchild.

engolfarse [engol'farse] *vr*: ~ en to bury o.s in, become deeply involved in.

engomar [engo'mar] *vt* to gum, glue, stick.

engordar [engor'δar] *vt* to fatten // *vi* to get fat, put on weight.

engranaje [engra'naxe] *nm* gear.

engranar [engra'nar] *vt* to put into gear // *vi* to interlock.

engrandecer [engrande'θer] *vt* to enlarge, magnify; (*alabar*) to praise, speak highly of; (*exagerar*) to exaggerate.

engrasar [engra'sar] *vt* (*TEC: poner grasa*) to grease; (: *lubricar*) to lubricate, oil; (*manchar*) to make greasy; (*animal*) to fatten.

engreído, a [engre'iδo, a] *a* vain, conceited; **engreírse** *vr* to become conceited.

engrosar [engro'sar] *vt* (*ensanchar*) to enlarge; (*aumentar*) to increase; (*hinchar*) to swell // *vi* to get fat; ~se *vr* to increase; to swell.

enhebrar [ene'βrar] *vt* to thread.

enhorabuena [enora'βwena] *nf* congratulations *pl* // *ad* well and good.

enigma [e'nixma] *nm* enigma; (*problema*) puzzle; (*misterio*) mystery.

enjabonar [enxaβo'nar] *vt* to soap; (*fam: adular*) to soft-soap; (: *regañar*) to scold.

enjambre [en'xamβre] *nm* swarm.

enjaular [enxau'lar] *vt* to put in a cage; (*fam*) to jail, lock up.

enjuagar [enxwa'xar] *vt* (*ropa*) to rinse (out).

enjugar [enxu'xar] *vt* to wipe (off); (*lágrimas*) to dry; (*déficit*) to wipe out.

enjuiciar [enxwi'θjar] *vt* (*JUR: procesar*) to prosecute, try; (*fig*) to judge.

enjuto, a [en'xuto, a] *a* dry, dried up; (*fig*) lean, skinny.

enlace [en'laθe] *nm* link, connection; (*relación*) relationship; (*casamiento*) marriage; (*de carretera, trenes*) connection; **agente**

de ~ broker; ~ **sindical** shop steward.
enlazar [enla'θar] vt (atar) to tie; (conectar) to link, connect; (AM) to lasso; ~**se** vr (novios) to get married; (dos familias) to become related by marriage; (conectarse) to link (up), be linked.
enlodar [enlo'ðar], **enlodazar** [enloða-'θar] vt to muddy, cover in mud; (fig: manchar) to stain; (: rebajar) to debase.
enloquecer [enloke'θer] vt to drive mad // vi, ~**se** vr to go mad.
enlutar [enlu'tar] vt to dress in mourning; ~**se** vr to go into mourning.
enmarañar [enmara'ɲar] vt (enredar) to tangle (up), entangle; (complicar) to complicate; (confundir) to confuse; ~**se** vr (enredarse) to become entangled; (confundirse) to get confused; (nublarse) to cloud over.
enmascarar [enmaska'rar] vt to mask; ~**se** vr to put on a mask; ~**se de** to masquerade as.
enmendar [enmen'dar] vt to emend, correct; (constitución etc) to amend; (compensar) to make good; (comportamiento) to reform; ~**se** vr to reform, mend one's ways; **enmienda** nf correction; amendment; reform; (compensación) compensation, indemnity.
enmohecerse [enmoe'θerse] vr (metal) to rust, go rusty; (muro, plantas) to get mouldy.
enmudecer [enmuðe'θer] vt to silence // vi, ~**se** vr (perder el habla) to go silent; (guardar silencio) to keep quiet.
ennegrecer [enneɣre'θer] vt (poner negro) to blacken; (oscurecer) to darken; ~**se** vr to turn black; (oscurecerse) to get dark.
ennoblecer [ennoβle'θer] vt to ennoble; (fig) to embellish, adorn.
enojadizo, a [enoxa'ðiθo, a] a irritable, short-tempered.
enojar [eno'xar] vt (encolerizar) to anger; (disgustar) to annoy, upset; ~**se** vr to get angry; to get annoyed.
enojo [e'noxo] nm (cólera) anger; (disgusto) annoyance; ~**s** nmpl trials, problems; ~**so, a** a annoying.
enorgullecerse [enorɣuʎe'θerse] vr to be proud; ~ **de** to pride o.s. on, be proud of.
enorme [e'norme] a enormous, huge; (fig) monstrous; **enormidad** nf hugeness, immensity; (despropósito) absurdity, piece of nonsense; (perversidad) monstrosity.
enraizar [enrai'θar] vi to take root.
enredadera [enreða'ðera] nf (BOT) creeper, climbing plant.
enredar [enre'ðar] vt (ovillo) to tangle (up), entangle; (peces) to net; (situación) to complicate, confuse; (meter cizaña) to sow discord among or between; (implicar) to embroil, implicate; ~**se** vr to get entangled, get tangled (up); (situación) to get complicated; (persona) to get embroiled; (AM: fam) to meddle.
enredo [en'reðo] nm (maraña) tangle;

(confusión) mix-up, confusion; (intriga) intrigue.
enrevesado, a [enreβe'saðo, a] a unruly, uncontrollable; (enredado) complicated, involved.
enriquecer [enrike'θer] vt to make rich, enrich; ~**se** vr to get rich.
enrojecer [enroxe'θer] vt to redden // vi, ~**se** vr (metal) to become red hot; (persona) to blush.
enrollar [enro'ʎar] vt to roll (up), wind (up).
enroscar [enros'kar] vt (torcer, doblar) to coil (round), wind; (tornillo, rosca) to screw in; ~**se** vr to coil, wind.
ensalada [ensa'laða] nf salad; **ensaladilla** nf Russian salad.
ensalzar [ensal'θar] vt (alabar) to praise, extol; (exaltar) to exalt.
ensambladura [ensambla'ðura] nf, **ensamblaje** [ensam'blaxe] nm assembly; (TEC) joint; **ensamblar** vt to assemble.
ensanchar [ensan'tʃar] vt (hacer más ancho) to widen; (agrandar) to enlarge, expand; ~**se** vr to get wider, expand; (pey) to give o.s. airs; **ensanche** nm (de vestido, calle) widening; (de negocio) expansion.
ensangrentar [ensangren'tar] vt to stain with blood; ~**se** vr (fig) to get angry.
ensañar [ensa'ɲar] vt to enrage; ~**se** vr: ~**se con** to delight in tormenting.
ensartar [ensar'tar] vt (gen) to string (together); (aguja) to thread.
ensayar [ensa'jar] vt to test, try (out); (TEATRO) to rehearse.
ensayista [ensa'jista] nm/f essayist.
ensayo [en'sajo] nm test, trial; (QUÍMICA) experiment; (TEATRO) rehearsal; (DEPORTE) try; (literaria) essay.
ensenada [ense'naða] nf inlet, cove.
enseñanza [ense'naθa] nf (educación) education; (acción) teaching; (doctrina) teaching, doctrine.
enseñar [ense'ɲar] vt (educar) to teach; (instruir) to teach, instruct; (mostrar, señalar) to show.
enseres [en'seres] nmpl goods and chattels, things.
ensimismarse [ensimis'marse] vr (abstraerse) to become lost in thought; (estar absorto) to be lost in thought; (AM) to become conceited.
ensoberbecerse [ensoβerβe'θerse] vr to become proud; (hacerse arrogante) to become arrogant; (mar) to get rough.
ensordecer [ensorðe'θer] vt to deafen // vi to go deaf.
ensortijar [ensorti'xar] vt, ~**se** vr (cabellos) to curl.
ensuciar [ensu'θjar] vt (manchar) to dirty, soil; (fig) to defile; ~**se** vr (mancharse) to get dirty; (fig) to dirty/wet o.s.
ensueño [en'sweɲo] nm (sueño) dream, fantasy; (ilusión) illusion; (soñando despierto) reverie.
entablado [enta'βlaðo] nm (piso)

floorboards *pl;* (*armazón*) boarding.

entablar [enta'ßlar] *vt* (*recubrir*) to board (up); (*AJEDREZ, DAMAS*) to set up; (*conversación*) to strike up; (*JUR*) to file // *vi* to draw.

entallar [enta'ʎar] *vt* (*piedra*) to sculpt; (*madera*) to carve; (*grabar*) to engrave; (*traje*) to tailor // *vi:* **el traje entalla bien** the suit fits well.

entender [enten'der] *vt* (*comprender*) to understand; (*darse cuenta*) to realize; (*creer, pensar*) to think, believe; (*querer decir*) to mean // *vi:* ~ **de** to know all about; ~ **en** to deal with, have to do with; ~**se** *vr* (*comprenderse*) to be understood; (*ponerse de acuerdo*) to understand one another, have an understanding; (*aliarse*) to agree, reach an agreement; (*fam*) to have an affair; **me entiendo con la mecánica** I'm (quite) good at mechanics.

entendido, a [enten'diðo, a] *a* (*comprendido*) understood; (*hábil*) skilled; (*inteligente*) knowledgeable // *nm/f* (*experto*) expert; (*docto*) knowledgeable person // *excl* agreed!; **entendimiento** *nm* (*comprensión*) understanding; (*facultad intelectual*) the mind, intellect; (*juicio*) judgement.

enterado, a [ente'raðo, a] *a* a well-informed; **estar** ~ **de** to know about, be aware of.

enteramente [entera'mente] *ad* entirely, completely.

enterar [ente'rar] *vt* (*informar*) to inform, tell; ~**se** *vr* to find out, get to know.

entereza [ente'reθa] *nf* (*totalidad*) entirety; (*fig: energía*) strength of mind; (*honradez*) integrity; (*severidad*) strictness, severity.

enternecer [enterne'θer] *vt* (*ablandar*) to soften; (*apiadar*) to touch, move; ~**se** *vr* to be touched, be moved.

entero, a [en'tero, a] *a* (*total*) whole, entire; (*fig: recto*) honest; (*: firme*) firm, resolute // *nm* (*COM: punto*) point; (*AM: pago*) payment.

enterrador [enterra'ðor] *nm* gravedigger.

enterrar [ente'rrar] *vt* to bury.

entibiar [enti'ßjar] *vt* to cool; (*fig*) to cool (down).

entidad [enti'ðað] *nf* (*empresa*) firm, company; (*organismo*) body; (*sociedad*) society; (*FILOSOFÍA*) entity.

entiendo *etc vb ver* **entender.**

entierro [en'tjerro] *nm* (*acción*) burial; (*funeral*) funeral.

entomología [entomolo'xia] *nf* entomology.

entonación [entona'θjon] *nf* (*LING*) intonation; (*fig*) conceit.

entonado, a [ento'naðo, a] *a* (*MUS*) in tune; (*fig*) conceited.

entonar [ento'nar] *vt* (*canción*) to intone; (*colores*) to tone; (*MED*) to tone up // *vi* to be in tune; ~**se** *vr* (*engreírse*) to give o.s. airs.

entonces [en'tonθes] *ad* then, at that time;

desde ~ since then; **en aquel** ~ at that time; (**pues**) ~ and so.

entornar [entor'nar] *vt* (*puerta, ventana*) to half close, leave ajar; (*los ojos*) to screw up.

entorpecer [entorpe'θer] *vt* (*adormecer los sentidos*) to dull, benumb; (*impedir*) to obstruct, hinder; (*: tránsito*) to slow down, delay; **entorpecimiento** *nm* numbness; slowing-down, delay; (*letargia*) lethargy.

entrado, a [en'traðo, a] *a:* ~ **en años** elderly; **una vez** ~ **el verano** in the summer(time), when summer comes // *nf* (*acción*) entry, access; (*sitio*) entrance, way in; (*COM*) receipts *pl*, takings *pl*; (*CULIN*) entree; (*DEPORTE*) innings *sg*; (*TEATRO*) house, audience; (*para el cine etc*) ticket; (*COM*): ~**as y salidas** income and expenditure; (*TEC*): ~**a de aire** air intake *or* inlet.

entrante [en'trante] *a* next, coming // *nm* inlet; **ser** ~ **en una casa** to have the run of a house.

entraña [en'traɲa] *nf* (*fig: centro*) heart, core; (*raíz*) root; ~**s** *nfpl* (*ANAT*) entrails; **entrañable** a close, intimate.

entrar [en'trar] *vt* (*introducir*) to bring in // *vi* (*meterse*) to go/come in, enter; (*comenzar*): ~ **diciendo** to begin by saying; **no me entra** I can't get the hang of it; **el año que entra** next year.

entre ['entre] *prep* (*dos*) between; (*más de dos*) among(st); **pensaba** ~ **mí** I thought to myself.

entreabrir [entrea'ßrir] *vt* to half-open, open halfway.

entrecejo [entre'θexo] *nm:* **fruncir el** ~ to frown.

entredicho [entre'ðitʃo] *nm* prohibition, ban; (*JUR*) injunction.

entrega [en'trexa] *nf* (*de mercancías*) delivery; (*rendición*) surrender; **novela por** ~**s** serial, novel in instalments.

entregar [entre'xar] *vt* (*dar*) to hand (over), deliver; (*ceder*) to give up; ~**se** *vr* (*rendirse*) to surrender, give in, submit; (*dedicarse*) to devote o.s.

entrelazar [entrela'θar] *vt* to entwine.

entremés [entre'mes] *nm* (*CULIN*) side-dish; **entremeses** *nmpl* hors d'œuvres.

entremeter [entreme'ter] *vt* to insert, put in; ~**se** *vr* to meddle, interfere; **entremetido, a** *a* meddling, interfering.

entremezclar [entremeθ'klar] *vt*, ~**se** *vr* to intermingle.

entrenador [entrena'ðor] *nm* trainer, coach; **entrenarse** *vr* to train.

entreoír [entreo'ir] *vt* to half hear.

entresacar [entresa'kar] *vt* to pick out, select.

entresuelo [entre'swelo] *nm* (*sótano*) basement.

entretanto [entre'tanto] *ad* meanwhile, meantime; **en el** ~ in the meantime.

entretejer [entrete'xer] *vt* to interweave.

entretener [entrete'ner] *vt* (*divertir*) to entertain, amuse; (*detener*) to hold up, delay; (*cuidar*) to maintain; ~**se** *vr* (*divertirse*) to amuse o.s.; (*retrasarse*) to delay, linger; **entretenido, a** *a* entertaining, amusing; **entretenimiento** *nm* entertainment, amusement; (*cuidado*) upkeep, maintenance.

entrever [entre'ßer] *vt* to glimpse, catch a glimpse of.

entreverar [entreße'rar] *vt* to mix (up).

entrevista [entre'ßista] *nf* interview; **entrevistar** *vt* to interview; **entrevistarse** *vr* to have an interview.

entristecer [entriste'θer] *vt* to sadden, grieve; ~**se** *vr* to grow sad.

entrometer [entrome'ter] *etc* = **entremeter** *etc.*

entroncar [entron'kar] *vi* to be connected *or* related.

entronque [en'tronke] *nm* connection, link.

entuerto [en'twerto] *nm* wrong, injustice.

entumecer [entume'θer] *vt* to numb, benumb; ~**se** *vr* (*por el frío*) to go *or* become numb; **entumecido, a** *a* numb, stiff.

enturbiar [entur'ßjar] *vt* (*el agua*) to disturb, make cloudy; (*fig*) to fog, confuse; ~**se** *vr* (*oscurecerse*) to become cloudy; (*fig*) to get confused, become obscure.

entusiasmar [entusjas'mar] *vt* to excite, fill with enthusiasm; (*gustar mucho*) to delight; ~**se** *vr:* ~**se con** *o* **por** to get enthusiastic *or* excited about.

entusiasmo [entu'sjasmo] *nm* enthusiasm; (*deleite*) delight; (*excitación*) excitement.

entusiasta [entu'sjasta] *a* enthusiastic // *nm/f* enthusiast.

enumerar [enume'rar] *vt* to enumerate.

enunciación [enunθja'θjon] *nf*, **enunciado** [enun'θjaðo] *nm* enunciation; (*declaración*) declaration, statement; **enunciar** *vt* to enunciate; to declare, state.

envainar [enßai'nar] *vt* to sheathe.

envalentonar [enßalento'nar] *vt* to give courage to; ~**se** *vr* to take courage, become bolder; (*pey: jactarse*) to boast, brag.

envanecer [enßane'θer] *vt* to make conceited; ~**se** *vr* to grow vain *or* conceited.

envasar [enßa'sar] *vt* (*empaquetar*) to pack, wrap; (*enfrascar*) to bottle; (*enlatar*) to tin; (*embolsar*) to pocket // *vi* (*fig: fam: vino*) to knock back; **envase** *nm* packing, wrapping; bottling; tinning, canning; pocketing; (*recipiente*) container; (*paquete*) package; (*botella*) bottle; (*lata*) tin, can.

envejecer [enßexe'θer] *vt* to make old, age // *vi*, ~**se** *vr* (*volverse viejo*) to grow old; (*fig*) to become old-fashioned.

envenenar [enßene'nar] *vt* to poison; (*fig*) to embitter.

envergadura [enßerxa'ðura] *nf* (*fig*) scope, compass.

envés [en'ßes] *nm* (*de tela*) back, wrong side.

enviar [en'ßjar] *vt* to send.

envidia [en'ßiðja] *nf* (*deseo ferviente*) envy; (*celos*) jealousy; **envidiar** *vt* (*desear*) to envy; (*tener celos de*) to be jealous of.

envilecer [enßile'θer] *vt* to debase, degrade; ~**se** *vr* to lower o.s.

envío [en'ßio] *nm* (*acción*) sending; (*de mercancías*) consignment; (*com*) remittance.

enviudar [enßju'ðar] *vi* to be widowed.

envoltura [enßol'tura] *nf* (*cobertura*) cover; (*embalaje*) wrapper, wrapping; (*funda*) case.

envolver [enßol'ßer] *vt* to wrap (up); (*cubrir*) to cover; (*enemigo*) to surround; (*implicar*) to involve, implicate; ~**se** *vr* (*cubrirse*) to wrap o.s. up; (*implicarse*) to become involved.

envuelto [en'ßwelto] *pp de* **envolver.**

enzarzar [enθar'θar] *vt* (*fig*) to involve (in a dispute).

épico, a ['epiko, a] *a* epic // *nf* epic.

epidemia [epi'ðemja] *nf* epidemic; **epidémico, a** *a* epidemic.

epifanía [epifa'nia] *nf* Epiphany.

epilepsia [epi'lepsja] *nf* epilepsy.

epílogo [e'piloxo] *nm* epilogue.

episodio [epi'soðjo] *nm* episode.

epístola [e'pistola] *nf* epistle; (*fam*) letter.

epitafio [epi'tafjo] *nm* epitaph.

época ['epoka] *nf* period, time; (*HISTORIA*) age, epoch; **hacer** ~ to be epoch-making.

equidad [eki'ðað] *nf* equity.

equilibrar [ekili'ßrar] *vt* to balance; **equilibrio** *nm* balance, equilibrium; **equilibrista** *nm/f* (*funámbulo*) tightrope walker; (*acróbata*) acrobat.

equipaje [eki'paxe] *nm* luggage; (*equipo*) equipment, kit; (*NAUT: tripulación*) crew; ~ **de mano** hand luggage.

equipar [eki'par] *vt* (*proveer*) to equip.

equipararse [ekipa'rarse] *vr:* ~ **con** to be on a level with.

equipo [e'kipo] *nm* (*materiales*) equipment; (*grupo*) team; (: *de obreros*) shift.

equis ['ekis] *nf* (the letter) X.

equitación [ekita'θjon] *nf* (*acto*) riding; (*arte*) horsemanship.

equitativo, a [ekita'tißo, a] *a* equitable, fair.

equivalente [ekißa'lente] *a, nm* equivalent; **equivaler** *vi* to be equivalent *or* equal.

equivocación [ekißoka'θjon] *nf* mistake, error; **equivocarse** *vr* to be wrong, make a mistake; **equivocarse de camino** to take the wrong road; **equívoco, a** *a* (*dudoso*) suspect; (*ambiguo*) ambiguous // *nm* ambiguity; (*juego de palabras*) play on words.

era *vb ver* **ser** // ['era] *nf* era, age.

erais *vb ver* **ser.**

éramos vb ver **ser.**

eran vb ver **ser.**

erario [e'rarjo] nm exchequer, treasury.

eras vb ver **ser.**

eres vb ver **ser.**

erguir [er'ʋir] vt to raise, lift; (poner derecho) to straighten; ~**se** vr to straighten up; (fig) to swell with pride.

erigir [eri'xir] vt to erect, build; ~**se** vr: ~**se en** to set o.s. up as.

erizado, a [eri'θaðo, a] a bristly.

erizarse [eri'θarse] vr to stand on end.

erizo [e'riθo] nm hedgehog; (~ de mar) sea-urchin.

ermitaño, a [ermi'taɲo, a] nm/f hermit.

erótico, a [e'rotiko, a] a erotic; **erotismo** nm eroticism.

erradicar [erraði'kar] vt to eradicate.

errado, a [e'rraðo, a] a mistaken, wrong.

errante [e'rrante] a wandering, errant.

errar [e'rrar] vi (vagar) to wander, roam; (equivocarse) to err, make a mistake // vt: ~ **el camino** to take the wrong road; ~ **el tiro** to miss.

erróneo, a [e'rroneo, a] a (equivocado) wrong, mistaken; (falso) false, untrue.

error [e'rror] nm error, mistake; ~ **de imprenta** misprint.

eructar [eruk'tar] vt to belch.

erudición [eruði'θjon] nf erudition, learning.

erudito, a [eru'ðito, a] a erudite, learned.

erupción [erup'θjon] nf eruption; (MED) rash.

es vb ver **ser.**

esa, esas det ver **ese.**

ésa, ésas pron ver **ése.**

esbelto, a [es'ßelto, a] a slim, slender.

esbozo [es'ßoθo] nm sketch, outline.

escabeche [eska'ßetʃe] nm brine; (de aceitunas etc) pickle; **pescado en** ~ pickled fish.

escabel [eska'ßel] nm (low) stool.

escabroso, a [eska'ßroso, a] a (accidentado) rough, uneven; (fig) tough, difficult; (: atrevido) risqué.

escabullirse [eskaßu'ʎirse] vr to slip away; (irse) to clear out.

escala [es'kala] nf (proporción, MUS) scale; (de mano) ladder; (AVIAT) stopover; **hacer** ~ **en** to stop or call in at; ~ **de colores** range of colours.

escalafón [eskala'fon] nm (escala de salarios) salary scale, wage scale; (lista etc) list; (registro) register.

escalar [eska'lar] vt (montaña etc) to climb, scale; (casa) to burgle, break into.

escalera [eska'lera] nf stairs pl, staircase; (escala) ladder; (NAIPES) run; ~ **mecánica** escalator; ~ **de caracol** spiral staircase.

escalinata [eskali'nata] nf outside staircase.

escalofrío [eskalo'frio] nm chill; ~s nmpl (fig) shivers; **escalofriante** a chilling.

escalón [eska'lon] nm step, stair; (de escalera) rung.

escama [es'kama] nf (de pez, serpiente) scale; (de jabón) flake; (fig) resentment.

escamado, a [eska'maðo, a] a wary, cautious.

escamotar [eskamo'tar], **escamotear** [eskamote'ar] vt (quitar) to lift, swipe (fam); (hacer desaparecer) to make disappear.

escampar [eskam'par] vb impersonal to stop raining; (del cielo) to clear (up).

escandalizar [eskandali'θar] vt to scandalize, shock; ~**se** vr to be shocked; (ofenderse) to be offended.

escándalo [es'kandalo] nm scandal; (alboroto, tumulto) row, uproar; **escandaloso, a** a scandalous, shocking.

escandinavo, a [eskandi'naßo, a] a, nm/f Scandinavian.

escaño [es'kaɲo] nm bench; (POL) seat.

escapar [eska'par] vi (gen) to escape, run away; (DEPORTE) to break away; ~**se** vr to escape, get away; (gas) to leak (out).

escaparate [eskapa'rate] nm shop window; (AM) wardrobe.

escape [es'kape] nm (de gas) leak; (de motor) exhaust; (de persona) escape.

escarabajo [eskara'ßaxo] nm beetle; ~s nmpl (fam) scribble sg.

escaramuza [eskara'muθa] nf skirmish; (fig) brush.

escarbar [eskar'ßar] vt (gallina) to scratch; (dientes) to pick; (orejas) to clean; (fig) to inquire into, investigate.

escarcha [es'kartʃa] nf frost.

escarlata [eskar'lata] a inv scarlet; **escarlatina** nf scarlet fever.

escarmentar [eskarmen'tar] vt to punish severely // vi to learn one's lesson; **escarmiento** nm (ejemplo) lesson, example; (castigo) punishment.

escarnecer [eskarne'θer] vt to mock, ridicule; **escarnio, escarnecimiento** nm mockery; (injuria) insult.

escarpado, a [eskar'paðo, a] a (abrupto) sheer; (inclinado) steep; (accidentado) craggy.

escasear [eskase'ar] vt to skimp (on) // vi to be scarce.

escasez [eska'seθ] nf (falta) shortage, scarcity; (pobreza) poverty; (mezquindad) meanness.

escaso, a [es'kaso, a] a (poco) scarce; (raro) rare; (ralo) thin, sparse; (limitado) limited.

escatimar [eskati'mar] vt (limitar) to skimp (on); (reducir) to curtail, cut down.

escena [es'θena] nf scene.

escenario [esθe'narjo] nm (TEATRO) stage; (CINE) set; (fig) scene.

escepticismo [esθepti'θismo] nm scepticism; **escéptico, a** a sceptical // nm/f sceptic.

esclarecer [esklare'θer] vt (iluminar) to light up, illuminate; (misterio, problema) to shed light on; (ennoblecer) to ennoble.

esclavitud [esklaβi'tuð] *nf* slavery.
esclavizar [esklaβi'θar] *vt* to enslave.
esclavo, a [es'klaβo, a] *nm/f* slave.
escoba [es'koβa] *nf* broom.
escocer [esko'θer] *vt* to annoy // *vi* to burn, sting; ~**se** *vr* to chafe, get chafed.
escocés, esa [esko'θes, esa] *a* Scottish // *nm/f* Scotsman/woman, Scot.
Escocia [es'koθja] *nf* Scotland.
escoger [esko'xer] *vt* to choose, pick, select; **escogido, a** *a* chosen, selected; (*calidad*) choice, select; **escogimiento** *nm* choice.
escolar [esko'lar] *a* school *cpd* // *nm/f* schoolboy/girl, pupil.
escolta [es'kolta] *nf* escort; **escoltar** *vt* to escort.
escombro [es'kombro] *nm* mackerel; ~**s** *nmpl* (*basura*) rubbish *sg*; (*restos*) debris *sg*.
esconder [eskon'der] *vt* to hide, conceal; ~**se** *vr* to hide; **escondite** *nm* hiding place; (*juego*) hide-and-seek.
escondrijo [eskon'drixo] *nm* hiding-place, hideout.
escopeta [esko'peta] *nf* shotgun.
escoplo [es'koplo] *nm* chisel.
Escorpio [es'korpjo] *nm* Scorpio.
escorpión [eskor'pjon] *nm* scorpion.
escote [es'kote] *nm* (*de vestido*) low neck; (*parte*) share; **pagar a** ~ to share the expenses.
escotillón [eskoti'ʎon] *nm* trapdoor.
escozor [esko'θor] *nm* (*dolor*) sting(ing); (*fig*) grief, heartache.
escribano, a [eskri'βano, a], **escribiente** [eskri'βjente] *nm/f* clerk.
escribir [eskri'βir] *vt, vi* to write; ~ **a máquina** to type; ¿**cómo se escribe?** how do you spell it?
escrito, a [es'krito, a] *pp de* **escribir** // *nm* (*documento*) document; (*manuscrito*) text, manuscript; **por** ~ in writing.
escritor, a [eskri'tor, a] *nm/f* writer.
escritorio [eskri'torjo] *nm* desk; (*oficina*) office.
escritura [eskri'tura] *nf* (*acción*) writing; (*caligrafía*) (hand)writing; (*JUR: documento*) deed.
escrúpulo [es'krupulo] *nm* scruple; (*minuciosidad*) scrupulousness; **escrupuloso, a** *a* scrupulous.
escrutar [eskru'tar] *vt* to scrutinize, examine; (*votos*) to count.
escrutinio [eskru'tinjo] *nm* (*examen atento*) scrutiny; (*recuento de votos*) poll; (*resultado de elección*) voting, ballot.
escuadra [es'kwaðra] *nf* (*MIL etc*) squad; (*NAUT*) squadron; (*de coches etc*) fleet; **escuadrilla** *nf* (*de aviones*) squadron; (*AM. de obreros*) gang.
escuadrón [eska'ðron] *nm* squadron.
escuálido, a [es'kwaliðo, a] *a* (*flaco, macilento*) pale, wan; (*sucio*) squalid.
escuchar [esku'tʃar] *vt* to listen to // *vi* to listen.

escudilla [esku'ðiʎa] *nf* bowl, basin.
escudo [es'kuðo] *nm* shield.
escudriñar [eskuðri'ɲar] *vt* (*examinar*) to investigate, examine closely; (*mirar de lejos*) to scan.
escuela [es'kwela] *nf* school.
escueto, a [es'kweto, a] *a* plain, unadorned.
esculpir [eskul'pir] *vt* to sculpt; (*grabar*) to engrave; (*tallar*) to carve; **escultor, a** *nm/f* sculptor/tress; **escultura** *nf* sculpture.
escupidora [eskupi'ðora], **escupidera** [eskupi'ðera] *nf* spittoon; (*orinal*) bedpan.
escupir [esku'pir] *vt, vi* to spit (out).
escurridero [eskurri'ðero] *nm* draining-board.
escurridizo, a [eskurri'ðiθo, a] *a* slippery.
escurrir [esku'rrir] *vt* (*ropa*) to wring out; (*verduras*) to strain; (*platos*) to drain // *vi* (*los líquidos*) to drip; (*resbalarse*) to slip, slide; ~**se** *vr* (*gotear*) to drip; (*secarse*) to drain; (*resbalarse*) to slip, slide; (*escaparse*) to slip away.
ese, esa, esos, esas ['ese, 'esa, 'esos, 'esas] *det* (*sg*) that; (*pl*) those.
ése, ésa, ésos, ésas ['ese, 'esa, 'esos, 'esas] *pron* (*sg*) that (one); (*pl*) those (ones); ~... **éste...** the former... the latter...; **¡no me vengas con** ~**as** don't give me any more of that nonsense.
esencia [e'senθja] *nf* essence; **esencial** *a* essential.
esfera [es'fera] *nf* sphere; (*de reloj*) face; **esférico, a** *a* spherical.
esforzado, a [esfor'θaðo, a] *a* (*enérgico*) energetic, vigorous; (*valiente*) brave.
esforzar [esfor'θar] *vt* (*fortalecer*) to strengthen; (*alentar*) to encourage; ~**se** *vr* to exert o.s., make an effort.
esfuerzo [es'fwerθo] *nm* effort; (*TEC*) stress; (*valor*) courage, spirit.
esfumarse [esfu'marse] *vr* to fade away.
esgrima [es'xrima] *nf* fencing.
esguince [es'xinθe] *nm* (*MED*) sprain; (*ademán*) swerve, dodge; (*ceño*) scowl, frown.
eslabón [esla'βon] *nm* link; **eslabonar** *vt* to link, connect.
esmaltar [esmal'tar] *vt* to enamel; (*las uñas*) to paint, varnish; **esmalte** *nm* enamel; **esmalte de uñas** nail varnish, nail polish.
esmerado, a [esme'raðo, a] *a* careful, neat.
esmeralda [esme'ralda] *nf* emerald.
esmerarse [esme'rarse] *vr* (*aplicarse*) to take great pains, exercise great care; (*brillar*) to shine, do well.
esmero [es'mero] *nm* (great) care.
esnob [es'nob] *a inv* (*persona*) snobbish; (*coche etc*) posh // *nm/f* snob; ~**ismo** *nm* snobbery.
eso ['eso] *pron* that, that thing *or* matter; ~ **de su coche** all that about his car; ~ **de ir al cine** all that about going to the cinema, the idea of going to the cinema; a ~ **de las cinco** at about five o'clock; **en**

~ thereupon, at that point; ~ **es** that's it; ¡~ **sí que es vida!** now this is really living!; **por** ~ **te lo dije** that's why I told you.

esos ['esos] *det ver* **ese.**

ésos ['esos] *pron ver* **ése.**

espabilar [espaßi'lar] *vt* (*vela*) to snuff; ~**se** *vr* (*despertarse*) to wake up; (*animarse*) to liven up, look lively.

espacial [espa'θjal] *a inv* (*del espacio*) space *cpd*.

espaciar [espa'θjar] *vt* to space (out); (*divulgar*) to spread; ~**se** *vr*: ~**se en un tema** to enlarge on a subject.

espacio [es'paθjo] *nm* space; (*MUS*) interval; (*emisión*) (short) programme, spot; **el** ~ space; ~**so, a** *a* spacious, roomy; (*lento*) slow.

espada [es'paða] *nf* sword; ~**s** *nfpl* (*NAIPES*) spades.

espaguetis [espa'ɣetis] *nmpl* spaghetti *sg*.

espalda [es'palda] *nf* (*gen*) back; ~**s** *nfpl* (*hombros*) shoulders; **a** ~**s de uno** behind sb's back; **cargado de** ~**s** round-shouldered; **tenderse de** ~**s** to lie (down) on one's back; **volver la** ~ **a alguien** to give sb the cold shoulder.

espaldar [espal'dar] *nm* (*de asiento*) back.

espaldilla [espal'ðiʎa] *nf* shoulder-blade.

espantadizo, a [espanta'ðiθo, a] *a* timid, easily frightened.

espantajo [espan'taxo] *nm,* **espanta-pájaros** [espanta'paxaros] *nmpl* scarecrow *sg*.

espantar [espan'tar] *vt* (*asustar*) to frighten, scare; (*ahuyentar*) to frighten off; (*asombrar*) to horrify, appal; ~**se** *vr* to get frightened *or* scared; to be appalled.

espanto [es'panto] *nm* (*susto*) fright; (*terror*) terror; (*fantasma*) ghost; (*asombro*) astonishment; ~**so, a** *a* frightening; terrifying; astonishing.

España [es'paɲa] *nf* Spain; **español, a** *a* Spanish // *nm/f* Spaniard // *nm* (*lengua*) Spanish.

esparadrapo [espara'ðrapo] *nm* sticking plaster.

esparcido, a [espar'θiðo, a] *a* scattered; (*fig*) jolly, cheerful.

esparcimiento [esparθi'mjento] *nm* (*de líquido*) spilling; (*dispersión*) spreading; (*derramamiento*) scattering; (*fig*) cheerfulness.

esparcir [espar'θir] *vt* to spread; (*derramar*) to scatter; (*líquido*) to spill; ~**se** *vr* to spread (out); to scatter; to spill; (*divertirse*) to enjoy o.s.

espárrago [es'parraɣo] *nm* asparagus.

espasmo [es'pasmo] *nm* spasm.

especia [es'peθja] *nf* spice.

especial [espe'θjal] *a* special; ~**idad** *nf* speciality.

especie [es'peθje] *nf* (*BIO*) species; (*clase*) kind, sort; (*asunto*) matter; (*comentario*) remark, comment; **en** ~ in kind.

especificar [espeθifi'kar] *vt* to specify; **específico, a** *a* specific.

espécimen [es'peθimen] (*pl* **especímenes**) *nm* specimen.

especioso, a [espe'θjoso, a] *a* (*perfecto*) perfect; (*fig*) deceitful.

espectáculo [espek'takulo] *nm* (*gen*) spectacle; (*TEATRO etc*) show.

espectador, a [espekta'ðor, a] *nm/f* spectator.

espectro [es'pektro] *nm* ghost; (*fig*) spectre.

especular [espeku'lar] *vt*, *vi* to speculate; **especulativo, a** *a* speculative.

espejismo [espe'xismo] *nm* mirage.

espejo [es'pexo] *nm* mirror; (*fig*) model; ~ **de retrovisión** rear-view mirror.

espeluznante [espeluθ'nante] *a inv* horrifying, hair-raising.

espera [es'pera] *nf* (*pausa, intervalo*) wait, period of waiting; (*JUR: plazo*) respite; **en** ~ **de** waiting for; (*con expectativa*) expecting.

esperanza [espe'ranθa] *nf* (*confianza*) hope; (*expectativa*) expectation; (*perspectiva*) prospect; **esperanzar** *vt* to give hope to.

esperar [espe'rar] *vt* (*aguardar*) to wait for; (*tener expectativa de*) to expect; (*desear*) to hope for // *vi* to wait; to expect; to hope.

esperma [es'perma] *nf* sperm.

espesar [espe'sar] *vt* to thicken; ~**se** *vr* to thicken, get thicker.

espeso, a [es'peso, a] *a* thick; **espesor** *nm* thickness.

espetar [espe'tar] *vt* (*pollo*) to put on a spit *or* skewer; (*pregunta*) to pop; (*dar: reto, sermón*) to give.

espetón [espe'ton] *nm* (*asador*) spit, skewer; (*aguja*) large pin; (*empujón*) jab, poke.

espía [es'pia] *nm/f* spy; **espiar** *vt* (*observar*) to spy on; (*acechar*) to watch out for.

espina [es'pina] *nf* thorn; (*de madera, astilla*) splinter; (*de pez*) bone; ~ **dorsal** spine.

espinaca [espi'naka] *nf* spinach.

espinar [espi'nar] *vt* (*herir*) to prick; (*fig*) to sting, hurt.

espinazo [espi'naθo] *nm* spine, backbone.

espino [es'pino] *nm* hawthorn.

espinoso, a [espi'noso, a] *a* (*planta*) thorny, prickly; (*fig*) bony.

espionaje [espjo'naxe] *nm* spying, espionage.

espiral [espi'ral] *a, nf* spiral.

espirar [espi'rar] *vt* to breathe out, exhale.

espiritista [espiri'tista] *a, nm/f* spiritualist.

espíritu [es'piritu] *nm* spirit; **espiritual** *a* spiritual.

espita [es'pita] *nf* tap; (*fig: fam*) drunkard.

esplendidez [esplendi'ðeθ] *nf* (*abundancia*) lavishness; (*magnificencia*) splendour.

esplendor [esplen'dor] *nm* splendour.

espolear [espole'ar] *vt* to spur on.
espolvorear [espolßore'ar] *vt* (*echar polvos*) to dust; (*esparcir*) to dust, sprinkle.
esponja [es'ponxa] *nf* sponge; (*fig*) sponger.
esponjarse [espon'xarse] *vr* (*fam: hincharse*) to swell with pride; (: *de salud*) to glow with health.
esponjoso, a [espon'xoso, a] *a* spongy, porous.
espontaneidad [espontanei'ðað] *nf* spontaneity; **espontáneo, a** *a* spontaneous.
esposa [es'posa] *nf* wife; **~s** *nfpl* handcuffs; **esposar** *vt* to handcuff.
esposo [es'poso] *nm* husband.
espuela [es'pwela] *nf* spur.
espuma [es'puma] *nf* foam; (*de cerveza*) froth, head; (*de jabón*) lather; **espumoso, a** *a* frothy, foamy; (*vino*) sparkling.
esqueleto [eske'leto] *nm* skeleton.
esquema [es'kema] *nm* (*diagrama*) diagram; (*dibujo*) plan; (*plan*) scheme; (*FILOSOFIA*) schema.
esquí [es'ki] (*pl* **esquís**) *nm* (*objeto*) ski; (*deporte*) skiing.
esquilar [eski'lar] *vt* to shear.
esquilmar [eskil'mar] *vt* (*cosechar*) to harvest; (*empobrecer: suelo*) to exhaust; (*fig*) to skin.
esquimal [eski'mal] *a, nm/f* Eskimo.
esquina [es'kina] *nf* corner.
esquirol [eski'rol] *nm* (*fam*) blackleg.
esquivar [eski'ßar] *vt* to avoid; (*evadir*) to dodge, elude; **~se** *vr* to withdraw.
esquivez [eski'ßeθ] *nf* (*altanería*) aloofness; (*desdeño*) scorn, disdain; **esquivo, a** *a* (*altanero*) aloof; (*desdeñoso*) scornful, disdainful.
esta ['esta] *det ver* **este.**
ésta ['esta] *pron ver* **éste.**
está *vb ver* **estar.**
estabilidad [estaßili'ðað] *nf* stability; **estable** *a* stable.
establecer [estaßle'θer] *vt* to establish; **~se** *vr* to establish o.s.; (*echar raíces*) to settle; **establecimiento** *nm* establishment.
estaca [es'taka] *nf* stake, post; (*para tiendas*) peg.
estacada [esta'kaða] *nf* (*cerca*) fence, fencing; (*palenque*) stockade.
estación [esta'θjon] *nf* station; (*del año*) season; **~ de autobuses** bus station.
estacionamiento [estaθjona'mjento] *nm* (*AUTO*) parking; (*MIL*) stationing; (*colocación*) placing.
estacionar [estaθjo'nar] *vt* (*AUTO*) to park; (*MIL*) to station; (*colocar*) to place; **~io, a** *a* stationary; (*COM: mercado*) slack.
estadio [es'taðjo] *nm* (*fase*) stage, phase; (*DEPORTE*) stadium.
estadista [esta'ðista] *nm* (*POL*) statesman; (*ESTADÍSTICA*) statistician.
estadística [esta'ðistika] *nf* (*una* **~**) figure, statistic; (*ciencia*) statistics *sg*.

estado [es'taðo] *nm* (*POL: condición*) state; (*social*) status; **~ de las cuentas** statement of accounts; **~ mayor** staff; **E~s Unidos (EE. UU.)** United States (USA).
estafa [es'tafa] *nf* swindle, trick; **estafar** *vt* to swindle, defraud.
estafeta [esta'feta] *nf* (*correo*) post; (*oficina de correos*) post office; **~ diplomática** diplomatic bag.
estallar [esta'ʎar] *vi* to burst; (*explotar*) to explode; (*epidemia, rebelión*) to break out; **~ en llanto** to burst into tears; **estallido** *nm* explosion; (*fig*) outbreak.
estampa [es'tampa] *nf* (*imagen*) image; (*impresión, imprenta*) print, engraving; (*imagen, figura: de persona*) appearance; (*fig: huella*) footprint.
estampado, a [estam'paðo, a] *a* printed // *nm* (*impresión: acción*) printing; (: *efecto*) print; (*marca*) stamping.
estampar [estam'par] *vt* (*imprimir*) to print; (*marcar*) to stamp; (*metal*) to engrave; (*poner sello en*) to stamp; (*fig*) to stamp, imprint.
estampida [estam'piða] *nf* stampede; (*estampido*) bang, report.
estampido [estam'piðo] *nm* bang, report.
estampilla [estam'piʎa] *nf* stamp.
están *vb ver* **estar.**
estancar [estan'kar] *vt* (*aguas*) to hold up, hold back; (*COM*) to monopolize; (*fig*) to block, hold up; **~se** *vr* to stagnate.
estancia [es'tanθja] *nf* (*permanencia*) stay; (*sala*) living-room; (*AM*) farm, ranch; **estanciero** *nm* farmer, rancher.
estanco, a [es'tanko, a] *a* watertight // *nm* (*monopolio*) state monopoly; (*tienda*) tobacconist's (shop).
estandarizar [estandari'θar] *vt* to standardize.
estandarte [estan'darte] *nm* banner, standard.
estanque [es'tanke] *nm* (*lago*) pool, pond; (*AGR*) reservoir.
estanquero, a [estan'kero, a], **estanquillero, a** [estanki'ʎero, a] *nm/f* tobacconist.
estante [es'tante] *nm* (*armario*) rack, stand; (*biblioteca*) bookcase; (*anaquel*) shelf; (*AM*) prop; **estantería** *nf* shelving, shelves *pl*.
estantigua [estan'tiɣwa] *nf* (*fantasma*) apparition.
estaño [es'taɲo] *nm* tin.
estar [es'tar] *vi* (*gen*) to be; (*en casa*) to be in; (*ubicarse*) to be found; (*presente*) to be present; **estamos a 2 de mayo** it is the 2nd May; **¿cómo está Ud?** how are you?; **~ enfermo** to be ill; **~ viejo/joven** (*parecerse*) to seem old/young; (*seguido de una preposición*): **¿a cuánto estamos de Madrid?** how far are we from Madrid?; **~ de fiesta** *o* **vacaciones** to be on holiday; **las uvas están a 5 pesetas** grapes are at 5 pesetas; **María no está** Maria isn't in; **~ por** (: *moción*) to be in

favour of; (: *persona*) to support, back; **está por hacer** it remains to be done; ¿**estamos?** are we agreed?
estas ['estas] *det ver* **este**.
éstas ['estas] *pron ver* **éste**.
estás *vb ver* **estar**.
estatal [esta'tal] *a inv* state *cpd.*
estático, a [es'tatiko, a] *a* static.
estatificar [estatifi'kar] *vt* to nationalize.
estatua [es'tatwa] *nf* statue.
estatuir [estatu'ir] *vt* (*establecer*) to establish; (*determinar*) to prove.
estatura [esta'tura] *nf* stature, height.
estatuto [esta'tuto] *nm* (*JUR*) statute; (*de ciudad*) bye-law; (*de comité*) rule.
este ['este] *nm* east.
este, esta, estos, estas ['este, 'esta, 'estos, 'estas] *det* (*sg*) this; (*pl*) these.
éste, ésta, éstos, éstas ['este, 'esta, 'estos, 'estas] *pron* (*sg*) this (one); (*pl*) these (ones); ~... **ése...** the latter... the former... .
esté *etc vb ver* **estar**.
estela [es'tela] *nf* wake, wash; (*fig*) trail.
estenografía [estenoxra'fia] *nf* shorthand, stenography.
estepa [es'tepa] *nf* (*GEO*) steppe.
estera [es'tera] *nf* mat(ting).
estereo... [estereo] *pref* stereo...; ~**fónico, a** *a* stereophonic; ~**tipar** *vt* to stereotype; ~**tipo** *nm* stereotype.
estéril [es'teril] *a* sterile, barren; (*fig*) vain, futile.
esterlina [ester'lina] *a.* **libra** ~ pound sterling.
estético, a [es'tetiko, a] *a* aesthetic // *nf* aesthetics *sg.*
estiércol [es'tjerkol] *nm* dung, manure.
estigma [es'tixma] *nm* stigma.
estilar [esti'lar] *vi,* ~**se** *vr* to be in fashion, be used, be worn.
estilo [es'tilo] *nm* style; (*TEC*) stylus; (*DEPORTE*) stroke; **algo por el** ~ something of the sort.
estima [es'tima] *nf* esteem, respect.
estimación [estima'θjon] *nf* (*evaluación*) estimation; (*aprecio, afecto*) esteem, regard.
estimar [esti'mar] *vt* (*evaluar*) to estimate; (*valorar*) to value; (*apreciar*) to esteem, respect; (*pensar, considerar*) to think, reckon; ¡**se estima!** thanks very much!
estimulante [estimu'lante] *a* stimulating // *nm* stimulant; **estimular** *vt* to stimulate; (*excitar*) to excite; (*animar*) to encourage; **estímulo** *nm* stimulus; (*ánimo*) encouragement.
estío [es'tio] *nm* summer.
estipulación [estipula'θjon] *nf* stipulation, condition; **estipular** *vt* to stipulate.
estirado, a [esti'raðo, a] *a* (*tenso*) (stretched *or* drawn) tight; (*fig*) stiff, pompous.
estirar [esti'rar] *vt* to stretch; (*conversa-*

ción, presupuesto) to stretch out; ~**se** *vr* to stretch.
estirón [esti'ron] *nm* pull, tug; (*crecimiento*) spurt, sudden growth; **dar un** ~ to shoot up.
estirpe [es'tirpe] *nf* stock, lineage.
estival [esti'βal] *a* summer *cpd.*
esto ['esto] *pron* this, this thing *or* matter; ~ **de la boda** this business about the wedding.
estofa [es'tofa] *nf* (*tela*) quilting; (*calidad, clase*) quality, class.
estofado, a [esto'faðo, a] *a* (*CULIN*) stewed; (*bordado*) quilted // *nm* stew.
estofar [esto'far] *vt* (*bordar*) to quilt; (*CULIN*) to stew.
estoico, a [es'toiko, a] *a* (*FILOSOFÍA*) stoic(al); (*fig*) cold, indifferent.
estólido, a [es'toliðo, a] *a* stupid.
estómago [es'tomaxo] *nm* stomach; **tener** ~ to be thick-skinned.
estorbar [estor'βar] *vt* to hinder, obstruct; (*fig*) to bother, disturb // *vi* to be in the way; **estorbo** *nm* (*molestia*) bother, nuisance; (*obstáculo*) hindrance, obstacle.
estornudar [estornu'ðar] *vi* to sneeze.
estos ['estos] *det ver* **este**.
éstos ['estos] *pron ver* **éste**.
estoy *vb ver* **estar**.
estrafalario, a [estrafa'larjo, a] *a* odd, eccentric; (*desarreglado*) slovenly, sloppy.
estragar [estra'xar] *vt* to deprave, corrupt; (*deteriorar*) to ruin; **estrago** *nm* ruin, destruction; **hacer estragos en** to wreak havoc among.
estragón [estra'xon] *nm* (*CULIN*) tarragon.
estrangul [estran'gul] *nm* mouthpiece.
estrangulación [estrangula'θjon] *nf* strangulation.
estrangulador, a [estrangula'ðor, a] *nm/f* strangler // *nm* (*TEC*) throttle; (*AUTO*) choke.
estrangulamiento [estrangula'mjento] *nm* (*AUTO*) bottleneck.
estrangular [estrangu'lar] *vt* (*persona*) to strangle; (*MED*) to strangulate.
estraperlo [estra'perlo] *nm* black market.
estratagema [estrata'xema] *nf* (*MIL*) stratagem; (*astucia*) cunning.
estrategia [estra'texja] *nf* strategy; **estratégico, a** *a* strategic.
estratificar [estratifi'kar] *vt* to stratify.
estrato [es'trato] *nm* stratum, layer.
estrechar [estre'tʃar] *vt* (*reducir*) to narrow; (*vestido*) to take in; (*persona*) to hug, embrace; ~**se** *vr* (*reducirse*) to narrow, grow narrow; (*apretarse*) to embrace; (*reducir los gastos*) to economize; ~ **la mano** to shake hands; ~ **amistad con alguien** to become very friendly with sb.
estrechez [estre'tʃeθ] *nf* narrowness; (*de ropa*) tightness; (*intimidad*) intimacy; (*COM*) want *or* shortage of money; **estrecheces** *nfpl* financial difficulties; ~ **de conciencia** small-mindedness; ~ **de miras** narrow-mindedness.

estrecho, a [es'tretʃo, a] *a* narrow; (*apretado*) tight; (*íntimo*) close, intimate; (*miserable*) mean // *nm* strait.

estregar [estre'xar] *vt* (*sobar*) to rub (hard); (*rascar*) to scrape.

estrella [es'treʎa] *nf* star; ~ **de mar** starfish.

estrellar [estre'ʎar] *vt* (*hacer añicos*) to smash (to pieces); (*huevos*) to fry; ~**se** *vr* to smash; (*chocarse*) to crash; (*fracasar*) to be smashed to pieces.

estremecer [estreme'θer] *vt* to shake; ~**se** *vr* to shake, tremble; **estremecimiento** *nm* (*conmoción*) tremor; (*sobresalto*) shock; (*temblor*) trembling, shaking.

estrenar [estre'nar] *vt* (*vestido*) to wear for the first time; (*casa*) to move into; (*película, obra de teatro*) to present for the first time; ~**se** *vr* (*persona*) to make one's début; **estreno** *nm* (*primer uso*) first use; (*en un empleo*) début, first appearance; (*CINE etc*) première.

estreñir [estre'pir] *vt* to constipate; ~**se** *vr* to become constipated.

estrépito [es'trepito] *nm* noise, racket; (*fig*) fuss; **estrepitoso, a** *a* noisy; (*fiesta*) rowdy, boisterous.

estría [es'tria] *nf* groove.

estribar [estri'ßar] *vi*: ~ **en** to rest on, be supported by.

estribo [es'trißo] *nm* (*de jinete*) stirrup; (*de coche, tren*) step; (*de puente*) support; (*fig*) basis, foundation; (*GEO*) spur.

estribor [estri'ßor] *nm* starboard.

estricnina [estrik'nina] *nf* strychnine.

estricto, a [es'trikto, a] *a* (*riguroso*) strict; (*severo*) severe.

estro ['estro] *nm* inspiration.

estropajo [estro'paxo] *nm* scourer.

estropear [estrope'ar] *vt* (*arruinar*) to spoil; (*dañar*) to damage; (*lisiar*) to maim; (*tullir*) to cripple; ~**se** *vr* (*objeto*) to get damaged; (*persona*) to be crippled.

estructura [estruk'tura] *nf* structure.

estruendo [es'trwendo] *nm* (*ruido*) racket, din; (*fig: alboroto*) uproar, turmoil; (*pompa*) pomp.

estrujar [estru'xar] *vt* (*apretar*) to squeeze; (*aplastar*) to crush; (*magullar*) to bruise; (*fig*) to drain, bleed.

estuario [es'twarjo] *nm* estuary.

estuche [es'tutʃe] *nm* box, case.

estudiante [estu'ðjante] *nm/f* student; **estudiantil** *a inv* student *cpd*.

estudiantina [estuðjan'tina] *nf* student music group.

estudiar [estu'ðjar] *vt* to study.

estudio [es'tuðjo] *nm* study; (*CINE, ARTE, RADIO*) studio; ~**s** *nmpl* studies; (*erudición*) learning *sg*; ~**so, a** *a* studious.

estufa [es'tufa] *nf* heater, fire.

estulticia [estul'tiθja] *nf* foolishness.

estupefacto, a [estupe'fakto, a] *a* speechless, thunderstruck.

estupendo, a [estu'pendo, a] *a* wonderful,

terrific; (*fam*) great; ¡~! that's great!, fantastic!

estupidez [estupi'ðeθ] *nf* (*torpeza*) stupidity; (*tontería*) piece of nonsense.

estúpido, a [es'tupiðo, a] *a* stupid, silly.

estupor [estu'por] *nm* stupor; (*fig*) astonishment, amazement.

estupro [es'tupro] *nm* rape.

estuve *etc vb ver* **estar.**

etapa [e'tapa] *nf* stage; (*DEPORTE*) leg; (*parada*) stopping place; (*fig*) stage, phase.

eternidad [eterni'ðað] *nf* eternity; **eterno, a** *a* eternal, everlasting.

ético, a ['etiko, a] *a* ethical // *nf* ethics *pl.*

etíope [e'tiope] *a, nm/f* Ethiopian.

Etiopía [etjo'pia] *nf* Ethiopia.

etiqueta [eti'keta] *nf* (*modales*) etiquette; (*papel*) label, tag.

eucalipto [euka'lipto] *nm* eucalyptus.

Eucaristía [eukaris'tia] *nf* Eucharist.

eufemismo [eufe'mismo] *nm* euphemism.

euforia [eu'forja] *nf* euphoria.

eugenesia [euxe'nesja] *nf*, **eugenismo** [euxe'nismo] *nm* eugenics *sg.*

eunuco [eu'nuko] *nm* eunuch.

Europa [eu'ropa] *nf* Europe; **europeo, a** *a, nm/f* European.

éuscaro, a ['euskaro, a] *a* Basque // *nm* (*lengua*) Basque.

Euskadi [eus'kaði] *nm* the Basque Provinces *pl.*

eutanasia [euta'nasja] *nf* euthanasia.

evacuación [eßakwa'θjon] *nf* evacuation; **evacuar** *vt* to evacuate.

evadir [eßa'ðir] *vt* to evade, avoid; ~**se** *vr* to escape.

evaluar [eßa'lwar] *vt* to evaluate.

evangélico, a [eßan'xeliko, a] *a* evangelic(al).

evangelio [eßan'xeljo] *nm* gospel.

evaporación [eßapora'θjon] *nf* evaporation.

evaporar [eßapo'rar] *vt* to evaporate; ~**se** *vr* to vanish.

evasión [eßa'sjon] *nf* escape, flight; (*fig*) evasion.

evasivo, a [eßa'sißo, a] *a* evasive, non-committal.

evento [e'ßento] *nm* unforeseen event; (*eventualidad*) eventuality; **a cualquier** ~ in any event.

eventual [eßen'twal] *a* possible, conditional (upon circumstances); (*trabajador*) casual, temporary.

evidencia [eßi'ðenθja] *nf* (*certidumbre*) evidence, proof; **evidenciar** *vt* (*hacer patente*) to make evident; (*probar*) to prove, show; **evidenciarse** *vr* to be evident.

evidente [eßi'ðente] *a* obvious, clear, evident.

evitar [eßi'tar] *vt* (*evadir*) to avoid; (*impedir*) to prevent.

evocar [eßo'kar] *vt* to evoke, call forth.

evolución [eßolu'θjon] *nf* (*desarrollo*) evolution, development; (*cambio*) change;

(*MIL*) manoeuvre; **evolucionar** *vi* to evolve; (*MIL, AVIAT*) to manoeuvre.
ex [eks] *a* ex-; **el ~ ministro** the former minister, the ex-minister.
exacerbar [eksaθer'ßar] *vt* to irritate, annoy; (*agravar*) to aggravate.
exactitud [eksakti'tuð] *nf* exactness; (*precisión*) accuracy; (*puntualidad*) punctuality; **exacto, a** *a* exact; accurate; punctual; **¡exacto!** exactly!
exageración [eksaxera'θjon] *nf* exaggeration; **exagerar** *vt, vi* to exaggerate.
exaltado, a [eksal'taðo, a] *a* (*apasionado*) over-excited, worked-up; (*exagerado*) extreme; (*excitado*) elated.
exaltar [eksal'tar] *vt* to exalt, glorify; **~se** *vr* (*excitarse*) to get excited *or* worked-up; (*arrebatarse*) to get carried away.
examen [ek'samen] *nm* examination.
examinar [eksami'nar] *vt* to examine; **~se** *vr* to be examined, sit an examination.
exangüe [ek'sangwe] *a* (*desangrado*) bloodless; (*sin fuerzas*) weak.
exasperar [eksaspe'rar] *vt* to exasperate; **~se** *vr* to get exasperated, lose patience.
Exca. *abr de* **Excelencia.**
excedente [eksθe'ðente] *a, nm* excess, surplus.
exceder [eksθe'ðer] *vt* to exceed, surpass; **~se** *vr* (*extralimitarse*) to go too far; (*sobrepasarse*) to excel o.s.
excelencia [eksθe'lenθja] *nf* excellence; **E~** Excellency; **excelente** *a* excellent.
exceiso, a [eks'θelso, a] *a* lofty, sublime.
excentricidad [eksθentriθi'ðað] *nf* eccentricity; **excéntrico, a** *a, nm/f* eccentric.
excepción [eksθep'θjon] *nf* exception; **excepcional** *a* exceptional.
excepto [eks'θepto] *ad* excepting, except (for).
exceptuar [eksθep'twar] *vt* to except, exclude.
excesivo, a [eksθe'sißo, a] *a* excessive.
exceso [eks'θeso] *nm* (*gen*) excess; (*COM*) surplus.
excitación [eksθita'θjon] *nf* (*sensación*) excitement; (*acción*) excitation.
excitado, a [eksθi'taðo, a] *a* excited; (*emociones*) aroused; **excitar** *vt* to excite; (*incitar*) to urge; **excitarse** *vr* to get excited.
exclamación [eksklama'θjon] *nf* exclamation; **exclamar** *vi* to exclaim.
excluir [eksklu'ir] *vt* to exclude; (*dejar fuera*) to shut out; (*descartar*) to reject; **exclusión** *nf* exclusion; (*descarte*) rejection; **con exclusión de** excluding.
exclusiva [eksklu'sißa], **exclusividad** [eksklusißi'ðað] *nf* exclusiveness; (*PRENSA*) exclusive; (*COM*) sole right *or* agency.
exclusivo, a [eksklu'sißo, a] *a* exclusive; (*único*) sole.
Excmo. *abr de* **excelentísimo.**
excomulgar [ekskomul'ɤar] *vt* (*REL*) to

excommunicate; (*excluir*) to ban, banish.
excomunión [ekskomu'njon] *nf* excommunication.
excoriar [eksko'rjar] *vt* to flay, skin.
excursión [ekskur'sjon] *nf* excursion, outing; **excursionismo** *nm* sightseeing.
excusa [eks'kusa] *nf* excuse; (*disculpa*) apology.
excusado, a [eksku'saðo, a] *a* unnecessary; (*disculpado*) excused, forgiven // *nm* lavatory, toilet.
excusar [eksku'sar] *vt* to excuse; (*evitar*) to avoid; (*impedir*) to prevent; **~se** *vr* (*rehusarse*) to decline a request; (*disculparse*) to apologize.
execrar [ekse'krar] *vt* to loathe.
exención [eksen'θjon] *nf* exemption.
exento, a [ek'sento, a] *pp de* **eximir** // *a* exempt; **~ de derechos** tax-free.
exequias [ek'sekjas] *nfpl* funeral rites, obsequies.
exhalación [eksala'θjon] *nf* (*del aire*) exhalation; (*vapor*) fumes *pl*, vapour; (*rayo*) shooting star.
exhalar [eksa'lar] *vt* to exhale, breathe out; (*olor etc*) to give off; (*suspiro*) to breathe, heave.
exhausto, a [ek'sausto, a] *a* exhausted.
exhibición [eksißi'θjon] *nf* exhibition, display, show.
exhibir [eksi'ßir] *vt* to exhibit, display, show.
exhortación [eksorta'θjon] *nf* exhortation; **exhortar** *vt*: **exhortar a** to exhort to.
exigencia [eksi'xenθja] *nf* demand, requirement; **exigente** *a* demanding.
exigir [eksi'xir] *vt* (*gen*) to demand, require; (*pago*) to exact.
exilio [ek'siljo] *nm* exile.
eximio, a [ek'simjo, a] *a* (*excelente*) choice, select; (*eminente*) distinguished, eminent.
eximir [eksi'mir] *vt* to exempt.
existencia [eksis'tenθja] *nf* existence; **~s** *nfpl* stock(s) (*pl*).
existir [eksis'tir] *vi* to exist, be.
éxito ['eksito] *nm* (*resultado*) result, outcome; (*triunfo*) success; **tener ~** to be successful.
exonerar [eksone'rar] *vt* to exonerate; **~ de una obligación** to free from an obligation.
exorcizar [eksorθi'θar] *vt* to exorcize.
exótico, a [ek'sotiko, a] *a* exotic.
expandir [ekspan'dir] *vt* to expand.
expansión [ekspan'sjon] *nf* expansion.
expatriarse [ekspa'trjarse] *vr* to emigrate; (*POL*) to go into exile.
expectativa [ekspekta'tißa] *nf* (*espera*) expectation; (*perspectiva*) prospect.
expedición [ekspeði'θjon] *nf* (*excursión*) expedition; (*envío*) shipment; (*rapidez*) speed.
expediente [ekspe'ðjente] *nm* expedient; (*JUR: procedimento*) action, proceedings *pl*; (*: papeles*) dossier, file, record.

expedir [ekspe'ðir] *vt* (*despachar*) to send, forward; (*libreta cívica, pasaporte*) to issue; (*fig*) to deal with.

expedito, a [ekspe'ðito, a] *a* (*libre*) clear, free; (*pronto*) prompt, speedy.

expendedor, a [ekspende'ðor, a] *nm/f* (*vendedor*) dealer; (*aparato*) (vending) machine; ~ **de cigarrillos** cigarette machine.

expendeduría [ekspendedu'ria] *nf* shop; (*estanco*) tobacconist's (shop).

expensas [eks'pensas] *nfpl* expenses; **a** ~ **de** at the expense of.

experiencia [ekspe'rjenθja] *nf* experience; (*científica*) experiment.

experimentado, a [eksperimen'taðo, a] *a* experienced.

experimentar [eksperimen'tar] *vt* (*en laboratorio*) to experiment with; (*probar*) to test, try out; (*notar, observar*) to experience; (*sufrir*) to suffer; **experimento** *nm* experiment.

experto, a [eks'perto, a] *a* (*práctico*) expert; (*diestro*) skilled, experienced // *nm/f* expert.

expiar [ekspi'ar] *vt* to atone for.

expirar [ekspi'rar] *vi* to expire.

explayar [ekspla'jar] *vt* to extend, expand; ~**se** *vr* to extend, spread; ~**se con uno** to confide in sb.

explicación [eksplika'θjon] *nf* explanation; **explicar** *vt* to explain; **explicarse** *vr* to explain (o.s.).

explícito, a [eks'pliθito, a] *a* explicit.

explorador, a [eksplora'ðor, a] *nm/f* (*pionero*) explorer; (*MIL*) scout // *nm* (*MED*) probe; (*TEC*) (radar) scanner; **los E~es** the Scouts.

explorar [eksplo'rar] *vt* to explore; (*MED*) to probe; (*radar*) to scan.

explosión [eksplo'sjon] *nf* explosion; **explosivo, a** *a* explosive.

explotación [eksplota'θjon] *nf* exploitation; (*de planta etc*) running, operation; **explotar** *vt* to exploit; to run, operate // *vi* to explode.

exponer [ekspo'ner] *vt* to expose; (*cuadro*) to display; (*vida*) to risk; (*idea*) to explain; ~**se** *vr* to expose o.s., leave o.s. open.

exportación [eksporta'θjon] *nf* (*acción*) export; (*mercancías*) exports *pl*; **exportar** *vt* to export.

exposición [eksposi'θjon] *nf* (*gen*) exposure; (*de arte*) show, exhibition; (*petición*) petition; (*explicación*) explanation; (*narración*) account, statement.

exposímetro [ekspo'simetro] *nm* (*FOTO*) exposure meter.

exprés [eks'pres] *nm* (*AM*) express (train).

expresar [ekspre'sar] *vt* to express; **expresión** *nf* expression; **expresiones** *nfpl* regards.

expreso, a [eks'preso, a] *pp de* **expresar** // *a* (*claro*) specific, clear; (*rápido*) fast // *nm*: **mandar por** ~ to send by express (delivery).

exprimir [ekspri'mir] *vt* (*fruta*) to squeeze (out); (*ropa*) to wring out; (*fig*) to express emphatically.

expropiar [ekspro'pjar] *vt* to expropriate.

expuesto, a [eks'pwesto, a] *a* exposed; (*cuadro etc*) on show, on display.

expugnar [ekspuɣ'nar] *vt* to take by storm.

expulsar [ekspul'sar] *vt* (*echar*) to eject; (*arrojar*) to throw out; (*expeler*) to expel; (*desalojar*) to drive out; (*despedir*) to sack, fire; (*a un futbolista*) to send off; **expulsión** *nf* expulsion; sending-off.

expurgar [ekspur'ɣar] *vt* to expurgate.

exquisito, a [ekski'sito, a] *a* exquisite; (*agradable*) delightful.

éxtasis ['ekstasis] *nm* ecstasy.

extender [eksten'der] *vt* (*gen*) to extend; (*los brazos*) to stretch out, hold out; (*mapa*) to spread (out), open (out); (*mantequilla*) to spread; (*certificado*) to issue; (*cheque, recibo*) to make out; (*documento*) to draw up; ~**se** *vr* (*gen*) to extend; (*en el suelo*) to stretch out; (*epidemia*) to spread; **extendido, a** *a* (*abierto*) spread out, open; (*brazos*) outstretched; (*prevaleciente*) widespread; **extensión** *nf* (*de país*) expanse, stretch; (*de libro*) extent; (*de tiempo*) length, duration; (*AM*) extension; **en toda la extensión de la palabra** in every sense of the word; **extenso, a** *a* extensive; (*prevaleciente*) widespread.

extenuar [ekste'nwar] *vi* (*agotar*) to exhaust; (*debilitar*) to weaken.

exterior [ekste'rjor] *a inv* (*de fuera*) external; (*afuera*) outside, exterior; (*apariencia*) outward; (*comercio*) foreign // *nm* (*gen*) exterior, outside; (*aspecto*) outward appearance; (*DEPORTE*) wing(er); **el** ~ foreign parts *pl*; **al** ~ outwardly, on the surface.

exterminar [ekstermi'nar] *vt* to exterminate; **exterminio** *nm* extermination.

externo, a [eks'terno, a] *a* (*exterior*) external, outside; (*superficial*) outward // *nm/f* day pupil.

extinguir [ekstin'gir] *vt* (*fuego*) to extinguish, put out; (*raza, población*) to wipe out; ~**se** *vr* (*fuego*) to go out; (*BIO*) to die out, become extinct.

extinto, a [eks'tinto, a] *a* extinct.

extintor [ekstin'tor] *nm* (fire) extinguisher.

extra ['ekstra] *a, nm/f* extra // *nm* extra; (*bono*) bonus.

extracción [ekstrak'θjon] *nf* extraction; (*en lotería*) draw.

extracto [eks'trakto] *nm* extract.

extraer [ekstra'er] *vt* to extract, take out.

extralimitarse [ekstralimi'tarse] *vr* to go too far.

extranjero, a [ekstran'xero, a] *a* foreign // *nm/f* foreigner // *nm* foreign lands *pl*; **en el** ~ abroad.

extrañar [ekstra'nar] *vt* (*desterrar*) to exile; (*sorprender*) to find strange *or* odd;

(*AM*) to miss; ~**se** *vr* (*sorprenderse*) to be amazed, be surprised; (*distanciarse*) to become estranged, grow apart.

extrañeza [ekstra'neθa] *nf* (*rareza*) strangeness, oddness; (*asombro*) amazement, surprise.

extraño, a [eks'traɲo, a] *a* (*extranjero*) foreign; (*raro, sorprendente*) strange, odd.

extraordinario, a [ekstraorði'narjo, a] *a* extraordinary; (*edición, número*) special // *nm* (*plato*) special dish; (*de periódico*) special edition; **horas** ~**as** overtime *sg*.

extravagancia [ekstraßa'ɣanθja] *nf* extravagance; **extravagante** *a* extravagant; (*extraño*) strange, odd; (*excéntrico*) eccentric; (*estrafalario*) outlandish.

extraviado, a [ekstra'ßjaðo, a] *a* lost, missing.

extraviar [ekstra'ßjar] *vt* (*desviar*) to mislead; (*perder*) to lose, misplace; ~**se** *vr* to lose one's way, get lost.

extravío [ekstra'ßio] *nm* loss; (*fig*) deviation.

extremar [ekstre'mar] *vt* to carry to extremes; ~**se** *vr* to do one's utmost, make every effort.

extremaunción [ekstremaun'θjon] *nf* extreme unction.

extremeño, a [ekstre'meɲo, a] *a, nm/f* Extremaduran.

extremidad [ekstremi'ðað] *nf* (*punta*) extremity; (*fila*) edge; ~**es** *nfpl* (*ANAT*) extremities.

extremo, a [eks'tremo, a] *a* extreme; (*último*) last // *nm* end; (*límite, grado sumo*) extreme; **en último** ~ as a last resort; ~ **derecho/izquierdo** outside-right/ outside-left.

extrínseco, a [eks'trinseko, a] *a* extrinsic.

extrovertido, a [ekstroßer'tiðo, a] *a, nm/f* extrovert.

exuberancia [eksuße'ranθja] *nf* exuberance; **exuberante** *a* exuberant; (*fig*) luxuriant, lush.

exvoto [eks'ßoto] *nm* votive offering.

eyacular [ejaku'lar] *vt, vi* to ejaculate.

F

f.a.b. *abr de* **franco a bordo** f.o.b. (free on board).

fábrica ['faßrika] *nf* factory; **marca de** ~ trademark; **precio de** ~ factory price.

fabricación [faßrika'θjon] *nf* (*manufactura*) manufacture; (*producción*) production; **de** ~ **casera** home-made; ~ **en serie** mass production.

fabricante [faßri'kante] *nm/f* manufacturer.

fabricar [faßri'kar] *vt* (*hacer*) to manufacture, make; (*construir*) to build; (*elaborar*) to fabricate, devise.

fabril [fa'ßril] *a*: **industria** ~ manufacturing industry.

fábula ['faßula] *nf* (*cuento*) fable; (*chisme*) rumour.

facción [fak'θjon] *nf* (*POL*) faction; (*del rostro*) feature.

fácil ['faθil] *a* (*simple*) easy; (*probable*) likely.

facilidad [faθili'ðað] *nf* (*capacidad*) ease; (*sencillez*) simplicity; (*de palabra*) fluency; ~**es** *nfpl* facilities.

facilitar [faθili'tar] *vt* (*hacer fácil*) to make easy; (*proporcionar*) to provide; (*hacer posible*) to arrange; (*hacer más fácil*) to facilitate.

fácilmente ['faθilmente] *ad* easily.

factible [fak'tißle] *a* feasible.

factor [fak'tor] *nm* factor.

factura [fak'tura] *nf* (*cuenta*) bill; (*hechura*) manufacture; **facturar** *vt* (*COM*) to invoice, charge for.

facultad [fakul'tað] *nf* (*aptitud, ESCOL etc*) faculty; (*poder*) power.

facha ['fatʃa] *nf* (*fam: aspecto*) look; (: *desagradable*) unpleasant sight.

fachada [fa'tʃaða] *nf* (*ARQ*) façade, front.

faena [fa'ena] *nf* (*trabajo*) work; (*quehacer*) task, job; ~**s de la casa** housework *sg*.

fagot [fa'got] *nm* (*MUS*) bassoon.

faisán [fai'san] *nm* pheasant.

faja ['faxa] *nf* (*para la cintura*) sash; (*de mujer*) corset; (*de tierra*) strip; (*venda*) bandage.

falange [fa'lanxe] *nf* (*POL*) Falange.

falda ['falda] *nf* (*prenda de vestir*) skirt.

falibilidad [falißili'ðað] *nf* fallibility.

fálico, a ['faliko, a] *a* phallic.

falo ['falo] *nm* phallus.

falsedad [false'ðað] *nf* (*hipocresía*) falseness; (*mentira*) falsehood.

falsificar [falsifi'kar] *vt* (*firma etc*) to forge; (*voto etc*) to rig; (*moneda*) to counterfeit.

falso, a ['falso, a] *a* (*gen*) false; (*erróneo*) mistaken; (*moneda etc*) fake; **en** ~ falsely.

falta ['falta] *nf* (*defecto*) fault, flaw; (*privación*) lack, want; (*ausencia*) absence; (*carencia*) shortage; (*equivocación*) mistake; (*DEPORTE*) foul; **hacer** ~ to be missing or lacking.

faltar [fal'tar] *vi* (*escasear*) to be lacking, be wanting; (*ausentarse*) to be absent, be missing; (*fallar: mecanismo*) to go wrong, break down; **faltan 2 horas para llegar** there are 2 hours to go till arrival; ~ **el respeto a alguien** to be disrespectful to sb; **echar a** ~ **a alguien** to miss sb; **¡no faltaba más!** that's the last straw!

falto, a ['falto, a] *a* (*desposeído*) deficient, lacking; (*necesitado*) poor, wretched.

falla ['faʎa] *nf* (*defecto*) fault, flaw; (*fracaso*) failure.

fallar [fa'ʎar] *vt* (*JUR*) to pronounce sentence on // *vi* (*memoria*) to fail; (*motor*) to miss.

fallecer [faʎe'θer] *vi* to pass away, die; **fallecimiento** *nm* decease, demise.

fallo ['faʎo] *nm* (*JUR*) verdict, ruling; (*fracaso*) failure.

fama ['fama] *nf* (*renombre*) fame; (*reputación*) reputation.
familia [fa'milja] *nf* family.
familiar [fami'ljar] *a* (*relativo a la familia*) family *cpd*; (*conocido, informal*) familiar // *nm* relative; **~idad** *nf* (*gen*) familiarity; (*informalidad*) homeliness; **~izarse** *vr* to familiarize o.s. with.
famoso, a [fa'moso, a] *a* (*renombrado*) famous; (*fam: fabuloso*) great.
fanático, a [fa'natiko, a] *a* fanatical // *nm/f* (*gen*) fanatic; (*CINE etc*) fan; (*de deportes*) supporter; **fanatismo** *nm* fanaticism.
fanfarrón, ona [fanfa'rron, ona] *a* boastful; (*pey*) showy.
fango ['fango] *nm* mud; **~ so, a** *a* muddy.
fantasía [fanta'sia] *nf* fantasy, imagination; (*fam*) conceit, vanity; **joyas de ~** imitation jewellery *sg*.
fantasma [fan'tasma] *nm* (*espectro*) ghost, apparition.
fantástico, a [fan'tastiko, a] *a* fantastic.
farmacéutico, a [farma'θeutiko, a] *a* pharmaceutical // *nm/f* chemist, pharmacist.
farmacia [far'maθja] *nf* chemist's (shop), pharmacy; **~ de turno** all-night chemist.
faro ['faro] *nm* (*NAUT: torre*) lighthouse; (*AUTO*) headlamp; **~s laterales** sidelights; **~s traseros** rear lights.
farol [fa'rol] *nm* (*luz*) lantern, lamp; (*de calle*) streetlamp.
farsa ['farsa] *nf* (*gen*) farce.
farsante [far'sante] *nm/f* fraud, fake.
fascinar [fasθi'nar] *vt* (*deslumbrar*) to fascinate.
fascismo [fas'θismo] *nm* fascism; **fascista** *a, nm/f* fascist.
fase ['fase] *nf* phase.
fastidiar [fasti'ðjar] *vt* (*disgustar*) to annoy, bother; (*estropear*) to spoil; (*aburrir*) to bore; **~se** *vr* (*dañarse*) to harm o.s.; (*disgustarse*) to get annoyed *or* cross.
fastidio [fas'tiðjo] *nm* (*disgusto*) annoyance; (*tedio*) boredom; **~so, a** *a* (*molesto*) annoying; (*aburrido*) tedious.
fatal [fa'tal] *a* (*gen*) fatal; (*inevitable*) unavoidable; (*desgraciado*) ill-fated; (*fam: malo, pésimo*) awful; **~idad** *nf* (*destino*) fate; (*mala suerte*) misfortune.
fatiga [fa'tixa] *nf* (*cansancio*) fatigue, weariness; **fatigar** *vt* to tire, weary; **fatigarse** *vr* to get tired; **fatigoso, a** *a* (*cansador*) tiring; (*aburrido*) tiresome.
fatuo, a ['fatwo, a] *a* (*vano*) fatuous; (*presuntuoso*) conceited.
fauces ['fauθes] *nfpl* jaws, mouth *sg*.
favor [fa'ßor] *nm* favour; **entrada de ~** complimentary ticket; **haga el ~ de...** would you be so good as to..., kindly...; **por ~** please; **~able** *a* favourable.
favorecer [faßore'θer] *vt* (*gen*) to favour; (*vestido etc*) to become, flatter; **este peinado le favorece** this hairstyle suits her.

favorito, a [faßo'rito, a] *a, nm/f* favourite.
faz [faθ] *nf*: **la ~ de la tierra** the face of the earth.
fe [fe] *nf* (*REL*) faith; (*confianza*) belief; (*documento*) certificate; (*lealtad*) fidelity, loyalty; **prestar ~ a** to believe, credit; **actuar con buena/mala ~** to act in good/bad faith; **dar ~ de** to bear witness to.
fealdad [feal'dað] *nf* ugliness.
febrero [fe'ßrero] *nm* February.
febril [fe'ßril] *a* feverish.
fecundar [fekun'dar] *vt* (*generar*) to fertilize, make fertile; **fecundo, a** *a* (*fértil*) fertile; (*prolífico*) prolific; (*fructífero*) fruitful; (*abundante*) abundant; (*productivo*) productive.
fecha ['fetʃa] *nf* date; **en ~ próxima** soon; **hasta la ~** to date, so far; **poner ~** to date; **con ~ adelantada** post-dated.
federación [federa'θjon] *nf* federation.
federal [feðe'ral] *a* federal; **~ismo** *nm* federalism.
felicidad [feliθi'ðað] *nf* (*satisfacción, contento*) happiness; (*suerte feliz*) (good) luck; **~es** *nfpl* best wishes, congratulations.
felicitación [feliθita'θjon] *nf* congratulation; **felicitar** *vt* to congratulate.
feligrés, esa [feli'xres, esa] *nm/f* parishioner.
feliz [fe'liθ] *a* (*contento*) happy; (*afortunado*) lucky.
felonía [felo'nia] *nf* felony, crime.
felpudo [fel'puðo] *nm* doormat.
femenino, a [feme'nino, a] *a, nm* feminine.
feminista [femi'nista] *nf* feminist.
fénix ['feniks] *nm* (*ave*) phoenix.
fenómeno [fe'nomeno] *nm* phenomenon; (*fig*) freak, accident // *a inv* great // *excl* smashing!, marvellous!
feo, a ['feo, a] *a* (*gen*) ugly; (*desagradable*) bad, nasty.
féretro ['feretro] *nm* (*ataúd*) coffin; (*sarcófago*) bier.
feria ['ferja] *nf* (*gen*) fair; (*AM*) village market; (*día de asueto*) holiday, rest day.
fermentar [fermen'tar] *vi* to ferment.
ferocidad [feroθi'ðað] *nf* fierceness, ferocity.
feroz [fe'roθ] *a* (*cruel*) cruel; (*salvaje*) fierce.
férreo, a ['ferreo, a] *a* iron.
ferretería [ferrete'ria], **ferrería** [ferre'ria] *nf* (*trastes*) ironmongery; (*tienda*) ironmonger's (shop), hardware store.
ferrocarril [ferroka'rril] *nm* railway; **~ de cremallera** rack railway.
fértil ['fertil] *a* (*productivo*) fertile; (*rico*) rich; **fertilidad** *nf* (*gen*) fertility; (*productividad*) fruitfulness; **fertilizar** *vt* to fertilize.
fervor [fer'ßor] *nm* fervour; **~oso, a** *a* fervent.
festejar [feste'xar] *vt* (*agasajar*) to

entertain lavishly; (*galantear*) to court; (*su cumpleaños*) to celebrate; **festejo** *nm* (*diversión*) entertainment; (*galanteo*) courtship; (*fiesta*) celebration.
festividad [festiβi'ðað] *nf* festivity.
festivo, a [fes'tiβo, a] *a* (*de fiesta*) festive; (*fig*) witty; (*CINE, LITERATURA*) humorous.
fétido, a ['fetiðo, a] *a* (*hediondo*) foul-smelling; (*podrido*) rotten.
fiado [fi'aðo] *nm*: **comprar al** ~ to buy on credit.
fiador, a [fia'ðor, a] *nm/f* (*JUR*) surety, guarantor; (*COM*) backer // *nm* (*de arma*) safety catch; (*cerrojo*) tumbler; **salir** ~ **por alguien** to go bail for sb.
fiambre ['fjambre] *nm* cold meat.
fianza ['fjanθa] *nf* surety; (*JUR*): **libertad bajo** ~ release on bail.
fiar [fi'ar] *vt* (*salir garante de*) to guarantee; (*vender a crédito*) to sell on credit // *vi* to trust; ~**se** *vr* to trust (in), rely on; ~**se de uno** to rely on sb.
fiasco ['fjasko] *nm* fiasco.
fibra ['fiβra] *nf* fibre.
ficción [fik'θjon] *nf* fiction.
ficticio, a [fik'tiθjo, a] *a* (*imaginario*) fictitious; (*falso*) fabricated.
ficha ['fitʃa] *nf* (*en juegos*) token, counter; (*tarjeta*) (index) card; (*ELEC*) plug; **fichar** *vt* (*archivar*) to file, index; **estar fichado** to have a record; **fichero** *nm* card index.
fidelidad [fiðeli'ðað] *nf* (*lealtad*) fidelity, loyalty; **alta** ~ high fidelity, hi-fi.
fideos [fi'ðeos] *nmpl* noodles.
fiebre ['fjeβre] *nf* (*MED*) fever; (*fig*) feverish excitement; ~ **amarilla/del heno** yellow/hay fever; ~ **palúdica** malaria; **tener** ~ to have a temperature.
fiel [fjel] *a* (*leal*) faithful, loyal; (*fiable*) reliable; (*exacto*) accurate, exact // *nm* inspector; (*aguja*) needle, pointer; **los** ~**es** the faithful.
fieltro ['fjeltro] *nm* felt.
fiereza [fje'reθa] *nf* (*bravura*) fierceness; (*fealdad*) ugliness.
fiero, a ['fjero, a] *a* (*cruel*) cruel; (*feroz*) fierce; (*duro*) harsh // *nf* (*animal feroz*) wild animal *or* beast.
fiesta ['fjesta] *nf* party; (*de pueblo*) festival; ~**s** *nfpl* (*caricias*) endearments; (*vacaciones*) holiday *sg*; (*broma*) jokes; (*juerga*) fun and games; (*REL*): ~ **de guardar** day of obligation.
figura [fi'ɣura] *nf* (*gen*) figure; (*forma, imagen*) shape, form; (*cara*) face; (*TEATRO*) marionette; (*NAIPES*) face card.
figurar [fiɣu'rar] *vt* (*representar*) to represent; (*fingir*) to figure // *vi* to figure; ~**se** *vr* (*imaginarse*) to imagine; (*suponer*) to suppose.
fijar [fi'xar] *vt* (*gen*) to fix; (*estampilla*) to affix, stick (on); (*fig*) to settle (on), decide; ~ **con hilos** to sew on; ~**se** *vr*: ~**se en** to notice.
fijo, a ['fixo, a] *a* (*gen*) fixed; (*firme*) firm; (*permanente*) permanent // *ad*: **mirar** ~ to stare.

fila ['fila] *nf* row; (*cola, columna*) queue; (*cadena*) line; **ponerse en** ~ to line up, get into line.
filántropo [fi'lantropo] *nm* philanthropist.
filatelia [fila'telja] *nf* philately.
filete [fi'lete] *nm* (*carne*) steak; (*pescado*) fillet.
filial [fi'ljal] *a* filial // *nf* subsidiary.
Filipinas [fili'pinas] *nfpl*: **las** ~ the Philippines.
filmar [fil'mar] *vt* to film, shoot.
filo ['filo] *nm* (*gen*) edge; **sacar** ~ **a** to sharpen; **al** ~ **del mediodía** at about midday; **de doble** ~ double-edged.
filosofía [filoso'fia] *nf* philosophy; **filósofo** *nm* philosopher.
filtrar [fil'trar] *vt*, *vi* to filter, strain; ~**se** *vr* to filter; (*fig*) to dwindle; **filtro** *nm* (*TEC, utensilio*) filter; (*CULIN*) strainer.
fin [fin] *nm* (*gen*) end; (*objetivo*) aim, purpose; **al** ~ **y al cabo** when all's said and done; **a** ~ **de** in order to; **por** ~ finally; **en** ~ in short; ~ **de semana** weekend; ~**al** *a* final // *nm* end, conclusion // *nf* final; ~**alista** *nm/f* finalist; ~**alizar** *vt* to end, finish // *vi*, ~**alizarse** *vr* to end, come to an end.
financiar [finan'θjar] *vt* to finance; **financiero, a** *a* financial.
finca ['finka] *nf* country estate; (*casa*) country house.
fingir [fin'xir] *vt* (*simular*) to simulate; (*pretextar*) to sham, fake // *vi* (*aparentar*) to pretend, feign; ~**se** *vr* to pretend to be.
finlandés, esa [finlan'des, esa] *a* Finnish // *nm/f* Finn // *nm* (*lengua*) Finnish.
Finlandia [fin'landja] *nf* Finland.
fino, a ['fino, a] *a* (*gen*) fine; (*delgado*) slender; (*puro*) pure; (*de buenas maneras*) polite, refined; (*inteligente*) shrewd.
firma ['firma] *nf* signature; (*COM*) firm, company; **firmar** *vt* to sign.
firme ['firme] *a* (*gen*) firm; (*estable*) stable; (*sólido*) solid; (*compacto*) compact; (*constante*) steady; (*decidido*) resolute // *nm* road (surface); ~**mente** *ad* firmly; ~**za** *nf* firmness; (*constancia*) steadiness; (*solidez*) solidity.
fiscal [fis'kal] *a* fiscal // *nm* Public Prosecutor.
fisgar [fis'xar] *vt* to pry into; (*pescar*) to spear, harpoon.
físico, a ['fisiko, a] *a* physical // *nm* physique // *nm/f* physicist // *nf* physics *sg*.
flaco, a ['flako, a] *a* (*muy delgado*) skinny, lean; (*débil*) weak, feeble.
flagrante [fla'xrante] *a* flagrant.
flamante [fla'mante] *a* brilliant; (*nuevo*) brand-new.
flamenco, a [fla'menko, a] *a* (*de Flandes*) Flemish; (*agitanado*) gipsy // *nm* (*canto y baile*) flamenco.
flan [flan] *nm* creme caramel.
flaqueza [fla'keθa] *nf* (*delgadez*) leanness; (*fig*) weakness.
flash [flaʃ] *nm* (*FOTO*) flash.
flauta ['flauta] *nf* flute.

fleco ['fleko] *nm* fringe.
flecha ['fletʃa] *nf* arrow.
flema ['flema] *nm* phlegm.
flequillo [fle'kiʎo] *nm* (*pelo*) fringe.
flete ['flete] *nm* (*carga*) freight; (*alquiler*) charter; (*precio*) freightage.
flexible [flek'siβle] *a* flexible.
flojo, a ['floxo, a] *a* (*gen*) loose; (*sin fuerzas*) limp; (*débil*) weak.
flor [flor] *nf* flower; (*piropo*) compliment; **a ~ de** on the surface of; **~ecer** *vi* (*bot*) to flower; (*fig*) to flourish; **~eciente** *a* (*bot*) in flower, flowering; (*fig*) thriving.
flota ['flota] *nf* fleet.
flotar [flo'tar] *vi* (*gen*) to float; (*colgar*) to hang; **flote** *nm*: **a flote** afloat; **sacar a flote** (*fig*) to get back on one's feet.
fluctuar [fluk'twar] *vi* (*oscilar*) to fluctuate; (*vacilar*) to waver.
fluidez [flui'ðeθ] *nf* fluidity; (*fig*) fluency.
flúido, a ['fluiðo, a] *a*, *nm* fluid.
fluir [flu'ir] *vi* to flow.
flujo ['fluxo] *nm* flow; **~ y reflujo** ebb and flow; **~ de sangre** (*med*) loss of blood.
foca ['foka] *nf* seal.
foco ['foko] *nm* focus; (*elec*) floodlight.
fogón [fo'xon] *nm* (*de cocina*) stove.
fogoso, a [fo'xoso, a] *a* spirited.
follaje [fo'ʎaxe] *nm* foliage.
folleto [fo'ʎeto] *nm* pamphlet.
fomentar [fomen'tar] *vt* (*med*) to foment; **fomento** *nm* (*med*) fomentation; (*promoción*) promotion; **Ministerio de Fomento** Ministry of Public Works.
fonda ['fonda] *nf* inn; (*restaurante*) buffet.
fondo ['fondo] *nm* (*de mar*) bottom; (*cuarto*) back; (*arte etc*) background; (*reserva*) fund; **~s** *nmpl* (*com*) funds, resources; **una investigación a ~ a** thorough investigation; **en el ~ at** bottom, deep down.
fontanería [fontane'ria] *nf* plumbing; **fontanero** *nm* plumber.
forastero, a [foras'tero, a] *a* (*extraño*) alien, strange // *nm/f* stranger.
forcejear [forθexe'ar] *vi* (*luchar*) to struggle; (*esforzarse*) to make violent efforts.
forjar [for'xar] *vt* to forge.
forma ['forma] *nf* (*figura*) form, shape; (*molde*) mould, pattern; (*med*) fitness; (*método*) way, means; **las ~s** the conventions.
formación [forma'θjon] *nf* (*gen*) formation; (*educación*) education.
formal [for'mal] *a* (*gen*) formal; (*fig: persona*) serious; **~idad** *nf* formality; seriousness.
formar [for'mar] *vt* (*componer*) to form, shape; (*constituir*) to make up, constitute; (*escol*) to train, educate; **~se** *vr* (*cobrar forma*) to form, take form; (*hacer línea*) to form up; (*desarrollarse*) to develop.
formidable [formi'ðaβle] *a* (*temible*) formidable; (*asombroso*) tremendous.
formulario [formu'larjo] *nm* form.

fornido, a [for'niðo, a] *a* strapping, well-built.
foro ['foro] *nm* (*gen*) forum; (*jur*) court.
forrar [fo'rrar] *vt* (*abrigo*) to line; (*libro*) to cover; **forro** *nm* (*de cuaderno*) cover; (*costura*) lining; (*de sillón*) upholstery; **forro de freno** brake lining.
fortalecer [fortale'θer] *vt* to strengthen.
fortaleza [forta'leθa] *nf* (*gen*) strength; (*determinación*) resolution.
fortuito, a [for'twito, a] *a* accidental.
fortuna [for'tuna] *nf* (*suerte*) fortune, (good) luck; (*riqueza, caudal*) fortune, wealth.
forzar [for'θar] *vt* (*puerta*) to force (open); (*casa*) to break into; (*compeler*) to compel.
forzoso, a [for'θoso, a] *a* necessary.
fosa ['fosa] *nf* (*sepultura*) grave; (*en tierra*) pit; (*med*) cavity.
fósforo ['fosforo] *nm* (*metaloide*) phosphorus; (*am*) match.
foso ['foso] *nm* ditch; (*teatro*) pit; (*auto*): **~ de reconocimiento** inspection pit.
foto ['foto] *nf* photo, snap(shot); **~copia** *nf* photocopy; **~copiador** *nm* photocopier; **~copiar** *vt* to photocopy.
fotografía [fotoxra'fia] *nf* (*gen*) photography; (*una ~*) photograph; **fotografiar** *vt* to photograph.
fotógrafo, a [fo'toxrafo, a] *nm/f* photographer.
fracaso [fra'kaso] *nm* (*desgracia, revés*) failure; **fracasar** *vi* (*gen*) to fail.
fracción [frak'θjon] *nf* fraction; (*pol*) faction; **fraccionar** *vt* to divide, break up.
fractura [frak'tura] *nf* fracture, break.
fragancia [fra'xanθja] *nf* (*olor*) fragrance; (*perfume*) perfume.
frágil ['fraxil] *a* (*débil*) fragile; (*quebradizo*) breakable; **fragilidad** *nf* fragility; (*de persona*) frailty.
fragmento [fraxː'mento] *nm* (*pedazo*) fragment.
fragor [fra'xor] *nm* (*ruido intenso*) din; (*de gente*) uproar.
fragua ['fraxwa] *nf* forge; **fraguar** *vt* to forge; (*fig*) to concoct // *vi* to harden.
fraile ['fraile] *nm* (*rel*) friar; (: *monje*) monk.
frambuesa [fram'bwesa] *nf* raspberry.
francés, esa [fran'θes, esa] *a* French // *nm/f* Frenchman/woman // *nm* (*lengua*) French.
Francia ['franθja] *nf* France.
franco, a ['franko, a] *a* (*leal, abierto*) frank, open; (*generoso, liberal*) generous, liberal; (*com: exento*) free // *nm* franc.
francotirador, a [frankotira'ðor, a] *nm/f* sniper.
franela [fra'nela] *nf* flannel.
franja ['franxa] *nf* fringe.
franquear [franke'ar] *vt* (*camino*) to clear; (*carta, paquete postal*) to frank, stamp; (*obstáculo*) to overcome; **~se** *vr* (*ceder*) to give way; (*confiarse a alguien*) to unburden o.s.

franqueo [fran'keo] *nm* postage.
franqueza [fran'keθa] *nf* (*candor*) frankness; (*generosidad*) generosity.
frasco ['frasko] *nm* bottle; (*al vacío*) (vacuum) flask.
frase ['frase] *nf* sentence; ~ **hecha** set phrase.
fraude ['frauðe] *nm* (*cualidad*) dishonesty; (*acto*) fraud; **fraudulento, a** *a* fraudulent.
frecuencia [fre'kwenθja] *nf* frequency; **con** ~ frequently, often.
fregador [freʁa'ðor] *nm* sink.
fregar [fre'ʁar] *vt* (*frotar*) to scrub; (*platos*) to wash (up); (*AM*) to annoy.
freír [fre'ir] *vt* to fry.
frenar [fre'nar] *vt* to brake; (*fig*) to check.
frenesí [frene'si] *nm* frenzy; **frenético, a** *a* frantic.
freno ['freno] *nm* (*TEC, AUTO*) brake; (*de cabalgadura*) bit; (*fig*) check.
frente ['frente] *nm* (*ARQ, POL*) front; (*de objeto*) front part // *nf* forehead, brow; **en** ~ **de** in front of; (*en situación opuesta de*) opposite; **chocar de** ~ to crash head-on; **hacer** ~ **a** to face up to.
fresa ['fresa] *nf* strawberry.
fresco, a ['fresko, a] *a* (*nuevo*) fresh; (*frío*) cool // *nm* (*aire*) fresh air; (*ARTE*) fresco; (*fam*) shameless person; (*persona insolente*) impudent person // *nf* cool part of the day; **tomar el** ~ to get some fresh air; **frescura** *nf* freshness; (*descaro*) cheek, nerve; (*calma*) calmness.
frialdad [frial'dað] *nf* (*gen*) coldness; (*indiferencia*) indifference.
fricción [frik'θjon] *nf* (*gen*) friction; (*acto*) rub(bing); (*MED*) massage.
frigidez [frixi'ðeθ] *nf* frigidity.
frigorífico [frixo'rifiko] *nm* refrigerator.
frijol [fri'xol] *nm* kidney bean.
frío, a ['frio, a] *a* cold // *nm* cold(ness).
frito, a ['frito, a] *a* fried; **me trae** ~ **ese hombre** I'm sick and tired of that man.
frívolo, a ['frißolo, a] *a* frivolous.
frontera [fron'tera] *nf* frontier; **fronterizo, a** *a* frontier *cpd*; (*contiguo*) bordering.
frontón [fron'ton] *nm* (*DEPORTE*) pelota court.
frotar [fro'tar] *vt* to rub; ~**se** *vr*: ~**se las manos** to rub one's hands.
fructífero, a [fruk'tifero, a] *a* fruitful.
frugal [fru'ʁal] *a* frugal.
fruncir [frun'θir] *vt* to pucker; (*costura*) to pleat; ~ **el ceño** to knit one's brow.
frustrar [frus'trar] *vt* to frustrate.
fruta ['fruta] *nf* fruit; **frutería** *nf* fruit shop.
fue *vb ver* **ser, ir.**
fuego ['fweʁo] *nm* (*gen*) fire; (*MED*) rash; **a** ~ **lento** on a low flame *or* gas; **¿tienes** ~**?** have you a light?
fuente ['fwente] *nf* (*de una plaza*) fountain; (*manantial, fig*) spring; (*origen*) source; (*plato*) large dish.
fuera *etc vb ver* **ser, ir** // ['fwera] *ad*

out(side); (*en otra parte*) away; (*excepto, salvo*) except, save // *prep*: ~ **de** outside; (*fig*) besides; ~ **de sí** beside o.s.
fuerte ['fwerte] *a* (*gen*) strong; (*golpe*) hard; (*ruido*) loud; (*comida*) rich; (*lluvia*) heavy; (*dolor*) intense // *ad* strongly; hard; loud(ly).
fuerza ['fwerθa] *nf* (*fortaleza*) strength; (*TEC, ELEC*) power; (*coacción*) force; (*MIL*) forces *pl*; **a** ~ **de** by dint of; **cobrar** ~**s** to recover one's strength; **tener** ~**s para** to have the strength to; **a la** ~, **por** ~ forcibly, by force.
fuga ['fuʁa] *nf* (*huida*) flight, escape; (*de gas*) leak; **fugarse** *vr* to flee, escape; **fugaz** *a* fleeting; **fugitivo, a** *a, nm/f* fugitive.
fui *vb ver* **ser, ir.**
fulano, a [fu'lano, a] *nm/f* so-and-so, what's-his-name.
fulgor [ful'xor] *nm* brilliance.
fumar [fu'mar] *vt, vi* to smoke; ~**se** *vr* (*disipar*) to squander; ~ **en pipa** to smoke a pipe.
funámbulo, a [fu'nambulo, a] *nm/f* tightrope-walker.
función [fun'θjon] *nf* function; (*de puesto*) duties *pl*; (*espectáculo*) show; **entrar en funciones** to take up one's duties; **funcionar** *vi* (*gen*) to function; (*máquina*) to work.
funcionario, a [funθjo'narjo, a] *nm/f* official; (*público*) civil servant.
funda ['funda] *nf* (*gen*) cover; (*de almohada*) pillowcase.
fundación [funda'θjon] *nf* foundation.
fundamental [fundamen'tal] *a* fundamental, basic.
fundamentar [fundamen'tar] *vt* (*poner base*) to lay the foundations of; (*establecer*) to found; (*fig*) to base; **fundamento** *nm* (*base*) foundation.
fundar [fun'dar] *vt* to found; (*dotar de fondos*) to endow; ~**se** *vr*: ~**se en** to be founded on.
fundición [fundi'θjon] *nf* fusing; (*fábrica*) foundry.
fundir [fun'dir] *vt* (*gen*) to fuse; (*metal*) to smelt, melt down; (*COM*) to merge; (*estatua*) to cast; ~**se** *vr* (*sólido*) to merge, blend; (*unirse*) to fuse together.
fúnebre ['funeßre] *a* funeral *cpd*, funereal.
funeral [fune'ral] *nm* funeral.
furgón [fur'xon] *nm* wagon.
furia ['furja] *nf* (*ira*) fury; (*violencia*) violence; **furibundo, a** *a* furious; **furioso, a** *a* (*iracundo*) furious; (*violento*) violent; **furor** *nm* (*cólera*) rage.
furtivo, a [fur'tißo, a] *a* furtive.
furúnculo [fu'runkulo] *nm* (*MED*) boil.
fusible [fu'sißle] *nm* fuse.
fusil [fu'sil] *nm* rifle; ~**ar** *vt* to shoot.
fusión [fu'sjon] *nf* (*gen*) melting; (*unión*) fusion; (*COM*) merger.
fútbol ['futßol] *nm* football; **futbolín** *nm* table football; **futbolista** *nm* footballer.

fútil ['futil] *a* trifling; **futilidad, futileza** *nf* triviality.

futuro, a [fu'turo, a] *a, nm* future.

G

gabacho, a [ga'ßatʃo, a] *a* Pyrenean; (*fam*) frenchified // *nm/f* Pyrenean villager.

gabán [ga'ßan] *nm* overcoat.

gabardina [gaßar'ðina] *nf* raincoat, gabardine.

gabinete [gaßi'nete] *nm* (*POL*) cabinet; (*estudio*) study; (*de abogados etc*) office.

gaceta [ga'θeta] *nf* gazette; **gacetilla** *nf* (*en periódico*) news in brief; (*de personalidades*) gossip column.

gacha ['gatʃa] *nf* mush; ~**s** *nfpl* porridge *sg*.

gafas ['gafas] *nfpl* glasses; ~ **oscuras** dark glasses.

gaita ['gaita] *nf* flute; (~ *gallega*) bagpipes *pl.*

gajes ['gaxes] *nmpl* (*salario*) pay; **los ~ del oficio** occupational hazards.

gajo ['gaxo] *nm* (*gen*) bunch; (*de árbol*) bough; (*de naranja*) segment.

gala ['gala] *nf* full dress; (*fig: lo mejor*) cream, flower; ~**s** *nfpl* finery *sg*; **estar de** ~ to be in one's best clothes; **hacer ~ de** to display, show off.

galán [ga'lan] *nm* lover, gallant; (*hombre atractivo*) ladies' man; (*TEATRO*): **primer** ~ leading man.

galano, a [ga'lano, a] *a* (*elegante*) elegant; (*bien vestido*) smart.

galante [ga'lante] *a* gallant; **galantear** *vt* (*hacer la corte a*) to court, woo; **galanteo** *nm* (*coqueteo*) flirting; (*de pretendiente*) wooing; **galantería** *nf* (*caballerosidad*) gallantry; (*cumplido*) politeness; (*comentario*) compliment.

galaxia [ga'laksja] *nf* galaxy.

galera [ga'lera] *nf* (*nave*) galley; (*carro*) wagon; (*MED*) hospital ward; (*IMPRENTA*) galley.

galería [gale'ria] *nf* (*gen*) gallery; (*balcón*) veranda(h); (*de casa*) corridor.

Gales ['gales] *nm* Wales; **galés, esa** *a* Welsh // *nm/f* Welshman/woman // *nm* (*lengua*) Welsh.

galgo, a ['galxo, a] *nm/f* greyhound.

galimatías [galima'tias] *nmpl* (*lenguaje*) gibberish *sg*, nonsense *sg*.

galón [ga'lon] *nm* (*MIL*) stripe; (*medida*) gallon.

galopar [galo'par] *vi* to gallop; **galope** *nm* gallop.

galvanizar [galßani'θar] *vt* to galvanize.

gallardía [gaʎar'ðia] *nf* (*galantería*) dash; (*valor*) bravery; (*elegancia*) elegance.

gallego, a [ga'ʎexo, a] *a, nm/f* Galician.

galleta [ga'ʎeta] *nf* biscuit.

gallina [ga'ʎina] *nf* hen // *nm* (*fam*) coward; ~ **ciega** blind man's buff.

gallo ['gaʎo] *nm* cock, rooster.

gama ['gama] *nf* (*MUS*) scale; (*fig*) range.

gamba ['gamba] *nf* prawn.

gamberro, a [gam'berro, a] *nm/f* hooligan, lout.

gamuza [ga'muθa] *nf* chamois.

gana ['gana] *nf* (*deseo*) desire, wish; (*apetito*) appetite; (*voluntad*) will; (*añoranza*) longing; **de buena** ~ willingly; **de mala** ~ reluctantly; **me da la** ~ **de** I feel like, I want to; **tener** ~**s de** to feel like.

ganadería [ganaðe'ria] *nf* (*ganado*) livestock; (*ganado vacuno*) cattle *pl*; (*cría, comercio*) cattle raising.

ganado [ga'naðo] *nm* livestock; ~ **lanar** sheep *pl*; ~ **vacuno** cattle *pl*; ~ **porcino** pigs *pl.*

ganador, a [gana'ðor, a] *a* winning // *nm/f* winner.

ganancia [ga'nanθja] *nf* (*lo ganado*) gain; (*aumento*) increase; (*beneficio*) profit; ~**s** *nfpl* (*ingresos*) earnings; (*beneficios*) profit *sg*, winnings.

ganapán [gana'pan] *nm* (*obrero casual*) odd-job man; (*individuo tosco*) lout.

ganar [ga'nar] *vt* (*obtener*) to get, obtain; (*sacar ventaja*) to gain; (*COM*) to earn; (*DEPORTE, premio*) to win; (*derrotar a*) to beat; (*alcanzar*) to reach // *vi* (*DEPORTE*) to win; ~**se** *vr*: ~**se la vida** to earn one's living.

gancho ['gantʃo] *nm* (*gen*) hook; (*colgador*) hanger.

gandul, a [gan'dul, a] *a, nm/f* good-for-nothing.

ganga ['ganga] *nf* (*cosa buena y barata*) bargain; (*buena situación*) cushy job.

gangrena [gan'grena] *nf* gangrene.

gansada [gan'saða] *nf* (*fam*) stupid thing to do.

ganso, a ['ganso, a] *nm/f* (*ZOOL*) gander/goose; (*fam*) idiot.

ganzúa [gan'θua] *nf* skeleton key // *nm/f* burglar.

gañán [ga'ɲan] *nm* farmhand, farm labourer.

garabato [gara'ßato] *nm* (*gancho*) hook; (*garfio*) grappling iron; (*escritura*) scrawl, scribble; (*fam*) sex appeal.

garaje [ga'raxe] *nm* garage.

garante [ga'rante] *a* responsible // *nm/f* guarantor.

garantía [garan'tia] *nf* guarantee.

garantizar [garanti'θar], **garantir** [garan'tir] *vt* (*hacerse responsable de*) to vouch for; (*asegurar*) to guarantee.

garbanzo [gar'ßanθo] *nm* chickpea.

garbo ['garßo] *nm* grace, elegance; ~**so, a** *a* graceful, elegant.

garfa ['garfa] *nf* claw.

garfio ['garfjo] *nm* grappling iron.

garganta [gar'xanta] *nf* (*interna*) throat; (*externa, de botella*) neck; **gargantilla** *nf* necklace.

gárgara ['garxara] *nf* gargle, gargling.

gárgola ['garxola] *nf* gargoyle.

garita [ga'rita] *nf* cabin, hut; (*MIL*) sentry box; (*de camión*) cab.

garra ['garra] *nf* (*de gato*, *TEC*) claw; (*de ave*) talon; (*fam*) hand, paw (*fam*).

garrafa [ga'rrafa] *nf* carafe, decanter.

garrido, a [ga'rriðo, a] *a* handsome.

garrote [ga'rrote] *nm* (*palo*) stick; (*porra*) cudgel; (*suplicio*) garrotte; (*MED*) tourniquet.

garrulería [garrule'ria] *nf* chatter.

gárrulo, a ['garrulo, a] *a* (*charlatán*) talkative; (*ave*) twittering; (*arroyo*) murmuring.

garzo, a ['garθo, a] *a* blue // *nf* heron.

gas [gas] *nm* gas.

gasa ['gasa] *nf* gauze.

gaseoso, a [gase'oso, a] *a* gassy, fizzy // *nf* lemonade, fizzy drink; (*fam*) pop.

gasolina [gaso'lina] *nf* petrol, gas(oline) (*US*); **gasolinera** *nf* petrol station.

gasómetro [ga'sometro] *nm* gasometer.

gastado, a [gas'taðo, a] *a* (*rendido*) spent; (*raído*) worn, threadbare; (*usado*: *frase etc*) trite.

gastar [gas'tar] *vt* (*dinero, tiempo*) to spend; (*fuerzas*) to use up; (*desperdiciar*) to waste; (*llevar*) to wear; ~**se** *vr* to wear out; (*estropearse*) to waste; ~ **bromas** to crack jokes.

gasto ['gasto] *nm* (*desembolso*) expenditure, spending; (*consumo, uso*) use; ~**s** *nmpl* (*desembolsos*) expenses; (*cargos*) charges, costs.

gatear [gate'ar] *vi* (*andar a gatas*) to go on all fours; (*trepar*) to climb // *vt* to scratch.

gatillo [ga'tiʎo] *nm* (*de arma de fuego*) trigger; (*de dentista*) forceps.

gato, a ['gato, a] *nm/f* cat // *nm* (*TEC*) jack; **andar a** ~**as** to go on all fours.

gatuno, a [ga'tuno, a] *a* feline.

gaucho ['gautʃo] *nm* gaucho.

gaveta [ga'ßeta] *nf* drawer.

gavilla [ga'ßiʎa] *nf* sheaf.

gaviota [ga'ßjota] *nf* seagull.

gay [ge] *a* gay, homosexual.

gayo, a ['gajo, a] *a* gay, merry.

gazapera [gaθa'pera] *nf* (*conejera*) rabbit warren; (*de gente*) den of thieves; **gazapo** *nm* young rabbit; (*fam*) sly fellow.

gazmoño, a [gaθ'moɲo, a], **gazmoñero, a** [gaθmo'ɲero, a] *nm/f* prude; (*pretencioso*) prig; (*hipócrita*) hypocrite.

gazpacho [gaθ'patʃo] *nm* gazpacho, cold vegetable soup.

gelatina [xela'tina] *nf* (*plato*) jelly; (*polvos etc*) gelatine.

gema ['xema] *nf* gem.

gemelo, a [xe'melo, a] *a*, *nm/f* twin; ~**s** *nmpl* (*de camisa*) cufflinks; **G**~**s** (*ASTRO*) Gemini *sg*; ~**s de campo** field glasses.

gemido [xe'miðo] *nm* (*quejido*) moan, groan; (*aullido*) howl.

gemir [xe'mir] *vi* (*quejarse*) to moan, groan; (*aullar*) to howl.

genealogía [xenealo'xia] *nf* genealogy.

generación [xenera'θjon] *nf* generation.

generador [xenera'ðor] *nm* generator.

general [xene'ral] *a* general // *nm* general; **por lo** *o* **en** ~ in general; ~**idad** *nf* generality; **G**~**itat** *nf* Catalan parliament; ~**ización** *nf* generalization; ~**izar** *vt* to generalize; ~**izarse** *vr* to become generalised, spread; ~**mente** *ad* generally.

generar [xene'rar] *vt* to generate.

genérico, a [xe'neriko, a] *a* generic.

género ['xenero] *nm* (*clase*) kind, sort; (*tipo*) type; (*BIO*) genus; (*LING*) gender; (*COM*) material; ~ **humano** human race.

generosidad [xenerosi'ðað] *nf* generosity; **generoso, a** *a* generous.

genial [xe'njal] *a* inspired; (*idea*) brilliant; (*afable*) genial.

genio ['xenjo] *nm* (*carácter*) nature, disposition; (*humor*) temper; (*facultad creadora*) genius; **de mal** ~ bad-tempered.

gente ['xente] *nf* (*personas*) people *pl*; (*raza*) race; (*nación*) nation; (*parientes*) relatives *pl*.

gentil [xen'til] *a* (*elegante*) graceful; (*encantador*) charming; ~**eza** *nf* grace; charm; (*cortesía*) courtesy.

gentío [xen'tio] *nm* crowd, throng.

genuflexión [xenuflek'sjon] *nf* genuflexion.

genuino, a [xe'nwino, a] *a* genuine.

geografía [xeoɤra'fia] *nf* geography.

geología [xeolo'xia] *nf* geology.

geometría [xeome'tria] *nf* geometry.

gerencia [xe'renθja] *nf* management; **gerente** *nm* (*supervisor*) manager; (*jefe*) director.

germen ['xermen] *nm* germ.

germinar [xermi'nar] *vi* to germinate.

gesticulación [xestikula'θjon] *nf* (*ademán*) gesticulation; (*mueca*) grimace.

gestión [xes'tjon] *nf* management; (*diligencia, acción*) negotiation; (*esfuerzo*) effort; **gestionar** *vt* (*lograr*) to try to arrange; (*llevar*) to manage; (*discutir*) to negotiate.

gesto ['xesto] *nm* (*mueca*) grimace; (*ademán*) gesture.

gestoría [xesto'ria] *nf* estate agent's.

Gibraltar [xißral'tar] *nm* Gibraltar.

gigante [xi'ɣante] *a*, *nm/f* giant.

gilipollas [xili'poʎas] *excl* (*fam*) bastard! (*fam*).

gimnasia [xim'nasja] *nf* gymnastics *pl*; **gimnasio** *nm* gymnasium; **gimnásta** *nm/f* gymnast.

gimotear [ximote'ar] *vi* to whine, whimper.

ginebra [xi'neßra] *nf* gin.

ginecólogo, a [xine'koloɤo, a] *nm/f* gynecologist.

gira ['xira] *nf* tour, trip.

girar [xi'rar] *vt* (*dar la vuelta*) to turn (around); (: *rápidamente*) to spin; (*COM*: *cheque*) to draw; (*comerciar*: *letra de cambio*) to issue // *vi* to turn (round); (*rápido*) to spin; (*COM*) to draw.

girasol [xira'sol] *nm* sunflower.
giratorio, a [xira'torjo, a] *a* (*gen*) revolving; (*puente*) swing.
giro ['xiro] *nm* (*movimiento*) turn, revolution; (*LING*) expression; (*COM*) draft; ~ **bancario/postal** money/ postal order.
gitano, a [xi'tano, a] *a, nm/f* gypsy.
glacial [gla'θjal] *a* icy, freezing.
glándula ['glandula] *nf* gland.
globo ['gloβo] *nm* (*esfera*) globe, sphere; (*aerostato, juguete*) balloon.
gloria ['glorja] *nf* glory; **gloriarse** *vr* to boast.
glorieta [glo'rjeta] *nf* (*de jardín*) bower, arbour; (*plazoleta*) roundabout.
glorificar [glorifi'kar] *vt* (*enaltecer*) to glorify, praise; ~**se** *vr*: ~**se de** to boast of.
glorioso, a [glo'rjoso, a] *a* glorious.
glosa ['glosa] *nf* comment; **glosar** *vt* (*comentar*) to comment on; (*fig*) to criticize.
glosario [glo'sarjo] *nm* glossary.
glotón, ona [glo'ton, ona] *a* gluttonous, greedy; **glotonería** *nf* gluttony, greed.
gobernación [goβerna'θjon] *nf* government, governing; **gobernador, a** *a* governing // *nm* governor; **gobernante** *a* governing.
gobernar [goβer'nar] *vt* (*dirigir*) to guide, direct; (*regir*) to rule, govern // *vi* to govern; (*NAUT*) to steer.
gobierno [go'βjerno] *nm* (*POL*) government; (*dirección*) guidance, direction; (*NAUT*) steering.
goce ['goθe] *nm* enjoyment.
gol [gol] *nm* goal.
gola ['gola] *nf* gullet; (*garganta*) throat.
golf [golf] *nm* golf.
golfa ['golfa] *nf* (*fam*) tart, whore.
golfo ['golfo] *nm* (*GEO*) gulf; (*fam*: *niño*) urchin; (*gamberro*) lout.
golondrina [golon'drina] *nf* swallow.
golosina [golo'sina] *nf* (*gen*) titbit; (*dulce*) sweet; **goloso, a** *a* sweet-toothed.
golpe ['golpe] *nm* (*gen*) blow; (*de puño*) punch; (*de mano*) smack; (*de corazón*) beat; (*de remo*) stroke; (*fig*: *choque*) clash; **no dar** ~ to be bone idle; **de un** ~ with one blow; **de** ~ suddenly; ~ **de estado** coup d'état; **golpear** *vt, vi* to strike, knock; (*asestar*) to beat; (*de puño*) to punch; (*golpetear*) to tap.
goma ['goma] *nf* (*caucho*) rubber; (*elástico*) elastic; ~ **espuma** foam rubber; ~ **de pegar** gum, glue.
gomita [go'mita] *nf* elastic band.
góndola ['gondola] *nf* (*barco*) gondola; (*de tren*) goods wagon.
gordo, a [gorðo, a] *a* (*gen*) fat; (*persona*) plump; (*tela*) coarse; (*fam*) enormous; **el premio** ~ (*en lotería*) first prize; **gordura** *nf* fat; (*corpulencia*) fatness, stoutness.
gorgojo [gor'xoxo] *nm* (*insecto*) grub; (*fam*) runt.

gorila [go'rila] *nm* gorilla.
gorjear [gorxe'ar] *vi* to twitter, chirp; **gorjeo** *nm* twittering, chirping.
gorra ['gorra] *nf* (*gen*) cap; (*de niño*) bonnet; (*militar*) bearskin // *nm* scrounger.
gorrión [go'rrjon] *nm* sparrow.
gorro ['gorro] *nm* (*gen*) cap; (*de niño, mujer*) bonnet.
gorrón [go'rron] *nm* pebble.
gota ['gota] *nf* (*gen*) drop; (*de sudor*) bead; (*MED*) gout; **gotear** *vi* to drip; (*lloviznar*) to drizzle; **gotera** *nf* leak.
gótico, a ['gotiko, a] *a* Gothic.
gozar [go'θar] *vi* to enjoy o.s.; ~ **de** (*disfrutar*) to enjoy; (*poseer*) to possess.
gozne ['goθne] *nm* hinge.
gozo ['goθo] *nm* (*alegría*) joy; (*placer*) pleasure; ~**so, a** *a* joyous, joyful.
grabación [graβa'θjon] *nf* recording.
grabado [gra'βaðo] *nm* print, engraving; **grabador** *nm* engraver.
grabadora [graβa'ðora] *nf* tape-recorder.
grabar [gra'βar] *vt* to engrave; (*discos, cintas*) to record.
gracejo [gra'θexo] *nm* (*humor*) wit, humour; (*elegancia*) grace.
gracia ['graθja] *nf* (*encanto*) grace, gracefulness; (*chiste*) joke; (*humor*) humour, wit; ¡~**s!** thanks!; ¡**muchas** ~**s!** thanks very much!; ~**s a** thanks to; **tener** ~ to be funny; (*ser divertido*) to be enjoyable; **no me hace** ~ I am not keen; **gracioso, a** *a* (*divertido*) funny, amusing; (*cómico*) comical // *nm* (*TEATRO*) comic character.
grada ['graða] *nf* (*de escalera*) step; (*de anfiteatro*) tier, row.
gradación [graða'θjon] *nf* gradation.
gradería [graðe'ria] *nf* (*gradas*) (flight of) steps *pl*; (*de anfiteatro*) tiers *pl*, rows *pl*; ~ **cubierta** covered stand.
grado ['graðo] *nm* degree; (*de aceite, vino*) grade; (*grada*) step; (*MIL*) rank; **de buen** ~ willingly.
graduación [graðwa'θjon] *nf* (*del alcohol*) proof, strength; (*ESCOL*) graduation.
gradual [gra'ðwal] *a* gradual.
graduar [gra'ðwar] *vt* (*gen*) to graduate; (*clasificar*) to grade; (*MIL*) to commission; ~**se** *vr* to graduate.
gráfico, a ['grafiko, a] *a* graphic // *nm* diagram // *nf* graph.
grajo ['graxo] *nm* rook.
Gral *abr de* **General.**
gramática [gra'matika] *nf* grammar.
gramo ['gramo] *nm* gramme.
gran [gran] *a ver* **grande.**
grana ['grana] *nf* (*BOT*) seedling; (*ZOOL*) cochineal; (*color, tela*) scarlet.
Granada [gra'naða] *n* Granada.
granada [gra'naða] *nf* pomegranate; (*MIL*) grenade; **granadina** *nf* grenadine.
granadino, a [grana'ðino, a] *a* of Granada // *nm/f* native *or* inhabitant of Granada.

granado, a [gra'naðo, a] a choice, select // nm pomegranate tree.

granar [gra'nar] vi to seed.

granate [gra'nate] nm garnet.

Gran Bretaña [granbre'taɲa] nf Great Britain.

grande ['grande], gran [gran] a (de tamaño) big, large; (alto) tall; (distinguido) great; (impresionante) grand // nm grandee; grandeza nf greatness.

grandioso, a [gran'djoso, a] a magnificent, grand.

grandor [gran'dor] nm size.

granel [gra'nel]: a ~ ad in abundance; (COM) in bulk.

granero [gra'nero] nm granary, barn.

granito [gra'nito] nm (AGR) small grain; (roca) granite; (MED) pimple.

granizado [grani'θaðo] nm iced drink; granizar vi to hail; granizo nm hail.

granja ['granxa] nf (gen) farm; (lechería) dairy; (café) milk bar.

granjear [granxe'ar] vt (cobrar) to earn; (ganar) to win; (avanzar) to gain; granjería nf (COM) profit; (AGR) farming.

grano ['grano] nm grain; (semilla) seed; (baya) berry; (MED) pimple; ~s nmpl cereals.

granoso, a [gra'noso, a] a granulated.

granuja [gra'nuxa] nf grape seed // nm rogue; (golfillo) urchin.

grapa ['grapa] nf staple; (TEC) clamp.

grasa ['grasa] nf (gen) grease; (de cocina) fat, lard; (sebo) suet; (mugre) filth; (escoria) dross; grasiento, a a greasy; (de aceite) oily.

gratificación [gratifika'θjon] nf (propina) tip; (bono) bonus; (recompensa) reward; gratificar vt to tip; to reward.

gratis ['gratis] ad free.

gratitud [grati'tuð] nf gratitude.

grato, a ['grato, a] a (agradable) pleasant, agreeable; (bienvenido) welcome.

gratuito, a [gra'twito, a] a (gratis) free; (sin razón) gratuitous.

gravamen [gra'ßamen] nm (carga) burden; (impuesto) tax.

gravar [gra'ßar] vt to burden.

grave ['graße] a heavy; (serio) grave, serious; ~ dad nf gravity.

grávido, a ['graßiðo, a] a (preñada) pregnant; (lleno, cargado) full.

gravitación [graßita'θjon] nf gravitation; gravitar vi to gravitate; gravitar sobre to rest on.

gravoso, a [gra'ßoso, a] a (pesado) burdensome; (costoso) costly.

graznar [graθ'nar] vi (cuervo) to squawk; (pato) to quack; (hablar ronco) to croak; graznido nm squawk; croak.

Grecia ['greθja] nf Greece.

greguería [greɣe'ria] nf hubbub.

gremio ['gremjo] nm (sindicato) trade union; (asociación) professional association.

greña ['greɲa] nf (cabellos) shock of hair;

(maraña) tangle; greñudo, a a (persona) dishevelled; (hair) tangled.

gresca ['greska] nf uproar.

grey [grei] nf flock.

griego, a ['grjexo, a] a, nm/f Greek.

grieta ['grjeta] nf crack; grietarse vr = agrietarse.

grifo, a ['grifo, a] a curly, kinky // nm tap.

grillo ['griʎo] nm (ZOOL) cricket; (BOT) shoot; ~s nmpl shackles, irons.

gripe ['gripe] nf flu, influenza.

gris [gris] a (color) grey.

grita ['grita] nf uproar; gritar vt, vi to shout, yell; grito nm shout, yell; (de horror) scream; a grito pelado at the top of one's voice.

grosella [gro'seʎa] nf (red)currant; ~ negra blackcurrant.

grosería [grose'ria] nf (actitud) rudeness; (comentario) vulgar comment; grosero, a a (poco cortés) rude; (ordinario) vulgar, crude.

grosor [gro'sor] nm thickness.

grotesco, a [gro'tesko, a] a grotesque.

grúa ['grua] nf (TEC) crane; (de petróleo) derrick.

grueso, a ['grweso, a] a thick; (voluminoso) stout // nm bulk // nf gross; el ~ de the bulk of.

grulla ['gruʎa] nf crane.

gruñido [gru'ɲiðo] nm grunt; (fig) grumble; gruñir vi (animal) to growl; (fam) to grumble.

grupa ['grupa] nf (ZOOL) rump.

grupo ['grupo] nm group; (TEC) unit, set.

gruta ['gruta] nf grotto.

guadamecí [gwaðame'θi], guadamecil [gwaðame'θil] nm embossed leather.

guadaña [gwa'ðaɲa] nf scythe; guadañar vt to scythe, mow.

guano ['gwano] nm (AM) guano.

guante ['gwante] nm glove.

guapo, a ['gwapo, a] a good-looking, attractive; (hombre) handsome; (elegante) smart // nm lover, gallant.

guarda ['gwarða] nm guard, keeper // nf guarding; (custodia) custody; ~ bosque nm gamekeeper; ~ costas nm inv coastguard vessel; ~ dor, a a protective // nm/f guardian, protector; ~ espaldas nm/f inv bodyguard; ~ polvo nm dust cover; (de niño) smock; (para el trabajo) overalls pl; guardar vt (gen) to keep; (vigilar) to guard, watch over; (dinero: ahorrar) to save, put by; guardarse vr (preservarse) to protect o.s.; (evitar) to avoid; guardarropa nm (armario) wardrobe; (en establecimiento público) cloakroom.

guardería [gwarðe'ria] nf (children's) nursery.

guardia ['gwarðja] nf (MIL) guard; (cuidado) care, custody // nm guard; (policía) policeman; estar de ~ to be on guard; montar ~ to mount guard; G ~ Civil Civil Guard; G ~ Nacional police; ~ urbano traffic policeman.

guardián, ana [gwar'ðjan, ana] *nm/f* (*gen*) guardian, keeper; (*sereno*) watchman.

guardilla [gwar'ðiʎa] *nf* attic.

guarecer [gware'θer] *vt* (*proteger*) to protect; (*abrigar*) to shelter; ~**se** *vr* to take refuge.

guarida [gwa'riða] *nf* (*de animal*) den, lair; (*refugio*) refuge.

guarismo [gwa'rismo] *nm* figure, number.

guarnecer [gwarne'θer] *vt* (*equipar*) to provide; (*adornar*) to adorn; (*TEC*) to reinforce; **guarnición** *nf* (*de vestimenta*) trimming; (*de piedra*) mount; (*CULIN*) garnish; (*arneses*) harness; (*MIL*) garrison.

guarro, a ['gwarro, a] *nm/f* pig.

guasa ['gwasa] *nf* joke; **guasón, ona** *a* witty; (*bromista*) joking // *nm/f* wit; joker.

Guatemala [gwate'mala] *nf* Guatemala.

gubernativo, a [guβerna'tiβo, a] *a* governmental.

guedeja [ge'ðexa] *nf* long hair; (*de león*) mane.

guerra ['gerra] *nf* war; (*pelea*) struggle; ~ **fría** cold war; **dar** ~ to annoy; **guerrear** *vi* to wage war; **guerrero, a** *a* fighting; (*carácter*) warlike // *nm/f* warrior.

guerrilla [ge'rriʎa] *nf* guerrilla warfare; (*tropas*) guerrilla band *or* group.

guía ['gia] *nm/f* guide // *nf* (*libro*) guidebook; ~ **de ferrocarriles** railway timetable; ~ **de teléfonos** telephone directory; **guiar** *vt* to guide, direct; (*AUT*) to steer; **guiarse** *vr*: **guiarse por** to be guided by.

guija ['gixa] *nf*, **guijarro** [gi'xarro] *nm* pebble; (*camino*) cobblestone.

guijo ['gixo] *nm* gravel; (*de playa*) shingle.

guillotina [giʎo'tina] *nf* guillotine.

guinda ['ginda] *nf* morello cherry.

guindar [gin'dar] *vt* to hoist.

guindilla [gin'diʎa] *nf* Guinea pepper.

guiñapo [gi'ɲapo] *nm* (*harapo*) rag; (*persona*) reprobate, rogue.

guiñar [gi'ɲar] *vi* to wink; (*parpadear*) to blink.

guión [gi'on] *nm* (*conductor*) leader; (*LING*) hyphen, dash; (*CINE*) script; **guionista** *nm/f* scriptwriter.

guirnalda [gir'nalda] *nf* garland.

guisa ['gisa] *nf*: **a** ~ **de** as, like, in the way of.

guisado [gi'saðo] *nm* stew.

guisante [gi'sante] *nm* pea; ~ **de olor** sweet pea.

guisar [gi'sar] *vt, vi* to cook; **guiso** *nm* cooked dish.

guita ['gita] *nf* twine.

guitarra [gi'tarra] *nf* guitar.

gula ['gula] *nf* gluttony, greed.

gusano [gu'sano] *nm* maggot; (*lombriz*) earthworm; ~ **de luz** glow-worm; ~ **de seda** silk-worm.

gustar [gus'tar] *vt* to taste, sample // *vi* to please, be pleasing; ~ **de algo** to like *or*

enjoy sth; **me gustan las uvas** I like grapes.

gusto ['gusto] *nm* (*sentido, sabor*) taste; (*placer*) pleasure; **tiene** ~ **a menta** it tastes of mint; **tener buen** ~ to have good taste; **sentirse a** ~ to feel at ease; **mucho** ~ **en conocerle** pleased to meet you; **el** ~ **es mío** the pleasure is mine; **con** ~ willingly, gladly; ~**so, a** *a* (*sabroso*) tasty; (*agradable*) pleasant.

gutural [gutu'ral] *a* guttural.

H

ha *vb ver* **haber.**

haba ['aβa] *nf* bean.

Habana [a'βana] *nf*: **la** ~ Havana.

habano [a'βano] *nm* Havana cigar.

haber [a'βer] *vb auxiliar* to have; **de** ~**lo sabido** if I had known (it); ~ **de** to have to // *vb impersonal*: **hay** there is/are; **hay que** it is necessary to, one must; **¿qué hay?** how's it going?; **no hay de qué** don't mention it // *nm* (*ingreso*) income; (*COM: crédito*) credit; ~**es** *nmpl* assets.

habichuela [aβi'tʃwela] *nf* kidney bean.

hábil ['aβil] *a* (*listo*) clever, smart; (*capaz*) fit, capable; (*experto*) expert; **día** ~ working day; **habilidad** *nf* (*gen*) skill, ability; (*inteligencia*) cleverness.

habilitación [aβilita'θjon] *nf* qualification; (*colocación de muebles*) fitting out; (*financiamiento*) financing.

habilitar [aβili'tar] *vt* (*capacitar*) to enable; (*dar instrumentos*) to equip; (*financiar*) to finance.

hábilmente [aβil'mente] *ad* skilfully, expertly.

habitación [aβita'θjon] *nf* (*cuarto*) room; (*casa*) dwelling, abode; (*BIO: morada*) habitat; ~ **sencilla** *o* **particular** single room; ~ **doble** *o* **matrimonial** double room.

habitante [aβi'tante] *nm/f* inhabitant.

habitar [aβi'tar] *vt* (*residir en*) to inhabit; (*ocupar*) to occupy // *vi* to live.

hábito ['aβito] *nm* habit; **habitual** *a* habitual.

habituar [aβi'twar] *vt* to accustom; ~**se** *vr*: ~**se a** to get used to.

habla ['aβla] *nf* (*capacidad de hablar*) speech; (*idioma*) language; (*dialecto*) dialect; **perder el** ~ to become speechless; **de** ~ **francesa** French-speaking; **estar al** ~ to be in contact; **¡González al** ~! Gonzalez speaking!

hablador, a [aβla'ðor, a] *a* talkative // *nm/f* chatterbox.

habladuría [aβlaðu'ria] *nf* rumour; (*sarcasmo*) sarcastic comment; ~**s** *nfpl* gossip *sg*.

hablar [a'βlar] *vt* to speak, talk // *vi* to speak; ~**se** *vr* to speak to each other; ~ **con** to speak to; ~ **de** to speak of *or* about; **'se habla inglés'** 'English spoken here'.

hablilla [a'βliʎa] *nf* story, rumour.

habré *etc vb ver* **haber.**

hacedero, a [aθe'ðero, a] *a* feasible.

hacedor, a [aθe'ðor, a] *nm/f* maker.

hacendoso, a [aθen'doso, a] *a* industrious.

hacer [a'θer] *vt* (*gen*) to make; (*crear*) to create; (*TEC*) to manufacture; (*preparar*) to prepare; (*ejecutar*) to do, execute; (*obligar*) to force, compel // *vi* (*comportarse*) to act, behave; (*disimular*) to pretend; (*importar*) to be important, matter; (*convenir, ser apto*) to be suitable; ~ **se** *vr* (*fabricarse*) to be made, be done; (*volverse*) to become; (*acostumbrarse a*) to get used to; ~ **la maleta** to pack; ~ **una pregunta** to ask a question; ~ **una visita** to visit; ~ **bien/mal** to act rightly/wrongly; **hace frío/calor** it's cold/hot; **hace dos años** two years ago; **hace poco** a little while ago; ~ **el malo** (*TEATRO*) to play (the part of) the villain; **¿qué** ~? what is to be done?; ~ **como que** *o* **como si** to act as though *or* as if; ~ **de** to act as; **me hice un traje** I had a suit made; ~**se el sordo** to turn a deaf ear; ~**se viejo** to grow old; ~**se con algo** to get hold of sth; ~**se a un lado** to stand aside.

hacia ['aθja] *prep* (*en dirección de*) towards; (*cerca de*) near; ~ **arriba/abajo** up(wards)/down(wards); ~ **mediodía** about noon.

hacienda [a'θjenda] *nf* (*propiedad*) property; (*estancia*) farm, ranch; (*AM*) plantation; ~ **pública** public finance; **(Ministerio de) H** ~ Treasury, Exchequer.

hacina [a'θina] *nf* pile, stack.

hacha ['atʃa] *nf* axe; (*antorcha*) torch.

hache ['atʃe] *nf* (the letter) H.

hada ['aða] *nf* fairy.

hago *etc vb ver* **hacer.**

Haití [ai'ti] *nm* Haiti.

halagar [ala'ɣar] *vt* (*mostrar afecto*) to show affection to; (*lisonjear*) to flatter.

halago [a'laɣo] *nm* pleasure, delight; (*atractivo*) attraction; (*adulación*) flattery; **halagüeño, a** *a* pleasing; attractive; flattering.

halcón [al'kon] *nm* falcon, hawk.

hálito ['alito] *nm* breath.

hallar [a'ʎar] *vt* (*gen*) to find; (*descubrir*) to discover; (*toparse con*) to run up against; ~ **se** *vr* to be (situated); **hallazgo** *nm* discovery; (*cosa*) find.

hamaca [a'maka] *nf* hammock; ~ **plegable** deckchair.

hambre ['ambre] *nf* hunger; (*carencia*) famine; (*fig*) longing; **tener** ~ to be hungry; ~**ar** *vi, vt* to starve; **hambriento, a** *a* hungry, starving.

hamburguesa [ambur'ɣesa] *nf* hamburger.

hampa ['ampa] *nf* underworld; **hampón** *nm* tough.

han *vb ver* **haber.**

haragán, ana [ara'ɣan, ana] *a, nm/f* good-

for-nothing; **haraganear** *vi* to idle, loaf about.

harapiento, a [ara'pjento, a] *a* tattered, in rags; **harapo** *nm* rag.

haré *etc vb ver* **hacer.**

harina [a'rina] *nf* flour; (*polvo*) powder; **harinero, a** *nm/f* flour merchant; **harinoso, a** *a* floury.

hartar [ar'tar] *vt* to satiate, glut; (*fig*) to tire, sicken; ~ **se** *vr* (*de comida*) to fill o.s., gorge o.s.; (*cansarse*) to get fed up (*de* with); **hartazgo** *nm* surfeit, glut; **harto, a** (*lleno*) full; (*cansado*) fed up // *ad* (*bastante*) enough; (*muy*) very; **estar harto de** to be fed up with; **hartura** *nf* (*exceso*) surfeit; (*abundancia*) abundance; (*satisfacción*) satisfaction.

has *vb ver* **haber.**

hasta ['asta] *ad* even // *prep* (*alcanzando a*) as far as, up/down to; (*de tiempo: a tal hora*) till, until; (*antes de*) before // *conj*: ~ **que** until; ~ **luego/la vista** see you soon.

hastiar [as'tjar] *vt* (*gen*) to weary; (*aburrir*) to bore; (*asquear*) to disgust; ~**se** *vr*: ~**se de** to get fed up with; **hastío** *nm* weariness; boredom; disgust.

hato ['ato], **hatillo** [a'tiʎo] *nm* belongings *pl*, kit; (*víveres*) provisions *pl*; (*banda*) gang, group; (*montón*) bundle, heap.

hay *vb ver* **haber.**

Haya ['aja] *nf*: **la** ~ The Hague.

haya *etc vb ver* **haber** // ['aja] *nf* beech tree; **hayal, hayedo** *nm* beech grove.

haz [aθ] *vb ver* **hacer** // *nm* bundle, bunch; (*rayo: de luz*) beam.

hazaña [a'θaɲa] *nf* feat, exploit.

hazmerreír [aθmerre'ir] *nm* laughing stock.

he *vb ver* **haber.**

hebilla [e'ßiʎa] *nf* buckle, clasp.

hebra ['eßra] *nf* thread; (*BOT: fibra*) fibre, grain; **tabaco de** ~ loose tobacco.

hebreo, a [e'ßreo, a] *a, nm/f* Hebrew // *nm* (*lengua*) Hebrew.

hectárea [ek'tarea] *nf* hectare.

hechizar [etʃi'θar] *vt* to cast a spell on, bewitch.

hechizo, a [e'tʃiθo, a] *a* (*gen*) false, artificial; (*removible*) detachable // *nm* witchcraft, magic; (*acto de magía*) spell, charm.

hecho, a ['etʃo, a] *pp de* **hacer** // *a* complete; (*maduro*) mature; (*costura*) ready-to-wear // *nm* deed, act; (*dato*) fact; (*cuestión*) matter; (*suceso*) event // *excl* agreed!, done!; **¡bien** ~! well done!; **de** ~ in fact, as a matter of fact.

hechura [e'tʃura] *nf* making, creation; (*producto*) product; (*forma*) form, shape; (*de persona*) build; (*TEC*) craftsmanship; ~**s** *nfpl* (*COSTURA*) cost of making up *sg*.

heder [e'ðer] *vi* to stink, smell; (*fig*) to be unbearable.

hediondez [eðjon'deθ] *nf* stench, stink; (*cosa*) stinking thing; **hediondo, a** *a* stinking; (*insoportable*) repulsive, unbearable.

hedor [e'ðor] *nm* stench.

helado, a [e'laðo, a] *a* frozen; (*glacial*) icy; (*fig*) chilly, cold // *nm* ice-cream // *nf* frost.

helar [e'lar] *vt* to freeze, ice (up); (*dejar atónito*) to amaze; (*desalentar*) to discourage // *vi*, ~**se** *vr* to freeze.

hélice ['eliθe] *nf* spiral; (*TEC*) propeller.

helicóptero [eli'koptero] *nm* helicopter.

hembra ['embra] *nf* (*BOT, ZOOL*) female; (*mujer*) woman; (*TEC*) nut.

hemorragia [emo'rraxja] *nf* haemorrhage.

hemorroides [emo'rroiðes] *nfpl* haemorrhoids.

hemos *vb ver* **haber.**

henchir [en'tʃir] *vt* to fill, stuff; ~**se** *vr* (*llenarse de comida*) to stuff o.s. (with food); (*inflarse*) to swell (up).

hender [en'der] *vt* to cleave, split; **hendidura** *nf* crack, split; (*GEO*) fissure.

heno ['eno] *nm* hay.

herbicida [erßi'θiða] *nm* weed-killer.

heredad [ere'ðað] *nf* landed property; (*granja*) farm.

heredar [ere'ðar] *vt* to inherit; **heredero, a** *nm/f* heir/heiress.

hereje [e'rexe] *nm/f* heretic; **herejía** *nf* heresy.

herencia [e'renθja] *nf* inheritance.

herido, a [e'riðo, a] *a* injured, wounded // *nm/f* casualty // *nf* wound, injury; (*insulto*) insult.

herir [e'rir] *vt* to wound, injure; (*fig*) to offend.

hermanar [erma'nar] *vt* to match; (*unir*) to join.

hermandad [erman'dað] *nf* brotherhood.

hermano, a [er'mano, a] *nm/f* brother/sister; ~ **gemelo** twin brother; ~ **político** brother-in-law; ~**a política** sister-in-law.

hermético, a [er'metiko, a] *a* hermetic; (*fig*) watertight.

hermoso, a [er'moso, a] *a* beautiful, lovely; (*estupendo*) splendid; (*guapo*) handsome; **hermosura** *nf* beauty.

héroe ['eroe] *nm* hero; **heroico, a** *a* heroic.

heroína [ero'ina] *nf* (*mujer*) heroine; (*droga*) heroin.

heroísmo [ero'ismo] *nm* heroism.

herrador [erra'ðor] *nm* blacksmith; **herradura** *nf*: **curva en herradura** hairpin bend.

herramienta [erra'mjenta] *nf* tool; (*conjunto*) set of tools.

herrería [erre'ria] *nf* smithy; (*TEC*) forge; **herrero** *nm* blacksmith.

herrumbre [e'rrumbre] *nf* rust.

hervidero [erßi'ðero] *nm* (*burbujeo*) boiling, seething; (*fuente*) hot spring.

hervir [er'ßir] *vi* (*gen*) to boil; (*burbujear*) to bubble; (*fig*): ~ **de** to teem with; ~ **a**

fuego lento to simmer; **hervor** *nm* boiling; (*fig*) ardour, fervour.

heterogéneo, a [etero'xeneo, a] *a* heterogeneous.

heterosexual [eterosek'swal] *a* heterosexual.

hice *etc vb ver* **hacer.**

hidráulico, a [i'ðrauliko, a] *a* hydraulic // *nf* hydraulics *sg*.

hidro... [iðro] *pref* hydro..., water-...; ~**ala** *nf* hovercraft; ~**avión** *nm* seaplane; ~**eléctrico, a** *a* hydroelectric; ~**fobia** *nf* hydrophobia, rabies; **hidrófugo, a** *a* damp-proof; **hidrógeno** *nm* hydrogen.

hiedra ['jeðra] *nf* ivy.

hiel [jel] *nf* gall, bile; (*fig*) bitterness.

hiela *etc vb ver* **helar.**

hielo ['jelo] *nm* (*gen*) ice; (*escarza*) frost; (*fig*) coldness, reserve.

hiena ['jena] *nf* hyena.

hierba ['jerßa] *nf* (*BOT*) grass; (*MED*) herb; **mala** ~ weed; (*fig*) evil influence; ~**buena** *nf* mint.

hierro ['jerro] *nm* (*metal*) iron; (*objeto*) iron object; (*herramienta*) tool; ~ **acanalado** corrugated iron; ~ **colado** *o* **fundido** cast iron.

hígado ['ixaðo] *nm* liver.

higiene [i'xjene] *nf* hygiene; **higiénico, a** *a* hygienic.

higo ['ixo] *nm* fig; ~ **paso** *o* **seco** dried fig; **higuera** *nf* fig tree.

hijastro, a [i'xastro, a] *nm/f* stepson/daughter.

hijo, a ['ixo, a] *nm/f* son/daughter, child; ~**s** *nmpl* children, sons and daughters; ~ **de papá/mamá** daddy's/mummy's boy; ~ **de puta** bastard, son of a bitch.

hilado, a [i'laðo, a] *a* spun // *nm* yarn.

hilandero, a [ilan'dero, a] *nm/f* spinner.

hilar [i'lar] *vt* to spin; ~ **delgado** to split hairs.

hilera [i'lera] *nf* row, file.

hilo ['ilo] *nm* (*gen*) thread; (*BOT*) fibre; (*metal*) wire; (*de agua*) trickle, thin stream; (*de luz*) beam, ray.

hilvanar [ilßa'nar] *vt* to tack; (*fig*) to do hurriedly.

Himalayas [ima'lajas] *nfpl*: **las** ~ the Himalayas.

himno ['imno] *nm* hymn; ~ **nacional** national anthem.

hincapié [inka'pje] *nm*: **hacer** ~ **en** to emphasize.

hincar [in'kar] *vt* to drive (in), thrust (in); ~**se** *vr*: ~**se de rodillas** to kneel down.

hinchado, a [in'tʃaðo, a] *a* (*gen*) swollen; (*persona*) pompous.

hinchar [in'tʃar] *vt* (*gen*) to swell; (*inflar*) to blow up, inflate; (*fig*) to exaggerate; ~**se** *vr* (*inflarse*) to swell up; (*fam: llenarse*) to stuff o.s.; **hinchazón** *nf* (*MED*) swelling; (*altivez*) arrogance.

hinojo [i'noxo] *nm* fennel.

hipar [i'par] *vi* to hiccup; (*perro*) to pant.

hipnotismo [ipno'tismo] *nm* hypnotism; **hipnotizar** *vt* to hypnotize.
hipo ['ipo] *nm* hiccups *pl.*
hipocresía [ipokre'sia] *nf* hypocrisy; **hipócrita** *a* hypocritical // *nm/f* hypocrite.
hipódromo [i'poðromo] *nm* racetrack.
hipopótamo [ipo'potamo] *nm* hippopotamus.
hipoteca [ipo'teka] *nf* mortgage.
hipótesis [i'potesis] *nf* hypothesis.
hiriente [i'rjente] *a* offensive, cutting.
hirsuto, a [ir'suto, a] *a* hairy; (*fig*) rough.
hispánico, a [is'paniko, a] *a* Hispanic.
hispano, a [is'pano, a] *a* Hispanic, Spanish, Hispano-; **H~américa** *nf* Spanish *or* Latin America; **~americano, a** *a, nm/f* Spanish *or* Latin American.
histeria [is'terja] *nf* hysteria.
historia [is'torja] *nf* (*gen*) history; (*cuento*) story, tale; **~s** *nfpl* (*chismes*) gossip *sg*; **dejarse de ~s** to come to the point; **pasar a la ~** to go down in history; **~dor, a** *nm/f* historian; **historiar** *vt* to chronicle, write the history of; **histórico, a** *a* historical; (*fig*) historic.
historieta [isto'rjeta] *nf* tale, anecdote; (*dibujos*) strip cartoon.
hito ['ito] *nm* (*gen*) landmark; (*objetivo*) goal, target.
hizo *vb ver* **hacer.**
hocico [o'θiko] *nm* snout; (*fig*) grimace; **caer** *o* **dar de ~s** to fall on one's face.
hockey ['xoki] *nm* hockey; **~ sobre patines** *o* **hielo** ice hockey.
hogar [o'ɣar] *nm* fireplace, hearth; (*casa*) home; (*vida familiar*) home life; **~eño, a** *a* home; (*persona*) home-loving.
hoguera [o'ɣera] *nf* (*gen*) bonfire; (*llamas*) blaze.
hoja ['oxa] *nf* (*gen*) leaf; (*de flor*) petal; (*de papel*) sheet; (*página*) page; **~ de afeitar** razor blade; **~ de estaño** tinfoil.
hojalata [oxa'lata] *nf* tin(plate).
hojear [oxe'ar] *vt* to leaf through, turn the pages of.
hola ['ola] *excl* hello!
Holanda [o'landa] *nf* Holland; **holandés, esa** *a* Dutch // *nm/f* Dutchman/woman // *nm* (*lengua*) Dutch.
holgado, a [ol'ɣaðo, a] *a* loose, baggy; (*libre*) free; (*desempleado*) idle; (*rico*) well-to-do.
holganza [ol'ɣanθa] *nf* (*ocio*) leisure; (*pereza*) idleness; (*diversión*) amusement.
holgar [ol'ɣar] *vi* (*descansar*) to rest; (*sobrar*) to be superfluous; **~se** *vr* to enjoy o.s.; **huelga decir que** it goes without saying that.
holgazán, ana [olɣa'θan, ana] *a* idle, lazy // *nm/f* loafer.
holgura [ol'ɣura] *nf* looseness, bagginess; (*TEC*) play, free movement; (*vida*) comfortable living, luxury.
hollar [o'ʎar] *vt* to tread (on), trample.
hollín [o'ʎin] *nm* soot.
hombradía [ombra'ðia] *nf* manliness.

hombre ['ombre] *nm* (*gen*) man(kind); (*uno*) man // *excl* (*claro*) of course!; (*para énfasis*) man, old boy; (*sorpresa*) you don't say!; **~ de negocios** businessman; **~-rana** frogman; **~ de pro** *o* **de provecho** honest man.
hombrera [om'brera] *nf* shoulder strap.
hombro ['ombro] *nm* shoulder.
hombruno, a [om'bruno, a] *a* mannish.
homenaje [ome'naxe] *nm* (*gen*) homage; (*lealtad*) allegiance; (*tributo*) tribute.
homicida [omi'θiða] *a* homicidal // *nm/f* murderer; **homicidio** *nm* murder, homicide.
homosexual [omosek'swal] *a, nm/f* homosexual.
hondo, a ['ondo, a] *a* deep; (*profundo*) low // *nm* depth(s) (*pl*); **~nada** *nf* hollow, depression; (*cañón*) ravine; (*GEO*) lowland; **hondura** *nf* depth, profundity.
Honduras [on'duras] *nf* Honduras.
hondureño, a [ondu'repo, a] *a, nm/f* Honduran.
honestidad [onesti'ðað] *nf* purity, chastity; (*decencia*) decency; **honesto, a** *a* chaste; decent, honest; (*justo*) just.
hongo ['ongo] *nm* (*BOT. gen*) fungus; (: *comestible*) mushroom; (: *venenoso*) toadstool.
honor [o'nor] *nm* (*gen*) honour; (*gloria*) glory; **en ~ a la verdad** to be fair; **~able** *a* honourable.
honorario, a [ono'rarjo, a] *a* honorary; **~s** *nmpl* fees.
honra ['onra] *nf* (*gen*) honour; (*nombre*) reputation; **~dez** *nf* honesty; (*de persona*) integrity; **~do, a** *a* honest, upright.
honrar [on'rar] *vt* to honour; **~se** *vr*: **~se con algo/de hacer algo** to be honoured by/to do sth.
honroso, a [on'roso, a] *a* (*honrado*) honourable; (*respetado*) respectable.
hora ['ora] *nf* (*gen*) time; (*específica*) hour; **¿qué ~ es?** what time is it?; **¿a qué ~?** at what time?; **media ~** half an hour; **a la ~ de recreo** at playtime; **a primera ~** first thing (in the morning); **a última ~** at the last moment; **en las altas ~s** in the small hours; **¡a buena ~!** it's high time!; **dar la ~** to strike the hour; **~s de oficina/de trabajo** office/working hours; **~s de visita** visiting times; **~s extras** *o* **extraordinarias** overtime *sg*; **~s punta** rush hours.
horadar [ora'ðar] *vt* to drill, bore.
horario, a [o'rarjo, a] *a* hourly, hour *cpd* // *nm* timetable.
horca ['orka] *nf* gallows *sg.*
horcajadas [orka'xaðas]: **a ~** *ad* astride.
horda ['orða] *nf* horde.
horizontal [oriθon'tal] *a* horizontal; **horizonte** *nm* horizon.
horma ['orma] *nf* mould.
hormiga [or'miɣa] *nf* ant; **~s** *nfpl* (*MED*) pins and needles.
hormigón [ormi'ɣon] *nm* concrete; **~**

armado/pretensado reinforced/pre-stressed concrete.

hormigueo [ormi'ɣeo] *nm* (*comezón*) itch; (*fig*) uneasiness; (*amontonamiento*) swarming.

hormona [or'mona] *nf* hormone.

hornillo [or'niʎo] *nm* small furnace; (*cocina*) portable stove.

horno ['orno] *nm* (*CULIN*) oven; (*TEC*) furnace; **alto** ~ blast furnace.

horóscopo [o'roskopo] *nm* horoscope.

horquilla [or'kiʎa] *nf* hairpin; (*AGR*) pitchfork.

horrendo, a [o'rrendo, a] *a* horrendous, frightful.

horrible [o'rriβle] *a* horrible, dreadful.

horripilante [orripi'lante] *a* hair-raising; (*espeluznante*) creepy.

horripilar [orripi'lar] *vt*: ~ **a uno** to horrify sb; ~**se** *vr* to be horrified.

horror [o'rror] *nm* horror, dread; (*atrocidad*) atrocity; ¡**qué** ~! (*fam*) oh, my God!; ~**izar** *vt* to horrify, frighten; ~**izarse** *vr* to be horrified; ~**oso, a** *a* horrifying, ghastly.

hortaliza [orta'liθa] *nf* vegetable.

hortelano, a [orte'lano, a] *nm/f* (market) gardener.

hosco, a ['osko, a] *a* dark; (*triste, ceñudo*) sullen, gloomy.

hospedar [ospe'ðar] *vt* to put up, lodge; ~**se** *vr* to stay, lodge.

hospital [ospi'tal] *nm* hospital.

hospitalario, a [ospita'larjo, a] *a* hospitable; **hospitalidad** *nf* hospitality.

hosquedad [oske'ðað] *nf* sullenness.

hostal [os'tal] *nm* small hotel.

hostelero, a [oste'lero, a] *nm/f* innkeeper, landlord/lady.

hostería [oste'ria] *nf* hostelry.

hostia ['ostja] *nf* host, consecrated wafer; (*fam: golpe*) whack, punch // *excl:* ¡~s! damn it!

hostigar [osti'ɣar] *vt* to whip; (*fig*) to harass, pester.

hostil [os'til] *a* hostile; ~**idad** *nf* hostility.

hotel [o'tel] *nm* hotel; ~**ero, a** *a* hotel *cpd* // *nm/f* hotelier.

hoy [oi] *ad* (*este día*) today; (*el ahora*) now(adays) // *nm* present time; ~ (**en**) **día** now(adays).

hoya ['oja] *nf* pit; (*sepulcro*) grave; (*GEO*) valley.

hoyo ['ojo] *nm* hole, pit; **hoyuelo** *nm* dimple.

hoz [oθ] *nf* sickle.

hube *etc vb ver* **haber.**

hucha ['utʃa] *nf* money box; (*fig*) nest egg.

hueco, a ['weko, a] *a* (*vacío*) hollow, empty; (*blanco: papel*) blank; (*resonante*) booming // *nm* hollow, cavity.

huelga *etc vb ver* **holgar** // ['welɣa] *nf* strike; **declararse en** ~ to go on strike, come out on strike; ~ **de brazos caídos/de hambre** sit-down/hunger strike; ~ **patronal** lockout.

huelgo *etc vb ver* **holgar** // ['welɣo] *nm* breath; (*espacio*) room, space.

huelguista [wel'ɣista] *nm/f* striker.

huelo *etc vb ver* **oler.**

huella ['weʎa] *nf* (*acto de pisar, pisada*) tread(ing); (*marca del paso*) footprint, footstep; (: *de animal, máquina*) track; ~ **digital** fingerprint; ~ **del sonido** sound track.

huérfano, a ['werfano, a] *a* orphan(ed) // *nm/f* orphan.

huerta ['werta] *nf* market garden; (*área de regadío*) irrigated region.

huerto ['werto] *nm* orchard.

hueso ['weso] *nm* (*ANAT*) bone; (*de fruta*) stone.

huésped, a ['wespeð, a] *nm/f* (*invitado*) guest; (*habitante*) resident; (*anfitrión*) host.

huesudo, a [we'suðo, a] *a* bony, big-boned.

huevo ['weβo] *nm* egg; ~ **en cáscara/escalfado/estrellado** *o* **frito/pasado por agua** boiled/poached/fried/soft-boiled egg; ~**s revueltos** scrambled eggs.

huida [u'iða] *nf* escape, flight.

huidizo, a [ui'ðiθo, a] *a* (*tímido*) shy; (*pasajero*) fleeting.

huir [u'ir] *vt* (*escapar*) to flee, escape (from); (*evadir*) to avoid; ~**se** *vr* (*escaparse*) to escape; (*el tiempo*) to fly.

hule ['ule] *nm* (*goma*) rubber; (*encerado*) oilskin.

humanidad [umani'ðað] *nf* (*los hombres*) man(kind); (*cualidad*) humanity.

humanizar [umani'θar] *vt* to humanize.

humano, a [u'mano, a] *a* (*gen*) human; (*humanitario*) humane // *nm* human; **ser** ~ human being.

humareda [uma'reða] *nf* cloud of smoke.

humear [ume'ar] *vi* to smoke.

humedad [ume'ðað] *nf* (*del clima*) humidity; (*de pared etc*) dampness; **a prueba de** ~ damp-proof; **humedecer** *vt* to moisten, wet; **humedecerse** *vr* to get wet.

húmedo, a ['umeðo, a] *a* (*mojado*) damp, wet; (*tiempo etc*) humid.

humildad [umil'dað] *nf* humility, humbleness; **humilde** *a* humble, modest; (*pequeño: voz*) small.

humillación [umiʎa'θjon] *nf* humiliation; **humillante** *a* humiliating; **humillar** *vt* to humiliate; **humillarse** *vr* to humble o.s., grovel.

humo ['umo] *nm* (*de fuego*) smoke; (*gas nocivo*) fumes *pl*; ~**s** *nmpl* (*fig*) conceit *sg*.

humor [u'mor] *nm* (*disposición*) mood, temper; (*lo que divierte*) humour; **de buen/mal** ~ in a good/bad mood; ~**ada** *nf* witticism; ~**ismo** *nm* humour; ~**ista** *nm/f* humorist; ~**ístico, a** *a* funny, humorous.

hundido, a [un'diðo, a] *a* (*de mejillas*) sunken; (*de ojos*) deep-set.

hundimiento [undi'mjento] *nm* (*gen*) sinking; (*colapso*) collapse.

hundir [un'dir] *vt* to sink; (*edificio, plan*) to

ruin, destroy; ~ **se** *vr* to sink, collapse.
húngaro, a ['ungaro, a] *a, nm/f* Hungarian.
Hungría [un'gria] *nf* Hungary.
huracán [ura'kan] *nm* hurricane.
huraño, a [u'raño, a] *a* shy; (*antisocial*) unsociable.
hurgar [ur'ɣar] *vt* to poke, jab; (*remover*) to stir (up).
hurgonear [urɣone'ar] *vt* to poke.
hurón, ona [u'ron, ona] *a* unsociable // *nm* (*zool*) ferret; (*persona tímida*) shy person; (*persona arisca*) unsociable person.
hurtadillas [urta'ðiʎas]: **a ~** *ad* stealthily, on the sly.
hurtar [ur'tar] *vt* to steal; ~ **se** *vr* to hide, withdraw; **hurto** *nm* theft, stealing.
husmear [usme'ar] *vt* (*oler*) to sniff out, scent; (*fam*) to pry into // *vi* to smell bad; **husmo** *nm* strong smell.
huyo *etc vb ver* **huir.**

I

iba *etc vb ver* **ir.**
ibérico, a [i'ßeriko, a] *a* Iberian.
iberoamericano, a [ißeroameri'kano, a] *a, nm/f* Spanish American.
íbice ['ißiθe] *nm* ibex.
ibicenco, a [ißi'θenko, a] *a* Ibizan.
Ibiza [i'ßiθa] *nf* Ibiza.
ibón [i'ßon] *nm* lake, tarn.
iceberg ['aisßerɣ] *nm* iceberg.
ícono ['ikono] *nm* ikon, icon.
iconoclasta [ikono'klasta] *a* iconoclastic // *nm/f* iconoclast.
ictericia [ikte'riθja] *nf* jaundice.
ida ['iða] *nf* going, departure; ~ **y vuelta** round trip, return.
idea [i'ðea] *nf* idea; **darse/hacerse una** ~ **de...** to get an idea of... .
ideal [iðe'al] *a, nm* ideal; ~ **ista** *nm/f* idealist; ~ **izar** *vt* to idealize.
idear [iðe'ar] *vt* to think up; (*aparato*) to invent; (*viaje*) to plan.
ídem ['iðem] *pron* ditto.
idéntico, a [i'ðentiko, a] *a* identical.
identidad [iðenti'ðað] *nf* identity; **carné de** ~ identity card.
identificación [iðentifika'θjon] *nf* identification; **identificar** *vt* to identify; **identificarse** *vr*: **identificarse con** to identify o.s. with.
ideología [iðeolo'xia] *nf* ideology; **ideológico, a** *a* ideological.
idioma [i'ðjoma] *nm* (*gen*) language; (*giro*) idiom.
idiota [i'ðjota] *a* idiotic // *nm/f* idiot; **idiotez** *nf* idiocy.
idólatra [i'ðolatra] *nm/f* idolater/tress; **idolatría** *nf* idolatry.
ídolo ['iðolo] *nm* idol.
idóneo, a [i'ðoneo, a] *a* (*apto*) fit; (*conveniente*) suitable.
iglesia [i'ɣlesja] *nf* church.
ignición [iɣni'θjon] *nf* ignition.

ignominia [iɣno'minja] *nf* ignominy; **ignominioso, a** *a* ignominious.
ignorado, a [iɣno'raðo, a] *a* unknown; (*dato*) obscure.
ignorancia [iɣno'ranθja] *nf* ignorance; **ignorante** *a* ignorant, uninformed // *nm/f* ignoramus.
ignorar [iɣno'rar] *vt* not to know, be ignorant of.
ignoto, a [iɣ'noto, a] *a* unknown.
igual [i'ɣwal] *a* (*gen*) equal; (*similar*) like, similar; (*mismo*) (the) same; (*constante*) constant; (*temperatura*) even // *nm/f* equal; **al** ~ **que** *prep, conj* like, just like.
igualada [iɣwa'laða] *nf* equaliser.
igualar [iɣwa'lar] *vt* (*gen*) to equalize, make equal; (*allanar, nivelar*) to level (off), even (out); ~ **se** *vr* (*platos de balanza*) to balance out; (*equivaler*) to be equal.
igualdad [iɣwal'dað] *nf* equality; (*similaridad*) sameness; (*uniformidad*) evenness, uniformity.
igualmente [iɣwal'mente] *ad* equally; (*también*) also, likewise // *excl* the same to you.
ikurriña [iku'rriɲa] *nf* Basque flag.
ilegal [ile'ɣal] *a* illegal.
ilegítimo, a [ile'xitimo, a] *a* illegitimate.
ileso, a [i'leso, a] *a* unhurt.
ilícito, a [i'liθito] *a* illicit.
ilimitado, a [ilimi'taðo, a] *a* unlimited.
ilógico, a [i'loxiko, a] *a* illogical.
iluminación [ilumina'θjon] *nf* (*gen*) illumination; (*alumbrado*) lighting.
iluminar [ilumi'nar] *vt* to illuminate, light (up); (*fig*) to enlighten.
ilusión [ilu'sjon] *nf* illusion; (*quimera*) delusion; (*esperanza*) hope; **ilusionado, a** *a* excited.
ilusionista [ilusjo'nista] *nm/f* conjurer.
iluso, a [i'luso, a] *a* easily deceived.
ilusorio, a [ilu'sorjo, a] *a* (*de ilusión*) illusory, deceptive; (*esperanza*) vain.
ilustración [ilustra'θjon] *nf* illustration; (*saber*) learning, erudition; **la I** ~ the Enlightenment; **ilustrado, a** *a* illustrated; learned.
ilustrar [ilus'trar] *vt* (*gen*) to illustrate; (*instruir*) to instruct; (*explicar*) to explain, make clear; ~ **se** *vr* to acquire knowledge.
ilustre [i'lustre] *a* famous, illustrious.
imagen [i'maxen] *nf* (*gen*) image; (*dibujo*) picture; (*semejanza*) likeness.
imaginación [imaxina'θjon] *nf* imagination.
imaginar [imaxi'nar] *vt* (*gen*) to imagine; (*idear*) to think up; (*suponer*) to suppose; ~ **se** *vr* to imagine; ~ **io, a** *a* imaginary; **imaginativo, a** *a* imaginative.
imán [i'man] *nm* magnet.
imbécil [im'beθil] *nm/f* imbecile, idiot; **imbecilidad** *nf* imbecility.
imbuir [imbu'ir] *vt* to imbue.
imitación [imita'θjon] *nf* imitation; **imitar**

vt to imitate; (*parodiar, remedar*) to mimic, ape.

impaciencia [impa'θjenθja] *nf* impatience; **impaciente** *a* impatient; (*nervioso*) anxious.

impacto [im'pakto] *nm* impact.

impar [im'par] *a* odd.

imparcial [impar'θjal] *a* impartial, fair; ~ **idad** *nf* impartiality, fairness.

impartir [impar'tir] *vt* to impart, give.

impasible [impa'siβle] *a* impassive.

impavidez [impaβi'δeθ] *nf* fearlessness, intrepidness; **impávido, a** *a* fearless, intrepid.

impecable [impe'kaβle] *a* impeccable.

impedimento [impeδi'mento] *nm* impediment, obstacle.

impedir [impe'δir] *vt* (*obstruir*) to impede, obstruct; (*estorbar*) to prevent.

impeler [impe'ler] *vt* to drive, propel; (*fig*) to impel.

impenetrabilidad [impenetraβili'δaδ] *nf* impenetrability; **impenetrable** *a* impenetrable; (*fig*) incomprehensible.

impenitente [impeni'tente] *a* unrepentant.

impensado, a [impen'saδo, a] *a* unexpected.

imperar [impe'rar] *vi* (*reinar*) to rule, reign; (*fig*) to prevail, reign; (*precio*) to be current.

imperativo, a [impera'tiβo, a] *a* (*persona*) imperious; (*urgente, LING*) imperative.

imperceptible [imperθep'tiβle] *a* imperceptible.

imperdible [imper'δiβle] *nm* safety pin.

imperdonable [imperδo'naβle] *a* unforgivable, inexcusable.

imperfección [imperfek'θjon] *nf* imperfection.

imperfecto, a [imper'fekto, a] *a* imperfect.

imperial [impe'rjal] *a* imperial; ~ **ismo** *nm* imperialism.

impericia [impe'riθja] *nf* (*torpeza*) unskilfulness; (*inexperiencia*) inexperience.

imperio [im'perjo] *nm* empire; (*reino, dominación*) rule, authority; (*fig*) pride, haughtiness; ~ **so, a** *a* imperious; (*urgente*) urgent; (*imperativo*) imperative.

impermeable [imperme'aβle] *a* impermeable; (*a prueba de agua*) waterproof // *nm* raincoat.

impersonal [imperso'nal] *a* impersonal.

impertérrito, a [imper'territo, a] *a* undaunted.

impertinencia [imperti'nenθja] *nf* (*inoportunidad*) irrelevant; (*insolencia*) impertinence; **impertinente** *a* irrelevant; impertinent.

imperturbable [impertur'βaβle] *a* imperturbable.

ímpetu ['impetu] *nm* (*impulso*) impetus, impulse; (*impetuosidad*) impetuosity; (*violencia*) violence.

impetuosidad [impetwosi'δaδ] *nf* impetuousness; (*violencia*) violence; **impetuoso, a** *a* impetuous; (*persona*) headstrong; (*río*) rushing, violent; (*acto*) hasty.

impío, a [im'pio, a] *a* impious, ungodly.

implacable [impla'kaβle] *a* implacable.

implicar [impli'kar] *vt* (*gen*) to implicate, involve; (*entrañar*) to imply.

implícito, a [im'pliθito, a] *a* (*tácito*) implicit; (*sobreentendido*) implied.

implorar [implo'rar] *vt* to beg, implore.

imponente [impo'nente] *a* (*impresionante*) impressive, imposing; (*solemne*) grand // *nm/f* investor.

imponer [impo'ner] *vt* (*gen*) to impose; (*informar*) to inform, instruct; (*exigir*) to exact, command; (*COM*) to invest; ~ **se** *vr* to assert o.s.; (*prevalecer*) to prevail.

impopular [impopu'lar] *a* unpopular.

importación [importa'θjon] *nf* (*acto*) importing; (*objetos*) imports *pl*.

importancia [impor'tanθja] *nf* importance; (*valor*) value, significance; (*extensión*) size, magnitude; **importante** *a* important; valuable, significant.

importar [impor'tar] *vt* (*del extranjero*) to import; (*valer*) to amount to, be worth // *vi* to be important, matter; **me importa el rábano** I don't give a damn; **no importa** it doesn't matter.

importe [im'porte] *nm* (*total*) amount; (*valor*) value.

importunar [importu'nar] *vt* to bother, pester.

importuno, a [impor'tuno, a] *a* (*inoportuno, molesto*) inopportune; (*indiscreto*) troublesome.

imposibilidad [imposiβili'δaδ] *nf* impossibility; **imposibilitar** *vt* to make impossible, prevent; (*incapacitar*) to disable, cripple.

imposible [impo'siβle] *a* (*gen*) impossible; (*insoportable*) unbearable, intolerable.

imposición [imposi'θjon] *nf* imposition; (*COM*) tax; (*enganche*) deposit.

impostor, a [impos'tor, a] *nm/f* impostor; **impostura** *nf* fraud, imposture.

impotencia [impo'tenθja] *nf* impotence; **impotente** *a* impotent, powerless.

impracticable [imprakti'kaβle] *a* (*irrealizable*) impracticable; (*intransitable*) impassable.

imprecar [impre'kar] *vi* to curse.

impregnar [impreɣ'nar] *vt* to impregnate; ~ **se** *vr* to become impregnated.

imprenta [im'prenta] *nf* (*gen*) printing; (*aparato*) press; (*casa*) printer's; (*letra*) print.

imprescindible [impresθin'diβle] *a* essential, indispensable.

impresión [impre'sjon] *nf* (*gen*) impression; (*IMPRENTA*) printing; (*edición*) edition; (*FOTO*) print; (*marca*) imprint; ~ **digital** fingerprint.

impresionable [impresjo'naβle] *a*

impresionante   98   incesto

(*sensible*) impressionable; (*excitable*) emotional.

impresionante [impresjo'nante] *a* impressive; (*tremendo*) tremendous; (*maravilloso*) great, marvellous.

impresionar [impresjo'nar] *vt* (*conmover*) to move; (*afectar*) to impress, strike; (*película fotográfica*) to expose; ~se *vr* to be impressed; (*conmoverse*) to be moved.

impreso, a [im'preso, a] *pp de* **imprimir** // *a* printed // *nm* printed paper/book *etc*.

impresor [impre'sor] *nm* printer.

imprevisto, a [impre'βisto, a] *a* (*gen*) unforeseen; (*inesperado*) unexpected.

imprimir [impri'mir] *vt* to imprint, impress, stamp; (*textos*) to print.

improbabilidad [improβaβili'ðað] *nf* (*sin seguridad*) improbability; (*inverosimilitud*) unlikelihood; **improbable** *a* improbable; unlikely.

improcedente [improθe'ðente] *a* (*inconveniente*) unsuitable; (*inadecuado*) inappropriate.

improductivo, a [improðuk'tiβo, a] *a* unproductive.

improperio [impro'perjo] *nm* insult, taunt.

impropiedad [impropje'ðað] *nf* impropriety (of language).

impropio, a [im'propjo, a] *a* improper.

impróvido, a [im'proβiðo, a] *a* improvident.

improvisación [improβisa'θjon] *nf* improvisation; **improvisado, a** *a* improvised; **improvisar** *vt* to improvise.

improviso, a [impro'βiso, a], **improvisto, a** [impro'βisto, a] *a* unexpected, unforeseen; **de** ~ unexpectedly, suddenly.

imprudencia [impru'ðenθja] *nf* imprudence; (*indiscreción*) indiscretion; (*descuido*) carelessness; **imprudente** *a* imprudent; indiscreet; (*irreflexivo*) unwise.

impúdico, a [im'puðiko, a] *a* shameless, immodest; (*lujurioso*) lecherous, lewd.

impudor [impu'ðor] *nm* shamelessness, immodesty; (*lujuria*) lechery, lewdness.

impuesto, a [im'pwesto, a] *a* imposed; (*informado*) informed // *nm* tax.

impugnar [impuɣ'nar] *vt* to oppose, contest; (*refutar*) to refute, impugn.

impulsar [impul'sar] *vt* = **impeler**.

impulsión [impul'sjon] *nf* (*TEC*) propulsion; (*fig*) impulse.

impulso [im'pulso] *nm* impulse; (*fuerza, empuje*) thrust, drive; (*rapto*) urge, impulse.

impune [im'pune] *a* unpunished; **impunidad** *nf* impunity.

impureza [impu'reθa] *nf* impurity; (*fig*) lewdness; **impuro, a** *a* impure; lewd.

imputación [imputa'θjon] *nf* imputation.

imputar [impu'tar] *vt* (*atribuir*) to attribute to; (*cargar*) to impute to.

inacabable [inaka'βaβle] *a* (*infinito*) endless; (*interminable*) interminable.

inaccesible [inakθe'siβle] *a* inaccessible.

inacción [inak'θjon] *nf* (*gen*) inaction; (*desocupación*) inactivity; (*ocio*) idleness.

inaceptable [inaθep'taβle] *a* inacceptable.

inactividad [inaktiβi'ðað] *nf* inactivity; (*pereza*) laziness, idleness; (*COM*) dullness; **inactivo, a** *a* inactive.

inadaptación [inaðapta'θjon] *nf* maladjustment.

inadecuado, a [inaðe'kwaðo, a] *a* (*insuficiente*) inadequate; (*inapto*) unsuitable.

inadmisible [inaðmi'siβle] *a* inadmissible.

inadvertencia [inaðβer'tenθja] *nf* oversight.

inadvertido, a [inaðβer'tiðo, a] *a* (*distraído*) inattentive; (*no visto*) unnoticed; (*descuidado*) careless.

inagotable [inaɣo'taβle] *a* inexhaustible.

inaguantable [inaɣwan'taβle] *a* unbearable.

inalterable [inalte'raβle] *a* immutable, unchangeable; (*permanente*) permanent.

inanición [inani'θjon] *nf* starvation.

inanimado, a [inani'maðo, a] *a* inanimate.

inapto, a [in'apto] *a* unsuited.

inaudito, a [inau'ðito, a] *a* unheard-of.

inauguración [inauɣura'θjon] *nf* inauguration; (*de exposición*) opening; **inaugurar** *vt* to inaugurate; to open.

I.N.B. *abr de* **Instituto Nacional de Bachillerato** ≈ secondary school.

inca ['inka] *nm/f* Inca; ~**ico, a** *a* Inca.

incalculable [inkalku'laβle] *a* incalculable.

incandescente [inkandes'θente] *a* incandescent.

incansable [inkan'saβle] *a* tireless, untiring.

incapacidad [inkapaθi'ðað] *nf* incapacity; (*incompetencia*) incompetence; ~ **física/mental** physical/mental incapacity *or* disability.

incapacitar [inkapaθi'tar] *vt* (*inhabilitar*) to incapacitate, render unfit; (*descalificar*) to disqualify.

incapaz [inka'paθ] *a* incapable.

incautación [inkauta'θjon] *nf* confiscation; **incautarse** *vr*: **incautarse de** to seize, confiscate.

incauto, a [in'kauto, a] *a* (*imprudente*) incautious, unwary.

incendiar [inθen'djar] *vt* to set on fire; (*fig*) to inflame; ~se *vr* to catch fire; ~**io, a** *a* incendiary; (*fig*) inflammatory.

incendio [in'θendjo] *nm* fire.

incentivo [inθen'tiβo] *nm* incentive.

incertidumbre [inθerti'ðumβre] *nf* (*inseguridad*) uncertainty; (*duda*) doubt.

incesante [inθe'sante], **incesable** [inθe'saβle] *a* incessant.

incesto [in'θesto] *nm* incest.

incidencia [inθi'ðenθja] nf (accidente) incident; (MAT) incidence.
incidente [inθi'ðente] a incidental // nm incident.
incidir [inθi'ðir] vi (influir) to influence; (afectar) to affect; ~ **en un error** to fall into error.
incienso [in'θjenso] nm incense.
incierto, a [in'θjerto, a] a uncertain.
incineración [inθinera'θjon] nf incineration; (de cadáveres) cremation; **incinerar** vt to burn; to cremate.
incipiente [inθi'pjente] a incipient.
incisión [inθi'sjon] nf incision.
incisivo, a [inθi'siβo, a] a sharp, cutting; (fig) incisive.
incitación [inθita'θjon] nf incitement.
incitante [inθi'tante] a (estimulante) exciting; (provocativo) provocative; **incitar** vt to incite, rouse.
incivil [inθi'βil] a rude, uncivil.
inclemencia [inkle'menθja] nf (severidad) harshness, severity; (del tiempo) inclemency; **inclemente** a harsh, severe; inclement.
inclinación [inklina'θjon] nf (gen) inclination; (de tierras) slope, incline; (de cabeza) nod, bow; (fig) leaning, bent.
inclinar [inkli'nar] vt to incline; (cabeza) to nod, bow; (tierras) to slope; (persuadir) to persuade; ~**se** vr to bow; (encorvarse) to stoop; ~**se a** to take after, resemble; ~**se ante** to bow down to; **me inclino a pensar que** I'm inclined to think that.
ínclito, a ['inklito, a] a illustrious, renowned.
incluir [inklu'ir] vt to include; (incorporar) to incorporate; (meter) to enclose.
inclusive [inklu'siβe] ad inclusive // prep including.
incluso, a [in'kluso, a] a included // ad inclusively; (hasta) even.
incógnito, a [in'koʏnito, a] a unknown // nm: **de** ~ incognito // nf unknown factor.
incoherente [inkoe'rente] a incoherent.
incoloro, a [inko'loro, a] a colourless.
incólume [in'kolume] a (gen) safe; (indemne) unhurt, unharmed.
incomodar [inkomo'ðar] vt to inconvenience; (molestar) to bother, trouble; (fastidiar) to annoy; ~**se** vr to put o.s. out; (fastidiarse) to get annoyed.
incomodidad [inkomoði'ðað] nf inconvenience; (fastidio, enojo) annoyance; (de vivienda) discomfort.
incómodo, a [in'komoðo, a] a (inconfortable) uncomfortable; (molesto) annoying; (inconveniente) inconvenient.
incomparable [inkompa'raβle] a incomparable.
incompatible [inkompa'tiβle] a incompatible.
incompetencia [inkompe'tenθja] nf incompetence; **incompetente** a incompetent.
incompleto, a [inkom'pleto, a] a incomplete, unfinished.

incomprensible [inkompren'siβle] a incomprehensible.
incomunicado, a [inkomuni'kaðo, a] a (aislado) cut off, isolated; (confinado) in solitary confinement.
inconcebible [inkonθe'βiβle] a inconceivable.
inconcluso, a [inkon'kluso, a] a (inacabado) unfinished; (incompleto) incomplete.
incondicional [inkondiθjo'nal] a unconditional; (apoyo) wholehearted; (partidario) staunch.
inconexo, a [inko'nekso, a] a (gen) unconnected; (desunido) disconnected.
inconfundible [inkonfun'diβle] a unmistakable.
incongruente [inkon'grwente] a incongruous.
inconmensurable [inkonmensu'raβle] a immeasurable, vast.
inconsciencia [inkons'θjenθja] nf unconsciousness; (fig) thoughtlessness; **inconsciente** a unconscious; thoughtless.
inconsecuencia [inkonse'kwenθja] nf inconsistency; **inconsecuente** a inconsistent.
inconsiderado, a [inkonsiðe'raðo, a] a inconsiderate.
inconsistente [inkonsis'tente] a weak; (tela) flimsy.
inconstancia [inkon'stanθja] nf (inconsecuencia, veleidad) inconstancy; (inestabilidad) unsteadiness; **inconstante** a inconstant.
incontestable [inkontes'taβle] a unanswerable; (innegable) undeniable.
incontinencia [inkonti'nenθja] nf incontinence; **incontinente** a incontinent.
inconveniencia [inkonβe'njenθja] nf unsuitability, inappropriateness; (incorrección) impoliteness; **inconveniente** a unsuitable; impolite // nm obstacle; (desventaja) disadvantage.
incorporación [inkorpora'θjon] nf incorporation; (del cuerpo) sitting/standing up; **incorporar** vt to incorporate; **incorporarse** vr to sit/stand up.
incorrección [inkorrek'θjon] nf (gen) incorrectness, inaccuracy; (descortesía) bad-mannered behaviour; **incorrecto, a** a (gen) incorrect, wrong; (facciones) irregular, odd; (comportamiento) bad-mannered.
incorregible [inkorre'xiβle] a incorrigible.
incorruptible [inkorrup'tiβle] a incorruptible; ~ **a la intemperie** rustproof.
incredulidad [inkreðuli'ðað] nf incredulity; (escepticismo) scepticism; **incrédulo, a** a incredulous, unbelieving; sceptical.
increíble [inkre'iβle] a incredible.
incremento [inkre'mento] nm increment; (aumento) rise, increase.
increpar [inkre'par] vt to reprimand.

incruento, a [in'krwento, a] a bloodless.
incrustar [inkrus'tar] vt to incrust;
(piedras: en joya) to inlay.
incubar [inku'ßar] vt to incubate; (fig) to
hatch.
inculcar [inkul'kar] vt to inculcate.
inculpar [inkul'par] vt (acusar) to accuse;
(achacar, atribuir) to charge, blame.
inculto, a [in'kulto, a] a (persona)
uneducated, uncultured; (terreno)
uncultivated // nm/f ignoramus.
incumplimiento [inkumpli'mjento] nm
non-fulfilment; ~ de contrato breach of
contract.
incurrir [inku'rrir] vi: ~ en to incur;
(crimen) to commit; ~ en un error to
fall into error.
indagación [indaxa'θjon] nf investigation;
(búsqueda) search; (JUR) inquest; **indagar**
vt to investigate; to search; (averiguar) to
ascertain.
indecente [inde'θente] a indecent,
improper; (lascivo) obscene.
indecible [inde'θißle] a unspeakable;
(indescriptible) indescribable.
indeciso, a [inde'θiso, a] a (por decidir)
undecided; (vacilante) hesitant; (resultado)
indecisive.
indefectible [indefek'tißle] a unfailing.
indefenso, a [inde'fenso, a] a defenceless.
indefinido, a [indefi'niðo, a] a indefinite;
(vago) vague, undefined.
indeleble [inde'leßle] a indelible.
indemnizar [indemni'θar] vt to
indemnify; (compensar) to compensate.
independencia [indepen'denθja] nf
independence.
independiente [indepen'djente] a (libre)
independent; (autónomo) self-sufficient.
indeterminado, a [indetermi'naðo, a] a
indefinite; (desconocido) indeterminate.
India ['indja] nf: la ~ India.
indicación [indika'θjon] nf indication;
(señal) sign; (sugerencia) suggestion, hint;
(de termómetro) reading.
indicador [indika'ðor] nm indicator; (TEC)
gauge, meter.
indicar [indi'kar] vt (mostrar) to indicate,
show; (termómetro etc) to read, register;
(señalar) to point to.
índice ['indiθe] nm index; (catálogo)
catalogue; (ANAT) index finger, forefinger;
(de cuadrante) pointer, needle; (de reloj)
hand.
indicio [in'diθjo] nm indication, sign;
(huella) trace; (pesquisa) clue.
indiferencia [indife'renθja] nf
indifference; (apatía) apathy; **indiferente**
a indifferent.
indígena [in'dixena] a indigenous, native;
(aborigen) aboriginal // nm/f native;
aborigine.
indigencia [indi'xenθja] nf poverty, need.
indigestión [indixes'tjon] nf indigestion.
indigesto, a [indi'xesto, a] a undigested;
(indigestible) indigestible; (fig) turgid.

indignación [indixna'θjon] nf indignation;
indignado, a a indignant.
indignar [indix'nar] vt to anger, make
indignant; ~se vr: ~se de o por to get
indignant about.
indignidad [indixni'ðað] nf (insulto)
indignity, insult; (ruindad) vile act;
indigno, a a (despreciable) low,
contemptible; (inmerecido) unworthy.
indio, a ['indjo, a] a, nm/f Indian.
indirecta [indi'rekta] nf insinuation,
innuendo; (sugerencia) hint.
indirecto, a [indi'rekto, a] a indirect.
indiscreción [indiskre'θjon] nf
(imprudencia) indiscretion; (irreflexión)
tactlessness; (acto) gaffe, tactless act.
indiscreto, a [indis'kreto, a] a indiscreet.
indiscutible [indisku'tißle] a indisputable,
unquestionable.
indispensable [indispen'saßle] a
indispensable.
indisponer [indispo'ner] vt to spoil, upset;
(salud) to make ill; ~se vr to fall ill; ~se
con uno to fall out with sb.
indisposición [indisposi'θjon] nf
indisposition.
indistinto, a [indis'tinto, a] a indistinct;
(vago) vague.
individual [indiβi'ðwal] a individual;
(habitación) single // nm (DEPORTE) singles
sg.
individuo, a [indi'βiðwo, a] a individual //
nm individual; (miembro, socio) member,
fellow.
indiviso, a [indi'βiso, a] a undivided.
índole ['indole] nf (naturaleza) nature;
(clase) sort, kind.
indolencia [indo'lenθja] nf indolence,
laziness.
indomable [indo'maßle] a indomitable;
(animal) untameable; (fig) unmanageable.
indómito, a [in'domito, a] a indomitable.
inducir [indu'θir] vt to induce; (inferir) to
infer; (persuadir) to persuade.
indudable [indu'ðaßle] a undoubted;
(incuestionable) unquestionable.
indulgencia [indul'xenθja] nf indulgence.
indultar [indul'tar] vt (perdonar) to
pardon, reprieve; (librar de pago) to
exempt; **indulto** nm pardon; exemption.
industria [in'dustrja] nf industry;
(habilidad) skill; **industrial** a industrial //
nm industrialist.
industrioso, a [indus'trjoso, a] a
industrious.
inédito, a [in'eðito, a] a (libro)
unpublished; (nuevo) unheard-of.
inefable [ine'faßle] a ineffable,
indescribable.
ineficaz [inefi'kaθ] a (inútil) ineffective;
(ineficiente) inefficient.
ineludible [inelu'ðißle] a inescapable,
unavoidable.
ineptitud [inepti'tuð] nf ineptitude,
incompetence; **inepto, a** a inept,
incompetent.

inequívoco, a [ine'kiβoko, a] *a* unequivocal; (*inconfundible*) unmistakable.

inercia [in'erθja] *nf* inertia; (*fig*) passivity.

inerme [in'erme] *a* (*sin armas*) unarmed; (*indefenso*) defenceless.

inerte [in'erte] *a* inert; (*fig*) passive.

inesperado, a [inespe'raðo, a] *a* unexpected, unforeseen.

inestable [ines'taβle] *a* unstable.

inevitable [ineβi'taβle] *a* inevitable.

inexactitud [ineksakti'tuð] *nf* inaccuracy; **inexacto, a** *a* inaccurate; (*falso*) untrue.

infamar [infa'mar] *vt* to dishonour; (*calumniar*) to defame, slander.

infame [in'fame] *a* infamous // *nm/f* vile person; **infamia** *nf* infamy; (*deshonra*) disgrace.

infancia [in'fanθja] *nf* infancy, childhood.

infante [in'fante] *nm* (*niño*) infant, child; (*hijo del rey*) prince.

infantería [infante'ria] *nf* infantry.

infantil [infan'til] *a* (*pueril, aniñado*) infantile; (*cándido*) childlike; (*literatura*) children's.

infarto [in'farto] *nm* heart attack.

infatigable [infati'xaβle] *a* tireless, untiring.

infausto, a [in'fausto, a] *a* unlucky.

infección [infek'θjon] *nf* infection; **infeccioso, a** *a* infectious.

infectar [infek'tar] *vt* to infect; ~**se** *vr* to become infected.

infelicidad [infeliθi'ðað] *nf* unhappiness.

infeliz [infe'liθ] *a* unhappy, wretched // *nm/f* wretch.

inferior [infe'rjor] *a* inferior; (*situación*) lower // *nm/f* inferior, subordinate.

inferir [infe'rir] *vt* (*deducir*) to infer, deduce; (*causar*) to cause.

infestar [infes'tar] *vt* (*infectar*) to infect; (*apestar*) to infest; (*fig*) to harass.

inficionar [infiθio'nar] *vt* to infect; (*fig*) to corrupt.

infidelidad [infiðeli'ðað] *nf* (*gen*) infidelity, unfaithfulness; (*REL*) lack of faith.

infiel [in'fjel] *a* unfaithful, disloyal; (*falso*) inaccurate // *nm/f* infidel, unbeliever.

infierno [in'fjerno] *nm* hell.

ínfimo, a ['infimo, a] *a* vile, mean.

infinidad [infini'ðað] *nf* infinity; (*abundancia*) great quantity.

infinito, a [infi'nito, a] *a, nm* infinite.

inflación [infla'θjon] *nf* (*hinchazón*) swelling; (*monetaria*) inflation; (*fig*) conceit; **inflacionario, a** *a* inflationary.

inflamar [infla'mar] *vt* to set on fire; (*MED*) to inflame; ~**se** *vr* to catch fire; (*fig*) to become inflamed.

inflar [in'flar] *vt* (*hinchar*) to inflate, blow up; (*fig*) to exaggerate; ~**se** *vr* to swell (up); (*fig*) to get conceited.

inflexible [inflek'siβle] *a* inflexible; (*irrompible*) unbending; (*fig*) strict.

infligir [infli'xir] *vt* to inflict.

influencia [influ'enθja] *nf* influence; **influenciar** *vt* to influence.

influir [influ'ir] *vt* to influence.

influjo [in'fluxo] *nm* influence.

influyente [influ'jente] *a* influential.

información [informa'θjon] *nf* information; (*noticias*) news *sg*; (*JUR*) inquiry.

informal [infor'mal] *a* (*gen*) irregular, incorrect; (*persona*) unreliable; (*poco serio*) frivolous; (*trabajo*) disorganized; (*comportamiento*) unconventional.

informalidad [informali'ðað] *nf* (*impuntualidad*) unpunctuality; (*incorrección*) bad manners *pl*; (*ligereza*) frivolity.

informante [infor'mante] *nm/f* informant.

informar [infor'mar] *vt* (*gen*) to inform; (*revelar*) to reveal, make known // *vi* (*JUR*) to plead; (*denunciar*) to inform; (*dar cuenta de*) to report on; ~**se** *vr* to find out; ~**se** *vr* to inquire into.

informe [in'forme] *a* shapeless // *nm* report.

infortunio [infor'tunjo] *nm* misfortune.

infracción [infrak'θjon] *nf* infraction, infringement; (*transgresión*) transgression.

infranqueable [infranke'aβle] *a* impassable; (*impracticable*) insurmountable.

infringir [infrin'xir] *vt* to infringe, contravene.

infructuoso, a [infruk'twoso, a] *a* fruitless, unsuccessful.

infundado, a [infun'daðo, a] *a* groundless, unfounded.

infundir [infun'dir] *vt* to infuse, instil.

ingeniar [inxe'njar] *vt* to think up, devise; ~**se** *vr*: ~**se para** to manage to.

ingeniería [inxenje'ria] *nf* engineering; **ingeniero, a** *nm/f* engineer; **ingeniero agrónomo/de sonido** agronomist/sound engineer.

ingenio [in'xenjo] *nm* (*talento*) talent; (*agudeza*) wit; (*habilidad*) ingenuity, inventiveness; (*TEC*): ~ **azucarero** sugar refinery.

ingenioso, a [inxe'njoso, a] *a* ingenious, clever; (*divertido*) witty.

ingénito, a [in'xenito, a] *a* innate.

ingenuidad [inxenwi'ðað] *nf* ingenuousness; (*candor*) candour; **ingenuo, a** *a* ingenuous.

ingerencia [inxe'renθja] *nf* = **injerencia.**

ingerir [inxe'rir] *vt* to ingest; (*tragar*) to swallow; (*consumir*) to consume.

Inglaterra [ingla'terra] *nf* England.

ingle ['ingle] *nf* groin.

inglés, esa [in'gles, esa] *a* English // *nm/f* Englishman/woman // *nm* (*lengua*) English.

ingratitud [ingrati'tuð] *nf* ingratitude; **ingrato, a** *a* (*gen*) ungrateful; (*desagradable*) unpleasant.

ingrediente [ingre'ðjente] *nm* ingredient.

ingresar [ingre'sar] *vt* (*dinero*) to deposit // *vi* to come in; ~ **en un club** to join a club; ~ **en el hospital** to go into hospital.

ingreso [in'greso] *nm* (*entrada*) entry; (: *en hospital etc*) admission; (*de dinero*) income, takings *pl.*

inhábil [in'aßil] *a* unskilful, clumsy; **día** ~ non-working day.

inhabitable [inaßi'taßle] *a* uninhabitable.

inherente [ine'rente] *a* inherent.

inhibir [ini'ßir] *vt* to inhibit; (*REL*) to restrain.

inhospitalario, a [inospita'larjo, a] *a* inhospitable.

inhumano, a [inu'mano, a] *a* inhuman.

I. N. I. ['ini] *nm abr de* **Instituto Nacional de Industria** = National Enterprise Board.

inicial [ini'θjal] *a, nf* initial.

iniciar [ini'θjar] *vt* (*persona*) to initiate; (*estudios*) to begin, commence; (*conversación*) to start up.

iniciativa [iniθja'tißa] *nf* initiative; **la** ~ **privada** private enterprise.

inicuo, a [in'ikwo, a] *a* iniquitous.

ininterrumpido, a [ininterrum'piðo, a] *a* uninterrupted.

injerencia [inxe'renθja] *nf* interference.

injertar [inxer'tar] *vt* to graft; (*inyectar*) to inject; **injerto** *nm* graft.

injuria [in'xurja] *nf* (*agravio, ofensa*) offence; (*insulto*) insult; (*daño*) harm; **injuriar** *vt* to insult; to harm; **injurioso, a** *a* offensive; insulting; harmful.

injusticia [inxus'tiθja] *nf* injustice.

injusto, a [in'xusto, a] *a* unjust, unfair.

inmadurez [inmaðu're θ] *nf* immaturity.

inmarcesible [inmarθe'sißle], **inmarchitable** [inmartʃi'taßle] *a* imperishable.

inmediaciones [inmeðja'θjones] *nfpl* neighbourhood *sg*, environs.

inmediato, a [inme'ðjato, a] *a* immediate; (*contiguo*) adjoining; (*rápido*) prompt; (*próximo*) close, next; **de** ~ immediately.

inmejorable [inmexo'raßle] *a* unsurpassable; (*precio*) unbeatable.

inmenso, a [in'menso, a] *a* immense, huge.

inmerecido, a [inmere'θiðo, a] *a* undeserved.

inmigración [inmiɣra'θjon] *nf* immigration.

inmiscuirse [inmisku'irse] *vr* to interfere, meddle.

inmobiliario, a [inmoßi'ljarjo, a] *a* real-estate *cpd* // *nf* estate agency.

inmoderado, a [inmoðe'raðo, a] *a* immoderate, excessive.

inmolar [inmo'lar] *vt* to immolate, sacrifice.

inmoral [inmo'ral] *a* immoral.

inmortal [inmor'tal] *a* immortal; ~ **izar** *vt* to immortalize.

inmotivado, a [inmoti'ßaðo, a] *a* motiveless.

inmóvil [in'moßil] *a* immobile;

(*inamovible*) immovable; (*invariable*) unchanging; (*parado*) still, stationary.

inmueble [in'mweßle] *nm* property.

inmundicia [inmun'diθja] *nf* filth; **inmundo, a** *a* filthy.

inmunidad [inmuni'ðað] *nf* immunity.

inmutar [inmu'tar] *vt* to alter; ~ **se** *vr* to turn pale.

innato, a [in'nato, a] *a* innate.

innecesario, a [inneθe'sarjo, a] *a* unnecessary.

innoble [in'noßle] *a* ignoble.

innocuo, a [in'nokwo, a] *a* innocuous.

innovación [innoßa'θjon] *nf* innovation; **innovar** *vt* to introduce.

inocencia [ino'θenθja] *nf* innocence.

inocentada [inoθen'taða] *nf* practical joke.

inocente [ino'θente] *a* (*ingenuo*) naive, simple; (*inculpable*) innocent // *nm/f* simpleton.

inodoro [ino'ðoro] *nm* toilet, lavatory.

inofensivo, a [inofen'sißo, a] *a* inoffensive.

inolvidable [inolßi'ðaßle] *a* unforgettable.

inoperante [inope'rante] *a* unworkable.

inopinado, a [inopi'naðo, a] *a* unexpected.

inoportuno, a [inopor'tuno, a] *a* untimely; (*molesto*) inconvenient.

inoxidable [inoksi'ðaßle] *a*: **acero** ~ stainless steel.

inquebrantable [inkeßran'taßle] *a* unbreakable.

inquietar [inkje'tar] *vt* to worry, trouble, disturb; ~ **se** *vr* to worry, get upset; **inquieto, a** *a* anxious, worried; **inquietud** *nf* anxiety, worry.

inquilino, a [inki'lino, a] *nm/f* tenant.

inquirir [inki'rir] *vt* to enquire into, investigate.

insaciable [insa'θjaßle] *a* insatiable.

insalubre [insa'lußre] *a* unhealthy.

inscribir [inskri'ßir] *vt* to inscribe; (*lista*) to list; (*censo*) to register; ~ **se** *vr* to register; (*ESCOL etc*) to enrol.

inscripción [inskrip'θjon] *nf* inscription; (*ESCOL etc*) enrolment; (*censo*) registration.

insecto [in'sekto] *nm* insect.

inseguridad [inseɣuri'ðað] *nf* insecurity.

inseguro, a [inse'ɣuro, a] *a* insecure; (*inconstante*) unsteady; (*incierto*) uncertain.

insensato, a [insen'sato, a] *a* foolish, stupid.

insensibilidad [insensißili'ðað] *nf* (*gen*) insensitivity; (*dureza de corazón*) callousness.

insensible [insen'sißle] *a* (*gen*) insensitive; (*duro*) callous; (*movimiento*) imperceptible; (*sin sentido*) numb.

insertar [inser'tar] *vt* to insert.

inservible [inser'ßißle] *a* useless.

insidioso, a [insi'ðjoso, a] *a* insidious.

insignia [in'siɣnja] *nf* (*señal distintivo*)

badge; (*estandarte*) flag; (*condecoración*) decoration.
insignificante [insiɣnifi'kante] *a* insignificant.
insinuar [insi'nwar] *vt* to insinuate, imply; ~**se** *vr*: ~**se con uno** to ingratiate o.s. with sb.
insípido, a [in'sipiðo, a] *a* insipid.
insistencia [insis'tenθja] *nf* (*obstinación*) insistence; (*porfía*) persistence.
insistir [insis'tir] *vi* to insist; ~ **en algo** to stress sth.
insolación [insola'θjon] *nf* (*MED*) sunstroke.
insolencia [inso'lenθja] *nf* insolence; **insolente** *a* insolent.
insólito, a [in'solito, a] *a* unusual.
insoluble [inso'luβle] *a* insoluble.
insolvencia [insol'βenθja] *nf* insolvency.
insomnio [in'somnjo] *nm* insomnia.
insondable [inson'daβle] *a* bottomless.
insoportable [insopor'taβle] *a* unbearable.
inspección [inspek'θjon] *nf* inspection, check; **inspeccionar** *vt* (*examinar*) to inspect, examine; (*controlar*) to check.
inspector, a [inspek'tor, a] *nm/f* inspector.
inspiración [inspira'θjon] *nf* inspiration; **inspirar** *vt* to inspire; (*MED*) to inhale; **inspirarse** *vr*: **inspirarse en** to be inspired by.
instalar [insta'lar] *vt* (*establecer*) to instal; (*erguir*) to set up, erect; ~**se** *vr* to establish o.s.
instancia [ins'tanθja] *nf* (*JUR*) petition; (*ruego*) request; **en última** ~ in the last resort.
instantáneo, a [instan'taneo, a] *a* instant, instantaneous // *nf* snap(shot).
instante [ins'tante] *nm* instant, moment.
instar [ins'tar] *vt* to press, urge // *vi* to be pressing *or* urgent.
instigar [insti'ɣar] *vt* to instigate.
instinto [ins'tinto] *nm* instinct; **por** ~ instinctively.
institución [institu'θjon] *nf* institution, establishment.
instituir [institu'ir] *vt* to establish; (*fundar*) to found; **instituto** *nm* (*gen*) institute; (*escuela*) high school.
instrucción [instruk'θjon] *nf* instruction.
instructivo, a [instruk'tiβo, a] *a* instructive.
instruir [instru'ir] *vt* (*gen*) to instruct; (*enseñar*) to teach, educate; (*MIL, DEPORTE*) to train.
instrumento [instru'mento] *nm* (*gen*) instrument; (*herramienta*) tool, implement.
insubordinarse [insuβorði'narse] *vr* to rebel.
insuficiencia [insufi'θjenθja] *nf* (*carencia*) lack; (*inadecuación*) inadequacy; **insuficiente** *a* (*gen*) insufficient; (*incompetente*) incompetent; (*nota*) inadequate.
insufrible [insu'friβle] *a* insufferable.

insular [insu'lar] *a* insular.
insulsez [insul'seθ] *nf* (*insipidez*) insipidity; (*fig*) dullness.
insultar [insul'tar] *vt* to insult; **insulto** *nm* insult.
insuperable [insupe'raβle] *a* (*excelente*) unsurpassable; (*arduo*) insurmountable.
insurgente [insur'xente] *a, nm/f* insurgent.
insurrección [insurrek'θjon] *nf* insurrection, rebellion.
intacto, a [in'takto, a] *a* intact.
intachable [inta'tʃaβle] *a* irreproachable.
integral [inte'ɣral] *a*: **pan** ~ wholemeal bread.
integrar [inte'ɣrar] *vt* to make up, compose; (*COM*) to repay; (*MAT*) to integrate.
integridad [inteɣri'ðað] *nf* wholeness; (*carácter*) integrity; **íntegro, a** *a* whole, entire; (*honrado*) honest.
intelectual [intelek'twal] *a, nm/f* intellectual.
inteligencia [inteli'xenθja] *nf* intelligence; (*ingenio*) ability; **inteligente** *a* intelligent.
intemperancia [intempe'ranθja] *nf* excess, intemperance.
intemperie [intem'perje] *nf* bad weather; **a la** ~ outdoors, in the open air.
intempestivo, a [intempes'tiβo, a] *a* untimely.
intención [inten'θjon] *nf* (*gen*) intention; (*propósito*) purpose; **con segundas intenciones** maliciously; **de primera** ~ provisionally; **con** ~ deliberately.
intencionado, a [intenθjo'naðo, a] *a* deliberate; **bien/mal** ~ well-meaning/ill-disposed.
intendencia [inten'denθja] *nf* management, administration.
intenso, a [in'tenso, a] *a* intense; (*impresión*) vivid; (*sentimiento*) profound, deep.
intentar [inten'tar] *vt* (*tratar*) to try, attempt; **intento** *nm* (*intención*) intention, purpose; (*tentativa*) attempt.
intercalar [interka'lar] *vt* to insert.
intercambio [inter'kambjo] *nm* exchange, swap.
interceder [interθe'ðer] *vi* to intercede.
intercesión [interθe'sjon] *nf* intercession.
interés [inte'res] *nm* (*gen*) interest; (*parte*) share, part; (*pey*) self-interest; **intereses creados** vested interests.
interesado, a [intere'saðo, a] *a* interested; (*prejuiciado*) prejudiced; (*pey*) mercenary, self-seeking.
interesar [intere'sar] *vt, vi* to interest, be of interest to; ~**se** *vr*: ~**se en** *o* **por** to take an interest in.
interferir [interfe'rir] *vt* to interfere with; (*TELEC*) to jam // *vi* to interfere.
interior [inte'rjor] *a* inner, inside; (*COM*) domestic, internal // *nm* interior, inside; (*fig*) soul, mind; **Ministerio del I**~ Home Office.

interjección [interxek'θjon] *nf* interjection.

interlocutor, a [interloku'tor] *nm/f* speaker.

intermediario, a [interme'ðjarjo, a] *nm/f* intermediary // *nm* middleman.

intermedio, a [inter'meðjo, a] *a* intermediate // *nm* interval.

interminable [intermi'naβle] *a* endless.

intermitente [intermi'tente] *a* intermittent // *nm* indicator.

internacional [internaθjo'nal] *a* international.

internar [inter'nar] *vt* to intern; (*loco*) to commit; ~**se** *vr* (*en un hospital*) to go into hospital; (*penetrar*) to penetrate.

interno, a [in'terno, a] *a* internal, interior; (*POL etc*) domestic // *nm/f* (*alumno*) boarder.

interpelar [interpe'lar] *vt* (*rogar*) to implore; (*hablar*) to speak to.

interponer [interpo'ner] *vt* to interpose, put in; ~**se** *vr* to intervene.

interposición [interposi'θjon] *nf* insertion.

interpretación [interpreta'θjon] *nf* interpretation; **interpretar** *vt* to interpret; **interprete** *nm/f* interpreter; (*traductor*) translator; (*músico, TEATRO*) performer, artist(e).

interrogación [interroxa'θjon] *nf* interrogation; (*LING*) question mark; **interrogar** *vt* to interrogate, question.

interrumpir [interrum'pir] *vt* to interrupt; (*ELEC*) to switch off, cut off.

interrupción [interrup'θjon] *nf* interruption.

interruptor [interrup'tor] *nm* (*ELEC*) switch.

intersección [intersek'θjon] *nf* intersection.

interurbano, a [interur'βano, a] *a*: **llamada** ~**a** trunk call.

intervalo [inter'βalo] *nm* interval; (*descanso*) break; **a** ~**s** at intervals, every now and then.

intervenir [interβe'nir] *vt* (*controlar*) to control, supervise; (*MED*) to operate on // *vi* (*participar*) to take part, participate; (*mediar*) to intervene.

interventor, a [interβen'tor, a] *nm/f* inspector; (*COM*) auditor.

interviú [inter'βju] *nf* interview.

intestino, a [intes'tino, a] *a* internal; (*doméstico*) domestic // *nm* intestine.

intimar [inti'mar] *vt* to intimate, announce // *vi* to become friendly.

intimidad [intimi'ðað] *nf* intimacy; (*confianza*) confidence; (*familiaridad*) familiarity; (*vida privada*) private life; (*soledad*) privacy.

íntimo, a ['intimo, a] *a* intimate.

intolerable [intole'raβle] *a* intolerable, unbearable.

intransitable [intransi'taβle] *a* impassable.

intrepidez [intrepi'ðeθ] *nf* courage, bravery; **intrépido, a** *a* intrepid.

intriga [in'triɣa] *nf* intrigue; (*plan*) plot; **intrigar** *vt, vi* to intrigue.

intrincado, a [intrin'kaðo, a] *a* intricate.

intrínseco, a [in'trinseko, a] *a* intrinsic.

introducción [introðuk'θjon] *nf* introduction.

introducir [introðu'θir] *vt* (*gen*) to introduce; (*hacer penetrar*) to insert.

intruso, a [in'truso, a] *a* intrusive // *nm/f* intruder.

intuición [intwi'θjon] *nf* intuition.

inundación [inunda'θjon] *nf* flood(ing); **inundar** *vt* to flood; (*fig*) to swamp, inundate.

inusitado, a [inusi'taðo, a] *a* unusual.

inútil [in'util] *a* useless; (*esfuerzo*) vain, fruitless; **inutilidad** *nf* uselessness.

inutilizar [inutili'θar] *vt* to make useless, render useless; ~**se** *vr* to become useless.

invadir [inβa'ðir] *vt* to invade.

inválido, a [in'βaliðo, a] *a* invalid // *nm/f* invalid.

invariable [inβa'rjaβle] *a* invariable.

invasión [inβa'sjon] *nf* invasion.

invasor, a [inβa'sor, a] *a* invading // *nm/f* invader.

invención [inβen'θjon] *nf* invention.

inventar [inβen'tar] *vt* to invent.

inventario [inβen'tarjo] *nm* inventory.

inventiva [inβen'tiβa] *nf* inventiveness.

inventor, a [inβen'tor, a] *nm/f* inventor.

inverosímil [inβero'simil] *a* implausible; (*improbable*) unlikely, improbable.

inversión [inβer'sjon] *nf* (*COM*) investment; (*AUTO*) reversing; **inversionista** *nm/f* investor.

inverso, a [in'βerso, a] *a* inverse, opposite; **en el orden** ~ in reverse order; **a la** ~**a** inversely, the other way round.

invertir [inβer'tir] *vt* (*COM*) to invest; (*volcar*) to turn upside down; (*tiempo etc*) to spend; (*AUTO*) to reverse.

investigación [inβestiɣa'θjon] *nf* investigation; (*estudio*) research; **investigar** *vt* to investigate; (*estudiar*) to do research into.

inveterado, a [inβete'raðo, a] *a* inveterate, confirmed.

invicto, a [in'βikto, a] *a* unconquered.

invierno [in'βjerno] *nm* winter.

invitar [inβi'tar] *vt* to invite; (*incitar*) to entice; (*pagar*) to buy, pay for.

invocar [inβo'kar] *vt* to invoke, call on.

inyección [injek'θjon] *nf* injection.

inyectar [injek'tar] *vt* to inject.

ir [ir] *vi* (*gen*) to go; (*viajar*) to travel; (*ropa*) to suit; ~ **caminando** to walk; ~ **en coche/bicicleta/caballo/a pie** to drive/cycle/ride/walk; ¡**voy**! I'm coming!; ~ **de viaje** to travel, go away; **voy para viejo** I'm getting on (in years); ~ **por/a por algo** to go for/go and get sth; ¡**qué va**! (*no diga*) you don't say!; (: ¡*no!*) no way!, rubbish!; ¡**vamos**! come on!; **vaya susto que me has dado** what a fright

you gave me; ~se *vr* to go away, leave; (*mano etc*) to slip; ¡vete! go away!
ira ['ira] *nf* anger, rage.
iracundo, a [ira'kundo, a] *a* irascible; (*colérico*) irate.
Irán [i'ran] *nm* Iran; **iraní, esa, iraní** *a, nm/f* Iranian.
iris ['iris] *nm* (*arco* ~) rainbow; (ANAT) iris.
Irlanda [ir'landa] *nf* Ireland; **irlandés, esa** *a* Irish // *nm/f* Irishman/woman.
ironía [iro'nia] *nf* irony; **irónico, a** *a* ironic(al).
irreal [irre'al] *a* unreal.
irreflexión [irreflek'sjon] *nf* thoughtlessness.
irremediable [irreme'ðjaβle] *a* incurable, hopeless.
irresoluto, a [irreso'luto, a] *a* irresolute, hesitant.
irrespetuoso, a [irrespe'twoso, a] *a* disrespectful.
irresponsable [irrespon'saβle] *a* irresponsible.
irrigar [irri'xar] *vt* to irrigate.
irrisorio, a [irri'sorjo, a] *a* derisory, ridiculous.
irritar [irri'tar] *vt* to irritate, annoy.
irrupción [irrup'θjon] *nf* irruption; (*invasión*) invasion.
isla ['isla] *nf* island.
islandés, esa [islan'des, esa] *a* Icelandic // *nm/f* Icelander.
Islandia [is'landja] *nf* Iceland.
isleño, a [is'leɲo, a] *a* island *cpd* // *nm/f* islander.
Israel [isra'el] *nm* Israel; **israelí** *a, nm/f* Israeli.
istmo ['istmo] *nm* isthmus.
Italia [i'talja] *nf* Italy; **italiano, a** *a, nm/f* Italian.
itinerario [itine'rarjo] *nm* itinerary, route.
izar [i'θar] *vt* to hoist.
izquierdista [iθkjer'ðista] *nm/f* left winger, leftist.
izquierdo, a [iθ'kjerðo, a] *a* left // *nf* left; **a la ~ a** on the left.

J

jabalí [xaβa'li] *nm* wild boar.
jabalina [xaβa'lina] *nf* javelin.
jabón [xa'βon] *nm* soap; **jabonar** *vt* to soap.
jaca ['xaka] *nf* pony.
jacinto [xa'θinto] *nm* hyacinth.
jactancia [xak'tanθja] *nf* boasting, boastfulness.
jactarse [xak'tarse] *vr* to boast, brag.
jadeante [xaðe'ante] *a* panting, gasping; **jadear** *vi* to pant, gasp for breath; **jadeo** *nm* panting, gasping.
jaez [xa'eθ] *nm* (*de caballerías*) harness; (*clase*) kind, sort.
jaguar [xa'xwar] *nm* jaguar.

jalar [xa'lar] *vt* to pull, haul.
jalbegue [xal'βexe] *nm* (*pintura*) whitewash; (*fig*) make-up.
jalea [xa'lea] *nf* jelly.
jaleo [xa'leo] *nm* racket, uproar; (*baile*) Andalusian popular dance; **estar de** ~ to be having a good time; **armar un** ~ to kick up a din.
Jamaica [xa'maika] *nf* Jamaica.
jamás [xa'mas] *ad* never; (*sin negación*) ever.
jamón [xa'mon] *nm* ham.
Japón [xa'pon] *nm*: **el** ~ Japan; **japonés, esa** *a, nm/f* Japanese.
jaque ['xake] *nm* cheque; (*fam*) bully; ~ **mate** checkmate.
jaqueca [xa'keka] *nf* (severe) headache, migraine.
jarabe [xa'raβe] *nm* syrup.
jarcia ['xarθja] *nf* (NAUT) ropes *pl*, rigging; (*para pescar*) (fishing) tackle; (*confusión, revoltijo*) jumble, mess.
jardín [xar'ðin] *nm* garden; **jardinería** *nf* gardening; **jardinero, a** *nm/f* gardener.
jarra ['xarra] *nf* jar.
jarro ['xarro] *nm* jug.
jaula ['xaula] *nf* cage.
jauría [xau'ria] *nf* pack of hounds.
J. C. *abr de* **Jesucristo.**
jefatura [xefa'tura] *nf*: ~ **de policía** police headquarters *sg*.
jefe ['xefe] *nm* (*gen*) chief, head; (*patrón*) boss; ~ **de camareros** head waiter; ~ **de cocina** chef; ~ **de estación** stationmaster; ~ **de estado** head of state; ~ **supremo** commander-in-chief; **ser el** ~ (*fig*) to be the boss.
jengibre [xen'xiβre] *nm* ginger.
jeque ['xeke] *nm* sheik.
jerarquía [xerar'kia] *nf* (*orden*) hierarchy; (*rango*) rank; **jerárquico, a** *a* hierarchic(al).
jerez [xe'reθ] *nm* sherry.
jerga ['xerxa] *nf* (*tela*) coarse cloth; (*lenguaje*) jargon, slang.
jerigonza [xeri'xonθa] *nf* (*jerga*) jargon, slang; (*galimatías*) nonsense, gibberish.
jeringa [xe'ringa] *nf* syringe; (AM) annoyance, bother; ~ **de engrase** grease gun; **jeringar** *vt* to syringe; (*inyectar*) to inject; (AM) to annoy, bother.
jeroglífico [xero'xlifiko] *nm* hieroglyphic.
jersé, jersey (*pl* **jerseys**) [xer'sei] *nm* jersey, pullover, jumper.
Jerusalén [xerusa'len] *n* Jerusalem.
Jesucristo [xesu'kristo] *n* Jesus Christ.
jesuita [xe'swita] *a, nm* Jesuit.
Jesús [xe'sus] *nm* Jesus; ¡~! good heavens!; (*al estornudar*) bless you!
jícara ['xikara] *nf* small cup.
jifero, a [xi'fero, a] *a* (*fam*) filthy // *nm* butcher's knife; (*matarife*) butcher, slaughterer.
jinete [xi'nete] *nm* (horse)rider.
jipijapa [xipi'xapa] *nm* (AM) straw hat.

jira ['xira] *nf* (*de tela*) strip; (*excursión*) picnic.

jirafa [xi'rafa] *nf* giraffe.

jirón [xi'ron] *nm* rag, shred.

jocosidad [xokosi'ðað] *nf* humour; (*chiste*) joke.

jocoso, a [xo'koso, a] *a* humorous, jocular.

jofaina [xo'faina] *nf* washbasin.

jornada [xor'naða] *nf* day's journey; (*camino o viaje entero*) journey; (*día de trabajo*) working day; (*fig*) lifetime.

jornal [xor'nal] *nm* (day's) wage; ~**ero** *nm* (day) labourer.

joroba [xo'roβa] *nf* hump, hunched back; (*fam*) nuisance; ~**do, a** *a* hunchbacked // *nm/f* hunchback.

jota ['xota] *nf* letter J; (*danza*) Aragonese dance; (*fam*) iota; **no saber** ~ to have no idea.

joven ['xoβen] *a* young // *nm* young man, youth // *nf* young woman, girl.

jovial [xo'βjal] *a* cheerful, jovial; ~**idad** *nf* cheerfulness, joviality.

joya ['xoja] *nf* jewel, gem; (*fig: persona*) gem; **joyería** *nf* (*joyas*) jewellery; (*tienda*) jeweller's (shop); **joyero** *nm* (*persona*) jeweller; (*caja*) jewel case.

juanete [xwa'nete] *nm* bunion.

jubilación [xuβila'θjon] *nf* (*retiro*) retirement; (*alegría*) jubilation.

jubilar [xuβi'lar] *vt* to pension off, retire; (*fam*) to discard // *vi* to rejoice; ~**se** *vr* to retire.

jubileo [xuβi'leo] *nm* (*indulgencia*) jubilee; (*fam*) comings and goings *pl*.

júbilo ['xuβilo] *nm* joy, jubilation, rejoicing; ~**so, a** *a* jubilant.

judaísmo [xuða'ismo] *nm* Judaism.

judía [xu'ðia] *nf* Jewess; (*CULIN*) bean.

judicatura [xuðika'tura] *nf* (*cargo de juez*) office of judge; (*magistratura*) judicature.

judicial [xuði'θjal] *a* judicial.

judío, a [xu'ðio, a] *a* Jewish // *nm/f* Jew/ess.

juego *etc vb ver* **jugar** // ['xweɣo] *nm* (*gen*) play; (*pasatiempo, partido*) game; (*en casino*) gambling; (*conjunto*) set; **fuera de** ~ (*persona*) offside; (*pelota*) out of play.

juerga ['xwerɣa] *nf* good time; (*fiesta*) party; **ir de** ~ to go out on a spree.

jueves ['xweβes] *nm inv* Thursday.

juez [xweθ] *nm* judge; ~ **de línea** linesman; ~ **de salida** starter.

jugada [xu'ɣaða] *nf* play; **buena** ~ good move/shot/stroke *etc*.

jugador, a [xuɣa'ðor, a] *nm/f* player; (*en casino*) gambler.

jugar [xu'ɣar] *vt, vi* to play; (*en casino*) to gamble; ~**se** *vr* to gamble (away).

juglar [xu'ɣlar] *nm* minstrel.

jugo ['xuɣo] *nm* (*BOT*) juice; (*fig*) essence, substance; ~**so, a** *a* juicy; (*fig*) substantial, important.

juguete [xu'ɣete] *nm* toy; (*TEATRO*) sketch; ~**ar** *vi* to play; ~**ría** *nf* toyshop.

juguetón, ona [xuɣe'ton, ona] *a* playful.

juicio ['xwiθjo] *nm* judgement; (*sana razón*) sanity, reason; (*opinión*) opinion; **estar fuera de** ~ to be out of one's mind; ~**so, a** *a* wise, sensible.

julio ['xuljo] *nm* July.

jumento, a [xu'mento, a] *nm/f* donkey.

junco ['xunko] *nm* rush, reed.

jungla ['xungla] *nf* jungle.

junio ['xunjo] *nm* June.

junta ['xunta] *nf ver* **junto**.

juntamente [xunta'mente] *ad* (*conjuntamente*) together; (*al mismo tiempo*) together, at the same time.

juntar [xun'tar] *vt* to join, unite; (*maquinaria*) to assemble, put together; (*dinero*) to collect; (*puerta*) to half-close, leave ajar; ~**se** *vr* to join, meet; (*reunirse: personas*) to meet, assemble; (*arrimarse*) to approach, draw closer; (*vivir juntos*) to live together; ~**se con uno** to join sb.

junto, a ['xunto, a] *a* (*unido*) joined, united; (*anexo*) near, close; (*continuo, próximo*) next, adjacent // *ad*: **todo** ~ all at once // *nf* (*asamblea*) meeting, assembly; (*comité, consejo*) board, council, committee; (*articulación*) joint; ~ **a** near (to), next to; ~**s** together.

juntura [xun'tura] *nf* (*punto de unión*) join, junction; (*articulación*) joint.

jurado [xu'raðo] *nm* (*JUR*) juror; (: *conjunto de* ~**s**) jury; (*de concurso*) panel (of judges); (: *individuo*) member of a panel.

juramentar [xuramen'tar] *vt* to swear in, administer the oath to; ~**se** *vr* to be sworn in, take the oath.

juramento [xura'mento] *nm* oath; (*maldición*) oath, curse; **prestar** ~ to take the oath; **tomar** ~ **a** to swear in, administer the oath to.

jurar [xu'rar] *vt, vi* to swear; ~ **en falso** to commit perjury; **jurárselas a uno** to have it in for sb.

jurídico, a [xu'riðiko, a] *a* legal.

jurisdicción [xurisðik'θjon] *nf* (*poder, autoridad*) jurisdiction; (*territorio*) district.

jurisprudencia [xurispru'ðenθja] *nf* jurisprudence.

jurista [xu'rista] *nm/f* jurist.

justamente [xusta'mente] *ad* justly, fairly; (*precisamente*) just, precisely, exactly.

justicia [xus'tiθja] *nf* justice; (*equidad*) fairness, justice; **justiciero, a** *a* just, righteous.

justificación [xustifika'θjon] *nf* justification; **justificar** *vt* to justify.

justo, a ['xusto, a] *a* (*equitativo*) just, fair, right; (*preciso*) exact, correct; (*ajustado*) tight // *ad* (*precisamente*) exactly, precisely.

juvenil [xuβe'nil] *a* youthful.

juventud [xuβen'tuð] *nf* (*adolescencia*) youth; (*jóvenes*) young people *pl*.

juzgado [xuθ'ɣaðo] *nm* tribunal; (*JUR*) court.

juzgar [xuθ'ɣar] *vt* to judge; **a** ~ **por...** to judge by..., judging by... .

K

kg *abr de* **kilogramo.**
kilo ['kilo] *nm* kilo // *pref:* ~**gramo** *nm* kilogramme; ~**litro** *nm* kilolitre; ~**metraje** *nm* distance in kilometres; **kilómetro** *nm* kilometre; ~**vatio** *nm* kilowatt.
kiosco ['kjosko] *nm* = **quiosco.**
km *abr de* **kilómetro.**
kv *abr de* **kilovatio.**

L

l *abr de* **litro.**
la [la] *det* the // *pron* her; (*Ud.*) you; (*cosa*) it // *nm* (*MUS*) la; ~ **del sombrero rojo** the girl in the red hat.
laberinto [laβe'rinto] *nm* labyrinth.
labia ['laβja] *nf* fluency; (*pey*) glibness.
labial [la'βjal] *a* labial; **lectura** ~ lip-reading.
labio ['laβjo] *nm* lip.
labor [la'βor] *nf* labour; (*AGR*) farm work; (*tarea*) job, task; (*costura*) needlework; ~**able** *a* workable; **día** ~**able** working day; ~**ar** *vi* to work; ~**eo** *nm* (*AGR*) cultivation; (*de minas*) working; ~**ioso, a** *a* (*persona*) hard-working; (*trabajo*) tough; ~**ista** *a:* **Partido L** ~**ista** Labour Party.
labrado, a [la'βraðo, a] *a* worked; (*cincelado*) carved; (*metal*) wrought // *nm* (*AGR*) cultivated field.
labrador, a [laβra'ðor, a] *a* farming // *nm/f* farmer.
labrantío, a [laβran'tio, a] *a* arable.
labranza [la'βranθa] *nf* (*AGR*) cultivation.
labrar [la'βrar] *vt* (*gen*) to work; (*madera etc*) to carve; (*fig*) to cause.
labriego, a [la'βrjexo, a] *nm/f* peasant.
laca ['laka] *nf* lacquer.
lacayo [la'kajo] *nm* lackey.
lacerar [laθe'rar] *vt* to lacerate.
lacio, a ['laθjo, a] *a* (*pelo*) lank; (*movimiento*) limp; (*BOT*) withered.
lacónico, a [la'koniko, a] *a* laconic.
lacrar [la'krar] *vt* (*MED*) to injure the health of; (*dañar*) to harm; (*cerrar*) to seal (with sealing wax); ~**se** *vr* to harm o.s.; **lacre** *nm* sealing wax.
lacrimoso, a [lakri'moso, a] *a* tearful.
lactar [lak'tar] *vt*, *vi* to suckle.
ladear [laðe'ar] *vt* to tip, tilt; (*ciudad, colina*) to skirt // *vi* to tilt; ~**se** *vr* to lean.
ladera [la'ðera] *nf* slope.
ladino, a [la'ðino, a] *a* cunning.
lado ['laðo] *nm* (*gen*) side; (*fig*) protection; (*MIL*) flank; **al** ~ **de** beside; **poner de** ~ to put on its side; **poner a un** ~ to put aside; **por todos** ~**s** on all sides, all round.
ladrar [la'ðrar] *vi* to bark; **ladrido** *nm* bark, barking.
ladrillo [la'ðriʎo] *nm* (*gen*) brick; (*azulejo*) tile; (*color*) brick red.

ladrón, ona [la'ðron, ona] *nm*
lagar [la'xar] *nm* (wine/oil) pre
lagarto [la'xarto] *nm* (*ZOOL*) liza
fam) sharp customer; ~ **de**
alligator.
lago ['laxo] *nm* lake.
lágrima ['laxrima] *nf* tear; **lagrimar** *vi* to weep.
laguna [la'xuna] *nf* (*lago*) lagoon; (*hueco*) gap.
laico, a ['laiko, a] *a* lay.
lamentable [lamen'taβle] *a* lamentable, regrettable; (*miserable*) pitiful.
lamentar [lamen'tar] *vt* (*sentir*) to regret; (*deplorar*) to lament; ~**se** *vr* to lament; **lamento** *nm* lament.
lamer [la'mer] *vt* to lick.
lámina ['lamina] *nf* (*plancha delgada*) sheet; (*para estampar, estampa*) plate; **laminar** *vt* (*en libro*) to laminate.
lámpara ['lampara] *nf* lamp; ~ **de alcohol/gas** spirit/gas lamp; ~ **de bolsillo** torch; ~ **de pie** standard lamp.
lampiño, a [lam'piɲo] *a* clean-shaven.
lana ['lana] *nf* wool.
lance ['lanθe] *nm* (*golpe*) stroke; (*suceso*) event, incident; (*riña*) quarrel; (*tirada*) throw; **libros de** ~ second-hand books.
lancha ['lantʃa] *nf* launch; ~ **automóvil** motorboat; ~ **de pesca** fishing boat; ~ **salvavidas/torpedera** lifeboat/torpedo boat; **lanchero** *nm* boatman.
lanero, a [la'nero, a] *a* woollen.
langosta [lan'gosta] *nf* (*insecto*) locust; (*crustáceo*) lobster; (*fig*) plague; **langostín, langostino** *nm* prawn.
languidecer [langiðe'θer] *vi* to languish; **languidez** *nf* languor; **lánguido, a** *a* (*gen*) languid; (*sin energía*) listless.
lanilla [la'niʎa] *nf* nap.
lanudo, a [la'nuðo, a] *a* woolly.
lanza ['lanθa] *nf* (*arma*) lance, spear; (*de vagón*) pole.
lanzadera [lanθa'ðera] *nf* shuttle.
lanzamiento [lanθa'mjento] *nm* (*gen*) throwing; (*NAUT, COM*) launch, launching; ~ **de pesos** putting the shot.
lanzar [lan'θar] *vt* (*gen*) to throw; (*DEPORTE*) to bowl; (*NAUT, COM*) to launch; (*JUR*) to evict; (*MED*) to vomit; ~**se** *vr* to throw o.s.
laña ['laɲa] *nf* clamp.
lapa ['lapa] *nf* limpet.
lapicero [lapi'θero] *nm* propelling pencil.
lápida ['lapiða] *nf* stone; ~ **mortuoria** headstone; ~ **conmemorativa** memorial stone; **lapidar** *vt* to stone; **lapidario, a** *a, nm* lapidary.
lápiz ['lapiθ] *nm* pencil; ~ **de color** coloured pencil; ~ **de labios** lipstick.
lapón, ona [la'pon, ona] *nm/f* Laplander, Lapp.
lapso ['lapso] *nm* (*de tiempo*) interval; (*error*) error.
largar [lar'xar] *vt* (*soltar*) to release; (*aflojar*) to loosen; (*lanzar*) to launch;

(*fam*) to let fly; (*pelota*) to throw; (*velas*) to unfurl; (*AM*) to throw; ~se *vr* (*fam*) to beat it; (*NAUT*) to set sail; ~se a (*AM*) to start to.

largo, a ['larxo, a] *a* (*longitud*) long; (*tiempo*) lengthy; (*persona: alta*) tall; (*fig*) generous // *nm* length; (*MUS*) largo // *ad* widely; **dos años** ~s two long years; **tiene 9 metros de** ~ it is 9 metres long; **a lo** ~ **de** along.

largueza [lar'xeθa] *nf* generosity.

lárice ['lariθe] *nm* larch.

laringe [la'rinxe] *nf* larynx; **laringitis** *nf* laryngitis.

larva ['larßa] *nf* larva.

las [las] *det* the // *pron* them; ~ **que cantan** the ones/women/girls who sing.

lascivo, a [las'θißo, a] *a* lewd.

láser ['laser] *nm* laser.

lasitud [lasi'tuð] *nf* lassitude, weariness.

lástima ['lastima] *nf* (*pena*) pity; (*queja*) complaint; **dar** ~ to be pitiful; **es** ~ **que** it's a pity that; **¡qué** ~! what a pity!; **ella está hecha una** ~ she looks pitiful.

lastimar [lasti'mar] *vt* (*herir*) to wound; (*ofender*) to offend; (*compadecer*) to pity; ~se *vr* to hurt o.s.; ~**se de** to feel sorry for; **lastimero, a, lastimoso, a** *a* pitiful, pathetic.

lastre ['lastre] *nm* (*TEC, NAUT*) ballast; (*fig*) dead weight.

lata ['lata] *nf* (*metal*) tin; (*caja*) tin, can; (*fam*) nuisance; **hoja de** ~ tin(plate); **en** ~ tinned; **dar (la)** ~ to be a nuisance.

latente [la'tente] *a* latent.

lateral [late'ral] *a* side, lateral // *nm* (*TEATRO*) wings.

latido [la'tiðo] *nm* (*del corazón*) beat; (*de perro*) yelp.

latifundio [lati'fundjo] *nm* large estate; **latifundista** *nm/f* owner of a large estate.

latigazo [lati'xaθo] *nm* (*golpe*) lash; (*sonido*) crack; (*fig: regaño*) sharp reproof; (*fam: bebida*) swig.

látigo ['latixo] *nm* whip.

latín [la'tin] *nm* Latin.

latino, a [la'tino, a] *a* Latin; ~**americano, a** *a, nm/f* Latin-American.

latir [la'tir] *vi* (*corazón, pulso*) to beat; (*perro*) to yelp.

latitud [lati'tuð] *nf* (*GEO*) latitude; (*fig*) breadth.

lato, a ['lato, a] *a* broad.

latón [la'ton] *nm* brass.

latoso, a [la'toso, a] *a* (*cansado*) annoying; (*aburrido*) boring.

latrocinio [latro'θinjo] *nm* robbery.

laúd [la'uð] *nm* lute.

laudo ['lauðo] *nm* (*JUR*) decision.

laureado, a [laure'aðo, a] *a* honoured // *nm* laureate.

laurel [lau'rel] *nm* (*BOT*) laurel; (*CULIN*) bay.

lava ['laßa] *nf* lava.

lavabo [la'ßaßo] *nm* washbasin.

lavadero [laßa'ðero] *nm* laundry.

lavado [la'ßaðo] *nm* washing; (*de ropa*) laundry; (*ARTE*) wash; ~ **de cerebro** brainwashing; ~ **en seco** dry cleaning.

lavadora [laßa'ðora] *nf* washing machine.

lavamanos [laßa'manos] *nm inv* washbasin.

lavandería [laßande'ria] *nf* laundry; ~ **automática** launderette.

lavaplatos [laßa'platos] *nm o f inv* dishwasher.

lavar [la'ßar] *vt* to wash; (*borrar*) to wipe away; ~se *vr* to wash o.s.; ~**se las manos** to wash one's hands; ~ **y marcar** (*pelo*) to shampoo and set; ~ **en seco** to dry clean.

lavavajillas [laßaßa'xiʎas] *nm inv* dishwasher.

laxante [lak'sante] *nm* laxative.

laya ['laja] *nf* spade; **de la misma** ~ (*fig*) of the same sort.

lazada [la'θaða] *nf* bow.

lazo ['laθo] *nm* knot; (*lazada*) bow; (*para animales*) lasso; (*trampa*) snare; (*de camino*) hairpin bend; (*vínculo*) tie.

lb(s) *abr de* **libra(s).**

le [le] *pron* (*directo*) him; (: *usted*) you; (*indirecto*) to him; (: *usted*) to you.

leal [le'al] *a* loyal; ~**tad** *nf* loyalty.

lebrel [le'ßrel] *nm* greyhound.

lección [lek'θjon] *nf* lesson.

lector, a [lek'tor, a] *nm/f* reader.

lectura [lek'tura] *nf* reading.

leche ['letʃe] *nf* milk; **tener mala** ~ to be nasty; ~ **condensada/en polvo** condensed/powdered milk; ~ **desnatada** skimmed milk; ~ **de magnesia** milk of magnesia; ~**ra** *nf* (*vendedora*) milkmaid; (*para hervir*) milk pan; (*para servir*) milkjug; (*AM*) cow; ~**ría** *nf* dairy.

lecho ['letʃo] *nm* (*cama*) bed; (*de río*) bottom; (*GEO*) layer.

lechón [le'tʃon] *nm* sucking pig.

lechoso, a [le'tʃoso, a] *a* milky.

lechuga [le'tʃuxa] *nf* lettuce.

lechuza [le'tʃuθa] *nf* owl.

leer [le'er] *vt* to read.

legación [lexa'θjon] *nf* legation.

legado [le'xaðo] *nm* (*don*) bequest; (*herencia*) legacy; (*enviado*) legate.

legajo [le'xaxo] *nm* file.

legal [le'xal] *a* (*gen*) legal; (*persona*) trustworthy; ~**idad** *nf* legality; ~**izar** *vt* to legalize; (*documento*) to authenticate.

légamo [le'xamo] *nm* (*cieno*) mud, ooze.

legar [le'xar] *vt* to bequeath, leave; **legatario, a** *nm/f* legatee.

legión [le'xjon] *nf* legion; **legionario, a** *a* legionary // *nm* legionnaire.

legislación [lexisla'θjon] *nf* legislation; **legislar** *vt* to legislate.

legitimar [lexiti'mar] *vt* to legitimize; **legítimo, a** *a* (*genuino*) authentic; (*legal*) legitimate.

lego, a ['lexo, a] *a* (*REL*) secular; (*ignorante*) ignorant // *nm* layman.

legua ['lexwa] *nf* league.

leguleyo [leʁu'lejo] *nm* (*pey*) petty lawyer.

legumbre [le'ʁumbre] *nf* vegetable.

leído, a [le'iðo, a] *a* well-read.

lejanía [lexa'nia] *nf* distance; **lejano, a** *a* far-off; (*en el tiempo*) distant; (*fig*) remote.

lejía [le'xia] *nf* bleach.

lejos ['lexos] *ad* far, far away; **a lo** ∼ in the distance; **de** *o* **desde** ∼ from afar; ∼ **de** *prep* far from.

lelo, a ['lelo, a] *a* silly; (*fig*) open-mouthed // *nm/f* idiot.

lema ['lema] *nm* motto; (*POL*) slogan.

lencería [lenθe'ria] *nf* drapery.

lengua ['lengwa] *nf* tongue; ∼ **moderna** modern language; **morderse la** ∼ to hold one's tongue.

lenguado [len'gwaðo] *nm* sole.

lenguaje [len'gwaxe] *nm* language.

lenguaraz [lengwa'raθ] *a* talkative; (*pey*) foul-mouthed.

lengüeta [len'gweta] *nf* (*ANAT*) epiglottis; (*de balanza, zapatos, MUS*) tongue; (*herramienta*) needle.

lenidad [leni'ðað] *nf* lenience.

lente ['lente] *nm o f* lens; (*lupa*) magnifying glass; ∼**s** *npl* glasses; ∼**s de contacto** contact lenses.

lenteja [len'texa] *nf* lentil; **lentejuela** *nf* sequin.

lentitud [lenti'tuð] *nf* slowness; **con** ∼ slowly.

lento, a ['lento, a] *a* slow.

leña ['leɲa] *nf* firewood; ∼**dor, a,** ∼**tero,** *a nm/f* woodcutter.

leño ['leɲo] *nm* (*trozo de árbol*) log; (*madera*) timber; (*fig*) blockhead.

Leo ['leo] *nm* Leo.

león [le'on] *nm* lion; (*AM*) puma; ∼ **marino** sea lion; **leonino, a** *a* leonine.

leontina [leon'tina] *nf* watch chain.

leopardo [leo'parðo] *nm* leopard.

lepra ['lepra] *nf* leprosy; **leproso, a** *nm/f* leper.

lerdo, a ['lerðo, a] *a* (*lento*) slow, (*patoso*) clumsy.

les [les] *pron* (*directo*) them; (: *ustedes*) you; (*indirecto*) to them; (: *ustedes*) to you.

lesbiana [les'ßjana] *a, nf* lesbian.

lesión [le'sjon] *nf* (*daño*) lesion; (*fig*) injury; **lesionado, a** *a* injured // *nm/f* injured person.

letal [le'tal] *a* lethal.

letanía [leta'nia] *nf* litany.

letargo [le'tarʁo] *nm* (*MED*) lethargy.

letra ['letra] *nf* letter; (*escritura*) handwriting; (*MUS*) lyrics *pl*; ∼ **de cambio** bill of exchange; ∼ **de imprenta** print; ∼**do,** *a a* learned; (*fam*) pedantic // *nm* lawyer; **letrero** *nm* (*cartel*) sign; (*etiqueta*) label.

leva ['leßa] *nf* (*NAUT*) weighing anchor; (*MIL*) levy; (*TEC*) lever.

levadizo [leßa'ðiθo] *a:* **puente** ∼ drawbridge.

levadura [leßa'ðura] *nf* (*para el pan*) yeast; (*de la cerveza*) brewer's yeast.

levantamiento [leßanta'mjento] *nm* raising, lifting; (*rebelión*) revolt, rising; ∼ **de pesos** weight-lifting.

levantar [leßan'tar] *vt* (*gen*) to raise; (*del suelo*) to pick up; (*hacia arriba*) to lift (up); (*plan*) to make, draw up; (*mesa*) to clear away; (*campamento*) to strike; (*fig*) to cheer up, hearten; ∼**se** *vr* to get up; (*enderezarse*) to straighten up; (*rebelarse*) to rebel; ∼ **el ánimo** to cheer up.

levante [le'ßante] *nm* east coast; **el L** ∼ the Near East, the Levant.

levar [le'ßar] *vi* to weigh anchor; ∼**se** *vr* to set sail.

leve ['leße] *a* light; (*fig*) trivial; ∼**dad** *nf* lightness.

levita [le'ßita] *nf* frock coat.

léxico ['leksiko] *nm* lexicon, dictionary.

ley [lei] *nf* (*gen*) law; (*fig*) loyalty; (*metal*) standard.

leyenda [le'jenda] *nf* legend.

leyó *etc vb ver* **leer.**

liar [li'ar] *vt* to tie (up); (*unir*) to bind; (*envolver*) to wrap (up); (*enredar*) to confuse; (*cigarrillo*) to roll; ∼**se** *vr* (*fam*) to get involved; ∼**se a palos** to get involved in a fight.

Líbano ['lißano] *nm:* **el** ∼ the Lebanon.

libar [li'ßar] *vt* to suck.

libelo [li'ßelo] *nm* satire, lampoon; (*JUR*) petition.

libélula [li'ßelula] *nf* dragonfly.

liberación [lißera'θjon] *nf* liberation; (*de la cárcel*) release.

liberal [liße'ral] *a, nm/f* liberal; ∼**idad** *nf* liberality; (*lujo*) lavishness.

liberar [liße'rar] *vt* to liberate.

libertad [lißer'tað] *nf* liberty; (*soltura*) freedom; ∼ **de culto/de prensa/de comercio** freedom of worship/the press/of trade; ∼ **condicional** probation; ∼ **bajo palabra** parole; ∼ **bajo fianza** bail.

libertar [lißer'tar] *vt* (*preso*) to set free; (*de una obligación*) to release; (*eximir*) to exempt.

libertino, a [lißer'tino, a] *a* loose-living // *nm/f* libertine.

libra ['lißra] *nf* pound; **L** ∼ (*ASTRO*) Libra; ∼ **esterlina** pound sterling.

librador, a [lißra'ðor, a] *nm/f* drawer.

libramiento [lißra'mjento] *nm* rescue; (*COM*) delivery.

libranza [li'ßranθa] *nf* (*COM*) draft; (*de letra de cambio*) bill of exchange.

librar [li'ßrar] *vt* (*de peligro*) to save; (*batalla*) to wage, fight; (*de impuestos*) to exempt; (*secreto*) to reveal; (*mercancías*) to draw; (*cheque*) to make out; (*JUR*) to exempt // *vi* to give birth; ∼**se** *vr:* ∼**se de** to escape from, free o.s. from.

libre ['lißre] *a* (*gen*) free; (*lugar*) unoccupied; (*asiento*) vacant; (*de impuestos*) tax-free; (*de deudas*) free of debts; (*pey*) outspoken; **tiro** ∼ free kick; **los 100 metros** ∼ the 100 metres freestyle (race); **al aire** ∼ in the open air.

librería [liβre'ria] *nf* (*biblioteca*) library; (*comercio*) bookshop; **librero, a** *nm/f* bookseller.

libreta [li'βreta] *nf* notebook; ~ **de ahorros** savings book; ~ **de banco** bank book.

libro ['liβro] *nm* book; ~ **en rústica/en pasta** *o* **encuadernado** paperback/hardback; ~ **de bolsillo** paperback; ~ **de caja** cashbook; ~ **de cheques** cheque book; ~ **de inventario** stock-list; ~ **de pedidos** order book; ~ **de texto** textbook.

Lic. *abr de* **licenciado, a.**

licencia [li'θenθja] *nf* (*gen*) licence; (*permiso*) permission; ~ **por enfermedad/con goce de sueldo** sick leave/paid leave; ~ **de caza/de conductor** game/driving licence; ~ **de derecho/de letras** law/arts degree; ~**do, a** *a* licensed // *nm/f* graduate; **licenciar** *vt* (*empleado*) to dismiss; (*permitir*) to permit, allow; (*soldado*) to discharge; (*estudiante*) to confer a degree upon; **licenciarse** *vr*: **licenciarse en letras** to graduate in arts.

licencioso, a [liθen'θjoso, a] *a* licentious.

liceo [li'θeo] *nm* (high) school.

licitador [liθita'ðor] *nm* bidder; (*AM*) auctioneer; **licitar** *vt* to bid for; (*AM*) to sell by auction.

lícito, a ['liθito, a] *a* (*legal*) lawful; (*justo*) fair, just; (*permisible*) permissible.

licor [li'kor] *nm* spirits *pl*; (*preparado*) liqueur.

licuadora [likwa'ðora] *nf* food-mixer, liquidizer; **licuar** *vt* to liquidize.

lid [lið] *nf* combat; (*fig*) controversy.

líder ['liðer] *nm/f* leader; **liderato** *nm* leadership.

lidia ['liðja] *nf* bullfight; **toros de** ~ fighting bulls; **lidiar** *vt*, *vi* to fight.

liebre ['ljeβre] *nf* hare.

lienzo ['ljenθo] *nm* linen; (*ARTE*) canvas; (*pañuelo*) handkerchief; (*ARQ*) wall.

liga ['li\va] *nf* (*de medias*) garter, suspender; (*confederación*) league; (*venda*) band; (*aleación*) alloy; (*BOT*) mistletoe.

ligadura [li\va'ðura] *nf* bond, tie; (*MED*, *MUS*) ligature.

ligamento [li\va'mento] *nm* (*ANAT*) ligament; (*atadura*) tie; (*unión*) bond.

ligar [li'\var] *vt* (*atar*) to tie; (*unir*) to join; (*MED*) to bind up; (*MUS*) to slur; (*metales*) to alloy // *vi* to mix, blend; (*fam*) to pick up; (*entenderse*) to get on (well); ~**se** *vr* to commit o.s.

ligereza [lixe're\va] *nf* lightness; (*rapidez*) swiftness; (*agilidad*) agility; (*superficialidad*) flippancy.

ligero, a [li'xero, a] *a* (*de peso*) light; (*tela*) thin; (*rápido*) swift, quick; (*ágil*) agile, nimble; (*de importancia*) slight; (*de carácter*) flippant, superficial // *ad*: **a la** ~**a** superficially.

lija ['lixa] *nf* (*ZOOL*) dogfish; (**papel de**) ~ sandpaper.

lila ['lila] *nf* lilac // *nm* (*fam*) twit.

lima ['lima] *nf* file; (*BOT*) lime; ~ **de carpintero** file; ~ **de uñas** nail-file; **limar** *vt* to file.

limitación [limita'θjon] *nf* limitation, limit.

limitar [limi'tar] *vt* to limit; (*reducir*) to reduce, cut down // *vi*: ~ **con** to border on; ~**se** *vr*: ~**se a** to limit o.s. to.

límite ['limite] *nm* (*gen*) limit; (*fin*) end; (*frontera*) border; ~ **de velocidad** speed limit.

limítrofe [li'mitrofe] *a* bordering, neighbouring.

limón [li'mon] *nm* lemon // *a*: **amarillo** ~ lemon-yellow; **limonada** *nf* lemonade; **limonero** *nm* lemon tree.

limosna [li'mosna] *nf* alms *pl*; **vivir de** ~ to live on charity.

limpiabotas [limpja'βotas] *nm inv* bootblack, shoeshine boy/girl.

limpiaparabrisas [limpjapara'βrisas] *nm inv* windscreen wiper.

limpiar [lim'pjar] *vt* (*gen*) to clean; (*con trapo*) to wipe; (*quitar*) to wipe away; (*zapatos*) to shine, polish; (*fig*) to clean up.

limpieza [lim'pjeθa] *nf* (*estado*) cleanliness; (*acto*) cleaning; (: *de las calles*) cleansing; (: *de zapatos*) polishing; (*habilidad*) skill; (*fig*) clean-up; (*pureza*) purity; (*MIL*): **operación de** ~ mopping-up operation; ~ **en seco** dry cleaning.

limpio, a ['limpjo, a] *a* clean; (*moralmente*) pure; (*COM*) clear, net; (*fam*) honest // *ad*: **jugar** ~ to play fair // *nm*: **pasar en** ~ to make a fair copy.

linaje [li'naxe] *nm* lineage, family; **linajudo, a** *a* highborn.

linaza [li'naθa] *nf* linseed; **aceite de** ~ linseed oil.

lince ['linθe] *nm* lynx.

linchar [lin'tʃar] *vt* to lynch.

lindante [lin'dante] *a* adjoining; ~ **con** bordering on.

lindar [lin'dar] *vi* to adjoin; ~ **con** to border on; **linde** *nm o f* boundary; **lindero, a** *a* adjoining // *nm* boundary.

lindo, a ['lindo, a] *a* pretty, lovely // *ad* (*AM*): **nos divertimos de lo** ~ we had a marvellous time; **canta muy** ~ he/she sings beautifully.

línea ['linea] *nf* (*gen*) line; ~ **aérea** airline; ~ **delantera** (*DEPORTE*) forward line; ~ **de meta** goal line; (*de carrera*) finishing line; ~ **de saque** service line, base line; ~ **recta** straight line.

lingüista [lin'gwista] *nm/f* linguist.

linimento [lini'mento] *nm* liniment.

lino ['lino] *nm* linen; (*BOT*) flax.

linóleo [li'noleo] *nm* lino, linoleum.

linterna [lin'terna] *nf* lantern, lamp; ~ **eléctrica** *o* **a pilas** torch.

lío ['lio] *nm* bundle; (*fam*) fuss; (*desorden*) muddle, mess; **armar un** ~ to make a fuss.

liquidación [likiða'θjon] *nf* liquidation; **venta de** ~ clearance sale.

liquidar [liki'ðar] *vt* (*licuar*) to liquidize; (*eliminar*) to liquidate; (*mercaderías*) to sell off; (*pagar*) to pay off; (*terminar*) to wind up; (*AM*) to ruin; ~**se** *vr* to liquefy.

líquido, a ['likiðo, a] *a* liquid; (*ganancia*) net; (*AM*) accurate // *nm* liquid; ~ **imponible** net taxable income.

lira ['lira] *nf* (*MUS*) lyre; (*moneda*) lira.

lirio ['lirjo] *nm* (*BOT*) iris.

Lisboa [lis'ßoa] *n* Lisbon.

lisiado, a [li'sjaðo, a] *a* injured // *nm/f* cripple.

lisiar [li'sjar] *vt* to maim; ~**se** *vr* to injure o.s.

liso, a ['liso, a] *a* (*terreno*) flat; (*cabello*) straight; (*superficie*) even; (*tela*) smooth.

lisonja [li'sonxa] *nf* flattery; **lisonjear** *vt* to flatter; (*fig*) to please; **lisonjero, a** *a* (*gen*) flattering; (*agradable*) gratifying, pleasing // *nm/f* flatterer.

lista ['lista] *nf* (*gen*) list; (*de alumnos*) school register; (*de libros*) catalogue; (*de correos*) poste restante; (*de platos*) menu; (*de precios*) price list; **pasar** ~ to call the roll; ~ **de espera** waiting list; **tela a** ~**s** striped material.

listado, a [lis'taðo, a] *a* striped.

listo, a ['listo, a] *a* (*perspicaz*) smart, clever; (*preparado*) ready.

listón [lis'ton] *nm* (*tela*) ribbon; (*de madera, metal*) strip.

litera [li'tera] *nf* (*en barco, tren*) berth; (*en dormitorio*) bunk, bunk bed.

literato, a [lite'rato, a] *a* literary // *nm/f* writer.

literatura [litera'tura] *nf* literature.

litigar [liti'xar] *vt* to fight // *vi* (*JUR*) to go to law; (*fig*) to dispute, argue.

litigio [li'tixjo] *nm* (*JUR*) lawsuit; (*fig*): **en** ~ **con** in dispute with.

litografía [litoxra'fia] *nf* lithography; (*una* ~) lithograph.

litoral [lito'ral] *a* coastal // *nm* coast, seaboard.

litro ['litro] *nm* litre.

liviano, a [li'ßjano, a] *a* (*persona*) fickle; (*cosa, objeto*) trivial.

lívido, a ['lißiðo, a] *a* livid; (*AM*) pale.

ll... *ver bajo la letra LL, después de L.*

lo [lo] *det neuter def art*; ~ **bueno** the good // *pron* (*persona*) him; (*cosa*) it.

loa ['loa] *nf* praise; **loable** *a* praiseworthy; **loar** *vt* to praise.

lobato [lo'ßato] *nm* wolf cub.

lobo ['loßo] *nm* wolf; ~ **de mar** sea dog; ~ **marino** seal.

lóbrego, a ['loßrexo, a] *a* dark; (*fig*) gloomy.

lóbulo ['loßulo] *nm* lobe.

locación [loca'θjon] *nf* lease.

local [lo'kal] *a* local // *nm* place, site; (*oficinas*) premises *pl*; ~**idad** *nf* (*barrio*) locality; (*lugar*) location; (*TEATRO*) seat, ticket; ~**izar** *vt* (*ubicar*) to locate, find; (*restringir*) to localize; (*situar*) to place.

loco, a ['loko, a] *a* mad // *nm/f* lunatic, mad person.

locomoción [lokomo'θjon] *nf* locomotion.

locomotora [lokomo'tora] *nf* engine.

locuaz [lo'kwaθ] *a* loquacious.

locución [loku'θjon] *nf* expression.

locura [lo'kura] *nf* madness; (*acto*) crazy act.

lodo ['loðo] *nm* mud; ~**s** *nmpl* (*MED*) mudbath *sg*.

lógico, a ['loxiko, a] *a* logical // *nf* logic.

logística [lo'xistika] *nf* logistics *pl*.

lograr [lo'xrar] *vt* to achieve; (*obtener*) to get, obtain; ~ **hacer** to manage to do; ~ **que uno venga** to manage to get sb to come.

logro ['loxro] *nm* achievement, success; **prestar a** ~ to lend at a high rate of interest.

loma ['loma] *nf* hillock.

lombriz [lom'briθ] *nf* worm; ~ **solitaria** tapeworm.

lomo ['lomo] *nm* (*de animal*) back; (*de cerdo*) pork loin; (*de vaca*) rib steak; (*de libro*) spine.

lona ['lona] *nf* canvas.

Londres ['londres] *n* London.

longaniza [longa'niθa] *nf* pork sausage.

longitud [lonxi'tuð] *nf* length; (*GEO*) longitude; **tener 3 metros de** ~ to be 3 metres long; ~ **de onda** wavelength.

lonja ['lonxa] *nf* slice; (*de jamón*) rasher; ~ **de pescado** fish market.

lontananza [lonta'nanθa] *nf* background.

loor [lo'or] *nm* praise.

loro ['loro] *nm* parrot.

los [los] *det* the // *pron* them; (*ustedes*) you; **mis libros y** ~ **de Ud** my books and yours.

losa ['losa] *nf* stone; ~ **sepulcral** gravestone.

lote ['lote] *nm* portion; (*COM*) lot.

lotería [lote'ria] *nf* lottery; (*juego*) lotto.

loza ['loθa] *nf* crockery.

lozanía [loθa'nia] *nf* (*lujo*) luxuriance; (*orgullo*) pride; **lozano, a** *a* luxuriant; (*animado*) lively; (*altanero*) haughty.

lubricante [lußri'kante] *nm* lubricant; **lubricar** *vt* to lubricate.

lucero [lu'θero] *nm* (*ASTRO*) bright star; (*fig*) brilliance.

lucidez [luθi'ðeθ] *nf* lucidity; **lúcido, a** *a* lucid.

luciente [lu'θjente] *a* shining.

luciérnaga [lu'θjernaxa] *nf* glow-worm.

lucimiento [luθi'mjento] *nm* (*brillo*) brilliance; (*éxito*) success.

lucir [lu'θir] *vt* to illuminate, light (up); (*fig*) to show off // *vi* (*brillar*) to shine; (*tener éxito*) to be successful; ~**se** *vr* to dress up.

lucrarse [lu'krarse] *vr* to enrich o.s.

lucro ['lukro] *nm* profit, gain.

luctuoso, a [luk'twoso, a] *a* mournful.

lucha ['lutʃa] *nf* fight, struggle; ~ **de**

clases class struggle; ~ **libre** wrestling; **luchar** vi to fight.
ludibrio [luˈðiβrjo] nm mockery.
luego [ˈlweɣo] ad (después) next; (más tarde) later, afterwards; (pronto) soon; **desde** ~ of course; **tan** ~ **como** as soon as.
lugar [luˈɣar] nm place; (sitio) spot; **en** ~ **de** instead of; **hacer** ~ to make room; **fuera de** ~ out of place; **tener** ~ to take place; ~ **común** commonplace.
lugareño, a [luɣaˈreɲo, a] a village cpd // nm/f villager.
lúgubre [ˈluɣuβre] a mournful.
lujo [ˈluxo] nm luxury; (fig) profusion, abundance; ~ **so, a** a luxurious.
lujuria [luˈxurja] nf lust; (fig) lewdness.
lumbre [ˈlumbre] nf (gen) light.
lumbrera [lumˈbrera] nf luminary; (en techo) skylight; (de barco) vent, port.
luminoso, a [lumiˈnoso, a] a luminous, shining.
luna [ˈluna] nf moon; (de un espejo) glass; (de gafas) lens; (fig) crescent; ~ **llena/nueva** full/new moon; **estar con** ~ to have one's head in the clouds.
lunar [luˈnar] a lunar // nm (ANAT) mole; **tela a** ~ **es** spotted material.
lunes [ˈlunes] nm inv Monday.
luneta [luˈneta] nf lens.
lupa [ˈlupa] nf magnifying glass.
lustrar [lusˈtrar] vt (mueble) to polish; (zapatos) to shine; **lustre** nm polish; (fig) lustre; **dar lustre a** to polish; **lustroso, a** a shining.
luterano, a [luteˈrano, a] a Lutheran.
luto [ˈluto] nm mourning; (congoja) grief, sorrow; ~ **s** nmpl mourning clothes; **llevar el** o **vestirse de** ~ to be in mourning.
Luxemburgo [luksemˈburɣo] nm Luxembourg.
luz [luθ] (pl **luces**) nf light; **dar a** ~ **un niño** to give birth to a child; **sacar a** ~ to bring to light; (ELEC): **dar** ~ to switch on the light; **prender/apagar la** ~ to put the light on/off; **a todas luces** by any reckoning; **hacer la** ~ **sobre** to shed light on; **tener pocas luces** to be dim or stupid; ~ **roja/verde** red/green light; (AUTO): ~ **de costado** sidelight; ~ **de freno** brake light; ~ **del relámpago** flashlight; **luces de tráfico** traffic lights; **traje de luces** bullfighter's costume.

LL

llaga [ˈʎaɣa] nf wound.
llama [ˈʎama] nf flame; (ZOOL) llama.
llamada [ʎaˈmaða] nf call; ~ **al orden** call to order; **toque de** ~ (MIL) call-up; ~ **a pie de página** reference note.
llamamiento [ʎamaˈmjento] nm call.
llamar [ʎaˈmar] vt to call; (atención) to attract // vi (por teléfono) to telephone; (a la puerta) to knock/ring; (por señas) to beckon; (MIL) to call up; ~ **se** vr to be

called, be named; ¿**cómo se llama Usted?** what's your name?
llamarada [ʎamaˈraða] nf (llamas) blaze; (rubor) flush; (fig) flare-up.
llamativo, a [ʎamaˈtiβo, a] a showy; (color) loud.
llamear [ʎameˈar] vi to blaze.
llaneza [ʎaˈneθa] nf (gen) simplicity; (honestidad) straightforwardness, frankness.
llano, a [ˈʎano, a] a (superficie) flat; (persona) straightforward; (estilo) clear // nm plain, flat ground.
llanta [ˈʎanta] nf (wheel) rim; (AM): ~ **de goma** tyre.
llanto [ˈʎanto] nm weeping.
llanura [ʎaˈnura] nf plain.
llave [ˈʎaβe] nf key; (del agua) tap; (MECÁNICA) spanner; (de la luz) switch; (MUS) key; ~ **inglesa** monkey wrench; ~ **de contacto** (AUTO) ignition key; **echar** ~ **a** to lock up; ~ **ro** nm keyring; **llavín** nm latchkey.
llegada [ʎeˈɣaða] nf arrival.
llegar [ʎeˈɣar] vi to arrive; (alcanzar) to reach; (bastar) to be enough; ~ **se** vr: ~ **se a** to approach; ~ **a** to manage to, succeed in; ~ **a ser** to become; ~ **a las manos de** to come into the hands of.
llenar [ʎeˈnar] vt (gen) to fill; (espacio) to cover; (formulario) to fill in or up; (deber) to fulfil; (fig) to heap.
lleno, a [ˈʎeno, a] a full, filled; (repleto) full up // nm (abundancia) abundance; (ASTRO) full moon; (TEATRO) full house; **dar de** ~ **contra un muro** to hit a wall head-on.
llevadero, a [ʎeβaˈðero, a] a bearable, tolerable.
llevar [ʎeˈβar] vt (gen) to take; (ropa) to wear; (cargar) to carry; (quitar) to take away; (conducir a alguien) to drive; (cargar hacia) to transport; (traer: dinero) to carry; (conducir) to lead; (MAT) to carry; ~ **se** vr to carry off, take away; **llevamos dos días aquí** we have been here for two days; **él me lleva 2 años** he's 2 years older than me; (COM): ~ **los libros** to keep the books; ~ **se bien** to get on well (together).
llorar [ʎoˈrar] vt, vi to weep; ~ **de risa** to cry with laughter.
lloriquear [ʎorikeˈar] vi to snivel, whimper.
lloro [ˈʎoro] nm weeping; **llorón, ona** a tearful // nm/f cry-baby; ~ **so, a** a (gen) weeping, tearful; (triste) sad, sorrowful.
llover [ʎoˈβer] vi to rain; ~ **se** vr (techo) to leak.
llovizna [ʎoˈβiθna] nf drizzle; **lloviznar** vi to drizzle.
llueve etc vb ver llover.
lluvia [ˈʎuβja] nf rain; ~ **radioactiva** radioactive fallout; **lluvioso, a** a rainy.

M

m *abr de* **metro; minuto.**

macarrones [makaˈrrones] *nmpl* macaroni *sg.*

macerar [maθeˈrar] *vt* to macerate; *(fig)* to mortify; ~**se** *vr* to mortify o.s.

maceta [maˈθeta] *nf (de flores)* pot of flowers; *(para plantas)* flowerpot; *(mazo pequeño)* mallet.

macilento, a [maθiˈlento, a] *a* wan; *(ojeroso)* haggard.

macis [ˈmaθis] *nf* mace.

macizo, a [maˈθiθo, a] *a* massive; *(puerta)* solid // *nm* mass, chunk; *(de edificios)* block; *(AUTO)* solid tyre.

mácula [ˈmakula] *nf* stain, blemish; *(ANAT)* blind spot.

machacar [matʃaˈkar] *vt* to crush, pound // *vi* to go on, keep on.

machamartillo [matʃamarˈtiʎo]: **a** ~ *ad*: **cumplir a** ~ to carry out a task to the letter; **eran cristianos a** ~ they were totally convinced Christians.

machete [maˈtʃete] *nm (AM)* machete, (large) knife.

macho [ˈmatʃo] *a* male; *(fig)* virile // *nm* male; *(fig)* he-man.

machucar [matʃuˈkar] *vt* to pound.

madeja [maˈðexa] *nf (de lana)* skein, hank; *(de pelo)* mop.

madera [maˈðera] *nf* wood; *(fig)* nature, character; **una** ~ a piece of wood.

madero [maˈðero] *nm* beam; *(fig)* ship.

madrastra [maˈðrastra] *nf* stepmother.

madre [ˈmaðre] *a* mother *cpd*; *(AM)* tremendous // *nf* mother; *(ANAT)* womb; *(AGR)* main channel; *(de vino etc)* dregs *pl*; *(de río)* bed; ~ **política/soltera** mother-in-law/unmarried mother.

madreperla [maðreˈperla] *nf* mother-of-pearl.

madreselva [maðreˈselβa] *nf* honeysuckle.

madriguera [maðriˈɣera] *nf* burrow.

madrileño, a [maðriˈleɲo, a] *a* of *or* from Madrid // *nm/f* native of Madrid.

madrina [maˈðrina] *nf (protectora)* godmother; *(ARQ)* prop, shore; *(TEC)* brace; ~ **de boda** bridesmaid.

madrugada [maðruˈɣaða] *nf* early morning; *(alba)* dawn, daybreak; **madrugador, a** *a* early-rising; **madrugar** *vi* to get up early; *(fig)* to get ahead.

madurar [maðuˈrar] *vt*, *vi (fruta)* to ripen; *(fig)* to mature; **madurez** *nf* ripeness; maturity; **maduro, a** *a* ripe; mature.

maestra [maˈestra] *nf ver* **maestro.**

maestría [maesˈtria] *nf* mastery; *(habilidad)* skill, expertise.

maestro, a [maˈestro, a] *a* masterly; *(perito)* skilled, expert; *(principal)* main; *(educado)* trained // *nm/f* master/mistress; *(que enseña)* teacher // *nm (autoridad)* authority; *(MUS)* maestro;

(AM) skilled workman; **obra** ~**a** masterpiece; ~ **albañil** master mason.

magia [ˈmaxja] *nf* magic; **mágico, a** *a* magic(al) // *nm/f* magician.

magisterio [maxisˈterjo] *nm (enseñanza)* teaching; *(profesión)* teaching profession; *(maestros)* teachers *pl.*

magistrado [maxisˈtraðo] *nm* magistrate.

magistral [maxisˈtral] *a* magisterial; *(fig)* masterly.

magnánimo, a [maɣˈnanimo, a] *a* magnanimous.

magnate [maɣˈnate] *nm* magnate, tycoon.

magnético, a [maɣˈnetiko, a] *a* magnetic; **magnetizar** *vt* to magnetize.

magnetofón [maɣnetoˈfon], **magnetófono** [maɣneˈtofono] *nm* tape recorder; **magnetofónico, a** *a*: **cinta magnetofónica** recording tape.

magnífico, a [maɣˈnifiko, a] *a* splendid, magnificent, wonderful.

magnitud [maɣniˈtuð] *nf* magnitude.

mago, a [ˈmaɣo, a] *nm/f* magician; **los Reyes M**~**s** the Magi, the Three Wise Men.

magro, a [ˈmaɣro, a] *a (persona)* thin, lean; *(carne)* lean.

magullar [maɣuˈʎar] *vt (amoratar)* to bruise; *(dañar)* to damage; *(fam: golpear)* to bash, beat.

mahometano, a [maomeˈtano, a] *a* Mohammedan.

maíz [maˈiθ] *nm* maize, sweet corn.

majada [maˈxaða] *nf (abrigo)* sheepfold; *(abono)* dung.

majadero, a [maxaˈðero, a] *a* silly, stupid // *nm (TEC)* pestle; *(canilla)* bobbin.

majar [maˈxar] *vt* to crush, grind; *(fig)* to bother, pester.

majestad [maxesˈtað] *nf* majesty; **majestuoso, a** *a* majestic.

majo, a [ˈmaxo, a] *a* nice; *(guapo)* attractive, good-looking; *(lujoso)* smart.

mal [mal] *ad* badly; *(equivocadamente)* wrongly, *(con dificultad)* with difficulty // *a* = **malo** // *nm* evil; *(desgracia)* misfortune; *(daño)* harm, hurt; *(MED)* illness; **¡menos** ~**!** just as well!; ~ **que bien** rightly or wrongly.

malabarismo [malaβaˈrismo] *nm* juggling; **malabarista** *nm/f* juggler.

malaconsejado, a [malakonseˈxaðo, a] *a* ill-advised.

malagueño, a [malaˈɣeɲo, a] *a* of *or* from Málaga.

malaria [maˈlarja] *nf* malaria.

malbaratar [malβaraˈtar] *vt (malgastar)* to squander; *(malvender)* to sell off cheap.

malcontento, a [malkonˈtento, a] *a* discontented.

malcriado, a [malˈkrjaðo, a] *a (grosero)* rude, bad-mannered; *(consentido)* spoiled.

maldad [malˈdað] *nf* evil, wickedness.

maldecir [maldeˈθir] *vt* to curse // *vi*: ~ **de** to speak ill of.

maldición [maldiˈθjon] *nf* curse.

maldito, a [mal'dito, a] *pp de* **maldecir** // *a* (*condenado*) damned; (*perverso*) wicked // *nf*: **soltar la ~a** to talk too much.

maleante [male'ante] *a* wicked // *nm/f* malefactor; **malear** *vt* to spoil; (*fig*) to corrupt.

malecón [male'kon] *nm* pier, jetty.

maledicencia [maleði'θenθja] *nf* slander, scandal.

maleficiar [malefi'θjar] *vt* to harm, damage; (*hechizar*) to bewitch; **maleficio** *nm* curse, spell.

malestar [males'tar] *nm* (*gen*) discomfort; (*fig*) uneasiness; (*POL*) unrest.

maleta [ma'leta] *nf* case, suitcase; (*AUTO*) boot; **maletín** *nm* small case, bag.

malevolencia [maleβo'lenθja] *nf* malice, spite; **malévolo, a** *a* malicious, spiteful.

maleza [ma'leθa] *nf* (*hierbas malas*) weeds *pl*; (*arbustos*) thicket.

malgastar [malxas'tar] *vt* (*tiempo, dinero*) to waste; (*salud*) to ruin.

malhechor, a [male'tʃor, a] *nm/f* malefactor; (*criminal*) criminal.

malicia [ma'liθja] *nf* (*maldad*) wickedness; (*astucia*) slyness, guile; (*mala intención*) malice, spite; (*carácter travieso*) mischievousness; **~s** *nfpl* suspicions; **malicioso, a** *a* wicked, evil; sly, crafty; malicious, spiteful; mischievous.

malignidad [malixni'ðað] *nf* (*MED*) malignancy; (*malicia*) malice.

maligno, a [ma'lixno, a] *a* evil; (*malévolo*) malicious; (*MED*) malignant.

malo, a ['malo, a] *a* bad; (*falso*) false // *nm/f* villain // *nf* spell of bad luck; **estar ~** to be ill; **estar de ~as** to be in a bad mood.

malograr [malo'xrar] *vt* to spoil; (*plan*) to upset; (*tiempo, ocasión*) to waste; **~se** *vr* (*plan etc*) to fail, come to grief; (*persona*) to die before one's time; **malogro** *nm* (*fracaso*) failure; (*pérdida*) waste; (*muerte*) early death.

malparado, a [malpa'raðo, a] *a*: **salir ~** to come off badly.

malparir [malpa'rir] *vi* to have a miscarriage.

malquistar [malkis'tar] *vt* to estrange, cause a rift with/between.

malsano, a [mal'sano, a] *a* unhealthy.

Malta ['malta] *nf* Malta.

maltratar [maltra'tar] *vt* to ill-treat; **maltrato** *nm* ill-treatment; (*ofensa*) abuse, insults *pl*.

maltrecho, a [mal'tretʃo, a] *a* battered, damaged.

malvado, a [mal'βaðo, a] *a* evil, villainous.

malvavisco [malβa'βisko] *nm* marshmallow.

malversar [malβer'sar] *vt* to embezzle, misappropriate.

Malvinas [mal'βinas]: **Islas ~** *nfpl* Falkland Islands.

malla ['maʎa] *nf* mesh; (*de baño*) bathing costume; **~s** *nfpl* tights; **~ de alambre**

wire mesh; **hacer ~** to knit.

Mallorca [ma'ʎorka] *nf* Majorca.

mama ['mama] *nf* (*de animal*) teat; (*de persona*) breast.

mamá [ma'ma] (*pl* **~s**) *nf* (*fam*) mum, mummy.

mamar [ma'mar] *vt* (*pecho*) to suck; (*fig*) to absorb, assimilate // *vi* to suck.

mamarracho [mama'rratʃo] *nm* sight, mess.

mampara [mam'para] *nf* (*entre habitaciones*) partition; (*biombo*) screen.

mampostería [mamposte'ria] *nf* masonry.

mampuesto [mam'pwesto] *nm* (*piedra*) rough stone; (*muro*) wall, parapet; **de ~** spare, emergency.

mamut [ma'mut] *nm* mammoth.

manada [ma'naða] *nf* (*rebaño*) herd; (*de ovejas*) flock; (*de lobos*) pack.

manantial [manan'tjal] *nm* spring; (*fuente*) fountain; (*fig*) source.

manar [ma'nar] *vt* to run with, flow with // *vi* to run, flow; (*abundar*) to abound.

mancebo [man'θeβo] *nm* (*joven*) young man; (*soltero*) bachelor; (*dependiente*) assistant.

mancilla [man'θiʎa] *nf* stain, blemish.

manco, a ['manko, a] *a* one-armed, one-handed; (*fig*) defective, faulty.

mancomún [manko'mun]: **de ~** *ad* jointly, together; **mancomunar** *vt* to unite, bring together; (*recursos*) to pool; (*JUR*) to make jointly responsible; **mancomunarse** *vr* to unite, merge; **mancomunidad** *nf* union, association; (*POL*) commonwealth; (*JUR*) joint responsibility.

mancha ['mantʃa] *nf* stain, mark; (*boceto*) sketch, outline; **manchar** *vt* (*gen*) to stain, mark; (*ensuciar*) to soil, dirty.

manchego, a [man'tʃexo, a] *a* of *or* from La Mancha.

mandadero [manda'ðero] *nm* messenger; (*niño*) errand boy.

mandado [man'daðo] *nm* (*orden*) order; (*comisión*) commission, errand.

mandamiento [manda'mjento] *nm* (*orden*) order, command; (*REL*) commandment; **~ judicial** warrant.

mandar [man'dar] *vt* (*ordenar*) to order; (*dirigir*) to lead, command; (*enviar*) to send; (*pedir*) to order, ask for // *vi* to be in charge; (*pey*) to be bossy; **~se** *vr* (*MED*) to get about by o.s.; ¿**mande?** pardon?; **~ hacer un traje** to have a suit made; **~se cambiar** to go away, leave.

mandarín [manda'rin] *nm* mandarin // *nf* tangerine, mandarin.

mandatario, a [manda'tarjo, a] *nm/f* (*representante*) agent; (*AM*) leader.

mandato [man'dato] *nm* (*orden*) order; (*POL*) term of office; (: *territorio*) mandate; **~ judicial** (*search*) warrant.

mandíbula [man'diβula] *nf* jaw.

mandil [man'dil] *nm* (*delantal*) apron; (*vestido*) pinafore dress.

mando ['mando] nm (MIL) command; (de país) rule; (el primer lugar) lead; (POL) term of office; (TEC) control; ~ a la izquierda left-hand drive; ~ remoto remote control.

mandolina [mando'lina] nf mandolin(e).

mandón, ona [man'don, ona] a bossy, domineering.

manea [ma'nea] nf hobble.

manejable [mane'xaβle] a manageable.

manejar [mane'xar] vt (gen) to manage; (máquina) to work, operate; (idioma, caballo etc) to handle; (casa) to run, manage; (AM) to drive; ~se vr (comportarse) to act, behave; (arreglárselas) to manage; (MED) to get about unaided; **manejo** nm management; handling; running; driving; (facilidad de trato) ease, confidence; **manejos** nmpl intrigues.

manera [ma'nera] nf way, manner, fashion; ~s nfpl manners; ~ de ser way of life; (aire) manner; **de ninguna** ~ no way, by no means; **de otra** ~ otherwise; **de todas** ~s at any rate; **no hay** ~ de **persuadirle** there's no way of convincing him.

manga ['manga] nf (de camisa) sleeve; (de riego) hose; (tromba) downpour; (filtro) filter; (NAUT) beam.

mangana [man'gana] nf lasso.

mango ['mango] nm handle; (BOT) mango.

mangonear [mangone'ar] vt to manage, boss about // vi (meterse) to meddle, interfere; (ser mandón) to boss people about.

manguera [man'gera] nf (de riego) hose; (tubo) pipe.

maní [ma'ni] nm (AM) peanut.

manía [ma'nia] nf (MED) mania; (capricho) rage, craze; (disgusto) dislike; (malicia) spite; **maníaco, a** a maniac(al) // nm/f maniac.

maniatar [manja'tar] vt to tie the hands of.

maniático, a [ma'njatiko, a] a maniac(al) // nm/f maniac.

manicomio [mani'komjo] nm asylum, mental hospital.

manifestación [manifesta'θjon] nf (declaración) statement, declaration; (demostración) show, manifestation; (POL) demonstration.

manifestar [manifes'tar] vt to show, manifest; (declarar) to state, declare; **manifiesto, a** a clear, manifest // nm manifesto.

manija [ma'nixa] nf handle.

manilla [ma'niʎa] nf: ~s de hierro handcuffs.

maniobra [ma'njoβra] nf manoeuvring; (maneja) handling; (fig) manoeuvre; (estratagema) stratagem; ~s nfpl manoeuvres; **maniobrar** vt to manoeuvre; (manejar) to handle.

manipulación [manipula'θjon] nf manipulation; **manipular** vt to manipulate; (manejar) to handle.

maniquí [mani'ki] nm dummy // nf model.

manirroto, a [mani'rroto, a] a lavish, extravagant // nm/f spendthrift.

manivela [mani'βela] nf crank.

manjar [man'xar] nm (tasty) dish; ~ blanco blancmange.

mano ['mano] nf hand; (ZOOL) foot, paw; (de pintura) coat; (serie) lot, series; **a** ~ by hand; **a la** ~ on hand, within reach; **a** ~ derecha/izquierda on the right(-hand side)/left(-hand side); **de primera** ~ (at) first hand; **de segunda** ~ (at) second hand; **robo a** ~ armada armed robbery; ~ de obra labour, manpower; **estrechar la** ~ a uno to shake sb's hand.

manojo [ma'noxo] nm handful, bunch; ~ de llaves bunch of keys.

manoseado, a [manose'aðo, a] a well-worn; **manosear** vt (tocar) to handle, touch; (desordenar) to mess up, rumple; (insistir en) to overwork; (AM) to caress, fondle.

manotazo [mano'taθo] nm slap, smack.

mansalva [man'salβa]: **a** ~ ad without risk, without any danger.

mansedumbre [manse'ðumbre] nf gentleness, meekness.

mansión [man'sjon] nf mansion.

manso, a ['manso, a] a gentle, mild, meek; (animal) tame.

manta ['manta] nf blanket; (abrigo) shawl.

manteca [man'teka] nf fat; ~ de cacahuete/cacao peanut/cocoa butter; ~ de cerdo lard.

mantecado [mante'kaðo] nm ice-cream.

mantel [man'tel] nm tablecloth.

mantener [mante'ner] vt (gen) to support, maintain; (alimentar) to sustain; (conservar) to keep; (TEC) to maintain, service; ~se vr (seguir de pie) to be still standing; (no ceder) to hold one's ground; (subsistir) to sustain o.s., keep going; **mantenimiento** nm maintenance; sustenance, (sustento) support.

mantequera [mante'kera] nf (para hacer) churn; (para servir) butter dish.

mantequilla [mante'kiʎa] nf butter.

mantilla [man'tiʎa] nf mantilla; ~s nfpl baby clothes.

manto ['manto] nm (capa) cloak; (chal) shawl; (de ceremonia) robe, gown.

mantón [man'ton] nm shawl.

manual [ma'nwal] a manual // nm manual, handbook.

manufactura [manufak'tura] nf manufacture; (fábrica) factory.

manuscrito, a [manus'krito, a] a hand-written // nm manuscript.

manutención [manuten'θjon] nf maintenance; (sustento) support.

manzana [man'θana] nf apple; (ARQ) block.

manzanilla [manθa'niʎa] nf (planta) camomile; (infusión) camomile tea; (vino) manzanilla.

manzano [man'θano] nm apple tree.

maña ['maɲa] *nf* (*gen*) skill, dexterity; (*pey*) guile; (*costumbre*) habit; (*una* ~) trick, knack.

mañana [ma'ɲana] *ad* tomorrow // *nm* future // *nf* morning; **de** *o* **por la** ~ in the morning; **¡hasta** ~**!** see you tomorrow!; ~ **por la** ~ tomorrow morning; **mañanero, a** *a* early-rising.

mañoso, a [ma'ɲoso, a] *a* (*hábil*) skilful; (*astuto*) smart, clever.

mapa ['mapa] *nm* map.

maque ['make] *nm* lacquer.

maqueta [ma'keta] *nf* (scale) model.

maquillaje [maki'ʎaxe] *nm* make-up; (*acto*) making up; **maquillar** *vt* to make up; **maquillarse** *vr* to put on (some) make-up.

máquina ['makina] *nf* machine; (*de tren*) locomotive, engine; (*cámara*) camera; (*fig*) machinery; (: *proyecto*) plan, project; **escrito a** ~ typewritten; ~ **de afeitar** (safety) razor; ~ **de escribir** typewriter; ~ **de coser/lavar** sewing/washing machine.

maquinación [makina'θjon] *nf* machination, scheme, plot.

maquinal [maki'nal] *a* (*fig*) mechanical, automatic.

maquinaria [maki'narja] *nf* (*máquinas*) machinery; (*mecanismo*) mechanism, works *pl*.

maquinista [maki'nista] *nm* (*de tren*) engine driver; (*TEC*) operator; (*NAUT*) engineer.

mar [mar] *nm o f* sea; (*marea*) tide; ~ **adentro** *o* **afuera** out at sea; **en alta** ~ on the high seas; **la** ~ **de** (*fam*) lots of; **el M** ~ **Negro/Báltico** the Black/Baltic Sea.

maraña [ma'raɲa] *nf* (*maleza*) thicket; (*confusión*) tangle.

maravilla [mara'ßiʎa] *nf* marvel, wonder; (*BOT*) marigold; **maravillar** *vt* to astonish, amaze; **maravillarse** *vr* to be astonished, be amazed; **maravilloso, a** *a* wonderful, marvellous.

marca ['marka] *nf* (*gen*) mark; (*sello*) stamp; (*COM*) make, brand; **de** ~ excellent, outstanding; ~ **de fábrica** trademark.

marcado, a [mar'kaðo, a] *a* marked, strong.

marcar [mar'kar] *vt* (*gen*) to mark; (*número de teléfono*) to dial; (*gol*) to score; (*números*) to record, keep a tally of; (*el pelo*) to set; (*fig*) to indicate, point to // *vi* (*DEPORTE*) to score; (*TELEC*) to dial; ~**se** *vr* (*NAUT*) to take one's bearings; (*fig*) to make one's mark, stand out.

marcial [mar'θjal] *a* martial, military.

marciano, a [mar'θjano, a] *a* Martian.

marco ['marko] *nm* frame; (*DEPORTE*) goal-posts *pl*; (*moneda*) mark; (*fig*) framework; ~ **de chimenea** mantelpiece.

marcha ['martʃa] *nf* march; (*TEC*) running, working; (*AUTO*) gear; (*velocidad*) speed;

(*fig*) progress; (*dirección*) course; **poner en** ~ to put into gear; **dar** ~ **atrás** to reverse, put into reverse; **estar en** ~ to be under way, be in motion.

marchante, a [mar'tʃante, a] *nm/f* dealer, merchant; (*AM: cliente*) client, customer; (: *buhonero*) pedlar.

marchar [mar'tʃar] *vi* to go; (*funcionar*) to work, go; ~**se** *vr* to go (away), leave.

marchitar [martʃi'tar] *vt* to wither, dry up; ~**se** *vr* (*BOT*) to wither; (*fig*) to go into a decline; **marchito, a** *a* withered, faded; (*fig*) in decline.

marea [ma'rea] *nf* tide; (*llovizna*) drizzle.

marear [mare'ar] *vt* (*NAUT*) to sail, navigate; (*fig*) to annoy, upset; (*MED*): ~ **a uno** to make sb feel sick; ~**se** *vr* (*tener náuseas*) to feel/be sick; (*desvanecerse*) to feel faint; (*aturdirse*) to feel dizzy; (*fam: emborracharse*) to get a bit drunk.

maremoto [mare'moto] *nm* tidal wave.

mareo [ma'reo] *nm* (*náusea*) sick feeling; (*aturdimiento*) dizziness; (*fam: lata*) nuisance.

marfil [mar'fil] *nm* ivory.

margarina [marɣa'rina] *nf* margarine.

margarita [marɣa'rita] *nf* (*BOT*) daisy; (*perla*) pearl.

margen ['marxen] *nm* (*borde*) edge, border; (*fig*) margin, space // *nf* bank; **dar** ~ **para** to give an opportunity for; **mantenerse al** ~ to keep out (of things).

marica [ma'rika] *nm* magpie; (*fam*) sissy.

maricón [mari'kon] *nm* (*fam*) queer (*fam*).

marido [ma'riðo] *nm* husband.

marijuana [mari'xwana] *nf* marijuana, cannabis.

marina [ma'rina] *nf* navy; ~ **mercante** merchant navy.

marinero, a [mari'nero, a] *a* sea *cpd*; (*barco*) seaworthy // *nm* sailor, seaman.

marino, a [ma'rino, a] *a* sea *cpd*, marine // *nm* sailor.

marioneta [marjo'neta] *nf* puppet.

mariposa [mari'posa] *nf* butterfly.

mariscos [ma'riskos] *nmpl* shellfish, seafood *sg*.

marisma [ma'risma] *nf* marsh, swamp.

marítimo, a [ma'ritimo, a] *a* sea *cpd*, maritime.

marmita [mar'mita] *nf* pot.

mármol ['marmol] *nm* marble; **marmóreo, a** *a* marble.

marqués, esa [mar'kes, esa] *nm/f* marquis/marchioness.

marrar [ma'rrar] *vi* to miss.

marrón [ma'rron] *a* brown.

marroquí [marro'ki] *a* Moroccan // *nm* Morocco (leather).

Marruecos [ma'rrwekos] *nm* Morocco.

Marsellas [mar'seʎas] *n* Marseille.

martes ['martes] *nm inv* Tuesday.

martillar [marti'ʎar] *vt* to hammer.

martillo [mar'tiʎo] *nm* hammer; ~

neumático pneumatic drill; ~ **de orejas** claw-hammer.

mártir ['martir] *nm/f* martyr; **martirio** *nm* martyrdom; (*fig*) torture, torment.

marxismo [mark'sismo] *nm* Marxism; **marxista** *nm/f* Marxist.

marzo ['marθo] *nm* March.

mas [mas] *conj* but.

más [mas] *a, ad* more; (*superlativo*) most // *conj* and, plus; **es** ~ **de medianoche** it's after midnight; **el libro** ~ **leído del año** the most-read book of the year; **¡qué perro** ~ **feo!** what an ugly dog!; ~ **de,** ~ **de lo que,** ~ **que** more than; ~ **bien** rather; ~ **o menos** more or less.

masa ['masa] *nf* (*mezcla*) dough; (*volumen*) volume, mass; (*FÍSICA*) mass; (*ELEC*) earth; **en** ~ **en masse; las** ~**s** the masses.

masacre [ma'sakre] *nm* massacre.

masaje [ma'saxe] *nm* massage.

mascar [mas'kar] *vt* to chew; (*fig*) to mumble, mutter.

máscara ['maskara] *nf* (*gen*) mask // *nm/f* masked person; **mascarada** *nf* masquerade.

masculino, a [masku'lino, a] *a* masculine; (*BIO*) male.

mascullar [masku'ʎar] *vt* to mumble, mutter.

masilla [ma'siʎa] *nf* putty.

masivo, a [ma'siβo, a] *a* (*enorme*) massive; (*en masa*) mass, en masse.

masón [ma'son] *nm* (free)mason.

masoquista [maso'kista] *nm/f* masochist.

masticar [masti'kar] *vt* to chew; (*fig*) to ponder.

mástil ['mastil] *nm* (*de navío*) mast; (*de guitarra*) neck; (*sostén*) post, support.

mastín [mas'tin] *nm* mastiff; ~ **danés** Great Dane.

masturbación [masturβa'θjon] *nf* masturbation; **masturbarse** *vr* to masturbate.

mata ['mata] *nf* bush, shrub; (*de hierbas*) tuft; (*campo*) field; (*AM*) clump (of trees).

matadero [mata'ðero] *nm* slaughterhouse, abattoir.

matador, a [mata'ðor, a] *a* killing // *nm/f* killer // *nm* (*TAUR*) matador, bullfighter.

matanza [ma'tanθa] *nf* (*de personas*) killing; (*de animales*) slaughter(ing).

matar [ma'tar] *vt, vi* to kill; ~**se** *vr* (*suicidarse*) to kill o.s., commit suicide; (*por otro*) to be killed; ~ **el hambre** to stave off hunger.

mate ['mate] *a* (*sin brillo: color*) dull // *nm* (*en ajedrez*) (check)mate; (*AM: hierba*) maté; (: *vasija*) gourd.

matemáticas [mate'matikas] *nfpl* mathematics; **matemático, a** *a* mathematical // *nm/f* mathematician.

materia [ma'terja] *nf* (*gen*) matter; (*TEC*) material; **en** ~ **de** on the subject of; ~ **prima** raw material; **material** *a* material; (*dolor*) physical // *nm* material; (*TEC*) equipment; **materialismo** *nm*

materialism; **materialista** *a* materialist(ic); **materialmente** *ad* materially; (*fig*) absolutely.

maternal [mater'nal] *a* motherly, maternal.

maternidad [materni'ðað] *nf* motherhood. maternity; **materno, a** *a* motherly, maternal; (*lengua*) mother *cpd*.

matinal [mati'nal] *a* morning *cpd*.

matiz [ma'tiθ] *nm* shade; ~**ar** *vt* (*dar tonos de*) to tinge, tint; (*variar*) to vary; (*ARTE*) to blend.

matón [ma'ton] *nm* bully.

matorral [mato'rral] *nm* thicket.

matraca [ma'traka] *nf* rattle.

matrícula [ma'trikula] *nf* (*registro*) register; (*AUTO*) registration number; (: *placa*) licence plate; **matricular** *vt* to register, enrol.

matrimonial [matrimo'njal] *a* matrimonial.

matrimonio [matri'monjo] *nm* (*boda*) wedding; (*pareja*) (married) couple; (*unión*) marriage.

matriz [ma'triθ] *nf* womb; (*TEC*) mould; **casa** ~ (*COM*) head office.

matrona [ma'trona] *nf* (*persona de edad*) matron; (*partera*) midwife.

matute [ma'tute] *nm* contraband.

maullar [mau'ʎar] *vi* to mew, miaow.

mausoleo [mauso'leo] *nm* mausoleum.

maxilar [maksi'lar] *nm* jaw(bone).

máxima ['maksima] *ver* **máximo.**

máxime ['maksime] *ad* especially.

máximo, a ['maksimo, a] *a* maximum; (*más alto*) highest; (*más grande*) greatest // *nm* maximum // *nf* maxim.

mayo ['majo] *nm* May.

mayonesa [majo'nesa] *nf* mayonnaise.

mayor [ma'jor] *a* (*gen*) main, chief; (*adulto*) adult; (*de edad avanzada*) elderly; (*MUS*) major; (*comparativo: de tamaño*) bigger; (: *de edad*) older; (*superlativo: de tamaño*) biggest; (: *de edad*) oldest // *nm* chief, boss; **al por** ~ wholesale; ~ **de edad** adult; ~**es** *nmpl* ancestors.

mayoral [majo'ral] *nm* foreman.

mayordomo [major'ðomo] *nm* (*criado*) butler; (*de hotel*) steward.

mayoría [majo'ria] *nf* majority, greater part.

mayorista [majo'rista] *nm/f* wholesaler.

mayúsculo, a [ma'juskulo, a] *a* (*fig*) big, tremendous // *nf* capital (letter).

mazapán [maθa'pan] *nm* marzipan.

mazo ['maθo] *nm* (*martillo*) mallet; (*de flores*) bunch; (*fig*) bore; (*DEPORTE*) bat; (*palo*) club.

me [me] *pron* (*directo*) me; (*indirecto*) (to) me; (*reflexivo*) (to) myself; **¡démelo!** give it to me!

mecánico, a [me'kaniko, a] *a* mechanical // *nm/f* mechanic // *nf* (*estudio*) mechanics *sg*; (*mecanismo*) mechanism.

mecanismo [meka'nismo] *nm* mechanism; (*marcha*) gear.

mecanografía [mekanoɤraˈfia] nf typewriting; **mecanógrafo, a** nm/f typist.
mecedor, a [meθeˈðor, a] a rocking // nm (columpio) swing // nf rocking chair.
mecer [meˈθer] vt (cuna) to rock; (líquido) to stir; ~**se** vr to rock; (ramo) to sway.
mechero [meˈtʃero] nm (cigarette) lighter.
mechón [meˈtʃon] nm (gen) tuft; (manojo) bundle; (de pelo) lock.
medalla [meˈðaʎa] nf medal.
media [ˈmeðja] nf ver **medio.**
mediado, a [meˈðjaðo, a] a half-full; (trabajo) half-complete; **a** ~**s de** in the middle of, halfway through.
mediano, a [meˈðjano, a] a (regular) medium, average; (mediocre) mediocre; (indiferente) indifferent.
medianoche [meðjaˈnotʃe] nf midnight.
mediante [meˈðjante] ad by (means of), through.
mediar [meˈðjar] vi (llegar a la mitad) to get to the middle, get halfway; (estar en medio) to be in the middle; (interceder) to mediate, intervene.
medicación [meðikaˈθjon] nf medication, treatment.
medicamento [meðikaˈmento] nm medicine, drug.
medicina [meðiˈθina] nf medicine.
medición [meðiˈθjon] nf measurement.
médico, a [ˈmeðiko, a] a medical // nm/f doctor.
medida [meˈðiða] nf (gen) measure; (medición) measurement; (prudencia) moderation, prudence; **en cierta/gran** ~ up to a point/to a great extent; **un traje a la** ~ made-to-measure suit; ~ **de cuello** collar size; **a** ~ **de** in proportion to; (de acuerdo con) in keeping with.
medio, a [ˈmeðjo, a] a half (a); (punto) mid, middle; (promedio) average // ad half // nm (centro) middle, centre; (promedio) average; (DEPORTE) half-back; (método) means, way; (ambiente) environment // nf (prenda de vestir) stocking; (promedio) average; ~**s** nmpl means, resources; ~ **litro** half a litre; **las tres y** ~**a** half past three; **M**~ **Oriente** Middle East; **a** ~ **terminar** half finished; **pagar a** ~**as** to share the cost; **hacer** ~**a** to knit.
mediocre [meˈðjokre] a middling, average; (pey) mediocre.
mediodía [meðjoˈðia] nm midday, noon.
medir [meˈðir] vt (gen) to measure; (pesar) to weigh up // vi to measure.
meditar [meðiˈtar] vt to ponder, think over, meditate (on); (planear) to think out.
mediterráneo, a [meðiteˈrraneo, a] a Mediterranean // nm: **el M**~ the Mediterranean.
medroso, a [meˈðroso, a] a fearful, timid.
medusa [meˈðusa] nf jellyfish.
megáfono [meˈɣafono] nm megaphone.
megalómano, a [meɤaˈlomano, a] nm/f megalomaniac.

mejicano, a [mexiˈkano, a] a, nm/f Mexican.
Méjico [ˈmexiko] nm Mexico.
mejilla [meˈxiʎa] nf cheek.
mejor [meˈxor] a, ad (comparativo) better; (superlativo) best; **a lo** ~ probably; (quizá) maybe; ~ **dicho** rather; **tanto** ~ so much the better.
mejora [meˈxora] nf improvement; **mejorar** vt to improve, make better // vi, **mejorarse** vr to improve, get better.
melancólico, a [melanˈkoliko, a] a (triste) sad, melancholy; (soñador) dreamy.
melena [meˈlena] nf (de persona) long hair; (del león) mane.
melocotón [melokoˈton] nm peach.
melodía [meloˈðia] nf melody; (aire) tune.
melodrama [meloˈðrama] nm melodrama; **melodramático, a** a a melodramatic.
melón [meˈlon] nm melon.
meloso, a [meˈloso, a] a honeyed, sweet.
mellizo, a [meˈʎiθo, a] a, nm/f twin.
membrete [memˈbrete] nm letterhead.
memorable [memoˈraβle] a memorable.
memorándum [memoˈrandum] nm (libro) notebook; (comunicación) memorandum.
memoria [meˈmorja] nf (gen) memory; (informe) report; ~**s** nfpl (de autor) memoirs.
mencionar [menθjoˈnar] vt to mention.
mendigar [mendiˈɤar] vt to beg (for).
mendigo, a [menˈdiɤo, a] nm/f beggar.
mendrugo [menˈdruɤo] nm crust.
menear [meneˈar] vt to move; (fig) to handle; ~**se** vr to shake; (balancearse) to sway; (moverse) to move; (fig) to get a move on.
menester [menesˈter] nm (necesidad) necessity; (ocupación) job; ~**es** nmpl (deberes) duties; (instrumentos) tackle sg, tools; **es** ~ it is necessary.
mengua [ˈmengwa] nf (disminución) decrease; (falta) lack; (pobreza) poverty; (fig) discredit; ~**do, a** a cowardly, timid; (cicatero) mean.
menguante [menˈgwante] a decreasing, diminishing; **menguar** vt to lessen, diminish; (fig) to discredit // vi to diminish, decrease; (fig) to decline.
menopausia [menoˈpausja] nf menopause.
menor [meˈnor] a (más pequeño: comparativo) smaller; (: superlativo) smallest; (más joven: comparativo) younger; (: superlativo) youngest; (MUS) minor // nm/f (joven) young person, juvenile; **no tengo la** ~ **idea** I haven't the slightest idea; **al por** ~ retail; ~ **de edad** person under age.
menos [ˈmenos] a (comparativo: sg) less; (: pl) fewer; (superlativo: sg) least; (: pl) fewest // ad (comparativo) less; (superlativo) least // conj except // nm (MAT) minus; **es lo** ~ **que puedo hacer**

it's the least I can do; **lo ~ posible** as little as possible; **a ~ que** unless; **te echo de ~** I miss you; **al o por lo ~** at least.

menoscabar [menoska'ßar] *vt* (*estropear*) to damage, harm; (*acortar*) to lessen, reduce; (*fig*) to discredit.

menospreciar [menospre'θjar] *vt* to underrate, undervalue; (*despreciar*) to scorn, despise; **menosprecio** *nm* underrating, undervaluation; scorn, contempt.

mensaje [men'saxe] *nm* message; **~ro, a** *nm/f* messenger.

menstruar [mens'trwar] *vi* to menstruate; **menstruo** *nm* menstruation, period.

mensual [men'swal] *a* monthly; **100 ptas ~es** 100 ptas. a month.

menta ['menta] *nf* mint.

mental [men'tal] *a* mental.

mentar [men'tar] *vt* to mention, name.

mente ['mente] *nf* mind.

mentecato, a [mente'kato, a] *a* silly, stupid // *nm/f* fool, idiot.

mentir [men'tir] *vi* to lie; **~a** *nf* (*una ~a*) lie; (*acto*) lying; (*invención*) fiction; **parece ~a que...** it seems incredible that..., I can't believe that...; **~oso, a** *a* lying; (*texto*) full of errors // *nm/f* liar.

mentis [men'tis] *nm*: **dar el ~ a** to deny.

menú [me'nu] *nm* menu.

menudeo [menu'ðeo] *nm*: **vender al ~** to sell retail.

menudo, a [me'nuðo, a] *a* (*pequeño*) small, tiny; (*sin importancia*) petty, insignificant; (*exacto*) exact, meticulous; **¡~ negocio!** (*fam*) some deal!; **a ~** often, frequently; **por ~** in detail.

meñique [me'ɲike] *nm* little finger.

meollo [me'oʎo] *nm* (*gen*) marrow; (*fig*) core.

mercadería [merkaðe'ria] *nf* commodity; **~s** *nfpl* goods, merchandise *sg*.

mercado [mer'kaðo] *nm* market; **M~ Común** Common Market.

mercadotecnia [merkaðo'teknja] *nf* marketing.

mercancía [merkan'θia] *nf* commodity; **~s** *nfpl* goods, merchandise *sg*.

mercantil [merkan'til] *a* mercantile, commercial.

mercenario, a [merθe'narjo, a] *a, nm* mercenary.

mercurio [mer'kurjo] *nm* mercury.

merecer [mere'θer] *vt* to deserve, merit // *vi* to be deserving, be worthy; **merece la pena** it's worthwhile; **merecido, a** *a* (well) deserved; **llevar su merecido** to get one's deserts.

merendar [meren'dar] *vt* to have for tea // *vi* to have tea; (*en el campo*) to have a picnic.

merengue [me'renge] *nm* meringue.

merienda [me'rjenda] *nf* (light) tea, afternoon snack; (*de campo*) picnic.

mérito ['merito] *nm* merit; (*valor*) worth, value.

merluza [mer'luθa] *nf* hake.

merma ['merma] *nf* decrease; (*pérdida*) wastage; **mermar** *vt* to reduce, lessen // *vi*, **mermarse** *vr* to decrease, dwindle; (*fig*) to waste away.

mermelada [merme'laða] *nf* jam.

mero, a ['mero, a] *a* mere.

mes [mes] *nm* month; (*salario*) month's pay.

mesa ['mesa] *nf* table; (*de trabajo*) desk; (*GEO*) plateau; (*ARQ*) landing; **~ directiva** board; **poner/quitar la ~** to lay/clear the table.

meseta [me'seta] *nf* (*GEO*) meseta, tableland; (*ARQ*) landing.

mesón [me'son] *nm* olde-worlde bar.

mestizo, a [mes'tiθo, a] *a* half-caste, of mixed race; (*ZOOL*) crossbred // *nm/f* half-caste, half-breed.

mesura [me'sura] *nf* (*moderación*) moderation, restraint; (*dignidad*) dignity, calm; (*cortesía*) courtesy.

meta ['meta] *nf* goal; (*de carrera*) finish.

metáfora [me'tafora] *nf* metaphor.

metal [me'tal] *nm* (*materia*) metal; (*MUS*) brass; (*fig*) quality; **metálico, a** *a* metallic; (*de metal*) metal // *nm* cash.

metalurgia [meta'lurxja] *nf* metallurgy.

meteoro [mete'oro] *nm* meteor.

meter [me'ter] *vt* (*colocar*) to put, place; (*introducir*) to put in, insert; (*añadir*) to add; (*involucrar*) to involve; (*causar*) to make, cause; **~se** *vr*: **~se en** to go into, enter; (*fig*) to interfere in, meddle in; **~se a** to start; **~se a escritor** to become a writer; **~se con alguien** to provoke sb, pick a quarrel with sb.

meticuloso, a [metiku'loso, a] *a* meticulous, thorough.

metódico, a [me'toðiko, a] *a* methodical.

metodismo [meto'ðismo] *nm* Methodism.

método ['metoðo] *nm* method.

metralleta [metra'ʎeta] *nf* submachine gun.

métrico, a ['metriko, a] *a* metric.

metro ['metro] *nm* metre; (*tren*) underground, subway.

México ['meksiko] *nm* Mexico.

mezcla ['meθkla] *nf* mixture; (*ARQ*) mortar; **mezclar** *vt* to mix (up); (*naipes*) to shuffle; **mezclarse** *vr* to mix, mingle; **mezclarse en** to get mixed up in, get involved in.

mezquino, a [meθ'kino, a] *a* (*cicatero*) mean; (*pobre*) miserable.

mezquita [meθ'kita] *nf* mosque.

mi [mi] *det* my.

mí [mi] *pron* me; myself.

miaja ['mjaxa] *nf* crumb.

microbús [mikro'ßus] *nm* minibus.

micrófono [mi'krofono] *nm* microphone.

microlentillas [mikrolen'tiʎas] *nfpl* contact lenses.

microscopio [mikro'skopjo] *nm* microscope.

miedo ['mjeðo] *nm* fear; (*nerviosismo*) apprehension, nervousness; **tener ~ to**

be afraid; **de** ~ wonderful, marvellous; **hace un frío de** ~ (*fam*) it's terribly cold; ~**so, a** *a* fearful, timid.

miel [mjel] *nf* honey.

miembro ['mjembro] *nm* limb; (*socio*) member; ~ **viril** penis.

mientes ['mjentes] *nfpl*: **no parar** ~ **en** to pay no attention to; **traer a las** ~ to recall.

mientras ['mjentras] *conj* while; (*duración*) as long as // *ad* meanwhile; ~ **tanto** meanwhile; ~ **más tiene, más quiere** the more he has, the more he wants.

miércoles ['mjerkoles] *nm inv* Wednesday.

mierda ['mjerða] *nf* (*fam*) shit.

miga ['miɣa] *nf* crumb; (*fig*) essence; **hacer buenas** ~**s** (*fam*) to get on well.

migración [miɣra'θjon] *nf* migration.

mil [mil] *num* thousand; **dos** ~ **libras** two thousand pounds.

milagro [mi'laɣro] *nm* miracle; ~**so, a** *a* miraculous.

mili ['mili] *nf*: **hacer la** ~ (*fam*) to do one's military service.

milicia [mi'liθja] *nf* (MIL) militia; (: *arte*) art of war; (*servicio militar*) military service.

milímetro [mi'limetro] *nm* millimetre.

militante [mili'tante] *a* militant.

militar [mili'tar] *a* (*del ejército*) military; (*guerrero*) warlike // *nm/f* soldier // *vi* to serve in the army; (*fig*) to be a member of a party.

milla ['miʎa] *nf* mile.

millar [mi'ʎar] *nm* thousand.

millón [mi'ʎon] *num* million; **millonario, a** *nm/f* millionaire.

mimar [mi'mar] *vt* (*gen*) to spoil, pamper; (*al poderoso*) to flatter.

mimbre ['mimbre] *nm* wicker.

mímica ['mimika] *nf* (*para comunicarse*) sign language; (*imitación*) mimicry.

mimo ['mimo] *nm* (*caricia*) affectionate caress; (*de niño*) spoiling; (TEATRO) mime.

mina ['mina] *nf* mine; **minar** *vt* to mine; (*fig*) to undermine.

mineral [mine'ral] *a* mineral // *nm* (GEO) mineral; (*mena*) ore.

minero, a [mi'nero, a] *a* mining // *nm/f* miner.

miniatura [minja'tura] *a inv*, *nf* miniature.

minifalda [mini'falda] *nf* miniskirt.

mínimo, a ['minimo, a] *a*, *nm* minimum.

ministerio [minis'terjo] *nm* Ministry; **M**~ **de Hacienda/del Exterior** Treasury/Foreign Office.

ministro [mi'nistro] *nm* minister.

minorar [mino'rar] *vt* to reduce.

minoría [mino'ria] *nf* minority.

minucioso, a [minu'θjoso, a] *a* thorough, meticulous; (*prolijo*) very detailed.

minúsculo, a [mi'nuskulo, a] *a* tiny, minute // *nf* small letter.

minuta [mi'nuta] *nf* (*de comida*) menu;

(*borrador*) rough draft; (*apunte*) note.

minutero [minu'tero] *nm* minute hand.

minuto [mi'nuto] *nm* minute.

mío, a ['mio, a] *pron*: **el** ~ mine; **un amigo** ~ a friend of mine; **lo** ~ what is mine.

miope [mi'ope] *a* short-sighted.

mira ['mira] *nf* (*de arma*) sight(s) (*pl*); (*fig*) aim, intention; **estar a la** ~ to be on the look-out, keep watch; ~**da** *nf* look, glance; (*expresión*) look, expression; **echar una** ~**da a** to glance at; ~**do, a** *a* (*sensato*) sensible; (*considerado*) considerate; **bien/mal** ~**do** well/not well thought of.

mirador [mira'ðor] *nm* viewpoint, vantage point.

mirar [mi'rar] *vt* to look at; (*observar*) to watch; (*considerar*) to consider, think over; (*vigilar, cuidar*) to watch, look after // *vi* to look; (ARQ) to face; ~**se** *vr* (*dos personas*) to look at each other; ~ **bien/mal** to think highly of/have a poor opinion of; ~**se al espejo** to look at o.s. in the mirror.

mirlo ['mirlo] *nm* blackbird.

misa ['misa] *nf* mass.

miserable [mise'raßle] *a* (*avaro*) mean, stingy; (*nimio*) miserable, paltry; (*lugar*) squalid; (*fam*) vile, despicable // *nm/f* (*indigente*) wretch, poor person; (*perverso*) rotter.

miseria [mi'serja] *nf* misery; (*pobreza*) poverty; (*tacañería*) meanness, stinginess; (*condiciones*) squalor; **una** ~ a pittance.

misericordia [miseri'korðja] *nf* (*compasión*) compassion, pity; (*piedad*) mercy.

misil [mi'sil] *nm* missile.

misión [mi'sjon] *nf* mission; **misionero, a** *nm/f* missionary.

mismo, a ['mismo, a] *a* (*semejante*) same; (*después de pronombre*) -self; (*para énfasis*) very; **el** ~ **traje** the same suit; **en ese** ~ **momento** at that very moment; **vino el** ~ **Ministro** the minister himself came; **yo** ~ **lo vi** I saw it myself; **lo** ~ the same (thing); **da lo** ~ it's all the same; **quedamos en las** ~**as** we're no further forward // *ad*: **aquí/hoy** ~ right here/this very day; **ahora** ~ right now // *conj*: **lo** ~ **que** just like, just as; **por lo** ~ for the same reason.

misterio [mis'terjo] *nm* (*gen*) mystery; (*lo secreto*) secrecy.

mitad [mi'tað] *nf* (*medio*) half; (*centro*) middle; **a** ~ **de precio** (at) half-price; **en o a** ~ **del camino** halfway along the road; **cortar por la** ~ to cut through the middle.

mitin ['mitin] *nm* meeting.

mito ['mito] *nm* myth.

mixto, a ['miksto, a] *a* mixed.

mobiliario [moßi'ljarjo] *nm* furniture.

mocedad [moθe'ðað] *nf* youth.

moción [mo'θjon] *nf* motion.

mochila [mo'tʃila] *nf* rucksack.

moda ['moða] *nf* (*gen*) fashion; (*estilo*) style: **de** *o* **a la** ~ in fashion, fashionable; **pasado** *o* **fuera de** ~ out of fashion.
modales [mo'ðales] *nmpl* manners.
modalidad [moðali'ðað] *nf* kind, variety.
modelar [moðe'lar] *vt* to model.
modelo [mo'ðelo] *a inv, nm/f* model.
moderado, a [moðe'raðo, a] *a* moderate.
moderar [moðe'rar] *vt* to moderate; (*violencia*) to restrain, control; (*velocidad*) to reduce; ~**se** *vr* to restrain o.s., control o.s.
modernizar [moðerni'θar] *vt* to modernize.
moderno, a [mo'ðerno, a] *a* modern; (*actual*) present-day.
modestia [mo'ðestja] *nf* modesty; **modesto, a** *a* modest.
módico, a ['moðiko, a] *a* moderate, reasonable.
modificar [moðifi'kar] *vt* to modify.
modista [mo'ðista] *nm/f* dressmaker.
modo ['moðo] *nm* (*manera, forma*) way, manner; (*MUS*) mode; ~**s** *nmpl* manners; **de ningún** ~ in no way; **de todos** ~**s** at any rate; ~ **de empleo** directions *pl* (for use).
modorra [mo'ðorra] *nf* drowsiness.
modular [moðu'lar] *vt* to modulate.
mofa ['mofa] *nf* mockery, ridicule; **hacer** ~ **de** to mock; **mofar** *vi* to mock, scoff; **mofarse** *vr*: **mofarse de** to mock, scoff at.
mohíno, a [mo'ino, a] *a* (*triste*) gloomy, depressed; (*enojado*) sulky.
moho ['moo] *nm* (*BOT*) mould; (*oxidación*) rust; ~ **so, a** *a* mouldy; rusty.
mojar [mo'xar] *vt* to wet; (*humedecer*) to damp(en), moisten; (*calar*) to soak // *vi*: ~ **en** to get involved in; ~**se** *vr* to get wet.
mojón [mo'xon] *nm* (*en un camino*) signpost; (*montón*) heap, pile.
molde ['molde] *nm* mould; (*de costura*) pattern; (*fig*) model; **el vestido le está de** ~ the dress is just right for her; ~**ar** *vt* to mould.
mole ['mole] *nf* mass, bulk.
moledora [mole'ðora] *nf* grinder, mill.
moler [mo'ler] *vt* to grind, crush; (*cansar*) to tire out, exhaust; (*irritar*) to annoy.
molestar [moles'tar] *vt* (*gen*) to bother; (*fastidiar*) to annoy; (*incomodar*) to inconvenience, put out // *vi* to be a nuisance; ~**se** *vr* to bother; (*incomodarse*) to go to trouble; (*ofenderse*) to take offence.
molestia [mo'lestja] *nf* (*gen*) bother, trouble; (*incomodidad*) inconvenience; (*MED*) discomfort; **es una** ~ it's a nuisance; **molesto, a** *a* (*que causa molestia*) annoying; (*incómodo*) inconvenient; (*inquieto*) uncomfortable, ill at ease; (*enfadado*) annoyed.
molinillo [moli'niʎo] *nm*: ~ **de café/carne** coffee grinder/mincer.

molino [mo'lino] *nm* (*edificio*) mill; (*máquina*) grinder.
momentáneo, a [momen'taneo, a] *a* momentary.
momento [mo'mento] *nm* (*gen*) moment; (*TEC*) momentum; **de** ~ at the moment, for the moment.
momia ['momja] *nf* mummy.
monarca [mo'narka] *nm/f* monarch, ruler; **monarquía** *nf* monarchy; **monarquista** *nm/f* royalist, monarchist.
monasterio [monas'terjo] *nm* monastery.
mondar [mon'dar] *vt* (*limpiar*) to clean; (*podar*) to prune, trim; (*pelar*) to peel; ~**se** *vr*: ~**se los dientes** to pick one's teeth.
moneda [mo'neða] *nf* (*tipo de dinero*) currency, money; (*pieza*) coin; **una** ~ **de 5p** a 5p piece; **monedero** *nm* purse; **monetario, a** *a* monetary, financial.
monja ['monxa] *nf* nun.
monje ['monxe] *nm* monk.
mono, a ['mono, a] *a* (*bonito*) lovely, pretty; (*gracioso*) nice, charming // *nm/f* monkey, ape // *nm* (*overoles*) overalls *pl*.
monopolio [mono'poljo] *nm* monopoly; **monopolizar** *vt* to monopolize.
monoriel [mono'riel] *nm* monorail.
monotonía [monoto'nia] *nf* (*sonido*) monotone; (*fig*) monotony.
monótono, a [mo'notono, a] *a* monotonous.
monstruo ['monstrwo] *nm* monster // *a* fantastic; ~**so, a** *a* monstrous.
monta ['monta] *nf* total, sum; **de poca** ~ unimportant, of little account.
montaje [mon'taxe] *nm* assembly; (*ARQ*) erection; (*TEATRO*) décor; (*CINE*) montage.
montaña [mon'tapa] *nf* (*monte*) mountain; (*sierra*) mountains *pl*, mountainous area; (*AM*) forest; ~ **rusa** roller coaster; **montañés, esa** *a* mountain *cpd* // *nm/f* highlander; (*de Santander*) native of the Santander region.
montar [mon'tar] *vt* (*subir a*) to mount, get on; (*caballo etc*) to ride; (*TEC*) to assemble, put together; (*ARQ*) to erect; (*negocio*) to set up; (*arma*) to cock; (*colocar*) to lift on to // *vi* to mount, get on; (*sobresalir*) to overlap; ~ **a** to amount to, come to; ~ **en cólera** to get angry.
montaraz [monta'raθ] *a* mountain *cpd*, highland *cpd*; (*salvaje*) wild, untamed; (*pey*) uncivilized.
monte ['monte] *nm* (*montaña*) mountain; (*bosque*) woodland; (*área sin cultivar*) wild area, wild country; ~ **de Piedad** pawnshop; ~ **alto** forest; ~ **bajo** scrub(land).
monto ['monto] *nm* total, amount.
montón [mon'ton] *nm* heap, pile; (*fig*): **un** ~ **de** heaps of, lots of.
monumento [monu'mento] *nm* monument.
monzón [mon'θon] *nm* monsoon.
moña ['mopa] *nf* hair ribbon.
moño ['mopo] *nm* bun.

morado, a [mo'raðo, a] *a* purple; (*violado*) violet // *nm* bruise // *nf* (*casa*) dwelling, abode; (*período*) stay.

moral [mo'ral] *a* moral // *nf* (*ética*) ethics; (*moralidad*) morals *pl*, morality; (*ánimo*) morale.

moraleja [mora'lexa] *nf* moral.

moralizar [morali'θar] *vt* to moralize.

morboso, a [mor'ßoso, a] *a* morbid.

morcilla [mor'θiʎa] *nf* blood sausage, black pudding.

mordaz [mor'ðaθ] *a* biting, scathing.

mordaza [mor'ðaθa] *nf* (*para la boca*) gag; (*TEC*) clamp.

morder [mor'ðer] *vt* to bite; (*mordisquear*) to nibble; (*consumir*) to eat away, eat into; **mordisco** *nm* bite.

moreno, a [mo'reno, a] *a* (*color*) (dark) brown; (*de tez*) dark; (*de pelo* ~) dark-haired; (*negro*) Negro.

moretón [more'ton] *nm* (*fam*) bruise.

morfina [mor'fina] *nf* morphine.

moribundo, a [mori'ßundo, a] *a* dying.

morir [mo'rir] *vi* (*gen*) to die; (*fuego*) to die down; (*luz*) to go out; ~**se** *vr* (*gen*) to die; (*pierna etc*) to go to sleep, go numb; (*fig*) to be dying; **fue muerto en un accidente** he was killed in an accident; ~**se por algo** to be dying for sth.

morisco, a [mo'risko, a], **moro, a** ['moro, a] *a* Moorish // *nm/f* Moor.

morral [mo'rral] *nm* haversack.

morsa ['morsa] *nf* walrus.

mortaja [mor'taxa] *nf* shroud; (*TEC*) mortise; (*AM*) cigarette paper.

mortal [mor'tal] *a* mortal; (*golpe*) deadly; ~**idad, mortandad** *nf* mortality.

mortero [mor'tero] *nm* mortar.

mortífero, a [mor'tifero, a] *a* deadly, lethal.

mortificar [mortifi'kar] *vt* (*MED*) to damage, affect seriously; (*fig*) to mortify; ~**se** *vr* to be (very) embarrassed.

mosca ['moska] *nf* fly.

Moscú [mos'ku] *n* Moscow.

mosquitero [moski'tero] *nm* mosquito net.

mosquito [mos'kito] *nm* mosquito.

mostaza [mos'taθa] *nf* mustard.

mostrador [mostra'ðor] *nm* (*de tienda*) counter; (*de café*) bar; (*de reloj*) face, dial.

mostrar [mos'trar] *vt* (*gen*) to show; (*exhibir*) to display, exhibit; (*explicar*) to explain; ~**se** *vr*: ~**se amable** to be kind, to prove to be kind; **no se muestra muy inteligente** he doesn't seem (to be) very intelligent.

mostrenco, a [mos'trenko, a] *a* ownerless, unclaimed; (*perro*) stray; (*persona*) homeless; (*fam*) dense, slow.

mota ['mota] *nf* speck, tiny piece; (*en diseño*) dot.

mote ['mote] *nm* (*apodo*) nickname; (*sentencia*) motto.

motín [mo'tin] *nm* (*del pueblo*) revolt, rising; (*del ejército*) mutiny.

motivar [moti'ßar] *vt* (*causar*) to cause, motivate; (*explicar*) to explain, justify; **motivo, a** *a* a motive // *nm* motive, reason.

moto ['moto] *nf*, **motocicleta** [motoθi-'kleta] *nf* motorbike.

motoniveladora [motonißela'ðora] *nf* bulldozer.

motor [mo'tor] *nm* motor, engine; ~ **a chorro** *o* **de reacción/de explosión** jet engine/internal combustion engine.

motora [mo'tora] *nf*, **motorbote** [motor-'ßote] *nm* motorboat.

motosierra [moto'sjerra] *nf* mechanical saw.

movedizo, a [moße'ðiθo, a] *a* easily moved, movable; (*inseguro*) unsteady; (*fig*) unsettled, changeable; (*persona*) fickle.

mover [mo'ßer] *vt* (*gen*) to move; (*cabeza*) to shake; (*accionar*) to drive; (*fig*) to cause, provoke; ~**se** *vr* to move; (*fig*) to get a move on.

móvil ['moßil] *a* mobile; (*pieza de máquina*) moving; (*mueble*) movable // *nm* motive; **movilidad** *nf* mobility; **movilizar** *vt* to mobilize.

movimiento [moßi'mjento] *nm* (*gen*) movement; (*TEC*) motion; (*actividad*) activity; **el M**~ the Falangist Movement.

mozo, a ['moθo, a] *a* (*joven*) young; (*soltero*) single, unmarried // *nm/f* (*joven*) youth, lad/girl; (*criado*) servant // *nm* (*camarero*) waiter.

muchacho, a [mu'tʃatʃo, a] *nm/f* (*niño*) boy/girl; (*criado*) servant/servant or maid.

muchedumbre [mutʃe'ðumbre] *nf* crowd.

mucho, a ['mutʃo, a] *a* (*sg*) a lot of; (*gen en frase negativa o interrogativa*) much; (*pl*) many, a lot of, lots of // *ad* (*en cantidad*) a lot, a great deal, much; (*del tiempo*) long; (*muy*) very // *pron*: **tengo** ~ **que hacer** I have a lot to do; ~**s dicen que** a lot of people say that; **ni** ~ **menos** far from it.

mudanza [mu'ðanθa] *nf* (*cambio*) change; (*de casa*) move; ~**s** *nfpl* (*fig*) moodiness *sg*.

mudar [mu'ðar] *vt* to change; (*ZOOL*) to shed // *vi* to change; ~**se** *vr* (*la ropa*) to change; (*de casa*) to move (house).

mudo, a ['muðo, a] *a* dumb; (*callado, CINE*) silent.

mueble ['mweßle] *nm* piece of furniture; ~**s** *nmpl* furniture *sg*; ~**ría** *nf* furniture shop.

mueca ['mweka] *nf* face, grimace; **hacer** ~**s a** to make faces at.

muela ['mwela] *nf* (*diente*) tooth; (: *de atrás*) molar.

muelle ['mweʎe] *a* (*blando*) soft; (*elástico*) springy; (*fig*) soft, easy // *nm* spring; (*NAUT*) wharf; (*malecón*) jetty.

muero *etc vb ver* **morir.**

muerte ['mwerte] *nf* death; (*homicidio*) murder; **dar** ~ **a** to kill.

muerto, a ['mwerto, a] *pp de* **morir** // *a* dead; (*color*) dull // *nm/f* dead man/woman; (*difunto*) deceased;

(*cadáver*) corpse; **estar** ~ **de cansancio** to be dead tired.

muestra ['mwestra] *nf* (*señal*) indication, sign; (*demostración*) demonstration; (*prueba*) proof; (*estadística*) sample; (*modelo*) model, pattern; (*testimonio*) token; **muestreo** *nm* sample, sampling.

muestro *etc vb ver* **mostrar.**

muevo *etc vb ver* **mover.**

mugir [mu'xir] *vi* (*vaca*) to moo; (*persona*) to roar, howl.

mugre ['muxre] *nf* dirt, filth; **mugriento, a** *a* dirty, filthy.

mujer [mu'xer] *nf* (*de sexo femenino*) woman; (*esposa*) wife; ~**iego** *nm* womaniser.

mula ['mula] *nf* mule.

muladar [mula'ðar] *nm* dungheap, dunghill.

muleta [mu'leta] *nf* (*para andar*) crutch; (*TAUR*) stick with red cape attached; (*fig*) prop, support.

multa ['multa] *nf* fine; **multar** *vt* to fine.

multicopista [multiko'pista] *nm* duplicator.

múltiple ['multiple] *a* multiple; (*pl*) many, numerous.

multiplicar [multipli'kar] *vt* (*MAT*) to multiply; (*fig*) to increase; ~**se** *vr* (*BIO*) to multiply; (*fig*) to attend to a lot of things at one time.

multitud [multi'tuð] *nf* (*gentío, muchedumbre*) crowd; ~ **de** lots of.

mullido, a [mu'ʎiðo, a] *a* (*cama*) soft; (*hierba*) soft, springy // *nm* stuffing, filling.

mundano, a [mun'dano, a] *a* worldly; (*de moda*) fashionable.

mundial [mun'djal] *a* world-wide, universal; (*guerra, récord*) world *cpd.*

mundo ['mundo] *nm* world; **todo el** ~ everybody; **tener** ~ to be experienced, know one's way around.

munición [muni'θjon] *nf* (*MIL*) stores *pl*, supplies *pl*; (*de arma*) ammunition.

municipio [muni'θipjo] *nm* (*ayuntamiento*) town council, corporation; (*comuna*) town, municipality.

muñeca [mu'ɲeka] *nf* (*ANAT*) wrist; (*juguete*) doll; (*maniquí*) dummy.

muñeco [mu'ɲeko] *nm* (*figura*) figure; (*marioneta*) puppet; (*maniquí*) dummy; (*fig*) puppet, pawn.

muralla [mu'raʎa] *nf* (city) wall(s) (*pl*).

murciélago [mur'θjelaxo] *nm* bat.

murmullo [mur'muʎo] *nm* murmur(ing); (*cuchicheo*) whispering; (*de arroyo*) murmur, rippling.

murmuración [murmura'θjon] *nf* gossip; **murmurar** *vi* to murmur, whisper; (*criticar*) to criticize; (*cotillear*) to gossip.

muro ['muro] *nm* wall.

muscular [musku'lar] *a* muscular.

músculo ['muskulo] *nm* muscle.

museo [mu'seo] *nm* museum.

musgo ['musxo] *nm* moss.

músico, a ['musiko, a] *a* musical // *nm/f* musician // *nf* music.

musitar [musi'tar] *vt, vi* to mutter, mumble.

muslo ['muslo] *nm* thigh.

mustio, a ['mustjo, a] *a* (*persona*) depressed, gloomy; (*planta*) faded, withered.

musulmán, ana [musul'man, ana] *nm/f* Moslem.

mutación [muta'θjon] *nf* (*BIO*) mutation; (*cambio*) (sudden) change.

mutilar [muti'lar] *vt* to mutilate; (*a una persona*) to maim.

mutuamente [mutwa'mente] *ad* mutually; **mutuo, a** *a* mutual.

muy [mwi] *ad* very; (*demasiado*) too; **M**~ **Señor mío** Dear Sir; ~ **de noche** very late at night; **eso es** ~ **de él** that's just like him.

N

N *abr de* **norte.**

n/ *abr de* **nuestro, a.**

nabo ['naßo] *nm* turnip; (*raíz*) root.

nácar ['nakar] *nm* mother-of-pearl.

nacer [na'θer] *vi* to be born; (*de huevo*) to hatch; (*vegetal*) to sprout; (*río*) to rise; ~ **al amor** to awaken to love; **nació una sospecha en su mente** a suspicion formed in her mind; **nacido, a** *a* born; **recién nacido** newborn; **naciente** *a* new, emerging; (*sol*) rising; **nacimiento** *nm* birth; (*fig*) birth, origin; (*de Navidad*) Nativity; (*linaje*) descent, family; (*de río*) source.

nación [na'θjon] *nf* nation; **nacional** *a* national; **nacionalismo** *nm* nationalism; **nacionalista** *nm/f* nationalist; **nacionalizar** *vt* to nationalize; **nacionalizarse** *vr* to become naturalized.

nada ['naða] *pron* nothing // *ad* not at all, in no way; **no decir** ~ to say nothing, not to say anything; **de** ~ don't mention it.

nadaderas [naða'ðeras] *nfpl* waterwings.

nadador, a [naða'ðor, a] *nm/f* swimmer.

nadar [na'ðar] *vi* to swim.

nadie ['naðje] *pron* nobody, no-one; ~ **habló** nobody spoke; **no había** ~ there was nobody there, there wasn't anybody there.

nado ['naðo]: **a** ~ *ad*: **pasar a** ~ to swim across.

naipe ['naipe] *nm* playing card; ~**s** *nmpl* cards.

nalgas ['nalxas] *nfpl* buttocks.

nana ['nana] *nf* (*fam: abuela*) grandma (*fam*), granny (*fam*); (: *canción*) lullaby.

naranja [na'ranxa] *a, nf* orange; **media** ~ (*fam*) better half (*fam*); ~**do, a** *a* orange // *nf* orangeade; **naranjo** *nm* orange tree.

narciso [nar'θiso] *nm* narcissus.

narcótico, a [nar'kotiko, a] *a, nm* narcotic; **narcotizar** *vt* to drug.

nardo ['narðo] *nm* lily.
narigón, ona [nari'ɣon, ona], **narigudo, a** [nari'ɣuðo, a] *a* big-nosed.
nariz [na'riθ] *nf* nose; **narices** *nfpl* nostrils; **en las narices de uno** under one's (very) nose.
narración [narra'θjon] *nf* narration; **narrador, a** *nm/f* narrator.
narrar [na'rrar] *vt* to narrate, recount; **narrativa** *nf* narrative, story.
nata ['nata] *nf* cream.
natación [nata'θjon] *nf* swimming.
natal [na'tal] *a:* **ciudad** ∼ home town; ∼**icio** *nm* birthday; ∼**idad** *nf* birth rate.
natillas [na'tiʎas] *nfpl* custard *sg.*
natividad [natiβi'ðað] *nf* nativity.
nativo, a [na'tiβo, a] *a* native; (*innato*) innate, natural // *nm/f* native.
nato, a ['nato, a] *a* born; **un músico** ∼ a born musician.
natural [natu'ral] *a* natural; (*fruta etc*) fresh // *nm/f* native // *nm* nature; ∼**eza** *nf* nature; (*género*) nature, kind; ∼**eza muerta** still life; ∼**idad** *nf* naturalness; ∼**ización** *nf* naturalization; ∼**izarse** *vr* to become naturalized; (*aclimatarse*) to become acclimatized; ∼**mente** *ad* naturally.
naufragar [naufra'ɣar] *vi* to sink; **naufragio** *nm* shipwreck; **náufrago, a** *nm/f* castaway, shipwrecked person.
náusea ['nausea] *nf* nausea; **me da** ∼ it makes me feel sick; **nauseabundo, a** *a* nauseating, sickening.
náutico, a ['nautiko, a] *a* nautical.
nava ['naβa] *nf* (*GEO*) level plain.
navaja [na'βaxa] *nf* (*cortaplumas*) clasp knife, penknife; (*de barbero, peluquero*) razor.
navarro, a [na'βarro, a] *a* Navarrese.
nave ['naβe] *nf* (*barco*) ship, vessel; (*ARQ*) nave; ∼ **espacial** spaceship.
navegación [naβeɣa'θjon] *nf* navigation; (*viaje*) sea journey; ∼ **aérea** air traffic; ∼ **costera** coastal shipping; **navegante** *nm/f* navigator; **navegar** *vi* (*barco*) to sail; (*avión*) to fly // *vt* to sail; to fly; (*dirigir el rumbo*) to navigate.
navidad [naβi'ðað] *nf* Christmas; **navideño, a** *a* Christmas *cpd.*
navío [na'βio] *nm* ship.
nazi ['naθi] *a, nm/f* Nazi.
neblina [ne'βlina] *nf* mist.
nebuloso, a [neβu'loso, a] *a* foggy; (*calinoso*) misty; (*cielo*) cloudy; (*indefinido*) nebulous, vague // *nf* nebula.
necedad [neθe'ðað] *nf* foolishness; (*una* ∼) foolish act.
necesario, a [neθe'sarjo, a] *a* necessary.
neceser [neθe'ser] *nm* vanity case; (*bolsa*) holdall; ∼ **de viaje** travelling case.
necesidad [neθesi'ðað] *nf* need; (*lo inevitable*) necessity; (*miseria*) poverty, need; **en caso de** ∼ in case of need *or* emergency; **hacer sus** ∼**es** to relieve o.s.

necesitado, a [neθesi'taðo, a] *a* needy, poor; ∼ **de** in need of.
necesitar [neθesi'tar] *vt* to need, require // *vi:* ∼ **de** to have need of.
necio, a ['neθjo, a] *a* foolish.
necrología [nekrolo'xia] *nf* obituary.
necrópolis [ne'kropolis] *nf* cemetery.
nectarina [nekta'rina] *nf* nectarine.
nefando, a [ne'fando, a] *a* unspeakable.
nefasto, a [ne'fasto, a] *a* ill-fated, unlucky.
negación [neɣa'θjon] *nf* negation; (*rechazo*) refusal, denial.
negar [ne'ɣar] *vt* (*renegar, rechazar*) to refuse; (*prohibir*) to refuse, deny; (*desmentir*) to deny; ∼**se** *vr:* ∼**se a** to refuse to.
negativo, a [neɣa'tiβo, a] *a, nm* negative // *nf* (*gen*) negative; (*rechazo*) refusal, denial.
negligencia [neɣli'xenθja] *nf* negligence; **negligente** *a* negligent.
negociable [neɣo'θjaβle] *a* (*COM*) negotiable.
negociado [neɣo'θjaðo] *nm* department, section.
negociante [neɣo'θjante] *nm/f* businessman/woman; (*comerciante*) merchant.
negociar [neɣo'θjar] *vt, vi* to negotiate; ∼ **en** to deal in, trade in.
negocio [ne'ɣoθjo] *nm* (*COM*) business; (*asunto*) affair, business; (*operación comercial*) deal, transaction; (*AM*) firm; (*lugar*) place of business; **los** ∼**s** business *sg;* **hacer** ∼ to do business.
negro, a ['neɣro, a] *a* black; (*suerte*) awful // *nm* black // *nm/f* Negro/Negress, black // *nf* (*MUS*) crotchet; **negrura** *nf* blackness.
nene, a ['nene, a] *nm/f* baby, small child; (*fam*) dear.
nenúfar [ne'nufar] *nm* water lily.
neologismo [neolo'xismo] *nm* neologism.
neoyorquino, a [neojor'kino, a] *a* (of) New York.
nepotismo [nepo'tismo] *nm* nepotism.
nervio ['nerβjo] *nm* (*ANAT*) nerve; (: *tendón*) tendon; (*fig*) vigour; ∼**sidad** *nf* nervousness, nerves *pl;* ∼**so, a, nervudo, a** *a* nervous.
neto, a ['neto, a] *a* clear; (*verdad etc*) pure; (*limpio*) clean; (*COM*) net.
neumático, a [neu'matiko, a] *a* pneumatic // *nm* tyre; ∼ **de recambio** spare tyre.
neuralgia [neu'ralxja] *nf* neuralgia.
neurastenia [neuras'tenja] *nf* nervous exhaustion.
neuritis [neu'ritis] *nf* neuritis.
neurólogo, a [neu'roloɣo, a] *nm/f* neurologist.
neurosis [neu'rosis] *nf inv* neurosis.
neutral [neu'tral] *a* neutral; ∼**izar** *vt* to neutralize; (*contrarrestar*) to counteract.
neutro, a ['neutro, a] *a* (*BIO*) neuter, sexless; (*LING*) neuter.

neutrón [neu'tron] *nm* neutron; **bomba de neutrones** neutron bomb.

nevada [ne'βaða] *nf* snowstorm; (*caída de nieve*) snowfall.

nevar [ne'βar] *vi* to snow; **nevasca** *nf* snowstorm.

nevera [ne'βera] *nf* refrigerator, icebox.

nevisca [ne'βiska] *nf* flurry of snow; (*aguanieve*) sleet; **neviscar** *vi* to snow lightly; to sleet.

ni [ni] *conj* nor, neither; (~ *siquiera*) not ... even; ~ **que** not even if; ~ **blanco** ~ **negro** neither white nor black.

Nicaragua [nika'raɣwa] *nf* Nicaragua; **nicaragüense** *a, nm/f* Nicaraguan.

nicotina [niko'tina] *nf* nicotine.

nicho ['nitʃo] *nm* niche.

nido ['niðo] *nm* nest; (*fig*) hiding place; (*lugar predilecto*) haunt.

niebla ['njeβla] *nf* fog; (*neblina*) mist.

niego *etc vb ver* **negar.**

nieto, a ['njeto, a] *nm/f* grandson/daughter; ~**s** *nmpl* grandchildren.

nieva *etc vb ver* **nevar.**

nieve ['njeβe] *nf* snow.

nigromancia [niɣro'manθja] *nf* necromancy, black magic.

nihilismo [nii'lismo] *nm* nihilism.

Nilo ['nilo] *nm*: **el** ~ the Nile.

nimbo ['nimbo] *nm* (*aureola*) halo; (*nube*) nimbus.

nimiedad [nimje'ðað] *nf* small-mindedness; (*prolijidad*) long-windedness; (*trivialidad*) triviality.

nimio, a ['nimjo, a] *a* (*insignificante*) trivial, insignificant; (*escrupuloso*) fussy, overparticular.

ninfa ['ninfa] *nf* nymph.

ninfómana [nin'fomana] *nf* nymphomaniac.

ninguno, a [nin'guno, a], **ningún** [nin'gun] *a* no // *pron* (*nadie*) nobody; (*ni uno*) none, not one; (*ni uno ni otro*) neither; **de ~a manera** by no means, not at all.

niña ['nina] *nf ver* **niño.**

niñera [ni'nera] *nf* nursemaid, nanny; **niñería** *nf* childish act.

niñez [ni'neθ] *nf* childhood; (*infancia*) infancy.

niño, a ['nino, a] *a* (*joven*) young; (*inmaduro*) immature // *nm* (*chico*) boy, child // *nf* (*chica*) girl, child; (*ANAT*) pupil.

nipón, ona [ni'pon, ona] *a, nm/f* Japanese.

níquel ['nikel] *nm* nickel; **niquelar** *vt* (*TEC*) to nickel-plate.

nitidez [niti'ðeθ] *nf* (*claridad*) clarity; (: *de atmósfera*) brightness; (: *de imagen*) sharpness; **nítido, a** *a* clear; sharp.

nitrato [ni'trato] *nm* nitrate.

nitrógeno [ni'troxeno] *nm* nitrogen.

nitroglicerina [nitroɣliθe'rina] *nf* nitroglycerine.

nivel [ni'βel] *nm* (*GEO*) level; (*norma*) level, standard; (*altura*) height; ~ **de aceite** oil level; ~ **de aire** spirit level; ~ **de vida** standard of living; ~**ar** *vt*

(*terreno*) to level out; (*equilibrar*: *mueble*) to even up; (*COM*) to balance.

NN. UU. *nfpl abr de* **Naciones Unidas** U.N. *sg* (United Nations).

no [no] *ad* no; not; (*con verbo*) not // *excl* no!; ~ **tengo nada** I don't have anything, I have nothing; ~ **es el mío** it's not mine; **ahora** ~ not now; ¿~ **lo sabes?** don't you know?; ~ **mucho** not much; ~ **bien termine, lo entregaré** as soon as I finish I'll hand it over; ¡**a que** ~ **lo sabes!** I bet you don't know!; ¡**cuándo** o **cómo** ~! of course!; **los países** ~ **alineados** the non-aligned countries; **el** ~ **conformismo** non-conformism; **la** ~ **intervención** non-intervention.

NO *abr de* **noroeste.**

no. *abr de* **número.**

noble ['noβle] *a, nm/f* noble; ~**za** *nf* nobility.

noción [no'θjon] *nf* notion.

nocivo, a [no'θiβo, a] *a* harmful.

noctambulismo [noktam'βulismo] *nm* sleepwalking; **noctámbulo, a** *nm/f* sleepwalker.

nocturno, a [nok'turno, a] *a* (*de la noche*) nocturnal, night *cpd*; (*de la tarde*) evening *cpd* // *nm* nocturne.

noche ['notʃe] *nf* night, night-time; (*la tarde*) evening; (*fig*) darkness; **de** ~, **por la** ~ at night.

nochebuena [notʃe'βwena] *nf* Christmas Eve.

nochevieja [notʃe'βjexa] *nf* New Year's Eve.

nodriza [no'ðriθa] *nf* wet nurse.

nogal [no'ɣal] *nm* walnut tree.

nómada ['nomaða] *a* nomadic // *nm/f* nomad.

nombradía [nombra'ðia] *nf* fame.

nombramiento [nombra'mjento] *nm* naming; (*a un empleo*) appointment.

nombrar [nom'brar] *vt* (*designar*) to name; (*mencionar*) to mention; (*dar puesto a*) to appoint.

nombre ['nombre] *nm* name; (*sustantivo*) noun; (*fama*) renown; ~ **y apellidos** name in full; ~ **común/propio** common/proper noun; ~ **de pila/de soltera** Christian/maiden name.

nomenclatura [nomenkla'tura] *nf* nomenclature.

nomeolvides [nomeol'βiðes] *nm inv* forget-me-not.

nómina ['nomina] *nf* (*lista*) list; (*COM*) payroll.

nominal [nomi'nal] *a* nominal.

nominativo, a [nomina'tiβo, a] *a* (*COM*): **cheque** ~ **a X** cheque made out to X.

non [non] *a* odd, uneven // *nm* odd number.

nonada [no'naða] *nf* trifle.

nono, a ['nono, a] *a* ninth.

nordeste [nor'ðeste] *a* north-east, north-eastern, north-easterly // *nm* north-east.

nórdico, a ['norðiko, a] *a* (*del norte*) northern, northerly; (*escandinavo*) Nordic.

noria ['norja] *nf* (*AGR*) waterwheel; (*de carnaval*) big wheel.

normal [nor'mal] *a* (*corriente*) normal; (*habitual*) usual, natural; **(gasolina)** ~ two-star petrol; ~**idad** *nf* normality; **restablecer la** ~**idad** to restore order; ~**izar** *vt* (*reglamentar*) to normalize; (*TEC*) to standardize; ~**izarse** *vr* to return to normal.

normando, a [nor'mando, a] *a, nm/f* Norman.

noroeste [noro'este] *a* north-west, north-western, north-westerly // *nm* north-west.

norte ['norte] *a* north, northern, northerly // *nm* north; (*fig*) guide.

norteamericano, a [norteameri'kano, a] *a, nm/f* (North) American.

noruego, [no'rweɣo, a] *a, nm/f* Norwegian; **N**~**a** *nf* Norway.

nos [nos] *pron* (*directo*) us; (*indirecto*) us; to us; for us; from us; (*reflexivo*) (to) ourselves; (*recíproco*) (to) each other; ~ **levantamos a las 7** we get up at 7.

nosotros [no'sotros] *pron* (*sujeto*) we; (*después de prep*) us.

nostalgia [nos'talxja] *nf* nostalgia.

nota ['nota] *nf* note; (*ESCOL*) mark.

notabilidad [notaβili'ðað] *nf* (*persona*) notable.

notable [no'taβle] *a, nm/f* notable.

notación [nota'θjon] *nf* (*nota*) note; (*MAT, MUS*) notation.

notar [no'tar] *vt* (*advertir*) to notice, note; (*anotar, asentar*) to note (down); (*censurar*) to criticize; ~**se** *vr* to be obvious.

notarial [nota'rjal] *a:* **acta** ~ affidavit.

notario [no'tarjo] *nm* notary.

noticia [no'tiθja] *nf* (*información*) piece of news; **las** ~**s** the news *sg*; **tener** ~**s de alguien** to hear from sb.

noticiar [noti'θjar] *vt* to notify; ~**io** *nm* (*CINE*) newsreel; (*TV*) news bulletin; **noticioso, a** *a* well-informed.

notificación [notifika'θjon] *nf* notification; **notificar** *vt* to notify, inform.

notoriedad [notorje'ðað] *nf* fame, renown; **notorio, a** *a* (*público*) well-known; (*evidente*) obvious.

novato, a [no'βato, a] *a* inexperienced // *nm/f* beginner.

novecientos [noβe'θjentos] *num* nine hundred.

novedad [noβe'ðað] *nf* (*calidad de nuevo*) newness; (*noticia*) piece of news; (*cambio*) change, (new) development.

novedoso, a [noβe'ðoso, a] *a* novel.

novel [no'βel] *a* new; (*inexperto*) inexperienced // *nm/f* beginner.

novela [no'βela] *nf* novel.

novelero, a [noβe'lero, a] *a* highly imaginative; (*voluble*) fickle; (*chismoso*) gossipy.

novelesco, a [noβe'lesko, a] *a* fictional; (*romántico*) romantic; (*fantástico*) fantastic.

noveno, a [no'βeno, a] *a* ninth.

noventa [no'βenta] *num* ninety.

novia ['noβja] *nf ver* **novio.**

noviazgo [no'βjaɸxo] *nm* engagement.

novicio, a [no'βiθjo, a] *nm/f* novice.

noviembre [no'βjembre] *nm* November.

novilla [no'βiʎa] *nf* heifer; ~**da** *nf* (*TAUR*) bullfight with young bulls; **novillero** *nm* novice bullfighter; **novillo** *nm* young bull; **hacer novillos** (*fam*) to play truant.

novio, a ['noβjo, a] *nm/f* boyfriend/girlfriend; (*prometido*) fiancé/fiancée; (*recién casado*) bridegroom/bride; **los** ~**s** the newly-weds.

N. S. *abr de* **Nuestro Señor.**

nubarrón [nuβa'rron] *nm* storm cloud.

nube ['nuβe] *nf* cloud.

nublado, a [nu'βlaðo, a] *a* cloudy // *nm* storm cloud; **nublar** *vt* (*oscurecer*) to darken; (*confundir*) to cloud; **nublarse** *vr* to grow dark.

nuca ['nuka] *nf* nape of the neck.

nuclear [nukle'ar] *a* nuclear.

núcleo ['nukleo] *nm* (*centro*) core; (*FÍSICA*) nucleus.

nudillo [nu'ðiʎo] *nm* knuckle.

nudo ['nuðo] *nm* (*gen*) knot; (*unión*) bond; (*de problema*) crux; (*de comunicaciones*) centre; ~**so, a** *a* knotty.

nuera ['nwera] *nf* daughter-in-law.

nuestro, a ['nwestro, a] *det* our // *pron* ours; ~ **padre** our father; **un amigo** ~ a friend of ours; **es el** ~ it's ours.

nueva ['nweβa] *nf ver* **nuevo.**

nuevamente [nweβa'mente] *ad* (*otra vez*) again; (*de nuevo*) anew.

nueve ['nweβe] *num* nine.

nuevo, a ['nweβo, a] *a* (*gen*) new // *nf* piece of news; **de** ~ again; **N**~**a York** *n* New York; **N**~**a Zelandia** *nf* New Zealand.

nuez [nweθ] (*pl* **nueces**) *nf* (*fruto*) nut; (*del nogal*) walnut; ~ **de Adán** Adam's apple; ~ **moscada** nutmeg.

nulidad [nuli'ðað] *nf* (*incapacidad*) incompetence; (*abolición*) nullity.

nulo, a ['nulo, a] *a* (*inepto, torpe*) useless; (*inválido*) (null and) void; (*DEPORTE*) drawn, tied.

núm. *abr de* **número.**

numen ['numen] *nm* inspiration.

numeración [numera'θjon] *nf* (*cifras*) numbers *pl*; (*arábiga, romana etc*) numerals *pl*.

numeral [nume'ral] *nm* numeral.

numerar [nume'rar] *vt* to number.

numerario [nume'rarjo] *nm* hard cash.

numérico, a [nu'meriko, a] *a* numerical.

número ['numero] *nm* (*gen*) number; (*tamaño: de zapato*) size; (*ejemplar: de diario*) number, issue; **sin** ~ numberless, unnumbered; ~ **de matrícula/telefónico** registration/telephone number; ~ **atrasado** back number.

numeroso, a [nume'roso, a] *a* numerous.

nunca ['nunka] *ad* (*jamás*) never; ~ **lo pensé** I never thought it; **no vino** ~ he

never came; ~ **más** never again.
nuncio ['nunθjo] *nm* (*REL*) nuncio.
nupcias ['nupθjas] *nfpl* wedding *sg*, nuptials.
nutria ['nutrja] *nf* otter.
nutrición [nutri'θjon] *nf* nutrition.
nutrido, a [nu'triðo, a] *a* (*alimentado*) nourished; (*fig: grande*) large; (*abundante*) abundant.
nutrir [nu'trir] *vt* (*alimentar*) to nourish; (*dar de comer*) to feed; (*alentar*) to encourage; (*esperanzas*) to cherish; **nutritivo, a** *a* nourishing, nutritious.
nylon [ni'lon] *nm* nylon.

Ñ

ñame ['name] *nm* yam.
ñaque ['nake] *nm* junk.
ñato, a ['nato, a] *a* (*AM*) snub-nosed.
ñoñería [none'ria], **ñoñez** [no'neθ] *nf* insipidness.
ñoño, a ['nono, a] *a* (*AM. tonto*) silly, stupid; (*soso*) insipid; (*persona*) spineless.

O

o [o] *conj* or.
O *abr de* **oeste.**
o/ *abr de* **orden.**
oasis [o'asis] *nm* oasis.
obcecar [oßθe'kar] *vt* to blind.
obedecer [oßeðe'θer] *vt* to obey; **obediencia** *nf* obedience; **obediente** *a* obedient.
obertura [oßer'tura] *nf* overture.
obesidad [oßesi'ðað] *nf* obesity; **obeso, a** *a* obese.
obispo [o'ßispo] *nm* bishop.
objeción [oßxe'θjon] *nf* objection; **objetar** *vt, vi* to object.
objetivo, a [oßxe'tißo, a] *a, nm* objective.
objeto [oß'xeto] *nm* (*cosa*) object; (*fin*) aim.
oblicuo, a [o'ßlikwo, a] *a* oblique; (*mirada*) sidelong.
obligación [oßlixa'θjon] *nf* obligation; (*COM*) bond.
obligar [oßli'xar] *vt* to force; ~**se** *vr* to bind o.s.; **obligatorio, a** *a* compulsory, obligatory.
oboe [o'ßoe] *nm* oboe.
obra ['oßra] *nf* (*gen*) work; (*hechura*) piece of work; (*ARQ*) construction, building; (*TEATRO*) play; ~ **maestra** masterpiece; (**Ministerio de**) **O~s Públicas** Ministry of Public Works; **en** ~ **de** in about; **por** ~ **de** thanks to (the efforts of); **obrar** *vt* to work; (*tener efecto*) to have an effect on // *vi* to act, behave; (*tener efecto*) to have an effect; **la carta obra en su poder** the letter is in his/her possession; **obrero, a** *a* working, labour *cpd*; **clase obrera** working class // *nm/f* (*gen*) worker; (*sin oficio*) labourer.

obscenidad [oßsθeni'ðað] *nf* obscenity; **obsceno, a** *a* obscene.
obscu... = oscu... .
obsequiar [oßse'kjar] *vt* (*ofrecer*) to present with; (*agasajar*) to make a fuss of, lavish attention on; **obsequio** *nm* (*regalo*) gift; (*cortesía*) courtesy, attention; **obsequioso, a** *a* attentive.
observación [oßserßa'θjon] *nf* observation; (*reflexión*) remark.
observancia [oßser'ßanθja] *nf* observance.
observar [oßser'ßar] *vt* to observe; (*anotar*) to notice; ~**se** *vr* to keep to, observe.
obsesión [oßse'sjon] *nf* obsession; **obsesionar** *vt* to obsess.
obstaculizar [oßstakuli'θar] *vt* (*dificultar*) to hinder; (*impedir*) to stand in the way of.
obstáculo [oß'stakulo] *nm* (*gen*) obstacle; (*impedimento*) hindrance, drawback.
obstante [oß'stante]: **no** ~ *ad* nevertheless // *prep* in spite of.
obstar [oß'star] *vi*: ~ **a** to hinder.
obstetricia [oßste'triθja] *nf* obstetrics *sg*; **obstétrico, a** *a* obstetric // *nm/f* obstetrician.
obstinado, a [oßsti'naðo, a] *a* (*gen*) obstinate; (*terco*) stubborn.
obstinarse [oßsti'narse] *vr* to be obstinate; ~ **en** to persist in.
obstrucción [oßstruk'θjon] *nf* obstruction; **obstruir** *vt* to obstruct.
obtener [oßte'ner] *vt* (*conseguir*) to obtain; (*ganar*) to gain.
obtuso, a [oß'tuso, a] *a* (*filo*) blunt; (*MAT, fig*) obtuse.
obviar [oß'ßjar] *vt* to clear away // *vi* to stand in the way.
obvio, a ['oßßjo, a] *a* obvious.
ocasión [oka'sjon] *nf* (*oportunidad*) opportunity, chance; (*momento*) occasion, time; (*causa*) cause; **de** ~ secondhand; **ocasionar** *vt* to cause.
ocaso [o'kaso] *nm* (*oeste*) west; (*fig*) decline.
occidente [okθi'ðente] *nm* west.
océano [o'θeano] *nm* ocean; **el** ~ **Índico** the Indian Ocean.
O.C.E.D. *nf abr de* **Organización de Cooperación Económica y Desarrollo** OECD (Organization for Economic Cooperation and Development).
ocio ['oθjo] *nm* (*tiempo*) leisure; (*pey*) idleness; ~**s** *nmpl* pastime *sg*; ~**sidad** *nf* idleness; ~**so, a** *a* (*inactivo*) idle; (*inútil*) useless.
octanaje [okta'naxe] *nm*: **de alto** ~ high octane; **octano** *nm* octane.
octavín [okta'ßin] *nm* piccolo.
octavo, a [ok'taßo, a] *a* eighth.
octogenario, a [oktoxe'narjo, a] *a* octogenarian.
octubre [ok'tußre] *nm* October.
ocular [oku'lar] *a* ocular, eye *cpd*; **testigo** ~ eyewitness.

oculista [oku'lista] *nm/f* oculist.
ocultar [okul'tar] *vt* (*esconder*) to hide; (*callar*) to withhold; **oculto, a** *a* hidden; (*fig*) secret.
ocupación [okupa'θjon] *nf* occupation.
ocupado, a [oku'paðo, a] *a* (*persona*) busy; (*sitio*) occupied; (*teléfono*) engaged; **ocupar** *vt* (*gen*) to occupy; **ocuparse** *vr*: **ocuparse con** *o* **de** *o* **en** (*gen*) to concern o.s. with; (*cuidar*) to look after.
ocurrencia [oku'rrenθja] *nf* (*ocasión*) occurrence; (*agudeza*) witticism.
ocurrir [oku'rrir] *vi* to happen; ~**se** *vr*: **se me ocurre que...** it occurs to me that... .
ochenta [o'tʃenta] *num* eighty. ☞
ocho ['otʃo] *num* eight.
odiar [o'ðjar] *vt* to hate; **odio** *nm* (*gen*) hate, hatred; (*disgusto*) dislike; **odioso, a** *a* (*gen*) hateful; (*malo*) nasty.
O.E.A. *nf abr de* **Organización de Estados Americanos** O.A.S. (Organization of American States).
oeste [o'este] *nm* west; **una película del** ~ a western.
ofender [ofen'der] *vt* (*agraviar*) to offend; (*ser ofensivo a*) to be offensive to; ~**se** *vr* to take offence; **ofensa** *nf* offence; **ofensivo, a** *a* (*insultante*) insulting; (*MIL*) offensive // *nf* offensive.
oferta [o'ferta] *nf* offer; (*propuesta*) proposal; **la** ~ **y la demanda** supply and demand; **artículos en** ~ goods on offer.
oficial [ofi'θjal] *a* official // *nm* official; (*MIL*) officer.
oficina [ofi'θina] *nf* office; **oficinista** *nm/f* clerk.
oficio [o'fiθjo] *nm* (*profesión*) profession; (*puesto*) post; (*REL*) service; **ser del** ~ to be an old hand; **tener mucho** ~ to have a lot of experience; ~ **de difuntos** funeral service; **de** ~ officially.
oficiosidad [ofiθjosi'ðað] *nf* helpfulness; (*pey*) officiousness.
oficioso, a [ofi'θjoso, a] *a* (*diligente*) attentive; (*pey*) officious; (*no oficial*) unofficial, informal.
ofrecer [ofre'θer] *vt* (*dar*) to offer; (*proponer*) to propose; ~**se** *vr* (*persona*) to offer o.s., volunteer; (*situación*) to present itself; **¿qué se le ofrece?, ¿se le ofrece algo?** what can I do for you?, can I get you anything?
ofrecimiento [ofreθi'mjento] *nm* offer, offering.
ofrendar [ofren'dar] *vt* to offer, contribute.
oftálmico, a [of'talmiko, a] *a* ophthalmic.
ofuscación [ofuska'θjon] *nf*, **ofuscamiento** [ofuska'mjento] *nm* (*fig*) bewilderment; **ofuscar** *vt* (*confundir*) to bewilder; (*enceguecer*) to dazzle, blind.
oída [o'iða] *nf* hearing; **de** ~**s** by hearsay.
oído [o'iðo] *nm* ear; (*sentido*) hearing.
oigo *etc vb ver* **oír**.
oír [o'ir] *vt* (*gen*) to hear; (*atender a*) to

listen to; **¡oiga!** listen!; ~ **misa** to attend mass.
O.I.T. *nf abr de* **Organización Internacional del Trabajo** I.L.O. (International Labour Organization).
ojal [o'xal] *nm* buttonhole.
ojalá [oxa'la] *excl* if only it were so!, some hope(s)! // *conj* if only...!, would that...!; ~ **que venga hoy** I hope he comes today.
ojeada [oxe'aða] *nf* glance; **ojear** *vt* (*mirar fijo*) to stare at; (*examinar*) to eye; (*mirar de reojo*) to glance at.
ojera [o'xera] *nf*: **tener** ~**s** to have rings or circles under the eyes.
ojeriza [oxe'riθa] *nf* ill-will.
ojeroso, a [oxe'roso, a] *a* haggard.
ojete [o'xete] *nm* eye(let).
ojo ['oxo] *nm* eye; (*de puente*) span; (*de cerradura*) keyhole // *excl* careful!; **tener** ~ **para** to have an eye for; ~ **de buey** porthole.
ola ['ola] *nf* wave.
olé [o'le] *excl* bravo!, olé!
oleada [ole'aða] *nf* big wave, swell; (*fig*) surge.
oleaje [ole'axe] *nm* swell.
óleo ['oleo] *nm* oil; **oleoducto** *nm* (oil) pipeline.
oler [o'ler] *vt* (*gen*) to smell; (*husmear*) to pry into; (*fig*) to sniff out // *vi*: ~ **a** to smell of.
olfatear [olfate'ar] *vt* to smell; (*fig*) to sniff out; (*husmear*) to pry into; **olfato** *nm* sense of smell.
oliente [o'ljente] *a* smelling; **bien/mal** ~ sweet-/foul-smelling.
oligarquía [olixar'kia] *nf* oligarchy.
olimpíada [olim'piaða] *nf*: **las O**~**s** the Olympics.
oliva [o'liβa] *nf* (*aceituna*) olive; (*árbol*) olive tree; **aceite de** ~ olive oil; **olivo** *nm* olive tree.
olmo ['olmo] *nm* elm (tree).
olor [o'lor] *nm* smell; ~**oso, a** *a* scented.
olvidadizo, a [olβiða'ðiθo, a] *a* (*desmemoriado*) forgetful; (*distraído*) absent-minded.
olvidar [olβi'ðar] *vt* to forget; (*omitir*) to omit; ~**se** *vr* to forget o.s.; **se me olvidó** I forgot.
olvido [ol'βiðo] *nm* oblivion.
olla ['oʎa] *nf* pan; (*comida*) stew; ~ **a presión** *o* **autopresión** pressure cooker; ~ **podrida** Spanish stew.
ombligo [om'blixo] *nm* navel.
ominoso, a [omi'noso, a] *a* ominous.
omisión [omi'sjon] *nf* (*abstención*) omission; (*descuido*) neglect.
omiso, a [o'miso, a] *a*: **hacer caso** ~ **de** to ignore, pass over.
omitir [omi'tir] *vt* to omit.
omnipotente [omnipo'tente] *a* omnipotent.
omnívoro, a [om'niβoro, a] *a* omnivorous.
omóplato [o'moplato] *nm* shoulder blade.
O.M.S. *nf abr de* **Organización Mundial**

de la Salud W.H.O. (World Health Organization).

once ['onθe] *num* eleven; **las** ~ (*fam*) elevenses.

onda ['onda] *nf* wave; ~ **corta/larga/media** short/long/ medium wave; ~**s acústicas/ hertzianas** acoustic/Hertzian waves; **ondear** *vt* to wave // *vi* to wave; (*tener ondas*) to be wavy; (*pelo*) to flow; (*agua*) to ripple; **ondearse** *vr* to swing, sway.

ondulación [ondula'θjon] *nf* undulation; **ondulado, a** *a* wavy // *nm* wave; **ondulante** *a* undulating; (*cartón, chapa*) corrugated.

ondular [ondu'lar] *vt* (*el pelo*) to wave // *vi*, ~**se** *vr* to undulate.

oneroso, a [one'roso, a] *a* onerous.

ONU *nf abr de* **Organización de las Naciones Unidas** UNO (United Nations Organization).

O.P. *nfpl. abr de* **Obras Públicas** Public Works.

opaco, a [o'pako, a] *a* opaque; (*fig*) dull.

opalescente [opales'θente] *a* opalescent.

ópalo ['opalo] *nm* opal.

opción [op'θjon] *nf* (*gen*) option; (*derecho*) right, option.

ópera ['opera] *nf* opera; ~ **bufa** *o* **cómica** comic opera.

operación [opera'θjon] *nf* (*gen*) operation; (*COM*) transaction, deal.

operador, a [opera'ðor, a] *nm/f* operator; (*en cine*) projectionist; (*de cine*) camera operator.

operante [ope'rante] *a* operating.

operar [ope'rar] *vt* (*producir*) to produce, bring about; (*MED*) to operate on // *vi* (*COM*) to operate, deal; ~**se** *vr* to occur; (*MED*) to have an operation.

opereta [ope'reta] *nf* operetta.

opinar [opi'nar] *vt* (*estimar*) to think // *vi* (*enjuiciar*) to give one's opinion; **opinión** *nf* (*creencia*) belief; (*criterio*) opinion.

opio ['opjo] *nm* opium.

oponente [opo'nente] *nm/f* opponent.

oponer [opo'ner] *vt* (*resistencia*) to put up, offer; (*negativa*) to raise; ~**se** *vr* (*objetar*) to object; (*estar frente a frente*) to be opposed; (*dos personas*) to oppose each other; ~ **A a B** to set A against B; **me opongo a pensar que...** I refuse to believe *or* think that... .

oportunidad [oportuni'ðað] *nf* (*ocasión*) opportunity; (*posibilidad*) chance.

oportunismo [oportu'nismo] *nm* opportunism; **oportunista** *nm/f* opportunist.

oportuno, a [opor'tuno, a] *a* (*apto*) appropriate, suitable; (*en su tiempo*) opportune; (*conveniente*) convenient; **en el momento** ~ at the right moment.

oposición [oposi'θjon] *nf* opposition; **oposiciones** *nfpl* public examinations.

opositor, a [oposi'tor, a] *nm/f* (*adversario*) opponent; (*concurrente*) competitor.

opresión [opre'sjon] *nf* oppression;

opresivo, a *a* oppressive; **opresor, a** *nm/f* oppressor.

oprimir [opri'mir] *vt* to squeeze; (*fig*) to oppress.

oprobio [o'proβjo] *nm* (*infamia*) ignominy; (*descrédito*) shame.

optar [op'tar] *vi* (*elegir*) to choose; ~ **a** *o* **por** to opt for.

óptico, a ['optiko, a] *a* optic(al) // *nm/f* optician.

optimismo [opti'mismo] *nm* optimism; **optimista** *nm/f* optimist.

óptimo, a ['optimo, a] *a* (*bueno*) very good; (*el mejor*) very best.

opuesto, a [o'pwesto, a] *a* (*contrario*) opposite; (*antagónico*) opposing.

opugnar [opuχ'nar] *vt* to attack.

opulencia [opu'lenθja] *nf* opulence; **opulento, a** *a* opulent.

oquedad [oke'ðað] *nf* (*fig*) void.

ora ['ora] *ad:* ~ **tú** ~ **yo** now you, now me.

oración [ora'θjon] *nf* (*discurso*) speech; (*REL*) prayer; (*LING*) sentence.

oráculo [o'rakulo] *nm* oracle.

orador, a [ora'ðor, a] *nm/f* (*predicador*) preacher; (*conferenciante*) speaker.

oral [o'ral] *a* oral.

orangután [orangu'tan] *nm* orang-utan.

orar [o'rar] *vi* (*REL*) to pray; (*hablar*) to make a speech.

oratoria [ora'torja] *nf* oratory.

órbita ['orβita] *nf* orbit.

orden ['orðen] *nm* (*gen*) order // *nf* (*gen*) order; ~ **del día** agenda; **de primer** ~ first-rate; **en** ~ **de prioridad** in order of priority.

ordenado, a [orðe'naðo, a] *a* (*metódico*) methodical; (*arreglado*) orderly.

ordenador [orðena'ðor] *nm* computer.

ordenanza [orðe'nanθa] *nf* ordinance.

ordenar [orðe'nar] *vt* (*mandar*) to order; (*poner orden*) to put in order, arrange; ~**se** *vr* (*REL*) to be ordained.

ordeñadora [orðeɲa'ðora] *nf* milking machine.

ordeñar [orðe'ɲar] *vt* to milk.

ordinario, a [orði'narjo, a] *a* (*común*) ordinary, usual; (*bajo*) vulgar, common.

orégano [o'reχano] *nm* oregano.

oreja [o'rexa] *nf* ear; (*de zapatos*) tongue; (*MECÁNICA*) lug, flange.

orfandad [orfan'dað] *nf* orphanhood.

orfebrería [orfeβre'ria] *nf* gold/silver work.

organillo [orχa'niʎo] *nm* barrel organ.

organismo [orχa'nismo] *nm* (*BIO*) organism; (*POL*) organization.

organista [orχa'nista] *nm/f* organist.

organización [orχaniθa'θjon] *nf* organization; **organizar** *vt* to organize.

órgano ['orχano] *nm* organ.

orgasmo [or'χasmo] *nm* orgasm.

orgía [or'xia] *nf* orgy.

orgullo [or'χuʎo] *nm* (*altanería*) pride; (*autorespeto*) self-respect; **orgulloso, a** *a*

orientación [orjenta'θjon] *nf* (*posición*) proud; (*altanero*) haughty.

orientación [orjenta'θjon] *nf* (*posición*) position; (*dirección*) direction; (*entrenamiento*) training.

orientar [orjen'tar] *vt* (*situar*) to orientate; (*señalar*) to point; (*dirigir*) to direct; (*informar*) to guide; ~**se** *vr* to get one's bearings; (*decidirse*) to decide on a course of action.

oriente [o'rjente] *nm* east; **Cercano/Medio/Lejano** O~ Near/Middle/Far East.

origen [o'rixen] *nm* (*germen*) origin; (*nacimiento*) lineage, birth.

original [orixi'nal] *a* (*nuevo*) original; (*extraño*) odd, strange; ~**idad** *nf* originality.

originar [orixi'nar] *vt* to originate; ~**se** *vr* to originate; ~**io, a** *a* (*nativo*) native; (*primordial*) original.

orilla [o'riʎa] *nf* (*borde*) border; (*de río*) bank; (*de bosque, tela*) edge; (*de taza etc*) rim, lip; (*de calle*) pavement; **orillar** *vt* (*bordear*) to skirt, go round; (*resolver*) to wind up; (*tocar: asunto*) to touch briefly on.

orín [o'rin] *nm* rust.

orina [o'rina] *nf* urine; **orinal** *nm* (chamber) pot; **orinar** *vi* to urinate; **orinarse** *vr* to wet o.s.; **orines** *nmpl* urine *sg*.

oriundo, a [o'rjundo, a] *a*: ~ **de** native of.

orlar [or'lar] *vt* (*adornar*) to adorn, decorate; (*encuadrar*) to frame.

ornamentar [ornamen'tar] *vt* (*adornar, ataviar*) to adorn; (*revestir*) to bedeck.

ornamento [orna'mento] *nm* ornament.

ornar [or'nar] *vt* to adorn.

oro ['oro] *nm* gold; ~**s** *nmpl* (*NAIPES*) hearts.

oropel [oro'pel] *nm* tinsel.

orozuz [oro'θuθ] *nm* liquorice.

orquesta [or'kesta] *nf* orchestra; ~ **de cámara/sinfónica** chamber/symphony orchestra.

orquídea [or'kiðea] *nf* orchid.

ortiga [or'tixa] *nf* nettle.

ortodoxo, a [orto'ðokso, a] *a* orthodox.

ortografía [ortoxra'fia] *nf* spelling.

ortopedia [orto'peðja] *nf* orthopaedics *sg*.

oruga [o'ruxa] *nf* caterpillar; (*BOT*) rocket.

orzuelo [or'θwelo] *nm* (*MED*) stye.

os [os] *pron* (*gen*) you; (*a vosotros*) to you.

osa ['osa] *nf* (she-)bear; O~ **Mayor/Menor** Great/Little Bear.

osadía [osa'ðia] *nf* daring.

osar [o'sar] *vi* to dare.

oscilación [osθila'θjon] *nf* (*movimiento*) oscillation; (*fluctuación*) fluctuation; (*vacilación*) hesitation; (*columpio*) swinging, movement to and fro; **oscilar** *vi* to oscillate; to fluctuate; to hesitate.

ósculo ['oskulo] *nm* kiss.

oscurecer [oskure'θer] *vt* to darken // *vi* to grow dark; ~**se** *vr* to grow *or* get dark.

oscuridad [oskuri'ðað] *nf* obscurity; (*tinieblas*) darkness.

oscuro, a [os'kuro, a] *a* dark; (*fig*) obscure; **a** ~**as** in the dark.

óseo, a ['oseo, a] *a* bony.

oso ['oso] *nm* bear; ~ **de peluche** teddy bear; ~ **hormiguero** anteater.

ostensible [osten'siβle] *a* obvious.

ostentación [ostenta'θjon] *nf* (*gen*) ostentation; (*acto*) display; **ostentar** *vt* (*gen*) to show; (*pey*) to flaunt, show off; (*poseer*) to have, possess; **ostentoso, a** *a* ostentatious, showy.

osteópata [oste'opata] *nm/f* osteopath.

ostra ['ostra] *nf* oyster.

ostracismo [ostra'θismo] *nm* ostracism.

osuno, a [o'suno, a] *a* bear-like.

OTAN ['otan] *nf abr de* **Organización del Tratado del Atlántico Norte** NATO (North Atlantic Treaty Organization).

otear [ote'ar] *vt* to observe; (*fig*) to look into.

otitis [o'titis] *nf* earache.

otoñal [oto'nal] *a* autumnal.

otoño [o'tono] *nm* autumn.

otorgamiento [otorxa'mjento] *nm* conferring, granting; (*JUR*) execution.

otorgar [otor'xar] *vt* (*conceder*) to concede; (*dar*) to grant.

otro, a ['otro, a] *a* (*sg*) another; (*pl*) other // *pron* another one; ~**s** others; ~**a cosa** something else; **de** ~**a manera** otherwise; **en** ~ **tiempo** formerly, once; **ni uno ni** ~ neither one nor the other; ~ **tanto** the same again.

ovación [oβa'θjon] *nf* ovation.

oval [o'βal], **ovalado, a** [oβa'laðo, a] *a* oval; **óvalo** *nm* oval.

oveja [o'βexa] *nf* sheep; **ovejuno, a** *a* sheep *cpd*.

overol [oβe'rol] *nm* overalls *pl*.

ovillar [oβi'ʎar] *vt* to wind (into a ball); ~**se** *vr* to curl up into a ball.

OVNI ['oβni] *nm abr de* **objeto volante no identificado** UFO (unidentified flying object).

ovulación [oβula'θjon] *nf* ovulation; **óvulo** *nm* ovum.

oxidación [oksiða'θjon] *nf* rusting; **oxidar** *vt* to rust; **oxidarse** *vr* to become rusty.

óxido ['oksiðo] *nm* oxide.

oxigenado, a [oksixe'naðo, a] *a* (*QUÍMICA*) oxygenated; (*pelo*) bleached // *nm* peroxide.

oxígeno [ok'sixeno] *nm* oxygen.

oyente [o'jente] *nm/f* listener, hearer.

oyes, oyó *etc vb ver* **oír.**

P

P *abr de* **padre.**

pabellón [paβe'ʎon] *nm* bell tent; (*ARQ*) pavilion; (*de hospital etc*) block, section; (*bandera*) flag.

pábilo ['paβilo] *nm* wick.

pacer [pa'θer] *vi* to graze // *vt* to graze on.

paciencia [pa'θjenθja] *nf* patience.

paciente [pa'θjente] *a, nm/f* patient.

pacificación [paθifika'θjon] *nf* pacification; **pacificar** *vt* to pacify; (*tranquilizar*) to calm.

pacífico, a [pa'θifiko, a] *a* (*persona*) peace-loving; (*existencia*) pacific; **el (océano) P**~ the Pacific (Ocean).

pacifismo [paθi'fismo] *nm* pacifism; **pacifista** *nm/f* pacifist.

pactar [pak'tar] *vt* to agree to, agree on // *vi* to come to an agreement.

pacto ['pakto] *nm* (*tratado*) pact; (*acuerdo*) agreement.

padecer [paðe'θer] *vt* (*sufrir*) to suffer; (*soportar*) to endure, put up with; (*ser victima de*) to be a victim of; **padecimiento** *nm* suffering.

padrastro [pa'ðrastro] *nm* stepfather.

padre ['paðre] *nm* father // *a* (*fam*): **un éxito** ~ a tremendous success; ~**s** *nmpl* parents.

padrino [pa'ðrino] *nm* (*REL*) godfather; (*fig*) sponsor, patron; ~**s** *nmpl* godparents; ~ **de boda** best man.

padrón [pa'ðron] *nm* (*censo*) census, roll; (*de socios*) register; (*TEC*) pattern.

paella [pa'eʎa] *nf* paella, *dish of rice with meat, shellfish etc.*

paga ['paxa] *nf* (*dinero pagado*) payment; (*sueldo*) pay, wages *pl.*

pagadero, a [paxa'ðero, a] *a* payable; ~ **a la entrega/a plazos** payable on delivery/in instalments.

pagador, a [paxa'ðor, a] *nm/f* (*quien paga*) payer; (*cajero*) cashier.

pagano, a [pa'xano, a] *a, nm/f* pagan, heathen.

pagar [pa'xar] *vt* (*gen*) to pay; (*las compras, crimen*) to pay for; (*fig: favor*) to repay // *vi* to pay; ~ **al contado/a plazos** to pay (in) cash/in instalments; ~**se** *vr*: ~**se con algo** to be content with sth; ~**se de sí mismo** to be conceited.

pagaré [paxa're] *nm* I.O.U.

página ['paxina] *nf* page.

pago ['paxo] *nm* (*dinero*) payment, (*fig*) return; (*barrio*) district; (*AM*) home region, home area; **estar** ~ to be even *or* quits; ~ **anticipado/a cuenta/a la entrega/en especie** advance payment/payment on account/cash on delivery/payment in kind.

país [pa'is] *nm* (*gen*) country; (*región*) land; (*paisaje*) landscape; **los P**~**es Bajos** the Low Countries; **el P**~ **Vasco** the Basque Country; **paisaje** *nm* countryside, scenery.

paisano, a [pai'sano, a] *a* of the same country // *nm/f* (*compatriota*) fellow countryman/woman; (*campesino*) peasant; **vestir de** ~ (*soldado*) to be in civvies (*fam*); (*guardia*) to be in plain clothes.

paja ['paxa] *nf* straw; (*fig*) trash, rubbish

pájara ['paxara] *nf* hen bird; (*cometa*) kite; (*mujer*) thief.

pájaro ['paxaro] *nm* bird.

pajita [pa'xita] *nf* (drinking) straw.

pala ['pala] *nf* (*de mango largo*) spade; (*de*

mango corto) shovel; (*raqueta etc*) bat; (*: de tenis*) racquet; (*CULIN*) slice; ~ **mata-moscas** fly swat.

palabra [pa'laβra] *nf* (*gen*) word; (*facultad*) (power of) speech; (*derecho de hablar*) right to speak; **palabrota** *nf* swearword.

palacio [pa'laθjo] *nm* palace; (*mansión*) mansion, large house; ~ **de justicia** courthouse; ~ **municipal** town/city hall.

paladar [pala'ðar] *nm* (*gen*) palate; **paladear** *vt* to taste.

palanca [pa'lanka] *nf* lever; (*fig*) pull, influence.

palangana [palan'gana] *nf* washbasin.

palco ['palko] *nm* box.

palenque [pa'lenke] *nm* (*cerca*) stockade, fence; (*área*) arena, enclosure; (*de gallos*) pit.

Palestina [pales'tina] *nf* Palestine.

paliar [pa'ljar] *vt* (*mitigar*) to mitigate; (*disfrazar*) to conceal; **paliativo** *nm* palliative.

palidecer [paliðe'θer] *vi* to turn pale; **palidez** *nf* paleness; **pálido, a** *a* pale.

palillo [pa'liʎo] *nm* small stick; (*para dientes*) toothpick.

paliza [pa'liθa] *nf* beating, thrashing.

palizada [pali'θaða] *nf* fence; (*lugar cercado*) enclosure.

palma ['palma] *nf* (*ANAT*) palm; (*árbol*) palm tree; **batir** *o* **dar** ~**s** to clap, applaud; ~**da** *nf* slap; ~**s** *nfpl* clapping *sg,* applause *sg.*

palmear [palme'ar] *vi* to clap.

palmo ['palmo] *nm* (*medida*) span; (*fig*) small amount; ~ **a** ~ inch by inch.

palmotear [palmote'ar] *vi* to clap, applaud; **palmoteo** *nm* clapping, applause; (*palmada*) slap.

palo ['palo] *nm* stick; (*poste*) post, pole; (*mango*) handle, shaft; (*golpe*) blow, hit; (*de golf*) club; (*de béisbol*) bat; (*NAUT*) mast; (*NAIPES*) suit; ~ **de tienda** tent pole.

paloma [pa'loma] *nf* dove, pigeon

palomilla [palo'miʎa] *nf* moth; (*TEC: tuerca*) wing nut; (*: hierro*) angle iron.

palomitas [palo'mitas] *nfpl* popcorn *sg.*

palpar [pal'par] *vt* to touch, feel; (*acariciar*) to caress, fondle; (*caminar a tientas*) to grope one's way along; (*fig*) to appreciate, understand; ~ **a uno** to frisk sb.

palpitación [palpita'θjon] *nf* palpitation; **palpitante** *a* palpitating; (*fig*) burning; **palpitar** *vi* to palpitate; (*latir*) to beat.

palúdico, a [pa'luðiko, a] *a* marshy.

paludismo [palu'ðismo] *nm* malaria.

pampa ['pampa] *nf* (*AM*) pampa(s), prairie.

pan [pan] *nm* (*en general*) bread; (*una barra*) loaf; (*trigo*) wheat; **de** ~ **llevar** arable; ~ **integral** wholemeal bread; ~ **molido** breadcrumbs *pl.*

pana ['pana] *nf* corduroy.

panadería [panaðe'ria] *nf* baker's (shop); **panadero, a** *nm/f* baker.

Panamá [pana'ma] *nm* Panama; **panameño, a** *a* Panamanian.

pancarta [pan'karta] *nf* placard, banner.

panda ['panda] *nf* panda.

pandereta [pande'reta] *nf* tambourine.

pandilla [pan'diʎa] *nf* set, group; (*de criminales*) gang; (*pey*) clique.

pando, a ['pando, a] *a* sagging.

panel [pa'nel] *nm* panel.

pánico ['paniko] *nm* panic.

panorama [pano'rama] *nm* panorama; (*vista*) view.

pantalones [panta'lones] *nmpl* trousers.

pantalla [pan'taʎa] *nf* (*de cine*) screen; (*cubre-luz*) lampshade.

pantano [pan'tano] *nm* (*ciénaga*) marsh, swamp; (*depósito: de agua*) reservoir; (*fig*) jam, fix, difficulty.

pantera [pan'tera] *nf* panther.

pantimedias [panti'meðjas] *nfpl* tights.

pantomima [panto'mima] *nf* pantomime.

pantorrilla [panto'rriʎa] *nf* calf (of the leg).

pantufla [pan'tufla] *nf* slipper.

panza ['panθa] *nf* belly, paunch; **panzudo, a, panzón, ona** *a* fat, potbellied.

pañal [pa'ɲal] *nm* nappy; ~**es** *nmpl* (*fig*) early stages, infancy *sg*.

pañería [paɲe'ria] *nf* drapery; **pañero, a** *nm/f* draper.

paño ['paɲo] *nm* (*tela*) cloth; (*pedazo de tela*) (piece of) cloth; (*trapo*) duster, rag; ~ **higiénico** sanitary towel; ~**s menores** underclothes.

pañuelo [pa'ɲwelo] *nm* handkerchief, hanky (*fam*); (*para la cabeza*) (head)scarf.

papa ['papa] *nf* (*AM*) potato // *nm*: **el P** ~ the Pope.

papá [pa'pa] (*pl* ~**s**) *nm* (*fam*) dad, daddy.

papagayo [papa'ɣajo] *nm* parrot.

papamoscas [papa'moskas] *nm inv* fly-catcher.

papanatas [papa'natas] *nm inv* (*fam*) sucker, simpleton.

papar [pa'par] *vt* to swallow, gulp (down).

paparrucha [papa'rrutʃa] *nf* (*tontería*) piece of nonsense; (*engaño*) hoax.

papaya [pa'paja] *nf* papaya.

papel [pa'pel] *nm* (*en general*) paper; (*hoja de papel*) sheet of paper; (*TEATRO*) part, role; ~ **de calcar/carbón/de cartas** tracing paper/carbon paper/stationery; ~ **de envolver/de empapelar** brown paper, wrapping paper/wallpaper; ~ **de estaño/higiénico** tinfoil/toilet paper; ~ **de lija** sandpaper; ~ **moneda** paper money; ~ **secante** blotting paper.

papeleo [pape'leo] *nm* red tape.

papelera [pape'lera] *nf* (*cesto*) wastepaper basket; (*escritorio*) desk.

papelería [papele'ria] *nf* (*papeles*) mass of papers; (*tienda*) stationer's (shop).

papeleta [pape'leta] *nf* (*pedazo de papel*) slip *or* bit of paper; (*tarjeta de archivo*) index card; (*POL*) ballot paper; (*ESCOL*) report.

paperas [pa'peras] *nfpl* mumps.

paquete [pa'kete] *nm* (*caja*) packet; (*bulto*) parcel; (*AM: fam*) nuisance, bore.

par [par] *a* (*igual*) like, equal; (*MAT*) even // *nm* equal; (*de guantes*) pair; (*de veces*) couple; (*dignidad*) peer; (*GOLF, COM*) par; **abrir de** ~ **en** ~ to open wide.

para ['para] *prep* (*gen*) for; **no es** ~ **comer** it's not for eating; **decir** ~ **sí** to say to o.s.; ¿~ **qué quieres?** what do you want it for?; **se casaron** ~ **separarse otra vez** they married only to separate again; **lo tendré** ~ **mañana** I'll have it for tomorrow; **ir** ~ **casa** to go home, head for home; ~ **profesor es muy estúpido** he's very stupid for a teacher; ¿**quién es usted** ~ **gritar así?** who are you to shout like that?; **tengo bastante** ~ **vivir** I have enough to live on; **estoy** ~ **cantar** I'm about to sing.

parabién [para'βjen] *nm* congratulations *pl*.

parábola [para'raβola] *nf* parable; (*MAT*) parabola.

parabrisas [para'βrisas] *nm inv* windscreen.

paracaídas [paraka'iðas] *nm inv* parachute; **paracaidista** *nm/f* parachutist; (*MIL*) paratrooper.

parachoques [para'tʃokes] *nm inv* bumper; (*en auto*) shock absorber.

parada [pa'raða] *nf ver* **parado.**

paradero [para'ðero] *nm* stopping-place; (*situación*) whereabouts; (*fin*) end.

parado, a [pa'raðo, a] *a* (*persona*) motionless, standing still; (*fábrica*) closed, at a standstill; (*coche*) stopped; (*AM*) standing (up); (*sin empleo*) unemployed, idle; (*confuso*) confused // *nf* (*gen*) stop; (*acto*) stopping; (*de industria*) shutdown, stoppage; (*de pagos*) suspension; (*lugar*) stopping-place; (*apuesta*) bet; ~**a de autobús** bus stop.

paradoja [para'ðoxa] *nf* paradox.

parador [para'ðor] *nm* (luxury) hotel.

paráfrasis [pa'rafrasis] *nm inv* paraphrase.

paragolpes [para'ɣolpes] *nm inv* bumper.

paraguas [pa'raɣwas] *nm inv* umbrella.

Paraguay [para'ɣwai] *nm*: **el** ~ Paraguay.

paraíso [para'iso] *nm* paradise, heaven.

paraje [pa'raxe] *nm* place, spot.

paralelo, a [para'lelo, a] *a* parallel.

parálisis [pa'ralisis] *nf* paralysis; **paralítico, a** *a, nm/f* paralytic; **paralizar** *vt* to paralyse; **paralizarse** *vr* to become paralysed; (*fig*) to come to a standstill.

paramilitar [paramili'tar] *a* para-military.

páramo ['paramo] *nm* bleak plateau.

parangón [paran'gon] *nm*: **sin** ~ incomparable.

paranoico, a [para'noiko, a] *nm/f* paranoiac.

parapléjico, a [para'plexiko, a] *a, nm/f* paraplegic.

parar [pa'rar] vt to stop; (golpe) to ward off // vi to stop; ~**se** vr to stop; (AM) to stand up; **ha parado de llover** it has stopped raining; **van a ~ en la comisaria** they're going to end up in the police station; ~**se en** to pay attention to.

parásito, a [pa'rasito, a] nm/f parasite.

parasol [para'sol] nm parasol, sunshade.

parcela [par'θela] nf plot, piece of ground.

parcial [par'θjal] a (pago) part-; (eclipse) partial; (juez) prejudiced, biased; ~**idad** nf (prejuicio) prejudice, bias; (partido, facción) party, faction.

parco, a ['parko, a] a (frugal) frugal; (mezquino) mean; (moderado) moderate.

parche ['partʃe] nm (MED) sticking plaster; (gen) patch.

parear [pare'ar] vt (juntar, hacer par) to match, put together; (calcetines) to put into pairs; (BIO) to mate, pair.

parecer [pare'θer] nm (opinión) opinion, view; (aspecto) looks pl // vi (tener apariencia) to seem, look; (asemejarse) to look like, seem like; (aparecer, llegar) to appear; ~**se** vr to look alike, resemble each other; ~**se a** to look like, resemble; **según o a lo que parece** evidently, apparently; **me parece que** I think (that), it seems to me that; **parecido, a** similar // nm similarity, likeness, resemblance; **bien parecido** good-looking, nice-looking.

pared [pa'reð] nf wall.

parejo, a [pa'rexo, a] a (igual) equal; (liso) smooth, even // nf (dos) pair; (: de personas) couple; (el otro: de un par) other one (of a pair); (: persona) partner.

parentela [paren'tela] nf relations pl.

parentesco [paren'tesko] nm relationship.

paréntesis [pa'rentesis] nm inv parenthesis; (digresión) digression; (en escrito) bracket.

parezco etc vb ver **parecer**.

pariente, a [pa'rjente, a] nm/f relative, relation.

parihuela [pari'wela] nf stretcher.

parir [pa'rir] vt to give birth to // vi (mujer) to give birth, have a baby.

Paris [pa'ris] n Paris.

parlamentar [parlamen'tar] vi (hablar) to talk, converse; (negociar) to parley.

parlamentario, a [parlamen'tarjo, a] a parliamentary // nm/f member of parliament.

parlamento [parla'mento] nm (POL) parliament; (conversación) parley.

parlanchín, ina [parlan'tʃin, ina] a loose-tongued, indiscreet // nm/f chatterbox.

parlar [par'lar] vi to chatter (away), talk (a lot); (chismear) to gossip; **parlero, a** a talkative; gossipy; (pájaro) singing.

paro ['paro] nm (huelga) stoppage (of work), strike; (desempleo) unemployment; **subsidio de** ~ unemployment benefit; **hay** ~ **en la industria** work in the industry is at a standstill.

parodia [pa'roðja] nf parody; **parodiar** vt to parody.

parpadear [parpaðe'ar] vi (los ojos) to blink; (luz) to flicker.

párpado ['parpaðo] nm eyelid.

parque ['parke] nm (lugar verde) park; (depósito) depot; ~ **de atracciones/de estacionamiento/zoológico** fairground/car park/zoo.

parquímetro [par'kimetro] nm parking meter.

párrafo ['parrafo] nm paragraph; **echar un** ~ (fam) to have a chat.

parranda [pa'rranda] nf (fam) spree, binge.

parrilla [pa'rriʎa] nf (CULIN) grill; (de coche) grille; (**carne de**) ~ barbecue; ~**da** nf barbecue.

párroco ['parroko] nm parish priest.

parroquia [pa'rrokja] nf parish; (iglesia) parish church; (COM) clientele, customers pl; ~**no, a** nm/f parishioner; client, customer.

parte ['parte] nm message; (informe) report // nf (gen) part; (lado, cara) side; (de reparto) share; (JUR) party; **en alguna** ~ **de Europa** somewhere in Europe; **en cualquier** ~ anywhere; **en gran** ~ to a large extent; **la mayor** ~ **de los españoles** most Spaniards; **de algún tiempo a esta** ~ for some time past; **de** ~ **de alguien** on sb's behalf; **por** ~ **de** on the part of; **yo por mi** ~ I for my part; **por otra** ~ on the other hand; **dar** ~ to inform; **tomar** ~ to take part.

partera [par'tera] nf midwife.

partición [parti'θjon] nf division, sharing-out; (POL) partition.

participación [partiθipa'θjon] nf (acto) participation, taking part; (parte, COM) share; (de lotería) small prize; (aviso) notice, notification.

participante [partiθi'pante] nm/f participant; **participar** vt to notify, inform // vi to take part, participate; (compartir) to share.

partícipe [par'tiθipe] nm/f participant.

particular [partiku'lar] a (especial) particular, special; (individual, personal) private, personal // nm (punto, asunto) particular, point; (individuo) individual; **tiene coche** ~ he has a car of his own; ~**izar** vt to distinguish; (especificar) to specify; (detallar) to give details about.

partida [par'tiða] nf (salida) departure; (COM) entry, item; (juego) game; (apuesta) bet; (grupo, bando) band, group; **mala** ~ dirty trick; ~ **de nacimiento/matrimonio/defunción** birth/marriage/death certificate.

partidario, a [parti'ðarjo, a] a partisan // nm/f (DEPORTE) supporter; (POL) partisan.

partido [par'tiðo] nm (POL) party; (encuentro) game, match; (apoyo) support; (equipo) team; **sacar** ~ **de** to profit from, benefit from; **tomar** ~ to take sides.

partir [par'tir] vt (dividir) to split, divide;

(compartir, distribuir) to share (out), distribute; (romper) to break open, split open; (rebanada) to cut (off) // vi (tomar camino) to set off, set out; (comenzar) to start (off or out); ~se vr to crack or split or break (in two etc); a ~ de (starting) from.

parto ['parto] nm birth; (fig) product, creation; **estar de** ~ to be in labour.

parvulario [parβu'larjo] nm nursery school, kindergarten.

pasa ['pasa] nf raisin; ~ **de Corinto/de Esmirna** currant/sultana.

pasada [pa'saða] nf ver **pasado**.

pasadizo [pasa'ðiθo] nm (pasillo) passage, corridor; (callejuela) alley.

pasado, a [pa'saðo, a] a past; (malo: comida, fruta) bad; (muy cocido) overdone; (anticuado) out of date // nm past // nf passing, passage; (acción de pulir) rub, polish; ~**s** nmpl ancestors; ~ **mañana** the day after tomorrow; **el mes** ~ last month; **de** ~**a** in passing, incidentally; **una mala** ~**a** a dirty trick.

pasador [pasa'ðor] nm (gen) bolt; (de pelo) pin, grip; ~**es** nmpl cufflinks.

pasaje [pa'saxe] nm (gen) passage; (pago de viaje) fare; (los pasajeros) passengers pl; (pasillo) passageway.

pasajero, a [pasa'xero, a] a passing; (calle) busy // nm/f passenger; (viajero) traveller.

pasamanos [pasa'manos] nm rail, handrail; (de escalera) banister.

pasaporte [pasa'porte] nm passport.

pasar [pa'sar] vt (gen) to pass; (tiempo) to spend; (durezas) to suffer, endure; (noticia) to give, pass on; (río) to cross; (barrera) to pass through; (falta) to overlook, tolerate; (contrincante) to surpass, do better than; (coche) to overtake; (enfermedad) to give, infect with // vi (gen) to pass; (terminarse) to be over; (ocurrir) to happen; ~**se** vr (flores) to fade; (comida) to go bad, go off; (fig) to overdo it, go too far; ~ **de** to go beyond, exceed; ¡**pase** come in!; ~**se al enemigo** to go over to the enemy; **se me pasó** I forgot; **no se le pasa nada** nothing escapes him, he misses nothing; **pase lo que pase** come what may.

pasarela [pasa'rela] nf footbridge; (en barco) gangway.

pasatiempo [pasa'tjempo] nm pastime; (distracción) amusement.

Pascua ['paskwa] nf: ~ (**de Resurrección**) Easter; ~ **de Navidad** Christmas; ~**s** nfpl Christmas time; ¡**felices** ~**s**! Merry Christmas.

pase ['pase] nm pass.

pasear [pase'ar] vt to take for a walk; (exhibir) to parade, show off // vi, ~**se** vr to walk, go for a walk; (holgazanear) to idle, loaf about; ~ **en coche** to go for a drive; **paseo** nm (avenida) avenue; (distancia corta) short walk; **dar un paseo** to go for a walk.

pasillo [pa'siʎo] nm passage, corridor.

pasión [pa'sjon] nf passion.

pasivo, a [pa'siβo, a] a passive; (inactivo) inactive // nm (COM) liabilities pl, debts pl.

pasmar [pas'mar] vt (asombrar) to amaze, astonish; (enfriar) to chill (to the bone); **pasmo** nm amazement, astonishment; chill; (fig) wonder, marvel; **pasmoso, a** a amazing, astonishing.

paso, a ['paso, a] a dried // nm (gen) step; (modo de andar) walk; (huella) footprint; (rapidez) speed, pace, rate; (camino accesible) way through, passage; (cruce) crossing; (pasaje) passing, passage; (GEO) pass; (estrecho) strait; **a ese** ~ (fig) at that rate; **salir al** ~ **de** o a to waylay; **estar de** ~ to be passing through; ~ **elevado** flyover; **prohibido el** ~ no entry; **ceda el** ~ give way.

pasta ['pasta] nf (gen) paste; (CULIN: masa) dough; (: de bizcochos etc) pastry; (cartón) cardboard; (fam) money, dough (fam); ~**s** nfpl (bizcochos) pastries, small cakes; (fideos, espaguetis etc) noodles, spaghetti sg etc; ~ **de dientes** o **dentífrica** toothpaste; ~ **de madera** wood pulp.

pastar [pas'tar], **pastear** [paste'ar] vt, vi to graze.

pastel [pas'tel] nm (dulce) cake; (de carne) pie; (pintura) pastel; ~**ería** nf cake shop, pastry shop.

pasteurizado, a [pasteuri'θaðo, a] a pasteurized.

pastilla [pas'tiʎa] nf (de jabón, chocolate) cake, bar; (píldora) tablet, pill.

pasto ['pasto] nm (hierba) grass; (lugar) pasture, field.

pastor, a [pas'tor, a] nm/f shepherd/ess // nm clergyman, pastor.

pata ['pata] nf (pierna) leg; (pie) foot; (de muebles) leg; ~**s arriba** upside down; **meter la** ~ to put one's foot in it; (TEC): ~ **de cabra** crowbar; **tener buena/mala** ~ to be lucky/unlucky; ~**da** nf stamp; (puntapié) kick.

patalear [patale'ar] vi to stamp one's feet.

patata [pa'tata] nf potato; ~**s fritas** o a **la española** chips, French fries; ~**s inglesas** crisps.

patear [pate'ar] vt (pisar) to stamp on, trample (on); (pegar con el pie) to kick // vi to stamp (with rage), stamp one's foot.

patente [pa'tente] a obvious, evident; (COM) patent // nf patent; **patentizar** vt to show, reveal, make evident.

paternal [pater'nal] a fatherly, paternal; **paterno, a** a paternal.

patético, a [pa'tetiko, a] a pathetic, moving.

patillas [pa'tiʎas] nfpl sideburns.

patín [pa'tin] nm skate; (de tobogán) runner; **patinaje** nm skating; **patinar** vi to skate; (resbalarse) to skid, slip; (fam) to slip up, blunder.

patio ['patjo] nm (de casa) patio, courtyard; ~ **de recreo** playground.

pato ['pato] nm duck; **pagar el** ~ (fam) to take the blame, carry the can.

patológico, a [pato'loxiko, a] *a* pathological.

patraña [pa'trapa] *nf* story, fib.

patria ['patrja] *nf* native land, mother country.

patrimonio [patri'monjo] *nm* inheritance; (*fig*) heritage.

patriota [pa'trjota] *nm/f* patriot; **patriotismo** *nm* patriotism.

patrocinar [patroθi'nar] *vt* to sponsor; (*apoyar*) to back, support; **patrocinio** *nm* sponsorship; backing, support.

patrón, ona [pa'tron, ona] *nm/f* (*jefe*) boss, chief, master/mistress; (*propietario*) landlord/lady; (*REL*) patron saint // *nm* (*TEC, costura*) pattern; **patronal** *a*: **la clase patronal** management; **patronato** *nm* sponsorship; (*acto*) patronage; (*COM*) employers' association.

patrulla [pa'truʎa] *nf* patrol.

pausa ['pausa] *nf* pause; (*intervalo*) break; (*interrupción*) interruption.

pausado, a [pau'saðo, a] *a* slow, deliberate.

pauta ['pauta] *nf* line, guide line.

pavo ['paβo] *nm* turkey; ~ **real** peacock.

pavor [pa'ßor] *nm* dread, terror.

payaso, a [pa'jaso, a] *nm/f* clown.

paz [paθ] *nf* peace; (*tranquilidad*) peacefulness, tranquillity; **hacer las paces** to make peace; (*fig*) to make up.

P.C.E. *abr de* **Partido Comunista Español.**

peaje [pe'axe] *nm* toll.

peatón [pea'ton] *nm* pedestrian.

peca ['peka] *nf* freckle.

pecado [pe'kaðo] *nm* sin; **pecador, a** *a* sinful // *nm/f* sinner.

pecaminoso, a [pekami'noso, a] *a* sinful.

pecar [pe'kar] *vi* (*REL*) to sin; (*fig*): **peca de generoso** he is too generous.

peculiar [peku'ljar] *a* special, peculiar; (*característico*) typical, characteristic; ~**idad** *nf* peculiarity; special feature, characteristic.

pecho ['petʃo] *nm* (*ANAT*) chest; (*de mujer*) breast(s) (*pl*), bosom; (*corazón*) heart, breast; (*valor*) courage, spirit; **dar el** ~ **a** to breast-feed; **tomar algo a** ~ to take sth to heart.

pechuga [pe'tʃuxa] *nf* breast (of chicken *etc*).

pedal [pe'ðal] *nm* pedal; ~**ear** *vi* to pedal.

pedante [pe'ðante] *a* pedantic // *nm/f* pedant; ~**ría** *nf* pedantry.

pedazo [pe'ðaθo] *nm* piece, bit; **hacerse** ~**s** to fall to pieces; (*romperse*) to smash, shatter.

pedernal [peðer'nal] *nm* flint.

pediatra [pe'ðjatra] *nm/f* pediatrician.

pedicuro, a [peði'kuro, a] *nm/f* chiropodist.

pedido [pe'ðiðo] *nm* (*COM. mandado*) order; (*petición*) request.

pedir [pe'ðir] *vt* to ask for, request; (*comida, COM. mandar*) to order; (*exigir:*

precio) to ask; (*necesitar*) to need, demand, require // *vi* to ask; **me pidió que cerrara la puerta** he asked me to shut the door; ¿**cuánto piden por el coche?** how much are they asking for the car?

pegadizo, a [peɣa'ðiθo, a] *a* sticky; (*MED*) infectious // *nm/f* sponger, hanger-on (*fam*).

pegajoso, a [peɣa'xoso, a] *a* sticky, adhesive; (*MED*) infectious.

pegamento [peɣa'mento] *nm* gum, sticky stuff.

pegar [pe'ɣar] *vt* (*papel, sellos*) to stick (on); (*cartel*) to post, stick up; (*coser*) to sew (on); (*unir: partes*) to join, fix together; (*MED*) to give, infect with; (*dar: golpe*) to give, deal // *vi* (*adherirse*) to stick, adhere; (*prender: fuego*) to catch; (*ir juntos: colores*) to match, go together; (*golpear*) to hit; (*quemar: el sol*) to strike hot, burn (*fig*); ~**se** *vr* (*gen*) to stick; (*dos personas*) to hit each other, fight; (*fam*): ~ **un grito** to let out a yell; ~ **un salto** to jump (with fright); ~ **en** to touch; ~**se un tiro** to shoot o.s.

peinado [pei'naðo] *nm* (*en peluquería*) hairdo; (*estilo*) hair style.

peinador, a [peina'ðor, a] *nm/f* hairdresser.

peinar [pei'nar] *vt* to comb; (*hacer estilo*) to style; ~**se** *vr* to comb one's hair.

peine ['peine] *nm* comb; ~**ta** *nf* ornamental comb.

Pekín [pe'kin] *n* Pekin(g).

pelado, a [pe'laðo, a] *a* (*cabeza*) shorn; (*fruta*) peeled; (*campo, fig*) bare // *nm* bare patch; (*fig*) wretch, poor devil.

pelaje [pe'laxe] *nm* (*ZOOL*) fur, coat; (*fig*) appearance.

pelambre [pe'lambre] *nm* (*pelo largo*) long hair, mop; (*piel de animal cortado*) fur; (: *de oveja*) fleece; (*parte sin piel*) bare patch.

pelar [pe'lar] *vt* (*cortar el pelo a*) to cut the hair of; (*quitar la piel: animal*) to skin; ~**se** *vr* (*la piel*) to peel off; (*persona*) to lose one's hair; **voy a** ~**me** I'm going to get my hair cut.

peldaño [pel'dapo] *nm* step.

pelea [pe'lea] *nf* (*lucha*) fight; (*discusión*) quarrel, row; **pelear** *vi* to fight; **pelearse** *vr* to fight; (*reñirse*) to fall out, quarrel.

peletería [pelete'ria] *nf* furrier's, fur shop.

pelicano [peli'kano], **pelícano** [pe'likano] *nm* pelican.

pelicorto, a [peli'korto, a] *a* short-haired.

película [pe'likula] *nf* film; (*cobertura ligera*) thin covering; (*FOTO. rollo*) roll or reel of film.

peligro [pe'lixro] *nm* danger; (*riesgo*) risk; **correr** ~ to be in danger of; ~**so, a** *a* dangerous; risky.

pelirrojo, a [peli'rroxo, a] *a* red-haired, red-headed.

pelo ['pelo] *nm* (*cabellos*) hair; (*de barba, bigote*) whisker; (*de animal: pellejo*) fur, coat; (*de perro etc*) hair, coat; **al** ~ just right; **venir al** ~ to be exactly what one needs; **un hombre de** ~ **en pecho** a brave man; **por los** ~**s** by the skin of one's teeth; **no tener** ~**s en la lengua** to be outspoken, not mince words; **tomar el** ~ **a uno** to pull sb's leg.

pelón, ona [pe'lon, ona] *a* hairless, bald; (*fig*) broke, skint (*fam*).

pelota [pe'lota] *nf* ball; (*fam: cabeza*) nut (*fam*); **en** ~ stark naked; ~ **vasca** pelota.

pelotón [pelo'ton] *nm* (*pelota*) big ball; (*muchedumbre*) crowd; (*MIL*) squad, detachment.

peluca [pe'luka] *nf* wig.

peluche [pe'lutʃe] *nm* felt.

peludo, a [pe'luðo, a] *a* hairy, shaggy.

peluquería [peluke'ria] *nf* hairdresser's; (*para hombres*) barber's (shop); **peluquero, a** *nm/f* hairdresser; barber.

pelleja [pe'ʎexa] *nf* skin, hide; (*fam*) whore.

pellejo [pe'ʎexo] *nm* (*de animal*) skin, hide; (*de fruta*) skin, peel.

pellizcar [peʎiθ'kar] *vt* to pinch, nip.

pena ['pena] *nf* (*congoja*) grief, sadness; (*ansia*) anxiety; (*remordimiento*) regret; (*dificultad*) trouble; (*dolor*) pain; **merecer** *o* **valer la** ~ to be worthwhile; **a duras** ~**s** with great difficulty; ~ **de muerte** death penalty; ~ **pecuniaria** fine; ¡**qué** ~! what a shame!

penal [pe'nal] *a* penal // *nm* (*cárcel*) prison; (*FÚTBOL*) penalty.

penalidad [penali'ðað] *nf* (*problema, dificultad*) trouble, hardship; (*JUR*) penalty, punishment.

penar [pe'nar] *vt* to penalize; (*castigar*) to punish // *vi* to suffer; ~**se** *vr* to grieve, mourn.

pender [pen'der] *vi* (*colgar*) to hang; (*JUR*) to be pending.

pendiente [pen'djente] *a* (*colgante*) hanging; (*por resolver*) pending, unsettled // *nm* earring // *nf* hill, slope.

pene ['pene] *nm* penis.

penetración [penetra'θjon] *nf* (*acto*) penetration; (*agudeza*) sharpness, insight.

penetrante [pene'trante] *a* (*herida*) deep; (*persona, arma*) sharp; (*sonido*) penetrating, piercing; (*mirada*) searching; (*viento, ironía*) biting.

penetrar [pene'trar] *vt* to penetrate, pierce; (*entender*) to grasp // *vi* to penetrate, go in; (*líquido*) to soak in; (*emoción*) to pierce.

penicilina [peniθi'lina] *nf* penicillin.

península [pe'ninsula] *nf* peninsula; **peninsular** *a* peninsular.

penitencia [peni'tenθja] *nf* (*remordimiento*) penitence; (*castigo*) penance; **penitencial** *a* penitential; ~**ría** *nf* prison, penitentiary.

penoso, a [pe'noso, a] *a* (*afligido*) painful, distressing; (*trabajoso*) laborious, difficult.

pensador, a [pensa'ðor, a] *nm/f* thinker.

pensamiento [pensa'mjento] *nm* (*gen*) thought; (*mente*) mind; (*idea*) idea; (*intento*) intention.

pensar [pen'sar] *vt* to think; (*considerar*) to think over, think out; (*proponerse*) to intend, plan, propose; (*imaginarse*) to think up, invent // *vi* to think; ~ **en** to aim at, aspire to; **pensativo, a** *a* thoughtful, pensive.

pensión [pen'sjon] *nf* (*casa*) boarding house, guest house; (*dinero*) pension; (*cama y comida*) board and lodging; (*beca*) scholarship; **pensionista** *nm/f* (*jubilado*) (old-age) pensioner; (*quien vive en pensión*) lodger.

penúltimo, a [pe'nultimo, a] *a* penultimate, second last.

penumbra [pe'numbra] *nf* half-light, semi-darkness.

penuria [pe'nurja] *nf* shortage, want.

peña ['peɲa] *nf* (*roca*) rock; (*cuesta*) cliff, crag; (*grupo*) group, circle.

peñascal [peɲas'kal] *nm* rocky place; **peñasco** *nm* large rock, boulder.

peñón [pe'ɲon] *nm* mass of rock; **el P**~ the Rock (of Gibraltar).

peón [pe'on] *nm* labourer; (*AM*) farm labourer, farmhand; (*eje*) spindle, shaft, axle; (*AJEDREZ*) pawn.

peor [pe'or] *a* (*comparativo*) worse; (*superlativo*) worst // *ad* worse; worst; **de mal en** ~ from bad to worse.

pepino [pe'pino] *nm* cucumber; **(no) me importa un** ~ I don't care two hoots.

pepita [pe'pita] *nf* (*BOT*) pip; (*MINERÍA*) nugget.

pequeñez [peke'ɲeθ] *nf* smallness, littleness; (*infancia*) infancy; (*trivialidad*) trifle, triviality.

pequeño, a [pe'keɲo, a] *a* small, little.

pera ['pera] *nf* pear; **peral** *nm* pear tree.

percance [per'kanθe] *nm* setback, misfortune.

percatarse [perka'tarse] *vr*: ~ **de** to notice, take note of.

percepción [perθep'θjon] *nf* (*vista*) perception; (*idea*) notion, idea; (*colecta de fondos*) collection.

perceptible [perθep'tiβle] *a* perceptible, noticeable; (*COM*) payable, receivable.

percibir [perθi'βir] *vt* to perceive, notice; (*COM*) to earn, receive, get.

percusión [perku'sjon] *nf* percussion.

percha ['pertʃa] *nf* (*poste*) pole, support; (*ganchos*) coat stand; (*colgador*) coat hanger; (*de ave*) perch.

perdedor, a [perðe'ðor, a] *a* (*que pierde*) losing; (*olvidadizo*) forgetful // *nm/f* loser.

perder [per'ðer] *vt* (*gen*) to lose; (*tiempo, palabras*) to waste; (*oportunidad*) to lose, miss; (*tren*) to miss // *vi* to lose; ~**se** *vr* (*extraviarse*) to get lost; (*desaparecer*) to disappear, be lost to view; (*arruinarse*) to be ruined; (*hundirse*) to sink; **echar a** ~ (*comida*) to spoil, ruin; (*oportunidad*) to waste.

perdición [perði'θjon] *nf* perdition, ruin.

pérdida ['perðiða] *nf* (*gen*) loss; (*de tiempo*) waste; ~**s** *nfpl* (*COM*) losses.
perdido, a [per'ðiðo, a] *a* lost; (*incorregible*) incorrigible; ~**so, a** *a* (*que pierde*) losing; (*fácilmente* ~) easily lost.
perdiz [per'ðiθ] *nf* partridge.
perdón [per'ðon] *nm* (*disculpa*) pardon, forgiveness; (*clemencia*) mercy; ¡~! sorry!, I beg your pardon!; **perdonar** *vt* to pardon, forgive; (*la vida*) to spare; (*excusar*) to exempt, excuse.
perdurable [perðu'raßle] *a* lasting; (*eterno*) everlasting; **perdurar** *vi* (*resistir*) to last, endure; (*seguir existiendo*) to stand, still exist.
perecer [pere'θer] *vi* (*morir*) to perish, die; (*objeto*) to shatter.
peregrinación [pereχrina'θjon] *nf* long tour, travels *pl*; (*REL*) pilgrimage; **peregrino, a** *a* travelling; (*nuevo*) newly-introduced // *nm/f* pilgrim.
perejil [pere'xil] *nm* parsley.
perenne [pe'renne] *a* everlasting, perennial.
perentorio, a [peren'torjo, a] *a* (*urgente*) urgent, peremptory; (*fijo*) set, fixed.
pereza [pe'reθa] *nf* (*flojera*) laziness; (*lentitud*) sloth, slowness; **perezoso, a** *a* lazy; slow, sluggish.
perfección [perfek'θjon] *nf* perfection; (*acto*) completion; **perfeccionar** *vt* to perfect; (*acabar*) to complete, finish.
perfecto, a [per'fekto, a] *a* perfect; (*terminado*) complete, finished.
perfidia [per'fiðja] *nf* perfidy, treachery.
perfil [per'fil] *nm* (*parte lateral*) profile; (*silueta*) silhouette, outline; (*ARQ*) (*cross*) section; ~**es** *nmpl* features; (*fig*) social graces; ~**ado, a** *a* (*bien formado*) well-shaped; (*largo: cara*) long; ~**ar** *vt* (*trazar*) to outline; (*dar carácter a*) to shape, give character to.
perforación [perfora'θjon] *nf* perforation; (*con taladro*) drilling; **perforadora** *nf* drill.
perforar [perfo'rar] *vt* to perforate; (*agujero*) to drill, bore; (*papel*) to punch a hole in // *vi* to drill, bore.
perfumado, a [perfu'maðo, a] *a* scented, perfumed.
perfume [per'fume] *nm* perfume, scent.
pericia [pe'riθja] *nf* skill, expertise.
periferia [peri'ferja] *nf* periphery; (*de ciudad*) outskirts *pl*.
perímetro [pe'rimetro] *nm* perimeter.
periódico, a [pe'rjoðiko, a] *a* periodic(al) // *nm* newspaper; **periodismo** *nm* journalism; **periodista** *nm/f* journalist.
periodo [pe'rjoðo], **período** [pe'rioðo] *nm* period.
perito, a [pe'rito, a] *a* (*experto*) expert; (*diestro*) skilled, skilful // *nm/f* expert; skilled worker; (*técnico*) technician.
perjudicar [perxuði'kar] *vt* (*gen*) to damage, harm; **ese vestido le perjudica** that dress doesn't suit her; **perjudicial** *a* damaging, harmful; (*en detrimento*) detri-

mental; **perjuicio** *nm* damage, harm; (*pérdidas*) financial loss.
perjurar [perxu'rar] *vi* to commit perjury.
perla ['perla] *nf* pearl; **me viene de** ~ it suits me fine.
permanecer [permane'θer] *vi* (*quedarse*) to stay, remain; (*seguir*) to continue to be.
permanencia [perma'nenθja] *nf* (*duración*) permanence; (*estancia*) stay.
permanente [perma'nente] *a* (*que queda*) permanent; (*constante*) constant // *nf* perm.
permisible [permi'siβle] *a* permissible, allowable.
permiso [per'miso] *nm* permission; (*licencia*) permit, licence; **con** ~ excuse me; **estar de** ~ (*MIL*) to be on leave; ~ **de conducir** *o* **conductor** driving licence.
permitir [permi'tir] *vt* to permit, allow.
pernicioso, a [perni'θjoso, a] *a* (*maligno, MED*) pernicious; (*persona*) wicked.
pernio ['pernjo] *nm* hinge.
perno ['perno] *nm* bolt.
pero ['pero] *conj* but; (*aún*) yet // *nm* (*defecto*) flaw, defect; (*reparo*) objection.
perorar [pero'rar] *vi* to make a speech.
perpendicular [perpendiku'lar] *a* perpendicular; **el camino es** ~ **al río** the road is at right angles to the river.
perpetrar [perpe'trar] *vt* to perpetrate.
perpetuamente [perpetwa'mente] *ad* perpetually; **perpetuar** *vt* to perpetuate; **perpetuo, a** *a* perpetual.
perplejo, a [per'plexo, a] *a* perplexed, bewildered.
perra ['perra] *nf* bitch; (*fam*) mania, crazy idea.
perrera [pe'rrera] *nf* kennel.
perrillo [pe'rriʎo] *nm* puppy.
perro ['perro] *nm* dog; ~ **caliente** hot dog.
persa ['persa] *a*, *nm/f* Persian.
persecución [perseku'θjon] *nf* pursuit, hunt, chase; (*REL, POL*) persecution.
perseguir [perse'ɣir] *vt* to pursue, hunt; (*cortejar*) to chase after; (*molestar*) to pester, annoy; (*REL, POL*) to persecute.
perseverante [perseße'rante] *a* persevering, persistent; **perseverar** *vi* to persevere, persist; **perseverar en** to persevere in, persist with.
persiana [per'sjana] *nf* (*Venetian*) blind.
persignarse [persiχ'narse] *vr* to cross o.s.
persistente [persis'tente] *a* persistant; **persistir** *vi* to persist.
persona [per'sona] *nf* person; **10** ~**s** 10 people.
personaje [perso'naxe] *nm* important person, celebrity; (*TEATRO*) character.
personal [perso'nal] *a* (*particular*) personal; (*para una persona*) single, for one person // *nm* personnel, staff; ~**idad** *nf* personality.
personarse [perso'narse] *vr* to appear in person.

personificar [personifi'kar] vt to personify.

perspectiva [perspek'tißa] nf perspective; (vista, panorama) view, panorama; (posibilidad futura) outlook, prospect.

perspicacia [perspi'kaθja] nf keen-sightedness; (fig) discernment, perspicacity.

perspicaz [perspi'kaθ] a (agudo: de la vista) keen; (fig) shrewd.

persuadir [perswa'ðir] vt (gen) to persuade; (convencer) to convince; ~se vr to become convinced; **persuasión** nf (acto) persuasion; (estado de mente) conviction; **persuasivo, a** a persuasive; convincing.

pertenecer [pertene'θer] vi to belong; (fig) to concern; **pertenencia** nf ownership; **pertenencias** nfpl possessions, property sg; **perteneciente** a: **perteneciente a** belonging to.

pertinaz [perti'naθ] a (persistente) persistent; (terco) obstinate.

pertinente [perti'nente] a relevant, pertinent; (apropiado) appropriate; ~ **a** concerning, relevant to.

perturbación [perturßa'θjon] nf (POL) disturbance; (MED) upset, disturbance.

perturbado, a [pertur'ßaðo, a] a mentally unbalanced.

perturbador, a [perturßa'ðor, a] a (que perturba) perturbing, disturbing; (subversivo) subversive.

perturbar [pertur'ßar] vt (el orden) to disturb; (MED) to upset, disturb; (mentalmente) to perturb.

Perú [pe'ru] nm: **el** ~ Peru; **peruano, a** a, nm/f Peruvian.

perversión [perßer'sjon] nf perversion; **perverso, a** a perverse; (depravado) depraved; **pervertido, a** a perverted // nm/f pervert; **pervertir** vt to pervert, corrupt; (distorsionar) to distort.

pesa ['pesa] nf weight; (DEPORTE) shot.

pesadez [pesa'ðeθ] nf (calidad de pesado) heaviness; (lentitud) slowness; (aburrimiento) tediousness.

pesadilla [pesa'ðiʎa] nf nightmare, bad dream.

pesado, a [pe'saðo, a] a (gen) heavy; (lento) slow; (difícil, duro) tough, hard; (aburrido) tedious, boring; (bochornoso) sultry.

pesadumbre [pesa'ðumbre] nf grief, sorrow.

pésame ['pesame] nm expression of condolence, message of sympathy.

pesar [pe'sar] vt to weigh // vi to weigh; (ser pesado) to weigh a lot, be heavy; (fig: opinión) to carry weight // nm (sentimiento) regret; (pena) grief, sorrow; **a** ~ **de** o **pese a (que)** in spite of, despite.

pesario [pe'sarjo] nm pessary.

pesca ['peska] nf (acto) fishing; (cantidad de pescado) catch; **ir de** ~ to go fishing.

pescadería [peskaðe'ria] nf fish shop.

pescado [pes'kaðo] nm fish.

pescador, a [peska'ðor, a] nm/f fisherman/woman.

pescar [pes'kar] vt (coger) to catch; (tratar de coger) to fish for; (conseguir: trabajo) to manage to get // vi to fish, go fishing; **viene a** ~ **un marido** she's come to get a husband.

pescuezo [pes'kweθo] nm neck.

pesebre [pe'seßre] nm manger.

peseta [pe'seta] nf peseta.

pesimista [pesi'mista] a pessimistic // nm/f pessimist.

pésimo, a ['pesimo, a] a abominable, vile.

peso ['peso] nm weight; (balanza) scales pl; (moneda) peso; ~ **bruto/neto** gross/net weight; **vender a** ~ to sell by weight.

pesquero, a [pes'kero, a] a fishing cpd.

pesquisa [pes'kisa] nf inquiry, investigation.

pestaña [pes'tapa] nf (ANAT) eyelash; (borde) rim; **pestañear, pestañar** vi to blink.

peste ['peste] nf (gen) plague; (mal olor) stink, stench.

pesticida [pesti'θiða] nm pesticide.

pestilencia [pesti'lenθja] nf (plaga) pestilence, plague; (mal olor) stink, stench.

pétalo ['petalo] nm petal.

petardista [petar'ðista] nm/f (tramposo) cheat; (rompehuelgas) blackleg.

petición [peti'θjon] nf (pedido) request, plea; (memorial) petition; (JUR) plea.

petrificar [petrifi'kar] vt to petrify.

petróleo [pe'troleo] nm oil, petroleum; **petrolero, a** a petroleum cpd // nm (COM) oil man; (extremista) extremist, revolutionary; (buque) (oil) tanker.

peyorativo, a [pejora'tißo, a] a pejorative.

pez [peθ] nm fish.

pezón [pe'θon] nm teat, nipple; (MECÁNICA) nipple, lubrication point.

piadoso, a [pja'ðoso, a] a (devoto) pious, devout; (misericordioso) kind, merciful.

pianista [pja'nista] nm/f pianist.

piano ['pjano] nm piano.

piar [pi'ar] vi to cheep.

picadillo [pika'ðiʎo] nm mince, minced meat.

picado, a [pi'kaðo, a] a pricked, punctured; (mar) choppy; (diente) bad; (tabaco) cut; (enfadado) cross // nf prick; (de abeja) sting; (de mosquito) bite.

picador [pika'ðor] nm (TAUR) picador; (entrenador de caballos) horse trainer; (minero) faceworker.

picadura [pika'ðura] nf (diente) bad tooth; (pinchazo) puncture; (de abeja) sting; (de mosquito) bite; (tabaco picado) cut tobacco.

picante [pi'kante] a hot; (comentario) racy, spicy.

picar [pi'kar] vt (agujerear, perforar) to prick, puncture; (abeja) to sting; (mosquito, serpiente) to bite; (incitar) to incite, goad; (dañar, irritar) to annoy, bother; (quemar:

lengua) to burn, sting // vi (pez) to bite, take the bait; (el sol) to burn, scorch; (abeja, MED) to sting; (mosquito) to bite; ~se vr (decaer) to decay; (agriarse) to turn sour, go off; (ofenderse) to take offence; ~ en (fig) to dabble in.

picardía [pikar'ðia] nf villainy; (astucia) slyness, craftiness; (una ~) dirty trick; (palabra) rude/bad word or expression.

pícaro, a ['pikaro, a] a (malicioso) villainous; (travieso) mischievous // nm (ladrón) crook; (astuto) sly sort; (sinvergüenza) rascal, scoundrel.

pico ['piko] nm (de ave) beak; (punto agudo) peak, sharp point; (TEC) pick, pickaxe; (GEO) peak, summit; y ~ and a bit.

picotear [pikote'ar] vt to peck // vi to nibble, pick; (fam) to chatter; ~se vr to squabble.

picudo, a [pi'kuðo, a] a pointed, with a point.

pichón [pi'tʃon] nm young pigeon.

pido, pidió etc vb ver **pedir.**

pie [pje] (pl ~s) nm (gen) foot; (fig: motivo) motive, basis; (: fundamento) foothold; **ir a** ~ to go on foot, walk; **estar de** ~ to be standing (up); **ponerse de** ~ to stand up; **al** ~ **de la letra** (citar) literally, verbatim; (copiar) exactly, word for word; **en** ~ **de guerra** on a war footing; **dar** ~ **a** to give cause for.

piedad [pje'ðað] nf (lástima) pity, compassion; (clemencia) mercy; (devoción) piety, devotion.

piedra ['pjeðra] nf stone; (roca) rock; (de mechero) flint; (METEOROLOGÍA) hailstone.

piel [pjel] nf (ANAT) skin; (ZOOL) skin, hide; (de oso) fur; (cuero) leather; (BOT) skin, peel; ~ **de ante** o **de Suecia** suede.

pienso etc vb ver **pensar.**

pierdo etc vb ver **perder.**

pierna ['pjerna] nf leg.

pieza ['pjeθa] nf piece; (habitación) room; ~ de recambio o repuesto spare (part).

pigmeo, a [pix'meo, a] a, nm/f pigmy.

pijama [pi'xama] nm pyjamas pl.

pila ['pila] nf (ELEC) battery; (montón) heap, pile; (fuente) sink.

píldora ['pildora] nf pill; **la** ~ **(anticonceptiva)** the pill.

pileta [pi'leta] nf basin, bowl; (AM) swimming pool.

pilón [pi'lon] nm pillar, post; (ELEC) pylon.

piloto [pi'loto] nm pilot; (de aparato) rear light, tail light; (AUTO) driver.

pillaje [pi'ʎaxe] nm pillage, plunder.

pillar [pi'ʎar] vt (saquear) to pillage, plunder; (fam: coger) to catch; (: agarrar) to grasp, seize; (: entender) to grasp, catch on to.

pillo, a ['piʎo, a] a villainous; (astuto) sly, crafty // nm/f rascal, rogue, scoundrel.

pimentón [pimen'ton] nm (polvo) paprika; (pimiento) red pepper.

pimienta [pi'mjenta] nf pepper.

pimiento [pi'mjento] nm pepper, pimiento.

pinacoteca [pinako'teka] nf art gallery.

pinar [pi'nar] nm pinewood.

pincel [pin'θel] nm paintbrush.

pinchar [pin'tʃar] vt (perforar) to prick, pierce; (neumático) to puncture; (incitar) to prod; (herir) to wound.

pinchazo [pin'tʃaθo] nm (perforación) prick; (de llanta) puncture; (fig) prod.

pinchitos [pin'tʃitos] nmpl bar snacks.

pingüino [pin'gwino] nm penguin.

pino ['pino] nm pine (tree); **en** ~ upright, vertical.

pinta ['pinta] nf spot; (medida) spot, drop; (aspecto) appearance, look(s) (pl); ~do, a a spotted; (de muchos colores) colourful.

pintar [pin'tar] vt to paint // vi to paint; (fam) to count, be important; ~se vr to put on make-up.

pintor, a [pin'tor, a] nm/f painter.

pintoresco, a [pinto'resko, a] a picturesque.

pintura [pin'tura] nf painting; ~ **a la acuarela** watercolour; ~ **al óleo** oil painting; ~ **rupestre** cave painting.

pinza ['pinθa] nf (ZOOL) claw; (para colgar ropa) clothes peg; (TEC) pincers pl; ~s nfpl (para depilar) tweezers pl.

piña ['piɲa] nf (fruto del pino) pine cone; (fruta) pineapple; (fig) group.

pío, a ['pio, a] a (devoto) pious, devout; (misericordioso) merciful // nm cheep, chirp.

piojo ['pjoxo] nm louse.

pionero, a [pjo'nero, a] a pioneering // nm/f pioneer.

pipa ['pipa] nf pipe; (BOT) edible sunflower seed.

pipí [pi'pi] nm (fam): **hacer** ~ to have a wee(wee).

pique ['pike] nm (resentimiento) pique, resentment; (rivalidad) rivalry, competition; **irse a** ~ to sink; (familia) to be ruined.

piquera [pi'kera] nf hole, vent.

piqueta [pi'keta] nf pick(axe).

piquete [pi'kete] nm (herida) prick, jab; (agujerito) small hole; (MIL) squad, party; (de obreros) picket.

piragua [pi'raɣwa] nf canoe; **piragüismo** nm (DEPORTE) canoeing.

pirámide [pi'ramiðe] nf pyramid.

pirata [pi'rata] a, nm pirate.

Pirineo(s) [piri'neo(s)] nm(pl) Pyrenees pl.

piropo [pi'ropo] nm compliment, (piece of) flattery.

pisada [pi'saða] nf (paso) footstep; (huella) footprint.

pisar [pi'sar] vt (caminar sobre) to walk on, tread on; (apretar con el pie) to press; (fig) to trample on, walk all over // vi to tread, step, walk.

piscina [pis'θina] nf swimming pool; (para peces) fishpond.

Piscis ['pisθis] *nm* Pisces.
piso ['piso] *nm* (*suelo, de edificio*) floor; (*apartamento*) flat, apartment.
pisotear [pisote'ar] *vt* to trample (on *or* underfoot).
pista ['pista] *nf* track, trail; (*indicio*) clue; ~ **de aterrizaje** runway; ~ **de baile** dance floor; ~ **de tenis** tennis court; ~ **de hielo** ice rink.
pistola [pis'tola] *nf* pistol; (*TEC*) spray-gun; **pistolero, a** *nm/f* gunman, gangster // *nf* holster.
pistón [pis'ton] *nm* (*TEC*) piston; (*MUS*) key.
pitar [pi'tar] *vt* (*hacer sonar*) to blow; (*rechiflar*) to whistle at, boo // *vi* to whistle; (*AUTO*) to sound *or* toot one's horn; (*AM*) to smoke.
pitillo [pi'tiʎo] *nm* cigarette.
pito ['pito] *nm* whistle; (*de coche*) horn.
pitón [pi'ton] *nm* (*ZOOL*) python; (*protuberancia*) bump, lump; (*de jarro*) spout.
pitonisa [pito'nisa] *nf* fortune-teller.
pizarra [pi'θarra] *nf* (*piedra*) slate; (*encerado*) blackboard.
pizca ['piθka] *nf* pinch, spot; (*fig*) spot, speck, trace; **ni** ~ not a bit.
placa ['plaka] *nf* plate; ~ **de matrícula** number plate.
placentero, a [plaθen'tero, a] *a* pleasant, agreeable.
placer [pla'θer] *nm* pleasure // *vt* to please.
plácido, a ['plaθiðo, a] *a* placid.
plaga ['plaɣa] *nf* pest; (*MED*) plague; (*abundancia*) abundance; **plagar** *vt* to infest, plague; (*llenar*) to fill.
plagio ['plaxjo] *nm* plagiarism.
plan [plan] *nm* (*esquema, proyecto*) plan; (*idea, intento*) idea, intention; **tener** ~ (*fam*) to have a date; **tener un** ~ (*fam*) to have an affair; **en** ~ **económico** (*fam*) on the cheap; **vamos en** ~ **de turismo** we're going as tourists; **si te pones en ese** ~... if that's your attitude... .
plana ['plana] *nf ver* **plano.**
plancha ['plantʃa] *nf* (*para planchar*) iron; (*rótulo*) plate, sheet; (*NAUT*) gangway; ~ **do** *nm* ironing; **planchar** *vt* to iron // *vi* to do the ironing.
planeador [planea'ðor] *nm* glider; ~ **a** *nf* bulldozer.
planear [plane'ar] *vt* to plan // *vi* to glide.
planeta [pla'neta] *nm* planet.
planicie [pla'niθje] *nf* plain.
planificación [planifika'θjon] *nf* planning; ~ **familiar** family planning.
plano, a ['plano, a] *a* flat, level, even // *nm* (*MAT, TEC, AVIAT*) plane; (*FOTO*) shot; (*ARQ*) plan; (*GEO*) map; (*de ciudad*) map, street plan // *nf* sheet (of paper), page; (*TEC*) trowel; **primer** ~ close-up; **caer de** ~ to fall flat; **en primera** ~ **a** on the front page; ~ **a mayor** staff.
planta ['planta] *nf* (*BOT, TEC*) plant; (*ANAT*) sole of the foot, foot; ~ **baja** ground floor.

plantación [planta'θjon] *nf* (*AGR*) plantation; (*acto*) planting.
plantar [plan'tar] *vt* (*BOT*) to plant; (*levantar*) to erect, set up; ~ **se** *vr* to stand firm; ~ **a uno en la calle** to chuck sb out; **dejar plantado a uno** (*fam*) to stand sb up.
plantear [plante'ar] *vt* (*problema*) to pose; (*dificultad*) to raise; (*planificar*) to plan; (*institución*) to set up, establish; (*reforma*) to implant.
plantilla [plan'tiʎa] *nf* (*de zapato*) insole; (*de media*) sole; (*personal*) personnel; **ser de** ~ to be on the staff.
plantío [plan'tio] *nm* (*acto*) planting; (*lugar*) plot, bed, patch.
plantón [plan'ton] *nm* (*MIL*) guard, sentry; (*fam*) long wait; **dar (un)** ~ **a uno** to stand sb up.
plañidero, a [plaɲi'ðero, a] *a* mournful, plaintive.
plañir [pla'ɲir] *vi* to mourn.
plasmar [plas'mar] *vt* (*dar forma*) to mould, shape; (*representar*) to represent // *vi*: ~ **en** to take the form of.
plasticina [plasti'θina] *nf* plasticine.
plástico, a ['plastiko, a] *a* plastic // *nf* (art of) sculpture, modelling // *nm* plastic.
plata ['plata] *nf* (*metal*) silver; (*cosas hechas de plata*) silverware; (*AM*) money; **hablar en** ~ to speak bluntly *or* frankly.
plataforma [plata'forma] *nf* platform; ~ **de lanzamiento/perforación** launch-(ing) pad/drilling rig.
plátano ['platano] *nm* (*fruta*) banana; (*árbol*) banana tree.
platea [pla'tea] *nf* (*TEATRO*) pit.
plateado, a [plate'aðo, a] *a* silver; (*TEC*) silver-plated.
platería [plate'ria] *nf* silversmith's.
plática ['platika] *nf* talk, chat; **platicar** *vi* to talk, chat.
platillo [pla'tiʎo] *nm* saucer; ~ **s** *nmpl* cymbals; ~ **volador** *o* **volante** flying saucer.
platino [pla'tino] *nm* platinum; ~ **s** *nmpl* (*AUTO*) contact points.
plato ['plato] *nm* plate, dish; (*parte de comida*) course; (*guiso*) dish.
playa ['plaja] *nf* beach; (*lugar veraniego*) seaside resort; (*costa*) seaside; ~ **de estacionamiento** (*AM*) car park.
playera [pla'jera] *nf* T-shirt.
plaza ['plaθa] *nf* square; (*mercado*) market(place); (*sitio*) room, space; (*en vehículo*) seat, place; (*colocación*) post, job.
plazco *etc vb ver* **placer.**
plazo ['plaθo] *nm* (*lapso de tiempo*) time, period, term; (*fecha de vencimiento*) expiry date; (*pago parcial*) instalment; **a corto/largo** ~ short-/long-term; **comprar a** ~ **s** to buy on hire purchase, pay for in instalments.
plazoleta [plaθo'leta], **plazuela** [pla-'θwela] *nf* small square.
pleamar [plea'mar] *nf* high tide.
plebe ['pleβe] *nf*: **la** ~ the common

people *pl*, the masses *pl*; (*pey*) the plebs *pl*; ~ **yo, a** *a* plebeian; (*pey*) coarse, common.

plebiscito [pleßis'θito] *nm* plebiscite.

plegable [ple'xaßle], **plegadizo, a** [plexa'ðiðo, a] *a* pliable; (*silla*) folding.

plegar [ple'xar] *vt* (*doblar*) to fold, bend; (*COSTURA*) to pleat; ~**se** *vr* to yield, submit.

pleito ['pleito] *nm* (*JUR*) lawsuit, case; (*fig*) dispute, feud.

plenilunio [pleni'lunjo] *nm* full moon.

plenitud [pleni'tuð] *nf* plenitude, fullness; (*abundancia*) abundance.

pleno, a ['pleno, a] *a* (*gen*) full; (*completo*) complete // *nm* plenum; **en** ~ **día** in broad daylight; **en** ~ **verano** at the height of summer; **en** ~ **a cara** full in the face.

pleuresía [pleure'sia] *nf* pleurisy.

plexiglás [pleksi'xlas] *nm* perspex.

pliego ['pljexo] *nm* (*hoja*) sheet (of paper); (*carta*) sealed letter/document; ~ **de condiciones** details *pl*, specifications *pl*.

pliegue ['pljexe] *nm* fold, crease; (*de vestido*) pleat.

plisado [pli'saðo] *nm* pleating; ~ **de acordeón** accordion pleats *pl*.

plomero [plo'mero] *nm* plumber.

plomo ['plomo] *nm* (*metal*) lead; (*ELEC*) fuse.

pluma ['pluma] *nf* (*gen*) feather; (*para escribir*) pen.

plural [plu'ral] *a* plural; ~**idad** *nf* plurality; **una** ~**idad de votos** a majority of votes.

plus [plus] *nm* bonus.

plutocracia [pluto'kraθja] *nf* plutocracy.

población [poßla'θjon] *nf* population; (*pueblo, ciudad*) town, city; **poblado, a** *a* inhabited // *nm* (*aldea*) village; (*pueblo*) (small) town; **densamente poblado** densely populated.

poblador, a [poßla'ðor, a] *nm/f* settler, colonist, (*fundador*) founder.

poblar [po'ßlar] *vt* (*colonizar*) to colonize; (*fundar*) to found; (*habitar*) to inhabit.

pobre ['poßre] *a* poor // *nm/f* poor person; ¡~! poor thing!; ~**za** *nf* poverty.

pocilga [po'θilxa] *nf* pigsty.

poción [po'θjon], **pócima** ['poθima] *nf* potion.

poco, a ['poko, a] *a* little; ~**s** few // *ad* (*no mucho*) little, not much // *nm*: **un** ~ a little, a bit; **tener a uno en** ~ to think little *or* not think much of sb; **por** ~ almost, nearly; ~ **a** ~ little by little, gradually; **dentro de** ~ (+ *presente o futuro*) shortly; (+ *pasado*) soon after; **hace** ~ a short time ago, not long ago.

podar [po'ðar] *vt* to prune.

podenco [po'ðenko] *nm* hound.

poder [po'ðer] *vi* can; (*sujeto: persona*) to be able to, can; (*permiso*) can, may; (*posibilidad, hipótesis*) may // *nm* (*gen*) power; (*autoridad*) authority; **puede que sea así** it may be, maybe; ¿**se puede?** may I come in?; ¿**puedes con eso?** can

you manage that?; **a más no** ~ to the utmost; **no** ~ **menos de hacer algo** not to be able to help doing sth; **no** ~ **más** to have had enough; ~**ío** *nm* power; (*autoridad*) authority; ~**oso, a** *a* powerful.

podrido, a [po'ðriðo, a] *a* rotten, bad; (*fig*) rotten, corrupt.

podrir [po'ðrir] = **pudrir.**

poema [po'ema] *nm* poem.

poesía [poe'sia] *nf* poetry.

poeta [po'eta] *nm* poet; **poético, a** *a* poetic(al).

póker ['poker] *nm* poker.

polaco, a [po'lako, a] *a* Polish // *nm/f* Pole.

polar [po'lar] *a* polar; ~**idad** *nf* polarity; ~**izarse** *vr* to polarize.

polea [po'lea] *nf* pulley.

polémica [po'lemika] *nf* (*gen*) polemics *sg*; (*una* ~) controversy.

policía [poli'θia] *nm/f* policeman/woman // *nf* police; ~**co, a** *a* police *cpd*; **novela** ~**ca** detective story.

poligamia [poli'xamja] *nf* polygamy.

polilla [po'liʎa] *nf* moth.

polio ['poljo] *nf* polio.

politécnico [poli'tekniko] *nm* polytechnic.

politene [poli'tene], **politeno** [poli'teno] *nm* polythene.

político, a [po'litiko, a] *a* political; (*discreto*) tactful; (*de familia*) in-law // *nm/f* politician // *nf* politics *sg*; (*económica, agraria*) policy; **padre** ~ father-in-law; **politicastro** *nm* (*pey*) politician, politico.

póliza ['poliθa] *nf* insurance policy.

polo ['polo] *nm* (*GEO, ELEC*) pole; (*helado*) iced lolly; (*DEPORTE*) polo; (*suéter*) polo-neck; ~ **Norte/Sur** North/South Pole.

Polonia [po'lonja] *nf* Poland.

poltrona [pol'trona] *nf* reclining chair, easy chair.

polución [polu'θjon] *nf* pollution.

polvera [pol'ßera] *nf* powder compact, vanity case.

polvo ['polßo] *nm* dust; (*QUIMICA, CULIN, MED*) powder; ~**s** *nmpl* powder *sg*; ~ **de talco** talcum powder; **estar hecho** ~ to be worn out *or* exhausted.

pólvora ['polßora] *nf* gunpowder; (*fuegos artificiales*) fireworks *pl*.

polvoriento, a [polßo'rjento, a] *a* (*superficie*) dusty; (*sustancia*) powdery.

pollería [poʎe'ria] *nf* poulterer's (shop).

pollo ['poʎo] *nm* chicken.

pomada [po'maða] *nf* pomade.

pomelo [po'melo] *nm* grapefruit.

pómez ['pomeθ] *nf*: **piedra** ~ pumice stone.

pompa ['pompa] *nf* (*burbuja*) bubble; (*bomba*) pump; (*esplendor*) pomp, splendour; **pomposo, a** *a* splendid, magnificent; (*pey*) pompous.

pómulo ['pomulo] *nm* cheekbone.

pon [pon] *vb ver* **poner.**

ponche ['pontʃe] *nm* punch.

poncho ['pontʃo] nm (AM) poncho, cape.

ponderado, a [ponde'raðo, a] a calm, steady, balanced.

ponderar [ponde'rar] vt (considerar) to weigh up, consider; (elogiar) to praise highly, speak in praise of.

pondré etc vb ver **poner.**

poner [po'ner] vt (gen) to put; (colocar) to place, set; (ropa) to put on; (problema, la mesa) to set; (telegrama) to send; (TELEC) to connect; (radio, TV) to switch on, turn on; (tienda) to open, set up; (nombre) to give; (añadir) to add; (TEATRO, CINE) to put on; (+ adjetivo) to make, turn; (suponer) to suppose // vi (ave) to lay (eggs); ~se vr to put or place o.s.; (ropa) to put on; (+ adjetivo) to turn, get, become; (el sol) to set; **póngame con el Señor X** get me Mr X, put me through to Mr X; ~**se de zapatero** to take a job as a shoemaker; ~**se a bien con uno** to get on good terms with sb; ~**se con uno** to quarrel with sb; ~**se rojo** to blush; ~**se a** to begin to.

pongo etc vb ver **poner.**

pontificado [pontifi'kaðo] nm papacy, pontificate; **pontífice** nm pope, pontiff.

pontón [pon'ton] nm pontoon.

ponzoña [pon'θoɲa] nf poison, venom; **ponzoñoso, a** a poisonous, venomous.

popa ['popa] nf stern.

popular [popu'lar] a popular; (del pueblo) of the people; ~**idad** nf popularity; ~**izarse** vr to become popular.

poquedad [poke'ðað] nf (escasez) scantiness; (una ~) small thing, trifle; (fig) timidity.

por [por] prep (con el fin de) in order to; (a favor de, hacia) for; (a causa de) out of, because of, from; (según) according to; (por agencia de) by; (a cambio de) for, in exchange for; (en lugar de) instead of, in place of; (durante) for; **10 ~ 10 son 100** 10 times 10 are 100; **será ~ poco tiempo** it won't be for long; ~ **correo/avión** by post/plane; ~ **centenares** by the hundred; **(el) 10 ~ ciento** 10 per cent; ~ **orden** in order; **ir a Bilbao ~ Santander** to go to Bilbao via Santander; **pasar ~ Madrid** to pass through Madrid; **camina ~ la izquierda** walk on the left; ~ **todo el país** throughout the country; **entra ~ delante/detrás** come/go in by the front/back (door); ~ **la calle** along the street; ~ **la mañana** in the morning; ~ **la noche** at night; **£2 ~ hora** £2 an hour; ~ **allí** over there; **está ~ el norte** it's somewhere in the north; ~ **mucho que quisiera, no puedo** much as I would like to, I can't; ~**que** because; ¿~ **qué?** why?; ~ (**lo**) **tanto** so, therefore; ~ **cierto** (seguro) certainly; (a propósito) by the way; ~ **ejemplo** for example; ~ **favor** please; ~ **fuera/dentro** outside/inside; ~ **si** (acaso) just in case; ~ **sí mismo** o **sólo** by o.s.

porcelana [porθe'lana] nf porcelain; (china) china.

porcentaje [porθen'taxe] nm percentage.

porción [por'θjon] nf (parte) portion, share; (cantidad) quantity, amount.

pordiosear [porðjose'ar] vi to beg; **pordiosero, a** nm/f beggar.

porfía [por'fia] nf persistence; (terquedad) obstinacy; **porfiado, a** a persistent; obstinate; **porfiar** vi to persist, insist; (disputar) to argue stubbornly.

pormenor [porme'nor] nm detail, particular.

pornografía [pornoxra'fia] nf pornography.

poro ['poro] nm pore; ~**so, a** a porous.

porque ['porke] conj (a causa de) because; (ya que) since; (con el fin de) so that, in order that.

porqué [por'ke] nm reason, cause.

porquería [porke'ria] nf (suciedad) filth, muck, dirt; (acción) dirty trick; (objeto) small thing, trifle; (fig) rubbish.

porro, a ['porro, a] a (fam) stupid // nf (arma) stick, club; (TEC) large hammer; (fam) bore.

porrón, ona [po'rron, ona] a slow, stupid // nm glass wine jar with a long spout.

portada [por'taða] nf (entrada) porch, doorway; (de revista) cover.

portador, a [porta'ðor, a] nm/f carrier, bearer.

portaequipajes [portaeki'paxes] nm inv boot; (arriba del coche) luggage rack.

portal [por'tal] nm (entrada) vestibule, hall; (portada) porch, doorway; (puerta de entrada) main door; (de ciudad) gate; (DEPORTE) goal.

portaligas [porta'lixas] nm inv suspender belt.

portamaletas [portama'letas] nm inv boot.

portamonedas [portamo'neðas] nm inv purse.

portarse [por'tarse] vr to behave, conduct o.s.

portátil [por'tatil] a portable.

portaviones [porta'βjones] nm inv aircraft carrier.

portavoz [porta'βoθ] nm (megáfono) megaphone, loudhailer; (vocero) spokesman/woman.

portazo [por'taθo] nm: **dar un ~** to slam the door.

porte ['porte] nm (COM) transport; (precio) transport charges pl; (comportamiento) conduct, behaviour.

portento [por'tento] nm marvel, wonder; ~**so, a** a marvellous, extraordinary.

porteño, a [por'teɲo, a] a of or from Buenos Aires.

portería [porte'ria] nf (oficina) porter's office; (gol) goal.

portero, a [por'tero, a] nm/f porter; (conserje) caretaker; (ujier) doorman // nm goalkeeper.

pórtico ['portiko] *nm* (*patio*) portico, porch; (*fig*) gateway; (*arcada*) arcade.

portilla [por'tiʎa] *nf* porthole.

portillo [por'tiʎo] *nm* (*abertura*) gap, opening; (GEO) narrow pass.

portorriqueño, a [portorri'keɲo, a] *a* Puerto Rican.

Portugal [portu'xal] *nm* Portugal; **portugués, esa** *a, nm/f* Portuguese.

porvenir [porβe'nir] *nm* future.

pos [pos] *prep:* **en ~ de** after, in pursuit of.

posada [po'saða] *nf* (*refugio*) shelter, lodging; (*mesón*) guest house; **dar ~ a** to give shelter to, take in.

posaderas [posa'ðeras] *nfpl* backside *sg*, buttocks.

posar [po'sar] *vt* (*en el suelo*) to lay down, put down; (*la mano*) to place, put gently // *vi* to sit, pose; **~se** *vr* to settle; (*pájaro*) to perch ; (*avión*) to land, come down.

posdata [pos'ðata] *nf* postscript.

pose ['pose] *nf* pose.

poseedor, a [posee'ðor, a] *nm/f* owner, possessor; (*de récord, puesto*) holder.

poseer [pose'er] *vt* to have, possess, own; (*ventaja*) to enjoy; (*récord, puesto*) to hold; **poseído, a** *a* possessed; **posesión** *nf* possession; **posesionarse** *vr:* **posesionarse de** to take possession of, take over; **posesivo, a** *a* possessive.

posibilidad [posiβili'ðað] *nf* possibility; (*oportunidad*) chance; **posibilitar** *vt* to make possible, permit; (*hacer factible*) to make feasible.

posible [po'siβle] *a* possible; (*factible*) feasible; **de ser ~** if possible; **en lo ~** as far as possible.

posición [posi'θjon] *nf* (*gen*) position; (*rango social*) status.

positivo, a [posi'tiβo, a] *a* positive // *nf* (FOTO) print.

poso ['poso] *nm* sediment.

posponer [pospo'ner] *vt* to put behind/below; (AM) to postpone.

posta ['posta] *nf* (*de caballos*) relay, team; (*pedazo*) slice // *nm* courier.

postal [pos'tal] *a* postal // *nf* postcard.

poste ['poste] *nm* (*de telégrafos*) post, pole; (*columna*) pillar; **dar ~ a uno** (*fam*) to keep sb hanging about.

postergar [poster'xar] *vt* (AM: *posponer*) to postpone, delay.

posteridad [posteri'ðað] *nf* posterity.

posterior [poste'rjor] *a* back, rear; (*siguiente*) following, subsequent; (*más tarde*) later; **~idad** *nf:* **con ~idad** later, subsequently.

postizo, a [pos'tiθo, a] *a* false, artificial // *nm* hairpiece.

postor, a [pos'tor, a] *nm/f* bidder.

postrado, a [pos'traðo, a] *a* prostrate; **postrar** *vt* (*derribar*) to cast down, overthrow; (*humillar*) to humble; (MED) to weaken, exhaust.

postre ['postre] *nm* sweet, dessert.

postremo, a [pos'tremo, a], **postrer,**

ero, a [pos'trer, ero, a] *a* (*último*) last; (*que viene detrás*) rear.

postulado [postu'laðo] *nm* postulate; **postular** *vt* (*empleo*) to apply for; (*pedir*) to seek, demand; (*proponer*) to postulate.

póstumo, a ['postumo, a] *a* posthumous.

postura [pos'tura] *nf* (*del cuerpo*) posture, position; (*fig*) attitude, position.

potable [po'taβle] *a* drinkable.

potaje [po'taxe] *nm* stew; **~s** *nmpl* mixed vegetables.

pote ['pote] *nm* pot, jar.

potencia [po'tenθja] *nf* power.

potencial [poten'θjal] *a, nm* potential.

potente [po'tente] *a* powerful.

pozo ['poθo] *nm* well; (*de río*) deep pool; (*de mina*) shaft.

práctica ['praktika] *nf ver* **práctico.**

practicable [prakti'kaβle] *a* practicable; (*camino*) passable, usable.

practicante [prakti'kante] *nm/f* (MED: *ayudante de doctor*) medical assistant; (: *enfermero*) male nurse; (*quien practica algo*) practitioner // *a* practising.

practicar [prakti'kar] *vt* to practise; (*deporte*) to go in for, play; (*realizar*) to carry out, perform.

práctico, a ['praktiko, a] *a* (*gen*) practical; (*conveniente*) handy; (*instruído: persona*) skilled, expert // *nf* practice; (*método*) method; (*arte, capacidad*) skill; **en la ~a** in practice.

pradera [pra'ðera] *nf* meadow; (*de Canadá*) prairie.

prado ['praðo] *nm* (*campo*) meadow, field; (*pastizal*) pasture.

Praga ['praxa] *n* Prague.

pragmático, a [prax'matiko, a] *a* pragmatic.

preámbulo [pre'ambulo] *nm* preamble, introduction.

precario, a [pre'karjo, a] *a* precarious.

precaución [prekau'θjon] *nf* (*medida preventiva*) preventive measure, precaution; (*prudencia*) caution, wariness.

precaver [preka'βer] *vt* to guard against; (*impedir*) to forestall; **~se** *vr:* **~se de** *o* **contra algo** to (be on one's) guard against sth; **precavido, a** *a* cautious, wary.

precedencia [preθe'ðenθja] *nf* precedence; (*prioridad*) priority; (*superioridad*) greater importance, superiority; **precedente** *a* preceding; (*anterior*) former // *nm* precedent; **preceder** *vt, vi* to precede, go/come before.

precepto [pre'θepto] *nm* precept.

preciado, a [pre'θjaðo, a] *a* (*estimado*) esteemed, valuable; (*vanidoso*) presumptuous; **preciar** *vt* to esteem, value; **preciarse** *vr* to boast; **preciarse de** to pride o.s. on, boast of being.

precio ['preθjo] *nm* (*de mercado*) price; (*costo*) cost; (*valor*) value, worth; (*de viaje*) fare; **~ al contado/de coste/de**

oportunidad cash/cost/bargain price; ~ **tope** top price.

preciosidad [preθjosi'ðað] *nf* (*valor*) (high) value, (great) worth; (*encanto*) charm; (*cosa bonita*) beautiful thing; **es una** ~ it's lovely, it's really beautiful; **precioso, a** *a* precious; (*de mucho valor*) valuable; (*fam*) lovely, beautiful.

precipicio [preθi'piθjo] *nm* cliff, precipice; (*fig*) abyss.

precipitación [preθipita'θjon] *nf* haste; (*lluvia*) rainfall.

precipitado, a [preθipi'taðo, a] *a* hasty, rash; (*salida*) hasty, sudden.

precipitar [preθipi'tar] *vt* (*arrojar*) to hurl down, throw; (*apresurar*) to hasten; (*acelerar*) to speed up, accelerate; ~ **se** *vr* to throw o.s.; (*apresurarse*) to rush; (*actuar sin pensar*) to act rashly.

precipitoso, a [preθipi'toso, a] *a* (*escarpado*) steep, sheer; (*a la carrera*, *imprudente*) hasty, rash.

precisamente [preθisa'mente] *ad* precisely; (*justo*) precisely, exactly, just.

precisar [preθi'sar] *vt* (*necesitar*) to need, require; (*fijar*) to determine exactly, fix; (*especificar*) to specify // *vi* to be necessary.

precisión [preθi'sjon] *nf* (*exactitud*) precision; (*necesidad*) need, necessity.

preciso, a [pre'θiso, a] *a* (*exacto*) precise; (*necesario*) necessary, essential.

preconcebido, a [prekonθe'ßiðo, a] *a* preconceived.

preconizar [prekoni'θar] *vt* (*aconsejar*) to advise; (*prever*) to foresee.

precoz [pre'koθ] *a* (*persona*) precocious; (*calvicie*) premature.

precursor, a [prekur'sor, a] *nm/f* precursor.

predecir [preðe'θir] *vt* to predict, foretell, forecast.

predestinado, a [preðesti'naðo, a] *a* predestined.

predeterminar [preðetermi'nar] *vt* to predetermine.

prédica ['preðika] *nf* sermon; **predicador, a** *nm/f* preacher; **predicar** *vt*, *vi* to preach.

predicción [preðik'θjon] *nf* prediction.

predilecto, a [preði'lekto, a] *a* favourite.

predio ['preðjo] *nm* property, estate.

predisponer [preðispo'ner] *vt* to predispose; (*pey*) to prejudice; **predisposición** *nf* predisposition, inclination; prejudice, bias.

predominante [preðomi'nante] *a* predominant.

predominar [preðomi'nar] *vt* to dominate // *vi* to predominate; (*prevalecer*) to prevail; **predominio** *nm* predominance; prevalence.

prefabricado, a [prefaßri'kaðo, a] *a* prefabricated.

prefacio [pre'faθjo] *nm* preface.

preferencia [prefe'renθja] *nf* preference; **de** ~ preferably, for preference;

preferible *a* preferable; **preferir** *vt* to prefer.

prefigurar [prefixu'rar] *vt* to foreshadow, prefigure.

pregonar [prexo'nar] *vt* to proclaim, announce.

pregunta [pre'xunta] *nf* question; **hacer una** ~ to ask *or* put a question.

preguntar [prexun'tar] *vt* to ask; (*cuestionar*) to question // *vi* to ask; ~ **se** *vr* to wonder; ~ **por alguien** to ask for sb; **preguntón, ona** *a* inquisitive.

prehistórico, a [preis'toriko, a] *a* prehistoric.

prejuicio [pre'xwiθjo] *nm* prejudgement; (*preconcepción*) preconception; (*pey*) prejudice, bias.

prelación [prela'θjon] *nf* priority.

preliminar [prelimi'nar] *a* preliminary.

preludio [pre'luðjo] *nm* prelude.

prematuro, a [prema'turo, a] *a* premature.

premeditación [premeðita'θjon] *nf* premeditation; **premeditar** *vt* to premeditate.

premiar [pre'mjar] *vt* to reward; (*en un concurso*) to give a prize to; **premio** *nm* reward; prize; (*COM*) premium.

premonición [premoni'θjon] *nf* premonition.

premura [pre'mura] *nf* (*aprieto*) pressure; (*prisa*) haste, urgency.

prenatal [prena'tal] *a* antenatal, prenatal.

prenda ['prenda] *nf* (*ropa*) garment, article of clothing; (*garantía*) pledge; ~ **s** *nfpl* talents, gifts.

prendar [pren'dar] *vt* to captivate, enchant; ~ **se de uno** to fall in love with sb.

prendedor [prende'ðor] *nm* brooch.

prender [pren'der] *vt* (*captar*) to catch, capture; (*detener*) to arrest; (*coser*) to pin, attach; (*sujetar*) to fasten // *vi* to catch; (*arraigar*) to take root; ~ **se** *vr* (*encenderse*) to catch fire; (*engalanarse*) to dress up.

prensa ['prensa] *nf* press; **la P** ~ the press; **prensar** *vt* to press.

preñado, a [pre'naðo, a] *a* (*mujer*) pregnant; ~ **de** pregnant with, full of; **preñez** *nf* pregnancy.

preocupación [preokupa'θjon] *nf* worry, concern; (*ansiedad*) anxiety; **preocupado, a** *a* worried, concerned; anxious.

preocupar [preoku'par] *vt* to worry; ~ **se** *vr* to worry; ~ **se de algo** (*hacerse cargo*) to worry about sth, take care of sth.

preparación [prepara'θjon] *nf* (*acto*) preparation; (*estado*) preparedness, readiness; (*entrenamiento*) training; **preparado, a** *a* (*dispuesto*) prepared; (*CULIN*) ready (to serve) // *nm* preparation.

preparador, a [prepara'ðor, a] *nm/f* trainer.

preparar [prepa'rar] *vt* (*disponer*) to prepare, get ready; (*TEC*: *tratar*) to

prepare, process, treat; (*entrenar*) to teach, train; ~**se** *vr*: ~**se a** *o* **para** to prepare to *or* for, get ready to *or* for;
preparativo, **a** *a* preparatory, preliminary; **preparativos** *nmpl* preparations; **preparatorio,** **a** *a* preparatory.
prerrogativa [prerroʋa'tiβa] *nf* prerogative, privilege.
presa ['presa] *nf* (*captura*) capture, seizure; (*cosa apresada*) catch; (*víctima*) victim; (*de animal*) prey; (*de agua*) dam.
presbítero [pres'βitero] *nm* priest.
prescindible [presθin'diβle] *a* dispensable.
prescindir [presθin'dir] *vi*: ~ **de** (*privarse de*) to do without, go without; (*descartar*) to dispense with.
prescribir [preskri'βir] *vt* to prescribe; **prescripción** *nf* prescription.
presencia [pre'senθja] *nf* presence; **presencial** *a*: **testigo presencial** eyewitness; **presenciar** *vt* to be present at; (*asistir a*) to attend; (*ver*) to see, witness.
presentación [presenta'θjon] *nf* presentation; (*introducción*) introduction.
presentador, a [presenta'ðor, a] *nm/f* compère.
presentar [presen'tar] *vt* to present; (*ofrecer*) to offer; (*mostrar*) to show, display; (*a una persona*) to introduce; ~**se** *vr* (*llegar inesperadamente*) to appear, turn up; (*ofrecerse: como candidato*) to run, stand; (*aparecer*) to show, appear; (*solicitar empleo*) to apply.
presente [pre'sente] *a* present // *nm* present; **hacer** ~ to state, declare; **tener** ~ to remember, bear in mind.
presentimiento [presenti'mjento] *nm* premonition, presentiment; **presentir** *vt* to have a premonition of.
preservación [preserβa'θjon] *nf* protection, preservation; **preservar** *vt* to protect, preserve; **preservativo** *nm* sheath, condom.
presidencia [presi'ðenθja] *nf* presidency; (*de comité*) chairmanship; **presidente** *nm/f* president; chairman/woman.
presidiario [presi'ðjarjo] *nm* convict; **presidio** *nm* (*penitenciaría*) prison, penitentiary; (*trabajo forzoso*) hard labour; (*MIL*) garrison.
presidir [presi'ðir] *vt* (*dirigir*) to preside at, preside over; (: *comité*) to take the chair at; (*dominar*) to dominate, rule // *vi* to preside; to take the chair.
presión [pre'sjon] *nf* pressure; **presionar** *vt* to press; (*fig*) to press, put pressure on // *vi*: **presionar para** *o* **por** to press for.
preso, a ['preso, a] *nm/f* prisoner; **tomar** *o* **llevar** ~ **a uno** to arrest sb, take sb prisoner.
prestado, a [pres'taðo, a] *a* on loan; **pedir** ~ to borrow.
prestamista [presta'mista] *nm/f* moneylender.
préstamo ['prestamo] *nm* loan.

prestar [pres'tar] *vt* to lend, loan; (*atención*) to pay; (*ayuda*) to give // *vi* to give, stretch.
prestatario, a [presta'tarjo, a] *nm/f* borrower.
presteza [pres'teθa] *nf* speed, promptness.
prestigio [pres'tixjo] *nm* prestige; ~**so, a** *a* (*honorable*) prestigious; (*famoso, renombrado*) renowned, famous.
presto, a ['presto, a] *a* (*rápido*) quick, prompt; (*dispuesto*) ready // *ad* at once, right away.
presumir [presu'mir] *vt* to presume // *vi* (*tener aires*) to be conceited; **según cabe** ~ as may be presumed, presumably; **presunción** *nf* presumption; **presunto, a** *a* (*supuesto*) supposed, presumed; (*así llamado*) so-called; **presuntuoso, a** *a* conceited, presumptuous.
presuponer [presupo'ner] *vt* to presuppose.
presupuesto [presu'pwesto] *nm* (*FINANZAS*) budget; (*estimación: de costo*) estimate.
presuroso, a [presu'roso, a] *a* (*rápido*) quick, speedy; (*que tiene prisa*) hasty.
pretencioso, a [preten'θjoso, a] *a* pretentious.
pretender [preten'der] *vt* (*intentar*) to try to, seek to; (*reivindicar*) to claim; (*buscar*) to seek, try for; (*cortejar*) to woo, court; ~ **que** to expect that; **pretendiente** *nm/f* (*candidato*) candidate, applicant; (*amante*) suitor; **pretensión** *nf* (*aspiración*) aspiration; (*reivindicación*) claim; (*orgullo*) pretension.
pretexto [pre'teksto] *nm* pretext; (*excusa*) excuse.
prevalecer [preβale'θer] *vi* to prevail; **prevaleciente** *a* prevailing, prevalent.
prevalerse [preβa'lerse] *vr*: ~ **de** to avail o.s. of.
prevención [preβen'θjon] *nf* (*preparación*) preparation; (*estado*) preparedness, readiness; (*el evitar*) prevention; (*previsión*) foresight, forethought; (*prejuicio*) bias, prejudice; (*precaución*) precaution.
prevenido, a [preβe'niðo, a] *a* prepared, ready; (*cauteloso*) cautious.
prevenir [preβe'nir] *vt* (*impedir*) to prevent; (*prever*) to foresee, anticipate; (*predisponer*) to prejudice, bias; (*avisar*) to warn; (*preparar*) to prepare, get ready; ~**se** *vr* to get ready, prepare; ~**se contra** to take precautions against; **preventivo, a** *a* preventive, precautionary.
prever [pre'βer] *vt* to foresee.
previo, a ['preβjo, a] *a* (*anterior*) previous; (*preliminar*) preliminary // *prep*: ~ **acuerdo de los otros** subject to the agreement of the others.
previsión [preβi'sjon] *nf* (*perspicacia*) foresight; (*predicción*) forecast; ~ **social** social security.
prieto, a ['prjeto, a] *a* (*oscuro*) dark; (*fig*) mean; (*comprimido*) tight, compressed.

prima ['prima] *nf ver* **primo.**
primacía [prima'θia] *nf* primacy.
primario, a [pri'marjo, a] *a* primary.
primavera [prima'ßera] *nf* (*temporada*) spring; (*período*) springtime.
primer, primero, a [pri'mer, pri'mero, a] *a* first; (*fig*) prime // *ad* first; (*más bien*) sooner, rather // *nf* (*AUTO*) first gear; (*FERRO*) first class; **de** ~**a** (*fam*) first-class, first-rate; ~**a plana** front page.
primitivo, a [primi'tißo, a] *a* primitive; (*original*) original.
primo, a ['primo, a] *nm/f* cousin; (*fam*) fool, dupe // *nf* (*COM*) bonus; ~ **hermano** first cousin; **materias** ~**as** raw materials.
primogénito, a [primo'xenito, a] *a* first-born.
primordial [primor'ðjal] *a* basic, fundamental.
primoroso, a [primo'roso, a] *a* exquisite, delicate.
princesa [prin'θesa] *nf* princess.
principal [prinθi'pal] *a* principal, main // *nm* (*jefe*) chief, principal.
príncipe ['prinθipe] *nm* prince.
principiante [prinθi'pjante] *nm/f* beginner; **principiar** *vt* to begin.
principio [prin'θipjo] *nm* (*comienzo*) beginning, start; (*origen*) origin; (*primera etapa*) rudiment, basic idea; (*moral*) principle; **a** ~**s de** at the beginning of; **tener** *o* **tomar en** ~ to start from, be based on.
pringue ['pringe] *nm* (*grasa*) grease, fat, dripping; (*mancha*) grease stain.
prioridad [priori'ðað] *nf* priority.
prisa ['prisa] *nf* (*apresuramiento*) hurry, haste; (*rapidez*) speed; (*urgencia*) (sense of) urgency; **a** *o* **de** ~ quickly; **correr** ~ to be urgent; **darse** ~ to hurry up; **estar de** *o* **tener** ~ to be in a hurry.
prisión [pri'sjon] *nf* (*cárcel*) prison; (*período de cárcel*) imprisonment; **prisionero, a** *nm/f* prisoner.
prismáticos [pris'matikos] *nmpl* binoculars.
privación [prißa'θjon] *nf* deprivation; (*falta*) want, privation.
privado, a [pri'ßaðo, a] *a* private.
privar [pri'ßar] *vt* to deprive; (*prohibir*) to forbid // *vi* (*gozar de favor*) to be in favour; (*prevalecer*) to prevail; **privativo, a** *a* exclusive.
privilegiado, a [prißile'xjaðo, a] *a* privileged; (*memoria*) very good; **privilegiar** *vt* to grant a privilege to; (*favorecer*) to favour.
privilegio [prißi'lexjo] *nm* privilege; (*concesión*) concession; ~ **de invención** patent.
pro [pro] *nm o f* profit, advantage // *prep*: **asociación** ~ **ciegos** association for the blind // *pref*: ~ **soviético/americano** pro-Soviet/American; **en** ~ **de** on behalf of, for; **los** ~**s y los contras** the pros and cons.

probabilidad [proßaßili'ðað] *nf* probability, likelihood; (*oportunidad, posibilidad*) chance, prospect; **probable** *a* probable, likely.
probanza [pro'ßanθa] *nf* proof, evidence.
probar [pro'ßar] *vt* (*demostrar*) to prove; (*someter a prueba*) to test, try out; (*ropa*) to try on; (*comida*) to taste // *vi* to try; ~**se un traje** to try on a suit.
probeta [pro'ßeta] *nf* test tube.
problema [pro'ßlema] *nm* problem.
procaz [pro'kaθ] *a* insolent, impudent.
procedente [proθe'ðente] *a* (*razonable*) reasonable; (*conforme a derecho*) proper, fitting; ~ **de** coming from, originating in.
proceder [proθe'ðer] *vi* (*avanzar*) to proceed; (*actuar*) to act; (*ser correcto*) to be right (and proper), be fitting // *nm* (*acción*) course of action; (*comportamiento*) behaviour, conduct; **procedimiento** *nm* procedure; (*proceso*) process; (*método*) means, method.
procesado, a [proθe'saðo, a] *nm/f* accused (person); **procesar** *vt* to try, put on trial.
procesión [proθe'sjon] *nf* procession.
proceso [pro'θeso] *nm* process; (*JUR*) trial; (*lapso*) course (of time).
proclama [pro'klama] *nf* (*acto*) proclamation; (*cartel*) poster; **proclamar** *vt* to proclaim.
procreación [prokrea'θjon] *nf* procreation; **procrear** *vt, vi* to procreate.
procurador, a [prokura'ðor, a] *nm/f* attorney.
procurar [proku'rar] *vt* (*intentar*) to try, endeavour; (*conseguir*) to get, obtain; (*asegurar*) to secure; (*producir*) to produce.
prodigio [pro'ðixjo] *nm* prodigy; (*milagro*) wonder, marvel; ~**so, a** a prodigious, marvellous.
pródigo, a ['proðixo, a] *a*: **hijo** ~ prodigal son.
producción [proðuk'θjon] *nf* production; (*suma de productos*) output; (*producto*) product; ~ **en serie** mass production.
producir [proðu'θir] *vt* to produce; (*generar*) to cause, bring about; ~**se** *vr* (*gen*) to come about, happen; (*hacerse*) to be produced, be made; (*estallar*) to break out.
productividad [proðuktißi'ðað] *nf* productivity; **productivo, a** *a* productive; (*provechoso*) profitable.
producto [pro'ðukto] *nm* product; (*producción*) production.
productor, a [proðuk'tor, a] *a* productive, producing // *nm/f* producer.
proeza [pro'eθa] *nf* exploit, feat.
profanar [profa'nar] *vt* to desecrate, profane; **profano, a** *a* profane // *nm/f* layman/woman.
profecía [profe'θia] *nf* prophecy.
proferir [profe'rir] *vt* (*palabra, sonido*) to utter; (*injuria*) to hurl, let fly.
profesar [profe'sar] *vt* (*declarar*) to profess; (*practicar*) to practise.

profesión [profe'sjon] *nf* profession; **profesional** *a* professional.
profesor, a [profe'sor, a] *nm/f* teacher; ~**ado** *nm* teaching profession.
profeta [pro'feta] *nm/f* prophet; **profetizar** *vt, vi* to prophesy.
prófugo, a ['profuxo, a] *nm/f* fugitive; (*desertor*) deserter.
profundidad [profundi'ðað] *nf* depth; **profundizar** *vt* (*fig*) to go deeply into; **profundo, a** *a* deep; (*misterio, pensador*) profound.
progenie [pro'xenje] *nf* offspring.
progenitor [proxeni'tor] *nm* ancestor; ~**es** *nmpl* (*fam*) parents.
programa [pro'xrama] *nm* programme; ~**ción** *nf* programming; ~**dor, a** *nm/f* programmer; **programar** *vt* to programme.
progresar [proxre'sar] *vi* to progress, make progress; **progresista** *a, nm/f* progressive; **progresivo, a** *a* progressive; (*gradual*) gradual; (*continuo*) continuous; **progreso** *nm* progress.
prohibición [proiβi'θjon] *nf* prohibition, ban; **prohibir** *vt* to prohibit, ban, forbid; **se prohibe fumar** no smoking.
prohijar [proi'xar] *vt* to adopt.
prójimo, a ['proximo, a] *nm/f* fellow man, neighbour.
proletariado [proleta'rjaðo] *nm* proletariat; **proletario, a** *a, nm/f* proletarian.
proliferación [prolifera'θjon] *nf* proliferation; **proliferar** *vi* to proliferate; **prolífico, a** *a* prolific.
prolijo, a [pro'lixo, a] *a* long-winded, tedious.
prólogo ['proloxo] *nm* prologue.
prolongación [prolonga'θjon] *nf* extension; **prolongado, a** *a* (*largo*) long; (*alargado*) lengthy; **prolongar** *vt* (*gen*) to extend; (*en el tiempo*) to prolong; (*calle, tubo*) to make longer, extend.
promedio [pro'meðjo] *nm* average; (*de distancia*) middle, mid point.
promesa [pro'mesa] *nf* promise.
prometer [prome'ter] *vt* to promise // *vi* to show promise; ~**se** *vr* (*dos personas*) to get engaged; **prometido, a** *a* promised; engaged // *nm/f* fiancé/fiancée.
prominente [promi'nente] *a* prominent.
promiscuo, a [pro'miskwo, a] *a* (*mezclado*) mixed(-up), in disorder; (*ambiguo*) ambiguous.
promoción [promo'θjon] *nf* promotion.
promotor [promo'tor] *nm* promoter; (*instigador*) instigator.
promover [promo'ßer] *vt* to promote; (*causar*) to cause; (*instigar*) to instigate, stir up.
promulgar [promul'xar] *vt* to promulgate; (*fig*) to proclaim.
pronosticar [pronosti'kar] *vt* to predict, foretell, forecast; **pronóstico** *nm* prediction, forecast.
prontitud [pronti'tuð] *nf* speed, quickness;

(*de ingenio*) quickness, sharpness.
pronto, a ['pronto, a] *a* (*rápido*) prompt, quick; (*preparado*) ready; (*astuto*) quick, sharp // *ad* quickly, promptly; (*en seguida*) at once, right away; (*dentro de poco*) soon; (*temprano*) early // *nm*: **tener** ~**s de enojo** to be quick-tempered; **al** ~ at first; **de** ~ suddenly; **por lo** ~ meanwhile, for the present.
pronunciación [pronunθja'θjon] *nf* pronunciation; **pronunciar** *vt* to pronounce; (*discurso*) to make, deliver; **pronunciarse** *vr* to revolt, rise, rebel; (*declararse*) to declare o.s.
propagación [propaxa'θjon] *nf* propagation.
propaganda [propa'ɣanda] *nf* (*política*) propaganda; (*comercial*) advertising.
propagar [propa'xar] *vt* to propagate.
propensión [propen'sjon] *nf* inclination, propensity; **propenso, a** *a* inclined to; **ser propenso a** to be inclined to, have a tendency to.
propiamente [propja'mente] *ad* properly; (*realmente*) really, exactly.
propicio, a [pro'piθjo, a] *a* favourable, propitious.
propiedad [propje'ðað] *nf* (*gen*) property; (*posesión*) possession, ownership; ~ **industrial** patent rights *pl*; ~ **literaria** copyright; ~ **particular** private property.
propietario, a [propje'tarjo, a] *nm/f* owner, proprietor.
propina [pro'pina] *nf* tip.
propio, a ['propjo, a] *a* own, of one's own; (*característico*) characteristic, typical; (*conveniente*) proper; (*mismo*) selfsame, very; **el** ~ **ministro** the minister himself; ¿**tienes casa** ~**a?** have you a house of your own?
proponer [propo'ner] *vt* to propose, put forward, (*problema*) to pose; ~**se** *vr* to propose, plan, intend.
proporción [propor'θjon] *nf* proportion; (*MAT*) ratio; (*oportunidad*) chance, opportunity; **proporciones** *nfpl* dimensions; (*fig*) size *sg*; **proporcionado, a** *a* proportionate; (*regular*) medium, middling; (*justo*) just right; **proporcionar** *vt* (*dar*) to give, supply, provide; (*adaptar*) to adjust, adapt.
proposición [proposi'θjon] *nf* proposition; (*propuesta*) proposal.
propósito [pro'posito] *nm* purpose; (*intento*) aim, intention // *a*: **a** ~ appropriate, suitable // *ad*: **a** ~ **de** by the way, incidentally; **a** ~ **de** about, with regard to; **de** ~ on purpose, deliberately.
propuesta [pro'pwesta] *nf* proposal.
propulsar [propul'sar] *vt* to drive, propel; (*fig*) to promote, encourage; **propulsión** *nf* propulsion; **propulsión a chorro** *o* **por reacción** jet propulsion.
prórroga ['prorroxa] *nf* (*gen*) extension; (*JUR*) stay; (*COM*) deferment; **prorrogar** *vt*

(*período*) to extend; (*decisión*) to defer, postpone.

prorrumpir [prorrum'pir] *vi* to burst forth, break out.

prosa ['prosa] *nf* prose.

proscribir [proskri'ßir] *vt* to prohibit, ban; (*desterrar*) to exile, banish; (*partido*) to proscribe; **proscripción** *nf* prohibition, ban; banishment; proscription.

prosecución [proseku'θjon] *nf* continuation; (*persecución*) pursuit.

proseguir [prose'xir] *vt* to continue, carry on, proceed with // *vi* to continue, go on.

prospección [prospek'θjon] *nf* exploration; (*del petróleo, del oro*) prospecting.

prospecto [pros'pekto] *nm* prospectus.

prosperar [prospe'rar] *vi* to prosper, thrive, flourish; **prosperidad** *nf* prosperity; (*éxito*) success; **próspero, a** *a* prosperous, thriving, flourishing; (*que tiene éxito*) successful.

prostíbulo [pros'tißulo] *nm* brothel.

prostitución [prostitu'θjon] *nf* prostitution; **prostituir** *vt* to prostitute; **prostituirse** *vr* to prostitute o.s., become a prostitute; **prostituta** *nf* prostitute.

protagonista [prota×o'nista] *nm/f* protagonist.

protección [protek'θjon] *nf* protection.

protector, a [protek'tor, a] *a* protective, protecting // *nm/f* protector.

proteger [prote'xer] *vt* to protect; **protegido, a** *nm/f* protégé/ protégée.

proteína [prote'ina] *nf* protein.

protesta [pro'testa] *nf* protest; (*declaración*) protestation.

protestante [protes'tante] *a* Protestant.

protestar [protes'tar] *vt* to protest, declare; (*fé*) to protest // *vi* to protest.

protocolo [proto'kolo] *nm* protocol.

prototipo [proto'tipo] *nm* prototype.

provecho [pro'ßetʃo] *nm* advantage, benefit; (*FINANZAS*) profit; ¡**buen** ~! bon appétit!; **en** ~ **de** to the benefit of; **sacar** ~ **de** to benefit from, profit by.

proveer [proße'er] *vt* to provide, supply; (*preparar*) to provide, get ready; (*vacante*) to fill; (*negocio*) to transact, dispatch // *vi*: ~ **a** to provide for.

provenir [proße'nir] *vi*: ~ **de** to come from, stem from.

proverbio [pro'ßerßjo] *nm* proverb.

providencia [proßi'ðenθja] *nf* providence; (*previsión*) foresight; ~s *nfpl* measures, steps.

provincia [pro'ßinθja] *nf* province; ~**no, a** *a* provincial; (*del campo*) country *cpd*.

provisión [proßi'sjon] *nf* provision; (*abastecimiento*) provision, supply; (*medida*) measure, step.

provisional [proßisjo'nal] *a* provisional.

provocación [proßoka'θjon] *nf* provocation; **provocar** *vt* to provoke; (*alentar*) to tempt, invite; (*causar*) to bring about, lead to; (*promover*) to promote;

(*estimular*) to rouse, stir, stimulate; **provocativo, a** *a* provocative.

próximamente [proksima'mente] *ad* shortly, soon.

proximidad [proksimi'ðað] *nf* closeness, proximity; **próximo, a** *a* near, close; (*vecino*) neighbouring; (*el que viene*) next.

proyectar [projek'tar] *vt* (*objeto*) to hurl, throw; (*luz*) to cast, shed; (*CINE*) to screen, show; (*planear*) to plan.

proyectil [projek'til] *nm* projectile, missile; (*MIL*) missile.

proyecto [pro'jekto] *nm* plan; (*estimación de costo*) detailed estimate.

proyector [projek'tor] *nm* (*CINE*) projector; (*MIL*) searchlight; (*de teatro*) spotlight.

prudencia [pru'ðenθja] *nf* (*sabiduría*) wisdom, prudence; (*cautela*) care; **prudente** *a* sensible, wise, prudent; (*conductor*) careful.

prueba ['prweßa] *nf* proof; (*ensayo*) test, trial; (*saboreo*) testing, sampling; (*de ropa*) fitting; ~**s** *nfpl* trials; **a** ~ on trial; **a** ~ **de** proof against; **a** ~ **de agua/fuego** waterproof/fireproof; **sala de** ~**s** fitting room; **someter a** ~ to put to the test.

prurito [pru'rito] *nm* itch; (*de bebé*) nappy rash.

psico... [siko] *pref* psycho...; ~**análisis** *nm* psychoanalysis; ~**logía** *nf* psychology; ~**lógico, a** *a* psychological; **psicólogo, a** *nm/f* psychologist; **psicópata** *nm/f* psychopath; ~**sis** *nf inv* psychosis.

psiquiatra [si'kjatra] *nm/f* psychiatrist; **psiquiátrico, a** *a* psychiatric.

psíquico, a ['sikiko, a] *a* psychic(al).

PSOE *abr de* **Partido Socialista Obrero Español.**

púa ['pua] *nf* sharp point; (*para guitarra*) plectrum; **alambre de** ~ barbed wire.

pubertad [pußer'tað] *nf* puberty.

publicación [pußlika'θjon] *nf* publication; **publicar** *vt* (*editar*) to publish; (*hacer público*) to publicize; (*vulgarizar*) to make public, divulge.

publicidad [pußliθi'ðað] *nf* publicity; (*COM*) advertising; **publicitario, a** *a* publicity *cpd*; advertising *cpd*.

público, a ['pußliko, a] *a* public // *nm* public; (*TEATRO etc*) audience.

puchero [pu'tʃero] *nm* stew; **hacer** ~**s** to pout.

pude *etc vb ver* **poder.**

púdico, a ['puðiko, a] *a* modest.

pudiera *etc vb ver* **poder.**

pudor [pu'ðor] *nm* modesty.

pudrir [pu'ðrir] *vt* to rot; (*fam*) to upset, annoy; ~**se** *vr* to rot, decay.

pueblo ['pweßlo] *nm* people; (*nación*) nation; (*aldea*) village.

puedo *etc vb ver* **poder.**

puente ['pwente] *nm* (*gen*) bridge; ~ **aéreo** airlift; ~ **colgante** suspension bridge; **hacer el** ~ (*fam*) to take an extra day off work between 2 public holidays.

puerco, a ['pwerko, a] *nm/f* pig/sow // *a*

(*sucio*) dirty, filthy; (*obsceno*) disgusting; ~ **de mar** porpoise; ~ **marino** dolphin.

pueril [pweˈril] a childish.

puerro [ˈpwerro] nm leek.

puerta [ˈpwerta] nf door; (*de jardín*) gate; (*portal*) doorway; (*fig*) gateway; (*gol*) goal; **a** ~ **cerrada** behind closed doors; ~ **giratoria** swing door, revolving door.

puertaventana [pwertaβenˈtana] nf shutter.

puerto [ˈpwerto] nm port; (*paso*) pass; (*fig*) haven, refuge.

Puerto Rico [pwertoˈriko] nm Puerto Rico; **puertorriqueño, a** a Puerto Rican.

pues [pwes] ad (*entonces*) then; (*¡entonces!*) well, well then; (*así que*) so // conj (*ya que*) since; ¡~! (*sí*) yes!, certainly!

puesto, a [ˈpwesto, a] pp de **poner** // a dressed // nm (*lugar, posición*) place; (*trabajo*) post, job; (*COM*) stall // conj: ~ **que** since, as // nf (*apuesta*) bet, stake; ~**a en marcha** starting; ~**a del sol** sunset.

púgil [ˈpuxil] nm boxer.

pugna [ˈpuɣna] nf battle, conflict; ~**cidad** nf pugnacity, aggressiveness; **pugnar** vi (*luchar*) to struggle, fight; (*pelear*) to fight.

pulcro, a [ˈpulkro, a] a neat, tidy; (*bello*) exquisite.

pulga [ˈpulɣa] nf flea.

pulgada [pulˈɣaða] nf inch.

pulgar [pulˈɣar] nm thumb.

pulir [puˈlir], **pulimentar** [pulimenˈtar] vt to polish; (*alisar*) to smooth; (*fig*) to polish up, touch up.

pulmón [pulˈmon] nm lung; **pulmonía** nf pneumonia.

pulpa [ˈpulpa] nf pulp; (*de fruta*) flesh, soft part.

púlpito [ˈpulpito] nm pulpit.

pulpo [ˈpulpo] nm octopus.

pulsación [pulsaˈθjon] nf beat, pulsation; (*ANAT*) throb(bing).

pulsador [pulsaˈðor] nm button, push button.

pulsar [pulˈsar] vt (*tecla*) to touch, tap, (*MUS*) to play; (*botón*) to press, push // vi to pulsate; (*latir*) to beat, throb; (*MED*): ~ **a uno** to take sb's pulse.

pulsera [pulˈsera] nf bracelet.

pulso [ˈpulso] nm (*ANAT*) pulse; (: *muñeca*) wrist; (*fuerza*) strength; (*firmeza*) steadiness, steady hand; (*tacto*) tact, good sense.

pulverizador [pulβeriθaˈðor] nm spray, spray gun; **pulverizar** vt to pulverize; (*líquido*) to spray.

pulla [ˈpuʎa] nf cutting remark; (*expresión grosera*) obscene remark.

pungir [punˈxir] vt to puncture, prick, pierce; (*fig*) to cause suffering to.

punición [puniˈθjon] nf punishment; **punitivo, a** a punitive.

punta [ˈpunta] nf point, tip; (*extremidad*) end; (*fig*) touch, trace; **horas** ~**s** peak hours, rush hours; **sacar** ~ **a** to sharpen; **estar de** ~ to be edgy.

puntada [punˈtaða] nf (*COSTURA*) stitch; (*fam*) hint; **no ha dado** ~ he hasn't done a stroke.

puntal [punˈtal] nm prop, support.

puntapié [puntaˈpje] nm kick.

puntear [punteˈar] vt (*marcar*) to tick, mark; (*coser*) to stitch (up).

puntería [punteˈria] nf (*de arma*) aim, aiming; (*destreza*) marksmanship.

puntiagudo, a [puntjaˈɣuðo, a] a sharp, pointed.

puntilla [punˈtiʎa] nf (*de pluma*) point, nib; (**andar) de** ~**s** (to walk) on tiptoe.

punto [ˈpunto] nm (*gen*) point; (*señal diminuta*) spot, dot; (*lugar*) spot, place; (*momento*) point, moment; **a** ~ ready; **estar a** ~ **de** to be on the point of or about to; **en** ~ on the dot; ~ **de arranque** starting point; ~ **muerto** dead centre; (*AUTO*) neutral (gear); ~ **y coma** semicolon; ~ **de interrogación** question mark.

puntuación [puntwaˈθjon] nf punctuation; (*puntos: en examen*) mark(s) (*pl*); (: *DEPORTE*) score.

puntual [punˈtwal] a (*a tiempo*) punctual; (*exacto*) exact, accurate; (*seguro*) reliable; ~**idad** nf punctuality; exactness, accuracy; reliability; ~**izar** vt to fix, specify; (*en la memoria*) to fix in one's mind/memory.

punzante [punˈθante] a (*dolor*) shooting, sharp; (*herramienta*) sharp; **punzar** vt to prick, pierce // vi to shoot, stab.

puñado [puˈɲaðo] nm handful.

puñal [puˈɲal] nm dagger; ~**ada** nf stab; ~**ada de misericordia** coup de grâce.

puñetazo [puɲeˈtaθo] nm punch.

puño [ˈpuɲo] nm (*ANAT*) fist; (*cantidad*) fistful, handful; (*COSTURA*) cuff; (*de herramienta*) handle.

pupila [puˈpila] nf pupil.

pupitre [puˈpitre] nm desk.

puré [puˈre] nm puree; (*sopa*) (thick) soup; ~ **de patatas** mashed potatoes.

pureza [puˈreθa] nf purity.

purga [ˈpurɣa] nf purge; **purgante** a, nm purgative; **purgar** vt to purge.

purgatorio [purɣaˈtorjo] nm purgatory.

purificar [purifiˈkar] vt to purify; (*refinar*) to refine.

puritano, a [puriˈtano, a] a (*actitud*) puritanical; (*iglesia, tradición*) puritan // nm/f puritan.

puro, a [ˈpuro, a] a pure; (*cielo*) clear; (*verdad*) simple, plain // ad: **de** ~ **cansado** out of sheer tiredness // nm cigar.

púrpura [ˈpurpura] nf purple; **purpúreo, a** a a purple.

puse, pusiera etc vb ver **poner.**

pústula [ˈpustula] nf pimple, sore.

puta [ˈputa] nf whore, prostitute.

putrefacción [putrefakˈθjon] nf rotting, putrefaction.

pútrido, a [ˈputriðo, a] a rotten.

Q

q.e.p.d. *abr de* **que en paz descanse.**
q.e.s.m. *abr de* **que estrecha su mano.**
que [ke] *pron* (*sujeto*) who, that; (: *cosa*) which, that; (*complemento*) whom, that; (: *cosa*) which, that // *conj* that; **el momento en** ~ **llegó** the moment he arrived; **lo** ~ **digo** what I say; **dar** ~ **hablar** to give cause to talk, cause talk; **le ruego** ~ **se calle** I'm asking you to keep quiet; **te digo** ~ **sí** I'm telling you, I assure you; **yo** ~ **tú** if I were you.
qué [ke] *a* what?, which? // *pron* what?; ¡~ **divertido!** how funny!; ¿~ **edad tiene** Ud? how old are you?; ¿**de** ~ **me hablas?** what are you saying to me?; ¿~ **tal?** how are you?, how are things?; ¿~ **hay (de nuevo)?** what's new?
quebrada [ke'ßraða] *nf ver* **quebrado.**
quebradizo, a [keßra'ðiθo, a] *a* fragile; (*persona*) frail.
quebrado, a [ke'ßraðo, a] *a* (*roto*) broken; (*pálido*) pale; (*COM*) bankrupt // *nm/f* bankrupt // *nf* ravine.
quebradura [keßra'ðura] *nf* (*fisura*) fissure; (*GEO*) gorge; (*MED*) rupture.
quebrantadura [keßranta'ðura] *nf*, **quebrantamiento** [keßranta'mjento] *nm* (*acto*) breaking; (*estado*) exhaustion.
quebrantar [keßran'tar] *vt* (*romper*) to break; (*infringir*) to violate, transgress; ~**se** *vr* (*persona*) to fail in health; (*deshacerse*) to break.
quebranto [ke'ßranto] *nm* damage, harm; (*decaimiento*) exhaustion; (*debilidad*) weakness; (*dolor*) grief, pain.
quebrar [ke'ßrar] *vt* to break, smash; (*interrumpir*) to interrupt // *vi* to go bankrupt; ~**se** *vr* to break, get broken; (*MED*) to be ruptured.
quedar [ke'ðar] *vi* (*permanecer*) to stay; (*seguir siendo*) to remain; (*encontrarse*) to be; (*restar*) to remain, be left; ~**se** *vr* to remain, stay (behind); ~**se con** to keep; ~ **en** (*acordar*) to agree on/to; (*acabar siendo*) to end up as; ~ **por hacer** to be still to be done; ~ **ciego/mudo** to be left blind/dumb; **no te queda bien ese vestido** that dress doesn't suit you; **quedamos a las seis** we agreed to meet at six.
quedo, a ['keðo, a] *a* still // *ad* softly, gently.
quehacer [kea'θer] *nm* task, job; (*doméstico*) chore.
queja ['kexa] *nf* complaint; **quejarse** *vr* (*enfermo*) to moan, groan; (*protestar*) to complain; **quejido** *nm* moan; **quejoso, a** *a* complaining.
quemado, a [ke'maðo, a] *a* burnt.
quemadura [kema'ðura] *nf* burn, scald.
quemar [ke'mar] *vt* to burn; (*fig*) to burn up, squander // *vi* to be burning hot; ~**se** *vr* to burn (up); (*del sol*) to get sunburnt.

quemarropa [kema'rropa]: **a** ~ *ad* point-blank.
quemazón [kema'θon] *nf* burn; (*calor*) intense heat; (*sensación*) itch.
quepo *etc vb ver* **caber.**
querella [ke'reʎa] *nf* (*JUR*) charge; (*disputa*) dispute.
querer [ke'rer] *vt* (*desear*) to want, wish; (*amar a*) to love; ~ **hacer algo** to want to do sth; **querido, a** *a* dear // *nm/f* darling // *nf* mistress.
quesería [kese'ria] *nf* dairy, cheese factory.
queso ['keso] *nm* cheese; ~ **crema** cream cheese; ~ **helado** ice-cream brick.
quicio ['kiθjo] *nm* hinge; **sacar a uno de** ~ to get on sb's nerves.
quiebra ['kjeßra] *nf* break, split; (*COM*) bankruptcy; (*ECON*) slump.
quiebro ['kjeßro] *nm* (*del cuerpo*) swerve.
quien [kjen] *pron* who; **hay** ~ **piensa que** there are those who think that; **no hay** ~ **lo haga** no-one will do it.
quién [kjen] *pron* who, whom; ¿~ **es?** who's there?
quienquiera [kjen'kjera] (*pl* **quienesquiera**) *pron* whoever.
quiero *etc vb ver* **querer.**
quieto, a ['kjeto, a] *a* still; (*carácter*) placid; **quietud** *nf* stillness.
quijada [ki'xaða] *nf* jaw, jawbone.
quilate [ki'late] *nm* carat.
quimera [ki'mera] *nf* chimera; **quimérico, a** *a* fantastic.
químico, a ['kimiko, a] *a* chemical // *nm/f* chemist // *nf* chemistry.
quincalla [kin'kaʎa] *nf* hardware, ironmongery.
quince ['kinθe] *num* fifteen; ~**na** *nf* fortnight; (*pago*) fortnightly pay; ~**nal** *a* fortnightly.
quiniela [ki'njela] *nf* pools coupon; ~**s** *nfpl* football pools.
quinientos [ki'njentos] *num* five hundred.
quinina [ki'nina] *nf* quinine.
quinqui ['kinki] *nm* gangster.
quinto, a ['kinto, a] *a* fifth // *nf* country house; (*MIL*) call-up, draft.
quiosco ['kjosko] *nm* (*de música*) bandstand; (*de periódicos*) news stand.
quirúrgico, a [ki'rurxiko, a] *a* surgical.
quise, quisiera *etc vb ver* **querer.**
quisquilloso, a [kiski'ʎoso, a] *a* touchy; (*fam*) pernickety.
quiste ['kiste] *nm* cyst.
quita ['kita] *nf* remission of debt; **de** ~ **y pon** detachable.
quitaesmalte [kitaes'malte] *nm* nail-polish remover.
quitamanchas [kita'mantʃas] *nm inv* stain remover.
quitar [ki'tar] *vt* to remove, take away; (*ropa*) to take off; (*dolor*) to kill, stop; **¡quita de ahí!** get away!; ~**se** *vr* to

withdraw; **se quitó el sombrero** he took off his hat.
quitasol [kita'sol] *nm* sunshade.
quite ['kite] *nm* (*esgrima*) parry; (*evasión*) dodge.
quizá(s) [ki'θa(s)] *ad* perhaps, maybe.

R

rábano ['raβano] *nm* radish; **me importa un** ~ I don't give a damn.
rabia ['raβja] *nf* (*MED*) rabies; (*fig*) fury, rage; **rabiar** *vi* to have rabies; to rage, be furious; **rabiar por algo** to be dying for *or* long for sth.
rabieta [ra'βjeta] *nf* tantrum, fit of temper.
rabino [ra'βino] *nm* rabbi.
rabioso, a [ra'βjoso, a] *a* rabid; (*fig*) furious.
rabo ['raβo] *nm* tail.
racial [ra'θjal] *a* racial, race *cpd.*
racimo [ra'θimo] *nm* bunch.
raciocinio [raθjo'θinjo] *nm* reason.
ración [ra'θjon] *nf* portion; **raciones** *nfpl* rations.
racional [raθjo'nal] *a* (*razonable*) reasonable; (*lógico*) rational; ~**izar** *vt* to rationalize.
racionar [raθjo'nar] *vt* to ration (out).
racismo [ra'θismo] *nm* racialism, racism; **racista** *a, nm/f* racist.
racha ['ratʃa] *nf* gust of wind.
radar [ra'ðar] *nm* radar.
radiador [raðja'ðor] *nm* radiator.
radiante [ra'ðjante] *a* radiant.
radical [raði'kal] *a, nm/f* radical.
radicar [raði'kar] *vi* to take root; ~ **en** to lie *or* consist in; ~**se** *vr* to establish o.s., put down (one's) roots.
radio ['raðjo] *nf* radio; (*aparato*) radio (set) // *nm* (*MAT*) radius; (*QUÍMICA*) radium; ~**activo, a** *a* radioactive; ~**difusión** *nf* broadcasting; ~**emisora** *nf* transmitter, radio station; ~**escucha** *nm/f* listener; ~**grafía** *nf* X-ray; ~**grafiar** *vt* to X-ray; ~**terapia** *nf* radiotherapy; **radioyente** *nm/f* listener.
raer [ra'er] *vt* to scrape (off).
ráfaga ['rafaxa] *nf* gust; (*de luz*) flash; (*de tiros*) burst.
raído, a [ra'iðo, a] *a* (*ropa*) threadbare; (*persona*) shameless.
raigambre [rai'xambre] *nf* (*BOT*) roots *pl*; (*fig*) tradition.
raíz [ra'iθ] (*pl* **raíces**) *nf* root; ~ **cuadrada** square root; **a** ~ **de** as a result of.
raja ['raxa] *nf* (*de melón etc*) slice; (*grieta*) crack; **rajar** *vt* to split; (*fam*) to slash; (*fruta etc*) to slice; **rajarse** *vr* to split, crack; (*AM*) to quit.
rajatabla [raxa'taβla]: **a** ~ *ad* (*estrictamente*) strictly, to the letter; (*cueste lo que cueste*) at all costs.
ralo, a ['ralo, a] *a* thin, sparse.

rallado, a [ra'ʎaðo, a] *a* grated; **rallador** *nm* grater; **rallar** *vt* to grate.
rama ['rama] *nf* branch; ~**da** *nf*, ~**je** *nm* branches *pl*, foliage; **ramal** *nm* (*de cuerda*) strand; (*FERRO*) branch line; (*AUTO*) branch (road).
rambla ['rambla] *nf* (*de agua*) stream; (*avenida*) avenue.
ramera [ra'mera] *nf* whore.
ramificación [ramifika'θjon] *nf* ramification; **ramificarse** *vr* to branch out.
ramillete [rami'ʎete] *nm* bouquet; (*fig*) select group.
ramo ['ramo] *nm* branch; (*COM*) department, section.
rampa ['rampa] *nf* (*MED*) cramp; (*plano*) ramp.
rampión, ona [ram'plon, ona] *a* uncouth, coarse.
rana ['rana] *nf* frog; ~ **toro** bullfrog; **salto de** ~ leapfrog.
rancio, a ['ranθjo, a] *a* rancid; (*vino*) aged, mellow; (*fig*) ancient.
rancho ['rantʃo] *nm* grub (*fam*); (*AM*) farm.
rango ['rango] *nm* rank, standing.
ranura [ra'nura] *nf* groove; (*de teléfono*) slot.
rapacidad [rapaθi'ðað] *nf* rapacity.
rapar [ra'par] *vt* to shave; (*los cabellos*) to crop; (*fam*) to pinch, nick (*fam*).
rapaz [ra'paθ] *a* (*ladrón*) thieving; (*ZOOL*) predatory.
rapaz, a [ra'paθ, a] *nm/f* young boy/girl.
rape ['rape] *nm* quick shave; **al** ~ cropped.
rapé [ra'pe] *nm* snuff.
rapidez [rapi'ðeθ] *nf* speed, rapidity; **rápido, a** *a* rapid, fast, quick // *ad* quickly // *nm* (*tren*) express; **rápidos** *nmpl* rapids.
rapiña [ra'piɲa] *nm* robbery; **ave de** ~ bird of prey.
raptar [rap'tar] *vt* to kidnap; **rapto** *nm* kidnapping; (*impulso*) sudden impulse; (*éxtasis*) ecstasy, rapture.
raqueta [ra'keta] *nf* racquet.
raquítico, a [ra'kitiko, a] *a* stunted; (*fig*) poor, inadequate; **raquitismo** *nm* rickets *sg*.
rareza [ra'reθa] *nf* rarity; (*fig*) eccentricity.
raro, a ['raro, a] *a* (*poco común*) rare; (*extraño*) odd, strange; (*excepcional*) remarkable.
ras [ras] *nm*: **a** ~ **de** level with; **a** ~ **de tierra** at ground level.
rasar [ra'sar] *vt* (*igualar*) to level; (*frotar*) to graze.
rascacielos [raska'θjelos] *nm inv* skyscraper.
rascar [ras'kar] *vt* (*con las uñas*) to scratch; (*raspar*) to scrape; ~**se** *vr* to scratch (o.s.).
rasgadura [rasxa'ðura] *nf* tear, rip; **rasgar** *vt* to tear, rip (up).
rasgo ['rasxo] *nm* stroke; ~**s** *nmpl*

features, characteristics; **a grandes** ~s in outline, broadly.
rasguñar [rasɣu'ɲar] *vt* to scratch; **rasguño** *nm* scratch.
raso, a ['raso, a] *a* (*liso*) flat, level; (*a baja altura*) very low // *nm* satin; **cielo** ~ clear sky; **soldado** ~ private.
raspador [raspa'ðor] *nm* scraper.
raspadura [raspa'ðura] *nf* scrape; (*marca*) scratch; ~s *nfpl* scrapings; **raspar** *vt* to scrape; (*arañar*) to scratch; (*limar*) to file.
rastra ['rastra] *nf* (*huella*) track; (*AGR*) rake; **a** ~**s** by dragging; (*fig*) unwillingly; **pescar a la** ~ to trawl.
rastreador [rastrea'ðor] *nm* tracker; (*NAUT*) trawler; ~ **de minas** minesweeper; **rastrear** *vt* to track; (*laguna, río*) to dredge, drag.
rastrero, a [ras'trero, a] *a* creeping; (*vestido*) trailing; (*fig*) despicable, mean.
rastrillar [rastri'ʎar] *vt* to rake; **rastrillo** *nm* rake.
rastro ['rastro] *nm* (*AGR*) rake; (*pista*) track, trail; (*curso*) course; (*vestigio*) trace; (*matadero*) slaughterhouse; **el R**~ the Madrid fleamarket.
rastrojo [ras'troxo] *nm* stubble.
rasurador [rasura'ðor] *nm*, **rasuradora** [rasura'ðora] *nf* electric shaver; **rasurarse** *vr* to shave.
rata ['rata] *nf* rat.
ratear [rate'ar] *vt* (*robar*) to steal; (*distribuir*) to share out.
ratería [rate'ria] *nf* petty theft.
ratero, a [ra'tero, a] *a* light-fingered // *nm/f* pickpocket.
ratificar [ratifi'kar] *vt* to ratify.
rato ['rato] *nm* while, short time; **a** ~**s** at times; **hay para** ~ there's still a long way to go; **pasar el** ~ to kill time; **pasar un buen/mal** ~ to have a good/rough time.
ratón [ra'ton] *nm* mouse; **ratonera** *nf* mousetrap.
raudal [rau'ðal] *nm* torrent; **a** ~**es** in abundance.
raya ['raja] *nf* line; (*marca*) scratch; (*en tela*) stripe; (*de pelo*) parting; (*límite*) boundary; **tener a** ~ to keep in check; **rayar** *vt* to line; to scratch; (*talón*) to cross; (*subrayar*) to underline // *vi*: **rayar en o con** to border on.
rayo ['rajo] *nm* (*del sol*) ray, beam; (*de luz*) shaft; (*en una tormenta*) lightning, flash of lightning; ~**s X** X-rays.
rayón [ra'jon] *nm* rayon.
raza ['raθa] *nf* race; ~ **humana** human race.
razón [ra'θon] *nf* (*gen*) reason; (*justicia*) right, justice; (*razonamiento*) reasoning; (*motivo*) course; (*MAT*) ratio; **a** ~ **de 10 cada día** at the rate of 10 a day; '~: ...' "inquiries to ..."; **en** ~ **de** with regard to; **dar** ~ **a uno** to agree that sb is right; **tener** ~ to be right; ~ **directa/inversa** direct/inverse proportion; ~ **de ser**

raison d'être; **razonable** *a* reasonable; (*justo, moderado*) fair; **razonamiento** *nm* (*juicio*) judgement; (*argumento*) reasoning; **razonar** *vt* to reason, argue; (*cuenta*) to itemize // *vi* to reason, argue.
reabastecer [reaβaste'θer] *vt* to refuel.
reabrir [rea'βrir] *vt* to reopen.
reacción [reak'θjon] *nf* reaction; **avión a** ~ jet plane; ~ **en cadena** chain reaction; **reaccionar** *vi* to react; **reaccionario, a** *a* reactionary.
reacio, a [re'aθjo, a] *a* stubborn.
reactor [reak'tor] *nm* reactor.
readaptación [reaðapta'θjon] *nf*: ~ **profesional** industrial retraining.
reafirmar [reafir'mar] *vt* to reaffirm.
reagrupar [reaɣru'par] *vt* to regroup.
reajuste [rea'xuste] *nm* readjustment.
real [re'al] *a* real; (*del rey, fig*) royal.
realce [re'alθe] *nm* (*TEC*) embossing; (*lustre, fig*) splendour; (*ARTE*) highlight; **poner de** ~ to emphasize.
realidad [reali'ðað] *nf* reality, fact; (*verdad*) truth.
realista [rea'lista] *nm/f* realist.
realización [realiθa'θjon] *nf* fulfilment; (*COM*) sale, selling-up.
realizador, a [realiθa'ðor, a] *nm/f* (*TV etc*) producer.
realizar [reali'θar] *vt* (*objetivo*) to achieve; (*plan*) to carry out; (*viaje*) to make, undertake; (*COM*) to sell up; ~**se** *vr* to come about, come true.
realmente [real'mente] *ad* really, actually.
realzar [real'θar] *vt* (*TEC*) to raise; (*embellecer*) to enhance; (*acentuar*) to highlight.
reanimar [reani'mar] *vt* to revive; (*alentar*) to encourage; ~**se** *vr* to revive.
reanudar [reanu'ðar] *vt* (*renovar*) to renew; (*retomar*) to resume.
reaparición [reapari'θjon] *nf* reappearance.
rearme [re'arme] *nm* rearmament.
reata [re'ata] *nf* rope, rein; **de** ~ in single file.
rebaja [re'βaxa] *nf* (*COM*) reduction; (*menoscabo*) lessening; **rebajar** *vt* (*bajar*) to lower; (*reducir*) to reduce; (*disminuir*) to lessen; (*humillar*) to humble.
rebanada [reβa'naða] *nf* slice.
rebaño [re'βaɲo] *nm* herd; (*de ovejas*) flock.
rebasar [reβa'sar] *vt* (*también* ~ **de**) to exceed; (*AUTO*) to overtake.
rebatir [reβa'tir] *vt* to refute; (*descontar*) to deduct.
rebato [re'βato] *nm* alarm; (*ataque*) surprise attack.
rebelarse [reβe'larse] *vr* to rebel, revolt.
rebelde [re'βelde] *a* rebellious; (*indócil*) unruly // *nm/f* rebel; **rebeldía** *nf* rebelliousness; (*desobediencia*) disobedience; **rebelión** *nf* rebellion.
reblandecer [reβlande'θer] *vt* to soften.

rebosante [reβo'sante] *a* overflowing; **rebosar** *vi* to overflow; (*abundar*) to abound, be plentiful.

rebotar [reβo'tar] *vt* to bounce; (*rechazar*) to repel; ~**se** *vr* (*pelota*) to rebound; (*bala*) to ricochet; **rebote** *nm* rebound; **de rebote** on the rebound.

rebozar [reβo'θar] *vt* to wrap up; (*CULIN*) to fry in batter; **rebozo** *nm* muffler; (*AM*) shawl; **decir algo sin rebozo** to call a spade a spade.

rebuscado, a [reβus'kaðo, a] *a* affected.

rebuscar [reβus'kar] *vt* to search carefully; (*objeto*) to search for carefully.

rebuznar [reβuθ'nar] *vi* to bray.

recabar [reka'βar] *vt* to manage to get.

recado [re'kaðo] *nm* errand; (*mensaje*) message; **tomar un** ~ (*TELEC*) to take a message.

recaer [reka'er] *vi* to relapse; ~ **en** to fall to *or* on; **recaída** *nf* relapse.

recalcar [rekal'kar] *vt* (*fig*) to stress, emphasize.

recalcitrante [rekalθi'trante] *a* recalcitrant.

recalcitrar [rekalθi'trar] *vi* (*echarse atrás*) to step back; (*resistir*) to resist, be stubborn.

recalentar [rekalen'tar] *vt* (*volver a calentar*) to reheat; (*demasiado*) to overheat.

recambio [re'kambjo] *nm* spare; (*de pluma*) refill.

recapacitar [rekapaθi'tar] *vt* to think over // *vi* to reflect.

recargado, a [rekar'xaðo, a] *a* overloaded; **recargar** *vt* to overload; (*batería*) to recharge; **recargar los precios** to increase prices; **recargo** *nm* surcharge; (*aumento*) increase.

recatado, a [reka'taðo, a] *a* modest, demure; (*prudente*) cautious.

recatar [reka'tar] *vt* to hide; ~**se** *vr* to hide o.s.

recato [re'kato] *nm* modesty, demureness; (*cautela*) caution.

recaudación [rekauða'θjon] *nf* collection; (*suma*) takings *pl*; (*en deporte*) gate; **recaudador** *nm* tax collector.

recelar [reθe'lar] *vt*: ~ **que** (*sospechar*) to suspect that; (*temer*) to fear that // *vi*, ~**se** *vr*: ~(**se**) **de** to distrust; **recelo** *nm* distrust, suspicion; **receloso, a** *a* distrustful, suspicious.

recepción [reθep'θjon] *nf* reception; **recepcionista** *nm/f* receptionist.

receptáculo [reθep'takulo] *nm* receptacle.

receptivo, a [reθep'tiβo, a] *a* receptive.

receptor, a [reθep'tor, a] *nm/f* recipient // *nm* receiver.

recesión [reθe'sjon] *nf* recession.

receta [re'θeta] *nf* (*CULIN*) recipe; (*MED*) prescription.

recibidor, a [reθiβi'ðor, a] *nm/f* receiver, recipient.

recibimiento [reθiβi'mjento] *nm*

(*recepción*) reception; (*acogida*) welcome.

recibir [reθi'βir] *vt* (*gen*) to receive; (*dar la bienvenida*) to welcome // *vi* to entertain; ~**se** *vr*: ~**se de** to qualify as; **recibo** *nm* receipt.

reciedumbre [reθje'ðumbre] *nf* strength; (*vigor*) vigour.

recién [re'θjen] *ad* recently, newly; **el** ~ **llegado** the newcomer; **el** ~ **nacido** the newborn child.

reciente [re'θjente] *a* recent; (*fresco*) fresh.

recinto [re'θinto] *nm* (*gen*) enclosure; (*área*) area, place.

recio, a ['reθjo, a] *a* strong, tough; (*voz*) loud; (*tiempo*) harsh // *ad* hard; loud(ly).

recipiente [reθi'pjente] *nm* receptacle.

reciprocidad [reθiproθi'ðað] *nf* reciprocity; **recíproco, a** *a* reciprocal.

recital [reθi'tal] *nm* (*MUS*) recital; (*LITERATURA*) reading; **recitar** *vt* to recite.

reclamación [reklama'θjon] *nf* claim, demand; (*queja*) complaint.

reclamar [rekla'mar] *vt* to claim, demand // *vi*: ~ **contra** to complain about; ~ **en justicia** to take to court; **reclamo** *nm* (*anuncio*) advertisement; (*tentación*) attraction.

reclinar [rekli'nar] *vt* to recline, lean; ~**se** *vr* to lean back.

recluir [reklu'ir] *vt* to intern, confine.

reclusión [reklu'sjon] *nf* (*prisión*) prison; (*refugio*) seclusion; ~ **perpetua** life imprisonment.

recluta [re'kluta] *nm/f* recruit // *nf* recruitment.

reclutamiento [rekluta'mjento] *nm* recruitment.

recobrar [reko'βrar] *vt* (*recuperar*) to recover; (*rescatar*) to get back; ~**se** *vr* to recover.

recodo [re'koðo] *nm* (*de río, camino*) bend.

recogedor, a [rekoxe'ðor, a] *nm/f* picker, harvester.

recoger [reko'xer] *vt* (*gen*) to collect; (*AGR*) to harvest; (*levantar*) to pick up; (*juntar*) to gather; (*pasar a buscar*) to come for, fetch; (*dar asilo*) to give shelter to; (*faldas*) to gather up; (*pelo*) to put up; ~**se** *vr* (*retirarse*) to retire; **recogido, a** *a* (*lugar*) quiet, secluded; (*persona*) modest, retiring; (*pequeño*) small // *nf* (*del correo*) collection; (*AGR*) harvest.

recolección [rekolek'θjon] *nf* (*de las mieses*) harvesting; (*colecta*) collection.

recomendación [rekomenda'θjon] *nf* (*sugerencia*) suggestion, recommendation; (*elogio*) praise; **recomendar** *vt* to suggest, recommend; to praise; (*confiar*) to entrust.

recompensa [rekom'pensa] *nf* reward, recompense; **recompensar** *vt* to reward, recompense; (*por pérdidas*) to compensate.

recomponer [rekompo'ner] *vt* to mend; ~**se** *vr* (*fam*) to doll up.

reconciliación [rekonθilja'θjon] *nf* reconciliation; **reconciliar** *vt* to reconcile; **reconciliarse** *vr* to become reconciled.

reconfortar [rekonfor'tar] *vt* to comfort; ~se *vr*: ~se con to fortify o.s. with.

reconocer [rekono'θer] *vt* to recognize; (*registrar*) to search; (*MED*) to examine; **reconocido, a** *a* recognized; (*agradecido*) grateful; **reconocimiento** *nm* recognition; search; examination; gratitude; (*confesión*) admission.

reconquista [rekon'kista] *nf* reconquest.

reconstituyente [rekonstitu'jente] *nm* tonic.

reconstruir [rekonstru'ir] *vt* to reconstruct.

recopilación [rekopila'θjon] *nf* (*sumario*) summary; (*compendio*) compilation; **recopilar** *vt* to compile.

récord ['rekorð] *a inv, nm* record.

recordar [rekor'ðar] *vt* (*acordarse de*) to remember; (*acordar a otro*) to remind // *vi* to remember.

recorrer [reko'rrer] *vt* (*país*) to cross, travel through; (*distancia*) to cover; (*repasar*) to go over, look over; **recorrido** *nm* run, journey; **tren de largo recorrido** main-line train.

recortado, a [rekor'taðo, a] *a* uneven, irregular.

recortar [rekor'tar] *vt* to cut out; **recorte** *nm* (*acción*) cutting; (*de prensa*) cutting, clipping; (*de telas, chapas*) trimming.

recostado, a [rekos'taðo, a] *a* leaning; **estar** ~ to be lying down.

recostar [rekos'tar] *vt* to lean; ~se *vr* to lie down.

recoveco [reko'ßeko] *nm* bend; (*en casa*) cubby hole.

recreación [rekrea'θjon] *nf* recreation; (*TEATRO, CINE*) interval, intermission.

recrear [rekre'ar] *vt* (*entretener*) to entertain; (*volver a crear*) to recreate; **recreativo, a** *a* recreational; **recreo** *nm* recreation; (*ESCOL*) break, playtime.

recriminar [rekrimi'nar] *vt* to reproach // *vi* to recriminate; ~se *vr* to reproach each other.

recrudecer [rekruðe'θer] *vt, vi,* ~se *vr* to worsen.

recrudecimiento [rekruðeθi'mjento] *nm,* **recrudescencia** [rekruðes'ßenθja] *nf* upsurge.

recta ['rekta] *nf ver* **recto.**

rectángulo, a [rek'tangulo, a] *a* rectangular // *nm* rectangle.

rectificar [rektifi'kar] *vt* to rectify; (*volverse recto*) to straighten // *vi* to correct o.s.

rectitud [rekti'tuð] *nf* (*exactitud*) correctness; (*fig*) rectitude.

recto, a ['rekto, a] *a* straight; (*persona*) honest, upright // *nm* rectum // *nf* straight line.

rector, a [rek'tor, a] *a* governing.

recua ['rekwa] *nf* mule train.

recuento [re'kwento] *nm* inventory; **hacer el** ~ **de** to count *or* reckon up.

recuerdo [re'kwerðo] *nm* souvenir; ~s *nmpl* memories; ¡~s **a tu madre!** give my regards to your mother.

recular [reku'lar] *vi* to fall back; (*fig*) to back down.

recuperable [rekupe'raßle] *a* recoverable; **recuperación** *nf* recovery.

recuperar [rekupe'rar] *vt* to recover; (*tiempo*) to make up; ~se *vr* to recuperate.

recurrir [reku'rrir] *vi* (*JUR*) to appeal; ~ **a** to resort to; (*persona*) to turn to; **recurso** *nm* resort; (*medios*) means *pl,* resources *pl*; (*JUR*) appeal.

recusar [reku'sar] *vt* to reject, refuse.

rechazar [retʃa'θar] *vt* to repel, drive back; (*idea*) to reject; (*oferta*) to turn down.

rechazo [re'tʃaθo] *nm* (*retroceso*) recoil; (*rebote*) rebound; (*negación*) rebuff.

rechifla [re'tʃifla] *nf* hissing, booing; (*fig*) derision; **rechiflar** *vt* to hiss, boo; **rechiflarse** *vr* to take things as a joke.

rechinar [retʃi'nar] *vi* to creak; (*gruñir*) to grumble; (*dientes*) to grind.

rechoncho, a [re'tʃontʃo, a] *a* (*fam*) chubby, thickset.

red [reð] *nf* net, mesh; (*de ferrocarriles etc*) network; (*trampa*) trap.

redacción [reðak'θjon] *nf* editing; (*oficina*) newspaper office; (*personal*) editorial staff.

redactar [reðak'tar] *vt* to draw up, draft; (*periódico*) to edit.

redada [re'ðaða] *nf*: ~ **policíaca** police raid, round-up.

rededor [reðe'ðor] *nm*: **al** *o* **en** ~ around, round about.

redención [reðen'θjon] *nf* redemption; **redentor, a** *a* redeeming.

redescubrir [reðesku'ßrir] *vt* to rediscover.

redicho, a [re'ðitʃo, a] *a* affected, stilted.

redil [re'ðil] *nm* sheepfold.

redimir [reði'mir] *vt* to redeem.

rédito ['reðito] *nm* interest, yield.

redoblar [reðo'ßlar] *vt* to redouble; (*plegar*) to fold back // *vi* (*tambor*) to play a roll on the drums.

redomado, a [reðo'maðo, a] *a* sly, crafty.

redonda [re'ðonda] *nf ver* **redondo.**

redondear [reðonde'ar] *vt* to round, round off; ~se *vr* to become wealthy.

redondel [reðon'del] *nm* (*círculo*) circle; (*TAUR*) bullring, arena.

redondo, a [re'ðondo, a] *a* (*circular*) round; (*directo*) straight; (*completo*) complete // *nf*: **a la** ~a around, round about.

reducción [reðuk'θjon] *nf* reduction; (*MED*) setting.

reducido, a [reðu'θiðo, a] *a* reduced; (*limitado*) limited; (*pequeño*) small; **reducir** *vt* to reduce; to limit; (*MED*) to set a bone; **reducirse** *vr* to diminish.

redundancia [reðun'danθja] *nf* redundancy.

reembolsar [reembol'sar] *vt* to reimburse; (*depósito*) to refund; **reembolso** *nm* reimbursement; refund.

reemplazar [reempla'θar] *vt* to replace; **reemplazo** *nm* replacement; **de reemplazo** (*MIL*) reserve.

refacción [refak'θjon] *nf* (*AM*) repair(s) (*pl*).

refajo [re'faxo] *nm* (*enagua*) flannel underskir'; (*falda*) short skirt.

referenc.a [refe'renθja] *nf* reference; (*informe*) ːeport; **con ~ a** with reference to.

referente [refe'rente] *a*: ~ **a** concerning, relating to.

referir [refe'rir] *vt* (*contar*) to tell, recount; (*relacionar*) to refer, relate; **~se** *vr*: **~se a** to refer to.

refilón [refi'lon]: **de ~** *ad* obliquely, aslant.

refinado, a [refi'naðo, a] *a* refined; **refinamiento** *nm* refinement; **refinar** *vt* to refine; (*fig*) to perfect, polish.

reflejar [refle'xar] *vt* (*gen*) to reflect; **reflejo, a** *a* reflected; (*movimiento*) reflex // *nm* reflection; (*ANAT*) reflex.

reflexión [reflek'sjon] *nf* reflection; **reflexionar** *vt* to reflect on // *vi* to reflect; (*detenerse*) to pause (to think).

reflexivo, a [reflek'siβo, a] *a* thoughtful; (*LING, fig*) reflexive.

reflujo [re'fluxo] *nm* ebb.

refocilar [refoθi'lar] *vt* to cheer up.

reforma [re'forma] *nf* reform; (*ARQ etc*) repair; **~ agraria** agrarian reform.

reformar [refor'mar] *vt* (*modificar*) to change, alter; (*formar de nuevo*) to reform; (*ARQ*) to repair; **~se** *vr* to mend one's ways.

reformatorio [reforma'torjo] *nm* reformatory.

reforzar [refor'θar] *vt* (*gen*) to strengthen; (*ARQ*) to reinforce; (*fig*) to encourage.

refractario, a [refrak'tarjo, a] *a* stubborn; (*TEC*) heat-resistant.

refrán [re'fran] *nm* proverb, saying.

refregar [refre'var] *vt* to scrub.

refrenar [refre'nar] *vt* to check, restrain.

refrendar [refren'dar] *vt* (*firma*) to endorse, countersign; (*pasaporte*) to stamp; (*ley*) to approve.

refrescar [refres'kar] *vt* (*gen*) to refresh // *vi* to cool down; **~se** *vr* to get cooler; (*tomar aire fresco*) to go out for a breath of fresh air.

refresco [re'fresko] *nm* soft drink, cool drink; "**~s**" "refreshments".

refriega [re'frjeva] *nf* scuffle, brawl.

refrigeración [refrixera'θjon] *nf* refrigeration; (*de casa*) air-conditioning; **refrigerador** *nm* refrigerator; **refrigerar** *vt* to refrigerate; to air-condition.

refuerzo [re'fwerθo] *nm* reinforcement; (*TEC*) support.

refugiado, a [refu'xjaðo, a] *nm/f* refugee; **refugiarse** *vr* to take refuge, shelter; **refugio** *nm* refuge; (*protección*) shelter.

refulgencia [reful'xenθja] *nf* brilliance; **refulgir** *vi* to shine, be dazzling.

refundición [refundi'θjon] *nf* recasting, revision; **refundir** *vt* to recast.

refunfuñar [refunfu'nar] *vi* to grunt, growl; (*quejarse*) to grumble.

refutación [refuta'θjon] *nf* refutation; **refutar** *vt* to refute.

regadera [reva'ðera] *nf* watering can.

regadío [reva'ðio] *nm* irrigated land.

regalado, a [reva'laðo, a] *a* comfortable, luxurious; (*gratis*) free, for nothing; (*pey*) soft.

regalar [reva'lar] *vt* (*dar*) to give, present; (*entregar*) to give away; (*mimar*) to pamper, make a fuss of.

regalía [reva'lia] *nf* privilege, prerogative; (*COM*) bonus; (*de autor*) royalty.

regaliz [reva'liθ] *nm*, **regaliza** [reva'liθa] *nf* liquorice.

regalo [re'valo] *nm* (*obsequio*) gift, present; (*gusto*) pleasure; (*comodidad*) comfort.

regalón, ona [reva'lon, ona] *a* spoiled, pampered.

regañadientes [revana'ðjentes]: **a ~** *ad* reluctantly.

regañar [reva'nar] *vt* to scold // *vi* to grumble; **regaño** *nm* scolding, telling-off; (*queja*) grumble; **regañón, ona** *a* grumbling; (*mujer*) nagging.

regar [re'var] *vt* to water, irrigate; (*fig*) to scatter, sprinkle.

regatear [revate'ar] *vt* to bargain over; (*guardar*) to be mean with // *vi* to bargain, haggle; (*DEPORTE*) to dribble; **regateo** *nm* bargaining; dribbling; (*del cuerpo*) swerve, dodge.

regazo [re'vaθo] *nm* lap.

regeneración [rexenera'θjon] *nf* regeneration; **regenerar** *vt* to regenerate.

regentar [rexen'tar] *vt* to direct, manage; **regente** *nm* manager; (*POL*) regent.

régimen ['reximen] (*pl* **regímenes**) *nm* regime; (*MED*) diet.

regimiento [rexi'mjento] *nm* regiment; (*organización*) administration.

regio, a ['rexjo, a] *a* royal, regal; (*fig: suntuoso*) splendid.

región [re'xjon] *nf* region; **regionalista** *nm/f* regionalist.

regir [re'xir] *vt* to govern, rule; (*dirigir*) to manage, run // *vi* to apply, be in force.

registrador [rexistra'ðor] *nm* registrar, recorder.

registrar [rexis'trar] *vt* (*buscar en cajón*) to look through, search; (*inspeccionar*) to inspect; (*anotar*) to register, record; **~se** *vr* to register; (*ocurrir*) to happen.

registro [re'xistro] *nm* registration; (*MUS, libro*) register; (*inspección*) inspection,

search; ~ **civil** registry office.
regla ['reχla] *nf* (*ley*) rule, regulation; (*de medir*) ruler, rule; **la** ~ (*MED*) periods *pl*; **salir de** ~ to step out of line.
reglamentación [reχlamenta'θjon] *nf* (*acto*) regulation; (*lista*) rules *pl*; **reglamentar** *vt* to regulate; **reglamentario, a** *a* statutory; **reglamento** *nm* rules *pl*, regulations *pl*.
reglar [re'χlar] *vt* (*papel*) to rule; (*actos*) to regulate.
regocijado, a [reχoθi'χaðo, a] *a* merry; **regocijar** *vt* to cheer up, gladden; **regocijarse** *vr* to have a good time, make merry; (*alegrarse*) to rejoice; **regocijo** *nm* joy, happiness.
regodearse [reχoðe'arse] *vr* to be glad, be delighted; **regodeo** *nm* delight.
regresar [reχre'sar] *vi* to come/go back, return; **regresivo, a** *a* backward; (*fig*) regressive; **regreso** *nm* return.
reguero [re'χero] *nm* irrigation ditch.
regulador [reχula'ðor] *nm* (*gen*) regulator; (*de radio etc*) knob, control.
regular [reχu'lar] *a* (*gen*) regular; (*normal*) normal, usual; (*común*) ordinary; (*organizado*) regular, orderly; (*mediano*) average; (*fam*) not bad, so-so // *ad* so-so, alright // *vt* (*controlar*) to control, regulate; (*TEC*) to adjust; **por lo** ~ as a rule; ~**idad** *nf* regularity; ~**izar** *vt* to regularize.
regusto [re'χusto] *nm* aftertaste.
rehabilitación [reaβilita'θjon] *nf* rehabilitation; (*ARQ*) restoration; **rehabilitar** *vt* to rehabilitate; to restore; (*reintegrar*) to reinstate.
rehacer [rea'θer] *vt* (*reparar*) to mend, repair; (*volver a hacer*) to redo, repeat; ~**se** *vr* (*MED*) to recover; (*dominarse*) to pull o.s. together.
rehén [re'en] *nm* hostage.
rehilete [rei'lete] *nm* (*dardo*) dart; (*DEPORTE*) badminton, shuttlecock.
rehuir [reu'ir] *vt* to avoid, shun.
rehusar [reu'sar] *vt, vi* to refuse.
reina ['reina] *nf* queen; ~**do** *nm* reign; **reinante** *a* (*fig*) prevailing; **reinar** *vi* to reign.
reincidir [reinθi'ðir] *vi* to relapse.
reincorporarse [reinkorpo'rarse] *vr*: ~ **a** to rejoin.
reino ['reino] *nm* kingdom; **el R** ~ **Unido** the United Kingdom.
reintegrar [reinte'χrar] *vt* (*reconstituir*) to reconstruct; (*persona*) to reinstate; (*dinero*) to return, pay back; ~**se** *vr*: ~**se a** to return to.
reír [re'ir] *vi*, ~**se** *vr* to laugh; ~**se de** to laugh at.
reiterar [reite'rar] *vt* to reiterate.
reivindicación [reiβindika'θjon] *nf* (*demanda*) claim, demand; (*justificación*) vindication; **reivindicar** *vt* to claim; (*restaurar*) to restore.
reja ['rexa] *nf* (*de ventana*) grille, bars *pl*;

(*en la calle*) grating; (*del arado*) ploughshare.
rejilla [re'xiλa] *nf* (*de ventana*) grille; (*de silla*) wickerwork; (*de ventilación*) vent; (*de coche*) luggage rack.
rejoneador [rexonea'ðor] *nm* mounted bullfighter.
rejuvenecer [rexuβene'θer] *vt, vi* to rejuvenate; ~**se** *vr* to be rejuvenated.
relación [rela'θjon] *nf* relation, relationship; (*MAT*) ratio; (*informe*) report; **relaciones públicas** public relations; **con** ~ **a** *o* **en** ~ **con** in relation to; **relacionar** *vt* to relate, connect; **relacionarse** *vr* to be connected, be linked.
relajación [relaxa'θjon] *nf* relaxation; **relajado, a** *a* (*disoluto*) loose; (*cómodo*) relaxed; (*MED*) ruptured; **relajar** *vt*, **relajarse** *vr* to relax.
relamer [rela'mer] *vt* to lick (repeatedly); ~**se** *vr* to lick one's lips.
relamido, a [rela'miðo, a] *a* (*pulcro*) overdressed; (*afectado*) affected.
relámpago [re'lampaχo] *nm* flash of lightning; **visita/huelga** ~ lightning visit/strike; **relampaguear** *vi* to flash.
relatar [rela'tar] *vt* to tell, relate.
relativo, a [rela'tiβo, a] *a* relative; **en lo** ~ **a** concerning.
relato [re'lato] *nm* (*narración*) story, tale; (*informe*) report.
relegar [rele'χar] *vt* to relegate.
relevante [rele'βante] *a* eminent, outstanding.
relevar [rele'βar] *vt* (*sustituir*) to relieve; ~**se** *vr* to relay; ~ **a uno de un cargo** to relieve sb of his post.
relevo [re'leβo] *nm* relief; **carrera de** ~**s** relay race.
relieve [re'ljeβe] *nm* (*ARTE, TEC*) relief; (*fig*) prominence, importance; ~**s** *nmpl* left-overs; **bajo** ~ bas-relief.
religión [reli'xjon] *nf* religion; **religiosidad** *nf* religiosity; **religioso, a** *a* religious // *nm/f* monk/nun // *nm* cleric.
relinchar [relin'tʃar] *vi* to neigh; **relincho** *nm* neigh; (*acto*) neighing.
reliquia [re'likja] *nf* relic; ~ **de familia** family heirloom.
reloj [re'lo(x)] *nm* watch; (*de iglesia etc*) clock; ~ **de pulsera** wristwatch; ~ **despertador** alarm clock; ~**ero, a** *nm/f* watchmaker; clockmaker.
reluciente [relu'θjente] *a* brilliant, shining; **relucir** *vi* to shine; (*fig*) to excel.
relumbrante [relum'brante] *a* dazzling; **relumbrar** *vi* to dazzle, shine brilliantly.
rellano [re'λano] *nm* (*ARQ*) landing.
rellenar [reλe'nar] *vt* (*llenar*) to fill up; (*CULIN*) to stuff; (*COSTURA*) to pad; **relleno, a** *a* full up; stuffed // *nm* stuffing; (*de tapicería*) padding.
remachar [rema'tʃar] *vt* to rivet; (*fig*) to hammer home, drive home; **remache** *nm* rivet.
remanente [rema'nente] *nm* remainder;

(COM) balance; (de producto) surplus.
remanso [re'manso] nm pool; (fig) quiet place.
remar [re'mar] vi to row.
rematado, a [rema'taðo, a] a complete, utter.
rematar [rema'tar] vt to finish off; (COM) to sell off cheap // vi to end, finish off.
remate [re'mate] nm end, finish; (punta) tip; (DEPORTE) shot; (ARQ) top; (COM) auction sale; **de** o **para** ~ to crown it all.
remedar [reme'ðar] vt to imitate.
remediar [reme'ðjar] vt (gen) to remedy; (subsanar) to make good, repair; (ayudar) to help; (evitar) to avoid.
remedio [re'meðjo] nm remedy; (alivio) relief, help; (JUR) recourse, remedy; **poner** ~ **a** to correct, stop; **no tener más** ~ to have no alternative; **¡qué** ~! there's no choice; **sin** ~ hopeless, incurable.
remedo [re'meðo] nm imitation; (pey) parody.
remendar [remen'dar] vt to repair; (con parche) to patch.
remesa [re'mesa] nf remittance; (COM) shipment; **remesar** vt to remit, send.
remiendo [re'mjendo] nm (gen) mend; (con parche) patch; (cosido) darn.
remilgado, a [remil'ɣaðo, a] a prim; (afectado) affected; **remilgo** nm primness; affectation.
reminiscencia [reminis'θenθja] nf reminiscence.
remisión [remi'sjon] nf (acto) sending, shipment.
remiso, a [re'miso, a] a remiss.
remitir [remi'tir] vt to remit, send; (perdonar) to pardon; (posponer) to postpone // vi to slacken; (en carta): **remite: X** sender: X; **remitente** nm/f sender.
remo ['remo] nm (de barco) oar; (deporte) rowing.
remoción [remo'θjon] nf removal.
remojar [remo'xar] vt to steep, soak; (galleta etc) to dip.
remojo [re'moxo] nm: **dejar la ropa a** ~ to leave clothes to soak.
remolacha [remo'latʃa] nf beet, beetroot.
remolcador [remolka'ðor] nm (NAUT) tug; (AUTO) breakdown lorry.
remolino [remoli'nar] vi to whirl, eddy; **remolino** nm (gen) eddy; (de agua) whirlpool; (de viento) whirlwind; (de gente) throng.
remolque [re'molke] nm tow, towing; (cuerda) towrope; **llevar a** ~ to tow.
remontar [remon'tar] vt to mend; ~**se** vr to soar; ~**se a** (COM) to amount to; ~ **el vuelo** to soar.
rémora ['remora] nf hindrance.
remorder [remor'ðer] vt to distress, disturb; ~**se** vr to suffer remorse; ~**se la conciencia** to have a troubled conscience; **remordimiento** nm remorse.
remoto, a [re'moto, a] a remote.

remover [remo'ßer] vt to stir; (tierra) to turn over; (objetos) to move around; (quitar) to remove.
remozar [remo'θar] vt to rejuvenate; ~**se** vr to be rejuvenated, look younger.
remuneración [remunera'θjon] nf remuneration; **remunerar** vt to remunerate; (premiar) to reward.
renacer [rena'θer] vi to be reborn; (fig) to revive; **renacimiento** nm rebirth; **el Renacimiento** the Renaissance.
renal [re'nal] a renal, kidney cpd.
rencilla [ren'θiʎa] nf quarrel.
rencor [ren'kor] nm rancour, bitterness; ~**oso, a** a spiteful.
rendición [rendi'θjon] nf surrender.
rendido, a [ren'diðo, a] a (sumiso) submissive; (cansado) worn-out.
rendimiento [rendi'mjento] nm (MIL) surrender; (producción) output; (agotamiento) exhaustion; (TEC, COM) efficiency.
rendir [ren'dir] vt (vencer) to defeat; (producir) to produce; (dar beneficio) to yield; (agotar) to exhaust; (dominar) to dominate // vi to pay; ~**se** vr (someterse) to surrender; (cansarse) to wear o.s. out; ~ **homenaje** o **culto a** to pay homage to.
renegado, a [rene'ɣaðo, a] a, nm/f renegade.
renegar [rene'ɣar] vi (renunciar) to renounce; (blasfemar) to blaspheme; (fam) to curse; (quejarse) to complain.
RENFE nf abr de **Red Nacional de los Ferrocarriles Españoles.**
renglón [ren'glon] nm (línea) line; (COM) item, article; **a** ~ **seguido** immediately after.
reniego [re'njexo] nm curse, oath; (queja) grumble, complaint.
renombrado, a [renom'braðo, a] a renowned; **renombre** nm renown.
renovación [renoßa'θjon] nf (de contrato) renewal; (ARQ) renovation; **renovar** vt to renew; to renovate.
renta ['renta] nf (ingresos) income; (beneficio) profit; (alquiler) rent; ~ **vitalicia** annuity; **rentable** a profitable; **rentar** vt to produce, yield.
rentero, a [ren'tero, a] nm/f tenant farmer.
rentista [ren'tista] nm/f stockholder.
renuencia [re'nwenθja] nf reluctance; **renuente** a inv reluctant.
renuncia [re'nunθja] nf (gen) resignation.
renunciar [renun'θjar] vt to renounce // vi to resign; ~ **a hacer algo** to give up doing sth.
reñido, a [re'niðo, a] a (batalla) bitter, hard-fought; **estar** ~ **con uno** to be on bad terms with sb.
reñir [re'nir] vt (regañar) to scold // vi (estar peleado) to quarrel, fall out; (combatir) to fight.
reo ['reo] nm/f culprit, offender; ~ **de muerte** prisoner condemned to death.
reojo [re'oxo] nm: **de** ~ ad out of the corner of one's eye; (fig) askance.

reorganizar [reorɣani'θar] *vt* to reorganize.

reorientar [reorjen'tar] *vt* to reorientate; (*reajustar*) to readjust.

reparación [repara'θjon] *nf* (*acto*) mending, repairing; (*TEC*) repair; (*fig*) amends, reparation; **reparar** *vt* to repair; to make amends for; (*suerte*) to retrieve; (*observar*) to observe // *vi*: **reparar en** (*darse cuenta de*) to notice; (*poner atención en*) to pay attention to.

reparo [re'paro] *nm* (*reparación*) repair; (*advertencia*) observation; (*duda*) doubt; (*dificultad*) difficulty; (*resguardo*) defence.

reparón, ona [repa'ron, ona] *a* carping.

repartición [reparti'θjon] *nf* distribution; (*división*) division; **repartidor, a** *nm/f* distributor.

repartir [repar'tir] *vt* to distribute, share out; (*correo*) to deliver; **reparto** *nm* distribution; delivery; (*TEATRO, CINE*) cast.

repasar [repa'sar] *vt* (*sitio*) to pass by again; (*lección*) to revise; (*MECÁNICA*) to check; **repaso** *nm* revision; overhaul, checkup; (*de ropa*) mending.

repatriar [repa'trjar] *vt* to repatriate.

repecho [re'petʃo] *nm* steep incline; **a ~** uphill.

repelente [repe'lente] *a* repellent, repulsive; **repeler** *vt* to repel.

repensar [repen'sar] *vt* to reconsider.

repente [re'pente] *nm*: **de ~** suddenly; **un ~ de ira** a fit of anger.

repentino, a [repen'tino, a] *a* sudden.

repercusión [reperku'sjon] *nf* repercussion.

repercutir [reperku'tir] *vi* to rebound; (*sonido*) to echo; **~se** *vr* to reverberate; **~ en** to have repercussions on.

repertorio [reper'torjo] *nm* list; (*TEATRO*) repertoire.

repetición [repeti'θjon] *nf* repetition; **repetir** *vt* to repeat; (*plato*) to have a second helping // *vi* to repeat; **repetirse** *vr* (*volver sobre tema*) to repeat o.s.; (*sabor*) to come back.

repicar [repi'kar] *vt* (*desmenuzar*) to chop up finely; (*campanas*) to ring; **~se** *vr* to boast.

repique [re'pike] *nm* pealing, ringing; **~teo** *nm* pealing; (*de tambor*) drumming.

repisa [re'pisa] *nf* ledge, shelf; **~ de chimenea** mantelpiece.

repito *etc vb ver* **repetir**.

replegar [reple'ɣar] *vt* to fold over; **~se** *vr* to fall back, retreat.

repleto, a [re'pleto, a] *a* replete, full up.

réplica ['replika] *nf* answer; (*ARTE*) replica.

replicar [repli'kar] *vi* to answer; (*objetar*) to argue, answer back.

repliegue [re'pljeɣe] *nm* (*MIL*) withdrawal.

repoblación [repoβla'θjon] *nf* repopulation; (*de río*) restocking; **~ forestal** reafforestation; **repoblar** *vt* to repopulate; to reafforest.

repollo [re'poʎo] *nm* cabbage.

reponer [repo'ner] *vt* to replace, put back; (*TEATRO*) to revive; **~se** *vr* to recover; **~ que** to reply that.

reportaje [repor'taxe] *nm* report, article.

reposacabezas [reposaka'βeθas] *nm inv* headrest.

reposado, a [repo'saðo, a] *a* (*descansado*) restful; (*tranquilo*) calm; **reposar** *vi* to rest, repose.

reposición [reposi'θjon] *nf* replacement; (*CINE*) remake.

repositorio [reposi'torjo] *nm* repository.

reposo [re'poso] *nm* rest.

repostar [repos'tar] *vt* to replenish; (*AUTO*) to fill up (with petrol).

repostería [reposte'ria] *nf* confectioner's (shop); (*depósito*) pantry, larder; **repostero, a** *nm/f* confectioner.

reprender [repren'der] *vt* to reprimand; **reprensión** *nf* rebuke, reprimand.

represa [re'presa] *nf* dam; (*lago artificial*) lake, pool.

represalia [repre'salja] *nf* reprisal.

representación [representa'θjon] *nf* representation; (*TEATRO*) performance; **representante** *nm/f* representative; performer.

representar [represen'tar] *vt* to represent; (*TEATRO*) to play; (*edad*) to look; **~se** *vr* to imagine; **representativo, a** *a* representative.

represión [repre'sjon] *nf* repression.

reprimir [repri'mir] *vt* to repress.

reprobar [repro'βar] *vt* to censure, reprove.

réprobo, a ['reproβo, a] *nm/f* reprobate.

reprochar [repro'tʃar] *vt* to reproach; **reproche** *nm* reproach.

reproducción [reproðuk'θjon] *nf* reproduction.

reproducir [reproðu'θir] *vt* to reproduce; **~se** *vr* to breed; (*situación*) to recur.

reptil [rep'til] *nm* reptile.

república [re'puβlika] *nf* republic; **republicano, a** *a, nm/f* republican.

repudiar [repu'ðjar] *vt* to repudiate; (*fe*) to renounce; **repudio** *nm* repudiation.

repuesto [re'pwesto] *nm* (*pieza de recambio*) spare (part); (*abastecimiento*) supply; **rueda de ~** spare wheel.

repugnancia [repuɣ'nanθja] *nf* repugnance; **repugnante** *a* repugnant, repulsive.

repugnar [repuɣ'nar] *vt* to disgust // *vi*, **~se** *vr* (*contradecirse*) to conflict; (*dar asco*) to be disgusting.

repujar [repu'xar] *vt* to emboss.

repulgar [repul'ɣar] *vt* to hem.

repulido, a [repu'liðo, a] *a* (*gen*) polished; (*persona*) dressed up, dolled up.

repulsa [re'pulsa] *nf* rebuff; (*fig*) reprimand.

repulsión [repul'sjon] *nf* repulsion, aversion; **repulsivo, a** *a* repulsive.

reputación [reputa'θjon] *nf* reputation.

reputar [repu'tar] *vt* to consider, deem.
requemado, a [reke'maðo, a] *a* (*quemado*) scorched; (*bronceado*) tanned.
requerimiento [rekeri'mjento] *nm* request; (*JUR*) summons.
requerir [reke'rir] *vt* (*rogar*) to ask, request; (*exigir*) to require; (*llamar*) to send for, summon.
requesón [reke'son] *nm* cottage cheese.
requete... [re'kete] *pref* extremely.
réquiem ['rekjem] *nm* requiem.
requisa [re'kisa] *nf* (*inspección*) survey, inspection; (*MIL*) requisition.
requisito [reki'sito] *nm* requirement, requisite.
res [res] *nf* beast, head of cattle.
resabio [re'saβjo] *nm* (*maña*) vice, bad habit; (*dejo*) aftertaste.
resaca [re'saka] *nf* (*en el mar*) undertow, undercurrent; (*fig*) backlash; (*fam*) hangover.
resalado, a [resa'laðo, a] *a* (*fam*) lively.
resaltar [resal'tar] *vi* to project, stick out; (*persona*) to stand out, be conspicuous.
resarcimiento [resarθi'mjento] *nm* compensation; **resarcir** *vt* to compensate; **resarcirse** *vr* to make up for.
resbaladero [resβala'ðero] *nm* (*gen*) slippery place; (*en parque infantil*) slide.
resbaladizo, a [resβala'ðiθo, a] *a* slippery.
resbalar [resβa'lar] *vi*, **~se** *vr* to slip, slide; (*fig*) to slip (up).
rescatar [reska'tar] *vt* (*heridos*) to save, rescue; (*objeto*) to get back, recover; (*cautivos*) to ransom.
rescate [res'kate] *nm* rescue, recovery; **pagar un ~** to pay a ransom.
rescindir [resθin'dir] *vt* to rescind.
rescisión [resθi'sjon] *nf* cancellation.
rescoldo [res'koldo] *nm* embers *pl*; (*fig*) scruple.
resecar [rese'kar] *vt* to dry thoroughly; (*MED*) to remove; **~se** *vr* to dry up.
reseco, a [re'seko, a] *a* very dry; (*fig*) skinny.
resentido, a [resen'tiðo, a] *a* resentful; **resentimiento** *nm* resentment, bitterness.
resentirse [resen'tirse] *vr* (*debilitarse*: *persona*) to suffer; **~ con** to resent; **~ de** (*consecuencias*) to feel the effects of.
reseña [re'seɲa] *nf* (*cuenta*) account; (*informe*) report; (*LITERATURA*) review; **reseñar** *vt* to describe; to review.
reserva [re'serβa] *nf* (*gen*) reserve; (*reservación*) reservation; **a ~ de** except for; **con toda ~** in strictest confidence.
reservado, a [reser'βaðo, a] *a* reserved; (*retraído*) cold, distant // *nm* private room.
reservar [reser'βar] *vt* (*guardar*) to keep; (*habitación, entrada*) to reserve; (*callar*) to keep to o.s.; **~se** *vr* to save o.s.
resfriado [resfri'aðo] *nm* cold; **resfriarse** *vr* to cool; (*MED*) to catch (a) cold.
resguardar [resɣwar'ðar] *vt* to protect,

shield; **~se** *vr*: **~se de** to guard against; **resguardo** *nm* defence; (*custodia*) protection; (*garantía*) guarantee; (*vale*) voucher.
residencia [resi'ðenθja] *nf* residence.
residente [resi'ðente] *a, nm/f* resident.
residir [resi'ðir] *vi* to reside, live; **~ en** to reside in, lie in.
residuo [re'siðwo] *nm* residue.
resignación [resiɣna'θjon] *nf* resignation; **resignar** *vt* to resign; **resignarse** *vr*: **resignarse a o con** to resign o.s. to, be resigned to.
resistencia [resis'tenθja] *nf* (*dureza*) endurance, strength; (*oposición, eléctrica*) resistance; **resistente** *a* strong, hardy; resistant.
resistir [resis'tir] *vt* (*soportar*) to bear; (*oponerse a*) to resist, oppose; (*aguantar*) to put up with // *vi* to resist; (*aguantar*) to last, endure; **~se** *vr*: **~se a** to refuse to, resist.
resma ['resma] *nf* ream.
resol [re'sol] *nm* glare of the sun.
resolución [resolu'θjon] *nf* (*gen*) resolution; (*decisión*) decision; **resoluto, a** *a* resolute.
resolver [resol'βer] *vt* to resolve; (*solucionar*) to solve, resolve; (*decidir*) to decide, settle; **~se** *vr* to make up one's mind.
resollar [reso'ʎar] *vi* to breathe noisily, wheeze.
resonancia [reso'nanθja] *nf* (*del sonido*) resonance; (*repercusión*) repercussion; **resonante** *a* resonant, resounding; (*fig*) tremendous; **resonar** *vi* to ring, echo.
resoplar [reso'plar] *vi* to snort; **resoplido** *nm* heavy breathing.
resorte [re'sorte] *nm* (*pieza*) spring; (*elasticidad*) elasticity; (*fig*) lever.
respaldar [respal'dar] *vt* to endorse; (*fig*) to back (up), support; **~se** *vr* to lean back; **~se con o en** to take one's stand on; **respaldo** *nm* (*de cama*) headboard; (*de sillón*) back; (*fig*) support, backing.
respectivo, a [respek'tiβo, a] *a* respective; **en lo ~ a** with regard to.
respecto [res'pekto] *nm*: **al ~** on this matter; **con ~ a, ~ de** with regard to, in relation to.
respetable [respe'taβle] *a* respectable; **respetar** *vt* to respect; **respeto** *nm* respect; (*acatamiento*) deference; **respetos** *nmpl* respects; **respetuoso, a** *a* respectful.
respingar [respin'gar] *vi* to shy; **respingo** *nm* start, jump; (*fig*) gesture of disgust.
respiración [respira'θjon] *nf* breathing; (*MED*) respiration; (*ventilación*) ventilation; **respirar** *vi* to breathe; (*inhalar*) to inhale; **respiratorio, a** *a* respiratory; **respiro** *nm* breathing; (*fig*) respite.
resplandecer [resplande'θer] *vi* to shine; **resplandeciente** *a* resplendent, shining;

resplandor *nm* brilliance, brightness; (*del fuego*) blaze.

responder [respon'der] *vt* to answer *;* / *vi* to answer; (*fig*) to respond; (*pey*) to answer back; ~ **de** *o* **por** to answer for.

responsabilidad [responsaβili'ðað] *nf* responsibility; **responsable** *a* responsible.

respuesta [res'pwesta] *nf* answer, reply.

resquebrajar [reskeβra'xar] *vt*, ~**se** *vr* to crack, split.

resquemor [reske'mor] *nm* resentment.

resquicio [res'kiθjo] *nm* chink; (*hendedura*) crack.

restablecer [restaβle'θer] *vt* to re-establish, restore; ~**se** *vr* to recover.

restallar [resta'ʎar] *vi* to crack.

restante [res'tante] *a* remaining; **lo** ~ the remainder.

restar [res'tar] *vt* (*MAT*) to subtract; (*fig*) to take away // *vi* to remain, be left.

restauración [restaura'θjon] *nf* restoration.

restaurán [restau'ran], **restaurante** [restau'rante] *nm* restaurant.

restaurar [restau'rar] *vt* to restore.

restitución [restitu'θjon] *nf* return, restitution.

restituir [restitu'ir] *vt* (*devolver*) to return, give back; (*rehabilitar*) to restore; ~**se** *vr*: ~**se a** to rejoin.

resto ['resto] *nm* (*residuo*) rest, remainder; (*apuesta*) stake; ~**s** *nmpl* remains.

restregar [restre'xar] *vt* to scrub, rub.

restricción [restrik'θjon] *nf* restriction.

restrictivo, a [restrik'tiβo, a] *a* restrictive.

restringir [restrin'xir] *vt* to restrict, limit.

resucitar [resuθi'tar] *vt*, *vi* to resuscitate, revive.

resuelto, a [re'swelto, a] *pp de* **resolver** // *a* resolute, determined.

resuello [re'sweʎo] *nm* breath.

resultado [resul'taðo] *nm* (*conclusión*) outcome; (*consecuencia*) result, consequence; **resultante** *a* resulting, resultant.

resultar [resul'tar] *vi* (*llegar a ser*) to turn out to be; (*salir bien*) to turn out well; (*COM*) to amount to; ~ **de** to stem from; **me resulta difícil hacerlo** it's difficult for me to do it.

resumen [re'sumen] *nm* summary, résumé; **en** ~ in short.

resumir [resu'mir] *vt* to sum up; (*cortar*) to abridge, cut down.

retablo [re'taβlo] *nm* altarpiece.

retaguardia [reta'xwarðja] *nf* rearguard.

retahíla [reta'ila] *nf* series, string.

retal [re'tal] *nm* remnant.

retama [re'tama] *nf* (*AM*) broom.

retar [re'tar] *vt* (*gen*) to challenge; (*desafiar*) to defy, dare.

retardar [retar'ðar] *vt* (*demorar*) to delay; (*hacer más lento*) to slow down; (*retener*) to hold back; **retardo** *nm* delay.

retazo [re'taθo] *nm* snippet.

rete... ['rete] *pref* very, extremely.

retén [re'ten] *nm* (*TEC*) catch; (*reserva*) store, reserve.

retener [rete'ner] *vt* (*guardar*) to retain, keep; (*intereses*) to withhold.

retina [re'tina] *nf* retina.

retintín [retin'tin] *nm* jangle.

retirada [reti'raða] *nf* (*MIL, refugio*) retreat; (*de dinero*) withdrawal; (*de embajador*) recall; **retirado, a** *a* (*distante*) remote; (*tranquilo*) quiet; (*jubilado*) retired.

retirar [reti'rar] *vt* to withdraw; (*quitar*) to remove; (*jubilar*) to retire, pension off; ~**se** *vr* to retreat, withdraw; to retire; (*acostarse*) to retire, go to bed; **retiro** *nm* retreat; retirement; (*pago*) pension.

reto ['reto] *nm* dare, challenge.

retocar [reto'kar] *vt* (*fotografía*) to touch up, retouch.

retoño [re'toɲo] *nm* sprout, shoot; (*fig*) offspring, child.

retoque [re'toke] *nm* retouching; (*MED*) symptom.

retorcer [retor'θer] *vt* (*gen*) to twist; (*manos, lavado*) to wring; ~**se** *vr* to become twisted; (*mover el cuerpo*) to writhe.

retorcimiento [retorθi'mjento] *nm* twist, twisting; (*fig*) deviousness.

retórica [re'torika] *nf* rhetoric; (*fig*) affectedness.

retornar [retor'nar] *vt* to return, give back // *vi* to return, go/come back; **retorno** *nm* return.

retortijón [retorti'xon] *nm* twist, twisting.

retozar [reto'θar] *vi* (*juguetear*) to frolic, romp; (*saltar*) to gambol; **retozón, ona** *a* playful.

retracción [retrak'θjon], **retractación** [retrakta'θjon] *nf* retraction.

retractar [retrak'tar] *vt* to retract; ~**se** *vr* to retract; **me retracto** I take that back.

retraer [retra'er] *vt* to dissuade; ~**se** *vr* to retreat, withdraw; **retraído, a** *a* shy, retiring; **retraimiento** *nm* (*gen*) retirement; (*timidez*) shyness; (*lugar*) retreat.

retransmisión [retransmi'sjon] *nf* repeat (broadcast); **retransmitir** *vt* (*mensaje*) to relay; (*TV etc*) to retransmit; (: *en vivo*) to broadcast live.

retrasado, a [retra'saðo, a] *a* late; (*MED*) mentally retarded; (*país etc*) backward, underdeveloped; **retrasar** *vt* (*demorar*) to postpone, put off; (*retardar*) to slow down // *vi*, **retrasarse** *vr* (*atrasarse*) to be late; (*reloj*) to be slow; (*producción*) to fall (away); (*quedarse atrás*) to lag behind.

retraso [re'traso] *nm* (*demora*) delay; (*lentitud*) slowness; (*tardanza*) lateness; (*atraso*) backwardness; **llegar con** ~ to arrive late; ~ **mental** mental deficiency.

retratar [retra'tar] *vt* (*ARTE*) to paint the portrait of; (*fotografiar*) to photograph; (*fig*) to depict; ~**se** *vr* to have one's portrait painted; to have one's photograph taken; **retrato** nm portrait; (fig) likeness; **retrato-robot** nm identikit picture.

retreta [re'treta] nf retreat.

retrete [re'trete] nm toilet, lavatory.

retribución [retriβu'θjon] nf (recompensa) reward; (pago) pay, payment; **retribuir** vt to reward; to pay.

retro... [retro] pref retro... .

retroactivo, a [retroak'tiβo, a] a retroactive, retrospective.

retroceder [retroθe'ðer] vi (echarse atrás) to move back(wards); (tropas) to fall back, retreat; (arma de fuego) to recoil; (fig) to back down.

retroceso [retro'θeso] nm backward movement; (MIL) withdrawal, retreat; (MED) relapse; (fig) backing down.

retrógrado, a [re'troxraðo, a] a (atrasado) retrograde; (POL) reactionary.

retropropulsión [retropropul'sjon] nf jet propulsion.

retrospectivo, a [retrospek'tiβo, a] a retrospective.

retrovisor [retroβi'sor] nm driving or rear-view mirror.

retumbante [retum'bante] a resounding; **retumbar** vi to echo, resound.

reuma ['reuma] nm rheumatism; **reumático, a** a rheumatic; **reumatismo** nm rheumatism.

reunificar [reunifi'kar] vt to reunify.

reunión [reu'njon] nf (asamblea) meeting; (fiesta) party; (reencuentro) reunion.

reunir [reu'nir] vt (juntar) to reunite, join; (recoger) to gather; (personas) to assemble; (cualidades) to combine; ~se vr to meet, gather.

revalidar [reβali'ðar] vt to confirm, ratify.

revalorar [reβalo'rar] vt to revalue, reassess.

revancha [re'βantʃa] nf revenge.

revelación [reβela'θjon] nf revelation.

revelado [reβe'laðo] nm developing.

revelar [reβe'lar] vt to reveal; (FOTO) to develop.

revendedor, a [reβende'ðor, a] nm/f retailer; (pey) ticket tout.

reventar [reβen'tar] vt to burst, explode; (fam: plan) to ruin // vi, ~se vr (estallar) to burst, explode; (fam: morirse) to kick the bucket (fam); ~ por to be bursting to.

reventón [reβen'ton] nm burst, explosion; (AUTO) blow-out, puncture.

reverberación [reβerβera'θjon] nf reverberation; **reverberar** vi to reverberate; **reverbero** nm reverberation.

reverdecer [reβerðe'θer] vi (fig) to revive, come to life again.

reverencia [reβe'renθja] nf reverence; **reverenciar** vt to revere.

reverendo, a [reβe'renðo, a] a reverend; **reverente** a reverent.

reversión [reβer'sjon] nf reversion.

reverso [re'βerso] nm back, wrong side; (de moneda) reverse.

revertir [reβer'tir] vi to revert.

revés [re'βes] nm back, wrong side; (fig) reverse, setback; (DEPORTE) backhand; **hacer al** ~ to do sth the wrong way round; **volver algo al** ~ to turn sth round; (ropa) to turn sth inside out.

revestir [reβes'tir] vt to put on; (cubrir) to cover, coat; ~ con o de to invest with.

revisar [reβi'sar] vt (examinar) to check; (rever) to revise; **revisión** nf revision.

revisor, a [reβi'sor, a] nm/f inspector; (FERRO) ticket collector.

revista [re'βista] nf magazine, review; (TEATRO) revue; (inspección) inspection; **pasar** ~ **a** to review, inspect.

revivir [reβi'βir] vi to revive.

revocación [reβoka'θjon] nf repeal; **revocar** vt to revoke.

revolcar [reβol'kar] vt to knock down, send flying; ~se vr to roll about.

revolotear [reβolote'ar] vi to flutter; **revoloteo** nm fluttering.

revoltijo [reβol'tixo] nm mess, jumble.

revoltoso, a [reβol'toso, a] a (travieso) naughty, unruly; (rebelde) rebellious.

revolución [reβolu'θjon] nf revolution; **revolucionar** vt to revolutionize; **revolucionario, a** a, nm/f revolutionary.

revólver [re'βolβer] nm revolver.

revolver [reβol'βer] vt (desordenar) to disturb, mess up; (mover) to move about; (poner al revés) to turn over; (investigar) to look through; (adentrarse en) to go into; (POL) to stir up; (hacer paquete) to wrap up // vi: ~ **en** to go through, rummage (about) in; ~se vr to turn round; (por dolor) to writhe; (volver contra) to turn on or against.

revuelco [re'βwelko] nm fall, tumble.

revuelo [re'βwelo] nm fluttering; (fig) commotion.

revuelto, a [re'βwelto, a] pp de **revolver** // a (mezclado) mixed-up; (huevos) scrambled; (descontento) discontented; (travieso) mischievous // nf (motín) revolt; (conmoción) commotion.

revulsivo [reβul'siβo] nm enema.

rey [rei] nm king.

reyerta [re'jerta] nf quarrel, brawl.

rezagado, a [reθa'xaðo, a] nm/f straggler.

rezagar [reθa'xar] vt (dejar atrás) to leave behind; (retrasar) to delay, postpone.

rezar [re'θar] vi to pray; ~ **con** (fam) to concern, have to do with; **rezo** nm prayer.

rezongar [reθon'gar] vi to grumble.

rezumar [reθu'mar] vt to ooze // vi to leak; ~se vr to leak out.

ría ['ria] nf estuary.

riada [ri'aða] nf flood.

ribera [ri'βera] nf (de río) bank; (: área) riverside; (del mar) shore.

ribete [ri'βete] nm (de vestido) border; (fig) addition; ~ar vt to edge, border.

rico, a ['riko, a] a (gen) rich; (adinerado)

wealthy; (*lujoso*) luxurious; (*comida*) tasty, delicious // *nm/f* rich person.

rictus ['riktus] *nm* (*mueca*) sneer, grin.

ridiculez [riðiku'leθ] *nf* absurdity; **ridiculizar** *vt* to ridicule.

ridículo, a [ri'ðikulo, a] *a* ridiculous; **hacer el** ~ to make o.s. ridiculous; **poner a uno en** ~ to ridicule sb.

riego ['rjexo] *nm* (*aspersión*) watering; (*irrigación*) irrigation.

riel [rjel] *nm* rail.

rienda ['rjenda] *nf* rein; **dar** ~ **suelta a** to give free rein to.

riente ['rjente] *a* laughing.

riesgo ['rjesxo] *nm* risk; **correr el** ~ **de** to run the risk of.

rifa ['rifa] *nf* (*lotería*) raffle; (*disputa*) quarrel; **rifar** *vt* to raffle // *vi* to quarrel; **rifarse** *vr:* **rifarse algo** to fight over sth.

rifle ['rifle] *nm* rifle.

rigidez [rixi'ðeθ] *nf* rigidity, stiffness; (*fig*) strictness; **rígido, a** *a* rigid, stiff; strict, inflexible.

rigor [ri'xor] *nm* strictness, rigour; (*inclemencia*) harshness; **de** ~ de rigueur, essential; **riguroso, a** *a* rigorous; harsh; (*severo*) severe.

rimar [ri'mar] *vi* to rhyme.

rimbombante [rimbom'bante] *a* resounding; (*fig*) pompous.

rincón [rin'kon] *nm* (inside) corner.

rinoceronte [rinoθe'ronte] *nm* rhinoceros.

riña ['riɲa] *nf* (*disputa*) argument; (*pelea*) brawl.

riñón [ri'ɲon] *nm* (*gen*) kidney; **tener riñones** to have guts.

río *etc vb ver* **reír** // ['rio] *nm* river; (*fig*) torrent, stream; ~ **abajo/arriba** downstream/upstream.

rioplatense [riopla'tense] *a* of the River Plate region.

ripio ['ripjo] *nm* (*residuo*) refuse, waste; (*cascotes*) rubble, debris.

riqueza [ri'keθa] *nf* wealth, riches *pl*; (*cualidad*) richness.

risa ['risa] *nf* (*una* ~) laugh; (*gen*) laughter.

risco ['risko] *nm* crag, cliff; ~**so, a** *a* steep.

risible [ri'sißle] *a* (*ridículo*) ludicrous; (*jocoso*) laughable.

risotada [riso'taða] *nf* guffaw.

ristra ['ristra] *nf* string.

risueño, a [ri'sweɲo, a] *a* (*sonriente*) smiling; (*contento*) cheerful.

ritmo ['ritmo] *nm* rhythm; **a** ~ **lento** slowly; **trabajar a** ~ **lento** to go slow.

rito ['rito] *nm* rite.

ritual [ri'twal] *a, nm* ritual.

rival [ri'ßal] *a, nm/f* rival; ~**idad** *nf* rivalry; ~**izar** *vi:* ~**izar con** to rival, vie with.

rizado, a [ri'θaðo, a] *a* curly // *nm* curls *pl*; **rizar** *vt* to curl; **rizarse** *vr* (*el pelo*) to

curl; (*el mar*) to ripple; **rizo** *nm* curl; ripple.

RNE *nf abr de* **Radio Nacional de España.**

robar [ro'ßar] *vt* to rob; (*objeto*) to steal; (*casa etc*) to break into; (*NAIPES*) to draw.

roble [ro'ßle] *nm* oak; ~**do,** ~**dal** *nm* oakwood.

roblón [ro'ßlon] *nm* rivet.

robo ['roßo] *nm* robbery, theft; ~ **relámpago** smash-and-grab raid.

robot [ro'ßo(t)] *nm* robot.

robustecer [roßuste'θer] *vt* to strengthen.

robusto, a [ro'ßusto, a] *a* robust, strong.

roca ['roka] *nf* rock.

rocalla [ro'kaʎa] *nf* pebbles *pl*.

roce ['roθe] *nm* (*caricia*) brush; (*TEC*) friction; (*en la piel*) graze; **tener** ~ **con** to be in close contact with.

rociada [ro'θjaða] *nf* (*aspersión*) sprinkling; (*fig*) hail, shower; **rociar** *vt* to spray.

rocín [ro'θin] *nm* nag, hack.

rocío [ro'θio] *nm* dew.

rocoso, a [ro'koso, a] *a* rocky.

rodado, a [ro'ðaðo, a] *a* (*con ruedas*) wheeled; (*redondo*) round // *nf* rut.

rodaja [ro'ðaxa] *nf* (*raja*) slice; (*rueda*) small wheel.

rodaje [ro'ðaxe] *nm* (*TEC*) wheels *pl*, set of wheels; (*CINE*) shooting, filming; (*AUTO*): **en** ~ running in.

rodar [ro'ðar] *vt* (*vehículo*) to wheel; (*escalera*) to roll down; (*viajar por*) to travel (over) // *vi* to roll; (*coche*) to go, run; (*CINE*) to shoot, film.

rodear [roðe'ar] *vt* to surround // *vi* to go round; ~**se** *vr:* ~**se de amigos** to surround o.s. with friends.

rodeo [ro'ðeo] *nm* (*ruta indirecta*) detour; (*evasión*) evasion; (*AM*) rodeo; **hablar sin** ~**s** to come to the point, speak plainly.

rodilla [ro'ðiʎa] *nf* knee; **de** ~**s** kneeling.

rodillo [ro'ðiʎo] *nm* roller; (*CULIN*) rolling-pin; ~ **apisonador** *o* **de vapor** steamroller.

rododendro [roðo'ðendro] *nm* rhododendron.

roedor, a [roe'ðor, a] *ε* gnawing // *nm* rodent.

roer [ro'er] *vt* (*masticar*) to gnaw; (*corroer, fig*) to corrode.

rogar [ro'xar] *vt, vi* (*pedir*) to ask for; (*suplicar*) to beg, plead; **se ruega no fumar** please do not smoke.

rojete [ro'xete] *nm* rouge.

rojizo, a [ro'xiθo, a] *a* reddish.

rojo, a ['roxo, a] *a, nm* red; **al** ~ **vivo** red-hot; ~ **de labios** lipstick.

rol [rol] *nm* list, roll; (*AM: papel*) role.

rollizo, a [ro'ʎiθo, a] *a* (*objeto*) cylindrical; (*persona*) plump.

rollo ['roʎo] *nm* (*gen*) roll; (*de cuerda*) coil; (*madera*) log; (*fam*) bore; ¡**qué** ~! what a carry-on!

Roma ['roma] *n* Rome.

romance [ro'manθe] *nm* Romance language; (*LITERATURA*) ballad; **hablar en** ~ to speak plainly.
romántico, a [ro'mantiko, a] *a* romantic.
romería [rome'ria] *nf* (*REL*) pilgrimage; (*excursión*) trip, outing.
romero, a [ro'mero, a] *nm/f* pilgrim // *nm* rosemary.
romo, a ['romo, a] *a* blunt; (*fig*) dull.
rompecabezas [rompeka'βeθas] *nm inv* riddle, puzzle; (*juego*) jigsaw.
rompehuelgas [rompe'welxas] *nm inv* strikebreaker, blackleg.
rompeolas [rompe'olas] *nm inv* breakwater.
romper [rom'per] *vt* (*gen*) to break; (*hacer pedazos*) to smash; (*papel etc*) to tear, rip // *vi* (*olas*) to break; (*sol, diente*) to break through; ~ **un contrato** to break a contract; ~ **a** to start (suddenly) to; ~ **en llanto** to burst into tears; ~ **con uno** to fall out with sb.
rompimiento [rompi'mjento] *nm* breaking; (*fig*) break; (*quiebra*) crack; ~ **de hostilidades** outbreak of hostilities.
ron [ron] *nm* rum.
roncar [ron'kar] *vi* to snore.
ronco, a ['ronko, a] *a* (*sin voz*) hoarse; (*áspero*) raucous.
roncha ['rontʃa] *nf* weal; (*contusión*) bruise.
ronda ['ronda] *nf* (*gen*) round; (*patrulla*) patrol; **rondar** *vt* to patrol // *vi* to patrol; (*fig*) to prowl round.
rondón [ron'don]: **de** ~ *ad* unexpectedly.
ronquear [ronke'ar] *vi* to be hoarse; **ronquedad** *nf* hoarseness.
ronquido [ron'kiðo] *nm* snore, snoring.
ronronear [ronrone'ar] *vi* to purr; **ronroneo** *nm* purr.
ronzal [ron'θal] *nm* halter.
roña ['roɲa] *nf* scab; (*mugre*) crust (of dirt).
roñoso, a [ro'ɲoso, a] *a* (*mugriento*) filthy; (*inútil*) useless, (*tacaño*) mean.
ropa ['ropa] *nf* clothes *pl*, clothing; ~ **blanca** linen; ~ **de cama** bed linen; ~ **interior** underwear; ~**je** *nm* gown, robes *pl*; ~**vejero, a** *nm/f* second-hand clothes dealer.
ropero [ro'pero] *nm* linen cupboard; (*guardarropa*) wardrobe.
roque ['roke] *nm* rook, castle.
roquedal [roke'ðal] *nm* rocky place.
rosa ['rosa] *a inv* pink // *nf* rose; (*ANAT*) red birthmark; ~ **de los vientos** the compass; ~**s** *nfpl* popcorn *sg*.
rosado, a [ro'saðo, a], **rosáceo, a** [ro-'saθeo, a] *a* pink // *nm* rosé.
rosal [ro'sal] *nm* rosebush.
rosario [ro'sarjo] *nm* (*REL*) rosary; **rezar el** ~ to say the rosary.
rosca ['roska] *nf* (*de tornillo*) thread; (*de humo*) coil, spiral; (*pan, postre*) ring-shaped roll/pastry.
rosetón [rose'ton] *nm* rosette; (*ARQ*) rose

window; (*AUTO*) cloverleaf (junction).
rostro ['rostro] *nm* (*cara*) face.
rotación [rota'θjon] *nf* rotation; ~ **de cultivos** crop rotation.
rotativo, a [rota'tiβo, a] *a* rotary.
roto, a ['roto, a] *pp de* **romper** // *a* broken; (*disipado*) debauched.
rótula ['rotula] *nf* kneecap; (*TEC*) ball-and-socket joint.
rotular [rotu'lar] *vt* (*titular, encabezar*) to head, entitle; (*etiquetar*) to label; **rótulo** *nm* heading, title; label.
rotundo, a [ro'tundo, a] *a* round; (*enfático*) emphatic.
rotura [ro'tura] *nf* (*rompimiento*) breaking; (*quiebra*) crack; (*MED*) fracture.
roturar [rotu'rar] *vt* to plough.
rozado, a [ro'θaðo, a] *a* worn.
rozadura [roθa'ðura] *nf* abrasion, graze.
rozar [ro'θar] *vt* (*frotar*) to rub; (*arañar*) to scratch; (*arrugar*) to crumple; (*AGR*) to graze; (*tocar ligeramente*) to shave, touch lightly; ~**se** *vr* to rub (together); (*trabarse*) to trip over one's own feet; ~ **con** (*fam*) to rub shoulders with.
roznar [roθ'nar] *vi* to bray.
rte *abr de* **remite, remitente** sender.
rubí [ru'βi] *nm* ruby.
rubicundo, a [ruβi'kundo, a] *a* ruddy; (*de salud*) rosy with health.
rubio, a ['ruβjo, a] *a* fair-haired // *nm/f* blond/blonde; **tabaco** ~ Virginia tobacco.
rubor [ru'βor] *nm* (*timidez*) bashfulness; (*sonrojo*) blush; ~**izarse** *vr* to blush; ~**oso, a** *a* blushing.
rúbrica ['ruβrika] *nf* title, heading; (*de la firma*) flourish; **rubricar** *vt* (*firmar*) to sign with a flourish; (*concluir*) to sign and seal.
rucio, a ['ruθjo, a] *a* grey.
rudeza [ru'ðeθa] *nf* (*tosquedad*) coarseness; (*sencillez*) simplicity.
rudimento [ruði'mento] *nm* rudiment.
rudo, a ['ruðo, a] *a* (*sin pulir*) unpolished; (*tosco*) coarse; (*violento*) violent; (*vulgar*) common; (*estúpido*) stupid.
rueda ['rweða] *nf* (*gen*) wheel; (*círculo*) ring, circle; (*rodaja*) slice, round; ~ **delantera/trasera/de repuesto** front/back/spare wheel; ~ **de prensa** press conference.
ruedo ['rweðo] *nm* (*contorno*) edge, border; (*de vestido*) hem; (*círculo*) circle; (*TAUR*) arena, bullring.
ruego *etc vb ver* **rogar** // ['rwexo] *nm* request.
rufián [ru'fjan] *nm* scoundrel.
rugby ['ruxβi] *nm* rugby.
rugido [ru'xiðo] *nm* roar; **rugir** *vi* to roar.
rugoso, a [ru'xoso, a] *a* (*arrugado*) wrinkled; (*áspero*) rough; (*desigual*) ridged.
ruibarbo [rui'βarβo] *nm* rhubarb.
ruido ['rwiðo] *nm* (*gen*) noise; (*sonido*) sound; (*alboroto*) racket, row; (*escándalo*)

commotion, rumpus; ~**so, a** *a* noisy, loud; (*fig*) sensational.
ruin [ru'in] *a* contemptible, mean.
ruina ['rwina] *nf* (*gen*) ruin; (*colapso*) collapse; (*de persona*) ruin, downfall; (*de imperio*) decline.
ruindad [rwin'dað] *nf* lowness, meanness; (*acto*) low *or* mean act.
ruinoso, a [rui'noso, a] *a* ruinous; (*destartalado*) dilapidated, tumbledown; (*COM*) disastrous.
ruiseñor [rwise'ɲor] *nm* nightingale.
rula ['rula], **ruleta** [ru'leta] *nf* roulette.
Rumania [ru'manja] *nf* Rumania.
rumba ['rumba] *nf* rumba.
rumbo ['rumbo] *nm* (*ruta*) route, direction; (*ángulo de dirección*) course, bearing; (*fig*) course of events.
rumboso, a [rum'boso, a] *a* generous.
rumiante [ru'mjante] *nm* ruminant.
rumiar [rumi'nar] *vt* to chew; (*fig*) to chew over // *vi* to chew the cud.
rumor [ru'mor] *nm* (*ruido sordo*) low sound; (*murmuración*) murmur, buzz; ~**earse** *vr*: **se ~ea que** it is rumoured that; ~**eo** *nm* murmur.
rupestre [ru'pestre] *a* rock *cpd*.
ruptura [rup'tura] *nf* (*MED*) fracture; (*fig*) rupture.
rural [ru'ral] *a* rural.
Rusia ['rusja] *nf* Russia; **ruso, a** *a, nm/f* Russian.
rústico, a ['rustiko, a] *a* rustic; (*ordinario*) coarse, uncouth // *nm/f* yokel // *nf*: **libro en ~a** paperback.
ruta ['ruta] *nf* route.
rutina [ru'tina] *nf* routine; ~**rio, a** *a* routine.

S

S *abr de* **santo, a; sur.**
s. *abr de* **siglo; siguiente.**
sábado ['saβaðo] *nm* Saturday.
sábana ['saβana] *nf* sheet.
sabandija [saβan'dixa] *nf* bug, insect.
sabañón [saβa'ɲon] *nm* chilblain.
sabelotodo [saβelo'toðo] *nm/f inv* know-all.
saber [sa'βer] *vt* to know; (*llegar a conocer*) to find out, learn; (*tener capacidad de*) to know how to // *vi*: ~ **a** to taste of, taste like // *nm* knowledge, learning; **a ~** namely; ¿**sabes nadar?** can you swim?; ¿**sabes ir?** do you know the way?
sabiduría [saβiðu'ria] *nf* (*conocimientos*) wisdom; (*instrucción*) knowledge, learning.
sabiendas [sa'βjendas]: **a ~** *ad* knowingly.
sabio, a ['saβjo,a] *a* (*docto*) learned; (*prudente*) wise, sensible.
sabor [sa'βor] *nm* taste, flavour; ~**ear** *vt* to savour, relish; (*dar ~ a*) to flavour.
sabotaje [saβo'taxe] *nm* sabotage; **sabotear** *vt* to sabotage.
sabré *etc vb ver* **saber.**

sabroso, a [sa'βroso, a] *a* tasty; (*fig*: *fam*) racy, salty.
sacacorchos [saka'kortʃos] *nm inv* corkscrew.
sacapuntas [saka'puntas] *nm inv* pencil sharpener.
sacar [sa'kar] *vt* (*gen*) to take out; (*fig*) to get (out); (*quitar*) to remove, get out; (*hacer salir*) to bring out; (*conclusión*) to draw; (*novela etc*) to publish, bring out; (*ropa*) to take off; (*obra*) to make; (*FOTO*) to take; (*premio*) to receive; (*entradas*) to get; ~ **adelante** to bring up; ~ **a alguien a bailar** to get sb up to dance; ~ **apuntes** to take notes; ~ **la cara por alguien** to stick up for sb; ~ **la lengua** to stick out one's tongue.
sacarina [saka'rina] *nf* saccharin(e).
sacerdote [saθer'ðote] *nm* priest.
saco ['sako] *nm* (*gen*) bag; (*grande*) sack; (*su contenido*) bagful; (*AM*) jacket; ~ **de dormir** sleeping bag.
sacramento [sakra'mento] *nm* sacrament.
sacrificar [sakrifi'kar] *vt* to sacrifice; **sacrificio** *nm* sacrifice.
sacrilegio [sakri'lexjo] *nm* sacrilege; **sacrílego, a** *a* sacrilegious.
sacristía [sakris'tia] *nf* sacristy.
sacro, a ['sakro, a] *a* sacred.
sacudida [saku'ðiða] *nf* (*zarandeada*) shake, shaking; (*sacudimiento*) jolt, bump; ~ **eléctrica** electric shock; **sacudir** *vt* to shake; (*golpear*) to hit.
sádico, a ['saðiko, a] *a* sadistic; **sadismo** *nm* sadism.
saeta [sa'eta] *nf* (*flecha*) arrow; (*de reloj*) hand; (*brújula*) magnetic needle.
sagacidad [saɣaθi'ðað] *nf* shrewdness, cleverness; **sagaz** *a* shrewd, clever; (*astuto*) astute.
sagrado, a [sa'ɣraðo, a] *a* sacred, holy // *nm* sanctuary, asylum.
Sáhara ['saara] *nm*: **el ~** the Sahara (desert).
sahumar [sau'mar] *vt* to fumigate.
sal [sal] *vb ver* **salir** // *nf* salt; ~ **de la Higuera** Epsom salts.
sala ['sala] *nf* (*cuarto grande*) large room; (~ **de estar**) living room; (*TEATRO*) house, auditorium; (*de hospital*) ward; ~ **de apelación** court; ~ **de espera** waiting room.
salado, a [sa'laðo, a] *a* salty; (*fig*) witty, amusing; **agua** ~**a** salt water; **salar** *vt* to salt, add salt to.
salario [sa'larjo] *nm* wage, pay.
salchicha [sal'tʃitʃa] *nf* pork sausage; **salchichón** *nm* (salami-type) sausage.
saldar [sal'dar] *vt* to pay; (*vender*) to sell off; (*fig*) to settle, resolve; **saldo** *nm* (*pago*) settlement; (*de una cuenta*) balance; (*lo restante*) remnant(s) (*pl*), remainder.
saldré *etc vb ver* **salir.**
salero [sa'lero] *nm* salt cellar.
salgo *etc vb ver* **salir.**

salida [sa'liða] nf exit, way out, (acto) leaving, going out; (de tren, AVIAT) departure; (TEC) output, production; (fig) way out; (COM) opening; (GEO, válvula) outlet; (de gas, aire) escape, leak; **calle sin** ~ cul-de-sac; ~ **de emergencia** emergency exit.

saliente [sa'ljente] a (ARQ) projecting; (que se retira) outgoing, retiring; (el sol) rising; (fig) outstanding.

salir [sa'lir] vi (gen) to come/go out; (resultar) to turn out; (partir) to leave, depart; (aparecer) to appear; (sobresalir) to project, jut out; ~**se** vr (vasija) to leak; (animal) to escape, get out; ~ **con** to go out with; ~ **a la superficie** to come to the surface; ~ **caro/barato** to work out expensive/cheap.

saliva [sa'liβa] nf saliva.

salmantino, a [salman'tino, a] a of Salamanca.

salmo ['salmo] nm psalm.

salmón [sal'mon] nm salmon.

salmuera [sal'mwera] nf pickle, brine.

salón [sa'lon] nm (de casa) living-room, lounge; (muebles) lounge suite; ~ **de belleza** beauty parlour; ~ **de pintura** art gallery; ~ **de baile** dance hall.

salpicadero [salpika'ðero] nm dashboard.

salpicar [salpi'kar] vt (rociar) to sprinkle, spatter; (esparcir) to scatter.

salsa ['salsa] nf sauce; (con carne asada) gravy; (fig) spice.

saltamontes [salta'montes] nm inv grasshopper.

saltar [sal'tar] vt to jump (over), leap (over); (dejar de lado) to skip, miss out // vi to jump, leap; (pelota) to bounce; (al aire) to fly up; (quebrarse) to break; (al agua) to dive; (fig) to explode, blow up.

saltear [salte'ar] vt (robar) to rob (in a holdup); (asaltar) to assault, attack; (CULIN) to sauté.

saltimbanqui [saltim'banki] nm/f acrobat.

salto ['salto] nm jump, leap; (al agua) dive; (DEPORTE) jump; ~ **de agua** waterfall.

saltón, ona [sal'ton, ona] a (ojos) bulging, popping; (dientes) protruding.

salubre [sa'luβre] a healthy, salubrious.

salud [sa'luð] nf health; ¡(a su) ~! good health!; ~**able** a (de buena ~) healthy; (provechoso) good, beneficial.

saludar [salu'ðar] vt to greet; (MIL) to salute; **saludo** nm greeting; **saludos** (en carta) best wishes, regards, greetings.

salvación [salβa'θjon] nf (gen) salvation; (rescate) rescue.

salvaguardar [salβaɣwar'ðar] vt to safeguard.

salvaje [sal'βaxe] a wild; (tribú) savage; **salvajismo** nm, **salvajez** nf savagery.

salvar [sal'βar] vt (rescatar) to save, rescue; (resolver) to overcome, resolve; (cubrir distancias) to cover, travel; (hacer excepción) to except, exclude; (un barco) to salvage.

salvavidas [salβa'βiðas] nm inv lifebelt // a: **bote/chaleco/cinturón** ~ lifeboat/jacket/belt.

salvia ['salβja] nf sage.

salvo, a ['salβo, a] a safe // ad except (for), save; a ~ out of danger; ~ **que** unless; ~**conducto** nm safe-conduct.

san [san] a saint; ~ **Juan** St. John.

sanar [sa'nar] vt (herida) to heal; (persona) to cure // vi (persona) to get well, recover; (herida) to heal.

sanatorio [sana'torjo] nm sanatorium.

sanción [san'θjon] nf sanction; **sancionar** vt to sanction.

sandalia [san'dalja] nf sandal.

sandía [san'dia] nf watermelon.

sandwich ['sandwitʃ] nm sandwich.

saneamiento [sanea'mjento] nm sanitation; (de la tierra) drainage; (indemnización) compensation; (fig) remedy; **sanear** vt to drain; to compensate; to remedy, repair; (garantizar) to guarantee; (asegurar) to insure.

sangrar [san'grar] vt, vi to bleed; **sangre** nf blood.

sangría [san'gria] nf sangria, sweetened drink of red wine with fruit.

sangriento, a [san'grjento, a] a (herido) bleeding; (batalla) bloody.

sanguinario, a [sangi'narjo, a] a bloodthirsty.

sanguíneo, a [san'gineo, a] a blood cpd.

sanidad [sani'ðað] nf sanitation; (calidad de sano) health, healthiness; ~ **pública** public health.

sanitario, a [sani'tarjo, a] a sanitary; (de la salud) health cpd.

sano, a ['sano, a] a healthy; (sin daños) sound; (comida) good; (entero) whole, intact; ~ **y salvo** safe and sound.

santidad [santi'ðað] nf holiness, sanctity; **santificar** vt to sanctify, make holy.

santiguar [santi'ɣwar] vt (fig) to slap, hit; ~**se** vr to make the sign of the cross.

santo, a ['santo, a] a holy; (fig) wonderful, miraculous // nm/f saint // nm saint's day; ~ **y seña** password.

santuario [san'twarjo] nm sanctuary, shrine.

saña ['saɲa] nf rage, fury.

sapo ['sapo] nm toad.

saque ['sake] nm (TENIS) service, serve; (FÚTBOL) throw-in; ~ **de esquina** corner (kick).

saquear [sake'ar] vt (MIL) to sack; (robar) to loot, plunder; (fig) to ransack; **saqueo** nm sacking; looting, plundering; ransacking.

sarampión [saram'pjon] nm measles sg.

sarcasmo [sar'kasmo] nm sarcasm; **sarcástico, a** a sarcastic.

sardina [sar'ðina] nf sardine.

sardónico, a [sar'ðoniko, a] a sardonic; (irónico) ironical, sarcastic.

sargento [sar'xento] nm sergeant.

sarna ['sarna] *nf* itch; (*MED*) scabies.
sartén [sar'ten] *nf* frying pan.
sastre ['sastre] *nm* tailor; ~**ría** *nf* (*arte*) tailoring; (*tienda*) tailor's (shop).
satélite [sa'telite] *nm* satellite.
sátira ['satira] *nf* satire.
satisfacción [satisfak'θjon] *nf* satisfaction; **satisfacer** *vt* to satisfy; (*gastos*) to meet; (*pérdida*) to make good; **satisfacerse** *vr* to satisfy o.s., be satisfied; (*vengarse*) to take revenge; **satisfecho, a** *a* satisfied; (*contento*) content(ed), happy; (*vanidoso*) self-satisfied, smug.
saturar [satu'rar] *vt* to saturate.
sauce ['sauθe] *nm* willow; ~ **llorón** weeping willow.
sauna ['sauna] *nf* sauna.
savia ['saβja] *nf* sap.
saxofón [sakso'fon], **saxófono** [sak-'sofono] *nm* saxophone.
sayo ['sajo] *nm* smock.
sazonado, a [saθo'naðo, a] *a* (*fruta*) ripe; (*CULIN*) flavoured, seasoned; **sazonar** *vt* to ripen; to flavour, season.
se [se] *pron reflexivo* oneself; (*sg: m*) himself; (: *f*) herself; (: *de una cosa*) itself; (: *de Ud*) yourself; (*pl*) themselves; (: *de Uds*) yourselves; (*de uno*) oneself; ~ **mira en el espejo** he looks at himself in the mirror; (*recíproco*) each other, one another; ~ **ayudan** they help each other; ~ **miraron (el uno al otro)** they looked at one another; (*uso impersonal*): ~ **compró hace 3 años** it was bought 3 years ago; **en esa parte** ~ **habla francés** in that area French is spoken *or* people speak French; (*dativo*): ~ **lo daré** I'll give it to him/her/you; **él** ~ **ha comprado un sombrero** he has bought himself a hat.
SE *abr de* **sudeste.**
sé *vb ver* **saber, ser.**
sea *etc vb ver* **ser.**
sebo ['seβo] *nm* fat, grease.
seca ['seka] *nf ver* **seco.**
secador [seka'ðor] *nm*: ~ **de cabello** *o* **para el pelo** hair-dryer.
secadora [seka'ðora] *nf* wringer; ~ **centrífuga** spin-dryer.
secar [se'kar] *vt* to dry; ~**se** *vr* to dry (off); (*río, planta*) to dry up.
sección [sek'θjon] *nf* section.
seco, a ['seko, a] *a* dry; (*carácter*) cold; (*respuesta*) sharp, curt; (*coñac*) straight // *nf* drought; **vivir a pan** ~ to live by bread alone; **habrá pan a** ~**as** there will be just bread; **decir algo a** ~**as** to say sth curtly; **parar en** ~ to stop dead.
secretaría [sekreta'ria] *nf* secretariat; **secretario, a** *nm/f* secretary.
secreto, a [se'kreto, a] *a* secret; (*persona*) secretive // *nm* secret; (*calidad*) secrecy.
secta ['sekta] *nf* sect; ~**rio, a** *a* sectarian.
sector [sek'tor] *nm* sector.
secuela [se'kwela] *nf* consequence.
secuestrar [sekwes'trar] *vt* to kidnap; (*bienes*) to seize, confiscate; **secuestro**

nm kidnapping; seizure, confiscation.
secular [seku'lar] *a* secular.
secundar [sekun'dar] *vt* to second, support.
secundario, a [sekun'darjo, a] *a* secondary.
sed [seð] *nf* thirst; **tener** ~ to be thirsty.
seda ['seða] *nf* silk.
sedal [se'ðal] *nm* fishing line.
sedante [se'ðante], **sedativo** [seða'tiβo] *nm* sedative.
sede ['seðe] *nf* (*de gobierno*) seat; (*de compañía*) headquarters *pl*; **Santa S**~ Holy See.
sediento, a [se'ðjento, a] *a* thirsty.
sedimentar [seðimen'tar] *vt* to deposit; ~**se** *vr* to settle; **sedimento** *nm* sediment.
seducción [seðuk'θjon] *nf* seduction; **seducir** *vt* to seduce; (*sobornar*) to bribe; (*cautivar*) to charm, fascinate; **seductor, a** *a* seductive; charming, fascinating; (*engañoso*) deceptive, misleading // *nm/f* seducer.
segadora-trilladora [seɣa'ðora triʎa-'ðora] *nf* combine harvester.
seglar [se'ɣlar] *a* secular, lay.
segregación [seɣreɣa'θjon] *nf* segregation; ~ **racial** racial segregation; **segregar** *vt* to segregate, separate.
seguido, a [se'ɣiðo, a] *a* (*continuo*) continuous, unbroken; (*recto*) straight; ~**s** consecutive, successive // *ad* (*directo*) straight (on); (*después*) after // *nf*: **en** ~**a** at once, right away; **5 días** ~**s** 5 days running, 5 days in a row.
seguimiento [seɣi'mjento] *nm* chase, pursuit; (*continuación*) continuation.
seguir [se'ɣir] *vt* (*gen*) to follow; (*venir después*) to follow on, come after; (*proseguir*) to continue; (*perseguir*) to chase, pursue // *vi* (*gen*) to follow; (*continuar*) to continue, carry *or* go on; ~**se** *vr* to follow; **sigo sin comprender** I still don't understand; **sigue lloviendo** it's still raining.
según [se'ɣun] *prep* according to // *ad* according to circumstances; ~ **y** **conforme** it all depends; ~ **esté el tiempo** depending on the weather.
segundo, a [se'ɣundo, a] *a* second // *nm* second // *nf* second meaning; **de** ~**a mano** second hand.
segur [se'ɣur] *nf* (*hacha*) axe; (*hoz*) sickle.
seguramente [seɣura'mente] *ad* surely; (*con certeza*) for sure, with certainty.
seguridad [seɣuri'ðað] *nf* (*gen*) safety; (*del estado, de casa etc*) security; (*certidumbre*) certainty; (*confianza*) confidence; (*estabilidad*) stability; ~ **social** social security.
seguro, a [se'ɣuro, a] *a* (*cierto*) sure, certain; (*fiel*) trustworthy; (*libre del peligro*) safe; (*bien defendido, firme*) secure // *ad* for sure, certainly // *nm* (*COM*) insurance; ~ **contra terceros/a todo riesgo** third party/comprehensive insurance; ~**s sociales** social security *sg*.

seis [seis] *num* six.
seismo ['seismo] *nm* tremor, earthquake.
selección [selek'θjon] *nf* selection; **seleccionar** *vt* to pick, choose, select; **selecto, a** *a* select, choice; (*escogido*) selected.
selva ['selßa] *nf* (*bosque*) forest, woods *pl*; (*jungla*) jungle.
sello ['seʌo] *nm* stamp; (*medicinal*) capsule, pill.
semáforo [se'maforo] *nm* (*AUTO*) traffic lights *pl*; (*FERRO*) signal.
semana [se'mana] *nf* week; **entre** ~ during the week; **semanal, semanario, a** *a* weekly.
semblante [sem'blante] *nm* face; (*fig*) face, appearance.
sembrar [sem'brar] *vt* to sow; (*objetos*) to sprinkle, scatter about; (*noticias*) to spread.
semejante [seme'xante] *a* (*parecido*) similar; ~**s** alike, similar // *nm* fellow man, fellow creature; **no he dicho cosa** ~ I have not said any such thing; **semejanza** *nf* similarity, resemblance.
semejar [seme'xar] *vi* to seem like, resemble; ~**se** *vr* to look alike, be similar.
semen ['semen] *nm* semen; ~**tal** *nm* stud.
semestral [semes'tral] *a* half-yearly, bi-annual.
semicírculo [semi'θirkulo] *nm* semicircle.
semiconsciente [semikons'θjente] *a* semiconscious.
semilla [se'miʌa] *nf* seed.
seminario [semi'narjo] *nm* (*REL*) seminary; (*en universidad*) seminar.
sémola ['semola] *nf* semolina.
sempiterno, a [sempi'terno, a] *a* everlasting // *nf* evergreen.
Sena ['sena] *nm*: **el** ~ the (river) Seine.
senado [se'naðo] *nm* senate; **senador, a** *nm/f* senator.
sencillez [senθi'ʎeθ] *nf* (*gen*) simplicity; (*naturalidad*) naturalness; **sencillo, a** *a* simple; natural, unaffected.
senda ['senda] *nf*, **sendero** [sen'dero] *nm* path, track.
sendos, as ['sendos, as] *apl*: **les dio** ~ **golpes** he hit both of them.
senil [se'nil] *a* senile.
seno ['seno] *nm* (*ANAT*) bosom, bust; (*fig*) bosom; (*vacío*) hollow; ~**s** breasts.
sensación [sensa'θjon] *nf* (*gen*) sensation; (*sentido*) sense; (*sentimiento*) feeling.
sensato, a [sen'sato, a] *a* sensible.
sensible [sen'sible] *a* sensitive; (*apreciable*) perceptible, appreciable; (*pérdida*) considerable.
sensitivo, a [sensi'tißo, a], **sensorio, a** [sen'sorjo, a], **sensorial** [senso'rjal] *a* sensory.
sensual [sen'swal] *a* sensual.
sentado, a [sen'taðo, a] *a* (*establecido*) settled; (*carácter*) sensible; **estar** ~ to sit, be sitting (down) // *nf* sitting; **dar por** ~ to take for granted, assume.

sentar [sen'tar] *vt* to sit, seat; (*fig*) to establish // *vi* (*vestido*) to suit; (*alimento*): ~ **bien/mal a** to agree/disagree with; ~**se** *vr* (*persona*) to sit, sit down; (*el tiempo*) to settle (down); (*los depósitos*) to settle.
sentencia [sen'tenθja] *nf* (*máxima*) maxim, saying; (*JUR*) sentence; **sentenciar** *vt* to sentence // *vi* to give one's opinion.
sentido, a [sen'tiðo, a] *a* (*pérdida*) regrettable; (*carácter*) sensitive // *nm* (*gen*) sense; (*sentimiento*) feeling; (*significado*) sense, meaning; (*dirección*) direction; **mi más** ~ **pésame** my deepest sympathy; ~ **del humor** sense of humour; ~ **único** one-way (street).
sentimental [sentimen'tal] *a* sentimental; **vida** ~ love life.
sentimiento [senti'mjento] *nm* (*emoción*) feeling, emotion; (*sentido*) sense; (*pesar*) regret, sorrow.
sentir [sen'tir] *vt* (*gen*) to feel; (*percibir*) to perceive, sense; (*lamentar*) to regret, be sorry for // *vi* (*tener la sensación*) to feel; (*lamentarse*) to feel sorry // *nm* opinion, judgement; ~**se bien/mal** to feel well/ill; **lo siento** I'm sorry.
seña ['seɲa] *nf* sign; (*MIL*) password; ~**s** *nfpl* address *sg*; ~**s personales** personal details.
señal [se'ɲal] *nf* (*gen*) sign; (*síntoma*) symptom; (*FERRO, TELEC*) signal; (*marca*) mark; (*COM*) deposit; **en** ~ **de** as a token of, as a sign of; ~**ar** *vt* to mark; (*indicar*) to point out, indicate; (*fijar*) to fix, settle; ~**arse** *vr* to make one's mark.
señor [se'ɲor] *nm* (*hombre*) man; (*caballero*) gentleman; (*dueño*) owner, master; (*trato: antes de nombre propio*) Mr; (: *directo*) sir; **muy** ~ **mío** Dear Sir; **el** ~ **alcalde/presidente** the mayor/president.
señora [se'ɲora] *nf* (*dama*) lady; (*trato*) Mrs; (*tratamiento de cortesía*) madam; (*esposa*) wife; **Nuestra S**~ Our Lady.
señorita [seɲo'rita] *nf* (*gen*) Miss; (*mujer joven*) young lady.
señuelo [se'ɲwelo] *nm* decoy.
sepa *etc vb ver* **saber**.
separación [separa'θjon] *nf* separation; (*división*) division; (*distancia*) gap, distance.
separar [sepa'rar] *vt* to separate; (*dividir*) to divide; ~**se** *vr* (*parte*) to come away; (*partes*) to come apart; (*persona*) to leave, go away; (*matrimonio*) to separate; **separatismo** *nm* separatism.
sepia ['sepja] *nf* cuttlefish.
séptico, a ['septiko, a] *a* septic.
septiembre [sep'tjembre] *nm* September.
séptimo, a ['septimo, a] *a, nm* seventh.
sepultar [sepul'tar] *vt* to bury; **sepultura** *nf* (*acto*) burial; (*tumba*) grave, tomb; **sepulturero, a** *nm/f* gravedigger.
sequedad [seke'ðað] *nf* dryness; (*fig*) brusqueness, curtness.

sequía [se'kia] *nf* drought.
séquito ['sekito] *nm* followers *pl*, retinue.
ser [ser] *vi* (*gen*) to be; (*devenir*) to become // *nm* being; ~ **de** (*origen*) to be from, come from; (*hecho de*) to be (made) of; (*pertenecer a*) to belong to; **es la una** it is one o'clock; **es de esperar que** it is to be hoped that; **era de ver** it was worth seeing, you should have seen it; **a no ~ que** unless; **de no ~ así** if it were not so, were it not so; **o sea** that is to say; **sea como sea** be that as it may.
serenarse [sere'narse] *vr* to calm down.
sereno, a [se'reno, a] *a* (*persona*) calm, unruffled; (*el tiempo*) fine, settled; (*ambiente*) calm, peaceful // *nm* night watchman.
serie ['serje] *nf* series; (*cadena*) sequence, succession; **fuera de** ~ out of order; **fabricación en** ~ mass production.
seriedad [serje'ðað] *nf* seriousness; (*formalidad*) reliability; (*de crisis*) gravity, seriousness; **serio, a** *a* serious; reliable, dependable; grave, serious; **en serio** *ad* seriously.
sermón [ser'mon] *nm* (*REL*) sermon.
serpentear [serpente'ar] *vi* to wriggle; (*fig*) to wind, snake.
serpentina [serpen'tina] *nf* streamer.
serpiente [ser'pjente] *nf* snake; ~ **boa** boa constrictor; ~ **pitón** python; ~ **de cascabel** rattlesnake.
serranía [serra'nia] *nf* mountainous area; **serrano, a** *a* highland *cpd*, hill *cpd* // *nm/f* highlander.
serrar [se'rrar] *vt* = **aserrar.**
serrín [se'rrin] *nm* = **aserrín.**
serrucho [se'rrutʃo] *nm* saw.
servicio [ser'βiθjo] *nm* service; ~**s** toilet(s).
servidor, a [serβi'ðor, a] *nm/f* servant; **su seguro** ~ (**s.s.s.**) yours faithfully; **servidumbre** *nf* (*sujeción*) servitude; (*criados*) servants *pl*, staff.
servil [ser'βil] *a* servile.
servilleta [serβi'ʎeta] *nf* serviette, napkin.
servir [ser'βir] *vt* to serve // *vi* to serve; (*tener utilidad*) to be of use, be useful; ~**se** *vr* to serve *or* help o.s.; ~**se de algo** to make use of sth, use sth; **sírvase pasar** please come in.
sesenta [se'senta] *num* sixty.
sesgado, a [ses'ɣaðo, a] *a* slanted, slanting; **sesgo** *nm* slant; (*fig*) slant, twist.
sesión [se'sjon] *nf* (*POL*) session, sitting; (*CINE*) showing.
seso ['seso] *nm* brain; **sesudo, a** *a* sensible, wise.
seta ['seta] *nf* mushroom.
setenta [se'tenta] *num* seventy.
seudo... ['seuðo] *pref* pseudo... .
seudónimo [seu'ðonimo] *nm* pseudonym.
severidad [seβeri'ðað] *nf* severity; **severo, a** *a* severe.
Sevilla [se'βiʎa] *n* Seville.

sexo ['sekso] *nm* sex.
sexto, a ['seksto, a] *a*, *nm* sixth.
sexual [sek'swal] *a* sexual; **vida** ~ **sex** life.
si [si] *conj* if; **me pregunto** ~ ... I wonder if *or* whether... .
sí [si] *ad* yes // *nm* consent // *pron* (*gen*) oneself; (*sg: m*) himself; (: *f*) herself; (: *de cosa*) itself; (*de usted*) yourself; (*pl*) themselves; (*de ustedes*) yourselves; (*recíproco*) each other; **él no quiere pero yo** ~ he doesn't want to but I do; **ella** ~ **vendrá** she will certainly come, she is sure to come; **claro que** ~ of course; **creo que** ~ I think so.
siderúrgico, a [siðe'rurxico, a] *a* iron and steel *cpd* // *nf*: **la** ~**a** the iron and steel industry.
sidra ['siðra] *nf* cider.
siembra ['sjembra] *nf* sowing.
siempre ['sjempre] *ad* (*gen*) always; (*todo el tiempo*) all the time; ~ **que** *conj* (*cada vez*) whenever; (*dado que*) provided that; **para** ~ for ever.
sien [sjen] *nf* temple.
siento *etc vb ver* **sentar, sentir.**
sierra ['sjerra] *nf* (*TEC*) saw; (*cadena de montañas*) mountain range.
siervo, a ['sjerβo, a] *nm/f* slave.
siesta ['sjesta] *nf* siesta, nap.
siete ['sjete] *num* seven.
sífilis ['sifilis] *nf* syphilis.
sifón [si'fon] *nm* syphon; **whisky con** ~ whisky and soda.
sigla ['siɣla] *nf* symbol.
siglo ['siɣlo] *nm* century; (*fig*) age.
significación [siɣnifika'θjon] *nf* significance.
significado [siɣnifi'kaðo] *nm* significance; (*de palabra*) meaning.
significar [siɣnifi'kar] *vt* to mean, signify; (*notificar*) to make known, express; ~**se** *vr* to become known, make a name for o.s.; **significativo, a** *a* significant.
signo ['siɣno] *nm* sign; ~ **de admiración** *o* **exclamación** exclamation mark; ~ **de interrogación** question mark.
sigo *etc vb ver* **seguir.**
siguiente [si'ɣjente] *a* next, following.
siguió *etc vb ver* **seguir.**
sílaba ['silaβa] *nf* syllable.
silbar [sil'βar] *vt*, *vi* to whistle; **silbato** *nm* whistle; **silbido** *nm* whistle, whistling.
silenciador [silenθja'ðor] *nm* silencer.
silenciar [silen'θjar] *vt* (*persona*) to silence; (*escándalo*) to hush up; **silencio** *nm* silence, quiet; **silencioso, a** *a* silent, quiet.
silicio [si'liθjo] *nm* silicon.
silueta [si'lweta] *nf* silhouette; (*de edificio*) outline; (*figura*) figure.
silvestre [sil'βestre] *a* rustic, rural; (*salvaje*) wild.
silla ['siʎa] *nf* (*asiento*) chair; (*de jinete*) saddle.

sillón [si'ʌon] *nm* armchair, easy chair; ~ **de ruedas** wheelchair.

simbólico, a [sim'boliko, a] *a* symbolic(al); **símbolo** *nm* symbol.

simetría [sime'tria] *nf* symmetry.

simiente [si'mjente] *nf* seed.

similar [simi'lar] *a* similar.

simio ['simjo] *nm* ape.

simpatía [simpa'tia] *nf* liking; (*afecto*) affection; (*amabilidad*) kindness; (*solidaridad*) mutual support, solidarity; **simpático, a** *a* nice, pleasant; kind; **simpatizante** *nm/f* sympathiser; **simpatizar** *vi*: **simpatizar con** to get on well with.

simple ['simple] *a* (*gen*) simple; (*elemental*) simple, easy; (*mero*) mere; (*puro*) pure, sheer // *nm/f* simpleton; ~**za** *nf* simpleness; (*necedad*) silly thing; **simplicidad** *nf* simplicity; **simplificar** *vt* to simplify.

simular [simu'lar] *vt* to simulate.

simultáneo, a [simul'taneo, a] *a* simultaneous.

sin [sin] *prep* without; **la ropa está** ~ **lavar** the clothes are unwashed; ~ **que** *conj* without; ~ **embargo** however, still.

sinagoga [sina'voxa] *nf* synagogue.

sinceridad [sinθeri'ðað] *nf* sincerity; **sincero, a** *a* sincere.

sincronizar [sinkroni'θar] *vt* to synchronize.

sindical [sindi'kal] *a* union *cpd*, trade-union *cpd*; ~**ista** *nm/f* trade-unionist; **sindicato** *nm* (*de trabajadores*) trade(s) union; (*de negociantes*) syndicate.

sinfín [sin'fin] *nm*: **un** ~ **de** a great many, no end of.

sinfonía [sinfo'nia] *nf* symphony.

singular [singu'lar] *a* singular; (*fig*) outstanding, exceptional; (*pey*) peculiar, odd; ~**idad** *nf* singularity, peculiarity; ~**izar** *vt* to single out; ~**izarse** *vr* to distinguish o.s., stand out.

siniestro, a [si'njestro, a] *a* left; (*fig*) sinister.

sinnúmero [sin'numero] *nm* = **sinfín**.

sino ['sino] *nm* fate, destiny // *conj* (*pero*) but; (*salvo*) except, save.

sinónimo [si'nonimo] *nm* synonym.

sinrazón [sinra'θon] *nf* wrong, injustice.

síntesis ['sintesis] *nf* synthesis; **sintético, a** *a* synthetic; **sintetizar** *vt* to synthesize.

sintió *vb ver* **sentir**.

síntoma ['sintoma] *nm* symptom.

sinvergüenza [sinßer'ɣwenθa] *nm/f* shameless person.

sionismo [sjo'nismo] *nm* Zionism.

siquiera [si'kjera] *conj* even if, even though // *ad* at least; **ni** ~ not even.

sirena [si'rena] *nf* siren.

sirviente, a [sir'ßjente, a] *nm/f* servant.

sirvo *etc vb ver* **servir**.

sisear [sise'ar] *vt, vi* to hiss.

sismógrafo [sis'moɣrafo] *nm* seismograph.

sistema [sis'tema] *nm* system; (*método*) method; **sistemático, a** *a* systematic.

sitiar [si'tjar] *vt* to beseige, lay seige to.

sitio ['sitjo] *nm* (*lugar*) place; (*espacio*) room, space; (*MIL*) siege.

situación [sitwa'θjon] *nf* situation, position; (*estatus*) position, standing.

situar [si'twar] *vt* to place, put; (*edificio*) to locate, situate.

slip [slip] *nm* pants *pl*, briefs *pl*.

smoking ['smokin] (*pl* ~**s**) *nm* dinner jacket.

so [so] *prep* under.

SO *abr de* **sudoeste**.

sobaco [so'ßako] *nm* armpit.

soberanía [soßera'nia] *nf* sovereignty; **soberano, a** *a* sovereign; (*fig*) supreme // *nm/f* sovereign.

soberbio, a [so'ßerßjo, a] *a* (*orgulloso*) proud; (*altivo*) haughty, arrogant; (*fig*) magnificent, superb // *nf* pride; haughtiness, arrogance; magnificence; (*cólera*) anger.

sobornar [soßor'nar] *vt* to bribe; **soborno** *nm* bribe.

sobra ['soßra] *nf* excess, surplus; ~**s** *nfpl* left-overs, scraps; **de** ~ surplus, extra; **tengo de** ~ I've more than enough; ~**do, a** (*de* ~) more than enough; (*excesivo*) excessive // *ad* too, exceedingly; **sobrante** *a* remaining, extra // *nm* surplus, remainder; **sobrar** *vt* to exceed, surpass // *vi* (*tener de más*) to be more than enough; (*quedar*) to remain, be left (over).

sobre ['soßre] *prep* (*gen*) on; (*encima*) on (top of); (*por encima de, arriba de*) over, above; (*más que*) more than; (*además*) in addition to, besides; (*alrededor de, tratando de*) about // *nm* envelope.

sobrecama [soßre'kama] *nf* bedspread.

sobrecargar [soßrekar'xar] *vt* (*camión*) to overload; (*com*) to surcharge.

sobrehumano, a [soßreu'mano, a] *a* superhuman.

sobrellevar [soßreʎe'ßar] *vt* (*fig*) to bear, endure.

sobremarcha [soßre'martʃa] *nf* (*AUTO*) overdrive.

sobrenatural [soßrenatu'ral] *a* supernatural.

sobrepasar [soßrepa'sar] *vt* to exceed, surpass.

sobreponer [soßrepo'ner] *vt* (*poner encima*) to put on top; (*añadir*) to add; ~**se** *vr*: ~**se a** to win through, pull through.

sobreprecio [soßre'preθjo] *nm* surcharge.

sobresaliente [soßresa'ljente] *a* projecting; (*fig*) outstanding, excellent; **sobresalir** *vi* to project, jut out; to stand out, excel.

sobresaltar [soßresal'tar] *vt* (*asustar*) to scare, frighten; (*sobrecoger*) to startle; **sobresalto** *nm* (*movimiento*) start; (*susto*) scare; (*turbación*) sudden shock; **de sobresalto** suddenly.

sobrescrito [soßres'krito] *nm* address.
sobretodo [soßre'toðo] *nm* overcoat.
sobreviviente [soßreßi'ßjente] *a* surviving // *nm/f* survivor; **sobrevivir** *vi* to survive.
sobriedad [soßrje'ðað] *nf* sobriety, soberness; (*moderación*) moderation, restraint.
sobrino, a [so'ßrino, a] *nm/f* nephew/niece.
sobrio, a ['soßrjo, a] *a* sober; (*moderado*) moderate, restrained.
socarrón, ona [soka'rron, ona] *a* (*sarcástico*) sarcastic, ironic(al); (*astuto*) crafty, cunning.
sociable [so'θjaßle] *a* (*persona*) sociable, friendly; (*animal*) social.
social [so'θjal] *a* social; (*COM*) company *cpd.*
socialdemócrata [soθjalde'mokrata] *nm/f* social democrat.
socialista [soθja'lista] *a, nm/f* socialist.
socializar [soθjali'θar] *vt* to socialize.
sociedad [soθje'ðað] *nf* (*gen*) society; (*COM*) company; ~ **anónima (SA)** limited company.
socio, a ['soθjo, a] *nm/f* (*miembro*) member; (*COM*) partner; ~ **comandatario** sleeping partner.
sociología [soθjolo'xia] *nf* sociology.
socorrer [soko'rrer] *vt* to help; **socorro** *nm* (*ayuda*) help, aid; (*MIL*) relief; ¡**socorro!** help!
soda ['soða] *nf* (*sosa*) soda; (*bebida*) soda water.
sofá [so'fa] (*pl* ~**s**) *nm* sofa, settee; ~-**cama** *nm* studio couch.
sofisticación [sofistika'θjon] *nf* sophistication.
sofocar [sofo'kar] *vt* to suffocate; (*apagar*) to smother, put out; ~**se** *vr* to suffocate; (*fig*) to blush, feel embarrassed; **sofoco** *nm* suffocation; embarrassment.
soga ['soxa] *nf* rope.
sois *vb ver* **ser.**
sojuzgar [soxuθ'xar] *vt* to subdue, rule despotically.
sol [sol] *nm* sun; (*luz*) sunshine, sunlight; **hace** ~ it is sunny.
solamente [sola'mente] *ad* only, just.
solapa [so'lapa] *nf* (*de ropa*) lapel; (*de libro*) jacket.
solar [so'lar] *a* solar, sun *cpd.*
solaz [so'laθ] *nm* recreation, relaxation; (*alivio*) solace; ~**ar** *vt* (*divertir*) to amuse; (*aliviar*) to console.
soldada [sol'daða] *nf* pay.
soldado [sol'daðo] *nm* soldier.
soldador [solda'ðor] *nm* soldering iron; (*persona*) welder; **soldar** *vt* to solder, weld; (*unir*) to join, unite.
soledad [sole'ðað] *nf* solitude; (*estado infeliz*) loneliness; (*nostalgia*) grieving, mourning.
solemne [so'lemne] *a* solemn; **solemnidad** *nf* solemnity.

soler [so'ler] *vi* to be in the habit of, be accustomed to.
solfa ['solfa] *nf*, **solfeo** [sol'feo] *nm* solfa; (*conjunto de signos*) musical notation.
solicitación [soliθita'θjon] *nf* request; (*de votos*) canvassing; **solicitar** *vt* (*permiso*) to ask for, seek; (*puesto*) to apply for; (*votos*) to canvass; (*atención*) to attract; (*persona*) to pursue, chase after.
solícito, a [so'liθito, a] *a* (*diligente*) diligent; (*cuidadoso*) careful; **solicitud** *nf* (*calidad*) great care; (*petición*) request; (*memorial*) petition; (*a un puesto*) application.
solidaridad [soliðari'ðað] *nf* solidarity; **solidario, a** *a* (*participación*) joint, common; (*compromiso*) mutually binding.
solidez [soli'ðeθ] *nf* solidity; **sólido, a** *a* solid.
soliloquio [soli'lokjo] *nm* soliloquy, monologue.
solista [so'lista] *nm/f* soloist.
solitario, a [soli'tarjo, a] *a* lonely, solitary // *nm/f* recluse; (*en la sociedad*) loner // *nm* solitaire.
soliviar [soli'ßjar] *vt* to lift.
solo, a ['solo, a] *a* (*único*) single, sole; (*sin compañía*) alone; (*solitario*) lonely; **hay una** ~**a dificultad** there is just one difficulty; **a** ~**as** alone, by o.s.
sólo ['solo] *ad* only, just.
solomillo [solo'miʎo] *nm* sirloin.
soltar [sol'tar] *vt* (*dejar ir*) to let go of; (*desprender*) to unfasten, loosen; (*librar*) to release, set free; (*estornudo, risa*) to let out.
soltero, a [sol'tero, a] *a* single, unmarried // *nm* bachelor // *nf* single woman, spinster.
soltura [sol'tura] *nf* looseness, slackness; (*de los miembros*) agility, ease of movement; (*en el hablar*) fluency, ease; (*MED*) diarrhoea.
soluble [so'lußle] *a* (*QUÍMICA*) soluble; (*problema*) solvable.
solución [solu'θjon] *nf* solution; **solucionar** *vt* (*problema*) to solve; (*asunto*) to settle.
solventar [solßen'tar] *vt* (*pagar*) to settle, pay; (*resolver*) to resolve.
sollozar [soʎo'θar] *vi* to sob; **sollozo** *nm* sob.
sombra ['sombra] *nf* shadow; (*como protección*) shade; ~**s** *nfpl* darkness *sg*; **tener buena/mala** ~ to be lucky/unlucky.
sombreador [sombrea'ðor] *nm*: ~ **de ojos** eyeshadow.
sombrero [som'brero] *nm* hat.
sombrilla [som'briʎa] *nf* parasol, sunshade.
sombrío, a [som'brio, a] *a* (*oscuro*) dark; (*sombreado*) shaded; (*fig*) sombre, sad; (*persona*) gloomy.
somero, a [so'mero, a] *a* superficial.
someter [some'ter] *vt* (*país*) to conquer; (*persona*) to subject to one's will; (*informe*) to present, submit; ~**se** *vr* to give in,

yield, submit; ~ **a** to subject to.
somnambulismo [somnambu'lismo] *nm* sleepwalking; **somnámbulo, a** *nm/f* sleepwalker.
somnífero [som'nifero] *nm* sleeping pill.
somos *vb ver* **ser.**
son [son] *vb ver* **ser** // *nm* sound; **en ~ de broma** as a joke.
sonar [so'nar] *vt* to ring // *vi* to sound; (*hacer ruido*) to make a noise; (*pronunciarse*) to be sounded, be pronounced; (*ser conocido*) to sound familiar; (*campana*) to ring; (*reloj*) to strike, chime; ~**se** *vr*: ~**se** (**las narices**) to blow one's nose; **me suena ese nombre** that name rings a bell.
sonda ['sonda] *nf* (*NAUT*) sounding; (*TEC*) bore, drill; (*MED*) probe; **sondear** *vt* to sound; to bore (into), drill; to probe, sound; (*fig*) to sound out; **sondeo** *nm* sounding; boring, drilling; (*fig*) poll, enquiry.
sónico, a ['soniko, a] *a* sonic, sound *cpd.*
sonido [so'niðo] *nm* sound.
sonoro, a [so'noro, a] *a* sonorous; (*resonante*) loud, resonant.
sonreír [sonre'ir] *vi*, ~**se** *vr* to smile; **sonriente** *a* smiling; **sonrisa** *nf* smile.
sonrojo [son'roxo] *nm* blush.
soñador, a [soɲa'ðor, a] *nm/f* dreamer; **soñar** *vt*, *vi* to dream; **soñar con** to dream about, dream of.
soñoliento, a [soɲo'ljento, a] *a* sleepy, drowsy.
sopa ['sopa] *nf* soup.
soplador [sopla'ðor] *nm* fan, ventilator.
soplar [so'plar] *vt* (*polvo*) to blow away, blow off; (*inflar*) to blow up; (*vela*) to blow out // *vi* to blow; ~**se** *vr* (*fam: ufanarse*) to get conceited; **soplo** *nm* blow, puff; (*de viento*) puff, gust.
soporífero [sopo'rifero] *nm* sleeping pill.
soportable [sopor'taßle] *a* bearable; **soportar** *vt* to bear, carry; (*fig*) to bear, put up with; **soporte** *nm* support; (*fig*) pillar, support.
soprano [so'prano] *nf* soprano.
sorber [sor'ßer] *vt* (*chupar*) to sip; (*inhalar*) to inhale; (*tragar*) to swallow (up); (*absorber*) to soak up, absorb.
sorbete [sor'ßete] *nm* iced fruit drink.
sorbo ['sorßo] *nm* (*trago*) gulp, swallow; (*chupada*) sip.
sordera [sor'ðera] *nf* deafness.
sórdido, a ['sorðiðo, a] *a* dirty, squalid; (*palabra*) nasty, dirty; (*fig*) mean.
sordo, a ['sorðo, a] *a* (*persona*) deaf; (*máquina*) quiet // *nm/f* deaf person; **a ~as** on the quiet; ~**mudo, a** *a* deaf and dumb.
sorprendente [sorpren'dente] *a* surprising; **sorprender** *vt* to surprise; **sorpresa** *nf* surprise.
sortear [sorte'ar] *vt* to draw lots for; (*objeto*) to raffle; (*dificultad*) to avoid; **sorteo** *nm* drawing lots; raffle.
sosegado, a [sose'ɣaðo, a] *a* quiet, calm; **sosegar** *vt* to quieten, calm; (*el ánimo*) to

reassure // *vi* to rest; **sosiego** *nm* quiet(ness), calm(ness).
soslayo [sos'lajo]: **al** *o* **de** ~ *ad* obliquely, sideways.
soso, a ['soso, a] *a* (*CULIN*) tasteless; (*fig*) dull, uninteresting.
sospecha [sos'petʃa] *nf* suspicion; **sospechar** *vt* to suspect; **sospechoso, a** *a* suspicious; (*testimonio, opinión*) suspect // *nm/f* suspect.
sostén [sos'ten] *nm* (*apoyo*) support; (*prenda femenina*) bra, brassière; (*alimentación*) sustenance, food.
sostener [soste'ner] *vt* to support; (*mantener*) to keep up, maintain; (*alimentar*) to sustain, keep going; ~**se** *vr* to support o.s.; (*seguir*) to continue, remain; **sostenido, a** *a* continuous, sustained; (*prolongado*) prolonged.
sótano ['sotano] *nm* basement.
soterrar [sote'rrar] *vt* to bury.
soviético, a [so'ßjetiko, a] *a* Soviet.
soy *vb ver* **ser.**
sport [sport] *nm* sport.
Sr *abr de* **Señor.**
Sra *abr de* **Señora.**
S.R.C. *abr de* **se ruega contestación** R.S.V.P.
Sta *abr de* **Santa; Señorita.**
status ['status] *nm inv* status.
Sto *abr de* **Santo.**
su [su] *pron* (*de él*) his; (*de ella*) her; (*de una cosa*) its; (*de ellos, ellas*) their; (*de usted, ustedes*) your.
suave ['swaße] *a* gentle; (*superficie*) smooth; (*trabajo*) easy; (*música, voz*) soft, sweet; **suavidad** *nf* gentleness; smoothness; softness, sweetness; **suavizar** *vt* to soften; (*quitar la aspereza*) to smooth (out).
subalimentado, a [sußalimen'taðo, a] *a* undernourished.
subasta [su'ßasta] *nf* auction; **subastar** *vt* to auction (off).
subconsciencia [sußkons'θjenθja] *nf* subconscious, **subconsciente** *a* subconscious.
subdesarrollado, a [sußðesarro'ʎaðo, a] *a* underdeveloped; **subdesarrollo** *nm* underdevelopment.
súbdito, a ['sußðito, a] *nm/f* subject.
subdividir [sußðiβi'ðir] *vt* to subdivide.
subestimar [sußesti'mar] *vt* to underestimate, underrate; (*propiedad*) to undervalue.
subexpuesto, a [sußeks'pwesto, a] *a* underexposed.
subido, a [su'ßiðo, a] *a* (*color*) bright, strong; (*precio*) high // *nf* (*gen*) ascent, climb; (*de precio*) rise, increase; (*camino*) way up; (*pendiente*) slope, hill.
subir [su'ßir] *vt* (*objeto*) to raise, lift up; (*cuesta, calle*) to go up; (*montaña*) to climb; (*precio*) to raise, put up // *vi* to go/come up; (*a un coche*) to get in; (*a un autobús*) to get on; (*precio*) to rise, go up; (*río*) to rise; ~**se** *vr* to get up, climb.

súbito, a ['suβito, a] a (*repentino*) sudden; (*imprevisto*) unexpected; (*precipitado*) hasty, rash // ad: (**de**) ~ suddenly.

sublevación [suβleβa'θjon] nf revolt, rising.

sublime [su'βlime] a sublime.

submarino, a [suβma'rino, a] a underwater // nm submarine.

subordinado, a [suβorði'naðo, a] a, nm/f subordinate.

subrayar [suβra'jar] vt to underline.

subrepticio, a [suβrep'tiθjo, a] a surreptitious.

subsanar [suβsa'nar] vt (*reparar*) to make good; (*perdonar*) to excuse; (*sobreponerse a*) to overcome.

subscribir [suβskri'βir] vt = **suscribir.**

subsidiario, a [suβsi'ðjarjo, a] a subsidiary.

subsidio [suβ'siðjo] nm (*ayuda*) aid, financial help; (*subvención*) subsidy, grant; (*de enfermedad, paro etc*) benefit.

subsistencia [suβsis'tenθja] nf subsistence; **subsistir** vi (*gen*) to subsist; (*vivir*) to live; (*sobrevivir*) to survive, endure.

subterráneo, a [suβte'rraneo, a] a underground, subterranean // nm underpass, underground passage.

suburbano, a [suβur'βano, a] a suburban.

suburbio [su'βurβjo] nm (*barrio*) slum quarter; (*afueras*) suburbs pl.

subvencionar [suββenθjo'nar] vt to subsidize.

subversión [suββer'sjon] nf subversion; **subversivo, a** a subversive.

subyugar [suβju'ɣar] vt (*país*) to subjugate, subdue; (*enemigo*) to overpower; (*voluntad*) to dominate.

suceder [suθe'ðer] vt, vi to happen; (*seguir*) to succeed, follow; **lo que sucede es que...** the fact is that...; **sucesión** nf succession; (*serie*) sequence, series.

sucesivamente [suθesiβa'mente] ad: **y así** ~ and so on.

sucesivo, a [suθe'siβo, a] a successive, following; **en lo** ~ in future, from now on.

suceso [su'θeso] nm (*hecho*) event, happening; (*incidente*) incident; (*resultado*) outcome.

suciedad [suθje'ðað] nf (*estado*) dirtiness; (*mugre*) dirt, filth.

sucinto, a [su'θinto, a] a succinct, concise.

sucio, a ['suθjo, a] a dirty.

suculento, a [suku'lento, a] a succulent.

sucumbir [sukum'bir] vi to succumb.

sucursal [sukur'sal] nf branch (office).

sudamericano, a [suðameri'kano, a] a South American.

sudar [su'ðar] vt, vi to sweat.

sudeste [su'ðeste] nm south-east; **sudoeste** nm south-west.

sudor [su'ðor] nm sweat; ~**oso, a**, **sudoso, a**, ~**iento, a** a sweaty, sweating.

Suecia ['sweθja] nf Sweden; **sueco, a** a Swedish // nm/f Swede.

suegro, a ['sweɣro, a] nm/f father-/mother-in-law.

suela ['swela] nf sole.

sueldo ['sweldo] nm pay, wage(s) (*pl*); **el** ~ **mínimo** the minimum wage.

suele etc vb ver **soler.**

suelo ['swelo] nm (*tierra*) ground; (*de casa*) floor.

suelto, a ['swelto, a] a loose; (*libre*) free; (*separado*) detached, individual; (*ágil*) quick, agile; (*corriente*) fluent, flowing // nm (loose) change, small change.

sueño etc vb ver **soñar** // ['sweɲo] nm sleep; (*somnolencia*) sleepiness, drowsiness; (*lo soñado, fig*) dream; **tener** ~ to be sleepy.

suero ['swero] nm serum.

suerte ['swerte] nf (*fortuna*) luck; (*azar*) chance; (*destino*) fate, destiny; (*condición*) lot; (*género*) sort, kind; **tener** ~ to be lucky; **de otra** ~ otherwise, if not; **de** ~ **que** so that, in such a way that.

suéter ['sweter] nm sweater.

suficiente [sufi'θjente] a enough, sufficient; (*capaz*) capable.

sufragio [su'fraxjo] nm (*voto*) vote; (*derecho de voto*) suffrage; (*ayuda*) help, aid.

sufrimiento [sufri'mjento] nm (*dolor*) suffering; (*paciencia*) patience; (*tolerancia*) tolerance.

sufrir [su'frir] vt (*padecer*) to suffer; (*soportar*) to bear, stand, put up with; (*apoyar*) to hold up, support // vi to suffer.

sugerencia [suxe'renθja] nf suggestion; **sugerir** vt to suggest; (*sutilmente*) to hint.

sugestión [suxes'tjon] nf suggestion; (*sutil*) hint; **sugestionar** vt to influence.

sugestivo, a [suxes'tiβo, a] a stimulating; (*fascinante*) fascinating.

suicida [sui'θiða] a suicidal // nm/f suicidal person; (*muerto*) suicide, person who has committed suicide; **suicidio** nm suicide.

Suiza ['swiθa] nf Switzerland; **suizo, a** a, nm/f Swiss.

sujeción [suxe'θjon] nf subjection.

sujetador [suxeta'ðor] nm fastener, clip; (*de papeles*) paper clip.

sujetar [suxe'tar] vt (*fijar*) to fasten; (*detener*) to hold down; (*fig*) to subject, subjugate; ~**se** vr to subject o.s.; **sujeto, a** a fastened, secure // nm subject; (*individuo*) individual; **sujeto a** a subject to.

suma ['suma] nf (*cantidad*) total, sum; (*de dinero*) sum; (*acto*) adding (up), addition; (*resumen*) summary; (*esencia*) essence; **en** ~ in short; ~**dora** nf adding machine.

sumamente [suma'mente] ad extremely, exceedingly.

sumar [su'mar] vt to add (up); (*reunir*) to collect, gather; (*abreviar*) to summarize, sum up // vi to add up.

sumario, a [su'marjo, a] a brief, concise // nm summary.

sumergir [sumer'xir] vt to submerge; (*hundir*) to sink; (*bañar*) to immerse, dip;

sumersión *nf* submersion; (*fig*) absorption.

sumidero [sumi'ðero] *nm* drain; (*TEC*) sump.

suministrador, a [suministra'ðor, a] *nm/f* supplier; **suministrar** *vt* to supply, provide; **suministro** *nm* supply; (*acto*) supplying, providing.

sumir [su'mir] *vt* to sink, submerge; (*fig*) to plunge.

sumisión [sumi'sjon] *nf* (*acto*) submission; (*calidad*) submissiveness, docility; **sumiso, a** *a* submissive, docile.

sumo, a ['sumo, a] *a* great, extreme; (*mayor*) highest, supreme.

supe *etc vb ver* **saber.**

super... [super] *pref* super..., over... // *nm* high-grade fuel.

superar [supe'rar] *vt* (*sobreponerse a*) to overcome; (*rebasar*) to surpass, do better than; (*pasar*) to go beyond; ~**se** *vr* to excel o.s.

superávit [supe'raßit] *nm* surplus.

supercarburante [superkarßu'rante] *nm* high-grade fuel.

superestructura [superestruk'tura] *nf* superstructure.

superficial [superfi'θjal] *a* superficial; (*medida*) surface *cpd*, of the surface.

superficie [super'fiθje] *nf* surface; (*área*) area.

superfluo, a [su'perflwo, a] *a* superfluous.

superintendente [superinten'dente] *nm/f* supervisor, superintendent.

superior [supe'rjor] *a* (*piso, clase*) upper; (*temperatura, número, nivel*) higher; (*mejor: calidad, producto*) superior, better // *nm/f* superior; ~**idad** *nf* superiority.

supermercado [supermer'kaðo] *nm* supermarket.

supersónico, a [super'soniko, a] *a* supersonic.

superstición [supersti'θjon] *nf* superstition; **supersticioso, a** *a* superstitious.

supervisor, a [superßi'sor, a] *nm/f* supervisor.

supervivencia [superßi'ßenθja] *nf* survival.

supiera *etc vb ver* **saber.**

suplementario, a [suplemen'tarjo, a] *a* supplementary; **suplemento** *nm* supplement.

suplente [su'plente] *a, nm/f* substitute.

súplica ['suplika] *nf* request; (*REL*) supplication.

suplicante [supli'kante] *nm/f* applicant.

suplicar [supli'kar] *vt* (*cosa*) to beg (for), plead for; (*persona*) to beg, plead with.

suplicio [su'pliθjo] *nm* torture.

suplir [su'plir] *vt* (*compensar*) to make good, make up for; (*reemplazar*) to replace, substitute // *vi*: ~ **a** *o* **por** to take the place of, substitute for.

suponer [supo'ner] *vt* to suppose // *vi* to have authority; **suposición** *nf* supposition; (*autoridad*) authority.

supremacía [suprema'θia] *nf* supremacy.

supremo, a [su'premo, a] *a* supreme.

supresión [supre'sjon] *nf* suppression; (*de derecho*) abolition; (*de dificultad*) removal; (*de palabra*) deletion; (*de restricción*) cancellation, lifting.

suprimir [supri'mir] *vt* to suppress; (*derecho, costumbre*) to abolish; (*dificultad*) to remove; (*palabra*) to delete; (*restricción*) to cancel, lift.

supuesto, a [su'pwesto, a] *a* (*hipotético*) supposed; (*falso*) false // *nm* assumption, hypothesis; ~ **que** *conj* since; **por** ~ of course.

sur [sur] *nm* south.

surcar [sur'kar] *vt* to plough, furrow; (*superficie*) to cut, score; **surco** *nm* groove; (*AGR*) furrow.

surgir [sur'xir] *vi* to arise, emerge; (*dificultad*) to come up, crop up.

surtido, a [sur'tiðo, a] *a* mixed, assorted // *nm* (*gen*) selection, assortment; (*abastecimiento*) supply, stock.

surtir [sur'tir] *vt* to supply, provide // *vi* to spout, spurt.

susceptible [susθep'tißle] *a* susceptible; (*sensible*) sensitive; ~ **de** capable of.

suscitar [susθi'tar] *vt* to cause, provoke; (*interés*) to arouse.

suscribir [suskri'ßir] *vt* (*firmar*) to sign; (*respaldar*) to subscribe to; endorse; ~**se** *vr* to subscribe; **suscripción** *nf* subscription.

suspender [suspen'der] *vt* (*objeto*) to hang (up), suspend; (*trabajo*) to stop, suspend; (*a estudiante*) to fail; **suspensión** *nf* suspension; (*fig*) stoppage, suspension.

suspenso, a [sus'penso, a] *a* hanging, suspended; (*estudiante*) failed; (*admirado*) astonished, amazed // *nm*: **quedar** *o* **estar en** ~ to be pending.

suspicacia [suspi'kaθja] *nf* suspicion, mistrust; **suspicaz** *a* suspicious, distrustful.

suspirar [suspi'rar] *vi* to sigh; **suspiro** *nm* sigh.

sustancia [sus'tanθja] *nf* substance.

sustentar [susten'tar] *vt* (*alimentar*) to sustain, nourish; (*objeto*) to hold up, support; (*idea, teoría*) to maintain, uphold; (*fig*) to sustain, keep going; **sustento** *nm* support; (*alimento*) sustenance, food.

sustituir [sustitu'ir] *vt* to substitute, replace; **sustituto, a** *nm/f* substitute, replacement.

susto ['susto] *nm* fright, scare.

sustraer [sustra'er] *vt* to remove, take away; (*MAT*) to subtract; ~**se** *vr* (*evitar*) to avoid; (*retirarse*) to withdraw.

susurrar [susu'rrar] *vi* to whisper; **susurro** *nm* whisper.

sutil [su'til] *a* subtle; (*tenue*) thin; ~**eza** *nf* subtlety; thinness.

suyo, a ['sujo, a] *a* (*con artículo o después del verbo ser: de él*) his; (: *de ella*) hers; (: *de ellos, ellas*) theirs; (: *de Ud, Uds*) yours; (*después de un nombre: de él*) of his; (: *de* *ella*) of hers; (: *de ellos, ellas*) of theirs; (: *de Ud, Uds*) of yours.

T

t *abr de* **tonelada.**

taba ['taßa] *nf* (ANAT) ankle bone; (*juego*) jacks *sg.*

tabaco [ta'ßako] *nm* tobacco; (*fam*) cigarettes *pl.*

taberna [ta'ßerna] *nf* bar; **tabernero, a** *nm/f* (*encargado*) publican; (*camarero*) barman.

tabique [ta'ßike] *nm* (*pared*) thin wall; (*para dividir*) partition.

tabla ['taßla] *nf* (*de madera*) plank; (*estante*) shelf; (*de anuncios*) board; (*lista, catálogo*) list; (*mostrador*) counter; (*de vestido*) pleat; (ARTE) panel; ~s (TAUR, TEATRO) boards; **hacer** ~s to draw; ~**do** *nm* (*plataforma*) platform; (*suelo*) plank floor; (TEATRO) stage.

tablero [ta'ßlero] *nm* (*de madera*) plank, board; (*pizarra*) blackboard; (*de ajedrez, damas*) board; (AUTO) dashboard.

tablilla [ta'ßliʎa] *nf* small board; (MED) splint.

tablón [ta'ßlon] *nm* (*de suelo*) plank; (*de techo*) beam; (*de anuncios*) notice board.

tabú [ta'ßu] *nm* taboo.

tabular [taßu'lar] *vt* to tabulate.

taburete [taßu'rete] *nm* stool.

tacaño, a [ta'kaɲo, a] *a* (*avaro*) mean; (*astuto*) crafty.

tácito, a ['taθito, a] *a* tacit.

taciturno, a [taθi'turno, a] *a* (*callado*) silent; (*malhumorado*) sullen.

taco ['tako] *nm* (BILLAR) cue; (*libro de billetes*) book; (*manojo de billetes*) wad; (AM) heel; (*tarugo*) peg; (*fam: bocado*) snack; (: *palabrota*) swear word; (: *trago de vino*) swig.

tacón [ta'kon] *nm* heel; **de** ~ **alto** high heeled; **taconeo** *nm* (heel) stamping.

táctico, a ['taktiko, a] *a* tactical // *nf* tactics *pl.*

tacto ['takto] *nm* touch; (*acción*) touching.

tacha ['tatʃa] *nf* flaw; (TEC) stud; **poner** ~ **a** to find fault with; **tachar** *vt* (*borrar*) to cross out; (*corregir*) to correct; (*criticar*) to criticize; **tachar de** to accuse of.

tafetán [tafe'tan] *nm* taffeta; **tafetanes** *nmpl* (*fam*) frills; ~ **adhesivo** *o* **inglés** sticking plaster.

tafilete [tafi'lete] *nm* morocco leather.

tahona [ta'ona] *nf* (*panadería*) bakery; (*molino*) flourmill.

tahur [ta'ur] *nm* gambler; (*pey*) cheat.

taimado, a [tai'maðo, a] *a* (*astuto*) sly; (*resentido*) sullen.

taja ['taxa] *nf* (*corte*) cut; (*repartición*) division; ~**da** *nf* slice; ~**dera** *nf* (*instrumento*) chopper; (*madera*) chopping block; **tajante** *a* sharp.

tajar [ta'xar] *vt* to cut; **tajo** *nm* (*corte*) cut; (*filo*) cutting edge; (GEO) cleft.

tal [tal] *a* such; ~ **vez** perhaps // *pron* (*persona*) someone, such a one; (*cosa*) something, such a thing; ~ **como** such as; ~ **para cual** tit for tat; (*dos iguales*) two of a kind // *ad*: ~ **como** (*igual*) just as; ~ **cual** (*como es*) just as it is; ~ **el padre, cual el hijo** like father, like son; ¿**qué** ~? how are things?; ¿**qué** ~ **te gusta?** how do you like it? // *conj*: **con** ~ **de que** provided that.

talabartero [talaßar'tero] *nm* saddler.

taladrar [tala'ðrar] *vt* to drill; **taladro** *nm* (*gen*) drill; (*hoyo*) drill hole; **taladro neumático** pneumatic drill.

talante [ta'lante] *nm* (*humor*) mood; (*voluntad*) will, willingness.

talar [ta'lar] *vt* to fell, cut down; (*fig*) to devastate.

talco ['talko] *nm* (*polvos*) talcum powder; (MINEROLOGÍA) talc.

talego [ta'leɣo] *nm,* **talega** [ta'leɣa] *nf* sack.

talento [ta'lento] *nm* talent; (*capacidad*) ability; (*don*) gift.

talidomida [taliðo'miða] *nm* thalidomide.

talismán [talis'man] *nm* talisman.

talmente [tal'mente] *ad* (*de esta forma*) in such a way; (*hasta tal punto*) to such an extent; (*exactamente*) exactly.

talón [ta'lon] *nm* (*gen*) heel; (COM) counterfoil.

talonario [talo'narjo] *nm* (*de cheques*) chequebook; (*de billetes*) book of tickets; (*de recibos*) receipt book.

talud [ta'luð] *nm* slope.

talla ['taʎa] *nf* (*estatura, fig,* MED) height, stature; (*palo*) measuring rod; (ARTE) carving.

tallado, a [ta'ʎaðo, a] *a* carved // *nm* carving; **tallar** *vt* (*trabajar*) to work, carve; (*grabar*) to engrave; (*medir*) to measure; (*repartir*) to deal // *vi* to deal.

tallarín [taʎa'rin] *nm* noodle.

talle ['taʎe] *nm* (ANAT) waist; (*medida*) size; (*física*) build; (: *de mujer*) figure; (*fig*) appearance.

taller [ta'ʎer] *nm* (TEC) workshop; (*de artista*) studio.

tallo ['taʎo] *nm* (*de planta*) stem; (*de hierba*) blade; (*brote*) shoot; (*col*) cabbage; (CULIN) candied peel.

tamaño, a [ta'maɲo, a] *a* such a (big/small) // *nm* size; **de** ~ **natural** full-size.

tamarindo [tama'rindo] *nm* tamarind.

tambalearse [tambale'arse] *vr* (*persona*) to stagger; (*vehículo*) to sway.

también [tam'bjen] *ad* (*igualmente*) also, too, as well; (*además*) besides.

tambor [tam'bor] *nm* drum; (ANAT) eardrum; ~ **del freno** brake drum.

tamiz [ta'miθ] *nm* sieve; ~**ar** *vt* to sieve.

tamo ['tamo] *nm* fluff.

tampoco [tam'poko] *ad* nor, neither; **yo** ~ **lo compré** I didn't buy it either.

tampón [tam'pon] *nm* plug; (MED) tampon.

tan [tan] *ad* so; ~ **es así que** so much so that.

tanda ['tanda] *nf* (*gen*) series; (*juego*) set; (*turno*) shift; (*grupo*) gang.

tangente [tan'xente] *nf* tangent.

Tánger ['tanxer] *n* Tangier(s).

tangible [tan'xißle] *a* tangible.

tanque ['tanke] *nm* (*gen*) tank; (*AUTO, NAUT*) tanker.

tantear [tante'ar] *vt* (*calcular*) to reckon (up); (*medir*) to take the measure of; (*probar*) to test, try out; (*tomar la medida: persona*) to take the measurements of; (*considerar*) to weigh up // *vi* (*DEPORTE*) to score; **tanteo** *nm* (*cálculo*) (rough) calculation; (*prueba*) test, trial; (*DEPORTE*) scoring; (*adivinanzas*) guesswork; **al tanteo** by trial and error.

tanto, a ['tanto, a] *a* (*cantidad*) so much, as much; ~**s** so many, as many; **20 y** ~**s** 20-odd // *ad* (*cantidad*) so much, as much; (*tiempo*) so long, as long; ~ **tú como yo** both you and I; ~ **como eso** it's not as bad as that; ~ **más ... cuanto que** it's all the more ... because; ~ **mejor/peor** so much the better/the worse; ~ **si viene como si va** whether he comes or whether he goes; ~ **es así que** so much so that; **por** *o* **por lo** ~ therefore; **me he vuelto ronco de** *o* **con** ~ **hablar** I have become hoarse with so much talking // *conj*: **con** ~ **que** provided (that); **en** ~ **que** while; **hasta** ~ **(que)** until such time as // *nm* (*suma*) certain amount; (*proporción*) so much; (*punto*) point; (*gol*) goal; **al** ~ **up to** date; **un** ~ **perezoso** somewhat lazy; **al** ~ **de que** because of the fact that // *pron*: **cada uno paga** ~ each one pays so much; **a** ~**s de agosto** on such and such a day in August.

tapar [ta'par] *vt* (*cubrir*) to cover; (*envolver*) to wrap *or* cover up; (*la vista*) to obstruct; (*persona, falta*) to conceal; (*AM*) to fill; ~**se** *vr* to wrap o.s. up.

taparrabo [tapa'rraßo] *nm* (*bañador*) (bathing *or* swimming) trunks *pl*.

tapete [ta'pete] *nm* table cover.

tapia ['tapja] *nf* (*garden*) wall; **tapiar** *vt* to wall in.

tapicería [tapiθe'ria] *nf* tapestry; (*para muebles*) upholstery; (*tienda*) upholsterer's (shop); **tapiz** *nm* (*alfombra*) carpet; (*tela tejida*) tapestry; **tapizar** *vt* (*pared*) to wallpaper; (*suelo*) to carpet; (*muebles*) to upholster.

tapón [ta'pon] *nm* (*corcho*) stopper; (*TEC*) plug; (*MED*) tampon; ~ **de rosca** *o* **de tuerca** screw-top.

taquigrafía [takiɣra'fia] *nf* shorthand; **taquígrafo, a** *nm/f* shorthand writer.

taquilla [ta'kiʎa] *nf* (*donde se compra*) booking office; (*suma recogida*) takings *pl*; **taquillero, a** *a*: **función taquillera** box office success // *nm/f* ticket clerk.

taquímetro [ta'kimetro] *nm* speedometer; (*de control*) tachymeter.

tara ['tara] *nf* (*defecto*) defect; (*COM*) tare.

tarántula [ta'rantula] *nf* tarantula.

tararear [tarare'ar] *vi* to hum.

tardanza [tar'ðanθa] *nf* (*demora*) delay; (*lentitud*) slowness.

tardar [tar'ðar] *vi* (*tomar tiempo*) to take a long time; (*llegar tarde*) to be late; (*demorar*) to delay; **¿tarda mucho el tren?** does the train take long?; **a más** ~ at the latest; **no tardes en venir** come soon, come before long.

tarde ['tarðe] *ad* (*hora*) late; (*después de tiempo*) too late // *nf* (*de día*) afternoon; (*al anochecer*) evening; **de** ~ **en** ~ from time to time; **¡buenas** ~**s!** (*de día*) good afternoon!; (*de noche*) good evening!; **a** *o* **por la** ~ in the afternoon; in the evening.

tardío, a [tar'ðio, a] *a* (*retrasado*) late; (*lento*) slow (to arrive).

tardo, a ['tarðo, a] *a* (*lento*) slow; (*torpe*) dull.

tarea [ta'rea] *nf* task; (*ESCOL*) homework; ~ **de ocasión** chore.

tarifa [ta'rifa] *nf* (*lista de precios*) price list; (*COM*) tariff; ~ **completa** all-in cost.

tarima [ta'rima] *nf* (*plataforma*) platform; (*taburete*) stool; (*litera*) bunk.

tarjeta [tar'xeta] *nf* card; ~ **postal/de crédito/de Navidad** postcard/credit card/Christmas card.

tarro ['tarro] *nm* jar, pot.

tarta ['tarta] *nf* (*pastel*) cake; (*torta*) tart.

tartamudear [tartamuðe'ar] *vi* to stammer; **tartamudo, a** *a* stammering // *nm/f* stammerer.

tartana [tar'tana] *nf* (*barco*) dinghy.

tartárico, a [tar'tariko, a] *a*: **ácido** ~ tartaric acid.

tártaro ['tartaro] *a, nm* Tartar.

tasa ['tasa] *nf* (*precio*) (fixed) price, rate; (*valoración*) valuation; (*medida, norma*) measure, standard; ~ **de interés** rate of interest; ~**ción** *nf* (*gen*) valuation; (*de oro etc*) appraisal; ~**dor** *nm* valuer.

tasajo [ta'saxo] *nm* dried beef.

tasar [ta'sar] *vt* (*arreglar el precio*) to fix a price for; (*valorar*) to value, assess; (*limitar*) to limit.

tasca ['taska] *nf* (*fam*) pub.

tatarabuelo [tatara'ßwelo] *nm* great-great-grandfather.

tatuaje [ta'twaxe] *nm* (*dibujo*) tattoo; (*acto*) tattooing; **tatuar** *vt* to tattoo.

taumaturgo [tauma'turxo] *nm* miracle-worker.

taurino, a [tau'rino, a] *a* bullfighting *cpd*.

Tauro ['tauro] *nm* Taurus.

tauromaquia [tauro'makja] *nf* tauromachy.

tautología [tautolo'xia] *nf* tautology.

taxi ['taksi] *nm* taxi.

taxidermia [taksi'ðermja] *nf* taxidermy.

taxista [tak'sista] *nm/f* taxi driver.

taza ['taθa] *nf* cup; (*de retrete*) bowl; ~ **para café** coffee cup; **tazón** *nm* (~ **grande**) large cup; (*escudilla*) basin.

te [te] *pron* (*complemento de objeto*) you; (*complemento indirecto*) (to) you; (*reflexivo*) (to) yourself; **¿**~ **duele**

mucho el brazo? does your arm hurt a lot?; **~ equivocas** you're wrong; **¡cálma~!** calm yourself!

té [te] *nm* tea.

tea ['tea] *nf* torch.

teatral [tea'tral] *a* theatre *cpd*; (*fig*) theatrical; **teatro** *nm* (*gen*) theatre; (*LITERATURA*) plays *pl*, drama.

tebeo [te'βeo] *nm* children's comic.

tecla ['tekla] *nf* key; **~do** *nm* keyboard; **teclear** *vi* to strum; (*fam*) to drum; **tecleo** *nm* (*MUS*; *sonido*) strumming; (*forma de tocar*) fingering; (*fam*) drumming.

técnico, a ['tekniko, a] *a* technical // *nm* technician; (*experto*) expert // *nf* (*procedimientos*) technique; (*arte, oficio*) craft.

tecnócrata [tek'nokrata] *nm/f* technocrat.

tecnología [teknolo'xia] *nf* technology; **tecnológico, a** *a* technological; **tecnólogo** *nm* technologist.

techo ['tetʃo] *nm* (*externo*) roof; (*interno*) ceiling; **techumbre** *nf* roof.

tedio ['teðjo] *nm* (*aburrimiento*) boredom; (*apatía*) apathy; (*fastidio*) depression; **~so, a** *a* boring; (*cansado*) wearisome, tedious.

teja ['texa] *nf* (*azulejo*) tile; (*BOT*) lime (tree); **~do** *nm* (tiled) roof.

tejanos [te'xanos] *nmpl* jeans.

tejemaneje [texema'nexe] *nm* (*bullicio*) bustle; (*lío*) fuss; (*aspaviento*) to-do; (*intriga*) intrigue.

tejer [te'xer] *vt* to weave; (*AM*) to knit; (*fig*) to fabricate; **tejido** *nm* fabric; (*telaraña*) web; (*estofa, tela*) (knitted) material; (*ANAT*) tissue; (*textura*) texture.

tel, teléf *abr de* **teléfono.**

tela ['tela] *nf* (*material*) material; (*telaraña*) web; (*de fruta, en líquido*) skin; (*del ojo*) film; **telar** *nm* (*máquina*) loom; (*de teatro*) gridiron; **telares** *nmpl* textile mill *sg*.

telaraña [tela'raɲa] *nf* cobweb.

tele ['tele] *nf* (*fam*) TV.

tele... [tele] *pref* tele...; **~comunicación** *nf* telecommunication; **~control** *nm* remote control; **~diario** *nm* television news; **~difusión** *nf* (television) broadcast; **~dirigido, a** *a* remote-controlled; **~férico** *nm* (*tren*) cable-railway; (*de esquí*) ski-lift; **~fonear** *vi* to telephone; **~fónico, a** *a* telephone *cpd*; **~fonista** *nm/f* telephonist; **teléfono** *nm* telephone; **~foto** *nf* telephoto; **~grafía** *nf* telegraphy; **telégrafo** *nm* telegraph; (*fam: persona*) telegraph boy; **~grama** *nm* telegram; **~impresor** *nm* teleprinter; **telémetro** *nm* rangefinder; **~objetivo** *nm* telephoto lens; **~pático, a** *a* telepathic; **~scópico, a** *a* telescopic; **~scopio** *nm* telescope; **~silla** *nf* chairlift; **~spectador, a** *nm/f* viewer; **~squí** *nm* ski-lift; **~tipista** *nm/f* teletypist; **~tipo** *nm* teletype; **~vidente** *nm/f* viewer; **~visar** *vt* to televise;

~visión *nf* television; **~visión en colores** colour television; **~visor** *nm* television set.

telex [te'leks] *nm* telex.

telón [te'lon] *nm* curtain; **~ de boca/seguridad** front/safety curtain; **~ de acero** (*POL*) iron curtain; **~ de fondo** backcloth, background.

tema ['tema] *nm* (*asunto*) subject, topic; (*MUS*) theme // *nf* (*obsesión*) obsession; (*manía*) ill-will; **tener ~ a uno** to have a grudge against sb; **temático, a** *a* thematic.

tembladera [tembla'ðera] *nf* shaking; (*AM*) quagmire.

temblar [tem'blar] *vi* to shake, tremble; (*de frío*) to shiver; **tembleque** *a* shaking // *nm* = **tembladera; temblón, ona** *a* shaking; **temblor** *nm* trembling; (*AM: de tierra*) earthquake; **tembloroso, a** *a* trembling.

temer [te'mer] *vt* to fear // *vi* to be afraid; **temo que llegue tarde** I am afraid he may be late.

temerario, a [teme'rarjo, a] *a* (*descuidado*) reckless; (*arbitrario*) hasty; **temeridad** *nf* (*imprudencia*) rashness; (*audacia*) boldness.

temeroso, a [teme'roso, a] *a* (*miedoso*) fearful; (*que inspira temor*) frightful.

temible [te'miβle] *a* fearsome.

temor [te'mor] *nm* (*miedo*) fear; (*duda*) suspicion.

témpano ['tempano] *nm* (*MUS*) kettledrum; **~ de hielo** ice-flow; **~ de tocino** flitch of bacon.

temperamento [tempera'mento] *nm* temperament.

temperatura [tempera'tura] *nf* temperature.

temperie [tem'perje] *nf* state of the weather.

tempestad [tempes'tað] *nf* storm; **tempestuoso, a** *a* stormy.

templado, a [tem'plaðo, a] *a* (*moderado*) moderate; (: *en el comer*) frugal; (: *en el beber*) abstemious; (*agua*) lukewarm; (*clima*) mild; (*MUS*) well-tuned; **templanza** *nf* moderation; abstemiousness; mildness.

templar [tem'plar] *vt* (*moderar*) to moderate; (*furia*) to restrain; (*calor*) to reduce; (*solución*) to dilute; (*afinar*) to tune (up); (*acero*) to temper; (*tuerca*) to tighten up // *vi* to moderate; **~se** *vr* to be restrained; **temple** *nm* (*humor*) mood; (*ajuste*) tempering; (*afinación*) tuning; (*clima*) temperature; (*pintura*) tempera.

templete [tem'plete] *nm* bandstand.

templo ['templo] *nm* (*iglesia*) church; (*pagano etc*) temple.

temporada [tempo'raða] *nf* time, period; (*estación*) season.

temporal [tempo'ral] *a* (*no permanente*) temporary; (*REL*) temporal // *nm* storm.

temprano, a [tempra'nero, a] *a* (*BOT*) early; (*persona*) early-rising.

temprano, a [tem'prano, a] *a* early;

(*demasiado pronto*) too soon, too early.
ten *vb ver* **tener.**
tenacidad [tenaθi'ðað] *nf* (*gen*) tenacity;
(*dureza*) toughness; (*terquedad*)
stubbornness.
tenacillas [tena'θiʎas] *nfpl* (*gen*) tongs;
(*para el pelo*) curling tongs; (*MED*) forceps.
tenaz [te'naθ] *a* (*material*) tough; (*persona*)
tenacious; (*pegajoso*) sticky; (*terco*)
stubborn.
tenaza(s) [te'naθa(s)] *nf(pl)* (*MED*)
forceps; (*TEC*) pliers; (*ZOOL*) pincers.
tendal [ten'dal] *nm* awning.
tendedero [tende'ðero] *nm* (*para ropa*)
drying-place; (*cuerda*) clothes line.
tendencia [ten'denθja] *nf* tendency;
(*proceso*) trend; **tener ~ a** to tend *or*
have a tendency to; **tendencioso, a** *a*
tendentious.
tender [ten'der] *vt* (*extender*) to spread
out; (*colgar*) to hang out; (*vía férrea, cable*)
to lay; (*cuerda*) to stretch // *vi* to tend;
~se *vr* to lie down; (*fig: dejarse llevar*) to
let o.s. go; (: *dejar ir*) to let things go; **~ la
cama/la mesa** (*AM*) to make the bed/lay
the table.
ténder ['tender] *nm* tender.
tenderete [tende'rete] *nm* (*puesto*) stall;
(*carretilla*) barrow; (*exposición*) display of
goods; (*jaleo*) mess.
tendero, a [ten'dero, a] *nm/f* shopkeeper.
tendido, a [ten'diðo, a] *a* (*acostado*) lying
down, flat; (*colgado*) hanging // *nm* (*ropa*)
washing; (*TAUR*) front rows of seats;
(*colocación*) laying; (*ARQ: enyesado*) coat of
plaster; **a galope ~** flat out.
tendón [ten'don] *nm* tendon.
tendré *etc vb ver* **tener.**
tenducho [ten'dutʃo] *nm* small dirty shop.
tenebroso, a [tene'βroso, a] *a* (*oscuro*)
dark; (*fig*) gloomy; (*siniestro*) sinister.
tenedor [tene'ðor] *nm* (*CULIN*) fork;
(*poseedor*) holder; **~ de libros** book-
keeper.
teneduría [teneðu'ria] *nf* keeping; **~ de
libros** book-keeping.
tenencia [te'nenθja] *nf* (*de casa*) tenancy;
(*de oficio*) tenure; (*de propiedad*)
possession.
tener [te'ner] *vt* (*poseer*) to have; (*en la
mano*) to hold; (*caja*) to hold, contain;
(*considerar*) to consider; **~ suerte** to be
lucky; **~ permiso** to have permission;
tiene 10 años he is 10 years old;
¿cuántos años tienes? how old are you?;
~ sed/hambre/frío/calor to be
thirsty/hungry/cold/hot; **~ ganas (de)**
to want (to); **~ celos** to be jealous; **~
cuidado** to be careful; **~ razón** to be
right; **~ un metro de ancho/de largo** to
be one metre wide/long; **~ a bien** to see
fit to; **~ en cuenta** to bear in mind, take
into account; **~ a menos** to consider it
beneath o.s.; **~ a uno en más (estima)**
to think all the more of sb; **~ a uno por...**
to think sb...; **~ por seguro** to be sure; **~
presente** to remember, bear in mind; **~**

que (*obligación*) to have to; **tiene que ser
así** it has to be this way; **nos tiene
preparada una sorpresa** he has
prepared a surprise for us; **¿qué tiene?**
what's the matter with him?; **¿ésas
tenemos?** what's all this?; **tiene un mes
de muerto** he has been dead for a month;
~se *vr* (*erguirse*) to stand; (*apoyarse*) to
lean (on); (*fig*) to control o.s.;
(*considerarse*) to consider o.s.
tenería [tene'ria] *nf* tannery.
tengo *etc vb ver* **tener.**
tenia ['tenja] *nf* tapeworm.
teniente [te'njente] *nm* (*rango*) lieutenant;
(*ayudante*) deputy.
tenis ['tenis] *nm* tennis; **~ta** *nm/f* tennis
player.
tenor [te'nor] *nm* (*tono*) tone; (*sentido*)
meaning; (*MUS*) tenor; **a ~ de** on the lines
of.
tensar [ten'sar] *vt* to tauten; (*arco*) to
draw.
tensión [ten'sjon] *nf* (*gen*) tension; (*TEC*)
stress; (*MED*): **~ arterial** blood pressure;
tener la ~ alta to have high blood
pressure; **tenso, a** *a* tense.
tentación [tenta'θjon] *nf* temptation.
tentáculo [ten'takulo] *nm* tentacle.
tentador, a [tenta'ðor, a] *a* tempting //
nm/f tempter/temptress.
tentar [ten'tar] *vt* (*tocar*) to touch, feel;
(*seducir*) to tempt; (*atraer*) to attract;
(*probar*) to try (out); (*lanzarse a*) to
venture; (*MED*) to probe; **tentativa** *nf*
attempt; **tentativa de asesinato**
attempted murder.
tentempié [tentem'pje] *nm* (*fam*) snack.
tenue ['tenwe] *a* (*delgado*) thin, slender;
(*alambre*) fine; (*insustancial*) tenuous;
(*sonido*) faint; (*neblina*) light; (*lazo, vínculo*)
slight; **tenuidad** *nf* thinness; fineness;
(*ligereza*) lightness; (*sencillez*) simplicity.
teñir [te'ɲir] *vt* to dye; (*fig*) to tinge; **~se**
vr to dye; **~se el pelo** to dye one's hair.
teología [teolo'xia] *nf* theology.
teorema [teo'rema] *nm* theorem.
teoría [teo'ria] *nf* theory; **en ~** in theory;
teóricamente *ad* theoretically; **teórico,
a** *a* theoretic(al) // *nm/f* theoretician,
theorist; **teorizar** *vi* to theorize.
terapéutico, a [tera'peutiko, a] *a*
therapeutic.
terapia [te'rapja] *nf* therapy; **~ laboral**
occupational therapy.
tercer [ter'θer] *a ver* **tercero.**
tercería [terθe'ria] *nf* (*mediación*)
mediation; (*arbitraje*) arbitration.
tercero, tercer, a [ter'θero, ter'θer, a] *a*
third // *nm* (*árbitro*) mediator; (*JUR*) third
party.
terceto [ter'θeto] *nm* trio.
terciado, a [ter'θjaðo, a] *a* slanting;
azúcar ~ brown sugar.
terciar [ter'θjar] *vt* (*MAT*) to divide into
three; (*inclinarse*) to slope; (*llevar*) to wear
(across the shoulder) // *vi* (*participar*) to
take part; (*hacer de árbitro*) to mediate;

~**se** *vr* to come up; ~**io, a** *a* tertiary.
tercio ['terθjo] *nm* third.
terciopelo [terθjo'pelo] *nm* velvet.
terco, a ['terko, a] *a* obstinate; (*material*) tough.
tergiversación [terxiβersa'θjon] *nf* (*deformación*) distortion; (*evasivas*) prevarication; **tergiversar** *vt* to distort // *vi* to prevaricate.
termas ['termas] *nfpl* hot springs.
terminación [termina'θjon] *nf* (*final*) end; (*conclusión*) conclusion, ending; **terminal** *a, nm, nf* terminal; **terminante** *a* (*final*) final, definitive; (*tajante*) categorical; **terminar** *vt* (*completar*) to complete, finish; (*concluir*) to end // *vi* (*llegar a su fin*) to end; (*parar*) to stop; (*acabar*) to finish; **terminarse** *vr* to come to an end; **terminar por hacer algo** to end up (by) doing sth; **término** *nm* end, conclusion; (*parada*) terminus; (*límite*) boundary; **término medio** average; (*fig*) middle way; **en último término** (*a fin de cuentas*) in the last analysis; (*como último recurso*) as a last resort; **en términos de** in terms of.
terminología [terminolo'xia] *nf* terminology.
termodinámico, a [termoði'namiko, a] *a* thermodynamic.
termómetro [ter'mometro] *nm* thermometer.
termonuclear [termonukle'ar] *a* thermonuclear.
termo(s) ['termo(s)] *nm* thermos.
termostato [termo'stato] *nm* thermostat.
ternero, a [ter'nero, a] *nm/f* (*animal*) calf // *nf* (*carne*) veal.
terneza [ter'neθa] *nf* tenderness.
terno ['terno] *nm* (*traje*) three-piece suit; (*conjunto*) set of three.
ternura [ter'nura] *nf* (*trato*) tenderness; (*palabra*) endearment; (*cariño*) fondness.
terquedad [terke'ðað] *nf* obstinacy; (*dureza*) harshness.
terrado [te'rraðo] *nm* terrace.
terraplén [terra'plen] *nm* (*AGR*) terrace; (*FERRO*) embankment; (*MIL*) rampart; (*cuesta*) slope.
terrateniente [terrate'njente] *nm* landowner.
terraza [te'rraθa] *nf* (*balcón*) balcony; (*techo*) flat roof; (*AGR*) terrace.
terremoto [terre'moto] *nm* earthquake.
terrenal [terre'nal] *a* earthly.
terreno [te'rreno] *nm* (*tierra*) land; (*parcela*) plot; (*suelo*) soil; (*fig*) field; **un** ~ a piece of land.
terrero, a [te'rrero, a] *a* (*de la tierra*) earthy; (*vuelo*) low; (*fig*) humble.
terrestre [te'rrestre] *a* terrestrial; (*ruta*) land *cpd*.
terrible [te'rriβle] *a* (*espantoso*) terrible; (*aterrador*) dreadful; (*tremendo*) awful.
territorio [terri'torjo] *nm* territory.
terrón [te'rron] *nm* (*de azúcar*) lump; (*de tierra*) clod, lump; **terrones** *nmpl* land *sg*.

terror [te'rror] *nm* terror; ~**ífico, a** *a* terrifying; ~**ista** *a, nm/f* terrorist.
terroso, a [te'rroso, a] *a* earthy.
terruño [te'rruɲo] *nm* (*pedazo*) clod; (*parcela*) plot; (*fig*) native soil.
terso, a ['terso, a] *a* (*liso*) smooth; (*pulido*) polished; (*fig: estilo*) flowing; **tersura** *nf* smoothness; (*brillo*) shine.
tertulia [ter'tulja] *nf* (*reunión informal*) social gathering; (*grupo*) group, circle; (*sala*) clubroom.
tesar [te'sar] *vt* to tighten up.
tesis ['tesis] *nf inv* thesis.
tesón [te'son] *nm* (*firmeza*) firmness; (*tenacidad*) tenacity.
tesorero, a [teso'rero, a] *nm/f* treasurer; **tesoro** *nm* (*gen*) treasure; (*FIN, POL*) treasury.
testaferro [testa'ferro] *nm* figurehead.
testamentaría [testamenta'ria] *nf* execution of a will.
testamentario, a [testamen'tarjo, a] *a* testamentary // *nm/f* executor/executrix; **testamento** *nm* will; **testar** *vi* to make a will.
testarudo, a [testa'ruðo, a] *a* stubborn.
testero, a [tes'tero, a] *nm/f* (*gen*) front // *nm* (*ARQ*) front wall.
testes ['testes] *nmpl* testes.
testículo [tes'tikulo] *nm* testicle.
testificar [testifi'kar] *vt* to testify; (*fig*) to attest // *vi* to give evidence.
testigo [tes'tixo] *nm/f* witness; ~ **de cargo/descargo** witness for the prosecution/defence; ~ **ocular** eye witness.
testimoniar [testimo'njar] *vt* to testify to; (*fig*) to show; **testimonio** *nm* testimony.
teta ['teta] *nf* (*de biberón*) teat; (*ANAT*) nipple; (*fam*) breast.
tétanos ['tetanos] *nm* tetanus.
tetera [te'tera] *nf* teapot.
tetilla [te'tiʎa] *nf* (*ANAT*) nipple; (*de biberón*) teat.
tétrico, a ['tetriko, a] *a* gloomy, dismal.
textil [teks'til] *a* textile; ~ **es** *nmpl* textiles.
texto ['teksto] *nm* text; **textual** *a* textual.
textura [teks'tura] *nf* (*de tejido*) texture; (*de mineral*) structure.
tez [teθ] *nf* (*cutis*) complexion; (*color*) colouring.
ti [ti] *pron* you; (*reflexivo*) yourself.
tía ['tia] *nf* (*pariente*) aunt; (*mujer cualquiera*) girl, bird (*col*); (*fam: pej: vieja*) old bag; (: *prostituta*) whore.
tibia ['tiβja] *nf* tibia.
tibieza [ti'βjeθa] *nf* (*temperatura*) tepidness; (*fig*) coolness; **tibio, a** *a* lukewarm.
tiburón [tiβu'ron] *nm* shark.
tic [tik] *nm* (*ruido*) click; (*de reloj*) tick; (*MED*): ~ **nervioso** nervous tic.
tictac [tik'tak] *nm* (*de reloj*) tick tock.
tiempo ['tjempo] *nm* (*gen*) time; (*época, período*) age, period; (*METEOROLOGÍA*) weather; (*LING*) tense; (*edad*) age; (*de

juego) half; **a** ~ in time; **a un** *o* **al mismo** ~ at the same time; **al poco** ~ very soon (after); **de** ~ **en** ~ from time to time; **hace buen/mal** ~ the weather is fine/bad; **estar a** ~ to be in time; **hace** ~ some time ago; **hacer** ~ to while away the time; **motor de 2** ~ **s** two-stroke engine.

tienda ['tjenda] *nf* (*gen*) shop; (*más grande*) store; (*NAUT*) awning; ~ **de campaña** tent.

tienes *etc vb ver* **tener.**

tienta ['tjenta] *nf* (*MED*) probe; (*fig*) tact; **andar a** ~ **s** to grope one's way along.

tiento ['tjento] *nm* (*tacto*) touch; (*precaución*) wariness; (*pulso*) steady hand; (*ZOOL*) feeler; (*de ciego*) blind man's stick.

tierno, a ['tjerno, a] *a* (*blando, dulce*) tender; (*fresco*) fresh.

tierra ['tjerra] *nf* earth; (*suelo*) soil; (*mundo*) world; (*país*) country, land; ~ **adentro** inland.

tieso, a ['tjeso, a] *a* (*rígido*) rigid; (*duro*) stiff; (*fig: testarudo*) stubborn; (*fam: orgulloso*) conceited // *ad* strongly.

tiesto ['tjesto] *nm* flowerpot; (*pedazo*) piece of pottery.

tiesura [tje'sura] *nf* rigidity; (*fig*) stubbornness; (*fam*) conceit.

tifo ['tifo] *nm* typhus.

tifoidea [tifoi'ðea] *nf* typhoid.

tifón [ti'fon] *nm* (*huracán*) typhoon; (*de mar*) tidal wave.

tifus ['tifus] *nm* typhus.

tigre ['tixre] *nm* tiger.

tijera [ti'xera] *nf* (*AM*) scissors *pl*; (*ZOOL*) claw; (*persona*) gossip; **de** ~ folding; ~ **s** *nfpl* scissors; (*para plantas*) shears; **tijeretear** *vt* to snip // *vi* (*fig*) to meddle.

tildar [til'dar] *vt*: ~ **de** to brand as.

tilde ['tilde] *nf* (*defecto*) defect; (*trivialidad*) triviality; (*TIPOGRAFÍA*) tilde.

tilín [ti'lin] *nm* tinkle.

tilo ['tilo] *nm* lime tree.

timar [ti'mar] *vt* (*robar*) to steal; (*estafar*) to swindle; ~ **se** *vr* (*fam*) to make eyes (*con uno* at sb).

timbal [tim'bal] *nm* small drum.

timbrar [tim'brar] *vt* to stamp.

timbre ['timbre] *nm* (*sello*) stamp; (*campanilla*) bell; (*tono*) timbre; (*COM*) stamp duty.

timidez [timi'ðeθ] *nf* shyness; **tímido, a** *a* shy.

timo ['timo] *nm* swindle.

timón [ti'mon] *nm* helm, rudder; **timonel** *nm* helmsman.

tímpano ['timpano] *nm* (*ANAT*) eardrum; (*MUS*) small drum.

tina ['tina] *nf* tub; (*baño*) bathtub; **tinaja** *nf* large jar.

tinglado [tin'glaðo] *nm* (*cobertizo*) shed; (*fig: truco*) trick; (*intriga*) intrigue.

tinieblas [ti'njeßlas] *nfpl* (*gen*) darkness *sg*; (*sombras*) shadows.

tino ['tino] *nm* (*habilidad*) skill; (*MIL*) marksmanship; (*juicio*) insight; (*moderación*) moderation.

tinta ['tinta] *nf* ink; (*TEC*) dye; (*ARTE*) colour.

tinte ['tinte] *nm* (*acto*) dyeing; (*carácter*) tinge; (*barniz*) veneer.

tinterillo [tinte'riʎo] *nm* penpusher.

tintero [tin'tero] *nm* inkwell.

tintinear [tintine'ar] *vt* to tinkle.

tinto, a ['tinto, a] *a* (*teñido*) dyed; (*manchado*) stained // *nm* red wine.

tintorera [tinto'rera] *nf* shark.

tintorería [tintore'ria] *nf* dry cleaner's.

tintura [tin'tura] *nf* (*acto*) dyeing; (*QUÍMICA*) dye; (*farmacéutico*) tincture.

tío ['tio] *nm* (*pariente*) uncle; (*fam: viejo*) old fellow; (: *individuo*) bloke, chap.

tiovivo [tio'ßißo] *nm* roundabout.

típico, a ['tipiko, a] *a* typical.

tiple ['tiple] *nm* soprano (voice) // *nf* soprano.

tipo ['tipo] *nm* (*clase*) type, kind; (*norma*) norm; (*patrón*) pattern; (*hombre*) fellow; (*ANAT*) build; (: *de mujer*) figure; (*IMPRENTA*) type; ~ **bancario/de descuento/de interés/de cambio** bank/discount/interest/exchange rate.

tipografía [tipoxra'fia] *nf* (*tipo*) printing; (*lugar*) printing press; **tipográfico, a** *a* printing; **tipógrafo, a** *nm/f* printer.

tiquismiquis [tikis'mikis] *nm* fussy person // *nmpl* (*querellas*) squabbling *sg*; (*escrúpulos*) silly scruples.

tira ['tira] *nf* strip; (*fig*) abundance; ~ **y afloja** give and take.

tirabuzón [tiraßu'θon] *nm* corkscrew.

tirado, a [ti'raðo, a] *a* (*barato*) dirt-cheap; (*fam: fácil*) very easy // *nf* (*acto*) cast, throw; (*distancia*) distance; (*serie*) series; (*TIPOGRAFÍA*) printing, edition; **de una** ~ **a** at one go.

tirador [tira'ðor] *nm* (*mango*) handle; (*ELEC*) flex.

tiranía [tira'nia] *nf* tyranny; **tirano, a** *a* tyrannical // *nm/f* tyrant.

tirante [ti'rante] *a* (*cuerda*) tight, taut; (*relaciones*) strained // *nm* (*ARQ*) brace; (*TEC*) stay; (*correa*) shoulder strap; ~ **s** *nmpl* braces; **tirantez** *nf* tightness; (*fig*) tension.

tirar [ti'rar] *vt* (*aventar*) to throw; (*dejar caer*) to drop; (*volcar*) to upset; (*derribar*) to knock down *or* over; (*jalar*) to pull; (*desechar*) to throw out *or* away; (*disipar*) to squander; (*imprimir*) to print; (*dar: golpe*) to deal // *vi* (*disparar*) to shoot; (*jalar*) to pull; (*fig*) to draw; (*fam: andar*) to go; (*tender a, buscar realizar*) to tend to; (*DEPORTE*) to shoot; ~ **se** *vr* to throw o.s.; (*fig*) to cheapen o.s.; ~ **abajo** to bring down, destroy; **tira más a su padre** he takes more after his father; **ir tirando** to manage; **a todo** ~ at the most.

tirita [ti'rita] *nf* (*sticking*) plaster.

tiritar [tiri'tar] *vi* to shiver.

tiro ['tiro] *nm* (*lanzamiento*) throw;

(*disparo*) shot; (*disparar*) shooting; (*DEPORTE*) drive; (*alcance*) range; (*de escalera*) flight (of stairs); (*golpe*) blow; (*engaño*) hoax; ~ **al blanco** target practice; **caballo de** ~ cart-horse; **andar de** ~**s largos** to be all dressed up; **al** ~ (*AM*) at once.

tirón [ti'ron] *nm* (*sacudida*) pull, tug; **de un** ~ in one go.

tirotear [tirote'ar] *vt* to shoot at; ~**se** *vr* to exchange shots; **tiroteo** *nm* exchange of shots, shooting.

tísico, a ['tisiko, a] *a* consumptive.

títere ['titere] *nm* puppet.

titilar [titi'lar] *vi* (*luz, estrella*) to twinkle; (*parpado*) to flutter.

titiritero, a [titiri'tero, a] *nm/f* puppeteer.

titubeante [tituße'ante] *a* (*inestable*) shaky, tottering; (*farfullante*) stammering; (*dudoso*) hesitant; **titubear** *vi* to stagger; (*fig*) to hesitate; **titubeo** *nm* staggering; stammering; hesitation.

titulado, a [titu'laðo, a] *a* (*libro*) entitled; (*persona*) titled; **titular** *a* titular // *nm/f* occupant // *nm* headline // *vt* to title; **titularse** *vr* to be entitled; **título** *nm* (*gen*) title; (*de diario*) headline; (*certificado*) professional qualification; (*universitario*) university degree; (*fig*) right; **a título de** in the capacity of.

tiza ['tiθa] *nf* chalk.

tizna ['tiθna] *nf* grime; **tiznar** *vt* to blacken; (*fig*) to tarnish.

tizón [ti'θon], **tizo** ['tiθo] *nm* brand; (*fig*) stain.

toalla [to'aʎa] *nf* towel.

tobillo [to'ßiʎo] *nm* ankle.

tobogán [toßo'ɤan] *nm* toboggan; (*montaña rusa*) switchback; (*resbaladilla*) chute, slide.

toca ['toka] *nf* headdress.

tocadiscos [toka'ðiskos] *nm inv* record player.

tocado, a [to'kaðo, a] *a* rotten; (*fam*) touched // *nm* headdress.

tocador [toka'ðor] *nm* (*mueble*) dressing table; (*cuarto*) boudoir; (*neceser*) toilet case; (*fam*) ladies' toilet.

tocante [to'kante]: ~ **a** *prep* with regard to.

tocar [to'kar] *vt* to touch; (*MUS*) to play; (*topar con*) to run into, strike; (*referirse a*) to allude to; (*padecer*) to suffer; (*el pelo*) to do // *vi* (*a la puerta*) to knock (on *or* at the door); (*ser de turno*) to fall to, be the turn of; (*ser hora*) to be due; (*barco, avión*) to call at; (*atañer*) to concern; ~**se** *vr* (*cubrirse la cabeza*) to cover one's head; (*tener contacto*) to touch (each other); **por lo que a mí me toca** as far as I am concerned; **esto toca en la locura** this verges on madness.

tocayo, a [to'kajo, a] *nm/f* namesake.

tocino [to'θino] *nm* bacon.

todavía [toða'ßia] *ad* (*aun*) still; (*aún*) yet; ~ **más** yet more; ~ **no** not yet.

todo, a ['toðo, a] *a* all; (*cada*) every;

(*entero*) whole; (*sentido negativo*): **en** ~ **el día lo he visto** I haven't seen him all day; ~**as las semanas**/~**s los martes** every week/Tuesday // *ad* all, completely // *nm* everything // *pron*: ~**s**/~**as** everyone; **a** ~**a velocidad** at full speed; **estaba** ~ **ojos** he was all eyes; **puede ser** ~ **lo honesto que quiera** he can be as honest as he likes; **ante** ~ above all; **en un** ~ as a whole; **corriendo y** ~, **no llegaron a tiempo** even though they ran, they still didn't arrive in time; **con** ~ still, even so; **del** ~ completely.

todopoderoso, a [toðopoðe'roso, a] *a* all powerful; (*REL*) almighty.

toga ['toɤa] *nf* toga; (*ESCOL*) gown.

Tokio ['tokjo] *n* Tokyo.

toldo ['toldo] *nm* (*para el sol*) sunshade; (*tienda*) marquee; (*fig*) pride.

tole ['tole] *nm* (*fam*) commotion.

tolerable [tole'raßle] *a* tolerable; **tolerancia** *nf* tolerance; **tolerar** *vt* to tolerate; (*resistir*) to endure.

toma ['toma] *nf* (*gen*) taking; (*MED*) dose.

tomar [to'mar] *vt* (*gen*) to take; (*aspecto*) to take on; (*beber*) to drink // *vi* to take; (*AM*) to drink; ~**se** *vr* to take; ~**se por** to consider o.s. to be; ~ **a bien/a mal** to take well/badly; ~ **en serio** to take seriously; ~ **el pelo a alguien** to pull sb's leg; ~**la con uno** to pick a quarrel with sb.

tomate [to'mate] *nm* tomato; ~**ra** *nf* tomato plant.

tomillo [to'miʎo] *nm* thyme.

tomo ['tomo] *nm* (*libro*) volume; (*tamaño*) size; (*fig*) importance.

ton [ton] *abr de* **tonelada** // *nm*: **sin** ~ **ni son** without rhyme or reason.

tonada [to'naða] *nf* tune.

tonalidad [tonali'ðað] *nf* tone.

tonel [to'nel] *nm* barrel.

tonelada [tone'laða] *nf* ton; **tonelaje** *nm* tonnage.

tonelero [tone'lero] *nm* cooper.

tónico, a ['toniko, a] *a* tonic // *nm* (*MED*) tonic // *nf* (*MUS*) tonic; (*fig*) keynote.

tonificar [tonifi'kar] *vt* to tone up.

tonillo [to'niʎo] *nm* monotonous voice.

tono ['tono] *nm* tone; **fuera de** ~ inappropriate; **darse** ~ to put on airs.

tontería [tonte'ria] *nf* (*estupidez*) foolishness; (*una* ~) stupid remark; ~**s** *nfpl* rubbish *sg*, nonsense *sg*.

tonto, a ['tonto, a] *a* stupid; (*sentimental*) silly // *nm/f* fool; (*payaso*) clown.

topacio [to'paθjo] *nm* topaz.

topar [to'par] *vt* (*tropezar*) to bump into; (*encontrar*) to find, come across; (*ZOOL*) to butt // *vi*: ~ **contra** *o* **en** to run into; ~ **con** to run up against; **el problema topa en eso** that's where the problem lies.

tope ['tope] *a* maximum // *nm* (*fin*) end; (*límite*) limit; (*riña*) quarrel; (*FERRO*) buffer; (*AUTO*) bumper; **al** ~ **end to end**.

tópico, a ['topiko, a] *a* topical // *nm* platitude.

topo ['topo] *nm* (*ZOOL*) mole; (*fig*) blunderer.

topografía [topoɣra'fia] *nf* topography; **topógrafo, a** *nm/f* topographer.

toque ['toke] *nm* touch; (*MUS*) beat; (*de campana*) peal; (*fig*) crux; **dar un** ~ **a** to test; ~ **de queda** curfew; ~**tear** *vt* to handle.

toquilla [to'kiʎa] *nf* (*bufanda*) headscarf; (*chal*) shawl.

torbellino [torbe'ʎino] *nm* whirlwind; (*fig*) whirl.

torcedura [torθe'ðura] *nf* twist; (*MED*) sprain.

torcer [tor'θer] *vt* to twist; (*la esquina*) to turn; (*MED*) to sprain; (*cuerda*) to plait; (*ropa, manos*) to wring; (*persona*) to corrupt // *vi* (*desviar*) to turn off; (*pelota*) to spin; ~**se** *vr* (*ladearse*) to bend; (*desviarse*) to go astray; (*fracasar*) to go wrong; **torcido, a** *a* twisted; (*fig*) crooked // *nm* curl.

tordo, a ['torðo, a] *a* dappled // *nm* thrush.

torear [tore'ar] *vt* (*fig: evadir*) to avoid; (*jugar con*) to tease // *vi* to fight bulls; **toreo** *nm* bullfighting; **torero, a** *nm/f* bullfighter.

tormenta [tor'menta] *nf* storm; (*fig: confusión*) turmoil; (*desgracia*) misfortune.

tormento [tor'mento] *nm* torture; (*fig*) anguish.

tornar [tor'nar] *vt* (*devolver*) to return, give back; (*transformar*) to transform // *vi* to go back; ~**se** *vr* (*ponerse*) to become; (*volver*) to return.

tornasol [torna'sol] *nm* (*BOT*) sunflower; **papel de** ~ litmus paper; ~**ado, a** *a* (*brillante*) iridescent; (*reluciente*) shimmering.

torneo [tor'neo] *nm* tournament.

tornero, a [tor'nero, a] *nm/f* machinist.

tornillo [tor'niʎo] *nm* screw.

torniquete [torni'kete] *nm* (*puerta*) turnstile; (*MED*) tourniquet.

torno ['torno] *nm* (*TEC*) winch, (*tambor*) drum; **en** ~ (**a**) round, about.

toro ['toro] *nm* bull; (*fam*) he-man; **los** ~**s** bullfighting.

toronja [to'ronxa] *nf* grapefruit.

torpe ['torpe] *a* (*poco hábil*) clumsy, awkward; (*necio*) dim; (*lento*) slow; (*indecente*) crude; (*no honrado*) dishonest.

torpedo [tor'peðo] *nm* torpedo.

torpeza [tor'peθa] *nf* (*falta de agilidad*) clumsiness; (*lentitud*) slowness; (*rigidez*) stiffness; (*error*) mistake; (*crudeza*) obscenity.

torre ['torre] *nf* tower; (*de petróleo*) derrick.

torrente [to'rrente] *nm* torrent.

tórrido, a ['torriðo, a] *a* torrid.

torrija [to'rrixa] *nf* fried bread; ~**s** French toast *sg*.

torsión [tor'sjon] *nf* twisting.

torso ['torso] *nm* torso.

torta ['torta] *nf* cake; (*fam*) slap.

tortícolis [tor'tikolis] *nm* stiff neck.

tortilla [tor'tiʎa] *nf* omelette; (*AM*) maize pancake; ~ **francesa/española** plain/potato omelette.

tórtola ['tortola] *nf* turtledove.

tortuga [tor'tuɣa] *nf* tortoise.

tortuoso, a [tor'twoso, a] *a* winding.

tortura [tor'tura] *nf* torture; **torturar** *vt* to torture.

tos [tos] *nf* cough; ~ **ferina** whooping cough.

tosco, a ['tosko, a] *a* coarse.

toser [to'ser] *vi* to cough.

tostado, a [tos'taðo, a] *a* toasted; (*por el sol*) dark brown; (*piel*) tanned // *nf* tan; **tostador** *nm* toaster; **tostar** *vt* to toast; (*café*) to roast; (*al sol*) to tan; **tostarse** *vr* to get brown.

total [to'tal] *a* total // *ad* in short; (*al fin y al cabo*) when all is said and done // *nm* total; ~ **que** to cut a long story short.

totalidad [totali'ðað] *nf* whole.

totalitario, a [totali'tarjo, a] *a* totalitarian.

tóxico, a ['toksiko, a] *a* toxic // *nm* poison.

tozudo, a [to'θuðo, a] *a* obstinate.

traba ['traβa] *nf* bond, tie; (*cadena*) fetter.

trabajador, a [traβaxa'ðor, a] *nm/f* worker // *a* hard-working.

trabajar [traβa'xar] *vt* to work; (*arar*) to till; (*empeñarse en*) to work at; (*empujar: persona*) to push; (*convencer*) to persuade // *vi* to work; (*esforzarse*) to strive; **trabajo** *nm* work; (*tarea*) task; (*POL*) labour; (*fig*) effort; **tomarse el trabajo de** to take the trouble to; **trabajo por turno/a destajo** shift work/ piecework; **trabajoso, a** *a* hard; (*MED*) pale.

trabalenguas [traβa'lengwas] *nm inv* tongue twister.

trabar [tra'βar] *vt* (*juntar*) to join, unite; (*atar*) to tie down, fetter; (*agarrar*) to seize; (*amistad*) to strike up; ~**se** *vr* to become entangled; (*reñir*) to squabble; **trabazón** *nf* (*TEC*) joining, assembly; (*fig*) bond, link.

trabucar [traβu'kar] *vt* (*confundir*) to confuse, mix up; (*palabras*) to misplace.

tracción [trak'θjon] *nf* traction; ~ **delantera/trasera** front-wheel/rear-wheel drive.

tractor [trak'tor] *nm* tractor.

tradición [traði'θjon] *nf* tradition; **tradicional** *a* traditional.

traducción [traðuk'θjon] *nf* translation; **traducir** *vt* to translate; **traductor, a** *nm/f* translator.

traer [tra'er] *vt* (*gen*) to bring; (*llevar*) to carry; (*ropa*) to wear; (*imán*) to draw; (*incluir*) to carry; (*fig*) to cause; ~**se** *vr*: ~**se algo** to be up to sth; ~**se bien/mal** to dress well/badly.

traficar [trafi'kar] *vi* to trade.

tráfico ['trafiko] *nm* (*COM*) trade; (*AUTO*) traffic.

tragaluz [traɣa'luθ] *nm* skylight.

tragamonedas [traɣamo'neðas] *nm inv*,

tragaperras [traɣa'perras] *nm inv* slot machine.

tragar [tra'ɣar] *vt* to swallow; (*devorar*) to devour, bolt down; ~**se** *vr* to swallow.

tragedia [tra'xeðja] *nf* tragedy; **trágico, a** *a* tragic.

trago ['traɣo] *nm* (*líquido*) drink; (*comido de golpe*) gulp; (*fam: de bebida*) swig; (*desgracia*) blow.

traición [trai'θjon] *nf* treachery; (*JUR*) treason; (*una* ~) act of treachery; **traicionar** *vt* to betray; **traidor, a, traicionero, a** *a* treacherous // *nm/f* traitor.

traigo *etc vb ver* **traer.**

traje ['traxe] *vb ver* **traer** // *nm* (*gen*) dress; (*de hombre*) suit; (*vestimenta típica*) costume; (*fig*) garb; ~ **de baño** swimsuit; ~ **de luces** bullfighter's costume.

trajera *etc vb ver* **traer.**

trajín [tra'xin] *nm* haulage; (*fam: movimiento*) bustle; **trajines** *nmpl* goings-on; **trajinar** *vt* (*llevar*) to carry, transport // *vi* (*moverse*) to bustle about; (*viajar*) to travel around.

trama ['trama] *nf* (*fig*) link; (: *intriga*) plot; (*de tejido*) weft; **tramar** *vt* to plot; (*TEC*) to weave.

tramitar [trami'tar] *vt* (*asunto*) to transact; (*negociar*) to negotiate; (*manejar*) to handle; **trámite** *nm* (*paso*) step; (*JUR*) transaction; **trámites** *nmpl* (*burocracia*) paperwork *sg*, procedures; (*JUR*) proceedings.

tramo ['tramo] *nm* (*de tierra*) plot; (*de escalera*) flight; (*de vía*) section.

tramoya [tra'moja] *nf* (*TEATRO*) piece of stage machinery; (*fig*) trick; **tramoyista** *nm/f* scene shifter; (*fig*) trickster.

trampa ['trampa] *nf* (*gen*) trap; (*en el suelo*) trapdoor; (*prestidigitación*) conjuring trick; (*engaño*) trick; (*fam*) fiddle; (*de pantalón*) fly; **trampear** *vt, vi* to cheat; **trampista** *nm/f* = **tramposo.**

trampolín [trampo'lin] *nm* trampoline; (*de piscina etc*) diving board.

tramposo, a [tram'poso, a] *a* crooked, cheating // *nm/f* crook, cheat.

tranca ['tranka] *nf* (*palo*) stick; (*viga*) beam; (*de puerta, ventana*) bar; **trancar** *vt* to bar // *vi* to stride along.

trance ['tranθe] *nm* (*momento difícil*) difficult moment; (*situación crítica*) critical situation; (*estado hipnotizado*) trance.

tranco ['tranko] *nm* stride.

tranquilidad [trankili'ðað] *nf* (*calma*) calmness, stillness; (*paz*) peacefulness; **tranquilizar** *vt* (*calmar*) to calm (down); (*asegurar*) to reassure; **tranquilo, a** *a* (*calmado*) calm; (*apacible*) peaceful; (*mar*) calm; (*mente*) untroubled.

transacción [transak'θjon] *nf* transaction.

transar [tran'sar] *vt* = **transigir.**

transbordador [transβorða'ðor] *nm* ferry.

transbordar [transβor'ðar] *vt* to transfer; ~**se** *vr* to change; **transbordo** *nm*

transfer; **hacer transbordo** to change (trains).

transcurrir [transku'rrir] *vi* (*tiempo*) to pass; (*hecho*) to turn out.

transcurso [trans'kurso] *nm*: ~ **del tiempo** lapse (of time).

transeúnte [transe'unte] *a* transient // *nm/f* passer-by.

transferencia [transfe'renθja] *nf* transference; (*COM*) transfer; **transferir** *vt* to transfer; (*de tiempo*) to postpone.

transfigurar [transfiɣu'rar] *vt* to transfigure.

transformador [transforma'ðor] *nm* transformer.

transformar [transfor'mar] *vt* to transform; (*convertirse*) to convert.

tránsfuga ['transfuɣa] *nm/f* (*MIL*) deserter; (*POL*) turncoat.

transgresión [transɣre'sjon] *nf* transgression.

transición [transi'θjon] *nf* transition.

transido, a [tran'siðo, a] *a* overcome.

transigir [transi'xir] *vi* to compromise, make concessions.

transistor [transis'tor] *nm* transistor.

transitar [transi'tar] *vi* to go (from place to place); **tránsito** *nm* transit; (*AUTO*) traffic; (*parada*) stop; **transitorio, a** *a* transitory.

transmisión [transmi'sjon] *nf* (*TEC*) transmission; (*transferencia*) transfer; ~ **en directo/exterior** live/outside broadcast; **transmitir** *vt* (*gen*) to transmit; (*RADIO, TV*) to broadcast.

transparencia [transpa'renθja] *nf* transparency; (*claridad*) clearness, clarity; (*foto*) slide; **transparentar** *vt* to reveal // *vi* to be transparent; **transparente** *a* transparent; clear; (*ligero*) diaphanous // *nm* curtain.

transpirar [transpi'rar] *vi* to perspire; (*fig*) to transpire.

transponer [transpo'ner] *vt* to transpose; (*cambiar de sitio*) to change the place of // *vi* (*desaparecer*) to disappear; (*ir más allá*) to go beyond; ~**se** *vr* to change places; (*ocultarse*) to hide; (*sol*) to go down.

transportación [transporta'θjon] *nf* transportation; **transportar** *vt* to transport; (*llevar*) to carry; **transporte** *nm* transport; (*COM*) haulage.

tranvía [tran'βia] *nm* tram.

trapecio [tra'peθjo] *nm* trapeze; **trapecista** *nm/f* trapeze artist.

trapero, a [tra'pero, a] *nm/f* ragman.

trapicheos [trapi'tʃeos] *nmpl* (*fam*) schemes, fiddles.

trapisonda [trapi'sonda] *nf* (*jaleo*) row; (*estafa*) swindle.

trapo ['trapo] *nm* (*tela*) rag; (*de cocina*) cloth.

traqueteo [trake'teo] *nm* (*crujido*) crack; (*golpeteo*) rattling.

tras [tras] *prep* (*detrás*) behind; (*después*) after; ~ **de** besides.

trascendencia [trasθen'denθja] *nf*

(*importancia*) importance; (*filosofía*) transcendence; **trascendental** *a* important; transcendental; **trascender** *vi* (*oler*) to smell; (*evocar*) to evoke, suggest; (*noticias*) to come out; (*suceso*) to have a wide effect; **trascender a** to smack of.

trasegar [trase'ɣar] *vt* (*moverse*) to move about; (*vino*) to decant.

trasero, a [tra'sero, a] *a* back // *nm* (ANAT) bottom; ~**s** *nmpl* ancestors.

trasfondo [tras'fondo] *nm* background.

trasgredir [trasɣre'ðir] *vt* to contravene.

trashumante [trasu'mante] *a* migrating.

trasladar [trasla'ðar] *vt* (*gen*) to move; (*persona*) to transfer; (*postergar*) to postpone; (*copiar*) to copy; (*interpretar*) to interpret; **traslado** *nm* (*gen*) move; (*mudanza*) move, removal; (*copia*) copy.

traslucir [traslu'θir] *vt* to show; ~**se** *vr* to be translucent; (*fig*) to be revealed.

trasluz [tras'luθ] *nm* reflected light; **al** ~ against *or* up to the light.

trasnochar [trasno'tʃar] *vi* (*acostarse tarde*) to stay up late; (*no dormir*) to have a sleepless night; (*pasar la noche*) to stay the night.

traspasar [traspa'sar] *vt* (*bala*) to pierce, go through; (*propiedad*) to sell, transfer; (*calle*) to cross over; (*límites*) to go beyond; (*ley*) to break; **traspaso** *nm* transfer; (*fig*) anguish.

traspié [tras'pje] *nm* (*caída*) stumble; (*tropezón*) trip; (*fig*) blunder.

trasplantar [trasplan'tar] *vt* to transplant.

traste ['traste] *nm* (MUS) fret; **dar al** ~ **con algo** to ruin sth.

trastienda [tras'tjenda] *nf* backshop; **obtener algo por la** ~ to get sth by underhand means.

trasto ['trasto] *nm* (*mueble*) piece of furniture; (*tarro viejo*) old pot; (*pey: cosa*) piece of junk; (: *persona*) dead loss; ~**s** *nmpl* (TEATRO) scenery *sg*.

trastornado, a [trastor'naðo, a] *a* (*loco*) mad; (*agitado*) crazy; **trastornar** *vt* to overturn, upset; (*fig: ideas*) to confuse; (: *nervios*) to shatter; (: *persona*) to drive crazy; **trastornarse** *vr* (*plan*) to fall through; **trastorno** *nm* (*acto*) overturning; (*confusión*) confusion.

trasunto [tra'sunto] *nm* copy.

tratable [tra'taβle] *a* friendly.

tratado [tra'taðo] *nm* (POL) treaty; (COM) agreement.

tratamiento [trata'mjento] *nm* treatment.

tratar [tra'tar] *vt* (*ocuparse de*) to treat; (*manejar*, TEC) to handle; (MED) to treat; (*dirigirse a: persona*) to address // *vi*: ~ **de** (*hablar sobre*) to deal with, be about; (*intentar*) to try to; ~ **con** (COM) to trade in; (*negociar*) to negotiate with; (*tener contactos*) to have dealings with; ~**se** *vr* to treat each other; **trato** *nm* dealings *pl*; (*relaciones*) relationship; (*comportamiento*)

manner; (COM) agreement; (*título*) (form of) address.

trauma ['trauma] *nm* trauma.

través [tra'ßes] *nm* (*fig*) reverse; **al** ~ *ad* across, crossways; **a** ~ **de** *prep* across; (*sobre*) over; (*por*) through.

travesaño [traße'saɲo] *nm* (ARQ) crossbeam; (DEPORTE) crossbar.

travesía [traße'sia] *nf* (*calle*) cross-street; (NAUT) crossing.

travesura [traße'sura] *nf* (*broma*) prank; (*ingenio*) wit; **travieso, a** *a* (*niño*) naughty; (*adulto*) restless; (*ingenioso*) witty // *nf* crossing; (ARQ) crossbeam.

trayecto [tra'jekto] *nm* (*ruta*) road, way; (*viaje*) journey; (*tramo*) stretch; (*curso*) course; ~**ria** *nf* trajectory; (*fig*) path.

traza ['traθa] *nf* (ARQ) plan, design; (*aspecto*) looks *pl*; (*señal*) sign; (*engaño*) trick; (*habilidad*) skill; ~**do, a** *a*: **bien** ~**do** shapely, well-formed // *nm* (ARQ) plan, design; (*fig*) outline; **trazar** *vt* (ARQ) to plan; (ARTE) to sketch; (*fig*) to trace; (*plan*) to follow; **trazo** *nm* (*línea*) line; (*bosquejo*) sketch.

trébol ['treßol] *nm* (BOT) clover.

trece ['treθe] *num* thirteen.

trecho ['tretʃo] *nm* (*distancia*) distance; (*de tiempo*) while; (*fam*) piece; **de** ~ **en** ~ at intervals.

tregua ['treɣwa] *nf* (MIL) truce; (*fig*) lull.

treinta ['treinta] *num* thirty.

tremendo, a [tre'mendo, a] *a* (*terrible*) terrible; (*imponente: cosa*) imposing; (*fam: fabuloso*) tremendous; (*divertido*) entertaining.

trémulo, a ['tremulo, a] *a* quivering.

tren [tren] *nm* train; ~ **de aterrizaje** undercarriage.

trenza ['trenθa] *nf* (*de pelo*) plait; **trenzar** *vt* (*el pelo*) to plait // *vi* (*en baile*) to weave in and out; **trenzarse** *vr* (AM) to become involved with.

trepadora [trepa'ðora] *nf* (BOT) climber; **trepar** *vt*, *vi* to climb; (TEC) to drill.

trepidación [trepiða'θjon] *nf* shaking, vibration; **trepidar** *vi* to shake, vibrate.

tres [tres] *num* three.

tresillo [tre'siʎo] *nm* three-piece suite; (MUS) triplet.

treta ['treta] *nf* (COM *etc*) gimmick; (*fig*) trick.

triángulo ['trjangulo] *nm* triangle.

tribu ['trißu] *nf* tribe.

tribuna [tri'ßuna] *nf* (*plataforma*) platform; (DEPORTE) stand; (*fig*) public speaking.

tribunal [trißu'nal] *nm* (*juicio*) court; (*comisión*, *fig*) tribunal.

tributar [trißu'tar] *vt* to pay; (*las gracias*) to give; (*cariño*) to show; **tributo** *nm* (COM) tax.

trigal [tri'ɣal] *nm* wheat field; **trigo** *nm* wheat; **trigos** *nmpl* wheat field(s) (*pl*).

trigueño, a [tri'ɣeɲo, a] *a* (*pelo*) corn-coloured; (*piel*) olive-skinned.

trillado, a [tri'ʎaðo, a] *a* threshed; (*fig*)

trite, hackneyed; **trilladora** *nf* threshing machine; **trillar** *vt* (*fig*) to frequent; (AGR) to thresh.

trimestral [trimes'tral] *a* quarterly; (ESCOL) termly; **trimestre** *nm* (ESCOL) term.

trincar [trin'kar] *vt* (*atar*) to tie up; (NAUT) to lash; (*agarrar*) to pinion.

trinchar [trin'tʃar] *vt* to carve.

trinchera [trin'tʃera] *nf* (*fosa*) trench; (*para vía*) cutting; (*impermeable*) trench-coat.

trineo [tri'neo] *nm* sledge.

trinidad [trini'ðað] *nf* trio; (REL): **la T**~ the Trinity.

trino ['trino] *nm* trill.

trinquete [trin'kete] *nm* (TEC) pawl; (NAUT) foremast.

tripa ['tripa] *nf* (ANAT) intestine; (*fam*) insides *pl.*

triple ['triple] *a* triple.

triplicado [tripli'kaðo] *a*: **por** ~ in triplicate.

tripulación [tripula'θjon] *nf* crew; **tripulante** *nm/f* crewman/woman; **tripular** *vt* (*barco*) to man; (AUTO) to drive.

triquiñuela [triki'ɲwela] *nf* trick.

tris [tris] *nm* crack; **en un** ~ in an instant.

triste ['triste] *a* (*afligido*) sad; (*sombrío*) melancholy, gloomy; (*desolado*) desolate; (*lamentable*) sorry, miserable; (*viejo*) old; ~**za** *nf* (*aflicción*) sadness; (*melancolía*) melancholy.

triturar [tritu'rar] *vt* (*moler*) to grind; (*mascar*) to chew.

triunfar [trjun'far] *vi* (*tener éxito*) to triumph; (*ganar*) to win; **triunfo** *nm* triumph.

trivial [tri'βjal] *a* trivial; ~**izar** *vt* to minimize, play down.

triza ['triθa] *nf* bit, piece; **hacer** ~**s** to smash to bits; **trizar** *vt* to smash to bits.

trocar [tro'kar] *vt* (COM) to exchange; (*dinero, de lugar*) to change; (*palabras*) to exchange; (*confundir*) to confuse; (*vomitar*) to vomit.

trocha ['trotʃa] *nf* (*sendero*) by-path; (*atajo*) short cut.

troche ['trotʃe]: **a** ~ **y moche** *ad* helter-skelter, pell-mell.

trofeo [tro'feo] *nm* (*premio*) trophy; (*éxito*) success.

troj(e) ['trox(e)] *nf* granary.

tromba ['tromba] *nf* whirlwind.

trombón [trom'bon] *nm* trombone.

trombosis [trom'bosis] *nf* thrombosis.

trompa ['trompa] *nf* horn; (*trompo*) humming top; (*hocico*) snout; (*fam*): **cogerse una** ~ to get tight.

trompeta [trom'peta] *nf* trumpet; (*clarín*) bugle.

trompo ['trompo] *nm* spinning top.

trompón [trom'pon] *nm* bump.

tronado, a [tro'naðo, a] *a* broken-down.

tronar [tro'nar] *vt* (AM) to shoot // *vi* to

thunder; (*fig*) to rage; (*fam*) to go broke.

tronco ['tronko] *nm* (*de árbol*, ANAT) trunk; (*de planta*) stem.

tronchar [tron'tʃar] *vt* (*árbol*) to chop down; (*fig: vida*) to cut short; (*esperanza*) to shatter; (*persona*) to tire out; ~**se** *vr* to fall down.

tronera [tro'nera] *nf* (MIL) loophole; (ARQ) small window.

trono ['trono] *nm* throne.

tropa ['tropa] *nf* (MIL) troop; (*soldados*) soldiers *pl*; (*gentío*) mob.

tropel [tro'pel] *nm* (*muchedumbre*) crowd; (*prisa*) rush; (*montón*) throng.

tropelía [trope'lia] *nm* outrage.

tropezar [trope'θar] *vi* to trip, stumble; (*fig*) to slip up; ~ **con** (*encontrar*) to run into; (*topar con*) to bump into; (*reñir*) to fall out with; **tropezón** *nm* trip; (*fig*) blunder.

tropical [tropi'kal] *a* tropical; **trópico** *nm* tropic.

tropiezo [tro'pjeθo] *nm* (*error*) slip, blunder; (*desgracia*) misfortune; (*obstáculo*) snag; (*discusión*) quarrel.

trotamundos [trota'mundos] *nm inv* globetrotter.

trotar [tro'tar] *vi* to trot; **trote** *nm* trot; (*fam*) travelling; **de mucho trote** hard-wearing.

trozo ['troθo] *nm* bit, piece.

truco ['truko] *nm* (*habilidad*) knack; (*engaño*) trick; ~**s** *nmpl* billiards *sg*.

trucha ['trutʃa] *nf* (*pez*) trout; (TEC) crane.

trueno ['trweno] *nm* (*gen*) thunder; (*estampido*) boom; (*de arma*) bang.

trueque ['trweke] *nm* exchange; (COM) barter.

trufa ['trufa] *nf* (BOT) truffle; (*fig: fam*) fib.

truhán, ana [tru'an, ana] *nm/f* rogue.

truncado, a [trun'kaðo, a] *a* truncated; **truncar** *vt* (*cortar*) to truncate; (*la vida etc*) to cut short; (*el desarrollo*) to stunt.

tu [tu] *a* your.

tú [tu] *pron* you.

tubérculo [tu'βerkulo] *nm* (BOT) tuber.

tuberculosis [tuβerku'losis] *nf* tuberculosis.

tubería [tuβe'ria] *nf* pipes *pl*; (*conducto*) pipeline; **tubo** *nm* tube, pipe; **tubo de ensayo** test-tube; **tubo de escape** exhaust (pipe).

tuerca ['twerka] *nf* nut.

tuerto, a ['twerto, a] *a* (*torcido*) twisted; (*ciego*) blind in one eye // *nm* one-eyed person; (*ofensa*) wrong; **a** ~**as** upside-down.

tuétano ['twetano] *nm* (*gen*) marrow; (BOT) pith.

tufo ['tufo] *nm* vapour; (*fig: pey*) stench.

tul [tul] *nm* tulle.

tulipán [tuli'pan] *nm* tulip.

tullido, a [tu'ʎiðo, a] *a* crippled; (*cansado*) exhausted.

tumba ['tumba] *nf* (*sepultura*) tomb; (*sacudida*) shake; (*voltereta*) somersault.

tumbar [tum'bar] *vt* to knock down; (*doblar*) to knock over; (*fam: suj: olor*) to overpower // *vi* to fall down; ~**se** *vr* (*echarse*) to lie down; (*extenderse*) to stretch out.

tumbo ['tumbo] *nm* (*caída*) fall; (*de vehículo*) jolt; (*momento crítico*) critical moment.

tumido, a [tu'miðo, a] *a* swollen.

tumor [tu'mor] *nm* tumour.

tumulto [tu'multo] *nm* turmoil.

tuna ['tuna] *nf ver* **tuno.**

tunante [tu'nante] *a* rascally.

tunda ['tunda] *nf* (*de tela*) shearing; (*golpeo*) beating; **tundir** *vt* (*tela*) to shear; (*hierba*) to mow; (*fig*) to exhaust; (*fam: golpear*) to beat.

túnel ['tunel] *nm* tunnel.

Túnez ['tuneθ] *nm* Tunisia; (*ciudad*) Tunis.

tuno, a ['tuno, a] *nm/f* (*fam*) rogue // *nf* (*BOT*) prickly pear; (*MUS*) student music group.

tuntún [tun'tun]: **al** ~ *ad* thoughtlessly.

tupido, a [tu'piðo, a] *a* (*denso*) dense; (*fig*) dim; (*tela*) close-woven.

turba ['turßa] *nf* crowd.

turbación [turßa'θjon] *nf* (*molestia*) disturbance; (*preocupación*) worry; **turbado, a** *a* (*molesto*) disturbed; (*preocupado*) worried; **turbar** *vt* (*molestar*) to disturb; (*incomodar*) to upset; **turbarse** *vr* to be disturbed.

turbina [tur'ßina] *nf* turbine.

turbio, a ['turßjo, a] *a* cloudy; (*lenguaje*) confused // *ad* indistinctly.

turbión [tur'ßjon] *nf* (*fig*) shower.

turbohélice [turßo'eliθe] *nm* turboprop.

turbulencia [turßu'lenθja] *nf* turbulence; (*fig*) restlessness; **turbulento, a** *a* turbulent; (*fig: intranquilo*) restless; (*: ruidoso*) noisy.

turco, a ['turko, a] *a* Turkish.

turismo [tu'rismo] *nm* tourism; (*coche*) saloon car; **turista** *nm/f* tourist; **turístico, a** *a* tourist *cpd*.

turnar [tur'nar] *vi*, ~**se** *vr* to take (it in) turns; **turno** *nm* (*INDUSTRIA*) shift; (*oportunidad, orden de prioridad*) opportunity; (*DEPORTE etc*) turn.

turquesa [tur'kesa] *nf* turquoise.

Turquía [tur'kia] *nf* Turkey.

turrón [tu'rron] *nm* (*dulce*) nougat; (*fam*) sinecure.

tutear [tute'ar] *vt* to address as familiar 'tú'; ~**se** *vr* to be on familiar terms.

tutela [tu'tela] *nf* (*legal*) guardianship; (*instrucción*) guidance; **tutelar** *a* tutelary // *vt* to protect.

tutor, a [tu'tor, a] *nm/f* (*legal*) guardian; (*ESCOL*) tutor.

tuve, tuviera *etc vb ver* **tener.**

tuyo, a ['tujo, a] *a* yours, of yours // *pron* yours; **los** ~**s** (*fam*) your relations, your family.

TVE *nf abr de* **Televisión Española.**

U

u [u] *conj* or.

ubérrimo, a [u'ßerrimo, a] *a* very rich, fertile.

ubicar [ußi'kar] *vt* (*AM*) to place, situate; (: *fig*) to install in a post; ~**se** *vr* to lie, be located.

ubicuo, a [u'ßikwo, a] *a* ubiquitous.

ubre ['ußre] *nf* udder.

U.C.D. *abr de* **Unión del Centro Democrático.**

Ud(s) *abr de* **usted(es).**

ufanarse [ufa'narse] *vr* to boast; ~ **de** to pride o.s. on; **ufano, a** *a* (*arrogante*) arrogant; (*presumido*) conceited.

U.G.T. *abr de* **Unión General de Trabajadores.**

ujier [u'xjer] *nm* usher; (*portero*) doorkeeper.

úlcera ['ulθera] *nf* ulcer; **ulcerar** *vt* to make sore; **ulcerarse** *vr* to ulcerate.

ulterior [ulte'rjor] *a* (*más allá*) farther, further; (*subsecuente, siguiente*) subsequent; ~**mente** *ad* later, subsequently.

últimamente [ultima'mente] *ad* (*recientemente*) lately, recently; (*finalmente*) finally; (*como último recurso*) as a last resort.

ultimar [ulti'mar] *vt* to finish; (*finalizar*) to finalize; (*AM: rematar*) to finish off.

último, a ['ultimo, a] *a* last; (*más reciente*) latest, most recent; (*más bajo*) bottom; (*más alto*) top; (*fig*) final, extreme; **en las** ~**as** on one's last legs; **por** ~ finally.

ultra ['ultra] *a* ultra // *nm/f* extreme right-winger.

ultrajar [ultra'xar] *vt* (*escandalizar*) to outrage; (*insultar*) to insult, abuse; **ultraje** *nm* outrage; insult.

ultramar [ultra'mar] *nm*: **de** *o* **en** ~ abroad, overseas; ~**ino, a** *a* overseas, foreign; ~**inos** *nmpl* groceries; **tienda de** ~**inos** grocer's (shop).

ultranza [ul'tranθa]: **a** ~ *ad* to the death; (*a todo trance*) at all costs; (*completo*) outright.

ultrasónico, a [ultra'soniko, a] *a* ultrasonic.

ulular [ulu'lar] *vi* to howl; (*búho*) to hoot.

umbral [um'bral] *nm* (*gen*) threshold.

umbroso, a [um'broso, a], **umbrío, a** [um'brio, a] *a* shady.

un, una [un, 'una] *det* a // *num* one; *ver* **uno.**

unánime [u'nanime] *a* unanimous; **unanimidad** *nf* unanimity.

unción [un'θjon] *nf* anointing; **extrema** ~ Extreme Unction.

undécimo, a [un'deθimo, a] *a* eleventh.

undular [undu'lar] *vi ver* **ondular.**

ungir [un'xir] *vt* to rub with ointment; (*REL*) to anoint.

ungüento [un'gwento] *nm* ointment; (*fig*) salve, balm.

únicamente ['unikamente] *ad* solely; (*solamente*) only; **único, a** *a* only; (*solo*) sole, single; (*sin par*) unique.

unidad [uni'ðað] *nf* unity; (*TEC*) unit.

unido, a [u'niðo, a] *a* joined, linked; (*fig*) united.

unificar [unifi'kar] *vt* to unite, unify.

uniformar [unifor'mar] *vt* to make uniform, level up; (*persona*) to put into uniform; **uniforme** *a* uniform, equal; (*superficie*) even // *nm* uniform; **uniformidad** *nf* uniformity; (*llaneza*) levelness, evenness.

unilateral [unilate'ral] *a* unilateral.

unión [u'njon] *nf* (*gen*) union; (*acto*) uniting, joining; (*calidad*) unity; (*TEC*) joint; (*fig*) closeness, togetherness; **la U~ Soviética** the Soviet Union.

unir [u'nir] *vt* (*juntar*) to join, unite; (*atar*) to tie, fasten; (*combinar*) to combine // *vi* to mix well; **~se** *vr* to join together, unite; (*empresas*) to merge.

unísono [u'nisono] *nm*: **al ~** in unison.

universal [uniβer'sal] *a* universal; (*mundial*) world *cpd*.

universidad [uniβersi'ðað] *nf* university.

universo [uni'βerso] *nm* universe.

uno ['uno] *num, det one* // *pron* one; (*alguien*) someone, somebody; **~s** some, a few; **~ a ~**, **~ por ~** one by one; **cada ~** each *or* every one; **estar en ~** to be at one; **~ que otro** some, a few; **~s y otros** all of them; **~ y otro** both.

untar [un'tar] *vt* (*gen*) to rub; (*engrasar*) to grease, oil; (*MED*) to rub with ointment; (*fig*) to bribe; **~se** *vr* to be crooked; **unto** *nm* animal fat; (*MED*) ointment; (*fam*) slush fund.

uña ['uɲa] *nf* (*ANAT*) nail; (*garra*) claw; (*casco*) hoof; (*arrancaclavos*) claw.

uranio [u'ranjo] *nm* uranium.

urbanidad [urβani'ðað] *nf* courtesy, politeness.

urbanismo [urβa'nismo] *nm* town planning.

urbanización [urβaniθa'θjon] *nf* housing scheme.

urbano, a [ur'βano, a] *a* (*de ciudad*) urban; (*cortés*) courteous, polite.

urbe ['urβe] *nf* large city.

urdimbre [ur'ðimbre] *nf* (*de tejido*) warp; (*intriga*) intrigue; **urdir** *vt* to warp; (*fig*) to plot, contrive.

urgencia [ur'xenθja] *nf* urgency; (*prisa*) haste, rush; **servicios de ~** emergency services; **urgente** *a* urgent; (*insistente*) insistent; **urgir** *vi* to be urgent.

urinario, a [uri'narjo, a] *a* urinary // *nm* urinal.

urna ['urna] *nf* urn; (*POL*) ballot box.

urraca [u'rraka] *nf* magpie.

URSS *nf*: **la ~** the USSR.

Uruguay [uru'ɣwai] *nm*: **el ~** Uruguay; **uruguayo, a** *a, nm/f* Uruguayan.

usado, a [u'saðo, a] *a* (*gen*) used; (*ropa etc*) worn.

usanza [u'sanθa] *nf* custom, usage.

usar [u'sar] *vt* to use; (*ropa*) to wear; (*tener costumbre*) to be in the habit of; **~se** *vr* to be used; **uso** *nm* use; wear; (*costumbre*) usage, custom; (*moda*) fashion; **al uso** in keeping with custom; **al uso de** in the style of.

usted [us'teð] *pron* you.

usual [u'swal] *a* usual.

usuario, a [usu'arjo, a] *nm/f* user.

usura [u'sura] *nf* usury; **usurero, a** *nm/f* usurer.

usurpar [usur'par] *vt* to usurp.

utensilio [uten'siljo] *nm* tool; (*CULIN*) utensil.

útero ['utero] *nm* uterus, womb.

útil ['util] *a* useful // *nm* tool; **utilidad** *nf* usefulness; (*COM*) profit; **utilizar** *vt* to use, utilize.

utopía [uto'pia] *nf* Utopia; **utópico, a** *a* Utopian.

uva ['uβa] *nf* grape.

V

v *abr de* **voltio.**

va *vb ver* **ir.**

vaca ['baka] *nf* (*animal*) cow; (*carne*) beef; (*cuero*) cowhide.

vacaciones [baka'θjones] *nfpl* holidays.

vacante [ba'kante] *a* vacant, empty // *nf* vacancy.

vacar [ba'kar] *vi* to fall vacant; **~ a o en** to devote o.s. to.

vaciado, a [ba'θjaðo, a] *a* (*hecho en molde*) cast in a mould; (*hueco*) hollow // *nm* cast.

vaciar [ba'θjar] *vt* to empty out; (*ahuecar*) to hollow out; (*moldear*) to cast // *vi* (*río*) to flow (*en into*); **~se** *vr* to empty; (*fig*) to blab, spill the beans.

vaciedad [baθje'ðað] *nf* emptiness.

vacilación [baθila'θjon] *nf* hesitation; **vacilante** *a* unsteady; (*habla*) faltering; (*fig*) hesitant; **vacilar** *vi* to be unsteady; to falter; to hesitate, waver; (*persona*) to stagger, stumble; (*memoria*) to fail.

vacío, a [ba'θio, a] *a* empty; (*puesto*) vacant; (*desocupado*) idle; (*vano*) vain // *nm* emptiness; (*FÍSICA*) vacuum; (*un ~*) (empty) space.

vacuna [ba'kuna] *nf* vaccine; **vacunar** *vt* to vaccinate.

vacuno, a [ba'kuno, a] *a* bovine.

vacuo, a ['bakwo, a] *a* empty.

vadear [baðe'ar] *vt* (*río*) to ford; (*problema*) to overcome; (*persona*) to sound out; **vado** *nm* ford; (*solución*) solution; (*descanso*) respite.

vagabundo, a [baɣa'βundo, a] *a* wandering; (*pey*) vagrant // *nm* tramp.

vagamente [baɣa'mente] *ad* vaguely.

vagancia [ba'ɣanθja] *nf* vagrancy; **vagar** *vi* (*gen*) to wander; (*no hacer nada*) to idle // *nm* leisure.

vagido [ba'xiðo] *nm* wail.
vagina [ba'xina] *nf* vagina.
vago, a ['baxo, a] *a* vague; (*perezoso*) lazy; (*ambulante*) wandering // *nm/f* (*vagabundo*) tramp; (*flojo*) lazybones *sg*, idler.
vagón [ba'xon] *nm* (*de pasajeros*) carriage; (*de mercancías*) wagon.
vaguedad [baxe'ðað] *nf* vagueness.
vaho ['bao] *nm* (*vapor*) vapour, steam; (*olor*) smell; (*respiración*) breath.
vaina ['baina] *nf* sheath.
vainilla [bai'niʎa] *nf* vanilla.
vais *vb ver* **ir.**
vaivén [bai'ßen] *nm* to-and-fro movement; (*de tránsito*) coming and going; **vaivenes** *nmpl* (*fig*) ups and downs.
vajilla [ba'xiʎa] *nf* crockery, dishes *pl.*
val, valdré *etc vb ver* **valer.**
vale ['bale] *nm* voucher; (*recibo*) receipt; (*pagaré*) I.O.U.
valedero, a [bale'ðero, a] *a* valid.
valenciano, a [balen'θjano, a] *a* Valencian.
valentía [balen'tia] *nf* courage, bravery; (*pey*) boastfulness; (*acción*) heroic deed; **valentón, ona** *a* blustering.
valer [ba'ler] *vt* to aid, protect; (*MAT*) to equal // *vi* to be worth; (*costar*) to cost; (*ser útil*) to be useful; (*ser válido*) to be valid; ~**se** *vr* to defend o.s.; ~**se de** to make use of, take advantage of // *nm* worth, value; ~ **la pena** to be worthwhile; ¿**vale?** O. K.?
valgo *etc vb ver* **valer.**
validar [bali'ðar] *vt* to validate; **validez** *nf* validity; **válido, a** *a* valid.
valiente [ba'ljente] *a* brave, valiant; (*pey*) boastful // *nm* hero.
valija [ba'lixa] *nf* case; (*mochila*) satchel.
valioso, a [ba'ljoso, a] *a* valuable; (*rico*) wealthy.
valor [ba'lor] *nm* value, worth; (*precio*) price; (*valentía*) valour, courage; (*importancia*) importancia; ~ *es nmpl* (*COM*) securities; ~**ación** *nf* valuation; ~**ar** *vt* to value.
vals [bals] *nm* waltz.
válvula ['balßula] *nf* valve.
valla ['baʎa] *nf* fence; (*DEPORTE*) hurdle; (*fig*) barrier; **vallar** *vt* to fence in.
valle ['baʎe] *nm* valley, vale.
vamos *vb ver* **ir.**
vampiro, resa [bam'piro, i'resa] *nm/f* vampire.
van *vb ver* **ir.**
vanagloriarse [banaxlo'rjarse] *vr* to boast.
vándalo, a ['bandalo, a] *nm/f* vandal; **vandalismo** *nm* vandalism.
vanguardia [ban'gwardja] *nf* vanguard; (*ARTE*) avant-garde.
vanidad [bani'ðað] *nf* vanity; (*irrealidad*) unreality; **vanidoso, a** *a* vain, conceited.
vano, a ['bano, a] *a* (*irreal*) unreal; (*irracional*) unreasonable; (*inútil*) useless;

(*persona*) vain, conceited; (*frívolo*) frivolous.
vapor [ba'por] *nm* vapour; (*vaho*) steam; (*neblina*) mist; ~**es** *nmpl* (*MED*) hysterics; **al** ~ (*CULIN*) steamed; ~**izar** *vt* to vaporize; ~**oso, a** *a* vaporous; (*vahoso*) steamy.
vaquero, a [ba'kero, a] *a* cattle *cpd* // *nm* cowboy; ~**s** *nmpl* jeans.
vara ['bara] *nf* stick, wand; (*TEC*) rod.
varear [bare'ar] *vt* to hit, beat.
variable [ba'rjaßle] *a*, *nf* variable; **variación** *nf* variation; **variar** *vt* to vary; (*modificar*) to modify; (*cambiar de posición*) to switch around // *vi* to vary; **variedad** *nf* variety.
varilla [ba'riʎa] *nf* stick; (*BOT*) twig; (*TEC*) rod; (*de rueda*) spoke.
vario, a ['barjo, a] *a* (*variado*) varied; (*multicolor*) motley; (*cambiable*) changeable; ~**s** various, several.
varón [ba'ron] *nm* male, man; **varonil** *a* manly.
Varsovia [bar'soßja] *n* Warsaw.
vas *vb ver* **ir.**
vascongado, a [baskon'xaðo, a], **vascuence** [bas'kwenθe], **vasco, a** ['basko, a] *a* Basque; **las Vascongadas** the Basque Country.
vaselina [base'lina] *nf* vaseline.
vasija [ba'sixa] *nf* container, vessel.
vaso ['baso] *nm* glass, tumbler; (*ANAT*) vessel.
vástago ['bastaxo] *nm* (*BOT*) shoot; (*TEC*) rod; (*fig*) offspring.
vasto, a ['basto, a] *a* vast, huge.
Vaticano [bati'kano] *nm*: **el** ~ the Vatican.
vaticinio [bati'θinjo] *nm* prophecy.
vatio ['batjo] *nm* (*ELEC*) watt.
vaya *etc vb ver* **ir.**
Vd(s) *abr de* **usted(es).**
ve *vb ver* **ir, ver.**
vecindad [beθin'dað] *nf*, **vecindario** [beθin'darjo] *nm* neighbourhood; (*habitantes*) residents *pl*; **vecino, a** *a* neighbouring // *nm/f* neighbour; (*residente*) resident.
veda ['beða] *nf* prohibition.
vedado [be'ðaðo] *nm* preserve.
vedar [be'ðar] *vt* (*prohibir*) to ban, prohibit; (*impedir*) to stop, prevent.
vegetación [bexeta'θjon] *nf* vegetation.
vegetal [bexe'tal] *a*, *nm* vegetable.
vehemencia [bee'menθja] *nf* (*insistencia*) vehemence; (*pasión*) passion; (*fervor*) fervour; (*violencia*) violence; **vehemente** *a* vehement; passionate; fervent.
vehículo [be'ikulo] *nm* vehicle; (*MED*) carrier.
veía *etc vb ver* **ver.**
veinte ['beinte] *num* twenty.
vejación [bexa'θjon] *nf* vexation; (*humillación*) humiliation.
vejamen [be'xamen] *nm* satire.

vejar [be'xar] vt (*irritar*) to annoy, vex; (*humillar*) to humiliate.
vejez [be'xeθ] nf old age.
vejiga [be'xiɤa] nf (*ANAT*) bladder.
vela ['bela] nf (*de cera*) candle; (*NAUT*) sail; (*insomnio*) sleeplessness; (*vigilia*) vigil; (*MIL*) sentry duty; (*fam*) snot; **estar a dos ~s** (*fam*) to be skint (*fam*).
velado, a [be'laðo, a] a veiled; (*sonido*) muffled; (*FOTO*) blurred // nf soirée.
velador [bela'ðor] nm watchman; (*candelero*) candlestick.
velar [be'lar] vt (*hacer guardia*) to keep watch over; (*cubrir*) to veil // vi to stay awake; **~ por** to watch over, look after.
veleidad [belei'ðað] nf (*ligereza*) fickleness; (*capricho*) whim.
velero [be'lero] nm (*NAUT*) sailing ship; (*AVIAT*) glider.
veleta [be'leta] nf weather vane.
velo ['belo] nm veil.
velocidad [beloθi'ðað] nf speed; (*TEC, AUTO*) gear.
velocímetro [belo'θimetro] nm speedometer.
velódromo [be'loðromo] nm cycle track.
veloz [be'loθ] a fast.
vello ['beʎo] nm down, fuzz; **vellón** nm fleece; **~so, a** a fuzzy; **velludo, a** a shaggy // nm plush, velvet.
ven vb ver **venir**.
vena ['bena] nf vein.
venablo [be'naβlo] nm javelin.
venado [be'naðo] nm deer.
venal [be'nal] a (*ANAT*) venous; (*pey*) venal; **~idad** nf venality.
vencedor, a [benθe'ðor, a] a victorious // nm/f victor, winner.
vencer [ben'θer] vt (*dominar*) to defeat, beat; (*derrotar*) to vanquish; (*superar, controlar*) to overcome, master // vi (*triunfar*) to win (through), triumph; (*plazo*) to expire; **vencido, a** a (*derrotado*) defeated, beaten; (*COM*) due // ad: **pagar vencido** to pay in arrears; **vencimiento** nm collapse; (*COM*) maturity.
venda ['benda] nf bandage; **~je** nm bandage, dressing; **vendar** vt to bandage; **vendar los ojos** to blindfold.
vendaval [benda'βal] nm (*viento*) gale; (*huracán*) hurricane.
vendedor, a [bende'ðor, a] nm/f seller.
vender [ben'der] vt to sell; **~ al contado/al por mayor/al por menor** to sell for cash/wholesale/retail.
vendimia [ben'dimja] nf grape harvest.
vendré etc vb ver **venir**.
veneno [be'neno] nm poison, venom; **~so, a** a poisonous.
venerable [bene'raβle] a venerable; **veneración** nf veneration; **venerar** vt (*reconocer*) to venerate; (*adorar*) to worship.
venéreo, a [be'nereo, a] a venereal.
venero [be'nero] nm (*veta*) seam, lode; (*fuente*) spring.

venezolano, a [beneθo'lano, a] a Venezuelan.
Venezuela [bene'θwela] nf Venezuela.
venganza [ben'ganθa] nf vengeance, revenge; **vengar** vt to avenge; **vengarse** vr to take revenge; **vengativo, a** a (*persona*) vindictive.
vengo etc vb ver **venir**.
venia ['benja] nf (*perdón*) pardon; (*permiso*) consent.
venial [be'njal] a venial.
venida [be'niða] nf (*llegada*) arrival; (*regreso*) return; (*fig*) rashness.
venidero, a [beni'ðero, a] a coming, future.
venir [be'nir] vi to come; (*llegar*) to arrive; (*fig*) to stem from; (*ocurrir*) to happen; **~ bien/mal** to be suitable/unsuitable; **el año que viene** next year; **~se abajo** to collapse.
venta ['benta] nf (*COM*) sale; **~ a plazos** hire purchase; **~ al contado/al por mayor/al por menor** o **al detalle** cash sale/ wholesale/retail; **~ de liquidación** clearance sale.
ventaja [ben'taxa] nf advantage; **ventajoso, a** a advantageous.
ventana [ben'tana] nf window; **~ de guillotina/saledizia** sash/bay window; **ventanilla** nf (*de taquilla*) window (*of booking office etc*).
ventear [bente'ar] vt (*ropa*) to hang out to dry; (*oler*) to sniff // vi (*investigar*) to investigate; (*soplar*) to blow; **~se** vr (*romperse*) to crack; (*ANAT*) to break wind.
ventilación [bentila'θjon] nf ventilation; (*corriente*) draught; **ventilar** vt to ventilate; (*a secar*) to put out to dry; (*fig*) to air, discuss.
ventisca [ben'tiska] nf, **ventisquero** [bentis'kero] nm blizzard; (*nieve amontonada*) snowdrift.
ventosear [bentose'ar] vi to break wind.
ventoso, a [ben'toso, a] a windy.
ventrílocuo, a [ben'trilokwo, a] nm/f ventriloquist; **ventriloquia** nf ventriloquism.
ventura [ben'tura] nf (*felicidad*) happiness; (*buena suerte*) luck; (*destino*) fortune; **a la (buena) ~** at random; **venturoso, a** a happy; (*afortunado*) lucky, fortunate.
veo etc vb ver **ver**.
ver [ber] vt, vi to see; (*mirar*) to look at, watch; (*investigar*) to look into; **~se** vr (*encontrarse*) to meet; (*dejarse ~*) to be seen; (*hallarse: en un apuro*) to find o.s., be // nm looks pl, appearance; **a ~** let's see; **dejarse ~** to become apparent; **no tener nada que ~ con** to have nothing to do with; **a mí modo de ~** as I see it.
vera ['bera] nf edge, verge; (*de río*) bank.
veracidad [beraθi'ðað] nf truthfulness.
veranear [berane'ar] vi to spend the summer; **veraneo** nm summer holiday; **veraniego, a** a summer cpd; **verano** nm summer.

veras ['beras] *nfpl* truth *sg*; **de** ~ really, truly.

veraz [be'raθ] *a* truthful.

verbal [ber'βal] *a* verbal.

verbena [ber'βena] *nf* street party.

verbigracia [berβi'ɣraθja] *ad* for example.

verbo ['berβo] *nm* verb; ~**so, a** *a* verbose.

verdad [ber'ðað] *nf* (*lo verídico*) truth; (*fiabilidad*) reliability // *ad* really; **de** ~ *a* real, proper; **a decir** ~ to tell the truth; ~**ero, a** *a* (*veraz*) true, truthful; (*fiable*) reliable; (*fig*) real.

verde ['berðe] *a* green; (*sucio*) blue, dirty // *nm* green; **viejo** ~ dirty old man; ~**ar**, ~**cer** *vi* to turn green; **verdor** *nm* (*lo* ~) greenness; (*BOT*) verdure; (*fig*) youthful vigour.

verdugo [ber'ðuɣo] *nm* executioner; (*BOT*) shoot; (*cardenal*) weal.

verdulero, a [berðu'lero, a] *nm/f* greengrocer.

verdura [ber'ðura] *nf* greenness; ~**s** *nfpl* (*CULIN*) greens.

vereda [be'reða] *nf* path.

veredicto [bere'ðikto] *nm* verdict.

vergonzoso, a [berɣon'θoso, a] *a* shameful; (*tímido*) timid, bashful.

vergüenza [ber'ɣwenθa] *nf* shame, sense of shame; (*timidez*) bashfulness; (*pudor*) modesty.

verídico, a [be'riðiko, a] *a* true, truthful.

verificar [berifi'kar] *vt* to check; (*corroborar*) to verify; (*llevar a cabo*) to carry out; ~**se** *vr* to occur, happen.

verja ['berxa] *nf* grating.

vermut [ber'mut] *nm* vermouth.

verosímil [bero'simil] *a* likely, probable; (*relato*) credible.

verruga [be'rruɣa] *nf* wart.

versado, a [ber'saðo, a] *a*: ~ **en** versed in.

versar [ber'sar] *vi* to go round, turn.

versátil [ber'satil] *a* versatile.

versión [ber'sjon] *nf* version; (*traducción*) translation.

verso ['berso] *nm* (*gen*) verse; **un** ~ a line of poetry.

vértebra ['berteβra] *nf* vertebra.

verter [ber'ter] *vt* (*vaciar*) to empty, pour (out); (*tirar*) to dump // *vi* to flow.

vertical [berti'kal] *a* vertical.

vértice ['bertiθe] *nm* vertex, apex.

vertiente [ber'tjente] *nf* slope.

vertiginoso, a [bertixi'noso, a] *a* giddy, dizzy; **vértigo** *nm* vertigo; (*mareo*) dizziness.

vesícula [be'sikula] *nf* blister.

vespertino, a [besper'tino, a] *a* evening *cpd*.

vestíbulo [bes'tiβulo] *nm* hall; (*de teatro*) foyer.

vestido [bes'tiðo] *nm* (*ropa*) clothes *pl*, clothing; (*de mujer*) dress, frock.

vestigio [bes'tixjo] *nm* (*trazo*) trace; (*señal*) sign; ~**s** *nmpl* remains.

vestimenta [besti'menta] *nf* clothing.

vestir [bes'tir] *vt* (*poner: ropa*) to put on; (*llevar: ropa*) to wear; (*cubrir*) to clothe, cover; (*pagar: la ropa*) to pay for the clothing of; (*sastre*) to make clothes for // *vi* (*ponerse: ropa*) to dress; (*verse bien*) to look good; ~**se** *vr* to get dressed, dress o.s.

vestuario [bes'twarjo] *nm* clothes *pl*, wardrobe; (*TEATRO*) dressing room; (*DEPORTE*) changing room.

veta ['beta] *nf* (*vena*) vein, seam; (*raya*) streak; (*de madera*) grain.

vetar [be'tar] *vt* to veto.

veterano, a [bete'rano, a] *a, nm* veteran.

veterinario, a [beteri'narjo, a] *nm/f* vet(erinary surgeon) // *nf* veterinary science.

veto ['beto] *nm* veto.

vetusto, a [be'tusto, a] *a* ancient.

vez [beθ] *nf* time; (*turno*) turn; **a la** ~ **que** at the same time as; **a su** ~ in its turn; **cada** ~ **más/menos** more and more/less and less; **una** ~ once; **de una** ~ in one go; **de una** ~ **para siempre** once and for all; **en** ~ **de** instead of; **a veces** sometimes; **una y otra** ~ repeatedly; **de** ~ **en cuando** from time to time; **7 veces 9** 7 times 9; **hacer las veces de** to stand in for; **tal** ~ perhaps.

v. g., v. gr. *abr de* **verbigracia.**

vía ['bia] *nf* track, route; (*FERRO*) line; (*fig*) way; (*ANAT*) passage, tube // *prep* via, by way of; **por** ~ **judicial** by legal means; **por** ~ **oficial** through official channels; **por** ~ **de** by way of; **en** ~**s de** in the process of; ~ **aérea** airway.

viaducto [bja'ðukto] *nm* viaduct.

viajante [bja'xante] *nm* commercial traveller.

viajar [bja'xar] *vi* to travel; **viaje** *nm* journey; (*gira*) tour; (*NAUT*) voyage; **estar de viaje** to be on a journey; **viaje de ida y vuelta** round trip; **viaje de novios** honeymoon; **viajero, a** *a* travelling; (*ZOOL*) migratory // *nm/f* (*quien viaja*) traveller; (*pasajero*) passenger.

vial [bjal] *a* road *cpd*, traffic *cpd*.

víbora ['biβora] *nf* viper.

vibración [biβra'θjon] *nf* vibration; **vibrador** *nm* vibrator; **vibrante** *a* vibrant; **vibrar** *vt*, *vi* to vibrate.

vicario [bi'karjo] *nm* curate.

vicepresidente [biθepresi'ðente] *nm/f* vice president.

viciado, a [bi'θjaðo, a] *a* (*corrompido*) corrupt; (*contaminado*) foul, contaminated; **viciar** *vt* (*pervertir*) to pervert; (*adulterar*) to adulterate; (*falsificar*) to falsify; (*JUR*) to nullify; (*estropear*) to spoil; (*sentido*) to twist; **viciarse** *vr* to become corrupted.

vicio ['biθjo] *nm* (*libertinaje*) vice; (*mala costumbre*) bad habit; (*mimo*) spoiling; (*alabeo*) warp, warping; ~**so, a** *a* (*muy malo*) vicious; (*corrompido*) depraved; (*mimado*) spoiled // *nm/f* depraved person.

vicisitud [biθisi'tuð] *nf* vicissitude.

víctima ['biktima] nf victim.
victoria [bik'torja] nf victory; **victorioso, a** a victorious.
vicuña [bi'kuɲa] nf vicuna.
vid [bið] nf vine.
vida ['biða] nf (gen) life; (duración) lifetime; **de por** ~ for life; **en la/mi** ~ never; **estar con** ~ to be still alive; **ganarse la** ~ to earn one's living.
vidriero, a [bi'ðrjero, a] nm/f glazier // nf (ventana) stained-glass window; (puerta) glass door.
vidrio ['biðrjo] nm glass; ~**so, a** a glassy; (frágil) fragile, brittle; (resbaladizo) slippery.
viejo, a ['bjexo, a] a old // nm/f old man/woman.
vienes etc vb ver **venir**.
vienés, esa [bje'nes, esa] a Viennese.
viento ['bjento] nm wind; (olfato) scent.
vientre ['bjentre] nm belly; (matriz) womb; ~**s** nmpl bowels.
viernes ['bjernes] nm inv Friday.
Vietnam [bjet'nam] nm: **el** ~ Vietnam; **vietnamita** a Vietnamese.
viga ['bixa] nf beam, rafter.
vigencia [bi'xenθja] nf validity; **estar en** ~ to be in force; **vigente** a valid, in force; (imperante) prevailing.
vigésimo, a [bi'xesimo, a] a twentieth.
vigía [bi'xia] nm look-out // nf (atalaya) watchtower; (acción) watching.
vigilancia [bixi'lanθja] nf vigilance; **vigilar** vt to watch over // vi (gen) to be vigilant; (hacer guardia) to keep watch.
vigilia [vi'xilja] nf wakefulness, being awake; (REL) fast; **comer de** ~ to fast.
vigor [bi'xor] nm vigour, vitality; **en** ~ in force; **entrar/poner en** ~ to take/put into effect; ~**oso, a** a vigorous.
vil [bil] a vile, low; ~**eza** nf vileness; (acto) base deed.
vilipendiar [bilipen'djar] vt to vilify, revile.
vilo ['bilo]: **en** ~ ad in the air, suspended.
villa ['biʎa] nf (pueblo) small town; (municipalidad) municipality.
villorrio [bi'ʎorrjo] nm one-horse town, dump (fam).
vinagre [bi'naxre] nm vinegar.
vinculación [binkula'θjon] nf (lazo) link, bond; (acción) linking; **vincular** vt to link, bind; **vínculo** nm link, bond.
vindicar [bindi'kar] vt to vindicate; (vengar) to avenge; (JUR) to claim.
vine etc vb ver **venir**.
vinicultura [binikul'tura] nf wine growing.
viniera etc vb ver **venir**.
vino ['bino] nm wine.
viña ['biɲa] nf, **viñedo** [bi'ɲeðo] nm vineyard.
violación [bjola'θjon] nf violation; ~ (**sexual**) rape; **violar** vt to violate; to rape.
violencia [bjo'lenθja] nf (fuerza) violence,

force; (embarazo) embarrassment; (acto injusto) unjust act; **violentar** vt to force; (casa) to break into; (agredir) to assault; (violar) to violate; **violento, a** a violent; (furioso) furious; (situación) embarrassing; (acto) forced, unnatural; (difícil) awkward.
violeta [bjo'leta] nf violet.
violín [bjo'lin] nm violin.
violón [bjo'lon] nm double bass.
viraje [bi'raxe] nm turn; (de vehículo) swerve; (de carretera) bend; (fig) change of direction; **virar** vt, vi to change direction.
virgen ['birxen] a, nf virgin.
Virgo ['birxo] nm Virgo.
viril [bi'ril] a virile; ~**idad** nf virility.
virtualmente [birtwal'mente] ad virtually.
virtud [bir'tuð] nf virtue; **virtuoso, a** a virtuous // nm/f virtuoso.
viruela [bi'rwela] nf smallpox; ~**s** nfpl pockmarks; ~**s locas** chickenpox.
virulento, a [biru'lento, a] a virulent.
virus ['birus] nm virus.
visado [bi'saðo] nm visa.
viscoso, a [bis'koso, a] a viscous.
visera [bi'sera] nf visor.
visibilidad [bisiβili'ðað] nf visibility; **visible** a visible; (fig) obvious.
visión [bi'sjon] nf (ANAT) vision, (eye)sight; (fantasía) vision, fantasy; (panorama) view; **visionario, a** a (que preve) visionary; (alucinado) deluded // nm/f visionary; (chalado) lunatic.
visita [bi'sita] nf call, visit; (persona) visitor; **visitar** vt to visit, call on; (inspeccionar) to inspect.
vislumbrar [bislum'brar] vt to glimpse, catch a glimpse of; **vislumbre** nf glimpse; (centelleo) gleam; (idea vaga) glimmer.
viso ['biso] nm (del metal) glint, gleam; (de tela) sheen; (aspecto) appearance.
visón [bi'son] nm mink.
visor [bi'sor] nm (FOTO) viewfinder.
víspera ['bispera] nf eve, day before.
vista ['bista] nf sight, vision; (capacidad de ver) (eye)sight; (mirada) look(s) (pl) // nm customs officer; **a primera** ~ at first glance; **hacer la** ~ **gorda** to turn a blind eye; **volver la** ~ to look back; **está a la** ~ que it's obvious that; **en** ~ **de** in view of; **en** ~ **de que** in view of the fact that; **¡hasta la** ~!** so long!, see you!; **con** ~**s a** with a view to; ~**zo** nm glance; **dar** o **echar un** ~**zo a** to glance at.
visto etc vb ver **vestir**.
visto, a ['bisto, a] pp de ver // a seen; (considerado) considered // nm: ~ **bueno** approval; '~ **bueno**' approved; **por lo** ~ evidently; **está** ~ **que** it's clear that; **está bien/mal** ~ it's acceptable/unacceptable; ~ **que** conj since, considering that.
vistoso, a [bis'toso, a] a colourful; (alegre) gay; (pey) gaudy.
vital [bi'tal] a life cpd, living cpd; (fig) vital; (persona) lively, vivacious; ~**icio, a** a for life.

vitamina [bita'mina] nf vitamin.
viticultor, a [bitikul'tor, a] nm/f vine grower; **viticultura** nf vine growing.
vitorear [bitore'ar] vt to cheer, acclaim.
vítreo, a ['bitreo, a] a vitreous.
vitrina [bi'trina] nf glass case.
vituperar [bitupe'rar] vt to condemn; **vituperio** nm (condena) condemnation; (censura) censure; (insulto) insult.
viudo, a ['bjuðo, a] nm/f widower/widow; **viudez** nf widowhood.
vivacidad [biβaθi'ðað] nf (vigor) vigour; (vida) vivacity.
vivaracho, a [biβa'ratʃo, a] a jaunty, lively; (ojos) bright, twinkling.
vivaz [bi'βaθ] a (que dura) enduring; (vigoroso) vigorous; (vivo) lively.
víveres ['biβeres] nmpl provisions.
viveza [bi'βeθa] nf liveliness; (agudeza) sharpness.
vivienda [bi'βjenda] nf (alojamiento) housing; (morada) dwelling.
viviente [bi'βjente] a living.
vivificar [biβifi'kar] vt to give life to.
vivir [bi'βir] vt, vi to live // nm life, living.
vivo, a ['biβo, a] a living, live, alive; (fig) vivid; (astuto) smart, clever; **llegar a lo** ~ to cut to the quick.
vocablo [bo'kaβlo] nm (palabra) word; (término) term.
vocabulario [bokaβu'larjo] nm vocabulary.
vocación [boka'θjon] nf vocation.
vocal [bo'kal] a vocal // nf vowel; ~**izar** vt to vocalize.
vocear [boθe'ar] vt (para vender) to cry; (aclamar) to acclaim; (fig) to proclaim // vi to yell; **vocerío** nm, **vocería** nf shouting.
vocero [bo'θero] nm/f spokesman/woman.
vociferar [boθife'rar] vt to shout; (jactarse) to proclaim boastfully // vi to yell.
vocinglero, a [boθin'glero, a] a vociferous, (garrulo) garrulous; (fig) blatant.
vodka ['boðka] nf vodka.
vol abr de volumen.
volador, a [bola'ðor, a] a flying.
volante [bo'lante] a flying // nm (de máquina, coche) steering wheel; (de reloj) balance.
volar [bo'lar] vt (demolir) to blow up, demolish // vi to fly.
volátil [bo'latil] a volatile; (fig) changeable.
volcán [bol'kan] nm volcano; ~**ico, a** a volcanic.
volcar [bol'kar] vt to upset, overturn; (tumbar, derribar) to knock over; (vaciar) to empty out // vi to overturn; ~**se** vr to tip over.
volibol [boli'βol] nm volleyball.
volición [boli'θjon] nf volition.
voltaje [bol'taxe] nm voltage.
volteador, a [boltea'ðor, a] nm/f acrobat.

voltear [bolte'ar] vt to turn over; (volcar) to turn upside down; (doblar) to peal // vi to roll over.
voltio ['boltjo] nm volt.
voluble [bo'luβle] a fickle.
volumen [bo'lumen] nm volume; **voluminoso, a** a voluminous; (enorme) massive.
voluntad [bolun'tað] nf will, willpower; (deseo) desire, wish; (afecto) fondness.
voluntario, a [bolun'tarjo, a] a voluntary // nm/f volunteer.
voluntarioso, a [bolunta'rjoso, a] a headstrong.
voluptuoso, a [bolup'twoso, a] a voluptuous.
volver [bol'βer] vt (gen) to turn; (dar vuelta) to turn (over); (voltear) to turn round, turn upside down; (poner al revés) to turn inside out; (devolver) to return; (transformar) to change, transform // vi to return, go/come back; ~**se** vr to turn round; (llegar a ser) to become; ~ **la espalda** to turn one's back; ~ **bien por mal** to return good for evil; ~ **a hacer** to do again; ~ **en sí** to come to; ~**se loco** to go mad.
vomitar [bomi'tar] vt, vi to vomit; **vómito** nm (acto) vomiting; (resultado) vomit.
voraz [bo'raθ] a voracious; (fig) fierce.
vórtice ['bortiθe] nm whirlpool; (de aire) whirlwind.
vosotros [bo'sotros] pron you.
votación [bota'θjon] nf (acto) voting; (voto) vote; **votar** vi to vote; **voto** nm vote; (promesa) vow; (maldición) oath, curse; **votos** (good) wishes.
voy vb ver **ir**.
voz [boθ] nf voice; (grito) shout; (chisme) rumour; (LING) word; **dar voces** to shout, yell; **a media** ~ in a low voice; **a** ~ **en cuello** o **en grito** at the top of one's voice; **de viva** ~ verbally; **en** ~ **alta** aloud; ~ **de mando** command.
vuelco ['bwelko] nm spill, overturning; (fig) collapse.
vuelo ['bwelo] vb ver **volar** // nm flight; (encaje) lace, frill; (fig) importance; **coger al** ~ to catch in flight.
vuelta ['bwelta] nf (gen) turn; (curva) bend, curve; (regreso) return; (revolución) revolution; (paseo) stroll; (circuito) lap; (de papel, tela) reverse; (cambio) change; **V**~ **de Francia** Tour de France; ~ **cerrada** hairpin bend; **a la** ~ on one's return; **a** ~ **de correo** by return of post; **dar** ~s to turn, revolve; **dar** ~s **a una idea** to turn over an idea (in one's head); **estar de** ~ (fam) to be back; **dar una** ~ to go for a walk.
vuelto pp de **volver**.
vuelvo etc vb ver **volver**.
vuestro, a ['bwestro, a] a your; **un amigo** ~ a friend of yours // pron: **el** ~/**la** ~/**los** ~s/**las** ~s as yours.
vulgar [bul'xar] a (ordinario) vulgar; (común) common; ~**idad** nf commonness; (acto) vulgarity; (expresión) coarse

expression; ~**idades** *nfpl* banalities; ~**izar** *vt* to popularize.
vulgo ['bulɣo] *nm* common people.
vulnerable [bulne'raßle] *a* vulnerable.
vulnerar [bulne'rar] *vt* to harm, damage.
vulpino, a [bul'pino, a] *a* vulpine; (*fig*) foxy.

W

wáter ['bater] *nm* lavatory.
wátman ['watman] *a inv* (*fam*) cool.
whisky ['wiski] *nm* whisky.

X

xenofobia [kseno'foßja] *nf* xenophobia.
xilófono [ksi'lofono] *nm* xylophone.

Y

y [i] *conj* and.
ya [ja] *ad* (*gen*) already; (*ahora*) now; (*en seguida*) at once; (*pronto*) soon // *excl* all right! // *conj* (*ahora que*) now that; ~ **lo sé** I know; ~ **dice que sí,** ~ **dice que no** first he says yes, then he says no; ~ **que** since.
yacer [ja'θer] *vi* to lie.
yacimiento [jaθi'mjento] *nm* bed, deposit.
yanqui ['janki] *a* Yankee.
yate ['jate] *nm* yacht.
yazco *etc vb ver* **yacer.**
yedra ['jeðra] *nf* ivy.
yegua ['jeɣwa] *nf* mare.
yema ['jema] *nf* (*del huevo*) yoke; (*BOT*) leaf bud; (*fig*) best part; ~ **del dedo** fingertip.
yergo *etc vb ver* **erguir.**
yermo, a ['jermo, a] *a* uninhabited // *nm* waste land.
yerno ['jerno] *nm* son-in-law.
yerro *etc vb ver* **errar.**
yerto, a ['jerto, a] *a* stiff.
yesca ['jeska] *nf* tinder.
yeso ['jeso] *nm* (*GEO*) gypsum; (*ARQ*) plaster.
yodo ['joðo] *nm* iodine.
yugo ['juɣo] *nm* yoke.
Yugoslavia [juɣos'laßja] *nf* Yugoslavia.
yugular [juɣu'lar] *a* jugular.
yunque ['junke] *nm* anvil.
yunta ['junta] *nf* yoke; **yuntero** *nm* ploughman.
yute ['jute] *nm* jute.
yuxtaponer [jukstapo'ner] *vt* to juxtapose; **yuxtaposición** *nf* juxtaposition.

Z

zafar [θa'far] *vt* (*soltar*) to untie; (*superficie*) to clear; ~**se** *vr* (*escaparse*) to escape; (*ocultarse*) to hide o.s. away; (*TEC*) to slip off.
zafio, a ['θafjo, a] *a* coarse.

zafiro [θa'firo] *nm* sapphire.
zaga ['θaɣa] *nf* rear; **a la** ~ behind, in the rear.
zagal, a [θa'ɣal, a] *nm/f* boy/girl, lad/lass.
zaguán [θa'ɣwan] *nm* hallway.
zahareño, a [θaa'reɲo, a] *a* (*salvaje*) wild; (*arisco*) unsociable.
zaherir [θae'rir] *vt* (*criticar*) to criticize; (*fig: herir*) to wound.
zahorí [θao'ri] *nm* clairvoyant.
zaino, a ['θaino, a] *a* (*color de caballo*) chestnut; (*pérfido*) treacherous; (*animal*) vicious.
zalamería [θala'merja] *nf* flattery; **zalamero, a** *a* flattering; (*relamido*) suave.
zamarra [θa'marra] *nf* (*piel*) sheepskin; (*saco*) sheepskin jacket.
zambra ['θambra] *nf* gypsy dance.
zambullirse [θambu'ʎirse] *vr* to dive; (*ocultarse*) to hide o.s.
zampar [θam'par] *vt* (*esconder*) to hide *or* put away (hurriedly); (*comer*) to gobble; (*arrojar*) to hurl // *vi* to eat voraciously; ~**se** *vr* (*chocar*) to bump; (*fig*) to gatecrash.
zanahoria [θana'orja] *nf* carrot.
zancada [θan'kaða] *nf* stride.
zancadilla [θanka'ðiʎa] *nf* trip; (*fig*) stratagem.
zancajo [θan'kaxo] *nm* (*ANAT*) heel; (*fig*) dwarf.
zanco ['θanko] *nm* stilt.
zancudo, a [θan'kuðo, a] *a* long-legged // *nm* (*AM*) mosquito.
zángano ['θangano] *nm* drone.
zanja ['θanxa] *nf* (*fosa*) ditch; (*tumba*) grave; **zanjar** *vt* (*fosa*) to ditch, trench; (*problema*) to surmount; (*conflicto*) to resolve.
zapapico [θapa'piko] *nm* pick, pickaxe.
zapata [θa'pata] *nf* half-boot; (*MECÁNICA*) shoe.
zapatear [θapate'ar] *vt* (*tocar*) to tap with one's foot; (*patear*) to kick; (*fam*) to ill-treat // *vi* to tap with one's feet.
zapatería [θapate'ria] *nf* (*oficio*) shoemaking; (*tienda*) shoe-shop; (*fábrica*) shoe factory; **zapatero, a** *nm/f* shoemaker.
zapatilla [θapa'tiʎa] *nf* slipper.
zapato [θa'pato] *nm* shoe.
zarabanda [θara'ßanda] *nf* saraband; (*fig*) whirl.
zaranda [θa'randa] *nf* sieve; **zarandear** *vt* to sieve; (*fam*) to shake vigorously.
zarcillo [θar'θiʎo] *nm* earring.
zarpa ['θarpa] *nf* (*garra*) claw.
zarpar [θar'par] *vi* to weigh anchor.
zarza ['θarθa] *nf* (*BOT*) bramble; **zarzal** *nm* (*matorral*) bramble patch.
zarzamora [θarθa'mora] *nf* blackberry.
zarzuela [θar'θwela] *nf* Spanish light opera.
zigzag [θiɣ'θaɣ] *a* zigzag; **zigzaguear** *vi* to zigzag.

zinc [θink] *nm* zinc.
zócalo ['θokalo] *nm* (*ARQ*) plinth, base.
zona ['θona] *nf* zone; ~ **fronteriza** border area.
zoología [θoolo'xia] *nf* zoology; **zoológico, a** *a* zoological // *nm* zoo; **zoólogo, a** *nm/f* zoologist.
zopilote [θopi'lote] *nm* (*AM*) buzzard.
zoquete [θo'kete] *nm* (*madera*) block; (*pan*) crust; (*fam*) blockhead.
zorro, a ['θorro, a] *a* crafty // *nm/f* fox/vixen.
zozobra [θo'θoβra] *nf* (*fig*) anxiety; **zozobrar** *vi* (*hundirse*) to capsize; (*fig*) to fail.
zueco ['θweko] *nm* clog.

zumbar [θum'bar] *vt* (*burlar*) to tease; (*golpear*) to hit // *vi* to buzz; (*fam*) to be very close; ~**se** *vr*: ~**se de** to tease; **zumbido** *nm* buzzing; (*fam*) punch.
zumo ['θumo] *nm* juice; (*ganancia*) profit.
zurcir [θur'θir] *vt* (*coser*) to darn; (*fig*) to put together.
zurdo, a ['θurðo, a] *a* (*mano*) left; (*persona*) left-handed.
zurrar [θu'rrar] *vt* (*TEC*) to dress; (*fam: pegar duro*) to wallop; (: *aplastar*) to flatten; (: *criticar*) to criticize harshly.
zurriago [θu'rrjaɣo] *nm* whip, lash.
zurrón [θu'rron] *nm* pouch.
zutano, a [θu'tano, a] *nm/f* so-and-so.

ENGLISH - SPANISH
INGLÉS - ESPAÑOL

A

a, an [eɪ, ə, æn, ən, n] *det* un(a); **3 a day/week** 3 por día/semana; **10 km an hour** 10 km por hora.

A.A. *n abbr of* **Automobile Association; Alcoholics Anonymous.**

aback [ə'bæk] *ad*: **to be taken ~** quedar desconcertado.

abandon [ə'bændən] *vt* abandonar; (*renounce*) renunciar a // *n* abandono; (*wild behaviour*) desenfreno.

abashed [ə'bæʃt] *a* avergonzado, confuso.

abate [ə'beɪt] *vi* moderarse; (*lessen*) disminuir; (*calm down*) calmarse.

abattoir ['æbətwɑ:*] *n* matadero.

abbey ['æbɪ] *n* monasterio.

abbot ['æbət] *n* abad *m.*

abbreviate [ə'bri:vɪeɪt] *vt* abreviar; **abbreviation** [-'eɪʃən] *n* (*short form*) abreviatura; (*act*) abreviación *f.*

abdicate ['æbdɪkeɪt] *vt, vi* abdicar; **abdication** [-'keɪʃən] *n* abdicación *f.*

abdomen ['æbdəmən] *n* abdomen *m.*

abduct [æb'dʌkt] *vt* raptar, secuestrar; **~ion** [-'dʌkʃən] *n* rapto, secuestro.

aberration [æbə'reɪʃən] *n* aberración *f.*

abet [ə'bɛt] *vt* (*incite*) incitar; (*aid*) ser cómplice de.

abeyance [ə'beɪəns] *n*: **in ~** (*law*) en desuso; (*matter*) en suspenso.

abhor [əb'hɔ:*] *vt* aborrecer, abominar (de); **~rent** *a* aborrecible, detestable.

abide [ə'baɪd], *pt, pp* **abode** *or* **abided** *vt* aguantar, soportar; **to ~ by** *vt fus* atenerse a.

ability [ə'bɪlɪtɪ] *n* habilidad *f*, capacidad *f*; (*talent*) talento.

ablaze [ə'bleɪz] *a* en llamas, ardiendo.

able ['eɪbl] *a* capaz; (*skilled*) hábil; **to be ~ to do sth** poder hacer algo; **~-bodied** *a* sano; **ably** *ad* hábilmente.

abnormal [æb'nɔ:məl] *a* anormal; **~ity** [-'mælɪtɪ] *n* anormalidad *f.*

aboard [ə'bɔ:d] *ad* a bordo // *prep* a bordo de.

abode [ə'bəud] *pt, pp of* **abide** // *n* domicilio.

abolish [ə'bɒlɪʃ] *vt* suprimir, abolir; **abolition** [æbəu'lɪʃən] *n* supresión *f*, abolición *f.*

abominable [ə'bɒmɪnəbl] *a* abominable.

aborigine [æbə'rɪdʒɪnɪ] *n* aborigen *m.*

abort [ə'bɔ:t] *vt* abortar; **~ion** [ə'bɔ:ʃən] *n* aborto (provocado); **to have an ~ion** abortarse, hacerse abortar; **~ive** *a* fracasado.

abound [ə'baund] *vi* abundar.

about [ə'baut] *prep* (*subject*) acerca de, sobre; (*place*) alrededor de, por // *ad* casi, más o menos, a eso de; **to walk ~ the town** andar por la ciudad; **it takes ~ 10 hours** es cosa de 10 horas más o menos; **at ~ 2 o'clock** a eso de las 2; **to be ~ to** estar a punto de; **what** *or* **how ~ doing this?** ¿qué tal si hacemos esto?; **~ turn** *n* media vuelta.

above [ə'bʌv] *ad* encima, por encima, arriba // *prep* encima de; **mentioned ~** susodicho; **~ all** sobre todo; **~ board** *a* legítimo.

abrasion [ə'breɪʒən] *n* (*on skin*) abrasión *f*; **abrasive** [ə'breɪzɪv] *a* abrasivo.

abreast [ə'brɛst] *ad* de frente; **to keep ~ of** mantenerse al corriente de.

abridge [ə'brɪdʒ] *vt* abreviar.

abroad [ə'brɔːd] *ad* (*to be*) en el extranjero; (*to go*) al extranjero.

abrupt [ə'brʌpt] *a* (*sudden*) brusco; (*gruff*) áspero.

abscess ['æbsɪs] *n* absceso.

abscond [əb'skɒnd] *vi* fugarse.

absence ['æbsəns] *n* ausencia.

absent ['æbsənt] *a* ausente; **~ee** [-'tiː] *n* ausente *m/f*; **~eeism** [-'tiːɪzəm] *n* absentismo; **~-minded** *a* distraído.

absolute ['æbsəluːt] *a* absoluto; **~ly** [-'luːtlɪ] *ad* absolutamente.

absolve [əb'zɒlv] *vt*: **to ~ sb (from)** absolver a alguien (de).

absorb [əb'zɔːb] *vt* absorber; **to be ~ed in a book** estar absorto en un libro; **~ent** *a* absorbente; **~ing** *a* absorbente.

abstain [əb'steɪn] *vi*: **to ~ (from)** abstenerse (de).

abstention [əb'stɛnʃən] *n* abstención *f.*

abstinence ['æbstɪnəns] *n* abstinencia.

abstract ['æbstrækt] *a* abstracto.

absurd [əb'sɔːd] *a* absurdo; **~ity** *n* absurdo.

abundance [ə'bʌndəns] *n* abundancia; **abundant** [-dənt] *a* abundante.

abuse [ə'bjuːs] *n* (*insults*) improperios *mpl*, injurias *fpl*; (*misuse*) abuso // *vt* [ə'bjuːz] (*ill-treat*) maltratar; (*take advantage of*) abusar de; **abusive** *a* ofensivo.

abysmal [ə'bɪzməl] *a* abismal; (*ignorance etc*) profundo.

abyss [ə'bɪs] *n* abismo.

academic [ækə'dɛmɪk] *a* académico, universitario; (*pej: issue*) puramente teórico.

academy [ə'kædəmɪ] *n* (*learned body*) academia; (*school*) instituto, colegio.

accede [æk'siːd] *vi*: **to ~ to** (*request*) consentir en; (*throne*) subir a.

accelerate [æk'sɛləreɪt] *vt* acelerar // *vi* acelerarse; **acceleration** [-'reɪʃən] *n* aceleración *f*; **accelerator** *n* acelerador *m*.

accent ['æksɛnt] *n* acento.

accept [ək'sɛpt] *vt* aceptar; (*approve*) aprobar; (*permit*) admitir; ~**able** *a* aceptable; admisible; ~**ance** *n* aceptación *f*; aprobación *f*.

access ['æksɛs] *n* acceso; **to have** ~ **to** tener libre acceso a; ~**ible** [-'sɛsəbl] *a* accesible.

accessory [æk'sɛsərɪ] *n* accesorio; **toilet accessories** *npl* artículos *mpl* de tocador.

accident ['æksɪdənt] *n* accidente *m*; (*chance*) casualidad *f*; **by** ~ (*unintentionally*) sin querer; (*by coincidence*) por casualidad; ~**al** [-'dɛntl] *a* accidental, fortuito; ~**ally** [-'dɛntəlɪ] *ad* sin querer; por casualidad; ~**-prone** *a* con tendencia a sufrir/causar accidentes.

acclaim [ə'kleɪm] *vt* aclamar, aplaudir // *n* aclamación *f*, aplausos *mpl*.

acclimatize [ə'klaɪmətaɪz] *vt*: **to become** ~**d** aclimatarse.

accommodate [ə'kɔmədeɪt] *vt* alojar, hospedar; (*reconcile*) componer; (*oblige, help*) complacer; (*adapt*): **to** ~ **one's plans to** acomodar sus proyectos a; **accommodating** *a* servicial, complaciente.

accommodation [əkɔmə'deɪʃən] *n* alojamiento; (*space*) sitio.

accompaniment [ə'kʌmpənɪmənt] *n* acompañamiento; **accompany** [-nɪ] *vt* acompañar.

accomplice [ə'kʌmplɪs] *n* cómplice *m/f*.

accomplish [ə'kʌmplɪʃ] *vt* (*finish*) acabar, alcanzar; (*achieve*) realizar, llevar a cabo; ~**ed** *a* experto, hábil; ~**ment** *n* (*ending*) conclusión *f*; (*bringing about*) realización *f*; (*skill*) talento.

accord [ə'kɔːd] *n* acuerdo // *vt* concordar; **of his own** ~ espontáneamente; ~**ance** *n*: **in** ~**ance with** de acuerdo con; ~**ing to** *prep* según; (*in accordance with*) conforme a; ~**ingly** *ad* (*thus*) por consiguiente.

accordion [ə'kɔːdɪən] *n* acordeón *m*.

accost [ə'kɔst] *vt* abordar, dirigirse a.

account [ə'kaunt] *n* (*COMM*) cuenta, factura; (*report*) informe *m*; **of little** ~ de poca importancia; **on** ~ a cuenta; **on no** ~ de ninguna manera, bajo ningún concepto; **on** ~ **of** a causa de, por motivo de; **to take into** ~, **take** ~ **of** tomar *o* tener en cuenta; **to** ~ **for** (*answer for*) responder de; (*explain*) dar cuenta *o* razón de; ~**able** *a* responsable.

accountancy [ə'kauntənsɪ] *n* contabilidad *f*; **accountant** [-tənt] *n* contador/a *m/f*.

accumulate [ə'kjuːmjuleɪt] *vt* acumular // *vi* acumularse; **accumulation** [-'leɪʃən] *n* acumulación *f*.

accuracy ['ækjurəsɪ] *n* exactitud *f*, precisión *f*; **accurate** [-rɪt] *a* (*number*) exacto; (*answer*) acertado; (*shot*) certero.

accusation [ækju'zeɪʃən] *n* acusación *f*; **accuse** [ə'kjuːz] *vt* acusar; (*blame*) echar la culpa a; **accused** [ə'kjuːzd] *n* acusado/a.

accustom [ə'kʌstəm] *vt* acostumbrar; ~**ed** *a*: ~**ed to** acostumbrado a.

ace [eɪs] *n* as *m*.

ache [eɪk] *n* dolor *m* // *vi* doler; **my head** ~**s** me duele la cabeza.

achieve [ə'tʃiːv] *vt* (*reach*) alcanzar; (*realize*) llevar a cabo; (*victory, success*) lograr, conseguir; ~**ment** *n* (*completion*) realización *f*; (*success*) éxito.

acid ['æsɪd] *a* ácido; (*bitter*) agrio // *n* ácido; ~**ity** [ə'sɪdɪtɪ] *n* acidez *f*; (*MED*) acedía.

acknowledge [ək'nɔlɪdʒ] *vt* (*letter*) acusar recibo de; (*fact*) reconocer; ~**ment** *n* acuse *m* de recibo; reconocimiento.

acne ['æknɪ] *n* acné *m*.

acorn ['eɪkɔːn] *n* bellota.

acoustic [ə'kuːstɪk] *a* acústico; ~**s** *n, npl* acústica *sg*.

acquaint [ə'kweɪnt] *vt*: **to** ~ **sb with sth** (*warn*) avisar a uno de algo; (*inform*) poner a uno al corriente de algo; **to be** ~**ed with** (*person*) conocer; (*fact*) estar al corriente de; ~**ance** *n* conocimiento; (*person*) conocido/a.

acquiesce [ækwɪ'ɛs] *vi*: **to** ~ **in** consentir en, conformarse con.

acquire [ə'kwaɪə*] *vt* adquirir; (*achieve*) conseguir; **acquisition** [ækwɪ'zɪʃən] *n* adquisición *f*; **acquisitive** [ə'kwɪzɪtɪv] *a* codicioso.

acquit [ə'kwɪt] *vt* absolver, exculpar; **to** ~ **o.s. well** defenderse, salir con éxito; ~**tal** *n* absolución *f*, exculpación *f*.

acre ['eɪkə*] *n* acre *m*.

acrimonious [ækrɪ'məunɪəs] *a* (*remark*) mordaz; (*argument*) reñido.

acrobat ['ækrəbæt] *n* acróbata *m/f*; ~**ics** [ækrəu'bætɪks] *n, npl* acrobacia *sg*.

across [ə'krɔs] *prep* (*on the other side of*) al otro lado de, del otro lado de; (*crosswise*) a través de // *ad* de un lado a otro, de una parte a otra; a través, al través; **to run/swim** ~ atravesar corriendo/nadando; ~ **from** enfrente de.

act [ækt] *n* acto, acción *f*; (*THEATRE*) acto; (*in music-hall etc*) número; (*LAW*) decreto, ley *f* // *vi* (*machine*) funcionar, marchar; (*person*) actuar, comportarse; (*THEATRE*) actuar, trabajar; (*pretend*) fingir; (*take action*) obrar // *vt* (*part*) hacer el papel de, representar; **to** ~ **as** actuar *o* hacer de; ~**ing** *a* suplente // *n*: **to do some** ~**ing** ser actor/actriz.

action ['ækʃən] *n* acción *f*, acto; (*MIL*) acción *f*, batalla; (*LAW*) proceso, demanda; **to take** ~ tomar medidas.

activate ['æktɪveɪt] *vt* (*mechanism*) activar.

active ['æktɪv] *a* activo, enérgico; (*volcano*) en actividad; **activity** [-'tɪvɪtɪ] *n* actividad *f*.

actor ['æktə*] *n* actor *m*; **actress** [-trɪs] *n* actriz *f*.

actual ['æktjuəl] *a* verdadero, real; ~**ly** *ad* realmente, en realidad.

acupuncture ['ækjupʌŋktʃə*] *n* acupuntura.

acute [ə'kju:t] *a* (*gen*) agudo.

ad [æd] *n abbr of* **advertisement.**

A.D. *ad abbr of* **Anno Domini** A.C. (año de Cristo).

Adam ['ædəm] *n* Adán; ~'s **apple** *n* nuez *f* de la garganta.

adamant ['ædəmənt] *a* firme, inflexible.

adapt [ə'dæpt] *vt* adaptar; (*reconcile*) acomodar // *vi*: **to** ~ **(to)** adaptarse (a), ajustarse (a); ~**able** *a* (*device*) adaptable; (*person*) que se adapta; ~**ation** [ædæp-'teɪʃən] *n* adaptación *f*; ~**er** *n* (*ELEC*) adaptador *m*.

add [æd] *vt* añadir, agregar; (*figures: also:* ~ **up**) sumar // *vi*: **to** ~ **to** (*increase*) aumentar, acrecentar; **it doesn't** ~ **up** no tiene sentido.

adder ['ædə*] *n* víbora.

addict ['ædɪkt] *n* (*enthusiast*) entusiasta *m/f*; (*to drugs etc*) adicto/a; ~**ed** [ə'dɪktɪd] *a*: **to be** ~**ed to** ser aficionado de; ser adicto a; **addiction** [ə'dɪkʃən] *n* (*enthusiasm*) afición *f*; (*dependence*) hábito morboso.

adding machine ['ædɪŋməʃiːn] *n* calculadora.

addition [ə'dɪʃən] *n* (*adding up*) adición *f*; (*thing added*) añadidura, añadido; **in** ~ además, por añadidura; **in** ~ **to** además de; ~**al** *a* adicional.

additive ['ædɪtɪv] *n* aditivo.

address [ə'drɛs] *n* dirección *f*, señas *fpl*; (*speech*) discurso // *vt* (*letter*) dirigir; (*speak to*) dirigirse a, dirigir la palabra a; ~**ee** [ædrɛ'siː] *n* destinatario/a.

adenoids ['ædɪnɔɪdz] *npl* vegetaciones *fpl* adenoideas.

adept ['ædɛpt] *a*: ~ **at** experto *o* hábil en.

adequate ['ædɪkwɪt] *a* (*apt*) adecuado; (*enough*) suficiente.

adhere [əd'hɪə*] *vi*: **to** ~ **to** pegarse a; (*fig: abide by*) observar; (: *hold to*) adherirse a; **adherent** *n* partidario/a.

adhesive [əd'hiːzɪv] *a*, *n* adhesivo.

adjacent [ə'dʒeɪsənt] *a*: ~ **to** contiguo a, inmediato a.

adjective ['ædʒɛktɪv] *n* adjetivo.

adjoining [ə'dʒɔɪnɪŋ] *a* contiguo, vecino.

adjourn [ə'dʒɜːn] *vt* aplazar; (*session*) suspender, levantar // *vi* suspenderse.

adjudicate [ə'dʒuːdɪkeɪt] *vi* sentenciar; **adjudicator** *n* juez *m*, árbitro.

adjust [ə'dʒʌst] *vt* (*change*) modificar; (*arrange*) arreglar; (*machine*) ajustar // *vi*: **to** ~ **(to)** adaptarse (a); ~**able** *a* ajustable; ~**ment** *n* modificación *f*; arreglo; (*of prices, wages*) ajuste *m*.

adjutant ['ædʒətənt] *n* ayudante *m*.

ad-lib [æd'lɪb] *vt*, *vi* improvisar; **ad lib** *ad* a voluntad, a discreción.

administer [əd'mɪnɪstə*] *vt* proporcionar;

(*justice*) administrar; **administration** [-'treɪʃən] *n* administración *f*; (*government*) gobierno; **administrative** [-trətɪv] *a* administrativo; **administrator** [-treɪtə*] *n* administrador/a *m/f*.

admirable ['ædmərəbl] *a* admirable.

admiral ['ædmərəl] *n* almirante *m*; **A**~**ty** *n* Ministerio de Marina, Almirantazgo.

admiration [ædmə'reɪʃən] *n* admiración *f*.

admire [əd'maɪə*] *vt* admirar; **admirer** *n* admirador/a *m/f*; (*suitor*) pretendiente *m*.

admission [əd'mɪʃən] *n* (*entry*) entrada; (*enrolment*) ingreso; (*confession*) confesión *f*.

admit [əd'mɪt] *vt* dejar entrar, dar entrada a; (*permit*) admitir; (*acknowledge*) reconocer; (*accept*) aceptar; **to** ~ **to** confesarse culpable de; ~**tance** *n* entrada; ~**tedly** *ad* de acuerdo que.

admonish [əd'mɔnɪʃ] *vt* amonestar; (*advise*) aconsejar.

ado [ə'duː] *n*: **without (any) more** ~ sin más (ni más).

adolescence [ædəu'lɛsns] *n* adolescencia; **adolescent** [-'lɛsnt] *a*, *n* adolescente *m/f*.

adopt [ə'dɔpt] *vt* adoptar; ~**ion** [ə'dɔpʃən] *n* adopción *f*; ~**ed** *a* adoptivo.

adore [ə'dɔ:*] *vt* adorar.

adorn [ə'dɔ:n] *vt* adornar.

adrenalin [ə'drɛnəlɪn] *n* adrenalina.

Adriatic [eɪdrɪ'ætɪk] *n*: **the** ~ **(Sea)** el (Mar) Adriático.

adrift [ə'drɪft] *ad* a la deriva; **to come** ~ desprenderse.

adult ['ædʌlt] *n* (*gen*) adulto.

adulterate [ə'dʌltəreɪt] *vt* adulterar.

adultery [ə'dʌltərɪ] *n* adulterio.

advance [əd'vɑ:ns] *n* (*gen*) adelanto, progreso; (*money*) anticipo, préstamo; (*MIL*) avance *m* // *vt* avanzar, adelantar; anticipar, prestar // *vi* avanzar, adelantarse; **in** ~ por adelantado; ~**d** *a* avanzado; (*SCOL: studies*) adelantado; ~**d in years** entrado en años; ~**ment** *n* progreso; (*in rank*) ascenso.

advantage [əd'vɑ:ntɪdʒ] *n* (*also TENNIS*) ventaja; **to take** ~ **of** (*use*) aprovecharse de; (*gain by*) sacar partido de; ~**ous** [ædvən'teɪdʒəs] *a* ventajoso, provechoso.

advent ['ædvənt] *n* advenimiento; **A**~ Adviento.

adventure [əd'vɛntʃə*] *n* aventura; **adventurous** [-tʃərəs] *a* aventurero.

adverb ['ædvɜːb] *n* adverbio.

adversary ['ædvəsərɪ] *n* adversario, contrario.

adverse ['ædvɜːs] *a* adverso, contrario; ~ **to** adverso a.

adversity [əd'vɜːsɪtɪ] *n* infortunio.

advert ['ædvɜːt] *n abbr of* **advertisement.**

advertise ['ædvətaɪz] *vi* hacer propaganda; (*in newspaper etc*) poner un anuncio // *vt* anunciar; ~**ment** [əd-'vɜːtɪsmənt] *n* (*COMM*) anuncio; **advertising** *n* publicidad *f*, propaganda; anuncios *mpl*.

advice [əd'vaɪs] *n* consejo, consejos *mpl*; (*notification*) aviso; **to take legal** ~ consultar a un abogado.
advisable [əd'vaɪzəbl] *a* aconsejable, conveniente.
advise [əd'vaɪz] *vt* aconsejar; (*inform*) avisar; **adviser** *n* consejero; (*business adviser*) asesor *m*; **advisory** *a* consultivo.
advocate ['ædvəkeɪt] *vt* (*argue for*) abogar por; (*give support to*) ser partidario de // *n* [-kɪt] abogado.
aerial ['ɛərɪəl] *n* antena // *a* aéreo.
aeroplane ['ɛərəpleɪn] *n* avión *m*.
aerosol ['ɛərəsɔl] *n* aerosol *m*.
aesthetic [iːs'θɛtɪk] *a* estético.
afar [ə'fɑ:*] *ad*: **from** ~ desde lejos.
affable ['æfəbl] *a* afable.
affair [ə'fɛə*] *n* asunto; (*also*: **love** ~) aventura *o* relación *f* (*amorosa*).
affect [ə'fɛkt] *vt* afectar, influir en; (*move*) conmover; ~**ation** [æfɛk'teɪʃən] *n* afectación *f*; ~**ed** *a* afectado.
affection [ə'fɛkʃən] *n* afecto, cariño; ~**ate** *a* afectuoso, cariñoso.
affiliated [ə'fɪlɪeɪtɪd] *a* afiliado.
affinity [ə'fɪnɪtɪ] *n* afinidad *f*.
affirmation [æfə'meɪʃən] *n* afirmación *f*.
affirmative [ə'fɔːmətɪv] *a* afirmativo.
affix [ə'fɪks] *vt* (*signature*) poner, añadir; (*stamp*) pegar.
afflict [ə'flɪkt] *vt* afligir; ~**ion** [ə'flɪkʃən] *n* enfermedad *f*, aflicción *f*.
affluence ['æfluəns] *n* opulencia, riqueza; **affluent** [-ənt] *a* opulento, acaudalado.
afford [ə'fɔːd] *vt* (*provide*) dar, proporcionar; **can we** ~ **it?** ¿tenemos bastante dinero para comprarlo?
affront [ə'frʌnt] *n* afrenta, ofensa.
afield [ə'fiːld] *ad*: **far** ~ muy lejos.
afloat [ə'fləut] *ad* (*floating*) a flote; (*at sea*) en el mar.
afoot [ə'fut] *ad*: **there is something** ~ algo se está tramando.
aforesaid [ə'fɔːsɛd] *a* susodicho.
afraid [ə'freɪd] *a*: **to be** ~ **of** (*person*) tener miedo a; (*thing*) tener miedo de; **to be** ~ **to** tener miedo de, temer; **I am** ~ **that** me temo que.
afresh [ə'frɛʃ] *ad* de nuevo, otra vez.
Africa ['æfrɪkə] *n* África; ~**n** *a*, *n* africano/a.
aft [ɑːft] *ad* (*to be*) en popa; (*to go*) a popa.
after ['ɑːftə*] *prep* (*time*) después de; (*place, order*) detrás de, tras // *ad* después // *conj* después (de) que; **what/who are you** ~? ¿qué/a quién busca Usted?; **to ask** ~ **sb** preguntar por alguien; ~ **all** después de todo, al fin y al cabo; ~ **you!** ¡pase Usted!; ~**birth** *n* secundinas *fpl*; ~-**effects** *npl* consecuencias *fpl*, efectos *mpl*; ~**life** *n* vida futura; ~**math** *n* consecuencias *fpl*, resultados *mpl*; ~**noon** *n* tarde *f*; ~-**shave** (**lotion**) *n* loción *f* para después del afeitado; ~**thought** *n* ocurrencia (tardía); ~**wards** *ad* después, más tarde.

again [ə'gɛn] *ad* otra vez, de nuevo; **to do sth** ~ volver a hacer algo; ~ **and** ~ una y otra vez; **now and** ~ de vez en cuando.
against [ə'gɛnst] *prep* (*opposed*) contra, en contra de; (*close to*) contra, junto a.
age [eɪdʒ] *n* (*gen*) edad *f*; (*old* ~) vejez *f*; (*period*) época // *vi* envejecer(se) // *vt* envejecer; **to come of** ~ llegar a la mayoría de edad; **it's been** ~**s since** hace muchísimo tiempo que; ~**d** *a* ['eɪdʒɪd] viejo, anciano // *a* [eɪdʒd]: ~**d 10** de 10 años de edad; ~ **group** *n*: **to be in the same** ~ **group** tener la misma edad; ~**less** *a* (*eternal*) eterno; (*ever young*) siempre joven; ~ **limit** *n* edad mínima/máxima.
agency ['eɪdʒənsɪ] *n* agencia; **through** *or* **by the** ~ **of** por medio de.
agenda [ə'dʒɛndə] *n* orden *m* del día.
agent ['eɪdʒənt] *n* (*gen*) agente *m/f*; (*representative*) representante *m/f*, delegado/a.
aggravate ['ægrəveɪt] *vt* agravar; (*annoy*) irritar, exasperar; **aggravation** [-'veɪʃən] *n* agravación *f*.
aggregate ['ægrɪgeɪt] *n* (*whole*) conjunto; (*collection*) agregado.
aggression [ə'grɛʃən] *n* agresión *f*; **aggressive** [ə'grɛsɪv] *a* agresivo; (*zealous*) enérgico.
aggrieved [ə'griːvd] *a* ofendido, agraviado.
aghast [ə'gɑːst] *a* horrorizado; **to be** ~ pasmarse.
agile ['ædʒaɪl] *a* ágil.
agitate ['ædʒɪteɪt] *vt* (*shake*) agitar; (*trouble*) inquietar; **to** ~ **for** hacer campaña pro *o* en favor de; **agitator** *n* agitador/a *m/f*.
ago [ə'gəu] *ad*: **2 days** ~ hace 2 días; **not long** ~ hace poco; **how long** ~? ¿hace cuánto tiempo?
agog [ə'gɔg] *a* (*anxious*) ansiado; (*excited*) emocionado.
agonizing ['ægənaɪzɪŋ] *a* (*pain*) atroz, agudo; (*suspense*) angustioso.
agony ['ægənɪ] *n* (*pain*) dolor *m* agudo; (*distress*) angustia; **to be in** ~ sufrir atrozmente.
agree [ə'griː] *vt* (*price*) acordar, quedar en // *vi* (*statements etc*) coincidir, concordar; **to** ~ (**with**) (*person*) estar de acuerdo (con), ponerse de acuerdo (con); **to** ~ **to do** aceptar hacer; **to** ~ **to sth** consentir en algo; **to** ~ **that** (*admit*) estar de acuerdo en que; **garlic doesn't** ~ **with me** el ajo no me sienta bien; ~**able** *a* agradable; (*person*) simpático; (*willing*) de acuerdo, conforme; ~**d** *a* (*time, place*) convenido; ~**ment** *n* acuerdo; (*comm*) contrato; **in** ~**ment** de acuerdo, conforme.
agricultural [ægrɪ'kʌltʃərəl] *a* agrícola; **agriculture** ['ægrɪkʌltʃə*] *n* agricultura.
aground [ə'graund] *ad*: **to run** ~ encallar, embarrancar.
ahead [ə'hɛd] *ad* delante; ~ **of** delante de;

(*fig*: *schedule etc*) antes de; ~ **of time** antes de la hora; **to be** ~ **of sb** (*fig*) llevar la ventaja a alguien; **go right** *or* **straight** ~ ¡siga adelante!

aid [eɪd] *n* ayuda, auxilio // *vt* ayudar, auxiliar; **in** ~ **of** a beneficio de; **to** ~ **and abet** (*LAW*) ser cómplice de.

aide [eɪd] *n* (*person*) edecán *m*.

ailment ['eɪlmənt] *n* enfermedad *f*, achaque *m*.

aim [eɪm] *vt* (*gun, camera*) apuntar; (*missile, remark*) dirigir; (*blow*) asestar // *vi* (*also*: **take** ~) apuntar // *n* puntería; (*objective*) propósito, meta; **to** ~ **at** (*objective*) aspirar a, pretender; **to** ~ **to do** tener la intención de hacer; ~**less** *a* sin propósito, sin objeto; ~**lessly** *ad* a la ventura, a la deriva.

air [ɛə*] *n* aire *m*; (*appearance*) aspecto // *vt* ventilar; (*grievances, ideas*) airear // *cpd* (*currents, attack etc*) aéreo, aeronáutico; ~**borne** *a* (*in the air*) en el aire; (*MIL*) aerotransportado; ~-**conditioned** *a* con aire acondicionado; ~ **conditioning** *n* aire acondicionado; ~**craft** *n*, *pl inv* avión *m*; ~**craft carrier** *n* porta(a)viones *m inv*; **A**~ **Force** *n* Fuerzas Aéreas *fpl*, aviación *f*; ~**gun** *n* escopeta de aire comprimido; ~ **hostess** *n* azafata; ~ **letter** *n* carta aérea; ~**lift** *n* puente *m* aéreo; ~**line** *n* línea aérea; ~**liner** *n* avión *m* de pasajeros; ~**lock** *n* esclusa de aire; ~**mail** *n*: **by** ~**mail** por avión; ~**port** *n* aeropuerto; ~ **raid** *n* ataque *m* aéreo; ~**sick** *a*: **to be** ~**sick** marearse (en un avión); ~**strip** *n* pista de aterrizaje; ~**tight** *a* hermético; ~**y** *a* (*room*) bien ventilado; (*manners*) ligero.

aisle [aɪl] *n* (*of church*) nave *f*; (*of theatre*) pasillo.

ajar [ə'dʒɑ:*] *a* entreabierto.

akin [ə'kɪn] *a*: ~ **to** relacionado con.

alarm [ə'lɑ:m] *n* alarma; (*anxiety*) inquietud *f* // *vt* asustar, inquietar; ~ **clock** *n* despertador *m*.

Albania [æl'heɪnɪə] *n* Albania.

album ['ælbəm] *n* álbum *m*; (*L.P.*) elepé *m*.

alcohol ['ælkəhɔl] *n* alcohol *m*; ~**ic** [-'hɔlɪk] *a*, *n* alcohólico/a; ~**ism** *n* alcoholismo.

alcove ['ælkəuv] *n* nicho, hueco.

alderman ['ɔːldəmən] *n*, *pl* -**men** concejal *m*.

ale [eɪl] *n* cerveza.

alert [ə'lɔːt] *a* alerta; (*sharp*) despierto, despabilado // *n* alerta *m*, alarma // *vt* poner sobre aviso; **to be on the** ~ estar alerta *o* sobre aviso.

algebra ['ældʒɪbrə] *n* álgebra.

Algeria [æl'dʒɪərɪə] *n* Argelia; ~**n** *a*, *n* argelino/a.

alias ['eɪlɪəs] *ad* alias, por otro nombre // *n* alias *m*.

alibi ['ælɪbaɪ] *n* coartada.

alien ['eɪlɪən] *n* extranjero/a // *a*: ~ **to** distinto de, ajeno a; ~**ate** *vt* enajenar, alejar; ~**ation** [-'neɪʃən] *n* enajenación *f*.

alight [ə'laɪt] *a* ardiendo, quemando // *vi* apearse, bajar.

align [ə'laɪn] *vt* alinear; ~**ment** *n* alineación *f*.

alike [ə'laɪk] *a* semejantes, iguales // *ad* igualmente, del mismo modo; **to look** ~ parecerse.

alimony ['ælɪmənɪ] *n* (*payment*) alimentos *mpl*.

alive [ə'laɪv] *a* (*gen*) vivo; (*lively*) activo, enérgico.

alkali ['ælkəlaɪ] *n* álcali *m*.

all [ɔːl] *a* todo; (*pl*) todos(as) // *pron* todo; (*pl*) todos(as) // *ad* completamente, del todo; ~ **alone** completamente solo; **at** ~ en absoluto, del todo; ~ **the time/his life** todo el tiempo/toda su vida; ~ **five** todos los cinco; ~ **of them** todos (ellos); ~ **of us went** fuimos todos; **not as hard as** ~ **that** no tan difícil; ~ **in** ~ con todo, así y todo.

allay [ə'leɪ] *vt* (*fears*) aquietar; (*pain*) aliviar.

allegation [ælɪ'geɪʃən] *n* aseveración *f*, alegación *f*.

allege [ə'lɛdʒ] *vt* afirmar, pretender.

allegiance [ə'liːdʒəns] *n* lealtad *f*.

allegory ['ælɪgərɪ] *n* alegoría.

allergic [ə'lɔːdʒɪk] *a*: ~ **to** alérgico a; **allergy** ['ælədʒɪ] *n* alergia.

alleviate [ə'liːvɪeɪt] *vt* aliviar, mitigar.

alley ['ælɪ] *n* (*street*) callejuela; (*in garden*) paseo.

alliance [ə'laɪəns] *n* alianza *f*; **allied** ['ælaɪd] *a* aliado; (*related*) relacionado.

alligator ['ælɪgeɪtə*] *n* caimán *m*.

all-in ['ɔːlɪn] *a* (*also ad*: *charge*) todo incluido; ~ **wrestling** *n* lucha libre.

alliteration [əlɪtə'reɪʃən] *n* aliteración *f*.

all-night ['ɔːl'naɪt] *a* (*café*) abierto toda la noche; (*party*) que dura toda la noche.

allocate ['æləkeɪt] *vt* (*share out*) repartir, distribuir; (*devote*) asignar; **allocation** [-'keɪʃən] *n* (*of money*) ración *f*, cuota; (*distribution*) reparto.

allot [ə'lɔt] *vt* asignar; ~**ment** *n* ración *f*, porción *f*; (*garden*) parcela.

all-out ['ɔːlaut] *a* (*effort etc*) máximo; **all out** *ad* con todas sus fuerzas; (*speed*) a máxima velocidad.

allow [ə'lau] *vt* (*practice, behaviour*) permitir, dejar; (*sum to spend etc*) pagar, dar; (*a claim*) admitir; (*sum, time estimated*) dar, conceder; (*concede*): **to** ~ **that** reconocer que; **to** ~ **sb to do** permitir a alguien hacer; **to** ~ **for** *vt fus* tener en cuenta, tomar en consideración; ~**ance** *n* (*gen*) concesión *f*; (*payment*) subvención *f*, pensión *f*; (*discount*) descuento, rebaja; **family** ~**ance** subsidio familiar; **to make** ~**ances for** ser indulgente con; tener en cuenta.

alloy ['ælɔɪ] *n* (*mix*) mezcla.

all: ~ **right** *ad* (*well*) bien; (*correct*) correcto; (*as answer*) ¡conforme!, ¡está bien!; ~-**round** *a* (*gen*) completo; (*view*) amplio; (*person*) que hace de todo;

~-time *a* (*record*) de todos los tiempos.
allude [ə'luːd] *vi*: **to** ~ **to** aludir a.
alluring [ə'ljuəriŋ] *a* seductor(a), atractivo.
allusion [ə'luːʒən] *n* referencia, alusión *f.*
ally ['ælaɪ] *n* aliado/a // *vr* [ə'laɪ]: **to** ~ **o.s.** with aliarse con.
almighty [ɔːl'maɪtɪ] *a* todopoderoso, omnipotente.
almond ['ɑːmənd] *n* (*fruit*) almendra; (*tree*) almendro.
almost ['ɔːlməust] *ad* casi, por poco.
alms [ɑːmz] *npl* limosna *sg.*
aloft [ə'lɔft] *ad* arriba, en alto.
alone [ə'ləun] *a* solo // *ad* sólo, solamente; **to leave sb** ~ dejar a uno solo o en paz; **to leave sth** ~ no tocar algo, dejar algo sin tocar; **let** ~ sin hablar de.
along [ə'lɔŋ] *prep* a lo largo de, por // *ad*: **is he coming** ~ **with us?** ¿nos acompaña?; **he was limping** ~ iba cojeando; ~ **with** junto con, además de; ~**side** *prep* junto a, al lado de // *ad* (*NAUT*) al costado.
aloof [ə'luːf] *a* reservado // *ad*: **to stand** ~ mantenerse a distancia.
aloud [ə'laud] *ad* en voz alta.
alphabet ['ælfəbɛt] *n* alfabeto; ~**ical** [-'bɛtɪkəl] *a* alfabético.
alpine ['ælpaɪn] *a* alpino, alpestre.
Alps [ælps] *npl*: **the** ~ los Alpes.
already [ɔːl'rɛdɪ] *ad* ya.
alright ['ɔːl'raɪt] *ad* = **all right.**
also ['ɔːlsəu] *ad* también, además.
altar ['ɔltə*] *n* altar *m.*
alter ['ɔltə*] *vt* cambiar, modificar // *vi* cambiarse, mudarse; (*worsen*) alterarse; ~**ation** [ɔltə'reɪʃən] *n* cambio, modificación *f*; alteración *f.*
alternate [ɔl'tɔːnɪt] *a* alterno, alternativo // *vi* ['ɔltɔːneɪt] alternarse; **on** ~ **days** un día sí y otro no; ~**ly** *ad* alternativamente, por turno; **alternating** [-'neɪtɪŋ] *a* (*current*) alterno.
alternative [ɔl'tɔːnətɪv] *a* alternativo // *n* alternativa; ~**ly** *ad*: ~**ly one could...** por otra parte se podría... .
alternator ['ɔltɔːneɪtə*] *n* (*AUT*) alternador *m.*
although [ɔːl'ðəu] *conj* aunque; (*given that*) si bien.
altitude ['æltɪtjuːd] *n* altitud *f*, altura.
alto ['æltəu] *n* (*female*) contralto *f*; (*male*) alto.
altogether [ɔːltə'gɛðə*] *ad* enteramente, del todo; (*on the whole, in all*) en total, en conjunto.
aluminium [ælju'mɪnɪəm], **aluminum** [ə'luːmɪnəm] (*US*) *n* aluminio.
always ['ɔːlweɪz] *ad* siempre.
am [æm] *vb see* **be.**
a.m. *ad abbr of* **ante meridiem** de la mañana, antes de mediodía.
amalgamate [ə'mælgəmeɪt] *vi* amalgamarse, unirse // *vt* amalgamar,

unir; **amalgamation** [-'meɪʃən] *n* (*COMM*) amalgamación *f*, unión *f.*
amass [ə'mæs] *vt* amontonar, acumular.
amateur ['æmətə*] *n* aficionado/a, amateur *m/f.*
amaze [ə'meɪz] *vt* asombrar, pasmar; ~**ment** *n* asombro, sorpresa.
Amazon ['æməzən] *n* (*GEO*) Amazonas *m.*
ambassador [æm'bæsədə*] *n* embajador *m.*
amber ['æmbə*] *n* ámbar *m*; **at** ~ (*AUT*) en el amarillo.
ambidextrous [æmbɪ'dɛkstrəs] *a* ambidextro.
ambiguity [æmbɪ'gjuɪtɪ] *n* ambigüedad *f*; (*of meaning*) doble sentido; **ambiguous** [-'bɪgjuəs] *a* ambiguo.
ambition [æm'bɪʃən] *n* ambición *f*; **ambitious** [-ʃəs] *a* ambicioso; (*plan*) grandioso.
ambivalent [æm'bɪvələnt] *a* ambivalente; (*pej*) equívoco.
amble ['æmbl] *vi* (*gen*: ~ **along**) deambular, andar sin prisa.
ambulance ['æmbjuləns] *n* ambulancia.
ambush ['æmbuʃ] *n* emboscada // *vt* tender una emboscada a; (*fig*) coger por sorpresa.
amenable [ə'miːnəbl] *a*: ~ **to** (*advice etc*) sensible a.
amend [ə'mɛnd] *vt* (*law, text*) enmendar; (*habits*) corregir, mejorar; **to make** ~**s** compensar, dar satisfacción por; ~**ment** *n* enmienda.
amenities [ə'miːnɪtɪz] *npl* conveniencias *fpl*, comodidades *fpl.*
America [ə'mɛrɪkə] *n* Estados Unidos *mpl*; ~**n** *a*, *n* norteamericano/a.
amiable ['eɪmɪəbl] *a* (*kind*) amable, simpático; (*hearty*) bonachón(ona).
amicable ['æmɪkəbl] *a* amistoso, amigable.
amid(st) [ə'mɪd(st)] *prep* entre, en medio de.
amiss [ə'mɪs] *ad*: **to take sth** ~ tomar algo a mal.
ammonia [ə'məunɪə] *n* amoníaco.
ammunition [æmju'nɪʃən] *n* municiones *fpl.*
amnesia [æm'niːzɪə] *n* amnesia.
amnesty ['æmnɪstɪ] *n* amnistía.
amok [ə'mɔk] *ad*: **to run** ~ enloquecerse, desbocarse.
among(st) [ə'mʌŋ(st)] *prep* entre, en medio de.
amoral [æ'mɔrəl] *a* amoral.
amorous ['æmərəs] *a* amoroso; (*in love*) enamorado.
amount [ə'maunt] *n* (*gen*) cantidad *f*; (*of bill etc*) suma, importe *m* // *vi*: **to** ~ **to** (*reach*) alcanzar; (*total*) sumar; (*be same as*) equivaler a, significar.
amp(ere) ['æmp(ɛə*)] *n* amperio.
amphibian [æm'fɪbɪən] *n* anfibio; **amphibious** [-bɪəs] *a* anfibio.
amphitheatre ['æmfɪθɪətə*] *n* anfiteatro.

ample ['æmpl] *a* (*spacious*) amplio, ancho; (*abundant*) abundante; (*enough*) bastante, suficiente.
amplifier ['æmplɪfaɪə*] *n* amplificador *m*.
amplify ['æmplɪfaɪ] *vt* amplificar, aumentar; (*explain*) explicar.
amputate ['æmpjuteɪt] *vt* amputar.
amuck [ə'mʌk] *ad* = **amok.**
amuse [ə'mjuːz] *vt* divertir; (*distract*) distraer, entretener; ~**ment** *n* diversión *f*; (*pastime*) pasatiempo; (*laughter*) risa.
an [æn, ən, n] *det see* **a.**
anaemia [ə'niːmɪə] *n* anemia; **anaemic** [-mɪk] *a* anémico; (*fig*) soso, insípido.
anaesthetic [ænɪs'θetɪk] *n* anestesia; **anaesthetist** [æ'niːsθɪtɪst] *n* anestesista *m/f*.
analgesic [ænæl'dʒiːsɪk] *a*, *n* analgésico.
analogy [ə'nælədʒɪ] *n* análogo.
analyse ['ænəlaɪz] *vt* analizar; **analysis** [ə'næləsɪs], *pl* **-ses** [-siːz] *n* análisis *m inv*; **analyst** [-lɪst] *n* (*US*) analista *m/f*; **analytic(al)** [-'lɪtɪk(əl)] *a* analítico.
anarchist ['ænəkɪst] *a*, *n* anarquista *m/f*; **anarchy** [-kɪ] *n* anarquía, desorden *m*.
anatomy [ə'nætəmɪ] *n* anatomía.
ancestor ['ænsɪstə*] *n* antepasado; **ancestry** [-trɪ] *n* ascendencia, abolengo.
anchor ['æŋkə*] *n* ancla, áncora // *vi* anclar // *vt* (*fig*) sujetar, asegurar; **to weigh** ~ levar anclas; ~**age** *n* ancladero.
anchovy ['æntʃəvɪ] *n* anchoa.
ancient ['eɪnʃənt] *a* antiguo.
and [ænd] *conj* y; (*before i, hi*) e; ~ **so on** etcétera, y así sucesivamente; **try** ~ **come** procure o intente venir; **better** ~ **better** cada vez mejor.
Andes ['ændiːz] *npl*: **the** ~ los Andes.
anecdote ['ænɪkdəut] *n* anécdota.
anew [ə'njuː] *ad* de nuevo, otra vez.
angel ['eɪndʒəl] *n* ángel *m*.
anger ['æŋgə*] *n* cólera, ira // *vt* enojar, provocar.
angina [æn'dʒaɪnə] *n* angina (de pecho).
angle ['æŋgl] *n* ángulo; **from their** ~ desde su punto de vista.
angler ['æŋglə*] *n* pescador/a *m/f* (de caña).
Anglican ['æŋglɪkən] *a*, *n* anglicano/a.
angling ['æŋglɪŋ] *n* pesca con caña.
Anglo- [æŋgləu] *pref* anglo... .
angrily ['æŋgrɪlɪ] *ad* con enojo, airadamente.
angry ['æŋgrɪ] *a* enfadado, enojado; **to be** ~ **with sb/at sth** estar enfadado con alguien/por algo; **to get** ~ enfadarse, enojarse.
anguish ['æŋgwɪʃ] *n* (*physical*) dolor *m* agudo; (*mental*) angustia.
angular ['æŋgjulə*] *a* (*shape*) angular; (*features*) anguloso.
animal ['ænɪml] *n* animal *m*, bestia; (*insect*) bicho // *a* animal.
animate ['ænɪmeɪt] *vt* (*enliven*) animar;

(*encourage*) estimular, alentar; ~**d** *a* vivo, animado.
animosity [ænɪ'mɔsɪtɪ] *n* animosidad *f*, rencor *m*.
aniseed ['ænɪsiːd] *n* anís *m*.
ankle ['æŋkl] *n* tobillo *m*.
annex ['æneks] *n* (*also*: **annexe**) (*edificio*) anexo, dependencia // *vt* [æ'neks] (*territory*) anexar; (*document*) adjuntar.
annihilate [ə'naɪəleɪt] *vt* aniquilar.
anniversary [ænɪ'vɔːsərɪ] *n* aniversario.
annotate ['ænəuteɪt] *vt* anotar, comentar.
announce [ə'nauns] *vt* comunicar, anunciar; ~**ment** *n* anuncio, aviso, declaración *f*; **announcer** *n* (*RADIO, TV*) locutor/a *m/f*.
annoy [ə'nɔɪ] *vt* molestar, fastidiar, irritar; **don't get** ~**ed!** ¡no se enfade!; ~**ance** *n* enojo; (*thing*) molestia; ~**ing** *a* molesto, fastidioso; (*person*) pesado.
annual ['ænjuəl] *a* anual // *n* (*BOT*) anual *m*; (*book*) anuario; ~**ly** *ad* anualmente, cada año.
annuity [ə'njuːɪtɪ] *n* renta o pensión *f* vitalicia.
annul [ə'nʌl] *vt* anular, cancelar; (*law*) revocar; ~**ment** *n* anulación *f*, cancelación *f*.
annum ['ænəm] *n see* **per.**
anoint [ə'nɔɪnt] *vt* untar.
anomaly [ə'nɔməlɪ] *n* anomalía.
anonymity [ænə'nɪmɪtɪ] *n* anonimato; **anonymous** [ə'nɔnɪməs] *a* anónimo.
anorak ['ænəræk] *n* anorak *m*.
anorexia [ænə'rɛksɪə] *n* (*MED*) anorexia
another [ə'nʌðə*] *a*: ~ **book** (*one more*) otro libro; (*a different one*) un libro distinto // *pron* otro; *see also* **one.**
answer ['ɑːnsə*] *n* contestación *f*, respuesta; (*to problem*) solución *f* // *vi* contestar, responder // *vt* (*reply to*) contestar a, responder a; (*problem*) resolver; **to** ~ **the phone** contestar el teléfono; **in** ~ **to your letter** contestando a o en contestación a su carta; **to** ~ **the bell** *or* **the door** acudir a la puerta; **to** ~ **back** *vi* replicar, ser respondón(ona); **to** ~ **for** *vt fus* responder de o por; **to** ~ **to** *vt fus* (*description*) corresponder a; (*needs*) satisfacer; ~**able** *a*: ~**able to sb for sth** responsable ante uno de algo.
ant [ænt] *n* hormiga.
antacid [ænt'æsɪd] *a* antiácido.
antagonist [æn'tægənɪst] *n* antagonista *m/f*, adversario/a; ~**ic** [-'nɪstɪk] *a* antagónico; (*opposed*) contrario, opuesto; **antagonize** [-naɪz] *vt* enemistarse con.
Antarctic [ænt'ɑːktɪk] *n*: **the** ~ el Antártico; ~**a** *n* Antártida.
antelope ['æntɪləup] *n* antílope *m*.
antenatal ['æntɪ'neɪtl] *a* antenatal, prenatal; ~ **clinic** *n* clínica prenatal.
antenna [æn'tɛnə], *pl* ~**e** [-niː] *n* antena.
anthem ['ænθəm] *n*: **national** ~ himno nacional.
anthology [æn'θɔlədʒɪ] *n* antología.

anthropologist [ænθrə'pɔlədʒ ɪst] *n* antropólogo; **anthropology** [-dʒɪ] *n* antropología.

anti... [æntɪ] *pref* anti...; ~**-aircraft** *a* antiaéreo.

antibiotic [æntɪbaɪ'ɔtɪk] *a, n* antibiótico.

anticipate [æn'tɪsɪpeɪt] *vt* (*foresee*) prever; (*expect*) esperar, contar con; (*forestall*) anticiparse a, adelantarse a; (*look forward to*) prometerse; **anticipation** [-'peɪʃən] *n* previsión *f*; esperanza; anticipación *f*, prevención *f*.

anticlimax [æntɪ'klaɪmæks] *n* decepción *f*.

anticlockwise [æntɪ'klɔkwaɪz] *ad* en dirección contraria a la de las agujas del reloj.

antics ['æntɪks] *npl* payasadas *fpl*; (*of child*) travesuras *fpl*.

anticyclone [æntɪ'saɪkləun] *n* anticiclón *m*.

antidote ['æntɪdəut] *n* antídoto.

antifreeze ['æntɪfriːz] *n* anticongelante *m*, solución *f* anticongelante.

antihistamine [æntɪ'hɪstəmiːn] *n* antihistamínico.

antiquated ['æntɪkweɪtɪd] *a* anticuado.

antique [æn'tiːk] *n* antigüedad *f*, antigualla // *a* antiguo, anticuado; ~ **dealer** *n* anticuario; ~ **shop** *n* tienda de antigüedades.

antiquity [æn'tɪkwɪtɪ] *n* antigüedad *f*.

antiseptic [æntɪ'septɪk] *a, n* antiséptico.

antisocial [æntɪ'səuʃəl] *a* antisocial.

antlers ['æntləz] *npl* cuernas *fpl*.

anus ['eɪnəs] *n* ano.

anvil ['ænvɪl] *n* yunque *m*.

anxiety [æŋ'zaɪətɪ] *n* (*worry*) inquietud *f*; (*eagerness*) ansia, anhelo; (*MED*) ansiedad *f*.

anxious ['æŋkʃəs] *a* (*worried*) inquieto; (*keen*) deseoso; ~**ly** *ad* con inquietud, de manera angustiada.

any ['enɪ] *a* (*in negative and interrogative sentences = some*) algún, alguno, alguna; (*negative sense*) ningún, ninguno, ninguna; (*no matter which*) cualquier(a); (*each and every*) todo; **I haven't ~ money/books** no tengo dinero/libros; **have you ~ butter/children?** ¿tiene mantequilla/hijos?; **at ~ moment** en cualquier momento; **in ~ case** de todas formas, de todas maneras; **at ~ rate** de todas formas, sea como sea // *pron* alguno; ninguno; (*anybody*) cualquiera; (*in negative and interrogative sentences*): **I haven't ~** no tengo ninguno; **have you got ~?** ¿tiene algunos?; **can ~ of you sing?** ¿alguno de Ustedes sabe cantar? // *ad* (*in negative sentences*) nada; (*in interrogative and conditional constructions*) algo; **I can't hear him ~ more** no le oigo más; **do you want ~ more soup?** ¿quiere más sopa?; ~**body** *pron* cualquiera, cualquier persona; (*in interrogative sentences*) alguien; (*in negative sentences*): **I don't see ~body** no veo a nadie; ~**how** *ad* de todos modos, de todas maneras;

(*carelessly*) de cualquier manera; ~**one** = ~**body**; ~**thing** *pron* (*see* ~**body**) algo, cualquier cosa; algo; (*in negative sentences*) nada; (*everything*) todo; ~**time** *ad* (*at any moment*) en cualquier momento, de un momento a otro; (*whenever*) no importa cuándo, cuando quiera; ~**way** *ad* de todas maneras; de cualquier modo; ~**where** *ad* (*see* ~**body**) dondequiera; en algún sitio; (*negative sense*) en ningún sitio; (*everywhere*) en *or* por todas partes; **I don't see him** ~**where** no le veo en ningún sitio.

apart [ə'pɑːt] *ad* aparte, separadamente; **10 miles** ~ separados por 10 millas; ~ **from** *prep* aparte de.

apartheid [ə'pɑːteɪt] *n* apartheid *m*.

apartment [ə'pɑːtmənt] *n* (*US*) piso, apartamento; (*room*) cuarto.

apathetic [æpə'θetɪk] *a* apático, indiferente; **apathy** ['æpəθɪ] *n* apatía, indiferencia.

ape [eɪp] *n* mono // *vt* imitar, remedar.

aperitif [ə'perɪtɪv] *n* aperitivo.

aperture ['æpətʃjuə*] *n* rendija, resquicio; (*PHOT*) abertura.

apex ['eɪpɛks] *n* ápice *m*; (*fig*) cumbre *f*.

aphrodisiac [æfrəu'dɪzɪæk] *a, n* afrodisíaco.

apiece [ə'piːs] *ad* cada uno.

apologetic [əpɔlə'dʒetɪk] *a* (*tone, letter*) lleno de disculpas.

apologize [ə'pɔlədʒaɪz] *vi*: **to ~ (for sth to sb)** disculparse (con alguien de algo); **apology** [-dʒɪ] *n* disculpa, excusa.

apostle [ə'pɔsl] *n* apóstol *m/f*.

apostrophe [ə'pɔstrəfɪ] *n* apóstrofe *m*.

appal [ə'pɔːl] *vt* horrorizar, espantar; ~**ling** *a* espantoso; (*awful*) pésimo.

apparatus [æpə'reɪtəs] *n* aparato.

apparent [ə'pærənt] *a* aparente; (*obvious*) manifiesto, claro; ~**ly** *ad* por lo visto, al parecer.

apparition [æpə'rɪʃən] *n* aparición *f*; (*ghost*) fantasma *m*.

appeal [ə'piːl] *vi* (*LAW*) apelar // *n* (*LAW*) apelación *f*; (*request*) llamamiento; (*plea*) súplica, ruego; (*charm*) atractivo, encanto; **to ~ for** suplicar, reclamar; **to ~ to** (*subj: person*) rogar a, suplicar a; (*subj: thing*) atraer, interesar; **to ~ to sb for mercy** rogarle misericordia a alguien; **it doesn't ~ to me** no me atrae, no me llama la atención; ~**ing** *a* (*nice*) atrayente, atractivo; (*touching*) conmovedor(a), emocionante.

appear [ə'pɪə*] *vi* aparecer, presentarse; (*LAW*) comparecer; (*publication*) salir (a luz), publicarse; (*seem*) parecer; **it would ~ that** parecería que; ~**ance** *n* aparición *f*; (*look, aspect*) apariencia, aspecto.

appease [ə'piːz] *vt* (*pacify*) apaciguar; (*satisfy*) satisfacer, saciar.

appendicitis [əpendɪ'saɪtɪs] *n* apendicitis *f*.

appendix [ə'pendɪks], *pl* **-dices** [-dɪsiːz] *n* apéndice *m*.

appetite ['æpɪtaɪt] n apetito; (fig) deseo, anhelo.
appetizing ['æpɪtaɪzɪŋ] a apetitoso.
applaud [ə'plɔːd] vt, vi aplaudir; **applause** [-ɔːz] n aplausos mpl.
apple ['æpl] n manzana; ~ **tree** n manzano.
appliance [ə'plaɪəns] n aparato.
applicable [ə'plɪkəbl] a aplicable, pertinente.
applicant ['æplɪkənt] n candidato/a, solicitante m/f.
application [æplɪ'keɪʃən] n aplicación f; (for a job, a grant etc) solicitud f, petición f; ~ **form** n formulario.
apply [ə'plaɪ] vt: **to** ~ **(to)** aplicar (a); (fig) emplear (para) // vi: **to** ~ **to** (ask) presentarse a, ser candidato a; (be suitable for) ser aplicable a; (be relevant to) tener que ver con; **to** ~ **for** (permit, grant, job) solicitar; **to** ~ **the brakes** aplicar los frenos; **to** ~ **o.s. to** aplicarse a, dedicarse a.
appoint [ə'pɔɪnt] vt (to post) nombrar; (date, place) fijar, señalar; ~**ment** n (engagement) cita; (date) compromiso; (act) nombramiento; (post) puesto.
apportion [ə'pɔːʃən] vt repartir, distribuir; (blame) dar.
appraisal [ə'preɪzl] n tasación f, valoración f.
appreciable [ə'priːʃəbl] a sensible.
appreciate [ə'priːʃɪeɪt] vt (like) apreciar, tener en mucho; (be grateful for) agradecer; (assess) valorar, apreciar; (be aware of) comprender, percibir // vi (comm) aumentar(se) en valor, subir; **appreciation** [-'eɪʃən] n aprecio; reconocimiento, agradecimiento; aumento en valor.
appreciative [ə'priːʃɪətɪv] a (person) agradecido; (comment) elogioso.
apprehend [æprɪ'hɛnd] vt percibir, comprender; (arrest) detener.
apprehension [æprɪ'hɛnʃən] n (fear) recelo, aprensión f; **apprehensive** [-'hɛnsɪv] a aprensivo.
apprentice [ə'prɛntɪs] n aprendiz/a m/f; ~**ship** n aprendizaje m.
approach [ə'prəutʃ] vi acercarse // vt acercarse a; (be approximate) aproximarse a; (ask, apply to) dirigirse a // n acercamiento; aproximación f; (access) acceso; (proposal) proposición f; ~**able** a (person) abordable; (place) accesible.
appropriate [ə'prəuprɪeɪt] vt (take) apropiarse; (allot): **to** ~ **sth for** destinar algo a // a [-rɪɪt] (apt) apropiado, conveniente; (relevant) competente.
approval [ə'pruːvəl] n aprobación f, visto bueno; **on** ~ (comm) a prueba.
approve [ə'pruːv] vt aprobar; ~**d school** n correccional m.
approximate [ə'prɔksɪmɪt] a aproximado // vt [-meɪt] aproximarse a, acercarse a;

approximation [-'meɪʃən] n aproximación f.
apricot ['eɪprɪkɔt] n albaricoque m.
April ['eɪprəl] n abril m; ~ **Fool's Day** n Día m de los Inocentes.
apron ['eɪprən] n delantal m.
apt [æpt] a (suitable) acertado, oportuno; (appropriate) conveniente; (likely): ~ **to do** con tendencia a hacer.
aptitude ['æptɪtjuːd] n aptitud f, capacidad f.
aqualung ['ækwəlʌŋ] n aparato de buceo autónomo.
aquarium [ə'kwɛərɪəm] n acuario.
Aquarius [ə'kwɛərɪəs] n Acuario.
aquatic [ə'kwætɪk] a acuático.
aqueduct ['ækwɪdʌkt] n acueducto.
Arab ['ærəb] n árabe m/f.
Arabia [ə'reɪbɪə] n Arabia; ~**n** a árabe.
Arabic ['ærəbɪk] n árabe m.
arable ['ærəbl] a cultivable.
arbitrary ['aːbɪtrərɪ] a arbitrario.
arbitrate ['aːbɪtreɪt] vi arbitrar; **arbitration** [-'treɪʃən] n arbitraje m; **arbitrator** n juez m árbitro.
arc [aːk] n arco.
arcade [aː'keɪd] n arcada; (round a square) soportales mpl; (passage with shops) galería, pasaje m.
arch [aːtʃ] n arco; (vault) bóveda; (of foot) empeine m // vt arquear.
archaeologist [aːkɪ'ɔlədʒɪst] n arqueólogo; **archaeology** [-dʒɪ] n arqueología.
archaic [aː'keɪɪk] a arcaico.
archbishop [aːtʃ'bɪʃəp] n arzobispo.
arch-enemy ['aːtʃ'ɛnɪmɪ] n enemigo jurado.
archer ['aːtʃə*] n arquero; ~**y** n tiro con arco.
archetype ['aːkɪtaɪp] n arquetipo.
archipelago [aːkɪ'pɛlɪgəu] n archipiélago.
architect ['aːkɪtɛkt] n arquitecto; ~**ural** [-'tɛktʃərəl] a arquitectónico; ~**ure** n arquitectura.
archives ['aːkaɪvz] npl archivo sg.
archway ['aːtʃweɪ] n arco, arcada.
Arctic ['aːktɪk] a ártico // n: **the** ~ el Ártico.
ardent ['aːdənt] a (passionate) ardiente, apasionado; (fervent) fervoroso; **ardour** ['aːdə*] n ardor m; fervor m.
arduous ['aːdjuəs] a (gen) arduo; (journey) penoso.
are [aː*] vb see **be**.
area ['ɛərɪə] n (gen) área; (math etc) superficie f, extensión f; (zone) región f, zona.
arena [ə'riːnə] n arena; (of circus) pista; (for bullfight) plaza, ruedo.
aren't [aːnt] = **are not**.
Argentina [aːdʒən'tiːnə] n Argentina; **Argentinian** [-'tɪnɪən] a, n argentino/a.
argue ['aːgjuː] vi (quarrel) discutir; (reason) argüir, discurrir; **to** ~ **that** sostener que; **argument** n (reasons)

argumento; (*quarrel*) discusión *f*; (*debate*) debate *m*, disputa; **argumentative** [-məntətɪv] *a* discutidor(a).
aria ['ɑːrɪə] *n* (*MUS*) aria.
arid ['ærɪd] *a* árido.
Aries ['ɛərɪz] *n* Aries *m*.
arise [ə'raɪz], *pt* **arose**, *pp* **arisen** [ə'rɪzn] *vi* (*rise up*) levantarse, alzarse; (*emerge*) surgir, presentarse; **to ~ from** resultar de.
aristocracy [ærɪs'tɔkrəsɪ] *n* aristocracia; **aristocrat** ['ærɪstəkræt] *n* aristócrata *m/f*.
arithmetic [ə'rɪθmətɪk] *n* aritmética.
ark [ɑːk] *n*: **Noah's A~** Arca de Noé.
arm [ɑːm] *n* (*ANAT*) brazo; (*weapon*, *MIL*: *branch*) arma // *vt* armar; **~s** *npl* (*weapons*) armas *fpl*; (*HERALDRY*) escudo *sg*; **~ race** carrera de armamentos; **~ in ~** cogidos del brazo; **~band** *n* brazalete *m*; **~chair** *n* sillón *m*; **~ed** *a* armado; **~ed robbery** *n* robo a mano armada; **~ful** *n* brazado, brazada.
armistice ['ɑːmɪstɪs] *n* armisticio.
armour ['ɑːmə*] *n* armadura; **~ed car** *n* coche *m* blindado; **~y** *n* armería, arsenal *m*.
armpit ['ɑːmpɪt] *n* sobaco, axila.
army ['ɑːmɪ] *n* ejército.
aroma [ə'rəumə] *n* aroma *m*, fragancia; **~tic** [ærə'mætɪk] *a* aromático, fragante.
arose [ə'rəuz] *pt of* **arise.**
around [ə'raund] *ad* alrededor; (*in the area*) a la redonda // *prep* alrededor de, en torno de; (*fig*: *about*) alrededor de.
arouse [ə'rauz] *vt* despertar.
arrange [ə'reɪndʒ] *vt* arreglar, ordenar; (*programme*) organizar; **~ment** *n* arreglo; (*agreement*) acuerdo; **~ments** *npl* (*plans*) planes *mpl*, medidas *fpl*; (*preparations*) preparativos *mpl*.
arrears [ə'rɪəz] *npl* atrasos *mpl*; **to be in ~ with one's rent** atrasarse en el arriendo.
arrest [ə'rɛst] *vt* detener; (*sb's attention*) llamar // *n* detención *f*; **under ~** detenido.
arrival [ə'raɪvəl] *n* llegada; **new ~** recién llegado.
arrive [ə'raɪv] *vi* llegar.
arrogance ['ærəgəns] *n* arrogancia; **arrogant** [-gənt] *a* arrogante.
arrow ['ærəu] *n* flecha.
arsenal ['ɑːsɪnl] *n* arsenal *m*.
arsenic ['ɑːsnɪk] *n* arsénico.
arson ['ɑːsn] *n* delito de incendiar.
art [ɑːt] *n* arte *m*; (*craft*) artes *fpl* y oficios *mpl*; (*skill*) destreza; (*technique*) técnica; **A~s** *npl* (*SCOL*) Letras *fpl*; **~ gallery** *n* museo de bellas artes; (*small and private*) galería de arte.
artery ['ɑːtərɪ] *n* (*MED*) arteria; (*fig*) vía principal.
arthritis [ɑː'θraɪtɪs] *n* artritis *f*.
artichoke ['ɑːtɪtʃəuk] *n* alcachofa; **Jerusalem ~** aguaturma.
article ['ɑːtɪkl] *n* artículo, objeto, cosa; (*in*

newspaper) artículo; (*LAW*: *training*): **~s** *npl* contrato *sg* de aprendizaje.
articulate [ɑː'tɪkjulɪt] *a* claro *o* distinto en el hablar // *vt* [-leɪt] articular; **~d lorry** *n* camión *m* articulado.
artificial [ɑːtɪ'fɪʃəl] *a* artificial; (*teeth etc*) postizo; **~ respiration** *n* respiración *f* artificial.
artillery [ɑː'tɪlərɪ] *n* artillería.
artisan ['ɑːtɪzæn] *n* artesano.
artist ['ɑːtɪst] *n* artista *m/f*; (*MUS*) intérprete *m/f*; **~ic** [ɑː'tɪstɪk] *a* artístico; **~ry** *n* arte *m*, habilidad *f* artística.
artless ['ɑːtlɪs] *a* (*innocent*) natural, sencillo; (*clumsy*) desmañado.
as [æz, əz] *conj* (*cause*) como, ya que; (*time*: *moment*) como, cuando; (: *duration*) mientras; (*manner*) como, lo mismo que, tal como; (*in the capacity of*) como; **~ big ~** tan grande como; **twice ~ big ~** dos veces más grande que; **~ she said** como ella dijo; **~ if** *or* **though** como si; **~ for** *or* **to that** en cuanto a eso, en lo que a eso se refiere; **~** *or* **so long ~** *conj* mientras (que); **~ much/many ~** tanto(s)... como; **~ soon ~** *conj* tan pronto como; **~ such** *ad* como tal; **~ well** *ad* también, además; **~ well ~** *conj* así como; *see also* **such.**
asbestos [æz'bɛstəs] *n* asbesto, amianto.
ascend [ə'sɛnd] *vt* subir; **~ancy** *n* ascendiente *m*, dominio.
ascent [ə'sɛnt] *n* subida; (*slope*) cuesta, pendiente *m*; (*promotion*) ascenso.
ascertain [æsə'teɪn] *vt* averiguar, determinar.
ascetic [ə'sɛtɪk] *a* ascético.
ascribe [ə'skraɪb] *vt*: **to ~ sth to** atribuir algo a.
ash [æʃ] *n* ceniza; (*tree*) fresno.
ashamed [ə'ʃeɪmd] *a* avergonzado; **to be ~ of** avergonzarse de.
ashen ['æʃn] *a* ceniciento, pálido.
ashore [ə'ʃɔː*] *ad* en tierra.
ashtray ['æʃtreɪ] *n* cenicero.
Asia ['eɪʃə] *n* Asia; **~n, ~tic** [eɪsɪ'ætɪk] *a*, *n* asiático/a.
aside [ə'saɪd] *ad* aparte, a un lado.
ask [ɑːsk] *vt* (*question*) preguntar; (*demand*) pedir; (*invite*) invitar; **to ~ sb sth/to do sth** preguntar algo a alguien/pedir a alguien que haga algo; **to ~ sb about sth** preguntar algo a alguien; **to ~ (sb) a question** hacer una pregunta (a alguien); **to ~ sb out to dinner** invitar a comer a uno; **to ~ for** *vt fus* pedir.
askance [ə'skɑːns] *ad*: **to look ~ at sb** mirar con recelo a uno.
askew [ə'skjuː] *ad* sesgado, ladeado, oblicuamente.
asleep [ə'sliːp] *a* dormido; **to fall ~** dormirse, quedarse dormido.
asparagus [əs'pærəgəs] *n* espárragos *mpl*.
aspect ['æspɛkt] *n* aspecto, apariencia; (*direction in which a building etc faces*) orientación *f*.

aspersions [əs'pəːʃənz] npl: **to cast ~ on** difamar a, calumniar a.

asphalt ['æsfælt] n asfalto; (place) pista asfaltada.

asphyxiate [æs'fıksıeıt] vt asfixiar // vi asfixiarse; **asphyxiation** [-'eıʃən] n asfixia.

aspiration [æspə'reıʃən] n (fig) anhelo, deseo, ambición f.

aspire [əs'paıə*] vi: **to ~ to** aspirar a, ambicionar.

aspirin ['æsprın] n aspirina.

ass [æs] n asno, burro; (col) imbécil m.

assailant [ə'seılənt] n asaltador/a m/f, agresor/a m/f.

assassin [ə'sæsın] n asesino; **~ate** vt asesinar; **~ation** [-'neıʃən] n asesinato.

assault [ə'sɔːlt] n (gen: attack) asalto, ataque m // vt asaltar, atacar; (sexually) violar.

assemble [ə'sɛmbl] vt reunir, juntar; (TECH) montar // vi reunirse, juntarse.

assembly [ə'sɛmblı] n (meeting) reunión f, asamblea; (people) concurrencia; (construction) montaje m; **~ line** n línea de producción.

assent [ə'sɛnt] n asentimiento, aprobación f // vi consentir, asentir.

assert [ə'səːt] vt afirmar; (claim etc) hacer valer; **~ion** [ə'səːʃən] n afirmación f.

assess [ə'sɛs] vt valorar, calcular; (tax, damages) fijar; (property etc: for tax) gravar; **~ment** n valoración f; gravamen m; **~or** n asesor/a m/f; (of tax) tasador/a m/f.

asset ['æsɛt] n posesión f; (quality) ventaja sg; **~s** npl (funds) activo sg, fondos mpl.

assiduous [ə'sıdjuəs] a asiduo.

assign [ə'saın] vt (date) fijar; (task) asignar; (resources) destinar; (property) traspasar; **~ment** n asignación f; (task) tarea.

assimilate [ə'sımıleıt] vt asimilar.

assist [ə'sıst] vt ayudar; (progress etc) fomentar; **~ance** n ayuda, auxilio; (welfare) subsidio; **~ant** n ayudante m/f, auxiliar m/f; (also: **shop ~ant**) dependiente/a m/f.

assizes [ə'saızız] npl sesión f de un tribunal.

associate [ə'səuʃııt] a asociado // n asociado, colega m; (in crime) cómplice m/f; (member) miembro // (vb: [-ʃıeıt]) vt asociar, relacionar // vi: **to ~ with sb** tratar con alguien.

association [əsəusı'eıʃən] n asociación f; (COMM) sociedad f.

assorted [ə'sɔːtıd] a surtido, variado.

assortment [ə'sɔːtmənt] n surtido.

assume [ə'sjuːm] vt (suppose) suponer, dar por sentado; (responsibilities etc) asumir; (attitude, name) adoptar, tomar.

assumption [ə'sʌmpʃən] n (supposition) suposición f, presunción f; (act) asunción f.

assurance [ə'ʃuərəns] n garantía, promesa; (confidence) confianza, aplomo; (certainty) certeza; (insurance) seguro.

assure [ə'ʃuə*] vt asegurar.

asterisk ['æstərısk] n asterisco.

astern [ə'stəːn] ad a popa, por la popa.

asteroid ['æstərɔıd] n asteroide m.

asthma ['æsmə] n asma; **~tic** [æs'mætık] a, n asmático/a.

astonish [ə'stɔnıʃ] vt asombrar, pasmar; **~ment** n asombro, sorpresa.

astound [ə'staund] vt asombrar, pasmar.

astray [ə'streı] ad: **to go ~** extraviarse; **to lead ~** llevar por mal camino.

astride [ə'straıd] ad a horcajadas // prep a caballo o horcajadas sobre.

astrologer [əs'trɔlədʒə*] n astrólogo; **astrology** [-dʒı] n astrología.

astronaut ['æstrənɔːt] n astronauta m/f.

astronomer [əs'trɔnəmə*] n astrónomo; **astronomical** [æstrə'nɔmıkəl] a astronómico; (fig) tremendo, enorme; **astronomy** [-mı] n astronomía.

astute [əs'tjuːt] a astuto.

asunder [ə'sʌndə*] ad: **to tear ~** romper en dos, hacer pedazos.

asylum [ə'saıləm] n (refuge) asilo; (hospital) manicomio.

at [æt] prep en, a; **~ the top** en la cumbre; **~ 4 o'clock** a las cuatro; **~ £1 a kilo** a libra el kilo; **~ night** de noche, por la noche; **~ a stroke** de un golpe; **two ~ a time** de dos en dos; **~ times** a veces.

ate [eıt] pt of **eat**.

atheist ['eıθııst] n ateo/a.

Athens ['æθınz] n Atenas f.

athlete ['æθliːt] n atleta m/f.

athletic [æθ'lɛtık] a atlético; **~s** n atletismo.

Atlantic [ət'læntık] n: **the ~ (Ocean)** el (Océano) Atlántico.

atlas ['ætləs] n atlas m.

atmosphere ['ætməsfıə*] n atmósfera; (fig) ambiente m.

atom ['ætəm] n átomo; **~ic** [ə'tɔmık] a atómico; **~(ic) bomb** n bomba atómica; **~izer** ['ætəmaızə*] n atomizador m.

atone [ə'təun] vi: **to ~ for** expiar.

atrocious [ə'trəuʃəs] a (very bad) atroz; (fig) horrible, infame.

atrocity [ə'trɔsıtı] n atrocidad f.

attach [ə'tætʃ] vt (gen) sujetar, pegar; (document, letter) adjuntar; **to be ~ed to sb/sth** (to like) tener cariño a alguien/algo.

attaché [ə'tæʃeı] n agregado; **~ case** n maletín m.

attachment [ə'tætʃmənt] n (tool) accesorio; (love): **~ (to)** cariño (a).

attack [ə'tæk] vt (MIL) atacar; (criminal) agredir, asaltar; (task etc) emprender // n ataque m, asalto; (on sb's life) atentado; **heart ~** ataque al corazón o cardíaco; **~er** n agresor/a m/f, asaltante m/f.

attain [ə'teın] vt (also: **~ to**) alcanzar; (achieve) lograr, conseguir; **~ments** npl dotes fpl, talento sg.

attempt [ə'tɛmpt] n tentativa, intento; (attack) atentado // vt intentar, tratar de.

attend [ə'tɛnd] vt asistir a; (patient) atender; **to ~ to** vt fus (needs, affairs etc) ocuparse de; (speech etc) prestar atención a; (customer) atender a; **~ance** n asistencia, presencia; (people present) concurrencia; **~ant** n sirviente/a m/f, mozo/a; (THEATRE) acomodador/a m/f // a concomitante.

attention [ə'tɛnʃən] n atención f // excl (MIL) ¡firme(s)!; **for the ~ of...** (ADMIN) atención... .

attentive [ə'tɛntɪv] a atento; (polite) cortés.

attest [ə'tɛst] vi: **to ~ to** dar fe de.

attic ['ætɪk] n desván m, ático.

attitude ['ætɪtjuːd] n (gen) actitud f; (disposition) disposición f.

attorney [ə'tɜːnɪ] n (lawyer) abogado; (having proxy) apoderado; **A~ General** n (Brit) fiscal m de la corona; (US) procurador m general.

attract [ə'trækt] vt atraer; (attention) llamar; **attraction** [ə'trækʃən] n (gen pl) encantos mpl; (amusements) diversiones fpl; (PHYSICS) atracción f; (fig: towards sth) atractivo; **~ive** a atractivo; (interesting) atrayente; (pretty) guapo, mono.

attribute ['ætrɪbjuːt] n atributo // vt [ə'trɪbjuːt]: **to ~ sth to** atribuir o achacar algo a.

aubergine ['əubəʒiːn] n berenjena.

auburn ['ɔːbən] a castaño rojizo.

auction ['ɔːkʃən] n (also: **sale by ~**) subasta // vt subastar; **~eer** [-'nɪə*] n subastador/a m/f.

audacious [ɔː'deɪʃəs] a audaz, atrevido; (pej) descarado; **audacity** [ɔː'dæsɪtɪ] n audacia, atrevimiento; (pej) descaro.

audible ['ɔːdɪbl] a audible, que se puede oír.

audience ['ɔːdɪəns] n auditorio, público; (interview) audiencia.

audio-visual [ɔːdɪəu'vɪzjuəl] a audiovisual.

audit ['ɔːdɪt] vt revisar, intervenir.

audition [ɔː'dɪʃən] n audición f.

auditor ['ɔːdɪtə*] n interventor/a m/f, censor/a m/f de cuentas.

auditorium [ɔːdɪ'tɔːrɪəm] n auditorio.

augment [ɔːg'mɛnt] vt aumentar // vi aumentarse.

augur ['ɔːgə*] vi: **it ~s well** es de buen agüero.

August ['ɔːgəst] n agosto.

aunt [aːnt] n tía; **~ie, ~y** n diminutive of **aunt**.

au pair ['əu'pɛə*] n (also: **~ girl**) au pair f.

aura ['ɔːrə] n emanación f; (atmosphere) ambiente m.

auspices ['ɔːspɪsɪz] npl: **under the ~ of** bajo los auspicios de.

auspicious [ɔːs'pɪʃəs] a propicio, de buen augurio.

austere [ɔs'tɪə*] a austero; (manner) adusto; **austerity** [ɔ'stɛrɪtɪ] n austeridad f.

Australia [ɔs'treɪlɪə] n Australia; **~n** a, n australiano/a.

Austria ['ɔstrɪə] n Austria; **~n** a, n austríaco/a.

authentic [ɔː'θɛntɪk] a auténtico.

author ['ɔːθə] n autor/a m/f.

authoritarian [ɔːθɔrɪ'tɛərɪən] a autoritario.

authoritative [ɔː'θɔrɪtətɪv] a autorizado; (manner) autoritario.

authority [ɔː'θɔrɪtɪ] n autoridad f; **the authorities** npl las autoridades.

authorize ['ɔːθəraɪz] vt autorizar.

auto ['ɔːtəu] n (US) coche m, automóvil m.

autobiography [ɔːtəbaɪ'ɔgrəfɪ] n autobiografía.

autocratic [ɔːtə'krætɪk] a autocrático.

autograph ['ɔːtəgrɑːf] n autógrafo // vt firmar; (photo etc) dedicar.

automatic [ɔːtə'mætɪk] a automático // n (gun) pistola automática.

automation [ɔːtə'meɪʃən] n automatización f.

automaton [ɔː'tɔmətən] pl **-mata** [-tə] n autómata m/f.

automobile ['ɔːtəməbiːl] n (US) coche m, automóvil m.

autonomous [ɔː'tɔnəməs] a autónomo.

autopsy ['ɔːtɔpsɪ] n autopsia.

autumn ['ɔːtəm] n otoño.

auxiliary [ɔːg'zɪlɪərɪ] a auxiliar.

Av. abbr of **avenue**.

avail [ə'veɪl] vt: **to ~ o.s. of** aprovechar(se) de, valerse de // n: **to no ~** en vano, sin resultado.

availability [əveɪlə'bɪlɪtɪ] n disponibilidad f.

available [ə'veɪləbl] a disponible; (usable) asequible.

avalanche ['ævəlɑːnʃ] n alud m, avalancha.

avant-garde ['ævãŋ'gɑːd] a de vanguardia.

avaricious [ævə'rɪʃəs] a avaro, avariento.

Ave. abbr of **avenue**.

avenge [ə'vɛndʒ] vt vengar.

avenue ['ævənjuː] n avenida; (path) camino.

average ['ævərɪdʒ] n promedio, término medio // a (mean) medio, de término medio; (ordinary) regular, corriente // vt calcular el promedio de, prorratear; **on ~** por regla general; **to ~ out** vi: **to ~ out** at resultar por promedio, ser por regla general.

averse [ə'vɜːs] a: **to be ~ to sth/doing** sentir aversión o antipatía por algo/por hacer; **aversion** [ə'vɜːʃən] n aversión f, repugnancia.

avert [ə'vɜːt] vt prevenir; (blow) desviar; (one's eyes) apartar.

aviary ['eɪvɪərɪ] n pajarera, avería.

aviation [eɪvɪ'eɪʃən] n aviación f.

avid ['ævɪd] a ávido, ansioso.

avocado [ævə'kɑːdəu] n (also: **~ pear**) aguacate m.

avoid [ə'vɔɪd] vt evitar, eludir; **~able** a

evitable, eludible; ~**ance** *n* el evitar, evitación *f*.
await [ə'weɪt] *vt* esperar, aguardar.
awake [ə'weɪk] *a* despierto // (*vb*: *pt* **awoke**, *pp* **awoken** *or* **awaked**) *vt* despertar // *vi* despertarse; ~**ning** *n* el despertar.
award [ə'wɔːd] *n* (*prize*) premio, condecoración *f*; (*LAW*) fallo, sentencia; (*act*) concesión *f* // *vt* (*prize*) otorgar, conceder; (*LAW: damages*) adjudicar, decretar.
aware [ə'wɛə*] *a* consciente; (*awake*) despierto; (*informed*) enterado; **to become** ~ **of** darse cuenta de, enterarse de; ~**ness** *n* conciencia, conocimiento.
awash [ə'wɔʃ] *a* inundado.
away [ə'weɪ] *ad* (*gen*) fuera; (*far* ~) lejos; **two kilometres** ~ a dos kilómetros de distancia; **two hours** ~ **by car** a dos horas en coche; **the holiday was two weeks** ~ faltaba dos semanas para las vacaciones; ~ **from** lejos de, fuera de; **he's** ~ **for a week** estará ausente una semana; **to take** ~ *vt* llevar(se); **to work/pedal** ~ seguir trabajando/pedaleando; **to fade** ~ desvanecerse; (*sound*) apagarse; ~ **match** *n* (*SPORT*) partido de fuera.
awe [ɔː] *n* pavor *m*, respeto, temor *m* reverencial; ~-**inspiring**, ~**some** *a* imponente, pasmoso; ~**struck** *a* pasmado.
awful ['ɔːfəl] *a* tremendo, terrible, pasmoso; ~**ly** *ad* (*very*) terriblemente.
awhile [ə'waɪl] *ad* durante un rato, un rato, algún tiempo.
awkward ['ɔːkwəd] *a* (*clumsy*) desmañado, torpe; (*shape*) incómodo; (*problem*) difícil; (*embarrassing*) delicado, desagradable.
awning ['ɔːnɪŋ] *n* (*of shop*) toldo; (*of window etc*) marquesina.
awoke [ə'wəuk], **awoken** [-kən] *pt*, *pp* of **awake**.
awry [ə'raɪ] *ad*: **to be** ~ estar de través o al soslayo; **to go** ~ salir mal, fracasar.
axe, **ax** (*US*) [æks] *n* hacha // *vt* (*employee*) despedir; (*project etc*) parar, cortar; (*jobs*) reducir.
axiom ['æksɪəm] *n* axioma *m*.
axis ['æksɪs], *pl* **axes** [-siːz] *n* eje *m*.
axle ['æksl] *n* eje *m*, árbol *m*.
ay(e) [aɪ] *excl* (*yes*) sí; **the ayes** *npl* los que votan a favor.
Aztec ['æztɛk] *n* azteca *m/f*.

B

B.A. *abbr of* **Bachelor of Arts** licenciado en letras.
babble ['bæbl] *vi* barbullar.
baboon [bə'buːn] *n* mandril *m*.
baby ['beɪbɪ] *n* nene/a *m/f*; ~ **carriage** *n* (*US*) cochecito; ~**ish** *a* infantil; ~-**sit** *vi* hacer de canguro; ~-**sitter** *n* canguro *m/f*.

bachelor ['bætʃələ*] *n* soltero.
back [bæk] *n* (*of person*) espalda; (*of animal*) lomo; (*of hand*) dorso; (*of house, car, train*) parte *f* de atrás; (*of chair*) respaldo; (*of page*) reverso; (*FOOTBALL*) defensa *m* // *vt* (*candidate: also:* ~ **up**) respaldar, apoyar; (*horse: at races*) apostar a; (*car*) dar marcha atrás a *o* con // *vi* (*car etc*) dar marcha atrás // *a* (*in compounds*) tras; ~ **seats/wheels** (*AUT*) asientos *mpl*/ruedas *fpl* de atrás; ~ **payments** pagos *mpl* con efecto retroactivo; ~ **rent** renta atrasada // *ad* (*not forward*) (hacia) atrás; (*returned*): **he's** ~ está de vuelta, ha vuelto; **he ran** ~ retrocedió corriendo; (*restitution*): **throw the ball** ~ devuelve la pelota; **can I have it** ~? ¿me lo devuelve?; (*again*): **he called** ~ llamó de nuevo; **to** ~ **down** *vi* echarse atrás; **to** ~ **out** *vi* (*of promise*) volverse atrás.
back: ~**ache** *n* dolor *m* de espalda; ~**bencher** *n* miembro del parlamento sin portafolio; ~**biting** *n* murmuración *f*; ~**bone** *n* columna vertebral; ~-**cloth** *n* telón *m* de foro; ~**date** *vt* (*letter*) poner fecha atrasada a; ~**dated pay rise** alza de sueldo con efecto retroactivo; ~**er** *n* partidario; (*COMM*) promotor *m*; ~**fire** *vi* (*AUT*) petardear; (*plans*) fallar, salir al revés; ~**gammon** *n* backgammon *m*; ~**ground** *n* fondo; (*of events*) antecedentes *mpl*; (*basic knowledge*) bases *fpl*; (*experience*) conocimientos *mpl*, educación *f*; **family** ~**ground** origen *m*, antecedentes *mpl*; ~**hand** *n* (*TENNIS: also:* ~**hand stroke**) revés *m*; ~**handed** *a* (*fig*) ambiguo, equívoco; ~**hander** *n* (*bribe*) soborno; ~**ing** *n* (*fig*) apoyo, respaldo; ~**lash** *n* reacción *f*, resaca; ~**log** *n*: ~**log of work** atrasos *mpl*; ~ **number** *n* (*of magazine etc*) número atrasado; ~ **pay** *n* pago atrasado; ~**side** *n* (*col*) trasero, culo; ~**stage** *ad* entre bastidores; ~**stroke** *n* braza de espaldas; ~**ward** *a* (*movement*) hacia atrás; (*person, country*) atrasado; (*shy*) tímido; ~**wards** *ad* (*move, go*) hacia atrás; (*read a list*) al revés; (*fall*) de espaldas; ~**water** *n* (*fig*) lugar *m* atrasado *o* apartado; ~**yard** *n* traspatio.
bacon ['beɪkən] *n* tocino.
bacteria [bæk'tɪərɪə] *npl* bacteria *sg*.
bad [bæd] *a* malo; (*serious*) grave; (*meat, food*) podrido, pasado; **to go** ~ echarse a perder.
badge [bædʒ] *n* insignia; (*of policeman*) chapa, placa.
badger ['bædʒə*] *n* tejón *m*.
badly ['bædlɪ] *ad* (*work, dress etc*) mal; ~ **wounded** gravemente herido; **he needs it** ~ le hace gran falta; **to be** ~ **off (for money)** andar mal de dinero.
badminton ['bædmɪntən] *n* badminton *m*.
bad-tempered ['bæd'tɛmpəd] *a* de mal genio *o* carácter; (*temporary*) de mal humor.

baffle ['bæfl] vt (*puzzle*) desconcertar, confundir.

bag [bæg] n bolsa, saco; (*handbag*) bolso; (*satchel*) mochila; (*case*) maleta; (*of hunter*) caza // vt (*col*: *take*) coger, pescar; ~**ful** n saco (lleno); ~**gage** n equipaje m; ~**gy** a que hace bolsas; ~**pipes** npl gaita sg.

bail [beɪl] n fianza, caución f // vt (*prisoner*: *gen*: **give** ~ **to**) poner en libertad bajo fianza; (*boat*: *also*: ~ **out**) achicar; **to** ~ **sb out** obtener la libertad de uno bajo fianza; *see also* **bale.**

bailiff ['beɪlɪf] n alguacil m.

bait [beɪt] n cebo // vt cebar, poner el cebo en.

bake [beɪk] vt cocer (al horno) // vi (*cook*) cocerse; (*be hot*) hacer un calor terrible; ~**d beans** npl judías fpl en salsa de tomate; **baker** n panadero; ~**ry** n (*for bread*) panadería; (*for cakes*) pastelería; **baking** n (*act*) cocción f; (*batch*) hornada; **baking powder** n polvos mpl de levadura.

balaclava [bælə'klɑːvə] n (*also*: ~ **helmet**) pasamontañas m inv.

balance ['bæləns] n equilibrio; (*COMM. sum*) balance m; (*remainder*) resto; (*scales*) balanza // vt equilibrar; (*budget*) nivelar; (*account*) saldar; (*compensate*) contrapesar; ~ **of trade/payments** balanza de comercio/pagos; ~**d** a (*personality, diet*) equilibrado; ~ **sheet** n balance m.

balcony ['bælkənɪ] n (*open*) balcón m; (*closed*) galería.

bald [bɔːld] a calvo; ~**ness** n calvicie f.

bale [beɪl] n (*AGR*) paca, fardo; **to** ~ **out** (*of a plane*) lanzarse en paracaídas; **to** ~ **sb out of a difficulty** sacar a uno de un problema.

baleful ['beɪlful] a (*look*) triste; (*sinister*) funesto, siniestro.

ball [bɔːl] n bola; (*football*) balón m; (*for tennis, golf*) pelota; (*dance*) baile m.

ballad ['bæləd] n balada, romance m.

ballast ['bæləst] n lastre m.

ballerina [bælə'riːnə] n bailarina.

ballet ['bæleɪ] n ballet m, baile m; ~ **dancer** n bailarín/ina m/f.

balloon [bə'luːn] n globo; ~**ist** n ascensionista m/f.

ballot ['bælət] n votación f; ~ **box** n urna (electoral); ~ **paper** n papeleta.

ball-point pen ['bɔːlpɔɪnt'-] n bolígrafo.

ballroom ['bɔːlrum] n salón m de baile.

balmy ['bɑːmɪ] a (*breeze, air*) suave, fragante; (*col*) = **barmy.**

Baltic ['bɔːltɪk] n: **the** ~ (**Sea**) el (Mar) Báltico.

balustrade ['bæləstreɪd] n barandilla.

bamboo [bæm'buː] n bambú m.

ban [bæn] n prohibición f, proscripción f // vt prohibir, proscribir; (*exclude*) excluir.

banal [bə'nɑːl] a banal, vulgar.

banana [bə'nɑːnə] n plátano.

band [bænd] n (*group*) banda; (*gang*) pandilla; (*strip*) faja, tira; (*at a dance*) orquesta; (*MIL*) banda; **to** ~ **together** vi juntarse, asociarse.

bandage ['bændɪdʒ] n venda, vendaje m // vt vendar.

bandit ['bændɪt] n bandido; **one-armed** ~ máquina tragaperras.

bandstand ['bændstænd] n quiosco.

bandwagon ['bændwægən] n: **to jump on the** ~ (*fig*) seguir la corriente o la moda.

bandy ['bændɪ] vt (*jokes, insults*) cambiar.

bandy-legged ['bændɪ'lɛgd] a estevado.

bang [bæŋ] n estallido; (*of door*) portazo; (*blow*) golpe m // vt hacer estallar; (*door*) cerrar de golpe // vi estallar.

banger ['bæŋə*] n (*car*: *gen*: **old** ~) chatarra.

bangle ['bæŋgl] n ajorca.

banish ['bænɪʃ] vt desterrar.

banister(s) ['bænɪstə(z)] n(pl) pasamanos m inv.

banjo ['bændʒəu], pl ~**es** or ~**s** n banjo.

bank [bæŋk] n (*COMM*) banco; (*of river, lake*) ribera, orilla; (*of earth*) terraplén m // vi (*AVIAT*) ladearse; **to** ~ **on** vt fus contar con; **to** ~ **with** tener la cuenta con; ~ **account** n cuenta de banco; ~**er** n banquero; **B**~ **holiday** n día m festivo; ~**ing** n banca; ~**note** n billete m de banco; ~ **rate** n tipo de interés bancario.

bankrupt ['bæŋkrʌpt] n quebrado/a // a quebrado, insolvente; **to go** ~ quebrar; **to be** ~ estar en quiebra; ~**cy** n quiebra; (*fraudulent*) bancarrota.

banner ['bænə*] n bandera; (*in demonstration*) pancarta.

banns [bænz] npl amonestaciones fpl.

banquet ['bæŋkwɪt] n banquete m.

baptism ['bæptɪzəm] n bautismo.

baptize [bæp'taɪz] vt bautizar.

bar [bɑː*] n barra; (*of window etc*) tranca; (*of soap*) pastilla; (*fig*: *hindrance*) obstáculo; (*prohibition*) proscripción f; (*pub*) bar m; (*counter*: *in pub*) mostrador m; (*MUS*) barra // vt (*road*) obstruir; (*window*) atrancar; (*person*) excluir; (*activity*) prohibir; **behind** ~**s** en la cárcel; **the B**~ (*LAW*) (*profession*) la abogacía; (*people*) el cuerpo de abogados; ~ **none** sin excepción.

barbaric [bɑː'bærɪk] a bárbaro.

barbarous ['bɑːbərəs] a bárbaro.

barbecue ['bɑːbɪkjuː] n barbacoa.

barbed wire ['bɑːbd-] n alambre m de púas.

barber ['bɑːbə*] n peluquero, barbero.

barbiturate [bɑː'bɪtjurɪt] n barbitúrico.

bare [bɛə*] a desnudo; (*head*) descubierto // vt desnudar; **to** ~ **one's teeth** enseñar los dientes; ~**back** ad sin montura; ~**faced** a descarado; ~**foot** a, ad descalzo; ~**ly** ad apenas.

bargain ['bɑːgɪn] n pacto, negocio; (*good buy*) ganga // vi negociar; (*haggle*) regatear; **into the** ~ además, por añadidura.

barge [bɑːdʒ] n barcaza; **to** ~ **in** vi

irrumpir, entrar sin permiso; **to ~ into** vt
fus dar contra.
baritone ['bærɪtəun] n barítono.
bark [bɑːk] n (of tree) corteza; (of dog)
ladrido // vi ladrar.
barley ['bɑːlɪ] n cebada.
barmaid ['bɑːmeɪd] n camarera.
barman ['bɑːmən] n camarero, barman m.
barmy ['bɑːmɪ] a (col) chiflado, lelo.
barn [bɑːn] n granero.
barnacle ['bɑːnəkl] n percebe m.
barometer [bə'rɔmɪtə*] n barómetro.
baron ['bærən] n barón m; **~ess** n
baronesa.
barracks ['bærəks] npl cuartel m.
barrage ['bærɑːʒ] n (MIL) descarga,
bombardeo; (dam) presa.
barrel ['bærəl] n tonel m, barril m; (of gun)
cañón m.
barren ['bærən] a estéril, árido.
barricade [bærɪ'keɪd] n barricada // vt
levantar barricadas.
barrier ['bærɪə*] n barrera.
barring ['bɑːrɪŋ] prep excepto, salvo.
barrister ['bærɪstə*] n abogado m/f.
barrow ['bærəu] n (cart) carretilla (de
mano).
bartender ['bɑːtɛndə*] n (US) camarero,
barman m.
barter ['bɑːtə*] vt: **to ~ sth for sth**
trocar algo por algo.
base [beɪs] n base f // vt: **to ~ sth on**
basar o fundar algo en // a bajo, infame;
~ball n béisbol m; **~ment** n sótano.
bash [bæʃ] vt (col) golpear.
bashful ['bæʃful] a tímido, vergonzoso.
bashing ['bæʃɪŋ] n (col) tunda.
basic ['beɪsɪk] a básico; **~ally** ad
fundamentalmente, en el fondo.
basil ['bæzl] n albahaca.
basin ['beɪsn] n (vessel) cuenco, tazón m;
(GEO) cuenca; (also: **wash~**) palangana,
jofaina.
basis ['beɪsɪs] pl **-ses** [-siːz] n base f.
bask [bɑːsk] vi: **to ~ in the sun** tomar el
sol.
basket ['bɑːskɪt] n cesta, cesto; (with
handle) canasta; **~ball** n baloncesto;
~work n cestería.
Basque [bæsk] a, n vasco/a; **~ Country**
Euskadi m, País m Vasco.
bass [beɪs] n (MUS) contrabajo.
bassoon [bə'suːn] n bajón m.
bastard ['bɑːstəd] n bastardo.
baste [beɪst] vt (CULIN) pringar.
bastion ['bæstɪən] n baluarte m.
bat [bæt] n (ZOOL) murciélago; (for ball
games) palo; (for cricket, baseball) bate m;
(for table tennis) raqueta; **he didn't ~ an
eyelid** ni pestañeó.
batch [bætʃ] n (of bread) hornada; (of
papers) colección f, lote m.
bated ['beɪtɪd] a: **with ~ breath** sin
respiración.
bath [bɑːθ, pl bɑːðz] n (~ tub) baño, bañera;
(also: **~s** pl) baño, piscina // vt bañar; **to**

have **a ~** bañarse, tomar un baño;
~chair n silla de ruedas.
bathe [beɪð] vi bañarse // vt bañar; **bather**
n bañista m/f.
bathing ['beɪðɪŋ] n el bañarse; **~ cap** n
gorro de baño; **~ costume** n traje m de
baño; **~ trunks** npl bañador m.
bath: **~mat** n estera de baño; **~room** n
(cuarto de) baño; **~s** npl piscina sg; **~
towel** n toalla de baño.
baton ['bætən] n (MUS) batuta.
battalion [bə'tælɪən] n batallón m.
batter ['bætə*] vt apalear, azotar // n
batido; **~ed** a (hat, pan) estropeado.
battery ['bætərɪ] n batería; (of torch) pila.
battle ['bætl] n batalla; (fig) lucha // vi
luchar; **~field** n campo m de batalla;
~ments npl almenas fpl; **~ship** n
acorazado.
bawdy ['bɔːdɪ] a indecente; (joke) verde.
bawl [bɔːl] vi chillar, gritar.
bay [beɪ] n (GEO) bahía; (BOT) laurel m // vi
aullar; **to hold sb at ~** mantener a
alguien a raya.
bayonet ['beɪənɪt] n bayoneta.
bay window ['beɪ-] n ventana saledizas.
bazaar [bə'zɑː*] n bazar m.
bazooka [bə'zuːkə] n bazuca.
b. & b., B. & B. abbr of **bed and
breakfast** cama y desayuno.
BBC n abbr of **British Broadcasting
Corporation.**
B.C. ad abbr of **before Christ** a. de J.C.
(antes de Jesucristo).
be [biː] pt **was, were,** pp **been** vi (of
state) ser; (of place, temporary condition)
estar; **I am English** soy inglés; **I am
tired** estoy cansado; **how are you?**
¿cómo está Usted?; **who is it?** ¿quién es?;
it is raining está lloviendo; **I am warm**
tengo calor; **it is cold** hace frío; **how
much is it?** ¿cuánto es o cuesta?; **he is
four (years old)** tiene cuatro años; **2 and
2 are 4** dos más dos son cuatro; **where
have you been?** ¿dónde has estado?, ¿de
dónde vienes?
beach [biːtʃ] n playa // vt varar.
beacon ['biːkən] n (lighthouse) faro;
(marker) guía.
bead [biːd] n cuenta, abalorio; (of sweat)
gota.
beak [biːk] n pico.
beaker ['biːkə*] n jarra.
beam [biːm] n (ARCH) viga, travesaño; (of
light) rayo, haz m de luz // vi brillar;
(smile) sonreír; **~ing** a (sun, smile)
radiante.
bean [biːn] n judía; **runner/broad ~**
habichuela/haba; **coffee ~** grano de
café.
bear [bɛə*] n oso // (vb: pt bore, pp borne)
vt (weight etc) llevar; (cost) pagar;
(responsibility) tener; (endure) soportar,
aguantar; (stand up to) resistir a; (children)
parir // vi: **to ~ right/left** torcer a la
derecha/izquierda; **~able** a soportable.
beard [bɪəd] n barba; **~ed** a barbado.

bearing ['bɛərɪŋ] *n* porte *m*, comportamiento; (*connection*) relación *f*; **(ball)** ~**s** *npl* cojinetes *mpl* a bolas; **to take a** ~ marcarse; **to find one's** ~**s** orientarse.

beast [bi:st] *n* bestia; (*col*) bruto, salvaje *m*; ~**ly** *a* bestial; (*awful*) horrible.

beat [bi:t] *n* (*of heart*) latido; (*MUS*) ritmo, compás *m*; (*of policeman*) ronda // (*vb*: *pt* **beat**, *pp* **beaten**) *vt* (*hit*) golpear; (*eggs*) batir; (*defeat*) vencer, derrotar; (*better*) sobrepasar; (*drum*) tocar; (*rhythm*) marcar // *vi* (*heart*) latir; **to** ~ **about the bush** ir por rodeos; **to** ~ **it** largarse; **to** ~ **off** *vt* rechazar; **to** ~ **up** *vt* (*col*: *person*) dar una paliza a; ~**er** *n* (*for eggs, cream*) batidora; ~**ing** *n* golpeo.

beautiful ['bju:tɪful] *a* hermoso, bello; ~**ly** *ad* maravillosamente; **beautify** [-faɪ] *vt* embellecer.

beauty ['bju:tɪ] *n* belleza, hermosura; (*person*) belleza; ~ **salon** *n* salón *m* de belleza; ~ **spot** *n* lunar *m* postizo; (*TOURISM*) lugar *m* de excepcional belleza.

beaver ['bi:və*] *n* castor *m*.

becalmed [bɪ'kɑ:md] *a* encalmado.

became [bɪ'keɪm] *pt of* **become.**

because [bɪ'kɔz] *conj* porque; ~ **of** *prep* debido a, a causa de.

beck [bɛk] *n*: **to be at the** ~ **and call of** estar a disposición de.

beckon ['bɛkən] *vt* (*also*: ~ **to**) llamar con señas.

become [bɪ'kʌm] (*irg*: *like* **come**) *vt* (*suit*) favorecer, sentar a // *vi* (+ *noun*) hacerse, llegar a ser; (+ *adj*) ponerse, volverse; **to** ~ **fat** engordarse.

becoming [bɪ'kʌmɪŋ] *a* (*behaviour*) decoroso; (*clothes*) favorecedor(a).

bed [bɛd] *n* cama; (*of flowers*) macizo; (*of coal, clay*) capa; **to go to** ~ acostarse; **single/double** ~ cama individual/matrimonial; ~**clothes** *npl* ropa *sg* de cama; ~**ding** *n* ropa de cama.

bedlam ['bɛdləm] *n* confusión *f.*

bedraggled [bɪ'drægld] *a* mojado, ensuciado.

bed: ~**ridden** *a* postrado (en cama); ~**room** *n* dormitorio, alcoba; ~**side** *n*: **at sb's** ~**side** a la cabecera de alguien; ~**sit(ter)** *n* apartamento; ~**spread** *n* sobrecama *m*, colcha.

bee [bi:] *n* abeja.

beech [bi:tʃ] *n* haya.

beef [bi:f] *n* carne *f* de vaca; **roast** ~ rosbif *m.*

bee: ~**hive** *n* colmena; ~**line** *n*: **to make a** ~**line for** ir derecho a.

been [bi:n] *pp of* **be.**

beer [bɪə*] *n* cerveza.

beetle ['bi:tl] *n* escarabajo.

beetroot ['bi:tru:t] *n* remolacha.

before [bɪ'fɔ:*] *prep* (*of time*) antes de; (*of space*) delante de // *conj* antes (de) que // *ad* (*time*) antes, anteriormente; (*space*) delante, adelante; **the week** ~ la semana

anterior; **I've never seen it** ~ no lo he visto nunca.

befriend [bɪ'frɛnd] *vt* ofrecer amistad a, ayudar.

beg [bɛg] *vi* pedir, rogar; (*as beggar*) pedir limosna // *vt* pedir, rogar; (*entreat*) suplicar.

began [bɪ'gæn] *pt of* **begin.**

beggar ['bɛgə*] *n* mendigo.

begin [bɪ'gɪn], *pt* **began**, *pp* **begun** *vt*, *vi* empezar, comenzar; ~**ner** *n* principiante *m/f*; ~**ning** *n* principio, comienzo.

begrudge [bɪ'grʌdʒ] *vt*: **to** ~ **sb sth** tenerle envidia a alguien por algo.

begun [bɪ'gʌn] *pp of* **begin.**

behalf [bɪ'hɑ:f] *n*: **on** ~ **of** en nombre de, por.

behave [bɪ'heɪv] *vi* (*person*) portarse, comportarse; (*thing*) funcionar; (*well*: *also*: ~ **o.s.**) portarse bien; **behaviour, behavior** (*US*) *n* comportamiento, conducta.

behind [bɪ'haɪnd] *prep* detrás de // *ad* detrás, por detrás, atrás // *n* trasero; ~ **time** atrasado.

behold [bɪ'həuld] (*irg*: *like* **hold**) *vt* contemplar.

beige [beɪʒ] *a* beige.

being ['bi:ɪŋ] *n* ser *m*; **to come into** ~ nacer, aparecer.

belated [bɪ'leɪtɪd] *a* atrasado, tardío.

belch [bɛltʃ] *vi* eructar // *vt* (*gen*: ~ **out**: *smoke etc*) arrojar.

belfry ['bɛlfrɪ] *n* campanario.

Belgian ['bɛldʒən] *a*, *n* belga *m/f.*

Belgium ['bɛldʒəm] *n* Bélgica.

belie [bɪ'laɪ] *vt* desmentir, contradecir.

belief [bɪ'li:f] *n* (*opinion*) opinión *f*; (*trust, faith*) fe *f*; (*acceptance as true*) creencia.

believable [bɪ'li:vəbl] *a* creíble.

believe [bɪ'li:v] *vt*, *vi* creer; **believer** *n* creyente *m/f*, fiel *m/f*; (*POL*) partidario/a.

belittle [bɪ'lɪtl] *vt* minimizar, despreciar.

bell [bɛl] *n* campana; (*small*) campanilla; (*on door*) timbre *m*; (*animal's*) cencerro; (*on toy etc*) cascabel *m.*

belligerent [bɪ'lɪdʒərənt] *a* (*at war*) beligerante; (*fig*) agresivo.

bellow ['bɛləu] *vi* bramar; (*person*) rugir // *vt* (*orders*) gritar, vociferar.

bellows ['bɛləuz] *npl* fuelle *m.*

belly ['bɛlɪ] *n* barriga, panza.

belong [bɪ'lɔŋ] *vi*: **to** ~ **to** pertenecer a; (*club etc*) ser socio de; ~**ings** *npl* pertenencias *fpl.*

beloved [bɪ'lʌvɪd] *a*, *n* querido/a, amado/a.

below [bɪ'ləu] *prep* bajo, debajo de // *ad* abajo, (por) debajo; **see** ~ véase más abajo.

belt [bɛlt] *n* cinturón *m*; (*MED*) faja; (*TECH*) correa, cinta // *vt* (*thrash*) golpear con correa.

bench [bɛntʃ] *n* banco; **the B~** (*LAW*) tribunal *m*; (*people*) judicatura.

bend [bɛnd], *pt*, *pp* **bent** *vt* doblar, inclinar;

(*leg, arm*) torcer // *vi* doblarse, inclinarse // *n* (*in road*) recodo, vuelta; (*in pipe, river*) ángulo, curva; **to ~ down** *vi* inclinar, doblar; **to ~ over** *vi* inclinarse.

beneath [bɪ'niːθ] *prep* bajo, debajo de; (*unworthy of*) indigno de // *ad* abajo, (por) debajo.

benefactor ['bɛnɪfæktə*] *n* bienhechor *m*.

beneficial [bɛnɪ'fɪʃəl] *a* provechoso, benéficioso.

benefit ['bɛnɪfɪt] *n* beneficio, provecho; (*profit*) utilidad *f*; (*money*) subsidio // *vt* beneficiar, aprovechar // *vi*: **he'll ~ from it** le sacará provecho.

Benelux ['bɛnɪlʌks] *n* Benelux *m*.

benevolent [bɪ'nɛvələnt] *a* benévolo.

bent [bɛnt] *pt, pp of* **bend** // *n* inclinación *f* // *a*: **to be ~ on** estar empeñado en.

bequeath [bɪ'kwiːð] *vt* legar.

bequest [bɪ'kwɛst] *n* legado.

bereaved [bɪ'riːvd] *n*: **the ~** los afligidos *mpl*; **bereavement** [-'riːvmənt] *n* aflicción *f*.

beret ['bɛreɪ] *n* boina.

berry ['bɛrɪ] *n* baya.

berserk [bə'səːk] *a*: **to go ~** perder los estribos.

berth [bəːθ] *n* (*bed*) litera; (*cabin*) camarote *m*; (*for ship*) amarradero // *vi* atracar, amarrar.

beseech [bɪ'siːtʃ], *pt, pp* **besought** [-'sɔːt] *vt* suplicar.

beset [bɪ'sɛt], *pt, pp* **beset** *vt* rodear; (*person*) acosar.

beside [bɪ'saɪd] *prep* junto a, al lado de; **to be ~ o.s. (with anger)** estar fuera de sí.

besides [bɪ'saɪdz] *ad* además // *prep* (*as well as*) además de; (*except*) fuera de, excepto.

besiege [bɪ'siːdʒ] *vt* (*town*) sitiar; (*fig*) asediar.

best [bɛst] *a* (el/la) mejor // *ad* (lo) mejor; **the ~ part of** (*quantity*) la mayor parte de; **at ~** en el mejor de los casos; **to make the ~ of sth** sacar el mejor partido de algo; **to the ~ of my knowledge** que yo sepa; **to the ~ of my ability** como mejor puedo; **~ man** *n* padrino de boda.

bestow [bɪ'stəu] *vt* otorgar; (*affection*) ofrecer.

bestseller ['bɛst'sɛlə*] *n* éxito de librería, bestseller *m*.

bet [bɛt] *n* apuesta // *vt, vi, pt, pp* **bet** *or* **betted** apostar, jugar.

betray [bɪ'treɪ] *vt* traicionar; (*denounce*) delatar; **~al** *n* traición *f*.

better ['bɛtə*] *a* mejor // *ad* mejor // *vt* mejorar; (*go above*) superar // *n*: **to get the ~ of** quedar por encima de alguien; **you had ~ do it** más vale que lo haga; **he thought ~ of it** cambió de parecer; **to get ~** mejorar(se); (MED) reponerse; **~ off** *a* más acomodado.

betting ['bɛtɪŋ] *n* juego, el apostar; **~ shop** *n* agencia de apuestas.

between [bɪ'twiːn] *prep* entre // *ad* en medio.

beverage ['bɛvərɪdʒ] *n* bebida.

bevy ['bɛvɪ] *n*: **a ~ of** una bandada de.

beware [bɪ'wɛə*] *vi*: **to ~ (of)** precaverse de, tener cuidado con // *excl* ¡cuidado!

bewildered [bɪ'wɪldəd] *a* aturdido, perplejo.

bewitching [bɪ'wɪtʃɪŋ] *a* hechicero, encantador(a).

beyond [bɪ'jɔnd] *prep* (*in space*) más allá de; (*exceeding*) además de, fuera de; (*above*) superior a // *ad* más allá, más lejos; **~ doubt** fuera de toda duda; **~ repair** irreparable.

bias ['baɪəs] *n* (*prejudice*) prejuicio, pasión *f*; (*preference*) predisposición *f*; **~(s)ed** *a* (*against*) con prejuicios; (*towards*) partidario.

bib [bɪb] *n* babero.

Bible ['baɪbl] *n* Biblia.

bibliography [bɪblɪ'ɔgrəfɪ] *n* bibliografía.

bicker ['bɪkə*] *vi* reñir.

bicycle ['baɪsɪkl] *n* bicicleta.

bid [bɪd] *n* (*at auction*) oferta, postura; (*attempt*) tentativa, conato // (*vb*: *pt* **bade** [bæd] *or* **bid**, *pp* **bidden** ['bɪdn] *or* **bid**) *vi* hacer una oferta // *vt* mandar, ordenar; **to ~ sb good day** dar a uno los buenos días; **~der** *n*: **the highest ~der** el mejor postor; **~ding** *n* (*at auction*) ofertas *fpl*; (*order*) orden *f*, mandato.

bide [baɪd] *vt*: **to ~ one's time** esperar el momento adecuado.

bidet ['biːdeɪ] *n* bidet *m*.

bier [bɪə*] *n* féretro.

big [bɪg] *a* grande.

bigamy ['bɪgəmɪ] *n* bigamia.

bigheaded ['bɪg'hɛdɪd] *a* engreído.

bigot ['bɪgət] *n* fanático, intolerante *m/f*; **~ed** *a* fanático, intolerante; **~ry** *n* fanatismo, intolerancia.

bike [baɪk] *n* bici *f*.

bikini [bɪ'kiːnɪ] *n* bikini *m*.

bile [baɪl] *n* bilis *f*.

bilingual [baɪ'lɪŋgwəl] *a* bilingüe.

bill [bɪl] *n* (*account*) cuenta; (*invoice*) factura; (POL) proyecto de ley; (*US*: *banknote*) billete *m*; (*of bird*) pico; **stick no ~s** prohibido fijar carteles.

billet ['bɪlɪt] *n* alojamiento.

billfold ['bɪlfəuld] *n* (*US*) cartera.

billiards ['bɪlɪədz] *n* billar *m*.

billion ['bɪliən] *n* (*Brit*) billón *m*; (*US*) mil millones.

billy goat ['bɪlɪ-] *n* macho cabrío.

bin [bɪn] *n* (*gen*) cubo; **bread/litter ~** nasa/papelera.

bind [baɪnd], *pt, pp* **bound** *vt* atar, liar; (*wound*) vendar; (*book*) encuadernar; (*oblige*) obligar; **~ing** *a* (*contract*) obligatorio.

binge [bɪndʒ] *n* borrachera, juerga.

bingo ['bɪŋgəu] *n* bingo *m*.

binoculars [bɪ'nɔkjuləz] *npl* gemelos *mpl*, prismáticos *mpl*.

bio... [baɪɔ] *pref*: ~**chemistry** *n* bioquímica; ~**graphy** [baɪ'ɔgrəfɪ] *n* biografía; ~**logical** *a* biológico; ~**logy** [baɪ'ɔlədʒɪ] *n* biología.
birch [bɔ:tʃ] *n* abedul *m*; (*cane*) vara.
bird [bɔ:d] *n* ave *f*, pájaro; (*col: girl*) chica; ~**cage** *n* jaula; ~**'s eye view** *n* vista de pájaro; ~ **watcher** *n* ornitólogo.
birth [bɔ:θ] *n* nacimiento; (*MED*) parto; **to give** ~ **to** parir, dar a luz; ~ **certificate** *n* partida de nacimiento; ~ **control** *n* control *m* de natalidad; (*methods*) métodos *mpl* anticonceptivos; ~**day** *n* cumpleaños *m*; ~**place** *n* lugar *m* de nacimiento; ~**rate** *n* (tasa de) natalidad *f*.
biscuit ['bɪskɪt] *n* galleta.
bisect [baɪ'sɛkt] *vt* bisecar.
bishop ['bɪʃəp] *n* obispo.
bit [bɪt] *pt of* **bite** // *n* trozo, pedazo, pedacito; (*of horse*) freno, bocado; **a** ~ **of** un poco de; **a** ~ **mad** algo loco; ~ **by** ~ poco a poco.
bitch [bɪtʃ] *n* (*dog*) perra.
bite [baɪt], *pt* **bit**, *pp* **bitten** *vt, vi* morder; (*insect etc*) picar // *n* mordedura; (*insect* ~) picadura; (*mouthful*) bocado; **let's have a** ~ **(to eat)** comamos algo.
biting ['baɪtɪŋ] *a* penetrante, cortante; (*sharp*) mordaz.
bitten ['bɪtn] *pp of* **bite**.
bitter ['bɪtə*] *a* amargo; (*wind, criticism*) cortante, penetrante; (*battle*) encarnizado // *n* (*beer*) cerveza clara; ~**ness** *n* amargura; (*anger*) rencor *m*.
bizarre [bɪ'za:*] *a* raro, estrafalario.
blab [blæb] *vi* chismear, soplar // *vt* (*also*: ~ **out**) revelar, contar.
black [blæk] *a* (*colour*) negro; (*dark*) oscuro // *n* negro; (*colour*) color *m* negro // *vt* (*shoes*) lustrar; (*INDUSTRY*) boicotear; **to give sb a** ~ **eye** darle a uno una bofetada (en el ojo); ~ **and blue** *a* amoratado; ~**berry** *n* zarzamora; ~**bird** *n* mirlo; ~**board** *n* pizarra; ~**currant** *n* grosella negra; ~**en** *vt* ennegrecer; (*fig*) denigrar; ~**leg** *n* esquirol *m*, rompehuelgas *m inv*; ~**list** *n* lista negra; ~**mail** *n* chantaje *m* // *vt* chantajear; ~**mailer** *n* chantajista *m/f*; ~ **market** *n* mercado negro; ~**out** *n* apagón *m*; (*fainting*) desmayo, pérdida de conocimiento; ~**smith** *n* herrero.
bladder ['blædə*] *n* vejiga.
blade [bleɪd] *n* hoja; (*cutting edge*) filo; **a** ~ **of grass** una brizna de hierba.
blame [bleɪm] *n* culpa // *vt*: **to** ~ **sb for sth** echar a uno la culpa de algo; **to be to** ~ tener la culpa de; ~**less** *a* (*person*) inocente.
bland [blænd] *a* suave; (*taste*) soso.
blank [blæŋk] *a* en blanco; (*shot*) sin bala; (*look*) sin expresión // *n* blanco, espacio en blanco; cartucho sin bala *o* de fogueo.
blanket ['blæŋkɪt] *n* manta // *vt* envolver.
blare [blɛə*] *vi* (*brass band, horns, radio*) resonar.
blasé ['bla:zeɪ] *a* hastiado.

blasphemy ['blæsfɪmɪ] *n* blasfemia.
blast [bla:st] *n* (*of wind*) ráfaga, soplo; (*of whistle*) toque *m*; (*of explosive*) carga explosiva; (*force*) choque *m* // *vt* (*blow up*) volar; (*blow open*) abrir con carga explosiva; ~**off** *n* (*SPACE*) lanzamiento.
blatant ['bleɪtənt] *a* descarado.
blaze [bleɪz] *n* (*fire*) fuego; (*flames*) llamarada; (*fig*) arranque *m* // *vi* (*fire*) arder en llamas; (*fig*) brillar // *vt*: **to** ~ **a trail** (*fig*) abrir (un) camino.
blazer ['bleɪzə*] *n* chaqueta ligera.
bleach [bli:tʃ] *n* (*also*: **household** ~) lejía // *vt* (*linen*) blanquear; ~**ed** *a* (*hair*) decolorado.
bleak [bli:k] *a* (*countryside*) desierto; (*prospect*) poco prometedor(a).
bleary-eyed ['blɪərɪ'aɪd] *a* de ojos legañosos.
bleat [bli:t] *vi* balar.
bleed [bli:d], *pt, pp* **bled** [blɛd] *vt, vi* sangrar.
blemish ['blɛmɪʃ] *n* mancha, tacha.
blend [blɛnd] *n* mezcla // *vt* mezclar // *vi* (*colours etc*) combinarse, mezclarse.
bless [blɛs], *pt, pp* **blessed** *or* **blest** [blɛst] *vt* bendecir; ~**ing** *n* bendición *f*; (*advantage*) beneficio, ventaja.
blew [blu:] *pt of* **blow**.
blight [blaɪt] *vt* (*hopes etc*) frustrar, arruinar.
blimey ['blaɪmɪ] *excl* (*col*) ¡caray!
blind [blaɪnd] *a* ciego // *n* (*for window*) persiana // *vt* cegar; (*dazzle*) deslumbrar; ~ **alley** *n* callejón *m* sin salida; ~ **corner** *n* esquina escondida; ~**fold** *n* venda // *a, ad* con los ojos vendados // *vt* vendar los ojos a; ~**ly** *ad* a ciegas, ciegamente; ~**ness** *n* ceguera; ~ **spot** *n* mácula.
blink [blɪŋk] *vi* parpadear, pestañear; (*light*) oscilar; ~**ers** *npl* anteojeras *fpl*.
blinking ['blɪŋkɪŋ] *a* (*col*): **this** ~**...** este condenado... .
bliss [blɪs] *n* felicidad *f*; (*fig*) éxtasis *m*.
blister ['blɪstə*] *n* (*on skin*) ampolla // *vi* (*paint*) ampollarse; ~**ing** *a* (*heat*) abrasador(a).
blithe [blaɪð] *a* alegre.
blithering ['blɪðərɪŋ] *a* (*col*): **this** ~ **idiot** este tonto perdido.
blitz [blɪts] *n* bombardeo aéreo.
blizzard ['blɪzəd] *n* ventisca.
bloated ['bləutɪd] *a* hinchado.
blob [blɔb] *n* (*drop*) gota; (*stain, spot*) mancha.
block [blɔk] *n* bloque *m*; (*in pipes*) obstáculo; (*of buildings*) manzana // *vt* (*gen*) obstruir, cerrar; (*progress*) estorbar; ~**ade** [-'keɪd] *n* bloqueo // *vt* bloquear; ~**age** *n* estorbo, obstrucción *f*; ~ **of flats** *n* bloque *m* de pisos; ~ **letters** *npl* letras *fpl* de molde.
bloke [bləuk] *n* (*col*) tipo, tío.
blond(e) [blɔnd] *a, n* rubio/a.
blood [blʌd] *n* sangre *f*; ~ **donor** *n*

donador/a *m/f* de sangre; ~ **group** *n* grupo sanguíneo; ~ **hound** *n* sabueso; ~ **pressure** *n* presión *f* sanguínea; ~**shed** *n* matanza; ~**shot** a inyectado en sangre; ~**stained** a manchado de sangre; ~**stream** *n* corriente *f* sanguínea; ~**thirsty** a sanguinario; ~ **transfusion** *n* transfusión *f* de sangre; ~**y** a sangriento; (*col!*): **this** ~**y...** este condenado/puñetero...; ~**y strong/ good** (*col!*) terriblemente fuerte/ bueno; ~**y-minded** a (*col*) malintencionado.

bloom [blu:m] *n* floración *f*; (*fig*) perfección *f*, plenitud *f* // *vi* florecer; ~**ing** a (*col*): **this** ~**ing...** este condenado... .

blossom ['blɔsəm] *n* flor *f* // *vi* florecer; (*fig*) desarrollarse.

blot [blɔt] *n* borrón *m* // *vt* secar; (*ink*) manchar; **to** ~ **out** *vt* (*view*) oscurecer, hacer desaparecer.

blotchy ['blɔtʃi] a (*complexion*) enrojecido, lleno de manchas.

blotting paper ['blɔtɪŋ-] *n* papel *m* secante.

blouse [blauz] *n* blusa.

blow [blau] *n* golpe *m* // (*vb: pt* **blew,** *pp* **blown** [blaun]) *vi* soplar // *vt* (*glass*) soplar; (*fuse*) quemar; (*instrument*) tocar; **to** ~ **one's nose** sonarse; **to** ~ **away** *vt* llevarse, arrancar; **to** ~ **down** *vt* derribar; **to** ~ **off** *vt* arrebatar; **to** ~ **out** *vi* apagarse; **to** ~ **over** *vi* pasar, quedar olvidado; **to** ~ **up** *vi* estallar // *vt* volar; (*tyre*) inflar; (*PHOT*) ampliar; ~**lamp** *n* soplete *m*, lámpara de soldar; ~**-out** *n* (*of tyre*) pinchazo.

blubber ['blʌbə*] *n* grasa de ballena // *vi* (*pej*) lloriquear.

blue [blu:] a azul; ~ **film/joke** film/chiste verde; **to have the** ~**s** estar melancólico; ~**bell** *n* campanilla, campánula azul; ~**bottle** *n* moscarda, mosca azul; ~ **jeans** *npl* bluejean *m inv*, vaqueros *mpl*; ~**print** *n* (*fig*) anteproyecto.

bluff [blʌf] *vi* hacer un bluff, farolear // *n* bluff *m*, farol *m*.

blunder ['blʌndə*] *n* error *m* garrafal, metedura de pata // *vi* cometer un error, meter la pata.

blunt [blʌnt] a embotado, desafilado; (*person*) franco, directo // *vt* embotar, desafilar; ~**ness** *n* (*of person*) franqueza, brusquedad *f*.

blur [blə:*] *n* aspecto borroso // *vt* hacer borroso, desdibujar.

blurt [blə:t]: ~ **out** *vt* (*say*) descolgarse con, dejar escapar.

blush [blʌʃ] *vi* ruborizarse, ponerse colorado // *n* rubor *m*.

blustering ['blʌstərɪŋ] a (*person*) fanfarrón(ona).

blustery ['blʌstəri] a (*weather*) tempestuoso, tormentoso.

board [bɔ:d] *n* tabla, tablero; (*on wall*) tablón *m*; (*for chess etc*) tablero; (*committee*) junta, consejo; (*in firm*) mesa *o* junta

directiva // *vt* (*ship*) embarcarse en; (*train*) subir a; **full** ~ pensión *f* completa; **to go by the** ~ (*fig*) ser abandonado/olvidado; **to** ~ **up** *vt* (*door*) entablar, enmaderar; ~ **and lodging** *n* pensión *f*; ~**er** *n* huésped/a *m/f*; (*SCOL*) interno; ~**ing house** *n* casa de huéspedes; ~**ing school** *n* internado; ~ **room** *n* sala de juntas.

boast [bəust] *vi* jactarse, presumir // *vt* ostentar // *n* alarde *m*, baladronada; ~**ful** a presumido, jactancioso.

boat [bəut] *n* barco, buque *m*; (*small*) barca, bote *m*; ~**er** *n* (*hat*) sombrero de paja; ~**ing** *n* canotaje *m*; ~**man** *n* barquero; ~**swain** ['bəusn] *n* contramaestre *m*.

bob [bɔb] *vi* (*boat, cork on water: also*: ~ **up and down**) menearse, balancearse; **to** ~ **up** *vi* aparecer, levantarse // *n* (*col*) = **shilling.**

bobbin ['bɔbɪn] *n* (*of sewing machine*) carrete *m*, bobina.

bobby ['bɔbi] *n* (*col*) poli *m/f.*

bobsleigh ['bɔbslei] *n* bob *m.*

bodice ['bɔdɪs] *n* corpiño.

bodily ['bɔdɪlɪ] a corpóreo, corporal // ad (*in person*) en persona; (*lift*) en peso.

body ['bɔdi] *n* cuerpo; (*corpse*) cadáver *m*; (*of car*) caja, carrocería; (*fig: society*) conjunto; (*fig: quantity*) parte *f* principal; **in a** ~ en bloque, en conjunto; ~**guard** *n* guardaespaldas *m inv*; ~**work** *n* carrocería.

bog [bɔg] *n* pantano, ciénaga // *vt*: **to get** ~**ged down** (*fig*) empantanarse, atascarse.

boggle ['bɔgl] *vi*: **the mind** ~**s** le deja boquiabierto a uno.

bogus ['bəugəs] a falso, fraudulento; (*person*) fingido.

boil [bɔil] *vt* cocer; (*eggs*) pasar por agua // *vi* hervir // *n* (*MED*) furúnculo, divieso; **to come to the** ~ comenzar a hervir; **to** ~ **down to** (*fig*) reducirse a; ~**er** *n* caldera; ~**er suit** *n* mono; ~**ing point** *n* punto de ebullición *f.*

boisterous ['bɔistərəs] a (*noisy*) bullicioso; (*excitable*) exuberante; (*crowd*) tumultuoso.

bold [bəuld] a (*brave*) valiente, audaz; (*excessively*) atrevido; (*pej*) descarado; (*outline, colour*) fuerte; ~**ness** *n* valor *m*, audacia; (*cheek*) descaro.

Bolivia [bə'lɪviə] *n* Bolivia.

bollard ['bɔləd] *n* (*AUT*) poste *m.*

bolster ['bəulstə*] *n* travesero, cabezal *m*; **to** ~ **up** *vt* reforzar; (*fig*) alentar.

bolt [bəult] *n* (*lock*) cerrojo; (*with nut*) perno, tornillo // *vt* (*door*) echar el cerrojo a; (*food*) engullir // *vi* fugarse; (*horse*) desbocarse.

bomb [bɔm] *n* bomba // *vt* bombardear; ~**ard** [-'bɑ:d] *vt* bombardear; (*fig*) asediar; ~**ardment** [-'bɑ:dmənt] *n* bombardeo.

bombastic [bɔm'bæstɪk] a rimbombante; (*person*) farolero.
bomb: ~ **disposal** n desmontaje m de explosivos; ~**er** n (*AVIAT*) bombardero; ~**shell** n obús m, granada; (*fig*) bomba.
bona fide ['bəunə'faɪdɪ] a genuino, auténtico.
bond [bɔnd] n (*binding promise*) fianza; (*FINANCE*) bono; (*link*) vínculo, lazo.
bondage [bɔndɪdʒ] n esclavitud f.
bone [bəun] n hueso; (*of fish*) espina // vt deshuesar; quitar las espinas a; ~-**dry** a completamente seco; ~ **idle** a gandul.
bonfire ['bɔnfaɪə*] n hoguera, fogata.
bonnet ['bɔnɪt] n gorra; (*Brit: of car*) capó m.
bonus ['bəunəs] n sobrepaga, prima.
bony ['bəunɪ] a (*arm, face*, MED. *tissue*) huesudo; (*meat*) lleno de huesos; (*fish*) lleno de espinas.
boo [buː] vt abuchear, rechiflar.
booby trap ['buːbɪ-] n trampa explosiva.
book [buk] n libro; (*notebook*) libreta; (*of stamps etc*) librito; (*COMM*): ~**s** las cuentas, el balance // vt (*ticket*) sacar; (*seat, room*) reservar; (*driver*) fichar; ~**case** n librería, estante m para libros; ~**ing office** n (*RAIL*) despacho de billetes; (*THEATRE*) taquilla; ~-**keeping** n teneduría de libros; ~**let** n folleto; ~**maker** n corredor m de apuestas; ~**seller** n librero; ~**shop** n librería; ~**stall** n quiosco de libros.
boom [buːm] n (*noise*) trueno, estampido; (*in prices etc*) alza rápida; (*ECON*) boom m, prosperidad f repentina.
boomerang ['buːməræŋ] n bumerang m.
boon [buːn] n favor m, beneficio.
boost [buːst] n estímulo, empuje m // vt estimular, empujar; ~**er** n (*MED*) reinyección f.
boot [buːt] n bota; (*Brit: of car*) maleta, maletero // vt dar un puntapié a; **to** ~ (*in addition*) además, por añadidura.
booth [buːð] n (*at fair*) barraca; (*telephone* ~, *voting* ~) cabina.
booty ['buːtɪ] n botín m.
booze [buːz] (*col*) n bebida, trago // vi emborracharse.
border ['bɔːdə*] n borde m, margen m, orilla; (*of a country*) frontera // a fronterizo; **the B**~**s** región fronteriza entre Escocia e Inglaterra; **to** ~ **on** vt fus lindar con; (*fig*) rayar en; ~**line** n (*fig*) frontera.
bore [bɔː*] pt of **bear** // vt (*hole*) taladrar, agujerear; (*person*) aburrir // n (*person*) pelmazo, pesado; (*of gun*) calibre m; ~**dom** n aburrimiento.
boring ['bɔːrɪŋ] a aburrido.
born [bɔːn] a: **to be** ~ nacer; **I was** ~ **in 1960** nací en 1960.
borne [bɔːn] pp of **bear.**
borough ['bʌrə] n municipio.
borrow ['bɔrəu] vt: **to** ~ **sth (from sb)** pedir algo prestado a alguien.
borstal ['bɔːstl] n reformatorio (de menores).

bosom ['buzəm] n pecho; (*fig*) seno; ~ **friend** n amigo del alma o íntimo.
boss [bɔs] n jefe m; (*employer*) patrón/ona m/f; (*political etc*) cacique m // vt regentar, dar órdenes a; ~**y** a mandón(ona).
bosun ['bəusn] n contramaestre m.
botanist ['bɔtənɪst] n botanista m/f; **botany** [-nɪ] n botánica.
botch [bɔtʃ] vt (*also*: ~ **up**) arruinar, estropear.
both [bəuθ] a, pron ambos(as), los dos; ~ **of us went, we** ~ **went** fuimos los dos, ambos fuimos // ad: ~ **A and B** tanto A como B.
bother ['bɔðə*] vt (*worry*) preocupar; (*disturb*) molestar, fastidiar // vi (*gen*: ~ **o.s.**) molestarse; **to** ~ **doing** tomarse la molestia de hacer // n: **what a** ~! ¡qué lata!
bottle ['bɔtl] n botella; (*small*) frasco; (*baby's*) biberón m // vt embotellar; **to** ~ **up** vt embotellar, contener; ~**neck** n embotellamiento; ~-**opener** n destapador m, abrebotellas m inv.
bottom ['bɔtəm] n (*of box, sea*) fondo; (*buttocks*) trasero, culo; (*of page, list*) pie m // a (*low*) inferior, más bajo; (*last*) último; ~**less** a sin fondo, insondable.
bough [bau] n rama.
bought [bɔːt] pt, pp of **buy.**
boulder ['bəuldə*] n canto rodado.
bounce [bauns] vi (*ball*) (re)botar; (*cheque*) ser rechazado o incobrable // vt hacer (re)botar // n (*rebound*) (re)bote m.
bound [baund] pt, pp of **bind** // n (*leap*) salto; (*gen pl: limit*) límite m // vi (*leap*) saltar // a: ~ **by** (*limited by*) rodeado de, confinado con; **to be** ~ **to do sth** (*obliged*) tener el deber de hacer algo; (*likely*) estar seguro de hacer algo; **out of** ~**s** prohibido el paso; ~ **for** con destino a.
boundary ['baundrɪ] n límite m, lindero.
boundless ['baundlɪs] a ilimitado.
bouquet ['bukeɪ] n (*of flowers*) ramo; (*of wine*) aroma m.
bout [baut] n (*of malaria etc*) ataque m; (*BOXING etc*) combate m, encuentro.
bow [bəu] n (*knot*) lazo; (*weapon, MUS*) arco // n [bau] (*of the head*) reverencia; (*NAUT*) proa // vi [bau] inclinarse, hacer una reverencia; (*yield*): **to** ~ **to** or **before** ceder ante, someterse a.
bowels [bauəlz] npl intestinos mpl, vientre m.
bowl [bəul] n tazón m, cuenco; (*for washing*) palangana, jofaina; (*ball*) bola // vi (*CRICKET*) arrojar la pelota; ~**s** n juego de las bochas, bolos mpl.
bow-legged ['bəulɛgɪd] a estevado.
bowler ['bəulə*] n (*CRICKET*) lanzador m (de la pelota); (*also*: ~ **hat**) hongo, bombín m.
bowling ['bəulɪŋ] n (*game*) bochas fpl, bolos mpl; ~ **alley** n bolera; ~ **green** n pista para bochas.

bow tie ['bəu-] *n* corbata de lazo.
box [bɔks] *n* (*also*: **cardboard** ~) caja, cajón *m*; (*for jewels*) estuche *m*; (*for money*) cofre *m*; (*THEATRE*) palco // *vt* encajonar // *vi* (*SPORT*) boxear; ~**er** *n* (*person*) boxeador *m*; (*dog*) boxer *m*; ~**ing** *n* (*SPORT*) boxeo; **B**~**ing Day** *n Día de San Esteban, 26 de diciembre*; ~**ing gloves** *npl* guantes *mpl* de boxeo; ~**ing ring** *n* ring *m*, cuadrilátero; ~ **office** *n* taquilla; ~**room** *n* trastero.
boy [bɔɪ] *n* (*young*) niño; (*older*) muchacho; (*servant*) criado.
boycott ['bɔɪkɔt] *n* boicot *m* // *vt* boicotear.
boyfriend ['bɔɪfrɛnd] *n* novio.
boyish ['bɔɪʃ] *a* muchachil.
B.R. *abbr of* **British Rail.**
bra [brɑ:] *n* sostén *m*.
brace [breɪs] *n* refuerzo, abrazadera; (*on teeth*) aparato; (*tool*) berbiquí *m* // *vt* asegurar, reforzar; ~**s** *npl* tirantes *mpl*; **to ~ o.s.** (*fig*) fortalecer el ánimo.
bracelet ['breɪslɪt] *n* pulsera, brazalete *m*.
bracing ['breɪsɪŋ] *a* vigorizante, tónico.
bracken ['brækən] *n* helecho.
bracket ['brækɪt] *n* (*TECH*) soporte *m*, puntal *m*; (*group*) clase *f*, categoría; (*also*: **brace** ~) soporte *m*, abrazadera; (*also*: **round** ~) paréntesis *m inv*; (*gen*: **square** ~) corchete *m* // *vt* (*group*) agrupar.
brag [bræg] *vi* jactarse.
braid [breɪd] *n* (*trimming*) galón *m*; (*of hair*) trenza.
Braille [breɪl] *n* Braille *m*.
brain [breɪn] *n* cerebro; ~**s** *npl* sesos *mpl*; ~**child** *n* parto del ingenio; ~**wash** *vt* lavar el cerebro a; ~**wave** *n* idea luminosa; ~**y** *a* muy listo o inteligente.
braise [breɪz] *vt* cocer a fuego lento.
brake [breɪk] *n* (*on vehicle*) freno // *vt, vi* frenar; ~ **drum** *n* tambor *m* de freno; ~ **fluid** *n* líquido para freno.
bramble ['bræmbl] *n* zarza.
branch [brɑ:ntʃ] *n* rama; (*fig*) ramo; (*road*) ramal *m*; (*COMM*) sucursal *f* // *vi* (*also*: ~ **out**) ramificarse; (: *fig*) extenderse.
brand [brænd] *n* marca; (*iron*) hierro de marcar // *vt* (*cattle*) marcar con hierro candente.
brandish ['brændɪʃ] *vt* blandir.
brand-new ['brænd'nju:] *a* flamante, completamente nuevo.
brandy ['brændɪ] *n* coñac *m*, brandy *m*.
brash [bræʃ] *a* (*rough*) tosco; (*cheeky*) descarado.
brass [brɑ:s] *n* latón *m*; ~ **band** *n* banda de metal.
brassière ['bræsɪə*] *n* sostén *m*.
brat [bræt] *n* (*pej*) mocoso.
bravado [brə'vɑ:dəu] *n* baladronada.
brave [breɪv] *a* valiente, valeroso // *vt* valiente *m* // *vt* (*challenge*) desafiar; (*resist*) aguantar; ~**ry** *n* valor *m*, valentía.
brawl [brɔ:l] *n* pendencia, reyerta // *vi* pelearse.

brawn [brɔ:n] *n* fuerza; (*meat*) carne *f* en gelatina; ~**y** *a* fornido, musculoso.
bray [breɪ] *n* rebuzno // *vi* rebuznar.
brazen ['breɪzn] *a* descarado, cínico // *vt*: **to ~ it out** defenderse con descaro.
brazier ['breɪzɪə*] *n* brasero.
Brazil [brə'zɪl] *n* (el) Brasil; ~**ian** *a, n* brasileño/a.
breach [bri:tʃ] *vt* abrir brecha en // *n* (*gap*) brecha; (*breaking*): ~ **of contract** infracción *f* de contrato; ~ **of the peace** perturbación *f* del órden público.
bread [brɛd] *n* pan *m*; ~ **and butter** *n* pan *m* con mantequilla; (*fig*) pan (de cada día) // *a* común y corriente; ~**crumbs** *npl* migajas *fpl*; (*CULIN*) pan molido.
breadth [brɛtθ] *n* anchura; (*fig*) amplitud *f*.
breadwinner ['brɛdwɪnə*] *n* sostén *m* de la familia.
break [breɪk] *pt* **broke**, *pp* **broken** *vt* (*gen*) romper; (*promise*) faltar a; (*fall*) amortiguar; (*journey*) interrumpir; (*law*) violar, infringir; (*record*) batir; (*news*) comunicar // *vi* romperse, quebrarse; (*storm*) estallar // *n* (*gap*) abertura; (*crack*) grieta; (*fracture*) fractura; (*breakdown*) ruptura, rompimiento; (*rest*) descanso; (*time*) intérvalo; (: *at school*) (período de) recreo; (*chance*) oportunidad *f*; (*escape*) evasión *f*, fuga; **to ~ down** *vt* (*figures, data*) analizar, descomponer; (*undermine*) acabar con // *vi* estropearse; (*MED*) sufrir un colapso; (*AUT*) averiarse; (*person*) romper a llorar; **to ~ even** *vi* salir sin ganar ni perder; **to ~ free** *or* **loose** *vi* abrirse paso; **to ~ in** *vt* (*horse etc*) domar // *vi* (*burglar*) forzar una entrada; **to ~ into** *vt fus* (*house*) forzar; **to ~ off** *vi* (*speaker*) pararse, detenerse; (*branch*) partir; **to ~ open** *vt* (*door etc*) abrir por la fuerza, forzar; **to ~ out** *vi* estallar; **to ~ out in spots** salir a uno granos; **to ~ up** *vi* romperse // *vt* romper, intervenir en; ~**able** *a* quebradizo; ~**age** *n* rotura; ~**down** *n* (*AUT*) avería; (*in communications*) interrupción *f*; (*MED*: *also*: **nervous** ~**down**) colapso, crisis *f* nerviosa; ~**down lorry** *n* grúa, camión *m* grúa; ~**er** *n* rompiente *m*, ola grande.
breakfast ['brɛkfəst] *n* desayuno.
break: ~**through** *n* ruptura; (*fig*) avance *m*, adelanto; ~**water** *n* rompeolas *m inv*.
breast [brɛst] *n* (*of woman*) pecho, seno; (*chest*) pecho; (*of bird*) pechuga; ~**-stroke** *n* braza de pecho.
breath [brɛθ] *n* aliento, respiración *f*; **out of** ~ sin aliento, sofocado; ~**alyser** *n* prueba de alcohol por el aliento.
breathe [bri:ð] *vt, vi* respirar; (*noisily*) resollar; **breather** *n* respiro.
breath: ~**less** *a* sin aliento, jadeante; ~**taking** *a* imponente, pasmoso.
breed [bri:d] *pt, pp* **bred** [brɛd] *vt* criar, engendrar // *vi* reproducirse, procrear // *n* raza, casta; ~**er** *n* (*person*) criador/a *m/f*; ~**ing** *n* (*of person*) educación *f*.

breeze [bri:z] n brisa.
breezy ['bri:zɪ] a de mucho viento, ventoso; (person) despreocupado.
brevity ['brɛvɪtɪ] n brevedad f.
brew [bru:] vt (tea) hacer; (beer) elaborar // vi hacerse, prepararse; (fig) amenazar; ~er n cervecero; ~ery n fábrica de cerveza.
bribe [braɪb] n soborno // vt sobornar, cohechar; ~ry n soborno, cohecho.
brick [brɪk] n ladrillo; ~layer n albañil m; ~works n ladrillar m.
bridal ['braɪdl] a nupcial.
bride [braɪd] n novia; ~groom n novio; **bridesmaid** n dama de honor.
bridge [brɪdʒ] n puente m; (NAUT) puente m de mando; (of nose) caballete m; (CARDS) bridge m // vt (river) tender un puente sobre; ~head n cabeza de puente.
bridle ['braɪdl] n brida, freno // vt poner la brida a; (fig) reprimir, refrenar; ~ path n camino de herradura.
brief [bri:f] a breve, corto // n (LAW) escrito // vt (inform) informar; (instruct) dar órdenes a; ~s npl (for men) calzoncillos mpl; (for women) bragas fpl; ~case n cartera; ~ing n (PRESS) informe m.
brigade [brɪ'geɪd] n (MIL) brigada.
brigadier [brɪgə'dɪə*] n general m de brigada.
bright [braɪt] a claro, luminoso; (weather) de sol; (person: clever) listo, inteligente; (: lively) alegre, animado; (colour) vivo; ~en vt (room) hacer más alegre // vi (weather) despejarse; (person: gen: ~en up) animarse, alegrarse.
brilliance ['brɪljəns] n brillo, brillantez f; **brilliant** [-ənt] a brillante; (clever) genial.
brim [brɪm] n borde m; (of hat) ala; ~ful a lleno hasta el borde; (fig) rebosante (de).
brine [braɪn] n (CULIN) salmuera.
bring [brɪŋ], pt, pp **brought** vt (thing) traer; (person) conducir; **to ~ about** vt ocasionar, producir; **to ~ back** vt volver a traer; (return) devolver; **to ~ down** vt bajar; (price) rebajar; **to ~ forward** vt adelantar; **to ~ in** vt (harvest) recoger; **to ~ off** vt (task, plan) lograr, conseguir; **to ~ out** vt (object) sacar; **to ~ round** vt (unconscious person) hacer volver en sí; (convince) convencer, ganar; **to ~ up** vt (person) educar, criar; (carry up) subir; (question) sacar a colación.
brink [brɪŋk] n borde m.
brisk [brɪsk] a enérgico, vigoroso; (speedy) rápido; (trade) activo.
brisket ['brɪskɪt] n carne f de vaca para asar.
bristle ['brɪsl] n cerda // vi erizarse.
Britain ['brɪtən] n Gran Bretaña.
British ['brɪtɪʃ] a británico; **the ~ npl** los británicos; **the ~ Isles** npl las Islas Británicas.
Briton ['brɪtən] n británico/a.
brittle ['brɪtl] a quebradizo, frágil.
broach [brəutʃ] vt (subject) abordar.

broad [brɔ:d] a ancho, amplio; (accent) cerrado; **in ~ daylight** en pleno día; ~cast n emisión f // (vb: pt, pp ~cast) vt (RADIO) emitir; (TV) transmitir // vi hablar o tocar por la radio; ~casting n radiodifusión f, difusión f; ~en vt ensanchar // vi ensancharse; ~ly ad en general; ~-minded a tolerante, liberal.
brochure ['brəuʃjuə*] n folleto.
broke [brəuk] pt of **break** // a (col) pelado, sin blanca.
broken ['brəukən] pp of **break** // a: ~ **leg** pierna rota; **in ~ English** en un inglés imperfecto; ~-hearted con el corazón partido.
broker ['brəukə*] n agente m/f, bolsista m/f.
bronchitis [brɔŋ'kaɪtɪs] n bronquitis f.
bronze [brɔnz] n bronce m.
brooch [brəutʃ] n prendedor m.
brood [bru:d] n camada, cría; (children) progenie f; (: pej) prole f // vi (hen) empollar; (obsessively) darle vueltas (a).
brook [bruk] n arroyo.
broom [brum] n escoba; (BOT) retama; ~stick n palo de escoba.
Bros. abbr of **Brothers.**
broth [brɔθ] n caldo.
brothel ['brɔθl] n burdel m.
brother ['brʌðə*] n hermano; ~-in-law n cuñado.
brought [brɔ:t] pt, pp of **bring.**
brow [brau] n ceja; (forehead) frente m; (of hill) cumbre f.
brown [braun] a moreno; (hair) castaño; (tanned) bronceado // n (colour) color m moreno o pardo // vt poner moreno; (tan) broncear; (CULIN) dorar; ~ie n niña Girl Guide.
browse [brauz] vi (among books) hojear libros.
bruise [bru:z] n cardenal m, contusión f // vt magullar.
brunette [bru:'nɛt] n morena.
brunt [brʌnt] n: **the ~ of** lo más fuerte de, lo peor de.
brush [brʌʃ] n cepillo; (large) escoba; (for painting, shaving etc) brocha; (artist's) pincel m; (BOT) maleza; (quarrel) escaramuza, encuentro // vt cepillar; (gen: ~ past, ~ against) rozar al pasar; **to ~ aside** vt rechazar, no hacer caso a; **to ~ up** vt (knowledge) repasar, refrescar; ~wood n (bushes) maleza; (sticks) leña.
brusque [bru:sk] a brusco, áspero.
Brussels ['brʌslz] n Bruselas; ~ **sprout** n colecilla de Bruselas.
brutal ['bru:tl] a brutal; ~ity [-'tælɪtɪ] n brutalidad f.
brute [bru:t] n bruto; (person) bestia.
B.Sc. abbr of **Bachelor of Science** licenciado en ciencias.
bubble ['bʌbl] n burbuja, ampolla // vi burbujear, borbotar; ~ **gum** n chicle m de globo.
buck [bʌk] n macho; (US: col) dólar m // vi

corcovear; **to pass the** ~ **(to sb)** echar (a uno) el muerto; **to** ~ **up** *vi* (*cheer up*) animarse, cobrar ánimo.
bucket ['bʌkɪt] *n* cubo, balde *m*.
buckle ['bʌkl] *n* hebilla // *vt* abrochar con hebilla // *vi* torcerse, combarse.
bud [bʌd] *n* brote *m*, yema; (*of flower*) capullo // *vi* brotar, echar brotes; (*fig*) florecer.
Buddhism ['budɪzm] *n* Budismo.
budding ['bʌdɪŋ] *a* en ciernes, en embrión.
buddy ['bʌdɪ] *n* (*US*) compañero, compinche *m*.
budge [bʌdʒ] *vt* mover; (*fig*) hacer ceder // *vi* moverse.
budgerigar ['bʌdʒərɪgɑ:*] *n* periquito.
budget ['bʌdʒɪt] *n* presupuesto.
budgie ['bʌdʒɪ] *n* = **budgerigar.**
buff [bʌf] *a* (*colour*) color *m* de ante // *n* (*enthusiast*) entusiasta *m/f.*
buffalo ['bʌfələu], *pl* ~ *or* ~**es** *n* búfalo.
buffer ['bʌfə*] *n* amortiguador *m*.
buffet ['bufeɪ] *n* (*bar*) bar *m*, cafetería; (*food*) buffet *m* // *vt* ['bʌfɪt] (*strike*) abofetear; (*wind etc*) golpear; ~ **car** *n* coche-comedor *m*.
buffoon [bə'fu:n] *n* bufón *m*.
bug [bʌg] *n* (*insect*) chinche *m*; (: *gen*) bicho, sabandija; (: *fig: germ*) microbio, bacilo; (*spy device*) micrófono oculto; (*tap*) intervención *f*; (*machine for tapping*) aparato de intervención // *vt* (*fam*) fastidiar; (*spy on*) poner micrófono oculto en.
bugle ['bju:gl] *n* corneta, clarín *m*.
build [bɪld] *n* (*of person*) talle *m*, tipo // *vt*, *pt*, *pp* **built** construir, edificar; ~**er** *n* constructor *m*; (*contractor*) contratista *m/f*; ~**ing** *n* (*act of*) construcción *f*; (*habitation, offices*) edificio; ~**ing society** *n* sociedad *f* inmobiliaria, cooperativa de construcciones; **to** ~ **up** *vt* (*MED*) fortalecer; (*stocks*) acumular.
built [bɪlt] *pt*, *pp of* **build** // *a*: ~-**in** (*cupboard*) empotrado; (*device*) interior, incorporado; ~-**up** (*area*) urbanizado.
bulb [bʌlb] *n* (*BOT*) bulbo; (*ELEC*) bombilla.
Bulgaria [bʌl'geərɪə] *n* Bulgaria; ~**n** *a*, *n* búlgaro/a.
bulge [bʌldʒ] *n* bombeo, pandeo // *vi* bombearse, pandearse; (*pocket etc*) hacer bulto.
bulk [bʌlk] *n* (*mass*) bulto, volumen *m*; (*major part*) grueso; **in** ~ (*COMM*) a granel; **the** ~ **of** la mayor parte de; ~**head** *n* mamparo; ~**y** *a* voluminoso, abultado.
bull [bul] *n* toro; ~**dog** *n* dogo.
bulldozer ['buldəuzə*] *n* aplanadora, motoniveladora.
bullet ['bulɪt] *n* bala; ~**proof** *a* a prueba de balas; ~ **wound** *n* balazo.
bulletin ['bulɪtɪn] *n* anuncio, parte *m*.
bullfight ['bulfaɪt] *n* corrida de toros; ~**er** *n* torero; ~**ing** *n* los toros *mpl*, el toreo; (*art of* ~*ing*) tauromaquia.
bullion ['buljən] *n* oro *o* plata en barras.

bullock ['bulək] *n* novillo.
bull's-eye ['bulzaɪ] *n* centro del blanco.
bully ['bulɪ] *n* valentón *m*, matón *m* // *vt* intimidar, tiranizar.
bum [bʌm] *n* (*col: backside*) culo, trasero; (*tramp*) vagabundo.
bumblebee ['bʌmblbi:] *n* (*ZOOL*) abejorro.
bump [bʌmp] *n* (*blow*) tope *m*, choque *m*; (*jolt*) sacudida; (*on road etc, on head*) bollo, abolladura // *vt* (*strike*) chocar contra, topetar // *vi* dar sacudidas; **to** ~ **into** *vt fus* chocar contra, tropezar con; (*person*) topar; ~**er** *n* (*Brit*) parachoques *m inv* // *a*: ~**er crop/harvest** cosecha abundante.
bumpy ['bʌmpɪ] *a* (*road*) lleno de baches; (*journey*) zarandeado.
bun [bʌn] *n* bollo; (*of hair*) moño.
bunch [bʌntʃ] *n* (*of flowers*) ramo; (*of keys*) manojo; (*of bananas*) piña; (*of people*) grupo; (*pej*) pandilla.
bundle ['bʌndl] *n* (*gen*) bulto, fardo; (*of sticks*) haz *f*; (*of papers*) legajo // *vt* (*also*: ~ **up**) atar, envolver; (*put*): **to** ~ **sth/sb into** meter algo/a alguien precipitadamente en.
bung [bʌŋ] *n* tapón *m*, bitoque *m* // *vt* (*throw: gen*: ~ **into**) arrojar.
bungalow ['bʌŋgələu] *n* bungalow *m*, chalé *m*.
bungle ['bʌŋgl] *vt* chapucear.
bunion ['bʌnjən] *n* juanete *m*.
bunk [bʌŋk] *n* tonterías *fpl*; ~ **beds** *npl* literas *fpl*.
bunker ['bʌŋkə*] *n* (*coal store*) carbonera; (*MIL*) refugio; (*GOLF*) bunker *m*.
bunny ['bʌnɪ] *n* (*also*: ~ **rabbit**) conejito.
bunting ['bʌntɪŋ] *n* empavesada, banderas *fpl.*
buoy [bɔɪ] *n* boya; **to** ~ **up** *vt* mantener a flote; (*fig*) animar; ~**ant** *a* boyante.
burden ['bə:dn] *n* carga // *vt* cargar.
bureau [hjuə'rəu], *pl* ~**x** [-z] *n* (*furniture*) escritorio, buró *m*; (*office*) oficina, agencia.
bureaucracy [bjuə'rɔkrəsɪ] *n* burocracia; **bureaucrat** ['bjuərəkræt] *n* burócrata *m/f.*
burglar ['bə:glə*] *n* ladrón/ona *m/f*; ~ **alarm** *n* alarma *f* de ladrones; ~**y** *n* robo con allanamiento, robo de una casa; **burgle** ['bə:gl] *vt* robar (con allanamiento).
burial ['bɛrɪəl] *n* entierro; ~ **ground** *n* cementerio.
burlesque [bə:'lɛsk] *n* parodia.
burly ['bə:lɪ] *a* fornido, membrudo.
Burma ['bə:mə] *n* Birmania.
burn [bə:n], *pt*, *pp* **burned** *or* **burnt** *vt* quemar; (*house*) incendiar // *vi* quemarse, arder; incendiarse; (*sting*) escocer // *n* quemadura; **to** ~ **down** *vt* incendiar; ~**er** *n* (*gas*) quemador *m*, fuego; ~**ing** *a* ardiente.
burp [bə:p] (*col*) *n* eructo // *vi* eructar.
burrow ['bʌrəu] *n* madriguera // *vt* hacer una madriguera.

bursar ['bɔːsə*] n tesorero; (student) becario; ~y n beca.

burst [bɔːst], pt, pp **burst** vt (balloon, pipe) reventar; (banks etc) romper // vi reventarse; romperse; (tyre) pincharse; (bomb) estallar // n (gen) reventón m; (explosion) estallido; (shots) ráfaga de tiros; **a ~ of energy** una explosión f de energía; **to ~ into flames** estallar en llamas; **to ~ into laughter** soltar la carcajada; **to ~ into tears** deshacerse en lágrimas; **to be ~ing with** reventar por o de; **to ~ into** vt fus (room etc) irrumpir en; **to ~ open** vi abrirse de golpe.

bury ['bɛrɪ] vt enterrar; (body) enterrar, sepultar.

bus [bʌs] n autobús m.

bush [buʃ] n arbusto; (scrub land) monte m; **to beat about the ~** ir por rodeos; **~y** a (thick) espeso, poblado.

busily ['bɪzɪlɪ] ad atareadamente, afanosamente.

business ['bɪznɪs] n (matter) negocio; (trading) comercio, negocios mpl; (firm) empresa, casa; (occupation) oficio; (affair) asunto; **it's my ~ to...** me toca o corresponde...; **it's none of my ~** yo no tengo nada que ver; **he means ~** habla en serio; **~like** a formal, metódico; **~man** n hombre m de negocios.

bus-stop ['bʌsstɔp] n parada de autobús.

bust [bʌst] n (ANAT) pecho // a (broken) roto, estropeado; **to go ~** quebrarse.

bustle ['bʌsl] n bullicio, movimiento // vi menearse, apresurarse; **bustling** a (town) animado, bullicioso.

busy ['bɪzɪ] a ocupado, atareado; (shop, street) concurrido, animado // vr: **to ~ o.s. with** ocuparse en; **~body** n entrometido.

but [bʌt] conj pero // prep excepto, menos; **nothing ~** nada más que; **~ for** a no ser por, si no fuera por; **all ~ finished** casi terminado.

butane ['bjuːteɪn] n butano.

butcher ['butʃə*] n carnicero // vt hacer una carnicería con; (cattle etc for meat) matar; **~'s (shop)** n carnicería.

butler ['bʌtlə*] n mayordomo.

butt [bʌt] n (cask) tonel m; (for rain) tina; (thick end) cabo, extremo; (of gun) culata; (of cigarette) colilla; (fig: target) blanco // vt dar cabezadas contra, topetar.

butter ['bʌtə*] n mantequilla // vt untar con mantequilla; **~ bean** n judía blanca; **~cup** n ranúnculo.

butterfly ['bʌtəflaɪ] n mariposa.

buttocks ['bʌtəks] npl nalgas fpl.

button ['bʌtn] n botón m // vt abotonar, abrochar // vi abrocharse; **~hole** n ojal m; (flower) flor f que se lleva en el ojal // vt obligar a escuchar.

buttress ['bʌtrɪs] n contrafuerte m; (fig) apoyo, sostén m.

buxom ['bʌksəm] a (baby) rollizo; (woman) frescachona.

buy [baɪ], pt, pp **bought** vt comprar // n compra; **to ~ sb sth/sth from sb** comprar algo para alguien/comprarle algo a alguien; **~er** n comprador/a m/f.

buzz [bʌz] n zumbido; (col: phone call) llamada (por teléfono) // vi zumbar.

buzzard ['bʌzəd] n águila ratonera.

buzzer ['bʌzə*] n zumbador m, vibrador m.

by [baɪ] prep por; (beside) junto a, cerca de; (according to) según, de acuerdo con; (before): ~ **4 o'clock** para las cuatro // ad see **pass, go** etc; ~ **bus/car** en autobús/coche; **paid ~ the hour** pagado por horas; ~ **night/day** de noche/día; **(all) ~ oneself** (completamente) solo; ~ **the way** a propósito, por cierto; ~ **and large** en general; ~ **and** ~ luego, más tarde.

bye(-bye) ['baɪ('baɪ)] excl adiós, hasta luego.

by(e)-law ['baɪlɔː] n ordenanza municipal.

by-election ['baɪɪlɛkʃən] n elección f parcial.

bygone ['baɪgɔn] a pasado, del pasado // n: **let ~s be ~s** lo pasado, pasado está.

bypass ['baɪpɑːs] n carretera de circunvalación // vt evitar.

by-product ['baɪprɔdʌkt] n subproducto, derivado.

bystander ['baɪstændə*] n espectador/a m/f.

byword ['baɪwɔːd] n: **to be a ~ for** ser conocidísimo por.

C

C. abbr of **centigrade**.

C.A. abbr of **chartered accountant**.

cab [kæb] n taxi m; (of truck) cabina.

cabaret ['kæbəreɪ] n cabaret m.

cabbage ['kæbɪdʒ] n col m, berza.

cabin ['kæbɪn] n cabaña; (on ship) camarote m; ~ **cruiser** n yate m de motor.

cabinet ['kæbɪnɪt] n (POL) consejo de ministros; (furniture) armario; (also: **display ~**) vitrina; **~-maker** n ebanista m.

cable ['keɪbl] n cable m // vt cablegrafiar; **~-car** n coche m de teleférico, tren m aéreo.

cackle ['kækl] vi cacarear.

cactus ['kæktəs], pl **-ti** [-taɪ] n cacto.

caddie ['kædɪ] n cadi m.

cadet [kə'dɛt] n (MIL) cadete m.

cadge [kædʒ] vt gorronear; **cadger** n gorrón/ona m/f.

Caesarean (section) [siː'zɛərɪən] n cesárea.

café ['kæfeɪ], **cafeteria** [kæfɪ'tɪərɪə] n café m.

caffein(e) ['kæfiːn] n cafeína.

cage [keɪdʒ] n jaula // vt enjaular.

cagey ['keɪdʒɪ] a (col) cauteloso, reservado.

Cairo ['kaɪərəu] n el Cairo.

cajole [kə'dʒəul] vt engatusar.
cake [keik] n (large) pastel m; (small) pasta, bizcocho; (of soap) pastilla; ~d with cubierto de.
calamitous [kə'læmitəs] a calamitoso; calamity [-iti] n calamidad f.
calcium ['kælsiəm] n calcio.
calculate ['kælkjuleit] vt calcular; calculating a (clever) astuto; (devious) calculador(a); calculation [-'leiʃən] n cálculo, cómputo; calculator n calculadora.
calculus ['kælkjuləs] n cálculo.
calendar ['kæləndə*] n calendario; ~ month/year mes m/año civil.
calf [kɑ:f], pl calves n (of cow) ternero, becerro; (of other animals) cría; (also: ~skin) piel m de becerro; (ANAT) pantorrilla.
calibre, caliber (US) ['kælibə*] n calibre m.
call [kɔ:l] vt (gen, also TEL) llamar // vi (shout) llamar; (telephone) llamar por teléfono; (visit: also: ~ in, ~ round) hacer una visita // n (shout, TEL) llamada; (of bird) canto; (appeal) llamamiento; to ~ for vt fus (demand) pedir, exigir; (fetch) venir por; to ~ off vt suspender; (cancel) cancelar; to ~ on vt fus (visit) visitar; (turn to) acudir a; to ~ out vi gritar, dar voces; to ~ up vt (MIL) llamar al servicio militar; ~box n cabina telefónica; ~er n visita m/f; (TEL) usuario; ~ girl n prostituta; ~ing n vocación f, profesión f.
callous ['kæləs] a insensible, cruel.
calm [kɑ:m] n calma, tranquilidad f // vt calmar, tranquilizar // a (gen) tranquilo; (sea) liso, en calma; ~ly ad tranquilamente, con calma; ~ness n calma; to ~ down vi calmarse, tranquilizarse // vt calmar, tranquilizar.
calorie ['kæləri] n caloría.
calve [kɑ:v] vi parir.
calves [kɑ:vz] pl of calf.
camber ['kæmbə*] n (of road) combadura, comba.
Cambodia [kæm'bəudjə] n Camboya.
came [keim] pt of come.
camel ['kæməl] n camello.
cameo ['kæmiəu] n camafeo.
camera ['kæmərə] n máquina fotográfica; (CINEMA, TV) cámara; in ~ en secreto; ~man n cámaraman m, cámara m/f.
camouflage ['kæməflɑ:ʒ] n camuflaje m // vt camuflar.
camp [kæmp] n campo, campamento // vi acampar // a afectado, afeminado.
campaign [kæm'pein] n (MIL, POL etc) campaña // vi hacer campaña.
camp: ~bed n cama de campaña; ~er n campista m/f; (vehicle) caravana; ~ing n camping m; to go ~ing hacer camping; ~site n camping m.
campus ['kæmpəs] n ciudad f universitaria.
can [kæn] auxiliary vb (gen) poder; (know

how to) saber; I ~ swim sé nadar // n (of oil, water) lata, bote m // vt enlatar; (preserve) conservar en lata.
Canada ['kænədə] n el Canadá; Canadian [kə'neidiən] a, n canadiense m/f.
canal [kə'næl] n canal m.
canary [kə'nɛəri] n canario; C~ Islands npl las (Islas) Canarias fpl.
cancel ['kænsəl] vt cancelar; (train) suprimir; (appointment) anular; (cross out) tachar, borrar; ~lation [-'leiʃən] n cancelación f; supresión f.
cancer ['kænsə*] n cáncer m; C~ (ASTRO) Cáncer m.
candid ['kændid] a franco, abierto.
candidate ['kændideit] n candidato.
candle ['kændl] n vela; (in church) cirio; ~stick n (also: ~ holder) (single) candelero; (low) palmatoria; (bigger, ornate) candelabro.
candour ['kændə*] n franqueza.
candy ['kændi] n azúcar m cande; (US) dulce m, caramelo.
cane [kein] n (BOT) caña; (stick) vara, palmeta // vt (SCOL) castigar (con palmeta).
canine ['kænain] a canino.
canister ['kænistə*] n bote m, lata.
cannabis ['kænəbis] n cáñamo, marijuana.
canned [kænd] a en lata, de lata.
cannibal ['kænibəl] n caníbal m/f; ~ism n canibalismo.
cannon ['kænən], pl ~ or ~s n cañón m; ~ball n bala (de cañón).
cannot ['kænɔt] = can not.
canny ['kæni] a astuto.
canoe [kə'nu:] n canoa; (SPORT) piragua; ~ing n (SPORT) piragüismo; ~ist n piragüista m/f.
canon ['kænən] n (clergyman) canónigo; (standard) canon m.
canonize ['kænənaiz] vt canonizar.
can opener ['kænəupnə*] n abrelatas m inv.
canopy ['kænəpi] n dosel m, toldo; (ARCH) baldaquín m.
can't [kænt] = can not.
cantankerous [kæn'tæŋkərəs] a arisco, malhumorado.
canteen [kæn'ti:n] n cantina; (bottle) cantimplora; (of cutlery) juego (de cubiertos).
canter ['kæntə*] n medio galope // vi ir a medio galope.
canvas ['kænvəs] n (gen) lona; (painting) lienzo; (NAUT) velas fpl; under ~ (camping) bajo lona.
canvass ['kænvəs] vt (POL) solicitar votos de.
canyon ['kænjən] n cañón m.
cap [kæp] n gorra; (of pen) capuchón m; (of bottle) tapa, cápsula; (MED) diafragma m // vt coronar, poner remate a; (outdo) superar; (FOOTBALL) seleccionar (para el equipo nacional).

capability [keɪpə'bɪlɪtɪ] *n* capacidad *f*; **capable** ['keɪpəbl] *a* capaz.

capacity [kə'pæsɪtɪ] *n* capacidad *f*; (*position*) calidad *f*.

cape [keɪp] *n* capa; (*GEO*) cabo.

caper ['keɪpə*] *n* (*CULIN*: *gen*: ~s) alcaparra; (*prank*) travesura.

capital ['kæpɪtl] *n* (*also*: ~ **city**) capital *f*; (*money*) capital *m*; (*also*: ~ **letter**) mayúscula; ~**ism** *n* capitalismo; ~**ist** *a*, *n* capitalista *m/f*; ~ **punishment** *n* pena de muerte.

capitulate [kə'pɪtjuleɪt] *vi* capitular, rendirse; **capitulation** [-'leɪʃən] *n* capitulación *f*, rendición *f*.

capricious [kə'prɪʃəs] *a* caprichoso.

Capricorn ['kæprɪkɔːn] *n* Capricornio.

capsize [kæp'saɪz] *vt* volcar, hacer zozobrar // *vi* volcarse, zozobrar.

capstan ['kæpstən] *n* cabrestante *m*.

capsule ['kæpsjuːl] *n* cápsula.

captain ['kæptɪn] *n* capitán *m* // *vt* capitanear, ser el capitán de.

caption ['kæpʃən] *n* (*heading*) título; (*to picture*) leyenda.

captivate ['kæptɪveɪt] *vt* cautivar, encantar.

captive ['kæptɪv] *a*, *n* cautivo/a; **captivity** [-'tɪvɪtɪ] *n* cautiverio.

capture ['kæptʃə*] *vt* prender, apresar; (*place*) tomar; (*attention*) captar, llamar // *n* apresamiento; toma; (*thing taken*) presa.

car [kɑː*] *n* coche *m*, automóvil *m*; (*RAIL*) vagón *m*.

carafe [kə'ræf] *n* garrafa.

caramel ['kærəməl] *n* caramelo.

carat ['kærət] *n* quilate *m*.

caravan ['kærəvæn] *n* caravana, rulota; (*of camels*) caravana.

caraway ['kærəweɪ] *n*: ~ **seed** carvi *m*.

carbohydrate [kɑːbəu'haɪdreɪt] *n* hidrato de carbono; (*food*) fécula.

carbon ['kɑːbən] *n* carbono; ~ **copy** *n* copia al carbón; ~ **paper** *n* papel *m* carbón.

carburettor [kɑːbju'rɛtə*] *n* carburador *m*.

carcass ['kɑːkəs] *n* cadáver *m* de animal.

card [kɑːd] *n* carta, naipe *m*; (*visiting* ~, *post*~ *etc*) tarjeta; ~**board** *n* cartón *m*, cartulina; ~ **game** *n* juego de naipes.

cardiac ['kɑːdɪæk] *a* cardíaco.

cardigan ['kɑːdɪgən] *n* rebeca.

cardinal ['kɑːdɪnl] *a* cardinal // *n* cardenal *m*.

card index *n* fichero.

care [kɛə*] *n* (*gen*) cuidado; (*worry*) inquietud *f*, solicitud *f*; (*charge*) cargo, custodia // *vi*: **to** ~ **about** preocuparse de, tener interés en; **in sb's** ~ a cargo de alguien; **to take** ~ **to** cuidarse *o* tener cuidado de; **to take** ~ **of** *vt* cuidar; **to** ~ **for** *vt fus* cuidar a; (*like*) querer; **I don't** ~ no me importa.

career [kə'rɪə*] *n* carrera // *vi* (*also*: ~

along) correr a toda velocidad.

carefree ['kɛəfriː] *a* despreocupado.

careful ['kɛəful] *a* cuidadoso; (*cautious*) cauteloso; (**be**) ~! ¡tenga cuidado!; ~**ly** *ad* con cuidado, cuidadosamente.

careless ['kɛəlɪs] *a* descuidado; (*heedless*) poco atento; ~**ly** *ad* sin cuidado, a la ligera; ~**ness** *n* descuido, falta de atención.

caress [kə'rɛs] *n* caricia // *vt* acariciar.

caretaker ['kɛəteɪkə*] *n* portero, conserje *m/f*.

car-ferry ['kɑːfɛrɪ] *n* transbordador *m* para coches.

cargo ['kɑːgəu], *pl* ~**es** *n* cargamento, carga.

Caribbean [kærɪ'biːən] *n*: **the** ~ (**Sea**) el Caribe.

caricature ['kærɪkətjuə*] *n* caricatura.

carnal ['kɑːnl] *a* carnal.

carnation [kɑː'neɪʃən] *n* clavel *m*.

carnival ['kɑːnɪvəl] *n* fiesta, feria, carnaval *m*.

carnivore ['kɑːnɪvɔː*] *n* carnívoro.

carol ['kærəl] *n*: (**Christmas**) ~ villancico.

carp [kɑːp] *n* (*fish*) carpa; **to** ~ **at** *vt fus* quejarse de.

car park *n* aparcamiento, parking *m*.

carpenter ['kɑːpɪntə*] *n* carpintero; **carpentry** [-trɪ] *n* carpintería.

carpet ['kɑːpɪt] *n* alfombra // *vt* alfombrar; ~ **slippers** *npl* zapatillas *fpl*.

carriage ['kærɪdʒ] *n* coche *m*; (*RAIL*) vagón *m*; (*for goods*) transporte *m*; (*bearing*) porte *m*; ~**way** *n* (*part of road*) carretera; **dual** ~**way** carretera de doble calzada.

carrier ['kærɪə*] *n* trajinista *m/f*; (*company*) empresa de transportes; ~ **bag** *n* bolsa (de papel).

carrot ['kærət] *n* zanahoria.

carry ['kærɪ] *vt* (*gen*) llevar; (*transport*) transportar; (*a motion*, *bill*) aprobar; (*involve*: *responsibilities etc*) entrañar, implicar // *vi* (*sound*) oírse; **to** ~ **on** *vi* (*continue*) seguir (adelante), continuar; (*fam*: *complain*) quejarse, protestar // *vt* proseguir, continuar; **to** ~ **out** *vt* (*orders*) cumplir; (*investigation*) llevar a cabo, realizar.

cart [kɑːt] *n* carro, carreta // *vt* acarrear, llevar (en carro).

cartilage ['kɑːtɪlɪdʒ] *n* cartílago.

cartographer [kɑː'tɔgrəfə*] *n* cartógrafo.

carton ['kɑːtən] *n* (*box*) caja (de cartón); (*of yogurt*) pote *m*.

cartoon [kɑː'tuːn] *n* (*PRESS*) caricatura; (*comic strip*) tira cómica; (*film*) dibujos *mpl* animados; ~**ist** *n* caricaturista *m/f*; dibujante *m/f*.

cartridge ['kɑːtrɪdʒ] *n* cartucho.

carve [kɑːv] *vt* (*meat*) trinchar; (*wood*, *stone*) cincelar, esculpir; (*on tree*) grabar; **to** ~ **up** dividir, repartir; **carving** *n* (*in wood etc*) escultura, (obra de) talla; **carving knife** *n* trinchante *m*.

car wash n lavado de coches.
cascade [kæs'keɪd] n salto de agua, cascada; (fig) chorro // vi caer a chorros o en forma de cascada.
case [keɪs] n (container) caja; (MED) caso; (for jewels etc) estuche m; (LAW) causa, proceso; (also: **suit**~) maleta; **in** ~ **(of)** en caso de (que), por si; **in any** ~ en todo caso; **just in** ~ por si acaso; **to make a good** ~ tener buenos argumentos.
cash [kæʃ] n (dinero en) efectivo, dinero contante // vt cobrar, hacer efectivo; **to pay (in)** ~ pagar al contado; ~ **on delivery** cóbrese al entregar; ~**book** n libro de caja; ~**desk** n caja.
cashew [kæ'ʃu:] n (also: ~ **nut**) anacardo.
cashier [kæ'ʃɪə*] n cajero.
cashmere [kæʃ'mɪə*] n casimir m, cachemira.
cash register n caja.
casing ['keɪsɪŋ] n envoltura; (of boiler etc) revestimiento.
casino [kə'si:nəʊ] n casino.
cask [kɑːsk] n tonel m, barril m.
casket ['kɑːskɪt] n cofre m, estuche m; (US: coffin) ataúd m.
casserole ['kæsərəʊl] n cacerola; (food) cazuela.
cassette [kæ'sɛt] n cassette m; ~ **player** n tocacassettes m inv.
cassock ['kæsək] n sotana.
cast [kɑːst], pt, pp **cast** vt (throw) echar, arrojar, lanzar; (skin) mudar, perder; (metal) fundir; (THEATRE) hacer el reparto de // vi (FISHING) lanzar // n (THEATRE) reparto; (mould) forma, molde m; (also: **plaster** ~) vaciado; **to** ~ **away** vt desechar; **to** ~ **down** vt derribar; **to** ~ **loose** soltar; **to** ~ **one's vote** dar el voto; **to** ~ **off** vi (NAUT) desamarrar.
castanets [kæstə'nɛts] npl castañuelas fpl.
castaway ['kɑːstəwəɪ] n náufrago.
caste [kɑːst] n casta.
casting vote ['kɑːstɪŋ-] n voto decisivo.
cast iron n hierro fundido.
castle ['kɑːsl] n castillo; (CHESS) torre f.
castor ['kɑːstə*] n (wheel) ruedecilla; ~ **oil** n aceite m de ricino; ~ **sugar** n azúcar m extrafino.
castrate [kæs'treɪt] vt castrar.
casual ['kæʒjul] a (by chance) fortuito; (irregular: work etc) eventual, temporero; (unconcerned) despreocupado; (informal: clothes) de sport; ~**ly** ad por casualidad; de manera despreocupada.
casualty ['kæʒjultɪ] n víctima m/f, herido; (dead) muerto; (MIL) baja; **casualties** npl pérdidas fpl.
cat [kæt] n gato.
Catalan ['kætəlæn] a, n Catalán/ana m/f.
catalogue, catalog (US) ['kætələg] n catálogo // vt catalogar.
Catalonia [kætə'ləʊnɪə] n Cataluña.
catalyst ['kætəlɪst] n catalizador m.
catapult ['kætəpʌlt] n tirador m.

cataract ['kætərækt] n (also MED) catarata.
catarrh [kə'tɑː*] n catarro.
catastrophe [kə'tæstrəfɪ] n catástrofe m; **catastrophic** [kætə'strɒfɪk] a catastrófico.
catch [kætʃ], pt, pp **caught** vt (gen) coger; (arrest) detener; (grasp) asir; (breath) suspender; (person: by surprise) sorprender; (attract: attention) ganar; (MED) contagiarse de, coger; (also: ~ **up**) alcanzar // vi (fire) encenderse; (in branches etc) enredarse // n (fish etc) pesca; (act of catching) cogida; (trick) trampa; (of lock) pestillo, cerradura; **to** ~ **on** vi (understand) caer en la cuenta; (grow popular) hacerse popular; **to** ~ **sight of** divisar; **to** ~ **up** vi (fig) ponerse al día.
catch: ~**ing** a (MED) contagioso; ~**ment area** n zona de captación; ~ **phrase** n lema m, slogan m; ~**y** a (tune) pegadizo.
catechism ['kætɪkɪzəm] n (REL) catequismo.
categoric(al) [kætɪ'gɒrɪk(əl)] a categórico, terminante.
categorize ['kætɪgəraɪz] vt clasificar; **category** [-rɪ] n categoría, clase f.
cater ['keɪtə*] vi: **to** ~ **for** abastecer a; (needs) atender a; (consumers) proveer a; ~**er** n abastecedor m, proveedor m; ~**ing** n servicio de comidas; (trade) abastecimiento.
caterpillar ['kætəpɪlə*] n oruga, gusano; ~ **track** n rodado de oruga.
cathedral [kə'θi:drəl] n catedral f.
catholic ['kæθəlɪk] a católico; **C**~ a, n (REL) católico/a.
cattle ['kætl] npl ganado sg.
catty ['kætɪ] a malicioso, rencoroso.
Caucasus ['kɔːkəsəs] n Cáucaso.
caught [kɔːt] pt, pp of **catch.**
cauliflower ['kɒlɪflaʊə*] n coliflor f.
cause [kɔːz] n causa, motivo, razón f // vt causar; (provoke) provocar.
causeway ['kɔːzweɪ] n (road) carretera elevada; (embankment) terraplén m
caustic ['kɔːstɪk] a cáustico; (fig) mordaz.
caution ['kɔːʃən] n cautela, prudencia; (warning) advertencia, amonestación f // vt amonestar.
cautious ['kɔːʃəs] a cauteloso, prudente, precavido; ~**ly** ad con cautela; ~**ness** n cautela.
cavalier [kævə'lɪə*] a arrogante, desdeñoso.
cavalry ['kævəlrɪ] n caballería.
cave [keɪv] n cueva, caverna; **to** ~ **in** vi (roof etc) derrumbarse, hundirse; ~**man** n cavernícola m/f, troglodita m/f.
cavern ['kævən] n caverna.
caviar(e) ['kævɪɑː*] n caviar m.
cavity ['kævɪtɪ] n hueco, cavidad f.
cavort [kə'vɔːt] vi dar cabriolas.
caw [kɔː] vi graznar.
CBI n abbr of **Confederation of British Industries.**

cc *abbr of* **cubic centimetres; carbon copy.**
cease [si:s] *vt, vi* cesar; ~**fire** *n* cese *m* de hostilidades *o* fuego; ~**less** *a* incesante; ~**lessly** *ad* sin cesar.
cedar ['si:də*] *n* cedro.
cede [si:d] *vt* ceder.
ceiling ['si:lɪŋ] *n* techo; (*fig*) límite *m*.
celebrate ['sɛlɪbreɪt] *vt* celebrar; (*marriage*) solemnizar // *vi* divertirse; ~**d** *a* célebre; **celebration** [-'breɪʃən] *n* fiesta, celebración *f.*
celebrity [sɪ'lɛbrɪtɪ] *n* celebridad *f.*
celery ['sɛlərɪ] *n* apio.
celestial [sɪ'lɛstɪəl] *a* (*of sky*) celeste; (*divine*) celestial.
celibacy ['sɛlɪbəsɪ] *n* celibato.
cell [sɛl] *n* celda; (*BIOL*) célula; (*ELEC*) elemento.
cellar ['sɛlə*] *n* sótano; (*for wine*) bodega.
'cello ['tʃɛləu] *n* violoncelo.
cellophane ['sɛləfeɪn] *n* celofán *m.*
cellular ['sɛljulə*] *a* celular.
cellulose ['sɛljuləus] *n* celulosa.
Celt [kɛlt, sɛlt] *a, n* celta *m/f;* ~**ic** *a* celta.
cement [sə'mɛnt] *n* cemento // *vt* cementar; (*fig*) cimentar, fortalecer.
cemetery ['sɛmɪtrɪ] *n* cementerio.
cenotaph ['sɛnətɑ:f] *n* cenotafio.
censor ['sɛnsə*] *n* censor // *vt* (*cut*) tachar, suprimir; ~**ship** *n* censura.
censure ['sɛnʃə*] *vt* censurar.
census ['sɛnsəs] *n* censo.
cent [sɛnt] *n* (*US: coin*) centavo, céntimo; *see also* **per.**
centenary [sɛn'ti:nərɪ] *n* centenario.
centi... [sɛntɪ] *pref:* ~**grade** *a* centígrado; ~**litre** *n* centilitro; ~**metre** *n* centímetro; ~**pede** *n* ciempiés *m.*
central ['sɛntrəl] *a* central; (*of town*) céntrico; **C**~ **American** *a* centroamericano; ~ **heating** *n* calefacción *f* central; ~**ize** *vt* centralizar.
centre ['sɛntə*] *n* centro; ~-**forward** *n* (*SPORT*) delantero centro; ~-**half** *n* (*SPORT*) medio centro.
century ['sɛntjurɪ] *n* siglo; **20th** ~ siglo veinte.
ceramic [sɪ'ræmɪk] *a* cerámico; ~**s** *n* cerámica.
cereal ['si:rɪəl] *n* cereal *m.*
ceremony ['sɛrɪmənɪ] *n* ceremonia.
certain ['sə:tən] *a* (*gen*) seguro; (*correct*) cierto; (*person*) seguro; (*a particular*) cierto; **for** ~ a ciencia cierta; ~**ly** *ad* desde luego, por cierto; ~**ty** *n* certeza, certidumbre *f,* seguridad *f.*
certificate [sə'tɪfɪkɪt] *n* certificado.
certify ['sə:tɪfaɪ] *vt* certificar.
cervix ['sə:vɪks] *n* cerviz *f.*
cessation [sə'seɪʃən] *n* cesación *f,* suspensión *f.*
cf. *abbr = * **compare** cfr.
chafe [tʃeɪf] *vt* (*rub*) rozar; (*wear*) desgastar; (*irritate*) irritar.
chaffinch ['tʃæfɪntʃ] *n* pinzón *m* vulgar.

chagrin ['ʃægrɪn] *n* disgusto, desazón *f.*
chain [tʃeɪn] *n* (*gen*) cadena // *vt* (*also:* ~ **up**) encadenar; ~ **reaction** *n* reacción *f* en cadena; ~ **store** *n* tienda de una cadena.
chair [tʃɛə*] *n* silla; (*armchair*) sillón *m*; (*of university*) cátedra // *vt* (*meeting*) presidir; ~**lift** *n* telesilla; ~**man** *n* presidente *m.*
chalet ['ʃæleɪ] *n* chalet *m.*
chalice ['tʃælɪs] *n* cáliz *m.*
chalk [tʃɔːk] *n* (*GEO*) creta; (*for writing*) tiza.
challenge ['tʃælɪndʒ] *n* desafío, reto // *vt* desafiar, retar; (*statement, right*) poner en duda, cuestionar; **to** ~ **sb to do sth** retar a uno a que haga algo; **challenger** *n* (*SPORT*) contrincante *m/f;* **challenging** *a* desafiante; (*tone*) de desafío.
chamber ['tʃeɪmbə*] *n* cámara, sala; ~ **of commerce** cámara de comercio; ~**maid** *n* camarera; ~ **music** *n* música de cámara.
chamois ['ʃæmwɑ:] *n* gamuza.
champagne [ʃæm'peɪn] *n* champaña *m,* champán *m.*
champion ['tʃæmpɪən] *n* campeón/ona *m/f;* ~**ship** *n* campeonato.
chance [tʃɑ:ns] *n* (*luck*) casualidad *f,* suerte *f;* (*fate*) azar *m;* (*opportunity*) ocasión *f,* oportunidad *f;* (*likelihood*) posibilidad *f;* (*risk*) riesgo // *vt* arriesgar, probar // *a* fortuito, casual; **to** ~ **it** aventurarse, arriesgarse; **to take a** ~ arriesgarse; **by** ~ por casualidad.
chancel ['tʃɑ:nsəl] *n* coro y presbiterio.
chancellor ['tʃɑ:nsələ*] *n* canciller *m;* **C**~ **of the Exchequer** *n* Ministro de Hacienda.
chandelier [ʃændə'lɪə*] *n* araña (de luces).
change [tʃeɪndʒ] *vt* (*gen*) cambiar; (*replace*) reemplazar; (*gear, clothes, house*) cambiar de, mudar de; (*exchange*) trocar; (*transform*) transformar // *vi* (*gen*) cambiar(se), mudar; (*trains*) hacer transbordo; **to** ~ **into** transformarse en // *n* cambio, modificación *f,* transformación *f;* (*coins*) moneda suelta, suelto; (*money returned*) vuelta; **for a** ~ para variar; ~**able** *a* (*weather*) cambiable, mudable; ~**less** *a* inmutable; ~**over** *n* (*to new system*) cambio.
changing ['tʃeɪndʒɪŋ] *a* cambiante; ~ **room** *n* vestuario.
channel ['tʃænl] *n* (*TV*) canal *m;* (*of river*) cauce *m;* (*of sea*) estrecho; (*groove, fig: medium*) conducto, medio // *vt* canalizar, encauzar; **the (English) C**~ el Canal (de la Mancha); **the C**~ **Islands** las Islas Normandas *fpl.*
chant [tʃɑ:nt] *n* canto // *vt* cantar; (*fig*) recitar en tono monótono.
chaos ['keɪɔs] *n* caos *m;* **chaotic** [keɪ'ɔtɪk] *a* caótico, desordenado.
chap [tʃæp] *n* (*col: man*) tío, tipo // *vi* (*skin*) agrietarse.

chapel ['tʃæpəl] n capilla.

chaperon ['ʃæpərəun] n carabina.

chaplain ['tʃæplɪn] n capellán m.

chapter ['tʃæptə*] n capítulo.

char [tʃɑ:*] vt (burn) carbonizar, chamuscar // n = **charlady.**

character ['kærɪktə*] n carácter m, naturaleza, índole f, calidad f; (in novel, film) personaje m; (role) papel m; ~**istic** [-'rɪstɪk] a característico // n característica; ~**ize** vt caracterizar.

charade [ʃə'rɑːd] n charada.

charcoal ['tʃɑːkəul] n carbón m vegetal; (ART) carboncillo.

charge [tʃɑːdʒ] n carga; (LAW) cargo, acusación f; (cost) precio, coste m; (responsibility) cargo; (task) encargo // vt (LAW) acusar (with de); (gun, battery, MIL: enemy) cargar; (price) pedir; (customer) cobrar; (sb with task) encargar // vi cargar, precipitarse; (make pay) cobrar; ~s npl: bank ~s suplemento cobrado por el banco; **free of** ~ gratis; **to reverse the** ~s (TEL) poner una conferencia por cobrar; **to take** ~ **of** hacerse cargo de, encargarse de; **to be in** ~ **of** estar a cargo de o encargado de; **how much do you** ~? ¿cuánto cobra Usted?; **to** ~ **an expense (up) to sb's account** cargar algo a cuenta de alguien.

charitable ['tʃærɪtəbl] a caritativo.

charity ['tʃærɪtɪ] n (gen) caridad f; (sympathy) compasión f; (organization) sociedad f benéfica.

charlady ['tʃɑːleɪdɪ] n mujer f de la limpieza.

charm [tʃɑːm] n encanto, atractivo; (spell) hechizo; (object) amuleto // vt encantar; hechizar; ~**ing** a encantador(a), simpático.

chart [tʃɑːt] n cuadro; (graph) gráfica; (map) carta de navegación // vt (course) trazar.

charter ['tʃɑːtə*] vt (plane) alquilar; (ship) fletar // n (document) carta; ~**ed accountant** n perito contable; ~ **flight** n vuelo charter.

charwoman ['tʃɑːwumən] n = **charlady.**

chase [tʃeɪs] vt (follow) perseguir; (hunt) cazar // n persecución f; caza; **to** ~ **after** correr tras.

chasm ['kæzəm] n abismo.

chassis ['ʃæsɪ] n chasis m.

chaste [tʃeɪst] a casto; **chastity** ['tʃæstɪtɪ] n castidad f.

chat [tʃæt] vi (also: **have a** ~) charlar // n charla.

chatter ['tʃætə*] vi (person) charlar; (teeth) castañetear // n (of birds) parloteo; (of people) charla, cháchara; ~**box** n parlanchín/ina m/f.

chatty ['tʃætɪ] a (style) familiar; (person) hablador(a), locuaz.

chauffeur ['ʃəufə*] n chófer m.

cheap [tʃiːp] a barato; (trick) malo; (poor quality) barato, de poca calidad // ad barato; ~**en** vt rebajar el precio.

abaratar; **to** ~**en o.s.** rebajarse; ~**ly** ad barato, a bajo precio.

cheat [tʃiːt] vi hacer trampa // vt defraudar, timar // n trampa, fraude m; (person) tramposo; ~**ing** n trampa, fraude m.

check [tʃek] vt (examine) controlar; (facts) comprobar; (count) contar; (halt) parar, detener; (restrain) refrenar, restringir // n (inspection) control m, inspección f; (curb) freno; (bill) nota, cuenta; (obstacle) impedimento, estorbo; (token) ficha; (pattern: gen pl) cuadro; **to** ~ **in** vi (in hotel, airport) registrarse // vt (luggage) facturar; **to** ~ **out** vi (of hotel) pagar la cuenta y marcharse; **to** ~ **up** vi: **to** ~ **up on sth** comprobar algo; **to** ~ **up on sb** investigar a una persona; ~**mate** n jaque m mate; ~**out** n caja; ~**point** n (punto de) control m; ~**up** n (MED) reconocimiento general; (of machine) repaso.

cheek [tʃiːk] n mejilla; (impudence) descaro; ~ **bone** n pómulo; ~**y** a fresco, descarado.

cheer [tʃɪə*] vt vitorear, aplaudir; (gladden) alegrar, animar // vi aplaudir, gritar con entusiasmo // n grito (de entusiasmo); ~**s** npl aplausos mpl; ~**s!** ¡salud!; **to** ~ **up** vi animarse, cobrar ánimos // vt alegrar, animar; ~**ful** a alegre; ~**fulness** n alegría; **cheerio** excl ¡hasta luego!; ~**less** a triste, sombrío.

cheese [tʃiːz] n queso.

chef [ʃef] n jefe/a m/f de cocina.

chemical ['kemɪkəl] a químico // n elemento químico.

chemist ['kemɪst] n farmacéutico; (scientist) químico; ~**ry** n química; ~'**s (shop)** n farmacia.

cheque [tʃek] n cheque m; ~**book** n libro de cheques, chequera.

chequered ['tʃekəd] a (fig) variado, accidentado.

cherish ['tʃerɪʃ] vt (love) querer, apreciar; (protect) cuidar; (hope etc) abrigar.

cherry ['tʃerɪ] n cereza.

chess [tʃes] n ajedrez m; ~**board** n tablero (de ajedrez); ~**man** n pieza, trebejo.

chest [tʃest] n (ANAT) pecho; (box) cofre m, cajón m; ~ **of drawers** n cómoda.

chestnut ['tʃesnʌt] n castaña; ~ (**tree**) n castaño.

chew [tʃuː] vt mascar, masticar; ~**ing gum** n chicle m.

chic [ʃiːk] a elegante.

chick [tʃɪk] n pollito, polluelo; (fam) chica.

chicken ['tʃɪkɪn] n gallina, pollo; (food) pollo; ~**pox** n varicela.

chickpea ['tʃɪkpiː] n garbanzo.

chicory ['tʃɪkərɪ] n (for coffee) achicoria; (salad) escarola.

chief [tʃiːf] n jefe/a m/f // a principal; ~**ly** ad principalmente.

chiffon ['ʃɪfɔn] n gasa.

chilblain ['tʃɪlbleɪn] n sabañón m.

child [tʃaɪld], pl ~ren ['tʃɪldrən] n niño/a; (offspring) hijo/a; ~birth n parto; ~hood n niñez f, infancia; ~ish a pueril, aniñado; ~like a como (de) niño; ~ minder n cuidadora de niños.

Chile ['tʃɪlɪ] n Chile m; ~an a, n chileno/a.

chill [tʃɪl] n frío; (MED) escalofrío, resfriado // vt enfriar; (CULIN) congelar; ~y a frío.

chime [tʃaɪm] n (peal) repique m, campanada // vi repicar, sonar.

chimney ['tʃɪmnɪ] n chimenea; ~ sweep n deshollinador m.

chimpanzee [tʃɪmpæn'ziː] n chimpancé m.

chin [tʃɪn] n barba, barbilla.

china ['tʃaɪnə] n porcelana; (gen) loza.

China ['tʃaɪnə] n China; Chinese [tʃaɪ'niːz] a chino // n chino/a; (LING) el chino.

chink [tʃɪŋk] n (opening) grieta, hendedura; (noise) tintineo.

chip [tʃɪp] n (gen pl: CULIN) patata frita; (of wood) astilla; (of glass, stone) lasca; (at poker) ficha // vt (cup, plate) astillar; to ~ in vi interrumpir; (contribute) compartir los gastos.

chiropodist [kɪ'rɔpədɪst] n pedicuro.

chirp [tʃəːp] vi gorjear, piar; (cricket) chirriar.

chisel ['tʃɪzl] n (for wood) formón m; (for stone) cincel m.

chit [tʃɪt] n nota.

chitchat ['tʃɪttʃæt] n chismes mpl, habladurías fpl.

chivalrous ['ʃɪvəlrəs] a caballeroso; chivalry [-rɪ] n caballerosidad f.

chives [tʃaɪvz] npl cebollino sg.

chlorine ['klɔːriːn] n cloro.

chock [tʃɔk]: ~-a-block, ~-full a de bote en bote, atestado.

chocolate ['tʃɔklɪt] n chocolate m.

choice [tʃɔɪs] n elección f, selección f; (preference) preferencia // a selecto, elegido.

choir ['kwaɪə*] n coro; ~boy n corista m.

choke [tʃəuk] vi sofocarse; (on food) atragantarse // vt ahogar, sofocar; (block) obstruir // n (AUT) estrangulador m; choker n (necklace) gargantilla.

cholera ['kɔlərə] n cólera m.

choose [tʃuːz], pt chose, pp chosen vt escoger, elegir; (team) seleccionar.

chop [tʃɔp] vt (wood) cortar, tajar; (CULIN: also: ~ up) desmenuzar; (meat) picar // n golpe m cortante; (CULIN) chuleta; ~s npl (jaws) boca sg, labios mpl; ~py a (sea) picado, agitado; ~sticks npl palillos mpl.

choral ['kɔːrəl] a coral.

chord [kɔːd] n (MUS) acorde m.

chore [tʃɔː*] n faena, tarea; (routine task) trabajo rutinario.

choreographer [kɔrɪ'ɔɡrəfə*] n coreógrafo.

chorister ['kɔrɪstə*] n corista m/f.

chortle ['tʃɔːtl] vi reír entre dientes.

chorus ['kɔːrəs] n coro; (repeated part of song) estribillo.

chose [tʃəuz], chosen ['tʃəuzn] pt, pp of choose.

Christ [kraɪst] n Cristo.

christen ['krɪsn] vt bautizar; ~ing n bautizo.

Christian ['krɪstɪən] a, n cristiano/a; ~ity [-'ænɪtɪ] n cristianismo; ~ name n nombre m de pila.

Christmas ['krɪsməs] n Navidad f; Merry ~! ¡Felices Pascuas!; ~ Eve n Nochebuena.

chrome [krəum], chromium ['krəumɪəm] n cromo.

chromosome ['krəuməsəum] n cromosoma m.

chronic ['krɔnɪk] a crónico.

chronicle ['krɔnɪkl] n crónica.

chronological [krɔnə'lɔdʒɪkəl] a cronológico.

chrysanthemum [krɪ'sænθəməm] n crisantemo.

chubby ['tʃʌbɪ] a rechoncho.

chuck [tʃʌk] vt lanzar, arrojar; to ~ out vt echar (fuera), tirar; to ~ (up) vt abandonar.

chuckle ['tʃʌkl] vi reírse entre dientes.

chug [tʃʌɡ] vi resoplar; to ~ along vi (fig) ir tirando.

chum [tʃʌm] n compinche m, compañero.

chunk [tʃʌŋk] n pedazo, trozo.

church [tʃəːtʃ] n iglesia; ~yard n campo santo.

churlish ['tʃəːlɪʃ] a grosero, hosco.

churn [tʃəːn] n (for butter) mantequera; (for milk) lechera // vt revolver, agitar.

chute [ʃuːt] n (also: rubbish ~) vertedero; (children's slide) tobogán m.

chutney ['tʃʌtnɪ] n salsa picante.

CID n abbr of Criminal Investigation Department B.I.C. (Brigada de Investigación Criminal).

cider ['saɪdə*] n sidra.

cigar [sɪ'ɡɑː*] n puro.

cigarette [sɪɡə'ret] n cigarrillo; (fam) pitillo; ~ case n pitillera; ~ end n colilla; ~ holder n boquilla.

Cinderella [sɪndə'relə] n la Cenicienta.

cinders ['sɪndəz] npl cenizas fpl.

cine [sɪnɪ]: ~-camera n cámara cinematográfica; ~-film n película cinematográfica.

cinema ['sɪnəmə] n cine m.

cinnamon ['sɪnəmən] n canela.

cipher ['saɪfə*] n cifra.

circle ['səːkl] n círculo; (in cinema) anfiteatro // vi dar vueltas // vt (surround) rodear, cercar; (move round) dar la vuelta a.

circuit ['səːkɪt] n circuito; (tour) gira; (track) pista; (lap) vuelta; ~ous [sə'kjuɪtəs] a tortuoso, indirecto.

circular ['səːkjulə*] a circular // n circular f.

circulate ['səːkjuleɪt] vi circular // vt poner en circulación, hacer circular;

circulation [-'leɪʃən] n circulación f; (of newspaper) tirada.

circumcise ['sɜːkəmsaɪz] vt circuncidar.

circumference [sə'kʌmfərəns] n circunferencia.

circumspect ['sɜːkəmspɛkt] a circunspecto, prudente.

circumstances ['sɜːkəmstənsɪz] npl circunstancias fpl; (financial condition) situación f económica.

circus ['sɜːkəs] n circo; (roundabout) glorieta.

cistern ['sɪstən] n tanque m, depósito; (in toilet) cisterna.

cite [saɪt] vt citar.

citizen ['sɪtɪzn] n (POL) ciudadano/a; (resident) vecino/a, habitante m/f; ~ship n ciudadanía.

citrus fruit ['sɪtrəs-] n agrios mpl.

city ['sɪtɪ] n ciudad f; the C~ centro financiero de Londres.

civic ['sɪvɪk] a cívico, municipal.

civil ['sɪvɪl] a civil; (polite) atento, cortés; (defence) pasivo; (well-bred) educado; ~ engineer n ingeniero civil; C~ Service administración f pública; ~ian [sɪ'vɪlɪən] a civil, de paisano // n civil m/f, paisano.

civilization [sɪvɪlaɪ'zeɪʃən] n civilización f.

civilized ['sɪvɪlaɪzd] a civilizado.

claim [kleɪm] vt exigir, reclamar; (rights etc) reivindicar; (assert) pretender // vi (for insurance) reclamar // n reclamación f; (LAW) demanda; (pretension) pretensión f; ~ant n (ADMIN, LAW) demandante m/f.

clairvoyant [klɛə'vɔɪənt] n clarividente m/f.

clam [klæm] n almeja.

clamber ['klæmbə*] vi subir gateando, trepar.

clammy ['klæmɪ] a (cold) frío y húmedo; (sticky) pegajoso.

clamp [klæmp] n abrazadera, grapa // vt afianzar (con abrazadera); to ~ down on vt fus suprimir, restringir.

clan [klæn] n clan m.

clang [klæŋ] n sonido metálico // vi sonar, hacer estruendo.

clap [klæp] vi aplaudir // vt (hands) batir; (put) poner // n (of hands) palmada; (of thunder) estampido (de trueno); ~ping n aplausos mpl.

claret ['klærət] n clarete m.

clarification [klærɪfɪ'keɪʃən] n aclaración f; **clarify** ['klærɪfaɪ] vt aclarar.

clarinet [klærɪ'nɛt] n clarinete m.

clarity ['klærɪtɪ] n claridad f.

clash [klæʃ] n estruendo; (fig) choque m // vi (meet) encontrarse; (battle) chocar; (disagree) estar en desacuerdo.

clasp [klɑːsp] n broche m; (on jewels) cierre m // vt abrochar; (hand) apretar, estrechar; (embrace) abrazar.

class [klɑːs] n (gen) clase f // a clasista, de clase // vt clasificar.

classic ['klæsɪk] a clásico // n (work) obra clásica; ~al a clásico.

classification [klæsɪfɪ'keɪʃən] n clasificación f; **classify** ['klæsɪfaɪ] vt clasificar.

class: ~mate n compañero de clase; ~room n aula.

clatter ['klætə*] n ruido, estruendo; (of hooves) trápala // vi hacer ruido o estruendo.

clause [klɔːz] n cláusula; (LING) oración f.

claustrophobia [klɔːstrə'fəubɪə] n claustrofobia.

claw [klɔː] n (of cat) uña; (of bird of prey) garra; (of lobster) pinza; (TECH) garfio // vt: to ~ at arañar; (tear) desgarrar.

clay [kleɪ] n arcilla.

clean [kliːn] a limpio; (clear) neto, bien definido // vt limpiar; to ~ out vt limpiar; to ~ up vt limpiar, asear; ~-cut a (person) de buen parecer; (clear) nítido; ~er n (person) asistenta; ~ing n (gen) limpieza; (clothes) limpieza en seco; ~liness ['klɛnlɪnɪs] n limpieza; ~-shaven a sin barba, lampiño.

cleanse [klɛnz] vt limpiar; **cleanser** n agente m de limpieza; (for face) desmaquillador m; **cleansing department** n departamento de limpieza.

clear [klɪə*] a claro; (road, way) limpio, libre; (complete) completo // vt (space) despejar, limpiar; (LAW: suspect) absolver; (obstacle) salvar, saltar por encima de; (debt) liquidar // vi (gen) aclararse; (fog etc) despejarse // ad: ~ of a distancia de; to ~ up vt limpiar; (mystery) aclarar, resolver; ~ance n (removal) despeje m; (permission) acreditación f; ~-cut a bien definido, nítido; ~ing n (in wood) claro; ~ing bank n cámara de compensación; ~ly ad claramente; ~way n (Brit) carretera donde no se puede aparcar.

cleaver ['kliːvə] n cuchilla (de carnicero).

clef [klɛf] n (MUS) clave f.

clemency ['klɛmənsɪ] n clemencia.

clench [klɛntʃ] vt apretar, cerrar.

clergy ['klɜːdʒɪ] n clero; ~man n clérigo.

clerical ['klɛrɪkəl] a oficinista, (REL) clerical.

clerk [klɑːk, (US) klɜːrk] n empleado, oficinista m/f.

clever ['klɛvə*] a (mentally) inteligente, listo; (deft, crafty) hábil; (device, arrangement) ingenioso.

cliché ['kliːʃeɪ] n cliché m, frase f hecha.

click [klɪk] vt (tongue) chasquear; (heels) taconear.

client ['klaɪənt] n cliente m/f; ~ele [kliːɑːn'tɛl] n clientela.

cliff [klɪf] n acantilado.

climate ['klaɪmɪt] n clima m; (fig) ambiente m.

climax ['klaɪmæks] n colmo, punto culminante; (sexual) clímax m.

climb [klaɪm] vi subir, trepar // vt (stairs) subir; (tree) trepar a; (hill) escalar // n subida; ~er n alpinista m/f, montañista m/f; ~ing n alpinismo.

clinch [klɪntʃ] vt (deal) cerrar; (argument) remachar.

cling [klɪŋ], pt, pp **clung** [klʌŋ] vi: **to ~ to** pegarse a, quedar pegado a; (of clothes) ajustarse a.

clinic ['klɪnɪk] n clínica; **~al** a clínico.

clink [klɪŋk] vi tintinar.

clip [klɪp] n (for hair) prendido; (also: **paper ~**) sujetapapeles m inv; (clamp) grapa // vt (cut) cortar; (shorten) acortar; (clamp) sujetar; **~pers** npl (for gardening) tijeras fpl; (for hair) maquinilla sg; (for nails) cortauñas m inv; **~ping** n recorte m.

clique [kliːk] n camarilla, pandilla.

cloak [kləuk] n capa, manto // vt (fig) encubrir, disimular; **~room** n guardarropa; (in station) consigna; (WC) lavabo, aseos mpl.

clock [klɔk] n reloj m; (in taxi) taxímetro; (fam) cara; **~wise** ad en el sentido de las agujas del reloj; **~work** n aparato de relojería // a de cuerda.

clog [klɔg] n zueco, chanclo // vt atascar // vi atascarse.

cloister ['klɔɪstə*] n claustro.

close a, ad and derivatives [kləus] a cercano, próximo; (print, weave) tupido, compacto; (friend) íntimo; (connection) estrecho; (examination) detallado, minucioso; (weather) bochornoso; (atmosphere) sofocante; (room) mal ventilado // ad cerca // vb and derivatives [kləuz] vt (shut) cerrar; (end) concluir, terminar // vi (shop etc) cerrarse; (end) concluirse, terminarse // n (end) fin m, final m, conclusión f; **to ~ down** vi cerrarse definitivamente; **to ~ up** vi (crowd) arrimarse; **~d** a (shop etc) cerrado; **~d shop** n acuerdo de emplear sólo trabajadores sindicados; **~ly** ad (exactly) fielmente; (carefully) atentamente.

closet ['klɔzɪt] n (cupboard) armario; (wc) lavabo.

close-up ['kləusʌp] n primer plano.

closure ['kləuʒə*] n (close-down) cierre m, clausura; (end) fin m.

clot [klɔt] n (gen: **blood ~**) embolia; (fam: idiot) imbécil m/f // vi (blood) cuajarse, coagularse.

cloth [klɔθ] n (material) tela, paño; (rag) trapo.

clothe [kləuð] vt vestir; (fig) revestir; **~s** npl ropa sg; **~s brush** n cepillo (para la ropa); **~s line** n cuerda (para tender la ropa); **~s peg** n pinza; **clothing** n = **clothes.**

cloud [klaud] n nube f; (storm~) nubarrón m; **~burst** n chaparrón m; **~y** a nublado, nubloso; (liquid) turbio.

clout [klaut] vt dar un tortazo a.

clove [kləuv] n clavo; **~ of garlic** diente m de ajo.

clover ['kləuvə*] n trébol m.

clown [klaun] n payaso // vi (also: **~ about, ~ around**) hacer el payaso.

club [klʌb] n (society) club m; (weapon) porra, cachiporra; (also: **golf ~**) palo // vt aporrear // vi: **to ~ together** hacer una colecta; **~s** npl (CARDS) tréboles mpl; **~ house** n sala de reunión.

cluck [klʌk] vi cloquear.

clue [kluː] n pista; (in crosswords) indicación f; **I haven't a ~** no tengo idea.

clump [klʌmp] n (of trees) grupo.

clumsy ['klʌmzɪ] a (person) torpe, desmañado; (movement) pesado.

cluster ['klʌstə*] n grupo; (BOT) racimo // vi agruparse, apiñarse.

clutch [klʌtʃ] n (grip, grasp) apretón m, agarro; (AUT) embrague m; (pedal) pedal m de embrague // vt sujetar, empuñar.

clutter ['klʌtə*] vt atestar, llenar desordenadamente.

Co. abbr of **county; company.**

c/o abbr of **care of** c/a (en casa de), a/c (a cuidado de).

coach [kəutʃ] n (bus) autocar m; (horse-drawn) coche m; (of train) vagón m, coche m; (SPORT) entrenador m, instructor m // vt (SPORT) entrenar; (student) preparar, enseñar.

coagulate [kəu'ægjuleɪt] vi coagularse.

coal [kəul] n carbón m; **~ face** n frente m de carbón; **~field** n yacimiento de carbón.

coalition [kəuə'lɪʃən] n coalición f.

coal: ~man, ~ merchant n carbonero; **~mine** n mina de carbón.

coarse [kɔːs] a basto, burdo; (vulgar) grosero, ordinario.

coast [kəust] n costa, litoral m // vi (AUT) ir en punto muerto; **~al** a costero, costanero; **~er** n buque m costero, barco de cabotaje; **~guard** n guardacostas m inv; **~line** n litoral m.

coat [kəut] n (jacket) chaqueta; (overcoat) abrigo; (of animal) pelo, lana; (of paint) mano f, capa // vt cubrir, revestir; **~ of arms** n escudo de armas; **~ hanger** n percha; **~ing** n capa, baño.

coax [kəuks] vt engatusar.

cob [kɔb] n see **corn.**

cobbler ['kɔblə] n zapatero remendón.

cobbles ['kɔblz], **cobblestones** ['kɔblstəunz] npl guijarros mpl.

cobra ['kəubrə] n cobra.

cobweb ['kɔbwɛb] n telaraña.

cocaine [kə'keɪn] n cocaína.

cock [kɔk] n (rooster) gallo; (male bird) macho // vt (gun) amartillar; **~atoo** n cacatúa; **~erel** n gallito.

cockle ['kɔkl] n berberecho.

cockney ['kɔknɪ] n habitante m/f de ciertos barrios bajos de Londres.

cockpit ['kɔkpɪt] n (in aircraft) carlinga, cabina.

cockroach ['kɔkrəutʃ] n cucaracha.

cocktail ['kɔkteɪl] n combinado, coctel m; **~ cabinet** n mueble-bar m; **~ party** n coctel m, cóctel m.

cocoa ['kəukəu] n cacao; (drink) chocolate m.

coconut ['kəukənʌt] n coco.
cocoon [kə'ku:n] n capullo.
cod [kɔd] n bacalao.
code [kəud] n código; (cipher) clave f;
codify vt codificar.
coerce [kəu'ə:s] vt forzar, obligar;
coercion [-'ə:ʃən] n coacción f.
coexistence ['kəuɪg'zɪstəns] n
coexistencia.
coffee ['kɔfɪ] n café m; ~ **bean** n grano de
café; ~ **grounds** npl heces fpl de café;
~**pot** n cafetera.
coffin ['kɔfɪn] n ataúd m.
cog [kɔg] n diente m; ~**wheel** n rueda
dentada.
cognac ['kɔnjæk] n coñac m.
coherent [kəu'hɪərənt] a coherente.
coil [kɔɪl] n rollo; (rope) adujada; (ELEC)
bobina, carrete m; (contraceptive) espiral f
// vi enrollarse, arrollarse.
coin [kɔɪn] n moneda // vt (word) inventar,
idear; ~**age** n moneda; ~**-box** n caja
recaudadora.
coincide [kəuɪn'saɪd] vi coincidir; (agree)
estar de acuerdo; **coincidence** [kəu-
'ɪnsɪdəns] n casualidad f.
coke [kəuk] n (coal) coque m.
Coke ® [kəuk] n (drink) Coca-Cola f.
colander ['kɔləndə*] n colador m,
escurridor m.
cold [kəuld] a frío // n frío; (MED) resfriado;
it's ~ hace frío; **to be** ~ tener frío; **to
catch** ~ resfriarse, acatarrarse; **to**
~**-shoulder** tratar con frialdad; ~**ly** a
fríamente; ~ **sore** n herpes m labial.
coleslaw ['kəulslɔ:] n ensalada de col.
colic ['kɔlɪk] n cólico.
collaborate [kə'læbəreɪt] vi colaborar;
collaboration [-'reɪʃən] n colaboración f.
collage [kɔ'lɑ:ʒ] n collage m.
collapse [kə'læps] vi (gen) hundirse,
derrumbarse; (MED) sufrir colapso // n
(gen) hundimiento; (MED) colapso;
collapsible a plegable.
collar ['kɔlə*] n (of coat, shirt) cuello;
~**bone** n clavícula.
collate [kə'leɪt] vt cotejar.
colleague ['kɔli:g] n colega m/f.
collect [kə'lɛkt] vt reunir; (as a hobby)
coleccionar; (call and pick up) recoger;
(wages) cobrar; (debts) recaudar;
(donations, subscriptions) colectar // vi
reunirse; coleccionar; ~**ion** [kə'lɛkʃən] n
colección f; cobro; (of people) grupo; (of
donations) recaudación f; (of post)
recogida.
collective [kə'lɛktɪv] a colectivo.
collector [kə'lɛktə*] n coleccionista m/f;
(of taxes etc) recaudador m.
college ['kɔlɪdʒ] n colegio.
collide [kə'laɪd] vi chocar.
collie ['kɔlɪ] n perro pastor.
collision [kə'lɪʒən] n choque m.
colloquial [kə'ləukwɪəl] a familiar,
coloquial.

colon ['kəulən] n (sign) dos puntos; (MED)
colón m.
colonel ['kɔ:nl] n coronel m.
colonial [kə'ləunɪəl] a colonial.
colonize ['kɔlənaɪz] vt colonizar.
colony ['kɔlənɪ] n colonia.
colossal [kə'lɔsl] a colosal.
colour, color (US) ['kʌlə*] n color m // vt
color(e)ar; (with crayons) pintar; (dye)
teñir // vi (blush) sonrojarse; ~**s** npl (of
party, club) colores mpl; ~**-blind** a
daltoniano; ~**ed** a de color; (photo) a
colores; ~**eds** npl gente f de color; ~
film n película en colores; ~**ful** a lleno de
color; (personality) animado; ~**ing** n
colorido; ~**less** a incoloro, sin color; ~
scheme n combinación f de colores; ~
television n televisión f en color(es).
colt [kəult] n potro.
column ['kɔləm] n columna; ~**ist**
['kɔləmnɪst] n columnista m/f.
coma ['kəumə] n coma m.
comb [kəum] n peine m; (ornamental)
peineta // vt (hair) peinar; (area)
registrar.
combat ['kɔmbæt] n combate m // vt
combatir.
combination [kɔmbɪ'neɪʃən] n (gen)
combinación f.
combine [kəm'baɪn] vt combinar;
(qualities) reunir // vi combinarse // n
['kɔmbaɪn] (ECON) asociación f; (pej)
monopolio; ~ **(harvester)** n
cosechadora.
combustion [kəm'bʌstʃən] n combustión f.
come [kʌm] pt **came**, pp **come** vi venir;
to ~ **about** vi suceder, ocurrir; **to** ~
across vt fus (person) topar; (thing) dar
con; **to** ~ **away** vi marcharse; **to** ~ **back**
vi volver; **to** ~ **by** vt fus (acquire)
conseguir; **to** ~ **down** vi bajar; (plane)
aterrizarse; (crash) estrellarse; (buildings)
desplomarse; **to** ~ **forward** vi
presentarse; **to** ~ **in** vi entrar; (train)
llegar; (fashion) ponerse de moda; **to** ~ **in
for** vt fus (criticism etc) merecer; **to** ~
into vt fus (money) heredar; **to** ~ **off** vi
(button) soltarse, desprenderse; (attempt)
tener lugar; **to** ~ **on** vi (pupil, undertaking)
crecer, desarrollarse // vt (find)
encontrar; **on!** ¡vamos!; **to** ~ **out** vi
salir, aparecer; (be revealed) salir a luz; **to**
~ **out for/against** declararse
por/contra; **to** ~ **to** vi volver en sí; (total)
sumar; **to** ~ **up** vi subir; (sun) salir;
(problem) surgir; **to** ~ **up against** vt fus
(resistance, difficulties) tropezar con; **to** ~
up with vt fus (idea) sugerir, proponer; **to**
~ **upon** vt fus dar o topar con; ~**back** n
(THEATRE) reaparición f.
comedian [kə'mi:dɪən] n cómico;
comedienne [-'ɛn] n cómica.
comedown ['kʌmdaun] n (fam) revés m,
bajón m.
comedy ['kɔmɪdɪ] n comedia.
comet ['kɔmɪt] n cometa m.
comfort ['kʌmfət] n comodidad f, confort

m; (*well-being*) bienestar *m*; (*solace*) consuelo; (*relief*) alivio // *vt* consolar; aliviar; ~**able** *a* cómodo.

comic ['kɔmɪk] *a* (*also*: ~**al**) cómico // *n* (*magazine*) tebeo; ~ **strip** *n* tira cómica.

coming ['kʌmɪŋ] *n* venida, llegada // *a* que viene; ~**(s) and going(s)** *n*(*pl*) ir y venir *m*, ajetreo.

comma ['kɔmə] *n* coma.

command [kə'mɑːnd] *n* orden *f*, mandato; (*MIL*: *authority*) mando; (*mastery*) dominio // *vt* (*troops*) mandar; (*give orders to*) mandar, ordenar; (*dispose of*) disponer de; (*deserve*) merecer; ~**eer** [kɔmən'dɪə*] *vt* requisar; ~**er** *n* (*MIL*) comandante *m/f*, jefe/a *m/f*.

commando [kə'mɑːndəu] *n* comando.

commemorate [kə'mɛmɔreɪt] *vt* conmemorar; **commemoration** [-'reɪʃɔn] *n* conmemoración *f*; **commemorative** [-rɔtɪv] *a* conmemorativo.

commence [kə'mɛns] *vt*, *vi* comenzar, empezar.

commend [kə'mɛnd] *vt* (*praise*) elogiar, alabar; (*recommend*) recomendar; (*entrust*) encomendar; ~**ation** [kɔmɛn'deɪʃɔn] *n* elogio, encomio; recomendación *f*.

commensurate [kə'mɛnʃɔrɪt] *a* equivalente (*with* a).

comment ['kɔmɛnt] *n* comentario // *vi* hacer comentarios; ~**ary** ['kɔmɔntɔrɪ] *n* comentario; ~**ator** ['kɔmɔnteɪtɔ*] *n* comentador *m*.

commerce ['kɔmɔːs] *n* comercio.

commercial [kə'mɔːʃɔl] *a* comercial // *n* (*TV*) anuncio (comercial); ~ **break** *n* emisión *f* publicitaria; ~**ize** *vt* comercializar.

commiserate [kə'mɪzɔreɪt] *vi*: **to** ~ **with** compadecerse de, condolerse de.

commission [kə'mɪʃɔn] *n* (*fee*) comisión *f*; (*act*) perpetración *f* // *vt* (*MIL*) nombrar; (*work of art*) encargar; **out of** ~ inutilizado; ~**aire** [kɔmɪʃɔ'nɛɔ*] *n* portero; ~**er** *n* comisario; (*POLICE*) jefe/a *m/f* de policía.

commit [kə'mɪt] *vt* (*act*) cometer; (*to sb's care*) entregar; **to** ~ **o.s.** (**to do**) comprometerse (a hacer); **to** ~ **suicide** suicidarse; ~**ment** *n* compromiso.

committee [kə'mɪtɪ] *n* comité *m*.

commodity [kə'mɔdɪtɪ] *n* mercancía.

common ['kɔmɔn] *a* (*gen*) común; (*pej*) ordinario // *n* campo común; **the C**~**s** *npl* (la Cámara de) los Comunes; **in** ~ en común; ~**er** *n* plebeyo; ~ **law** *n* ley *f* consuetudinaria; ~**ly** *ad* comúnmente; **C**~ **Market** *n* Mercado Común; ~**place** *a* vulgar, trivial; ~**room** *n* salón *m* común; ~ **sense** *n* sentido común; **the C**~**wealth** *n* la Mancomunidad.

commotion [kə'mɔuʃɔn] *n* tumulto, confusión *f*.

communal ['kɔmjuːnl] *a* comunal.

commune ['kɔmjuːn] *n* (*group*) comuna //

vi [kə'mjuːn]: **to** ~ **with** comulgar *o* conversar con.

communicate [kə'mjuːnɪkeɪt] *vt* comunicar // *vi*: **to** ~ (**with**) comunicarse (con).

communication [kəmjuːnɪ'keɪʃɔn] *n* comunicación *f*; ~ **cord** *n* timbre *m* de alarma.

communion [kə'mjuːnɪɔn] *n* (*also*: **Holy C** ~) comunión *f*.

communiqué [kə'mjuːnɪkeɪ] *n* comunicado, parte *m*.

communism ['kɔmjunɪzɔm] *n* comunismo; **communist** *a*, *n* comunista *m/f*.

community [kə'mjuːnɪtɪ] *n* comunidad *f*; (*large group*) colectividad *f*; (*locals*) vecindario; ~ **centre** *n* centro social.

commute [kə'mjuːt] *vi* viajar a diario // *vt* conmutar; **commuter** *n* persona que viaja a menudo.

compact [kɔm'pækt] *a* compacto; (*style*) conciso; (*packed*) apretado // *n* ['kɔmpækt] (*pact*) pacto; (*for powder*) polvera.

companion [kɔm'pænɪɔn] *n* compañero; ~**ship** *n* compañerismo.

company ['kʌmpɔnɪ] *n* (*gen*) compañía; (*COMM*) sociedad *f*, compañía; **to keep sb** ~ acompañar a uno; **limited** ~ sociedad *f* anónima.

comparable ['kɔmpɔrɔbl] *a* comparable.

comparative [kɔm'pærɔtɪv] *a* relativo.

compare [kɔm'pɛɔ*] *vt* comparar; (*set side by side*) cotejar // *vi*: **to** ~ (**with**) compararse (con); **comparison** [-'pærɪsn] *n* comparación *f*; cotejo; **in comparison** (**with**) en comparación (con).

compartment [kɔm'pɑːtmɔnt] *n* (*also RAIL*) departamento.

compass ['kʌmpɔs] *n* brújula; ~**es** *npl* compás *m*.

compassion [kɔm'pæʃɔn] *n* compasión *f*; ~**ate** *a* compasivo.

compatible [kɔm'pætɪbl] *a* compatible.

compel [kɔm'pɛl] *vt* obligar; ~**ling** *a* (*fig*: *argument*) convincente.

compendium [kɔm'pɛndɪɔm] *n* compendio.

compensate ['kɔmpɔnseɪt] *vt* compensar // *vi*: **to** ~ **for** compensar; **compensation** [-'seɪʃɔn] *n* (*for loss*) indemnización *f*.

compère ['kɔmpɛɔ*] *n* presentador *m*.

compete [kɔm'piːt] *vi* (*take part*) tomar parte, concurrir; (*vie with*) competir, hacer competencia.

competence ['kɔmpɪtɔns] *n* capacidad *f*, aptitud *f*; **competent** [-ɔnt] *a* competente, capaz.

competition [kɔmpɪ'tɪʃɔn] *n* (*contest*) concurso; (*ECON*) competencia; (*rivalry*) competencia.

competitive [kɔm'pɛtɪtɪv] *a* (*ECON*) competitivo; (*spirit*) competidor(a), de competencia.

competitor [kɔm'pɛtɪtɔ*] *n* (*rival*)

competidor/a *m/f*; (*participant*) concursante *m/f*.
compile [kəm'paıl] *vt* recopilar, compilar.
complacency [kəm'pleısnsı] *n* satisfacción *f* de sí mismo; **complacent** [-sənt] *a* complacido.
complain [kəm'pleın] *vi* (*gen*) quejarse; ~**t** *n* (*gen*) queja; (*JUR*) demanda, querella; (*MED*) enfermedad *f*.
complement ['komplımənt] *n* complemento; (*esp ship's crew*) dotación *f*; ~**ary** [komplı'mentərı] *a* complementario.
complete [kəm'pli:t] *a* (*full*) completo; (*finished*) acabado // *vt* (*fulfil*) completar; (*finish*) acabar; (*a form*) llenar; ~**ly** *ad* completamente; **completion** *n* (*gen*) conclusión *f*, terminación *f*; (*of contract etc*) realización *f*.
complex ['kompleks] *a* complejo // *n* (*gen*) complejo.
complexion [kəm'plekʃən] *n* (*of face*) tez *f*, cutis *m*; (*fig*) aspecto.
complexity [kəm'pleksıtı] *n* complejidad *f*.
compliance [kəm'plaıəns] *n* (*submission*) sumisión *f*; (*agreement*) conformidad *f*; **in** ~ **with** de acuerdo con; **compliant** [-ənt] *a* sumiso; conforme.
complicate ['komplıkeıt] *vt* complicar; ~**d** *a* complicado; **complication** [-'keıʃən] *n* complicación *f*.
compliment *n* ['komplımənt] (*formal*) cumplido; (*lovers'*) piropo; ~**s** *npl* saludos *mpl*; **to pay sb a** ~ (*amorously*) piropear, echar piropos a alguien; ~**ary** [-'mentərı] *a* lisonjero; (*free*) de favor.
comply [kəm'plaı] *vi*: **to** ~ **with** cumplir con.
component [kəm'pəunənt] *a* componente // *n* (*TECH*) pieza.
compose [kəm'pəuz] *vt* componer; **to be** ~**d of** componerse de, constar de; **to** ~ **o.s.** tranquilizarse; ~**d** *a* sosegado; **composer** *n* (*MUS*) compositor *m*.
composite ['kompəzıt] *a* compuesto.
composition [kompə'zıʃən] *n* composición *f*.
compost ['kompost] *n* abono compuesto.
composure [kəm'pəuʒə*] *n* serenidad *f*, calma.
compound ['kompaund] *n* (*CHEM, LING*) compuesto; (*enclosure*) recinto // *a* (*gen*) compuesto; (*fracture*) complicado.
comprehend [komprı'hend] *vt* comprender; **comprehension** [-'henʃən] *n* comprensión *f*.
comprehensive [komprı'hensıv] *a* (*broad*) extenso; (*general*) de conjunto; (*INSURANCE*) contra todo riesgo; ~ (**school**) *n* integrado.
compress [kəm'pres] *vt* comprimir // *n* ['kompres] (*MED*) compresa; ~**ion** [-'preʃən] *n* compresión *f*.
comprise [kəm'praız] *vt* (*also*: **be** ~**d of**) comprender, constar de.
compromise ['komprəmaız] *n*

(*agreement*) componenda, arreglo; (*midpoint*) término medio // *vt* comprometer // *vi* transigir.
compulsion [kəm'pʌlʃən] *n* obligación *f*.
compulsive [kəm'pʌlsıv] *a* compulsivo; (*PSYCH*) empedernido.
compulsory [kəm'pʌlsərı] *a* obligatorio.
computer [kəm'pju:tə*] *n* ordenador *m*, computador *m*, computadora; ~**ize** *vt* computerizar; ~ **programmer** *n* programador/a *m/f*; ~ **programming** *n* programación *f*; ~ **science** *n* ciencia de computadoras.
comrade ['komrıd] *n* camarada *m/f*; ~**ship** *n* camaradería, compañerismo.
con [kon] *vt* estafar // *n* estafa.
concave ['kon'keıv] *a* cóncavo.
conceal [kən'si:l] *vt* ocultar.
concede [kən'si:d] *vt* conceder // *vi* ceder, darse por vencido.
conceit [kən'si:t] *n* presunción *f*; ~**ed** *a* presumido.
conceivable [kən'si:vəbl] *a* concebible.
conceive [kən'si:v] *vt, vi* concebir.
concentrate ['konsəntreıt] *vi* concentrarse // *vt* concentrar.
concentration [konsən'treıʃən] *n* concentración *f*; ~ **camp** *n* campo de concentración.
concept ['konsept] *n* concepto.
conception [kən'sepʃən] *n* (*idea*) concepto, idea; (*BIOL*) concepción *f*.
concern [kən'sə:n] *n* (*matter*) asunto; (*COMM*) empresa; (*anxiety*) preocupación *f* // *vt* tener que ver con; **to be** ~**ed** (**about**) interesarse (por), preocuparse (por); ~**ing** *prep* sobre, acerca de.
concert ['konsət] *n* concierto; ~ **hall** *n* sala de conciertos.
concertina [konsə'ti:nə] *n* concertina.
concerto [kon'tʃə:təu] *n* concierto.
concession [kən'seʃən] *n* concesión *f*; **tax** ~ privilegio fiscal.
conciliation [kənsılı'eıʃən] *n* conciliación *f*; **conciliatory** [-'sılıətrı] *a* conciliador(a).
concise [kən'saıs] *a* conciso.
conclude [kən'klu:d] *vt* (*finish*) concluir; (*treaty etc*) firmar; (*agreement*) llegar a; (*decide*) llegar a la conclusión de; **conclusion** [-'klu:ʒən] *n* conclusión *f*; **conclusive** [-'klu:sıv] *a* decisivo, concluyente.
concoct [kən'kokt] *vt* (*gen*) confeccionar; (*plot*) tramar.
concrete ['konkri:t] *n* hormigón *m* // *a* concreto.
concur [kən'kə:*] *vi* estar de acuerdo, asentir.
concurrently [kən'kʌrntlı] *ad* al mismo tiempo.
concussion [kən'kʌʃən] *n* conmoción *f* cerebral.
condemn [kən'dem] *vt* condenar; ~**ation** [kondem'neıʃən] *n* (*gen*) condenación *f*; (*blame*) censura.

condensation [kɔndɛn'seɪʃən] n condensación f.

condense [kən'dɛns] vi condensarse // vt condensar, abreviar; ~d milk n leche f condensada.

condescend [kɔndɪ'sɛnd] vi condescender, dignarse; ~ing a condescendiente.

condition [kən'dɪʃən] n condición f // vt condicionar; on ~ that a condición (de) que.

condolences [kən'dəulənsɪz] npl pésame m.

condone [kən'dəun] vt condonar.

conducive [kən'djuːsɪv] a: ~ to conducente a.

conduct ['kɔndʌkt] n conducta, comportamiento // vt [kən'dʌkt] (lead) conducir; (manage) llevar, dirigir; (MUS) dirigir // vi (MUS) llevar la batuta; to ~ o.s. comportarse; ~or n (of orchestra) director m; (on bus) cobrador m; (ELEC) conductor m; ~ress n (on bus) cobradora.

cone [kəun] n cono; (for ice-cream) barquillo.

confectioner [kən'fɛkʃənə*] n pastelero; ~'s (shop) n pastelería; (sweet shop) confitería; ~y n (cakes) pasteles mpl; (sweets) dulces mpl.

confederation [kənfɛdə'reɪʃən] n confederación f.

confer [kən'fɔː*] vt otorgar (on a) // vi conferenciar.

conference ['kɔnfərns] n (meeting) congreso.

confess [kən'fɛs] vt confesar // vi confesarse; ~ion [-'fɛʃən] n confesión f; ~ional [-'fɛʃənl] n confesionario; ~or n confesor m.

confetti [kən'fɛtɪ] n confeti m.

confide [kən'faɪd] vi: to ~ in confiar en, fiarse de.

confidence ['kɔnfɪdns] n (gen) confianza; (secret) confidencia; ~ trick n timo; **confident** a seguro de sí mismo; **confidential** [kɔnfɪ'dɛnʃəl] a confidencial; (secretary) de confianza.

confine [kən'faɪn] vt (limit) limitar; (shut up) encerrar; ~d a (space) reducido; ~ment n (prison) prisión f; (enclosure) encierro; (MED) parto, sobreparto; ~s ['kɔnfaɪnz] npl confines mpl.

confirm [kən'fɔːm] vt confirmar; ~ation [kɔnfə'meɪʃən] n confirmación f; ~ed a empedernido.

confiscate ['kɔnfɪskeɪt] vt confiscar; **confiscation** [-'keɪʃən] n incautación f.

conflict ['kɔnflɪkt] n conflicto // vi [kən-'flɪkt] (opinions) chocar; ~ing a contrario.

conform [kən'fɔːm] vi conformarse; to ~ to ajustarse a, cuadrar con; ~ist m/f.

confound [kən'faund] vt confundir; ~ed a condenado.

confront [kən'frʌnt] vt (problems) encararse con; (enemy, danger)

enfrentarse con; ~ation [kɔnfrən'teɪʃən] n enfrentamiento.

confuse [kən'fjuːz] vt (perplex) aturdir, desconcertar; (mix up) confundir; ~d a confuso; (person) perplejo, despistado; **confusing** a confuso; **confusion** [-'fjuːʒən] n confusión f.

congeal [kən'dʒiːl] vi (freeze) congelarse; (coagulate) coagularse.

congenial [kən'dʒiːnɪəl] a simpático, agradable.

congenital [kən'dʒɛnɪtl] a congénito.

congested [kən'dʒɛstɪd] a (gen) lleno; (area) superpoblado; **congestion** [-'dʒɛstʃən] n congestión f.

conglomeration [kənglɔmə'reɪʃən] n conglomeración f.

congratulate [kən'grætjuleɪt] vt felicitar; **congratulations** [-'leɪʃənz] npl felicidades fpl.

congregate ['kɔŋgrɪgeɪt] vi congregarse; **congregation** [-'geɪʃən] n (in church) fieles mpl; (assembly) reunión f.

congress ['kɔŋgrɛs] n congreso; ~man n (US) diputado.

conical ['kɔnɪkl] a cónico.

conifer ['kɔnɪfə*] n conífera; ~ous [kə'nɪfərəs] a (forest) conífero.

conjecture [kən'dʒɛktʃə*] n conjetura.

conjugal ['kɔndʒugl] a conyugal.

conjugate ['kɔndʒugeɪt] vt conjugar.

conjunction [kən'dʒʌŋkʃən] n conjunción f.

conjure ['kʌndʒə*] vi hacer juegos de manos; to ~ up vt (ghost, spirit) hacer aparecer; (memories) evocar; **conjurer** n ilusionista m/f; **conjuring trick** n ilusionismo, juego de manos.

conk [kɔŋk]: ~ out vi (col) estropearse.

con man ['kɔn-] n timador m.

connect [kə'nɛkt] vt juntar, unir; (ELEC) conectar; (fig) relacionar, asociar // vi: to ~ with (train) enlazar con; ~ion [-ʃən] n juntura, unión f; (ELEC) conexión f; (RAIL) correspondencia; (TEL) comunicación f; (fig) relación f.

connive [kə'naɪv] vi: to ~ at hacer la vista gorda a.

connoisseur [kɔnɪ'sə*] n experto, entendido.

connotation [kɔnə'teɪʃən] n connotación f.

conquer ['kɔŋkə*] vt (gen) conquistar; (enemy) vencer; (feelings) dominar; ~or n conquistador m.

conquest ['kɔŋkwɛst] n conquista.

cons [kɔnz] npl see pro.

conscience ['kɔnʃəns] n conciencia.

conscientious [kɔnʃɪ'ɛnʃəs] a concienzudo; (objection) de conciencia.

conscious ['kɔnʃəs] a consciente; ~ness n conciencia; (MED) conocimiento.

conscript ['kɔnskrɪpt] n recluto m/f; ~ion [kən'skrɪpʃən] n servicio militar (obligatorio).

consecrate ['kɔnsɪkreɪt] vt consagrar.

consecutive [kɔn'sɛkjutɪv] a sucesivo, seguido.
consensus [kɔn'sɛnsɔs] n consenso.
consent [kɔn'sɛnt] n consentimiento // vi: **to ~ to** consentir en.
consequence ['kɔnsɪkwɔns] n consecuencia.
consequently ['kɔnsɪkwɔntlɪ] ad por consiguiente.
conservation [kɔnsɔ'veɪʃɔn] n conservación f.
conservative [kɔn'sɔ:vɔtɪv] a conservador(a); (cautious) cauteloso; **C~** a, n conservador/a m/f.
conservatory [kɔn'sɔ:vɔtrɪ] n (greenhouse) invernadero.
conserve [kɔn'sɔ:v] vt conservar // n conserva.
consider [kɔn'sɪdɔ*] vt (gen) considerar; (take into account) tomar en cuenta; (study) estudiar, examinar; **~able** a considerable; (sum) importante.
considerate [kɔn'sɪdɔrɪt] a considerado; **consideration** [-'reɪʃɔn] n consideración f; (reward) retribución f.
considering [kɔn'sɪdɔrɪŋ] prep en consideración a.
consign [kɔn'saɪn] vt consignar; **~ment** n envío.
consist [kɔn'sɪst] vi: **to ~ of** consistir en.
consistency [kɔn'sɪstɔnsɪ] n (of person etc) consecuencia; (thickness) consistencia.
consistent [kɔn'sɪstɔnt] a (person) consecuente; (even) constante.
consolation [kɔnsɔ'leɪʃɔn] n consuelo.
console [kɔn'sɔul] vt consolar // n ['kɔnsɔul] consola.
consolidate [kɔn'sɔlɪdeɪt] vt consolidar.
consommé [kɔn'sɔmeɪ] n consomé m, caldo.
consonant ['kɔnsɔnɔnt] n consonante f.
consortium [kɔn'sɔ:tɪɔm] n consorcio.
conspicuous [kɔn'spɪkjuɔs] a (visible) visible; (garish etc) llamativo; (outstanding) notable.
conspiracy [kɔn'spɪrɔsɪ] n conjura, complot m.
conspire [kɔn'spaɪɔ*] vi conspirar.
constable ['kʌnstɔbl] n policía m/f; **chief ~** jefe m de policía.
constabulary [kɔn'stæbjulɔrɪ] n policía.
constant ['kɔnstɔnt] a (gen) constante; (loyal) leal, fiel.
constellation [kɔnstɔ'leɪʃɔn] n constelación f.
consternation [kɔnstɔ'neɪʃɔn] n consternación f.
constipated ['kɔnstɪpeɪtɔd] a estreñido.
constituency [kɔn'stɪtjuɔnsɪ] n (POL) distrito electoral; **constituent** [-ɔnt] n (POL) elector/a m/f; (part) componente m.
constitute ['kɔnstɪtju:t] vt constituir.
constitution [kɔnstɪ'tju:ʃɔn] n constitución f; **~al** a constitucional.
constrain [kɔn'streɪn] vt obligar; **~ed** a:

to feel ~ed to... sentirse en la necesidad de...; **~t** n (force) fuerza; (confinement) encierro; (shyness) reserva.
constrict [kɔn'strɪkt] vt apretar, estrechar.
construct [kɔn'strʌkt] vt construir; **~ion** [-ʃɔn] n construcción f; **~ive** a constructivo.
construe [kɔn'stru:] vt interpretar.
consul ['kɔnsl] n cónsul m/f; **~ate** ['kɔnsjulɪt] n consulado.
consult [kɔn'sʌlt] vt, vi consultar; **~ant** n (MED) especialista m/f; (other specialist) asesor m; **~ation** [kɔnsɔl'teɪʃɔn] n consulta; **~ing room** n consultorio.
consume [kɔn'sju:m] vt (eat) comerse; (drink) beberse; (fire etc, COMM) consumir; **consumer** n consumidor/a m/f; **consumer goods** npl bienes mpl de consumo; **consumer society** n sociedad f de consumo.
consummate ['kɔnsʌmeɪt] vt consumar.
consumption [kɔn'sʌmpʃɔn] n consumo.
cont. abbr of **continued**.
contact ['kɔntækt] n contacto; (pej) enchufe m // vt ponerse en contacto con; **he has good ~s** tiene buenas relaciones; **~ lenses** npl lentes fpl de contacto, microlentillas fpl.
contagious [kɔn'teɪdʒɔs] a contagioso.
contain [kɔn'teɪn] vt contener; **to ~ o.s.** contenerse; **~er** n recipiente m; (for shipping etc) contenedor m.
contaminate [kɔn'tæmɪneɪt] vt contaminar; **contamination** [-'neɪʃɔn] n contaminación f.
cont'd abbr of **continued**.
contemplate ['kɔntɔmpleɪt] vt (gen) contemplar; (expect) contar con; (intend)· pensar; **contemplation** [-'pleɪʃɔn] n contemplación f.
contemporary [kɔn'tɛmpɔrɔrɪ] a, n contemporáneo/a.
contempt [kɔn'tɛmpt] n desprecio; **~ible** a despreciable; **~uous** a despectivo, desdeñoso.
contend [kɔn'tɛnd] vt (argue) afirmar // vi (struggle) luchar; **~er** n contendiente m/f.
content [kɔn'tɛnt] a (happy) contento; (satisfied) satisfecho // vt contentar; satisfacer // n ['kɔntɛnt] contento; satisfacción f; **~s** npl contenido sg; **~ed** a contento; satisfecho.
contention [kɔn'tɛnʃɔn] n contienda; (argument) argumento.
contentment [kɔn'tɛntmɔnt] n contento.
contest ['kɔntɛst] n contienda; (competition) concurso // vt [kɔn'tɛst] (dispute) impugnar; (legal case) defender; (POL) ser candidato en; **~ant** [kɔn'tɛstɔnt] n concursante m/f; (in fight) contendiente m/f.
context ['kɔntɛkst] n contexto.
continent ['kɔntɪnɔnt] n continente m; **the C~** el continente europeo; **~al** [-'nɛntl] a continental.

Page

contingency [kən'tɪndʒənsɪ] *n* contingencia; **contingent** [-ənt] *n* contingente *m*.
continual [kən'tɪnjuəl] *a* continuo; ~**ly** *ad* constantemente.
continuation [kəntɪnju'eɪʃən] *n* prolongación *f*; (*after interruption*) continuación *f*.
continue [kən'tɪnjuː] *vi* seguir, continuar // *vt* seguir, continuar; (*start again*) proseguir.
continuity [kɒntɪ'njuɪtɪ] *n* continuidad *f*.
continuous [kən'tɪnjuəs] *a* continuo.
contort [kən'tɔːt] *vt* retorcer; ~**ion** [-'tɔːʃən] *n* contorsión *f*; ~**ionist** [-'tɔːʃənɪst] *n* contorsionista *m/f*.
contour ['kɒntuə*] *n* contorno; (*also*: ~ **line**) curva de nivel.
contraband ['kɒntrəbænd] *n* contrabando.
contraception [kɒntrə'sɛpʃən] *n* contracepción *f*; **contraceptive** [-'sɛptɪv] *a*, *n* anticonceptivo.
contract ['kɒntrækt] *n* contrato // (*vb*: [kən'trækt]) *vi* (*COMM*): **to** ~ **to do sth** comprometerse por contrato a hacer algo; (*become smaller*) contraerse, encogerse // *vt* contraer; ~**ion** [-ʃən] *n* contracción *f*; ~**or** *n* contratista *m/f*.
contradict [kɒntrə'dɪkt] *vt* (*deny*) desmentir; (*be contrary to*) contradecir; ~**ion** [-ʃən] *n* contradicción *f*.
contralto [kən'træltəu] *n* contralto.
contraption [kən'træpʃən] *n* (*pej*) armatoste *m*.
contrary ['kɒntrərɪ] *a*, *n* contrario.
contrast ['kɒntrɑːst] *n* contraste *m* // *vt* [kən'trɑːst] comparar; ~**ing** *a* opuesto.
contravene [kɒntrə'viːn] *vt* oponerse a; (*law*) contravenir.
contribute [kən'trɪbjuːt] *vi* contribuir // *vt*: **to** ~ **to** (*gen*) contribuir a; (*newspaper*) escribir para; **contribution** [kɒntrɪ'bjuːʃən] *n* (*money*) aportación *f*; (*to debate*) intervención *f*; (*to journal*) colaboración *f*; **contributor** *n* (*to newspaper*) colaborador *m*.
contrive [kən'traɪv] *vt* (*invent*) idear; (*carry out*) efectuar; (*plot*) tramar // *vi*: **to** ~ **to do** lograr hacer.
control [kən'trəul] *vt* (*gen*) controlar; (*traffic etc*) dirigir; (*machinery*) regular; (*temper*) dominar // *n* (*command*) control *m*; (*of car*) conducción *f*; (*check*) freno; ~**s** *npl* mando *sg*; ~ **panel** *n* tablero de instrumentos; ~ **room** *n* sala de mando; ~ **tower** *n* (*AVIAT*) torre *f* de control.
controversial [kɒntrə'vɜːʃl] *a* discutible; **controversy** ['kɒntrəvɜːsɪ] *n* controversia.
convalesce [kɒnvə'lɛs] *vi* convalecer; **convalescence** *n* convalecencia; **convalescent** *a*, *n* convaleciente *m/f*.
convector [kən'vɛktə*] *n* (*heater*) calentador *m* de convección.
convene [kən'viːn] *vt* convocar // *vi* reunirse.
convenience [kən'viːnɪəns] *n* (*comfort*) comodidad *f*; (*advantage*) ventaja; **at your** ~ cuando le sea conveniente; **public** ~ aseos públicos *mpl*; **convenient** [-ənt] *a* cómodo; (*useful*) útil; (*place*) accesible; (*time*) oportuno, conveniente.
convent ['kɒnvənt] *n* convento; ~ **school** *n* colegio de monjas.
convention [kən'vɛnʃən] *n* convención *f*; (*meeting*) asamblea; ~**al** *a* convencional.
converge [kən'vɜːdʒ] *vi* converger.
conversant [kən'vɜːsnt] *a*: **to be** ~ **with** ser enterado de.
conversation [kɒnvə'seɪʃən] *n* conversación *f*; ~**al** *a* (*familiar*) familiar; (*talkative*) locuaz.
converse ['kɒnvɜːs] *n* inversa // *vi* [kən'vɜːs] conversar; ~**ly** [-'vɜːslɪ] *ad* a la inversa.
conversion [kən'vɜːʃən] *n* conversión *f*; ~ **table** *n* tabla de conversión.
convert [kən'vɜːt] *vt* (*REL*, *COMM*) convertir; (*alter*) transformar // *n* ['kɒnvɜːt] converso/a; ~**ible** *a* convertible // *n* descapotable *m*.
convex ['kɒn'vɛks] *a* convexo.
convey [kən'veɪ] *vt* (*gen*) llevar; (*thanks*) comunicar; (*idea*) expresar; ~**or belt** *n* cinta transportadora.
convict [kən'vɪkt] *vt* (*gen*) condenar; (*sentence*) declarar culpable // *n* ['kɒnvɪkt] presidiario; ~**ion** [-ʃən] *n* condena; (*belief*) creencia, convicción *f*.
convince [kən'vɪns] *vt* convencer; **convincing** *a* convincente.
convoy ['kɒnvɔɪ] *n* convoy *m*.
convulse [kən'vʌls] *vt* convulsionar; (*laughter*) hacer morir de la risa; **convulsion** [-'vʌlʃən] *n* convulsión *f*; (*laughter*) paroxismo.
coo [kuː] *vi* arrullar.
cook [kuk] *vt* (*gen*) cocinar; (*stew etc*) guisar; (*meal*) preparar // *vi* cocer; (*person*) cocinar // *n* cocinero; ~**er** *n* cocina; ~**ery** *n* (*dishes*) cocina; (*art*) arte *m* de cocinar; ~**ery book** *n* libro de cocina; ~**ie** *n* (*US*) bizcocho; ~**ing** *n* cocina.
cool [kuːl] *a* fresco; (*not hot*) tibio; (*not afraid*) tranquilo; (*unfriendly*) frío // *vt* enfriar // *vi* enfriarse; ~**ness** *n* frescura; tranquilidad *f*; (*hostility*) frialdad *f*; (*indifference*) falta de entusiasmo.
coop [kuːp] *n* gallinero // *vt*: **to** ~ **up** (*fig*) encerrar.
co-op ['kəuɒp] *n abbr of* **Cooperative** (**Society**).
cooperate [kəu'ɒpəreɪt] *vi* cooperar, colaborar; **cooperation** [-'reɪʃən] *n* cooperación *f*, colaboración *f*; **cooperative** [-rətɪv] *a* cooperativo // *n* cooperativa.
coordinate [kəu'ɔːdɪneɪt] *vt* coordinar; **coordination** [-'neɪʃən] *n* coordinación *f*.
cop [kɒp] *n* (*col*) poli *m*.
cope [kəup] *vi*: **to** ~ **with** poder con; (*problem*) hacer frente a.
co-pilot ['kəu'paɪlət] *n* copiloto.
copious ['kəupɪəs] *a* copioso, abundante.

copper ['kɔpə*] n (metal) cobre m; (col: policeman) poli m; ~s npl monedas fpl de poco valor.
coppice ['kɔpɪs], **copse** [kɔps] n bosquecillo.
copulate ['kɔpjuleɪt] vi copularse; **copulation** [-'leɪʃən] n cópula.
copy ['kɔpɪ] n copia; (of book etc) ejemplar m; (of writing) original m // vt copiar; ~right n derechos mpl de autor.
coral ['kɔrəl] n coral m; ~ reef n arrecife m (de coral).
cord [kɔːd] n cuerda; (ELEC) cordón m; (fabric) pana.
cordial ['kɔːdɪəl] a afectuoso // n cordial m.
cordon ['kɔːdn] n cordón m; to ~ off vt acordonar.
corduroy ['kɔːdərɔɪ] n pana.
core [kɔː*] n (gen) centro, núcleo; (of fruit) corazón m // vt quitar el corazón de.
coriander [kɔrɪ'ændə*] n culantro.
cork [kɔːk] n corcho; (tree) alcornoque m; ~screw n sacacorchos m inv.
cormorant ['kɔːmərnt] n cormorán m grande.
corn [kɔːn] n (wheat) trigo; (US: maize) maíz m; (cereals) granos mpl; (on foot) callo; ~ on the cob (CULIN) maíz en la mazorca.
corned beef ['kɔːnd-] n carne f de vaca acecinada.
corner ['kɔːnə*] n (gen) ángulo; (outside) esquina; (inside) rincón m; (in road) curva; (FOOTBALL) córner m // vt (trap) arrinconar; (COMM) acaparar // vi (in car) tomar una curva; ~stone n piedra angular.
cornet ['kɔːnɪt] n (MUS) corneta; (of icecream) barquillo.
cornflour ['kɔːnflauə*] n harina de maíz.
Cornwall ['kɔːnwəl] n Cornualles m.
corny ['kɔːnɪ] a (col) viejo, gastado.
corollary [kə'rɔlərɪ] n corolario.
coronary ['kɔrənərɪ] n: ~ (thrombosis) trombosis f coronaria.
coronation [kɔrə'neɪʃən] n coronación f.
coroner ['kɔrənə*] n juez m de primera instancia.
coronet ['kɔrənɪt] n corona.
corporal ['kɔːpərl] n cabo // a corporal.
corporate ['kɔːpərɪt] a corporativo.
corporation [kɔːpə'reɪʃən] n (of town) ayuntamiento; (COMM) corporación f.
corps [kɔː*], pl **corps** [kɔːz] n cuerpo.
corpse [kɔːps] n cadáver m.
corpuscle ['kɔːpʌsl] n corpúsculo.
corral [kə'rɑːl] n corral m.
correct [kə'rɛkt] a (accurate) justo, exacto; (proper) correcto // vt corregir; (exam) calificar; ~ion [-ʃən] n rectificación f; (erasure) tachadura.
correlate ['kɔrɪleɪt] vt correlacionar.
correspond [kɔrɪs'pɔnd] vi (write) escribirse; (be equal to) corresponder; ~ence n correspondencia; ~ence

course n curso por correspondencia; ~ent n corresponsal m/f; ~ing a correspondiente.
corridor ['kɔrɪdɔː*] n pasillo.
corroborate [kə'rɔbəreɪt] vt corroborar.
corrode [kə'rəud] vt corroer // vi corroerse; **corrosion** [-'rəuʒən] n corrosión f.
corrugated ['kɔrəgeɪtɪd] a ondulado; ~ iron n chapa ondulada.
corrupt [kə'rʌpt] a corrompido; (person) venal // vt corromper; (bribe) sobornar; ~ion [-ʃən] n corrupción f.
corset ['kɔːsɪt] n faja.
Corsica ['kɔːsɪkə] n Córcega.
cortège [kɔː'teːʒ] n cortejo, desfile m.
cortisone ['kɔːtɪzəun] n cortisona.
cosh [kɔʃ] n cachiporra.
cosiness ['kəuzɪnɪs] n comodidad f; (atmosphere) lo holgado.
cos lettuce [kɔs-] n lechuga cos.
cosmetic [kɔz'mɛtɪk] n cosmético.
cosmic ['kɔzmɪk] a cósmico.
cosmonaut ['kɔzmənɔːt] n cosmonauta m/f.
cosmopolitan [kɔzmə'pɔlɪtn] a cosmopolita.
cosmos ['kɔzmɔs] n cosmos m.
cost [kɔst] n (gen) coste m, costo; (price) precio; ~s npl costes mpl // vi, pt, pp cost costar, valer // vt preparar el presupuesto de; at the ~ of a costa de; how much does it ~? ¿cuánto cuesta?
co-star ['kəustɑː*] n colega m/f de reparto.
Costa Rican ['kɔstə'riːkən] a costarriqueño.
costly ['kɔstlɪ] a (expensive) costoso; (valuable) suntuoso.
cost price n precio de coste.
costume ['kɔstjuːm] n traje m; (also: swimming ~) traje de baño.
cosy ['kəuzɪ] a cómodo; (atmosphere) acogedor(a); (life) holgado.
cot [kɔt] n (child's) cuna.
cottage ['kɔtɪdʒ] n casita de campo; (rustic) barraca; ~ cheese n requesón m.
cotton ['kɔtn] n algodón m; (thread) hilo; to ~ on to vt (col) caer en la cuenta de; ~ wool n algodón m (hidrófilo).
couch [kautʃ] n sofá m.
cough [kɔf] vi toser // n tos f; to ~ up vt escupir; ~ drop n pastilla para la tos.
could [kud] pt of can; ~n't = could not.
council ['kaunsl] n consejo; city or town ~ consejo municipal; ~ estate n polígono de renta limitada; ~ house n vivienda de renta limitada; ~lor n concejal m/f.
counsel ['kaunsl] n (advice) consejo; (lawyer) abogado // vt aconsejar; ~lor n consejero.
count [kaunt] vt (gen) contar; (include) incluir // vi contar // n (gen) cuenta; (of votes) escrutinio; (nobleman) conde m; (sum) total m, suma; to ~ on vt fus contar con; that doesn't ~! ¡eso no vale!;

~**down** n cuenta hacia atrás.
counter ['kauntə*] n (in shop) mostrador m; (in games) ficha // vt contrarrestar; (blow) parar; (attack) contestar a // ad: ~ **to** contrario a; ~**act** vt contrarrestar; ~**attack** n contrataque m // vi contratacar; ~**balance** n contrapeso; ~-**espionage** n contraespionaje m.
counterfeit ['kauntəfɪt] n moneda falsa // vt falsificar // a falso, falsificado.
counterfoil ['kauntəfɔɪl] n talón m.
counterpart ['kauntəpɑ:t] n (of person) colega m/f.
counter-revolution [kauntərɛvə'lu:ʃən] n contrarrevolución f.
countersign ['kauntəsaɪn] vt refrendar.
countess ['kauntɪs] n condesa.
countless ['kauntlɪs] a incontable.
country ['kʌntrɪ] n país m; (native land) patria; (as opposed to town) campo; (region) región f, tierra; ~ **dancing** n baile m regional; ~ **house** n quinta, finca; ~**side** n campo.
county ['kauntɪ] n condado; ~ **town** n cabeza de partido.
coup [ku:], pl ~**s** [-z] n golpe m; ~ **d'état/de grâce** golpe de estado/de gracia.
coupé ['ku:peɪ] n cupé m.
couple ['kʌpl] n (of things) par m; (of people) pareja; (married ~) matrimonio // vt (ideas, names) unir, juntar; (machinery) acoplar; **a** ~ **of** un par de.
coupling ['kʌplɪŋ] n (RAIL) enganche m.
coupon ['ku:pɔn] n cupón m; (pools ~) boleto.
courage ['kʌrɪdʒ] n valor m, valentía; ~**ous** [kə'reɪdʒəs] a valiente.
courier ['kurɪə*] n estafeta; (diplomatic) correo; (for tourists) agente m/f de turismo.
course [kɔ:s] n (direction) dirección f; (of river, ESCOL) curso; (of ship) rumbo, derrota; (of bullet) trayectoria; (fig) proceder m; (GOLF) campo; (part of meal) plato; **of** ~ ad desde luego, naturalmente; **of** ~! ¡claro!; **in due** ~ en el momento oportuno.
court [kɔ:t] n (royal) corte m; (LAW) tribunal m, juzgado; (TENNIS) pista, cancha // vt (woman) cortejar, hacer la corte a; (danger etc) buscar; **to take to** ~ demandar.
courteous ['kɔ:tɪəs] a cortés.
courtesan [kɔ:tɪ'zæn] n cortesana.
courtesy ['kɔ:təsɪ] n cortesía; **by** ~ **of** con permiso de.
court-house ['kɔ:thaus] n (US) palacio de justicia.
courtier ['kɔ:tɪə*] n cortesano.
court: ~-**martial**, pl ~**s-martial** n consejo de guerra // vt someter a consejo de guerra; ~**room** n sala de justicia; ~**yard** n patio.
cousin ['kʌzn] n primo/a; **first** ~ primo carnal.
cove [kəuv] n cala, ensenada.

covenant ['kʌvənənt] n convenio.
cover ['kʌvə*] vt (gen) cubrir; (with lid) tapar; (chairs etc) revestir; (distance) recorrer; (include) abarcar; (protect) abrigar; (journalist) investigar; (issues) tratar // n (gen) cubierta; (lid) tapa; (for chair etc) funda; (for bed) cobertor m; (envelope) sobre m; (for book) forro; (of magazine) portada; (shelter) abrigo; (insurance) cobertura; **under** ~ (indoors) bajo techo; **under** ~ **of** al abrigo de; (fig) so capa de; **to** ~ **up for sb** encubrir a uno; ~**age** n alcance m; ~ **charge** n precio del cubierto; ~**ing** n cubierta, envoltura; ~**ing letter** n carta explicatoria.
covet ['kʌvɪt] vt codiciar.
cow [kau] n vaca // vt intimidar.
coward ['kauəd] n cobarde m/f; ~**ice** [-ɪs] n cobardía; ~**ly** a cobarde.
cowboy ['kaubɔɪ] n vaquero.
cower ['kauə*] vi encogerse (de miedo).
cowshed ['kauʃɛd] n establo.
coxswain ['kɔksn] n (abbr: **cox**) timonel m/f.
coy [kɔɪ] a tímido.
coyote [kɔɪ'əutɪ] n coyote m.
crab [kræb] n cangrejo; ~ **apple** n manzana silvestre.
crack [kræk] n grieta; (noise) crujido; (: of whip) chasquido; (fam) chiste m // vt agrietar, romper; (nut) cascar; (safe) forzar; (whip etc) chasquear; (knuckles) crujir; (joke) contar // a (expert) experto; **to** ~ **up** vi (MED) sufrir un colapso nervioso; ~**er** n (biscuit) cracker m; (Christmas cracker) sorpresa.
crackle ['krækl] vi crepitar; **crackling** n (of fire) crepitación f; (of leaves etc) crujido; (of pork) chicharrón m.
cradle ['kreɪdl] n cuna.
craft [krɑ:ft] n (skill) arte m; (trade) oficio; (cunning) astucia; (boat) barco.
craftsman ['krɑ:ftsmən] n artesano; ~**ship** n artesanía.
crafty ['krɑ:ftɪ] a astuto.
crag [kræg] n peñasco; ~**gy** a escarpado.
cram [kræm] vt (fill) llenar, henchir; ~**med** a atestado.
cramp [kræmp] n (MED) calambre m; (TECH) grapa // vt (limit) restringir; (annoy) estorbar; ~**ed** a apretado, estrecho.
crampon ['kræmpən] n crampón m.
cranberry ['krænbərɪ] n arándano agrio.
crane [kreɪn] n (TECH) grúa; (bird) grulla.
crank [kræŋk] n manivela; (person) chiflado; ~**shaft** n eje m del cigüeñal.
cranky ['kræŋkɪ] a (eccentric) maniático; (bad-tempered) irritable.
cranny ['krænɪ] n see **nook**.
crash [kræʃ] n (noise) estruendo; (of cars etc) choque m; (of plane) accidente m de avión; (COMM) quiebra // vt (plane) estrellar // vi (plane) estrellarse; (two cars) chocar; (fall noisily) caer con estrépito; ~ **course** n curso acelerado; ~

helmet n casco (protector); ~ **landing** n aterrizaje m forzoso.

crate [kreɪt] n cajón m de embalaje; (fam) armatoste m.

crater ['kreɪtə*] n cráter m.

cravat(e) [krə'væt] n pañuelo.

crave [kreɪv] vt: **to** ~ **for** ansiar, anhelar; **craving** n (of pregnant woman) antojo.

crawl [krɔːl] vi (gen) arrastrarse; (child) andar a gatas, gatear; (vehicle) avanzar a paso de tortuga // n (swimming) crol m.

crayfish ['kreɪfɪʃ] n, pl inv langostino.

crayon ['kreɪən] n pastel m, lápiz m de color.

craze [kreɪz] n manía; (fashion) moda.

crazy ['kreɪzɪ] a (person) loco; (idea) disparatado.

creak [kriːk] vi chirriar, rechinar; (door etc) crujir.

cream [kriːm] n (of milk) nata; (gen) crema; (fig) flor y nata // a (colour) color m (de) crema; ~ **cake** n pastel m de nata; ~ **cheese** n queso de nata; ~**y** a cremoso.

crease [kriːs] n (fold) pliegue m; (in trousers) raya; (wrinkle) arruga // vt (fold) doblar, plegar; (wrinkle) arrugar // vi (wrinkle up) arrugarse.

create [kriː'eɪt] vt crear; **creation** [-ʃən] n creación f; **creative** a creador(a); **creator** n creador m.

creature ['kriːtʃə*] n (animal) animal m, bicho; (living thing) criatura.

crèche, creche [krɛʃ] n guardería infantil.

credentials [krɪ'dɛnʃlz] npl credenciales fpl.

credibility [krɛdɪ'bɪlɪtɪ] n credibilidad f.

credible ['krɛdɪbl] a creíble.

credit ['krɛdɪt] n (gen) crédito; (merit) honor m, mérito // vt (comm) abonar; (believe) creer, prestar fe a // a creditício; ~**s** npl (cinema) fichas técnicas; ~**able** a estimable, digno de elogio; ~ **card** n tarjeta de crédito; ~**or** n acreedor m.

credulity [krɪ'djuːlɪtɪ] n credulidad f.

creed [kriːd] n credo.

creek [kriːk] n cala, ensenada; (US) riachuelo.

creep [kriːp] pt, pp **crept** vi (animal) deslizarse; (gen) arrastrarse; (plant) trepar; ~**er** n enredadera; ~**y** a (frightening) horripilante.

cremate [krɪ'meɪt] vt incinerar; **cremation** [-ʃən] n incineración f.

crematorium [krɛmə'tɔːrɪəm], pl **-ria** [-rɪə] n (horno) crematorio.

creosote ['krɪəsəut] n creosota.

crêpe [kreɪp] n (fabric) crespón m; (rubber) crepé m; ~ **bandage** n venda de crepé.

crept [krɛpt] pt, pp of **creep.**

crescent ['krɛsnt] n media luna; (street) calle f en semicírculo.

cress [krɛs] n mastuerzo.

crest [krɛst] n (of bird) cresta; (of hill)

cima, cumbre f; (of helmet) cimera; (of coat of arms) blasón m; ~**fallen** a alicaído.

Crete [kriːt] n Creta.

crevasse [krɪ'væs] n grieta.

crevice ['krɛvɪs] n grieta, hendedura.

crew [kruː] n (of ship etc) tripulación f; (gang) banda; (mil) dotación f; ~**-cut** n corte m al rape; ~**-neck** n cuello plano.

crib [krɪb] n pesebre m // vt (col) plagiar.

crick [krɪk] n (in neck) tortícolis m.

cricket ['krɪkɪt] n (insect) grillo; (game) críquet m.

crime [kraɪm] n crimen m; (less serious) delito; **criminal** ['krɪmɪnl] n criminal m, delincuente m // a criminal, delictivo; (law) penal; **the Criminal Investigation Department (CID)** Brigada de Investigación Criminal (B.I.C.).

crimson ['krɪmzn] a carmesí.

cringe [krɪndʒ] vi agacharse, encogerse.

crinkle ['krɪŋkl] vt arrugar.

cripple ['krɪpl] n lisiado, mutilado // vt lisiar, tullir.

crisis ['kraɪsɪs], pl **-ses** [-siːz] n crisis f.

crisp [krɪsp] a fresco; (cooked) tostado; (hair) crespo; (manner) seco; ~**s** npl papas fritas fpl.

criss-cross ['krɪskrɔs] a entrelazado.

criterion [kraɪ'tɪərɪən], pl **-ria** [-rɪə] n criterio.

critic ['krɪtɪk] n (gen) criticón/ona m/f; (paper) crítico; ~**al** a (gen) crítico; (illness) grave; ~**ally** ad (ill) gravemente; ~**ism** ['krɪtɪsɪzm] n crítica; ~**ize** ['krɪtɪsaɪz] vt criticar.

croak [krəuk] vi (frog) croar; (raven) graznar // n graznido.

crochet ['krəuʃeɪ] n ganchillo.

crockery ['krɔkərɪ] n loza, vajilla.

crocodile ['krɔkədaɪl] n cocodrilo.

crocus ['krəukəs] n azafrán m.

croft [krɔft] n granja pequeña; ~**er** n pequeño granjero.

croissant ['krwasã] n croissant m, medialuna.

crone [krəun] n bruja.

crony ['krəunɪ] n compinche m/f.

crook [kruk] n (fam) maleante m/f; (of shepherd) cayado; (of arm) pliegue m; ~**ed** ['krukɪd] a torcido; (path) tortuoso; (action) poco limpio.

crop [krɔp] n (species) cultivo; (quantity) cosecha // vt cortar, recortar; **to** ~ **up** vi surgir, presentarse.

croquet ['krəukeɪ] n croquet m.

croquette [krə'kɛt] n croqueta.

cross [krɔs] n cruz f // vt (street etc) cruzar, atravesar // a de mal humor, malhumorado; **to** ~ **o.s.** santiguarse; **to** ~ **out** vt tachar; **to** ~ **over** vi cruzar; ~**bar** n travesaño; (sport) larguero; ~**country (race)** n carrera a campo traviesa, cross m; ~**-examination** n repregunta, interrogatorio; ~**-examine** vt repreguntar; ~**-eyed** a bizco; ~**ing** n

crotch [krɔtʃ] *n* (*of garment*) entrepierna.
crotchet ['krɔtʃit] *n* (*MUS*) negra.
crotchety ['krɔtʃiti] *a* (*person*) arisco.
crouch [krautʃ] *vi* agacharse, acurrucarse.
croupier ['kru:piə] *n* crupier *m/f*.
crow [krəu] *n* (*bird*) cuervo; (*of cock*) canto, cacareo // *vi* (*cock*) cantar, cacarear.
crowbar ['krəubɑ:*] *n* palanca.
crowd [kraud] *n* muchedumbre *f*; (*SPORT*) público; (*unruly*) tropel *m*; (*common herd*) vulgo // *vt* (*gather*) amontonar; (*fill*) llenar // *vi* (*gather*) reunirse; (*pile up*) amontonarse; ~ed *a* (*full*) atestado; (*well-attended*) concurrido.
crown [kraun] *n* corona; (*of head*) coronilla; (*of hat*) copa; (*of hill*) cumbre *f* // *vt* coronar; ~ jewels *npl* joyas *fpl* reales; ~ prince *n* príncipe *m* heredero.
crucial ['kru:ʃl] *a* decisivo.
crucifix ['kru:sifiks] *n* crucifijo; ~ion [-'fikʃən] *n* crucifixión *f*; **crucify** [-fai] *vt* crucificar.
crude [kru:d] *a* (*materials*) bruto; (*fig: basic*) tosco; (: *vulgar*) ordinario; ~ (oil) *n* aceite *m* crudo.
cruel ['kruəl] *a* cruel; ~ty *n* crueldad *f*.
cruet ['kru:it] *n* angarillas *fpl*.
cruise [kru:z] *n* crucero, viaje *m* por mar // *vi* (*ship*) hacer un crucero; (*car*) circular lentamente; **cruiser** *n* crucero.
crumb [krʌm] *n* miga, migaja.
crumble ['krʌmbl] *vt* desmenuzar // *vi* (*gen*) desmenuzarse; (*building*) desmoronarse; **crumbly** *a* desmenuzable.
crumpet ['krʌmpit] *n* bollo blando.
crumple ['krʌmpl] *vt* (*paper*) estrujar; (*material*) arrugar.
crunch [krʌntʃ] *vt* (*food etc*) mascar; (*underfoot*) hacer crujir // *n* (*fig*) crisis *f*; ~y *a* crujiente.
crusade [kru:'seid] *n* cruzada.
crush [krʌʃ] *n* (*people*) agolpamiento; (*crowd*) aglomeración *f*; (*drink*): **lemon** ~ limonada // *vt* (*gen*) aplastar; (*paper*) estrujar; (*cloth*) arrugar; (*fruit*) exprimir; ~ing *a* aplastante; (*burden*) agobiador(a).
crust [krʌst] *n* corteza; (*MED*) costra.
crutch [krʌtʃ] *n* muleta.
crux [krʌks] *n* lo esencial.
cry [krai] *vi* llorar; (*shout*) gritar // *n* grito.
crypt [kript] *n* cripta.
cryptic ['kriptik] *a* enigmático, secreto.
crystal ['kristl] *n* cristal *m*; ~-clear *a* transparente, claro como el agua; **crystallize** *vt* cristalizar // *vi* cristalizarse.

cub [kʌb] *n* cachorro.
Cuba ['kju:bə] *n* Cuba; ~n *a, n* cubano/a.
cubbyhole ['kʌbihəul] *n* chiribitil *m*.
cube [kju:b] *n* cubo; (*of sugar*) terrón *m* // *vt* (*MATH*) cubicar; ~ root *n* raíz *f* cúbica; **cubic** *a* cúbico.
cubicle ['kju:bikl] *n* (*at pool*) caseta; (*for bed*) camarilla.
cuckoo ['kuku:] *n* cuco; ~ clock *n* reloj *m* de cuclillo.
cucumber ['kju:kʌmbə*] *n* pepino.
cuddle ['kʌdl] *vt* abrazar amorosamente // *vi* abrazarse; **cuddly** *a* mimoso.
cue [kju:] *n* (*snooker*) taco; (*THEATRE etc*) entrada, apunte *m*.
cuff [kʌf] *n* (*of shirt, coat etc*) puño; (*blow*) bofetada; **off the** ~ *ad* de improviso; ~links *npl* gemelos *mpl*.
cuisine [kwi'zi:n] *n* cocina.
cul-de-sac ['kʌldəsæk] *n* callejón *m* sin salida.
culinary ['kʌlinəri] *a* culinario.
cull [kʌl] *vt* (*flowers*) coger; (*select*) entresacar.
culminate ['kʌlmineit] *vi*: **to** ~ **in** terminar en; **culmination** [-'neiʃən] *n* culminación *f*, colmo.
culpable ['kʌlpəbl] *a* culpable.
culprit ['kʌlprit] *n* (*persona*) culpable, delincuente *m/f*.
cult [kʌlt] *n* culto.
cultivate ['kʌltiveit] *vt* (*also fig*) cultivar; **cultivation** [-'veiʃən] *n* cultivo; (*fig*) cultura.
cultural ['kʌltʃərəl] *a* cultural.
culture ['kʌltʃə*] *n* (*also fig*) cultura; ~d *a* culto.
cumbersome ['kʌmbəsəm] *a* molesto, incómodo.
cumulative ['kju:mjulətiv] *a* cumulativo.
cunning ['kʌniŋ] *n* astucia // *a* astuto.
cup [kʌp] *n* taza; (*prize, event*) copa.
cupboard ['kʌbəd] *n* armario; (*on wall*) alacena.
Cupid ['kju:pid] *n* Cupido.
cupola ['kju:pələ] *n* cúpula.
cup-tie ['kʌptai] *n* partido de copa.
cur [kə:] *n* perro de mala raza; (*person*) canalla *m/f*.
curable ['kjuərəbl] *a* curable.
curate ['kjuə:rit] *n* cura *m*.
curator [kjuə'reitə*] *n* director *m*.
curb [kə:b] *vt* refrenar // *n* freno.
curdle ['kə:dl] *vi* cuajarse.
curds [kə:dz] *npl* requesón *m*.
cure [kjuə*] *vt* curar // *n* cura, curación *f*.
curfew ['kə:fju:] *n* toque *m* de queda.
curio ['kjuəriəu] *n* curiosidad *f*.
curiosity [kjuəri'ɔsiti] *n* curiosidad *f*; **curious** ['kjuəriəs] *a* curioso.
curl [kə:l] *n* rizo, bucle *m* // *vt* (*hair*) rizar; (*paper*) arrollar; (*lip*) fruncir // *vi* rizarse; arrollarse; **to** ~ **up** *vi* arrollarse; (*person*) hacer un ovillo; (*fam*) morirse de risa; ~er *n* bigudí *m*, chincho; ~y *a* rizado.

currant ['kʌrnt] n pasa; (black, red) grosella.
currency ['kʌrnsɪ] n moneda.
current ['kʌrnt] n corriente f // a corriente, actual; ~ **account** n cuenta corriente; ~ **affairs** npl actualidades fpl; ~ **ly** ad actualmente.
curriculum [kə'rɪkjuləm], pl ~s or **-la** [-lə] n plan m de estudios; ~ **vitae** n currículum m.
curry ['kʌrɪ] n curry m // vt: **to** ~ **favour with** buscar favores con; ~ **powder** n polvos mpl de curry.
curse [kə:s] vi echar pestes // vt maldecir, echar pestes de // n maldición f; (swearword) palabrota.
cursory ['kə:sərɪ] a rápido, superficial.
curt [kə:t] a corto, seco.
curtail [kə:'teɪl] vt (visit etc) acortar; (expenses etc) restringir.
curtain ['kə:tn] n cortina; (THEATRE) telón m; ~ **ring** n anilla.
curts(e)y ['kə:tsɪ] n reverencia // vi hacer una reverencia.
curve [kə:v] n curva // vt encorvar, torcer // vi encorvarse, torcerse; (road) hacer (una) curva.
cushion ['kuʃən] n cojín m; (SNOOKER) banda // vt (seat) acolchar; (shock) amortiguar.
custard ['kʌstəd] n (for pouring) natilla.
custodian [kʌs'təudɪən] n custodio.
custody ['kʌstədɪ] n custodia; **to take into** ~ detener.
custom ['kʌstəm] n costumbre f; (COMM) clientela; ~ **ary** a acostumbrado.
customer ['kʌstəmə*] n cliente m/f.
custom-made ['kʌstəm'meɪd] a hecho a la medida.
customs ['kʌstəmz] npl aduana sg; ~ **duty** n derechos mpl de aduana; ~ **officer** n aduanero.
cut [kʌt], pt, pp **cut** vt cortar; (price) rebajar; (record) grabar; (reduce) reducir // vi cortar; (intersect) cruzarse // n (gen) corte m; (in skin) cortadura; (with sword) tajo; (of knife) cuchillada; (in salary etc) rebaja; (of meat) tajada; **power** ~ apagón m; **to** ~ **a tooth** salirle a uno un diente; **to** ~ **down** vt (tree) derribar; (reduce) reducir; **to** ~ **off** vt (gen) cortar; (retreat) impedir; (troops) cercar; **to** ~ **out** vt (shape) recortar; (delete) suprimir; **to** ~ **through** vi abrirse camino; ~ **back** n reducción f.
cute [kju:t] a lindo; (shrewd) listo.
cuticle ['kju:tɪkl] n cutícula.
cutlery ['kʌtlərɪ] n cubiertos mpl.
cutlet ['kʌtlɪt] n chuleta.
cut: ~ **out** n recortable m; ~ **-price** a a precio reducido; ~ **throat** n asesino // a intenso.
cutting ['kʌtɪŋ] a (gen) cortante; (remark) mordaz // n (PRESS) recorte m; (RAIL) desmonte m.
cwt abbr of **hundredweight(s).**
cyanide ['saɪənaɪd] n cianuro.

cyclamen ['sɪkləmən] n ciclamen m.
cycle ['saɪkl] n ciclo; (bicycle) bicicleta // vi ir en bicicleta; **cycling** n ciclismo; **cyclist** n ciclista m/f.
cyclone ['saɪkləun] n ciclón m.
cygnet ['sɪgnɪt] n pollo de cisne.
cylinder ['sɪlɪndə*] n cilindro; ~ **block** n bloque m de cilindros; ~ **capacity** n cilindrada; ~ **head** n culata de cilindro; ~ **-head gasket** n junta de culata.
cymbals ['sɪmblz] npl platillos mpl.
cynic ['sɪnɪk] n cínico; ~ **al** a cínico; ~ **ism** ['sɪnɪsɪzəm] n cinismo.
cypress ['saɪprɪs] n ciprés m.
Cypriot ['sɪprɪət] a, n chipriota m/f.
Cyprus ['saɪprəs] n Chipre f.
cyst [sɪst] n quiste m; ~ **itis** n cistitis f.
czar [zɑ:*] n zar m.
Czech [tʃɛk] a, n checo/a.
Czechoslovakia [tʃɛkəslə'vækɪə] n Checoslovaquia.

D

dab [dæb] vt (eyes, wound) tocar (ligeramente); (paint, cream) mojar ligeramente // n (of paint) brochazo; (of liquid) gota; (amount) pequeña cantidad f.
dabble ['dæbl] vi: **to** ~ **in** interesarse por.
dad [dæd], **daddy** ['dædɪ] n papá m; **daddy-long-legs** n típula.
daffodil ['dæfədɪl] n narciso trompón.
daft [dɑ:ft] a estúpido, tonto.
dagger ['dægə*] n puñal m, daga; **to look** ~ **s at sb** apuñalar a alguien con la mirada.
daily ['deɪlɪ] a diario, cotidiano // n (paper) diario; (domestic help) asistenta // ad a diario, cada día.
dainty ['deɪntɪ] a delicado; (tasteful) elegante, primoroso.
dairy ['dɛərɪ] n (shop) lechería; (on farm) vaquería // a lechero; ~ **farm** n granja; ~ **produce** n productos mpl lácteos.
daisy ['deɪzɪ] n margarita.
dale [deɪl] n valle m.
dam [dæm] n presa // vt represar.
damage ['dæmɪdʒ] n daño, perjuicio; (to machine) avería // vt dañar, perjudicar; averiar; ~ **s** npl (LAW) daños y perjuicios.
damn [dæm] vt condenar; (curse) maldecir // n (col): **I don't give a** ~ me trae sin cuidado // a (col) maldito; ~ **(it)!** ¡mecachis!; ~ **ing** a (evidence) irrecusable.
damp [dæmp] a húmedo, mojado // n humedad f // vt (also: ~ **en**) (cloth, rag) mojar; (enthusiasm etc) desalentar; ~ **ness** n humedad f.
damson ['dæmzən] n ciruela damascena.
dance [dɑ:ns] n baile m // vi bailar; ~ **hall** n salón m de baile; **dancer** n bailador/a m/f; (professional) bailarín/ina m/f; **dancing** n baile m.
dandelion ['dændɪlaɪən] n diente m de león.

dandruff ['dændrɔf] n caspa.
Dane [deɪn] n danés/esa m/f.
danger ['deɪndʒə*] n peligro; (risk) riesgo;
~! (on sign) ¡peligro de muerte!; to be in
~ of correr riesgo de; ~ous a peligroso;
~ously ad peligrosamente.
dangle ['dæŋgl] vt colgar // vi pender,
estar colgado.
Danish ['deɪnɪʃ] a, n danés/esa m/f.
dare [dɛə*] vt: to ~ sb to do desafiar a
uno a hacer algo // vi: to ~ (to) do sth
atreverse a hacer algo; ~devil n
temerario, atrevido; **daring** a atrevido,
osado // n atrevimiento, osadía.
dark [dɑ:k] a (gen) oscuro; (hair,
complexion) moreno; (cheerless) triste,
sombrío; (fig) secreto, escondido // n
(gen) oscuridad f; (night) tinieblas fpl; to
be left in the ~ about (fig) quedar sin
saber nada de; **after** ~ después del
anochecer; ~en vt oscurecer; (colour)
hacer más oscuro // vi oscurecerse; (sky)
anublarse; ~ **glasses** npl gafas fpl
oscuras; ~ness n oscuridad f, tinieblas
fpl; ~ **room** n cuarto oscuro.
darling ['dɑ:lɪŋ] a, n querido/a.
darn [dɑ:n] vt zurcir.
dart [dɑ:t] n dardo; (in game) rehilete m;
(in sewing) sisa // vi precipitarse; to ~
away/along irse/seguir precipitado;
~board n blanco; ~s n juego de
rehiletes.
dash [dæʃ] n (sign) guión m; (: long) raya;
(rush) carrera // vt (break) romper,
estrellar; (hopes) defraudar // vi
precipitarse, ir de prisa; to ~ away or off
vi marcharse apresuradamente; ~board
n tablero de instrumentos; ~ing a
gallardo.
data ['deɪtə] npl datos mpl; ~ **processing**
n procesamiento de datos.
date [deɪt] n (day) fecha; (with friend) cita;
(fruit) dátil m; (tree) palmera // vt fichar;
citar; to ~ ad hasta la fecha; out of ~
fuera de moda; up to ~ moderno, al día;
~d a anticuado.
daub [dɔ:b] vt manchar.
daughter ['dɔ:tə*] n hija; ~-in-law n
nuera, hija política.
daunting ['dɔ:ntɪŋ] a desalentador(a).
dawdle ['dɔ:dl] vi (waste time) perder el
tiempo; (go slow) andar muy despacio.
dawn [dɔ:n] n alba, amanecer m // vi
(day) amanecer; (fig): it ~ed on him
that... cayó en la cuenta de que....
day [deɪ] n día m; (working ~) jornada; the
~ before el día anterior; the following
~ el día siguiente; by ~ de día; ~break
n amanecer m; ~dream n ensueño // vi
soñar despierto; ~light n luz f (del día);
~time n día m // a de día.
daze [deɪz] vt (stun) aturdir // n: in a ~
aturdido.
dazzle ['dæzl] vt deslumbrar; **dazzling** a
deslumbrante.
dead [dɛd] a (gen) muerto; (deceased)
difunto; (telephone) cortado; (ELEC) sin

corriente // ad (gen) totalmente; (exactly)
justo; ~ **tired** muerto de cansancio; to
stop ~ parar en seco; the ~ los
muertos; ~en vt (blow, sound)
amortiguar; (make numb) calmar, aliviar;
~ end n callejón m sin salida; ~ heat n
(SPORT) empate m; ~line n fecha o hora
tope; ~lock n punto muerto; ~ly a
mortal, fatal; ~pan a sin expresión.
deaf [dɛf] a sordo; ~-aid n audífono; ~en
vt ensordecer; ~ening a
ensordecedor(a); ~ness n sordera;
~-mute n sordomudo/a.
deal [di:l] n (agreement) pacto, convenio;
(business) negocio, trato; (CARDS) reparto
// vt, pt, pp dealt [dɛlt] (gen) dar; a great
~ (of) bastante, mucho; to ~ in tratar
en, comerciar en; to ~ with vt fus
(people) tratar con; (problem) ocuparse
de; (subject) tratar de; (punish) castigar;
~er n comerciante m, tratante m; (CARDS)
mano f; ~ings npl transacciones fpl;
(relations) relaciones fpl.
dear [dɪə*] a querido; (expensive) caro //
n: my ~ mi querido/a // excl: ~ me!
¡Dios mío!; D~ Sir/Madam (in letter)
Muy Señor Mío, estimado Señor/estimada
Señora; ~ly ad (love) tiernamente; (pay)
caro.
death [dɛθ] n muerte f; ~bed n lecho de
muerte; ~ **certificate** n partida de
defunción; ~ **duties** npl (Brit) derechos
mpl de herencia; ~ly a mortal; (silence)
profundo; ~ **penalty** n pena de muerte;
~ **rate** n mortalidad f.
debar [dɪ'bɑ:*] vt (exclude) excluir.
debase [dɪ'beɪs] vt degradar.
debate [dɪ'beɪt] n debate m // vt discutir.
debauchery [dɪ'bɔ:tʃərɪ] n libertinaje m.
debit ['dɛbɪt] n debe m // vt: to ~ a sum
to sb or to sb's account cargar una suma
en cuenta a alguien.
debris ['dɛbri:] n escombros mpl.
debt [dɛt] n deuda; to be in ~ tener
deudas; ~or n deudor/a m/f.
début ['deɪbju:] n presentación f.
decade ['dɛkeɪd] n decenio.
decadence ['dɛkədəns] n decadencia.
decay [dɪ'keɪ] n decadencia; (of building)
desmoronamiento; (fig) deterioro;
(rotting) pudrición f; (of tooth) caries f //
vi (rot) pudrirse; (fig) decaer.
deceased [dɪ'si:st] a difunto.
deceit [dɪ'si:t] n engaño; ~ful a engañoso.
deceive [dɪ'si:v] vt engañar.
decelerate [di:'sɛləreɪt] vt moderar la
marcha de // vi decelerar.
December [dɪ'sɛmbə*] n diciembre m.
decency ['di:sənsɪ] n decencia.
decent ['di:sənt] a (proper) decente;
(person) amable, bueno.
decentralize [di:'sɛntrəlaɪz] vt
descentralizar.
deception [dɪ'sɛpʃən] n engaño;
deceptive [-tɪv] a engañoso.
decibel ['dɛsɪbɛl] n decibel(io) m.
decide [dɪ'saɪd] vt (person) decidir;

(*question, argument*) resolver // *vi* decidir;
to ~ on sth decidir por algo; **~d** *a*
(*resolute*) decidido; (*clear, definite*)
indudable; **~dly** [-dɪdlɪ] *ad* decididamente.
deciduous [dɪ'sɪdjuəs] *a* de hoja caduca.
decimal ['dɛsɪməl] *a* decimal // *n* decimal
f; **~ point** *n* coma de decimales.
decimate ['dɛsɪmeɪt] *vt* diezmar.
decipher [dɪ'saɪfə*] *vt* descifrar.
decision [dɪ'sɪʒən] *n* decisión *f*.
decisive [dɪ'saɪsɪv] *a* decisivo; (*conclusive*)
terminante; (*manner*) tajante.
deck [dɛk] *n* (*NAUT*) cubierta; (*of bus*) piso;
(*of cards*) baraja; **~chair** *n* tumbona,
hamaca.
declaration [dɛklə'reɪʃən] *n* declaración *f*;
declare [dɪ'klɛə*] *vt* (*gen*) declarar.
decline [dɪ'klaɪn] *n* decaimiento,
decadencia; (*lessening*) disminución *f* // *vt*
rehusar // *vi* decaer; disminuir; (*fall*)
bajar.
declutch ['di:'klʌtʃ] *vi* desembragar.
decode [di:'kəud] *vt* descifrar.
decompose [di:kəm'pəuz] *vi*
descomponerse; **decomposition**
[di:kəmpə'zɪʃən] *n* descomposición *f*.
decontaminate [di:kən'tæmɪneɪt] *vt*
descontaminar.
décor ['deɪkɔ:*] *n* decoración *f*; (*THEATRE*)
decorado.
decorate ['dɛkəreɪt] *vt* adornar, decorar;
(*paint*) pintar; (*paper*) empapelar;
decoration [-'reɪʃən] *n* adorno; (*act*)
decoración *f*; (*medal*) condecoración *f*;
decorator *n* (*painter*) pintor *m*.
decoy ['di:kɔɪ] *n* señuelo.
decrease ['di:kri:s] *n* disminución *f* // (*vb*:
[di:'kri:s]) *vt* disminuir, reducir // *vi*
reducirse.
decree [dɪ'kri:] *n* decreto; **~ nisi** *n* orden
f provisional de divorcio.
decrepit [dɪ'krɛpɪt] *a* decrépito.
dedicate ['dɛdɪkeɪt] *vt* dedicar;
dedication [-'keɪʃən] *n* (*devotion*)
dedicación *f*; (*in book*) dedicatoria.
deduce [dɪ'dju:s] *vt* deducir.
deduct [dɪ'dʌkt] *vt* restar; (*from wage etc*)
descontar; **~ion** [dɪ'dʌkʃən] *n* descuento;
(*conclusion*) deducción *f*, conclusión *f*.
deed [di:d] *n* hecho, acto; (*feat*) hazaña;
(*LAW*) escritura.
deem [di:m] *vt* juzgar.
deep [di:p] *a* (*gen*) profundo; (*voice*) bajo;
(*breath*) profundo, a pleno pulmón;
(*person*) insondable // *ad*: **the spectators
stood 20 ~** los espectadores se formaron
de 20 en fondo; **to be 4 metres ~** tener 4
metros de profundo; **~en** *vt* ahondar,
profundizar // *vi* (*darkness*) intensificarse;
~-freeze *n* congeladora; **~-fry** *vt* freír
en aceite abundante; **~-sea diving** *n*
buceo de altura; **~-seated** *a* (*beliefs*)
(profundamente) arraigado; **~-set** *a*
(*eyes*) hundido.
deer [dɪə*] *n, pl inv* ciervo; **~skin** *n*
gamuza, piel *f* de ciervo.
deface [dɪ'feɪs] *vt* desfigurar, mutilar.

defamation [dɛfə'meɪʃən] *n* difamación *f*.
default [dɪ'fɔ:lt] *vi* no pagar; (*SPORT*) dejar
de presentarse // *n*: **by ~** (*LAW*) en
rebeldía; (*SPORT*) por no presentarse el
adversario; **~er** *n* (*in debt*) moroso/a.
defeat [dɪ'fi:t] *n* derrota // *vt* derrotar,
vencer; (*fig: efforts*) frustrar; **~ist** *a, n*
derrotista *m/f*.
defect ['di:fɛkt] *n* defecto // *vi* [dɪ'fɛkt]
desertar; **~ive** [dɪ'fɛktɪv] *a* (*gen*)
defectuoso; (*person*) anormal.
defence [dɪ'fɛns] *n* defensa; **~less** *a*
indefenso.
defend [dɪ'fɛnd] *vt* defender; **~ant** *n*
acusado/a; (*in civil case*) demandado/a;
~er *n* defensor *m*.
defensive [dɪ'fɛnsɪv] *a* defensivo; **on the
~** a la defensiva.
defer [dɪ'fɔ:*] *vt* (*postpone*) aplazar; **to ~
to** diferir a; **~ence** ['dɛfərəns] *n*
deferencia, respeto.
defiance [dɪ'faɪəns] *n* desafío; **in ~ of** en
contra de; **defiant** [-ənt] *a* (*insolent*)
insolente; (*challenging*) retador(a).
deficiency [dɪ'fɪʃənsɪ] *n* (*lack*) falta;
(*defect*) defecto; **deficient** [-ənt] *a*
(*lacking*) insuficiente; (*incomplete*)
incompleto; (*defective*) defectuoso;
(*mentally*) anormal; **deficient in** falto de.
deficit ['dɛfɪsɪt] *n* déficit *m*.
defile [dɪ'faɪl] *vt* manchar, deshonrar.
define [dɪ'faɪn] *vt* definir.
definite ['dɛfɪnɪt] *a* (*fixed*) determinado;
(*clear, obvious*) claro, categórico; **he was
~ about it** no dejó lugar a dudas (sobre
ello); **~ly** *ad* claramente.
definition [dɛfɪ'nɪʃən] *n* definición *f*.
definitive [dɪ'fɪnɪtɪv] *a* definitivo.
deflate [di:'fleɪt] *vt* (*gen*) desinflar;
(*person*) quitar los humos a.
deflect [dɪ'flɛkt] *vt* desviar.
deform [dɪ'fɔ:m] *vt* deformar; **~ed** *a*
deformado; **~ity** *n* deformación *f*.
defraud [dɪ'frɔ:d] *vt* estafar; **to ~ sb of
sth** estafar algo a uno.
defrost [di:'frɔst] *vt* (*fridge*) deshelar,
descongelar.
deft [dɛft] *a* diestro, hábil.
defunct [dɪ'fʌŋkt] *a* difunto.
defuse [di:'fju:z] *vt* quitar el fusible a.
defy [dɪ'faɪ] *vt* (*resist*) oponerse
resueltamente a; (*challenge*) desafiar;
(*order*) contravenir.
degenerate [dɪ'dʒɛnəreɪt] *vi* degenerar //
a [dɪ'dʒɛnərɪt] degenerado.
degradation [dɛgrə'deɪʃən] *n* degradación
f; **degrading** [dɪ'greɪdɪŋ] *a* degradante.
degree [dɪ'gri:] *n* grado; (*SCOL*) título; **~ in
maths** licencia en matemáticas.
dehydrated [di:haɪ'dreɪtɪd] *a*
deshidratado; (*milk*) en polvo.
de-ice [di:'aɪs] *vt* (*windscreen*) deshelar.
deign [deɪn] *vi*: **to ~ to do** dignarse
hacer.
deity ['di:ɪtɪ] *n* deidad *f*, divinidad *f*.
dejected [dɪ'dʒɛktɪd] *a* abatido,

desanimado; (*face*) cariacontecido; **dejection** [-ʃən] *n* abatimiento.
delay [dɪ'leɪ] *vt* demorar, aplazar; (*person*) entretener; (*trains*) retrasar // *vi* tardar // *n* (*gen*) dilación *f*; (*a* ~) demora, retraso; **without** ~ en seguida, sin tardar.
delegate ['dɛlɪgɪt] *n* delegado/a // *vt* ['dɛlɪgeɪt] delegar; **delegation** [-'geɪʃən] *n* delegación *f*.
delete [dɪ'liːt] *vt* suprimir, tachar.
deliberate [dɪ'lɪbərɪt] *a* (*intentional*) intencionado; (*slow*) pausado, lento // *vi* [dɪ'lɪbəreɪt] deliberar; ~**ly** *ad* (*on purpose*) a propósito; (*slowly*) pausadamente.
delicacy ['dɛlɪkəsɪ] *n* delicadeza; (*choice food*) golosina.
delicate ['dɛlɪkɪt] *a* (*gen*) delicado; (*fragile*) frágil; (*skilled*) fino.
delicatessen [dɛlɪkə'tɛsn] *n* tienda especializada en comida exótica.
delicious [dɪ'lɪʃəs] *a* delicioso, rico.
delight [dɪ'laɪt] *n* (*feeling*) placer *m*, deleite *m*; (*object*) encanto, delicia // *vt* encantar, deleitar; **to take** ~ **in** deleitarse con; ~**ful** *a* encantador(a), delicioso.
delinquency [dɪ'lɪŋkwənsɪ] *n* delincuencia; **delinquent** [-ənt] *a*, *n* delincuente *m/f*.
delirious [dɪ'lɪrɪəs] *a* delirante; **delirium** [-ɪəm] *n* delirio.
deliver [dɪ'lɪvə*] *vt* (*distribute*) repartir; (*hand over*) entregar; (*message*) comunicar; (*speech*) pronunciar; (*blow*) lanzar, dar; (*MED*): **to be** ~**ed** dar a luz; ~**y** *n* reparto; entrega; (*distribution*) distribución *f*; (*of speaker*) modo de expresarse; (*MED*) parto, alumbramiento; (*saving*) liberación *f*; **to take** ~**y of** recibir.
delta ['dɛltə] *n* delta *m*.
delude [dɪ'luːd] *vt* engañar.
deluge ['dɛljuːdʒ] *n* diluvio // *vt* inundar.
delusion [dɪ'luːʒən] *n* ilusión *f*, engaño.
de luxe [də'lʌks] *a* de lujo.
delve [dɛlv] *vi*: **to** ~ **into** ahondar en.
demand [dɪ'mɑːnd] *vt* (*gen*) exigir; (*rights*) reclamar // *n* (*gen*) exigencia; (*claim*) reclamación *f*; (*ECON*) demanda; **to be in** ~ ser muy solicitado; **on** ~ a solicitud; ~**ing** *a* (*boss*) exigente; (*work*) absorbente.
demarcation [diːmɑː'keɪʃən] *n* demarcación *f*.
demean [dɪ'miːn] *vt*: **to** ~ **o.s.** rebajarse.
demeanour [dɪ'miːnə*] *n* porte *m*, conducta.
demented [dɪ'mɛntɪd] *a* demente.
demister [diː'mɪstə*] *n* (*AUT*) de(s)fuminador *m* de vapores.
democracy [dɪ'mɒkrəsɪ] *n* democracia; **democrat** ['dɛmɒkræt] *n* demócrata *m/f*; **democratic** [dɛmə'krætɪk] *a* democrático.
demolish [dɪ'mɒlɪʃ] *vt* derribar, demoler; **demolition** [dɛmə'lɪʃən] *n* derribo, demolición *f*.
demonstrate ['dɛmənstreɪt] *vt* demostrar

// *vi* manifestarse; **demonstration** [-'streɪʃən] *n* (*POL*) manifestación *f*; (*proof*) prueba, demostración *f*; **demonstrator** *n* (*POL*) manifestante *m/f*.
demoralize [dɪ'mɒrəlaɪz] *vt* desmoralizar.
demote [dɪ'məut] *vt* degradar.
demure [dɪ'mjuə*] *a* recatado.
den [dɛn] *n* (*of animal*) guarida; (*study*) estudio.
denial [dɪ'naɪəl] *n* (*refusal*) negativa; (*of report etc*) desmentimiento; **self-**~ abnegación *f*.
denim ['dɛnɪm] *n* dril *m*; ~**s** *npl* vaqueros *mpl*.
Denmark ['dɛnmɑːk] *n* Dinamarca.
denomination [dɪnɒmɪ'neɪʃən] *n* valor *m*; (*REL*) confesión *f*.
denominator [dɪ'nɒmɪneɪtə*] *n* denominador *m*.
denote [dɪ'nəut] *vt* indicar, significar.
denounce [dɪ'nauns] *vt* denunciar.
dense [dɛns] *a* (*thick*) espeso; (: *foliage etc*) tupido; (*stupid*) torpe, duro de mollera; ~**ly** *ad*: ~**ly populated** con gran densidad de población.
density ['dɛnsɪtɪ] *n* densidad *f*.
dent [dɛnt] *n* abolladura // *vt* (*also:* **make a** ~ **in**) abollar.
dental ['dɛntl] *a* dental; ~ **surgeon** *n* odontólogo.
dentist ['dɛntɪst] *n* dentista *m/f*; ~**ry** *n* odontología.
dentures ['dɛntʃəz] *npl* dentadura *sg* (postiza).
deny [dɪ'naɪ] *vt* (*gen*) negar; (*charge*) rechazar; (*report*) desmentir; **to** ~ **o.s.** privarse (de).
deodorant [diː'əudərənt] *n* desodorante *m*.
depart [dɪ'pɑːt] *vi* irse, marcharse; (*train*) salir; **to** ~ **from** (*fig: differ from*) apartarse de.
department [dɪ'pɑːtmənt] *n* (*COMM*) sección *f*; (*SCOL*) ramo; (*POL*) ministerio; ~ **store** *n* gran almacén *m*.
departure [dɪ'pɑːtʃə*] *n* partida, ida; (*of train*) salida; **a new** ~ un nuevo rumbo.
depend [dɪ'pɛnd] *vi*: **to** ~ **on** depender de; (*rely on*) contar con; **it** ~**s** ¡depende!, ¡según!; ~**able** *a* (*person*) formal, serio; ~**ence** *n* dependencia; ~**ant,** ~**ent** *n* dependiente *m/f*.
depict [dɪ'pɪkt] *vt* (*in picture*) pintar; (*describe*) representar.
depleted [dɪ'pliːtɪd] *a* reducido.
deplorable [dɪ'plɔːrəbl] *a* lamentable, deplorable; **deplore** [dɪ'plɔː*] *vt* lamentar, deplorar.
deploy [dɪ'plɔɪ] *vt* desplegar.
depopulation ['diːpɒpjuˈleɪʃən] *n* despoblación *f*.
deport [dɪ'pɔːt] *vt* deportar; ~**ation** [-'teɪʃən] *n* deportación *f*; ~**ment** *n* comportamiento.
depose [dɪ'pəuz] *vt* deponer.
deposit [dɪ'pɒzɪt] *n* (*gen*) depósito; (*CHEM*) sedimento; (*of ore, oil*) yacimiento // *vt*

(gen) depositar; ~ account n cuenta de ahorros; ~or n cuentacorrentista m/f.

depot ['dɛpəu] n (storehouse) depósito; (for vehicles) parque m.

depraved [dɪ'preɪvd] a depravado, vicioso; depravity [-'prævɪtɪ] n depravación f, vicio.

depreciate [dɪ'pri:ʃɪeɪt] vi depreciarse, perder valor; depreciation [-'eɪʃən] n depreciacion f.

depress [dɪ'prɛs] vt deprimir; (press down) presionar; ~ed a deprimido; ~ing a deprimente; ~ion [dɪ'prɛʃən] n depresión f.

deprivation [dɛprɪ'veɪʃən] n privación f; (loss) pérdida.

deprive [dɪ'praɪv] vt: to ~ sb of privar a alguien de; ~d a pobre.

depth [dɛpθ] n (gen) profundidad f; (of room etc) fondo; in the ~s of en lo más hondo de.

deputation [dɛpju'teɪʃən] n delegación f.

deputize ['dɛpjutaɪz] vi: to ~ for sb sustituir por uno.

deputy ['dɛpjutɪ] a: ~ head subdirector/a m/f // n sustituto/a, suplente m; (POL) diputado; (agent) representante m.

derail [dɪ'reɪl] vt: to be ~ed descarrilarse; ~ment n descarrilamiento.

deranged [dɪ'reɪndʒd] a (person) vuelto loco, trastornado (mentalmente).

derelict ['dɛrɪlɪkt] a abandonado.

deride [dɪ'raɪd] vt ridiculizar, mofarse de; derision [-'rɪʒən] n irrisión f, mofas fpl.

derivative [dɪ'rɪvətɪv] n derivado // a derivado; (work) poco original.

derive ['dɪ'raɪv] vt derivar // vi: to ~ from derivarse de.

dermatitis [də:mə'taɪtɪs] n dermatitis f; dermatology [-'tɔlədʒɪ] n dermatología.

derogatory [dɪ'rɔgətərɪ] a despectivo.

derrick ['dɛrɪk] n torre f de perforación.

descend [dɪ'sɛnd] vt, vi descender, bajar; to ~ from descender de; ~ant n descendiente m/f.

descent [dɪ'sɛnt] n descenso; (GEO) pendiente m, declive m; (origin) descendencia.

describe [dɪs'kraɪb] vt describir; description [-'krɪpʃən] n descripción f; (sort) clase f, género; descriptive [-'krɪptɪv] a descriptivo.

desecrate ['dɛsɪkreɪt] vt profanar.

desert ['dɛzət] n desierto // (vb: [dɪ'zə:t]) vt abandonar, desamparar // vi (MIL) desertar; ~er n desertor m; ~ion [dɪ'zə:ʃən] n deserción f.

deserve [dɪ'zə:v] vt merecer, ser digno de; deserving a (person) digno, (action, cause) meritorio.

design [dɪ'zaɪn] n (sketch) bosquejo; (layout, shape) diseño; (pattern) dibujo; (intention) propósito, intención f // vt (gen) diseñar; (plan) proyectar.

designate ['dɛzɪgneɪt] vt (point to) señalar; (appoint) nombrar; (destine)

designar // a ['dɛzɪgnɪt] designado; designation [-'neɪʃən] n (appointment) nombramiento; (name) denominación f.

designer [dɪ'zaɪnə*] n (ART) dibujante m; (TECH) diseñador m; (fashion ~) modista m/f.

desirable [dɪ'zaɪərəbl] a (proper) deseable; (attractive) atractivo.

desire [dɪ'zaɪə*] n deseo // vt desear.

desk [dɛsk] n (in office) escritorio; (for pupil) pupitre m; (in hotel, at airport) recepción f.

desolate ['dɛsəlɪt] a (place) desierto; (person) afligido; desolation [-'leɪʃən] n (of place) desolación f; (of person) aflicción f.

despair [dɪs'pɛə*] n desesperación f // vi: to ~ of desesperarse de.

despatch [dɪs'pætʃ] n, vt = dispatch.

desperate ['dɛspərɪt] a desesperado; (fugitive) peligroso; ~ly ad desesperadamente; (very) terriblemente, gravemente.

desperation [dɛspə'reɪʃən] n desesperación f; in ~ desesperado.

despicable [dɪs'pɪkəbl] a vil, despreciable.

despise [dɪs'paɪz] vt despreciar.

despite [dɪs'paɪt] prep a pesar de, pese a.

despondent [dɪs'pɔndənt] a deprimido, abatido.

dessert [dɪ'zə:t] n postre m; ~spoon n cuchara (de postre).

destination [dɛstɪ'neɪʃən] n destino.

destiny ['dɛstɪnɪ] n destino.

destitute ['dɛstɪtju:t] a desamparado, indigente.

destroy [dɪs'trɔɪ] vt (gen) destruir; (finish) acabar con; ~er n (NAUT) destructor m.

destruction [dɪs'trʌkʃən] n destrucción f; (fig) ruina; destructive [-tɪv] a destructivo, destructor(a).

detach [dɪ'tætʃ] vt separar; (unstick) despegar; ~able a separable; (TECH) desmontable; ~ed a (attitude) objetivo, imparcial; (house) independiente, sólo; ~ment n (gen) separación f; (MIL) destacamento; (fig) objetividad f, imparcialidad f.

detail ['di:teɪl] n detalle m // vt (gen) detallar; (MIL) destacar; in ~ en detalle; ~ed a detallado.

detain [dɪ'teɪn] vt retener; (in captivity) detener.

detect [dɪ'tɛkt] vt (gen) descubrir; (MED, POLICE) identificar; (MIL, RADAR, TECH) detectar; ~ion [dɪ'tɛkʃən] n descubrimiento; identificación f; ~ive n detective m; ~ive story n novela policíaca; ~or n detector m.

détente [deɪ'tɑ:nt] n detente f.

detention [dɪ'tɛnʃən] n detención f, arresto.

deter [dɪ'tə:*] vt (discourage) desalentar; (dissuade) disuadir; (prevent) impedir.

detergent [dɪ'tə:dʒənt] n detergente m.

deteriorate [dɪ'tɪərɪəreɪt] vi deteriorarse; deterioration [-'reɪʃən] n deterioro.

determination [dɪtə:mɪ'neɪʃən] n (gen)

determinación *f*; (*resolve*) resolución *f*.
determine [dɪ'tɜ:mɪn] *vt* (*gen*) determinar; (*limits etc*) definir; (*dispute*) resolver; ~**d** *a* (*person*) resuelto.
deterrent [dɪ'tɛrənt] *n* fuerza de disuasión.
detest [dɪ'tɛst] *vt* aborrecer; ~**able** *a* aborrecible.
detonate ['dɛtəneɪt] *vi* estallar // *vt* hacer detonar; **detonator** *n* detonador *m*, fulminante *m*.
detour ['di:tuə*] *n* rodeo.
detract [dɪ'trækt] *vt*: **to** ~ **from** quitar mérito a, desvirtuar.
detriment ['dɛtrɪmənt] *n*: **to the** ~ **of** en perjuicio de; ~**al** [dɛtrɪ'mɛntl] *a* perjudicial (*to* a).
devaluation [dɪvælju'eɪʃən] *n* devaluación *f*; **devalue** [-'vælju:] *vt* devaluar.
devastate ['dɛvəsteɪt] *vt* devastar; **he was** ~**d by the news** las noticias le dejaron desolado; **devastating** *a* devastador(a); (*fig*) arrollador(a).
develop [dɪ'vɛləp] *vt* (*gen*) desarrollar; (*PHOT*) revelar; (*disease*) coger; (*engine trouble*) empezar a tener // *vi* desarrollarse; (*advance*) progresar; (*appear*) aparecer; ~**ing country** país *m* en desarrollo; ~**ment** *n* desarrollo; (*advance*) progreso; (*of affair, case*) desenvolvimiento; (*of land*) urbanización *f*.
deviate ['di:vɪeɪt] *vi* desviarse; **deviation** [-'eɪʃən] *n* desviación *f*.
device [dɪ'vaɪs] *n* (*scheme*) estratagema *f*, recurso; (*apparatus*) aparato, mecanismo.
devil ['dɛvl] *n* diablo, demonio; ~**ish** *a* diabólico.
devious ['di:vɪəs] *a* intricado, enrevesado; (*person*) taimado.
devise [dɪ'vaɪz] *vt* idear, inventar.
devoid [dɪ'vɔɪd] *a*: ~ **of** desprovisto de.
devote [dɪ'vəut] *vt*: **to** ~ **sth to** dedicar algo a; ~**d** *a* (*loyal*) leal, fiel; **the book is** ~**d to politics** el libro trata de la política; **devotee** [dɛvəu'ti:] *n* devoto/a.
devotion [dɪ'vəuʃən] *n* dedicación *f*; (*REL*) devoción *f*.
devour [dɪ'vauə*] *vt* devorar.
devout [dɪ'vaut] *a* devoto.
dew [dju:] *n* rocío.
dexterity [dɛks'tɛrɪtɪ] *n* destreza.
diabetes [daɪə'bi:ti:z] *n* diabetes *f*; **diabetic** [-'bɛtɪk] *a*, *n* diabético/a.
diagnose [daɪəg'nəuz] *vt* diagnosticar; **diagnosis** [-'nəusɪs], *pl* -**ses** [-'nəusi:z] *n* diagnóstico.
diagonal [daɪ'ægənl] *a* diagonal // *n* diagonal *f*.
diagram ['daɪəgræm] *n* diagrama *m*, esquema *m*.
dial ['daɪəl] *n* esfera, cuadrante *m* // *vt* (*number*) marcar; ~**ling tone** *n* tono de marcar.
dialect ['daɪəlɛkt] *n* dialecto.
dialogue ['daɪəlɔg] *n* diálogo.
diameter [daɪ'æmɪtə*] *n* diámetro.

diamond ['daɪəmənd] *n* diamante *m*; ~**s** *npl* (*CARDS*) oros *mpl*.
diaper ['daɪəpə*] *n* (*US*) pañal *m*.
diaphragm ['daɪəfræm] *n* diafragma *m*.
diarrhoea, diarrhea (*US*) [daɪə'ri:ə] *n* diarrea.
diary ['daɪərɪ] *n* (*daily account*) diario; (*book*) agenda *m*.
dice [daɪs] *n*, *pl inv* dados *mpl* // *vt* (*CULIN*) cortar en cuadritos.
dictate [dɪk'teɪt] *vt* dictar; ~**s** ['dɪkteɪts] *npl* dictados *mpl*; **dictation** [-'teɪʃən] *n* dictado.
dictator [dɪk'teɪtə*] *n* dictador *m*; ~**ship** *n* dictadura.
diction ['dɪkʃən] *n* dicción *f*.
dictionary ['dɪkʃənrɪ] *n* diccionario.
did [dɪd] *pt of* **do**.
die [daɪ] *vi* morir; **to** ~ **away** *vi* (*sound, light*) extinguirse lentamente; **to** ~ **down** *vi* (*gen*) apagarse; (*wind*) amainar; **to** ~ **out** *vi* desaparecer, extinguirse.
diesel ['di:zəl]: ~ **engine** *n* motor *m* Diesel; ~ (**oil**) *n* gas-oil *m*.
diet ['daɪət] *n* dieta; (*restricted food*) régimen *m* // *vi* (*also*: **be on a** ~) estar a dieta, hacer régimen.
differ ['dɪfə*] *vi* (*be different*) ser distinto, diferenciarse; (*disagree*) discrepar; ~**ence** *n* diferencia; (*quarrel*) desacuerdo; ~**ent** *a* diferente, distinto; ~**entiate** [-'rɛnʃɪeɪt] *vt* distinguir // *vi* diferenciarse; **to** ~**entiate between** distinguir entre; ~**ently** *ad* de otro modo, en forma distinta.
difficult ['dɪfɪkəlt] *a* difícil; ~**y** *n* dificultad *f*.
diffidence ['dɪfɪdəns] *n* timidez *f*; **diffident** [-ənt] *a* tímido.
diffuse [dɪ'fju:s] *a* difuso // *vt* [dɪ'fju:z] difundir.
dig [dɪg], *pt*, *pp* **dug** *vt* (*hole*) cavar; (*garden*) cultivar; (*coal*) extraer; (*nails etc*) hincar // *n* (*prod*) empujón *m*; (*archaeological*) excavación *f*; (*remark*) indirecta; **to** ~ **in** *vi* atrincherarse; **to** ~ **into** *vt* (*savings*) consumir; **to** ~ **out** *vt* (*hole*) excavar; (*fig*) sacar; **to** ~ **up** *vt* desenterrar; (*plant*) desarraigar.
digest [daɪ'dʒɛst] *vt* (*food*) digerir; (*facts*) asimilar // *n* ['daɪdʒɛst] resumen *m*; ~**ion** [dɪ'dʒɛstʃən] *n* digestión *f*.
digital ['dɪdʒɪtəl] *a* digital.
dignified ['dɪgnɪfaɪd] *a* grave, solemne; (*action*) decoroso.
dignity ['dɪgnɪtɪ] *n* dignidad *f*.
digress [daɪ'grɛs] *vi*: **to** ~ **from** apartarse de; ~**ion** [daɪ'grɛʃən] *n* digresión *f*.
digs [dɪgz] *npl* (*Brit*: *col*) pensión *f*, alojamiento.
dilapidated [dɪ'læpɪdeɪtɪd] *a* desmoronado, ruinoso.
dilate [daɪ'leɪt] *vt* dilatar // *vi* dilatarse.
dilemma [daɪ'lɛmə] *n* dilema *m*.
diligent ['dɪlɪdʒənt] *a* diligente.
dilute [daɪ'lu:t] *vt* diluir // *a* diluido.

dim [dɪm] a (*light*) débil; (*sight*) turbio; (*outline*) indistinto; (*stupid*) lerdo; (*room*) oscuro // vt (*light*) bajar; (*AUT*) poner a media luz.

dime [daɪm] n (*US*) *moneda de diez centavos.*

dimension [dɪ'menʃən] n dimensión f.

diminish [dɪ'mɪnɪʃ] vi disminuirse.

diminutive [dɪ'mɪnjutɪv] a diminuto // n (*LING*) diminutivo.

dimly ['dɪmlɪ] ad débilmente; (*not clearly*) indistintamente.

dimple ['dɪmpl] n hoyuelo.

din [dɪn] n estruendo, estrépito.

dine [daɪn] vi cenar; **diner** n (*person*) comensal m/f; (*RAIL*) = **dining car.**

dinghy ['dɪŋgɪ] n bote m; **rubber** ~ lancha (neumática).

dingy ['dɪndʒɪ] a (*room*) sombrío; (*dirty*) sucio; (*dull*) deslucido.

dining ['daɪnɪŋ]: ~ **car** n coche-comedor m; ~ **room** n comedor m.

dinner ['dɪnə*] n (*evening meal*) cena; (*lunch*) comida; (*public*) cena, banquete m; ~ **jacket** n smoking m; ~ **party** n cena; ~ **time** n hora de cenar o comer.

diocese ['daɪəsɪs] n diócesis f.

dip [dɪp] n (*slope*) pendiente m; (*in sea*) baño // vt (*in water*) mojar; (*ladle etc*) meter; (*AUT: lights*) poner a media luz // vi inclinarse hacia abajo.

diphtheria [dɪf'θɪərɪə] n difteria.

diploma [dɪ'pləumə] n diploma m.

diplomacy [dɪ'pləuməsɪ] n diplomacia; **diplomat** ['dɪpləmæt] n diplomático; **diplomatic** [dɪplə'mætɪk] a diplomático.

dipstick ['dɪpstɪk] n (*AUT*) varilla graduada, indicador m de nivel (del aceite).

dire [daɪə*] a calamitoso.

direct [daɪ'rɛkt] a (*gen*) directo // vt dirigir; **can you** ~ **me to...?** ¿puede indicarme dónde está...?

direction [dɪ'rɛkʃən] n dirección f; ~**s** npl (*advice*) órdenes fpl, instrucciones fpl; ~**s for use** modo de empleo.

directly [dɪ'rɛktlɪ] ad (*in straight line*) directamente; (*at once*) en seguida.

director [dɪ'rɛktə*] n director m; **managing** ~ director gerente.

directory [dɪ'rɛktərɪ] n (*TEL*) guía (telefónica).

dirt [dɔːt] n suciedad f; ~-**cheap** a tirado, muy barato; ~**y** a sucio; (*joke*) verde // vt ensuciar; (*stain*) manchar; ~**y trick** n juego sucio.

disability [dɪsə'bɪlɪtɪ] n incapacidad f; **disabled** [dɪs'eɪbld] a disminuido, minusválido.

disadvantage [dɪsəd'vɑːntɪdʒ] n desventaja, inconveniente m.

disagree [dɪsə'griː] vi (*differ*) discrepar; (*be against, think otherwise*): **to** ~ (**with**) no estar de acuerdo (con); ~**able** a desagradable; ~**ment** n (*gen*) desacuerdo; (*quarrel*) riña.

disallow ['dɪsə'lau] vt (*goal*) anular.

disappear [dɪsə'pɪə*] vi desaparecer; ~**ance** n desaparición f.

disappoint [dɪsə'pɔɪnt] vt decepcionar; (*hopes*) defraudar; ~**ing** a decepcionante; ~**ment** n decepción f.

disapproval [dɪsə'pruːvəl] n desaprobación f.

disapprove [dɪsə'pruːv] vi: **to** ~ **of** desaprobar.

disarm [dɪs'ɑːm] vt desarmar; ~**ament** n desarme m; ~**ing** a encantador(a).

disaster [dɪ'zɑːstə*] n desastre m; **disastrous** a desastroso.

disband [dɪs'bænd] vt disolver // vi desbandarse.

disbelief [dɪsbə'liːf] n incredulidad f.

disc [dɪsk] n disco.

discard [dɪs'kɑːd] vt (*old things*) tirar; (*fig*) descartar.

discern [dɪ'sɜːn] vt percibir, discernir; ~**ing** a perspicaz.

discharge [dɪs'tʃɑːdʒ] vt (*duties*) cumplir, desempeñar; (*ship etc*) descargar; (*patient*) dar de alta; (*employee*) despedir; (*soldier*) licenciar; (*defendant*) poner en libertad // n ['dɪstʃɑːdʒ] (*ELEC*) descarga; (*dismissal*) despedida; (*of duty*) desempeño; (*of debt*) pago, descargo.

disciple [dɪ'saɪpl] n discípulo.

discipline ['dɪsɪplɪn] n disciplina // vt disciplinar.

disclaim [dɪs'kleɪm] vt negar.

disclose [dɪs'kləuz] vt revelar; **disclosure** [-'kləuʒə*] n revelación f.

disco ['dɪskəu] n abbr of **discothèque.**

discoloured [dɪs'kʌləd] a descolorado.

discomfort [dɪs'kʌmfət] n incomodidad f; (*unease*) inquietud f; (*physical*) malestar m.

disconcert [dɪskən'sɜːt] vt desconcertar.

disconnect [dɪskə'nɛkt] vt (*gen*) separar; (*ELEC etc*) desconectar.

discontent [dɪskən'tɛnt] n descontento; ~**ed** a descontento.

discontinue [dɪskən'tɪnjuː] vt interrumpir; (*payments*) suspender.

discord ['dɪskɔːd] n discordia; (*MUS*) disonancia; ~**ant** [dɪs'kɔːdənt] a disonante.

discothèque ['dɪskəutɛk] n discoteca.

discount ['dɪskaunt] n descuento // vt [dɪs'kaunt] descontar.

discourage [dɪs'kʌrɪdʒ] vt desalentar; (*oppose*) oponerse a; **discouraging** a desalentador(a).

discourteous [dɪs'kɔːtɪəs] a descortés.

discover [dɪs'kʌvə*] vt descubrir; ~**y** n descubrimiento.

discredit [dɪs'krɛdɪt] vt desacreditar.

discreet [dɪ'skriːt] a (*tactful*) discreto; (*careful*) circunspecto, prudente; ~**ly** ad discretamente.

discrepancy [dɪ'skrɛpənsɪ] n (*difference*) diferencia; (*disagreement*) discrepancia.

discretion [dɪ'skrɛʃən] n (*tact*) discreción f; (*care*) prudencia, circunspección f.

discriminate [dɪ'skrɪmɪneɪt] vi: to ~ between distinguir entre; to ~ against discriminar contra; discriminating a perspicaz; discrimination [-'neɪʃən] n (discernment) perspicacia; (bias) discriminación f.

discuss [dɪ'skʌs] vt (gen) discutir; (a theme) tratar; ~ion [dɪ'skʌʃən] n discusión f.

disdain [dɪs'deɪn] n desdén m // vt desdeñar.

disease [dɪ'ziːz] n enfermedad f.

disembark [dɪsɪm'bɑːk] vt, vi desembarcar.

disengage [dɪsɪn'geɪdʒ] vt soltar; (clutch) desembragar.

disentangle [dɪsɪn'tæŋgl] vt desenredar.

disfigure [dɪs'fɪgə*] vt desfigurar.

disgrace [dɪs'greɪs] n ignominia; (downfall) caída; (shame) vergüenza, escándalo // vt deshonrar; ~ful a vergonzoso; (behaviour) escandaloso.

disgruntled [dɪs'grʌntld] a disgustado, malhumorado.

disguise [dɪs'gaɪz] n disfraz m // vt disfrazar; in ~ disfrazado.

disgust [dɪs'gʌst] n repugnancia // vt repugnar, dar asco a; ~ing a repugnante, asqueroso.

dish [dɪʃ] n (gen) plato; to do or wash the ~es fregar los platos; to ~ up vt servir; to ~ out vt repartir; ~cloth n paño de cocina, bayeta.

dishearten [dɪs'hɑːtn] vt desalentar.

dishevelled [dɪ'ʃevəld] a despeinado, desmelenado.

dishonest [dɪs'ɒnɪst] a (person) poco honrado, tramposo; (means) fraudulento; ~y n falta de honradez.

dishonour [dɪs'ɒnə*] n deshonra; ~able a deshonroso.

dishwasher ['dɪʃwɒʃə*] n lavaplatos m inv; (person) friegaplatos m/f inv.

disillusion [dɪsɪ'luːʒən] vt desilusionar.

disinfect [dɪsɪn'fɛkt] vt desinfectar; ~ant n desinfectante m.

disintegrate [dɪs'ɪntɪgreɪt] vi disgregarse, desintegrarse.

disinterested [dɪs'ɪntrəstɪd] a desinteresado.

disjointed [dɪs'dʒɔɪntɪd] a inconexo.

disk [dɪsk] n = disc.

dislike [dɪs'laɪk] n antipatía, aversión f // vt tener antipatía a.

dislocate ['dɪsləkeɪt] vt dislocar.

dislodge [dɪs'lɒdʒ] vt sacar; (enemy) desalojar.

disloyal [dɪs'lɔɪəl] a desleal.

dismal ['dɪzml] a (dark) sombrío; (depressing) triste; (depressed) abatido; (very bad) fatal.

dismantle [dɪs'mæntl] vt desmontar, desarmar.

dismay [dɪs'meɪ] n consternación f // vt consternar.

dismiss [dɪs'mɪs] vt (worker) despedir;

(official) destituir; (idea, LAW) rechazar; (possibility) descartar // vi (MIL) romper filas; ~al n despedida; destitución f.

dismount [dɪs'maunt] vi apearse.

disobedience [dɪsə'biːdɪəns] n desobediencia; disobedient [-ənt] a desobediente.

disobey [dɪsə'beɪ] vt desobedecer.

disorder [dɪs'ɔːdə*] n desorden m; (rioting) disturbio; (MED) trastorno; (disease) enfermedad f; ~ly a (untidy) desordenado; (meeting) alborotado; (conduct) escandaloso.

disorganized [dɪs'ɔːgənaɪzd] a desorganizado.

disorientated [dɪs'ɔːrɪenteɪtəd] a desorientado.

disown [dɪs'əun] vt desconocer.

disparaging [dɪs'pærɪdʒɪŋ] a despreciativo.

disparity [dɪs'pærɪtɪ] n disparidad f.

dispatch [dɪs'pætʃ] vt enviar; (kill) despachar // n (sending) envío; (speed) prontitud f; (PRESS) informe m; (MIL) parte m.

dispel [dɪs'pɛl] vt disipar, dispersar.

dispensary [dɪs'pɛnsərɪ] n dispensario, farmacia.

dispense [dɪs'pɛns] vt dispensar, repartir; to ~ with vt fus prescindir de; dispenser n (container) distribuidor m automático; dispensing chemist n farmacéutico.

dispersal [dɪs'pɔːsl] n dispersión f; disperse [-'pɔːs] vt dispersar // vi dispersarse.

displace [dɪs'pleɪs] vt (shift) sacar de su sitio; ~d person n (POL) desplazado/a; ~ment n cambio de sitio.

display [dɪs'pleɪ] n (exhibition) exposición f; (MIL) alarde m; (of feeling) manifestación f; (pej) aparato, pompa // vt exponer; manifestar; (ostentatiously) lucir.

displease [dɪs'pliːz] vt (offend) ofender; (annoy) enojar, enfadar; (be unpleasant to) desagradar; ~d with disgustado con; displeasure [-'plɛʒə*] n disgusto.

disposable [dɪs'pəuzəbl] a para (usar y) tirar.

disposal [dɪs'pəuzl] n (sale) venta; (of house) traspaso; (arrangement) colocación f; (of rubbish) destrucción f; at one's ~ a disposición de uno.

dispose [dɪs'pəuz] vt: to ~ of (time, money) disponer de; (unwanted goods) deshacerse de; (throw away) tirar; ~d a: ~d to do dispuesto a hacer; disposition [-'zɪʃən] n disposición f.

disproportionate [dɪsprə'pɔːʃənət] a desproporcionado.

disprove [dɪs'pruːv] vt refutar.

dispute [dɪs'pjuːt] n disputa; (verbal) discusión f; (also: industrial ~) conflicto (laboral) // vt (argue) disputar; (question) cuestionar.

disqualification [dɪskwɒlɪfɪ'keɪʃən] n

inhabilitación *f*; (*SPORT, from driving*) descalificación *f*.

disqualify [dis'kwɔlifai] *vt* (*SPORT*) descalificar; **to ~ sb for sth/from doing sth** inhabilitar a alguien para algo/hacer algo.

disregard [disri'gɑːd] *vt* desatender; (*ignore*) no hacer caso de.

disrepair [disri'pɛə*] *n*: **to fall into ~** desmoronarse.

disreputable [dis'rɛpjutəbl] *a* (*person*) de mala fama; (*behaviour*) vergonzoso.

disrespectful [disri'spɛktful] *a* irrespetuoso.

disrupt [dis'rʌpt] *vt* (*plans*) desbaratar; (*conversation*) interrumpir; **~ion** [-'rʌpʃən] *n* trastorno; desbaratamiento; interrupción *f*.

dissatisfaction [dissætis'fækʃən] *n* disgusto, descontento; **dissatisfied** [-'sætisfaid] *a* insatisfecho.

dissect [di'sɛkt] *vt* disecar.

dissent [di'sɛnt] *n* disensión *f*.

disservice [dis'sɑːvis] *n*: **to do sb a ~** perjudicar a alguien.

dissident ['disidnt] *a, n* disidente *m/f*.

dissipate ['disipeit] *vt* disipar; (*waste*) desperdiciar.

dissociate [di'səuʃieit] *vt* disociar.

dissolute ['disəluːt] *a* disoluto.

dissolve [di'zɔlv] *vt* disolver // *vi* disolverse.

dissuade [di'sweid] *vt*: **to ~ sb (from)** disuadir a alguien (de).

distance ['distns] *n* distancia; **in the ~** *a* lo lejos.

distant ['distnt] *a* lejano; (*manner*) reservado, frío.

distaste [dis'teist] *n* repugnancia; **~ful** *a* repugnante, desagradable.

distil [dis'til] *vt* destilar; **~lery** *n* destilería.

distinct [dis'tiŋkt] *a* (*different*) distinto; (*clear*) claro; (*unmistakeable*) inequívoco; **as ~ from** a diferencia de; **~ion** [dis-'tiŋkʃən] *n* distinción *f*; (*in exam*) sobresaliente *m*; **~ive** *a* distintivo; **~ly** *ad* claramente.

distinguish [dis'tiŋgwiʃ] *vt* distinguir; **~ed** *a* (*eminent*) distinguido; **~ing** *a* (*feature*) distintivo.

distort [dis'tɔːt] *vt* torcer, retorcer; **~ion** [dis'tɔːʃən] *n* deformación *f*; (*of sound*) distorsión *f*.

distract [dis'trækt] *vt* distraer; (*attention*) apartar; (*bewilder*) aturdir; **~ed** *a* distraído; **~ion** [dis'trækʃən] *n* distracción *f*; (*confusion*) aturdimiento; (*amusement*) diversión *f*.

distraught [dis'trɔːt] *a* turbado, enloquecido.

distress [dis'trɛs] *n* (*anguish*) angustia; (*misfortune*) desgracia; (*want*) miseria; (*pain*) dolor *m*; (*danger*) peligro // *vt* (*cause anguish*) apenar, afligir; (*pain*) doler; **~ing** *a* doloroso; **~ signal** *n* señal *f* de socorro.

distribute [dis'tribjuːt] *vt* (*gen*) distribuir; (*share out*) repartir; **distribution** [-'bjuːʃən] *n* distribución *f*; **distributor** *n* (*AUT*) distribuidor *m*; (*COMM*) distribuidora.

district ['distrikt] *n* (*of country*) zona, región *f*; (*of town*) barrio; (*ADMIN*) distrito; **~ attorney** *n* (*US*) fiscal *m/f*; **~ nurse** *n* (*Brit*) enfermera que asiste a domicilio.

distrust [dis'trʌst] *n* desconfianza // *vt* desconfiar de.

disturb [dis'tɔːb] *vt* (*gen*) perturbar; (*bother*) molestar; (*interrupt*) interrumpir; (*upset*) trastornar; (*disorganize*) desordenar; **~ance** *n* (*gen*) perturbación *f*; (*political etc*) disturbio; (*violence*) alboroto; (*of mind*) trastorno; **~ing** *a* inquietante, perturbador(a).

disuse [dis'juːs] *n*: **to fall into ~** caer en desuso.

disused [dis'juːzd] *a* abandonado.

ditch [ditʃ] *n* zanja; (*irrigation ~*) acequia // *vt* (*col*) deshacerse de.

dither ['diðə*] *vi* vacilar.

ditto ['ditəu] *ad* ídem, lo mismo.

divan [di'væn] *n* diván *m*.

dive [daiv] *n* (*from board*) salto; (*underwater*) buceo; (*of submarine*) sumersión *f*; (*AVIAT*) picada // *vi* saltar; bucear; sumergirse; picar; **diver** *n* (*SPORT*) saltador/a *m/f*; (*underwater*) buzo.

diverge [dai'vɔːdʒ] *vi* divergir.

diverse [dai'vɔːs] *a* diversos(as), varios(as).

diversify [dai'vɔːsifai] *vt* diversificar.

diversion [dai'vɔːʃən] *n* (*AUT*) desviación *f*; (*distraction, MIL*) diversión *f*.

diversity [dai'vɔːsiti] *n* diversidad *f*.

divert [dai'vɔːt] *vt* (*turn aside*) desviar; (*amuse*) divertir.

divest [dai'vɛst] *vt*: **to ~ sb of sth** despojar a alguien de algo.

divide [di'vaid] *vt* dividir; (*separate*) separar // *vi* dividirse; (*road*) bifurcarse.

dividend ['dividɛnd] *n* dividendo; (*fig*) beneficio.

divine [di'vain] *a* divino.

diving ['daiviŋ] *n* (*SPORT*) salto; (*underwater*) buceo; **~ board** *n* trampolín *m*; **~ suit** *n* escafandra.

divinity [di'viniti] *n* divinidad *f*; (*SCOL*) teología.

division [di'viʒən] *n* división *f*; (*sharing out*) repartimiento; (*disagreement*) discordia; (*POL*) votación *f*.

divorce [di'vɔːs] *n* divorcio // *vt* divorciarse de; **~d** *a* divorciado; **divorcee** [-'siː] *n* divorciado/a.

divulge [dai'vʌldʒ] *vt* divulgar, revelar.

D.I.Y. *a, n abbr of* **do-it-yourself.**

dizziness ['dizinis] *n* vértigo.

dizzy ['dizi] *a* (*person*) mareado; (*height*) vertiginoso; **to feel ~** marearse, estar mareado.

DJ *n abbr of* **disc jockey.**

do [duː] *pt* **did**, *pp* **done** *vt, vi* (*gen*) hacer; (*speed*) ir a; (*THEATRE*) representar // *n* (col) fiesta; **he didn't laugh** no se rió; **she swims better than I** ~ nada mejor que yo; **he laughed, didn't he?** se rió ¿no?; **that will ~!** ¡basta!; **to make ~ with** contentarse con; **~ you agree?** ¿está Usted de acuerdo?; **to ~ one's hair** (comb) peinarse; (style) arreglarse el pelo; **will it ~?** ¿sirve?, ¿conviene?; **to ~ well** prosperar, tener éxito; **to ~ without sth** prescindir de algo; **to ~ away with** vt fus (kill) exterminar; (suppress) suprimir; **to ~ up** vt (laces) liar, atar; (room) renovar.

docile ['dəusaıl] a dócil.

dock [dɔk] n (NAUT) muelle m; (LAW) banquillo (de los acusados); **~s** npl muelles mpl, puerto // vi (arrive) llegar; (enter ~) atracar el muelle; (pay etc) rebajar; **~er** n trabajador m portuario, estibador m; **~yard** n astillero.

doctor ['dɔktə*] n médico; (Ph.D. etc) doctor/a m/f // vt (fig) arreglar, falsificar; (drink etc) adulterar.

doctrine ['dɔktrın] n doctrina.

document ['dɔkjumənt] n documento; **~ary** [-'mɛntərı] a documental // n documental m; **~ation** [-'teıʃən] n documentación f.

dodge [dɔdʒ] n (of body) regate m; (fig) truco // vt (gen) evadir; (blow) esquivar.

dodgems ['dɔdʒəmz] npl coches mpl de choque.

dog [dɔg] n perro // vt seguir los pasos de; **~ biscuits** npl galletas fpl de perro; **~ collar** n collar m de perro; (fig) cuello de cura.

dogged ['dɔgıd] a tenaz, obstinado.

dogma ['dɔgmə] n dogma m; **~tic** [-'mætık] a dogmático.

doings ['duıŋz] npl (events) sucesos mpl; (acts) hechos mpl.

do-it-yourself [du:ıtjɔ:'sɛlf] n bricolaje m.

doldrums ['dɔldrəmz] npl: **to be in the ~** (person) estar abatido; (business) estar encalmado.

dole [dəul] n (Brit) (payment) subsidio de paro; **on the ~** parado; **to ~ out** vt repartir.

doleful ['dəulful] a triste, lúgubre.

doll [dɔl] n muñeca; **to ~ o.s. up** ataviarse.

dollar ['dɔlə*] n dólar m.

dolphin ['dɔlfın] n delfín m.

domain [də'meın] n campo, competencia; (empire) dominio.

dome [dəum] n (ARCH) cúpula; (shape) bóveda.

domestic [də'mɛstık] a (gen) doméstico; (national) nacional; (home-loving) hogareño; (internal: trade) interior; (: strife) interno; **~ated** a domesticado; (home-loving) casero, hogareño.

dominant ['dɔmınənt] a dominante.

dominate ['dɔmıneıt] vt dominar; **domination** [-'neıʃən] n dominación f.

domineering [dɔmı'nıərıŋ] a dominante.

dominion [də'mınıən] n dominio.

domino ['dɔmınəu], pl **~es** n ficha de dominó; **~es** n (game) dominó.

donate [də'neıt] vt donar; **donation** [də'neıʃən] n donativo.

done [dʌn] pp of **do.**

donkey ['dɔŋkı] n burro.

donor ['dəunɔ*] n donante m/f.

don't [dəunt] = **do not.**

doom [du:m] n (fate) suerte f; (death) muerte f // vt: **to be ~ed to failure** ser condenado al fracaso.

door [dɔ:*] n puerta; (entry) entrada; **next ~** en la casa de al lado; **~bell** n timbre m; **~ handle** n tirador m; (of car) manija; **~ knocker** n aldaba; **~man** n (in hotel) portero; **~mat** n felpudo, estera; **~step** n peldaño.

dope [dəup] n (col: person) imbécil m/f // vt (horse etc) drogar.

dopey ['dəupı] a (dizzy) mareado.

dormant ['dɔ:mənt] a inactivo; (latent) latente.

dormitory ['dɔ:mıtrı] n dormitorio.

dormouse ['dɔ:maus], pl **-mice** [-maıs] n lirón m.

dosage ['dəusıdʒ] n dósis f inv.

dose [dəus] n dósis f inv // vt: **to ~ o.s.** medicinarse.

doss house ['dɔss-] n pensión f de mala muerte.

dot [dɔt] n punto; **~ted with** salpicado de; **on the ~** en punto.

dote [dəut]: **to ~ on** vt fus adorar, idolatrar.

double ['dʌbl] a doble // ad (twice): **to cost ~** costar el doble // n (game) doble m // vt doblar; (efforts) redoblar // vi doblarse; **at the ~** coːriendo; **~s** n (TENNIS) juego de dobles; **~ bass** n contrabajo; **~ bed** n cama matrimonial; **~ bend** n doble curva; **~-breasted** a cruzado; **~cross** vt (trick) engañar; (betray) traicionar; **~decker** n autobús m de dos pisos; **~ room** n cuarto para dos; **doubly** ad doblemente.

doubt [daut] n duda // vt dudar; (suspect) dudar de; **to ~ that** dudar que; **there is no ~ that** no cabe duda de que; **~ful** a dudoso; (person) sospechoso; **~less** ad sin duda.

dough [dəu] n masa, pasta; **~nut** n buñuelo.

dove [dʌv] n paloma; **~tail** vi (fig) encajar.

dowdy ['daudı] a desaliñado; (inelegant) poco elegante.

down [daun] n (fluff) pelusa; (feathers) plumón m, flojel m // ad (~ wards) abajo, hacia abajo; (on the ground) por/en tierra // prep abajo // vt (col: drink) beberse; (: food) devorar; **the D~s** zona de colinas del sur de Inglaterra; **~ with X!** ¡abajo X!; **~-at-heel** a venido a menos; (appearance) desaliñado; **~cast** a abatido; **~fall** n caída, ruina; **~hearted** a desanimado; **~hill** ad: **to go ~hill** ir cuesta abajo; **~ payment** n enganche m, pago al contado; ~**pour** n aguacero; ~**right** a (clear) manifiesto; (out-and-out) terminante, definitivo; ~**stairs** ad (below) (en la casa) de abajo; (~ wards) escaleras abajo; ~**stream** ad aguas o río abajo; ~**-to-earth** a práctico; ~**town** ad en el centro de la ciudad; ~**ward** a, ad, ~**wards** ad hacia abajo.

dowry ['dauri] n dote f.

doz. abbr of **dozen.**

doze [dəuz] vi dormitar; **to** ~ **off** vi quedarse medio dormido.

dozen ['dʌzn] n docena.

Dr. abbr of **doctor; drive.**

drab [dræb] a gris, monótono.

draft [drɑːft] n (first copy) borrador m; (COMM) giro; (US: call-up) quinta // vt (plan) redactar; (send) mandar; (conscript) quintar; (write roughly) hacer un borrador de; see also **draught.**

drag [dræg] vt arrastrar; (river) dragar, rastrear // vi arrastrarse por el suelo // n (col) lata; **to** ~ **on** vi ser interminable.

dragonfly ['drægənflaɪ] n libélula.

drain [dreɪn] n desaguadero; (in street) sumidero; (source of loss) desagüe m; (loss) pérdida; (on resources) sumidero // vt (land, marshes) desaguar; (MED) drenar; (reservoir) desecar; (fig) agotar // vi escurrirse; ~**age** n (act) desagüe m; (MED, AGR) drenaje m; (sewage) alcantarillado; ~**ing board,** ~**board** (US) n escurridera, escurridor m; ~**pipe** n tubo de desagüe.

dram [dræm] n (drink) trago.

drama ['drɑːmə] n (art) teatro; (play) drama m; ~**tic** [drə'mætɪk] a dramático; ~**tist** ['dræmətɪst] n dramaturgo.

drank [dræŋk] pt of **drink.**

drape [dreɪp] vt cubrir; ~**s** npl (US) cortinas fpl; **draper** n pañero.

drastic ['dræstɪk] a (measure) severo; (change) radical; (forceful) enérgico.

draught [drɑːft] n (of air) corriente f; (drink) trago; (NAUT) calado; ~**s** n juego de damas; **on** ~ (beer) de barril; ~**board** n tablero de damas.

draughtsman ['drɑːftsmən] n proyectista m, delineante m.

draw [drɔː], pt **drew,** pp **drawn** vt (pull) tirar; (take out) sacar; (attract) atraer; (picture) dibujar; (money) retirar // vi (SPORT) empatar // n (SPORT) empate m; (lottery) sorteo; (attraction) atracción f; **to** ~ **near** vi acercarse; **to** ~ **out** vi (lengthen) alargar; **to** ~ **up** vi (stop) pararse // vt (document) redactar; ~**back** n inconveniente m, desventaja; ~**bridge** n puente m levadizo.

drawer [drɔː*] n cajón m.

drawing ['drɔːɪŋ] n dibujo; ~ **board** n tablero (de dibujante); ~ **pin** n chinche m; ~ **room** n salón m.

drawl [drɔːl] n habla lenta y cansina.

drawn [drɔːn] pp of **draw.**

dread [dred] n pavor m, terror m // vt

temer, tener miedo o pavor a; ~**ful** a espantoso.

dream [driːm] n sueño // vt, vi, pt, pp **dreamed** or **dreamt** [drɛmt] soñar; ~**er** n soñador/a m/f; ~**y** a (distracted) soñador(a), distraído; (music) de sueño.

dreary ['drɪəri] a monótono, aburrido.

dredge [drɛdʒ] vt dragar; **dredger** n (ship) draga; (also: **sugar dredger**) espolvoreador m.

dregs [drɛgz] npl heces fpl.

drench [drɛntʃ] vt empapar; **to get** ~**ed** mojarse hasta los huesos.

dress [drɛs] n vestido; (clothing) ropa // vt vestir; (wound) vendar; (CULIN) aliñar // vi vestirse; **to** ~ **up** vi vestirse de etiqueta; (in fancy dress) disfrazarse; ~ **circle** n principal m; ~**er** n (furniture) aparador m; (: US) cómoda con espejo; ~**ing** n (MED) vendaje m; (CULIN) aliño; ~**ing gown** n bata; ~**ing room** n (THEATRE) camarín m; (SPORT) vestidor m; ~**ing table** n tocador m; ~**maker** n modista, costurera; ~**making** n costura; ~ **rehearsal** n ensayo general; ~ **shirt** n camisa de frac.

drew [druː] pt of **draw.**

dribble ['drɪbl] vi gotear, caer gota a gota; (baby) babear // vt (ball) regatear.

dried [draɪd] a (gen) seco; (fruit) paso; (milk) en polvo.

drift [drɪft] n (of current etc) velocidad f; (of sand etc) montón m; (distance off course) deriva; (meaning) significado // vi (boat) ir a la deriva; (sand, snow) amontonarse; ~**wood** n madera de deriva.

drill [drɪl] n taladro; (bit) broca; (of dentist) fresa; (for mining etc) perforadora, barrena; (MIL) instrucción f // vt perforar, taladrar // vi (for oil) perforar.

drink [drɪŋk] n bebida // vt, vi, pt **drank,** pp **drunk** beber; **to have a** ~ tomar; ~**er** n bebedor/a m/f; ~**ing water** n agua potable.

drip [drɪp] n (act) goteo; (one ~) gota; (MED) gota a gota m // vi gotear, caer gota a gota; ~**-dry** a (shirt) de lava y pon; ~**ping** n pringue m; ~**ping wet** a calado.

drive [draɪv] n paseo (en coche); (journey) viaje m; (also: ~**way**) entrada; (energy) energía, vigor m; (PSYCH) impulso; (SPORT) ataque m // (vb: pt **drove,** pp **driven** ['drɪvn] vt (car) conducir; (urge) hacer trabajar; (by power) mover; (nail) clavar; (push) empujar; (TECH. motor) impulsar // vi (AUT. at controls) conducir; (: travel) pasearse en coche; **left-/right-hand** ~ conducción f a la izquierda/derecha.

driver ['draɪvə*] n conductor m; (of taxi, bus) chofer m; ~'**s license** n (US) permiso de conducir.

driving ['draɪvɪŋ] n el conducir, automovilismo; ~ **instructor** n instructor m de conducción; ~ **lesson** n clase f de conducción; ~ **licence** n (Brit) permiso

de conducir; ~ **mirror** *n* retrovisor *m*; ~ **school** *n* autoescuela; ~ **test** *n* examen *m* de conducción.
drizzle ['drɪzl] *n* llovizna // *vi* lloviznar.
drone [drəun] *n* zumbido; (*male bee*) zángano.
drool [dru:l] *vi* babear; **to** ~ **over sth** extasiarse ante algo.
droop [dru:p] *vi* colgar; (*fig*) decaer, desanimarse.
drop [drɔp] *n* (*of water*) gota; (*lessening*) baja; (*fall*) caída; (*of cliff*) pendiente *m*, declive *m* // *vt* (*allow to fall*) dejar caer; (*voice, eyes, price*) bajar; (*set down from car*) dejar; (*omit*) omitir // *vi* caer; (*price, temperature*) bajar; (*wind*) amainar; **to** ~ **off** *vi* (*sleep*) dormirse // *vt* (*passenger*) bajar; **to** ~ **out** *vi* (*withdraw*) retirarse; ~**-out** *n* marginado; ~**per** *n* cuentagotas *m inv*; ~**pings** *npl* excremento *sg* (de animal).
drought [draut] *n* sequía.
drove [drəuv] *pt of* **drive.**
drown [draun] *vt* ahogar // *vi* ahogarse.
drowsy ['drauzɪ] *a* soñoliento; **to be** ~ tener sueño.
drudgery ['drʌdʒərɪ] *n* trabajo monótono.
drug [drʌg] *n* medicamento; (*narcotic*) droga // *vt* drogar; ~ **addict** *n* drogadicto/a; ~**gist** *n* (*US*) farmacéutico; ~**store** *n* (*US*) farmacia.
drum [drʌm] *n* tambor *m*; (*large*) bombo; (*for oil, petrol*) bidón *m*; ~**s** *npl* batería *sg* // *vi* tocar el tambor; (*with fingers*) tamborilear; ~**mer** *n* tambor *m*; ~**stick** *n* (*MUS*) palillo; (*of chicken*) muslo.
drunk [drʌŋk] *pp of* **drink** // *a* borracho // *n* (*also:* ~**ard**) borracho/a; ~**en** *a* borracho; ~**enness** *n* embriaguez *f.*
dry [draɪ] *a* seco; (*day*) sin lluvia; (*climate*) árido, seco // *vt* secar; (*tears*) enjugarse // *vi* secarse; **to** ~ **up** *vi* agotarse; (*in speech*) atascarse; ~**-cleaner's** *n* tintorería; ~**-cleaning** *n* lavado en seco; ~**er** *n* lavadora; ~**ness** *n* sequedad *f*; ~ **rot** *n* putrefacción *f* fungoide.
dual ['djuəl] *a* doble; ~**-control** *a* de doble mando; ~ **nationality** *n* doble nacionalidad *f*; ~**-purpose** *a* de doble uso.
dubbed [dʌbd] *a* (*CINEMA*) doblado.
dubious ['dju:bɪəs] *a* dudoso; (*reputation, company*) sospechoso.
duchess ['dʌtʃɪs] *n* duquesa.
duck [dʌk] *n* pato // *vi* agacharse; ~**ling** *n* patito.
duct [dʌkt] *n* conducto, canal *m.*
dud [dʌd] *n* (*shell*) obús *m* que no estalla; (*object, tool*): **it's a** ~ es una filfa // *a:* ~ **cheque** cheque *m* sin fondos.
due [dju:] *a* (*proper*) debido; (*expected*) esperado; (*fitting*) conveniente, oportuno // *n* (*debt*) deuda; (*desert*) lo que merece uno // *ad:* ~ **north** derecho al norte; ~**s** *npl* (*for club, union*) cuota *sg*; (*in harbour*) derechos *mpl*; **in** ~ **course** a su debido tiempo; ~ **to** debido a.

duel ['djuəl] *n* duelo.
duet [dju:'ɛt] *n* dúo.
dug [dʌg] *pt, pp of* **dig.**
duke [dju:k] *n* duque *m.*
dull [dʌl] *a* (*light*) apagado; (*slow*) torpe; (*boring*) pesado; (*sound, pain*) sordo; (*weather, day*) gris // *vt* (*pain, grief*) aliviar; (*mind, senses*) entorpecer.
duly ['dju:lɪ] *ad* debidamente; (*on time*) a su debido tiempo.
dumb [dʌm] *a* mudo; (*stupid*) estúpido; ~**founded** [dʌm'faundɪd] *a* pasmado.
dummy ['dʌmɪ] *n* (*tailor's model*) maniquí *m*; (*for baby*) chupete *m* // *a* falso, postizo.
dump [dʌmp] *n* (*heap*) montón *m*; (*place*) basurero, vaciadero; (*col*) casucha; (*MIL*) depósito // *vt* (*put down*) verter, vaciar; (*get rid of*) deshacerse de; (*goods*) inundar el mercado con; ~**ing** *n* (*ECON*) dumping *m*; (*of rubbish*): 'no ~**ing**' prohibido verter basura'.
dumpling ['dʌmplɪŋ] *n* bola de masa hervida.
dunce [dʌns] *n* zopenco.
dune [dju:n] *n* duna.
dung [dʌŋ] *n* estiércol *m.*
dungarees [dʌŋgə'ri:z] *npl* mono *sg.*
dungeon ['dʌndʒən] *n* calabozo.
dupe [dju:p] *n* (*victim*) víctima // *vt* engañar.
duplicate ['dju:plɪkət] *n* duplicado // *vt* ['dju:plɪkeɪt] duplicar; (*on machine*) multicopiar; **in** ~ por duplicado; **duplicator** *n* multicopista *m.*
durable ['djuərəbl] *a* duradero.
duration [djuə'reɪʃən] *n* duración *f.*
duress [djuə'rɛs] *n:* **under** ~ por compulsión.
during ['djuərɪŋ] *prep* durante.
dusk [dʌsk] *n* crepúsculo, anochecer *m.*
dust [dʌst] *n* polvo // *vt* (*furniture*) desempolvorar; (*cake etc*): **to** ~ **with** espolvorear de; ~**bin** *n* (*Brit*) cubo de la basura; ~**er** *n* paño, trapo, bayeta; (*feather* ~) plumero; ~ **jacket** *n* sobrecubierta; ~**man** *n* (*Brit*) basurero; ~**y** *a* polvoriento.
Dutch [dʌtʃ] *a* holandés(esa) // *n* (*LING*) holandés *m*; ~**man/woman** *n* holandés/esa *m/f.*
duty ['dju:tɪ] *n* deber *m*; (*tax*) derechos *mpl* de aduana; **on** ~ de servicio; (*at night etc*) de guardia; **off** ~ libre (de servicio); ~**-free** *a* libre de derechos de aduana.
dwarf [dwɔ:f], *pl* **dwarves** [dwɔ:vz] *n* enano // *vt* empequeñecer.
dwell [dwɛl], *pt, pp* **dwelt** [dwɛlt] *vi* morar; **to** ~ **on** *vt fus* explayarse en; ~**ing** *n* vivienda.
dwindle ['dwɪndl] *vi* menguar, disminuir.
dye [daɪ] *n* tinte *m* // *vt* teñir.
dying ['daɪɪŋ] *a* moribundo, agonizante; (*moments*) final; (*words*) último.
dynamic [daɪ'næmɪk] *a* dinámico; ~**s** *n, npl* dinámica *sg.*
dynamite ['daɪnəmaɪt] *n* dinamita.

dynamo ['daɪnəməu] *n* dinamo *f.*
dynasty ['dɪnəstɪ] *n* dinastía.

E

each [i:tʃ] *det* cada *inv* // *pron* cada uno; ~ **other** el uno al otro; **they hate** ~ **other** se odian (entre ellos *o* mutuamente); **they have 2 books** ~ tiene 2 libros por persona.
eager ['i:gə*] *a* (*gen*) impaciente; (*hopeful*) ilusionado; (*ambitious*) ambicioso; **to be** ~ **to do sth** ansiar hacer algo, impacientarse por hacer algo; **to be** ~ **for** ansiar, anhelar.
eagle ['i:gl] *n* águila.
ear [ɪə*] *n* oreja; (*MUS*) oído; (*of corn*) espiga; ~**ache** *n* dolor *m* de oídos; ~**drum** *n* tímpano.
earl [ɔ:l] *n* conde *m.*
early ['ɔ:lɪ] *ad* (*gen*) temprano; (*before time*) con tiempo, con anticipación // *a* (*gen*) temprano; (*reply*) pronto; (*first*) primero; (*work*) juvenil; **have an** ~ **night** acuéstate temprano; **in the** ~ *or* ~ **in the spring/19th century** a principios de primavera/del siglo diez y nueve; **as** ~ **as possible** cuánto antes, lo más pronto posible.
earmark ['ɪəmɑ:k] *vt* reservar (*for* para), destinar (*for* a).
earn [ɔ:n] *vt* (*gen*) ganar; (*salary*) percibir; (*interest*) devengar; (*praise*) merecerse.
earnest ['ɔ:nɪst] *a* serio, formal; **in** ~ *ad* en serio.
earnings ['ɔ:nɪŋz] *npl* (*personal*) sueldo, ingresos *mpl*; (*company*) ganancias *fpl.*
ear: ~**phones** *npl* auriculares *mpl*; ~**ring** *n* pendiente *m*, arete *m*; ~**shot** *n*: **within** ~**shot** al alcance del oído.
earth [ɔ:θ] *n* (*gen*) tierra; (*ELEC*) cable *m* de toma de tierra // *vt* (*ELEC*) conectar a tierra; ~**enware** *n* loza de barro; ~**quake** *n* terremoto; ~**y** *a* (*fig*: *vulgar*) grosero; (: *sensual*) sensual.
earwig ['ɪəwɪg] *n* tijereta.
ease [i:z] *n* (*gen*) facilidad *f*; (*relief*) alivio; (*calm*) tranquilidad *f*; (*relaxed state*) comodidad *f* // *vt* facilitar; aliviar; tranquilizar; (*loosen*) soltar; (*relieve: pressure*) aflojar; (*weight*) aligerar; (*help pass*): **to** ~ **sth in/out** meter/sacar con cuidado; **at** ~! (*MIL*) ¡descanso!; **to** ~ **off** *or* **up** *vi* (*gen*) suavizarse; (*at work*) dejar de trabajar tanto; (*wind*) amainar; (*rain*) moderarse.
easel ['i:zl] *n* caballete *m.*
east [i:st] *n* este *m*, oriente *m* // *a* del este, oriental // *ad* al este, hacia el este; **the** E~ el Oriente.
Easter ['i:stə*] *n* Pascua (de Resurrección).
easterly ['i:stəlɪ] *a* (*to the east*) al este; (*from the east*) del este.
eastern ['i:stən] *a* del este, oriental.
East Germany *n* Alemania Oriental.
eastward(s) ['i:stwəd(z)] *ad* hacia el este.

easy ['i:zɪ] *a* (*gen*) fácil; (*simple*) sencillo; (*slow*) lento, pausado; (*comfortable*) holgado, cómodo; (*relaxed*) natural, llano // *ad*: **to take it** *or* **things** ~ (*not worry*) tomarlo con calma; (*go slowly*) ir despacio; (*rest*) descansar; ~ **chair** *n* sillón *m*; ~**going** *a* acomodadizo.
eat [i:t] *pt* **ate**, *pp* **eaten** ['i:tn] *vt* (*gen*) comer; (*supper*) cenar; **to** ~ **into, to** ~ **away at** *vt fus* corroer; ~**able** *a* comestible.
eau de Cologne [əudəkə'ləun] *n* (agua de) Colonia.
eaves [i:vz] *npl* alero *sg.*
eavesdrop ['i:vzdrɔp] *vi* escuchar a escondidas (*on sb* a uno).
ebb [ɛb] *n* reflujo // *vi* bajar; (*fig: also*: ~ **away**) decaer; ~ **tide** *n* marea menguante.
ebony ['ɛbənɪ] *n* ébano.
eccentric [ɪk'sɛntrɪk] *a*, *n* excéntrico/a.
ecclesiastical [ɪkli:zɪ'æstɪkəl] *a* eclesiástico.
echo ['ɛkəu], *pl* ~**es** *n* eco *m* // *vt* (*sound*) repetir // *vi* resonar, hacer eco.
eclipse [ɪ'klɪps] *n* eclipse *m* // *vt* eclipsar.
ecology [ɪ'kɔlədʒɪ] *n* ecología.
economic [i:kə'nɔmɪk] *a* económico; (*business etc*) rentable; ~**al** *a* económico; ~**s** *n* (la) economía; **economist** [ɪ'kɔnəmɪst] *n* economista *m/f.*
economize [ɪ'kɔnəmaɪz] *vi* economizar, ahorrar.
economy [ɪ'kɔnəmɪ] *n* economía.
ecstasy ['ɛkstəsɪ] *n* éxtasis *m*; **ecstatic** [-'tætɪk] *a* extático.
ecumenical [i:kju'mɛnɪkl] *a* ecuménico.
eczema ['ɛksɪmə] *n* eczema *m.*
edge [ɛdʒ] *n* (*of knife etc*) filo; (*of object*) borde *m*; (*of lake etc*) orilla // *vt* (*SEWING*) ribetear; **on** ~ (*fig*) = **edgy**; **to** ~ **away from** alejarse poco a poco; ~**ways** *ad*: **he couldn't get a word in** ~**ways** no pudo meter baza; **edging** *n* (*SEWING*) ribete *m*; (*of path*) borde *m.*
edgy ['ɛdʒɪ] *a* nervioso, inquieto.
edible ['ɛdɪbl] *a* comestible.
edict ['i:dɪkt] *n* edicto.
edifice ['ɛdɪfɪs] *n* edificio.
edit ['ɛdɪt] *vt* (*be editor of*) dirigir; (*cut*) cortar; ~**ion** [ɪ'dɪʃən] *n* (*gen*) edición *f*; (*number printed*) tirada; ~**or** *n* (*of newspaper*) director *m*; (*of book*) autor *m* de la edición; ~**orial** [-'tɔːrɪəl] *a* editorial, de la dirección // *n* editorial *m.*
educate ['ɛdjukeɪt] *vt* (*gen*) educar; (*instruct*) instruir.
education [ɛdju'keɪʃən] *n* educación *f*; (*schooling*) enseñanza; (*ESCOL*) pedagogía; ~**al** *a* (*policy etc*) educacional; (*teaching*) docente; (*instructive*) educativo.
EEC *n* abbr of **European Economic Community** CEE (Comunidad Económica Europea).
eel [i:l] *n* anguila.
eerie ['ɪərɪ] *a* (*strange*) extraño; (*mysterious*) misterioso.

effect [ɪ'fɛkt] *n* efecto // *vt* efectuar, llevar a cabo; ~**s** *npl* efectos *mpl*; **to take** ~ (*drug*) surtir efecto; **in** ~ en realidad; ~**ive** *a* (*gen*) eficaz; (*striking*) impresionante; (*real*) efectivo; **to become** ~**ive** entrar en vigor; ~**iveness** *n* eficacia.

effeminate [ɪ'fɛmɪnɪt] *a* afeminado.

effervescent [ɛfə'vɛsnt] *a* efervescente.

efficiency [ɪ'fɪʃənsɪ] *n* (*gen*) eficiencia; (*of machine*) rendimiento.

efficient [ɪ'fɪʃənt] *a* eficiente.

effigy ['ɛfɪdʒɪ] *n* efigie *f*.

effort ['ɛfət] *n* esfuerzo; **to make an** ~ **to** esforzarse por; ~**less** *a* sin esfuerzo (alguno).

effrontery [ɪ'frʌntərɪ] *n* descaro.

effusive [ɪ'fjuːsɪv] *a* efusivo.

e.g. *ad abbr of* **exempli gratia** p. ej. (por ejemplo).

egg [ɛg] *n* huevo; **hard-boiled/poached/soft-boiled** ~ huevo duro/escalfado/pasado por agua; **scrambled** ~**s** huevos revueltos; **to** ~ **on** *vt* incitar; ~**cup** *n* huevera; ~**shell** *n* cáscara de huevo.

ego ['iːgəu] *n* ego; ~**ism** *n* egoísmo; ~**ist** *n* egoísta *m/f*.

Egypt ['iːdʒɪpt] *n* Egipto; ~**ian** [ɪ'dʒɪpʃən] *a*, *n* egipcio/a.

eiderdown ['aɪdədaun] *n* edredón *m*.

eight [eɪt] *num* ocho; **eighteen** *num* diez y ocho, dieciocho; **eighth** *a*, *n* octavo; ~**y** *num* ochenta.

Eire ['ɛərə] *n* Eire *m*.

either ['aɪðə*] *det* cualquier ... de los dos; (*both*, *each*) uno u otro; **on** ~ **side** en ambos lados // *pron*: ~ (**of them**) cualquiera (de los dos); **I don't like** ~ no me gusta ni el uno ni otro // *ad* tampoco; **no, I don't** ~ no, yo tampoco // *conj*: ~ **yes or no** o sí o no.

eject [ɪ'dʒɛkt] *vt* echar; (*tenant*) desahuciar; ~**or seat** *n* asiento proyectable.

eke [iːk]: **to** ~ **out** *vt* (*make last*) escatimar; (*add to*) suplir las deficiencias de.

elaborate [ɪ'læbərɪt] *a* complicado; (*decorated*) rebuscado // (*vb*: [ɪ'læbəreɪt]) *vt* elaborar // *vi* explicarse con muchos detalles.

elapse [ɪ'læps] *vi* transcurrir.

elastic [ɪ'læstɪk] *a*, *n* elástico; ~ **band** *n* gomita.

elated [ɪ'leɪtɪd] *a*: **to be** ~ regocijarse; **elation** [ɪ'leɪʃən] *n* regocijo.

elbow ['ɛlbəu] *n* codo.

elder ['ɛldə*] *a* mayor // *n* (*tree*) saúco; (*person*) mayor; (*of tribe*) anciano; ~**ly** *a* de edad, mayor // *n*: **the** ~**ly** la gente mayor.

eldest ['ɛldɪst] *a*, *n* el/la mayor.

elect [ɪ'lɛkt] *vt* elegir; **to** ~ **to do** optar por hacer // *a*: **the president** ~ el presidente electo; ~**ion** [ɪ'lɛkʃən] *n* elección *f*; ~**ioneering** [ɪlɛkʃə'nɪərɪŋ] *n* campaña electoral; ~**or** *n* elector/a *m/f*;

~**oral** *a* electoral; ~**orate** *n* electorado.

electric [ɪ'lɛktrɪk] *a* eléctrico; ~**al** *a* eléctrico; ~ **blanket** *n* manta eléctrica; ~ **chair** *n* silla eléctrica; ~ **cooker** *n* cocina eléctrica; ~ **fire** *n* estufa eléctrica.

electrician [ɪlɛk'trɪʃən] *n* electricista *m/f*.

electricity [ɪlɛk'trɪsɪtɪ] *n* electricidad *f*.

electrify [ɪ'lɛktrɪfaɪ] *vt* (*RAIL*) electrificar; (*audience*) electrizar.

electro... [ɪlɛktrəu] *pref*: ~**cute** [-kjuːt] *vt* electrocutar; **electrode** [ɪ'lɛktrəud] *n* electrodo; ~**magnetic** *a* electromagnético.

electron [ɪ'lɛktrɔn] *n* electrón *m*.

electronic [ɪlɛk'trɔnɪk] *a* electrónico; ~**s** *n* electrónica.

elegance ['ɛlɪgəns] *n* elegancia; **elegant** [-gənt] *a* elegante.

element ['ɛlɪmənt] *n* (*gen*) elemento; **to brave the** ~**s** salir a la intemperie; ~**ary** [-'mɛntərɪ] *a* (*gen*) elemental; (*primitive*) rudimentario; (*school, education*) de primera enseñanza.

elephant ['ɛlɪfənt] *n* elefante *m*.

elevate ['ɛlɪveɪt] *vt* (*gen*) elevar; (*in rank*) ascender.

elevation [ɛlɪ'veɪʃən] *n* elevación *f*; (*rank*) ascenso; (*height*) altura.

elevator ['ɛlɪveɪtə*] *n* (*US*) ascensor *m*.

eleven [ɪ'lɛvn] *num* once; ~**ses** *npl* las once; ~**th** *a* undécimo.

elf [ɛlf], *pl* **elves** [ɛlvz] *n* duende *m*.

elicit [ɪ'lɪsɪt] *vt*: **to** ~ (**from**) sacar (de).

eligible ['ɛlɪdʒəbl] *a* elegible; **to be** ~ **for sth** llenar los requisitos para algo.

eliminate [ɪ'lɪmɪneɪt] *vt* eliminar; (*strike out*) suprimir; (*suspect*) descartar; **elimination** [-'neɪʃən] *n* eliminación *f*; supresión *f*.

élite [eɪ'liːt] *n* élite *f*.

elm [ɛlm] *n* olmo.

elocution [ɛlə'kjuːʃən] *n* elocución *f*.

elongated ['iːlɔŋgeɪtɪd] *a* alargado, estirado.

elope [ɪ'ləup] *vi* fugarse con su amante; ~**ment** *n* fuga.

eloquence ['ɛləkwəns] *n* elocuencia; **eloquent** [-wənt] *a* elocuente.

else [ɛls] *ad* lo(s) demás; **something** ~ otra cosa; **somewhere** ~ en otra parte; **everywhere** ~ en todas partes (menos aquí); **where** ~? ¿dónde más?, ¿en qué otra parte?; **there was little** ~ **to do** apenas quedaba otra cosa que hacer; **nobody** ~ **spoke** no habló nadie más; ~**where** *ad* (*be*) en otra parte; (*go*) a otra parte.

elucidate [ɪ'luːsɪdeɪt] *vt* aclarar, elucidar.

elude [ɪ'luːd] *vt* (*gen*) eludir; (*blow*) esquivar; (*pursuer*) escaparse de, zafarse de.

elusive [ɪ'luːsɪv] *a* esquivo; (*answer*) difícil de encontrar.

emaciated [ɪ'meɪsɪeɪtɪd] *a* demacrado.

emanate ['ɛməneɪt] *vi* emanar, proceder.

emancipate [ɪ'mænsɪpeɪt] vt emancipar;
~d a liberado; emancipation [-'peɪʃən] n
emancipación f, liberación f.
embalm [ɪm'baːm] vt embalsamar.
embankment [ɪm'bæŋkmənt] n terraplén
m; (riverside) dique m.
embargo [ɪm'baːgəu], pl ~es n
prohibición f.
embark [ɪm'baːk] vi embarcarse // vt
embarcar; to ~ on (fig) emprender,
lanzarse a; ~ation [ɛmbaː'keɪʃən] n
(people) embarco; (goods) embarque m.
embarrass [ɪm'bærəs] vt desconcertar,
azorar; (financially etc) poner en un
aprieto; ~ing a embarazoso; ~ment n
desconcierto, azoramiento; (financial)
apuros mpl.
embassy ['ɛmbəsɪ] n embajada.
embed [ɪm'bɛd] vt (gen) empotrar; (teeth
etc) clavar.
embellish [ɪm'bɛlɪʃ] vt embellecer; (fig)
adornar.
embers ['ɛmbəz] npl rescoldo sg, ascua sg.
embezzle [ɪm'bɛzl] vt desfalcar,
malversar; ~ment n desfalco,
malversación f.
embitter [ɪm'bɪtə*] vt amargar; (fig)
envenenar; ~ed a resentido, amargado.
emblem ['ɛmbləm] n emblema m.
embody [ɪm'bɔdɪ] vt (features) encarnar;
(ideas) expresar.
embossed [ɪm'bɔst] a realzado; ~ with
con grabado en relieve.
embrace [ɪm'breɪs] vt abrazar, dar un
abrazo a; (include) abarcar; (adopt: idea)
adherirse a // vi abrazarse // n abrazo.
embroider [ɪm'brɔɪdə*] vt bordar; (fig:
story) adornar, embellecer; ~y n
bordado.
embryo ['ɛmbrɪəu] n (also fig) embrión m.
emerald ['ɛmərəld] n esmeralda.
emerge [ɪ'məːdʒ] vi (gen) salir, aparecer;
(arise) surgir; emergence n salida,
aparición f; surgimiento.
emergency [ɪ'məːdʒənsɪ] n (event)
emergencia; (crisis) crisis f; (need)
necesidad f urgente; in an ~ en caso de
urgencia; state of ~ estado de
emergencia; ~ exit n salida de
emergencia; ~ landing n aterrizaje m
forzoso; ~ meeting n reunión f
extraordinaria.
emery ['ɛmərɪ] ~ board n lima de uñas;
~ paper n papel m de esmeril.
emetic [ɪ'mɛtɪk] n emético.
emigrant ['ɛmɪgrənt] n emigrante m/f.
emigrate ['ɛmɪgreɪt] vi emigrarse;
emigration [-'greɪʃən] n emigración f.
eminence ['ɛmɪnəns] n eminencia;
eminent [-ənt] a eminente.
emission [ɪ'mɪʃən] n emisión f.
emit [ɪ'mɪt] vt (gen) emitir; (smoke)
arrojar; (smell) despedir; (sound) producir.
emotion [ɪ'məuʃən] n emoción f; ~al a
(person) sentimental; (scene)
conmovedor(a), emocionante; ~ally ad
con emoción.

emotive [ɪ'məutɪv] a emotivo.
emperor ['ɛmpərə*] n emperador m.
emphasis ['ɛmfəsɪs], pl -ses [-siːz] n
énfasis m inv.
emphasize ['ɛmfəsaɪz] vt (word, point)
subrayar, recalcar; (feature) hacer
resaltar.
emphatic [ɛm'fætɪk] a (strong) enérgico;
(unambiguous, clear) enfático; ~ally ad
con énfasis.
empire ['ɛmpaɪə*] n imperio.
empirical [ɛm'pɪrɪkl] a empírico.
employ [ɪm'plɔɪ] vt emplear; ~ee [-'iː] n
empleado/a; ~er n patrón/ona m/f,
empresario; ~ment n (gen) empleo;
(work) trabajo; full ~ment pleno
empleo; ~ment agency n agencia de
colocaciones; ~ment exchange n bolsa
de trabajo.
empower [ɪm'pauə*] vt: to ~ sb to do
sth autorizar a uno a hacer algo.
empress ['ɛmprɪs] n emperatriz f.
emptiness ['ɛmptɪnɪs] n (gen) vacío; (of
life etc) vaciedad f.
empty ['ɛmptɪ] a vacío; (place) desierto;
(house) desocupado; (threat) vano // n
(bottle) envase m // vt vaciar; (place)
dejar vacío // vi vaciarse; (house) quedar
desocupado; (place) quedar desierto;
~-handed a con las manos vacías.
emulate ['ɛmjuleɪt] vt emular.
emulsion [ɪ'mʌlʃən] n emulsión f.
enable [ɪ'neɪbl] vt: to ~ sb to do sth
(allow) permitir a uno hacer algo;
(prepare) capacitar a uno para hacer algo.
enact [ɪn'ækt] vt (law) promulgar; (play)
representar; (role) hacer.
enamel [ɪ'næməl] n esmalte m.
enamoured [ɪ'næməd] a: to be ~ of
(person) estar enamorado de; (activity etc)
tener gran afición a; (idea) aferrarse a.
encased [ɪn'keɪst] a: ~ in (enclosed)
encerrado en; (covered) revestido de.
enchant [ɪn'tʃaːnt] vt encantar; ~ing a
encantador(a).
encircle [ɪn'səːkl] vt (gen) rodear; (waist)
ceñir.
encl. abbr of enclosed adj. (adjunto).
enclose [ɪn'kləuz] vt (land) cercar; (with
letter etc) adjuntar; (in receptacle)
encerrar; please find ~d le adjunto.
enclosure [ɪn'kləuʒə*] n cercado, recinto;
(comm) carta adjunta.
encore [ɔŋ'kɔː*] excl ¡otra!, ¡bis! // n bis m.
encounter [ɪn'kauntə*] n encuentro // vt
encontrar, encontrarse con; (difficulty)
tropezar con.
encourage [ɪn'kʌrɪdʒ] vt alentar, animar;
(growth) estimular; ~ment n estímulo; (of
industry) fomento.
encroach [ɪn'krəutʃ] vi: to ~ (up)on
(gen) invadir; (time) ocupar.
encrusted [ɪn'krʌstəd] a: ~ with
incrustado de.
encumber [ɪn'kʌmbə*] vt: to be ~ed
with (carry) tener que cargar con; (debts)
estar gravado de.

encyclop(a)edia [ɛnsaıklɔu'piːdıə] n enciclopedia.

end [ɛnd] n (gen, also aim) fin m; (of table) extremo; (of street) final m; (SPORT) lado // vt terminar, acabar; (also: **bring to an ~, put an ~ to**) acabar con // vi terminar, acabar; **in the ~** al fin, por fin, finalmente; **on ~** (object) de punta, de cabeza; **to stand on ~** (hair) erizarse; **for hours on ~** horas seguidas; **to ~ up** vi: **to ~ up in** terminar en; (piace) ir a parar en.

endanger [ın'deındʒə*] vt poner en peligro.

endear [ın'dıə*] vr: **to ~ o.s. to** hacerse querer de; **~ing** a simpático, atractivo; **~ment** n cariño, palabra cariñosa.

endeavour [ın'dɛvə*] n esfuerzo; (attempt) tentativa; (striving) empeño // vi: **to ~ to do** esforzarse por hacer; (try) procurar hacer.

ending ['ɛndıŋ] n fin m, conclusión f; (of book) desenlace m; (LING) terminación f.

endless ['ɛndlıs] a interminable, inacabable.

endorse [ın'dɔːs] vt (cheque) endosar; (approve) aprobar; **~ment** n (on driving licence) nota de inhabilitación.

endow [ın'dau] vt (provide with money) dotar; (: institution) fundar; **to be ~ed with** estar dotado de.

endurance [ın'djuərəns] n resistencia; **endure** vt (bear) aguantar, soportar; (resist) resistir // vi (last) durar; (resist) resistir.

enemy ['ɛnəmı] a, n enemigo/a.

energetic [ɛnə'dʒɛtık] a enérgico.

energy ['ɛnədʒı] n energía.

enforce [ın'fɔːs] vt (LAW) hacer cumplir; **~d** a forzoso, forzado.

engage [ın'geıdʒ] vt (attention) llamar; (in conversation) abordar; (worker) contratar; (taxi) alquilar; (clutch) embragar // vi (TECH) engranar con; **to ~ in** dedicarse a, ocuparse en; **~d** a (busy, in use) ocupado; (betrothed) prometido; **to get ~d** prometerse; **he is ~d in research** se dedica a la investigación; **~d tone** n señal f de comunicando; **~ment** n (appointment) compromiso, cita; (battle) combate m; (to marry) compromiso; (period) noviazgo; **~ment ring** n alianza, anillo de prometida.

engaging [ın'geıdʒıŋ] a atractivo, simpático.

engender [ın'dʒɛndə*] vt engendrar.

engine ['ɛndʒın] n (AUT) motor m; (RAIL) locomotora; **~ driver** n maquinista m.

engineer [ɛndʒı'nıə*] n ingeniero; (US: RAIL) maquinista m; **~ing** n ingeniería.

England ['ıŋglənd] n Inglaterra.

English ['ıŋglıʃ] a inglés(esa) // n (LING) el inglés; **the ~** los ingleses; **~man/woman** n inglés/esa m/f.

engrave [ın'greıv] vt grabar; **engraving** n grabado.

engrossed [ın'grəust] a: **~ in** absorto en.

engulf [ın'gʌlf] vt sumergir, hundir.

enhance [ın'hɑːns] vt (gen) intensificar, aumentar; (beauty) realzar.

enigma [ı'nıgmə] n enigma m; **~tic** [ɛnıg'mætık] a enigmático.

enjoy [ın'dʒɔı] vt (possess) poseer; (have: health, fortune) disfrutar de, gozar de; (food) comer con gusto; **to ~ o.s.** divertirse, pasarlo bien; **~able** a (pleasant) agradable; (amusing) divertido; **~ment** n (use) disfrute m; (joy) placer m.

enlarge [ın'lɑːdʒ] vt aumentar; (broaden) extender; (PHOT) ampliar // vi: **to ~ on** (subject) tratar con más detalles; **~ment** n (PHOT) ampliación f.

enlighten [ın'laıtn] vt (inform) informar, instruir; **~ed** a (cultured) culto; (knowledgeable) bien informado; (tolerant) comprensivo; **~ment** n (HISTORY): **the E~ment** la Ilustración, el Siglo de las Luces.

enlist [ın'lıst] vt alistar; (support) conseguir // vi alistarse.

enmity ['ɛnmıtı] n enemistad f.

enormity [ı'nɔːmıtı] n enormidad f; **enormous** [-məs] a enorme.

enough [ı'nʌf] a: **~ time/books** bastante tiempo/bastantes libros // n: **have you got ~?** ¿tiene Usted bastante? // ad: **big ~** bastante grande; **he has not worked ~** no ha trabajado bastante; **~!** ¡basta ya!; **that's ~, thanks** con eso basta, gracias; **I've had ~ of him** estoy harto de él; **... which, funnily ~ ... ...** lo que, por extraño que parezca... .

enquire [ın'kwaıə*] vt, vi = **inquire.**

enrage [ın'reıdʒ] vt enfurecer, hacer rabiar.

enrich [ın'rıtʃ] vt enriquecer.

enrol [ın'rəul] vt inscribir; (SCOL) matricular // vi inscribirse; matricularse; **~ment** n inscripción f; matriculación f.

en route [ɔn'ruːt] ad (on the way to) camino de; (on the way) en camino.

ensign ['ɛnsaın] n (flag) bandera; (MIL) alférez m.

enslave [ın'sleıv] vt esclavizar.

ensue [ın'sjuː] vi seguirse; (result) resultar; (happen) sobrevenir.

ensure [ın'ʃuə*] vt asegurar.

entail [ın'teıl] vt (imply) suponer; (result in) acarrear.

entangle [ın'tæŋgl] vt enredar, enmarañar; **~ment** n enredo.

enter ['ɛntə*] vt (room) entrar en; (club) hacerse socio de; (army) alistarse en; (sb for a competition) inscribir; (write down) anotar, apuntar // vi entrar; **to ~ for** vt fus presentarse para; **to ~ into** vt fus (relations) establecer; (plans) formar parte de; (debate) tomar parte en; (agreement) llegar a, firmar; **to ~ (up)on** vt fus (career) emprender.

enteritis [ɛntə'raıtıs] n enteritis f.

enterprise ['ɛntəpraız] n empresa; (spirit) iniciativa; **free ~** la libre empresa; **private ~** la iniciativa privada;

enterprising a emprendedor(a).

entertain [ɛntə'teɪn] vt (amuse) divertir; (receive: guest) recibir (en casa); (idea) abrigar; (plan) estudiar; ~**er** n artista m/f; ~**ing** a divertido, entretenido; ~**ment** n (amusement) diversión f; (show) espectáculo; (party) fiesta.

enthralled [ɪn'θrɔːld] a encantado, cautivado.

enthusiasm [ɪn'θuːzɪæzəm] n entusiasmo.

enthusiast [ɪn'θuːzɪæst] n entusiasta m/f; ~**ic** [-'æstɪk] a entusiasta inv; **to be** ~**ic about** entusiasmarse por.

entice [ɪn'taɪs] vt tentar; (seduce) seducir; **enticing** a atractivo, tentador(a).

entire [ɪn'taɪə*] a entero, completo; (in total) total, todo; ~**ly** ad totalmente; ~**ty** [ɪn'taɪərətɪ] n: **in its** ~**ty** en su totalidad.

entitle [ɪn'taɪtl] vt: **to** ~ **sb to sth** dar a uno derecho a algo; ~**d** a (book) que se titula; **to be** ~**d to do** tener derecho a hacer.

entourage [ɔntu'rɑːʒ] n séquito.

entrails ['ɛntreɪlz] npl entrañas fpl.

entrance ['ɛntrəns] n entrada // vt [ɪn'trɑːns] encantar, hechizar; **to gain** ~ **to** (university etc) ingresar en; ~ **examination** n examen m de ingreso; ~ **fee** n cuota.

entrant ['ɛntrənt] n participante m/f.

entreat [ɛn'triːt] vt rogar, suplicar; ~**y** n ruego, súplica.

entrée ['ɔntreɪ] n (CULIN) entrada.

entrenched [ɛn'trɛntʃd] a atrincherado.

entrepreneur [ɔntrəprə'nɜː] n empresario; (of works) contratista m/f.

entrust [ɪn'trʌst] vt: **to** ~ **sth to sb** confiar algo a uno.

entry ['ɛntrɪ] n entrada; (permission to enter) acceso; (in register) apunte m; (in account) partida; ~ **form** n boleto de inscripción; **no** ~ prohibido el paso; (AUT) dirección prohibida.

enumerate [ɪ'njuːməreɪt] vt enumerar.

enunciate [ɪ'nʌnsɪeɪt] vt pronunciar; (principle etc) enunciar.

envelop [ɪn'vɛləp] vt envolver.

envelope ['ɛnvələup] n sobre m.

envious ['ɛnvɪəs] a envidioso; (look) de envidia.

environment [ɪn'vaɪərnmənt] n medio ambiente; ~**al** [-'mɛntl] a ambiental.

envisage [ɪn'vɪzɪdʒ] vt (foresee) prever; (imagine) concebir, representarse.

envoy ['ɛnvɔɪ] n enviado.

envy ['ɛnvɪ] n envidia // vt tener envidia a; **to** ~ **sb sth** envidiar algo a uno.

enzyme ['ɛnzaɪm] n enzima.

ephemeral [ɪ'fɛmərl] a efímero.

epic ['ɛpɪk] n épica // a épico.

epidemic [ɛpɪ'dɛmɪk] n epidemia.

epilepsy ['ɛpɪlɛpsɪ] n epilepsia; **epileptic** [-'lɛptɪk] a, n epiléptico/a.

episode ['ɛpɪsəud] n episodio.

epistle [ɪ'pɪsl] n epístola.

epitaph ['ɛpɪtɑːf] n epitafio.

epitome [ɪ'pɪtəmɪ] n epítome m; **epitomize** vt epitomar, resumir.

epoch ['iːpɔk] n época.

equable ['ɛkwəbl] a uniforme, igual; (character) tranquilo, afable.

equal ['iːkwl] a (gen) igual; (treatment) equitativo // n igual m/f // vt ser igual a; **to be** ~ **to** (task) estar a la altura de; ~**ity** [iː'kwɔlɪtɪ] n igualdad f; ~**ize** vt, vi igualar; (SPORT) lograr el empate; ~**izer** n igualada; ~**ly** ad igualmente; (share etc) por igual.

equanimity [ɛkwə'nɪmɪtɪ] n ecuanimidad f.

equate [ɪ'kweɪt] vt: **to** ~ **sth with** considerar algo equivalente a; **equation** [ɪ'kweɪʃən] n (MATH) ecuación f.

equator [ɪ'kweɪtə*] n ecuador m; ~**ial** [ɛkwə'tɔːrɪəl] a ecuatorial.

equilibrium [iːkwɪ'lɪbrɪəm] n equilibrio.

equinox ['iːkwɪnɔks] n equinoccio.

equip [ɪ'kwɪp] vt (gen) equipar; (person) proveer; **to be well** ~**ped** estar bien dotado; ~**ment** n equipo; (tools) avíos mpl.

equitable ['ɛkwɪtəbl] a equitativo.

equivalent [ɪ'kwɪvəlnt] a equivalente; **to be** ~ **to** equivaler a // n equivalente m.

equivocal [ɪ'kwɪvəkl] a equívoco; (open to suspicion) ambiguo.

era ['ɪərə] n era, época.

eradicate [ɪ'rædɪkeɪt] vt erradicar, extirpar.

erase [ɪ'reɪz] vt borrar; **eraser** n goma de borrar.

erect [ɪ'rɛkt] a erguido // vt erigir, levantar; (assemble) montar.

erection [ɪ'rɛkʃən] n construcción f; (assembly) montaje m; (structure) edificio; (MED) erección f.

ermine ['ɜːmɪn] n armiño.

erode [ɪ'rəud] vt (GEO) erosionar; (metal) corroer, desgastar; **erosion** [ɪ'rəuʒən] n erosión f; desgaste m.

erotic [ɪ'rɔtɪk] a erótico; ~**ism** [ɪ'rɔtɪsɪzm] n erotismo.

err [ɜː*] vi errar, equivocarse; (REL) pecar.

errand ['ɛrnd] n recado, mandado; ~ **boy** n recadero.

erratic [ɪ'rætɪk] a irregular; (uneven) desigual, poco uniforme.

erroneous [ɪ'rəunɪəs] a erróneo.

error ['ɛrə*] n error m, equivocación f.

erupt [ɪ'rʌpt] vi estar en erupción; (MED) hacer erupción; (fig) estallar; ~**ion** [ɪ'rʌpʃən] n erupción f; (fig) explosión f.

escalate ['ɛskəleɪt] vi extenderse, intensificarse; **escalation** [-'leɪʃən] n escalamiento, intensificación f.

escalator ['ɛskəleɪtə*] n escalera móvil.

escapade [ɛskə'peɪd] n travesura.

escape [ɪ'skeɪp] n (gen) fuga; (from duties) escapatoria; (from chase) fuga, evasión f // vi (gen) escaparse; (flee) huir, evadirse; (leak) fugarse // vt evitar, eludir; (consequences) escapar a; **to** ~ **from**

(*place*) escaparse de; (*person*) escaparse a; (*clutches*) librarse de; **escapism** *n* escapismo.

escort ['ɛskɔːt] *n* acompañante *m/f*; (*MIL*) escolta; (*NAUT*) convoy *m* // *vt* [ɪ'skɔːt] acompañar; (*MIL, NAUT*) escoltar.

Eskimo ['ɛskɪməu] *n* esquimal *m/f*.

especially [ɪ'spɛʃlɪ] *ad* (*gen*) especialmente; (*above all*) sobre todo; (*particularly*) en particular.

espionage ['ɛspɪɒnɑːʒ] *n* espionaje *m*.

esplanade [ɛsplə'neɪd] *n* (*by sea*) paseo marítimo.

espouse [ɪ'spauz] *vt* adherirse a.

Esquire [ɪ'skwaɪə] *n* (*abbr* **Esq.**): **J. Brown,** ~ Sr. Don J. Brown.

essay ['ɛseɪ] *n* (*SCOL*) ensayo.

essence ['ɛsns] *n* esencia.

essential [ɪ'sɛnʃl] *a* (*necessary*) imprescindible; (*basic*) esencial; ~**ly** *ad* esencialmente.

establish [ɪ'stæblɪʃ] *vt* establecer; (*facts*) verificar; (*proof*) demostrar; (*relations*) entablar; ~**ed** *a* (*business*) de buena reputación; (*staff*) de plantilla; ~**ment** *n* establecimiento; **the E~ment** la clase dirigente.

estate [ɪ'steɪt] *n* (*land*) finca, hacienda; (*property*) propiedad *f*; (*inheritance*) herencia; (*POL*) estado; **housing** ~ urbanización *f*; **industrial** ~ polígono industrial; ~ **agent** *n* agente *m/f* inmobiliario; ~ **car** *n* (*Brit*) furgoneta.

esteem [ɪ'stiːm] *n*: **to hold sb in high** ~ estimar en mucho a uno // *vt* estimar.

estimate ['ɛstɪmət] *n* estimación *f*, apreciación *f*; (*assessment*) tasa, cálculo; (*COMM*) presupuesto // *vt* [-meɪt] estimar; tasar, calcular; **estimation** [-'meɪʃən] *n* opinión *f*, juicio; (*esteem*) aprecio.

estrange [ɪ'streɪndʒ] *vt* enajenar.

estuary ['ɛstjuərɪ] *n* estuario, ría.

etching ['ɛtʃɪŋ] *n* aguafuerte *f*.

eternal [ɪ'tɜːnl] *a* eterno.

eternity [ɪ'tɜːnɪtɪ] *n* eternidad *f*.

ether ['iːθə*] *n* éter *m*.

ethical ['ɛθɪkl] *a* ético; (*honest*) honrado; **ethics** ['ɛθɪks] *n* ética // *npl* moralidad *f*.

ethnic ['ɛθnɪk] *a* étnico.

etiquette ['ɛtɪkɛt] *n* etiqueta.

eucalyptus [juːkə'lɪptəs] *n* eucalipto.

euphemism ['juːfəmɪzm] *n* eufemismo.

euphoria [juː'fɔːrɪə] *n* euforia.

Europe ['juərəp] *n* Europa; **European** [-'piːən] *a*, *n* europeo/a.

euthanasia [juːθə'neɪzɪə] *n* eutanasia.

evacuate [ɪ'vækjueɪt] *vt* desocupar; **evacuation** [-'eɪʃən] *n* evacuación *f*.

evade [ɪ'veɪd] *vt* evadir, eludir.

evaluate [ɪ'væljueɪt] *vt* evaluar; (*value*) tasar; (*evidence*) interpretar.

evangelist [ɪ'vændʒəlɪst] *n* evangelizador *m*, evangelista *m/f*.

evaporate [ɪ'væpəreɪt] *vi* evaporarse, desvanecerse // *vt* evaporar; ~**d milk** *n*

leche *f* evaporada; **evaporation** [-'reɪʃən] *n* evaporación *f*.

evasion [ɪ'veɪʒən] *n* evasiva, evasión *f*; **evasive** [-sɪv] *a* evasivo.

eve [iːv] *n*: **on the** ~ **of** en vísperas de.

even ['iːvn] *a* (*level*) llano; (*smooth*) liso; (*speed, temperature*) uniforme; (*number*) par; (*nature*) ecuánime; (*SPORT*) igual(es) // *ad* hasta, aun, siquiera; ~ **more** aun más; ~ **so** aun así; **not** ~ ni siquiera; ~ **he was there** hasta él estuvo allí; ~ **on Sundays** incluso los domingos; **to** ~ **out** *vi* nivelarse; **to get** ~ **with sb** ajustar cuentas con uno.

evening ['iːvnɪŋ] *n* tarde *f*; (*dusk*) atardecer *m*; (*night*) noche *f*; (*event*) velada; **in the** ~ por la tarde; ~ **class** *n* clase *f* nocturna; ~ **dress** *n* (*man's*) traje *m* de etiqueta; (*woman's*) traje *m* de noche.

event [ɪ'vɛnt] *n* suceso, acontecimiento; (*SPORT*) prueba; **in the** ~ **of** en caso de (que); ~**ful** *a* accidentado; (*game etc*) lleno de emoción.

eventual [ɪ'vɛntʃuəl] *a* (*last*) final; (*resulting*) consiguiente; ~**ity** [-'ælɪtɪ] *n* eventualidad *f*; ~**ly** *ad* (*finally*) finalmente, al fin y al cabo; (*in time*) a la larga.

ever ['ɛvə*] *ad* nunca, jamás; (*at all times*) alguna vez; **the best** ~ el/la mejor que se ha visto jamás; **have you** ~ **seen it?** ¿lo ha visto Usted jamás?; **better than** ~ mejor que nunca; ~ **since** *ad* desde entonces // *conj* después de que; ~**green** *n* árbol *m* de hoja perenne; ~**lasting** *a* eterno, perpetuo.

every ['ɛvrɪ] *det* (*each*) cada; (*all*) todo; ~ **day** cada día; ~ **other car** cada dos coches; ~ **now and then** de vez en cuando; ~**body** *pron* todos *pl*, todo el mundo; ~**day** *a* (*daily*) diario, cotidiano; (*usual*) corriente; (*common*) vulgar; (*routine*) rutinario; ~**one** = ~**body**; ~**thing** *pron* todo; ~**where** *ad* (*be*) en todas partes; (*go*) a o por todas partes.

evict [ɪ'vɪkt] *vt* desahuciar; ~**ion** [ɪ'vɪkʃən] *n* desahucio.

evidence ['ɛvɪdəns] *n* (*proof*) prueba; (*of witness*) testimonio; (*facts*) datos *mpl*, hechos *mpl*; **to give** ~ prestar declaración, dar testimonio.

evident ['ɛvɪdənt] *a* evidente, manifiesto; ~**ly** *ad* naturalmente.

evil ['iːvl] *a* malo; (*influence*) funesto; (*smell*) horrible // *n* mal *m*, maldad *f*; ~**doer** *n* malhechor/a *m/f*.

evocative [ɪ'vɒkətɪv] *a* sugestivo, evocador(a).

evoke [ɪ'vəuk] *vt* evocar.

evolution [iːvə'luːʃən] *n* evolución *f*, desarrollo.

evolve [ɪ'vɒlv] *vt* desarrollar // *vi* evolucionar, desarrollarse.

ewe [juː] *n* oveja.

ex-... [ɛks] *pref* ex.

exact [ɪg'zækt] *a* exacto // *vt*: **to** ~ **sth**

(from) exigir algo (de); ~**ing** a exigente; (conditions) arduo; ~**itude** n exactitud f; ~**ly** ad exactamente; (time) en punto.
exaggerate [ig'zædʒəreit] vt, vi exagerar; **exaggeration** [-'reiʃən] n exageración f.
exalted [ig'zɔːltid] a exaltado, elevado.
exam [ig'zæm] n abbr of **examination.**
examination [igzæmi'neiʃən] n (gen) examen m; (LAW) interrogación f; (inquiry) investigación f.
examine [ig'zæmin] vt (gen) examinar; (inspect) inspeccionar, escudriñar; (SCOL, LAW: person) interrogar; (at customs: luggage) registrar; **examiner** n inspector m.
example [ig'zɑːmpl] n ejemplo; (copy) ejemplar m; **for** ~ por ejemplo.
exasperate [ig'zɑːspəreit] vt exasperar, irritar; **exasperating** a irritante.
excavate ['ekskəveit] vt excavar; **excavation** [-'veiʃən] n excavación f.
exceed [ik'siːd] vt exceder; (number) pasar de; (speed limit) sobrepasar; (limits) rebasar; (powers) excederse en; (hopes) superar; ~**ingly** ad sumamente, sobremanera.
excel [ik'sɛl] vi sobresalir.
excellence ['eksələns] n excelencia.
Excellency ['eksələnsi] n: **His** ~ Su Excelencia.
excellent ['eksələnt] a excelente.
except [ik'sɛpt] prep (also: ~ **for,** ~**ing**) excepto, salvo, con excepción de // vt exceptuar, excluir; ~ **if/when** excepto si/cuando; ~ **that** salvo que; ~**ion** [ik-'sɛpʃən] n excepción f; **to take** ~**ion to** ofenderse por; ~**ional** [ik'sɛpʃənl] a excepcional.
excerpt ['eksəːpt] n extracto.
excess [ik'sɛs] n exceso; (COMM) excedente m; ~ **baggage** n exceso de equipaje; ~ **fare** n suplemento; ~**ive** a excesivo.
exchange [iks'tʃeindʒ] n cambio; (of goods) canje m; (of ideas) intercambio; (also: **telephone** ~) central f (telefónica) // vt cambiar; canjear.
exchequer [iks'tʃekə*] n hacienda.
excise ['eksaiz] n impuestos mpl sobre el comercio exterior // vt [ek'saiz] suprimir.
excite [ik'sait] vt (stimulate) excitar; (awaken) despertar; (move) entusiasmar; **to get** ~**d** emocionarse; ~**ment** n emoción f; (anticipation) ilusión f; (agitation) agitación f; **exciting** a emocionante.
exclaim [ik'skleim] vi exclamar; **exclamation** [eksklə'meiʃən] n exclamación f; **exclamation mark** n punto de admiración.
exclude [ik'skluːd] vt excluir; (except) exceptuar; **exclusion** [ik'skluːʒən] n exclusión f.
exclusive [ik'skluːsiv] a exclusivo; (club, district) selecto; ~ **of tax** excluyendo impuestos; ~**ly** ad únicamente.
excommunicate [ekskə'mjuːnikeit] vt excomulgar.

excrement ['ekskrəmənt] n excremento.
excrete [ik'skriːt] vi excretar.
excruciating [ik'skruːʃieitiŋ] a agudísimo, atroz.
excursion [ik'skəːʃən] n excursión f.
excusable [ik'skjuːzəbl] a perdonable.
excuse [ik'skjuːs] n disculpa, excusa; (evasion) pretexto // vt [ik'skjuːz] disculpar, perdonar; **to** ~ **sb from doing sth** dispensar a uno de hacer algo; ~ **me!** ¡perdón!; **if you will** ~ **me** con su permiso.
execute ['eksikjuːt] vt (plan) realizar; (order) cumplir; (person) ajusticiar, ejecutar; **execution** n realización f; cumplimiento; ejecución f; **executioner** n verdugo.
executive [ig'zekjutiv] n (COMM, POL) ejecutivo // a ejecutivo.
executor [ig'zekjutə*] n albacea m, testamentario.
exemplary [ig'zempləri] a ejemplar.
exemplify [ig'zemplifai] vt ejemplificar.
exempt [ig'zempt] a: ~ **from** exento de // vt. **to** ~ **sb from** eximir a uno de; ~**ion** [ig'zempʃən] n exención f; (immunity) inmunidad f.
exercise ['eksəsaiz] n ejercicio // vt ejercer; (right) valerse de; (dog) llevar de paseo // vi hacer ejercicio(s); ~ **book** n cuaderno.
exert [ig'zəːt] vt ejercer; **to** ~ **o.s.** esforzarse, afanarse; (overdo things) trabajar demasiado; ~**ion** n esfuerzo.
exhaust [ig'zɔːst] n (pipe) escape m; (fumes) gases mpl de escape // vt agotar; ~**ion** [ig'zɔːstʃən] n agotamiento; **nervous** ~**ion** postración f nerviosa; ~**ive** a exhaustivo.
exhibit [ig'zibit] n (ART) obra expuesta; (LAW) objeto expuesto // vt (show) manifestar; (emotion) acusar; (film) presentar; (paintings) exponer; ~**ion** [eksi'biʃən] n exposición f; ~**ionist** [eksi'biʃənist] n exhibicionista m/f.
exhilarating [ig'ziləreitiŋ] a estimulante, tónico.
exhort [ig'zɔːt] vt exhortar.
exile ['eksail] n exilio; (person) exiliado/a // vt desterrar, exiliar.
exist [ig'zist] vi existir; (live) vivir; ~**ence** n existencia; (life) vida; ~**ing** a existente, actual.
exit ['eksit] n salida.
exonerate [ig'zɔnəreit] vt: **to** ~ **from** exculpar de.
exorcize ['eksɔːsaiz] vt exorcizar.
exotic [ig'zɔtik] a exótico.
expand [ik'spænd] vt (widen) ensanchar; (number) aumentar // vi (trade etc) expandirse; (gas, metal) dilatarse.
expanse [ik'spæns] n extensión f; (of wings) envergadura.
expansion [ik'spænʃən] n (of town) ensanche m; (of trade) expansión f.
expatriate [eks'pætriət] n expatriado/a.
expect [ik'spekt] vt (gen) esperar; (count

on) contar con; (*suppose*) suponer // *vi*: **to be** ~**ing** estar encinta; ~**ant mother** *n* mujer *f* encinta; ~**ation** [ɛkspɛk'teɪʃən] *n* esperanza, expectativa.

expedience [ɛk'spiːdɪəns] **expediency** [ɛk'spiːdɪənsɪ] *n* conveniencia; **expedient** *a* conveniente, oportuno // *n* recurso, expediente *m*.

expedition [ɛkspə'dɪʃən] *n* expedición *f*.

expel [ɪk'spɛl] *vt* arrojar; (*SCOL*) expulsar.

expend [ɪk'spɛnd] *vt* gastar; (*use up*) consumir; ~**able** *a* prescindible; ~**iture** *n* gastos *mpl*, desembolso.

expense [ɪk'spɛns] *n* gasto, gastos *mpl*; (*high cost*) costa; ~**s** *npl* (*COMM*) gastos *mpl*; **at the** ~ **of** a costa o expensas de; ~ **account** *n* cuenta de gastos.

expensive [ɪk'spɛnsɪv] *a* caro, costoso.

experience [ɪk'spɪərɪəns] *n* experiencia // *vt* experimentar; (*suffer*) sufrir; ~**d** *a* experimentado.

experiment [ɪk'spɛrɪmənt] *n* experimento // *vi* hacer experimentos; ~**al** [-'mɛntl] *a* experimental.

expert ['ɛkspəːt] *a* experto, perito // *n* experto, perito; (*specialist*) especialista *m/f*; ~**ise** [-'tiːz] *n* pericia.

expire [ɪk'spaɪə*] *vi* (*gen*) expirar; (*end*) terminar; (*run out*) caducar, vencerse; **expiry** *n* expiración *f*; terminación *f*; vencimiento.

explain [ɪk'spleɪn] *vt* explicar; (*clarify*) aclarar; (*demonstrate*) exponer; **explanation** [ɛksplə'neɪʃən] *n* explicación *f*; aclaración *f*; **explanatory** [ɪk'splænətrɪ] *a* explicativo; aclaratorio.

explicit [ɪk'splɪsɪt] *a* explícito.

explode [ɪk'spləud] *vi* estallar, explotar; (*with anger*) reventar // *vt* volar, explotar.

exploit ['ɛksplɔɪt] *n* hazaña // *vt* [ɪk'splɔɪt] explotar; ~**ation** [-'teɪʃən] *n* explotación *f*.

exploration [ɛksplə'reɪʃən] *n* exploración *f*; **exploratory** [ɪk'splɔrətrɪ] *a* (*fig: talks*) exploratorio, de sondaje.

explore [ɪk'splɔː*] *vt* explorar; (*fig*) examinar, sondar; **explorer** *n* explorador *m*.

explosion [ɪk'spləuʒən] *n* explosión *f*; **explosive** [-sɪv] *a, n* explosivo.

exponent [ɪk'spəunənt] *n* exponente *m/f*, intérprete *m/f*.

export [ɛk'spɔːt] *vt* exportar // *n* ['ɛkspɔːt] exportación *f* // *cpd* de exportación; ~**ation** [-'teɪʃən] *n* exportación *f*; ~**er** *n* exportador *m*.

expose [ɪk'spəuz] *vt* exponer; (*unmask*) desenmascarar; ~**d** *a* expuesto; (*position*) desabrigado.

exposure [ɪk'spəuʒə*] *n* exposición *f*; (*PHOT*) revelación *f*; (: *shot*) fotografía; **to die from** ~ (*MED*) morir de frío; ~ **meter** *n* fotómetro.

expound [ɪk'spaund] *vt* exponer, explicar.

express [ɪk'sprɛs] *a* (*definite*) expreso, explícito; (*letter etc*) urgente // *n* (*train*) rápido // *ad* (*send*) por carta urgente // *vt* expresar; (*squeeze*) exprimir; ~**ion** [ɪk-

'spɛʃən] *n* expresión *f*; ~**ive** *a* expresivo; ~**ly** *ad* expresamente.

expulsion [ɪk'spʌlʃən] *n* expulsión *f*.

exquisite [ɛk'skwɪzɪt] *a* exquisito.

extend [ɪk'stɛnd] *vt* (*visit, street*) prolongar; (*building*) ensanchar; (*offer*) ofrecer // *vi* (*land*) extenderse.

extension [ɪk'stɛnʃən] *n* extensión *f*; (*building*) ampliación *f*; (*TEL: line*) línea derivada; (: *telephone*) extensión *f*; (*of deadline*) prórroga.

extensive [ɪk'stɛnsɪv] *a* (*gen*) extenso; (*broad*) vasto, ancho; (*frequent*) general, común; **he's travelled** ~**ly** ha viajado por muchos países.

extent [ɪk'stɛnt] *n* (*breadth*) extensión *f*; (*scope*) alcance *m*; **to some** ~ hasta cierto punto; **to the** ~ **of...** hasta el punto de...; **to such an** ~ **that...** hasta tal punto que...; **to what** ~? ¿hasta qué punto?

exterior [ɛk'stɪərɪə*] *a* exterior, externo // *n* exterior *m*; (*appearance*) aspecto.

exterminate [ɪk'stəːmɪneɪt] *vt* exterminar; **extermination** [-'neɪʃən] *n* exterminación *f*.

external [ɛk'stəːnl] *a* externo, exterior; ~**ly** *ad* por fuera.

extinct [ɪk'stɪŋkt] *a* extinto; ~**ion** [ɪk-'stɪŋkʃən] *n* extinción *f*.

extinguish [ɪk'stɪŋgwɪʃ] *vt* extinguir, apagar; ~**er** *n* extintor *m*.

extort [ɪk'stɔːt] *vt* sacar a la fuerza (*from sb* de uno); ~**ion** [ɪk'stɔːʃən] *n* exacción *f*; ~**ionate** [ɪk'stɔːʃnət] *a* excesivo, exorbitante.

extra ['ɛkstrə] *a* adicional; (*excessive*) de más, de sobra; (*bonus: payment*) extraordinario // *ad* (*in addition*) especialmente // *n* (*addition*) extra *m*, suplemento; (*THEATRE*) extra *m/f*, comparsa *m/f*; (*newspaper*) edición *f* extraordinaria.

extra... [ɛkstrə] *pref* extra... .

extract [ɪk'strækt] *vt* sacar, extraer; (*confession*) arrancar, obtener // *n* ['ɛkstrækt] extracto.

extradite ['ɛkstrədaɪt] *vt* (*from country*) conceder la extradición de; (*to country*) obtener la extradición de; **extradition** [-'dɪʃən] *n* extradición *f*.

extramarital [ɛkstrə'mærɪtl] *a* extra-matrimonial.

extramural [ɛkstrə'mjuərl] *a* de extramuros.

extraordinary [ɪk'strɔːdnrɪ] *a* extra-ordinario; (*odd*) raro.

extravagant [ɪk'strævəgənt] *a* (*lavish*) pródigo; (*wasteful*) derrochador(a); (*price*) exorbitante; (*praise*) excesivo; (*odd*) raro.

extreme [ɪk'striːm] *a* extremo; (*poverty etc*) extremado; (*case*) excepcional // *n* extremo, extremidad *f*; ~**ly** *ad* sumamente, extremadamente; **extremist** *a, n* extremista *m/f*.

extremity [ɪk'strɛmətɪ] *n* extremidad *f*, punta; (*need*) apuro, necesidad *f*.

extricate ['ɛkstrɪkeɪt] *vt* librar.

extrovert ['ɛkstrəvɔːt] n extrovertido/a.
exuberant [ɪgˈzjuːbərnt] a (person) eufórico; (style) exuberante.
exude [ɪgˈzjuːd] vt rezumar, sudar.
exult [ɪgˈzʌlt] vi regocijarse.
eye [aɪ] n ojo // vt mirar de soslayo, ojear; to keep an ~ on vigilar, estar pendiente de; ~ball n globo del ojo; ~bath n ojera; ~brow n ceja; ~brow pencil n lápiz m de cejas; ~-catching a llamativo; ~drops npl gotas fpl para los ojos; ~lash n pestaña; ~lid n párpado; ~-opener n revelación f, gran sorpresa; ~shadow n sombreador m de ojos; ~sight n vista; ~sore n monstruosidad f; ~wash n (fig) disparates mpl, tonterías fpl; ~ witness n testigo m/f presencial.
eyrie [ˈɪərɪ] n aguilera.

F

F. abbr of Fahrenheit.
fable [ˈfeɪbl] n fábula.
fabric [ˈfæbrɪk] n tejido, tela.
fabrication [fæbrɪˈkeɪʃən] n invención f.
fabulous [ˈfæbjuləs] a fabuloso.
façade [fəˈsɑːd] n fachada.
face [feɪs] n cara; (ANAT) cara, rostro; (of clock) esfera; (side, surface) superficie f // vt (person) encararse con; (building) dar a; to lose ~ desprestigiarse; in the ~ of (difficulties etc) en vista de; on the ~ of it a primera vista; ~ to ~ cara a cara; to ~ up to vt fus hacer frente a, arrostrar; ~ cloth n paño; ~ cream n crema (de belleza); ~ lift n cirugía estética; ~ powder n polvos mpl; ~-saving a para salvar las apariencias.
facet [ˈfæsɪt] n faceta.
facetious [fəˈsiːʃəs] a chistoso.
face value [ˈfeɪsˈvæljuː] n (of stamp) valor m nominal; to take sth at ~ (fig) tomar algo en sentido literal, aceptar las apariencias de algo.
facial [ˈfeɪʃəl] a de la cara.
facile [ˈfæsaɪl] a superficial, ligero.
facilitate [fəˈsɪlɪteɪt] vt facilitar.
facilities [fəˈsɪlɪtɪz] npl facilidades fpl.
facing [ˈfeɪsɪŋ] prep frente a // a de enfrente.
fact [fækt] n hecho; in ~ en realidad.
faction [ˈfækʃən] n facción f.
factor [ˈfæktə*] n factor m.
factory [ˈfæktərɪ] n fábrica.
factual [ˈfæktjuəl] a objetivo.
faculty [ˈfækəltɪ] n facultad f; (US: teaching staff) profesorado.
fade [feɪd] vi desteñirse; (sound, hope) desvanecerse; (light) apagarse; (flower) marchitarse.
fag [fæg] n (col: cigarette) pitillo; ~ end n colilla; ~ged out a (col) agotado.
fail [feɪl] vt (candidate) suspender; (exam) no aprobar // vi acabarse; (engine) fallar; (voice) desfallecer; (patient) debilitarse; to ~ to do sth (neglect) dejar de hacer algo;

(be unable) no poder hacer algo; without ~ sin falta; ~ing n falta, defecto // prep a falta de; ~ure ['feɪljə*] n fracaso; (person) fracasado/a; (mechanical etc) fallo.
faint [feɪnt] a débil; (recollection) vago; (mark) apenas visible // n desmayo // vi desmayarse; to feel ~ estar mareado, marearse; ~-hearted a pusilánime; ~ly ad débilmente; vagamente; ~ness n debilidad f.
fair [fɛə*] a justo; (colour) rubio; (weather) bueno; (good enough) suficiente; (sizeable) considerable // ad (play) limpio // n feria; (funfair) parque m de atracciones; ~ly ad (justly) con justicia; (equally) equitativamente; (quite) bastante; ~ness n justicia; (impartiality) imparcialidad f.
fairy [ˈfɛərɪ] n hada; ~ tale n cuento de hadas.
faith [feɪθ] n fe f; (trust) confianza; (sect) religión f; ~ful a fiel; ~fully ad fielmente; yours ~fully le saluda atentamente.
fake [feɪk] n (painting etc) falsificación f; (person) impostor m // a falso // vt fingir; (painting etc) falsificar; his illness is a ~ su enfermedad es una invención.
falcon [ˈfɔːlkən] n halcón m.
fall [fɔːl] n caída; (US: autumn) otoño // vi, pt fell, pp fallen [ˈfɔːlən] caer, caerse; (price) bajar; ~s npl (waterfall) cascada, salto de agua; to ~ flat vi (on one's face) caerse (boca abajo); (plan) fracasar; to ~ back vi retroceder; to ~ back on vt fus (remedy etc) recurrir a; to ~ backwards vi caer de espaldas; to ~ behind vi quedarse atrás; to ~ down vi (person) caerse; (building, hopes) derrumbarse; to ~ for vt fus (trick) dejarse engañar por; (person) enamorarse de; to ~ in vi (roof) hundirse; (MIL) alinearse; to ~ off vi caerse; (diminish) disminuir; to ~ out vi (friends etc) reñir; (MIL) romper filas; to ~ through vi (plan, project) fracasar.
fallacy [ˈfæləsɪ] n (error) error m; (lie) mentira.
fallible [ˈfæləbl] a falible.
fallout [ˈfɔːlaut] n lluvia radioactiva; ~ shelter n refugio contra ataques nucleares.
false [fɔːls] a (gen) falso; (hair, teeth etc) postizo; (disloyal) desleal, traidor(a); under ~ pretences con engaños; ~hood n (lie) mentira; (falseness) falsedad f; ~ly ad (accuse) falsamente; ~ teeth npl dentadura postiza sg.
falter [ˈfɔːltə*] vi vacilar.
fame [feɪm] n fama.
familiar [fəˈmɪlɪə*] a familiar; (well-known) conocido; (tone) de confianza; to be ~ with (subject) estar enterado de; ~ity [fəmɪlɪˈærɪtɪ] n familiaridad f; ~ize [fəˈmɪlɪəraɪz] vr: to ~ize o.s. with familiarizarse con.
family [ˈfæmɪlɪ] n familia; ~ business n

negocio familiar; ~ **doctor** *n* médico de cabecera.
famine ['fæmɪn] *n* hambre *f.*
famished ['fæmɪʃt] a hambriento.
famous ['feɪməs] *a* famoso, célebre; ~ly *ad* (*get on*) estupendamente.
fan [fæn] *n* abanico; (*ELEC*) ventilador *m*; (*person*) aficionado/a // *vt* abanicaɪ; (*fire, quarrel*) atizar; **to** ~ **out** *vi* desparramarse.
fanatic [fə'nætɪk] *n* fanático/a; ~al *a* fanático.
fan belt ['fænbɛlt] *n* correa de ventilador.
fanciful ['fænsɪful] *a* (*gen*) fantástico; (*imaginary*) imaginario.
fancy ['fænsɪ] *n* (*whim*) capricho, antojo; (*taste*) afición *f*, gusto; (*imagination*) imaginación *f*; (*delusion*) quimera // *a* (*decorative*) hermoso; (*luxury*) de lujo; (*as decoration*) de adorno // *vt* (*feel like, want*) tener ganas de; (*imagine*) imaginarse; (*think*) creer; **to take a** ~ **to** encapricharse por, tomar afición a; **it took** *or* **caught my** ~ me cayó en gracia; **to** ~ **that...** imaginarse que...; **he fancies her** le gusta (ella); ~ **dress** *n* disfraz *m*; ~**-dress ball** *n* baile *m* de disfraces.
fang [fæŋ] *n* colmillo.
fantastic [fæn'tæstɪk] *a* fantástico.
fantasy ['fæntəzɪ] *n* fantasía.
far [fɑ:*] *a* (*distant*) lejano // *ad* lejos; ~ **away**, ~ **off** (a lo) lejos; ~ **better** mucho mejor; ~ **from** lejos de; **by** ~ con mucho; **go as** ~ **as the farm** vaya hasta la granja; **as** ~ **as I know** que yo sepa; **how** ~? ¿hasta dónde?; (*fig*) ¿hasta qué punto?; **the F** ~ **East** el Extremo Oriente; ~**away** *a* remoto.
farce [fɑ:s] *n* farsa; **farcical** *a* absurdo.
fare [fɛə*] *n* (*on trains, buses*) precio (del billete); (*in taxi: cost*) tarifa; (: *passenger*) pasajero; (*food*) comida.
farewell [fɛə'wɛl] *excl, n* adiós *m.*
farm [fɑ:m] *n* granja, finca, estancia (*AM*) // *vt* cultivar; ~**er** *n* granjero, estanciero (*AM*); ~**hand** *n* peón *m*; ~**house** *n* casa de labranza; ~**ing** *n* (*gen*) agricultura; (*tilling*) cultivo; ~**land** *n* tierra de cultivo; ~ **worker** *n* = ~**hand**; ~**yard** *n* corral *m.*
far-sighted ['fɑ:'saɪtɪd] *a* previsor(a).
fart [fɑ:t] (*col!*) n pedo // *vi* tirarse un pedo.
farther ['fɑ:ðə*] *ad* más lejos, más allá.
farthest ['fɑ:ðɪst] *superlative of* **far.**
fascinate ['fæsɪneɪt] *vt* fascinar; **fascination** [-'neɪʃən] *n* fascinación *f.*
fascism ['fæʃɪzəm] *n* fascismo; **fascist** [-ɪst] *a, n* fascista *m/f.*
fashion ['fæʃən] *n* moda; (*manner*) manera // *vt* formar; **in** ~ a la moda; **out of** ~ pasado de moda; ~**able** *a* de moda; ~ **show** *n* desfile *m* de modelos.
fast [fɑ:st] *a* rápido; (*dye, colour*) sólido; (*clock*): **to be** ~ estar adelantado // *ad* rápidamente, de prisa; (*stuck, held*) firmemente // *n* ayuno // *vi* ayunar; ~

asleep profundamente dormido.
fasten ['fɑ:sn] *vt* asegurar, sujetar; (*coat, belt*) abrochar // *vi* cerrarse; ~**er**, ~**ing** *n* (*gen*) cierre *m*; (*of door etc*) cerrojo; **zip** ~**er** cremallera.
fastidious [fæs'tɪdɪəs] *a* (*fussy*) delicado; (*demanding*) exigente.
fat [fæt] *a* gordo; (*meat*) con mucha grasa; (*greasy*) grasiento // *n* grasa; (*on person*) carnes *fpl*; (*lard*) manteca.
fatal ['feɪtl] *a* (*gen*) fatal; (*injury*) mortal; (*consequence*) funesto; ~**ism** *n* fatalismo; ~**ity** [fə'tælɪtɪ] *n* (*road death etc*) víctima *m/f*; ~**ly** *ad*: ~**ly injured** herido a muerte.
fate [feɪt] *n* destino; (*of person*) suerte *f*; ~**ful** *a* fatídico.
father ['fɑ:ðə*] *n* padre *m*; ~**hood** *n* paternidad *f*; ~**-in-law** *n* suegro; ~**ly** *a* paternal.
fathom ['fæðəm] *n* braza // *vt* (*NAUT*) sondear; (*unravel*) desentrañar; (*understand*) lograr comprender.
fatigue [fə'ti:g] *n* fatiga, cansancio.
fatten ['fætn] *vt, vi* engordar.
fatty ['fætɪ] *a* (*food*) graso // *n* (*fam*) gordito/a, gordinflón/ona *m/f.*
faucet ['fɔ:sɪt] *n* (*US*) grifo.
fault [fɔ:lt] *n* (*error*) falta; (*blame*) culpa; (*defect*: *in character*) defecto; (*in manufacture*) desperfecto; (*GEO*) falla // *vt* tachar; **it's my** ~ es culpa mía; **to find** ~ **with** criticar, poner peros a; **at** ~ culpable; ~**less** *a* (*action*) intachable; (*person*) sin defectos; ~**y** *a* defectuoso.
fauna ['fɔ:nə] *n* fauna.
faux pas ['fəu'pɑ:] *n* paso en falso; (*gaffe*) plancha.
favour, favor (*US*) ['feɪvə*] *n* favor *m*; (*support*) apoyo; (*approval*) aprobación *f* // *vt* (*proposition*) estar a favor de, aprobar; (*person etc*) favorecer; (*assist*) ser propicio a; **to ask a** ~ **of** pedir un favor a; **to do sb a** ~ hacer un favor a uno; **to find** ~ **with** caer en gracia de; **in** ~ **of** a favor de; ~**able** *a* favorable; ~**ite** [-rɪt] *a, n* favorito, preferido; ~**itism** *n* favoritismo.
fawn [fɔ:n] *n* cervato // *a* (*also*: ~**-coloured**) color de cervato, leonado.
fear [fɪə*] *n* miedo, temor *m* // *vt* tener miedo a *o* de, temer; **for** ~ **of** por temor a; ~**ful** *a* temeroso, miedoso; (*cowardly*) tímido; (*awful*) terrible; ~**less** *a* (*gen*) sin miedo *o* temor; (*bold*) audaz.
feasible ['fi:zəbl] *a* factible.
feast [fi:st] *n* banquete *m*; (*REL*: *also*: ~ **day**) fiesta // *vt, vi* banquetear.
feat [fi:t] *n* hazaña.
feather ['fɛðə*] *n* pluma; ~**-weight** *n* (*BOXING*) peso pluma.
feature ['fi:tʃə*] *n* (*gen*) característica; (*ANAT*) rasgo; (*article*) crónica // *vt* (*subj: film*) presentar // *vi* figurar; ~**s** *npl* (*of face*) facciones *fpl*; ~ **film** *n* película (de largo metraje).
February ['fɛbruərɪ] *n* febrero.

fed [fɛd] *pt, pp of* **feed**.
federal ['fɛdərəl] *a* federal; **federation** [-'reɪʃən] *n* federación *f.*
fed-up [fɛd'ʌp] *a*: **to be** ~ estar harto.
fee [fi:] *n* derechos *mpl*, honorarios *mpl*; (*of school*) matrícula; (*of club*) cuota.
feeble ['fi:bl] *a* débil; ~**-minded** *a* imbécil.
feed [fi:d] *n* (*gen*) comida; (*of baby*) alimento infantil; (*of animal*) pienso // *vt, pt, pp* **fed** (*gen*) alimentar; (*baby: breastfeed*) dar el pecho a; (*animal*) dar de comer a; (*data, information*): **to** ~ **into** suministrar a; **to** ~ **on** *vt fus* alimentarse de; ~**ing bottle** *n* biberón *m.*
feel [fi:l] *n* (*sensation*) sensación *f*; (*sense of touch*) tacto // *vt, pt, pp* **felt** tocar, palpar; (*cold, pain etc*) sentir; (*think, believe*) creer; **to** ~ **hungry/cold** tener hambre/frío; **to** ~ **lonely/better** sentirse solo/ mejor; **it** ~**s soft** es suave al tacto; **to** ~ **like** (*want*) tener ganas de; **to** ~ **about** *or* **around** tantear; ~**er** *n* (*of insect*) antena; **to put out** ~**ers** (*fig*) sondear; ~**ing** *n* (*gen*) sensación *f*; (*foreboding*) presentimiento; (*opinion*) opinión *f*; (*emotion*) sentimiento.
feet [fi:t] *pl of* **foot**.
feign [feɪn] *vt* fingir.
feline ['fi:laɪn] *a* felino.
fell [fɛl] *pt of* **fall** // *vt* (*tree*) talar.
fellow ['fɛləu] *n* (*gen*) tipo; (*fam*) tío; (*of learned society*) socio; ~ **students** compañeros *mpl* de curso, condiscípulos *mpl*; ~ **citizen** *n* conciudadano; ~ **countryman** *n* compatriota *m/f*; ~ **men** *npl* semejantes *mpl*; ~**ship** *n* compañerismo; (*grant*) beca.
felony ['fɛlənɪ] *n* crimen *m.*
felt [fɛlt] *pt, pp of* **feel** // *n* fieltro; ~**-tip pen** *n* rotulador *m.*
female ['fi:meɪl] *n* (*woman*) mujer *f*; (*zool*) hembra // *a* femenino.
feminine ['fɛmɪnɪn] *a* femenino.
feminist ['fɛmɪnɪst] *n* feminista.
fence [fɛns] *n* valla, cerca // *vt* (*also*: ~ **in**) cercar // *vi* hacer esgrima; **fencing** *n* esgrima.
fend [fɛnd] *vi*: **to** ~ **for o.s.** arreglárselas por su cuenta.
fender ['fɛndə*] *n* guardafuego; (*US*: *AUT*) parachoques *m inv*; (: *RAIL*) trompa.
ferment [fə'mɛnt] *vi* fermentar // *n* ['fə:mɛnt] (*fig*) agitación *f*; ~**ation** [-'teɪʃən] *n* fermentación *f.*
fern [fə:n] *n* helecho.
ferocious [fə'rəuʃəs] *a* feroz; **ferocity** [-'rɔsɪtɪ] *n* ferocidad *f.*
ferret ['fɛrɪt] *n* hurón *m* // *vt*: **to** ~ **out** descubrir.
ferry ['fɛrɪ] *n* (*small*) barca (de pasaje), balsa; (*large: also*: ~**boat**) transbordador *m* // *vt* transportar.
fertile ['fə:taɪl] *a* fértil; (*BIOL*) fecundo; **fertility** [fə'tɪlɪtɪ] *n* fertilidad *f*; fecundidad *f*; **fertilize** ['fə:tɪlaɪz] *vt* fertilizar;

fecundar; (*AGR*) abonar; **fertilizer** *n* fertilizante *m.*
fervent ['fə:vənt] *a* ardiente, apasionado.
fester ['fɛstə*] *vi* ulcerarse.
festival ['fɛstɪvəl] *n* (*REL*) fiesta; (*ART, MUS*) festival *m.*
festive ['fɛstɪv] *a* festivo; **the** ~ **season** (*Christmas*) las Navidades.
festivities [fɛs'tɪvɪtɪz] *npl* fiestas *fpl.*
fetch [fɛtʃ] *vt* ir a buscar; (*sell for*) venderse por.
fetching ['fɛtʃɪŋ] *a* atractivo.
fête [feɪt] *n* fiesta.
fetish ['fɛtɪʃ] *n* fetiche *m.*
fetters ['fɛtəz] *npl* grillos *mpl.*
feud [fju:d] *n* (*hostility*) enemistad *f*; (*quarrel*) disputa.
feudal ['fju:dl] *a* feudal; ~**ism** *n* feudalismo.
fever ['fi:və*] *n* fiebre *f*; ~**ish** *a* febril.
few [fju:] *a* (*not many*) pocos; (*some*) algunos, unos; **a** ~ a unos pocos // *pron* algunos; ~**er** *a* menos; ~**est** *a* los/las menos.
fiancé [fɪ'ã:ŋseɪ] *n* novio, prometido; ~**e** *n* novia, prometida.
fiasco [fɪ'æskəu] *n* fiasco.
fibre, fiber (*US*) ['faɪbə*] *n* fibra; ~**-glass** *n* fibra de vidrio.
fickle ['fɪkl] *a* inconstante.
fiction ['fɪkʃən] *n* (*gen*) ficción *f*; ~**al** *a* novelesco; **fictitious** [fɪk'tɪʃəs] *a* ficticio.
fiddle ['fɪdl] *n* (*MUS*) violín *m*; (*cheating*) trampa; (*swindle*) estafa // *vt* (*accounts*) falsificar; **to** ~ **with** *vt fus* jugar con; **fiddler** *n* violinista *m/f.*
fidelity [fɪ'dɛlɪtɪ] *n* fidelidad *f.*
fidget ['fɪdʒɪt] *vi* moverse nerviosamente; ~**y** *a* nervioso.
field [fi:ld] *n* campo; (*ELEC*) prado; (*fig*) esfera, especialidad *f*; (*competitors*) competidores *mpl*; (*entrants*) concurrentes *mpl*; ~ **glasses** *npl* gemelos *mpl*; ~ **marshal** *n* mariscal *m*; ~**work** *n* trabajo de campo.
fiend [fi:nd] *n* demonio; ~**ish** *a* diabólico.
fierce [fɪəs] *a* feroz; (*wind, attack*) violento; (*heat*) intenso; (*fighting, enemy*) encarnizado.
fiery ['faɪərɪ] *a* (*burning*) ardiente; (*temperament*) apasionado.
fifteen [fɪf'ti:n] *num* quince.
fifth [fɪfθ] *a, n* quinto.
fiftieth ['fɪftɪɪθ] *a* quincuagésimo.
fifty ['fɪftɪ] *num* cincuenta.
fig [fɪg] *n* higo.
fight [faɪt] *n* (*gen*) pelea; (*MIL*) combate *m*; (*struggle*) lucha // (*vb: pt, pp* **fought**) *vt* luchar contra; (*cancer, alcoholism*) combatir // *vi* pelear, luchar; ~**er** *n* combatiente *m/f*; (*fig*) luchador/a *m/f*; (*plane*) caza; ~**ing** *n* (*gen*) el luchar; (*battle*) combate *m.*
figment ['fɪgmənt] *n*: **a** ~ **of the imagination** una quimera.
figurative ['fɪgjurətɪv] *a* figurado.

figure 260 **fit**

figure ['fɪgə*] n (DRAWING, GEOM) figura, dibujo; (number, cipher) cifra; (body, outline) talle m, tipo // vt (esp US) imaginar // vi (appear) figurar; **to ~ out** vt (understand) comprender; **~head** n mascarón m de proa; **~ skating** n patinaje m de figuras.

file [faɪl] n (tool) lima; (dossier) expediente m; (folder) carpeta; (row) fila // vt limar; (papers) clasificar; (LAW: claim) presentar; (store) archivar; **to ~ in/out** vi entrar/salir en fila; **to ~ past** vt fus desfilar ante; **filing** n el archivar; **filing cabinet** n fichero, archivo.

fill [fɪl] vt llenar // n: **to eat one's ~** llenarse; **to ~ in** vt rellenar; **to ~ up** vt llenar (hasta el borde) // vi (AUT) poner gasolina.

fillet ['fɪlɪt] n filete m.

filling ['fɪlɪŋ] n (CULIN) relleno; (for tooth) empaste m; **~ station** n estación f de servicio.

film [fɪlm] n película // vt (scene) filmar // vi rodar (una película); **~ star** n astro, estrella de cine; **~strip** n tira de película.

filter ['fɪltə*] n filtro // vt filtrar; **~ tip** n boquilla.

filth [fɪlθ] n suciedad f; **~y** a sucio; (language) obsceno.

fin [fɪn] n (gen) aleta.

final ['faɪnl] a (last) final, último; (definitive) definitivo, terminante // n (SPORT) final f; **~s** npl (SCOL) exámenes mpl finales.

finale [fɪ'nɑːlɪ] n final m.

final: ~ist n (SPORT) finalista m/f; **~ize** vt concluir, completar; **~ly** ad (lastly) por último, finalmente; (eventually) por fin; (irrevocably) de modo definitivo.

finance [faɪ'næns] n (money) fondos mpl; **~s** npl finanzas fpl // vt financiar; **financial** [-'nænʃəl] a financiero; (economic) económico; **financier** n (gen) financiero; (investor) inversionista m/f.

find [faɪnd], pt, pp **found** vt (gen) encontrar, hallar; (come upon) descubrir // n hallazgo; descubrimiento; **to ~ sb guilty** (LAW) declarar culpable a uno; **to ~ out** vt averiguar; (truth, secret) descubrir; **to ~ out about** (by chance) enterarse de; **~ings** npl (LAW) veredicto sg, fallo sg; (of report) recomendaciones fpl.

fine [faɪn] a (delicate) fino; (good) bueno; (beautiful) bonito // ad (well) bien; (small) delgado // n (LAW) multa // vt (LAW) multar; **to be ~** (weather) hacer buen tiempo; **~ arts** npl bellas artes fpl.

finery ['faɪnərɪ] n adornos mpl.

finesse [fɪ'nɛs] n sutileza.

finger ['fɪŋgə*] n dedo // vt (touch) manosear; (MUS) tocar (distraídamente); **little/index ~** dedo meñique/índice; **~nail** n uña; **~print** n huella dactilar; **~ tip** n yema del dedo.

finicky ['fɪnɪkɪ] a (fussy) delicado.

finish ['fɪnɪʃ] n (end) fin m; (goal) meta; (polish etc) acabado // vt, vi terminar; **to ~ off** vt acabar, terminar; (kill) acabar con; **to ~ third** llegar el tercero; **~ing line** n línea de llegada o meta.

finite ['faɪnaɪt] a finito.

Finland ['fɪnlənd] n Finlandia.

Finn [fɪn] n finlandés/esa m/f; **~ish** a finlandés(esa) // n (LING) finlandés m.

fiord [fjɔːd] n fiordo.

fir [fəː*] n abeto.

fire ['faɪə*] n (gen) fuego; (accidental) incendio // vt (gun) disparar; (set fire to) incendiar; (excite) exaltar; (interest) despertar; (dismiss) despedir // vi encenderse; **on ~** ardiendo, en llamas; **~ alarm** n alarma de incendios; **~arm** n arma de fuego; **~ brigade** n (cuerpo de) bomberos mpl; **~ engine** n coche m de bomberos; **~ escape** n escalera de incendios; **~ extinguisher** n extintor m (de fuego); **~man** n bombero; **~place** n chimenea; **~proof** a a prueba de fuego; **~side** n hogar m; **~ station** n parque m de bomberos; **~wood** n leña; **~works** npl fuegos mpl artificiales.

firing ['faɪərɪŋ] n (MIL) disparos mpl, tiroteo; **~ squad** n pelotón m de ejecución.

firm [fəːm] a firme // n firma; **~ly** ad firmemente; **~ness** n firmeza.

first [fəːst] a primero // ad (before others) primero; (when listing reasons etc) en primer lugar, primeramente // n (person: in race) primero; (AUT) primera; **at ~** al principio; **~ of all** ante todo; **~-aid kit** n botiquín m; **~-class** a de primera clase; **~-hand** a de primera mano; **~ly** ad en primer lugar; **~ name** n nombre m de pila; **~-rate** a de primera clase.

fir tree n abeto.

fiscal ['fɪskəl] a fiscal.

fish [fɪʃ] n, pl inv pez m; (food) pescado // vt, vi pescar; **to go ~ing** ir de pesca; **~erman** n pescador m; **~ery** n pesquería; **~ fingers** npl dedos mpl de pescado; **~ing boat** n barca de pesca; **~ing line** n sedal m; **~ing rod** n caña (de pescar); **~ing tackle** n aparejo (de pescar); **~ market** n mercado de pescado; **~monger** n pescadero; **~monger's (shop)** n pescadería; **~y** a (fig) sospechoso.

fission ['fɪʃən] n fisión f.

fissure ['fɪʃə*] n fisura.

fist [fɪst] n puño.

fit [fɪt] a (MED, SPORT) en (buena) forma; (proper) adecuado, apropiado // vt (clothes) sentar bien a; (try on: clothes) probar; (facts) cuadrar o corresponder con; (accommodate) ajustar, adaptar; (correspond exactly) encajar en // vi (clothes) entallar; (in space, gap) caber; (correspond) corresponder // n (MED) ataque m; **~ to** apto para; **~ for** apropiado para; **this dress is a good ~** este vestido me sienta bien; **to ~ in** vi (gen) encajarse en; (fig: person) llevarse bien (con todos); **to ~ out** (*also:* ~ **up**) *vt* equipar; **~ful** *a* espasmódico, intermitente; **~ment** *n* mueble *m*; **~ness** *n* (*MED*) salud *f*; (*of remark*) conveniencia; **~ter** *n* ajustador *m*; **~ting** *a* apropiado // *n* (*of dress*) prueba; **~tings** *npl* instalaciones *fpl*.

five [faiv] *num* cinco; **fiver** *n* (*Brit: col*) billete *m* de cinco libras.

fix [fiks] *vt* (*secure*) fijar, asegurar; (*mend*) arreglar // *n*: **to be in a ~** estar en un aprieto; **~ed** [fikst] *a* (*prices etc*) fijo; **~ture** ['fikstʃə*] *n* cosa fija; (*furniture*) mueble *m* fijo; (*SPORT*) partido.

fizz [fiz] *vi* hacer efervescencia.

fizzle ['fizl]: **~ out** *vi* apagarse.

fizzy ['fizi] *a* (*drink*) gaseoso; (*gen*) efervescente.

fjord [fjɔːd] = **fiord**.

flabbergasted ['flæbəgɑːstɪd] *a* pasmado.

flabby ['flæbi] *a* flojo; (*fat*) gordo.

flag [flæg] *n* bandera; (*stone*) losa // *vi* acabarse, decaer; **to ~ sb down** hacer signos a uno para que se detenga; **~pole** *n* asta de bandera.

flagrant ['fleigrənt] *a* flagrante.

flair [flɛə*] *n* aptitud *f* especial.

flake [fleik] *n* (*of rust, paint*) escama; (*of snow, soap powder*) copo // *vi* (*also:* ~ **off**) desprenderse en escamas.

flamboyant [flæm'bɔiənt] *a* (*dress*) vistoso; (*person*) extravagante.

flame [fleim] *n* llama.

flamingo [flə'miŋgəu] *n* flamenco.

flammable ['flæməbl] *a* inflamable.

flan [flæn] *n* tarta.

flank [flæŋk] *n* flanco; (*of person*) costado // *vt* flanquear.

flannel ['flænl] *n* (*also:* **face ~**) paño; (*fabric*) franela; (*col*) coba; **~s** *npl* pantalones *mpl* de franela.

flap [flæp] *n* (*of pocket*) cartera; (*of envelope*) solapa; (*of table*) hoja (plegadiza); (*wing movement*) aletazo // *vt* (*wings*) aletear // *vi* (*sail, flag*) ondear.

flare [flɛə*] *n* llamarada; (*Mil*) bengala; (*in skirt etc*) vuelo; **to ~ up** *vi* encenderse; (*fig: person*) encolerizarse; (: *revolt*) estallar.

flash [flæʃ] *n* relámpago; (*also:* **news ~**) noticias *fpl* de última hora; (*PHOT*) flash *m* // *vt* (*light, headlights*) encender y apagar (la luz); (*torch*) encender // *vi* brillar, relampaguear; **in a ~** en un instante; **he ~ed by** *or* **past** pasó como un rayo; **~back** *n* flashback *m*; **~ bulb** *n* bombilla fusible; **~er** *n* (*AUT*) intermitente *m*.

flashy ['flæʃi] *a* (*pej*) ostentoso.

flask [flɑːsk] *n* frasco; (*also:* **vacuum ~**) termo.

flat [flæt] *a* llano; (*smooth*) liso; (*tyre*) desinflado; (*beer*) muerto; (*MUS*) desafinado // *n* (*apartment*) piso, apartamento; (*MUS*) bemol *m*; (*AUT*) pinchazo; **~ly** *ad* terminantemente, de plano; **~ness** *n* (*of land*) llanura, lo llano; **~ten** *vt* (*also:* **~ten out**) allanar;

(*smooth out*) alisar; (*demolish*) aplastar.

flatter ['flætə*] *vt* adular, halagar; **~er** *n* adulador/a *m/f*; **~ing** *a* halagüeño; **~y** *n* adulación *f*.

flatulence ['flætjuləns] *n* flatulencia.

flaunt [flɔːnt] *vt* ostentar, lucir.

flavour, flavor (*US*) ['fleivə*] *n* sabor *m*, gusto // *vt* sazonar, condimentar; **~ed with** con sabor a; **~ing** *n* condimento.

flaw [flɔː] *n* defecto; **~less** *a* intachable.

flax [flæks] *n* lino; **~en** *a* rubio.

flea [fliː] *n* pulga; **~pit** *n* cine *m* de baja categoría.

flee [fliː], *pt, pp* **fled** [flɛd] *vt* huir de, abandonar // *vi* huir, fugarse.

fleece [fliːs] *n* vellón *m*; (*wool*) lana // *vt* (*col*) pelar.

fleet [fliːt] *n* (*gen*) flota; (*of lorries etc*) escuadra.

fleeting ['fliːtiŋ] *a* fugaz.

Flemish ['flɛmiʃ] *a* flamenco.

flesh [flɛʃ] *n* carne *f*; (*of fruit*) pulpa; **of ~ and blood** de carne y hueso.

flew [fluː] *pt of* **fly**.

flex [flɛks] *n* cordón *m* // *vt* (*muscles*) tensar; **~ibility** [-i'biliti] *n* flexibilidad *f*; **~ible** *a* flexible.

flick [flik] *n* golpecito; (*with finger*) capirotazo; (*with whip*) chasquido // *vt* dar un golpecito a; **to ~ through** *vt fus* hojear.

flicker ['flikə*] *vi* (*light*) parpadear; (*flame*) vacilar // *n* parpadeo.

flier ['flaiə*] *n* aviador/a *m/f*.

flight [flait] *n* vuelo; (*escape*) huida, fuga; (*also:* **~ of steps**) tramo (de escaleras); **to take ~** huir, darse a la fuga; **to put to ~** ahuyentar; **~ deck** *n* (*AVIAT*) cabina.

flimsy ['flimzi] *a* (*thin*) muy ligero; (*weak*) débil.

flinch [flintʃ] *vi* acobardarse.

fling [fliŋ], *pt, pp* **flung** *vt* arrojar.

flint [flint] *n* pedernal *m*; (*in lighter*) piedra.

flip [flip] *vt* dar la vuelta a; (*coin*) echar a cara o cruz.

flippant ['flipənt] *a* poco serio.

flirt [flɜːt] *vi* coquetear, flirtear // *n* coqueta *m/f*; **~ation** [-'teiʃən] *n* coqueteo, flirteo.

flit [flit] *vi* revolotear.

float [fləut] *n* flotador *m*; (*in procession*) carroza // *vi* flotar; (*swimmer*) hacer la plancha // *vt* (*gen*) hacer flotar; (*company*) lanzar.

flock [flɔk] *n* (*of sheep*) rebaño; (*of birds*) bandada; (*of people*) multitud *f*.

flog [flɔg] *vt* azotar; (*col*) vender.

flood [flʌd] *n* inundación *f*; (*of words, tears etc*) torrente *m* // *vt* inundar; **~ing** *n* inundación *f*; **~light** *n* foco.

floor [flɔː*] *n* suelo; (*storey*) piso; (*of sea*) fondo; (*dance* ~) pista // *vt* (*fig*) dejar sin respuesta; **ground ~** (*Brit*), **first ~** (*US*) planta baja; **first ~** (*Brit*), **second ~**

(*US*) primer piso; ~**board** *n* tabla; ~
show *n* cabaret *m*.
flop [flɔp] *n* fracaso // *vi* (*fail*) fracasar.
floppy ['flɔpɪ] *a* flojo.
flora ['flɔːrə] *n* flora; **floral** ['flɔːrl] *a* floral.
florid ['flɔrɪd] *a* (*style*) florido.
florist ['flɔrɪst] *n* florista *m/f*; ~'s (**shop**)
n florería.
flounce [flauns] *n* volante *m*; **to** ~ **out** *vi*
salir enfadado.
flounder ['flaundə*] *vi* tropezar.
flour ['flauə*] *n* harina.
flourish ['flʌrɪʃ] *vi* florecer; ~**ing** *a*
floreciente.
flout [flaut] *vt* burlarse de.
flow [fləu] *n* (*movement*) flujo; (*direction*)
curso; (*tide*) corriente *f* // *vi* correr, fluir;
(*blood*) derramarse.
flower ['flauə*] *n* flor *f* // *vi* florecer; ~
bed *n* macizo; ~**pot** *n* tiesto; ~**y** *a*
florido.
flown [fləun] *pp of* **fly**.
flu [fluː] *n* gripe *f*.
fluctuate ['flʌktjueɪt] *vi* fluctuar;
fluctuation [-'eɪʃən] *n* fluctuación *f*.
fluent ['fluːənt] *a* (*speech*) elocuente; **he**
speaks ~ **French, he's** ~ **in French**
domina el francés; ~**ly** *ad* con fluidez.
fluff [flʌf] *n* pelusa; ~**y** *a* velloso.
fluid ['fluːɪd] *a, n* fluido, líquido.
fluke [fluːk] *n* (*col*) chiripa.
flung [flʌŋ] *pt, pp of* **fling**.
fluorescent [fluə'rɛsnt] *a* fluorescente.
fluoride ['fluəraɪd] *n* fluoruro.
flurry ['flʌrɪ] *n* (*of snow*) ráfago; (*haste*)
agitación *f*; ~ **of activity** frenesí *m* de
actividad.
flush [flʌʃ] *n* (*on face*) rubor *m*; (*plenty*)
plenitud *f*, abundancia // *vt* limpiar con
agua // *vi* ruborizarse // *a*: ~ **with** a ras
de; **to** ~ **the toilet** hacer funcionar el
WC; ~**ed** *a* ruborizado.
flustered ['flʌstəd] *a* aturdido.
flute [fluːt] *n* flauta.
flutter ['flʌtə*] *n* emoción *f*; (*of wings*)
revoloteo, aleteo; (*fam: bet*) apuesta // *vi*
revolotear.
flux [flʌks] *n* flujo; **in a state of** ~
cambiando continuamente.
fly [flaɪ] *n* (*insect*) mosca; (*on trousers: also*:
flies) bragueta // (*vb: pt* **flew**, *pp* **flown**)
vt (*gen*) hacer volar; (*plane*) pilot(e)ar;
(*cargo*) transportar (en avión); (*distances*)
recorrer (en avión) // *vi* volar;
(*passengers*) ir *o* subir en avión; (*escape*)
evadirse; (*flag*) ondear; **to let** ~
desahogarse; ~**ing** *n* (*activity*) (el) volar
// *a*: ~**ing visit** visita relámpago; **with**
~**ing colours** con lucimiento; ~**ing**
saucer *n* platillo volante; ~**over** *n* (*Brit*:
bridge) paso a desnivel *o* superior; ~**past**
n desfile *m* aéreo; ~**sheet** *n* (*for tent*)
doble techo.
foal [fəul] *n* potro.
foam [fəum] *n* espuma // *vi* echar espuma;
~ **rubber** *n* espuma de caucho.

fob [fɔb] *vt*: **to** ~ **sb off** deshacerse de
alguien con excusas.
focal ['fəukəl] *a* focal.
focus ['fəukəs], *pl* ~**es** *n* foco // *vt* (*field*
glasses etc) enfocar; **to** ~ **on** enfocar a;
in/out of ~ enfocado/desenfocado.
fodder ['fɔdə*] *n* pienso.
foe [fəu] *n* enemigo.
foetus ['fiːtəs] *n* feto.
fog [fɔg] *n* niebla; ~**gy** *a*: **it's** ~**gy** hay
niebla, está brumoso.
foil [fɔɪl] *vt* frustrar // *n* hoja; (*also*:
kitchen ~) papel *m* (de) aluminio;
(*FENCING*) florete *m*.
fold [fəuld] *n* (*bend, crease*) pliegue *m*; (*of*
skin) arruga; (*AGR*) redil *m* // *vt* doblar; **to**
~ **up** *vi* (*map etc*) plegarse, doblarse;
(*business*) quebrar // *vt* (*map etc*) plegar;
~**er** *n* (*for papers*) carpeta; (*brochure*)
folleto; ~**ing** *a* (*chair, bed*) plegable.
foliage ['fəulɪɪdʒ] *n* follaje *m*.
folk [fəuk] *npl* gente *f* // *a* popular,
folklórico; ~**s** *npl* familia, parientes *mpl*;
~**lore** ['fəuklɔː*] *n* folklore *m*; ~**song** *n*
canción *f* popular *o* folklórica.
follow ['fɔləu] *vt* seguir // *vi* seguir; (*result*)
resultar; **he** ~**ed suit** hizo lo mismo; **to**
~ **up** *vt* (*letter, offer*) responder a; (*case*)
investigar; ~**er** *n* seguidor/a *m/f*; (*POL*)
partidario/a; ~**ing** *a* siguiente // *n*
afición *f*, partidarios *mpl*.
folly ['fɔlɪ] *n* locura.
fond [fɔnd] *a* (*loving*) cariñoso; **to be** ~ **of**
tener cariño a.
fondle ['fɔndl] *vt* acariciar.
fondness ['fɔndnɪs] *n* (*for things*) gusto;
(*for people*) cariño.
font [fɔnt] *n* pila bautismal.
food [fuːd] *n* comida; ~ **mixer** *n* batidora;
~ **poisoning** *n* botulismo; ~**stuffs** *npl*
comestibles *mpl*.
fool [fuːl] *n* tonto/a; (*CULIN*) puré *m* de
frutas con nata // *vt* engañar // *vi* (*gen*:
~ **around**) bromear; (*waste time*) perder
el tiempo; ~**hardy** *a* temerario; ~**ish** *a*
tonto; (*stupid*) estúpido; (*careless*)
imprudente; ~**proof** *a* (*plan etc*) infalible.
foot [fut], *pl* **feet** *n* pie *m*; (*measure*) pie *m*
(= *304 mm*); (*of animal*) pata // *vt* (*bill*)
pagar; **on** ~ a pie; ~**ball** *n* balón *m*;
(*game*) fútbol *m*; ~**baller** *n* futbolista *m*;
~**brake** *n* freno de pie; ~**bridge** *n*
puente *m* para peatones; ~**hills** *npl*
estribaciones *fpl*; ~**hold** *n* pie *m* firme;
~**ing** *n* (*fig*) posición *f*; **to lose one's**
~**ing** perder el pie; **on an equal** ~**ing**
en pie de igualdad; ~**lights** *npl* candilejas
fpl; ~**man** *n* lacayo; ~**note** *n* nota de pie;
~**path** *n* sendero; (*pavement*) acera;
~**sore** *a* con los pies adoloridos; ~**step** *n*
paso; ~**wear** *n* calzado.
for [fɔː*] *prep* (*gen*) para; (*as, in exchange*
for, because of) por; (*during*) durante; (*in*
spite of) a pesar de // *conj* pues, ya que; **it**
was sold ~ **100 pesetas** se vendió por
100 pesetas; **what** ~? ¿para qué?; **what's**
it ~? ¿para qué sirve?; **he was away** ~

2 years estuvo fuera 2 años; **he went** ~ **the paper** fue a buscar el periódico; ~ **sale** se vende.
forage ['fɔrɪdʒ] n forraje m.
foray ['fɔreɪ] n incursión f.
forbid [fə'bɪd], pt **forbad(e)** [fə'bæd], pp **forbidden** [fə'bɪdn] vt prohibir; ~**ding** a (gloomy) lúgubre; (severe) severo.
force [fɔːs] n fuerza // vt forzar; **to** ~ **o.s.** to hacer un esfuerzo por; **the F**~**s** npl las Fuerzas Armadas; **in** ~ en vigor; ~**d** [fɔːst] a forzado; ~**ful** a enérgico.
forceps ['fɔːsɛps] npl fórceps m inv.
forcibly ['fɔːsəblɪ] ad a la fuerza.
ford [fɔːd] n vado // vt vadear.
forearm ['fɔːrɑːm] n antebrazo.
foreboding [fɔː'bəudɪŋ] n presagio.
forecast ['fɔːkɑːst] n pronóstico // vt (irg: like cast) pronosticar.
forefathers ['fɔːfɑːðəz] npl antepasados mpl.
forefinger ['fɔːfɪŋgə*] n (dedo) índice m.
forego = **forgo.**
foregone ['fɔːgɔn] a: **it's a** ~ **conclusion** es una conclusión inevitable.
foreground ['fɔːgraund] n primer plano.
forehead ['fɔrɪd] n frente f.
foreign ['fɔrɪn] a extranjero; (trade) exterior; ~**er** n extranjero; ~ **exchange** n divisas fpl; **F**~ **Minister** n Ministro de Asuntos Exteriores; **F**~ **Office** n Ministerio de Asuntos Exteriores.
foreleg ['fɔːlɛg] n pata delantera.
foreman ['fɔːmən] n capataz m; (in construction) maestro de obras.
foremost ['fɔːməust] a principal.
forensic [fə'rɛnsɪk] a forense.
forerunner ['fɔːrʌnə*] n precursor/a m/f.
foresee [fɔː'siː] (irg: like see) vt prever; ~**able** a previsible.
foresight ['fɔːsaɪt] n previsión f.
forest ['fɔrɪst] n bosque m.
forestall [fɔː'stɔːl] vt prevenir.
forestry ['fɔrɪstrɪ] n silvicultura.
foretaste ['fɔːteɪst] n (gen) anticipo; (sample) muestra.
foretell [fɔː'tɛl] (irg: like tell) vt predecir, pronosticar.
forever [fə'rɛvə*] ad para siempre.
foreword ['fɔːwəːd] n prefacio.
forfeit ['fɔːfɪt] n pérdida; (fine) multa // vt perder (derecho a).
forgave [fə'geɪv] pt of **forgive.**
forge [fɔːdʒ] n fragua; (smithy) herrería // vt (signature, money) falsificar; (metal) forjar; **to** ~ **ahead** vi avanzar constantemente; ~**r** n falsificador/a m/f; ~**ry** n falsificación f.
forget [fə'gɛt], pt **forgot**, pp **forgotten** vt olvidar // vi olvidarse; ~**ful** a olvidadizo; ~**fulness** n (gen) olvido; (thoughtlessness) descuido; (oblivion) falta de memoria.
forgive [fə'gɪv], pt **forgave**, pp **forgiven** vt perdonar; **to** ~ **sb for sth** perdonar algo a uno; ~**ness** n perdón m.
forgo [fɔː'gəu] (irg: like go) (give up)

renunciar a; (go without) privarse de.
forgot [fə'gɔt] pt of **forget.**
forgotten [fə'gɔtn] pp of **forget.**
fork [fɔːk] n (for eating) tenedor m; (for gardening) horca; (of roads) bifurcación f; (in tree) horcadura // vi (road) bifurcarse; **to** ~ **out** vt (col: pay) desembolsar; ~**ed** [fɔːkt] a (lightning) en zigzag; ~-**lift truck** n elevadora-transportadora de horquilla.
form [fɔːm] n forma; (SCOL) clase f; (questionnaire) formulario // vt formar; **in** ~ **top** ~ en plena forma.
formal ['fɔːməl] a (offer, receipt) oficial; (person etc) ceremonioso; (occasion, dinner) oficial, protocolario; (dress) de etiqueta; ~**ity** [-'mælɪtɪ] n ceremonia; ~**ities** npl formalidades fpl; ~**ly** ad oficialmente.
format ['fɔːmæt] n formato.
formation [fɔː'meɪʃən] n formación f.
formative ['fɔːmətɪv] a (years) formativo.
former ['fɔːmə*] a anterior; (earlier) antiguo; (ex) ex; **the** ~ ... **the latter** ... aquél ... éste ...; ~**ly** ad antiguamente.
formidable ['fɔːmɪdəbl] a formidable.
formula ['fɔːmjulə] n fórmula.
formulate ['fɔːmjuleɪt] vt formular.
forsake [fə'seɪk], pt **forsook** [fə'suk], pp **forsaken** [fə'seɪkən] vt (gen) abandonar; (plan) renunciar a.
fort [fɔːt] n fuerte m.
forte ['fɔːtɪ] n fuerte m.
forth [fɔːθ] ad en adelante; **back and** ~ de acá para allá; **and so** ~ y así sucesivamente; ~**coming** a próximo, venidero; (character) comunicativo; ~**right** a franco.
fortieth ['fɔːtɪɪθ] a cuadragésimo.
fortification [fɔːtɪfɪ'keɪʃən] n fortificación f; **fortify** ['fɔːtɪfaɪ] vt fortalecer.
fortitude ['fɔːtɪtjuːd] n fortaleza.
fortnight ['fɔːtnaɪt] n quincena; ~**ly** a quincenal // ad quincenalmente.
fortress ['fɔːtrɪs] n fortaleza.
fortuitous [fɔː'tjuːɪtəs] a fortuito.
fortunate ['fɔːtʃənɪt] a: **to be** ~ tener suerte; **it is** ~ **that...** es afortunado que...; ~**ly** ad afortunadamente.
fortune ['fɔːtʃən] n suerte f; (wealth) fortuna; ~-**teller** n adivina.
forty ['fɔːtɪ] num cuarenta.
forum ['fɔːrəm] n foro.
forward ['fɔːwəd] a (movement, position) avanzado; (front) delantero; (not shy) atrevido // n (SPORT) delantero // vt (letter) remitir; (career) progresar; **to move** ~ avanzar; ~**(s)** ad (hacia) adelante.
fossil ['fɔsl] n fósil m.
foster ['fɔstə*] vt fomentar; ~ **brother** n hermano de leche; ~ **child** n hijo adoptivo; ~ **mother** n madre f adoptiva.
fought [fɔːt] pt, pp of **fight.**
foul [faul] a (gen) sucio, puerco; (weather) horrible; (smell etc) asqueroso // n (FOOTBALL) falta (en contra) // vt (dirty)

ensuciar; (*block*) atascar; (*football player*) cometer una falta contra; ~ **play** *n* (*SPORT*) mala jugada; (*LAW*) muerte *f* violenta.

found [faund] *pt, pp of* **find** // *vt* (*establish*) fundar; ~**ation** [-'deiʃən] *n* (*act*) fundación *f*; (*basis*) base *f*; (*also:* ~**ation cream**) crema base; ~**ations** *npl* (*of building*) cimientos *mpl.*

founder ['faundə*] *n* fundador/a *m/f* // *vi* hundirse.

foundry ['faundri] *n* fundición *f.*

fountain ['fauntin] *n* fuente *f*; ~ **pen** *n* pluma-fuente *f.*

four [fɔ:*] *num* cuatro; **on all** ~**s** a gatas; ~**-poster** *n* cama a columnas; ~**some** ['fɔ:səm] *n* grupo de cuatro personas; ~ **teen** *num* catorce; ~**teenth** *a* décimocuarto; ~**th** *a* cuarto.

fowl [faul] *n* ave *f* (de corral).

fox [fɔks] *n* zorro // *vt* confundir; ~**trot** *n* fox *m.*

foyer ['fɔiei] *n* vestíbulo.

fracas ['fræka:] *n* gresca, riña.

fraction ['frækʃən] *n* fracción *f.*

fracture ['fræktʃə*] *n* fractura // *vt* fracturar.

fragile ['frædʒail] *a* frágil.

fragment ['frægmənt] *n* fragmento; ~**ary** *a* fragmentario.

fragrance ['freigrəns] *n* fragancia; **fragrant** [-ənt] *a* fragante, oloroso.

frail [freil] *a* (*fragile*) frágil, quebradizo; (*weak*) delicado.

frame [freim] *n* (*gen*) estructura; (*body*) talle *m*; (*TECH*) armazón *m*; (*of picture, door etc*) marco; (*of spectacles: also:* ~**s**) montura // *vt* encuadrar; (*reply*) formular; (*fam*) incriminar; ~ **of mind** *n* estado de ánimo; ~**work** *n* marco.

France [frɑ:ns] *n* Francia.

franchise ['fræntʃaiz] *n* (*POL*) derecho de votar, sufragio.

frank [fræŋk] *a* franco // *vt* (*letter*) franquear; ~**ly** *ad* francamente; ~**ness** *n* franqueza.

frantic ['fræntik] *a* frenético.

fraternal [frə'tə:nl] *a* fraterno; **fraternity** [-niti] *n* (*club*) fraternidad *f*; (*US*) club *m* de estudiantes; (*guild*) cofradía; **fraternize** ['frætənaiz] *vi* confraternizar.

fraud [frɔ:d] *n* fraude *m*; (*person*) impostor *m*; ~**ulent** *a* fraudulento.

fraught [frɔ:t] *a*: ~ **with** cargado de.

fray [frei] *n* combate *m*, lucha // *vi* deshilacharse; **tempers were** ~**ed** tenían los nervios a punto.

freak [fri:k] *n* (*person*) fenómeno; (*event*) suceso anormal; (*thing*) cosa insólita.

freckle ['frɛkl] *n* peca.

free [fri:] *a* (*gen*) libre; (*not fixed*) suelto; (*gratis*) gratuito; (*unoccupied*) desocupado; (*liberal*) generoso // *vt* (*prisoner etc*) poner en libertad; (*jammed object*) soltar; ~ (**of charge**) *ad* gratis; ~**dom** ['fri:dəm] *n* libertad *f*; ~**-for-all** *n* riña general; ~ **kick** *n* tiro libre; ~**lance** *a*

independiente; ~**ly** *ad* libremente; generosamente; ~**mason** *n* francmasón *m*; ~ **trade** *n* libre comercio; ~**way** *n* (*US*) autopista; ~**wheel** *vi* ir en punto muerto; ~ **will** *n* libre albedrío; **of one's own** ~ **will** por su propia voluntad.

freeze [fri:z], *pt* **froze**, *pp* **frozen** *vi* helarse, congelarse // *vt* helar; (*prices, food, salaries*) congelar // *n* helada; congelación *f*; **freezer** *n* congelador *m.*

freezing ['fri:ziŋ] *a* helado; ~ **point** *n* punto de congelación; **3 degrees below** ~ tres grados bajo cero.

freight [freit] *n* (*goods*) carga; (*money charged*) flete *m*; ~ **car** *n* (*US*) vagón *m* de mercancías.

French [frɛntʃ] *a* francés(esa) // *n* (*LING*) francés *m*; **the** ~ los franceses; ~ **fried (potatoes)** *npl* patatas *fpl* fritas; ~**man/woman** *n* francés/esa *m/f*; ~ **window** *n* puertaventana.

frenzy ['frɛnzi] *n* frenesí *m.*

frequency ['fri:kwənsi] *n* frecuencia; **frequent** [-ənt] *a* frecuente // *vt* [fri'kwent] frecuentar; **frequently** [-əntli] *ad* frecuentemente, a menudo.

fresco ['freskəu] *n* fresco.

fresh [frɛʃ] *a* (*gen*) fresco; (*new*) nuevo; (*water*) dulce; ~**en** *vi* (*wind, air*) soplar más recio; **to** ~**en up** *vi* (*person*) lavarse, arreglarse; ~**ly** *ad* (*newly*) nuevamente; (*recently*) recientemente; ~**ness** *n* frescura.

fret [frɛt] *vi* inquietarse.

friar ['fraiə*] *n* fraile *m*; (*before name*) fray.

friction ['frikʃən] *n* fricción *f.*

Friday ['fraidi] *n* viernes *m.*

fridge [fridʒ] *n* nevera.

friend [frɛnd] *n* amigo/a; ~**liness** *n* simpatía; ~**ly** *a* simpático; ~**ship** *n* amistad *f.*

frieze [fri:z] *n* friso.

frigate ['frigit] *n* fragata.

fright [frait] *n* susto; **to take** ~ asustarse; ~**en** *vt* asustar; ~**ening** *a* espantoso; ~**ful** *a* espantoso, horrible; ~**fully** *ad* terriblemente.

frigid ['fridʒid] *a* (*MED*) frígido, frío; ~**ity** [fri'dʒiditi] *n* frialdad *f*; (*MED*) frigidez *f.*

frill [fril] *n* volante *m.*

fringe [frindʒ] *n* flequillo; (*edge: of forest etc*) borde *m*, margen *m*; ~ **benefits** *npl* ventajas *fpl* supletorias.

frisky ['friski] *a* juguetón(ona), fogoso.

fritter ['fritə*] *n* buñuelo; **to** ~ **away** *vt* desperdiciar.

frivolous ['frivələs] *a* frívolo.

frizzy ['frizi] *a* rizado.

fro [frəu] *see* **to.**

frock [frɔk] *n* vestido.

frog [frɔg] *n* rana; ~**man** *n* hombre-rana *m.*

frolic ['frɔlik] *vi* juguetear.

from [frɔm] *prep* de; ~ **January (on)** *a* partir de enero; ~ **what he says** por lo que dice.

front [frʌnt] *n* (*foremost part*) parte *f* delantera; (*of house*) fachada; (*promenade*: *also*: **sea** ~) paseo marítimo; (*MIL, POL, METEOROLOGY*) frente *m*; (*fig*: *appearances*) apariencias *fpl* // a delantero, primero; **in** ~ **(of)** delante (de); ~**al** a frontal; ~ **door** *n* puerta principal; ~**ier** ['frʌntɪə*] *n* frontera; ~ **page** *n* primera plana; ~ **room** *n* (*Brit*) salón *m*, sala; ~**-wheel drive** *n* tracción *f* delantera.

frost [frɔst] *n* (*gen*) helada; (*visible*) escarcha; ~**bite** *n* congelación *f*; ~**ed** a (*glass*) deslustrado; ~**y** a (*window*) cubierto de escarcha; (*welcome*) glacial.

froth [frɔθ] *n* espuma.

frown [fraun] *n* ceño // *vi* fruncir el ceño.

froze [frəuz] *pt of* **freeze.**

frozen ['frəuzn] *pp of* **freeze.**

frugal ['fru:gəl] a frugal.

fruit [fru:t] *n, pl inv* fruta; ~**erer** *n* frutero; ~**erer's (shop)** *n* frutería; ~**ful** a provechoso; ~**ion** [fru:'ɪʃən] *n*: **to come to** ~**ion** realizarse; ~ **machine** *n* máquina tragaperras.

frustrate [frʌs'treɪt] *vt* frustrar; ~**d** a frustrado; **frustration** [-'treɪʃən] *n* frustración *f*.

fry [fraɪ], *pt, pp* **fried** *vt* freír; **small** ~ gente *f* menuda; ~**ing pan** *n* sartén *f*.

ft. *abbr of* **foot, feet.**

fuchsia ['fju:ʃə] *n* fucsia.

fudge [fʌdʒ] *n* (*CULIN*) dulce *m* de azúcar, manjar *m*.

fuel [fjuəl] *n* (*for heating*) combustible *m*; (*coal*) carbón *m*; (*wood*) leña; (*for propelling*) carburante *m*; ~ **oil** *n* aceite *m* combustible; ~ **tank** *n* depósito de combustible.

fugitive ['fju:dʒɪtɪv] *n* fugitivo.

fulfil [ful'fɪl] *vt* (*function*) cumplir con; (*condition*) satisfacer; (*wish, desire*) realizar; ~**ment** *n* satisfacción *f*, realización *f*.

full [ful] a lleno; (*fig*) pleno; (*complete*) completo; (*information*) detallado // ad: ~ **well** perfectamente; **I'm** ~ estoy lleno; ~ **employment** pleno empleo; ~ **fare** pasaje *m* completo; **a** ~ **two hours** dos horas completas; **at** ~ **speed** a máxima velocidad; **in** ~ (*reproduce, quote*) íntegramente; ~**-length** a (*portrait*) de cuerpo entero; ~ **moon** *n* luna llena; ~**-sized** a (*portrait etc*) de tamaño natural; ~ **stop** *n* punto; ~**-time** a (*work*) de tiempo completo // *n* (*SPORT*) final *m*; ~**y** ad completamente; ~**y-fledged** a (*teacher, barrister*) diplomado.

fumble ['fʌmbl]: **to** ~ **with** *vt fus* revolver, manosear.

fume [fju:m] *vi* humear, echar humo; ~**s** *npl* humo *sg*, gases *mpl*.

fumigate ['fju:mɪgeɪt] *vt* fumigar.

fun [fʌn] *n* (*amusement*) diversión *f*; (*joy*) alegría; **to have** ~ divertirse; **for** ~ en broma; **to make** ~ **of** *vt fus* burlarse de.

function ['fʌŋkʃən] *n* función *f* // *vi* funcionar; ~**al** a funcional.

fund [fʌnd] *n* fondo; (*source, store*) fuente *f*; ~**s** *npl* fondos *mpl*.

fundamental [fʌndə'mɛntl] a fundamental.

funeral ['fju:nərəl] *n* (*burial*) entierro; (*ceremony*) funerales *mpl*; ~ **service** *n* misa de difuntos.

funfair ['fʌnfɛə*] *n* parque *m* de atracciones.

fungus ['fʌŋgəs], *pl* **-gi** [-gaɪ] *n* hongo.

funnel ['fʌnl] *n* embudo; (*of ship*) chimenea.

funnily ['fʌnɪlɪ] ad de modo divertido.

funny ['fʌnɪ] a gracioso, divertido; (*strange*) curioso, raro.

fur [fə:*] *n* piel *f*; (*in kettle etc*) sarro; ~ **coat** *n* abrigo de pieles.

furious ['fjuərɪəs] a furioso; (*effort*) violento; ~**ly** ad con furia.

furlong ['fə:lɔŋ] *n* octava parte de una milla.

furlough ['fə:ləu] *n* (*US*) licencia.

furnace ['fə:nɪs] *n* horno.

furnish ['fə:nɪʃ] *vt* amueblar; (*supply*) suministrar; ~**ings** *npl* muebles *mpl*.

furniture ['fə:nɪtʃə*] *n* muebles *mpl*; **piece of** ~ mueble *m*; ~ **polish** *n* cera de lustrar.

furrier ['fʌrɪə*] *n* peletero.

furrow ['fʌrəu] *n* surco.

furry ['fə:rɪ] a peludo.

further ['fə:ðə*] a (*new*) nuevo, adicional; (*place*) más lejano // ad más lejos; (*more*) más; (*moreover*) además // *vt* promover, adelantar; ~ **education** *n* educación *f* superior; ~ **more** [fə:ðə'mɔ:*] ad además.

furthest ['fə:ðɪst] *superlative of* **far.**

furtive ['fə:tɪv] a furtivo.

fury ['fjuərɪ] *n* furia.

fuse, fuze (*US*) [fju:z] *n* fusible *m*; (*for bomb etc*) mecha // *vt* (*metal*) fundir; (*fig*) fusionar // *vi* fundirse; fusionarse; (*ELEC*): **to** ~ **the lights** fundir los plomos; ~ **box** *n* caja de fusibles.

fuselage ['fju:zəlɑ:ʒ] *n* fuselaje *m*.

fusion ['fju:ʒən] *n* fusión *f*.

fuss [fʌs] *n* (*noise*) bulla; (*dispute*) lío; (*complaining*) protesta; (*ceremony*) ceremonias *fpl*; **to make a** ~ armar un lío o jaleo; ~**y** a (*person*) exigente.

futile ['fju:taɪl] a vano; **futility** [-'tɪlɪtɪ] *n* inutilidad *f*.

future ['fju:tʃə*] a (*gen*) futuro; (*coming*) venidero // *n* futuro; **futuristic** [-'rɪstɪk] a futurístico.

fuzzy ['fʌzɪ] a (*PHOT*) borroso; (*hair*) muy rizado.

G

gabble ['gæbl] *vi* hablar atropelladamente; (*gossip*) cotorrear.

gable ['geɪbl] *n* aguilón *m*.

gadget ['gædʒɪt] *n* aparato.

Gaelic ['geɪlɪk] *n* (*LING*) gaélico.

gag [gæg] *n* (*joke*) chiste *m* // *vt* amordazar.

gaiety ['geɪɪtɪ] *n* alegría.
gaily ['geɪlɪ] *ad* alegremente.
gain [geɪn] *n* ganancia // *vt* ganar // *vi* (*watch*) adelantarse; **to ~ by sth** sacar provecho de algo; **to ~ on sb** ir ganando terreno a uno.
gait [geɪt] *n* modo de andar.
gala ['gɑːlə] *n* fiesta.
galaxy ['gæləksɪ] *n* galaxia.
gale [geɪl] *n* (*wind*) vendaval *m*.
gallant ['gælənt] *a* valiente; (*towards ladies*) atento; **~ry** *n* valentía; (*courtesy*) cortesía.
gall-bladder ['gɔːlblædə*] *n* vesícula biliar.
gallery ['gælərɪ] *n* galería; (*also*: **art ~**) museo.
galley ['gælɪ] *n* (*ship's kitchen*) cocina; (*ship*) galera.
gallon ['gæln] *n* galón *m* (*4.543 litros*).
gallop ['gæləp] *n* galope *m* // *vi* galopar.
gallows ['gæləuz] *n* horca.
gallstone ['gɔːlstəun] *n* cálculo biliario.
gamble ['gæmbl] *n* (*risk*) riesgo; (*bet*) apuesta // *vt*: **to ~ on** apostar a; (*fig*) confiar en que // *vi* jugar; (*COMM*) especular; **gambler** *n* jugador/a *m/f*; **gambling** *n* el juego.
game [geɪm] *n* (*gen*) juego; (*match*) partido; (*of cards*) partida; (*HUNTING*) caza // *a* valiente; (*ready*): **to be ~ for anything** atreverse a todo; **~ bird** *n* ave *f* de caza; **~keeper** *n* guardabosques *m inv*.
gammon ['gæmən] *n* (*bacon*) tocino ahumado; (*ham*) jamón *m* ahumado.
gang [gæŋ] *n* pandilla; (*of workmen*) brigada // *vi*: **to ~ up on sb** conspirar contra uno.
gangrene ['gæŋgriːn] *n* gangrena.
gangster ['gæŋstə*] *n* gángster *m*.
gangway ['gæŋweɪ] *n* (*in theatre etc*) pasillo; (*on ship*) pasarela; (*on dock*) pasadera.
gaol [dʒeɪl] = **jail.**
gap [gæp] *n* vacío, hueco; (*in trees, traffic*) claro; (*in time*) intervalo.
gape [geɪp] *vi* estar *o* quedarse boquiabierto; **gaping** *a* (*hole*) muy abierto.
garage ['gærɑːʒ] *n* garaje *m*.
garbage ['gɑːbɪdʒ] *n* basura; **~ can** *n* (*US*) cubo de la basura.
garbled ['gɑːbld] *a* (*distorted*) falsificado, amañado.
garden ['gɑːdn] *n* jardín *m*; **~er** *n* jardinero; **~ing** *n* jardinería.
gargle ['gɑːgl] *vi* hacer gárgaras.
gargoyle ['gɑːgɔɪl] *n* gárgola.
garish ['gɛərɪʃ] *a* chillón(ona).
garland ['gɑːlənd] *n* guirnalda.
garlic ['gɑːlɪk] *n* ajo.
garment ['gɑːmənt] *n* prenda (de vestir).
garnish ['gɑːnɪʃ] *vt* adornar; (*CULIN*) aderezar.

garrison ['gærɪsn] *n* guarnición *f* // *vt* guarnecer.
garrulous ['gærjuləs] *a* gárrulo.
garter ['gɑːtə*] *n* liga; **~ belt** portaligas *m inv*.
gas [gæs] *n* gas *m*; (*US*: *gasoline*) gasolina // *vt* asfixiar con gas; **~ cooker** *n* cocina de gas; **~ cylinder** *n* bombona de gas; **~ fire** *n* estufa de gas.
gash [gæʃ] *n* raja; (*on face*) cuchillada // *vt* (*gen*) rajar; (*with knife*) acuchillar.
gasket ['gæskɪt] *n* (*AUT*) junta.
gas: ~mask *n* careta antigás; **~ meter** *n* contador *m* de gas.
gasoline ['gæsəliːn] *n* (*US*) gasolina.
gasp [gɑːsp] *n* grito sofocado // *vi* (*pant*) jadear; **to ~ out** *vt* (*say*) decir con voz entrecortada.
gas: ~ ring *n* hornillo de gas; **~ stove** *n* cocina de gas; **~sy** *a* gaseoso; **~ tap** *n* llave *f* del gas.
gastric ['gæstrɪk] *a* gástrico; **~ ulcer** *n* úlcera gástrica.
gate [geɪt] *n* puerta; (*RAIL*) barrera; **~crash** *vt* colarse de gorra en; **~way** *n* puerta.
gather ['gæðə*] *vt* (*flowers, fruit*) coger; (*assemble*) reunir; (*pick up*) recoger; (*SEWING*) fruncir; (*understand*) entender // *vi* (*assemble*) reunirse; **~ing** *n* reunión *f*, asamblea.
gauche [gəuʃ] *a* torpe.
gaudy ['gɔːdɪ] *a* chillón(ona).
gauge [geɪdʒ] *n* medida; (*RAIL*) entrevía; (*instrument*) indicador *m* // *vt* medir.
gaunt [gɔːnt] *a* descarnado; (*grim, desolate*) desolado.
gauntlet ['gɔːntlɪt] *n* (*fig*): **to run the ~** correr baquetas; **to throw down the ~** arrojar el guante.
gauze [gɔːz] *n* gasa.
gave [geɪv] *pt of* **give.**
gay [geɪ] *a* (*person*) alegre; (*colour*) vistoso, vivo; (*homosexual*) gay.
gaze [geɪz] *n* mirada fija; **to ~ at sth** mirar algo con fijeza.
gazelle [gə'zɛl] *n* gacela.
gazetteer [gæzə'tɪə*] *n* diccionario geográfico.
G.B. *abbr of* **Great Britain.**
G.C.E. *n abbr of* **General Certificate of Education.**
gear [gɪə*] *n* equipo, herramientas *fpl*; (*TECH*) engranaje *m*; (*AUT*) velocidad *f*, marcha; **top/low ~** tercera (*o* cuarta)/primera velocidad; **in ~** en marcha; **~ box** *n* caja de cambios; **~ lever, ~ shift** (*US*) *n* palanca de velocidades; **~ wheel** *n* rueda dentada.
geese [giːs] *pl of* **goose.**
gelatin(e) ['dʒɛlətiːn] *n* gelatina.
gelignite ['dʒɛlɪgnaɪt] *n* gelignita.
gem [dʒɛm] *n* joya.
Gemini ['dʒɛmɪnaɪ] *n* Géminis *m*, Gemelos *mpl*.
gender ['dʒɛndə*] *n* género.

general ['dʒenərl] n general m // a general; **in** ~ en general; ~ **election** n elecciones fpl generales; ~**ization** [-aɪ'zeɪʃən] n generalización f; ~**ize** vi generalizar; ~**ly** ad generalmente, en general; ~ **practitioner (G.P.)** n médico general.

generate ['dʒenəreɪt] vt (ELEC) generar; (fig) producir.

generation [dʒenə'reɪʃən] n generación f.

generator ['dʒenəreɪtə*] n generador m.

generosity [dʒenə'rɔsɪtɪ] n generosidad f; **generous** ['dʒenərəs] a generoso; (helping etc) abundante.

genetics [dʒɪ'nɛtɪks] n genética.

Geneva [dʒɪ'niːvə] n Ginebra.

genial ['dʒiːnɪəl] a afable, simpático.

genitals ['dʒenɪtlz] npl órganos mpl genitales.

genius ['dʒiːnɪəs] n genio.

genocide ['dʒenəusaɪd] n genocidio.

gent [dʒent] n abbr of **gentleman**.

genteel [dʒen'tiːl] a fino, elegante.

gentle ['dʒentl] a (sweet) amable, dulce; (touch etc) ligero, suave; (animal) manso.

gentleman ['dʒentlmən] n señor m; (well-bred man) caballero.

gentleness ['dʒentlnɪs] n dulzura; (of touch) suavidad f; (of animal) mansedumbre f.

gently ['dʒentlɪ] ad suavemente.

gentry ['dʒentrɪ] n alta burguesía.

gents [dʒents] n (aseos de) caballeros mpl.

genuine ['dʒenjuɪn] a auténtico; (person) sincero.

geographic(al) [dʒɪə'græfɪk(l)] a geográfico; **geography** [dʒɪ'ɔgrəfɪ] n geografía.

geological [dʒɪə'lɔdʒɪkl] a geológico; **geologist** [dʒɪ'ɔlədʒɪst] n geólogo; **geology** [dʒɪ'ɔlədʒɪ] n geología.

geometric(al) [dʒɪə'mɛtrɪk(l)] a geométrico; **geometry** [dʒɪ'ɔmətrɪ] n geometría.

geranium [dʒɪ'reɪnjəm] n geranio.

germ [dʒɔːm] n (gen) microbio, bacteria; (BIO, fig) germen m.

German ['dʒɔːmən] a alemán(ana) // n alemán/ana m/f; (LING) alemán m; ~ **measles** n rubéola.

Germany ['dʒɔːmənɪ] n Alemania.

germination [dʒɔːmɪ'neɪʃən] n germinación f.

gesticulate [dʒes'tɪkjuleɪt] vi gesticular.

gesture ['dʒestjə*] n gesto.

get [gɛt], pt, pp **got**, pp **gotten** (US) vt (obtain) obtener; (receive) recibir; (achieve) conseguir; (find) encontrar; (catch) coger; (fetch) traer, ir a buscar; (understand) entender // vi (become) hacerse, volverse; **to** ~ **old** hacerse viejo, envejecer; **to** ~ **to** (place) llegar a; **he got under the fence** pasó por debajo de la barrera; **to** ~ **ready/washed** prepararse/lavarse; **to** ~ **sb to do sth** hacer que alguien haga algo; **to** ~ **sth**

out of sth sacar algo de algo; **to** ~ **about** vi salir mucho, viajar mucho; (news) divulgarse; **to** ~ **along** vi (agree) entenderse; (depart) marcharse; (manage) = **to get by**; **to** ~ **at** vt fus (attack) atacar; (reach) llegar a; (the truth) descubrir; **to** ~ **away** vi marcharse; (on holiday) irse de vacaciones; (escape) escaparse; **to** ~ **away with** vt fus hacer impunemente; **to** ~ **back** vi (return) volver // vt recobrar; **to** ~ **by** vi (pass) lograr pasar; (manage) arreglárselas; **to** ~ **down** vi bajarse // vt (object) bajar; (depress) deprimir; **to** ~ **down to** vt fus (work) ponerse a (hacer); **to** ~ **in** vi (train) llegar; (arrive home) volver a casa, regresar; **to** ~ **off** vi (from train etc) bajar; (depart: person, car) marcharse // vt fus (train, bus) bajar de; **to** ~ **on** vi (at exam etc) tener éxito; (agree) entenderse // vt (horse) subir; **to** ~ **out** vi salir; (of vehicle) bajar; (news) saberse // vt (take out) sacar; **to** ~ **out of** vt fus (duty etc) escaparse de; **to** ~ **over** vt (illness) recobrarse de; (put across) hacer comprender; **to** ~ **round** vt fus rodear; (fig: person) engatusar a; **to** ~ **through to** vt fus (TEL) comunicar con; **to** ~ **together** vi reunirse; **to** ~ **up** vi (rise) levantarse // vt fus levantar; **to** ~ **up to** vt fus (reach) llegar a; (prank etc) hacer; ~**away** n fuga, escape m.

geyser ['giːzə*] n calentador m de agua; (GEO) géiser m.

Ghana ['gɑːnə] n Ghana.

ghastly ['gɑːstlɪ] a horrible; (pale) pálido.

gherkin ['gəːkɪn] n pepinillo.

ghetto ['gɛtəu] n ghetto.

ghost [gəust] n fantasma m; ~**ly** a fantasmal.

giant ['dʒaɪənt] n gigante m // a gigantesco, gigante.

gibberish ['dʒɪbərɪʃ] n galimatías m.

gibe [dʒaɪb] n pulla.

giblets ['dʒɪblɪts] npl menudillos mpl.

giddiness ['gɪdɪnɪs] n vértigo; **giddy** a (dizzy) mareado; (speed) vertiginoso; (frivolous) atolondrado; **it makes me giddy** me marea.

gift [gɪft] n (gen) regalo; (offering) obsequio; (ability) talento; ~**ed** a dotado.

gigantic [dʒaɪ'gæntɪk] a gigantesco.

giggle ['gɪgl] vi reírse con risa tonta // n risilla tonta.

gill [dʒɪl] n (measure) = 0.14 l // n [gɪl] (of fish) agalla, branquia.

gilt [gɪlt] a, n dorado; ~**-edged** a (COMM) del Estado.

gimmick ['gɪmɪk] n truco.

gin [dʒɪn] n (liquor) ginebra.

ginger ['dʒɪndʒə*] n jengibre m; ~ **ale** n cerveza de jengibre; ~**bread** n pan m de jengibre; ~**-haired** a pelirrojo.

gingerly ['dʒɪndʒəlɪ] ad con pies de plomo.

gipsy ['dʒɪpsɪ] n gitano/a.

giraffe [dʒɪ'rɑːf] n jirafa.

girder ['gəːdə*] n viga.

girdle ['gɔːdl] n (corset) faja // vt ceñir.
girl [gɔːl] n (small) niña; (young woman) chica, joven f, muchacha; **an English ~** una (chica) inglesa; **~friend** n (of girl) amiga; (of boy) novia; **~ish** a de niña.
girth [gɔːθ] n circunferencia; (stoutness) gordura.
gist [dʒɪst] n lo esencial.
give [gɪv], pt **gave**, pp **given** vt (gen) dar; (deliver) entregar; (as gift) regalar // vi (break) romperse; (stretch: fabric) dar de sí; **to ~ sb sth, ~ sth to sb** dar algo a uno; **to ~ away** vt (give free) regalar; (betray) traicionar; (disclose) revelar; **to ~ back** vt devolver; **to ~ in** vi ceder // vt entregar; **to ~ off** vt despedir; **to ~ out** vt distribuir; **to ~ up** vi renunciar, darse por vencido // vt renunciar a; **to ~ up smoking** dejar de fumar; **to ~ way** vi ceder; (AUT) ceder el paso.
glacier ['glæsiə*] n glaciar m.
glad [glæd] a contento; **~den** vt alegrar.
gladioli [glædɪˈəʊlaɪ] npl gladíolos mpl.
gladly ['glædlɪ] ad con mucho gusto.
glamorous ['glæmərəs] a encantador(a), atractivo; **glamour** n encanto, atractivo.
glance [glɑːns] n ojeada, mirada // vi: **to ~ at** echar una ojeada a; **to ~ off** (bullet) rebotar; **glancing** a (blow) oblicuo.
gland [glænd] n glándula.
glare [glɛə*] n luz f deslumbradora, brillo // vi deslumbrar; **to ~ at** mirar ferozmente a; **glaring** a (mistake) notorio.
glass [glɑːs] n vidrio, cristal m; (for drinking) vaso; (: with stem) copa; (also: **looking ~**) espejo; **~es** npl gafas fpl; **~house** n invernadero; **~ware** n cristalería; **~y** a (eyes) vidrioso.
glaze [gleɪz] vt (door) poner cristal a; (pottery) barnizar // n barniz m; **~d** a (eye) vidrioso; (pottery) barnizado.
glazier ['gleɪzɪə*] n vidriero.
gleam [gliːm] n destello // vi brillar; **~ing** a reluciente.
glee [gliː] n alegría, regocijo.
glen [glɛn] n cañada, valle m estrecho.
glib [glɪb] a de mucha labia; **~ness** n labia.
glide [glaɪd] vi deslizarse; (AVIAT, birds) planear // n deslizamiento; (AVIAT) vuelo sin motor; **glider** n (AVIAT) planeador m; **gliding** n (AVIAT) vuelo sin motor.
glimmer ['glɪmə*] n luz f trémula.
glimpse [glɪmps] n vista momentánea, vislumbre m // vt vislumbrar, entrever.
glint [glɪnt] n destello; (in the eye) chispa // vi centellear.
glisten ['glɪsn] vi relucir, brillar.
glitter ['glɪtə*] vi relucir, brillar // n brillo.
gloat [gləʊt] vi: **to ~ (over)** recrearse en, saborear.
global ['gləʊbl] a mundial; (sum) global.
globe [gləʊb] n globo, esfera.
gloom [gluːm] n tinieblas fpl, oscuridad f; (sadness) tristeza, melancolía; **~y** a

(dark) oscuro; (sad) triste; (pessimistic) pesimista.
glorify ['glɔːrɪfaɪ] vt glorificar; (praise) alabar.
glorious ['glɔːrɪəs] a glorioso; **glory** n gloria.
gloss [glɔs] n (shine) brillo; (paint) pintura brillante o esmalte; **to ~ over** vt fus encubrir.
glossary ['glɔsərɪ] n glosario.
glossy ['glɔsɪ] a lustroso.
glove [glʌv] n guante m; **~ compartment** n (AUT) guantera.
glow [gləʊ] vi (shine) brillar; (fire) arder // n brillo.
glower ['glauə*] vi: **to ~ at** mirar con ceño.
glucose ['gluːkəʊs] n glucosa.
glue [gluː] n goma (de pegar) // vt pegar.
glum [glʌm] a (mood) abatido; (person, tone) melancólico.
glut [glʌt] n superabundancia.
glutton ['glʌtn] n glotón/ona m/f; **a ~ for work** un trabajador incansable; **~y** n gula, glotonería.
glycerin(e) ['glɪsəriːn] n glicerina.
gnarled [nɑːld] a nudoso.
gnat [næt] n mosquito.
gnaw [nɔː] vt roer.
gnome [nəʊm] n gnomo.
go [gəʊ], pt **went**, pp **gone** vi ir; (travel) viajar; (depart) irse, marcharse; (work) funcionar, marchar; (be sold) venderse; (time) pasar; (fit, suit): **to ~ with** hacer juego con; (become) ponerse; (break etc) estropearse, romperse // n, pl **~es**: **to have a ~ (at)** probar suerte (con); **to be on the ~** moverse, estar trabajando; **whose ~ is it?** ¿a quién le toca?; **he's going to do it** va a hacerlo; **to ~ for a walk** ir de paseo; **to ~ dancing** ir a bailar; **how did it ~?** ¿qué tal salió o resultó?, ¿cómo ha ido?; **to ~ about** vi (rumour) propagarse // vt fus: **how do I ~ about this?** ¿cómo me las arreglo para hacer esto?; **to ~ ahead** vi (make progress) avanzar; (get going) seguir; **to ~ along** vi ir // vt fus bordear; **to ~ along with** estar de acuerdo con; **to ~ away** vi irse, marcharse; **to ~ back** vi volver; (fall back) retroceder; **to ~ back on** vt fus (promise) faltar a; **to ~ by** vi (years, time) pasar // vt fus guiarse por; **to ~ down** vi bajar; (ship) hundirse; (sun) ponerse // vt fus bajar por; **to ~ for** vt fus (fetch) ir por; (like) gustar; (attack) atacar; **to ~ in** vi entrar; **to ~ in for** vt fus (competition) presentarse a; **to ~ into** vt fus entrar en; (investigate) investigar; (embark on) embarcarse en; **to ~ off** vi irse, marcharse; (food) pasarse; (explode) estallar; (event) realizarse // vt fus dejar de gustar; **to ~ on** vi seguir, continuar; (happen) pasar, ocurrir; **to ~ on doing sth** seguir haciendo algo; **to ~ out** vi salir; (fire, light) apagarse; **to ~ over** vi (ship) zozobrar // vt fus (check) revisar; **to**

~ **through** vt fus (town etc) atravesar; **to** ~ **up** vi subir; **to** ~ **without** vt fus pasarse sin.

goad [gəud] vt aguijonear.

go-ahead ['gəuəhɛd] a emprendedor(a) // n luz f verde.

goal [gəul] n meta; (score) gol m; ~**keeper** n portero; ~-**post** n poste m de la portería.

goat [gəut] n cabrío, cabra m/f.

gobble ['gɔbl] vt (also: ~ **down**, ~ **up**) engullirse (ávidamente).

goblet ['gɔblɪt] n copa.

goblin ['gɔblɪn] n duende m.

go-cart ['gəukɑ:t] n go-cart m.

god [gɔd] n dios m; **G**~ n Dios m; ~**child** n ahijado/a; ~**dess** n diosa; ~**father** n padrino; ~-**forsaken** a dejado de la mano de Dios; ~**mother** n madrina; ~**send** n don m del cielo; ~**son** n ahijado.

goggles ['gɔglz] npl gafas fpl submarinas.

going ['gəuɪŋ] n (conditions) estado del terreno // a: **the** ~ **rate** la tarifa corriente o en vigor.

gold [gəuld] n oro // a de oro; ~**en** a (made of ~) de oro; (~ in colour) dorado; ~**fish** n pez m de colores; ~**mine** n mina de oro.

golf [gɔlf] n golf m; ~ **club** n club m de golf; (stick) palo (de golf); ~ **course** n campo de golf; ~**er** n jugador/a m/f de golf.

gondola ['gɔndələ] n góndola.

gone [gɔn] pp of **go**.

gong [gɔŋ] n gong m.

gonorrhea [gɔnə'rɪə] n gonorrea.

good [gud] a (gen) bueno; (kind) bueno, amable; (well-behaved) educado; (useful) útil // n bien m, provecho; ~**s** npl bienes mpl; (COMM) mercancías fpl; **to be** ~ **at** tener aptitud para; **to be** ~ **for** servir para; **it's** ~ **for you** te hace bien; **would you be** ~ **enough to...?** ¿podría hacerme el favor de...?, ¿sería tan amable de...?; **a** ~ **deal (of)** mucho; **a** ~ **many** muchos; **to make** ~ reparar; **for** ~ para siempre, definitivamente; ~ **morning/afternoon!** ¡buenos días/buenas tardes!; ~ **evening!** ¡buenas noches!; ~ **night!** ¡buenas noches!; ~**bye!** ¡adiós!; **to say** ~**bye** despedirse; **G**~ **Friday** n Viernes m Santo; ~-**looking** a guapo; ~**ness** n (of person) bondad f; **for** ~**ness sake!** ¡Por Dios!; ~**ness gracious!** ¡Dios mío!; ~**will** n buena voluntad f.

goose [gu:s], pl **geese** n ganso, oca.

gooseberry ['guzbərɪ] n grosella espinosa.

gooseflesh ['gu:sflɛʃ] n, **goose pimples** npl carne f de gallina.

gore [gɔ:*] vt cornear // n sangre f.

gorge [gɔ:dʒ] n barranco // vr: **to** ~ **o.s. (on)** atracarse (de).

gorgeous ['gɔ:dʒəs] a magnífico, maravilloso.

gorilla [gə'rɪlə] n gorila m.

gorse [gɔ:s] n aulaga.

gory ['gɔ:rɪ] a sangriento.

go-slow ['gəu'sləu] n huelga de trabajo lento.

gospel ['gɔspl] n evangelio.

gossip ['gɔsɪp] n (scandal) chismorreo, chismes mpl; (chat) charla; (scandalmonger) chismoso/a; (talker) hablador/a m/f // vi cotillear.

got [gɔt] pt, pp of **get**; ~**ten** (US) pp of **get**.

gout [gaut] n gota.

govern ['gʌvən] vt (gen) gobernar; (dominate) dominar.

governess ['gʌvənɪs] n institutriz f.

government ['gʌvnmənt] n gobierno; ~**al** [-'mɛntl] a gubernamental.

governor ['gʌvənə*] n gobernador m; (of jail) director/a m/f.

gown [gaun] n traje m; (of teacher, judge) toga.

G.P. n abbr of **general practitioner**.

GPO n abbr of **General Post Office**.

grab [græb] vt coger, arrebatar.

grace [greɪs] n (REL) gracia; (gracefulness) elegancia, finura // vt (favour) honrar; (adorn) adornar; **5 days'** ~ un plazo de 5 días; **to say** ~ bendecir la mesa; ~**ful** a elegante, gracioso; **gracious** ['greɪʃəs] a amable.

grade [greɪd] n (quality) clase f, calidad f; (degree) grado; (US: SCOL) clase f // vt clasificar.

gradient ['greɪdɪənt] n pendiente f.

gradual ['grædjuəl] a paulatino; ~**ly** ad paulatinamente.

graduate ['grædjuɪt] n graduado, licenciado // vi ['grædjueɪt] graduarse, licenciarse; **graduation** [-'eɪʃən] n graduación f.

graft [grɑ:ft] n (AGR, MED) injerto; (bribery) corrupción f // vt injertar.

grain [greɪn] n grano; (corn) granos mpl, cereales mpl; (in wood) fibra.

gram [græm] n gramo.

grammar ['græmə*] n gramática; **grammatical** [grə'mætɪkl] a gramatical.

gramme [græm] n = **gram**.

gramophone ['græməfəun] n tocadiscos m inv.

granary ['grænərɪ] n granero, troj f.

grand [grænd] a magnífico, imponente; ~**children** npl nietos mpl; ~**dad** n yayo, abuelito; ~**daughter** n nieta; ~**eur** ['grændjə*] n magnificencia, lo grandioso; ~**father** n abuelo; ~**iose** ['grændɪəuz] a grandioso; (pej) pomposo; ~**ma** n yaya, abuelita; ~**mother** n abuela; ~**pa** n = ~**dad**; ~ **piano** n piano de cola; ~**son** n nieto; ~**stand** n (SPORT) tribuna.

granite ['grænɪt] n granito.

granny ['grænɪ] n abuelita, yaya.

grant [grɑ:nt] vt (concede) conceder; (admit) asentir // n (SCOL) beca; **to take sth for** ~**ed** dar algo por sentado.

granulated sugar ['grænjuleɪtɪd-] n azúcar m granulado.

granule ['grænju:l] n gránulo.

grape [greɪp] *n* uva; **sour** ~**s** (*fig*) envidia.

grapefruit ['greɪpfruːt] *n* pomelo, toronja (*AM*).

graph [grɑːf] *n* gráfica; ~**ic** *a* gráfico.

grapple ['græpl] *vi:* **to** ~ **with sth** esforzarse por resolver algo.

grasp [grɑːsp] *vt* agarrar, asir; (*understand*) comprender // *n* (*grip*) asimiento; (*reach*) alcance *m*; (*understanding*) comprensión *f*; ~**ing** *a* avaro.

grass [grɑːs] *n* hierba; (*lawn*) césped *m*; ~**hopper** *n* saltamontes *m inv*; ~**land** *n* pradera; ~**-roots** *a* popular; ~ **snake** *n* culebra; ~**y** *a* cubierto de hierba.

grate [greɪt] *n* (*fireplace*) chimenea; (*of iron*) parrilla // *vi* rechinar // *vt* (*CULIN*) rallar.

grateful ['greɪtful] *a* agradecido.

grater ['greɪtə*] *n* rallador *m*.

gratify ['grætɪfaɪ] *vt* complacer; (*whim*) satisfacer; ~**ing** *a* grato.

grating ['greɪtɪŋ] *n* (*iron bars*) rejilla // *a* (*noise*) áspero.

gratitude ['grætɪtjuːd] *n* agradecimiento.

gratuity [grəˈtjuːɪtɪ] *n* gratificación *f*.

grave [greɪv] *n* tumba // *a* serio, grave; ~ **digger** *n* sepulturero.

gravel ['grævl] *n* grava.

grave: ~**stone** *n* lápida; ~**yard** *n* cementerio, camposanto.

gravity ['grævɪtɪ] *n* gravedad *f*; (*seriousness*) seriedad *f*.

gravy ['greɪvɪ] *n* salsa.

gray [greɪ] *a* = **grey.**

graze [greɪz] *vi* pacer // *vt* (*touch lightly*) rozar; (*scrape*) raspar // *n* (*MED*) rasguño.

grease [griːs] *n* (*fat*) grasa; (*lubricant*) lubricante *m* // *vt* engrasar; ~**proof** *a* a prueba de grasa; (*paper*) apergaminado; **greasy** *a* grasiento.

great [greɪt] *a* grande; (*col*) magnífico, estupendo; **G**~ **Britain** *n* Gran Bretaña; ~**-grandfather/mother** *n* bisabuelo/a; ~**ly** *ad* sumamente, mucho, muy; ~**ness** *n* grandeza.

Greece [griːs] *n* Grecia.

greed [griːd] *n* (*also:* ~**iness**) codicia, avaricia; (*for food*) gula; ~**ily** *ad* con avidez; ~**y** *a* avaro; (*for food*) glotón(ona).

Greek [griːk] *a* griego // *n* griego/a; (*LING*) griego.

green [griːn] *a* verde; (*inexperienced*) novato // *n* verde *m*; (*stretch of grass*) césped *m*; ~**s** *npl* verduras *fpl*; ~**gage** *n* claudia; ~**grocer** *n* verdulero; ~**house** *n* invernadero; ~**ish** *a* verdoso.

Greenland ['griːnlənd] *n* Groenlandia.

greet [griːt] *vt* saludar; (*welcome*) dar la bienvenida a; ~**ing** *n* (*gen*) saludo; (*welcome*) bienvenida.

gregarious [grəˈgɛərɪəs] *a* gregario.

grenade [grəˈneɪd] *n* granada.

grew [gruː] *pt of* **grow.**

grey [greɪ] *a* gris; ~**-haired** *a* canoso; ~**hound** *n* galgo.

grid [grɪd] *n* reja; (*ELEC*) red *f*.

grief [griːf] *n* dolor *m*, pena.

grievance ['griːvəns] *n* motivo de queja, agravio.

grieve [griːv] *vi* afligirse, acongojarse // *vt* dar pena a; **to** ~ **for** llorar por.

grievous ['griːvəs] *a* penoso.

grill [grɪl] *n* (*on cooker*) parrilla // *vt* asar a la parrilla; (*question*) interrogar duramente.

grille [grɪl] *n* reja; (*AUT*) rejilla.

grim [grɪm] *a* siniestro; (*fam*) horrible.

grimace [grɪˈmeɪs] *n* mueca // *vi* hacer muecas.

grime [graɪm] *n* mugre *f*; **grimy** *a* mugriento.

grin [grɪn] *n* sonrisa abierta // *vi* sonreír abiertamente.

grind [graɪnd], *pt, pp* **ground** *vt* (*coffee, pepper etc*) moler; (*make sharp*) afilar // *n* (*work*) trabajo pesado y aburrido; **to** ~ **one's teeth** rechinar los dientes.

grip [grɪp] *n* (*hold*) asimiento; (*of hands*) apretón *m*; (*handle*) asidero; (*of racquet etc*) mango; (*holdall*) maletín *m*; (*understanding*) comprensión *f* // *vt* agarrar; **to come to** ~**s with** luchar a brazo partido con; ~**ping** *a* absorbente.

grisly ['grɪzlɪ] *a* horripilante, horrible.

gristle ['grɪsl] *n* cartílago.

grit [grɪt] *n* gravilla; (*courage*) valor *m* // *vt* (*road*) poner gravilla en; **to** ~ **one's teeth** apretar los dientes.

groan [grəun] *n* gemido, quejido // *vi* gemir, quejarse.

grocer ['grəusə*] *n* tendero de ultramarinos; ~**ies** *npl* comestibles *mpl*; ~**'s (shop)** *n* tienda de ultramarinos.

groggy ['grɔgɪ] *a* aturdido; (*BOXING*) grogui.

groin [grɔɪn] *n* ingle *f*.

groom [gruːm] *n* mozo de caballos; (*also:* **bride**~) novio // *vt* (*horse*) cuidar; **well-**~**ed** acicalado.

groove [gruːv] *n* ramura, surco.

grope [grəup] *vi* ir a tientas; **to** ~ **for** *vt fus* buscar a tientas.

gross [grəus] *a* grueso; (*COMM*) bruto; ~**ly** *ad* (*greatly*) enormemente.

grotesque [grəˈtɛsk] *a* grotesco.

grotto ['grɔtəu] *n* gruta.

ground [graund] *pt, pp of* **grind** // *n* suelo, tierra; (*SPORT*) campo, terreno; (*reason: gen pl*) causa, razón *f* // *vt* (*plane*) mantener en tierra; (*US: ELEC*) conectar con tierra // *vi* (*ship*) varar, encallar; ~**s** *npl* (*of coffee etc*) poso *sg*; (*gardens etc*) jardines *mpl*, parque *m*; **on the** ~ en el suelo; **to the** ~ al suelo; ~ **floor** *n* planta baja; ~**ing** *n* (*in education*) conocimientos *mpl* básicos; ~**less** *a* infundado; ~**sheet** *n* tela impermeable; ~ **staff** *n* personal *m* de tierra; ~**work** *n* preparación *f*.

group [gruːp] *n* grupo; (*musical*) conjunto

// (*vb*: *also*: ~ **together**) *vt* agrupar // *vi* agruparse.
grouse [graus] *n, pl inv* (*bird*) urogallo // *vi* (*complain*) quejarse.
grove [grəuv] *n* arboleda.
grovel ['grɔvl] *vi* (*fig*) humillarse.
grow [grəu], *pt* **grew**, *pp* **grown** *vi* (*gen*) crecer; (*plants*) cultivarse; (*increase*) aumentarse; (*spread*) extenderse, desarrollarse; (*become*) volverse; **to ~ rich/weak** enriquecerse/debilitarse // *vt* cultivar, dejar crecer; **to ~ up** *vi* crecer, hacerse hombre/mujer; **~er** *n* cultivador/a *m/f*, productor/a *m/f*; **~ing** *a* creciente.
growl [graul] *vi* gruñir.
grown [grəun] *pp of* **grow**; **~-up** *n* adulto, persona mayor.
growth [grəuθ] *n* crecimiento, desarrollo; (*what has grown*) brote *m*; (*MED*) acceso, tumor *m*.
grub [grʌb] *n* gusano; (*col: food*) comida.
grubby ['grʌbɪ] *a* sucio, mugriento.
grudge [grʌdʒ] *n* motivo de rencor // *vt*: **to ~ sb sth** dar algo a uno de mala gana, escatimar algo a uno; **to bear sb a ~** guardar rencor a uno; **he ~s (giving) the money** da el dinero de mala gana.
gruelling ['gruəlɪŋ] *a* penoso, duro.
gruesome ['gru:səm] *a* horrible.
gruff [grʌf] *a* (*voice*) bronco; (*manner*) brusco.
grumble ['grʌmbl] *vi* refunfuñar, quejarse.
grumpy ['grʌmpɪ] *a* gruñón(ona).
grunt [grʌnt] *vi* gruñir // *n* gruñido.
guarantee [gærən'ti:] *n* garantía // *vt* garantizar.
guarantor [gærən'tɔ:*] *n* garante *m/f*, fiador/a *m/f*.
guard [gɑ:d] *n* guardia; (*RAIL*) jefe *m* de tren // *vt* guardar; **~ed** *a* (*fig*) cauteloso; **~ian** *n* guardián/ana *m/f*; (*of minor*) tutor/a *m/f*; **~'s van** *n* (*RAIL*) furgón *m*.
guerrilla [gə'rɪlə] *n* guerrillero; **~ warfare** *n* guerra de guerrillas.
guess [gɛs] *vi, vt* (*gen*) adivinar; (*suppose*) suponer // *n* suposición *f*, conjetura; **to take** *or* **have a ~** tratar de adivinar; **~ work** *n* conjeturas *fpl*.
guest [gɛst] *n* invitado/a; (*in hotel*) huésped/a *m/f*; **~-house** *n* casa de huéspedes, pensión *f*; **~ room** *n* cuarto de huéspedes.
guffaw [gʌ'fɔ:] *n* carcajada // *vi* reírse a carcajadas.
guidance ['gaɪdəns] *n* (*gen*) dirección *f*; (*advice*) consejos *mpl*.
guide [gaɪd] *n* (*person*) guía *m/f*; (*book, fig*) guía // *vt* guiar; **(girl) ~** *n* exploradora; **~book** *n* guía; **~ dog** *n* perro guía; **~ lines** *npl* (*fig*) principios *mpl* generales.
guild [gɪld] *n* gremio; **~hall** *n* (*Brit*) ayuntamiento.
guile [gaɪl] *n* astucia; **~less** *a* cándido.
guillotine ['gɪləti:n] *n* guillotina.
guilt [gɪlt] *n* culpabilidad *f*; **~y** *a* culpable.

guinea pig ['gɪnɪpɪg] *n* conejillo de Indias.
guise [gaɪz] *n*: **in** *or* **under the ~ of** so capa de.
guitar [gɪ'tɑ:*] *n* guitarra; **~ist** *n* guitarrista *m/f*.
gulf [gʌlf] *n* golfo; (*abyss*) abismo.
gull [gʌl] *n* gaviota.
gullet ['gʌlɪt] *n* esófago; (*fam*) garganta.
gullible ['gʌlɪbl] *a* crédulo.
gully ['gʌlɪ] *n* barranco.
gulp [gʌlp] *vi* tragar saliva // *vt* (*also*: **~ down**) tragarse // *n*: **at one ~** de un trago.
gum [gʌm] *n* (*ANAT*) encía; (*glue*) goma; (*sweet*) caramelo de goma; (*also*: **chewing-~**) chiclé *m* // *vt* engomar, pegar con goma; **~boots** *npl* botas *fpl* de goma.
gun [gʌn] *n* (*gen*) arma de fuego; (*small*) pistola; (*shotgun*) escopeta; (*rifle*) fusil *m*; (*cannon*) cañón *m*; **~boat** *n* cañonero; **~fire** *n* fuego, disparos *mpl*; **~man** *n* pistolero; **~ner** *n* artillero; **at ~point** bajo la amenaza de un arma; **~powder** *n* pólvora; **~shot** *n* escopetazo, cañonazo; **~smith** *n* armero.
gurgle ['gə:gl] *vi* gorgotear.
gush [gʌʃ] *vi* chorrear; (*fig*) deshacerse en efusiones.
gusset ['gʌsɪt] *n* escudete *m*.
gust [gʌst] *n* (*of wind*) ráfaga.
gusto ['gʌstəu] *n* entusiasmo.
gut [gʌt] *n* intestino, tripa; (*MUS etc*) cuerda de tripa; **~s** *npl* (*courage*) valor *m*.
gutter ['gʌtə*] *n* (*of roof*) canalón *m*; (*in street*) arroyo.
guttural ['gʌtərl] *a* gutural.
guy [gaɪ] *n* (*also*: **~rope**) cuerda; (*col: man*) tío, tipo.
guzzle ['gʌzl] *vi* tragar // *vt* engullir.
gym [dʒɪm] *n* (*also*: **gymnasium**) gimnasio; (*also*: **gymnastics**) gimnasia; **~nast** *n* gimnasta *m/f*; **~nastics** *n* gimnasia; **~ shoes** *npl* zapatillas *fpl* de gimnasia; **~ slip** *n* túnica de colegiala.
gynaecologist, gynecologist (*US*) [gaɪnɪ'kɔlədʒɪst] *n* ginecólogo; **gynaecology, gynecology** (*US*) [-nə'kɔlədʒɪ] *n* ginecología.
gypsy ['dʒɪpsɪ] *n* = **gipsy**.
gyrate [dʒaɪ'reɪt] *vi* girar.

H

haberdashery ['hæbə'dæʃərɪ] *n* mercería.
habit ['hæbɪt] *n* hábito, costumbre *f*; (*costume*) hábito.
habitable ['hæbɪtəbl] *a* habitable.
habitual [hə'bɪtjuəl] *a* acostumbrado, habitual; (*drinker, liar*) empedernido; **~ly** *ad* por costumbre.
hack [hæk] *vt* (*cut*) cortar; (*slice*) tajar // *n* corte *m*; (*axe blow*) hachazo.
hackneyed ['hæknɪd] *a* trillado, gastado.
had [hæd] *pt, pp of* **have**.

haddock ['hædək], pl ~ or ~s n especie de merluza.
hadn't ['hædnt] = **had not**.
haemorrhage, hemorrhage (US) ['hɛmərɪdʒ] n hemorragia.
haemorrhoids, hemorrhoids (US) ['hɛmərɔɪdz] npl hemorroides fpl.
haggard ['hægəd] a ojeroso.
haggle ['hægl] vi (argue) discutir; (bargain) regatear.
Hague [heɪg] n: **The** ~ La Haya.
hail [heɪl] n (weather) granizo // vt saludar; (call) llamar a // vi granizar; ~**stone** n (piedra de) granizo.
hair [hɛə*] n (gen) pelo, cabellos mpl; (one ~) pelo, cabello; (head of ~) cabellera; (on legs) vello; **grey** ~ canas fpl; ~**brush** n cepillo (del pelo); ~**cut** n corte m de pelo; ~**do** n peinado; ~**dresser** n peluquero; ~**dresser's** n peluquería; ~**-drier** n secador m de pelo; ~**net** n redecilla; ~**piece** n trenza postiza; ~**pin** n horquilla; ~**pin bend** n curva de horquilla; ~**raising** a espeluznante; ~ **remover** n depilador m; (cream) crema depilatoria; ~ **spray** n laca; ~**style** n peinado; ~**y** a peludo; velludo.
half [hɑːf], pl **halves** n mitad f // a medio // ad medio, a medias; ~**-an-hour** media hora; **two and a** ~ dos y media; ~ **a pound** media libra; **to cut sth in** ~ cortar algo por la mitad; ~ **asleep** medio dormido; ~**-price** a mitad de precio; ~**-back** n (SPORT) medio; ~**-breed,** ~**-caste** n mestizo; ~**-hearted** a indiferente, poco entusiasta; ~**-hour** n media hora; ~**penny** ['heɪpnɪ] n medio penique; ~**-time** n medio tiempo; ~**way** ad a medio camino.
halibut ['hælɪbət] n, pl inv halibut m.
hall [hɔːl] n (for concerts) sala; (entrance way) hall m, vestíbulo; **town** ~ palacio municipal; ~ **of residence** n residencia (universitaria).
hallmark ['hɔːlmɑːk] n (mark) marca; (seal) sello.
hallo [hə'ləu] excl = **hello**.
hallucination [həluːsɪ'neɪʃən] n alucinación f.
halo ['heɪləu] n (of saint) aureola.
halt [hɔːlt] n (stop) alto, parada; (RAIL) apeadero // vt parar // vi pararse; (process) interrumpirse.
halve [hɑːv] vt partir por la mitad.
halves [hɑːvz] pl of **half**.
ham [hæm] n jamón m (cocido); (actor) comicastro.
hamburger ['hæmbɔːgə*] n hamburguesa.
hamlet ['hæmlɪt] n aldea.
hammer ['hæmə*] n martillo // vt amartillar // vi (on door) golpear.
hammock ['hæmək] n hamaca.
hamper ['hæmpə*] vt estorbar // n cesto.
hand [hænd] n mano f; (of clock) manecilla; (writing) letra; (applause) aplausos mpl; (worker) obrero; (measure) palmo // vt

(give) dar, pasar; (deliver) entregar; **to give sb a** ~ dar una mano a uno, ayudar a uno; **at** ~ a la mano; **in** ~ entre manos; **on the one** ~ ..., **on the other** ~ ... por una parte ... por otra (parte) ...; **to** ~ **in** vt entregar; **to** ~ **out** vt distribuir; **to** ~ **over** vt (deliver) entregar; (surrender) ceder; ~**bag** n bolso; ~**basin** n lavabo; ~**book** n manual m; ~**brake** n freno de mano; ~**cuffs** npl esposas fpl; ~**ful** n puñado.
handicap ['hændɪkæp] n handicap m, desventaja // vt estorbar; **mentally/physically** ~**ped** incapacitado mentalmente/físicamente.
handicraft ['hændɪkrɑːft] n artesanía.
handkerchief ['hæŋkətʃɪf] n pañuelo.
handle ['hændl] n (of door etc) tirador m, manija; (of cup etc) asa; (of knife etc) mango; (for winding) manivela; (fam: name) título // vt (touch) tocar; (deal with) encargarse de; (treat: people) manejar; '~ **with care'** 'tratar con cuidado'; **to fly off the** ~ perder los estribos; ~**bar(s)** n(pl) manillar m.
hand-luggage ['hændlʌgɪdʒ] n equipaje m de mano.
handmade ['hændmeɪd] a hecho a mano.
handout ['hændaut] n (distribution) repartición f; (charity) limosna; (leaflet) folleto.
handshake ['hændʃeɪk] n apretón m de manos.
handsome ['hænsəm] a guapo.
handwriting ['hændraɪtɪŋ] n letra.
handy ['hændɪ] a (close at hand) a mano; (convenient) práctico; (skilful) hábil, diestro; ~ **man** n (hombre) mañoso.
hang [hæŋ], pt, pp **hung** vt colgar; (criminal: pt, pp **hanged**) ahorcar; (head) bajar // vi colgar; **to** ~ **about** vi haraganear; **to** ~ **on** vi (wait) esperar; **to** ~ **up** vi (TEL) colgar.
hangar ['hæŋə*] n hangar m.
hanger ['hæŋə*] n percha; ~**-on** n parásito.
hangover ['hæŋəuvə*] n (after drinking) resaca.
hang-up ['hæŋʌp] n complejo.
hanker ['hæŋkə*] vi: **to** ~ **after** (miss) echar de menos; (long for) añorar.
hankie, hanky ['hæŋkɪ] n abbr of **handkerchief**.
haphazard [hæp'hæzəd] a fortuito.
happen ['hæpən] vi suceder, ocurrir; (take place) tener lugar, realizarse; **to** ~ **upon** tropezar con; ~**ing** n suceso, acontecimiento.
happily ['hæpɪlɪ] ad (luckily) afortunadamente; (cheerfully) alegremente.
happiness ['hæpɪnɪs] n (gen) felicidad f; (joy) alegría.
happy ['hæpɪ] a feliz, alegre; **to be** ~ (**with**) estar contento (con); **to be** ~ **ser** feliz.
harass ['hærəs] vt acosar, hostigar;

~**ment** n persecución f; (worry) preocupación f.

harbour, harbor (US) ['hɑ:bə*] n puerto // vt (hope etc) abrigar; (hide) esconder.

hard [hɑ:d] a (gen) duro; (difficult) difícil; (work) arduo; (person) severo // ad (work) mucho, duro, duramente; (think, try) seriamente; **to look** ~ mirar fijo o fijamente; **no** ~ **feelings!** sin rencor; **to be** ~ **of hearing** ser duro de oído; **to be** ~ **done by** ser tratado injustamente; ~**back** n libro encuadernado; ~**board** n chapa de madera; ~**en** vt endurecer; (fig) curtir // vi endurecerse; ~-**headed** a poco sentimental, práctico; ~ **labour** n trabajos mpl forzados.

hardly ['hɑ:dlɪ] ad (scarcely) apenas; **that can** ~ **be true** difícilmente puede ser cierto; ~ **ever** casi nunca.

hardness ['hɑ:dnɪs] n dureza.

hardship ['hɑ:dʃɪp] n (troubles) penas fpl; (financial) apuro.

hard-up [hɑ:d'ʌp] a (col) pelado.

hardware ['hɑ:dwɛə*] n ferretería; (COMPUTERS) material m; ~ **shop** n ferretería.

hard-wearing [hɑ:d'wɛərɪŋ] a resistente, duradero.

hard-working [hɑ:d'wə:kɪŋ] a trabajador(a).

hardy ['hɑ:dɪ] a fuerte; (plant) resistente.

hare [hɛə*] n liebre f; ~-**brained** a casquivano.

harem [hɑ:'ri:m] n harén m.

haricot (bean) ['hærɪkəu] n alubia.

harm [hɑ:m] n daño, mal m // vt (person) hacer daño a, perjudicar; (thing) dañar; **out of** ~'s **way** a salvo; ~**ful** a perjudicial; (pest) dañino; ~**less** a inofensivo.

harmonica [hɑ:'mɔnɪkə] n armónica.

harmonious [hɑ:'məunɪəs] a armonioso; **harmonize** ['hɑ:mənaɪz] vt, vi armonizar; **harmony** ['hɑ:mənɪ] n armonía.

harness ['hɑ:nɪs] n arreos mpl // vt (horse) enjaezar; (resources) aprovechar.

harp [hɑ:p] n arpa // vi: **to** ~ **on about** hablar constantemente de; ~**ist** n arpista m/f.

harpoon [hɑ:'pu:n] n arpón m.

harrowing ['hærəuɪŋ] a horroroso.

harsh [hɑ:ʃ] a (hard) duro, cruel; (severe) severo; (unpleasant) desagradable; (: colour) chillón(ona); (contrast) violento; ~**ness** n dureza.

harvest ['hɑ:vɪst] n cosecha; (of grapes) vendimia // vt, vi cosechar; ~**er** n (machine) cosechadora.

has [hæz] vb see **have.**

hash [hæʃ] n (CULIN) picadillo; (fig: mess) lío.

hashish ['hæʃɪʃ] n hachís m, hachich m.

hasn't ['hæznt] = **has not.**

hassle ['hæsl] n pelea // vt molestar a.

haste [heɪst] n prisa; **hasten** ['heɪsn] vt acelerar // vi darse prisa; **hastily** ad de prisa; **hasty** a apresurado.

hat [hæt] n sombrero.

hatch [hætʃ] n (NAUT. also: ~**way**) escotilla // vi salir del cascarón // vt incubar; (plot) tramar.

hatchback ['hætʃbæk] n (AUT) coche m con puerta trasera.

hatchet ['hætʃɪt] n hacha.

hate [heɪt] vt odiar, aborrecer // n odio; ~**ful** a odioso; **hatred** n odio.

hat trick ['hættrɪk] n (SPORT, also fig) tres triunfos seguidos.

haughty ['hɔ:tɪ] a altanero, arrogante.

haul [hɔ:l] vt tirar; (by lorry) transportar // n (of fish) redada; (of stolen goods etc) botín m; ~**age** n transporte m; (costs) gastos mpl de transporte; ~**ier** n contratista m de transportes.

haunch [hɔ:ntʃ] n anca; (of meat) pierna.

haunt [hɔ:nt] vt (subj: ghost) aparecer en; (frequent) frecuentar; (obsess) obsesionar // n guarida; ~**ed house** casa de fantasmas.

have [hæv], pt, pp **had** vt (gen) tener; (possess) poseer; (meal, shower) tomar; **to** ~ **sth done** hacer hacer algo; **she has to do it** tiene que hacerlo; **I had better leave** más vale que me marche; **I won't** ~ **it** no lo tolero; **he has gone** se ha ido; **to** ~ **it out with sb** ajustar cuentas con alguien; **to** ~ **a baby** parir, dar a luz.

haven ['heɪvn] n puerto; (fig) refugio.

haven't ['hævnt] = **have not.**

haversack ['hævəsæk] n mochila.

havoc ['hævək] n estragos mpl.

hawk [hɔ:k] n halcón m.

hay [heɪ] n heno; ~ **fever** n fiebre f del heno; ~**stack** n almiar m.

haywire ['heɪwaɪə*] a (col): **to go** ~ (person) volverse loco; (plan) embarullarse.

hazard ['hæzəd] n riesgo // vt aventurar; ~**ous** a (dangerous) peligroso; (risky) arriesgado.

haze [heɪz] n neblina.

hazelnut ['heɪzlnʌt] n avellana.

hazy ['heɪzɪ] a brumoso; (idea) vago.

he [hi:] pron él; ~ **who...** él que..., quien...; ~-**man** n macho.

head [hɛd] n cabeza; (leader) jefe/a m/f // vt (list) encabezar; (group) capitanear; ~**s (or tails)** cara (o cruz); ~ **first** de cabeza; ~ **over heels** patas arriba; **to** ~ **the ball** cabecear (la pelota); **to** ~ **for** vt fus dirigirse a; ~**ache** n dolor m de cabeza; ~**ing** n título; ~**lamp** n faro; ~**land** n promontorio; ~**light** = ~**lamp**; ~**line** n titular m; ~**long** ad (fall) de cabeza; (rush) precipitadamente; ~**master/ mistress** n director/a m/f (de escuela); ~ **office** n oficina central, central f; ~-**on** a (collision) de frente; ~**phones** npl auriculares mpl; ~**quarters (HQ)** npl sede f central; (MIL) cuartel m general; ~-**rest** n reposacabezas m inv; ~**room** n (in car) espacio para la cabeza; (under bridge) luz f; ~**scarf** n pañuelo (de cabeza); ~**stone** n lápida mortuoria; ~**strong** *a* voluntarioso; ~ **waiter** *n* jefe *m* de camareros; ~**way** *n* progreso; **to make** ~**way** avanzar; ~**wind** *n* viento contrario.

heal [hi:l] *vt* curar // *vi* cicatrizarse.

health [hɛlθ] *n* salud *f*; **good** ~! ¡salud y pesetas!; ~ **food** *n* comida natural; **H**~ **Service** *n* Seguro de Enfermedad; ~**y** *a* (*gen*) sano.

heap [hi:p] *n* montón *m* // *vt* amontonar; (*plate*) colmar.

hear [hɪə*], *pt, pp* **heard** [hɔːd] *vt* oír; (*perceive*) sentir; (*listen to*) escuchar; (*lecture*) asistir a // *vi* oír; **to** ~ **about** oír hablar de; **to** ~ **from sb** tener noticias de alguien; ~**ing** *n* (*sense*) oído; (*LAW*) vista; ~**ing aid** *n* audífono; ~**say** *n* rumores *mpl*, hablillas *fpl*.

hearse [hɔːs] *n* coche *m* fúnebre.

heart [hɑːt] *n* corazón *m*; ~**s** *npl* (*CARDS*) corazones *mpl*; **at** ~ en el fondo; **by** ~ (*learn, know*) de memoria; ~ **attack** *n* ataque *m* cardíaco; ~**beat** *n* latido (del corazón); ~**breaking** *a* desgarrador(a); **to be** ~**broken** estar angustiado; ~**burn** *n* acedía; ~ **failure** *n* fallo cardíaco; ~**felt** *a* (*cordial*) cordial; (*deeply felt*) más sentido.

hearth [hɑːθ] *n* (*gen*) hogar *m*; (*fireplace*) chimenea.

heartily [ˈhɑːtɪlɪ] *ad* sinceramente, cordialmente; (*laugh*) a carcajadas; (*eat*) con buen apetito.

heartless [ˈhɑːtlɪs] *a* cruel.

hearty [ˈhɑːtɪ] *a* cordial.

heat [hiːt] *n* (*gen*) calor *m*; (*ardour*) ardor *m*; (*SPORT. also*: **qualifying** ~) prueba eliminatoria // *vt* calentar; (*fig*) acalorar; **to** ~ **up** *vi* (*gen*) calentarse; ~**ed** *a* caliente; (*fig*) acalorado; ~**er** *n* calentador *m*.

heath [hiːθ] *n* (*Brit*) brezal *m*.

heathen [ˈhiːðn] *a, n* pagano/a.

heather [ˈhɛðə*] *n* brezo.

heating [ˈhiːtɪŋ] *n* calefacción *f*.

heatstroke [ˈhiːtstrəuk] *n* insolación *f*.

heatwave [ˈhiːtweɪv] *n* ola de calor.

heave [hiːv] *vt* (*pull*) tirar de; (*push*) empujar con esfuerzo; (*lift*) levantar (con esfuerzo) // *vi* (*water*) agitarse // *n* tirón *m*; empujón *m*; (*effort*) esfuerzo; (*throw*) echada.

heaven [ˈhɛvn] *n* cielo; (*REL*) paraíso; ~**ly** *a* celestial; (*REL*) divino.

heavily [ˈhɛvɪlɪ] *ad* pesadamente; (*drink, smoke*) con exceso; (*sleep, sigh*) profundamente.

heavy [ˈhɛvɪ] *a* pesado; (*work*) duro; (*sea, rain, meal*) fuerte; (*drinker, smoker*) gran; (*eater*) comilón(ona); ~**weight** *n* (*SPORT*) peso pesado.

Hebrew [ˈhiːbruː] *a* hebreo.

heckle [ˈhɛkl] *vt* interrumpir.

hectic [ˈhɛktɪk] *a* febril, agitado.

he'd [hiːd] = **he would; he had.**

hedge [hɛdʒ] *n* seto // *vt* cercar (con un seto) // *vi* contestar con evasivas; **to** ~ **one's bets** (*fig*) cubrirse.

hedgehog [ˈhɛdʒhɔg] *n* erizo.

heed [hiːd] *vt* (*also*: **take** ~ **of**) (*attend to*) hacer caso de; (*bear in mind*) tener en cuenta; ~**less** *a* desatento.

heel [hiːl] *n* talón *m* // *vt* (*shoe*) poner tacón a.

hefty [ˈhɛftɪ] *a* (*person*) fornido; (*piece*) grande; (*price*) gordo.

heifer [ˈhɛfə*] *n* novilla, ternera.

height [haɪt] *n* (*of person*) talle *m*; (*of building*) altura; (*high ground*) cerro; (*altitude*) altitud *f*; ~**en** *vt* elevar; (*fig*) aumentar.

heir [ɛə*] *n* heredero; ~**ess** *n* heredera; ~**loom** *n* reliquia de familia.

held [hɛld] *pt, pp of* **hold.**

helicopter [ˈhɛlɪkɔptə*] *n* helicóptero.

hell [hɛl] *n* infierno; ~! ¡demonios!

he'll [hiːl] = **he will, he shall.**

hellish [ˈhɛlɪʃ] *a* infernal; (*fam*) horrible.

hello [həˈləu] *excl* ¡hola!; (*surprise*) ¡caramba!

helm [hɛlm] *n* (*NAUT*) timón *m*.

helmet [ˈhɛlmɪt] *n* casco.

help [hɛlp] *n* ayuda; (*charwoman*) criada, asistenta; (*assistant etc*) empleado // *vt* ayudar; ~! ¡socorro!; ~ **yourself** sírvete; **he can't** ~ **it** no es culpa suya; ~**er** *n* ayudante *m/f*; ~**ful** *a* útil, servicial; ~**ing** *n* ración *f*; ~**less** *a* (*incapable*) incapaz; (*defenceless*) indefenso.

hem [hɛm] *n* dobladillo; **to** ~ **in** *vt* cercar.

hemisphere [ˈhɛmɪsfɪə*] *n* hemisferio.

hen [hɛn] *n* gallina.

hence [hɛns] *ad* (*therefore*) por lo tanto; **2 years** ~ de aquí a 2 años; ~**forth** *ad* de hoy en adelante.

henchman [ˈhɛntʃmən] *n* (*pej*) secuaz *m*.

henpecked [ˈhɛnpɛkt] *a* dominado por su mujer.

her [hɔː*] *pron* (*direct*) la; (*indirect*) le; (*stressed, after prep*) ella // *a* su.

herald [ˈhɛrəld] *n* (*forerunner*) precursor/a *m/f* // *vt* anunciar.

heraldry [ˈhɛrəldrɪ] *n* heráldica.

herb [hɔːb] *n* hierba.

herd [hɔːd] *n* rebaño.

here [hɪə*] *ad* aquí; ~! (*present*) presente; ~ **she is** aquí está; ~**after** *ad* en el futuro // *n*: **the** ~**after** (la vida de) ultratumba; ~**by** *ad* (*in letter*) por la presente.

hereditary [hɪˈrɛdɪtrɪ] *a* hereditario; **heredity** [-tɪ] *n* herencia.

heresy [ˈhɛrəsɪ] *n* herejía.

heretic [ˈhɛrətɪk] *n* hereje *m/f*; ~**al** [hɪˈrɛtɪkl] *a* herético.

heritage [ˈhɛrɪtɪdʒ] *n* (*gen*) herencia; (*fig*) patrimonio.

hermit [ˈhɔːmɪt] *n* ermitaño.

hernia [ˈhɔːnɪə] *n* hernia.

hero [ˈhɪərəu], *pl* ~**es** *n* héroe *m*; (*in book, film*) protagonista *m*; ~**ic** [hɪˈrəuɪk] *a* heroico.

heroin ['hɛrəuɪn] *n* heroína.
heroine ['hɛrəuɪn] *n* heroína; (*in book, film*) protagonista.
heroism ['hɛrəuɪzm] *n* heroísmo.
heron ['hɛrən] *n* garza.
herring ['hɛrɪŋ] *n* arenque *m*.
hers [hɔːz] *pron* (el) suyo/(la) suya *etc*.
herself [hɔːˈsɛlf] *pron* (*reflexive*) se; (*emphatic*) ella misma; (*after prep*) sí (misma).
he's [hiːz] = **he is; he has.**
hesitant ['hɛzɪtənt] *a* vacilante, dudoso.
hesitate ['hɛzɪteɪt] *vi* dudar, vacilar; **hesitation** ['-teɪʃən] *n* indecisión *f.*
hew [hjuː] *vt* cortar con hacha.
hexagon ['hɛksəgən] *n* hexágono; ~al [-'sægənl] *a* hexagonal.
hi [haɪ] *excl* ¡oye!, ¡hola!
hibernate ['haɪbəneɪt] *vi* invernar.
hiccough, hiccup ['hɪkʌp] *vi* hipar; ~s *npl* hipo *sg.*
hid [hɪd] *pt of* **hide.**
hidden ['hɪdn] *pp of* **hide.**
hide [haɪd] *n* (*skin*) piel *f* // (*vb*: *pt* **hid**, *pp* **hidden**) *vt* esconder, ocultar // *vi*: **to ~ (from sb)** esconderse *o* ocultarse (de alguien); ~-**and-seek** *n* escondite *m*; ~**away** *n* escondite *m.*
hideous ['hɪdɪəs] *a* horrible.
hiding ['haɪdɪŋ] *n* (*beating*) paliza; **to be in ~** (*concealed*) estar escondido; ~ **place** *n* escondrijo.
hierarchy ['haɪərɑːkɪ] *n* jerarquía.
high [haɪ] *a* (*gen*) alto; (*speed, number*) grande; (*price*) elevado; (*wind*) fuerte; (*voice*) agudo // *ad* alto, a gran altura; **it is 20 m ~** tiene 20 m de altura; **~ in the air** en las alturas; ~**brow** *a* culto; ~**chair** *n* silla alta; ~-**handed** *a* despótico; ~-**heeled** *a* de tacón alto; ~**jack** = **hijack;** ~ **jump** *n* (*SPORT*) salto de altura; ~**light** *n* (*fig*: *of event*) punto culminante // *vt* subrayar; ~**ly** *ad* sumamente; ~**ly strung** *a* hipertenso; **H~ Mass** *n* misa mayor; ~**ness** *n* altura; **Her H~ness** Su Alteza; ~-**pitched** *a* agudo; ~-**rise block** *n* torre *f* de pisos; ~ **school** *n* colegio de segunda enseñanza, Instituto; ~ **street** *n* calle *f* mayor; ~ **way** *n* carretera.
hijack ['haɪdʒæk] *vt* secuestrar; ~**er** *n* secuestrador/a *m/f.*
hike [haɪk] *vi* (*go walking*) ir de excursión; (*tramp*) caminar // *n* caminata; **hiker** *n* excursionista *m/f.*
hilarious [hɪˈlɛərɪəs] *a* (*behaviour, event*) regocijante.
hill [hɪl] *n* colina; (*high*) montaña; (*slope*) cuesta; ~**side** *n* ladera; ~**y** *a* montañoso; (*uneven*) accidentado.
hilt [hɪlt] *n* (*of sword*) empuñadura; **to the ~** completamente.
him [hɪm] *pron* (*direct*) le, lo; (*indirect*) le; (*stressed, after prep*) él; ~**self** *pron* (*reflexive*) se; (*emphatic*) él mismo; (*after prep*) sí (mismo).
hind [haɪnd] *a* posterior // *n* cierva.

hinder ['hɪndə*] *vt* estorbar, impedir; **hindrance** ['hɪndrəns] *n* estorbo, obstáculo.
Hindu ['hɪnduː] *n* hindú *m/f.*
hinge [hɪndʒ] *n* bisagra, gozne *m* // *vi* (*fig*): **to ~ on** depender de.
hint [hɪnt] *n* indirecta; (*advice*) consejo // *vt*: **to ~ that** insinuar que // *vi* soltar indirectas; **to ~ at** hacer una alusión a.
hip [hɪp] *n* cadera; ~ **pocket** *n* bolsillo de atrás.
hippopotamus [hɪpəˈpɔtəməs], *pl* ~**es** *or* -**mi** [-maɪ] *n* hipopótamo.
hire ['haɪə*] *vt* (*car, equipment*) alquilar; (*worker*) contratar // *n* alquiler *m*; (*of person*) salario; **for ~** se alquila; (*taxi*) libre; ~ **purchase (H.P.)** *n* compra a plazos.
his [hɪz] *pron* (el) suyo/(la) suya *etc* // *a* su.
Hispanic [hɪsˈpænɪk] *a* hispánico.
hiss [hɪs] *vi* silbar, sisear // *n* silbido, siseo.
historian [hɪˈstɔːrɪən] *n* historiador/a *m/f.*
historic(al) [hɪˈstɔrɪk(l)] *a* histórico.
history ['hɪstərɪ] *n* historia.
hit [hɪt], *pt, pp* **hit** *vt* (*strike*) golpear, pegar; (*reach*: *target*) alcanzar; (*collide with*: *car*) chocar contra // *n* golpe *m*; (*success*) éxito, sensación *f*; **to ~ it off with sb** hacer buenas migas con alguien.
hitch [hɪtʃ] *vt* (*fasten*) atar, amarrar; (*also*: ~ **up**) alzar // *n* (*difficulty*) dificultad *f*; **to ~ a lift** hacer autostop.
hitch-hike ['hɪtʃhaɪk] *vi* hacer autostop; **hitch-hiker** *n* autostopista *m/f.*
hive [haɪv] *n* colmena.
hoard [hɔːd] *n* acumulación *f* // *vt* acumular; ~**ing** *n* acumulación *f*; (*for posters*) cartelera.
hoarfrost ['hɔːfrɔst] *n* escarcha.
hoarse [hɔːs] *a* ronco.
hoax [həuks] *n* trampa.
hobble ['hɔbl] *vi* cojear // *vt* (*horse*) manear.
hobby ['hɔbɪ] *n* pasatiempo, afición *f*; ~-**horse** *n* (*fig*) tema, manía.
hobo ['həubəu] *n* (*US*) vagabundo.
hockey ['hɔkɪ] *n* hockey *m.*
hoe [həu] *n* azadón *m* // *vt* azadonar.
hog [hɔg] *n* cerdo, puerco // *vt* (*fig*) acaparar; **to go the whole ~** liarse la manta a la cabeza.
hoist [hɔɪst] *n* (*lift*) montacargas *m inv*; (*crane*) grúa.
hold [həuld], *pt, pp* **held** *vt* tener; (*contain*) contener; (*keep back*) retener; (*believe*) sostener; (*take ~ of*) coger; (*take weight*) soportar; (*meeting*) celebrar // *vi* (*withstand pressure*) resistir; (*be valid*) valer; (*stick*) pegarse // *n* (*handle*) asidero; (*grasp*) asimiento; (*fig*) dominio; (*WRESTLING*) presa; (*NAUT*) bodega; ~ **the line!** (*TEL*) no cuelgue; **to ~ one's own** (*fig*) defenderse; **to catch** *or* **get (a) ~ of** agarrarse, asirse de; **to ~ back** *vt* retenerse; (*secret*) guardarse; **to ~ down** *vt* (*person*) sujetar; (*job*) conservar; **to ~ off** *vt* (*enemy*) rechazar; **to ~ on** *vi*

agarrarse bien; (*wait*) esperar; ~ on! (*TEL*) no cuelgue; **to** ~ **on to** *vt fus* agarrarse a; (*keep*) guardar; **to** ~ **out** *vt* alargar // *vi* (*resist*) resistir; **to** ~ **up** *vt* (*raise*) levantar; (*support*) apoyar; (*delay*) atrasar; (*rob*) asaltar; ~**all** *n* funda, neceser *m*; ~**er** *n* (*of ticket, record*) poseedor/a *m/f*; (*of office, title etc*) titular *m/f*; ~**ing** *n* (*share*) interés *m*; ~**up** *n* (*robbery*) atraco; (*delay*) parada; (*in traffic*) embotellamiento.

hole [həul] *n* agujero // *vt* agujerear.

holiday ['hɔlədɪ] *n* vacaciones *fpl*; (*day off*) (día de) fiesta, feriado; ~-**maker** *n* veraneante *m/f*; ~ **resort** *n* punto de veraneo.

holiness ['həulɪnɪs] *n* santidad *f.*

Holland ['hɔlənd] *n* Holanda.

hollow ['hɔləu] *a* hueco, vacío; (*eyes*) hundido; (*sound*) sordo; (*doctrine*) falso // *n* (*gen*) hueco; (*in ground*) hoyo // *vt*: **to** ~ **out** ahuecar.

holly ['hɔlɪ] *n* acebo; ~**hock** *n* malva loca.

holster ['həulstə*] *n* pistolera.

holy ['həulɪ] *a* (*gen*) santo, sagrado; (*water*) bendito; **H**~ **Ghost** *or* **Spirit** *n* Espíritu *m* Santo.

homage ['hɔmɪdʒ] *n* homenaje *m*; **to pay** ~ **to** rendir homenaje a.

home [həum] *n* casa; (*country*) patria; (*institution*) asilo // *a* (*domestic*) casero, de casa; (*ECON, POL*) nacional // *ad* (*direction*) a casa; **at** ~ en casa; **to go/come** ~ ir/volver a casa; **make yourself at** ~ ¡estás en tu casa!; ~ **address** *n* señas *fpl*; ~ **land** *n* tierra natal; ~**less** *a* sin hogar, sin casa; ~**ly** *a* (*domestic*) casero; (*simple*) sencillo; ~-**made** *a* hecho en casa; ~ **rule** *n* autonomía; **H**~ **Secretary** *n* (*Brit*) Ministro del Interior; ~**sick** *a*: **to be** ~**sick** tener morriña, tener nostalgia; ~ **town** *n* ciudad *f* natal; ~**ward** ['həumwəd] *a* (*journey*) hacia casa; ~ **work** *n* tarea.

homicide ['hɔmɪsaɪd] *n* (*US*) homicidio.

homosexual [hɔməu'sɛksjuəl] *a*, *n* homosexual *m*.

honest ['ɔnɪst] *a* honrado; (*sincere*) franco, sincero; ~**ly** *ad* honradamente; francamente; ~**y** *n* honradez *f.*

honey ['hʌnɪ] *n* miel *f*; ~**comb** *n* panal *m*; (*pattern*) nido de abejas; ~**moon** *n* luna de miel; (*trip*) viaje *m* de novios.

honk [hɔŋk] *vi* (*AUT*) tocar la bocina.

honorary ['ɔnərərɪ] *a* no remunerado; (*duty, title*) honorario.

honour, honor (*US*) ['ɔnə*] *vt* honrar // *n* honor *m*, honra; ~**able** *a* honorable; ~**s degree** *n* (*SCOL*) título universitario.

hood [hud] *n* capucha; (*Brit: AUT*) capota; (*US: AUT*) capó *m*.

hoodlum ['hu:dləm] *n* matón *m*.

hoof [hu:f], *pl* **hooves** *n* pezuña.

hook [huk] *n* gancho; (*on dress*) corchete *m*, broche *m*; (*for fishing*) anzuelo // *vt* enganchar.

hooligan ['hu:lɪgən] *n* gamberro.

hoop [hu:p] *n* aro.

hoot [hu:t] *vi* (*AUT*) tocar la bocina; (*siren*) tocar la sirena // *n* bocinazo; toque *m* de sirena; **to** ~ **with laughter** morirse de risa; ~**er** *n* (*AUT*) bocina; (*NAUT*) sirena.

hooves [hu:vz] *pl of* **hoof.**

hop [hɔp] *vi* saltar, brincar; (*on one foot*) saltar con un pie // *n* salto, brinco.

hope [həup] *vt, vi* esperar // *n* esperanza; **I** ~ **so/not** espero que sí/no; ~**ful** *a* (*person*) optimista, lleno de esperanzas; (*situation*) prometedor(a); ~**fully** *ad* con optimismo, con esperanza; ~**less** *a* desesperado.

hops [hɔps] *npl* lúpulo *sg.*

horde [hɔːd] *n* horda.

horizon [hə'raɪzn] *n* horizonte *m*; ~**tal** [hɔrɪ'zɔntl] *a* horizontal.

hormone ['hɔːməun] *n* hormona.

horn [hɔːn] *n* cuerno; (*MUS*) trompa; (*AUT*) bocina; ~-**rimmed** de concha; ~**ed** *a* (*animal*) con cuernos.

hornet ['hɔːnɪt] *n* avispón *m*.

horny ['hɔːnɪ] *a* (*material*) córneo; (*hands*) calloso.

horoscope ['hɔrəskəup] *n* horóscopo.

horrible ['hɔrɪbl] *a* horrible.

horrid ['hɔrɪd] *a* horrible, horroroso.

horrify ['hɔrɪfaɪ] *vt* horrorizar.

horror ['hɔrə*] *n* horror *m*; ~ **film** *n* película de horror.

hors d'œuvre [ɔː'dəːvrə] *n* entremeses *mpl.*

horse [hɔːs] *n* caballo; **on** ~**back** *a* caballo; ~**man/woman** *n* jinete *m*/amazona; ~**power (h.p.)** *n* caballo (de fuerza); ~-**racing** *n* carreras *fpl* de caballos; ~**radish** *n* rábano picante; ~**shoe** *n* herradura.

horticulture ['hɔːtɪkʌltʃə*] *n* horticultura.

hose [həuz] *n* (*also*: ~ **pipe**) manga.

hosiery ['həuzɪərɪ] *n* calcetería.

hospitable ['hɔspɪtəbl] *a* hospitalario.

hospital ['hɔspɪtl] *n* hospital *m*.

hospitality [hɔspɪ'tælɪtɪ] *n* hospitalidad *f.*

host [həust] *n* anfitrión *m*; (*in hotel etc*) huésped *m*; (*large number*): **a** ~ **of** multitud de; (*REL*) hostia.

hostage ['hɔstɪdʒ] *n* rehén *m*.

hostel ['hɔstl] *n* hostal *m*; **youth** ~ *n* albergue *m* de juventud.

hostess ['həustɪs] *n* anfitriona; (*air* ~) azafata; (*in night-club*) cabaretera.

hostile ['hɔstaɪl] *a* hostil; **hostility** [-'stɪlɪtɪ] *n* hostilidad *f.*

hot [hɔt] *a* caliente; (*weather*) caluroso, de calor; (*as opposed to only warm*) muy caliente; (*spicy*) picante; (*fig*) ardiente, acalorado; ~ **dog** *n* perro caliente.

hotel [həu'tɛl] *n* hotel *m*; ~**ier** *n* hotelero.

hot: ~-**headed** *a* exaltado; ~**house** *n* invernadero; ~**ly** *ad* con pasión, apasionadamente; ~-**water bottle** *n* bolsa de agua caliente.

hound [haund] *vt* acosar // *n* perro de caza.

hour ['auə*] n hora; ~ly ad cada hora.
house [haus, pl: 'hauzɪz] n (also: firm) casa; (POL) cámara; (THEATRE) sala // vt [hauz] (person) alojar; **on the** ~ (fig) la casa invita; ~ **arrest** n arresto domiciliario; ~**boat** n casa flotante; ~**breaking** n robo (en una casa); ~**coat** n bata; ~**hold** n familia; ~**keeper** n ama de llaves; ~**keeping** n (work) trabajos domésticos mpl; ~**keeping** (**money**) dinero para gastos domésticos; ~-**warming party** n fiesta de estreno de casa; ~**wife** n ama de casa; ~**work** n faenas fpl (de la casa).
housing ['hauzɪŋ] n (act) alojamiento; (houses) viviendas fpl; ~ **estate** n bloque m de viviendas.
hovel ['hɔvl] n pocilga.
hover ['hɔvə*] vi flotar (en el aire); ~**craft** n hidroala m, aerodeslizador m.
how [hau] ad cómo; ~ **are you?** ¿cómo está Vd?, ¿cómo estás?; ~ **long have you been here?** ¿cuánto tiempo hace que estás aquí?; ~ **lovely!** ¡qué bonito!; ~ **many/much?** ¿cuántos/cuánto?; ~ **old are you?** ¿cuántos años tienes?; ~**ever** ad de cualquier manera; (+ adjective) por muy ... que; (in questions) cómo // conj sin embargo, no obstante.
howl [haul] n aullido // vi aullar.
h.p., H.P. abbr of **hire purchase; horse power.**
HQ abbr of **headquarters.**
hub [hʌb] n (of wheel) centro.
hubbub ['hʌbʌb] n barahúnda, barullo.
hubcap ['hʌbkæp] n tapacubo.
huddle ['hʌdl] vi: **to** ~ **together** amontonarse.
hue [hju:] n color m, matiz m; ~ **and cry** n alarma.
huff [hʌf] n: **in a** ~ con rabieta.
hug [hʌg] vt abrazar // n abrazo.
huge [hju:dʒ] a enorme.
hulk [hʌlk] n (wreck) barco viejo; (hull) casco.
hull [hʌl] n (of ship) casco.
hullo [hə'ləu] excl = **hello.**
hum [hʌm] vt tararear, canturrear // vi tararear, canturrear; (insect) zumbar // n zumbido.
human ['hju:mən] a, n humano.
humane [hju:'meɪn] a humano, humanitario.
humanity [hju:'mænɪtɪ] n humanidad f.
humble ['hʌmbl] a humilde // vt humillar; **humbly** ad humildemente.
humbug ['hʌmbʌg] n embustes mpl; (sweet) caramelo de menta.
humdrum ['hʌmdrʌm] a (boring) monótono, aburrido; (routine) rutinario.
humid ['hju:mɪd] a húmedo; ~**ity** [-'mɪdɪtɪ] n humedad f.
humiliate [hju:'mɪlɪeɪt] vt humillar; **humiliation** [-'eɪʃən] n humillación f.
humility [hju:'mɪlɪtɪ] n humildad f.
humorist ['hju:mərɪst] n humorista m/f.

humorous ['hju:mərəs] a gracioso, divertido.
humour, humor (US) ['hju:mə*] n humorismo, sentido del humor; (mood) humor m // vt (person) complacer.
hump [hʌmp] n (in ground) montículo; (camel's) giba.
hunch [hʌntʃ] n (premonition) presentimiento; ~**back** n joroba; ~**ed** a jorobado.
hundred ['hʌndrəd] num ciento; (before n) cien; ~**weight** n (Brit) = 50.8 kg; 112 lb; (US) = 45.3 kg; 100 lb.
hung [hʌŋ] pt, pp of **hang.**
Hungarian [hʌŋ'gɛərɪən] a, n húngaro/a.
Hungary ['hʌŋgərɪ] n Hungría.
hunger ['hʌŋgə*] n hambre f // vi: **to** ~ **for** (gen) tener hambre de; (desire) anhelar; ~ **strike** n huelga de hambre; **hungrily** [-grəlɪ] ad ávidamente, con ganas; **hungry** [-grɪ] a hambriento; **to be hungry** tener hambre.
hunt [hʌnt] vt (seek) buscar; (SPORT) cazar // vi cazar // n caza, cacería; ~**er** n cazador m; ~**ing** n caza.
hurdle ['hɜ:dl] n (SPORT) valla; (fig) obstáculo.
hurl [hɜ:l] vt lanzar, arrojar.
hurrah [hu'rɑ:], **hurray** [hu'reɪ] n ¡viva!, ¡vítor!
hurricane ['hʌrɪkən] n huracán m.
hurried ['hʌrɪd] a (fast) apresurado; (rushed) hecho de prisa; ~**ly** ad con prisa, apresuradamente.
hurry ['hʌrɪ] n prisa // vi apresurarse, darse prisa // vt (person) dar prisa a; (work) apresurar; **to be in a** ~ tener prisa.
hurt [hɜ:t], pt, pp **hurt** vt hacer daño a // vi doler // a lastimado; ~**ful** a (gen) dañoso; (remark) hiriente.
hurtle ['hɜ:tl] vi: **to** ~ **past** pasar como un rayo; **to** ~ **down** caer con violencia.
husband ['hʌzbənd] n marido.
hush [hʌʃ] n silencio // vt hacer callar; (cover up) encubrir; ~! ¡chitón!, ¡cállate!
husk [hʌsk] n (of wheat) cáscara.
husky ['hʌskɪ] a ronco; (burly) fornido // n perro esquimal.
hustle ['hʌsl] vt (push) empujar; (hurry) dar prisa a // n bullicio, actividad f febril; ~ **and bustle** n vaivén m.
hut [hʌt] n cabaña; (shed) cobertizo.
hutch [hʌtʃ] n conejera.
hyacinth ['haɪəsɪnθ] n jacinto.
hybrid ['haɪbrɪd] a, n híbrido.
hydrant ['haɪdrənt] n (also: **fire** ~) boca de incendios.
hydraulic [haɪ'drɔ:lɪk] a hidráulico.
hydroelectric [haɪdrəu'lɛktrɪk] a hidroeléctrico.
hydrogen ['haɪdrədʒən] n hidrógeno.
hyena [haɪ'i:nə] n hiena.
hygiene ['haɪdʒi:n] n higiene f; **hygienic** [-'dʒi:nɪk] a higiénico.
hymn [hɪm] n himno.

hyphen ['haɪfn] n guión m.

hypnosis [hɪp'nəusɪs] n hipnosis f; **hypnotic** [-'nɔtɪk] a hipnótico; **hypnotism** ['hɪpnətɪzm] n hipnotismo; **hypnotist** ['hɪpnətɪst] n hipnotista m/f; **hypnotize** ['hɪpnətaɪz] vt hipnotizar.

hypocrisy [hɪ'pɔkrɪsɪ] n hipocresía; **hypocrite** ['hɪpəkrɪt] n hipócrita m/f; **hypocritical** [hɪpə'krɪtɪkl] a hipócrita.

hypothesis [haɪ'pɔθɪsɪs], pl -ses [-si:z] n hipótesis f; **hypothetic(al)** [-pəu'θεtɪk(l)] a hipotético.

hysteria [hɪ'stɪərɪə] n histeria; **hysterical** [-'stεrɪkl] a histérico; **hysterics** [-'stεrɪks] npl histeria sg, histerismo sg.

I

I [aɪ] pron yo.

ice [aɪs] n hielo // vt (cake) alcorzar; (drink) helar // vi (also: ~ over, ~ up) helarse; ~ **age** n período glacial; ~ **axe** n piolet m; ~**berg** n iceberg m; ~**box** n (US) nevera; ~**-cold** a helado; ~ **cream** n helado; ~ **cube** n cubito de hielo; ~ **hockey** n hockey m sobre hielo.

Iceland ['aɪslənd] n Islandia; ~**er** n islandés/esa m/f; ~**ic** [-'lændɪk] a islandés(esa).

ice: ~ **rink** n pista de hielo; ~ **skating** n patinaje m sobre hielo.

icicle ['aɪsɪkl] n carámbano.

icing ['aɪsɪŋ] n (CULIN) alcorza, garapiña; (AVIAT etc) formación f de hielo; ~ **sugar** n azúcar m de alcorza.

icon ['aɪkɔn] n ícono.

icy ['aɪsɪ] a (road) helado; (fig) glacial.

I'd [aɪd] = **I would; I had.**

idea [aɪ'dɪə] n idea.

ideal [aɪ'dɪəl] n ideal m // a ideal; ~**ist** n idealista m/f.

identical [aɪ'dεntɪkl] a idéntico.

identification [aɪdεntɪfɪ'keɪʃən] n identificación f; **means of** ~ documentos mpl personales.

identify [aɪ'dεntɪfaɪ] vt identificar.

identikit picture [aɪ'dεntɪkɪt-] n retrato-robot m.

identity [aɪ'dεntɪtɪ] n identidad f.

ideological [aɪdɪə'lɔdʒɪkəl] a ideológico; **ideology** [-dɪ'ɔlədʒɪ] n ideología.

idiocy ['ɪdɪəsɪ] n idiotez f; (stupid act) estupidez f.

idiom ['ɪdɪəm] n modismo; (style of speaking) lenguaje m.

idiosyncrasy [ɪdɪəu'sɪŋkrəsɪ] n idiosincrasia.

idiot ['ɪdɪət] n (gen) idiota m/f; (fool) tonto/a; ~**ic** [-'ɔtɪk] a idiota; tonto.

idle ['aɪdl] a (gen) ocioso; (lazy) holgazán(ana); (unemployed) desocupado; (pointless) inútil // vi (machine) marchar en vacío // vt: **to** ~ **away the time** malgastar el tiempo; ~**ness** n ociosidad f; holgazanería; desocupación f.

idol ['aɪdl] n ídolo; ~**ize** vt idolatrar.

if [ɪf] conj si.

igloo ['ɪglu:] n iglú m.

ignite [ɪg'naɪt] vt encender; (set fire to) incendiar // vi encenderse.

ignition [ɪg'nɪʃən] n (AUT) encendido; **to switch on/off the** ~ encender/apagar el motor; ~ **key** n (AUT) llave f de contacto.

ignorance ['ɪgnərəns] n ignorancia; **ignorant** [-ənt] a ignorante; **to be ignorant of** ignorar.

ignore [ɪg'nɔ:*] vt (person) no hacer caso de; (fact) pasar por alto.

I'll [aɪl] = **I will, I shall.**

ill [ɪl] a enfermo, malo; (bad) malo // n mal m; (fig) infortunio // ad mal; **to take** or **be taken** ~ ponerse enfermo, enfermar; ~**-advised** a poco recomendable; (misled) mal aconsejado; ~**-at-ease** a incómodo.

illegal [ɪ'li:gl] a ilegal.

illegible [ɪ'lεdʒɪbl] a ilegible.

illegitimate [ɪlɪ'dʒɪtɪmət] a ilegítimo.

ill: ~**-fated** a malogrado; ~ **feeling** n rencor m.

illicit [ɪ'lɪsɪt] a ilícito.

illiterate [ɪ'lɪtərət] a analfabeto.

ill-mannered [ɪl'mænəd] a mal educado.

illness ['ɪlnɪs] n enfermedad f.

illogical [ɪ'lɔdʒɪkl] a ilógico.

ill-treat [ɪl'tri:t] vt maltratar.

illuminate [ɪ'lu:mɪneɪt] vt (room, street) iluminar, alumbrar; (subject) aclarar; **illumination** [-'neɪʃən] n alumbrado; **illuminations** npl luminarias fpl.

illusion [ɪ'lu:ʒən] n ilusión f; **to be under the** ~ **that...** estar bajo la ilusión de que...; **illusory** [-səri] a ilusorio.

illustrate ['ɪləstreɪt] vt (gen) ilustrar; (subject) aclarar; (point) poner ejemplos a; **illustration** [-'streɪʃən] n (example) ejemplo; (explanation) aclaración f; (in book) lámina.

illustrious [ɪ'lʌstrɪəs] a ilustre.

ill will [ɪl'wɪl] n rencor m.

I'm [aɪm] = **I am.**

image ['ɪmɪdʒ] n imagen f.

imaginary [ɪ'mædʒɪnərɪ] a imaginario; **imagination** [-'neɪʃən] n imaginación f; (inventiveness) inventiva; (illusion) fantasía; **imaginative** [-nətɪv] a imaginativo; **imagine** vt imaginarse; (delude o.s.) hacerse la ilusión (de que).

imbalance [ɪm'bæləns] n (gen) desequilibrio; (inequality) falta de correspondencia.

imbecile ['ɪmbəsi:l] n imbécil m/f.

imbue [ɪm'bju:] vt: **to** ~ **sth with** imbuir algo de.

imitate ['ɪmɪteɪt] vt imitar; **imitation** [-'teɪʃən] n imitación f; (copy) copia; (mimicry) mímica.

immaculate [ɪ'mækjulət] a perfectamente limpio; (REL) inmaculado.

immaterial [ɪmə'tɪərɪəl] a incorpóreo; **it is** ~ **whether...** no importa si... .

immature [ɪmə'tjuə*] a (person) poco
maduro; (of one's youth) juvenil.
immediate [ɪ'miːdɪət] a inmediato;
(pressing) urgente, apremiante; ~ly ad
(at once) en seguida; ~ly next to muy
junto a.
immense [ɪ'mɛns] a inmenso, enorme.
immerse [ɪ'məːs] vt (submerge) sumergir;
(sink) hundir; to be ~d in (fig) estar
absorto en.
immersion heater [ɪ'məːʃn-] n
calentador m de inmersión.
immigrant ['ɪmɪgrənt] n inmigrante m/f;
immigrate [-greɪt] vi inmigrar;
immigration [-'greɪʃən] n inmigración f.
imminent ['ɪmɪnənt] a inminente.
immobile [ɪ'məubaɪl] a inmóvil;
immobilize [-bɪlaɪz] vt inmovilizar.
immoral [ɪ'mɔrl] a inmoral; ~ity [-'rælɪtɪ]
n inmoralidad f.
immortal [ɪ'mɔːtl] a inmortal; ~ize vt
inmortalizar.
immune [ɪ'mjuːn] a: ~ (to) inmune
(contra); immunity n (MED) inmunidad f;
(COMM) exención f.
immunization [ɪmjunaɪ'zeɪʃən] n
inmunización f; immunize ['ɪmjunaɪz] vt
inmunizar.
imp [ɪmp] n diablillo.
impact ['ɪmpækt] n (gen) impacto.
impair [ɪm'pɛə*] vt perjudicar.
impale [ɪm'peɪl] vt atravesar.
impart [ɪm'pɑːt] vt comunicar.
impartial [ɪm'pɑːʃl] a imparcial; ~ity
[ɪmpɑːʃɪ'ælɪtɪ] n imparcialidad f.
impassable [ɪm'pɑːsəbl] a (barrier)
infranqueable; (river) invadeable; (road)
intransitable.
impatience [ɪm'peɪʃəns] n impaciencia;
impatient [-ənt] a impaciente; to get or
grow impatient impacientarse.
impeccable [ɪm'pɛkəbl] a impecable.
impede [ɪm'piːd] vt estorbar, dificultar.
impediment [ɪm'pɛdɪmənt] n obstáculo,
estorbo; (also: speech ~) defecto (del
habla).
impending [ɪm'pɛndɪŋ] a (near) próximo.
impenetrable [ɪm'pɛnɪtrəbl] a (gen)
impenetrable; (unfathomable) insondable.
imperative [ɪm'pɛrətɪv] a (tone)
imperioso; (necessary) indispensable;
(pressing) urgente // n (LING) imperativo.
imperceptible [ɪmpə'sɛptɪbl] a
imperceptible, insensible.
imperfect [ɪm'pəːfɪkt] a imperfecto;
(goods etc) defectuoso; ~ion [-'fɛkʃən] n
(blemish) desperfecto; (state)
imperfección f.
imperial [ɪm'pɪərɪəl] a imperial; ~ism n
imperialismo.
imperil [ɪm'pɛrɪl] vt arriesgar, poner en
peligro.
impersonal [ɪm'pəːsənl] a impersonal.
impersonate [ɪm'pəːsəneɪt] vt hacerse
pasar por; (THEATRE) imitar.

impertinent [ɪm'pəːtɪnənt] a impertinente, insolente.
impervious [ɪm'pəːvɪəs] a impermeable;
(fig): ~ to insensible a.
impetuous [ɪm'pɛtjuəs] a impetuoso,
irreflexivo.
impetus ['ɪmpətəs] n ímpetu m; (fig)
impulso.
impinge [ɪm'pɪndʒ]: to ~ on vt fus
invadir, abusar de; (affect) afectar a.
implausible [ɪm'plɔːzɪbl] a inverosímil.
implement ['ɪmplɪmənt] n instrumento,
herramienta // vt ['ɪmplɪmɛnt] hacer
efectivo; (carry out) realizar.
implicate ['ɪmplɪkeɪt] vt (compromise)
comprometer; (involve) enredar;
implication [-'keɪʃən] n consecuencia,
implicancia (AM).
implicit [ɪm'plɪsɪt] a (gen) implícito;
(complete) absoluto.
implore [ɪm'plɔː*] vt (person) suplicar.
imply [ɪm'plaɪ] vt (involve) implicar;
(mean) significar; (hint) dar a entender
que; it is implied se sobreentiende.
impolite [ɪmpə'laɪt] a mal educado.
import [ɪm'pɔːt] vt importar // n ['ɪmpɔːt]
(COMM) importación f; (: article) artículo
importado; (meaning) significado, sentido.
importance [ɪm'pɔːtəns] n importancia;
important [-ənt] a importante; it's not
important no importa, no tiene
importancia.
importer [ɪm'pɔːtə*] n importador/a m/f.
impose [ɪm'pəuz] vt imponer // vi: to ~
on sb abusar de uno; imposing a
imponente, impresionante.
impossible [ɪm'pɔsɪbl] a imposible;
(person) insoportable.
impostor [ɪm'pɔstə*] n impostor/a m/f.
impotence ['ɪmpətəns] n impotencia;
impotent [-ənt] a impotente.
impound [ɪm'paund] vt embargar.
impoverished [ɪm'pɔvərɪʃt] a necesitado;
(land) agotado.
impracticable [ɪm'præktɪkəbl] a no
factible, irrealizable.
impractical [ɪm'præktɪkl] a (person) poco
práctico.
imprecise [ɪmprɪ'saɪs] a impreciso.
impregnable [ɪm'prɛgnəbl] a
invulnerable; (castle) inexpugnable.
impregnate ['ɪmprɛgneɪt] vt (gen)
impregnar; (soak) empapar; (fertilize)
fecundar.
impresario [ɪmprɪ'sɑːrɪəu] n empresario.
impress [ɪm'prɛs] vt impresionar; (mark)
estampar // vi hacer buena impresión; to
~ sth on sb convencer a uno de algo; it
~ed itself on me se me grabó (en la
memoria).
impression [ɪm'prɛʃən] n impresión f;
(footprint etc) huella; (print run) edición f;
to be under the ~ that tener la
impresión de que; ~able a influenciable;
(sensitive) sensible; ~ist n impresionista
m/f.
impressive [ɪm'prɛsɪv] a impresionante.

imprint ['ımprınt] *n* impresión *f*, huella.
imprison [ım'prızn] *vt* encarcelar;
~ment *n* encarcelamiento, cárcel *f*.
improbable [ım'prɔbəbl] *a* improbable,
inverosímil.
impromptu [ım'prɔmptju:] *a* improvisado
// *ad* de improviso.
improper [ım'prɔpə*] *a* (*incorrect*)
impropio; (*unseemly*) indecoroso;
(*indecent*) indecente.
impropriety [ımprə'praıətı] *n* falta de
decoro; (*indecency*) indecencia; (*of
language*) impropiedad *f*.
improve [ım'pru:v] *vt* mejorar // *vi*
mejorarse; (*become perfect*) per-
feccionarse; (*pupils*) hacer progresos;
~ment *n* mejoramiento; perfección *f*;
progreso.
improvise ['ımprəvaız] *vt, vi* improvisar.
imprudent [ım'pru:dnt] *a* imprudente.
impudent ['ımpjudnt] *a* descarado,
insolente.
impulse ['ımpʌls] *n* impulso; **to act on** ~
obrar sin reflexión; **impulsive** [-'pʌlsıv] *a*
irreflexivo.
impunity [ım'pju:nıtı] *n*: **with** ~
impunemente.
impure [ım'pjuə*] *a* (*adulterated*)
adulterado; (*not pure*) impuro; **impurity** *n*
(*gen*) impureza.
in [ın] *prep* en; (*within*) dentro de; (*with
time: during, within*): ~ **2 days** en 2 días;
(: *after*): ~ **2 weeks** dentro de 2
semanas; (*with town, country*): **it's** ~
France está en Francia // *ad* dentro,
adentro; (*fashionable*) de moda; **is he** ~?
¿está en casa?; ~ **the country** en el
campo; ~ **the distance** a lo lejos; ~
town en el centro (de la ciudad); ~ **the
sun** al sol, bajo el sol; ~ **the rain** bajo la
lluvia; ~ **French** en francés; 1 ~ 10 uno
sobre 10, uno de cada 10; ~ **hundreds**
por centenares; **the best pupil** ~ **the
class** el mejor alumno de la clase;
written ~ **pencil** escrito con lápiz; ~
saying this al decir esto; **their party is**
~ su partido ha llegado al poder; **to ask
sb** ~ invitar a uno a entrar; **to run/limp**
~ entrar corriendo/cojeando; **the** ~**s
and outs** los recovecos.
in., ins *abbr of* **inch(es)**.
inability [ınə'bılıtı] *n* incapacidad *f*.
inaccessible [ınək'sɛsıbl] *a* inaccesible.
inaccuracy [ın'ækjurəsı] *n* inexactitud *f*;
inaccurate [-rət] *a* inexacto, incorrecto.
inactivity [ınæk'tıvıtı] *n* inactividad *f*.
inadequate [ın'ædıkwət] *a* (*insufficient*)
insuficiente; (*unsuitable*) inadecuado;
(*person*) incapaz.
inadvertently [ınəd'və:tntlı] *ad* por
equivocación *o* descuido.
inadvisable [ınəd'vaızəbl] *a* no
aconsejable.
inane [ı'neın] *a* necio, fatuo.
inanimate [ın'ænımət] *a* inanimado.
inapplicable [ın'æplıkəbl] *a* inaplicable.
inappropriate [ınə'prəuprıət] *a*

inoportuno, inconveniente; (*word,
expression*) impropio.
inapt [ın'æpt] *a* impropio; ~**itude** *n*
incapacitad *f*.
inarticulate [ına:'tıkjulət] *a* (*person*)
incapaz de expresarse; (*speech*)
inarticulado.
inasmuch as [ınəz'mʌtʃæz] *ad* (*given that*)
puesto que; (*since*) ya que.
inattentive [ınə'tɛntıv] *a* distraído.
inaudible [ın'ɔ:dıbl] *a* inaudible.
inaugural [ı'nɔ:gjurəl] *a* (*speech*) de
apertura; **inaugurate** [-reıt] *vt* inaugurar;
inauguration [-'reıʃən] *n* ceremonia de
apertura.
in-between [ınbı'twi:n] *a* intermedio, de
entre medio.
inborn [ın'bɔ:n] *a* (*feeling*) innato.
inbred [ın'brɛd] *a* innato; (*family*)
engendrado por endogamia.
incalculable [ın'kælkjuləbl] *a*
incalculable.
incapable [ın'keıpəbl] *a* incapaz.
incapacitate [ınkə'pæsıteıt] *vt*: **to** ~ **sb**
incapacitar a uno.
incapacity [ınkə'pæsıtı] *n* (*inability*)
incapacidad *f*.
incarcerate [ın'ka:səreıt] *vt* encarcelar.
incarnate [ın'ka:nıt] *a* en persona // *vt*
['ınka:neıt] encarnar; **incarnation**
[-'neıʃən] *n* encarnación *f*.
incendiary [ın'sɛndıərı] *a* incendiario.
incense ['ınsɛns] *n* incienso // *vt* [ın'sɛns]
(*anger*) indignar, encolerizar.
incentive [ın'sɛntıv] *n* incentivo, estímulo.
incessant [ın'sɛsnt] *a* incesante, continuo;
~**ly** *ad* constantemente.
incest ['ınsɛst] *n* incesto.
inch [ıntʃ] *n* pulgada; **to be within an** ~
of estar a dos dedos de; **he didn't give an**
~ no dio concesión alguna; **to** ~
forward avanzar palmo a palmo.
incidence ['ınsıdns] *n* (*of crime, disease*)
frecuencia.
incident ['ınsıdnt] *n* incidente *m*, suceso;
(*in book*) episodio.
incidental [ınsı'dɛntl] *a* no esencial,
accesorio; (*unplanned*) fortuito; ~ **to** al
margen de; ~**ly** [-'dɛntəlı] *ad* (*by the way*)
a propósito.
incinerator [ın'sınəreıtə*] *n* incinerador
m.
incipient [ın'sıpıənt] *a* incipiente.
incision [ın'sıʒən] *n* corte *m*.
incisive [ın'saısıv] *a* (*mind*) penetrante;
(*tone*) mordaz; (*remark etc*) tajante.
incite [ın'saıt] *vt* provocar.
inclination [ınklı'neıʃən] *n* (*tendency*)
tendencia, inclinación *f*.
incline ['ınklaın] *n* pendiente *m*, cuesta //
(*vb*: [ın'klaın]) *vt* (*slope*) inclinar; (*head*)
poner de lado // *vi* inclinarse; **to be** ~**d
to** (*tend*) ser propenso a; (*be willing*) estar
dispuesto a.
include [ın'klu:d] *vt* incluir, comprender;

(*in letter*) adjuntar; **including** *prep* incluso, inclusive.

inclusion [ɪn'kluː3ən] *n* inclusión *f*; **inclusive** [-sɪv] *a* inclusivo // *ad* inclusive.

incognito [ɪnkɒg'niːtəʊ] *ad* de incógnito.

incoherent [ɪnkəʊ'hɪərənt] *a* incoherente.

income ['ɪŋkʌm] *n* (*personal*) ingresos *mpl*; (*from property etc*) renta; (*profit*) rédito; ~ **tax** *n* impuesto sobre la renta; ~ **tax inspector** *n* inspector/a *m/f* fiscal; ~ **tax return** *n* registro fiscal.

incoming ['ɪnkʌmɪŋ] *a*: ~ **flight** vuelo entrante.

incomparable [ɪn'kɒmpərəbl] *a* incomparable, sin par.

incompatible [ɪnkəm'pætɪbl] *a* incompatible.

incompetence [ɪn'kɒmpɪtəns] *n* incompetencia; **incompetent** [-ənt] *a* incompetente.

incomplete [ɪnkəm'pliːt] *a* incompleto; (*unfinished*) sin terminar.

incomprehensible [ɪnkɒmprɪ'hɛnsɪbl] *a* incomprensible.

inconceivable [ɪnkən'siːvəbl] *a* inconcebible.

inconclusive [ɪnkən'kluːsɪv] *a* sin resultado (definitivo); (*argument*) poco convincente.

incongruous [ɪn'kɒŋgruəs] *a* (*foolish*) absurdo, estrafalario; (*remark, act*) disonante, nada lógico.

inconsiderate [ɪnkən'sɪdərət] *a* desconsiderado; **how ~ of him!** ¡qué falta de consideración (de su parte)!

inconsistent [ɪnkən'sɪstnt] *a* inconsecuente; ~ **with** (que) no concuerda con.

inconspicuous [ɪnkən'spɪkjuəs] *a* poco llamativo, modesto; **to make o.s.** ~ no llamar la atención.

inconstant [ɪn'kɒnstnt] *a* inconstante.

incontinent [ɪn'kɒntɪnənt] *a* incontinente.

inconvenience [ɪnkən'viːnjəns] *n* (*gen*) inconvenientes *mpl*; (*trouble*) molestia, incomodidad *f* // *vt* incomodar; **inconvenient** [-ənt] *a* incómodo, poco práctico; (*time, place*) inoportuno.

incorporate [ɪn'kɔːpəreɪt] *vt* incorporar; (*contain*) comprender; (*add*) agregar; ~**d** *a*: ~**d company** (*US: abbr* **Inc.**) Sociedad Anónima (S.A.).

incorrect [ɪnkə'rɛkt] *a* incorrecto.

incorruptible [ɪnkə'rʌptɪbl] *a* (*gen*) incorruptible; (*not open to bribes*) insobornable.

increase ['ɪnkriːs] *n* aumento // *vi* [ɪn-'kriːs] aumentarse; (*grow*) crecer; (*price*) subir; **increasing** *a* (*number*) creciente, en aumento; **increasingly** *ad* de más en más, cada vez más.

incredible [ɪn'krɛdɪbl] *a* increíble.

incredulous [ɪn'krɛdjuləs] *a* incrédulo.

increment ['ɪnkrɪmənt] *n* aumento, incremento.

incriminate [ɪn'krɪmɪneɪt] *vt* incriminar.

incubation [ɪnkju'beɪʃən] *n* incubación *f*;

incubator ['ɪnkjubeɪtə*] *n* incubadora.

incumbent [ɪn'kʌmbənt] *n* ocupante *m/f* // *a*: **it is** ~ **on him to...** le incumbe... .

incur [ɪn'kə:*] *vt* (*expenses*) contraer; (*gen*) incurrir en.

incurable [ɪn'kjuərəbl] *a* incurable; (*fig*) irremediable.

incursion [ɪn'kə:ʃən] *n* incursión *f*.

indebted [ɪn'dɛtɪd] *a*: **to be** ~ **to sb** estar en deuda con uno.

indecent [ɪn'diːsnt] *a* indecente; ~ **assault** *n* atentado contra el pudor; ~ **exposure** *n* exhibicionismo.

indecisive [ɪndɪ'saɪsɪv] *a* indeciso; (*discussion*) no resuelto, inconcluyente.

indeed [ɪn'diːd] *ad* de hecho, realmente; **yes** ~! claro que sí.

indefinite [ɪn'dɛfɪnɪt] *a* indefinido; (*uncertain*) incierto; ~**ly** *ad* (*wait*) indefinidamente.

indelible [ɪn'dɛlɪbl] *a* imborrable.

indemnify [ɪn'dɛmnɪfaɪ] *vt* indemnizar, resarcir.

indentation [ɪndɛn'teɪʃən] *n* mella; (*TYP*) sangría.

independence [ɪndɪ'pɛndns] *n* independencia; **independent** [-ənt] *a* independiente; **to become independent** independizarse.

index ['ɪndɛks] *n* (*pl*: ~**es**: *in book*) índice *m*; (: *in library etc*) catálogo; (*pl*: **indices** ['ɪndɪsiːz]: *ratio, sign*) exponente *m*; ~ **card** *n* ficha; ~ **finger** *n* índice *m*; ~**-linked** *a* vinculado al índice del coste de la vida.

India ['ɪndɪə] *n* la India; ~**n** *a, n* indio/a; **Red** ~**n** piel roja *m/f*.

indicate ['ɪndɪkeɪt] *vt* indicar; **indication** [-'keɪʃən] *n* indicio, señal *f*; **indicator** *n* (*gen*) indicador *m*.

indices ['ɪndɪsiːz] *pl of* **index**.

indict [ɪn'daɪt] *vt* acusar; ~**ment** *n* acusación *f*.

indifference [ɪn'dɪfrəns] *n* indiferencia; **indifferent** [-ənt] *a* indiferente, (*poor*) regular.

indigenous [ɪn'dɪdʒɪnəs] *a* indígena *inv*.

indigestion [ɪndɪ'dʒɛstʃən] *n* indigestión *f*, empacho.

indignant [ɪn'dɪgnənt] *a*: **to be** ~ **about sth** indignarse por algo; **indignation** [-'neɪʃən] *n* indignación *f*.

indignity [ɪn'dɪgnɪtɪ] *n* indignidad *f*; (*insult*) ultraje *m*, afrenta.

indigo ['ɪndɪgəʊ] *a* color de añil // *n* añil *m*.

indirect [ɪndɪ'rɛkt] *a* indirecto; ~**ly** *ad* indirectamente.

indiscreet [ɪndɪ'skriːt] *a* indiscreto; (*rash*) imprudente; **indiscretion** [-'skrɛʃən] *n* indiscreción *f*; imprudencia.

indiscriminate [ɪndɪ'skrɪmɪnət] *a* indistinto.

indispensable [ɪndɪ'spɛnsəbl] *a* indispensable, imprescindible.

indisposed [ɪndɪ'spəʊzd] *a* (*unwell*) indispuesto.

indisputable [ɪndɪ'spju:təbl] *a* incontestable.

indistinct [ɪndɪ'stɪŋkt] *a* indistinto; (*memory, noise*) confuso.

individual [ɪndɪ'vɪdjuəl] *n* individuo // *a* individual; (*personal*) personal; (*for/of one only*) particular; ~**ist** *n* individualista *m/f*; ~**ity** [-'ælɪtɪ] *n* individualidad *f*; ~**ly** *ad* individualmente; particularmente.

indoctrinate [ɪn'dɔktrɪneɪt] *vt* adoctrinar; **indoctrination** [-'neɪʃən] *n* adoctrinamiento.

indolent ['ɪndələnt] *a* indolente, perezoso.

indoor ['ɪndɔ:*] *a* (*inner*) interior; (*household*) de casa; (*inside*) de puertas adentro; (*swimming-pool*) cubierto; (*games*) de salón; (*sport*) bajo cubierta; ~**s** [ɪn'dɔ:z] *ad* dentro; (*at home*) en casa.

induce [ɪn'dju:s] *vt* inducir; (*bring about*) producir; (*provoke*) provocar; ~**ment** *n* (*incentive*) incentivo, aliciente *m*.

induction [ɪn'dʌkʃən] *n* (MED. *of birth*) inducción *f*; ~ **course** *n* curso de inducción.

indulge [ɪn'dʌldʒ] *vt* (*desire*) dar rienda suelta a; (*whim*) condescender con; (*person*) complacer; (*child*) consentir // *vi*: **to** ~ **in** darse el lujo de; **indulgence** *n* (*of desire*) gratificación *f*; (*leniency*) complacencia; **indulgent** *a* indulgente.

industrial [ɪn'dʌstrɪəl] *a* industrial; ~ **action** *n* huelga; ~ **estate** *n* zona industrial; ~**ist** *n* industrial *m/f*; ~**ize** *vt* industrializar.

industrious [ɪn'dʌstrɪəs] *a* (*gen*) trabajador(a); (*student*) aplicado.

industry ['ɪndəstrɪ] *n* industria; (*diligence*) aplicación *f*.

inebriated [ɪ'ni:brɪeɪtɪd] *a* borracho.

inedible [ɪn'ɛdɪbl] *a* incomible; (*plant etc*) no comestible.

ineffective [ɪnɪ'fɛktɪv] *a* ineficaz, inútil.

inefficiency [ɪnɪ'fɪʃənsɪ] *n* ineficacia; **inefficient** [-ənt] *a* ineficaz, ineficiente.

ineligible [ɪn'ɛlɪdʒɪbl] *a* (*candidate*) inelegible; **to be** ~ **for sth** no tener derecho a algo.

inept [ɪ'nɛpt] *a* incompetente, incapaz.

inequality [ɪnɪ'kwɔlɪtɪ] *n* desigualdad *f*.

inert [ɪ'nə:t] *a* inerte, inactivo; (*immobile*) inmóvil; ~**ia** [ɪ'nə:ʃə] *n* inercia; (*laziness*) pereza.

inescapable [ɪnɪ'skeɪpəbl] *a* ineludible.

inestimable [ɪn'ɛstɪməbl] *a* inestimable.

inevitable [ɪn'ɛvɪtəbl] *a* inevitable; (*necessary*) forzoso.

inexcusable [ɪnɪks'kju:zəbl] *a* imperdonable.

inexhaustible [ɪnɪg'zɔ:stɪbl] *a* inagotable.

inexorable [ɪn'ɛksərəbl] *a* inexorable, implacable.

inexpensive [ɪnɪk'spɛnsɪv] *a* económico.

inexperience [ɪnɪk'spɪərɪəns] *n* falta de experiencia; ~**d** *a* inexperto.

inexplicable [ɪnɪk'splɪkəbl] *a* inexplicable.

inextricable [ɪnɪk'strɪkəbl] *a* inextricable.

infallible [ɪn'fælɪbl] *a* infalible.

infamous ['ɪnfəməs] *a* infame; **infamy** [-mɪ] *n* infamia.

infancy ['ɪnfənsɪ] *n* infancia.

infant ['ɪnfənt] *n* (*baby*) criatura; (*young child*) niño/a; ~**ile** *a* infantil; (*pej*) aniñado; ~ **school** *n* escuela de párvulos.

infantry ['ɪnfəntrɪ] *n* infantería; ~**man** *n* soldado (de infantería).

infatuated [ɪn'fætjueɪtɪd] *a*: ~ **with** (*gen*) encaprichado por; (*in love*) enamorado de; **infatuation** [-'eɪʃən] *n* encaprichamiento; enamoramiento.

infect [ɪn'fɛkt] *vt* (*wound*) infectar; (*person*) contagiar; (*fig: pej*) corromper; ~**ed with** (*illness*) contagiado de; ~**ion** [ɪn'fɛkʃən] *n* infección *f*; (*fig*) contagio; ~**ious** [ɪn'fɛkʃəs] *a* contagioso; (*also: fig*) infeccioso.

infer [ɪn'fə:*] *vt* deducir, inferir; ~**ence** ['ɪnfərəns] *n* deducción *f*, inferencia.

inferior [ɪn'fɪərɪə*] *a, n* inferior *m/f*; ~**ity** [-rɪ'ɔrətɪ] *n* inferioridad *f*; ~**ity complex** *n* complejo de inferioridad.

infernal [ɪn'fə:nl] *a* infernal.

inferno [ɪn'fə:nəu] *n* infierno; (*fig*) hoguera.

infertile [ɪn'fə:taɪl] *a* estéril, infecundo; **infertility** [-'tɪlɪtɪ] *n* esterilidad *f*, infecundidad *f*.

infested [ɪn'fɛstɪd] *a*: ~ **(with)** plagado (de).

infidelity [ɪnfɪ'dɛlɪtɪ] *n* infidelidad *f*.

in-fighting ['ɪnfaɪtɪŋ] *n* (*fig*) luchas *fpl* internas.

infiltrate ['ɪnfɪltreɪt] *vt* (*troops etc*) infiltrarse en // *vi* infiltrarse.

infinite ['ɪnfɪnɪt] *a* infinito.

infinitive [ɪn'fɪnɪtɪv] *n* infinitivo.

infinity [ɪn'fɪnɪtɪ] *n* (*also* MATH) infinito; (*an* ~) infinidad *f*.

infirm [ɪn'fə:m] *a* enfermo, débil; ~**ary** *n* hospital *m*; ~**ity** *n* debilidad *f*; (*illness*) enfermedad *f*, achaque *m*.

inflame [ɪn'fleɪm] *vt* inflamar.

inflammable [ɪn'flæməbl] *a* inflamable; (*explosive*) explosivo.

inflammation [ɪnflə'meɪʃən] *n* inflamación *f*.

inflate [ɪn'fleɪt] *vt* (*tyre, balloon*) inflar; (*fig*) hinchar; ~**d** *a* (*style*) exagerado; (*value*) excesivo; **inflation** [ɪn'fleɪʃən] *n* (ECON) inflación *f*; **inflationary** [ɪn'fleɪʃnərɪ] *a* inflacionario.

inflexible [ɪn'flɛksɪbl] *a* inflexible.

inflict [ɪn'flɪkt] *vt*: **to** ~ **on** infligir en; (*tax etc*) imponer a; ~**ion** [ɪn'flɪkʃən] *n* imposición *f*.

inflow ['ɪnfləu] *n* afluencia *f*.

influence ['ɪnfluəns] *n* influencia // *vt* influir en, influenciar; (*persuade*) sugestionar; **under the** ~ **of alcohol** en estado de embriaguez; **influential** [-'ɛnʃl] *a* influyente.

influenza [ɪnflu'ɛnzə] *n* gripe *f*.

influx ['ɪnflʌks] *n* afluencia.

inform [ɪn'fɔːm] vt: to ~ sb of sth informar a uno sobre o de algo; (warn) avisar a uno de algo; (communicate) comunicar algo a uno // vi soplar; to ~ on sb delatar a uno.

informal [ɪn'fɔːml] a (person, manner) desenvuelto; (tone) familiar; (visit, discussion) extraoficial; (intimate) de confianza; ~ity [-'mælɪtɪ] n falta de ceremonia; (intimacy) intimidad f; (familiarity) familiaridad f; (ease) afabilidad f.

information [ɪnfə'meɪʃən] n información f, informes mpl; (news) noticias fpl; (knowledge) conocimientos mpl; (LAW) delatación f; **a piece of** ~ un dato.

informative [ɪn'fɔːmətɪv] a informativo.

informer [ɪn'fɔːmə*] n delator/a m/f; (also: **police** ~) soplón/ona m/f.

infra-red [ɪnfrə'rɛd] a infrarrojo.

infrequent [ɪn'friːkwənt] a infrecuente.

infringe [ɪn'frɪndʒ] vt infringir, violar // vi: **to** ~ **on** invadir, abusar de; ~**ment** n infracción f; (of rights) invasión f; (SPORT) falta.

infuriate [ɪn'fjuərɪeɪt] vt enfurecer; **infuriating** a enloquecedor(a).

ingenious [ɪn'dʒiːnjəs] a ingenioso; **ingenuity** [-dʒɪ'njuːɪtɪ] n ingeniosidad f.

ingenuous [ɪn'dʒɛnjuəs] a ingenuo.

ingot ['ɪŋgət] n lingote m, barra.

ingrained [ɪn'greɪnd] a arraigado.

ingratiate [ɪn'greɪʃɪeɪt] vt: **to** ~ **o.s. with** congraciarse con.

ingratitude [ɪn'grætɪtjuːd] n ingratitud f.

ingredient [ɪn'griːdɪənt] n ingrediente m.

inhabit [ɪn'hæbɪt] vt habitar, vivir en; (occupy) ocupar; ~**ant** n habitante m/f.

inhale [ɪn'heɪl] vt inhalar // vi (in smoking) aspirar.

inherent [ɪn'hɪərənt] a: ~ **in** or **to** inherente a.

inherit [ɪn'hɛrɪt] vt heredar; ~**ance** n herencia; (fig) patrimonio.

inhibit [ɪn'hɪbɪt] vt inhibir, impedir; **to** ~ **sb from doing sth** impedir a uno hacer algo; ~**ion** [-'bɪʃən] n inhibición f.

inhospitable [ɪnhɔs'pɪtəbl] a (person) inhospitalario; (place) inhóspito.

inhuman [ɪn'hjuːmən] a inhumano.

inimitable [ɪ'nɪmɪtəbl] a inimitable.

iniquity [ɪ'nɪkwɪtɪ] n inicuidad f; (injustice) injusticia.

initial [ɪ'nɪʃl] a inicial; (first) primero // n inicial f // vt firmar con las iniciales; ~**s** npl iniciales fpl; (abbreviation) siglas fpl; ~**ly** ad al principio, en primer lugar.

initiate [ɪ'nɪʃɪeɪt] vt (start) iniciar, dar comienzo a; **to** ~ **sb into a secret** iniciar a uno en un secreto; **to** ~ **proceedings against sb** (LAW) entablar proceso contra uno; **initiation** [-'eɪʃən] n (into secret etc) iniciación f; (beginning) comienzo.

initiative [ɪ'nɪʃətɪv] n iniciativa.

inject [ɪn'dʒɛkt] vt (liquid) inyectar; (fig) injertar; ~**ion** [ɪn'dʒɛkʃən] n inyección f.

injunction [ɪn'dʒʌŋkʃən] n interdicto.

injure ['ɪndʒə*] vt herir, lastimar; (fig) perjudicar; (offend) ofender; **injury** n herida, lesión f; (wrong) perjuicio, daño; **injury time** n (SPORT) descuento.

injustice [ɪn'dʒʌstɪs] n injusticia.

ink [ɪŋk] n tinta.

inkling ['ɪŋklɪŋ] n sospecha; (idea) idea, atisbo.

inlaid ['ɪnleɪd] a taraceado, entarimado.

inland ['ɪnlənd] a interior, del interior // ad [ɪn'lænd] tierra adentro; **I**~ **Revenue** n (Brit) el fisco.

in-laws ['ɪnlɔːz] npl parientes mpl políticos.

inlet ['ɪnlɛt] n (GEO) ensenada, cala; (TECH) admisión f, entrada.

inmate ['ɪnmeɪt] n (in prison) presidiario; (in asylum) internado/a.

inn [ɪn] n posada, mesón m.

innate [ɪ'neɪt] a innato.

inner ['ɪnə*] a interior, interno; ~ **city** n centro de la ciudad; ~ **tube** n (of tyre) cámara.

innocence ['ɪnəsns] n inocencia; **innocent** [-nt] a inocente.

innocuous [ɪ'nɔkjuəs] a innocuo.

innovation [ɪnəu'veɪʃən] n novedad f.

innuendo [ɪnju'ɛndəu], pl ~**es** n indirecta.

innumerable [ɪ'njuːmrəbl] a innumerable.

inoculation [ɪnɔkju'leɪʃən] n inoculación f.

inopportune [ɪn'ɔpətjuːn] a inoportuno.

inordinately [ɪ'nɔːdɪnətlɪ] ad desmesuradamente.

inorganic [ɪnɔː'gænɪk] a inorgánico.

in-patient ['ɪnpeɪʃənt] n paciente m/f interno/a.

input ['ɪnput] n (ELEC) entrada; (COMM) inversión f.

inquest ['ɪnkwɛst] n pesquisa judicial; (coroner's) encuesta judicial.

inquire [ɪn'kwaɪə*] vi pedir informes // vt (ask) preguntar; (seek information about) pedir informes sobre; **to** ~ **about** vt fus (person) preguntar por; (fact) informarse de; **to** ~ **into** vt fus investigar, indagar; **inquiring** a (mind) penetrante; (look) interrogativo; **inquiry** n pregunta; (LAW) investigación f, pesquisa; (commission) comisión f investigadora; **inquiry office** n oficina de informaciones.

inquisitive [ɪn'kwɪzɪtɪv] a (curious) activo, inquiridor(a); (prying) preguntón(ona), fisgón(ona).

inroad ['ɪnrəud] n incursión f; (fig) invasión f.

insane [ɪn'seɪn] a loco; (MED) demente.

insanitary [ɪn'sænɪtərɪ] a insalubre.

insanity [ɪn'sænɪtɪ] n demencia, locura.

insatiable [ɪn'seɪʃəbl] a insaciable.

inscribe [ɪn'skraɪb] vt inscribir; (book etc): **to** ~ **(to sb)** dedicar (a uno).

inscription [ɪn'skrɪpʃən] n (gen) inscripción f; (in book) dedicatoria.

inscrutable [ɪn'skruːtəbl] a inescrutable, insondable.

insect ['ɪnsɛkt] *n* insecto; ~**icide** [ɪn-'sɛktɪsaɪd] *n* insecticida *m*.
insecure [ɪnsɪ'kjuə⁺] *a* inseguro; **insecurity** *n* inseguridad *f*.
insensible [ɪn'sɛnsɪbl] *a* impasible, insensible; (*unconscious*) inconsciente.
insensitive [ɪn'sɛnsɪtɪv] *a* insensible.
inseparable [ɪn'sɛprəbl] *a* inseparable; **they were ~ friends** les unía una estrecha amistad.
insert [ɪn'sɔːt] *vt* (*between things*) intercalar; (*into sth*) introducir; (*in paper*) publicar; (: *advert*) poner // *n* ['ɪnsɔːt] hoja suelta (intercalada); ~**ion** [ɪn'sɔːʃən] *n* inserción *f*; (*publication*) publicación *f*; (*of pages*) materia añadida.
inshore [ɪn'ʃɔː⁺] *a* cercano a la orilla *o* costa // *ad* (*be*) cerca de la orilla; (*move*) hacia la orilla.
inside ['ɪn'saɪd] *n* interior *m*; (*lining*) forro // *a* interior, interno; (*secret*) secreto // *ad* (*within*) (por) dentro; (*with movement*) hacia dentro; (*fam: in prison*) en la cárcel // *prep* dentro de; (*of time*): ~ **10 minutes** en menos de 10 minutos; ~**s** *npl* (*col*) tripas *fpl*; ~ **forward** *n* (*SPORT*) delantero interior; ~ **lane** *n* (*AUT: in Britain*) el lado *o* carril izquierdo; ~ **out** *ad* (*turn*) al revés; (*know*) a fondo.
insidious [ɪn'sɪdɪəs] *a* insidioso; (*underground*) clandestino.
insight ['ɪnsaɪt] *n* perspicacia.
insignificant [ɪnsɪg'nɪfɪknt] *a* insignificante.
insincere [ɪnsɪn'sɪə⁺] *a* poco sincero; **insincerity** [-'sɛrɪtɪ] *n* falta de sinceridad, doblez *f*.
insinuate [ɪn'sɪnjueɪt] *vt* insinuar; **insinuation** [-'eɪʃən] *n* insinuación *f*; (*hint*) indirecta.
insipid [ɪn'sɪpɪd] *a* soso, insulso.
insist [ɪn'sɪst] *vi* insistir; **to ~ on doing** empeñarse en hacer; **to ~ that** insistir en que; (*claim*) exigir que; ~**ence** *n* insistencia; (*stubbornness*) empeño; ~**ent** *a* insistente; empeñado.
insole ['ɪnsəul] *n* plantilla.
insolence ['ɪnsələns] *n* insolencia, descaro; **insolent** [-ənt] *a* insolente, descarado.
insoluble [ɪn'sɔljubl] *a* insoluble.
insolvent [ɪn'sɔlvənt] *a* insolvente.
insomnia [ɪn'sɔmnɪə] *n* insomnio.
inspect [ɪn'spɛkt] *vt* inspeccionar, examinar; (*troops*) pasar revista a; ~**ion** [ɪn'spɛkʃən] *n* inspección *f*, examen *m*; ~ **or** *n* inspector/a *m/f*; (*RAIL*) revisor *m*.
inspiration [ɪnspə'reɪʃən] *n* inspiración *f*; **inspire** [ɪn'spaɪə⁺] *vt* inspirar.
instability [ɪnstə'bɪlɪtɪ] *n* inestabilidad *f*.
install [ɪn'stɔːl] *vt* instalar; ~**ation** [ɪnstə'leɪʃən] *n* instalación *f*.
instalment, installment (*US*) [ɪn-'stɔːlmənt] *n* plazo; (*of story*) entrega; (*of TV serial etc*) episodio.
instance ['ɪnstəns] *n* ejemplo, caso; **for ~**

por ejemplo; **in the first ~** en primer lugar.
instant ['ɪnstənt] *n* instante *m*, momento // *a* instantáneo, inmediato; (*coffee*) en polvo; ~**ly** *ad* en seguida.
instead [ɪn'stɛd] *ad* en cambio; ~ **of** en lugar de, en vez de.
instep ['ɪnstɛp] *n* empeine *m*.
instigation [ɪnstɪ'geɪʃən] *n* instigación *f*.
instil [ɪn'stɪl] *vt*: **to ~ into** infundir a, inculcar en.
instinct ['ɪnstɪŋkt] *n* instinto; ~**ive** [-'stɪŋktɪv] *a* instintivo; ~**ively** [-'stɪŋktɪvlɪ] *ad* por instinto.
institute ['ɪnstɪtjuːt] *n* instituto; (*professional body*) colegio // *vt* (*inquiry*) iniciar, empezar; (*proceedings*) entablar.
institution [ɪnstɪ'tjuːʃən] *n* (*gen*) institución *f*; (*beginning*) iniciación *f*; (*organization*) instituto; (*MED: home*) asilo; (*asylum*) manicomio; (*custom*) costumbre *f*.
instruct [ɪn'strʌkt] *vt*: **to ~ sb in sth** instruir a uno en *o* sobre algo; **to ~ sb to do sth** dar instrucciones a uno de hacer algo; ~**ion** [ɪn'strʌkʃən] *n* (*teaching*) instrucción *f*; ~**ions** *npl* órdenes *fpl*; ~**ions (for use)** modo *sg* de empleo; ~**ive** *a* aleccionador(a); ~**or** *n* instructor/a *m/f*.
instrument ['ɪnstrumənt] *n* instrumento; ~**al** [-'mɛntl] *a* (*MUS*) instrumental; **to be ~al in** contribuir materialmente a; ~ **panel** *n* tablero (de instrumentos).
insubordinate [ɪnsə'bɔːdənɪt] *a* insubordinado; **insubordination** [-'neɪʃən] *n* insubordinación *f*; (*disobedience*) desobediencia.
insufferable [ɪn'sʌfrəbl] *a* insufrible.
insufficient [ɪnsə'fɪʃənt] *a* insuficiente.
insular ['ɪnsjulə⁺] *a* insular; (*outlook*) de miras estrechas.
insulate ['ɪnsjuleɪt] *vt* aislar; **insulating tape** *n* cinta aislante; **insulation** [-'leɪʃən] *n* aislamiento.
insulin ['ɪnsjulɪn] *n* insulina.
insult ['ɪnsʌlt] *n* insulto; (*offence*) ofensa // *vt* [ɪn'sʌlt] insultar, injuriar; ofender; ~**ing** *a* insultante; ofensivo.
insuperable [ɪn'sjuːprəbl] *a* insuperable.
insurance [ɪn'ʃuərəns] *n* seguro; **fire/life ~** seguro sobre la vida/contra incendios; ~ **agent** *n* agente *m/f* de seguros; ~ **policy** *n* póliza (de seguros).
insure [ɪn'ʃuə⁺] *vt* asegurar.
insurrection [ɪnsə'rɛkʃən] *n* insurrección *f*.
intact [ɪn'tækt] *a* íntegro; (*unharmed*) ileso, sano.
intake ['ɪnteɪk] *n* (*TECH*) entrada, toma; (: *pipe*) tubo de admisión; (*of food*) cantidad admitida; (*SCOL*): **an ~ of 200 a year** 200 matriculados al año.
intangible [ɪn'tænzɪbl] *a* intangible.
integral ['ɪntɪgrəl] *a* (*whole*) íntegro; (*part*) integrante.

integrate ['ıntıgreıt] vt integrar // vi integrarse.

integrity [ın'tɛgrıtı] n honradez f, rectitud f.

intellect ['ıntəlɛkt] n intelecto; ~ual [-'lɛktjuəl] a, n intelectual m/f.

intelligence [ın'tɛlıdʒəns] n inteligencia; (MIL etc) informes mpl; I~ Service n Servicio de Inteligencia; **intelligent** [-ənt] a inteligente.

intelligible [ın'tɛlıdʒıbl] a inteligible, comprensible.

intend [ın'tɛnd] vt (gift etc): to ~ sth for destinar algo a; to ~ to do sth tener intención de o proponerse hacer algo; ~ed a (effect) deseado // n prometido/a.

intense [ın'tɛns] a intenso; (person) nervioso; ~ly ad intensamente; (very) sumamente.

intensify [ın'tɛnsıfaı] vt intensificar; (increase) aumentar.

intensity [ın'tɛnsıtı] n intensidad f; (strength) fuerza.

intensive [ın'tɛnsıv] a intensivo; ~ care unit n centro de cuidados intensivos.

intent [ın'tɛnt] n propósito // a (absorbed) absorto; (attentive) atento; to all ~s and purposes prácticamente; to be ~ on doing sth estar resuelto a hacer algo.

intention [ın'tɛnʃən] n intento, propósito; (plan) proyecto; ~al a intencional, deliberado; ~ally ad a propósito.

intently [ın'tɛntlı] ad atentamente, fijamente.

inter [ın'tə:*] vt enterrar.

interact [ıntər'ækt] vi influirse mutuamente; ~ion [-'ækʃən] n influencia mútua, acción f recíproca.

intercede [ıntə'si:d] vi: to ~ (with) interceder (con).

intercept [ıntə'sɛpt] vt interceptar; (stop) detener; ~ion [-'sɛpʃən] n interceptación f; detención f.

interchange ['ıntətʃeındʒ] n intercambio; (exchange) canje m; (on motorway) paso a desnivel // vt [ıntə'tʃeındʒ] intercambiar; canjear; ~able a intercambiable.

intercom ['ıntəkɔm] n sistema m de intercomunicación.

interconnect [ıntəkə'nɛkt] vi (rooms) conectarse.

intercourse ['ıntəkɔ:s] n (sexual) relaciones fpl; (social) trato.

interest ['ıntrıst] n (also COMM) interés m; (profit) ventaja, provecho // vt interesar; to be ~ed in interesarse por; ~ing a interesante.

interfere [ıntə'fıə*] vi: to ~ in (quarrel, other people's business) entrometerse o mezclarse en; to ~ with (hinder) estorbar; (damage) estropear; (radio) interferir con.

interference [ıntə'fıərəns] n (gen) intromisión f; (RADIO, TV) interferencia f.

interim ['ıntərım] n: in the ~ entretanto, en el interino.

interior [ın'tıərıə*] n interior m // a interior.

interject [ıntə'dʒɛkt] vt interponerse; ~ion [-'dʒɛkʃən] n interyección f.

interlock [ıntə'lɔk] vi entrelazarse; (wheels etc) endentarse.

interloper ['ıntələupə*] n intruso.

interlude ['ıntəlu:d] n intérvalo; (rest) descanso; (THEATRE) intermedio.

intermarry [ıntə'mærı] vi casarse (parientes).

intermediary [ıntə'mi:dıərı] n intermediario.

intermediate [ıntə'mi:dıət] a intermedio, medio.

intermission [ıntə'mıʃən] n (THEATRE) descanso.

intermittent [ıntə'mıtnt] a intermitente.

intern [ın'tə:n] vt internar; (enclose) encerrar // n ['ıntə:n] (US) interno.

internal [ın'tə:nl] a interno, interior; ~ly ad interiormente; 'not to be taken ~ly' 'uso externo'; ~ revenue n (US) rentas fpl públicas.

international [ıntə'næʃənl] a internacional; ~ game partido internacional; ~ player jugador/a m/f internacional.

interplay ['ıntəpleı] n interacción f.

interpret [ın'tə:prıt] vt interpretar; (translate) traducir; (understand) entender // vi hacer de intérprete; ~ation [-'teıʃən] n interpretación f; traducción f; entendimiento; ~er n intérprete m/f.

interrelated [ıntərı'leıtıd] a interrelacionado.

interrogate [ın'tɛrəugeıt] vt interrogar; **interrogation** [-'geıʃən] n interrogatorio; **interrogative** [ıntə'rɔgətıv] a interrogativo.

interrupt [ıntə'rʌpt] vt, vi interrumpir; ~ion [-'rʌpʃən] n interrupción f.

intersect [ıntə'sɛkt] vt cruzar // vi (roads) cruzarse; ~ion [-'sɛkʃən] n intersección f; (of roads) cruce m.

intersperse [ıntə'spə:s] vt esparcir, entremezclar.

intertwine [ıntə'twaın] vt entrelazar // vi entrelazarse.

interval ['ıntəvl] n intérvalo; (SCOL) recreo; (THEATRE, SPORT) descanso; at ~s a ratos, de vez en cuando.

intervene [ıntə'vi:n] vi (gen) intervenir; (take part) participar; (occur) sobrevenir; **intervention** [-'vɛnʃən] n intervención f.

interview ['ıntəvju:] n (RADIO, TV etc) entrevista // vt entrevistarse con; ~ee [-'i:] n entrevistado/a; ~er n entrevistador/a m/f.

intestine [ın'tɛstın] n: large/small ~ intestino grueso/delgado.

intimacy ['ıntıməsı] n intimidad f; (relations) relaciones fpl íntimas.

intimate ['ıntımət] a íntimo; (friendship) estrecho; (knowledge) profundo // vt ['ıntımeıt] (announce) dar a entender.

intimidate [ın'tımıdeıt] vt intimidar,

amedrentar; **intimidation** [-'deɪʃən] *n* intimidación *f.*

into ['ɪntu] *prep* (*gen*) en; (*towards*) a; (*inside*) hacia el interior de; ~ **3 pieces/French** en 3 pedazos/ francés.

intolerable [ɪn'tɔlərəbl] *a* intolerable, insufrible; **intolerance** [-rəns] *n* intolerancia; **intolerant** [-rənt] *a*: **intolerant of** intolerante con *o* para.

intonation [ɪntəu'neɪʃən] *n* entonación *f.*

intoxicate [ɪn'tɔksɪkeɪt] *vt* embriagar; ~**d** *a* embriagado; **intoxication** [-'keɪʃən] *n* embriaguez *f.*

intractable [ɪn'træktəbl] *a* (*child*) intratable; (*material*) difícil de trabajar; (*problem*) espinoso.

intransigent [ɪn'trænsɪdʒənt] *a* intransigente.

intransitive [ɪn'trænsɪtɪv] *a* intransitivo.

intravenous [ɪntrə'viːnəs] *a* intravenoso.

intrepid [ɪn'trepɪd] *a* intrépido.

intricate ['ɪntrɪkət] *a* intrincado; (*complex*) complejo.

intrigue [ɪn'triːg] *n* intriga // *vt* interesar, fascinar // *vi* andar en intrigas; **intriguing** *a* intrigante.

intrinsic [ɪn'trɪnsɪk] *a* intrínseco.

introduce [ɪntrə'djuːs] *vt* introducir, meter; **to** ~ **sb (to sb)** presentar uno (a otro); **to** ~ **sb to** (*pastime, technique*) introducir a uno a; **introduction** [-'dʌkʃən] *n* introducción *f*; (*of person*) presentación *f*; **introductory** [-'dʌktərɪ] *a* preliminar.

introspective [ɪntrəu'spektɪv] *a* introspectivo.

introvert ['ɪntrəuvəːt] *a, n* introvertido/a.

intrude [ɪn'truːd] *vi* (*person*) entrometerse; **to** ~ **on** *or* **into** estorbar; **intruder** *n* intruso/a; **intrusion** [-ʒən] *n* invasión *f*; **intrusive** [-sɪv] *a* intruso.

intuition [ɪntjuː'ɪʃən] *n* intuición *f*; **intuitive** [-'tjuːɪtɪv] *a* intuitivo.

inundate ['ɪnʌndeɪt] *vt*: **to** ~ **with** inundar de.

invade [ɪn'veɪd] *vt* invadir; **invader** *n* invasor/a *m/f.*

invalid ['ɪnvəlɪd] *n* inválido/a // *a* [ɪn-'vælɪd] (*not valid*) inválido, nulo; ~**ate** [ɪn-'vælɪdeɪt] *vt* invalidar, anular.

invaluable [ɪn'væljuəbl] *a* inestimable.

invariable [ɪn'vɛərɪəbl] *a* invariable.

invasion [ɪn'veɪʒən] *n* invasión *f.*

invent [ɪn'vent] *vt* inventar; ~**ion** [ɪn-'venʃən] *n* invento; (*inventiveness*) inventiva; (*lie*) ficción *f*, mentira; ~**ive** *a* ingenioso; ~**iveness** *n* ingenio, inventiva; ~**or** *n* inventor/a *m/f.*

inventory ['ɪnvəntrɪ] *n* inventario.

inverse [ɪn'vəːs] *a, n* inverso; ~**ly** *ad* a la inversa.

invert [ɪn'vəːt] *vt* invertir, volver al revés; ~**ed commas** *npl* comillas *fpl.*

invertebrate [ɪn'vəːtɪbrət] *n* invertebrado.

invest [ɪn'vest] *vt, vi* invertir.

investigate [ɪn'vestɪgeɪt] *vt* investigar; (*study*) estudiar, examinar; **investigation**

[-'geɪʃən] *n* investigación *f*, pesquisa; examen *m*; **investigator** *n* investigador/a *m/f.*

investiture [ɪn'vestɪtʃə*] *n* investidura.

investment [ɪn'vestmənt] *n* inversión *f.*

investor [ɪn'vestə*] *n* inversionista *m/f.*

inveterate [ɪn'vetərət] *a* empedernido.

invigorating [ɪn'vɪgəreɪtɪŋ] *a* vigorizante.

invincible [ɪn'vɪnsɪbl] *a* invencible.

inviolate [ɪn'vaɪələt] *a* inviolado.

invisible [ɪn'vɪzɪbl] *a* invisible; ~ **ink** *n* tinta simpática.

invitation [ɪnvɪ'teɪʃən] *n* invitación *f.*

invite [ɪn'vaɪt] *vt* (*gen*) invitar; (*to drink, food*) convidar; (*opinions etc*) solicitar, pedir; (*trouble*) buscarse; **inviting** *a* atractivo; (*look*) incitante; (*food*) apetitoso.

invoice ['ɪnvɔɪs] *n* factura // *vt* facturar.

invoke [ɪn'vəuk] *vt* invocar; (*aid*) implorar; (*law*) recurrir a.

involuntary [ɪn'vɔləntrɪ] *a* involuntario.

involve [ɪn'vɔlv] *vt* (*entail*) suponer, implicar; **to** ~ **sb (in)** comprometer a uno (con); ~**d** *a* complicado; ~**ment** *n* (*gen*) enredo; (*obligation*) compromiso; (*difficulty*) apuro.

invulnerable [ɪn'vʌlnərəbl] *a* invulnerable.

inward ['ɪnwəd] *a* (*movement*) interior, interno; (*thought, feeling*) íntimo; ~**ly** *ad* (*feel, think etc*) para sí, para dentro; ~(**s**) *ad* hacia dentro.

iodine ['aɪəudiːn] *n* yodo.

iota [aɪ'əutə] *n* (*fig*) jota, ápice *m.*

IOU *n abbr of* **I owe you** pagaré *m.*

IQ *n abbr of* **intelligence quotient** cociente *m* intelectual.

Iran [ɪ'rɑːn] *n* Irán *m*; ~**ian** [ɪ'reɪnɪən] *a, n* iraní *m/f.*

Iraq [ɪ'rɑːk] *n* El Irak; ~**i** *a, n* irakí *m/f.*

irascible [ɪ'ræsɪbl] *a* irascible.

irate [aɪ'reɪt] *a* enojado, indignado.

Ireland ['aɪələnd] *n* Irlanda.

iris ['aɪrɪs], *pl* ~**es** *a* (ANAT) iris *m*; (BOT) lirio.

Irish ['aɪrɪʃ] *a* irlandés(esa) // *npl*: **the** ~ los irlandeses; ~**man/ woman** *n* irlandés/esa *m/f.*

irk [əːk] *vt* fastidiar; ~**some** *a* fastidioso.

iron ['aɪən] *n* hierro; (*for clothes*) plancha // *a* de hierro // *vt* (*clothes*) planchar; ~**s** *npl* (*chains*) grillos *mpl*; **to** ~ **out** *vt* (*crease*) quitar; (*fig*) allanar.

ironic(al) [aɪ'rɔnɪk(l)] *a* irónico.

ironing ['aɪənɪŋ] *n* (*act*) planchado; (*ironed clothes*) ropa planchada; (*to be ironed*) ropa por planchar; ~ **board** *n* tabla de planchar.

ironmonger ['aɪənmʌŋgə*] *n* ferretero; ~**'s (shop)** *n* ferretería, quincallería.

iron ore ['aɪən'ɔː*] *n* mineral *m* de hierro.

irony ['aɪrənɪ] *n* ironía; **the** ~ **of it is that...** lo irónico es que...

irrational [ɪ'ræʃənl] *a* irracional.

irreconcilable [ɪrekən'saɪləbl] *a*

inconciliable, irreconciliable.
irrefutable [ɪrɪˈfjuːtəbl] a irrefutable.
irregular [ɪˈrɛgjulə*] a irregular; (surface) desigual; (illegal) ilegal; ~**ity** [-ˈlærɪtɪ] n irregularidad f; desigualdad f.
irrelevant [ɪˈrɛləvənt] a fuera de lugar, inoportuno.
irreparable [ɪˈrɛprəbl] a irreparable.
irreplaceable [ɪrɪˈpleɪsəbl] a irremplazable.
irrepressible [ɪrɪˈprɛsəbl] a irrefrenable.
irreproachable [ɪrɪˈprəutʃəbl] a irreprochable.
irresistible [ɪrɪˈzɪstɪbl] a irresistible.
irresolute [ɪˈrɛzəluːt] a indeciso.
irrespective [ɪrɪˈspɛktɪv]: ~ **of** prep sin tener en cuenta, no importa.
irresponsible [ɪrɪˈspɔnsɪbl] a (act) irresponsable; (person) poco serio.
irreverent [ɪˈrɛvərnt] a irreverente, irrespetuoso.
irrevocable [ɪˈrɛvəkəbl] a irrevocable.
irrigate [ˈɪrɪgeɪt] vt regar; **irrigation** [-ˈgeɪʃən] n riego.
irritable [ˈɪrɪtəbl] a irritable; (mood) de mal humor.
irritate [ˈɪrɪteɪt] vt irritar; (MED) picar; **irritation** [-ˈteɪʃən] n irritación f, enojo; picazón m, picor m.
is [ɪz] vb see **be.**
Islam [ˈɪzlɑːm] n Islam m.
island [ˈaɪlənd] n isla; (also: **traffic** ~) refugio; ~**er** n isleño/a.
isle [aɪl] n isla.
isn't [ˈɪznt] = **is not.**
isolate [ˈaɪsəleɪt] vt aislar; ~**d** a aislado; **isolation** [-ˈleɪʃən] n aislamiento.
isotope [ˈaɪsəutəup] n isótopo.
Israel [ˈɪzreɪl] n Israel m; ~**i** [ɪzˈreɪlɪ] a, n israelí m/f.
issue [ˈɪsjuː] n cuestión f, asunto; (outcome) resultado; (of banknotes etc) emisión f; (of newspaper etc) número; (offspring) sucesión f, descendencia // vt (rations, equipment) distribuir, repartir; (orders) dar; (certificate) expedir; (decree) promulgar; (book) publicar; (cheques) extender; (banknotes, stamps) emitir.
isthmus [ˈɪsməs] n istmo.
it [ɪt] pron (subject) él/ella; (direct object) lo/la; (indirect object) le; (impersonal) ello; (after prep) él/ella/ello; ~**'s raining** llueve, está lloviendo; **where is** ~? ¿dónde está?; **he's proud of** ~ le enorgullece; **he agreed to** ~ está de acuerdo (con ello).
Italian [ɪˈtæljən] a italiano // n italiano/a; (LING) el italiano.
italic [ɪˈtælɪk] a cursivo; ~**s** npl cursiva sg.
Italy [ˈɪtəlɪ] n Italia.
itch [ɪtʃ] n comezón m; (fig) prurito // vi (person) sentir o tener comezón; (part of body) picar; **I'm** ~**ing to do sth** rabio por hacer algo; ~**ing** n comezón m; ~**y** a: **to be** ~**y** picar.
it'd [ˈɪtd] = **it would; it had.**

item [ˈaɪtəm] n (gen) artículo; (detail) detalle m; (on agenda) asunto a tratar; (in programme) número; (also: **news** ~) noticia; ~**ize** vt detallar.
itinerant [ɪˈtɪnərənt] a ambulante.
itinerary [aɪˈtɪnərərɪ] n itinerario.
it'll [ˈɪtl] = **it will, it shall.**
its [ɪts] a su // pron (el) suyo/(la) suya.
it's [ɪts] = **it is; it has.**
itself [ɪtˈsɛlf] pron (reflexive) sí mismo/a; (emphatic) él mismo/ella misma.
ITV n abbr of **Independent Television.**
I.U.D. n abbr of **intra-uterine device** DIU.
I've [aɪv] = **I have.**
ivory [ˈaɪvərɪ] n marfil m; ~ **tower** n (fig) torre f de marfil.
ivy [ˈaɪvɪ] n hiedra.

J

jab [dʒæb] vt (elbow) dar un codazo a; (punch) dar un golpe rápido a; **to** ~ **sth into sth** clavar algo en algo // n codazo; golpe m (rápido); (MED: col) pinchazo.
jabber [ˈdʒæbə*] vt, vi farfullar.
jack [dʒæk] n (AUT) gato; (BOWLS) boliche m; (CARDS) sota; **to** ~ **up** vt (AUT) alzar con gato.
jackdaw [ˈdʒækdɔː] n grajilla.
jacket [ˈdʒækɪt] n chaqueta, americana; (of boiler etc) camisa; (of book) sobrecubierta; **potatoes in their** ~**s** patatas con su piel.
jack-knife [ˈdʒæknaɪf] n navaja.
jackpot [ˈdʒækpɔt] n premio gordo.
jade [dʒeɪd] n (stone) jade m.
jaded [ˈdʒeɪdɪd] a (tired) cansado; (fed-up) hastiado.
jagged [ˈdʒægɪd] a dentado.
jail [dʒeɪl] n cárcel f; ~**break** n fuga o evasión f (de la cárcel); ~**er** n carcelero.
jam [dʒæm] n mermelada; (also: **traffic** ~) embotellamiento; (difficulty) apuro // vt (passage etc) obstruir, cerrar; (mechanism, drawer etc) atascar; (RADIO) interferir // vi atascarse, trabarse; **to** ~ **sth into sth** meter algo por la fuerza en algo.
Jamaica [dʒəˈmeɪkə] n Jamaica.
jangle [ˈdʒæŋgl] vi sonar (de manera) discordante.
janitor [ˈdʒænɪtə*] n (caretaker) portero, conserje m.
January [ˈdʒænjuərɪ] n enero.
Japan [dʒəˈpæn] n (el) Japón; ~**ese** [dʒæpəˈniːz] a japonés(esa) // n, pl inv japonés/esa m/f; (LING) japonés m.
jar [dʒɑː*] n (glass: large) jarra; (: small) tarro // vi (sound) chirriar; (colours) desentonar.
jargon [ˈdʒɑːgən] n jerga.
jasmin(e) [ˈdʒæzmɪn] n jazmín m.
jaundice [ˈdʒɔːndɪs] n ictericia; ~**d** a (fig: embittered) amargado; (: disillusioned) desilusionado.

jaunt [dʒɔːnt] *n* excursión *f*; ~**y** *a* alegre.
javelin ['dʒævlɪn] *n* jabalina.
jaw [dʒɔː] *n* mandíbula.
jaywalker ['dʒeɪwɔːkə*] *n* peatón *m* imprudente.
jazz [dʒæz] *n* jazz *m*; **to** ~ **up** *vt* (*liven up*) animar, avivar; ~**y** *a* de colores llamativos.
jealous ['dʒɛləs] *a* (*gen*) celoso; (*envious*) envidioso; **to be** ~ tener celos; ~**y** *n* celos *mpl*; envidia.
jeans [dʒiːnz] *npl* (pantalones) vaqueros *o* tejanos *mpl*.
jeep [dʒiːp] *n* jeep *m*.
jeer [dʒɪə*] *vi*: **to** ~ (**at**) (*boo*) abuchear; (*mock*) mofarse (de).
jelly ['dʒɛlɪ] *n* jalea, gelatina; ~**fish** *n* medusa.
jeopardize ['dʒɛpədaɪz] *vt* arriesgar, poner en peligro; **jeopardy** [-dɪ] *n*: **to be in jeopardy** estar en peligro *o* a riesgo.
jerk [dʒɔːk] *n* (*jolt*) sacudida; (*wrench*) tirón *m* // *vt* dar una sacudida a // *vi* (*vehicle*) traquetear.
jerkin ['dʒɔːkɪn] *n* cazadora.
jerky ['dʒɔːkɪ] *a* espasmódico.
jersey ['dʒɔːzɪ] *n* jersey *m*.
jest [dʒɛst] *n* broma.
jet [dʒɛt] *n* (*of gas, liquid*) chorro; (AVIAT) avión *m* a reacción; ~-**black** *a* de azabache; ~ **engine** *n* motor *m* a reacción.
jettison ['dʒɛtɪsn] *vt* desechar.
jetty ['dʒɛtɪ] *n* muelle *m*, embarcadero.
Jew [dʒuː] *n* judío; ~**ess** *n* judía.
jewel ['dʒuːəl] *n* joya; (*in watch*) rubí *m*; ~**ler** *n* joyero; ~**ler's** (**shop**) *n* joyería; ~**lery** *n* joyas *fpl*, alhajas *fpl*.
Jewish ['dʒuːɪʃ] *a* judío.
jibe [dʒaɪb] *n* pulla.
jiffy ['dʒɪfɪ] *n* (*col*): **in a** ~ en un instante.
jig [dʒɪg] *n* jiga.
jigsaw ['dʒɪgsɔː] *n* (*also*: ~ **puzzle**) rompecabezas *m inv*.
jilt [dʒɪlt] *vt* dar calabazas a.
jingle ['dʒɪŋgl] *n* (*advert*) estribillo // *vi* tintinear.
jinx [dʒɪŋks] *n* (*col*) gafe *m*, maldición *f*.
jitters ['dʒɪtəz] *npl* (*col*): **to get the** ~ ponerse nervioso.
job [dʒɔb] *n* (*gen*) trabajo; (*task*) tarea; (*duty*) deber *m*; (*post*) empleo; (*fam: difficulty*) dificultad *f*; **it's a good** ~ **that...** menos mal que...; **just the** ~! ¡estupendo!; ~**less** *a* sin trabajo.
jockey ['dʒɔkɪ] *n* jockey *m* // *vi*: **to** ~ **for position** maniobrar para conseguir una posición.
jocular ['dʒɔkjulə*] *a* (*humorous*) jocoso; (*merry*) alegre.
jog [dʒɔg] *vt* empujar (ligeramente) // *vi* (*run*) hacer footing; **to** ~ **along** ir tirando; **to** ~ **sb's memory** refrescar la memoria a uno; ~**ging** *n* footing *m*.
join [dʒɔɪn] *vt* (*things*) juntar, unir; (*become member of*) inscribirse en, afiliarse a;

(*meet: people*) reunirse *o* encontrarse con // *vi* (*roads, rivers*) confluir // *n* juntura; **to** ~ **up** *vi* unirse; (MIL) alistarse.
joiner ['dʒɔɪnə*] *n* carpintero; ~**y** *n* carpintería.
joint [dʒɔɪnt] *n* (TECH) junta, unión *f*; (*wood*) ensambladura; (ANAT) articulación *f*; (CULIN) asado; (*col: place*) garito // *a* (*common*) común; (*combined*) combinado; (*committee*) mixto; **by** ~ **agreement** por común acuerdo; ~**ly** *ad* (*gen*) mutuamente, en común; (*collectively*) colectivamente; (*together*) conjuntamente.
joke [dʒəuk] *n* chiste *m*; (*also*: **practical** ~) broma // *vi* bromear; **to play a** ~ **on** gastar una broma a; **joker** *n* chistoso/a, bromista *m/f*; (CARDS) comodín *m*.
jolly ['dʒɔlɪ] *a* (*merry*) alegre; (*enjoyable*) divertido // *ad* (*col*) muy, terriblemente.
jolt [dʒəult] *n* (*shake*) sacudida; (*blow*) golpe *m*; (*shock*) susto // *vt* sacudir; asustar.
Jordan ['dʒɔːdən] *n* Jordania.
jostle ['dʒɔsl] *vt* dar empellones a, codear.
jot [dʒɔt] *n*: **not one** ~ ni jota, ni pizca; **to** ~ **down** *vt* apuntar; ~**ter** *n* bloc *m*; (SCOL) cuaderno.
journal ['dʒɔːnl] *n* (*paper*) periódico; (*magazine*) revista; (*diary*) diario; ~**ese** [-'liːz] *n* (*pej*) lenguaje *m* periodístico; ~**ism** *n* periodismo; ~**ist** *n* periodista *m/f*.
journey ['dʒɔːnɪ] *n* viaje *m*; (*distance covered*) trayecto // *vi* viajar; **return** ~ viaje de regreso.
joy [dʒɔɪ] *n* alegría; ~**ful**, ~**ous** *a* alegre; ~ **ride** *n* paseo en coche; (*illegal*) paseo en coche robado.
J.P. *n abbr of* **Justice of the Peace.**
Jr, Jun., Junr *abbr of* **junior.**
jubilant ['dʒuːbɪlnt] *a* jubiloso; **jubilation** [-'leɪʃən] *n* júbilo.
jubilee ['dʒuːbɪliː] *n* aniversario.
judge [dʒʌdʒ] *n* juez *m* // *vt* (*gen*) juzgar; (*estimate*) considerar; **judg(e)ment** *n* juicio; (*punishment*) sentencia, fallo.
judicial [dʒuː'dɪʃl] *a* judicial.
judicious [dʒuː'dɪʃəs] *a* juicioso.
judo ['dʒuːdəu] *n* judo.
jug [dʒʌg] *n* jarro.
juggernaut ['dʒʌgənɔːt] *n* (*huge truck*) mastodonte *m*.
juggle ['dʒʌgl] *vi* hacer juegos malabares; **juggler** *n* malabarista *m/f*.
Jugoslav ['juːgəu'slɑːv] *a*, *n* = **Yugoslav.**
juice [dʒuːs] *n* zumo, jugo; **juicy** *a* jugoso.
jukebox ['dʒuːkbɔks] *n* rocola.
July [dʒuː'laɪ] *n* julio.
jumble ['dʒʌmbl] *n* revoltijo // *vt* (*also*: ~ **up**: *mix up*) revolver; (: *disarrange*) mezclar; ~ **sale** *n* (*Brit*) venta de objetos usados.
jumbo (jet) ['dʒʌmbəu] *n* jumbo-jet *m*.
jump [dʒʌmp] *vi* saltar, dar saltos; (*start*) asustarse, sobresaltarse; (*increase*) aumentar // *vt* saltar // *n* salto; aumento; **to** ~ **the queue** colarse.

jumper ['dʒʌmpə*] n suéter m, jersey m.
jumpy ['dʒʌmpi] a nervioso.
junction ['dʒʌŋkʃən] n (of roads) cruce m; (RAIL) empalme m.
juncture ['dʒʌŋktʃə*] n: **at this** ~ en este momento, en esta coyuntura.
June [dʒu:n] n junio.
jungle ['dʒʌŋgl] n selva, jungla.
junior ['dʒu:niə*] a (in age) menor, más joven; (competition) juvenil; (position) subalterno // n menor m/f, joven m/f; ~ **school** n escuela primaria.
junk [dʒʌŋk] n (cheap goods) baratijas fpl; (lumber) trastos viejos mpl; (rubbish) basura; (ship) junco; ~**shop** n tienda de objetos usados.
jurisdiction [dʒuəris'dikʃən] n jurisdicción f.
jurisprudence [dʒuəris'pru:dəns] n jurisprudencia.
jury ['dʒuəri] n jurado.
just [dʒʌst] a justo // ad (exactly) exactamente; (only) sólo, solamente; **he's** ~ **done it/left** acaba de hacerlo/irse; ~ **right** perfecto, perfectamente; ~ **two o'clock** las dos en punto; ~ **as well that...** menos mal que...; ~ **as he was leaving** en el momento en que se marchaba; ~ **before/enough** justo antes/lo suficiente; ~ **here** aquí mismo; **he** ~ **missed** ha fallado por poco; ~ **listen** escucha (solamente).
justice ['dʒʌstis] n justicia; **J**~ **of the Peace (J.P.)** n juez m de paz.
justifiable [dʒʌsti'faiəbl] a justificable; **justifiably** ad justificadamente.
justification [dʒʌstifi'keiʃən] n justificación f; **justify** ['dʒʌstifai] vt justificar.
justly ['dʒʌstli] ad (gen) justamente; (with reason) con razón.
justness ['dʒʌstnis] n justicia.
jut [dʒʌt] vi (also: ~ **out**) sobresalir.
juvenile ['dʒu:vənail] a juvenil; (court) de menores; (books) para jóvenes // n joven m/f, menor m/f de edad.
juxtapose ['dʒʌkstəpəuz] vt yuxtaponer.

K

kaleidoscope [kə'laidəskəup] n calidoscopio.
kangaroo [kæŋgə'ru:] n canguro.
keel [ki:l] n quilla; **on an even** ~ (fig) en equilibrio.
keen [ki:n] a (interest, desire) grande, vivo; (eye, intelligence) agudo; (competition) intenso; (edge) afilado; (eager) entusiasta inv; **to be** ~ **to do** or **on doing sth** tener muchas ganas de hacer algo; **to be** ~ **on sth/sb** interesarse por algo/alguien; ~**ness** n (eagerness) entusiasmo, interés m.
keep [ki:p], pt, pp **kept** vt (retain, preserve) guardar; (hold back) quedarse con; (shop, diary) llevar; (feed: family etc) mantener; (promise) cumplir; (chickens, bees etc)

criar // vi (food) conservarse; (remain) seguir, continuar // n (of castle) torreón m; (food etc) comida, subsistencia; **to** ~ **doing sth** seguir haciendo algo; **to** ~ **sb from doing sth** impedir a alguien hacer algo; **to** ~ **sth from happening** impedir que algo ocurra; **to** ~ **sb happy** hacer a alguien feliz; **to** ~ **a place tidy** mantener un lugar limpio; **to** ~ **sth to o.s.** guardar algo para sí mismo; **to** ~ **sth (back) from sb** ocultar algo a alguien; **to** ~ **time** (clock) mantener la hora exacta; **to** ~ **on** vi seguir, continuar; **to** ~ **out** vi (stay out) permanecer fuera; '~ **out**' prohibida la entrada; **to** ~ **up** vt mantener, conservar // vi no retrasarse; **to** ~ **up with** (pace) ir al paso de; (level) mantenerse a la altura de; ~**er** n guardián m; ~**ing** n (care) cuidado; **in** ~**ing with** de acuerdo con; ~**sake** n recuerdo.
keg [kɛg] n barrilete m, barril m.
kennel ['kɛnl] n perrera; ~**s** npl criadero sg de perros.
Kenya ['kɛnjə] n Kenia.
kept [kɛpt] pt, pp of **keep.**
kerb [kə:b] n bordillo.
kernel ['kə:nl] n almendra.
kerosene ['kɛrəsi:n] n keroseno.
ketchup ['kɛtʃəp] n salsa de tomate, catsup m.
kettle ['kɛtl] n hervidor m, olla.
key [ki:] n (gen) llave f; (MUS) tono; (of piano, typewriter) tecla; ~**board** n teclado; ~**hole** n ojo (de la cerradura); ~**note** n (MUS) tónica; ~**ring** n llavero; ~**stone** n piedra clave.
khaki ['kɑ:ki] n caqui.
kick [kik] vt (person) dar una patada a; (ball) dar un puntapié a // vi (horse) dar coces // n patada; puntapié m; (of rifle) culetazo; (thrill): **he does it for** ~**s** lo hace para divertirse; **to** ~ **off** vi (SPORT) hacer el saque inicial; ~-**off** n (SPORT) saque m inicial.
kid [kid] n (child) chiquillo, (animal) cabrito; (leather) cabritilla // vi (col) bromear.
kidnap ['kidnæp] vt secuestrar; ~**per** n secuestrador/a m/f; ~**ping** n secuestro.
kidney ['kidni] n riñón m.
kill [kil] vt (gen) matar; (murder) asesinar; (destroy) destruir; (finish off) acabar con // n acto de matar; ~**er** n asesino; ~**ing** n (one) asesinato; (several) matanza // a (funny) divertido.
kiln [kiln] n horno.
kilo ['ki:ləu] n kilo; ~**gram(me)** ['kiləugræm] n kilo, kilogramo; ~**metre,** ~**meter** (US) ['kiləmi:tə*] n kilómetro; ~**watt** ['kiləuwɔt] n kilovatio.
kilt [kilt] n falda escocesa.
kimono [ki'məunəu] n quimono.
kin [kin] n parientes mpl.
kind [kaind] a (generous) bondadoso; (good) bueno, amable // n clase f, especie f; (species) género; **in** ~ (COMM) en

especie; **a** ~ **of** una especie de; **two of a** ~ dos de la misma especie.

kindergarten ['kɪndəgɑːtn] *n* jardín *m* de infancia.

kind-hearted [kaɪnd'hɑːtɪd] *a* bondadoso, de buen corazón.

kindle ['kɪndl] *vt* encender.

kindly ['kaɪndlɪ] *a* (*gen*) bondadoso; (*good*) bueno; (*gentle*) cariñoso // *ad* bondadosamente, amablemente; **will you** ~... sea Usted tan amable de... .

kindness ['kaɪndnɪs] *n* bondad *f*, amabilidad *f*.

kindred ['kɪndrɪd] *n* familia, parientes *mpl* // *a*: ~ **spirit** espíritu *m* afín.

king [kɪŋ] *n* rey *m*; ~**dom** *n* reino; ~**fisher** *n* martín *m* pescador; ~-**size** *a* de tamaño extra.

kink [kɪŋk] *n* (*of rope*) enroscadura.

kinky ['kɪŋkɪ] *a* (*odd*) excéntrico; (*pej*) pervertido.

kiosk ['kiːɔsk] *n* quiosco; (*TEL*) cabina.

kipper ['kɪpə*] *n* arenque *m* ahumado.

kiss [kɪs] *n* beso // *vt* besar; **to** ~ **(each other)** besarse.

kit [kɪt] *n* (*gen*) avíos *mpl*; (*equipment*) equipo; (*set of tools etc*) (caja de) herramientas *fpl*; (*for assembly*) mecano.

kitchen ['kɪtʃɪn] *n* cocina; ~ **garden** *n* huerto; ~ **sink** *n* fregadero; ~**ware** *n* batería de cocina.

kite [kaɪt] *n* (*toy*) cometa.

kitten ['kɪtn] *n* gatito.

kitty ['kɪtɪ] *n* (*pool of money*) fondo común; (*CARDS*) polla.

kleptomaniac [klɛptəu'meɪnɪæk] *n* cleptómano/a.

knack [næk] *n*: **to have the** ~ **of doing sth** tener el don de hacer algo.

knapsack ['næpsæk] *n* mochila.

knead [niːd] *vt* amasar.

knee [niː] *n* rodilla; ~**cap** *n* rótula.

kneel [niːl], *pt, pp* **knelt** *vi* arrodillarse.

knell [nɛl] *n* toque *m* de difuntos.

knelt [nɛlt] *pt, pp of* **kneel.**

knew [njuː] *pt of* **know.**

knickers ['nɪkəz] *npl* bragas *fpl*.

knife [naɪf], *pl* **knives** *n* cuchillo // *vt* acuchillar.

knight [naɪt] *n* caballero; (*CHESS*) caballo; ~**hood** *n* caballería; (*title*): **to get a** ~**hood** recibir el título de sir.

knit [nɪt] *vt* hacer a punto; (*brows*) fruncir // *vi* hacer punto; (*bones*) soldarse; **to** ~ **together** (*fig*) unir, juntar; ~**ting** *n* labor *f* de punto; ~**ting machine** *n* máquina de tricotar; ~**ting needle** *n* aguja de hacer punto; ~**wear** *n* géneros *mpl* de punto.

knives [naɪvz] *pl of* **knife.**

knob [nɔb] *n* (*of door*) tirador *m*; (*of stick*) puño; (*lump*) bulto; (*fig*): **a** ~ **of butter** una porción de mantequilla.

knock [nɔk] *vt* (*strike*) golpear; (*bump into*) chocar contra; (*fig: col*) denigrar // *n* golpe *m*; (*on door*) llamada; **to** ~ **at or on the door** llamar a la puerta; **to** ~ **down**

vt atropellar; **to** ~ **off** *vi* (*col*: *finish*) despachar // *vt* (*col*: *steal*) birlar; **to** ~ **out** *vt* dejar sin sentido; (*BOXING*) poner fuera de combate, dejar K.O.; ~**er** *n* (*on door*) aldaba; ~-**kneed** *a* patizambo; ~**out** *n* (*BOXING*) K.O. *m*, knockout *m*.

knot [nɔt] *n* (*gen*) nudo // *vt* anudar; ~**ty** *a* (*fig*) complicado.

know [nəu], *pt* **knew,** *pp* **known** *vt* (*gen*) saber; (*person, author, place*) conocer; **to** ~ **that...** saber que...; **to** ~ **how to swim** saber nadar; ~-**all** *n* sabelotodo *m/f*; ~-**how** *n* habilidad *f*; ~**ing** *a* (*look*: *of complicity*) de complicidad; (: *spiteful*) malicioso; ~**ingly** *ad* (*purposely*) adrede; (*spitefully*) maliciosamente.

knowledge ['nɔlɪdʒ] *n* (*gen*) conocimiento; (*range of learning*) saber *m*, conocimientos *mpl*; (*learning*) erudición *f*, ciencia; ~**able** *a* entendido, erudito.

known [nəun] *pp of* **know.**

knuckle ['nʌkl] *n* nudillo.

K.O. *n abbr of* **knockout.**

Koran [kɔ'rɑːn] *n* Corán *m*.

L

l. *abbr of* **litre.**

lab [læb] *n abbr of* **laboratory.**

label ['leɪbl] *n* etiqueta; (*brand: of record*) marca // *vt* poner etiqueta a.

laboratory [lə'bɔrətərɪ] *n* laboratorio.

laborious [lə'bɔːrɪəs] *a* penoso.

labour, labor (*US*) ['leɪbə*] *n* (*task*) trabajo; (~ *force*) mano *f* de obra; (*workers*) trabajadores *mpl*; (*MED*) (dolores *mpl* del) parto // *vi*: **to** ~ (**at**) trabajar (en) // *vt* insistir en; **in** ~ (*MED*) de parto; **L**~, **the L**~ **party** el partido laborista; ~ **hard** ~ trabajos *mpl* forzados; ~**ed** *a* (*movement*) penoso; (*style*) pesado; ~**er** *n* peón *m*; (*on farm*) peón *m*, bracero; (*day* ~*er*) jornalero.

labyrinth ['læbɪrɪnθ] *n* laberinto.

lace [leɪs] *n* encaje *m*; (*of shoe etc*) cordón *m* // *vt* (*shoe*) atar.

lack [læk] *n* (*absence*) falta; (*scarcity*) escasez *f* // *vt* no tener, carecer de; **through** *or* **for** ~ **of** por falta de; **to be** ~**ing** faltar, no haber.

lackadaisical [lækə'deɪzɪkl] *a* (*careless*) descuidado; (*indifferent*) indiferente.

laconic [lə'kɔnɪk] *a* lacónico.

lacquer ['lækə*] *n* laca.

lad [læd] *n* muchacho, chico; (*in stable etc*) mozo.

ladder ['lædə*] *n* escalera (de mano); (*in tights*) carrera // *vt* (*tights*) hacer una carrera en.

laden ['leɪdn] *a*: ~ (**with**) cargado (de).

ladle ['leɪdl] *n* cucharón *m*.

lady ['leɪdɪ] *n* señora; (*distinguished, noble*) dama; **young** ~ señorita; **'ladies' (toilets)'** 'señoras'; ~**bird,** ~**bug** (*US*) *n* mariquita; ~-**in-waiting** *n* dama de honor; ~**like** *a* fino.

lag [læg] *vi* (*also*: ~ **behind**) retrasarse,

quedarse atrás // vt (pipes) calorifugar.
lager ['lɑːgɔ*] n cerveza (rubia).
lagging ['lægɪŋ] n revestimiento.
lagoon [lɔ'guːn] n laguna.
laid [leɪd] pt, pp of **lay**.
lain [leɪn] pp of **lie**.
lair [lɛɔ*] n guarida.
lake [leɪk] n lago.
lamb [læm] n cordero; (meat) carne f de cordero; ~ **chop** n chuleta de cordero; **lambswool** n lana de cordero.
lame [leɪm] a cojo; (weak) débil, poco convincente.
lament [lɔ'mɛnt] n lamento // vt lamentarse de; ~**able** ['læmɔntɔbl] a lamentable.
laminated ['læmɪneɪtɪd] a laminado.
lamp [læmp] n lámpara.
lampoon [læm'puːn] vt satirizar.
lamp: ~**post** n farol m; ~**shade** n pantalla.
lance [lɑːns] n lanza // vt (MED) abrir con lanzeta; ~ **corporal** n soldado de primera clase.
lancet ['lɑːnsɪt] n lanceta.
land [lænd] n (gen) tierra; (country) país m; (piece of ~) terreno; (estate) tierras fpl, finca; (AGR) campo // vi (from ship) desembarcar; (AVIAT) aterrizar; (fig: fall) caer, terminar // vt (obtain) conseguir; (passengers, goods) desembarcar; to ~ up in/at ir a parar a/en; ~**ing** n desembarco; aterrizaje m; (of staircase) rellano; ~**ing craft** n barca de desembarco; ~**ing gear** n tren m de aterrizaje; ~**ing stage** n desembarcadero; ~**ing strip** n pista de aterrizaje; ~**lady** n (of boarding house) patrona; (owner) dueña; ~**locked** a cercado de tierra; ~**lord** n propietario; (of pub etc) patrón m; ~**lubber** n hombre m de tierra; ~**mark** n lugar m conocido; to be a ~**mark** (fig) hacer época; ~**owner** n terrateniente m/f.
landscape ['lænskeɪp] n paisaje m; ~**d** a reformado artísticamente.
landslide ['lændslaɪd] n (GEO) corrimiento de tierras; (fig: POL) victoria arrolladora.
lane [leɪn] n (in country) vereda; (in town) callejón m; (AUT) carril m; (in race) calle f; (for air or sea traffic) ruta.
language ['læŋgwɪdʒ] n lenguaje m; (national tongue) idioma m, lengua; **bad** ~ lenguaje indecente.
languid ['læŋgwɪd] a lánguido.
languish ['læŋgwɪʃ] vi languidecer.
lank [læŋk] a (hair) lacio.
lanky ['læŋkɪ] a larguirucho.
lantern ['læntn] n linterna; (NAUT) farol m.
lap [læp] n (of track) vuelta; (of body): to sit on sb's ~ sentarse en las rodillas de uno // vt (also: ~ up) lamer // vi (waves) chapotear; ~**dog** n perro faldero.
lapel [lɔ'pɛl] n solapa.
Lapland ['læplænd] n Laponia; **Lapp** [læp] a, n lapón/ona m/f.
lapse [læps] n error m, equivocación f;

(moral) desliz m // vi (expire) caducar; (LAW) equivocarse; (morally) caer en un desliz; (time) pasar, transcurrir; to ~ **into bad habits** volver a las andadas; ~ **of time** lapso, período.
larceny ['lɑːsɔnɪ] n latrocinio; **petty** ~ robo de menor cuantía.
lard [lɑːd] n manteca (de cerdo).
larder ['lɑːdɔ*] n despensa.
large [lɑːdʒ] a (gen) grande; (fat) gordo; **at** ~ (free) en libertad; (generally) en general; ~**ly** ad en gran parte; ~**-scale** a (map) en gran escala; (fig) importante.
lark [lɑːk] n (bird) alondra; (joke) travesura, broma; to ~ **about** vi bromear, divertirse tontamente
larva ['lɑːvɔ], pl -**vae** [-viː] n larva.
laryngitis [lærɪn'dʒaɪtɪs] n laringitis f.
larynx ['lærɪŋks] n laringe f.
lascivious [lɔ'sɪvɪɔs] a lascivo.
laser ['leɪzɔ*] n laser m.
lash [læʃ] n latigazo; (punishment) azote m; (gen: eyelash) pestaña // vt azotar; (tie) atar; to ~ **out** vi: to ~ **out at** or **against sb** atacar violentamente a alguien; to ~ **out** (col: spend) gastar generosamente.
lass [læs] n chica.
lasso [læ'suː] n lazo // vt coger con lazo.
last [lɑːst] a (gen) último; (final) último, final // ad por último // vi (endure) durar; (continue) continuar, seguir; ~ **week** la semana pasada; ~ **night** anoche; **at** ~ por fin; ~ **but one** penúltimo; ~**ing** a duradero; ~**-minute** a de última hora.
latch [lætʃ] n picaporte m, pestillo; ~**key** n llavín m.
late [leɪt] a (not on time) tarde, atrasado; (far on in day etc) tardío; (hour) avanzado; (recent) reciente; (former) antiguo, ex; (dead) fallecido // ad tarde; (behind time, schedule) con retraso; **of** ~ últimamente; **in** ~ **May** hacia fines de mayo; **the** ~ **Mr X** el difunto Sr X; ~**comer** n recién llegado; ~**ly** ad últimamente; ~**ness** n (of person) retraso; (of event) lo tardío.
latent ['leɪtnt] a latente.
later ['leɪtɔ*] a (date etc) posterior; (version etc) más reciente // ad más tarde, después.
lateral ['lætɔrl] a lateral.
latest ['leɪtɪst] a último; **at the** ~ a más tardar.
lathe [leɪð] n torno.
lather ['lɑːðɔ*] n espuma (de jabón) // vt enjabonar // vi hacer espuma.
Latin ['lætɪn] n latín m // a latino; ~ **America** n América latina; ~**-American** a latinoamericano.
latitude ['lætɪtjuːd] n latitud f.
latrine [lɔ'triːn] n letrina.
latter ['lætɔ*] a último; (of two) segundo // n: **the** ~ el último, éste; ~**ly** ad últimamente.
lattice ['lætɪs] n enrejado; (on window) reja.
laudable ['lɔːdɔbl] a loable.
laugh [lɑːf] n risa; (loud) carcajada // vi

reírse, reír; reírse a carcajadas; **to** ~ **at**
vt fus reírse de; **to** ~ **off** *vt* tomar algo a
risa; ~**able** *a* risible, ridículo; **to be the**
~**ing stock of the town** ser el
hazmerreír de la ciudad; ~**ter** *n* risa.
launch [lɔːntʃ] *n* (*boat*) lancha; *see also*
~**ing** // *vt* (*ship, rocket, plan*) lanzar;
~**ing** *n* (*of rocket etc*) lanzamiento;
(*inauguration*) estreno; ~(**ing**) **pad** *n*
plataforma de lanzamiento.
launder ['lɔːndə*] *vt* lavar.
launderette [lɔːn'drɛt] *n* lavandería
(automática).
laundry ['lɔːndrɪ] *n* lavandería; (*clothes*)
ropa sucia; **to do the** ~ hacer la colada.
laureate ['lɔːrɪət] *a see* **poet.**
laurel ['lɔrl] *n* laurel *m*.
lava ['lɑːvə] *n* lava.
lavatory ['lævətərɪ] *n* lavabo; **lavatories**
npl servicios *mpl*, aseos *mpl*.
lavender ['lævəndə*] *n* lavanda.
lavish ['lævɪʃ] *a* abundante; (*giving freely*):
~ **with** pródigo en // *vt*: **to** ~ **sth on sb**
colmar a uno de algo.
law [lɔː] *n* ley *f*; (*study*) derecho; (*of game*)
regla; ~-**abiding** *a* que cumple la ley; ~
and order *n* órden *m* público; ~**breaker**
n infractor *m* (de la ley); ~ **court** *n*
tribunal *m* (de justicia); ~**ful** *a* legítimo,
lícito; ~**fully** *ad* legalmente; ~**less** *a*
(*act*) ilegal; (*person*) rebelde; (*country*)
desordenado.
lawn [lɔːn] *n* césped *m*; ~**mower** *n*
cortacésped *m*; ~ **tennis** [-'tɛnɪs] *n* tenis
m.
law: ~ **school** *n* facultad *f* de derecho; ~
student *n* estudiante *m/f* de derecho.
lawsuit ['lɔːsuːt] *n* pleito.
lawyer ['lɔːjə*] *n* abogado; (*for sales, wills
etc*) notario.
lax [læks] *a* flojo; (*negligent*) negligente.
laxative ['læksətɪv] *n* laxante *m*.
laxity ['læksɪtɪ] *n* flojedad *f*; (*moral*)
relajamiento; (*negligence*) negligencia.
lay [leɪ] *pt of* **lie** // *a* laico; (*not expert*)
profano // *vt, pt, pp* **laid** (*place*) colocar;
(*eggs, table*) poner; (*trap*) tender; **to** ~
aside *or* **by** *vt* dejar a un lado; **to** ~ **down**
vt (*pen etc*) dejar; (~ *flat*) acostar; (*arms*)
rendir; (*policy*) asentar; **to** ~ **down the
law** imponer la ley; **to** ~ **off** *vt* (*workers*)
despedir, poner en paro; **to** ~ **on** *vt*
(*water, gas*) instalar; (*provide*) proveer; **to**
~ **out** *vt* (*design*) diseñar; (*display*)
disponer; (*spend*) gastar; **to** ~ **up** *vt*
(*store*) guardar; (*ship*) desarmar; (*subj:
illness*) obligar a guardar cama; ~**about**
n vago/a; ~-**by** *n* apartadero.
layer ['leɪə*] *n* capa.
layette [leɪ'ɛt] *n* canastilla, ajuar *m* (de
niño).
layman ['leɪmən] *n* persona no experta;
(*REL*) lego.
layout ['leɪaut] *n* (*design*) plan *m*, trazado;
(*disposition*) disposición *f*; (*PRESS*)
composición *f*.
laze [leɪz] *vi* no hacer nada; (*pej*)

holgazanear; **laziness** *n* pereza; **lazy** *a*
perezoso, vago.
lb. *abbr of* **pound** (*weight*).
lead [liːd] *n* (*front position*) delantera;
(*SPORT*) liderato; (*distance, time ahead*)
ventaja; (*clue*) pista; (*ELEC*) cable *m*; (*for
dog*) correa; (*THEATRE*) papel *m* principal
// *n* [lɛd] plomo; (*in pencil*) mina // (*vb: pt,
pp* **led**) *vt* conducir; (*induce*) llevar; (*be
leader of*) dirigir; (*SPORT*) ir en cabeza de
// *vi* ir primero; **to** ~ **to** llevar a, salir a;
to ~ **astray** *vt* llevar por mal camino; **to**
~ **away** *vt* llevar; **to** ~ **back** *vt* hacer
volver; **to** ~ **on** *vt* (*tease*) coquetear con;
to ~ **on to** *vt* (*induce*) incitar a; **to** ~ **up
to** conducir a.
leader ['liːdə*] *n* (*gen*) jefe *m*, líder *m*; (*of
union etc*) dirigente *m/f*; (*of gang*)
cabecilla *m*; (*guide*) guía *m/f*; (*of
newspaper*) artículo de fondo; ~**ship** *n*
dirección *f*; (*quality*) dotes *fpl* de mando.
leading ['liːdɪŋ] *a* (*main*) principal;
(*outstanding*) destacado; (*first*) primero;
(*front*) delantero; ~ **lady** *n* (*THEATRE*)
primera actriz *f*; ~ **light** *n* (*person*)
figura principal.
leaf [liːf], *pl* **leaves** *n* hoja // *vi*: **to** ~
through hojear; **to turn over a new** ~
reformarse.
leaflet ['liːflɪt] *n* folleto.
league [liːg] *n* sociedad *f*; (*FOOTBALL*) liga;
to be in ~ **with** estar de manga con.
leak [liːk] *n* (*of liquid, gas*) escape *m*, fuga;
(*hole*) agujero; (*in roof*) gotera; (*of money*)
filtración *f* // *vi* (*shoes, ship*) hacer agua;
(*pipe*) tener (un) escape; (*roof*) gotear;
(*container*) salirse; (*gas*) escaparse; (*fig:
news*) filtrarse // *vt* (*gen*) dejar escapar;
(*exude*) rezumar; **the information was**
~**ed to the enemy** las informaciones se
pasaron al enemigo; **the news** ~**ed out**
trascendió la noticia.
lean [liːn] *a* (*thin*) flaco; (*meat*) magro //
(*vb: pt, pp* **leaned** *or* **leant** [lɛnt]) *vt*: **to** ~
sth on apoyar algo en // *vi* (*slope*)
inclinarse; (*rest*): **to** ~ **against** apoyarse
contra; **to** ~ **on** apoyarse en; (*fig: rely on*)
contar con (el apoyo de); **to** ~
back/forward *vi* inclinarse hacia
atrás/hacia adelante; **to** ~ **over** *vi*
ladearse; ~**ing** *a* inclinado // *n*: ~**ing**
(**towards**) inclinación *f* (hacia); ~-**to** *n*
colgadizo.
leap [liːp] *n* salto // *vi, pt, pp* **leaped** *or*
leapt [lɛpt] saltar; ~**frog** *n* pídola; ~
year *n* año bisiesto.
learn [lɜːn], *pt, pp* **learned** *or* **learnt** *vt*
(*gen*) aprender; (*come to know of*)
enterarse de // *vi* aprender; **to** ~ **how to
do sth** aprender a hacer algo; ~**ed**
['lɜːnɪd] *a* erudito; ~**er** *n* principiante *m/f*;
~**ing** *n* el saber *m*, conocimientos *mpl*.
lease [liːs] *n* arriendo // *vt* arrendar.
leash [liːʃ] *n* cuerda.
least [liːst] *a* (*slightest*) menor; (*smallest*)
más pequeño; (*smallest amount of*) mínimo
// *ad* menos // *n*: **the** ~ lo menos; **the** ~

possible effort el mínimo de esfuerzo posible; **at** ~ por lo menos, al menos; **not in the** ~ en absoluto.
leather ['lɛðə*] n cuero.
leave [li:v], pt, pp **left** vt dejar; (go away from) abandonar // vi irse; (train) salir // n permiso; **to be left** quedar, sobrar; **there's some milk left over** sobra o queda algo de leche; **on** ~ de permiso; **to take one's** ~ **of** despedirse de; **to** ~ **out** vt omitir.
leaves [li:vz] pl of **leaf**.
Lebanon ['lɛbənən] n Líbano.
lecherous ['lɛtʃərəs] a lascivo.
lecture ['lɛktʃə*] n conferencia; (SCOL) clase f // vi dar una clase // vt (scold) sermonear; **to give a** ~ **on** dar una conferencia sobre; **lecturer** n conferenciante m/f; (at university) profesor adjunto/profesora adjunta m/f.
led [lɛd] pt, pp of **lead**.
ledge [lɛdʒ] n (of window, on wall) repisa, reborde m; (of mountain) plataforma.
ledger ['lɛdʒə*] n libro mayor.
lee [li:] n sotavento.
leek [li:k] n puerro.
leer [liə*] vi: **to** ~ **at sb** mirar impúdicamente a alguien.
leeway ['li:wei] n (fig): **to have some** ~ tener cierta libertad de acción.
left [lɛft] pt, pp of **leave** // a izquierdo; (POL) de izquierda // n izquierda // ad la izquierda; **the L**~ (POL) la izquierda; ~**-handed** a zurdo; **the** ~**-hand side** n la izquierda; ~**-luggage (office)** n consigna; ~**-overs** npl sobras fpl; ~**-wing** a (POL) de izquierdas, izquierdista.
leg [lɛg] n pierna; (of animal) pata; (of chair) pie m; (CULIN. of meat) pierna; (of journey) etapa; **lst/2nd** ~ (SPORT) partido de ida/de vuelta; **to pull sb's** ~ bromear con uno.
legacy ['lɛgəsi] n legado.
legal ['li:gl] a (gen) lícito; (of law) legal; (enquiry etc) jurídico; ~**ize** vt legalizar; ~**ly** ad legalmente; ~ **tender** n moneda corriente.
legend ['lɛdʒənd] n leyenda; ~**ary** a legendario.
legible ['lɛdʒəbl] a legible.
legion ['li:dʒən] n legión f.
legislate ['lɛdʒisleit] vi legislar; **legislation** [-'leiʃən] n legislación f; **legislative** [-lətiv] a legislativo; **legislature** [-lətʃə*] n cuerpo legislativo.
legitimacy [li'dʒitiməsi] n legitimidad f; **legitimate** [-mət] a legítimo.
leg-room ['lɛgru:m] n espacio para las piernas.
leisure ['lɛʒə*] n ocio, tiempo libre; **at** ~ con tranquilidad; ~ **centre** n centro de diversiones; ~**ly** a pausado, lento.
lemon ['lɛmən] n limón m; ~**ade** [-'neid] n (fruit juice) limonada; (fizzy) gaseosa.
lend [lɛnd] pt, pp **lent** vt: **to** ~ **sth to sb** prestar algo a alguien; ~**er** n prestador/a

m/f; ~**ing library** n biblioteca circulante.
length [lɛŋθ] n largo, longitud f; (section: of road, pipe etc) tramo; **at** ~ (at last) por fin, finalmente; (lengthily) largamente; ~**en** vt alargar // vi alargarse; ~**ways** ad de largo; ~**y** a largo, extenso; (meeting) prolongado.
leniency ['li:niənsi] n indulgencia; **lenient** [-ənt] a indulgente.
lens [lɛnz] n (of spectacles) lente f; (of camera) objetivo.
lent [lɛnt] pt, pp of **lend**.
Lent [lɛnt] n Cuaresma.
lentil ['lɛntl] n lenteja.
Leo ['li:əu] n Leo.
leopard ['lɛpəd] n leopardo.
leotard ['li:ətɑ:d] n leotardo.
leper ['lɛpə*] n leproso/a; **leprosy** [-prəsi] n lepra.
lesbian ['lɛzbiən] n lesbiana.
less [lɛs] det a (in size, degree etc) menor; (in quantity) menos // pron, ad menos; ~ **than half** menos de la mitad; ~ **and** ~ cada vez menos; **the** ~ **he works...** cuanto menos trabaja... .
lessen ['lɛsn] vi disminuir, menguar // vt disminuir, reducir.
lesson ['lɛsn] n lección f; **a maths** ~ una clase o una lección de matemáticas.
lest [lɛst] conj: ~ **it happen** para que no pase.
let [lɛt] pt, pp **let** vt (allow) dejar, permitir; (lease) alquilar; ~**'s go** ¡vamos!; ~ **him come** que venga; **'to** ~' 'se alquila'; **to** ~ **down** vt (lower) bajar; (dress) alargar; (tyre) desinflar; (hair) soltar; (disappoint) defraudar; **to** ~ **go** vi soltar; (fig) dejarse ir // vt abandonar; **to** ~ **in** vt dejar entrar; (visitor etc) hacer pasar; **to** ~ **off** vt dejar libre; (firework etc) disparar; (smell etc) despedir; **to** ~ **on** vt (col) divulgar (that que); **to** ~ **out** vt dejar salir; (dress) ensanchar; **to** ~ **up** vi amainar, disminuir.
lethal ['li:θl] a mortífero; (wound) mortal.
lethargic [lɛ'θɑ:dʒik] a letárgico; **lethargy** ['lɛθədʒi] n letargo.
letter ['lɛtə*] n (of alphabet) letra; (correspondence) carta; ~ **bomb** n carta con bomba explosiva; ~**box** n buzón m; ~**ing** n letras fpl.
lettuce ['lɛtis] n lechuga.
let-up ['lɛtʌp] n descanso, tregua.
leukaemia, leukemia (US) [lu:'ki:miə] n leucemia.
level ['lɛvl] a (flat) llano; (flattened) nivelado; (uniform) igual // ad a nivel // n nivel m; (flat place) llano // vt nivelar, allanar; **to be** ~ **with** estar a nivel de; **'A'** ~**s** npl Bachillerato Superior, B.U.P.; **'O'** ~**s** npl bachillerato elemental, octavo de básica; **on the** ~ (fig: honest) en serio; **to** ~ **off** or **out** vi (prices etc) estabilizarse; ~ **crossing** n paso a nivel; ~**-headed** a sensato.
lever ['li:və*] n palanca // vt: **to** ~ **up**

alzar con palanca; ~**age** n (fig: influence) influencia.

levity ['lɛvɪtɪ] n frivolidad f, informalidad f.

levy ['lɛvɪ] n impuesto // vt exigir, recaudar.

lewd [lu:d] a impúdico, obsceno.

liability [laɪə'bɪlətɪ] n responsabilidad f; (handicap) desventaja; (risk) riesgo; **liabilities** npl obligaciones fpl; (COMM) deudas fpl, pasivo sg.

liable ['laɪəbl] a (subject): ~ **to** sujeto a; **to be** ~ **for** ser responsable de; **to be** ~ **to** (likely) tener tendencia a.

liaison [li:'eɪzɔn] n (coordination) enlace m; (affair) relaciones fpl amorosas.

liar ['laɪə*] n mentiroso/a.

libel ['laɪbl] n calumnia // vt calumniar.

liberal ['lɪbərl] a (gen) liberal; (generous): ~ **with** generoso con.

liberate ['lɪbəreɪt] vt liberar; **liberation** [-'reɪʃən] n liberación f.

liberty ['lɪbətɪ] n libertad f; **to be at** ~ **to** tener permiso para; **to take the** ~ **of doing sth** tomarse la libertad de hacer algo.

Libra ['li:brə] n Libra.

librarian [laɪ'brɛərɪən] n bibliotecario/a.

library ['laɪbrərɪ] n biblioteca.

libretto [lɪ'brɛtəu] n libreto.

Libya ['lɪbɪə] n Libia; ~**n** a, n libio/a.

lice [laɪs] pl of **louse**.

licence, license (US) ['laɪsns] n (gen) licencia; (permit) permiso; (also: **driving** ~) carnet m de conducir; (excessive freedom) libertinaje m; ~ **number** n matrícula; ~ **plate** n placa (de matrícula).

license ['laɪsns] n (US) = **licence** // vt autorizar, licenciar; ~**d** a (for alcohol) autorizado para la venta de bebidas alcohólicas.

licensee [laɪsən'si:] n (in a pub) patrón/ona m/f.

licentious [laɪ'sɛnʃəs] a licencioso.

lichen ['laɪkən] n líquen m.

lick [lɪk] vt lamer // n lamedura; **a** ~ **of paint** una mano de pintura.

licorice ['lɪkərɪs] n = **liquorice**.

lid [lɪd] n (of box, case) tapa; (of pan) cobertera.

lido ['laɪdəu] n piscina.

lie [laɪ] n mentira // vi mentir // vi, pt **lay**, pp **lain** (act) echarse; (state) estar echado, estar acostado; (of object: be situated) estar, encontrarse; **to** ~ **low** (fig) esconderse; **to** ~ **about** vi (things) estar en desorden; (people) gandulear; **to have a** ~**-down** echarse (una siesta); **to have a** ~**-in** quedarse pegado a las sábanas.

lieu [lu:]: **in** ~ **of** prep en lugar de.

lieutenant [lɛf'tɛnənt] n lugarteniente m; (MIL) teniente m.

life [laɪf], pl **lives** n (gen) vida; (way of ~) modo de vivir; (of licence etc) vigencia; ~ **assurance** n seguro de vida; ~**belt** n cinturón m salvavidas; ~**boat** n bote m salvavidas; ~**guard** n vigilante m; ~

jacket n chaleco salvavidas; ~**less** a sin vida; (dull) soso; ~**like** a natural; ~**line** n cuerda salvavidas; ~**long** a de toda la vida; ~**-saver** n bañero, socorrista m/f; ~ **sentence** n condena perpetua; ~**-sized** a de tamaño natural; ~ **span** n vida; ~ **support system** n (MED) respirador m artificial; ~**time** n: **in his** ~**time** durante su vida; **once in a** ~**time** una vez en la vida.

lift [lɪft] vt levantar; (steal) robar // vi (fog) levantarse, disiparse // n (elevator) ascensor m; **to give sb a** ~ llevar a uno en el coche; ~**-off** n despegue m.

ligament ['lɪgəmənt] n ligamento.

light [laɪt] n (gen) luz f; (flame) lumbre f; (lamp) luz f, lámpara; (daylight) luz del día; (headlight) faro; (rear ~) luz trasera; (for cigarette etc): **have you got a** ~? ¿tiene fuego? // vt, pt, pp **lighted** or **lit** (candle, cigarette, fire) encender; (room) alumbrar // a (colour) claro; (not heavy, also fig) ligero; (room) alumbrado; **to** ~ **up** vi (smoke) encender un cigarrillo; (face) iluminarse // vt (illuminate) iluminar, alumbrar; ~ **bulb** n bombilla; ~**en** vi (grow ~) clarear // vt (give light to) iluminar; (make lighter) aclarar; (make less heavy) aligerar; ~**er** n (also: **cigarette** ~**er**) encendedor m, mechero; ~**-headed** a (dizzy) mareado; (excited) exaltado; (by nature) casquivano; ~**-hearted** a alegre; ~**house** n faro; ~**ing** n (act) iluminación f; (system) alumbrado; ~**ly** ad (touch) ligeramente; (thoughtlessly) a la ligera; (slightly) levemente; (not seriously) con poca seriedad; **to get off** ~**ly** ser castigado con poca severidad; ~ **meter** n (PHOT) fotómetro; ~**ness** n claridad f; (in weight) ligereza.

lightning ['laɪtnɪŋ] n relámpago, rayo; ~ **conductor** n pararrayos m inv.

light: ~**weight** a (suit) ligero // n (BOXING) peso ligero; ~ **year** n año luz.

like [laɪk] vt (person) querer, tener cariño a; (things) gustarle a uno // prep como // a parecido, semejante // n: **the** ~ semejante m/f; **his** ~**s and dislikes** sus gustos y aversiones; **I would** ~, **I'd** ~ me gustaría; (for purchase) quisiera; **would you** ~ **a coffee?** ¿te apetece un café?; **to be** or **look** ~ **sb/sth** parecerse a alguien/algo; **that's just** ~ **him** es muy de él, es característico de él; **it is nothing** ~**...** no tiene parecido alguno con...; ~**able** a simpático, agradable.

likelihood ['laɪklɪhud] n probabilidad f;

likely [-lɪ] a probable; **he's likely to leave** es probable que se vaya.

like-minded [laɪk'maɪndɪd] a de la misma opinión.

liken ['laɪkən] vt: **to** ~ **sth to sth** comparar algo con algo.

likewise ['laɪkwaɪz] ad igualmente.

liking ['laɪkɪŋ] n: **to his** ~ para su gusto.

lilac ['laɪlək] n lila // a (colour) de color lila.

lily ['lɪlɪ] n lirio, azucena; ~ **of the valley** n lirio de los valles.

limb [lɪm] n miembro.

limber ['lɪmbə*]: **to** ~ **up** vi (fig) entrenarse; (SPORT) desentumecerse.

limbo ['lɪmbəu] n: **to be in** ~ (fig) caer en el olvido.

lime [laɪm] n (tree) limero; (fruit) lima; (GEO) cal f.

limelight ['laɪmlaɪt] n: **to be in the** ~ (fig) ser el centro de atención.

limerick ['lɪmərɪk] n quintilla humorística.

limestone ['laɪmstəun] n piedra caliza.

limit ['lɪmɪt] n límite m // vt limitar; ~**ation** [-'teɪʃən] n limitación f; ~**ed** a limitado; **to be** ~**ed to** limitarse a; ~**ed (liability) company (Ltd)** n sociedad f anónima; ~**less** a sin límites.

limousine ['lɪməziːn] n limusina.

limp [lɪmp] n: **to have a** ~ tener cojera // vi cojear // a flujo.

limpet ['lɪmpɪt] n lapa.

limpid ['lɪmpɪd] a límpido, cristalino.

line [laɪn] n (gen) línea; (straight ~) raya; (rope) cuerda; (for fishing) sedal m; (wire) hilo; (row, series) fila, hilera; (of writing) renglón m; (on face) arruga; (specialty) rama // vt (SEWING) forrar (with de); **to** ~ **the streets** ocupar las aceras; **in** ~ **with** de acuerdo con; **to** ~ **up** vi hacer cola // vt alinear, poner en fila; ~**d** a (face) arrugado; (paper) rayado.

linear ['lɪnɪə*] a lineal.

linen ['lɪnɪn] n ropa blanca; (cloth) lino.

liner ['laɪnə*] n vapor m de línea, transatlántico.

linesman ['laɪnzmən] n (SPORT) juez m de línea.

line-up ['laɪnʌp] n alineación f.

linger ['lɪŋgə*] vi retrasarse, tardar en marcharse; (smell, tradition) persistir.

lingerie ['lænʒəriː] n ropa interior (de mujer).

lingering ['lɪŋgərɪŋ] a persistente; (death) lento.

lingo ['lɪŋgəu], pl ~**es** n (pej) jerga.

linguist ['lɪŋgwɪst] n lingüista m/f; ~**ic** a lingüístico; ~**ics** n lingüística.

lining ['laɪnɪŋ] n forro.

link [lɪŋk] n (of a chain) eslabón m; (connection) conexión f; (bond) vínculo, lazo // vt vincular, unir; ~**s** npl campo sg de golf; **to** ~ **up** vt acoplar // vi unirse; ~-**up** n (gen) unión f; (in space) acoplamiento.

lino ['laɪnəu], **linoleum** [lɪ'nəuliəm] n linóleo.

lintel ['lɪntl] n dintel m.

lion ['laɪən] n león m; ~**ess** n leona.

lip [lɪp] n labio; (of jug) pico; (of cup etc) borde m; ~**read** vi leer los labios; ~ **service** n: **to pay** ~ **service to sth** alabar algo pero sin hacer nada; ~**stick**

n lápiz m labial, barra de labios.

liquefy ['lɪkwɪfaɪ] vt liquidar.

liqueur [lɪ'kjuə*] n licor m.

liquid ['lɪkwɪd] a, n líquido.

liquidate ['lɪkwɪdeɪt] vt liquidar; **liquidation** [-'deɪʃən] n liquidación f; **liquidator** n liquidador/a m/f.

liquidize ['lɪkwɪdaɪz] vt (CULIN) licuar.

liquor ['lɪkə*] n licor m, bebidas alcohólicas fpl.

liquorice ['lɪkərɪs] n regaliz m.

lisp [lɪsp] n ceceo.

list [lɪst] n lista; (of ship) inclinación f // vt (write down) hacer una lista de; (enumerate) catalogar // vi (ship) inclinarse.

listen ['lɪsn] vi escuchar, oír; (pay attention) atender; ~**er** n oyente m/f.

listless ['lɪstlɪs] a apático, indiferente.

lit [lɪt] pt, pp of **light.**

litany ['lɪtənɪ] n letanía.

literacy ['lɪtərəsɪ] n capacidad f de leer y escribir; ~ **campaign** campaña de alfabetización.

literal ['lɪtərl] a literal; ~**ly** ad literalmente.

literary ['lɪtərərɪ] a literario.

literate ['lɪtərət] a que sabe leer y escribir; (fig) culto.

literature ['lɪtərɪtʃə*] n literatura; (brochures etc) folletos mpl.

lithe [laɪð] a ágil.

litigation [lɪtɪ'geɪʃən] n litigio.

litre, liter (US) ['liːtə*] n litro.

litter ['lɪtə*] n (rubbish) basura; (paper) papel m tirado; (young animals) camada, cría; (stretcher) camilla; ~ **bin** n papelera; ~**ed** a: ~**ed with** (scattered) esparcido con; (covered with) lleno de.

little ['lɪtl] a (small) pequeño; (not much) poco; often translated by suffix: eg ~ **house** casita // ad poco; **a** ~ un poco (de); ~ **by** ~ poco a poco.

liturgy ['lɪtədʒɪ] n liturgia.

live [lɪv] vi vivir // vt (a life) llevar; (experience) vivir // a [laɪv] (animal) vivo; (wire) conectado; (broadcast) en directo; (shell) cargado; **to** ~ **down** vt hacer olvidar; **to** ~ **on** vt fus (food) vivirse de, alimentarse de; **to** ~ **up to** vt fus (fulfil) cumplir con; (justify) justificar.

livelihood ['laɪvlɪhud] n sustento.

lively ['laɪvlɪ] a (gen) vivo; (talk) animado; (pace) rápido; (party, tune) alegre.

liver ['lɪvə*] n (ANAT) hígado; ~**ish** a (fig) rezongón(ona).

livery ['lɪvərɪ] n librea.

lives [laɪvz] pl of **life.**

livestock ['laɪvstɔk] n ganado.

livid ['lɪvɪd] a lívido; (furious) furioso.

living ['lɪvɪŋ] a (alive) vivo // n: **to earn** or **make a** ~ ganarse la vida; ~ **conditions** npl condiciones fpl de vida; ~ **room** n sala (de estar); ~ **standards** npl nivel m de vida; ~ **wage** n sueldo suficiente para vivir.

lizard ['lɪzəd] n lagartija.
llama ['lɑːmə] n llama.
load [ləud] n (gen) carga; (weight) peso // vt: **to ~ (with)** cargar (con); (fig) colmar (de); **a ~ of, ~s of** (fig) (gran) cantidad de, montones de; **~ed** a (dice) cargado; (question, word) intencionado; (col: rich) forrado (de dinero); (: drunk) trompa.
loaf [ləuf], pl **loaves** n (barra de) pan m // vi (also: **~ about, ~ around**) holgazanear.
loan [ləun] n préstamo; (COMM) empréstito // vt prestar; **on ~** prestado.
loath [ləuθ] a: **to be ~ to do sth** estar poco dispuesto a hacer algo.
loathe [ləuð] vt aborrecer; (person) odiar; **loathing** n aversión f; odio; **it fills me with loathing** me da asco.
loaves [ləuvz] pl of **loaf**.
lobby ['lɔbɪ] n vestíbulo, sala de espera; (POL: pressure group) grupo de presión // vt presionar.
lobe [ləub] n lóbulo.
lobster ['lɔbstə*] n langosta; (large) bogavante m.
local ['ləukl] a local // n (pub) bar m; **the ~s** npl los vecinos, los del lugar; **~ity** [-'kælɪtɪ] n localidad f; **~ly** [-kəlɪ] ad en la vecindad.
locate [ləu'keɪt] vt (find) localizar; (situate) colocar.
location [ləu'keɪʃən] n situación f; **on ~** (CINEMA) en exteriores, fuera del estudio.
loch [lɔx] n lago.
lock [lɔk] n (of door, box) cerradura; (of canal) esclusa; (stop) tope m; (of hair) mechón m // vt (with key) cerrar con llave; (immobilize) inmovilizar // vi (door etc) cerrarse con llave; (wheels) bloquearse, trabarse.
locker ['lɔkə*] n casillero.
locket ['lɔkɪt] n medallón m.
lockout ['lɔkaut] n paro patronal, lockout m.
locomotive [ləukə'məutɪv] n locomotora.
locum ['ləukəm] n (MED) (médico) interino.
locust ['ləukəst] n langosta.
lodge [lɔdʒ] n casa del guarda; (porter's) portería; (FREEMASONRY) logia // vi (person): **to ~ (with)** alojarse (en casa de) // vt (complaint) presentar; **lodger** n huésped/a m/f.
lodgings ['lɔdʒɪŋz] npl alojamiento sg; (house) casa sg de huéspedes.
loft [lɔft] n desván m.
lofty ['lɔftɪ] a alto; (haughty) orgulloso.
log [lɔg] n (of wood) leño, tronco; (book) = **logbook.**
logarithm ['lɔgərɪðəm] n logaritmo.
logbook ['lɔgbuk] n (NAUT) diario de a bordo; (AVIAT) libro de vuelo; (of car) documentación f (del coche).
loggerheads ['lɔgəhɛdz] npl: **at ~ (with)** de pique (con).
logic ['lɔdʒɪk] n lógica; **~al** a lógico.

logistics [lɔ'dʒɪstɪks] n logística.
loin [lɔɪn] n (CULIN) lomo, solomillo; **~s** npl lomos mpl; **~ cloth** n taparrobo.
loiter ['lɔɪtə*] vi perder el tiempo; (pej) merodear.
loll [lɔl] vi (also: **~ about**) repantigarse.
lollipop ['lɔlɪpɔp] n pirulí m; (iced) polo; **~ man/lady** n persona encargada de ayudar a los niños a cruzar la calle.
London ['lʌndən] n Londres; **~er** n londinense m/f.
lone [ləun] a solitario.
loneliness ['ləunlɪnɪs] n soledad f, aislamiento; **lonely** [-lɪ] a solitario, solo.
loner ['ləunə*] n solitario.
long [lɔŋ] a largo // ad mucho tiempo, largamente // vi: **to ~ for sth** anhelar o suspirar por algo; **in the ~ run** a la larga; **so** or **as ~ as** mientras, con tal que; **don't be ~!** ¡no tardes!, ¡vuelve pronto!; **how ~ is the street?** ¿cuánto tiene la calle de largo?; **how ~ is the lesson?** ¿cuánto dura la lección?; **6 metres ~** que mide 6 metros, de 6 metros de largo; **6 months ~** que dura 6 meses, de 6 meses de duración; **all night ~** toda la noche; **~ before** mucho antes; **before ~** (+ future) dentro de poco; (+ past) poco tiempo después; **at ~ last** al fin, por fin; **~-distance** a (race) de larga distancia; (call) interurbano; **~-haired** a de pelo largo; **~-hand** n escritura (corriente); **~-ing** n anhelo, ansia; (nostalgia) nostalgia // a anhelante.
longitude ['lɔŋgɪtjuːd] n longitud f.
long: ~ jump n salto de longitud; **~-lost** a desaparecido hace mucho tiempo; **~-playing record (L.P.)** n elepé m, disco de larga duración; **~-range** a de gran alcance; **~-sighted** a (fig) previsor(a); **~-standing** a de mucho tiempo; **~-suffering** a sufrido; **~-term** a a largo plazo; **~ wave** a de onda larga; **~-winded** a prolijo.
loo [luː] n (col) wáter m.
loofah ['luːfə] n esponja de lufa.
look [luk] vi mirar; (seem) parecer; (building etc): **to ~ south/on to the sea** dar al sur/al mar // n mirada; (glance) vistazo; (appearance) aire m, aspecto; **~s** npl físico, apariencia; **to ~ like sb** parecerse a alguien; **to ~ after** vt fus cuidar a; **to ~ at** vt fus mirar; (consider) considerar; **to ~ back** vi mirar hacia atrás; **to ~ down on** vt fus (fig) despreciar, mirar con desprecio; **to ~ for** vt fus buscar; **to ~ forward to** vt fus esperar con ilusión; **to ~ into** vt investigar; **to ~ on** vi mirar (como espectador); **to ~ out** vi (beware): **to ~ out (for)** tener cuidado (de); **to ~ out for sth** (seek) buscar; (await) esperar; **to ~ round** vi volver la cabeza; **to ~ to** vt fus ocuparse de; (rely on) contar con; **to ~ up** vi mirar hacia arriba; (improve) mejorar // vt (word) buscar; (friend) visitar; **to ~ up to** vt fus admirar; **~-out**

n (*tower etc*) puesto de observación; (*person*) vigía *m*; **to be on the ~-out for sth** estar al acecho de algo.
loom [lu:m] *n* telar *m* // *vi* asomarse; (*threaten*) amenazar.
loony ['lu:nɪ] *n* (*col*) loco/a; ~ **bin** *n* (*col*) manicomio.
loop [lu:p] *n* lazo; (*bend*) vuelta, recodo; (*contraceptive*) espiral *f*; ~**hole** *n* escapatoria.
loose [lu:s] *a* (*gen*) suelto; (*not tight*) flojo; (*wobbly etc*) movedizo; (*clothes*) ancho; (*morals, discipline*) relajado; **to be at a** ~ **end** no saber qué hacer; ~**ly** *ad* libremente, aproximadamente; **loosen** *vt* (*free*) soltar; (*untie*) desatar; (*slacken*) aflojar.
loot [lu:t] *n* botín *m* // *vt* saquear; ~**ing** *n* pillaje *m*.
lop [lɔp]: **to** ~ **off** *vt* cortar; (*branches*) podar.
lop-sided ['lɔp'saɪdɪd] *a* desequilibrado.
lord [lɔ:d] *n* señor *m*; **L**~ **Smith** Lord Smith; **the** ľ ~ **el** Señor; **the (House of) L**~**s** la Cámara de los Lores; ~**ly** *a* señorial; (*arrogant*) arrogante; ~**ship** *n*: **your L**~**ship** su señoría.
lore [lɔ:*] *n* saber *m* popular, tradiciones *fpl*.
lorry ['lɔrɪ] *n* camión *m*; ~ **driver** *n* camionero.
lose [lu:z], *pt, pp* **lost** *vt* perder // *vi* perder, ser vencido; **to** ~ (**time**) (*clock*) atrasarse; **loser** *n* perdedor/a *m/f*.
loss [lɔs] *n* pérdida; **to be at a** ~ no saber qué hacer; **to be a dead** ~ ser completamente inútil.
lost [lɔst] *pt, pp of* **lose** // *a* perdido; ~ **property** *n* objetos *mpl* perdidos.
lot [lɔt] *n* (*at auctions*) lote *m*; (*destiny*) suerte *f*; **the** ~ el todo, todos; **a** ~ mucho, bastante; **a** ~ **of**, ~**s of** mucho(s) (*pl*); **to draw** ~**s (for sth)** echar suertes (para decidir algo); **I read a** ~ leo bastante.
lotion ['ləuʃən] *n* loción *f*.
lottery ['lɔtərɪ] *n* lotería.
loud [laud] *a* (*voice*) alto; (*shout*) fuerte; (*noisy*) estrepitoso; (*gaudy*) chillón(ona) // *ad* (*speak etc*) en alta voz; ~**hailer** *n* megáfono; ~**ly** *ad* (*noisily*) ruidosamente; (*aloud*) en alta voz; ~**speaker** *n* altavoz *m*.
lounge [laundʒ] *n* salón *m*, sala (de estar) // *vi* reposar, holgazanear; ~ **suit** *n* traje *m* de calle.
louse [laus], *pl* **lice** *n* piojo.
lousy ['lauzɪ] *a* (*fig*) vil, asqueroso.
lout [laut] *n* gamberro.
lovable ['lʌvəbl] *a* amable, simpático.
love [lʌv] *n* amor *m* // *vt* amar, querer; **to** ~ **to do** gustar(le a uno) mucho hacer; **to be in** ~ **with** estar enamorado de; **to make** ~ hacer el amor; **for the** ~ **of** por amor de; **'15** ~' (*TENNIS*) 15 a cero; **I** ~ **paella** me gusta mucho la paella; **'with** ~' con cariño; ~ **affair** *n* aventura

sentimental; ~ **letter** *n* carta de amor; ~ **life** *n* vida sentimental.
lovely ['lʌvlɪ] *a* (*delightful*) precioso, encantador(a); (*beautiful*) hermoso.
lover ['lʌvə*] *n* amante *m/f*; (*amateur*): **a** ~ **of** un aficionado a *o* un amante de.
lovesong ['lʌvsɔŋ] *n* canción *f* de amor.
loving ['lʌvɪŋ] *a* amoroso, cariñoso.
low [ləu] *a, ad* bajo // *n* (*METEOROLOGY*) área de baja presión // *vi* (*cow*) mugir; **to feel** ~ sentirse deprimido; **to turn (down)** ~ *vt* bajar; ~**-cut** *a* (*dress*) escotado.
lower ['ləuə*] *vt* bajar; (*reduce*) reducir // *vr*: **to** ~ **o.s. to** (*fig*) rebajarse a.
low: ~**-grade** *a* de baja calidad; ~**ly** *a* humilde; ~**-lying** *a* de bajo nivel.
loyal ['lɔɪəl] *a* leal; ~**ty** *n* lealtad *f*.
lozenge ['lɔzɪndʒ] *n* (*MED*) pastilla.
L.P. *n* *abbr of* **long-playing record**.
L-plates ['ɛlpleɪts] *npl* placa de aprendiz de conductor.
Ltd *abbr of* **limited company** S.A.
lubricant ['lu:brɪkənt] *n* lubricante *m*; **lubricate** [-keɪt] *vt* lubricar, engrasar.
lucid ['lu:sɪd] *a* lúcido; ~**ity** [-'sɪdɪtɪ] *n* lucidez *f*.
luck [lʌk] *n* suerte *f*; **bad** ~ mala suerte; **good** ~! ¡que tengas suerte!, ¡suerte!; ~**ily** *ad* afortunadamente; ~**y** *a* afortunado.
lucrative ['lu:krətɪv] *a* lucrativo.
ludicrous ['lu:dɪkrəs] *a* absurdo.
ludo ['lu:dəu] *n* parchís *m*.
lug [lʌg] *vt* (*drag*) arrastrar; (*pull*) tirar de.
luggage ['lʌgɪdʒ] *n* equipaje *m*; ~ **rack** *n* (*in train*) rejilla, redecilla; (*on car*) vaca, portaequipajes *m inv*.
lukewarm ['lu:kwɔ:m] *a* tibio, templado.
lull [lʌl] *n* tregua // *vt* (*child*) acunar; (*person, fear*) calmar.
lullaby ['lʌləbaɪ] *n* canción *f* de cuna.
lumbago [lʌm'beɪgəu] *n* lumbago.
lumber ['lʌmbə*] *n* (*junk*) trastos viejos *mpl*; (*wood*) maderos *mpl*; ~**jack** *n* maderero.
luminous ['lu:mɪnəs] *a* luminoso.
lump [lʌmp] *n* terrón *m*; (*fragment*) trozo; (*in sauce*) grumo; (*in throat*) nudo; (*swelling*) bulto // *vt* (*also*: ~ **together**) amontonar; **a** ~ **sum** suma global; ~**y** *a* (*sauce*) lleno de grumos.
lunacy ['lu:nəsɪ] *n* locura.
lunar ['lu:nə*] *a* lunar.
lunatic ['lu:nətɪk] *a, n* loco/a; ~ **asylum** *n* manicomio.
lunch [lʌntʃ] *n* almuerzo, comida // *vi* almorzar; ~ **time** *n* hora del almuerzo *o* de comer.
luncheon ['lʌntʃən] *n* almuerzo; ~ **meat** *n* pastel *m* de carne.
lung [lʌŋ] *n* pulmón *m*; ~ **cancer** *n* cáncer *m* de pulmón.
lunge [lʌndʒ] *vi* (*also*: ~ **forward**) abalanzarse; **to** ~ **at** arremeter contra.
lurch [lə:tʃ] *vi* dar sacudidas // *n* sacudida;

to leave sb in the ~ dejar a uno plantado.
lure [luə*] n (*bait*) cebo; (*decoy*) señuelo // vt atraer, seducir.
lurid ['luərɪd] a (*light*) misterioso; (*dress*) chillón(ona); (*account*) sensacional; (*detail*) horrible.
lurk [lɔːk] vi (*hide*) esconderse; (*wait*) estar al acecho.
luscious ['lʌʃəs] a delicioso.
lush [lʌʃ] a exuberante.
lust [lʌst] n lujuria; (*greed*) codicia; **to** ~ **after** vt fus codiciar; ~**ful** a lascivo, lujurioso.
lustre, luster (*US*) ['lʌstə*] n lustre m, brillo.
lusty ['lʌstɪ] a robusto, fuerte.
lute [luːt] n laúd m.
Luxembourg ['lʌksəmbɔːg] n Luxemburgo.
luxuriant [lʌg'zjuərɪənt] a exuberante.
luxurious [lʌg'zjuərɪəs] a lujoso; **luxury** ['lʌkʃərɪ] n lujo // cpd de lujo.
lying ['laɪɪŋ] n mentiras fpl // a mentiroso.
lynch [lɪntʃ] vt linchar; ~**ing** n linchamiento.
lynx [lɪŋks] n lince m.
lyre ['laɪə*] n lira.
lyric ['lɪrɪk] a lírico; ~**s** npl (*of song*) letra sg; ~**al** a lírico.

M

m. *abbr of* **metre; mile; million.**
M.A. *abbr of* **Master of Arts** licenciado en letras.
mac [mæk] n impermeable m.
macaroni [mækə'rəunɪ] n macarrones mpl.
mace [meɪs] n (*BOT*) macis f.
machine [mə'ʃiːn] n máquina // vt (*dress etc*) coser a máquina; ~ **gun** n ametralladora; ~**ry** n maquinaria; (*fig*) mecanismo; **machinist** n operario (de máquina).
mackerel ['mækrl] n, pl inv caballa.
mackintosh ['mækɪntɔʃ] n impermeable m.
mad [mæd] a (*gen*) loco; (*crazed*) demente; (*angry*) furioso.
madam ['mædəm] n señora.
madden ['mædn] vt volver loco.
made [meɪd] pt, pp of **make**; ~**-to-measure** a hecho a la medida.
madly ['mædlɪ] ad locamente.
madman ['mædmən] n loco.
madness ['mædnɪs] n locura.
magazine [mægə'ziːn] n revista; (*MIL: store*) almacén m; (*of firearm*) recámara.
maggot ['mægət] n gusano.
magic ['mædʒɪk] n magia // a mágico; ~**al** a mágico; ~**ian** [mə'dʒɪʃən] n mago; (*conjurer*) prestidigitador m.
magistrate ['mædʒɪstreɪt] n juez m/f (municipal).

magnanimous [mæg'nænɪməs] a magnánimo.
magnate ['mægneɪt] n magnate m.
magnet ['mægnɪt] n imán m; ~**ic** [-'nɛtɪk] a magnético; ~**ism** n magnetismo.
magnification [mægnɪfɪ'keɪʃən] n aumento.
magnificence [mæg'nɪfɪsns] n magnificencia; **magnificent** [-nt] a magnífico.
magnify ['mægnɪfaɪ] vt aumentar; (*fig*) exagerar; ~**ing glass** n lupa.
magnitude ['mægnɪtjuːd] n magnitud f.
magnolia [mæg'nəulɪə] n magnolia.
magpie ['mægpaɪ] n urraca.
mahogany [mə'hɔgənɪ] n caoba // cpd de caoba.
maid [meɪd] n criada; **old** ~ (*pej*) solterona.
maiden ['meɪdn] n doncella // a (*aunt etc*) solterona; (*speech, voyage*) inaugural; ~ **name** n nombre m de soltera.
mail [meɪl] n correo; (*letters*) cartas fpl // vt (*post*) echar al correo; (*send*) mandar por correo; ~**box** n (*US*) buzón m; ~**-order** n pedido postal; (*business*) venta por correo.
maim [meɪm] vt mutilar, lisiar.
main [meɪn] a principal, mayor // n (*pipe*) cañería maestra; **the** ~**s** (*ELEC*) la red eléctrica; **in the** ~ en general; ~**land** n continente m; ~**stay** n (*fig*) pilar m; ~**stream** n corriente f principal.
maintain [meɪn'teɪn] vt mantener; (*keep up*) conservar (en buen estado); (*affirm*) sostener; **maintenance** ['meɪntənəns] n mantenimiento.
maisonette [meɪzə'nɛt] n apartamento de dos pisos.
maize [meɪz] n maíz m.
majestic [mə'dʒɛstɪk] a majestuoso; **majesty** ['mædʒɪstɪ] n majestad f.
major ['meɪdʒə*] n (*MIL*) comandante m // a principal; (*MUS*) mayor.
Majorca [mə'jɔːkə] n Mallorca.
majority [mə'dʒɔrɪtɪ] n mayoría.
make [meɪk], pt, pp **made** vt hacer; (*manufacture*) hacer, fabricar; (*cause to be*): **to** ~ **sb sad** hacer o poner triste a alguien; (*force*): **to** ~ **sb do sth** obligar a uno a hacer algo; (*equal*): **2 and 2** ~ **4** 2 y 2 son 4 // n marca; **to** ~ **do with** contentarse con; **to** ~ **for** vt fus (*place*) dirigirse a; **to** ~ **out** vt (*decipher*) descifrar; (*understand*) entender; (*see*) distinguir; **to** ~ **up** vt (*invent*) inventar; (*parcel*) envolver // vi reconciliarse; (*with cosmetics*) maquillarse; **to** ~ **up for** vt fus compensar; ~**-believe** a fingido; **maker** n fabricante m/f; ~**shift** a improvisado; ~**-up** n maquillaje m.
making ['meɪkɪŋ] n (*fig*): **in the** ~ en vías de formación.
malaise [mæ'leɪz] n malestar m.
malaria [mə'lɛərɪə] n malaria.
Malay [mə'leɪ] a, n malayo/a.
Malaysia [mə'leɪzɪə] n Malaysia.

male [meɪl] *n* (*BIOL, ELEC*) macho // *a* (*sex, attitude*) masculino; (*child etc*) varón.
malevolent [mə'lɛvələnt] *a* malévolo.
malfunction [mæl'fʌŋkʃən] *n* funcionamiento defectuoso.
malice ['mælɪs] *n* (*ill will*) malevolencia; (*rancour*) rencor *m*; **malicious** [mə'lɪʃəs] *a* malévolo; rencoroso.
malign [mə'laɪn] *vt* difamar, calumniar // *a* maligno.
malignant [mə'lɪgnənt] *a* (*MED*) maligno.
malingerer [mə'lɪŋgərə*] *n* enfermo fingido.
malleable ['mælɪəbl] *a* maleable.
mallet ['mælɪt] *n* mazo.
malnutrition [mælnju:'trɪʃən] *n* desnutrición *f*.
malpractice [mæl'præktɪs] *n* falta profesional.
malt [mɔ:lt] *n* malta.
Malta ['mɔ:ltə] *n* Malta; **Maltese** [-'ti:z] *a*, *n*, *pl inv* maltés/esa *m/f*.
maltreat [mæl'tri:t] *vt* maltratar.
mammal ['mæml] *n* mamífero.
mammoth ['mæməθ] *n* mamut *m* // *a* gigantesco.
man [mæn], *pl* **men** *n* hombre *m*; (*CHESS*) pieza // *vt* (*NAUT*) tripular; (*MIL*) guarnecer; **an old** ~ un viejo; ~ **and wife** marido y mujer.
manacle ['mænəkl] *n* manilla; ~**s** *npl* grillos *mpl*.
manage ['mænɪdʒ] *vi* arreglárselas, ir tirando // *vt* (*be in charge of*) dirigir; (*person etc*) manejar; ~**able** *a* manejable; ~**ment** *n* dirección *f*, administración *f*; **manager/ess** *n* director/a *m/f*; (*SPORT*) entrenador/a *m/f*; **managerial** [-ə'dʒɪərɪəl] *a* directivo; **managing director** *n* director *m* general.
mandarin ['mændərɪn] *n* (*also:* ~ **orange**) mandarina; (*person*) mandarín *m*.
mandate ['mændeɪt] *n* mandato.
mandatory ['mændətərɪ] *a* obligatorio.
mandolin(e) ['mændəlɪn] *n* mandolina.
mane [meɪn] *n* (*of horse*) crin *f*; (*of lion*) melena.
manfully ['mænfəlɪ] *ad* violentemente.
mangle ['mæŋgl] *vt* mutilar, magullar // *n* rodillo.
mango ['mæŋgəu], *pl* ~**es** *n* mango.
mangy ['meɪndʒɪ] *a* roñoso, sarnoso.
manhandle ['mænhændl] *vt* maltratar.
manhole ['mænhəul] *n* pozo de visita.
manhood ['mænhud] *n* edad *f* viril.
man-hour ['mæn'auə*] *n* hora-hombre *f*.
manhunt ['mænhʌnt] *n* caza de hombre.
mania ['meɪnɪə] *n* manía; **maniac** ['meɪnɪæk] *n* maníaco; (*fig*) maniático.
manicure ['mænɪkjuə*] *n* manicura // *vt* (*person*) hacer la manicura a; ~ **set** *n* estuche *m* de manicura.
manifest ['mænɪfɛst] *vt* manifestar, mostrar // *a* manifiesto; ~**ation** [-'teɪʃən] *n* manifestación *f*.

manifesto [mænɪ'fɛstəu] *n* manifiesto.
manipulate [mə'nɪpjuleɪt] *vt* manipular, manejar.
mankind [mæn'kaɪnd] *n* la humanidad, el género humano.
manly ['mænlɪ] *a* varonil.
man-made ['mæn'meɪd] *a* artificial.
manner ['mænə*] *n* manera, modo; (*behaviour*) conducta, manera de ser; (*type*) clase *f*; ~**s** *npl* modales *mpl*, educación *f*; **bad** ~**s** mala educación; ~**ism** *n* hábito, peculiaridad *f*.
manoeuvre, maneuver (*US*) [mə'nu:və*] *vt*, *vi* maniobrar // *n* maniobra.
manor ['mænə*] *n* (*also:* ~ **house**) casa solariega.
manpower ['mænpauə*] *n* mano *f* de obra.
mansion ['mænʃən] *n* palacio, casa grande.
manslaughter ['mænslɔ:tə*] *n* homicidio no premeditado.
mantelpiece ['mæntlpi:s] *n* repisa, chimenea.
mantle ['mæntl] *n* manto; (*fig*) capa.
manual ['mænjuəl] *a* manual // *n* manual *m*; (*MUS*) teclado.
manufacture [mænju'fæktʃə*] *vt* fabricar // *n* fabricación *f*; **manufacturer** *n* fabricante *m/f*.
manure [mə'njuə*] *n* estiércol *m*, abono.
manuscript ['mænjuskrɪpt] *n* manuscrito.
Manx [mæŋks] *a* de la Isla de Man.
many ['mɛnɪ] *det* muchos(as) // *pron* muchos/as; **a great** ~ muchísimos, buen número de; ~ **a time** muchas veces.
map [mæp] *n* mapa *m* // *vt* trazar el mapa de; **to** ~ **out** *vt* proyectar.
maple ['meɪpl] *n* arce *m*.
mar [mɑ:*] *vt* estropear.
marathon ['mærəθən] *n* maratón *m*.
marauder [mə'rɔ:də*] *n* merodeador *m*; (*intruder*) intruso.
marble ['mɑ:bl] *n* mármol *m*; (*toy*) canica.
March [mɑ:tʃ] *n* marzo.
march [mɑ:tʃ] *vi* (*MIL*) marchar; (*fig*) caminar con resolución // *n* marcha; (*demonstration*) manifestación *f*, marcha; ~-**past** *n* desfile *m*.
mare [mɛə*] *n* yegua.
margarine [mɑ:dʒə'ri:n] *n* margarina.
margin ['mɑ:dʒɪn] *n* margen *m*; ~**al** *a* marginal.
marigold ['mærɪgəuld] *n* caléndula.
marijuana [mærɪ'wɑ:nə] *n* marijuana.
marina [mə'ri:nə] *n* marina.
marine [mə'ri:n] *a* marino // *n* soldado de marina.
marital ['mærɪtl] *a* matrimonial; ~ **status** estado civil.
maritime ['mærɪtaɪm] *a* marítimo.
marjoram ['mɑ:dʒərəm] *n* orégano.
mark [mɑ:k] *n* marca, señal *f*; (*imprint*) huella; (*stain*) mancha; (*SCOL*) puntuación *f*, nota; (*currency*) marco // *vt* marcar;

manchar; (*SCOL*) calificar; **to** ～ **time** marcar el paso; **to** ～ **out** *vt* trazar; ～**ed** *a* marcado, acusado; ～**er** *n* (*sign*) marcador *m*; (*bookmark*) registro.

market ['mɑːkɪt] *n* mercado // *vt* (*COMM*) vender; **black** ～ mercado negro; **Common M** ～ Mercado Común; ～ **day** *n* día de mercado; ～ **garden** *n* (*Brit*) huerto; ～**ing** *n* márketing *m*, mercadotecnia; ～**-place** *n* mercado; ～ **research** *n* análisis *m inv* de mercados.

marksman ['mɑːksmɔn] *n* tirador *m*; ～**ship** *n* puntería.

marmalade ['mɑːmɔleɪd] *n* mermelada (de naranjas).

maroon [mɔ'ruːn] *vt* (*fig*): **to be** ～**ed** (*shipwrecked*) naufragarse; (*fig*) quedar abandonado // *a* marrón.

marquee [mɑːˈkiː] *n* entoldado.

marquess, marquis ['mɑːkwɪs] *n* marqués *m*.

marriage ['mærɪdʒ] *n* (*state*) matrimonio; (*wedding*) boda; (*act*) casamiento; ～ **bureau** *n* agencia matrimonial; ～ **certificate** *n* partida de casamiento.

married ['mærɪd] *a* casado; (*life, love*) conyugal.

marrow ['mærɔu] *n* médula; (*vegetable*) calabacín *m*.

marry ['mærɪ] *vt* casarse con; (*subj: father, priest etc*) casar // *vi* (*also*: **get married**) casarse.

marsh [mɑːʃ] *n* pantano; (*salt* ～) marisma.

marshal ['mɑːʃl] *n* (*MIL*) mariscal *m*; (*at sports meeting etc*) oficial *m* // *vt* (*facts*) ordenar; (*soldiers*) formar.

marshmallow [mɑːʃˈmælɔu] *n* malvavisco.

marshy ['mɑːʃɪ] *a* pantanoso.

martial ['mɑːʃl] *a* marcial; ～ **law** *n* ley *f* marcial.

martyr ['mɑːtɔ*] *n* mártir *m/f* // *vt* martirizar; ～**dom** *n* martirio.

marvel ['mɑːvl] *n* maravilla, prodigio // *vi*: **to** ～ **(at)** maravillarse (de); ～**lous,** ～**ous** (*US*) *a* maravilloso.

Marxism ['mɑːksɪzɔm] *n* marxismo; **Marxist** [-sɪst] *a, n* marxista *m/f*.

marzipan ['mɑːzɪpæn] *n* mazapán *m*.

mascara [mæsˈkɑːrɔ] *n* rimel *m*.

mascot ['mæskɔt] *n* mascota.

masculine ['mæskjulɪn] *a* masculino; **masculinity** [-ˈlɪnɪtɪ] *n* masculinidad *f*.

mash [mæʃ] *n* (*mix*) mezcla; (*pulp*) amasijo; ～**ed potatoes** puré *m* de patatas.

mask [mɑːsk] *n* máscara // *vt* enmascarar.

masochist ['mæsɔukɪst] *n* masoquista *m/f*.

mason ['meɪsn] *n* (*also*: **stone**～) albañil *m*; (*also*: **free**～) masón *m*; ～**ic** [mɔˈsɔnɪk] *a* masónico; ～**ry** *n* masonería; (*building*) mampostería.

masquerade [mæskɔˈreɪd] *n* baile *m* de máscaras; (*fig*) farsa // *vi*: **to** ～ **as** disfrazarse de, hacerse pasar por.

mass [mæs] *n* (*people*) muchedumbre *f*; (*PHYSICS*) masa; (*REL*) misa; (*great quantity*)

montón *m* // *vi* reunirse; (*MIL*) concentrarse; **the** ～**es** las masas.

massacre ['mæsɔkɔ*] *n* masacre *f* // *vt* masacrar.

massage ['mæsɑːʒ] *n* masaje *m* // *vt* dar masaje a.

masseur [mæˈsɔː*] *n* masajista *m*; **masseuse** [-ˈsɔːz] *n* masajista *f*.

massive ['mæsɪv] *a* (*solid*) sólido; (*head etc*) grande; (*support, intervention*) masivo.

mass media ['mæsˈmiːdɪɔ] *npl* medios *mpl* de comunicación masiva.

mass-production ['mæsprɔˈdʌkʃɔn] *n* fabricación *f* en serie.

mast [mɑːst] *n* (*NAUT*) mástil *m*; (*RADIO etc*) torre *f*.

master ['mɑːstɔ*] *n* maestro; (*landowner*) señor *m*, amo; (*in secondary school*) profesor *m*; (*title for boys*): **M** ～ **X** Señorito X // *vt* dominar; (*learn*) aprender a fondo; ～ **key** *n* llave *f* maestra; ～**ly** *a* magistral; ～**mind** *n* inteligencia superior // *vt* dirigir, planear; **M** ～ **of Arts** *n* Licenciado en Letras; ～**piece** *n* obra maestra; ～ **plan** *n* plan *m* rector; ～ **stroke** *n* golpe *m* maestro; ～**y** *n* maestría.

masturbate ['mæstɔbeɪt] *vi* masturbarse; **masturbation** [-ˈbeɪʃɔn] *n* masturbación *f*.

mat [mæt] *n* estera; (*also*: **door**～) felpudo // *a* = **matt**.

match [mætʃ] *n* cerilla; (*game*) partido; (*fig*) igual *m/f* // *vt* emparejar; (*go well with*) hacer juego con; (*equal*) igualar, ser igual a // *vi* hacer juego; **to be a good** ～ hacer una buena pareja; ～**box** *n* caja de cerillas; ～**ing** *a* que hace juego; ～**less** *a* sin par, incomparable.

mate [meɪt] *n* compañero; (*assistant*) ayudante *m/f*; (*CHESS*) mate *m*; (*in merchant navy*) segundo de a bordo // *vi* acoplarse, parearse // *vt* acoplar, parear.

material [mɔˈtɪɔrɪɔl] *n* (*substance*) materia; (*equipment*) material *m*; (*cloth*) tela, tejido; (*data*) datos *mpl* // *a* material; (*important*) importante; ～**s** *npl* materiales *mpl*; ～**istic** [-ɔˈlɪstɪk] *a* materialista; ～**ize** *vi* materializarse.

maternal [mɔˈtɔːnl] *a* maternal.

maternity [mɔˈtɔːnɪtɪ] *n* maternidad *f*; ～ **dress** vestido premamá; ～ **hospital** *n* hospital *m* de maternidad.

mathematical [mæθɔˈmætɪkl] *a* matemático; **mathematician** [-mɔˈtɪʃɔn] *n* matemático; **mathematics** [-tɪks], **maths** [mæθs] *n* matemáticas *fpl*.

matinée ['mætɪneɪ] *n* función *f* de tarde.

mating ['meɪtɪŋ] *n* apareamiento; ～ **call** *n* llamada del macho; ～ **season** *n* época de celo.

matriarchal [meɪtrɪˈɑːkl] *a* matriarcal.

matrices ['meɪtrɪsiːz] *pl of* **matrix.**

matrimonial [mætrɪˈmɔunɪɔl] *a* matrimonial.

matrimony ['mætrɪmɔnɪ] *n* matrimonio.

matrix ['meɪtrɪks], *pl* **matrices** *n* matriz *f*.

matron ['meitrən] n (in hospital)
enfermera jefe; (in school) ama de llaves;
~ ly a de matrona; (fig: figure) corpulento.
matt [mæt] a mate.
matted ['mætɪd] a enmarañado.
matter ['mætə*] n cuestión f, asunto;
(PHYSICS) sustancia, materia; (content)
contenido; (MED: pus) pus m // vi importar;
it doesn't ~ no importa; **what's the** ~?
¿qué pasa?; **no** ~ **what** pase lo que pase;
as a ~ **of course** por rutina; **as a** ~ **of
fact** de hecho; ~-**of-fact** a prosaico,
práctico.
mattress ['mætrɪs] n colchón m.
mature [mə'tjuə*] a maduro // vi
madurar; **maturity** n madurez f.
maudlin ['mɔːdlɪn] a llorón(ona).
maul [mɔːl] vt magullar.
mausoleum [mɔːsə'lɪəm] n mausoleo.
mauve [məuv] a de color malva.
maxim ['mæksɪm] n máxima.
maxima ['mæksɪmə] pl of **maximum.**
maximum ['mæksɪməm] a máximo // n,
pl **maxima** máximo.
May [meɪ] n mayo.
may [meɪ] vi (conditional: **might**)
(indicating possibility): **he** ~ **come** puede
que venga; (be allowed to): ~ **I smoke?**
¿puedo fumar?; (wishes): ~ **God bless
you!** que Dios le bendiga.
maybe ['meɪbiː] ad quizá(s).
mayday ['meɪdeɪ] n S.O.S. m (llamada de
socorro internacional).
mayhem ['meɪhɛm] n mutilación f
criminal.
mayonnaise [meɪə'neɪz] n mayonesa.
mayor [mɛə*] n alcalde m; ~**ess** n
alcaldesa.
maypole ['meɪpəul] n mayo.
maze [meɪz] n laberinto.
M.D. abbr of **Doctor of Medicine.**
me [miː] pron me; (stressed, after prep) mí;
with ~ conmigo; **it's** ~ soy yo.
meadow ['mɛdəu] n prado, pradera.
meagre, meager (US) ['miːgə*] a escaso,
pobre.
meal [miːl] n comida; (flour) harina;
~ **time** n hora de comer.
mean [miːn] a (with money) tacaño;
(unkind) mezquino, malo; (shabby)
humilde, vil; (of poor quality) inferior;
(average) medio // vt, pt, pp **meant**
(signify) querer decir, significar; (intend):
to ~ **to do sth** pensar o pretender hacer
algo // n medio, término medio; ~**s** npl
medio sg, manera sg; (resource) recursos
mpl, medios mpl; **by** ~**s of** mediante, por
medio de; **by all** ~**s!** ¡naturalmente!,
¡claro que sí!; **do you** ~ **it?** ¿lo dices en
serio?; **what do you** ~? ¿qué quiere
decir?
meander [mɪ'ændə*] vi (river)
serpentear; (person) vagar.
meaning ['miːnɪŋ] n significado, sentido;
~ **ful** a significativo; ~ **less** a sin sentido.
meanness ['miːnnɪs] n (with money)

tacañería; (shabbiness) vileza, bajeza;
(unkindness) maldad f, mezquindad f.
meant [mɛnt] pt, pp of **mean.**
meantime ['miːntaɪm], **meanwhile**
['miːnwaɪl] ad (also: **in the** ~) mientras
tanto.
measles ['miːzlz] n sarampión m;
German ~ rubéola.
measly ['miːzlɪ] a (col) miserable.
measure ['mɛʒə*] vt medir; (for clothes
etc) tomar las medidas a; (consider) pesar
// vi medir // n medida; (ruler) regla; ~**d**
a moderado; (tone) mesurado; ~**ments**
npl medidas fpl.
meat [miːt] n carne f; **cold** ~ fiambre m;
~**ball** n albóndiga; ~ **pie** n pastel m de
carne; ~**y** a carnoso; (fig) sustancioso.
mechanic [mɪ'kænɪk] n mecánico; ~**s** n
mecánica // npl mecanismo sg; ~**al** a
mecánico.
mechanism ['mɛkənɪzəm] n mecanismo.
mechanization [mɛkənaɪ'zeɪʃən] n
mecanización f.
medal ['mɛdl] n medalla; ~**lion**
[mɪ'dælɪən] n medallón m; ~**list**, ~**ist**
(US) n (SPORT) ganador/a m/f.
meddle ['mɛdl] vi: **to** ~ **in** entrometerse
en; **to** ~ **with sth** manosear algo;
~**some** a entrometido.
media ['miːdɪə] npl medios mpl de
comunicación.
mediaeval [mɛdɪ'iːvl] a = **medieval.**
mediate ['miːdɪeɪt] vi mediar; **mediation**
[-'eɪʃən] n mediación f; **mediator** n
intermediario, mediador/a m/f.
medical ['mɛdɪkl] a médico // n
reconocimiento médico.
medicated ['mɛdɪkeɪtɪd] a medicinal.
medicinal [mɛ'dɪsɪnl] a medicinal.
medicine ['mɛdsɪn] n medicina; (drug)
medicamento; ~ **chest** n botiquín m.
medieval [mɛdɪ'iːvl] a medieval.
mediocre [miːdɪ'əukə*] a mediocre;
mediocrity [ˈblɪrɪtɪ] n mediocridad f.
meditate ['mɛdɪteɪt] vi meditar;
meditation [-'teɪʃən] n meditación f.
Mediterranean [mɛdɪtə'reɪnɪən] a
mediterráneo; **the** ~ **(Sea)** el (Mar)
Mediterráneo.
medium ['miːdɪəm] a mediano, regular //
n (pl **media**: means) medio; (pl **mediums**:
person) médium m/f.
medley ['mɛdlɪ] n mezcla; (MUS) popurrí
m.
meek [miːk] a manso, dócil.
meet [miːt] pt, pp **met** vt (gen) encontrar;
(accidentally) encontrarse con, tropezar
con; (by arrangement) reunirse con; (for
the first time) conocer; (go and fetch) ir a
buscar; (opponent) enfrentarse con;
(obligations) cumplir // vi encontrarse; (in
session) reunirse; (join: objects) unirse; (get
to know) conocerse; **to** ~ **with** vt fus
reunirse con; (face: difficulty) tropezar
con; ~**ing** n encuentro; (session: of club
etc) reunión f; (interview) entrevista;
(COMM) junta, sesión f; (POL) mítin m.

megalomaniac [mɛgəlɔu'meɪnɪæk] a, n megalómano/a.

megaphone ['mɛgəfɔun] n megáfono.

melancholy ['mɛlənkɔlɪ] n melancolía // a melancólico.

melee ['mɛleɪ] n refriega.

mellow ['mɛlɔu] a (sound) dulce; (colour) suave; (fruit) maduro // vi (person) madurar.

melodious [mɪ'lɔudɪəs] a melodioso.

melodrama ['mɛlɔudraːmə] n melodrama m.

melody ['mɛlədɪ] n melodía.

melon ['mɛlən] n melón m.

melt [mɛlt] vi (metal) fundirse; (snow) derretirse; (fig) ablandarse // vt (also: ~ down) fundir; to ~ away vi desvanecerse; ~ing point n punto de fusión; ~ing pot n (fig) crisol m.

member ['mɛmbə*] n (gen) miembro; (of club) socio; M~ of Parliament (M.P.) diputado; ~ship n (members) número de miembros; to seek ~ship of pedir el ingreso a; ~ship card carnet m de socio.

membrane ['mɛmbreɪn] n membrana.

memento [mə'mɛntəu] n recuerdo.

memo ['mɛməu] n apunte m, nota.

memoirs ['mɛmwaːz] npl memorias fpl.

memorable ['mɛmərəbl] a memorable.

memorandum [mɛmə'rændəm], pl -da [-də] n apunte m, nota; (POL) memorándum m.

memorial [mɪ'mɔːrɪəl] n monumento conmemorativo // a conmemorativo.

memorize ['mɛməraɪz] vt aprender de memoria.

memory ['mɛmərɪ] n memoria; (recollection) recuerdo.

men [mɛn] pl of man.

menace ['mɛnəs] n amenaza // vt amenazar; **menacing** a amenazador(a).

menagerie [mɪ'næd ʒ ərɪ] n casa de fieras.

mend [mɛnd] vt reparar, arreglar; (darn) zurcir // vi reponerse // n (gen) remiendo; (darn) zurcido; to be on the ~ ir mejorando; ~ing n reparación f; (clothes) ropa por remendar.

menial ['miːnɪəl] a doméstico; (pej) bajo // n criado.

meningitis [mɛnɪn'dʒaɪtɪs] n meningitis f.

menopause ['mɛnəupɔːz] n menopausia.

menstruate ['mɛnstrueɪt] vi menstruar; **menstruation** [-'eɪʃən] n menstruación f.

mental ['mɛntl] a mental; ~ity [-'tælɪtɪ] n mentalidad f.

mention ['mɛnʃən] n mención f // vt mencionar; (speak of) hablar de; don't ~ it! ¡de nada!

menu ['mɛnjuː] n (set ~) menú m; (printed) carta.

mercenary ['mɔːsɪnərɪ] a, n mercenario.

merchandise ['mɔːtʃəndaɪz] n mercancías fpl.

merchant ['mɔːtʃənt] n comerciante m/f; ~ bank n banco comercial; ~ navy n marina mercante.

merciful ['mɔːsɪful] a compasivo; (fortunate) afortunado.

merciless ['mɔːsɪlɪs] a despiadado.

mercury ['mɔːkjurɪ] n mercurio.

mercy ['mɔːsɪ] n compasión f; (REL) misericordia; at the ~ of a la merced de.

mere [mɪə*] a simple, mero; ~ly ad simplemente, sólo.

merge [mɔːdʒ] vt (join) unir; (mix) mezclar; (fuse) fundir // vi unirse; (COMM) fusionarse; **merger** n (COMM) fusión f.

meridian [mə'rɪdɪən] n meridiano.

meringue [mə'ræŋ] n merengue m.

merit ['mɛrɪt] n mérito // vt merecer.

mermaid ['mɔːmeɪd] n sirena.

merriment ['mɛrɪmənt] n alegría.

merry ['mɛrɪ]38 a alegre; ~-go-round n tiovivo.

mesh [mɛʃ] n malla; (TECH) engranaje m // vi (gears) engranar.

mesmerize ['mɛzməraɪz] vt hipnotizar.

mess [mɛs] n (gen) confusión f; (of objects) revoltijo; (tangle) lío; (MIL) comedor m; to ~ about vi (col) perder el tiempo; (pass the time) entretenerse; to ~ about with vt fus (col) (play with) divertirse con; (handle) manosear; to ~ up vt (disarrange) desordenar; (spoil) estropear; (dirty) ensuciar.

message ['mɛsɪdʒ] n recado, mensaje m.

messenger ['mɛsɪndʒə*] n mensajero/a.

messy ['mɛsɪ] a (dirty) sucio; (untidy) desordenado.

met [mɛt] pt, pp of **meet.**

metabolism [mɛ'tæbəlɪzəm] n metabolismo.

metal ['mɛtl] n metal m; ~lic [-'tælɪk] a metálico; ~lurgy [-'tælədʒɪ] n metalurgia.

metamorphosis [mɛtə'mɔːfəsɪs], pl -ses [-siːz] n metamorfosis f inv.

metaphor ['mɛtəfə*] n metáfora.

metaphysics [mɛtə'fɪzɪks] n metafísica.

mete [miːt]: to ~ out vt fus (gen) repartir; (punishment) imponer.

meteor ['miːtɪə*] n meteoro.

meteorological [miːtɪərə'lɔdʒɪkl] a meteorológico; **meteorology** [-'rɔlədʒɪ] n meteorología.

meter ['miːtə*] n (instrument) contador m; (US) = **metre.**

method ['mɛθəd] n método; ~ical [mɪ'θɔdɪkl] a metódico.

Methodist ['mɛθədɪst] a, n metodista m/f.

meths [mɛθs], **methylated spirit** ['mɛθɪleɪtɪd-] n alcohol m metilado o desnaturalizado.

meticulous [mɛ'tɪkjuləs] a meticuloso.

metre, meter (US) ['miːtə*] n metro.

metric ['mɛtrɪk] a métrico.

metronome ['mɛtrənəum] n metrónomo.

metropolis [mɪ'trɔpəlɪs] n metrópoli f.

mettle ['mɛtl] n (spirit) valor m, ánimo; (tone) temple m.

mew [mjuː] vi (cat) maullar.

mews [mjuːz] n: ~ cottage casa

acondicionada en antiguos establos o cocheras.

Mexican ['mɛksɪkən] a, n mejicano/a, mexicano/a (AM).

Mexico ['mɛksɪkəu] n Méjico, México (AM).

mezzanine ['mɛtsəni:n] n entresuelo.

miaow [mi:'au] vi maullar.

mice [maɪs] pl of **mouse**.

microbe ['maɪkrəub] n microbio.

micro... [maɪkrəu] pref micro...; ~**film** n microfilm m; ~**phone** n micrófono; ~**processor** n microprocesador m; ~**scope** n microscopio; ~**scopic** [-'skɔpɪk] a microscópico; ~**wave** a de microonda.

mid [mɪd] a: **in** ~ **May** a mediados de mayo; **in** ~ **afternoon** a media tarde; **in** ~ **air** en el aire; ~**day** n mediodía m.

middle ['mɪdl] n medio, centro; (half) mitad f; (waist) cintura // a medio; (quantity, size) mediano; ~**-aged** a de mediana edad; **the M**~ **Ages** npl la Edad Media; ~**-class** a de clase media; **M**~ **East** n Oriente m Medio; ~**man** n intermediario; ~ **name** n segundo nombre.

middling ['mɪdlɪŋ] a mediano.

midge [mɪdʒ] n mosca.

midget ['mɪdʒɪt] n enano // a minúsculo.

Midlands ['mɪdləndz] npl la región central de Inglaterra.

midnight ['mɪdnaɪt] n medianoche f.

midriff ['mɪdrɪf] n diafragma m.

midst [mɪdst] n: **in the** ~ **of** entre, en medio de.

midsummer [mɪd'sʌmə*] n: **a** ~ **day** un día de pleno verano.

midway [mɪd'weɪ] a, ad: ~ **(between)** a mitad de camino, a medio camino (entre).

midweek [mɪd'wi:k] ad entre semana.

midwife ['mɪdwaɪf], pl **-wives** [-waɪvz] n comadrona, partera; ~**ry** [-wɪfərɪ] n partería.

midwinter [mɪd'wɪntə*] n: **in** ~ en pleno invierno.

might [maɪt] vb: **he** ~ **be there** podría estar allí, puede que está allí; **I** ~ **as well go** más vale que vaya; **you** ~ **like to try** podría intentar // n fuerza, poder m; ~**y** a fuerte, poderoso.

migraine ['mi:greɪn] n jaqueca.

migrant ['maɪgrənt] n (bird) ave f migratoria; (person) emigrante m/f; (fig) nómada m/f // a migratorio; (worker) emigrante.

migrate [maɪ'greɪt] vi emigrar; **migration** [-'greɪʃən] n emigración f.

mike [maɪk] n abbr of **microphone** micro.

mild [maɪld] a (character) pacífico; (climate) templado; (slight) ligero; (taste) suave; (illness) benigno, leve.

mildew ['mɪldju:] n moho.

mildness ['maɪldnɪs] n (softness) suavidad f; (gentleness) dulzura; (quiet character) apacibilidad f.

mile [maɪl] n milla; ~**age** n número de millas; (AUT) kilometraje m; ~**stone** n mojón m.

milieu ['mi:ljɔ:] n medio, medio ambiente.

militant ['mɪlɪtnt] a, n militante m/f.

military ['mɪlɪtərɪ] a militar.

militate ['mɪlɪteɪt] vi: **to** ~ **against** militar contra.

militia [mɪ'lɪʃə] n milicia.

milk [mɪlk] n leche f // vt (cow) ordeñar; (fig) chupar; ~**man** n lechero; ~ **shake** n batido de leche; ~**y** a lechoso; **M**~**y Way** n Vía Láctea.

mill [mɪl] n (windmill etc) molino; (coffee ~) molinillo; (factory) fábrica; (spinning ~) hilandería // vt moler // vi (also: ~ **about**) moverse por todas partes, apiñarse.

millennium [mɪ'lɛnɪəm], pl ~**s** or **-ia** [-nɪə] n milenio, milenario.

miller ['mɪlə*] n molinero.

millet ['mɪlɪt] n mijo.

milli... ['mɪlɪ] pref: ~**gram(me)** n miligramo; ~**litre** n mililitro; ~**metre** n milímetro.

milliner ['mɪlɪnə*] n modista de sombreros; ~**y** n sombrerería.

million ['mɪljən] n millón m; **a** ~ **times** un millón de veces; ~**aire** n millonario.

millstone ['mɪlstəun] n piedra de molino.

milometer [maɪ'lɔmɪtə*] n cuenta-kilómetros m inv.

mime [maɪm] n mímica; (actor) mimo // vt remedar // vi actuar de mimo.

mimic ['mɪmɪk] n imitador/a m/f // a mímico // vt remedar, imitar; ~**ry** n imitación f.

min. abbr of **minute(s); minimum.**

minaret [mɪnə'rɛt] n alminar m.

mince [mɪns] vt picar // vi (in walking) andar con pasos menudos // n (CULIN) carne f picada, picadillo; ~**meat** n conserva de fruta picada; ~ **pie** n empanadilla rellena de fruta picada; **mincer** n máquina de picar carne.

mind [maɪnd] n (gen) mente f; (intellect) inteligencia; (contrasted with matter) espíritu // vt (attend to, look after) ocuparse de, cuidar; (be careful of) tener cuidado con; (object to): **I don't** ~ **the noise** no me importa el ruido; **it is on my** ~ me preocupa; **to my** ~ en mi opinión; **to be out of one's** ~ estar fuera de juicio; **never** ~! ¡es igual!, ¡no importa!; (don't worry) ¡no se preocupe!; **to bear sth in** ~ tomar o tener algo en cuenta; **to make up one's** ~ decidirse; '~ **the step'** cuidado con el escalón; ~**ful** a: ~**ful of** consciente de; ~**less** a estúpido.

mine [maɪn] pron (el) mío/(la) mía etc // a: **this book is** ~ este libro es mío // n mina // vt (coal) extraer, explotar; (ship, beach) minar; ~**field** n campo de minas; **miner** n minero.

mineral ['mɪnərəl] a mineral // n mineral m; ~**s** npl (soft drinks) aguas fpl minerales, gaseosa sg.

minesweeper ['maɪnswiːpə*] n dragaminas m inv.

mingle ['mɪŋgl] vi: to ~ with mezclarse con.

mingy ['mɪndʒɪ] a (col) tacaño.

miniature ['mɪnətʃə*] a (en) miniatura // n miniatura.

minibus ['mɪnɪbʌs] n microbús m.

minicab ['mɪnɪkæb] n microtaxi m.

minim ['mɪnɪm] n (MUS) blanca.

minimal ['mɪnɪml] a mínimo.

minimize ['mɪnɪmaɪz] vt minimizar.

minimum ['mɪnɪməm] n, pl **minima** ['mɪnɪmə] mínimo // a mínimo.

mining ['maɪnɪŋ] n explotación f minera // a minero.

miniskirt ['mɪnɪskəːt] n minifalda.

minister ['mɪnɪstə*] n (POL) ministro; (REL) pastor m // vi atender; ~ial [-'tɪərɪəl] a (POL) ministerial.

ministry ['mɪnɪstrɪ] n ministerio.

mink [mɪŋk] n visón m; ~ coat n abrigo de visón.

minnow ['mɪnəu] n pececillo (de agua dulce).

minor ['maɪnə*] a menor; (unimportant) sin importancia; (inferior) secundario; (MUS) menor // n (LAW) menor m/f de edad.

minority [maɪ'nɔrɪtɪ] n minoría; (age) minoridad f.

minster ['mɪnstə*] n catedral f.

minstrel ['mɪnstrəl] n juglar m.

mint [mɪnt] n (plant) menta, herbabuena; (sweet) caramelo de menta // vt (coins) acuñar; **the (Royal) M** ~ la (Real) Casa de la Moneda; **in** ~ **condition** en perfecto estado.

minuet [mɪnjuˈɛt] n minué m.

minus ['maɪnəs] n (also: ~ **sign**) signo de menos // prep menos.

minute ['mɪnɪt] n minuto; (fig) momento; ~s npl actas fpl // a [maɪ'njuːt] diminuto; (search) minucioso; **at the last** ~ a última hora.

miracle ['mɪrəkl] n milagro; **miraculous** [mɪ'rækjuləs] a milagroso.

mirage ['mɪrɑːʒ] n espejismo.

mirror ['mɪrə*] n espejo; (in car) retrovisor m // vt reflejar.

mirth [məːθ] n alegría; (laughter) risa, risas fpl.

misadventure [mɪsəd'vɛntʃə*] n desgracia, accidente m.

misanthropist [mɪ'zænθrəpɪst] n misántropo.

misapprehension ['mɪsæprɪ'hɛnʃən] n equivocación f.

misbehave [mɪsbɪ'heɪv] vi portarse mal; **misbehaviour** n mala conducta.

miscalculate [mɪs'kælkjuleɪt] vt calcular mal; **miscalculation** [-'leɪʃən] n error m (de cálculo).

miscarriage ['mɪskærɪdʒ] n (MED) aborto; (failure) fracaso; ~ **of justice** error m judicial.

miscellaneous [mɪsɪ'leɪnɪəs] a vario(s), diverso(s).

mischance [mɪs'tʃɑːns] n desgracia, mala suerte f.

mischief ['mɪstʃɪf] n (naughtiness) travesura; (harm) mal m, daño; (maliciousness) malicia; **mischievous** [-ʃɪvəs] a travieso; dañoso; (playful) malicioso.

misconception ['mɪskən'sɛpʃən] n concepto erróneo, equivocación f.

misconduct [mɪs'kɔndʌkt] n mala conducta; **professional** ~ falta profesional.

miscount [mɪs'kaunt] vt, vi contar mal.

misdeed [mɪs'diːd] n delito.

misdemeanour, misdemeanor (US) [mɪsdɪ'miːnə*] n delito, ofensa.

misdirect [mɪsdɪ'rɛkt] vt (person) informar mal; (letter) poner señas incorrectas en.

miser ['maɪzə*] n avaro/a.

miserable ['mɪzərəbl] a (unhappy) triste, desgraciado; (wretched) miserable; (despicable) despreciable.

miserly ['maɪzəlɪ] a avariento, tacaño.

misery ['mɪzərɪ] n (unhappiness) tristeza, sufrimiento; (wretchedness) miseria, desdicha.

misfire [mɪs'faɪə*] vi fallar.

misfit ['mɪsfɪt] n (person) inadaptado/a, desplazado/a.

misfortune [mɪs'fɔːtʃən] n desgracia.

misgiving(s) [mɪs'gɪvɪŋ(z)] n(pl) (mistrust) recelo; (apprehension) presentimiento.

misguided [mɪs'gaɪdɪd] a equivocado.

mishandle [mɪs'hændl] vt (treat roughly) maltratar; (mismanage) manejar mal.

mishap ['mɪshæp] n desgracia, contratiempo.

mishear [mɪs'hɪə*] (irg: like **hear**) vt oír mal.

misinform [mɪsɪn'fɔːm] vt informar mal.

misinterpret [mɪsɪn'təːprɪt] vt interpretar mal.

misjudge [mɪs'dʒʌdʒ] vt juzgar mal.

mislay [mɪs'leɪ] (irg: like **lay**) vt extraviar, perder.

mislead [mɪs'liːd] (irg: like **lead**) vt llevar a conclusiones erróneas; ~**ing** a engañoso, erróneo.

mismanage [mɪs'mænɪdʒ] vt administrar mal; ~**ment** n mala administración f.

misnomer [mɪs'nəumə*] n nombre m inapropiado o equivocado.

misogynist [mɪ'sɔdʒɪnɪst] n misógino.

misplace [mɪs'pleɪs] vt (lose) extraviar, perder.

misprint ['mɪsprɪnt] n errata, error m de imprenta.

mispronounce [mɪsprə'nauns] vt pronunciar mal.

misread [mɪs'riːd] (irg: like **read**) vt leer mal.

misrepresent [mɪsrɛprɪ'zɛnt] *vt* falsificar.

miss [mɪs] *vt* (*train etc*) perder; (*fail to hit*) errar, fallar; (*regret the absence of*): **I** ~ **him** (yo) le echo de menos *o* a faltar // *vi* fallar /*;* *n* (*shot*) tiro fallido *o* perdido; (*fig*): **that was a near** ~ (*near accident*) faltó poco para que chocáramos; **to** ~ **out** *vt* omitir.

Miss [mɪs] *n* Señorita.

missal ['mɪsl] *n* misal *m*.

misshapen [mɪs'ʃeɪpən] *a* deforme.

missile ['mɪsaɪl] *n* (*AVIAT*) mísil *m*; (*object thrown*) proyectil *m*.

missing ['mɪsɪŋ] *a* (*pupil*) ausente; (*thing*) perdido; (*MIL*) desaparecido; **to go** ~ desaparecer.

mission ['mɪʃən] *n* misión *f*; ~**ary** *n* misionero.

misspent ['mɪs'spɛnt] *a*: **his** ~ **youth** su juventud disipada.

mist [mɪst] *n* (*light*) neblina; (*heavy*) niebla; (*at sea*) bruma // *vi* (*also*: ~ **over,** ~ **up**) empañarse.

mistake [mɪs'teɪk] *n* error *m* // *vt* (*irg*: *like* **take**) entender mal, equivocarse sobre; **to** ~ **A for B** confundir A con B; **mistaken** *a* (*idea etc*) equivocado; **to be mistaken** equivocarse, engañarse.

mister ['mɪstə*] *n* (*col*) señor *m*; *see* **Mr.**

mistletoe ['mɪsltəu] *n* muérdago.

mistook [mɪs'tuk] *pt of* **mistake.**

mistreat [mɪs'triːt] *vt* maltratar; ~**ment** *n* maltrato.

mistress ['mɪstrɪs] *n* (*lover*) amante *f*; (*of house*) señora (de la casa); (*in primary school*) maestra; (*in secondary school*) profesora; *see* **Mrs.**

mistrust [mɪs'trʌst] *vt* desconfiar de, dudar de.

misty ['mɪstɪ] *a* nebuloso, brumoso; (*day*) de niebla; (*glasses*) empañado.

misunderstand [mɪsʌndə'stænd] (*irg*: *like* **understand**) *vt*, *vi* entender mal; ~**ing** *n* malentendido.

misuse [mɪs'juːs] *n* mal uso, (*of power*) abuso // *vt* [mɪs'juːz] abusar de; (*funds*) malversar.

mitigate ['mɪtɪgeɪt] *vt* mitigar.

mitre, miter (*US*) ['maɪtə*] *n* mitra; (*CARPENTRY*) inglete *m*.

mitt(en) ['mɪt(n)] *n* mitón *m*.

mix [mɪks] *vt* (*gen*) mezclar; (*combine*) unir // *vi* mezclarse; (*people*) llevarse bien // *n* mezcla; **to** ~ **up** *vt* mezclar; (*confuse*) confundir; ~**ed** *a* (*assorted*) variado, surtido; (*school etc*) mixto; ~**ed-up** *a* (*confused*) confuso, revuelto; ~**er** *n* (*for food*) licuadora; (*person*) persona sociable; ~**ture** *n* mezcla; ~**-up** *n* confusión *f*.

moan [məun] *n* gemido // *vi* gemir; (*col*: *complain*): **to** ~ (**about**) quejarse (de).

moat [məut] *n* foso.

mob [mɔb] *n* multitud *f*; (*pej*): **the** ~ el populacho // *vt* acosar.

mobile ['məubaɪl] *a* móvil // *n* móvil *m*; ~ **home** *n* caravana.

mobility [məu'bɪlɪtɪ] *n* movilidad *f*.

mobilize ['məubɪlaɪz] *vt* movilizar.

moccasin ['mɔkəsɪn] *n* mocasín *m*.

mock [mɔk] *vt* (*make ridiculous*) ridiculizar; (*laugh at*) burlarse de // *a* fingido; ~**ery** *n* burla; ~**ing** *a* burlón(ona); ~**-up** *n* maqueta.

mode [məud] *n* modo; (*fashion*) moda.

model ['mɔdl] *n* (*gen*) modelo; (*ARCH*) maqueta; (*person: for fashion, ART*) modelo *m/f* // *a* modelo // *vt* modelar // *vi* servir de modelo; ~ **railway** ferrocarril *m* de juguete; **to** ~ **clothes** pasar modelos, ser modelo.

moderate ['mɔdərət] *a*, *n* moderado/a // (*vb*: [-reɪt]) *vi* moderarse, calmarse // *vt* moderar; **moderation** [-'reɪʃən] *n* moderación *f*.

modern ['mɔdən] *a* moderno; ~**ize** *vt* modernizar.

modest ['mɔdɪst] *a* modesto; ~**y** *n* modestia.

modicum ['mɔdɪkəm] *n*: **a** ~ **of** un mínimo de.

modification [mɔdɪfɪ'keɪʃən] *n* modificación *f*; **modify** ['mɔdɪfaɪ] *vt* modificar.

modulation [mɔdju'leɪʃən] *n* modulación *f*.

mohair ['məuhɛə*] *n* moer *m*.

moist [mɔɪst] *a* húmedo; ~**en** ['mɔɪsn] *vt* humedecer; ~**ure** ['mɔɪstʃə*] *n* humedad *f*; ~**urizer** ['mɔɪstʃəraɪzə*] *n* crema hidratante.

molar ['məulə*] *n* muela.

molasses [məu'læsɪz] *n* melaza.

mole [məul] *n* (*animal*) topo; (*spot*) lunar *m*.

molecule ['mɔlɪkjuːl] *n* molécula.

molehill ['məulhɪl] *n* topera.

molest [məu'lɛst] *vt* importunar.

mollusc [məulæsk] *n* molusco.

mollycoddle ['mɔlɪkɔdl] *vt* mimar.

molten ['məultən] *a* fundido; (*lava*) líquido.

moment ['məumənt] *n* momento; ~**ary** *a* momentáneo; ~**-ous** ['mɛntəs] *a* trascendental, importante.

momentum [məu'mɛntəm] *n* momento; (*fig*) ímpetu *m*; **to gather** ~ cobrar velocidad.

monarch ['mɔnək] *n* monarca *m/f*; ~**y** *n* monarquía.

monastery ['mɔnəstərɪ] *n* monasterio.

monastic [mə'næstɪk] *a* monástico.

Monday ['mʌndɪ] *n* lunes *m*.

monetary ['mʌnɪtərɪ] *a* monetario.

money ['mʌnɪ] *n* dinero; **to make** ~ ganar dinero; ~**lender** *n* prestamista *m/f*; ~ **order** *n* giro.

mongol ['mɔŋgəl] *a*, *n* (*MED*) mongólico.

mongrel ['mʌŋgrəl] *n* (*dog*) perro cruzado.

monitor ['mɔnɪtə*] *n* (*SCOL*) monitor *m*; (*also*: **television** ~) receptor *m* de control // *vt* controlar.

monk [mʌŋk] *n* monje *m*.

monkey ['mʌŋkɪ] *n* mono; ~ **nut** *n*

cacahuete *m*; ~ **wrench** *n* llave *f* inglesa.
mono... [mɔnəu] *pref*: ~**chrome** *a* monocromo.
monocle ['mɔnəkl] *n* monóculo.
monogram ['mɔnəgræm] *n* monograma *m*.
monologue ['mɔnəlɔg] *n* monólogo.
monopoly [mə'nɔpəlɪ] *n* monopolio.
monorail ['mɔnəureɪl] *n* monorriel *m*.
monosyllabic [mɔnəusɪ'læbɪk] *a* monosilábico.
monotone ['mɔnətəun] *n* monotonía; **to speak in a** ~ hablar en un solo tono.
monotonous [mə'nɔtənəs] *a* monótono; **monotony** [-nɪ] *n* monotonía.
monsoon [mɔn'suːn] *n* monzón *m/f*.
monster ['mɔnstə*] *n* monstruo.
monstrosity [mɔns'trɔsɪtɪ] *n* monstruosidad *f*.
monstrous ['mɔnstrəs] *a* (*huge*) enorme; (*atrocious*) monstruoso.
montage [mɔn'tɑːʒ] *n* montaje *m*.
month [mʌnθ] *n* mes *m*; ~**ly** *a* mensual // *ad* mensualmente // *n* (*magazine*) revista mensual.
monument ['mɔnjumənt] *n* monumento; ~**al** [-'mɛntl] *a* monumental.
moo [muː] *vi* mugir.
mood [muːd] *n* humor *m*; **to be in a good/bad** ~ estar de buen/mal humor; ~**y** *a* (*variable*) de humor variable; (*sullen*) melancólico.
moon [muːn] *n* luna; ~**beam** *n* rayo de luna; ~**light** *n* luz *f* de la luna; ~**lit** *a*: **a** ~**lit night** una noche de luna.
moor [muə*] *n* páramo // *vt* (*ship*) amarrar // *vi* echar las amarras.
Moor [muə*] *n* moro/a.
moorings ['muərɪŋz] *npl* (*chains*) amarras *fpl*; (*place*) amarradero *sg*.
Moorish ['muərɪʃ] *a* moro; (*architecture*) árabe, morisco.
moorland ['muələnd] *n* páramo, brezal *m*.
moose [muːs] *n*, *pl inv* alce *m*.
mop [mɔp] *n* fregona; (*of hair*) greña, melena // *vt* fregar; **to** ~ **up** *vt* limpiar.
mope [məup] *vi* estar *o* andar deprimido.
moped ['məupɛd] *n* (*Brit*) ciclomotor *m*.
moral ['mɔrl] *a* moral // *n* moraleja; ~**s** *npl* moralidad *f*, moral *f*.
morale [mɔ'rɑːl] *n* moral *f*.
morality [mə'rælɪtɪ] *n* moralidad *f*.
morass [mə'ræs] *n* pantano.
morbid ['mɔːbɪd] *a* (*depressed*) melancólico; (*MED*) mórbido; **don't be** ~! ¡no seas morboso!
more [mɔː*] *det*, *ad* más; **once** ~ otra vez, una vez más; **I want** ~ quiero más; ~ **dangerous than** más peligroso que; ~ **or less** más o menos; ~ **than ever** más que nunca.
moreover [mɔː'rəuvə*] *ad* además, por otra parte.
morgue [mɔːg] *n* depósito de cadáveres.
moribund ['mɔrɪbʌnd] *a* moribundo.
Mormon ['mɔːmən] *n* mormón/ona *m/f*.

morning ['mɔːnɪŋ] *n* (*gen*) mañana; (*early* ~) madrugada; **good** ~ buenas días; **in the** ~ por la mañana; **7 o'clock in the** ~ las 7 de la mañana; **tomorrow** ~ mañana por la mañana.
Moroccan [mə'rɔkən] *a*, *n* marroquí *m/f*.
Morocco [mə'rɔkəu] *n* Marruecos *m*.
moron ['mɔːrɔn] *n* imbécil *m/f*; ~**ic** [mə'rɔnɪk] *a* imbécil.
morose [mə'rəus] *a* hosco, malhumorado.
morphine ['mɔːfiːn] *n* morfina.
Morse [mɔːs] *n* (*also:* ~ **code**) (alfabeto) morse.
morsel ['mɔːsl] *n* (*of food*) bocado.
mortal ['mɔːtl] *a*, *n* mortal *m/f*; ~**ity** [-'tælɪtɪ] *n* mortalidad *f*.
mortar ['mɔːtə*] *n* argamasa; (*dish*) mortero.
mortgage ['mɔːgɪdʒ] *n* hipoteca // *vt* hipotecar.
mortify ['mɔːtɪfaɪ] *vt* mortificar, humillar.
mortuary ['mɔːtjuərɪ] *n* depósito de cadáveres.
mosaic [məu'zeɪɪk] *n* mosaico.
Moscow ['mɔskəu] *n* Moscú *m*.
Moslem ['mɔzləm] *a*, *n* = **Muslim.**
mosque [mɔsk] *n* mezquita.
mosquito [mɔs'kiːtəu] *pl* ~**es** *n* mosquito.
moss [mɔs] *n* musgo.
most [məust] *det* la mayor parte de, la mayoría de // *pron* la mayor parte, la mayoría // *ad* el más; (*very*) muy; **the** ~ (*also:* + *adjective*) el más; ~ **of them** la mayor parte de ellos; **I saw the** ~ yo vi el que más; **at the (very)** ~ a lo sumo, todo lo más; **to make the** ~ **of** aprovechar (al máximo); ~**ly** *ad* en su mayor parte, principalmente; **a** ~ **interesting book** un libro interesantísimo.
MOT *n abbr of* **Ministry of Transport: the** ~ (**test**) inspección (anual) obligatoria de coches y camiones.
motel [məu'tɛl] *n* motel *m*.
moth [mɔθ] *n* mariposa nocturna; (*clothes* ~) polilla; ~**ball** *n* bola de naftalina; ~**-eaten** *a* apolillado.
mother ['mʌðə*] *n* madre *f* // *a* materno // *vt* (*care for*) cuidar (como a una madre); ~**hood** *n* maternidad *f*; ~**-in-law** *n* suegra; ~**ly** *a* maternal; ~**-of-pearl** *n* nácar *m*; ~**-to-be** *n* futura madre; ~ **tongue** *n* lengua materna.
motif [məu'tiːf] *n* motivo; (*theme*) tema *m*.
motion ['məuʃən] *n* movimiento; (*gesture*) ademán *m*, señal *f*; (*at meeting*) moción *f* // *vt*, *vi*: **to** ~ (**to**) **sb to do sth** hacer señas a uno para que haga algo; ~**less** *a* inmóvil; ~ **picture** *n* película.
motivated ['məutɪveɪtɪd] *a* motivado; **motivation** [-'veɪʃən] *n* motivación *f*.
motive ['məutɪv] *n* motivo // *a* motor (*f*: motora, motriz).
motley ['mɔtlɪ] *a* variado.
motor ['məutə*] *n* motor *m*; (*col: vehicle*) coche *m*, automóvil *m* // *a* motor (*f*:

motora, motriz); ~**bike** n moto f; ~**boat** n lancha motora; ~**car** n coche m, automóvil m; ~**cycle** n motocicleta; ~**cyclist** n motorista m/f; ~**ing** n automovilismo; ~**ist** n conductor/a m/f, automovilista m/f; ~ **oil** n aceite m de coche; ~ **racing** n carreras fpl de coches, automovilismo; ~ **scooter** n moto f; ~ **vehicle** n automóvil m; ~**way** n (Brit) autopista.

mottled ['mɔtld] a abigarrado, multicolor.

motto ['mɔtəu], pl ~**es** n lema m; (watchword) consigna.

mould, mold (US) [məuld] n molde m; (mildew) moho // vt moldear; (fig) formar; ~**er** vi (decay) decaer; ~**ing** n moldura; ~**y** a enmohecido.

moult, molt (US) [məult] vi mudar (la piel/la pluma).

mound [maund] n montón m, montículo.

mount [maunt] n monte m; (horse) montura; (for jewel etc) engaste m; (for picture) marco // vt montar, subir a // vi (also: ~ **up**) subirse, montarse.

mountain ['mauntɪn] n montaña // cpd de montaña; ~**eer** [-'nɪə*] n alpinista m/f, montañero/a; ~**eering** [-'nɪərɪŋ] n alpinismo, montañismo; **to go** ~**eering** hacer alpinismo; ~**ous** a montañoso; ~**side** n ladera de la montaña.

mourn [mɔːn] vt llorar, lamentar // vi: **to** ~ **for** llorar la muerte de, lamentarse por; ~**er** n pariente m/f/amigo del difunto; ~**ful** a triste, lúgubre; ~**ing** n luto // cpd (dress) de luto; **in** ~**ing** de luto.

mouse [maus], pl **mice** n ratón m; ~**trap** n ratonera.

moustache [məs'tɑːʃ] n bigote m.

mousy ['mausɪ] a (person) tímido; (hair) pardusco.

mouth [mauθ], pl ~**s** [-ōz] n boca; (of river) desembocadura; ~**ful** n bocado; ~ **organ** n armónica; ~**piece** n (of musical instrument) boquilla; (spokesman) portavoz m; ~**wash** n enjuague m; ~-**watering** a apetitoso.

movable ['muːvəbl] a movible.

move [muːv] n (movement) movimiento; (in game) jugada; (: turn to play) turno; (change of house) mudanza // vt mover; (emotionally) conmover; (POL: resolution etc) proponer // vi (gen) moverse; (traffic) circular; (also: ~ **house**) trasladarse, mudarse; **to** ~ **sb to do sth** mover a uno a hacer algo; **to get a** ~ **on** darse prisa; **to** ~ **about** vi ir de acá para allá; (travel) viajar; **to** ~ **along** vi avanzar, adelantarse; **to** ~ **away** vi alejarse; **to** ~ **back** vi retroceder; **to** ~ **forward** vi avanzar // vt adelantar; **to** ~ **in** vi (to a house) instalarse (en una casa); **to** ~ **on** vi ponerse en camino; **to** ~ **out** vi (of house) abandonar (una casa); **to** ~ **up** vi subir; (employee) ser ascendido.

movement ['muːvmənt] n movimiento; (TECH) mecanismo.

movie ['muːvɪ] n película; **to go to the** ~**s** ir al cine; ~ **camera** n cámara cinematográfica.

moving ['muːvɪŋ] a (emotional) conmovedor(a); (that moves) móvil.

mow [məu], pt **mowed**, pp **mowed** or **mown** vt (grass) cortar; (corn: also: ~ **down**) segar; ~**er** n segadora; (for lawn) cortacéspedes m inv.

M.P. n abbr of **Member of Parliament**.

m.p.h. abbr of **miles per hour**.

Mr ['mɪstə*] n: ~ **Smith** (el) Sr. Smith.

Mrs ['mɪsɪz] n: ~ **Smith** (la) Sra. Smith.

Ms [mɪz] n = **Miss** or **Mrs**: ~ **Smith** (la) Sa. Smith.

M.Sc. abbr of **Master of Science**.

much [mʌtʃ] det mucho // ad, n or pron mucho; (before pp) muy; **how** ~ **is it?** ¿cuánto es?, ¿cuánto cuesta?; **too** ~ demasiado; **it's not** ~ no es mucho; **as** ~ **as** tanto como; **however** ~ **he tries** por mucho que se esfuerce.

muck [mʌk] n (dirt) suciedad f; (fig) porquería; **to** ~ **about** vi (col) perder el tiempo; (enjoy o.s.) entretenerse; **to** ~ **up** vt (col: ruin) arruinar, estropear; ~**y** a (dirty) sucio.

mucus ['mjuːkəs] n moco.

mud [mʌd] n barro, lodo.

muddle ['mʌdl] n desorden m, confusión f; (mix-up) embrollo, lío // vt (also: ~ **up**) embrollar, confundir; **to** ~ **through** vi salir del paso sin saber cómo.

mud: ~**dy** a fangoso, cubierto de lodo; ~**guard** n guardabarros m inv; ~**pack** n mascarilla (de belleza); ~-**slinging** n injurias fpl, difamación f.

muff [mʌf] n manguito // vt (chance) desperdiciar; (lines) estropear.

muffin ['mʌfɪn] n mollete m.

muffle ['mʌfl] vt (sound) amortiguar; (against cold) embozar; ~**d** a sordo, apagado.

mufti ['mʌftɪ] n: **in** ~ vestido de paisano.

mug [mʌg] n (cup) taza (alta, sin platillo); (: for beer) jarra; (col: face) jeta; (: fool) bobo // vt (assault) asaltar; ~**ging** n asalto.

muggy ['mʌgɪ] a bochornoso.

mule [mjuːl] n mula.

mull [mʌl]: **to** ~ **over** vt meditar sobre.

mulled [mʌld] a: ~ **wine** vino calentado y con especias.

multi... [mʌltɪ] pref multi...; ~**coloured**, ~**colored** (US) a multicolor.

multifarious [mʌltɪ'fɛərɪəs] a múltiple.

multiple ['mʌltɪpl] a, n múltiplo; ~ **sclerosis** n esclerósis f múltiple; ~ **store** n (cadena de) grandes almacenes.

multiplication [mʌltɪplɪ'keɪʃən] n multiplicación f; **multiply** ['mʌltɪplaɪ] vt multiplicar // vi multiplicarse.

multitude ['mʌltɪtjuːd] n multitud f.

mum [mʌm] n mamá // a: **to keep** ~ callarse.

mumble ['mʌmbl] vt, vi hablar entre dientes, refunfuñar.

mummy ['mʌmɪ] n (mother) mamá; (embalmed) momia.

mumps [mʌmps] n paperas fpl.

munch [mʌntʃ] vt, vi mascar.

mundane [mʌn'deɪn] a mundano.

municipal [mju:'nɪsɪpl] a municipal; ~ity [-'pælɪtɪ] n municipio.

munitions [mju:'nɪʃənz] npl municiones fpl.

mural ['mjuərl] n (pintura) mural m.

murder ['mɜːdə*] n asesinato; (in law) homicidio // vt asesinar, matar; (spoil) estropear; ~er n asesino; ~ess n asesina; ~ous a homicida.

murky ['mɜːkɪ] a oscuro; (fig) tenebroso.

murmur ['mɜːmə*] n murmullo // vt, vi murmurar.

muscle ['mʌsl] n músculo; (fig: strength) fuerza (muscular); **to ~ in** vi introducirse por fuerza; **muscular** ['muskjulə*] a muscular; (person) musculoso.

muse [mju:z] vi meditar // n musa.

museum [mju:'zɪəm] n museo.

mushroom ['mʌʃrum] n (gen) seta, hongo; (food) champiñón m // vi (fig) crecer de la noche a la mañana.

mushy ['mʌʃɪ] a triturado; (pej) sensiblero.

music ['mju:zɪk] n música; ~al a melodioso; (person) musical // n (show) (comedia) musical; ~al **instrument** n instrumento musical; ~ **hall** n teatro de variedades; ~ian [-'zɪʃən] n músico/a.

musket ['mʌskɪt] n mosquete m.

Muslim ['mʌzlɪm] a, n musulmán/ana m/f.

muslin ['mʌzlɪn] n muselina.

mussel ['mʌsl] n mejillón m.

must [mʌst] auxiliary vb (obligation): **I ~ do it** debo hacerlo, tengo que hacerlo; (probability): **he ~ be there by now** ya debe estar allí // n necesidad f; **it's a ~** es imprescindible.

mustard ['mʌstəd] n mostaza.

muster ['mʌstə*] vt juntar, reunir.

mustn't ['mʌsnt] = **must not**.

musty ['mʌstɪ] a mohoso, que huele a humedad.

mute [mju:t] a, n mudo/a.

muted ['mju:tɪd] a callado; (MUS) apagado.

mutilate ['mju:tɪleɪt] vt mutilar; **mutilation** [-'leɪʃən] n mutilación f.

mutinous ['mju:tɪnəs] a (troops) amotinado; (attitude) rebelde.

mutiny ['mju:tɪnɪ] n motín m // vi amotinarse.

mutter ['mʌtə*] vt, vi murmurar, hablar entre dientes.

mutton ['mʌtn] n carne f de cordero.

mutual ['mju:tʃuəl] a mutuo; (gen: shared) común; ~ly ad mutuamente.

muzzle ['mʌzl] n hocico; (protective device) bozal m; (of gun) boca // vt amordazar; (dog) poner un bozal a.

my [maɪ] a mi // interj: ~! ¡caramba!

mynah bird ['maɪnə*] n mainat m.

myopic [maɪ'ɔpɪk] a miope.

myself [maɪ'sɛlf] pron (reflexive) me; (emphatic) yo mismo; (after prep) mí (mismo).

mysterious [mɪs'tɪərɪəs] a misterioso; **mystery** ['mɪstərɪ] n misterio.

mystic ['mɪstɪk] a, n místico/a; ~al a místico.

mystify ['mɪstɪfaɪ] vt (perplex) dejar perplejo; (disconcert) desconcertar.

myth [mɪθ] n mito; ~ical a mítico; ~ological [mɪθə'lɔdʒɪkl] a mitológico; ~ology [mɪ'θɔlədʒɪ] n mitología.

N

nab [næb] vt (col: grab) coger; (: catch out) pillar.

nag [næg] n (pej: horse) rocín m // vt (scold) regañar; (annoy) fastidiar; ~ging a (doubt) persistente; (pain) continuo // n quejas fpl.

nail [neɪl] n (human) uña; (metal) clavo // vt clavar; (fig: catch) coger, pillar; **to ~ sb down to doing sth** comprometer a uno a que haga algo; ~brush n cepillo para las uñas; ~file n lima para las uñas; ~ **polish** n esmalte m o laca para las uñas; ~ **scissors** npl tijeras fpl para las uñas.

naïve [naɪ'i:v] a ingenuo; (simple) sencillo.

naked ['neɪkɪd] a (nude) desnudo; (fig) inerme, indefenso; (flame) expuesto al aire; ~ness n desnudez f.

name [neɪm] n (gen) nombre m; (surname) apellido; (reputation) fama, renombre m // vt (child) poner nombre a; (criminal) dar el nombre de; (appoint) nombrar; **by ~** de nombre; **maiden ~** nombre de soltera; **in the ~ of** en nombre de; **what's your ~?** ¿cómo se llama?; **to give one's ~ and address** dar las señas; ~less a anónimo, sin nombre; ~ly ad a saber; ~sake n tocayo/a.

nanny ['nænɪ] n niñera; ~ **goat** n cabra.

nap [næp] n (sleep) sueñecito, siesta.

napalm ['neɪpɑ:m] n nápalm m.

nape [neɪp] n: **the ~ of the neck** la nuca, el cogote.

napkin ['næpkɪn] n (also: **table ~**) servilleta; (Brit: for baby) pañal m.

nappy ['næpɪ] n pañal m; ~ **liner** n gasa; ~ **rash** n prurito.

narcissus [nɑ:'sɪsəs], pl **-si** [-saɪ] n narciso.

narcotic [nɑ:'kɔtɪk] a, n narcótico.

narrate [nə'reɪt] vt narrar, contar; **narrative** ['nærətɪv] n narrativa // a narrativo; **narrator** n narrador/a m/f.

narrow ['nærəu] a estrecho, angosto; (fig) de miras estrechas, intolerante // vi estrecharse, angostarse; (diminish) reducirse; **to ~ down the possibilities to** reducir las posibilidades a; ~ly ad (miss) por poco; ~-**minded** a de miras estrechas.

nasal ['neɪzl] a nasal.

nastiness ['nɑ:stɪnɪs] n (malice)

malevolencia; (*rudeness*) grosería.

nasty ['nɑːstɪ] a (*unpleasant*: *remark*) feo, horrible; (: *person*) antipático; (*malicious*) rencoroso; (*rude*) grosero; (*revolting*: *taste, smell*) asqueroso, repugnante; (*wound, disease etc*) peligroso, grave.

nation ['neɪʃən] n nación f.

national ['næʃənl] a, n nacional m/f; ~**ism** n nacionalismo; ~**ist** a, n nacionalista m/f; ~**ity** [-'nælɪtɪ] n nacionalidad f; ~**ization** [-aɪ'zeɪʃən] n nacionalización f; ~**ize** vt nacionalizar; ~**ly** ad (*nationwide*) en escala nacional; (*as a nation*) nacionalmente, como nación.

nationwide ['neɪʃənwaɪd] a en escala o a nivel nacional.

native ['neɪtɪv] n (*local inhabitant*) natural m/f, nacional m/f; (*in colonies*) indígena m/f, nativo/a // a (*indigenous*) indígena; (*of one's birth*) natal; (*innate*) natural, innato.

NATO ['neɪtəu] n abbr of **North Atlantic Treaty Organization** OTAN (Organización del Tratado del Atlántico del Norte).

natter ['nætə*] vi charlar.

natural ['nætʃrəl] a natural; (*unaffected*: *manner*) inafectado, sin afectación; ~**ist** n naturalista m/f; ~**ize** vt: **to become** ~**ized** (*person*) naturalizarse; (*plant*) aclimatarse; ~**ly** ad naturalmente; (*of course*) desde luego, por supuesto; (*instinctively*) por instinto, por naturaleza; ~**ness** n naturalidad f.

nature ['neɪtʃə*] n naturaleza; (*group, sort*) género, clase f; (*character*) carácter m, genio; **by** ~ por o de naturaleza.

naughty ['nɔːtɪ] a (*child*) travieso; (*story, film*) verde, escabroso.

nausea ['nɔːsɪə] n náusea; **nauseate** [-sɪeɪt] vt dar náuseas a; (*fig*) dar asco a; **nauseating** [-sɪeɪtɪŋ] a nauseabundo; (*fig*) asqueroso.

nautical ['nɔːtɪkl] a náutico, marítimo; (*mile*) marino.

naval ['neɪvl] a naval, de marina; ~ **officer** n oficial m/f de marina.

nave [neɪv] n nave f.

navel ['neɪvl] n ombligo.

navigable ['nævɪgəbl] a navegable.

navigate ['nævɪgeɪt] vt (*guide*) gobernar; (*sail along*) navegar por; (*fig*) guiar // vi navegar; **navigation** [-'geɪʃən] n (*action*) navegación f; (*science*) náutica; **navigator** n navegador/a m/f, navegante m/f.

navvy ['nævɪ] n peón m caminero.

navy ['neɪvɪ] n marina de guerra; (*ships*) armada, flota; ~**(-blue)** a azul marino.

Nazi ['nɑːtsɪ] n nazi m/f; **nazism** n nazismo.

neap tide [niːp-] n marea muerta.

near [nɪə*] a (*place*) cercano, vecino; (*time*) próximo; (*relation*) estrecho, íntimo // ad cerca // prep (*also*: ~ **to**) (*space*) cerca de, junto a; (*time*) cerca de, casi // vt acercarse a, aproximarse a; ~**by**

[nɪə'baɪ] a cercano, próximo // ad cerca; **N** ~ **East** n Cercano Oriente m; ~**ly** ad casi, por poco; **I** ~**ly fell** por poco me caigo; ~ **miss** n tiro cercano; ~**ness** n proximidad f, cercanía; (*relationship*) intimidad f; ~**side** n (*AUT: in Britain*) lado izquierdo; (: *in Spain*) lado derecho; ~**-sighted** a miope, corto de vista.

neat [niːt] a (*place*) bien arreglado o cuidado; (*person*) pulcro, esmerado; (*skilful*) diestro; (: *plan*) hábil, ingenioso; (*spirits*) solo.

nebulous ['nɛbjuləs] a nebuloso; (*fig*) vago, confuso.

necessarily ['nɛsɪsrɪlɪ] ad necesariamente.

necessary ['nɛsɪsrɪ] a necesario, preciso; **he did all that was** ~ hizo todo lo necesario.

necessitate [nɪ'sɛsɪteɪt] vt necesitar, exigir.

necessity [nɪ'sɛsɪtɪ] n (*thing needed*) necesidad f, requisito; (*compelling circumstances*) la necesidad; **necessities** npl artículos mpl de primera necesidad.

neck [nɛk] n (*ANAT*) cuello; (*of animal*) pescuezo // vi besuquearse, abrazarse; ~ **and** ~ parejos; **to stick one's** ~ **out** arriesgarse.

necklace ['nɛklɪs] n collar m.

neckline ['nɛklaɪn] n escote m.

necktie ['nɛktaɪ] n corbata.

née [neɪ] a: ~ **Scott** de soltera Scott.

need [niːd] n (*lack*) escasez f, falta; (*necessity*) necesidad f; (*thing needed*) requisito, necesidad f // vt (*require*) necesitar; **I** ~ **to do it** tengo que o debo hacerlo, hay que hacerlo; **you don't** ~ **to go** no hace falta que vayas.

needle ['niːdl] n aguja // vt (*fig: fam*) picar, fastidiar.

needless ['niːdlɪs] a innecesario, inútil; ~ **to say** huelga decir que.

needlework ['niːdlwɜːk] n (*activity*) costura, labor f de aguja.

needy ['niːdɪ] a necesitado.

negation [nɪ'geɪʃən] n negación f.

negative ['nɛgətɪv] n (*PHOT*) negativo; (*answer*) negativa // a negativo.

neglect [nɪ'glɛkt] vt (*one's duty*) faltar a, no cumplir con; (*child*) descuidar, desatender // n (*gen*) negligencia, abandono; (*personal*) dejadez f; (*of duty*) incumplimiento.

negligee ['nɛglɪʒeɪ] n (*nightdress*) salto de cama; (*housecoat*) bata.

negligence ['nɛglɪdʒəns] n negligencia, descuido; **negligent** [-ənt] a (*careless*) descuidado, negligente; (*forgetful*) olvidadizo.

negligible ['nɛglɪdʒɪbl] a insignificante, despreciable.

negotiable [nɪ'gəuʃɪəbl] a (*cheque*) negociable; (*road*) transitable.

negotiate [nɪ'gəuʃɪeɪt] vi negociar // vt (*treaty*) negociar; (*transaction*) gestionar, tramitar; (*obstacle*) franquear;

negotiation [-'eɪʃɔn] n negociación f,
gestión f; **negotiator** n negociador/a m/f.
Negress ['niːgrɪs] n negra.
Negro ['niːgrəu] a, n negro.
neigh [neɪ] n relincho // vi relinchar.
neighbour, neighbor (US) ['neɪbə*] n
vecino/a; ~**hood** n (place) vecindad f,
barrio; (people) vecindario; ~**ing** a
vecino; ~**ly** a amistoso, de buen vecino.
neither ['naɪðə*] a ni // conj: **I didn't
move and** ~ **did John** no me he movido,
ni Juan tampoco // pron ninguno // ad: ~
good nor bad ni bueno ni malo.
neo... [niːəu] pref neo-.
neon ['niːɔn] n neón m; ~ **light** n lámpara
de neón.
nephew ['nɛvjuː] n sobrino.
nerve [nɔːv] n (ANAT) nervio; (courage)
valor m; (impudence) descaro, frescura;
~-**racking** a que crispa los nervios; ~**s**
npl (fig: anxiety) nerviosidad f,
nerviosismo.
nervous ['nɔːvəs] a (anxious, ANAT)
nervioso; (timid) tímido, miedoso; ~
breakdown n crisis f nerviosa; ~**ly** ad
nerviosamente; tímidamente; ~**ness** n
nerviosidad f, nerviosismo; timidez f.
nest [nɛst] n (of bird) nido; (of wasp)
avispero // vi anidar.
nestle ['nɛsl] vi: **to** ~ **up to sb** arrimarse
a uno.
net [nɛt] n (gen) red f; (fig) trampa // a
(COMM) neto, líquido // vt coger con red;
(SPORT) marcar; ~**ball** n básquet m.
Netherlands ['nɛðələndz] npl: **the** ~ los
Países Bajos.
nett [nɛt] a = **net.**
netting ['nɛtɪŋ] n red f, redes fpl.
nettle ['nɛtl] n ortiga.
network ['nɛtwɔːk] n red f.
neurosis [njuə'rəusɪs], pl **-ses** [-siːz] n
neurosis f; **neurotic** [-'rɔtɪk] a, n
neurótico/a.
neuter ['njuːtə*] a (sexless) castrado, sin
sexo; (LING) neutro // vt castrar, capar.
neutral ['njuːtrəl] a (person) neutral;
(colour etc, ELEC) neutro // n (AUT) punto
muerto; ~**ity** [-'trælɪti] n neutralidad f.
neutron ['njuːtrɔn] n neutrón m; ~ **bomb**
n bomba de neutrones.
never ['nɛvə*] ad nunca, jamás; **I** ~ **went**
no fui nunca; ~ **in my life** jamás en la
vida; ~-**ending** a interminable, sin fin;
~**theless** [nɛvəðə'lɛs] ad sin embargo, no
obstante.
new [njuː] a (brand ~) nuevo; (recent)
reciente; (different) nuevo, distinto;
(inexperienced) tierno, nuevo; ~-**born** a
recién nacido; ~**comer** ['njuːkʌmə*] n
recién venido o llegado; ~**ly** ad nuevamente, recién; ~ **moon** n luna nueva;
~**ness** n novedad f; (fig) inexperiencia.
news [njuːz] n noticias fpl; **a piece of** ~
una noticia; **the** ~ (RADIO, TV) las noticias
fpl, telediario; ~ **agency** n agencia de
noticias; ~**agent** n vendedor/a m/f de
periódicos; ~**caster** n presentador/a m/f

de noticias; ~ **flash** n noticia de última
hora; ~**letter** n hoja informativa, boletín
m; ~**paper** n periódico, diario; ~**reel** n
noticiario; ~ **stand** n quiosco o puesto de
periódicos.
New Year ['njuː'jɪə*] n Año Nuevo; ~**'s
Day** n Día m de Año Nuevo; ~**'s Eve** n
Nochevieja.
New York ['njuː'jɔːk] n Nueva York.
New Zealand [njuː'ziːlənd] n Nueva
Zelanda.
next [nɛkst] a (in space) próximo, vecino;
(in time) próximo, siguiente // ad (place)
después; (time) después, luego; ~ **time** la
próxima vez; ~ **year** el año próximo o
que viene; ~ **door** ad en la casa de al lado
// a vecino, de al lado; ~-**of-kin** n
pariente(s) m(pl) cercano(s); ~ **to** prep
junto a, al lado de.
N.H.S. n abbr of **National Health
Service.**
nib [nɪb] n plumilla.
nibble ['nɪbl] vt mordisquear, mordiscar;
(ZOOL) roer.
nice [naɪs] a (likeable) simpático, majo;
(kind) amable; (pleasant) agradable;
(attractive) bonito, mono; (subtle) fino,
preciso; ~-**looking** a atractivo, guapo;
~**ly** ad amablemente, bien.
niche [niːʃ] n nicho.
nick [nɪk] n (wound) rasguño; (cut,
indentation) mella, muesca // vt (col)
birlar, robar; **in the** ~ **of time** a última
hora.
nickel ['nɪkl] n níquel m.
nickname ['nɪkneɪm] n apodo, mote m //
vt apodar.
nicotine ['nɪkətiːn] n nicotina.
niece [niːs] n sobrina.
Nigeria [naɪ'dʒɪərɪə] n Nigeria; ~**n** a, n
nigeriano/a.
niggardly ['nɪgədlɪ] a (person) avaro,
tacaño; (amount) miserable.
niggling ['nɪglɪŋ] a (trifling) nimio,
insignificante; (annoying) molesto.
night [naɪt] n (gen) noche f; (evening)
tarde f; **last** ~ anoche; **the** ~ **before
last** anteanoche; **good** ~! ¡buenas
noches!; **at** or **by** ~ de noche, por la
noche; ~**cap** n (drink) resopón m; ~
club n cabaret m; ~**dress** n camisón m;
~**fall** n anochecer m; ~**ie** ['naɪtɪ] n
camisón m.
nightingale ['naɪtɪŋgeɪl] n ruiseñor m.
nightly ['naɪtlɪ] a de noche, nocturno // ad
todas las noches, cada noche.
night: ~**mare** n pesadilla; ~ **school** n
clase(s) f(pl) nocturna(s); ~ **shift** n turno
nocturno o de noche; ~-**time** n noche f;
~ **watchman** n sereno.
nil [nɪl] n cero, nada.
nimble ['nɪmbl] a (agile) ágil, ligero;
(skilful) diestro.
nine [naɪn] num nueve; ~**teen** num
diecinueve, diez y nueve; ~**ty** num
noventa.
ninth [naɪnθ] a noveno.

nip [nɪp] *vt* (*pinch*) pellizcar; (*bite*) morder // *n* (*drink*) trago, gota.

nipple ['nɪpl] *n* (*ANAT*) pezón *m*; (*of bottle*) tetilla; (*TECH*) boquilla, manguito.

nippy ['nɪpɪ] *a* (*person*) ágil, rápido; (*taste*) picante.

nitrate ['naɪtreɪt] *n* nitrato.

nitrogen ['naɪtrədʒən] *n* nitrógeno.

no [nəu] *ad* no // *a* ninguno, no ... alguno // *n* no.

nobility [nəu'bɪlɪtɪ] *n* nobleza.

noble ['nəubl] *a* (*person*) noble; (*title*) de nobleza; (*generous*) noble; ~**man** *n* noble *m*, aristócrata *m*.

nobody ['nəubədɪ] *pron* nadie.

nod [nɔd] *vi* saludar con la cabeza; (*in agreement*) decir que sí con la cabeza; (*doze*) cabecear // *vt* inclinar // *n* inclinación *f* de cabeza; **to** ~ **off** *vi* cabecear.

noise [nɔɪz] *n* ruido; (*din*) escándalo, estrépito; **noisily** *ad* ruidosamente; **noisy** *a* (*gen*) ruidoso; (*child*) escandaloso.

nomad ['nəumæd] *n* nómada *m/f*; ~**ic** [-'mædɪk] *a* nómada.

nominal ['nɔmɪnl] *a* nominal.

nominate ['nɔmɪneɪt] *vt* (*propose*) proponer; (*appoint*) nombrar; **nomination** [-'neɪʃən] *n* propuesta; nombramiento.

nominee [nɔmɪ'niː] *n* candidato/a.

non... [nɔn] *pref* no, des..., in...; ~**-alcoholic** *a* no alcohólico; ~**-aligned** *a* no alineado; ~**-committal** ['nɔnkə'mɪtl] *a* (*reserved*) reservado; (*uncommitted*) evasivo; ~**conformist** *a* no conformista; ~**descript** ['nɔndɪskrɪpt] *a* indeterminado; (*pej*) mediocre.

none [nʌn] *pron* (*person*) nadie; (*thing*) ninguno, nada // *ad* de ninguna manera.

nonentity [nɔ'nentɪtɪ] *n* cero a la izquierda, nulidad *f*.

nonetheless [nʌnðə'lɛs] *ad* sin embargo, no obstante.

non- ~**-fiction** *n* literatura no novelesca; ~**plussed** *a* perplejo.

nonsense ['nɔnsəns] *n* tonterías *fpl*, disparates *fpl*.

non-stop ['nɔn'stɔp] *a* continuo; (*RAIL*) directo // *ad* sin parar.

noodles ['nuːdlz] *npl* tallarines *mpl*.

nook [nuk] *n* rincón *m*; ~**s and crannies** escondrijos *mpl*.

noon [nuːn] *n* mediodía *m*.

no-one ['nəuwʌn] *pron* = **nobody.**

noose [nuːs] *n* lazo corredizo; (*hangman's*) dogal *m*.

nor [nɔ:*] *conj* = **neither** // *ad see* **neither.**

norm [nɔːm] *n* norma.

normal ['nɔːml] *a* (*usual*) normal; (*ordinary*) corriente, regular; ~**ly** *ad* normalmente.

north [nɔːθ] *n* norte *m* // *a* del norte, norteño // *ad* al o hacia el norte; **N~ America** *n* América del Norte; ~**-east** *n* nor(d)este *m*; ~**ern** ['nɔːðən] *a* norteño,

del norte; **N~ern Ireland** *n* Irlanda del Norte; **N~ Pole** *n* Polo Norte; **N~ Sea** *n* Mar *m* del Norte; ~**ward(s)** ['nɔːθwəd(z)] *ad* hacia el norte; ~**-west** *n* nor(d)oeste *m*.

Norway ['nɔːweɪ] *n* Noruega; **Norwegian** [-'wiːdʒən] *a*, *n* noruego/a.

nose [nəuz] *n* (*ANAT*) nariz *f*; (*ZOOL*) hocico; (*sense of smell*) olfato // *vi*: **to** ~ **about** curiosear; ~**bleed** *n* hemorragia nasal; ~**-dive** *n* (*deliberate*) picado vertical; (*involuntary*) caída de narices; ~**y** *a* curioso, fisgón(ona).

nostalgia [nɔs'tældʒɪə] *n* nostalgia; **nostalgic** *a* nostálgico.

nostril ['nɔstrɪl] *n* ventana de la nariz; ~**s** *npl* narices *fpl*.

nosy ['nəuzɪ] *a* = **nosey.**

not [nɔt] *ad* no; ~ **at all** no ... en absoluto; ~ **that...** no es que...; ~ **yet** todavía no; ~ **now** ahora no; **why** ~**?** ¿por qué no?

notable ['nəutəbl] *a* notable.

notary ['nəutərɪ] *n* notario.

notch [nɔtʃ] *n* muesca, corte *m*.

note [nəut] *n* (*MUS*) nota; (*banknote*) billete *m*; (*letter*) nota, carta; (*record*) nota, apunte *m*; (*fame*) importancia, renombre *m*; (*tone*) tono // *vt* (*observe*) notar, observar; (*write down*) apuntar, anotar; ~**book** *n* libreta, cuaderno; ~**-case** *n* cartera, billetero; ~**d** ['nəutɪd] *a* célebre, conocido; ~**paper** *n* papel *m* para cartas.

nothing ['nʌθɪŋ] *n* nada; (*zero*) cero; **for** ~ (*free*) gratis, sin pago; (*in vain*) en balde.

notice ['nəutɪs] *n* (*announcement*) anuncio; (*attention*) atención *f*, interés *m*; (*warning*) aviso; (*dismissal*) despido; (*resignation*) dimisión *f*; (*period of time*) plazo // *vt* (*observe*) notar, observar; **to take** ~ **of** tomar nota de, prestar atención a; **at short** ~ a corto plazo, con poco anticipación; **until further** ~ hasta nuevo aviso; ~**able** *a* evidente, obvio; ~**board** *n* (*Brit*) tablón *m* de anuncios.

notification [nəutɪfɪ'keɪʃən] *n* aviso; **notify** ['nəutɪfaɪ] *vt* avisar, notificar.

notion ['nəuʃən] *n* noción *f*, concepto; (*opinion*) opinión *f*.

notorious [nəu'tɔːrɪəs] *a* notorio, célebre.

notwithstanding [nɔtwɪθ'stændɪŋ] *ad* no obstante, sin embargo; ~ **this** a pesar de esto.

nougat ['nuːgɑː] *n* turrón *m*.

nought [nɔːt] *n* cero.

noun [naun] *n* nombre *m*, sustantivo.

nourish ['nʌrɪʃ] *vt* nutrir, alimentar; (*fig*) fomentar, nutrir; ~**ing** *a* nutritivo, rico; ~**ment** *n* alimento, sustento.

novel ['nɔvl] *n* novela // *a* (*new*) nuevo, original; (*unexpected*) insólito; ~**ist** *n* novelista *m/f*; ~**ty** *n* novedad *f*.

November [nəu'vɛmbə*] *n* noviembre *m*.

novice ['nɔvɪs] *n* principiante *m/f*, novato/a; (*REL*) novicio/a.

now [nau] *ad* (*at the present time*) ahora; (*these days*) actualmente, hoy día; **right**

~ ahora mismo; ~ **and then,** ~ **and again** de vez en cuando; **from** ~ **on** de ahora en adelante; ~ **adays** ['nauədeɪz] ad hoy (en) día, actualmente.

nowhere ['nəuwɛə*] ad (direction) a ninguna parte; (location) en ninguna parte.

nozzle ['nɔzl] n (gen) boquilla; (TECH) tobera, inyector m.

nuance ['njuːɑːns] n matiz m.

nuclear ['njuːklɪə*] a nuclear.

nucleus ['njuːklɪəs], pl **-lei** [-lɪaɪ] n núcleo.

nude [njuːd] a. n desnudo/a; **in the** ~ desnudo.

nudge [nʌdʒ] vt dar un codazo a.

nudist ['njuːdɪst] n nudista m/f.

nudity ['njuːdɪtɪ] n desnudez f.

nuisance ['njuːsns] n molestia, fastidio; (person) pesado, latoso; **what a** ~! ¡qué lata!

null [nʌl] a: ~ **and void** nulo y sin efecto; ~**ify** ['nʌlɪfaɪ] vt anular, invalidar.

numb [nʌm] a entumecido; (fig) insensible // vt entumecer, entorpecer.

number ['nʌmbə*] n número; (numeral) número, cifra // vt (pages etc) numerar, poner número a; (amount to) sumar, ascender a; **to be** ~**ed among** figurar entre; **a** ~ **of** varios, algunos; **they were ten in** ~ eran diez; ~ **plate** n placa de matrícula.

numbness ['nʌmnɪs] n entumecimiento; (fig) insensibilidad f.

numeral ['njuːmərəl] n número, cifra.

numerical ['njuː'mɛrɪkl] a numérico.

numerous ['njuːmərəs] a numeroso, muchos.

nun [nʌn] n monja, religiosa.

nurse [nəːs] n enfermero/a; (nanny) niñera // vt (patient) cuidar, atender; (baby) criar, amamantar; (fig) guardar; **wet** ~ nodriza.

nursery ['nəːsərɪ] n (institution) guardería infantil; (room) cuarto de los niños; (for plants) criadero, semillero; ~ **rhyme** n canción f infantil; ~ **school** n parvulario, escuela de párvulos; ~ **slope** n (SKI) cuesta para principiantes.

nursing ['nəːsɪŋ] n (profession) profesión f de enfermera; (care) asistencia, cuidado; ~ **home** n clínica de reposo.

nut [nʌt] n (TECH) tuerca; (BOT) nuez f; ~**s** a (col) loco; ~**case** n (col) loco/a, chalado/a; ~**crackers** npl cascanueces m inv; ~**meg** ['nʌtmɛg] n nuez f moscada.

nutrient ['njuːtrɪənt] n nutrimento.

nutrition [njuː'trɪʃən] n nutrición f, alimentación f; **nutritious** [-ʃəs] a nutritivo, rico.

nutshell ['nʌtʃɛl] n cáscara de nuez; **in a** ~ en resumidas cuentas.

nylon ['naɪlɔn] n nilón m // a de nilón; ~**s** npl medias fpl (de nilón).

nymph [nɪmf] n ninfa.

O

oaf [əuf] n zoquete m.

oak [əuk] n roble m // a de roble.

O.A.P. abbr of **old-age pensioner.**

oar [ɔː*] n remo; **oarsman** n remero.

oasis [əu'eɪsɪs], pl **-ses** [-siːz] n oasis m.

oath [əuθ] n juramento; (swear word) palabrota; **on** ~ bajo juramento.

oatmeal ['əutmiːl] n harina de avena.

oats [əuts] n avena.

obedience [ə'biːdɪəns] n obediencia; **in** ~ **to** de acuerdo con; **obedient** [-ənt] a obediente.

obesity [əu'biːsɪtɪ] n obesidad f.

obey [ə'beɪ] vt obedecer; (instructions, regulations) cumplir.

obituary [ə'bɪtjuərɪ] n necrología.

object ['ɔbdʒɪkt] n (gen) objeto; (purpose) objeto, propósito; (LING) complemento // vi [əb'dʒɛkt]: **to** ~ **to** (attitude) protestar contra; (proposal) oponerse a; **I** ~! ¡yo protesto!; ~**ion** [əb'dʒɛkʃən] n protesta; **I have no** ~**ion to...** no tengo inconveniente en que...; ~**ionable** [əb'dʒɛkʃənəbl] a (gen) desagradable; (conduct) censurable; ~**ive** a, n objetivo; ~**ivity** [ɔbdʒɪk'tɪvɪtɪ] n objetividad f; ~**or** n objetor/a m/f.

obligation [ɔblɪ'geɪʃən] n obligación f; (debt) deber m; **without** ~ sin compromiso.

obligatory [ə'blɪgətərɪ] a obligatorio.

oblige [ə'blaɪdʒ] vt (force): **to** ~ **sb to do sth** forzar o obligar a uno a hacer algo; (do a favour for) complacer, hacer un favor a; **I should be** ~**d if...** le agradecería que...; **obliging** a servicial, atento.

oblique [ə'bliːk] a oblicuo; (allusion) indirecto.

obliterate [ə'blɪtəreɪt] vt borrar.

oblivion [ə'blɪvɪən] n olvido; **oblivious** [-ɪəs] a: **oblivious of** inconsciente de.

oblong ['ɔblɔŋ] a rectangular // n rectángulo.

obnoxious [əb'nɔkʃəs] a odioso, detestable; (smell) nauseabundo.

oboe ['əubəu] n oboe m.

obscene [əb'siːn] a obsceno; **obscenity** [-'sɛnɪtɪ] n obscenidad f.

obscure [əb'skjuə*] a oscuro // vt oscurecer; (hide: sun) esconder; **obscurity** n oscuridad f.

obsequious [əb'siːkwɪəs] a obsequioso.

observance [əb'zəːvns] n observancia, cumplimiento; (ritual) práctica.

observant [əb'zəːvnt] a observador(a).

observation [ɔbzə'veɪʃən] n observación f; (by police etc) vigilancia; (MED) examen m.

observatory [əb'zəːvətrɪ] n observatorio.

observe [əb'zəːv] vt (gen) observar; (rule) cumplir; **observer** n observador/a m/f.

obsess [əb'sɛs] vt obsesionar; ~**ion** [əb-

'sɛʃən] n obsesión f, idea fija; ~ive a obsesivo, obsesionante.
obsolescence [ɔbsə'lɛsns] n caída en desuso; **obsolete** ['ɔbsəli:t] a (que está) en desuso.
obstacle ['ɔbstəkl] n obstáculo; (nuisance) estorbo; ~ **race** n carrera de obstáculos.
obstetrician [ɔbstə'trɪʃən] n obstétrico; **obstetrics** [-'stɛtrɪks] n obstetricia.
obstinate ['ɔbstɪnɪt] a terco, porfiado; (determined) tenaz.
obstruct [əb'strʌkt] vt (block) obstruir; (hinder) estorbar, obstaculizar; ~**ion** [əb-'strʌkʃən] n obstrucción f; estorbo, obstáculo.
obtain [əb'teɪn] vt (get) obtener; (achieve) conseguir; ~**able** a asequible.
obtrusive [əb'tru:sɪv] a (person) importuno, entrometido; (building etc) demasiado visible.
obvious ['ɔbvɪəs] a (clear) obvio, evidente; (unsubtle) poco sutil; ~**ly** ad evidentemente, naturalmente.
occasion [ə'keɪʒən] n (gen) oportunidad f, ocasión f; (reason) motivo; (time) ocasión f, vez f; (event) acontecimiento // vt ocasionar, causar; ~**ally** ad de vez en cuando.
occult [ɔ'kʌlt] a (gen) oculto.
occupant ['ɔkjupənt] n (of house) inquilino/a; (of car) ocupante m/f.
occupation [ɔkju'peɪʃən] n (of house) tenencia; (job) trabajo; (: calling) oficio; **unfit for** ~ (house) inhabitable; ~**al hazard** n riesgo profesional.
occupier ['ɔkjupaɪə*] n inquilino/a.
occupy ['ɔkjupaɪ] vt (gen) ocupar; (house) habitar, vivir en; (time) emplear, pasar; (attention) entretener; **to ~ o.s. with** or **by doing** (as job) dedicarse a hacer; (to pass time) pasar el tiempo haciendo.
occur [ə'kə:*] vi pasar, suceder; **to ~ to sb** ocurrírsele a uno; **it ~s to me that...** se me ocurre que...; ~**rence** n (event) acontecimiento; (existence) existencia.
ocean ['əuʃən] n océano; ~**-going** a de alta mar; ~ **liner** n transatlántico.
o'clock [ə'klɔk] ad: **it is 5** ~ son las 5.
octagonal [ɔk'tægənl] a octagonal.
octane ['ɔkteɪn] n octano.
octave ['ɔktɪv] n octava.
October [ɔk'təubə*] n octubre m.
octopus ['ɔktəpəs] n pulpo.
odd [ɔd] a (strange) extraño, raro; (number) impar; (left over) sobrante, suelto; **60-**~ 60 y pico; **at** ~ **times** de vez en cuando; **to be the** ~ **one out** estar de más; ~**ity** n rareza; (person) excéntrico; ~**-job man** n hombre m que hace de todo; ~ **jobs** npl bricolaje m; ~**ly** ad curiosamente, extrañamente; ~**ments** npl (COMM) retales mpl; ~**s** npl (in betting) puntos mpl de ventaja; **it makes no** ~**s** no importa, lo mismo da; **at** ~**s** reñidos(as).
ode [əud] n oda.
odious ['əudɪəs] a odioso.

odour, odor (US) ['əudə*] n olor m; (perfume) perfume m; ~**less** a inodoro.
of [ɔv, əv] prep de; **a friend** ~ **ours** un amigo nuestro; **3** ~ **them** 3 de ellos; **the 5th** ~ **July** el 5 de julio; **a boy** ~ **10** un niño de 10 años; **made** ~ **wood** hecho de madera.
off [ɔf] a, ad (engine) desconectado; (light) apagado; (tap) cerrado; (food: bad) pasado, malo; (milk) cortado; (cancelled) anulado // prep de; **to be** ~ (to leave) irse, marcharse; **to be 5 km** ~ estar a 5 kilómetros; **a day** ~ un día libre o sin trabajar; **to have an** ~ **day** tener un día malo; **he had his coat** ~ se había quitado el abrigo; **10%** ~ (COMM) (con el) 10% de descuento; **5 km** ~ **(the road)** a 5 km (de la carretera); ~ **the coast** frente a la costa; **on the** ~ **chance** por si acaso.
offal ['ɔfl] n (CULIN) menudencias fpl.
off-colour ['ɔf'kʌlə*] a (ill) indispuesto.
offence, offense (US) [ə'fɛns] n (crime) delito; (insult) ofensa; **to take** ~ **at** ofenderse por.
offend [ə'fɛnd] vt (person) ofender; ~**er** n delincuente m/f; (against regulations) infractor/a m/f.
offensive [ə'fɛnsɪv] a ofensivo; (smell etc) repugnante // n (MIL) ofensiva.
offer ['ɔfə*] n (gen) oferta, ofrecimiento; (proposal) propuesta // vt ofrecer; (opportunity) facilitar; **'on** ~' (COMM) 'en oferta'; ~**ing** n ofrenda; ~**tory** n (REL) ofertorio.
offhand [ɔf'hænd] a informal // ad de improviso.
office ['ɔfɪs] n (place) oficina; (room) despacho; (position) carga, oficio; **to take** ~ entrar en funciones; ~ **block** n bloque m de oficinas; ~ **boy** n mozo (de oficina); **officer** n (MIL etc) oficial m; (of organization) director m; (also: **police officer**) agente m/f de policía; ~ **worker** n oficinista m/f.
official [ə'fɪʃl] a (authorized) oficial, autorizado // n funcionario, oficial m; ~**dom** n burocracia.
officious [ə'fɪʃəs] a oficioso.
offing ['ɔfɪŋ] n: **in the** ~ (fig) en perspectiva.
off: ~**-licence** n (Brit: shop) bodega, tienda de vinos y bebidas alcohólicas; ~**-peak** a de temporada de poca actividad; ~**-putting** a que desanima; ~**-season** a, ad fuera de temporada.
offset ['ɔfsɛt] (irg: like set) vt (counteract) contrarrestar, compensar // n (also: ~ **printing**) offset m.
offshore [ɔf'ʃɔ:*] a (que está) cerca de la costa.
offside ['ɔf'saɪd] a (SPORT) fuera de juego.
offspring ['ɔfsprɪŋ] n descendencia, descendientes mpl or fpl.
off: ~**-stage** ad entre bastidores; ~**-the-peg** ad confeccionado; ~**-white** a blanco grisáceo.
often ['ɔfn] ad a menudo, con frecuencia.

ogle ['əugl] *vt* echar miradas a.

oil [ɔıl] *n* aceite *m*; (*petroleum*) petróleo // *vt* (*machine*) engrasar; ~**can** *n* lata de aceite; ~**field** *n* campo petrolífero; ~**-fired** *a* que quema aceite combustible; ~ **painting** *n* pintura de óleo; ~ **refinery** *n* refinería de petróleo; ~ **rig** *n* torre *f* de perforación; ~**skins** *npl* impermeables *mpl* de hule, chubasquero *sg*; ~ **tanker** *n* petrolero; ~ **well** *n* pozo (de petróleo); ~**y** *a* aceitoso; (*food*) grasiento.

ointment ['ɔıntmənt] *n* ungüento.

O.K., okay ['əu'keı] *excl* O.K., ¡está bien!, ¡vale! // *a* bien // *vt* dar el visto bueno a.

old [əuld] *a* viejo; (*former*) antiguo; **how** ~ **are you?** ¿cuántos años tienes?, ¿qué edad tienes?; **he's 10 years** ~ tiene 10 años; ~**er brother** hermano mayor; ~ **age** *n* la vejez; ~**-age pensioner (O.A.P.)** *n* jubilado/a; ~**-fashioned** *a* anticuado, pasado de moda.

olive ['ɔlıv] *n* (*fruit*) aceituna; (*tree*) olivo // *a* (*also*: ~**-green**) verde oliva; ~ **oil** *n* aceite *m* de oliva.

Olympic [əu'lımpık] *a* olímpico; **the** ~ **Games, the** ~**s** los Juegos Olímpicos.

omelet(te) ['ɔmlıt] *n* tortilla (de huevo).

omen ['əumən] *n* presagio.

ominous ['ɔmınəs] *a* de mal agüero, amenazador(a).

omission [əu'mıʃən] *n* omisión *f*; (*error*) descuido.

omit [əu'mıt] *vt* omitir; (*by mistake*) olvidar, descuidar.

on [ɔn] *prep* en, sobre // *ad* (*machine*) conectado; (*light, radio*) encendido; (*tap*) abierto; **is the meeting still** ~? ¿todavía hay reunión?; **when is this film** ~? ¿cuándo van a poner esta película?; ~ **the wall** en la pared, colgado de la pared; ~ **television** en la televisión; ~ **horseback** a caballo; ~ **seeing this** al ver esto; ~ **arrival** al llegar; ~ **the left** a la izquierda; ~ **Friday** el viernes; **a week** ~ **Friday** el viernes en ocho días; **to have one's coat** ~ tener el abrigo puesto; **to go** ~ seguir adelante; **it's not** ~! ¡eso no se hace!

once [wʌns] *ad* una vez; (*formerly*) antiguamente // *conj* una vez que; **at** ~ en seguida, inmediatamente; (*simultaneously*) a la vez; ~ **a week** una vez por semana; ~ **more** otra vez; ~ **and for all** de una vez por todas; ~ **upon a time** érase una vez.

oncoming ['ɔnkʌmıŋ] *a* (*traffic*) que viene de frente.

one [wʌn] *det, num* un, uno, una // *pron* uno; (*impersonal*) se // *a* (*sole*) único; (*same*) mismo; **this** ~ éste/a; **that** ~ ése/a, aquél/aquella; ~ **by** ~ uno por uno; ~ **never knows** nunca se sabe; ~ **another** el uno al otro; ~**-man** *a* (*business*) individual; ~**-man band** *n* un hombre-orquesta; ~**self** *pron* uno mismo; (*after*

prep, also emphatic) sí (mismo/a); '~**-way**' 'dirección única'.

ongoing ['ɔngəuıŋ] *a* continuo.

onion ['ʌnjən] *n* cebolla.

onlooker ['ɔnlukə*] *n* espectador/a *m/f*.

only ['əunlı] *ad* solamente, sólo // *a* único, solo // *conj* solamente que, pero; **an** ~ **child** un hijo único; **not** ~ ... **but also...** no sólo ... sino también... .

onset ['ɔnsɛt] *n* (*beginning*) comienzo; (*attack*) ataque *m*.

onslaught ['ɔnslɔːt] *n* ataque *m*, embestida.

onto ['ɔntu] *prep* = **on to.**

onus ['əunəs] *n* responsabilidad *f*.

onward(s) ['ɔnwəd(z)] *ad* (*move*) (hacia) adelante; **from this time** ~ de ahora en adelante.

onyx ['ɔnıks] *n* ónice *m*, onyx *m*.

ooze [uːz] *vi* rezumar.

opal ['əupl] *n* ópalo.

opaque [əu'peık] *a* opaco.

open ['əupn] *a* abierto; (*car*) descubierto; (*road, view*) despejado; (*meeting*) público; (*admiration*) manifiesto // *vt* abrir // *vi* (*flower, eyes, door, debate*) abrirse; (*book etc: commence*) comenzar; **to** ~ **on to** *vt fus* (*subj: room, door*) dar a; **to** ~ **up** *vt* abrir; (*blocked road*) despejar // *vi* abrirse, empezar; **in the** ~ (**air**) al aire libre; ~**ing** *n* abertura, comienzo; (*opportunity*) oportunidad *f*; (*job*) puesto vacante, vacante *f*; ~**ly** *ad* abiertamente; ~**-minded** *a* imparcial; ~**-necked** *a* sin corbata.

opera ['ɔpərə] *n* ópera; ~ **glasses** *npl* gemelos *mpl*; ~ **house** *n* teatro de la ópera.

operate ['ɔpəreıt] *vt* (*machine*) hacer funcionar; (*company*) dirigir // *vi* funcionar; (*drug*) hacer efecto; **to** ~ **on sb** (*MED*) operar a uno.

operatic [ɔpə'rætık] *a* de ópera.

operating ['ɔpəreıtıŋ]: ~ **table** *n* mesa de operaciones; ~ **theatre** *n* sala de operaciones.

operation [ɔpə'reıʃən] *n* (*gen*) operación *f*; (*of machine*) funcionamiento; **to be in** ~ estar en funcionamiento o funcionando; ~**al** *a* operacional, en buen estado.

operative ['ɔpərətıv] *a* (*measure*) en vigor.

operator ['ɔpəreıtə*] *n* (*of machine*) maquinista *m/f*, operario; (*TEL*) operador/a *m/f*, telefonista *m/f*.

operetta [ɔpə'rɛtə] *n* opereta; (*in Spain*) zarzuela.

ophthalmic [ɔf'θælmık] *a* oftálmico.

opinion [ə'pınıən] *n* (*gen*) opinión *f*; (*point of view*) parecer *m*, juicio; ~**ated** *a* testarudo; ~ **poll** *n* encuesta, sondeo.

opium ['əupıəm] *n* opio.

opponent [ə'pəunənt] *n* adversario/a, contrincante *m/f*.

opportune ['ɔpətjuːn] *a* oportuno; **opportunist** [-'tjuːnıst] *n* oportunista *m/f*.

opportunity [ɔpə'tjuːnıtı] *n* oportunidad *f*.

oppose [ə'pəuz] *vt* oponerse a; **to be** ～**d to sth** oponerse a algo, resistirse a aceptar algo; **opposing** *a* (*side*) opuesto, contrario.

opposite ['ɔpəzit] *a* opuesto; (*house etc*) de enfrente // *ad* en frente // *prep* en frente de, frente a // *n* lo contrario.

opposition [ɔpə'ziʃən] *n* oposición *f.*

oppress [ə'prɛs] *vt* oprimir; ～**ion** [ə'prɛʃən] *n* opresión *f*; ～**ive** *a* opresivo.

opt [ɔpt] *vi*: **to** ～ **for** elegir; **to** ～ **to do** optar por hacer; **to** ～ **out of** optar por no hacer.

optical ['ɔptikl] *a* óptico.

optician [ɔp'tiʃən] *n* óptico.

optimism ['ɔptimizəm] *n* optimismo.

optimist ['ɔptimist] *n* optimista *m/f*; ～**ic** [-'mistik] *a* optimista.

optimum ['ɔptiməm] *a* óptimo.

option ['ɔpʃən] *n* opción *f*; **to keep one's** ～**s open** (*fig*) mantener las opciones abiertas; ～**al** *a* facultativo, discrecional.

opulent ['ɔpjulənt] *a* opulento.

or [ɔ:*] *conj* o; (*before o, ho*) u; (*with negative*): **he hasn't seen** ～ **heard anything** no ha visto ni oído nada; ～ **else** si no.

oracle ['ɔrəkl] *n* oráculo.

oral ['ɔ:rəl] *a* oral // *n* examen *m* oral.

orange ['ɔrindʒ] *n* (*fruit*) naranja // *a* color naranja.

oration [ɔ:'reiʃən] *n* oración *f*; **orator** ['ɔrətə*] *n* orador/a *m/f*.

orbit ['ɔ:bit] *n* órbita // *vt, vi* orbitar.

orchard ['ɔ:tʃəd] *n* huerto.

orchestra ['ɔ:kistrə] *n* orquesta; **orchestral** [-'kɛstrəl] *a* orquestral.

orchid ['ɔ:kid] *n* orquídea.

ordain [ɔ:'dein] *vt* (*REL*) ordenar, decretar; (*decide*) mandar.

ordeal [ɔ:'di:l] *n* experiencia penosa.

order ['ɔ:də*] *n* orden *m*; (*command*) orden *f*; (*type, kind*) clase *f*; (*state*) estado; (*COMM*) pedido, encargo // *vt* (*also, put in* ～) arreglar, poner en orden; (*COMM*) encargar, pedir; (*command*) mandar, ordenar; **in** ～ (*of document*) en regla; **in** ～ **to do** para hacer; **to** ～ **sb to do sth** mandar a uno hacer algo; ～**ly** *n* (*MIL*) ordenanza *m*; (*MED*) enfermero (auxiliar) // *a* (*room*) en orden, ordenado; (*person*) ordenado.

ordinary ['ɔ:dnri] *a* corriente, normal; (*pej*) ordinario, vulgar; **out of the** ～ fuera de lo común.

ordnance ['ɔ:dnəns] *n* (*MIL: unit*) artillería; **O**～ **Survey** *n* servicio oficial de topografía y cartografía.

ore [ɔ:*] *n* mineral *m*.

organ ['ɔ:gən] *n* órgano; ～**ic** [ɔ:'gænik] *a* orgánico.

organism ['ɔ:gənizəm] *n* organismo.

organist ['ɔ:gənist] *n* organista *m/f*.

organization [ɔ:gənai'zeiʃən] *n* organización *f*; **organize** ['ɔ:gənaiz] *vt*

organizar; **organizer** ['ɔ:gənaizə*] *n* organizador/a *m/f.*

orgasm ['ɔ:gæzəm] *n* orgasmo.

orgy ['ɔ:dʒi] *n* orgía.

Orient ['ɔ:riənt] *n* Oriente *m*; **oriental** [-'ɛntl] *a* oriental.

orientate ['ɔ:riənteit] *vt* orientar.

origin ['ɔridʒin] *n* origen *m*; (*point of departure*) procedencia.

original [ə'ridʒinl] *a* original; (*first*) primero; (*earlier*) primitivo // *n* original *m*; ～**ity** [-'næliti] *n* originalidad *f*; ～**ly** *ad* (*at first*) al principio; (*with originality*) con originalidad.

originate [ə'ridʒineit] *vi*: **to** ～ **from** *or* **in** surgir de, tener su origen en.

ornament ['ɔ:nəmənt] *n* adorno; (*trinket*) chuchería; ～**al** [-'mɛntl] *a* decorativo, de adorno.

ornate [ɔ:'neit] *a* muy ornado, vistoso.

ornithologist [ɔ:ni'θɔlədʒist] *n* ornitólogo; **ornithology** [-dʒi] *n* ornitología.

orphan ['ɔ:fn] *n* huérfano // *vt*: **to be** ～**ed** quedar huérfano; ～**age** *n* orfelinato.

orthodox ['ɔ:θədɔks] *a* ortodoxo; ～**y** *n* ortodoxia.

orthopaedic, orthopedic (*US*) [ɔ:θə'pi:dik] *a* ortopédico; ～**s** *n* ortopedia.

oscillate ['ɔsileit] *vi* oscilar; (*person*) vacilar.

ostensibly [ɔs'tɛnsibli] *ad* aparentemente.

ostentatious [ɔstɛn'teiʃəs] *a* pretencioso, aparatoso; (*person*) ostentativo.

osteopath ['ɔstiəpæθ] *n* osteópata *m/f.*

ostracize ['ɔstrəsaiz] *vt* condenar al ostracismo.

ostrich ['ɔstritʃ] *n* avestruz *m*.

other ['ʌðə*] *a* otro; ～ **than** (*in another way*) de otra manera que; (*apart from*) aparte de; ～**wise** *ad, conj* de otra manera; (*if not*) si no.

otter ['ɔtə*] *n* nutria.

ought [ɔ:t], *pt* **ought** *auxiliary vb*: **I** ～ **to do it** debería hacerlo; **this** ～ **to have been corrected** esto debiera de haberse corregido; **he** ～ **to win** (*probability*) debe *o* debiera ganar.

ounce [auns] *n* onza (*28.35g*).

our ['auə*] *a* nuestro; ～**s** *pron* (el) nuestro/(la) nuestra *etc*; ～**selves** *pron pl* (*reflexive, after prep*) nosotros; (*emphatic*) nosotros mismos.

oust [aust] *vt* desalojar.

out [aut] *ad* fuera, afuera; (*not at home*) fuera (de casa); (*light, fire*) apagado; ～ **there** allí, allí fuera; **he's** ～ (*absent*) no está, ha salido; **to be** ～ **in one's calculations** equivocarse (en sus cálculos); **to run** ～ salir corriendo; ～ **loud** en alta voz; ～ **of** (*outside*) fuera de; (*because of: anger etc*) por; ～ **of petrol** sin gasolina; "～ **of order**" "no funciona"; ～**-of-the-way** (*fig*) insólito.

outback ['autbæk] *n* interior *m*.

outboard ['autbɔ:d] *a*: ～ **motor** motor *m* de fuera de borda.

outbreak ['autbreik] *n* (*of war*) comienzo;

(of disease) epidemia; (of violence etc) arranque m.
outburst ['autbɔːst] n explosión f, arranque m.
outcast ['autkɑːst] n paria m/f.
outcome ['autkʌm] n resultado.
outcry ['autkraɪ] n protesta ruidosa.
outdated [aut'deɪtɪd] a anticuado, fuera de moda.
outdo [aut'duː] (irg: like do) vt exceder.
outdoor [aut'dɔː*] a, ~s ad al aire libre.
outer ['autə*] a exterior, externo; ~ space n el espacio.
outfit ['autfɪt] n equipo; (clothes) traje m; ~ter's n camisería.
outgoing ['autgəʊɪŋ] a (character) extrovertido; ~s npl gastos mpl.
outgrow [aut'grəu] (irg: like grow) vt: he has ~n his clothes su ropa le queda pequeña ya.
outing ['autɪŋ] n excursión f, paseo.
outlandish [aut'lændɪʃ] a estrafalario.
outlaw ['autlɔː] n proscrito // vt (person) declarar fuera de la ley; (practice) declarar ilegal.
outlay ['autleɪ] n inversión f.
outlet ['autlɛt] n salida; (of pipe) desagüe m; (for emotion) desahogo; (also: retail ~) lugar m de venta.
outline ['autlaɪn] n (shape) contorno, perfil m; (of plan) trazado; (sketch) esbozo, idea general.
outlive [aut'lɪv] vt sobrevivir.
outlook ['autluk] n perspectiva; (opinion) punto de vista.
outlying ['autlaɪɪŋ] a remoto, aislado.
outmoded [aut'məʊdɪd] a anticuado, pasado de moda.
outnumber [aut'nʌmbə*] vt exceder en número.
outpatient ['autpeɪʃənt] n paciente m/f de consulta externa.
outpost ['autpəʊst] n puesto avanzado.
output ['autput] n (volumen m de) producción f, rendimiento.
outrage ['autreɪdʒ] n (scandal) escándalo; (atrocity) atrocidad f // vt ultrajar; ~ous [-'reɪdʒəs] a monstruoso.
outright [aut'raɪt] ad completamente // a ['autraɪt] completo.
outset ['autsɛt] n principio.
outside [aut'saɪd] n exterior m; (surface) superficie f; (aspect) aspecto // a exterior, externo // ad fuera // prep fuera de; (beyond) más allá de; at the ~ (fig) a lo sumo; ~ lane n (AUT: in Britain) carril m de la derecha; ~-left n (FOOTBALL) extremo izquierdo; **outsider** n (stranger) extraño, forastero.
outsize ['autsaɪz] a (clothes) de talla grande.
outskirts ['autskɜːts] npl alrededores mpl, afueras fpl.
outspoken [aut'spəʊkən] a muy franco.
outstanding [aut'stændɪŋ] a excepcional, destacado; (unfinished) pendiente.

outstay [aut'steɪ] vt: to ~ one's welcome quedarse más tiempo de lo indicado.
outstretched [aut'strɛtʃt] a (hand) extendido.
outward ['autwəd] a (sign, appearances) externo; (journey) de ida; ~ly ad por fuera.
outweigh [aut'weɪ] vt pesar más que.
outwit [aut'wɪt] vt ser más listo que, burlar.
oval ['əuvl] a ovalado // n óvalo.
ovary ['əuvərɪ] n ovario.
ovation [əu'veɪʃən] n ovación f.
oven ['ʌvn] n horno; ~proof a refractario.
over ['əuvə*] ad encima, por encima // a (or ad) (finished) terminado // prep (por) encima de; (above) sobre; (on the other side of) al otro lado de; (more than) más de; (during) durante; ~ here (por) aquí; ~ there (por) allí o allá; all ~ (everywhere) por todas partes; ~ and ~ (again) una y otra vez; ~ and above más de; to ask sb ~ invitar a uno; to bend ~ inclinarse.
over... [əuvə*] pref sobre..., super...; ~abundant a superabundante.
overall ['əuvərɔːl] a (length) total; (study) de conjunto // ad [əuvər'ɔːl] en conjunto; ~s npl mono sg o bata sg (de trabajo).
overbalance [əuvə'bæləns] vi perder el equilibrio.
overbearing [əuvə'bɛərɪŋ] a autoritario, imperioso.
overboard ['əuvəbɔːd] ad (NAUT) por la borda; man ~! ¡hombre al agua!
overcast ['əuvəkɑːst] a encapotado.
overcharge [əuvə'tʃɑːdʒ] vt: to ~ sb cobrar un precio excesivo a uno.
overcoat ['əuvəkəut] n abrigo, sobretodo.
overcome [əuvə'kʌm] (irg: like come) vt (gen) vencer; (difficulty) superar.
overcrowded [əuvə'kraudɪd] a atestado de gente; (country) superpoblado.
overdo [əuvə'duː] (irg: like do) vt exagerar; (overcook) cocer demasiado.
overdose ['əuvədəus] n dosis f excesiva.
overdraft ['əuvədrɑːft] n saldo deudor.
overdrawn [əuvə'drɔːn] a (account) en descubierto.
overdue [əuvə'djuː] a retrasado; (recognition) tardío.
overestimate [əuvər'ɛstɪmeɪt] vt sobreestimar.
overexcited [əuvərɪk'saɪtɪd] a sobreexcitado.
overexpose [əuvərɪk'spəuz] vt (PHOT) sobreexponer.
overflow [əuvə'fləu] vi desbordarse // n ['əuvəfləu] (excess) exceso; (of river) desbordamiento; (also: ~ pipe) (cañería de) desagüe m.
overgrown [əuvə'grəun] a (garden) cubierto de hierba.
overhaul [əuvə'hɔːl] vt revisar, repasar // n ['əuvəhɔːl] revisión f.
overhead [əuvə'hɛd] ad por lo alto // a

['ɔuvəhɛd] de arriba; (*railway*) elevado, aéreo; ~s *npl* gastos *mpl* generales.

overhear [ɔuvə'hıə*] (*irg*: *like* **hear**) *vt* oír por casualidad.

overjoyed [ɔuvə'dʒɔıd] *a* encantado, lleno de alegría.

overland ['ɔuvəlænd] *a, ad* por tierra.

overlap [ɔuvə'læp] *vi* traslaparse // *n* ['ɔuvəlæp] traslapo.

overleaf [ɔuvə'liːf] *ad* al dorso.

overload [ɔuvə'ləud] *vt* sobrecargar.

overlook [ɔuvə'luk] *vt* (*have view on*) dar a, tener vistas a; (*miss*: *by mistake*) pasar por alto; (: *deliberately*) no hacerse caso de; (*forgive*) perdonar.

overnight [ɔuvə'naıt] *ad* durante la noche; (*fig*) de la noche a la mañana // *a* de noche; **to stay** ~ pasar la noche.

overpass ['ɔuvəpɑːs] *n* paso superior.

overpower [ɔuvə'pauə*] *vt* dominar; ~**ing** *a* (*heat, stench*) abrumador(a).

overrate [ɔuvə'reıt] *vt* sobreestimar.

override [ɔuvə'raıd] (*irg*: *like* **ride**) *vt* (*order, objection*) no hacer caso de; **overriding** *a* predominante.

overrule [ɔuvə'ruːl] *vt* (*decision*) anular; (*claim*) denegar.

overseas [ɔuvə'siːz] *ad* en ultramar; (*abroad*) en el extranjero // *a* (*trade*) exterior; (*visitor*) extranjero.

overseer ['ɔuvəsıə*] *n* (*in factory*) superintendente *m/f*; (*foreman*) capataz *m*.

overshadow [ɔuvə'ʃædəu] *vt* (*fig*) eclipsar.

overshoot [ɔuvə'ʃuːt] (*irg*: *like* **shoot**) *vt* excederse.

oversight ['ɔuvəsaıt] *n* descuido.

oversleep [ɔuvə'sliːp] (*irg*: *like* **sleep**) *vi* despertarse (muy) tarde.

overspend [ɔuvə'spɛnd] (*irg*: *like* **spend**) *vi* gastar demasiado.

overspill ['ɔuvəspıl] *n* exceso de población.

overstate [ɔuvə'steıt] *vt* exagerar; ~**ment** *n* exageración *f*.

overt [əu'vɔːt] *a* abierto.

overtake [ɔuvə'teık] (*irg*: *like* **take**) *vt* sobrepasar; (*AUT*) adelantar; **overtaking** *n* (*AUT*) adelantamiento.

overthrow [ɔuvə'θrəu] (*irg*: *like* **throw**) *vt* (*government*) derrocar.

overtime ['ɔuvətaım] *n* horas *fpl* extraordinarias.

overtone ['ɔuvətəun] *n* (*fig*) sugestión *f*, alusión *f*.

overture ['ɔuvətʃuə*] *n* (*MUS*) obertura; (*fig*) propuesta.

overturn [ɔuvə'tɔːn] *vt, vi* volcar.

overweight [ɔuvə'weıt] *a* demasiado gordo *o* pesado.

overwhelm [ɔuvə'wɛlm] *vt* aplastar; ~**ing** *a* (*victory, defeat*) arrollador(a); (*desire*) irresistible.

overwork [ɔuvə'wɔːk] *n* trabajo excesivo // *vt* hacer trabajar demasiado // *vi* trabajar demasiado.

overwrought [ɔuvə'rɔːt] *a* sobreexcitado.

owe [əu] *vt* deber; **to** ~ **sb sth, to** ~ **sth to sb** deber algo a uno; **owing to** *prep* debido a, por causa de.

owl [aul] *n* búho, lechuza.

own [əun] *vt* tener, poseer // *a* propio; **a room of my** ~ una habitación propia; **to get one's** ~ **back** tomar revancha; **on one's** ~ solo, a solas; **to** ~ **up** *vi* confesar; ~**er** *n* dueño; ~**ership** *n* posesión *f*.

ox [ɔks], *pl* ~**en** ['ɔksn] *n* buey *m*.

oxide ['ɔksaıd] *n* óxido.

oxtail ['ɔksteıl] *n*: ~ **soup** sopa de rabo de buey.

oxygen ['ɔksıdʒən] *n* oxígeno; ~ **mask/tent** máscara/tienda de oxígeno.

oyster ['ɔıstə*] *n* ostra.

oz. *abbr of* **ounce(s)**.

ozone ['əuzəun] *n* ozono.

P

p [piː] *abbr of* **penny, pence**.

p.a. *abbr of* **per annum**.

pa [pɑː] *n* (*col*) papá *m*.

pace [peıs] *n* paso; (*rhythm*) ritmo // *vi*: **to** ~ **up and down** pasarse de un lado a otro; **to keep** ~ **with** llevar el mismo paso que; (*events*) mantenerse a la altura de *o* al corriente de; ~**maker** *n* (*MED*) regulador *m* cardíaco, marcapasos *m inv*.

pacific [pə'sıfık] *a* pacífico // *n*: **the P**~ **(Ocean)** el (Océano) Pacífico.

pacifist ['pæsıfıst] *n* pacifista *m/f*.

pacify ['pæsıfaı] *vt* (*soothe*) apaciguar; (*country*) pacificar.

pack [pæk] *n* (*gen*) paquete *m*; (*of hounds*) jauría; (*of thieves etc*) manada, bando; (*of cards*) baraja; (*bundle*) fardo; (*back* ~) mochila // *vt* (*wrap*) empaquetar; (*fill*) llenar; (*in suitcase etc*) meter *o* poner (en maleta); (*cram*) llenar, atestar; (*fig*: *meeting etc*) llenar de partidarios; **to** ~ **sb off** despachar a uno; ~ **it in!** (*col*) ¡déjalo!; **to** ~ **one's case** hacerse la maleta.

package ['pækıdʒ] *n* paquete *m*; (*bulky*) bulto; (*also*: ~ **deal**) acuerdo global; ~ **tour** *n* viaje *m* todo incluido.

packet ['pækıt] *n* paquete *m*; (*NAUT*) paquebote *m*.

packing ['pækıŋ] *n* embalaje *m*; (*external*) envase *m*; (*internal*) relleno; ~ **case** *n* cajón *m* de embalaje.

pact [pækt] *n* pacto.

pad [pæd] *n* (*of paper*) bloc *m*; (*cushion*) cojinete *m*; (*launching* ~) plataforma (de lanzamiento); (*foot*) pata; (*col*: *flat*) casa // *vi* andar (sin hacer ruido); ~**ding** *n* relleno; (*fig*) paja.

paddle ['pædl] *n* (*oar*) canalete *m* // *vt* impulsar con canalete // *vi* (*with feet*) chapotear; ~ **steamer** *n* vapor *m* de ruedas; **paddling pool** *n* estanque *m* de juegos.

paddock ['pædək] *n* corral *m*.

paddy field ['pædɪ-] n arrozal m.
padlock ['pædlɔk] n candado // vt cerrar con candado.
padre ['pɑːdrɪ] n capellán m.
paediatrics, pediatrics (US) [piːdɪ'ætrɪks] n pediatría.
pagan ['peɪgɔn] a, n pagano/a.
page [peɪdʒ] n (of book) página; (of newspaper) plana; (also: ~ boy) paje m // vt (in hotel etc) buscar (a uno) llamando su nombre.
pageant ['pædʒɔnt] n (procession) desfile m; (show) espectáculo; ~ry n pompa.
pagoda [pɔ'gɔudɔ] n pagoda.
paid [peɪd] pt, pp of **pay** // a (work) remunerado; (official) asalariado; **to put** ~ **to** acabar con.
pail [peɪl] n cubo, balde m.
pain [peɪn] n dolor m; **to be in** ~ sufrir; **on** ~ **of death** so pena de muerte; **to take** ~**s to do sth** tomarse trabajo en hacer algo; ~**ed** a (expression) afligido; ~**ful** a doloroso; (difficult) penoso; (disagreeable) desagradable; ~**fully** ad (fig: very) terriblemente; ~**killer** n calmante m; ~**less** a que no causa dolor; **painstaking** ['peɪnzteɪkɪŋ] a (person) concienzudo, esmerado.
paint [peɪnt] n pintura // vt pintar; **to** ~ **one's face** pintarse (la cara); **to** ~ **the door blue** pintar la puerta de azul; ~**brush** n (artist's) pincel m; (decorator's) brocha; ~**er** n pintor/a m/f; ~**ing** n pintura.
pair [pɛɔ*] n (of shoes, gloves etc) par m; (of people) pareja; **a** ~ **of scissors** unas tijeras; **a** ~ **of trousers** unos pantalones, un pantalón.
pajamas [pɪ'dʒɑːmɔz] npl (US) pijama m.
Pakistan [pɑːkɪ'stɑːn] n Paquistán m; ~**i** a, n paquistani.
pal [pæl] n (col) compinche m/f, compañero/a.
palace ['pælɔs] n palacio.
palatable ['pælɪtɔbl] a sabroso; (acceptable) aceptable.
palate ['pælɪt] n paladar m.
palaver [pɔ'lɑːvɔ*] n (fuss) lío; (hindrances) molestias fpl.
pale [peɪl] a (gen) pálido; (colour) claro; **to grow** ~ palidecer; **to be beyond the** ~ estar excluido; ~**ness** n palidez f.
Palestine ['pælɪstaɪn] n Palestina; **Palestinian** [-'tɪnɪɔn] a, n palestino/a.
palette ['pælɪt] n paleta.
paling ['peɪlɪŋ] n (stake) estaca; (fence) valla.
palisade [pælɪ'seɪd] n palizada.
pall [pɔːl] n (of smoke) capa (de humo) // vi perder el sabor.
pallid ['pælɪd] a pálido.
palm [pɑːm] n (gen) palma; (also: ~ tree) palmera, palma // vt: **to** ~ **sth off on sb** (col) encajar algo a uno; ~**ist** n quiromántico/a; **P**~ **Sunday** n Domingo de Ramos.
palpable ['pælpɔbl] a palpable.

palpitation [pælpɪ'teɪʃɔn] n palpitación f; **to have** ~**s** tener vahidos.
paltry ['pɔːltrɪ] a (insignificant) baladí; (miserable) vil.
pamper ['pæmpɔ*] vt mimar.
pamphlet ['pæmflɔt] n folleto.
pan [pæn] n (also: **sauce**~) cacerola, cazuela; (also: **frying** ~) sartén m; (of lavatory) taza // vi (CINEMA) tomar una vista panorámica.
panacea [pænɔ'sɪɔ] n panacea.
Panama ['pænɔmɑː] n Panamá m.
pancake ['pænkeɪk] n canapé m.
panda ['pændɔ] n panda m/f; ~ **car** n coche m de la policía.
pandemonium [pændɪ'mɔunɪɔm] n (noise) estruendo; (mess) caos m.
pander ['pændɔ*] vi: **to** ~ **to** complacer a.
pane [peɪn] n cristal m.
panel ['pænl] n (of wood) panel m; (of cloth) paño; (RADIO, TV) tablero; ~**ling,** ~**ing** (US) n paneles mpl, entrepaños mpl.
pang [pæŋ] n: ~**s of conscience** remordimiento sg; ~**s of hunger** dolores mpl del hambre.
panic ['pænɪk] n (terror) pánico // vi aterrarse; ~**ky** a (person) asustadizo; ~-**stricken** a preso de pánico.
pannier ['pænɪɔ*] n (on bicycle) cartera; (on mule etc) alforja.
panorama [pænɔ'rɑːmɔ] n panorama m.
pansy ['pænzɪ] n (BOT) pensamiento; (col) maricón m.
pant [pænt] vi jadear.
panther ['pænθɔ*] n pantera.
panties ['pæntɪz] npl bragas fpl, pantis mpl.
pantomime ['pæntɔmaɪm] n revista musical representada en Navidad, basada en cuentos de hadas.
pantry ['pæntrɪ] n despensa.
pants [pænts] n (woman's) bragas fpl; (man's) calzoncillos mpl; (US: trousers) pantalones mpl.
papal ['peɪpɔl] a papal.
paper ['peɪpɔ*] n papel m; (also: **news**~) periódico, diario; (study, article) artículo; (exam) examen m // a de papel // vt empapelar; (identity) ~**s** npl papeles mpl, documentos mpl; ~-**back** n libro de bolsillo; ~ **bag** n saco de papel; ~ **clip** n grapa; ~ **hankie** n pañuelo de papel; ~ **money** n papel moneda; ~**weight** n pisapapeles m inv; ~**work** n trabajo administrativo; (pej) papeleo.
papier-mâché ['pæpɪeɪ'mæʃeɪ] n cartón m piedra.
paprika ['pæprɪkɔ] n pimienta húngara o roja.
par [pɑː*] n par f; (GOLF) par m; **to be on a** ~ **with** correr parejas con.
parable ['pærɔbl] n parábola.
parachute ['pærɔʃuːt] n paracaídas m inv // vi lanzarse en paracaídas; ~ **jump** n salto en paracaídas.
parade [pɔ'reɪd] n desfile m // vt (gen)

recorrer, desfilar por; (*show off*) hacer alarde de // *vi* desfilar; (*MIL*) pasar revista.
paradise ['pærədaɪs] *n* paraíso.
paradox ['pærədɔks] *n* paradoja; ~**ical** [-'dɔksɪkl] *a* paradójico.
paraffin ['pærəfɪn] *n*: ~ (**oil**) petróleo.
paragraph ['pærəgrɑːf] *n* párrafo.
parallel ['pærəlɛl] *a* en paralelo; (*fig*) semejante // *n* (*line*) paralela; (*fig, GEO*) paralelo.
paralysis [pə'rælɪsɪs] *n* parálisis *f*; **paralyze** ['pærəlaɪz] *vt* paralizar.
paramount ['pærəmaunt] *a*: **of** ~ **importance** de la mayor importancia, primordial.
paranoia [pærə'nɔɪə] *n* paranoia; **paranoiac** *a* paranoico.
paraphernalia [pærəfə'neɪlɪə] *n* (*gear*) avíos *mpl*.
paraplegic [pærə'pliːdʒɪk] *n* parapléjico.
parasite ['pærəsaɪt] *n* parásito.
parasol [pærə'sɔl] *n* sombrilla, quitasol *m*.
paratrooper ['pærətruːpə*] *n* paracaidista *m/f*.
parcel ['pɑːsl] *n* paquete *m* // *vt* (*also*: ~ **up**) empaquetar, embalar.
parch [pɑːtʃ] *vt* secar, resecar; ~**ed** *a* (*person*) muerto de sed.
parchment ['pɑːtʃmənt] *n* pergamino.
pardon ['pɑːdn] *n* perdón *m*; (*LAW*) indulto // *vt* perdonar; indultar; ~! ¡perdone!; ~ **me!, I beg your** ~! ¡perdone Usted!; (**I beg your**) ~? ¿cómo?
parent ['pɛərənt] *n* padre *m*/madre *f*; ~**s** *npl* padres *mpl*; ~**al** [pə'rɛntl] *a* paternal/maternal.
parenthesis [pə'rɛnθɪsɪs], *pl* -**theses** [-θɪsiːz] *n* paréntesis *m inv*.
Paris ['pærɪs] *n* París.
parish ['pærɪʃ] *n* parroquia; ~**ioner** [pə'rɪʃənə*] *n* feligrés/esa *m/f*.
Parisian [pə'rɪzɪən] *a, n* parisino/a, parisiense *m/f*.
parity ['pærɪtɪ] *n* paridad *f*, igualdad *f*.
park [pɑːk] *n* parque *m* // *vt* estacionar // *vi* aparcar, estacionarse; ~**ing** *n* aparcamiento, estacionamiento; '**no** ~**ing**' 'prohibido estacionarse'; ~**ing lot** *n* (*US*) parking *m*; ~**ing meter** *n* parquímetro.
parliament ['pɑːləmənt] *n* parlamento; (*Spanish*) Cortes *mpl*; ~**ary** [-'mɛntərɪ] *a* parlamentario.
parlour, parlor (*US*) ['pɑːlə*] *n* sala de recibo, salón *m*.
parochial [pə'rəukɪəl] *a* parroquial; (*pej*) de miras estrechas.
parody ['pærədɪ] *n* parodia // *vt* parodiar.
parole [pə'rəul] *n*: **on** ~ libre bajo palabra.
parquet ['pɑːkeɪ] *n*: ~ **floor(ing)** parquet *m*.
parrot ['pærət] *n* loro, papagayo; ~ **fashion** *ad* mecánicamente.
parry ['pærɪ] *vt* parar.

parsimonious [pɑːsɪ'məunɪəs] *a* parco.
parsley ['pɑːslɪ] *n* perejil *m*.
parsnip ['pɑːsnɪp] *n* chirivia.
parson ['pɑːsn] *n* (*parish*) párroco; (*gen*) cura *m*.
part [pɑːt] *n* (*gen, MUS*) parte *f*; (*bit*) trozo; (*of machine*) pieza; (*THEATRE etc*) papel *m*; (*of serial*) entrega // **ad** = **partly** // *vt* dividir; (*break*) partir // *vi* (*people*) separarse; (*roads*) bifurcarse; (*crowd*) apartarse; (*break*) romperse; **to take** ~ **in** participar *o* tomar parte en; **to take sth in good** ~ tomar algo en buena parte; **to take sb's** ~ defender a uno; **for my** ~ por mi parte; **for the most** ~ en la mayor parte; **to** ~ **with** *vt fus* ceder, entregar; (*money*) pagar; (*get rid of*) deshacerse de; **in** ~ **exchange** como parte del pago; **spare** ~ pieza de recambio.
partial ['pɑːʃl] *a* parcial; **to be** ~ **to** ser aficionado a; ~**ly** *ad* en parte.
participant [pɑː'tɪsɪpənt] *n* (*in competition*) concursante *m/f*; **participate** [-peɪt] *vi*: **to participate in** participar en; **participation** [-'peɪʃən] *n* participación *f*.
participle ['pɑːtɪsɪpl] *n* participio.
particle ['pɑːtɪkl] *n* partícula; (*of dust*) grano; (*fig*) pizca.
particular [pə'tɪkjulə*] *a* (*special*) particular; (*concrete*) concreto; (*given*) determinado; (*detailed*) detallado, minucioso; (*fussy*) quisquilloso, exigente; ~**s** *npl* (*information*) datos *mpl*, detalles *mpl*; (*details*) pormenores *mpl*; ~**ly** *ad* especialmente, en particular.
parting ['pɑːtɪŋ] *n* (*act of*) separación *f*; (*farewell*) despedida; (*in hair*) raya // *a* de despedida.
partisan [pɑːtɪ'zæn] *a, n* partidario/a.
partition [pɑː'tɪʃən] *n* (*POL*) división *f*; (*wall*) tabique *m* // *vt* dividir; dividir con tabique.
partly ['pɑːtlɪ] *ad* en parte.
partner ['pɑːtnə*] *n* (*COMM*) socio/a; (*SPORT, at dance*) pareja; (*spouse*) cónyuge *m/f*; (*friend etc*) compañero/a // *vt* acompañar; ~**ship** *n* (*gen*) asociación *f*; (*COMM*) sociedad *f*.
partridge ['pɑːtrɪdʒ] *n* perdiz *f*.
part-time ['pɑːt'taɪm] *a, ad* de medio tiempo *o* media jornada.
party ['pɑːtɪ] *n* (*POL*) partido; (*celebration*) fiesta; (*group*) grupo; (*LAW*) parte *f*, interesado // *a* (*POL*) de partido; (*dress etc*) de fiesta, de gala.
pass [pɑːs] *vt* (*time, object*) pasar; (*place*) pasar por; (*exam*) aprobar; (*overtake, surpass*) rebasar; (*approve*) aprobar // *vi* pasar; (*SCOL*) aprobar, ser aprobado // *n* (*permit*) permiso; (*membership card*) carnet *m*; (*in mountains*) puerto, desfiladero; (*SPORT*) pase *m*; (*SCOL: also*: ~ **mark**): **to get a** ~ **in** aprobar en; **to** ~ **sth through sth** pasar algo por algo; **to** ~ **away** *vi* fallecer; **to** ~ **by** *vi* pasar //

vt (*ignore*) pasar por alto; **to** ~ **for** pasar por; **to** ~ **out** vi desmayarse; **to** ~ **up** vt renunciar a; ~**able** a (*road*) transitable; (*work*) pasable.

passage ['pæsɪdӡ] n (*also*: ~**way**) pasillo; (*act of passing*) tránsito; (*fare, in book*) pasaje m; (*by boat*) travesía; (*MECH, MED*) tubo.

passenger ['pæsɪndӡə*] n pasajero, viajero.

passer-by [pɑːsə'baɪ] n transeúnte m/f.

passing ['pɑːsɪŋ] a (*fleeting*) pasajero; **in** ~ de paso.

passion ['pæʃən] n pasión f; (*anger*) cólera; ~**ate** a apasionado; colérico.

passive ['pæsɪv] a (*also LING*) pasivo.

Passover ['pɑːsəuvə*] n Pascua (de los judíos).

passport ['pɑːspɔːt] n pasaporte m.

password ['pɑːswɔːd] n santo y seña.

past [pɑːst] prep (*further than*) más allá de; (*later than*) después de // a pasado; (*president etc*) ex, antiguo // n el pasado; (*antecedents*) antecedentes mpl; **he's** ~ **forty** tiene más de cuarenta años; **for the** ~ **few/3 days** durante los últimos/3 días; **to run** ~ pasar a la carrera por.

pasta ['pæstə] n pastas fpl.

paste [peɪst] n (*gen*) pasta; (*glue*) engrudo // vt (*stick*) pegar; (*glue*) engomar.

pastel ['pæstl] a pastel; (*painting*) al pastel.

pasteurized ['pæstəraɪzd] a pasteurizado.

pastille ['pæstl] n pastilla.

pastime ['pɑːstaɪm] n pasatiempo.

pastor ['pɑːstə*] n pastor m.

pastoral ['pɑːstərl] a pastoral.

pastry ['peɪstrɪ] n pasta; (*cakes*) pastas fpl, pasteles mpl.

pasture ['pɑːstʃə*] n (*grass*) pasto; (*land*) prado, pasto.

pasty ['pæstɪ] n empanada // a ['peɪstɪ] pastoso; (*complexion*) pálido.

pat [pæt] vt dar una palmadita a; (*dog etc*) acariciar // n (*of butter*) pastelillo; **to give sb a** ~ **on the back** felicitar a uno.

patch [pætʃ] n (*of material*) parche m; (*piece*) pedazo; (*mend*) remiendo; (*of land*) terreno // vt (*clothes*) remendar; **to** ~ **up** vt (*mend temporarily*) componer de modo provisional; (*quarrel*) hacer las paces con; ~**work** n labor m de retazos; ~**y** a desigual.

pâté ['pæteɪ] n pastel m de carne.

patent ['peɪtnt] n patente f // vt patentar // a patente, evidente; ~ **leather** n charol m.

paternal [pə'tɜːnl] a paternal; (*relation*) paterno; **paternity** [-nɪtɪ] n paternidad f.

path [pɑːθ] n senda, sendero; (*trail, track*) pista; (*of missile*) trayectoria.

pathetic [pə'θetɪk] a (*pitiful*) patético, lastimoso; (*very bad*) malísimo; (*moving*) conmovedor(a).

pathologist [pə'θɒlədӡɪst] n patólogo; **pathology** [-dӡɪ] n patología.

pathos ['peɪθɒs] n patetismo, lo patético.

pathway ['pɑːθweɪ] n sendero, vereda.

patience ['peɪʃns] n paciencia; (*CARDS*) solitario.

patient ['peɪʃnt] n paciente m/f // a paciente, sufrido.

patio ['pætɪəu] n patio.

patriot ['peɪtrɪət] n patriota m/f; ~**ic** [pætrɪ'ɒtɪk] a patriótico.

patrol [pə'trəul] n patrulla // vt patrullar por; ~ **car** n coche m patrulla; ~**man** n (*US*) policía m.

patron ['peɪtrən] n (*in shop*) cliente m/f; (*of charity*) patrocinador/a m/f; ~ **of the arts** mecenas m; ~**age** ['pætrənɪdӡ] n mecenazgo, protección f; ~**ize** ['pætrənaɪz] vt (*shop*) ser cliente de; (*business*) patrocinar; (*look down on*) tratar con condescendencia; ~ **saint** n patrono.

patter ['pætə*] n golpeteo; (*of feet*) pasos mpl ligeros; (*sales talk*) jerga // vi andar con pasos ligeros; (*rain*) tamborilear.

pattern ['pætən] n modelo; (*SEWING*) patrón m; (*design*) dibujo; (*sample*) muestra.

paunch [pɔːntʃ] n panza, barriga.

pauper ['pɔːpə*] n pobre m/f.

pause [pɔːz] n pausa; (*interval*) intérvalo // vi hacer una pausa.

pave [peɪv] vt pavimentar; **to** ~ **the way for** preparar el terreno para.

pavement ['peɪvmənt] n (*Brit*) acera.

pavilion [pə'vɪlɪən] n pabellón m; (*for band etc*) quiosco; (*SPORT*) caseta.

paving ['peɪvɪŋ] n pavimento, enlosado; ~ **stone** n losa.

paw [pɔː] n pata; (*of cat*) garra // vt tocar con la pata; (*touch*) tocar, manosear; (*amorously*) sobar.

pawn [pɔːn] n (*CHESS*) peón m; (*fig*) instrumento // vt empeñar; ~**broker** n prestamista m/f; ~**shop** n monte m de piedad.

pay [peɪ] n paga; (*wage etc*) sueldo // (*vb: pt, pp* **paid**) vt pagar; (*debt*) liquidar; (*visit*) hacer; (*respect*) ofrecer // vi pagar; (*be profitable*) rendir; **to** ~ **attention (to)** prestar atención (a); **to** ~ **back** vt (*money*) devolver; (*person*) pagar; **to** ~ **for** vt pagar por; **to** ~ **in** vt ingresar; **to** ~ **off** vt liquidar; **to** ~ **up** vt pagar (de mala gana); ~**able** a pagadero; ~ **day** n día m de paga; ~**ee** n portador/a m/f; ~**ing** a provechoso; ~**ment** n pago; **advance** ~**ment** anticipo; **monthly** ~**ment** mensualidad f; ~ **packet** n sobre m de paga; ~**roll** n nómina; ~ **slip** n hoja de paga.

p.c. abbr of **per cent**.

pea [piː] n guisante m; **sweet** ~ guisante de olor.

peace [piːs] n paz f; (*calm*) paz f, tranquilidad f; ~**able** a pacífico; ~**ful** a (*gentle*) pacífico; (*calm*) tranquilo, sosegado; ~-**keeping** n pacificación f; ~ **offering** n prenda de paz.

peach [piːtʃ] n melocotón m, durazno (*AM*).

peacock ['piːkɒk] n pavo real.

peak [piːk] n (of mountain: top) cumbre f, cima; (: point) pico; (of cap) visera; (fig) cumbre f; ~ **hours** npl horas fpl punta.

peal [piːl] n (of bells) repique m, toque m de campanas; ~ **of laughter** carcajada.

peanut ['piːnʌt] n cacahuete m, maní m (AM); ~ **butter** n manteca de cacahuete.

pear [pɛə*] n pera; ~ **tree** n peral m.

pearl [pɜːl] n perla; **mother-of-** ~ n nácar m.

peasant ['pɛznt] n campesino/a.

peat [piːt] n turba.

pebble ['pɛbl] n guijarro.

peck [pɛk] vt (also: ~ **at**) picotear; (food) comer sin ganas // n picotazo; (kiss) beso ligero; ~**ing order** n orden m de jerarquía; ~**ish** a (col) con hambre.

peculiar [pɪ'kjuːlɪə*] a (odd) extraño, raro; (typical) propio, característico; (marked) especial; ~ **to** propio de; ~**ity** [pɪkjuːlɪ'ærɪtɪ] n peculiaridad f; (feature) característica; (oddity) rareza, singularidad f.

pedal ['pɛdl] n pedal m // vi pedalear.

pedantic [pɪ'dæntɪk] a pedante.

peddle ['pɛdl] vt vender (de puerta en puerta); **peddler** n vendedor/a m/f ambulante.

pedestal ['pɛdəstl] n pedestal m.

pedestrian [pɪ'dɛstrɪən] n peatón m // a pedestre; ~ **crossing** n paso de peatones.

pedigree ['pɛdɪgriː] n genealogía; (of animal) raza // cpd (animal) de raza, de casta.

peek [piːk] vi mirar a hurtadillas.

peel [piːl] n piel f; (of orange, lemon) peladuras fpl // vt pelar // vi (paint etc) desconcharse; (wallpaper) despegarse, desprenderse.

peep [piːp] n (look) mirada furtiva; (sound) pío // vi piar; **to** ~ **out** vi asomar la cabeza; ~**hole** n mirilla.

peer [pɪə*] vi: **to** ~ **at** mirar con ojos de miope // n (noble) par m; (equal) igual m; ~**age** n nobleza; ~**less** a sin par.

peeved [piːvd] a enojado.

peevish ['piːvɪʃ] a malhumorado.

peg [pɛg] n clavija; (for coat etc) gancho, colgadero; (also: **clothes** ~) pinza; (tent ~) estaca // vt (prices) fijar; **off the** ~ ad de confección.

pejorative [pɪ'dʒɔrətɪv] a peyorativo.

pekingese [piːkɪ'niːz] n pequinés/esa m/f.

pelican ['pɛlɪkən] n pelícano.

pellet ['pɛlɪt] n bolita; (bullet) perdigón m.

pelmet ['pɛlmɪt] n galería.

pelt [pɛlt] vt: **to** ~ **sb with sth** tirar algo a uno // vi (rain) llover a cántaros // n pellejo.

pelvis ['pɛlvɪs] n pelvis f.

pen [pɛn] n pluma; (for sheep) redil m; **play** ~ parque m de niño; ~ **name** n seudónimo.

penal ['piːnl] a penal; ~**ize** vt penar; (SPORT) castigar.

penalty ['pɛnltɪ] n (gen) pena; (fine) multa; (SPORT) castigo; ~ (**kick**) n (FOOTBALL) penalty m.

penance ['pɛnəns] n penitencia.

pence [pɛns] pl of **penny**.

pencil ['pɛnsl] n lápiz m; (for eyebrows) lapiz de cejas; **propelling** ~ lapicero; ~ **sharpener** n sacapuntas m inv.

pendant ['pɛndnt] n pendiente m.

pending ['pɛndɪŋ] prep antes de // a pendiente.

pendulum ['pɛndjuləm] n péndulo.

penetrate ['pɛnɪtreɪt] vt penetrar; **penetrating** a penetrante; **penetration** [-'treɪʃən] n penetración f.

penfriend ['pɛnfrɛnd] n amigo/a por correspondencia.

penguin ['pɛŋgwɪn] n pingüino.

penicillin [pɛnɪ'sɪlɪn] n penicilina.

peninsula [pə'nɪnsjulə] n península.

penis ['piːnɪs] n pene m.

penitence ['pɛnɪtns] n penitencia; **penitent** [-nt] a (gen) arrepentido; (REL) penitente.

penitentiary [pɛnɪ'tɛnʃərɪ] n (US) cárcel f, presidio.

penknife ['pɛnnaɪf] n navaja.

pennant ['pɛnənt] n banderola.

penniless ['pɛnɪlɪs] a sin dinero.

penny ['pɛnɪ], pl **pennies** ['pɛnɪz] or **pence** [pɛns] n penique m.

pension ['pɛnʃən] n (gen) pensión f; (old-age) jubilación f; (MIL) retiro; ~**er** n jubilado; ~ **fund** n caja de jubilaciones.

pensive ['pɛnsɪv] a pensativo; (withdrawn) preocupado.

pentagon ['pɛntəgən] n pentágono.

Pentecost ['pɛntɪkɔst] n Pentecostés m.

penthouse ['pɛnthaus] n ático.

pent-up ['pɛntʌp] a (feelings) reprimido.

penultimate [pɛ'nʌltɪmət] a penúltimo.

people ['piːpl] npl gente f; (citizens) pueblo sg, ciudadanos mpl // n (nation, race) pueblo, nación f // vt poblar; **several** ~ **came** vinieron varias personas; ~ **say that...** dice la gente que... .

pep [pɛp] n (col) energía; **to** ~ **up** vt animar.

pepper ['pɛpə*] n pimienta; (vegetable) pimiento // vt (fig) salpicar; ~**mint** n menta; (sweet) pastilla de menta.

peptalk ['pɛptɔːk] n (col) palabras fpl para levantar los ánimos.

per [pɜː*] prep por; ~ **day/person** por día/persona; ~ **cent** por ciento; ~ **annum** al año.

perceive [pə'siːv] vt percibir; (realize) darse cuenta de.

percentage [pə'sɛntɪdʒ] n porcentaje m.

perception [pə'sɛpʃən] n percepción f; (insight) perspicacia; **perceptive** [-'sɛptɪv] a perspicaz.

perch [pɜːtʃ] n (fish) perca; (for bird) percha // vi posarse.

percolator ['pɜːkəleɪtə*] n cafetera filtradora.

percussion [pə'kʌʃən] n percusión f.

peremptory [pə'rɛmptərɪ] a perentorio; (person: imperious) imperioso.
perennial [pə'rɛnɪəl] a perenne.
perfect ['pə:fɪkt] a perfecto // n (also: ~ tense) perfecto // vt [pə'fɛkt] perfeccionar; ~ion [-'fɛkʃən] n perfección f; ~ionist n perfeccionista m/f.
perforate ['pə:fəreɪt] vt perforar; ~d a (stamp) dentado; **perforation** [-'reɪʃən] n perforación f.
perform [pə'fɔ:m] vt (carry out) realizar, cumplir; (concert etc) representar; (piece of music) interpretar // vi (animal) hacer trucos; (THEATRE) actuar; (TECH) funcionar; ~ance n (of task) cumplimiento, realización f; (of an artist) representación f; (of player etc) actuación f; (of car, engine) funcionamiento; (of function) desempeño; ~er n (actor) actor/actriz m/f; (MUS) interprete m/f; ~ing a (animal) amaestrado.
perfume ['pə:fju:m] n perfume m // vt perfumar.
perhaps [pə'hæps] ad quizá(s), tal vez.
peril ['pɛrɪl] n peligro, riesgo.
perimeter [pə'rɪmɪtə*] n perímetro.
period ['pɪərɪəd] n período; (HISTORY) época; (time limit) plazo; (SCOL) clase f; (full stop) punto; (MED) regla, reglas fpl // a (costume, furniture) de época; ~ic [-'ɔdɪk] a periódico; ~ical [-'ɔdɪkl] n periódico; ~ically [-'ɔdɪklɪ] ad de vez en cuando, cada cierto tiempo.
peripheral [pə'rɪfərəl] a periférico; **periphery** [-rɪ] n periferia.
periscope ['pɛrɪskəup] n periscopio.
perish ['pɛrɪʃ] vi perecer; (decay) echarse a perder, deteriorar(se); ~able a perecedero; ~ing a (col: cold) helado, glacial.
perjure ['pə:dʒə*] vt: to ~ o.s. perjurarse; **perjury** n (LAW) perjurio.
perk [pə:k] n pago encima del sueldo; **to** ~ **up** vi (cheer up) animarse; (in health) sentirse mejor; ~y a (cheerful) alegre, despabilado.
perm [pə:m] n permanente f.
permanent ['pə:mənənt] a permanente.
permissible [pə'mɪsɪbl] a permisible, lícito.
permission [pə'mɪʃən] n permiso; (authorization) licencia.
permissive [pə'mɪsɪv] a permisivo.
permit ['pə:mɪt] n permiso, licencia // vt [pə'mɪt] permitir; (authorize) autorizar; (accept) tolerar.
permutation [pə:mju'teɪʃən] n permutación f.
pernicious [pə:'nɪʃəs] a nocivo; (MED) pernicioso.
perpendicular [pə:pən'dɪkjulə*] a perpendicular.
perpetrate ['pə:pɪtreɪt] vt cometer.
perpetual [pə'pɛtjuəl] a perpetuo.
perpetuate [pə'pɛtjueɪt] vt perpetuar.
perplex [pə'plɛks] vt dejar perplejo.
persecute ['pə:sɪkju:t] vt (pursue)

perseguir; (harass) acosar; **persecution** [-'kju:ʃən] n persecución f.
persevere [pə:sɪ'vɪə*] vi persistir.
Persian ['pə:ʃən] a, n persa m/f.
persist [pə'sɪst] vi: to ~ (in doing sth) persistir (en hacer algo); ~ence n empeño; (of disease) pertinacia; ~ent a persistente; (determined) porfiado; (disease) pertinaz.
person ['pə:sn] n persona; ~able a atractivo; ~al a personal; (private) particular; (visit) en persona; (TEL) persona a persona; (column) de anuncios personales; ~ality [-'nælɪtɪ] n personalidad f; ~ally ad personalmente; ~ify [-'sɔnɪfaɪ] vt encarnar.
personnel [pə:sə'nɛl] n personal m.
perspective [pə'spɛktɪv] n perspectiva.
perspex ['pə:spɛks] n plexiglás m.
perspiration [pə:spɪ'reɪʃən] n transpiración f, sudor m; **perspire** [-'spaɪə*] vi transpirar, sudar.
persuade [pə'sweɪd] vt persuadir; **persuasion** [-'sweɪʒən] n persuasión f; (persuasiveness) persuasiva; (creed) creencia; **persuasive** [-'sweɪsɪv] a persuasivo.
pert [pə:t] a impertinente, fresco.
pertaining [pə:'teɪnɪŋ]: ~ **to** prep relacionado con.
pertinent ['pə:tɪnənt] a pertinente, a propósito.
perturb [pə'tə:b] vt perturbar.
Peru [pə'ru:] n el Perú.
peruse [pə'ru:z] vt leer con detención, examinar.
Peruvian [pə'ru:vjən] a, n peruano/a.
pervade [pə'veɪd] vt impregnar, saturar.
perverse [pə'və:s] a perverso; (stubborn) terco; (wayward) travieso; **perversion** [-'və:ʃən] n perversión f.
pervert ['pə:və:t] n pervertido/a // vt [pə'və:t] pervertir.
pessary ['pɛsərɪ] n pesario.
pessimism ['pɛsɪmɪzəm] n pesimismo; **pessimist** [-mɪst] n pesimista m/f; **pessimistic** [-'mɪstɪk] a pesimista.
pest [pɛst] n plaga; (insect) insecto nocivo; (fig) lata, molestia.
pester ['pɛstə*] vt molestar, acosar.
pesticide ['pɛstɪsaɪd] n pesticida m.
pet [pɛt] n animal doméstico; (favourite) favorito // vt acariciar // vi (col) besuquearse, sobarse.
petal ['pɛtl] n pétalo.
peter ['pi:tə*]: **to** ~ **out** vi agotarse, acabarse.
petite [pə'ti:t] a chiquita.
petition [pə'tɪʃən] n petición f.
petrified ['pɛtrɪfaɪd] a (fig) pasmado, horrorizado; **petrify** vt petrificar; (frighten) pasmar.
petrol ['pɛtrəl] n (Brit) gasolina; (for lighter) bencina.
petroleum [pə'trəulɪəm] n petróleo.
petrol: ~ **pump** n (in car) bomba de

gasolina; (in garage) surtidor m de
gasolina; ~ **station** n gasolinera; ~ **tank**
n depósito de gasolina.
petticoat ['pɛtıkɔut] n enagua; (slip)
combinación f.
pettiness ['pɛtınıs] n mezquindad f.
petty ['pɛtı] a (mean) mezquino;
(unimportant) nimio; ~ **cash** n dinero
suelto; ~ **officer** n contramaestre m.
petulant ['pɛtjulənt] a malhumorado.
pew [pju:] n banco.
pewter ['pju:tə*] n peltre m.
phallic ['fælık] a fálico.
phantom ['fæntəm] n fantasma m.
Pharaoh ['fɛərəu] n Faraón m.
pharmacist ['fɑːməsıst] n farmacéutico;
pharmacy [-sı] n farmacia.
phase [feız] n fase f // vt: **to** ~ **sth in/out**
introducir/reducir algo por etapas.
Ph.D. abbr of **Doctor of Philosophy.**
pheasant ['fɛznt] n faisán m.
phenomenon [fə'nɔmınɔn], pl -**mena**
[-mınə] n fenómeno.
phial ['faıəl] n ampolla.
philanthropist [fı'lænθrɔpıst] n
filántropo/a.
philately [fı'lætəlı] n filatelia.
Philippines ['fılıpi:nz] npl (also:
Philippine Islands) (Islas) Filipinas fpl.
philosopher [fı'lɔsɔfə*] n filósofo;
philosophical [fılə'sɔfıkl] a filosófico;
philosophy [-fı] n filosofía.
phlegm [flɛm] n flema; ~**atic** [flɛg-
'mætık] a flemático.
phobia ['fəubjə] n fobia.
phone [fəun] n teléfono // vt telefonear,
llamar (por teléfono); **to be on the** ~
tener teléfono; (be calling) estar llamando;
to ~ **back** vt, vi devolver la llamada.
phonetics [fə'nɛtıks] n fonética.
phoney ['fəunı] a falso; (person) insincero
// n (person) farsante m/f.
phosphate ['fɔsfeıt] n fosfato.
phosphorus ['fɔsfərəs] n fósforo.
photo ['fəutəu] n fotografía.
photo... [fəutəu] pref: ~**copier** n
fotocopiador m; ~**copy** n fotocopia // vt
fotocopiar; ~**genic** [-'dʒɛnık] a
fotogénico; ~**graph** n fotografía // vt
fotografiar; ~**grapher** [fə'tɔgrəfə*] n
fotógrafo; ~**graphic** [-'græfık] a
fotográfico; ~**graphy** [fə'tɔgrəfı] n
fotografía; ~**stat** ['fəutəustæt] n fotóstato.
phrase [freız] n frase f // vt expresar;
~**book** n libro de frases.
physical ['fızıkl] a físico.
physician [fı'zıʃən] n médico.
physicist ['fızısıst] n físico.
physics ['fızıks] n física.
physiology [fızı'ɔlədʒı] n fisiología.
physiotherapy [fızıəu'θɛrəpı] n
fisioterapia.
physique [fı'zi:k] n físico.
pianist ['pi:ənıst] n pianista m/f.
piano [pı'ænəu] n piano; **grand** ~ piano
de cola.

pick [pık] n (tool: also: ~-**axe**) pico,
piqueta // vt (select) elegir, escoger;
(gather) recoger; (lock) forzar; **take your**
~ escoja lo que quiera; **the** ~ **of** lo
mejor de; **to** ~ **one's teeth** limpiarse los
dientes; **to** ~ **pockets** ratear, ser
carterista; **to** ~ **off** vt (kill) matar de un
tiro; **to** ~ **on** vt fus (person) meterse con;
to ~ **out** vt escoger; (distinguish) lograr
ver; **to** ~ **up** vi (improve) reponerse // vt
(from floor) recoger; (telephone)
descolgar; (buy) comprar; (find)
encontrar; (learn) aprender; **to** ~ **up**
speed acelerarse; **to** ~ **o.s. up**
levantarse.
picket ['pıkıt] n (in strike) guardia, piquete
m // vt piquetear; ~ **line** n línea de
huelgistas.
pickle ['pıkl] n (also: ~**s**: as condiment)
escabeche m; (fig: mess) apuro // vt
encurtir; (in vinegar) conservar en
vinagre.
pickpocket ['pıkpɔkıt] n carterista m/f.
pickup ['pıkʌp] n (on record player) pickup
m; (small truck) furgoneta.
picnic ['pıknık] n picnic m, merienda de
campo // vi merendar en el campo.
pictorial [pık'tɔ:rıəl] a pictórico;
(magazine etc) ilustrado.
picture ['pıktʃə*] n cuadro; (painting)
pintura; (photograph) fotografía; (film)
película // vt pintar; **the** ~**s** el cine; ~
book n libro de imágenes.
picturesque [pıktʃə'rɛsk] a pintoresco.
pidgin ['pıdʒın] a: ~ **English** el inglés
macarrónico.
pie [paı] n pastel m; (open) tarta; (of meat)
empanada.
piebald ['paıbɔ:ld] a pío.
piece [pi:s] n pedazo, trozo; (of land)
terreno; (of cake) porción f; (item): **a** ~ **of**
furniture/advice un mueble/un consejo
// vt: **to** ~ **together** juntar; (TECH)
montar; **to take to** ~**s** desmontar;
~**meal** ad poco a poco; ~**work** n trabajo
a destajo.
pier [pıə*] n muelle m; (jetty)
embarcadero, malecón m.
pierce [pıəs] vt penetrar, atravesar;
(puncture) pinchar.
piercing ['pıəsıŋ] a (cry) penetrante.
piety ['paıətı] n piedad f.
pig [pıg] n cerdo, puerco; (fig) cochino.
pigeon ['pıdʒən] n paloma; (as food)
pichón m; ~**hole** n casilla.
piggy bank ['pıgıbæŋk] n hucha en forma
de cerdito.
pigheaded ['pıg'hɛdıd] a terco, testarudo.
pigment ['pıgmənt] n pigmento; ~**ation**
[-'teıʃən] n pigmentación f.
pigmy ['pıgmı] n = **pygmy.**
pigsty ['pıgstaı] n pocilga.
pigtail ['pıgteıl] n (girl's) trenza; (Chinese)
coleta.
pike [paık] n (spear) pica; (fish) lucio.
pilchard ['pıltʃəd] n sardina arenque.
pile [paıl] n (heap) montón m; (of carpet)

pelo; (of cloth) pelillo // (vb: also: ~ **up**) vt amontonar; (fig) acumular // vi amontonarse.

piles [paɪlz] npl (MED) almorranas fpl, hemorroides mpl.

pile-up ['paɪlʌp] n (AUT) accidente m múltiple.

pilfer ['pɪlfə*] vt ratear; ~ing n ratería.

pilgrim ['pɪlgrɪm] n peregrino/a; ~age n peregrinaje m, romería.

pill [pɪl] n píldora; **the** ~ la píldora.

pillage ['pɪlɪdʒ] n saqueo, pillaje m.

pillar ['pɪlə*] n (gen) pilar m; (concrete) columna; ~ **box** n (Brit) buzón m.

pillion ['pɪljən] n (of motor cycle) asiento de atrás.

pillory ['pɪlərɪ] vt poner en ridículo.

pillow ['pɪləu] n almohada; ~**case** n funda.

pilot ['paɪlət] n piloto // a (scheme etc) piloto // vt pilotar; (fig) guiar, conducir; ~ **light** n piloto.

pimp [pɪmp] n alcahuete m, chulo.

pimple ['pɪmpl] n grano.

pin [pɪn] n alfiler m; (TECH) perno; (: wooden) clavija // vt prender (con alfiler); sujetar con perno; ~**s and needles** hormigueo sg; **rolling/ safety** ~ rodillo/imperdible m; **to** ~ **sb down** (fig) hacer que uno concrete; **to** ~ **sth on sb** (fig) acusar (falsamente) a uno de algo.

pinafore ['pɪnəfɔ:*] n delantal m; ~ **dress** n mandil m.

pinball ['pɪnbɔ:l] n billar m automático.

pincers ['pɪnsəz] npl pinzas fpl, tenazas fpl.

pinch [pɪntʃ] n pellizco; (of salt etc) pizca // vt pellizcar; (col: steal) birlar; (: arrest) coger, pescar // vi (shoe) apretar; **to feel the** ~ pasar apuros.

pincushion ['pɪnkuʃən] n acerico.

pine [paɪn] n (also: ~ **tree**) pino // vi: **to** ~ **for** suspirar por; **to** ~ **away** languidecer.

pineapple ['paɪnæpl] n piña, ananás m.

ping [pɪŋ] n (noise) tintineo; (of bullet through air) subido; ~-**pong** n pingpong m.

pink [pɪŋk] a rosado, color de rosa // n (colour) color m de rosa; (BOT) clavel m, clavellina.

pinnacle ['pɪnəkl] n cumbre f.

pinpoint ['pɪnpɔɪnt] vt poner el dedo en.

pint [paɪnt] n pinta (0.57 litros): **to go for a** ~ ir a tomar una cerveza.

pin-up ['pɪnʌp] n fotografía de mujer bonita.

pioneer [paɪə'nɪə*] n pionero.

pious ['paɪəs] a piadoso, devoto.

pip [pɪp] n (seed) pepita; (time signal on radio) señal f.

pipe [paɪp] n tubo, caño; (for smoking) pipa // vt conducir en cañerías; ~**s** npl (gen) cañería sg; (also: **bag**~**s**) gaita sg; **to** ~ **down** vi (col) callarse; ~ **dream** n sueño imposible; ~**line** n tubería, cañería; (for oil) oleoducto; (for gas) gasoducto; **piper** n

(gen) flautista m/f; (with bagpipes) gaitero.

piping ['paɪpɪŋ] ad: ~ **hot** bien caliente.

piquant ['pi:kənt] a picante.

pique [pi:k] n pique m, resentimiento.

pirate ['paɪərət] n pirata m; ~ **radio** n emisora ilegal.

pirouette [pɪru'ɛt] n pirueta // vi piruetear.

Pisces ['paɪsi:z] n Piscis m.

piss [pɪs] vi (col) mear; ~**ed** a (col: drunk) trompa.

pistol ['pɪstl] n pistola.

piston ['pɪstən] n pistón m, émbolo.

pit [pɪt] n hoyo; (also: **coal** ~) mina; (in garage) foso de inspección; (also: **orchestra** ~) platea; (quarry) cantera // vt: **to** ~ **A against B** oponer A a B; ~**s** npl (AUT) box m.

pitch [pɪtʃ] n (throw) lanzamiento; (MUS) tono; (SPORT) campo, terreno; (tar) brea; (in market etc) puesto // vt (throw) arrojar, lanzar // vi (fall) caer(se); (NAUT) cabecear; **to** ~ **a tent** armar una tienda (de campaña); ~-**black** a negro como boca de lobo; ~**ed battle** n batalla campal.

pitcher ['pɪtʃə*] n cántaro, jarro.

pitchfork ['pɪtʃfɔ:k] n horca.

piteous ['pɪtɪəs] a lastimoso.

pitfall ['pɪtfɔ:l] n escollo, peligro.

pith [pɪθ] n (of orange) médula; (fig) meollo.

pithy ['pɪθɪ] a jugoso.

pitiable ['pɪtɪəbl] a lastimoso.

pitiful ['pɪtɪful] a (touching) lastimoso, conmovedor(a); (contemptible) lamentable, miserable.

pitiless ['pɪtɪlɪs] a despiadado.

pittance ['pɪtns] n miseria.

pity ['pɪtɪ] n (compassion) compasión f, piedad f; (shame) lástima // vt tener lástima a, compadecer(se de); **what a** ~! ¡qué lástima!

pivot ['pɪvət] n eje m // vi: **to** ~ **on** girar sobre; (fig) depender de.

pixie ['pɪksɪ] n duende m.

placard ['plækɑ:d] n (sign) letrero; (in march etc) pancarta.

placate [plə'keɪt] vt apaciguar.

place [pleɪs] n lugar m, sitio; (rank) rango; (seat) plaza, asiento; (post) puesto; (home): **at/to his** ~ en/a su casa // vt (object) poner, colocar; (identify) reconocer, ubicar; (find a post for) dar un puesto a, colocar; **to take** ~ tener lugar; **to be** ~**d** (in race, exam) colocarse; **out of** ~ (not suitable) fuera de lugar; **in the first** ~ en primer lugar; **to change** ~**s with sb** trocarse con uno.

placid ['plæsɪd] a apacible.

plagiarism ['pleɪdʒərɪzm] n plagio.

plague [pleɪg] n plaga; (MED) peste f // vt (fig) acosar, atormentar; **to** ~ **sb** fastidiar a uno.

plaice [pleɪs] n, pl inv platija.

plaid [plæd] n (material) tela a cuadros; (pattern) plaid m.

plain [pleɪn] a (clear) claro, evidente; (simple) sencillo, llano; (frank) franco, abierto; (not handsome) sin atractivo; (pure) natural, puro // ad claro, claramente // n llano, llanura; **in** ~ **clothes** (police) de paisano; ~**ly** ad claramente, evidentemente; (frankly) francamente, con franqueza; ~**ness** n claridad f; sencillez f; franqueza.

plaintiff ['pleɪntɪf] n demandante m/f.

plait [plæt] n trenza // vt trenzar.

plan [plæn] n (drawing) plano; (scheme) plan m, proyecto; (schedule) programa m // vt (think in advance) proyectar; (prepare) planear, planificar // vi hacer proyectos; **to** ~ **to do** proponerse hacer.

plane [pleɪn] n (AVIAT) avión m; (tree) plátano; (tool) cepillo; (MATH) plano.

planet ['plænɪt] n planeta m; ~**arium** [-'tɛərɪəm] n planetario.

plank [plæŋk] n tabla; (POL) punto.

planner ['plænə*] n planificador/a m/f.

planning ['plænɪŋ] n planificación f; **family** ~ planificación familiar.

plant [plɑːnt] n planta; (machinery) maquinaria; (factory) fábrica // vt plantar; (field) sembrar; (bomb) colocar; (fam) colocar a escondidas.

plantation [plæn'teɪʃən] n plantación f; (estate) hacienda.

plaque [plæk] n placa.

plasma ['plæzmə] n plasma m.

plaster ['plɑːstə*] n (for walls) yeso; (also: **sticking** ~) curitas m inv, parche m // vt enyesar; (cover): **to** ~ **with** llenar o cubrir de; ~**ed** a (col) trompa; ~**er** n yesero.

plastic ['plæstɪk] n plástico // a de plástico.

plasticine ['plæstɪsiːn] n plasticina.

plastic surgery ['plæstɪk'sɔːdʒərɪ] n cirujía plástica.

plate [pleɪt] n (dish) plato; (metal, in book) lámina; (PHOT, dental) placa.

plateau ['plætəu], pl ~**s** or ~**x** [-z] n meseta, altiplanicie f.

plateful ['pleɪtful] n plato.

plate glass [pleɪt'glɑːs] n vidrio cilindrado.

platform ['plætfɔːm] n (RAIL) andén m; (stage) plataforma; (at meeting) tribuna; (POL) programa m electoral; ~ **ticket** n billete m de andén.

platinum ['plætɪnəm] n platino.

platitude ['plætɪtjuːd] n lugar m común, tópico.

platoon [plə'tuːn] n pelotón m.

platter ['plætə*] n fuente f, platón m.

plausible ['plɔːzɪbl] a verosímil, admisible; (person) convincente.

play [pleɪ] n (gen) juego; (also: ~**time**) recreo; (THEATRE) obra, comedia // vt (game) jugar; (instrument) tocar; (THEATRE) representar; (: part) hacer (el papel de); (fig) desempeñar // vi jugar;

(amuse o.s.) divertirse; (frolic) juguetear; **to** ~ **down** vt quitar importancia a; **to** ~ **up** vt (cause trouble to) fastidiar a; ~**-acting** n teatro; ~**er** n jugador/a m/f; (THEATRE) actor/actriz m/f; (MUS) músico/a; ~**ful** a juguetón(ona); ~**ground** n (in park) parque m de juegos; (in school) patio de recreo; ~**group** n jardín m de niños; ~**ing card** n naipe m, carta; ~**ing field** n campo de deportes; ~**mate** n compañero de juego; ~**-off** n (SPORT) partido de desempate; ~**pen** n corral m; ~**thing** n juguete m; ~**wright** n dramaturgo.

plea [pliː] n (request) súplica, petición f; (excuse) pretexto, disculpa; (LAW) alegato, defensa.

plead [pliːd] vt (LAW) interceder; (give as excuse) poner como pretexto // vi (LAW) declarar; (beg): **to** ~ **with sb** suplicar o rogar a uno.

pleasant ['plɛznt] a agradable; (surprise) grato; (person) simpático; ~**ness** n (of person) simpatía, amabilidad f; (of place) lo agradable; ~**ries** npl (polite remarks) cortesías fpl.

please [pliːz] vt (give pleasure to) dar gusto a, agradar; (get on well with) caer en gracia a // vi (think fit): **do as you** ~ haga lo que quiera o lo que le da la gana; ~**!** ¡por favor!; ~ **yourself!** ¡como Usted guste!, ¡como quiera!; ~**d** a (happy) alegre, contento; ~**d** (**with**) satisfecho (de); **pleasing** a (gen) agradable; (surprise) grato; (flattering) halagüeño.

pleasure ['plɛʒə*] n placer m, gusto; (will) voluntad f // cpd de recreo; **'it's a** ~' el gusto es mío; **it's a** ~ **to see him** da gusto verle.

pleat [pliːt] n pliegue m.

plebs [plɛbz] npl (pej) la plebe.

plectrum ['plɛktrəm] n plectro.

pledge [plɛdʒ] n (object) prenda; (promise) promesa, voto // vt (pawn) empeñar; (promise) prometer.

plentiful ['plɛntɪful] a copioso, abundante.

plenty ['plɛntɪ] n abundancia; ~ **of** (enough) bastante; (many) muchos.

pleurisy ['pluərɪsɪ] n pleuresía.

pliable ['plaɪəbl] a flexible; (fig) manejable.

pliers ['plaɪəz] npl alicates mpl, tenazas fpl.

plight [plaɪt] n condición f, situación f difícil.

plimsolls ['plɪmsəlz] npl zapatos mpl de tenis.

plod [plɔd] vi caminar penosamente; (fig) trabajar laboriosamente; ~**der** n empollón/ona m/f; ~**ding** a laborioso.

plonk [plɔŋk] (col) n (wine) vino corriente // vt: **to** ~ **sth down** dejar caer algo (pesadamente).

plot [plɔt] n (scheme) complot m, conjura; (of story, play) argumento; (of land) terreno // vt (mark out) trazar; (conspire) tramar, urdir // vi conspirar; ~**ter** n conspirador/a m/f.

plough, plow (*US*) [plau] *n* arado // *vt* (*earth*) arar; **to ~ back** *vt* (*COMM*) reinvertir; **to ~ through** *vt fus* (*crowd*) abrirse paso por la fuerza.

ploy [plɔɪ] *n* truco, estratagema.

pluck [plʌk] *vt* (*fruit*) coger; (*musical instrument*) puntear; (*bird*) desplumar // *n* valor *m*, ánimo; **to ~ up courage** hacer de tripas corazón; **~y** *a* valiente, valeroso.

plug [plʌg] *n* tapón *m*; (*ELEC*) enchufe *m*, clavija; (*AUT. also*: **sparking ~**) bujía // *vt* (*hole*) tapar; (*col: advertise*) dar publicidad a.

plum [plʌm] *n* (*fruit*) ciruela // *a* (*col: job*) breva, chollo.

plumage ['plu:mɪdʒ] *n* plumaje *m*.

plumb [plʌm] *ad* (*exactly*) exactamente, en punto // *vt* sondar, sondear.

plumber ['plʌmə*] *n* fontanero; **plumbing** [-mɪŋ] *n* (*trade*) fontanería; (*piping*) instalación *f* de cañerías.

plume [plu:m] *n* (*gen*) pluma; (*on helmet*) penacho.

plummet ['plʌmɪt] *vi*: **to ~ (down)** caer a plomo.

plump [plʌmp] *a* rechoncho, rollizo // *vt*: **to ~ sth (down) on** dejar caer algo en; **to ~ for** (*col: choose*) optar por.

plunder ['plʌndə*] *n* pillaje *m*; (*loot*) botín *m* // *vt* pillar, saquear; (*tomb*) robar.

plunge [plʌndʒ] *n* (*dive*) salto; (*submersion*) zambullida; (*bath*) baño // *vt* sumergir, hundir // *vi* (*fall*) caer; (*dive*) saltar; (*person*) arrojarse; (*sink*) hundirse; **to take the ~** resolverse; **plunger** *n* émbolo; **plunging** *a* (*neckline*) escotado.

pluperfect [plu:'pɜ:fɪkt] *n* pluscuamperfecto.

plural ['pluərl] *n* plural *m*.

plus [plʌs] *n* (*also*: **~ sign**) signo más // *prep* más, y, además de; **ten/twenty ~** diez/veinte y pico.

plush [plʌʃ] *a* de felpa.

ply [plaɪ] *vt* (*a trade*) ejercer // *vi* (*ship*) ir y venir; (*for hire*) ofrecerse (para alquilar); **three ~** (*wool*) de tres cordones; **to ~ sb with drink** ofrecer bebidas a alguien muchas veces; **~ wood** *n* madera contrachapada.

P.M. *abbr of* **Prime Minister.**

p.m. *ad abbr of* **post meridiem** de la tarde *o* noche.

pneumatic [nju:'mætɪk] *a* neumático.

pneumonia [nju:'məunɪə] *n* pulmonía.

poach [pəutʃ] *vt* (*cook*) escalfar; (*steal*) cazar en vedado // *vi* cazar/pescar en finca ajena; **~ed** *a* (*egg*) escalfado; **~er** *n* cazador *m* furtivo; **~ing** *n* caza/pesca furtiva.

pocket ['pɒkɪt] *n* bolsillo; (*of air, GEO, fig*) bolsa; (*BILLIARDS*) tronera // *vt* meter en el bolsillo; (*steal*) embolsar; (*BILLIARDS*) entronerar; **to be out of ~** salir perdiendo; **~ book** *n* (*US: wallet*) cartera; **~ knife** *n* navaja; **~ money** *n* dinero para gastos personales.

pod [pɒd] *n* vaina.

podgy ['pɒdʒɪ] *a* gordinflón(ona).

poem ['pəuɪm] *n* poema *m*.

poet ['pəuɪt] *n* poeta *m/f*; **~ess** *n* poetisa; **~ic** [-'ɛtɪk] *a* poético; **~ laureate** *n* poeta laureado; **~ry** *n* poesía.

poignant ['pɔɪnjənt] *a* conmovedor(a); (*sharp*) agudo.

point [pɔɪnt] *n* (*gen*) punto; (*tip*) punta; (*purpose*) fin *m*, finalidad *f*; (*use*) utilidad *f*; (*significant part*) lo significativo; (*characteristic*) rasgo; (*also*: **decimal ~**): **2 ~ 3 (2.3)** dos punto tres // *vt* (*show*) subrayar; (*gun etc*): **to ~ sth at sb** apuntar algo a uno // *vi* señalar con el dedo; **~s** *npl* (*AUT*) contactos *mpl*; (*RAIL*) agujas *fpl*; **to make a ~ of** no dejar de; **to get the ~** comprender; **to come to the ~** ir al grano; **there's no ~ (in doing)** no hay para qué (hacer); **to ~ out** *vt* señalar; **to ~ to** indicar con el dedo; (*fig*) indicar, señalar; **~-blank** *ad* (*also*: **at ~-blank range**) a quemarropa; **~ed** *a* (*shape*) puntiagudo, afilado; (*remark*) directo, enfático; **~edly** *ad* directamente, con énfasis; **~er** *n* (*stick*) puntero; (*needle*) aguja, indicador *m*; **~less** *a* (*useless*) inútil; (*senseless*) sin sentido; (*motiveless*) sin motivo; **~ of view** *n* punto de vista.

poise [pɔɪz] *n* (*balance*) equilibrio; (*of head, body*) aire *m*, porte *m*; (*calmness*) confianza.

poison ['pɔɪzn] *n* veneno // *vt* envenenar; **~ing** *n* envenenamiento; **~ous** *a* venenoso; (*fumes etc*) tóxico; (*fig*) pernicioso.

poke [pəuk] *vt* (*fire*) hurgar, atizar; (*jab with finger, stick etc*) empujar; (*put*): **to ~ sth in(to)** introducir algo en // *n* (*to fire*) hurgonada; (*push*) empujón *m*; (*with elbow*) codazo; **to ~ about** *vi* fisgar.

poker ['pəukə*] *n* badila, atizador *m*; (*CARDS*) póker *m*; **~-faced** *a* de cara impasible.

poky ['pəukɪ] *a* estrecho.

Poland ['pəulənd] *n* Polonia.

polar ['pəulə*] *a* polar; **~ bear** *n* oso polar.

polarize ['pəulɔraɪz] *vt* polarizar.

pole [pəul] *n* palo; (*GEO*) polo; (*TEL*) poste *m*; (*flag~*) asta; (*tent ~*) mástil *m*.

Pole [pəul] *n* polaco/a.

pole vault ['pəulvɔ:lt] *n* salto con pértiga.

police [pə'li:s] *n* policía // *vt* mantener el orden en; **~ car** *n* coche-patrulla *m*; **~man** *n* policía *m*, guardia *m*; **~ state** *n* estado policíaco; **~ station** *n* comisaría; **~woman** *n* mujer *f* policía.

policy ['pɒlɪsɪ] *n* política; (*also*: **insurance ~**) póliza.

polio ['pəulɪəu] *n* polio *f*.

Polish ['pəulɪʃ] *a, n* polaco.

polish ['pɒlɪʃ] *n* (*for shoes*) betún *m*; (*for floor*) cera (de lustrar); (*for nails*) esmalte *m*; (*shine*) brillo, lustre *m*; (*fig: refinement*) cultura, urbanidad *f* // *vt* (*shoes*) limpiar;

(*make shiny*) pulir, sacar brillo a; (*fig: improve*) refinar, repasar; **to** ~ **off** *vt* (*work*) terminar; (*food*) despachar; ~**ed** *a* (*fig: person*) culto; (: *manners*) fino.

polite [pə'lait] *a* cortés, atento; (*formal*) correcto; ~**ness** *n* cortesía.

politic ['politik] *a* prudente; ~**al** [pə'litikl] *a* político; ~**ian** [-'tiʃən] *n* político; ~**s** *npl* política *sg*.

polka ['polkə] *n* polca; ~ **dot** *n* punto.

poll [pəul] *n* (*votes*) votación *f*, votos *mpl*; (*also:* **opinion** ~) sondeo, encuesta // *vt* (*votes*) recibir, obtener.

pollen ['polən] *n* polen *m*.

pollination [poli'neiʃən] *n* polinización *f*.

polling ['pəuliŋ]: ~ **booth** *n* cabina de votar; ~ **day** *n* día *m* de elecciones; ~ **station** *n* centro electoral.

pollute [pə'lu:t] *vt* contaminar; **pollution** [-'lu:ʃən] *n* polución *f*, contaminación *f*.

polo ['pəuləu] *n* (*sport*) polo; ~-**neck** *a* de cuello vuelto.

polyester [poli'estə*] *n* poliester *m*.

polygamy [pə'ligəmi] *n* poligamia.

Polynesia [poli'ni:ziə] *n* Polinesia.

polytechnic [poli'teknik] *n* politécnico, escuela de formación profesional.

polythene ['poliθi:n] *n* politeno.

pomegranate ['pomigrænit] *n* granada.

pommel ['poml] *n* pomo // *vt* dar de puñetazos.

pomp [pomp] *n* pompa.

pompous ['pompəs] *a* pomposo.

pond [pond] *n* (*natural*) charca; (*artificial*) estanque *m*.

ponder ['pondə*] *vt* meditar; ~**ous** *a* pesado.

pontiff ['pontif] *n* pontífice *m*.

pontificate [pon'tifikeit] *vi* (*fig*): **to** ~ (**about**) pontificar (sobre).

pontoon [pon'tu:n] *n* pontón *m*; (*card game*) veintiuna.

pony ['pəuni] *n* poney *m*, jaca; ~ **tail** *n* cola de caballo; ~ **trekking** *n* excursión *f* a caballo.

poodle ['pu:dl] *n* perro de lanas.

pool [pu:l] *n* (*of rain*) charca; (*pond*) estanque *m*; (*also:* **swimming** ~) piscina; (*billiards*) trucos *mpl* // *vt* juntar; (**football**) ~**s** quinielas *fpl*.

poor [puə*] *a* pobre; (*bad*) de baja calidad // *npl*: **the** ~ los pobres; ~**ly** *a* mal, enfermo.

pop [pop] *n* ¡pum!; (*sound*) ruido seco; (*MUS*) pop *m*; (*US: col: father*) papá *m*; (*lemonade*) gaseosa // *vt* (*put*) poner // *vi* reventar; (*cork*) saltar; **to** ~ **in** *vi* entrar de sopetón; **to** ~ **out** *vi* salir un momento; **to** ~ **up** *vi* aparecer inesperadamente; ~ **concert** *n* concierto pop; ~**corn** *n* palomitas *fpl*.

pope [pəup] *n* papa *m*.

poplar ['poplə*] *n* álamo.

poplin ['poplin] *n* popelina.

poppy ['popi] *n* amapola.

populace ['popjuləs] *n* pueblo, plebe *f*.

popular ['popjulə*] *a* popular; (*fashionable*) de moda; ~**ity** [-'læriti] *n* popularidad *f*; ~**ize** *vt* popularizar; (*disseminate*) vulgarizar.

populate ['popjuleit] *vt* poblar; **population** [-'leiʃən] *n* población *f*.

populous ['popjuləs] *a* populoso.

porcelain ['po:slin] *n* porcelana.

porch [po:tʃ] *n* pórtico, entrada.

porcupine ['po:kjupain] *n* puerco espín.

pore [po:*] *n* poro // *vi*: **to** ~ **over** estar absorto en.

pork [po:k] *n* carne *f* de cerdo.

pornographic [po:nə'græfik] *a* pornográfico; **pornography** [-'nogrəfi] *n* pornografía.

porous ['po:rəs] *a* poroso.

porpoise ['po:pəs] *n* marsopa.

porridge ['poridʒ] *n* avena.

port [po:t] *n* (*harbour*) puerto; (*NAUT: left side*) babor *m*; (*wine*) (vino de) oporto.

portable ['po:təbl] *a* portátil.

portend [po:'tend] *vt* presagiar, anunciar; **portent** ['po:tent] *n* presagio, augurio.

porter ['po:tə*] *n* (*for luggage*) mozo; (*doorkeeper*) portero, conserje *m*.

porthole ['po:thəul] *n* portilla.

portion ['po:ʃən] *n* porción *f*; (*helping*) ración *f*.

portly ['po:tli] *a* corpulento.

portrait ['po:treit] *n* retrato.

portray [po:'trei] *vt* retratar; (*in writing*) describir, representar; ~**al** *n* representación *f*.

Portugal ['po:tjugl] *n* Portugal *m*.

Portuguese [po:tju'gi:z] *a* portugués(esa) // *n*, *pl inv* portugués/esa *m/f*; (*LING*) portugués *m*.

pose [pəuz] *n* postura, actitud *f*; (*pej*) afectación *f*, pose *f* // *vi* posar; (*pretend*): **to** ~ **as** darse tono de // *vt* (*question*) plantear.

posh [poʃ] *a* (*col*) elegante, de lujo.

position [pə'ziʃən] *n* posición *f*; (*job*) puesto // *vt* colocar.

positive ['pozitiv] *a* positivo; (*certain*) seguro; (*definite*) definitivo.

posse ['posi] *n* (*US*) pelotón *m*.

possess [pə'zes] *vt* poseer; ~**ion** [pə'zeʃən] *n* posesión *f*; ~**ive** *a* posesivo.

possibility [posi'biliti] *n* posibilidad *f*; **possible** ['posibl] *a* posible; **as big as possible** lo más grande posible; **possibly** ['posibli] *ad* (*perhaps*) posiblemente, tal vez; **I cannot possibly come** me es imposible venir.

post [pəust] *n* (*letters, delivery*) correo; (*job, situation*) puesto; (*pole*) poste *m* // *vt* (*send by post*) echar al correo; (*MIL*) apostar; (*bills*) fijar, pegar; (*appoint*): **to** ~ **to** enviar a; ~ **age** *n* porte *m*, franqueo; ~ **al** *a* postal, de correos; ~**al order** *n* giro postal; ~ **box** *n* buzón *m*; ~**card** *n* tarjeta postal.

postdate [pəust'deit] *vt* (*cheque*) poner fecha adelantada a.

poster ['pəustə*] n cartel m.
posterior [pɔs'tɪərɪə*] n (col) culo, trasero.
posterity [pɔs'tɛrɪtɪ] n posteridad f.
postgraduate ['pəust'grædjuət] n postgraduado.
posthumous ['pɔstjuməs] a póstumo.
post: ~**man** n cartero; ~**mark** n matasellos m inv; ~**master** n administrador/a m/f de correos.
post-mortem [pəust'mɔ:təm] n autopsia.
post office ['pəustɔfɪs] n (building) correos f; (organization) Administración General de Correos; ~ **box (P.O. box)** n apartado postal.
postpone [pɔs'pəun] vt aplazar; ~**ment** n aplazamiento.
postscript ['pəustskrɪpt] n posdata.
postulate ['pɔstjuleɪt] vt postular.
posture ['pɔstʃə*] n postura, actitud f.
postwar [pəust'wɔ:*] a de posguerra.
posy ['pəuzɪ] n ramillete m (de flores).
pot [pɔt] n (for cooking) olla; (for flowers) maceta; (for jam) tarro, pote m; (col: marijuana) mota // vt (plant) poner en tiesto; (conserve) conservar.
potato [pə'teɪtəu], pl ~**es** n patata, papa (AM).
potent ['pəutnt] a potente, poderoso; (drink) fuerte.
potential [pə'tɛnʃl] a potencial, en potencial // n potencial m, potencialidad f.
pothole ['pɔthəul] n (in road) bache m; (underground) caverna; **potholer** n espeleólogo; **potholing** n: **to go potholing** dedicarse a la espeleología.
potion ['pəuʃən] n poción f, pócima.
potluck [pɔt'lʌk] n: **to take** ~ contentarse con lo que haya.
potshot ['pɔtʃɔt] n: **to take a** ~ **at sth** tirar a algo sin apuntar.
potted ['pɔtɪd] a (food) en conserva; (plant) en tiesto o maceta.
potter ['pɔtə*] n (artistic) ceramista m/f; (artisan) alfarero // vi: **to** ~ **around,** ~ **about** ocuparse en fruslerías; ~**y** n cerámica; alfarería.
potty ['pɔtɪ] a (col: mad) chiflado // n orinal m de niño.
pouch [pautʃ] n (ZOOL) bolsa; (for tobacco) petaca.
pouf(fe) [pu:f] n pouf m.
poultice ['pəultɪs] n cataplasma, emplasto.
poultry ['pəultrɪ] n aves fpl de corral; (dead) pollos mpl; ~ **farm** n granja avícola.
pounce [pauns] vi: **to** ~ **on** precipitarse sobre // n salto, ataque m.
pound [paund] n (gen) libra; (for dogs) corral m; (for cars) depósito // vt (beat) golpear; (crush) machacar // vi (beat) dar golpes; ~ **sterling** n (libra) esterlina.
pour [pɔ:*] vt echar; (tea) servir // vi correr, fluir; (rain) llover a cántaros; **to** ~ **away** or **off** vt vaciar, verter; **to** ~ **in** vi (people) entrar en tropel; **to** ~ **out** vi (people) salir en tropel // vt (drink) echar, servir; ~**ing** a: ~**ing rain** lluvia torrencial.
pout [paut] vi hacer pucheros.
poverty ['pɔvətɪ] n pobreza, miseria; (fig) falta, escasez f; ~**-stricken** a necesitado.
powder ['paudə*] n polvo; (face ~) polvos mpl; (gun~) pólvora // vt polvorear; **to** ~ **one's face** empolvarse; ~ **compact** n polvera; ~ **room** n aseos mpl; ~**y** a polvoriento.
power ['pauə*] n (gen) poder m; (strength) fuerza; (nation) potencia; (ability, POL: of party, leader) poder m, poderío; (drive) empuje m; (TECH) potencia; (ELEC) fuerza, energía // vt impulsar; ~ **cut** n apagón m; ~**ed** a: ~**ed by** impulsado por; ~**ful** a poderoso; (engine) potente; (build) fuerte; (emotion) intenso; ~**less** a impotente, ineficaz; ~ **line** n línea de conducción eléctrica; ~ **point** n enchufe m; ~ **station** n central f eléctrica.
p.p. abbr of **per procurationem:** ~ **J. Smith** p.p. (por poder de) J. Smith.
practicable ['præktɪkəbl] a (scheme) factible.
practical ['præktɪkl] a práctico; ~ **joke** n broma pesada; ~**ly** ad (almost) prácticamente.
practice ['præktɪs] n (habit) costumbre f; (exercise) práctica, ejercicio; (training) adiestramiento; (MED) clientela // vt, vi (US) = **practise; in** ~ (in reality) en la práctica; **out of** ~ desentrenado.
practise, practice (US) ['præktɪs] vt (carry out) practicar; (be in the habit of) tener por costumbre; (profession) ejercer; (train at) hacer ejercicios de // vi ejercer (profesión); (train) entrenar, adiestrarse; **practising** a (Christian etc) practicante; (lawyer) que ejerce.
practitioner [præk'tɪʃənə*] n practicante m/f; (MED) médico/a.
pragmatic [præg'mætɪk] a pragmático.
prairie ['prɛərɪ] n pradera, pampa.
praise [preɪz] n alabanza, elogio, alabanzas fpl, elogios mpl; ~**worthy** a loable, digno de elogios.
pram [præm] n cochecito de niño.
prance [prɑ:ns] vi (horse) hacer cabriolas.
prank [præŋk] n travesura.
prattle ['prætl] vi parlotear; (child) balbucear.
prawn [prɔ:n] n gamba; (small) quisquilla.
pray [preɪ] vi rezar; ~**er** n oración f, rezo; (entreaty) ruego, súplica; ~**er book** n devocionario, misal m.
preach [pri:tʃ] vi predicar; ~**er** n predicador/a m/f; (US) pastor m.
preamble [prɪ'æmbl] n preámbulo.
prearranged [pri:ə'reɪndʒd] a arreglado de antemano.
precarious [prɪ'kɛərɪəs] a precario.
precaution [prɪ'kɔ:ʃən] n precaución f.
precede [prɪ'si:d] vt, vi preceder.
precedence ['prɛsɪdəns] n precedencia;

(*priority*) prioridad *f;* **precedent** [-ɔnt] *n* precedente *m.*
preceding [prɪ'si:dɪŋ] *a* precedente.
precept ['pri:sɛpt] *n* precepto.
precinct ['pri:sɪŋkt] *n* recinto; ~**s** *npl* contornos *mpl;* **pedestrian** ~ zona reservada para peatones; **shopping** ~ zona comercial.
precious ['prɛʃəs] *a* precioso; (*stylized*) afectado.
precipice ['prɛsɪpɪs] *n* precipicio, despeñadero.
precipitate [prɪ'sɪpɪtɪt] *a* (*hasty*) precipitado, apresurado // *vt* [prɪ'sɪpɪteɪt] (*hasten*) acelerar; (*bring about*) causar; **precipitation** [-'teɪʃən] *n* precipitación *f.*
precipitous [prɪ'sɪpɪtəs] *a* (*steep*) escarpado.
precise [prɪ'saɪs] *a* preciso, exacto; (*person*) escrupuloso; ~**ly** *ad* exactamente, precisamente; **precision** [-'sɪʒən] *n* precisión *f.*
preclude [prɪ'klu:d] *vt* excluir.
precocious [prɪ'kəuʃəs] *a* precoz.
preconceived [pri:kən'si:vd] *a* (*idea*) preconcebido.
precursor [pri:'kə:sə*] *n* precursor/a *m/f.*
predator ['prɛdətə*] *n* animal *m* de rapiña; ~**y** *a* rapaz, de rapiña.
predecessor ['pri:dɪsɛsə*] *n* antecesor/a *m/f.*
predestination [pri:dɛstɪ'neɪʃən] *n* predestinación *f.*
predetermine [pri:dɪ'tə:mɪn] *vt* predeterminar.
predicament [prɪ'dɪkəmənt] *n* apuro.
predict [prɪ'dɪkt] *vt* pronosticar; ~**ion** [-'dɪkʃən] *n* pronóstico.
predominant [prɪ'dɔmɪnənt] *a* predominante; **predominate** [-neɪt] *vi* predominar.
pre-eminent [pri:'ɛmɪnənt] *a* preeminente.
pre-empt [pri:'ɛmt] *vt* apropiarse de antemano.
preen [pri:n] *vt:* **to** ~ **itself** (*bird*) limpiarse (las plumas); **to** ~ **o.s.** pavonearse.
prefab ['pri:fæb] *n* casa prefabricada.
prefabricated [pri:'fæbrikeɪtɪd] *a* prefabricado.
preface ['prɛfəs] *n* prefacio.
prefect ['pri:fɛkt] *n* (*Brit: in school*) tutor *m,* monitor *m.*
prefer [prɪ'fə:*] *vt* preferir; ~**able** ['prɛfrəbl] *a* preferible; ~**ably** ['prɛfrəblɪ] *ad* de preferencia; ~**ence** ['prɛfrəns] *n* preferencia, prioridad *f;* ~**ential** [prɛfə'rɛnʃəl] *a* preferente.
prefix ['pri:fɪks] *n* prefijo.
pregnancy ['prɛgnənsɪ] *n* embarazo; **pregnant** [-ɔnt] *a* embarazada; **to be pregnant** estar encinta; **pregnant with** preñado de.
prehistoric ['pri:hɪs'tɔrɪk] *a* prehistórico.
prejudge [pri:'dʒʌdʒ] *vt* prejuzgar.

prejudice ['prɛdʒudɪs] *n* (*bias*) prejuicio; (*harm*) perjuicio // *vt* (*predispose*) predisponer; (*harm*) perjudicar; ~**d** *a* (*person*) predispuesto, con prejuicios; (*view*) parcial, interesado.
prelate ['prɛlət] *n* prelado.
preliminary [prɪ'lɪmɪnərɪ] *a* preliminar.
prelude ['prɛlju:d] *n* preludio.
premarital ['pri:'mærɪtl] *a* premarital.
premature ['prɛmətʃuə*] *a* prematuro.
premeditated [pri:'mɛdɪteɪtɪd] *a* premeditado.
premier ['prɛmɪə*] *a* primero, principal // *n* (*POL*) primer ministro.
première ['prɛmɪɛə*] *n* estreno.
premise ['prɛmɪs] *n* premisa; ~**s** *npl* local *m;* (*house*) casa *sg;* (*shop*) tienda *sg;* **on the** ~**s** en el local.
premium ['pri:mɪəm] *n* premio; (*COMM*) prima; **to be at a** ~ ser muy solicitado.
premonition [prɛmə'nɪʃən] *n* presentimiento.
preoccupation [pri:ɔkju'peɪʃən] *n* preocupación *f;* **preoccupied** [-'ɔkjupaɪd] *a* (*worried*) preocupado; (*absorbed*) absorto.
prep [prɛp] *n* (*SCOL: study*) deberes *mpl;* ~ **school** *n* = **preparatory school.**
prepaid [pri:'peɪd] *a* con porte pagado.
preparation [prɛpə'reɪʃən] *n* preparación *f;* ~**s** *npl* preparativos *mpl.*
preparatory [prɪ'pærətərɪ] *a* preparatorio, preliminar; ~ **to** con miras a; ~ **school** *n* escuela preparatoria.
prepare [prɪ'pɛə*] *vt* preparar, disponer // *vi:* **to** ~ **for** prepararse o disponerse para; (*make preparations*) hacer preparativos para; ~**d to** dispuesto a.
preponderance [prɪ'pɔndərns] *n* preponderancia, predominio.
preposition [prɛpə'zɪʃən] *n* preposición *f.*
preposterous [prɪ'pɔstərəs] *a* absurdo, ridículo.
prerequisite [pri:'rɛkwɪzɪt] *n* requisito (previo).
prerogative [prɪ'rɔgətɪv] *n* prerrogativa.
presbyterian [prɛzbɪ'tɪərɪən] *a, n* presbiteriano/a.
preschool ['pri:'sku:l] *a* preescolar.
prescribe [prɪ'skraɪb] *vt* prescribir; (*MED*) recetar.
prescription [prɪ'skrɪpʃən] *n* prescripción *f;* (*MED*) receta.
presence ['prɛzns] *n* presencia; (*attendance*) asistencia; ~ **of mind** *n* presencia de ánimo.
present ['prɛznt] *a* (*in attendance*) presente; (*current*) actual // *n* (*gift*) regalo; (*actuality*) actualidad *f,* presente *m* // *vt* [prɪ'zɛnt] (*introduce*) presentar; (*expound*) exponer; (*give*) presentar, dar, ofrecer; (*THEATRE*) representar; **at** ~ actualmente; ~**able** [prɪ'zɛntəbl] *a* presentable; ~**ation** [-'teɪʃən] *n* presentación *f;* (*gift*) obsequio; (*of case*) exposición *f;* (*THEATRE*) representación *f;*

~-**day** a actual; ~**ly** ad (soon) dentro de poco.
preservation [prɛzə'veɪʃən] n conservación f.
preservative [prɪ'zɔːvətɪv] n preservativo.
preserve [prɪ'zɔːv] vt (keep safe) preservar, proteger; (maintain) conservar; (food) hacer una conserva de; (in salt) salar // n (for game) coto, vedado; (often pl: jam) conserva, confitura.
preside [prɪ'zaɪd] vi presidir.
presidency ['prɛzɪdənsɪ] n presidencia; **president** [-ənt] n presidente m/f; **presidential** [-'dɛnʃl] a presidencial.
press [prɛs] n (tool, machine, newspapers) prensa; (printer's) imprenta; (crowd) apiñamiento, agolpamiento; (of hand) apretón m // vt (push) empujar; (squeeze) apretar; (clothes: iron) planchar; (harry) acosar; (insist): **to ~ sth on sb** insistir en que uno acepte algo // vi (squeeze) apretar; (pressurize) ejercer presión; **we are ~ed for time** tenemos poco tiempo; **to ~ on** vi avanzar; (hurry) apretar el paso; ~ **agency** n agencia de prensa; ~ **conference** n conferencia de prensa; ~ **cutting** n recorte m (de periódico); ~**ing** a apremiante; ~ **stud** n botón m de presión.
pressure ['prɛʃə*] n presión f; (urgency) apremio, urgencia; (influence) influencia; (MED) tensión f nerviosa; ~ **cooker** n olla a presión; ~ **gauge** n manómetro; ~ **group** n grupo de presión; **pressurized** a a presión.
prestige [prɛs'tiːʒ] n prestigio; **prestigious** [-'tɪdʒəs] a prestigioso.
presumably [prɪ'zjuːməblɪ] ad se supone que, cabe presumir que.
presume [prɪ'zjuːm] vt presumir, suponer; **to ~ to do** (dare) atreverse a; (set out to) pretender.
presumption [prɪ'zʌmpʃən] n suposición f; (pretension) pretensión f; (boldness) atrevimiento.
presuppose [priːsə'pəuz] vt presuponer.
pretence, pretense (US) [prɪ'tɛns] n (claim) pretensión f; (display) ostentación f; (pretext) pretexto; (make-believe) fingimiento; **on the ~ of** so pretexto de.
pretend [prɪ'tɛnd] vt (feign) fingir // vi (feign) fingir; (claim): **to ~ to sth** pretender a algo.
pretension [prɪ'tɛnʃən] n (presumption) presunción f; (claim) pretensión f.
pretentious [prɪ'tɛnʃəs] a presumido; (ostentacious) ostenso, aparatoso.
pretext ['priːtɛkst] n pretexto.
pretty ['prɪtɪ] a (gen) hermoso; (person) guapo; (dress) bonito; (sum) importante // ad (quite) bastante; (nearly) casi.
prevail [prɪ'veɪl] vi (win) imponerse; (be current) imperar; (be in fashion) estar de moda; (be usual) prevalecer; (persuade): **to ~ (up)on sb to do sth** persuadir a uno a hacer algo; ~**ing** a (dominant)

imperante; (usual) corriente.
prevalent ['prɛvələnt] a (dominant) predominante; (usual) corriente; (fashionable) en boga; (present-day) actual.
prevent [prɪ'vɛnt] vt: **to ~ (sb) from doing sth** impedir (a uno) hacer algo; ~**able** a evitable; ~**ative** a preventivo; ~**ion** [-'vɛnʃən] n prevención f; ~**ive** a preventivo.
preview ['priːvjuː] n (of film) preestreno; (fig) anticipo.
previous ['priːvɪəs] a previo, anterior; (hasty) prematuro; ~**ly** ad previamente, con anticipación; (in earlier times) antes.
prewar [priː'wɔː*] a de preguerra, prebélico.
prey [preɪ] n presa // vi: **to ~ on** vivir a costa de; (feed on) alimentarse de; (plunder) robar, pillar; **it was ~ing on his mind** le agobiaba, le preocupaba.
price [praɪs] n precio // vt (goods) fijar el precio de; ~**less** a inapreciable.
prick [prɪk] n pinchazo; (with pin) alfilerazo; (sting) picadura // vt pinchar; picar; **to ~ up one's ears** aguzar el oído.
prickle ['prɪkl] n (sensation) escozor m; (BOT) espina; (ZOOL) púa; **prickly** a espinoso; (fig: person) malhumorado; (: touchy) quisquilloso.
pride [praɪd] n orgullo; (pej) soberbia // vt: **to ~ o.s. on** enorgullecerse de, ufanarse de.
priest [priːst] n sacerdote m; ~**ess** n sacerdotisa; ~**hood** n (practice) sacerdocio; (priests) clero.
prig [prɪg] n presumido/a, pedante m/f.
prim [prɪm] a (formal) estirado; (affected) remilgado; (prudish) gazmoño.
primarily ['praɪmərɪlɪ] ad (above all) ante todo; (firstly) en primer lugar.
primary ['praɪmərɪ] a primario; (first in importance) principal; ~ **school** n escuela primaria.
primate ['praɪmɪt] n (REL) primado // n ['praɪmeɪt] (ZOOL) primate m.
prime [praɪm] a primero, principal; (basic) fundamental; (excellent) selecto, de primera clase // vt (gun, pump) cebar; (fig) preparar, aprestar; **in the ~ of life** en la flor de la vida; ~ **minister** n primer ministro; **primer** n (book) libro de texto; (paint) pintura de base.
primitive ['prɪmɪtɪv] a primitivo; (crude) rudimentario; (uncivilized) inculto.
primrose ['prɪmrəuz] n primavera, prímula.
primus (stove) ['praɪməs] n hornillo de campaña a presión.
prince [prɪns] n príncipe m.
princess [prɪn'sɛs] n princesa.
principal ['prɪnsɪpl] a principal, mayor // n director/a m/f.
principality [prɪnsɪ'pælɪtɪ] n principado.
principle ['prɪnsɪpl] n principio.
print [prɪnt] n (impression) marca, impresión f; (letters) letra de molde; (fabric) estampado; (ART) estampa,

grabado; (*PHOT*) positiva // *vt* (*gen*) imprimir; (*on mind*) grabar; (*write in capitals*) escribir en letras de molde; **out of** ~ agotado; ~**ed matter** *n* impresos *mpl*; ~**er** *n* impresor/a *m/f*; ~**ing** *n* (*art*) imprenta; (*act*) impresión *f*; (*quantity*) tirada; ~**ing press** *n* (prensa de) imprenta.

prior ['praɪə*] *a* anterior, previo // *n* prior *m*; ~ **to doing** antes de *o* hasta hacer.

priority [praɪ'ɔrɪtɪ] *n* prioridad *f*.

prise [praɪz] *vt*: **to** ~ **open** abrir con palanca.

prism ['prɪzəm] *n* prisma *m*.

prison ['prɪzn] *n* cárcel *f*, prisión *f* // *a* carcelario; ~**er** *n* (*in prison*) preso; (*under arrest*) detenido; (*in dock*) acusado.

privacy ['prɪvəsɪ] *n* (*seclusion*) aislamiento, soledad *f*; (*intimacy*) intimidad *f*.

private ['praɪvɪt] *a* (*personal*) particular; (*confidential*) secreto, reservado; (*intimate*) privado, íntimo; (*sitting etc*) a puertas cerradas // *n* soldado raso; '~' (*on envelope*) 'privado'; (*on door*) 'uso particular *o* privado'; **in** ~ en privado; ~ **enterprise** *n* la empresa privada; ~ **eye** *n* detective *m* privado; ~**ly** *ad* en privado; (*in o.s.*) en el fondo.

privet ['prɪvɪt] *n* alheña.

privilege ['prɪvɪlɪdʒ] *n* privilegio; (*prerogative*) prerrogativa; ~**d** *a* privilegiado.

privy ['prɪvɪ] *a*: **to be** ~ **to** estar enterado de; **P** ~ **Council** *n* Consejo Privado.

prize [praɪz] *n* premio // *a* premiado; (*first class*) de primera clase // *vt* apreciar, estimar; ~-**giving** *n* distribución *f* de premios; ~ **winner** *n* premiado/a.

pro [prəu] *n* (*SPORT*) profesional *m/f*; **the** ~**s and cons** los pros y los contras.

probability [prɔbə'bɪlɪtɪ] *n* probabilidad *f*; **probable** ['prɔbəbl] *a* probable; (*plausible*) verosímil; **probably** ['prɔbəblɪ] *ad* probablemente.

probation [prə'beɪʃən] *n*: **on** ~ (*employee*) de prueba; (*LAW*) en libertad condicional.

probe [prəub] *n* (*MED, SPACE*) sonda; (*enquiry*) encuesta, sondeo // *vt* sondar; (*investigate*) indagar.

problem ['prɔbləm] *n* problema *m*; ~**atic** [-'mætɪk] *a* problemático.

procedure [prə'si:dʒə*] *n* (*ADMIN, LAW*) procedimiento; (*method*) proceder *m*; (*bureaucratic*) trámites *mpl*.

proceed [prə'si:d] *vi* proceder; (*continue*): **to** ~ (**with**) continuar *o* seguir (con); ~**ings** *npl* acto *sg*, actos *mpl*; (*LAW*) medidas *fpl*; (*meeting*) función *f*; (*records*) actas *fpl*; ~**s** ['prəusi:dz] *npl* ganancias *fpl*, ingresos *mpl*.

process ['prəuses] *n* proceso; (*method*) método, sistema *m*; (*proceeding*) procedimiento // *vt* tratar, elaborar; **in** ~ en curso; ~**ing** *n* elaboración *f*.

procession [prə'seʃən] *n* desfile *m*; **funeral** ~ cortejo fúnebre.

proclaim [prə'kleɪm] *vt* proclamar; (*announce*) anunciar; **proclamation** [prɔklə'meɪʃən] *n* proclamación *f*; (*written*) proclama.

procreation [prəukrɪ'eɪʃən] *n* procreación *f*.

procure [prə'kjuə*] *vt* conseguir, obtener.

prod [prɔd] *vt* (*push*) empujar; (*with elbow*) dar un codazo a; (*jab*) pinchar // *n* empuje *m*; codazo; pinchazo.

prodigal ['prɔdɪgl] *a* pródigo.

prodigious [prə'dɪdʒəs] *a* prodigioso.

prodigy ['prɔdɪdʒɪ] *n* prodigio.

produce ['prɔdju:s] *n* (*AGR*) productos *mpl* agrícolas // *vt* [prə'dju:s] (*gen*) producir; (*profit*) rendir; (*show*) presentar, mostrar; (*THEATRE*) presentar, poner en escena; (*offspring*) dar a luz; **producer** *n* (*THEATRE*) director/a *m/f*; (*AGR, CINEMA*) productor/a *m/f*.

product ['prɔdʌkt] *n* (*thing*) producto; (*result*) fruto, resultado.

production [prə'dʌkʃən] *n* (*act*) producción *f*; (*thing*) producto; (*THEATRE*) representación *f*, obra; ~ **line** *n* línea *o* cadena de montaje.

productive [prə'dʌktɪv] *a* productivo; **productivity** [prɔdʌk'tɪvɪtɪ] *n* productividad *f*.

profane [prə'feɪn] *a* profano; (*language etc*) fuerte.

profess [prə'fɛs] *vt* profesar; (*regret*) manifestar.

profession [prə'fɛʃən] *n* profesión *f*; ~**al** *n* profesional *m/f*; (*expert*) perito // *a* profesional; perito, experto; (*by profession*) de oficio.

professor [prə'fɛsə*] *n* catedrático/a.

proficiency [prə'fɪʃənsɪ] *n* pericia, habilidad *f*; **proficient** [-ənt] *a* perito, hábil.

profile ['prəufaɪl] *n* perfil *m*.

profit ['prɔfɪt] *n* (*COMM*) ganancia; (*fig*) provecho // *vi*: **to** ~ **by** *or* **from** aprovechar *o* sacar provecho de; ~**ability** [-ə'bɪlɪtɪ] *n* rentabilidad *f*; ~**able** *a* (*ECON*) rentable; (*useful*) provechoso; ~**eering** [-'tɪərɪŋ] *n* (*pej*) ganancias *fpl* excesivas.

profound [prə'faund] *a* profundo.

profuse [prə'fju:s] *a* profuso, pródigo; ~**ly** *ad* profusamente, pródigamente; **profusion** [-'fju:ʒən] *n* profusión *f*, abundancia.

progeny ['prɔdʒɪnɪ] *n* progenie *f*, prole *f*.

programme, program (*US*) ['prəugræm] *n* programa *m* // *vt* programar; **programming, programing** (*US*) *n* programación *f*.

progress ['prəugrɛs] *n* progreso; (*development*) desarrollo // *vi* [prə'grɛs] progresar, avanzar; desarrollarse; **in** ~ en marcha; ~**ion** [-'grɛʃən] *n* progresión *f*; ~**ive** [-'grɛsɪv] *a* progresivo; (*person*) progresista *m/f*.

prohibit [prə'hıbıt] vt prohibir; **to ~ sb from doing sth** prohibir a uno hacer algo; **~ion** [prəuı'bıʃən] n (US) prohibicionismo; **~ive** a (price etc) excesivo.

project ['prɔdʒɛkt] n proyecto // (vb: [prə'dʒɛkt]) vt proyectar // vi (stick out) salir, sobresalir.

projectile [prə'dʒɛktaıl] n proyectil m.

projection [prə'dʒɛkʃən] n proyección f; (overhang) saliente m.

projector [prə'dʒɛktə*] n proyector m.

proletarian [prəulı'tɛərıən] a, n proletario/a; **proletariat** [-rıət] n proletariado.

proliferate [prə'lıfəreıt] vi proliferar, multiplicarse; **proliferation** [-'reıʃən] n proliferación f.

prolific [prə'lıfık] a prolífico.

prologue ['prəulɔg] n prólogo.

prolong [prə'lɔŋ] vt prolongar, extender.

prom [prɔm] n abbr of **promenade** baile m de gala.

promenade [prɔmə'nɑːd] n (by sea) paseo marítimo; **~ concert** n concierto (en que parte del público permanece de pie).

prominence ['prɔmınəns] n (fig) eminencia, importancia; **prominent** [-ənt] a (standing out) saliente; (important) eminente, importante.

promiscuous [prə'mıskjuəs] a (sexually) libertino.

promise ['prɔmıs] n promesa // vt, vi prometer; **promising** a prometedor(a).

promontory ['prɔməntrı] n promontorio.

promote [prə'məut] vt (gen) promover; (new product) hacer propaganda por; (MIL) ascender; **promoter** n (of sporting event) promotor/a m/f; **promotion** [-'məuʃən] n (gen) promoción f; (MIL) ascenso.

prompt [prɔmpt] a pronto // ad (punctually) puntualmente // vt (urge) mover, incitar; (THEATRE) apuntar; **to ~ sb to do sth** mover a uno a hacer algo; **~er** n (THEATRE) apuntador/a m/f; **~ly** ad (punctually) puntualmente; (rapidly) rápidamente; **~ness** n puntualidad f; rapidez f.

prone [prəun] a (lying) postrado; **~ to** propenso a.

prong [prɔŋ] n diente m, púa.

pronoun ['prəunaun] n pronombre m.

pronounce [prə'nauns] vt pronunciar; (declare) declarar // vi: **to ~ (up)on** pronunciarse sobre; **~d** a (marked) marcado; **~ment** n declaración f.

pronunciation [prənʌnsı'eıʃən] n pronunciación f.

proof [pruːf] n prueba; (of alcohol) graduación f normal // a: **~ against** a prueba de; **~reader** n corrector/a m/f de pruebas.

prop [prɔp] n apoyo; (fig) sostén m // vt (also: **~ up**) apoyar; (lean): **to ~ sth against** apoyar algo contra.

propaganda [prɔpə'gændə] n propaganda.

propagate ['prɔpəgeıt] vt propagar.

propel [prə'pɛl] vt impulsar, propulsar; **~ler** n hélice f; **~ling pencil** n lapicero.

proper ['prɔpə*] a (suited, right) propio; (exact) justo; (apt) apropiado, conveniente; (timely) oportuno; (seemly) correcto, decente; (authentic) verdadero; (col: real) auténtico.

property ['prɔpətı] n (gen) propiedad f; (goods) bienes mpl; (estate) hacienda; **it's their ~** es suyo, les pertenece.

prophecy ['prɔfısı] n profecía; **prophesy** [-saı] vt profetizar; (fig) predecir.

prophet ['prɔfıt] n profeta m/f; **~ic** [prə'fɛtık] a profético.

proportion [prə'pɔːʃən] n proporción f; (share) parte f, porción f; **~al a**, **~ate** a proporcional; a proporcionado.

proposal [prə'pəuzl] n propuesta; (offer) oferta; (plan) proyecto; (of marriage) declaración f; (suggestion) sugerencia.

propose [prə'pəuz] vt proponer; (offer) ofrecer // vi declararse; **to ~ to do** proponerse hacer.

proposition [prɔpə'zıʃən] n propuesta, proposición f.

proprietor [prə'praıətə*] n propietario, dueño.

propulsion [prə'pʌlʃən] n propulsión f.

pro rata [prəu'rɑːtə] ad a prorrateo.

prosaic [prəu'zeıık] a prosaico.

prose [prəuz] n prosa.

prosecute ['prɔsıkjuːt] vt (LAW) procesar; **prosecution** [-'kjuːʃən] n procesa, causa; (accusing side) parte f actora; **prosecutor** n acusador/a m/f; (also: **public prosecutor**) fiscal m.

prospect ['prɔspɛkt] n (view) vista; (chance) posibilidad f; (outlook) perspectiva; (hope) esperanza // (vb: [prə'spɛkt]) vt explorar // vi buscar; **~s** npl (for work etc) perspectivas fpl; **~ing** n prospección f; **~ive a** (possible) probable, esperado; (certain) futuro; (heir) presunto; (legislation) en perspectiva; **~or** n explorador/a m/f.

prospectus [prə'spɛktəs] n prospecto.

prosper ['prɔspə*] vi prosperar; **~ity** [-'spɛrıtı] n prosperidad f; **~ous** a próspero.

prostitute ['prɔstıtjuːt] n prostituta.

prostrate ['prɔstreıt] a postrado; (fig) abatido.

protagonist [prə'tægənıst] n protagonista m/f.

protect [prə'tɛkt] vt proteger; **~ion** n protección f; **~ive a** protector(a); **~or** n protector/a m/f.

protégé ['prəutɛʒeı] n protegido.

protein ['prəutiːn] n proteína.

protest ['prəutɛst] n protesta // (vb: [prə'tɛst]) vi protestar // vt (affirm) afirmar, declarar.

Protestant ['prɔtıstənt] a, n protestante m/f.

protocol ['prəutəkɔl] n protocolo.

prototype ['prəutətaıp] n prototipo.

protracted [prə'træktıd] a prolongado.

protrude [prɔ'truːd] *vi* salir fuera, sobresalir.

proud [praud] *a* orgulloso; (*pej*) soberbio, altanero; (*imposing*) imponente.

prove [pruːv] *vt* probar; (*verify*) comprobar; (*show*) demostrar // *vi*: **to ~ correct** resultar correcto; **to ~ o.s.** ponerse a prueba.

proverb ['prɔvɔːb] *n* refrán *m*; **~ial** [prɔ'vɔːbɪəl] *a* proverbial.

provide [prɔ'vaɪd] *vt* proporcionar, dar; **to ~ sb with sth** proveer a uno de algo; **to ~ for** *vt* (*person*) mantener a; (*emergency*) prevenir; **~d (that)** *conj* con tal que, siempre que.

providing [prɔ'vaɪdɪŋ] *conj* a condición de que, siempre que.

province ['prɔvɪns] *n* provincia; (*fig*) esfera; **provincial** [prɔ'vɪnʃəl] *a* de provincia; (*pej*) provinciano.

provision [prɔ'vɪʒən] *n* (*gen*) provisión *f*; (*supply*) suministro; (*supplying*) abastecimiento; **~s** *npl* (*food*) comestibles *mpl*; **~al** *a* provisional; (*temporary*) interino.

proviso [prɔ'vaɪzɔu] *n* condición *f*, estipulación *f*.

provocation [prɔvɔ'keɪʃən] *n* provocación *f*.

provocative [prɔ'vɔkɔtɪv] *a* provocativo; (*stimulating*) sugestivo.

provoke [prɔ'vɔuk] *vt* (*arouse*) provocar, incitar; (*cause*) causar, producir; (*anger*) irritar.

prow [prau] *n* proa.

prowess ['prauɪs] *n* (*skill*) destreza, habilidad *f*; (*courage*) valor *m*.

prowl [praul] *vi* (*also*: **~ about, ~ around**) rondar // *n*: **on the ~** de ronda; **~er** *n* rondador/a *m/f*; (*thief*) ladrón/ona *m/f*.

proximity [prɔk'sɪmɪtɪ] *n* proximidad *f*.

proxy ['prɔksɪ] *n* poder *m*; (*person*) apoderado/a; **by ~** por poder *o* poderes.

prudence ['pruːdns] *n* prudencia; **prudent** [-ɔnt] *a* prudente.

prudish ['pruːdɪʃ] *a* gazmoño.

prune [pruːn] *n* ciruela pasa // *vt* podar.

pry [praɪ] *vi*: **to ~ into** entrometerse en.

psalm [sɑːm] *n* salmo.

pseudo- [sjuːdəu] *pref* seudo...; **~nym** *n* seudónimo.

psychiatric [saɪkɪ'ætrɪk] *a* psiquiátrico; **psychiatrist** [-'kaɪɔtrɪst] *n* psiquiatra *m/f*; **psychiatry** [-'kaɪɔtrɪ] *n* psiquiatría.

psychic ['saɪkɪk] *a* (*also*: **~al**) psíquico // *n* medium *m/f*.

psychoanalyse [saɪkəu'ænəlaɪz] *vt* psicoanalizar; **psychoanalysis** [-kəuə'nælɪsɪs] *n* psicoanálisis *m inv*; **psychoanalyst** [-'ænəlɪst] *n* psicoanalista *m/f*.

psychological [saɪkə'lɔdʒɪkl] *a* psicológico.

psychologist [saɪ'kɔlɔdʒɪst] *n* psicólogo; **psychology** [-dʒɪ] *n* psicología.

psychopath ['saɪkəupæθ] *n* psicópata *m/f*.

psychosomatic ['saɪkəusə'mætɪk] *a* psicosomático.

psychotic [saɪ'kɔtɪk] *a*, *n* psicótico.

pub [pʌb] *n abbr of* **public house** pub *m*, taberna.

puberty ['pjuːbətɪ] *n* pubertad *f*.

public ['pʌblɪk] *a*, *n* público.

publican ['pʌblɪkən] *n* tabernero.

publication [pʌblɪ'keɪʃən] *n* publicación *f*.

public: ~ convenience *n* aseos *mpl* públicos; **~ house** *n* bar *m*, pub *m*.

publicity [pʌb'lɪsɪtɪ] *n* publicidad *f*.

publicly ['pʌblɪklɪ] *ad* públicamente, en público.

public: ~ opinion *n* opinión *f* pública; **~ relations** *n* relaciones *fpl* públicas; **~ school** *n* (*Brit*) escuela privada; **~-spirited** *a* de buen ciudadano.

publish ['pʌblɪʃ] *vt* publicar; **~er** *n* editor/a *m/f*; **~ing** *n* (*industry*) la industria editorial.

puce [pjuːs] *a* de color pardo rojizo.

pucker ['pʌkə*] *vt* (*pleat*) arrugar; (*brow etc*) fruncir.

pudding ['pudɪŋ] *n* pudín *m*; (*sweet*) postre *m*; **black ~** morcilla.

puddle ['pʌdl] *n* charco.

puff [pʌf] *n* soplo; (*from mouth*) bocanada; (*sound*) resoplido; (*also*: **powder ~**) borla // *vt*: **to ~ one's pipe** chupar la pipa // *vi* (*gen*) soplar; (*pant*) jadear; **to ~ out smoke** echar humo; **to ~ up** *vt* hinchar, inflar; **~ed** *a* (*col*: *out of breath*) sin aliento.

puffin ['pʌfɪn] *n* frailecillo.

puffy ['pʌfɪ] *a* hinchado.

pull [pul] *n* (*tug*): **to give sth a ~** dar un tirón a algo; (*fig*: *advantage*) ventaja; (: *influence*) influencia // *vt* tirar de; (*tug*) jalar; (*muscle*) torcerse; (*haul*) tirar, arrastrar // *vi* tirar, dar un tirón; **to ~ a face** hacer muecas; **to ~ to pieces** hacer pedazos; **to ~ one's punches** no emplear toda la fuerza; **to ~ one's weight** hacer su parte; **to ~ o.s. together** serenarse; **to ~ sb's leg** tomarle el pelo a uno; **to ~ apart** *vt* (*break*) romper (en dos); **to ~ down** *vt* (*house*) derribar; **to ~ in** *vi* (*AUT*: *at the kerb*) parar (junto a la acera); (*RAIL*) llegar (al andén); **to ~ off** *vt* (*deal etc*) cerrar, concluir con éxito; **to ~ out** *vi* irse, marcharse; (*AUT*: *from kerb*) salir // *vt* sacar, arrancar; **to ~ through** *vi* salir (de un apuro); (*MED*) recobrar la salud; **to ~ up** *vi* (*stop*) parar // *vt* (*uproot*) arrancar, desarraigar; (*stop*) parar.

pulley ['pulɪ] *n* polea.

pullover ['puləuvə*] *n* jersey *m*.

pulp [pʌlp] *n* (*of fruit*) pulpa; (*for paper*) pasta.

pulpit ['pulpɪt] *n* púlpito.

pulsate [pʌl'seɪt] *vi* pulsar, latir.

pulse [pʌls] *n* (*ANAT*) pulso; (*of music, engine*) pulsación *f*; (*BOT*) legumbre *f*.

pulverize ['pʌlvəraɪz] *vt* pulverizar; (*fig*) hacer polvo.

puma ['pju:mə] n puma.
pummel ['pʌml] vt dar de puñetazos.
pump [pʌmp] n bomba; (shoe) zapato de tenis // vt sacar con una bomba; (fig: col) sonsacar; **to ~ up** vt inflar.
pumpkin ['pʌmpkın] n calabaza.
pun [pʌn] n juego de palabras.
punch [pʌntʃ] n (blow) golpe m, puñetazo; (tool) punzón m; (for tickets) taladro; (drink) ponche m // vt (hit): **to ~ sb/sth** dar un puñetazo o golpear a uno/algo; (make a hole in) punzar; **~card** n tarjeta perforada; **~line** n palabras que rematan un chiste; **~-up** n (col) riña.
punctual ['pʌŋktjuəl] a puntual; **~ity** [-'ælıtı] n puntualidad f.
punctuate ['pʌŋktjueıt] vt interrumpir; **punctuation** [-'eıʃən] n puntuación f.
puncture ['pʌŋktʃə*] n pinchazo // vt pinchar.
pundit ['pʌndıt] n sabio.
pungent ['pʌndʒənt] a acre.
punish ['pʌnıʃ] vt castigar; **~ment** n castigo.
punt [pʌnt] n (boat) batea.
punter ['pʌntə*] n (gambler) jugador/a m/f.
puny ['pju:nı] a débil.
pup [pʌp] n cachorro.
pupil ['pju:pl] n alumno/a.
puppet ['pʌpıt] n títere m.
puppy ['pʌpı] n cachorro, perrito.
purchase ['pə:tʃıs] n compra; (grip) pie m firme // vt comprar; **purchaser** n comprador/a m/f.
pure [pjuə*] a puro.
purée ['pjuəreı] n puré m.
purge [pə:dʒ] n (MED) purgante m; (POL) purga // vt purgar.
purification [pjuərıfı'keıʃən] n purificación f, depuración f; **purify** ['pjuərıfaı] vt purificar, depurar.
purist ['pjuərıst] n purista m/f.
puritan ['pjuərıtən] n puritano/a; **~ical** [-'tænıkl] a puritano.
purity ['pjuərıtı] n pureza.
purl [pə:l] n punto del revés.
purple ['pə:pl] a purpúreo; (bruise) morado.
purport [pə:'pɔ:t] vi: **to ~ to be/do** dar a entender que es/hace.
purpose ['pə:pəs] n propósito; **on ~** a propósito, adrede; **~ful** a resuelto, determinado.
purr [pə:*] n ronroneo // vi ronronear.
purse [pə:s] n monedero; (bag) bolsa // vt fruncir.
purser ['pə:sə*] n (NAUT) contador m de navío.
pursue [pə'sju:] vt seguir, perseguir; (profession) ejercer; **pursuer** n perseguidor/a m/f.
pursuit [pə'sju:t] n (chase) caza; (persecution) persecución f; (occupation) carrera; (pastime) pasatiempo.
purveyor [pə'veıə*] n proveedor/a m/f.

pus [pʌs] n pus m.
push [puʃ] n (gen) empuje m; (shove) empujón m; (attack) ataque m; (advance) avance m // vt empujar; (button) apretar; (promote) promover; (thrust): **to ~ sth (into)** meter algo a la fuerza (en) // vi empujar; (fig) hacer esfuerzos; **to ~ aside** vt apartar con la mano; **to ~ off** vi (col) largarse; **to ~ on** vi (continue) seguir adelante; **to ~ through** vt (measure) despachar; **to ~ up** vt (total, prices) hacer subir; **~chair** n sillita de ruedas; **~ing** a emprendedor(a), enérgico; **~over** n (col): **it's a ~over** está tirado; **~y** a (pej) agresivo.
puss [pus], **pussy(-cat)** ['pusı(kæt)] n minino.
put [put], pt, pp put vt (place) poner, colocar; (~ into) meter; (say) declarar, expresar; (a question) hacer; (estimate) calcular; **to ~ about** vi (NAUT) virar // vt (rumour) diseminar; **to ~ across** vt (ideas etc) comunicar; **to ~ away** vt (store) guardar; **to ~ back** vt (replace) devolver a su lugar; (postpone) posponer; **to ~ by** vt (money) guardar; **to ~ down** vt (on ground) poner en el suelo; (animal) sacrificar; (in writing) apuntar; (suppress: revolt etc) sofocar; (attribute) atribuir; **to ~ forward** vt (ideas) presentar, proponer; (date) adelantar; **to ~ in** vt (application, complaint) presentar; **to ~ off** vt (postpone) aplazar; (discourage) desanimar; **to ~ on** vt (clothes, lipstick etc) ponerse; (light etc) encender; (play etc) presentar; (weight) ganar; (brake) echar; (attitude) adoptar postura de; **to ~ out** vt (fire, light) apagar; (one's hand) alargar; (news, rumour) sacar a luz, diseminar; (tongue etc) sacar; (person: inconvenience) molestar, fastidiar; **to ~ up** vt (raise) levantar, alzar; (hang) colgar; (build) construir; (increase) aumentar; (accommodate) alojar; **to ~ up with** vt fus aguantar.
putrid ['pju:trıd] a podrido.
putt [pʌt] vt golpear con poca fuerza // n put m, golpe m corto; **~er** n (GOLF) putter m; **~ing green** n campo de golf en miniatura.
putty ['pʌtı] n masilla.
puzzle ['pʌzl] n (riddle) acertijo; (jigsaw) rompecabezas m inv; (crossword) crucigrama m; (mystery) misterio, problema m // vt dejar perplejo, confundir // vi devanarse los sesos; **puzzling** a misterioso, enigmático.
pygmy ['pıgmı] n pigmeo.
pyjamas [pı'dʒɑ:məz] npl pijama m.
pylon ['paılən] n pilón m, poste m.
pyramid ['pırəmıd] n pirámide m.
python ['paıθən] n pitón m.

Q

quack [kwæk] n (of duck) graznido; (pej: doctor) curandero // vi graznar.
quad [kwɔd] abbr of **quadrangle; quadruplet.**
quadrangle ['kwɔdræŋgl] n (courtyard: abbr: **quad**) patio.
quadruple [kwɔ'drupl] a cuádruple // n cuádruplo // vt, vi cuadruplicar.
quadruplets [kwɔ:'dru:plɪts] npl cuatrillizos mpl.
quagmire ['kwægmaɪə*] n lodazal m, cenegal m.
quail [kweɪl] n (bird) codorniz f // vi amedrentarse.
quaint [kweɪnt] a curioso; (picturesque) pintoresco.
quake [kweɪk] vi temblar // n abbr of **earthquake.**
Quaker ['kweɪkə*] n cuáquero/a.
qualification [kwɔlɪfɪ'keɪʃən] n (reservation) reserva; (modification) modificación f; (act) calificación f; (degree) título; **qualified** ['kwɔlɪfaɪd] a (trained) cualificado; (fit) apto, competente; (limited) limitado; (professionally) con título.
qualify ['kwɔlɪfaɪ] vt calificar; (capacitate) capacitar; (modify) modificar; (limit) moderar // vi (SPORT) clasificarse; **to ~ (as)** calificarse (de), graduarse (en); **to ~ (for)** reunir los requisitos (para).
quality ['kwɔlɪtɪ] n calidad f; (moral) cualidad f.
qualm [kwɑ:m] n escrúpulo.
quandary ['kwɔndrɪ] n: **to be in a ~** estar en un dilema.
quantity ['kwɔntɪtɪ] n cantidad f.
quarantine ['kwɔrntiːn] n cuarentena.
quarrel ['kwɔrl] n (argument) riña; (fight) pelea // vi reñir; pelearse; **~some** a pendenciero.
quarry ['kwɔrɪ] n (for stone) cantera; (animal) presa.
quart [kwɔ:t] n cuarto de galón = 1.136 litros.
quarter ['kwɔ:tə*] n cuarto, cuarta parte f; (of year) trimestre m; (district) barrio // vt dividir en cuartos; (MIL: lodge) alojar; **~s** npl (barracks) cuartel m; (living **~s**) alojamiento sg; **a ~ of an hour** un cuarto de hora; **~ final** n cuarto de final; **~ly** a trimestral // ad cada 3 meses, trimestralmente; **~master** n (MIL) comisario, intendente m militar.
quartet(te) [kwɔ:'tɛt] n cuarteto.
quartz [kwɔ:ts] n cuarzo.
quash [kwɔʃ] vt (verdict) anular.
quasi- ['kweɪzaɪ] pref cuasi.
quaver ['kweɪvə*] n (MUS) corchea // vi temblar.
quay [ki:] n (also: **~side**) muelle m.
queasy ['kwi:zɪ] a (sickly) delicado.
queen [kwi:n] n (gen) reina; (CARDS etc) dama; **~ mother** n reina madre.
queer [kwɪə*] a (odd) raro, extraño; (suspect) sospechoso // n (col) maricón m.
quell [kwɛl] vt calmar; (put down) sofocar.
quench [kwɛntʃ] vt apagar.
query ['kwɪərɪ] n (question) pregunta; (doubt) duda; (fig) interrogante f // vt preguntar; poner en duda.
quest [kwɛst] n busca, búsqueda.
question ['kwɛstʃən] n pregunta; (matter) asunto, cuestión f // vt (gen) preguntar; (doubt) dudar de; (interrogate) interrogar, hacer preguntas a; **beyond ~** fuera de toda duda; **out of the ~** imposible, ni hablar; **~able** a discutible; (doubtful) dudoso; **~ mark** n punto de interrogación; **~naire** [-'nɛə*] n cuestionario.
queue [kju:] n cola // vi hacer cola.
quibble ['kwɪbl] vi sutilizar.
quick [kwɪk] a rápido; (temper) vivo; (agile) ágil; (mind) listo; (eye) agudo; (ear) fino; **be ~!** ¡date prisa!; **~en** vt apresurar // vi apresurarse, darse prisa; **~ly** ad rápidamente, de prisa; **~ness** n rapidez f; agilidad f; (liveliness) viveza; **~sand** n arenas fpl movedizas; **~step** n (dance) fox-trot m, quickstep m; **~-witted** a perspicaz.
quid [kwɪd] n, pl inv (Brit: col) libra.
quiet [kwaɪət] a tranquilo; (silent) callado; (ceremony) discreto // n silencio, tranquilidad f; **keep ~!** ¡cállate!, ¡silencio!; **~en** (also: **~en down**) vi (grow calm) calmarse; (grow silent) callarse // vt calmar; hacer callar; **~ly** ad (gen) tranquilamente; (silently) silenciosamente; **~ness** n (silence) silencio; (calm) tranquilidad f.
quilt [kwɪlt] n edredón m; (continental) **~** n edredón m.
quin [kwɪn] abbr of **quintuplet.**
quinine [kwɪ'niːn] n quinina.
quintet(te) [kwɪn'tɛt] n quinteto.
quintuplets [kwɪn'tju:plɪts] npl quintillizos mpl.
quip [kwɪp] n pulla.
quirk [kwɔ:k] n peculiaridad f.
quit [kwɪt], pt, pp **quit** or **quitted** vt dejar, abandonar; (premises) desocupar // vi (give up) retirarse; (go away) irse; (resign) dimitir; (stop work) abandonar (una empresa).
quite [kwaɪt] ad (rather) bastante; (entirely) completamente; **~ a few of them** un buen número de ellos; **~ (so)!** ¡así es!, ¡exactamente!
quits [kwɪts] a: **~ (with)** en paz (con).
quiver ['kwɪvə*] vi estremecerse // n (for arrows) carcaj m.
quiz [kwɪz] n (game) concurso; (questioning) interrogatorio // vt interrogar; **~zical** a burlón(ona).
quoits [kwɔɪts] npl juego de aros.
quorum ['kwɔ:rəm] n quórum m.
quota ['kwəutə] n cuota.
quotation [kwəu'teɪʃən] n cita; (estimate)

presupuesto; ~ **marks** *npl* comillas *fpl.*
quote [kwəut] *n* cita // *vt* (*sentence*) citar;
(*price*) fijar // *vi*: **to** ~ **from** citar de.
quotient ['kwəuʃənt] *n* cociente *m.*

R

rabbi ['ræbaɪ] *n* rabino.
rabbit ['ræbɪt] *n* conejo; ~ **hole** *n* hura
(de conejos); ~ **hutch** *n* conejera.
rabble ['ræbl] *n* (*pej*) chusma, populacho.
rabies ['reɪbiːz] *n* rabia.
RAC *n abbr of* **Royal Automobile Club.**
raccoon [rə'kuːn] *n* mapache *m.*
race [reɪs] *n* (*gen*) carrera; (*species*) raza,
estirpe *f* // *vt* (*horse*) presentar (en
carrera); (*engine*) acelerar // *vi* (*compete*)
competir; (*run*) correr; (*pulse*) latir a
ritmo acelerado; ~ **course** *n* hipódromo;
~ **horse** *n* caballo de carreras; ~ **track** *n*
hipódromo; (*for cars*) autódromo.
racial ['reɪʃl] *a* racial; ~ **ism** *n* racismo;
~ **ist** *a, n* racista *m/f.*
racing ['reɪsɪŋ] *n* carreras *fpl*; ~ **car** *n*
coche *m* de carreras; ~ **driver** *n*
corredor/a *m/f* de coches.
racist ['reɪsɪst] *a, n* (*pej*) racista *m/f.*
rack [ræk] *n* (*also*: **luggage** ~) rejilla;
(*shelf*) estante *m*; (*also*: **roof** ~) baca,
portaequipajes *m inv*; (*clothes* ~) percha
// *vt* (*cause pain to*) atormentar.
racket ['rækɪt] *n* (*for tennis*) raqueta;
(*noise*) ruido, estrépito; (*swindle*) estafa,
timo.
racoon [rə'kuːn] *n* = **raccoon.**
racquet ['rækɪt] *n* raqueta.
racy ['reɪsɪ] *a* picante, salado.
radar ['reɪdɑ:*] *n* radar *m.*
radiance ['reɪdɪəns] *n* brillantez *f,*
resplandor *m*; **radiant** [-ənt] *a* brillante,
resplandeciente.
radiate ['reɪdɪeɪt] *vt* (*heat*) radiar,
irradiar // *vi* (*lines*) extenderse.
radiation [reɪdɪ'eɪʃən] *n* radiación *f.*
radiator ['reɪdɪeɪtə*] *n* radiador *m*; ~
cap *n* tapón *m* de radiador.
radical ['rædɪkl] *a* radical.
radio ['reɪdɪəu] *n* radio *f*; **on the** ~ por
radio; ~ **station** *n* emisora.
radio... [reɪdɪəu] *pref*: ~ **active** *a*
radioactivo; ~ **activity** *n* radioactividad *f*;
~ **-controlled** *a* teledirigido; ~ **graphy**
[-'ɔgrəfɪ] *n* radiografía; ~ **logy** [-'ɔlədʒɪ] *n*
radiología; ~ **telephone** *n* radioteléfono;
~ **therapy** *n* radioterapia.
radish ['rædɪʃ] *n* rábano.
radius ['reɪdɪəs], *pl* **radii** [-ɪaɪ] *n* radio.
raffia ['ræfɪə] *n* rafia.
raffle ['ræfl] *n* rifa, sorteo // *vt* rifar.
raft [rɑ:ft] *n* (*also*: **life** ~) balsa.
rafter ['rɑ:ftə*] *n* viga.
rag [ræg] *n* (*piece of cloth*) trapo; (*torn
cloth*) harapo; (*pej*: *newspaper*)
periodicucho; (*for charity*) actividades
estudiantiles benéficas // *vt* tomar el pelo
a; ~ **s** *npl* harapos *mpl*; ~ **-and-bone man**

n trapero; ~ **doll** *n* muñeca de trapo.
rage [reɪdʒ] *n* (*fury*) rabia, furor *m*;
(*fashion*) boga // *vi* (*person*) rabiar, estar
furioso; (*storm*) bramar.
ragged ['rægɪd] *a* (*edge*) desigual,
mellado; (*cuff*) roto; (*appearance*)
andrajoso, harapiento; (*coastline*)
accidentado.
raid [reɪd] *n* (*MIL*) incursión *f*; (*criminal*)
asalto; (*attack*) ataque *m*; (*by police*)
redada // *vt* invadir, atacar; asaltar; ~ **er**
n invasor/a *m/f*; (*criminal*) asaltante *m/f.*
rail [reɪl] *n* (*on stair*) barandilla,
pasamanos *m inv*; (*on bridge, balcony*)
pretil *m*; (*of ship*) borda; (*for train*) riel *m*,
carril *m*; ~ **s** *npl* vía *sg*; **by** ~ por
ferrocarril; ~ **ing(s)** *n(pl)* verja *sg,*
enrejado *sg*; ~ **road** (*US*), ~ **way** *n*
ferrocarril *m*, vía férrea; ~ **wayman** *n*
ferroviario; ~ **way station** *n* estación *f* de
ferrocarril.
rain [reɪn] *n* lluvia // *vi* llover; **in the** ~
bajo la lluvia; **it's** ~ **ing** llueve, está
lloviendo; ~ **bow** *n* arco iris; ~ **coat** *n*
impermeable *m*; ~ **drop** *n* gota de lluvia;
~ **fall** *n* lluvia; ~ **y** *a* lluvioso.
raise [reɪz] *n* aumento // *vt* (*lift*) levantar;
(*build*) erigir, edificar; (*increase*)
aumentar; (*doubts*) suscitar; (*a question*)
plantear; (*cattle, family*) criar; (*crop*)
cultivar; (*army*) reclutar; (*funds*) reunir;
(*loan*) obtener; **to** ~ **one's voice** alzar la
voz.
raisin ['reɪzn] *n* paso de Corinto.
rake [reɪk] *n* (*tool*) rastrillo; (*person*)
libertino // *vt* (*garden*) rastrillar; (*fire*)
hurgar; (*with machine gun*) barrer.
rakish ['reɪkɪʃ] *a* (*suave*) gallardo; **at a** ~
angle echado al lado.
rally ['rælɪ] *n* (*POL etc*) reunión *f*, mitin *m*;
(*AUT*) rallye *m*; (*TENNIS*) peloteo // *vt*
reunir; (*encourage*) reanimar // *vi*
reunirse; (*sick person, Stock Exchange*)
recuperarse; **to** ~ **round** *vt fus* (*fig*) dar
apoyo a.
ram [ræm] *n* carnero; (*TECH*) pisón *m* // *vt*
(*crash into*) dar contra, chocar con; (*tread
down*) apisonar.
ramble ['ræmbl] *n* caminata, excursión *f*
en el campo // *vi* (*pej*: *also*: ~ **on**)
divagar; **rambler** *n* excursionista *m/f*;
(*BOT*) trepadora; **rambling** *a* (*speech*)
divagador(a); (*BOT*) trepador(a) // *n* excursionismo.
ramp [ræmp] *n* rampa.
rampage [ræm'peɪdʒ] *n*: **to be on the** ~
desbocarse // *vi*: **they went rampaging
through the town** corrieron como locos
por la ciudad.
rampant ['ræmpənt] *a* (*disease etc*)
violento.
rampart ['ræmpɑ:t] *n* terraplén *m*; (*wall*)
muralla.
ramshackle ['ræmʃækl] *a* destartalado.
ran [ræn] *pt of* **run.**
ranch [rɑ:ntʃ] *n* hacienda, estancia; ~ **er** *n*
ganadero.

rancid ['rænsɪd] a rancio.
rancour, rancor (US) ['ræŋkə*] n rencor m.
random ['rændəm] a fortuito, sin orden // n: **at** ~ al azar.
randy ['rændɪ] a (col) cachondo.
rang [ræŋ] pt of **ring**.
range [reɪndʒ] n (of mountains) cadena, cordillera; (of missile) alcance m; (of voice) extensión f; (series) serie f; (of products) surtido; (MIL: also: **shooting** ~) campo de tiro; (also: **kitchen** ~) fogón m // vt (place) colocar; (arrange) arreglar // vi: **to** ~ **over** (wander) recorrer; (extend) extenderse por; **to** ~ **from ... to...** oscilar entre ... y...; **ranger** n guardabosques m inv.
rank [ræŋk] n (row) fila; (MIL) rango; (status) categoría; (also: **taxi** ~) parada // vi: **to** ~ **among** figurar entre // a (stinking) fétido, rancio; **the** ~ **and file** (fig) la base.
rankle ['ræŋkl] vi (insult) doler.
ransack ['rænsæk] vt (search) registrar; (plunder) saquear.
ransom ['rænsəm] n rescate m; **to hold sb to** ~ (fig) poner a uno entre la espada y la pared.
rant [rænt] vi divagar, desvariar; ~**ing** n lenguaje m declamatorio.
rap [ræp] n golpecito, golpe m seco // vt tocar, dar un golpecito en.
rape [reɪp] n violación f // vt violar.
rapid ['ræpɪd] a rápido; ~**s** npl (GEO) rápidos mpl; ~**ity** [rə'pɪdɪtɪ] n rapidez f.
rapist ['reɪpɪst] n violador m.
rapport [ræ'pɔ:*] n armonía, relación f amistosa.
rapture ['ræptʃə*] n éxtasis m, rapto; **rapturous** a extático; (applause) entusiasta.
rare [rɛə*] a raro, poco común; (CULIN: steak) poco hecho.
rarely ['rɛəlɪ] ad rara vez.
rarity ['rɛərɪtɪ] n rareza.
rascal ['rɑːskl] n pillo, pícaro.
rash [ræʃ] a imprudente, precipitado // n (MED) salpullido, erupción f (cutánea).
rasher ['ræʃə*] n lonja.
rasp [rɑːsp] n (tool) escofina.
raspberry ['rɑːzbərɪ] n frambuesa; ~ **bush** n frambueso.
rasping ['rɑːspɪŋ] a: **a** ~ **noise** un ruido áspero.
rat [ræt] n rata.
ratchet ['rætʃɪt] n (TECH) trinquete m.
rate [reɪt] n (ratio) razón f; (percentage) tanto por ciento; (price) precio; (: of hotel) tarifa; (of interest) tipo; (speed) velocidad f // vt (value) tasar; (estimate) estimar; **to** ~ **as** ser considerado como; ~**s** npl (Brit) impuesto sg municipal; (fees) tarifa sg; ~**able value** n valor m impuesto; ~**payer** n contribuyente m/f.
rather ['rɑːðə*] ad antes, más bien; (in speech) mejor dicho; **it's** ~ **expensive** es algo caro; (too much) es demasiado caro;

there's ~ **a lot** hay bastante; **I would** or **I'd** ~ **go** preferiría ir.
ratify ['rætɪfaɪ] vt ratificar.
rating ['reɪtɪŋ] n (valuation) tasación f; (value) valor m; (standing) posición f; (NAUT: category) clase f; (: sailor) marinero.
ratio ['reɪʃɪəu] n razón f; **in the** ~ **of 100 to 1** a razón de 100 a 1.
ration ['ræʃən] n ración f; ~**s** npl víveres mpl // vt racionar.
rational ['ræʃənl] a racional; (solution, reasoning) lógico, razonable; (person) cuerdo, sensato; **rationale** [-'nɑːl] n razón f fundamental; ~**ize** vt organizar lógicamente, racionalizar; ~**ly** ad racionalmente; (logically) lógicamente.
rationing ['ræʃnɪŋ] n racionamiento.
rattle ['rætl] n golpeteo; (of train etc) traqueteo; (of hail) tamborileo; (object: of baby) sonaja, sonajero; (: of sports fan) matraca; (of snake) cascabel m // vi sonar, golpear; traquetear; tamborilear; (small objects) castañetear // vt agitar, sacudir; ~**snake** n serpiente f de cascabel.
raucous ['rɔːkəs] a estridente, ronco.
ravage ['rævɪdʒ] vt hacer estragos, destrozar; ~**s** npl estragos mpl.
rave [reɪv] vi (in anger) encolerizarse; (with enthusiasm) entusiasmarse; (MED) delirar, desvariar.
raven ['reɪvən] n cuervo.
ravenous ['rævənəs] a hambriento, famélico.
ravine [rə'viːn] n barranco.
raving ['reɪvɪŋ] a: ~ **lunatic** loco de atar.
ravioli [rævɪ'əulɪ] n raviolis mpl.
ravish ['rævɪʃ] vt encantar; ~**ing** a encantador(a).
raw [rɔː] a (uncooked) crudo; (not processed) bruto; (sore) vivo; (inexperienced) novato, inexperto; ~ **material** n materia prima.
ray [reɪ] n rayo; ~ **of hope** (rayo de) esperanza.
rayon ['reɪɔn] n rayón m.
raze [reɪz] vt arrasar.
razor ['reɪzə*] n (open) navaja; (safety ~) máquina de afeitar; ~ **blade** n hoja de afeitar.
Rd abbr of **road**.
re [riː] prep con referencia a.
reach [riːtʃ] n alcance m; (BOXING) envergadura; (of river etc) extensión f entre dos recodos // vt alcanzar, llegar a; (achieve) lograr; (stretch out) alargar, extender // vi alcanzar, extenderse; **within** ~ (object) al alcance (de la mano); **out of** ~ fuera del alcance; **to** ~ **out for sth** alargar o tender la mano para tomar algo.
react [riː'ækt] vi reaccionar; ~**ion** [-'ækʃən] n reacción f; ~**ionary** [-'ækʃənrɪ] a, n reaccionario/a.
reactor [riː'æktə*] n reactor m.
read [riːd], pt, pp **read** [rɛd] vi leer // vt

leer; (*understand*) entender; (*study*) estudiar; **to ~ out** *vt* leer en alta voz; **~able** *a* (*writing*) legible; (*book*) que merece leerse; **~er** *n* lector/a *m/f*; (*book*) libro de lecturas; (*at university*) profesor/a *m/f*; **~ership** *n* (*of paper etc*) número de lectores.

readily ['rɛdɪlɪ] *ad* (*willingly*) de buena gana; (*easily*) fácilmente; (*quickly*) en seguida.

readiness ['rɛdɪnɪs] *n* buena voluntad; (*preparedness*) preparación *f*; **in ~** (*prepared*) listo, preparado.

reading ['riːdɪŋ] *n* lectura; (*understanding*) comprensión *f*; (*on instrument*) indicación *f*.

readjust [riːə'dʒʌst] *vt* reajustar // *vi* (*person*): **to ~ to** reorientarse a.

ready ['rɛdɪ] *a* listo, preparado; (*willing*) dispuesto; (*available*) disponible // *ad*: **~-cooked** listo para comer // *n*: **at the ~** (*MIL*) listo para tirar; **~-made** *a* confeccionado; **~ reckoner** *n* libro de cálculos hechos.

reaffirm [riːə'fɜːm] *vt* reafirmar.

real [rɪəl] *a* verdadero, auténtico; **in ~ terms** en términos reales; **~ estate** *n* bienes *mpl* raíces; **~ism** *n* (*also ART*) realismo; **~ist** *n* realista *m/f*; **~istic** [-'lɪstɪk] *a* realista.

reality [riː'ælɪtɪ] *n* realidad *f*; **in ~** en realidad.

realization [rɪəlaɪ'zeɪʃən] *n* comprensión *f*; (*COMM*) realización *f*.

realize ['rɪəlaɪz] *vt* (*understand*) darse cuenta de; (*a project, COMM: asset*) realizar.

really ['rɪəlɪ] *ad* verdaderamente, realmente; **~?** ¿de veras?

realm [rɛlm] *n* reino; (*fig*) esfera.

reap [riːp] *vt* segar; (*fig*) cosechar, recoger; **~er** *n* segadora.

reappear [riːə'pɪə*] *vi* reaparecer; **~ance** *n* reaparición *f*.

reapply [riːə'plaɪ] *vi*: **to ~ for** aplicar de nuevo.

rear [rɪə*] *a* trasero // *n* parte *f* trasera // *vt* (*cattle, family*) criar // *vi* (*also*: **~ up**) (*animal*) encabritarse; **~-engined** *a* (*AUT*) con motor trasero; **~guard** *n* retaguardia.

rearm [riː'ɑːm] *vt, vi* rearmar; **~ament** *n* rearme *m*.

rearrange [riːə'reɪndʒ] *vt* ordenar *o* arreglar de nuevo.

rear-view ['rɪəvjuː] *a*: **~ mirror** (*AUT*) espejo retrovisor.

reason ['riːzn] *n* (*gen*) razón *f*; (*cause*) motivo, causa; (*sense*) sensatez *f* // *vi*: **to ~ with sb** alegar razones para convencer a uno; **it stands to ~ that** es lógico que; **~able** *a* razonable; (*sensible*) sensato; **~ably** *ad* razonablemente; **~ed** *a* (*argument*) razonado; **~ing** *n* razonamiento, argumentos *mpl*.

reassemble [riːə'sɛmbl] *vt* (*machine*) montar de nuevo // *vi* reunirse de nuevo.

reassure [riːə'ʃuə*] *vt* tranquilizar,

alentar; **to ~ sb of** tranquilizar a uno diciendo que; **reassuring** *a* alentador(a).

rebate ['riːbeɪt] *n* (*on product*) rebaja; (*on tax etc*) descuento.

rebel ['rɛbl] *n* rebelde *m/f* // *vi* [rɪ'bɛl] rebelarse, sublevarse; **~lion** *n* rebelión *f*, sublevación *f*; **~lious** *a* rebelde; (*child*) revoltoso.

rebirth [riː'bɜːθ] *n* renacimiento.

rebound [rɪ'baund] *vi* (*ball*) rebotar // *n* ['riːbaund] rebote *m*.

rebuff [rɪ'bʌf] *n* desaire *m*, rechazo // *vt* rechazar.

rebuild [riː'bɪld] (*irg: like* **build**) *vt* reconstruir.

rebuke [rɪ'bjuːk] *n* reprimenda // *vt* reprender.

recalcitrant [rɪ'kælsɪtrənt] *a* reacio.

recall [rɪ'kɔːl] *vt* (*remember*) recordar; (*ambassador etc*) retirar // *n* aviso, llamada.

recant [rɪ'kænt] *vi* retractarse.

recap ['riːkæp] *vt, vi* recapitular.

recapture [riː'kæptʃə*] *vt* (*town*) reconquistar; (*atmosphere*) hacer revivir.

recede [rɪ'siːd] *vi* retroceder; **receding** *a* (*forehead, chin*) huidizo.

receipt [rɪ'siːt] *n* (*document*) recibo; (*act of receiving*) recepción *f*; **~s** *npl* (*COMM*) ingresos *mpl*.

receive [rɪ'siːv] *vt* recibir; (*guest*) acoger; (*wound*) sufrir; **receiver** *n* (*TEL*) auricular *m*; (*of stolen goods*) receptador/a *m/f*; (*COMM*) recibidor/a *m/f*.

recent ['riːsnt] *a* reciente; **~ly** *ad* recién, recientemente.

receptacle [rɪ'sɛptɪkl] *n* receptáculo.

reception [rɪ'sɛpʃən] *n* (*gen*) recepción *f*; (*welcome*) acogida; **~ desk** *n* recepción *f*; **~ist** *n* recepcionista *m/f*.

receptive [rɪ'sɛptɪv] *a* receptivo.

recess [rɪ'sɛs] *n* (*in room*) hueco; (*for bed*) nicho; (*secret place*) escondrijo; (*POL etc*) holiday) vacaciones *fpl*; **~ion** *n* recesión *f*.

recharge [riː'tʃɑːdʒ] *vt* (*battery*) recargar.

recipe ['rɛsɪpɪ] *n* receta.

recipient [rɪ'sɪpɪənt] *n* recibidor/a *m/f*; (*of letter*) destinatario/a.

reciprocal [rɪ'sɪprəkl] *a* recíproco.

recital [rɪ'saɪtl] *n* recital *m*.

recite [rɪ'saɪt] *vt* (*poem*) recitar; (*complaints etc*) enumerar.

reckless ['rɛkləs] *a* temerario, imprudente; (*speed*) excesivo, peligroso; **~ly** *ad* imprudentemente; de modo peligroso.

reckon ['rɛkən] *vt* (*count*) contar; (*consider*) considerar; (*think*): **I ~ that...** me parece que...; **~ing** *n* (*calculation*) cálculo; **the day of ~ing** el día del juicio (final).

reclaim [rɪ'kleɪm] *vt* (*land*) recuperar; (: *from sea*) rescatar; (*demand back*) reclamar; **reclamation** [rɛklə'meɪʃən] *n* recuperación *f*; rescate *m*.

recline [rɪ'klaɪn] *vi* reclinarse; (*lean*) apoyarse; **reclining** *a* (*seat*) reclinable.

recluse [rɪˈkluːs] n recluso.
recognition [rɛkəgˈnɪʃən] n reconocimiento; **transformed beyond** ~ tan transformado que resulta irreconocible.
recognizable [ˈrɛkəgnaɪzəbl] a: ~ **(by)** reconocible (por).
recognize [ˈrɛkəgnaɪz] vt reconocer, conocer; **to** ~ **by/as** reconocer de/por.
recoil [rɪˈkɔɪl] vi (gun) retroceder; (person): **to** ~ **from doing sth** sentir repugnancia por hacer algo.
recollect [rɛkəˈlɛkt] vt recordar, acordarse de; ~**ion** [-ˈlɛkʃən] n recuerdo.
recommend [rɛkəˈmɛnd] vt recomendar; ~**ation** [-ˈdeɪʃən] n recomendación f.
recompense [ˈrɛkəmpɛns] vt recompensar // n recompensa.
reconcile [ˈrɛkənsaɪl] vt (two people) reconciliar; (two facts) conciliar; **to** ~ **o.s. to sth** resignarse a algo, conformarse a algo; **reconciliation** [-sɪlɪˈeɪʃən] n reconciliación f.
reconnaissance [rɪˈkɒnɪsns] n (MIL) reconocimiento.
reconnoitre, reconnoiter (US) [rɛkəˈnɔɪtə*] vt, vi (MIL) reconocer.
reconsider [riːkənˈsɪdə*] vt repensar.
reconstitute [riːˈkɒnstɪtjuːt] vt reconstituir.
reconstruct [riːkənˈstrʌkt] vt reconstruir; ~**ion** [-kʃən] n reconstrucción f.
record [ˈrɛkɔːd] n (MUS) disco; (of meeting etc) relación f; (register) registro, partida; (file) archivo; (also: **police** ~) antecedentes mpl; (written) expediente m; (SPORT) récord m // vt [rɪˈkɔːd] (set down) registrar; (relate) hacer constar; (MUS: song etc) grabar; **in** ~ **time** en un tiempo récord; **off the** ~ a no oficial // ad confidencialmente; ~ **card** n (in file) ficha; ~**er** n (MUS) flauta de pico; (TECH) contador m; ~ **holder** n (SPORT) recordman m; ~**ing** n (MUS) grabación f; ~ **player** n tocadiscos m inv.
recount [rɪˈkaunt] vt contar.
re-count [ˈriːkaunt] n (POL: of votes) segundo escrutinio // vt [riːˈkaunt] volver a contar.
recoup [rɪˈkuːp] vt: **to** ~ **one's losses** recuperar las pérdidas.
recourse [rɪˈkɔːs] n recurso; **to have** ~ **to** recurrir a.
recover [rɪˈkʌvə*] vt recobrar, recuperar; (rescue) rescatar // vi (from illness) reponerse; (from shock) sobreponerse; ~**y** n recuperación f; rescate m; (MED) mejora.
recreate [riːkrɪˈeɪt] vt recrear.
recreation [rɛkrɪˈeɪʃən] n recreación f; (play) recreo; ~**al** a de recreo.
recrimination [rɪkrɪmɪˈneɪʃən] n recriminación f.
recruit [rɪˈkruːt] n recluta m/f // vt reclutar; ~**ment** n reclutamiento.
rectangle [ˈrɛktæŋgl] n rectángulo; **rectangular** [-ˈtæŋgjulə*] a rectangular.
rectify [ˈrɛktɪfaɪ] vt rectificar.

rector [ˈrɛktə*] n (REL) párroco; (SCOL) rector/a m/f; ~**y** n casa del párroco.
recuperate [rɪˈkuːpəreɪt] vi reponerse, restablecerse.
recur [rɪˈkəː*] vi repetirse; (opportunity) producirse de nuevo; ~**rence** n repetición f; ~**rent** a repetido.
red [rɛd] n rojo // a rojo; **to be in the** ~ deber dinero; **R**~ **Cross** n Cruz f Roja; ~**currant** n grosella; ~**den** vt enrojecer // vi enrojecerse; ~**dish** a (hair) rojizo.
redecorate [riːˈdɛkəreɪt] vt decorar de nuevo; **redecoration** [-ˈreɪʃən] n renovación f.
redeem [rɪˈdiːm] vt (gen) redimir; (sth in pawn) desempeñar; (fig, also REL) rescatar; ~**ing** a: ~**ing feature** rasgo bueno o favorable.
redeploy [riːdɪˈplɔɪ] vt (resources) disponer de nuevo.
red: ~-**haired** a pelirrojo; ~-**handed** a: **to be caught** ~-**handed** cogerse con las manos en la masa; ~-**head** n pelirrojo/a; ~-**hot** a candente.
redirect [riːdaɪˈrɛkt] vt (mail) reexpedir.
redness [ˈrɛdnɪs] n lo rojo; (of hair) rojez f.
redo [riːˈduː] (irg: like do) vt rehacer.
redouble [riːˈdʌbl] vt: **to** ~ **one's efforts** intensificar los esfuerzos.
redress [rɪˈdrɛs] n reparación f // vt reajustar.
red tape n (fig) trámites mpl, papeleo.
reduce [rɪˈdjuːs] vt reducir; (lower) rebajar; '~ **speed now'** (AUT) 'reduzca la velocidad'; **at a** ~**d price** (of goods) (a precio) rebajado; **reduction** [rɪˈdʌkʃən] n reducción f; (of price) rebaja; (discount) descuento.
redundancy [rɪˈdʌndənsɪ] n desempleo.
redundant [rɪˈdʌndnt] a (worker) parado, sin trabajo; (detail, object) superfluo; **to be made** ~ quedarse sin trabajo.
reed [riːd] n (BOT) junco, caña; (MUS: of clarinet etc) lengüeta.
reef [riːf] n (at sea) arrecife m.
reek [riːk] vi: **to** ~ **(of)** oler o heder a.
reel [riːl] n (gen) carrete m, bobina; (of film) rollo, película // vt (TECH) devanar; (also: ~ **in**) cobrar // vi (sway) tambalear.
re-election [riːɪˈlɛkʃən] n reelección f.
re-enter [riːˈɛntə*] vt reingresar en; **re-entry** n reingreso.
ref [rɛf] n (col) abbr of **referee.**
refectory [rɪˈfɛktərɪ] n refectorio, comedor m.
refer [rɪˈfəː*] vt (send) remitir; (ascribe) referir a, relacionar con // vi: **to** ~ **to** (allude to) referirse a, aludir a; (apply to) relacionarse con; (consult) remitirse a.
referee [rɛfəˈriː] n árbitro; (for job application) persona que recomienda a otro // vt arbitrar.
reference [ˈrɛfrəns] n (mention) referencia; (sending) remisión f; (relevance) relación f; (for job application: letter) referencia, carta de

recomendación; **with** ~ **to** con referencia a; (*COMM: in letter*) me remito a; ~ **book** *n* libro de consulta.
referendum [rɛfə'rɛndəm], *pl* -**da** [-də] *n* referéndum *m*.
refill [ri:'fɪl] *vt* rellenar // *n* ['ri:fɪl] repuesto, recambio.
refine [rɪ'faɪn] *vt* (*sugar, oil*) refinar; ~**d** *a* (*person, taste*) refinado, culto; ~**ment** *n* (*of person*) cultura, educación *f*; ~**ry** *n* refinería.
reflect [rɪ'flɛkt] *vt* (*light, image*) reflejar // *vi* (*think*) reflexionar, pensar; **it** ~**s badly/well on him** le perjudica/le hace honor; ~**ion** [-'flɛkʃən] *n* (*act*) reflexión *f*; (*image*) reflejo; (*criticism*) reproche *m*, crítica; **on** ~**ion** pensándolo bien; ~**or** *n* (*also AUT*) captafaros *m inv*, reflector *m*.
reflex ['ri:flɛks] *a, n* reflejo; ~**ive** [rɪ'flɛksɪv] *a* (*LING*) reflexivo.
reform [rɪ'fɔ:m] *n* reforma // *vt* reformar; **the R** ~**ation** [rɛfə'meɪʃən] *n* la Reforma; ~**er** *n* reformador/a *m/f*; ~**ist** *n* reformista *m/f*.
refrain [rɪ'freɪn] *vi*: **to** ~ **from doing** abstenerse de hacer // *n* estribillo.
refresh [rɪ'frɛʃ] *vt* refrescar; ~**er course** *n* curso de repaso; ~**ments** *npl* (*drinks*) refrescos *mpl*.
refrigeration [rɪfrɪdʒə'reɪʃən] *n* refrigeración *f*; **refrigerator** [-'frɪdʒəreɪtə*] *n* refrigeradora, nevera.
refuel [ri:'fjuəl] *vi* repostar combustible.
refuge ['rɛfju:dʒ] *n* refugio, asilo; **to take** ~ **in** refugiarse en.
refugee [rɛfju'dʒi:] *n* refugiado/a.
refund ['ri:fʌnd] *n* reembolso // *vt* [rɪ'fʌnd] devolver, reembolsar.
refurbish [ri:'fɔ:bɪʃ] *vt* restaurar, renovar.
refusal [rɪ'fju:zəl] *n* negativa; **first** ~ primera opción.
refuse ['rɛfju:s] *n* basura // (*vb*: [rɪ'fju:z]) *vt* (*reject*) rehusar; (*say no to*) negarse a // *vi* negarse; (*horse*) rehusar; ~ **bin** *n* cubo de la basura; ~ **tip** *n* vertedero.
refute [rɪ'fju:t] *vt* refutar, rebatir.
regain [rɪ'geɪn] *vt* recobrar, recuperar.
regal ['ri:gl] *a* regio, real.
regalia [rɪ'geɪlɪə] *n, npl* insignias *fpl* reales.
regard [rɪ'gɑ:d] *n* (*gaze*) mirada; (*aspect*) respecto; (*attention*) atención *f*; (*esteem*) respeto, consideración *f* // *vt* (*consider*) considerar; (*look at*) mirar; '**with kindest** ~**s**' con muchos recuerdos; ~**ing, as** ~**s, with** ~ **to** con respecto a, en cuanto a; ~**less** *ad* a pesar de todo.
regatta [rɪ'gætə] *n* regata.
regent ['ri:dʒənt] *n* regente *m/f*.
régime [reɪ'ʒi:m] *n* régimen *m*.
regiment ['rɛdʒɪmənt] *n* regimiento // *vt* reglamentar; ~**al** [-'mɛntl] *a* militar; ~**ation** [-'teɪʃən] *n* regimentación *f*.
region ['ri:dʒən] *n* región *f*; **in the** ~ **of** (*fig*) alrededor de; ~**al** a regional.
register ['rɛdʒɪstə*] *n* (*gen*) registro; (*list*) lista // *vt* registrar; (*birth*) declarar; (*letter*) certificar; (*subj: instrument*)

marcar, indicar // *vi* (*at hotel*) registrarse; (*sign on*) inscribirse; (*make impression*) producir impresión; ~**ed** *a* (*design*) registrado; (*letter*) certificado.
registrar ['rɛdʒɪstrɑ:*] *n* secretario (del registro civil).
registration [rɛdʒɪs'treɪʃən] *n* (*act*) inscripción *f*; (*AUT: also:* ~ **number**) matrícula.
registry ['rɛdʒɪstrɪ] *n* registro, archivo; ~ **office** *n* registro civil; **to get married in a** ~ **office** casarse por lo civil.
regret [rɪ'grɛt] *n* sentimiento, pesar *m*; (*remorse*) remordimiento // *vt* sentir, lamentar; (*repent of*) arrepentirse de; ~**fully** *ad* con pesar, sentidamente; ~**table** *a* lamentable; (*loss*) sensible.
regroup [ri:'gru:p] *vt* reagrupar // *vi* reagruparse.
regular ['rɛgjulə*] *a* (*gen*) regular; (*usual*) corriente, normal; (*soldier*) de línea; (*intensive*) verdadero // *n* (*client etc*) cliente *m/f* habitual; ~**ity** [-'lærɪtɪ] *n* regularidad *f*; ~**ly** *ad* con regularidad.
regulate ['rɛgjuleɪt] *vt* regular; (*TECH*) arreglar, ajustar; **regulation** [-'leɪʃən] *n* (*rule*) regla, reglamento; (*adjustment*) ajuste *m*.
rehabilitation ['ri:həbɪlɪ'teɪʃən] *n* rehabilitación *f*.
rehearsal [rɪ'hə:səl] *n* ensayo; **rehearse** *vt* ensayar.
reign [reɪn] *n* reinado; (*fig*) dominio // *vi* reinar; (*fig*) imperar; ~**ing** *a* (*monarch*) reinante, actual; (*predominant*) imperante.
reimburse [ri:ɪm'bə:s] *vt* reembolsar; ~**ment** *n* reembolso.
rein [reɪn] *n* (*for horse*) rienda; **to give** ~ **to** dar rienda suelta a.
reincarnation [ri:ɪnkɑ:'neɪʃən] *n* reencarnación *f*.
reindeer ['reɪndɪə*] *n, pl inv* reno.
reinforce [ri:ɪn'fɔ:s] *vt* reforzar; ~**d** *a* (*concrete*) armado; ~**ment** *n* (*action*) reforzamiento; ~**ments** *npl* (*MIL*) refuerzos *mpl*.
reinstate [ri:ɪn'steɪt] *vt* (*worker*) reintegrar a su puesto.
reiterate [ri:'ɪtəreɪt] *vt* reiterar, repetir.
reject ['ri:dʒɛkt] *n* (*COMM*) artículo defectuoso // *vt* [rɪ'dʒɛkt] rechazar; (*plan*) desechar; (*solution*) descartar; ~**ion** [rɪ'dʒɛkʃən] *n* rechazo.
rejoice [rɪ'dʒɔɪs] *vi*: **to** ~ **at** *or* **over** regocijarse *o* alegrarse de.
rejuvenate [rɪ'dʒu:vəneɪt] *vt* rejuvenecer.
rekindle [ri:'kɪndl] *vt* reencender; (*fig*) despertar.
relapse [rɪ'læps] *n* (*MED*) recaída; (*into crime*) reincidencia.
relate [rɪ'leɪt] *vt* (*tell*) contar, relatar; (*connect*) relacionar // *vi* relacionarse; ~**d** *a* afín, conexo; (*person*) emparentado; ~**d to** con referencia a, relacionado con; **relating to** *prep* acerca de.
relation [rɪ'leɪʃən] *n* (*person*) pariente *m/f*; (*link*) relación *f*; ~**ship** *n* relación *f*;

(*personal ties*) relaciones *fpl*; (*also*: **family ~ship**) parentesco.
relative ['rɛlətɪv] *n* pariente *m/f*, familiar *m/f* // *a* relativo.
relax [rɪ'læks] *vi* descansar; (*person: unwind*) relajarse // *vt* relajar; (*mind, person*) descansar; **~ation** [ri:læk'seɪʃən] *n* (*rest*) descanso; (*ease*) relajación *f*, relax *m*; (*amusement*) recreo; (*entertainment*) diversión *f*; **~ed** *a* relajado; (*tranquil*) tranquilo; **~ing** *a* enervante.
relay ['ri:leɪ] *n* (*race*) carrera de relevos // *vt* (*message*) retransmitir.
release [rɪ'li:s] *n* (*from prison, obligation*) liberación *f*, libertad *f*; (*of shot*) disparo; (*of gas etc*) escape *m*; (*of film etc*) estreno // *vt* (*prisoner*) poner en libertad; (*book, film*) estrenar; (*report, news*) publicar; (*gas etc*) despedir, arrojar; (*free: from wreckage etc*) soltar; (*TECH*. catch, spring *etc*) desenganchar; (*let go*) soltar, aflojar.
relegate ['rɛləgeɪt] *vt* relegar; (*SPORT*): **to be ~d** descender.
relent [rɪ'lɛnt] *vi* ablandarse, ceder; **~less** a implacable.
relevance ['rɛləvəns] *n* relación *f*; **relevant** [-ənt] *a* relacionado; (*fact*) pertinente; (*apt*) oportuno.
reliable [rɪ'laɪəbl] *a* (*person, firm*) de confianza, de fiar; (*method, machine*) seguro; (*news*) fidedigno; **reliably** ad: **to be reliably informed that...** saber de fuente fidedigna que... .
reliance [rɪ'laɪəns] *n*: **~ (on)** dependencia (de).
relic ['rɛlɪk] *n* (*REL*) reliquia; (*of the past*) vestigio.
relief [rɪ'li:f] *n* (*from pain, anxiety*) alivio, desahogo; (*help, supplies*) socorro, ayuda; (*ART, GEO*) relieve *m*.
relieve [rɪ'li:v] *vt* (*pain, patient*) aliviar; (*bring help to*) ayudar, socorrer; (*burden*) aligerar; (*take over from: gen*) sustituir a; (: *guard*) relevar; **to ~ sb of sth** quitar algo a uno; **to ~ o.s.** hacer sus necesidades.
religion [rɪ'lɪdʒən] *n* religión *f*; **religious** a religioso.
relinquish [rɪ'lɪŋkwɪʃ] *vt* abandonar; (*plan, habit*) renunciar a.
relish ['rɛlɪʃ] *n* (*CULIN*) salsa, condimento; (*enjoyment*) entusiasmo; (*flavour*) sabor *m*, gusto // *vt* (*food etc*) saborear; **to ~ doing** gustar de hacer.
reload [ri:'ləʊd] *vt* recargar.
reluctance [rɪ'lʌktəns] *n* renuencia; **reluctant** [-ənt] *a* renuente; **reluctantly** [-əntlɪ] ad con renuencia.
rely [rɪ'laɪ]: **to ~ on** *vt fus* confiar en, fiarse de; (*be dependent on*) depender de.
remain [rɪ'meɪn] *vi* (*survive*) quedar; (*be left*) sobrar; (*continue*) quedar(se), permanecer; **~der** *n* resto; **~ing** *a* sobrante; **~s** *npl* restos *mpl*; (*leftovers*) desperdicios *mpl*.
remand [rɪ'mɑːnd] *n*: **on ~** detenido (en espera del juicio) // *vt*: **to ~ in custody**

reencarcelar, mantener bajo custodia; **~ home** *n* reformatorio.
remark [rɪ'mɑːk] *n* comentario // *vt* comentar; (*notice*) observar, notar; **~able** *a* notable; (*outstanding*) extraordinario.
remarry [ri:'mærɪ] *vi* casarse por segunda vez.
remedial [rɪ'miːdɪəl] *a* (*tuition, classes*) de niños atrasados.
remedy ['rɛmədɪ] *n* remedio // *vt* remediar, curar.
remember [rɪ'mɛmbə*] *vt* recordar, acordarse de; (*bear in mind*) tener presente; **remembrance** *n* (*memory*) memoria; (*souvenir*) recuerdo.
remind [rɪ'maɪnd] *vt*: **to ~ sb to do sth** recordar a uno que haga algo; **to ~ sb of sth** recordar algo a uno; **she ~s me of her mother** me recuerda a su madre; **~er** *n* advertencia; (*souvenir*) recuerdo.
reminisce [rɛmɪ'nɪs] *vi* recordar viejas historias; **reminiscent** *a*: **to be reminiscent of sth** recordar algo
remiss [rɪ'mɪs] *a* descuidado; **it was ~ of him** fue un descuido suyo.
remission [rɪ'mɪʃən] *n* remisión *f*; (*of debt, sentence*) perdón *m*.
remit [rɪ'mɪt] *vt* (*send: money*) remitir, enviar; **~tance** *n* remesa, envío.
remnant ['rɛmnənt] *n* resto; (*of cloth*) retazo.
remorse [rɪ'mɔːs] *n* remordimientos *mpl*; **~ful** *a* arrepentido; **~less** *a* (*fig*) implacable, despiadado.
remote [rɪ'məʊt] *a* (*distant*) lejano; (*person*) distante; **~ control** *n* telecontrol *m*; **~ly** *ad* remotamente; (*slightly*) levemente; **~ness** *n* alejamiento; distancia.
remould ['ri:məʊld] *vt* (*tyre*) recauchutar.
removable [rɪ'muːvəbl] *a* (*detachable*) amovible, separable.
removal [rɪ'muːvəl] *n* (*taking away*) el quitar; (*from house*) mudanza; (*from office: sacking*) destitución *f*; (*MED*) extirpación *f*; **~ van** *n* camión *m* de mudanzas.
remove [rɪ'muːv] *vt* quitar; (*employee*) destituir; (*name: from list*) tachar, borrar; (*doubt, abuse*) disipar; (*TECH*) retirar, separar; (*MED*) extirpar; **removers** *npl* (*company*) agencia de mudanzas.
remuneration [rɪmjuːnə'reɪʃən] *n* remuneración *f*.
rend [rɛnd], *pt*, *pp* **rent** *vt* rasgar, desgarrar.
render ['rɛndə*] *vt* (*give*) dar, prestar; (*hand over*) entregar; (*reproduce*) reproducir; (*make*) hacer, volver; (*return*) devolver; **~ing** *n* (*MUS etc*) interpretación *f*.
rendez-vous ['rɔndɪvuː] *n* cita.
renegade ['rɛnɪgeɪd] *n* renegado.
renew [rɪ'njuː] *vt* renovar; (*resume*) reanudar; (*loan etc*) prorrogar; (*negotiations*) volver a; (*acquaintance*) entablar de

nuevo; ~al n renovación f; reanudación f; prórroga.
renounce [rɪ'naʊns] vt renunciar a; (disown) renunciar.
renovate ['rɛnəveɪt] vt renovar; **renovation** [-'veɪʃən] n renovación f.
renown [rɪ'naʊn] n renombre m; ~**ed** a renombrado.
rent [rɛnt] pt, pp of rend // n alquiler m, arriendo // vt alquilar; ~**al** n (for television, car) alquiler m.
renunciation [rɪnʌnsɪ'eɪʃən] n renuncia.
reorganize [riː'ɔːgənaɪz] vt reorganizar.
rep [rɛp] n abbr of **representative; repertory**.
repair [rɪ'pɛə*] n reparación f, compostura; (patch) remiendo // vt reparar, componer; (shoes) remendar; **in good/bad** ~ en buen/mal estado; ~ **kit** n caja de herramientas para reparaciones.
repartee [rɛpɑː'tiː] n dimes y diretes.
repay [riː'peɪ] (irg: like **pay**) vt (money) devolver, reembolsar; (person) pagar; (debt) liquidar; (sb's efforts) devolver, corresponder a; ~**ment** n reembolso, devolución f; (of debt) pago.
repeal [rɪ'piːl] n (of law) abrogación f; (of sentence) anulación f // vt abrogar, revocar.
repeat [rɪ'piːt] n (RADIO, TV) retransmisión f // vt repetir // vi repetirse; ~**edly** ad repetidas veces.
repel [rɪ'pɛl] vt (lit, fig) repugnar; ~**lent** a repugnante // n: **insect** ~**lent** crema/loción f anti-insectos.
repent [rɪ'pɛnt] vi: **to** ~ **(of)** arrepentirse (de); ~**ance** n arrepentimiento.
repercussion [riːpə'kʌʃən] n (consequence) repercusión f; **to have** ~**s** repercutir.
repertoire ['rɛpətwɑː*] n repertorio.
repertory ['rɛpətərɪ] n (also: ~ **theatre**) teatro de repertorio.
repetition [rɛpɪ'tɪʃən] n repetición f.
repetitive [rɪ'pɛtɪtɪv] a (movement, work) reiterativo; (speech) lleno de repeticiones.
replace [rɪ'pleɪs] vt (put back) devolver a su sitio; (take the place of) reemplazar, sustituir; ~**ment** n (gen) reemplazo; (act) reposición f; (person) suplente m/f.
replenish [rɪ'plɛnɪʃ] vt (glass) rellenar; (stock etc) reponer; (with fuel) repostar.
replete [rɪ'pliːt] a repleto; (well-fed) lleno.
replica ['rɛplɪkə] n copia, reproducción f.
reply [rɪ'plaɪ] n respuesta, contestación f // vi contestar, responder.
report [rɪ'pɔːt] n informe m; (PRESS etc) reportaje m; (also: **school** ~) nota; (of gun) estallido // vt informar sobre; (PRESS etc) hacer un reportaje sobre; (bring to notice: occurrence) dar cuenta de // vi (make a report) presentar un informe; (present o.s.): **to** ~ **(to sb)** presentarse (ante uno); ~**er** n periodista m.f.
reprehensible [rɛprɪ'hɛnsɪbl] a reprensible, censurable.

represent [rɛprɪ'zɛnt] vt representar; (fig) hablar en nombre de; (COMM) ser agente de; ~**ation** [-'teɪʃən] n representación f; (petition) petición f; ~**ations** npl (protest) quejas fpl; ~**ative** n representante m/f // a representativo.
repress [rɪ'prɛs] vt reprimir; ~**ion** [-'prɛʃən] n represión f; ~**ive** a represivo.
reprieve [rɪ'priːv] n (LAW) indulto; (fig) alivio // vt indultar, suspender la pena de.
reprimand ['rɛprɪmɑːnd] n reprimenda // vt reprender.
reprint ['riːprɪnt] n reimpresión f // vt [riː'prɪnt] reimprimir.
reprisal [rɪ'praɪzl] n represalia.
reproach [rɪ'prəʊtʃ] n reproche m // vt: **to** ~ **sb with sth** reprochar algo a uno; **beyond** ~ intachable; ~**ful** a lleno de reproches.
reproduce [riːprə'djuːs] vt reproducir // vi reproducirse; **reproduction** [-'dʌkʃən] n reproducción f; **reproductive** [-'dʌktɪv] a reproductor(a).
reprove [rɪ'pruːv] vt: **to** ~ **sb for sth** reprender algo a uno.
reptile ['rɛptaɪl] n reptil m.
republic [rɪ'pʌblɪk] n república; ~**an** a, n republicano/a.
repudiate [rɪ'pjuːdɪeɪt] vt (accusation) rechazar; (friend) repudiar; (obligation) desconocer.
repugnant [rɪ'pʌgnənt] a repugnante.
repulse [rɪ'pʌls] vt rechazar, repulsar; **repulsive** a repulsivo.
reputable ['rɛpjutəbl] a (make etc) de toda confianza; (person) formal.
reputation [rɛpju'teɪʃən] n reputación f.
repute [rɪ'pjuːt] n reputación f, fama; ~**d** a supuesto; ~**dly** ad según dicen o se dice.
request [rɪ'kwɛst] n petición f; (formal) solicitud f // vt: **to** ~ **sth of** or **from sb** pedir algo a uno; (formally) solicitar algo a uno.
requiem ['rɛkwɪəm] n réquiem m.
require [rɪ'kwaɪə*] vt (need: subj: person) necesitar, tener necesidad de; (: thing, situation) exigir; (want) pedir; (order) insistir en que; ~**ment** n requisito; (need) necesidad f.
requisite ['rɛkwɪzɪt] n requisito // a preciso, imprescindible; **toilet** ~**s** artículos mpl de aseo personal.
requisition [rɛkwɪ'zɪʃən] n: ~ **(for)** solicitud f (de) // vt (MIL) requisar.
reroute [riː'ruːt] vt (train etc) desviar.
resale ['riː'seɪl] n reventa.
rescue ['rɛskjuː] n rescate m // vt rescatar; **to** ~ **from** librar de; ~ **party** n expedición f de salvamento; **rescuer** n salvador/a m/f.
research [rɪ'sɔːtʃ] n investigaciones fpl // vt investigar; ~**er** n investigador/a m/f; ~ **work** n investigación f.
resell [riː'sɛl] vt revender.
resemblance [rɪ'zɛmbləns] n parecido; **to**

bear a ~ to parecerse a; **resemble** vt parecerse a.
resent [rɪ'zɛnt] vt resentirse de; ~**ful** a resentido; ~**ment** n resentimiento.
reservation [rɛzə'veɪʃən] n (gen) reserva; (on road: also: **central** ~) faja intermedia.
reserve [rɪ'zəːv] n reserva; (SPORT) suplente m/f; (game ~) coto // vt (seats etc) reservar; ~**s** npl (MIL) reserva sg; **in** ~ de reserva; ~**d** a reservado.
reservoir ['rɛzəvwɑː*] n (large) embalse m; (small) depósito.
reshape [riː'ʃeɪp] vt (policy) reformar, rehacer.
reshuffle [riː'ʃʌfl] n: **Cabinet** ~ (POL) reconstrucción f del gabinete.
reside [rɪ'zaɪd] vi residir, vivir.
residence ['rɛzɪdəns] n residencia; (formal: home) domicilio; (length of stay) permanencia; **resident** [-ənt] n vecino; (in hotel) huésped/a m/f // a (population) permanente; (doctor) interno; **residential** [-'dɛnʃəl] a residencial.
residue ['rɛzɪdjuː] n resto, residuo; (COMM) saldo.
resign [rɪ'zaɪn] vt (one's post) renunciar a // vi dimitir; **to** ~ **o.s. to** (endure) resignarse a; ~**ation** [rɛzɪg'neɪʃən] n renuncia; (state of mind) resignación f; ~**ed** a resignado.
resilience [rɪ'zɪlɪəns] n (of material) elasticidad f; (of person) resistencia; **resilient** [-ənt] a (person) resistente.
resin ['rɛzɪn] n resina.
resist [rɪ'zɪst] vt resistir, oponerse a; ~**ance** n resistencia.
resolute ['rɛzəluːt] a resuelto.
resolution [rɛzə'luːʃən] n (gen) resolución f; (purpose) propósito.
resolve [rɪ'zɔlv] n resolución f; (purpose) propósito // vt resolver // vi resolverse; **to** ~ **to do** resolver hacer; ~**d** a resuelto.
resonant ['rɛzənənt] a resonante.
resort [rɪ'zɔːt] n (town) centro de turismo; (recourse) recurso // vi: **to** ~ **to** recurrir a; **in the last** ~ en último caso.
resound [rɪ'zaund] vi resonar, retumbar; **the room** ~**ed with shouts** los gritos resonaron en el cuarto; ~**ing** a sonoro; (fig) clamoroso.
resource [rɪ'sɔːs] n recurso; ~**s** npl recursos mpl; ~**ful** a inventivo, ingenioso.
respect [rɪs'pɛkt] n (consideration) respeto; (relation) respecto; ~**s** npl recuerdos mpl, saludos mpl // vt respetar; **with** ~ **to** con respecto a; **in this** ~ en cuanto a eso; ~**ability** [-ə'bɪlɪtɪ] n respetabilidad f; ~**able** a respetable; (large) apreciable; (passable) tolerable; ~**ful** a respetuoso.
respective [rɪs'pɛktɪv] a respectivo; ~**ly** ad respectivamente.
respiration [rɛspɪ'reɪʃən] n respiración f.
respiratory [rɛs'pɪrətərɪ] a respiratorio.
respite ['rɛspaɪt] n respiro; (LAW) prórroga.

resplendent [rɪs'plɛndənt] a resplandeciente.
respond [rɪs'pɔnd] vi responder; (react) reaccionar; **response** [-'pɔns] n respuesta; reacción f.
responsibility [rɪspɔnsɪ'bɪlɪtɪ] n responsabilidad f.
responsible [rɪs'pɔnsɪbl] a (liable): ~ (for) responsable (de); (character) serio, formal; (job) de confianza.
responsive [rɪs'pɔnsɪv] a sensible.
rest [rɛst] n descanso, reposo; (MUS) pausa, silencio; (support) apoyo; (remainder) resto // vi descansar; (be supported): **to** ~ **on** posar(se) en // vt (lean): **to** ~ **sth on/against** apoyar algo en o sobre/contra.
restart [riː'stɑːt] vt (engine) volver a arrancar; (work) volver a empezar.
restaurant ['rɛstərɔŋ] n restorán m, restaurante m; ~ **car** n coche-comedor m.
restful ['rɛstful] a descansado, reposado.
rest home n residencia para jubilados.
restitution [rɛstɪ'tjuːʃən] n: **to make** ~ **to sb for sth** indemnizar a uno por algo.
restive ['rɛstɪv] a inquieto; (horse) rebelón(ona).
restless ['rɛstlɪs] a inquieto; ~**ly** ad inquietamente.
restoration [rɛstə'reɪʃən] n restauración f; **restore** [rɪ'stɔː*] vt (building) restaurar; (sth stolen) devolver; (health) restablecer.
restrain [rɪs'treɪn] vt (feeling) contener, refrenar; (person): **to** ~ (**from doing**) disuadir (de hacer); ~**ed** a (style) moderado; ~**t** n (restriction) freno, control m; (moderation) moderación f; (of style) reserva.
restrict [rɪs'trɪkt] vt restringir, limitar; ~**ion** [-kʃən] n restricción f, limitación f; ~**ive** a restrictivo.
rest room n (US) aseos mpl.
result [rɪ'zʌlt] n resultado // vi: **to** ~ **in** terminar en, dar por resultado; **as a** ~ **of** a consecuencia de.
resume [rɪ'zjuːm] vt, vi (work, journey) reanudar.
résumé ['reɪzjuːmeɪ] n resumen m.
resumption [rɪ'zʌmpʃən] n reanudación f.
resurgence [rɪ'səːdʒəns] n resurgimiento.
resurrection [rɛzə'rɛkʃən] n resurrección f.
resuscitate [rɪ'sʌsɪteɪt] vt (MED) resucitar; **resuscitation** [-'teɪʃn] n resucitación f.
retail ['riːteɪl] n venta al por menor // cpd al por menor // vt vender al por menor o al detalle; ~**er** n detallista m/f.
retain [rɪ'teɪn] vt (keep) retener, conservar; (employ) contratar; ~**er** n (servant) criado; (fee) anticipo.
retaliate [rɪ'tælɪeɪt] vi: **to** ~ (**against**) tomar represalias (contra); **retaliation** [-'eɪʃn] n represalias fpl.
retarded [rɪ'tɑːdɪd] a retrasado.
retch [rɛtʃ] vi dar arcadas.

retentive [rı'tɛntıv] a (*memory*) retentivo.
reticent ['rɛtısnt] a reservado.
retina ['rɛtınə] n retina.
retinue ['rɛtınjuː] n séquito, comitiva.
retire [rı'taıə*] vi (*give up work*) jubilarse; (*withdraw*) retirarse; (*go to bed*) (ir a) acostarse; ~**d** a (*person*) jubilado; ~**ment** n (*state*) retiro; (*act*) jubilación f; **retiring** a (*leaving*) saliente; (*shy*) retraído.
retort [rı'tɔːt] n (*reply*) réplica // vi contestar.
retrace [riː'treıs] vt: **to ~ one's steps** volver sobre sus pasos, desandar lo andado.
retract [rı'trækt] vt (*statement*) retirar; (*claws*) retraer; (*undercarriage, aerial*) replegar // vi retractarse; ~**able** a replegable.
retrain [riː'treın] vt reeducar; ~**ing** n readaptación f profesional.
retreat [rı'triːt] n (*place*) retiro; (*act*) retraimiento; (*MIL*) retirada // vi retirarse; (*flood*) bajar.
retribution [rɛtrı'bjuːʃən] n desquite m.
retrieve [rı'triːv] vt (*gen*) recobrar; (*situation, honour*) salvar; (*error, loss*) recuperar; **retriever** n perro cobrador, perdiguero.
retrospect ['rɛtrəspɛkt] n: **in ~** retrospectivamente, mirando hacia atrás; ~**ive** [-'spɛktıv] a (*law*) retroactivo.
return [rı'tɔːn] n (*going or coming back*) vuelta, regreso; (*of sth stolen etc*) devolución f; (*recompense*) recompensa; (*FINANCE: from land, shares*) ganancia, ingresos mpl; (*report*) informe m // cpd (*journey*) de regreso; (*ticket*) de ida y vuelta; (*match*) de vuelta // vi (*person etc: come or go back*) volver, regresar; (*symptoms etc*) reaparecer // vt devolver; (*favour, love etc*) corresponder a; (*verdict*) declarar; (*POL: candidate*) elegir; ~**s** npl (*COMM*) ingresos mpl; **in ~** en cambio; **many happy ~s (of the day)!** ¡muchas felicidades!, ¡feliz cumpleaños!
reunion [riː'juːnıən] n reunión f.
reunite [riːjuː'naıt] vt reunir; (*reconcile*) reconciliar.
rev [rɛv] n abbr of **revolution** (*AUT*) // (*vb: also:* ~ **up**) vt girar (el motor de) // vi acelerarse.
reveal [rı'viːl] vt (*make known*) revelar; ~**ing** a revelador(a).
reveille [rı'vælı] n (*MIL*) diana.
revel ['rɛvl] vi: **to ~ in sth/in doing sth** deleitarse en algo/en hacer algo.
revelation [rɛvə'leıʃən] n revelación f.
reveller ['rɛvlə*] n jaranero, juergista m/f; **revelry** [-rı] n jarana, juerga.
revenge [rı'vɛndʒ] n venganza; (*in sport*) revancha; **to take ~ on** vengarse de.
revenue ['rɛvənjuː] n ingresos mpl, renta; (*on investment*) rédito; (*profit*) ganancia.
reverberate [rı'vɔːbəreıt] vi (*sound*) resonar, retumbar; **reverberation** [-'reıʃən] n retumbo, eco.
revere [rı'vıə*] vt reverenciar, venerar;

reverence ['rɛvərəns] n reverencia; **reverent** ['rɛvərənt] a reverente.
reverie ['rɛvərı] n ensueño.
reversal [rı'vɔːsl] n (*of order*) inversión f; (*of direction*) cambio completo; (*of decision*) revocación f.
reverse [rı'vɔːs] n (*opposite*) contrario; (*back: of cloth*) revés m; (: *of coin*) reverso, (: *of paper*) dorso; (*AUT: also:* ~ **gear**) marcha atrás, contramarcha // a (*order*) inverso; (*direction*) contrario // vt (*turn over*) volver al revés; (*invert*) invertir; (*change: opinion*) cambiar (completamente) de // vi (*AUT*) poner en marcha atrás.
revert [rı'vɔːt] vi: **to ~ to** volver a.
review [rı'vjuː] n (*magazine, MIL*) revista; (*of book, film*) reseña; (*examination*) repaso, examen m // vt repasar, examinar; (*MIL*) pasar revista a; (*book, film*) reseñar; ~**er** n crítico/a.
revile [rı'vaıl] vt injuriar, vilipendiar.
revise [rı'vaız] vt (*manuscript*) corregir; (*opinion*) modificar; (*study: subject*) repasar; (*look over*) revisar; **revision** [rı'vıʒən] n corrección f; modificación f; repaso; revisión f.
revitalize [riː'vaıtəlaız] vt revivificar.
revival [rı'vaıvəl] n (*recovery*) restablecimiento; (*of interest*) renacimiento; (*THEATRE*) reestreno; (*of faith*) despertar m.
revive [rı'vaıv] vt (*gen*) resucitar; (*custom*) restablecer; (*hope, courage*) reanimar; (*play*) reestrenar // vi (*person*) volver en sí, restablecerse; (*from faint*) revivir; (*activity*) recobrarse.
revoke [rı'vəuk] vt revocar.
revolt [rı'vəult] n rebelión f, sublevación f // vi rebelarse, sublevarse // vt dar asco a, repugnar; ~**ing** a asqueroso, repugnante.
revolution [rɛvə'luːʃən] n revolución f; ~**ary** a, n revolucionario/a; ~**ize** vt revolucionar.
revolve [rı'vɔlv] vi dar vueltas, girar.
revolver [rı'vɔlvə*] n revólver m.
revolving [rı'vɔlvıŋ] a (*chair etc*) giratorio; ~ **door** n puerta giratoria.
revue [rı'vjuː] n (*THEATRE*) revista.
revulsion [rı'vʌlʃən] n asco, repugnancia.
reward [rı'wɔːd] n premio, recompensa // vt: **to ~ (for)** recompensar o premiar (por); ~**ing** a (*fig*) provechoso, valioso.
rewire [riː'waıə*] vt (*house*) renovar el alambrado de.
reword [riː'wɔːd] vt expresar en otras palabras.
rewrite [riː'raıt] (*irg: like* **write**) vt volver a escribir o redactar.
rhapsody ['ræpsədı] n (*MUS*) rapsodia; (*fig*) transporte m (de admiración).
rhetoric ['rɛtərık] n retórica; ~**al** [rı'tɔrıkl] a retórico.
rheumatic [ruː'mætık] a reumático; **rheumatism** ['ruːmətızəm] n reumatismo, reúma.

Rhine [raɪn] *n*: the ~ el (río) Rin.
rhinoceros [raɪ'nɔsərəs] *n* rinoceronte *m*.
rhododendron [rəudə'dɛndrn] *n* rododendro.
Rhone [rəun] *n*: the ~ el (río) Ródano.
rhubarb ['ru:bɑ:b] *n* ruibarbo.
rhyme [raɪm] *n* rima; (*verse*) poesía.
rhythm ['rɪðm] *n* ritmo; ~ **method** método de Ojino; ~**ic(al)** *a* rítmico.
rib [rɪb] *n* (ANAT) costilla // *vt* (*mock*) tomar el pelo a.
ribald ['rɪbəld] *a* escabroso.
ribbon ['rɪbən] *n* cinta; **in** ~**s** (*torn*) hecho trizas.
rice [raɪs] *n* arroz *m*; ~**field** *n* arrozal *m*; ~ **pudding** *n* arroz *m* con leche.
rich [rɪtʃ] *a* rico; (*banquet*) suntuoso; (*soil*) fértil; (*food*) fuerte; (: *sweet*) empalagoso; **the** ~ los ricos; ~**es** *npl* riqueza *sg*; ~**ness** *n* riqueza; suntuosidad *f*; fertilidad *f*.
rickets ['rɪkɪts] *n* raquitismo.
rickety ['rɪkɪtɪ] *a* desvencijado; (*shaky*) tambaleante.
rickshaw ['rɪkʃɔ:] *n* rikisha.
ricochet ['rɪkəʃeɪ] *n* rebote *m* // *vi* rebotar.
rid [rɪd], *pt, pp* **rid** *vt*: **to** ~ **sb of sth** librar a uno de algo; **to get** ~ **of** deshacerse o desembarazarse de.
ridden ['rɪdn] *pp of* **ride**.
riddle ['rɪdl] *n* (*conundrum*) acertijo; (*mystery*) enigma *m*, misterio; (*sieve*) criba // *vt*: **to be** ~**d with** ser lleno o plagado de.
ride [raɪd] *n* (*gen*) paseo; (*on horse*) cabalgata; (*distance covered*) viaje *m*, recorrido // (*vb*: *pt* **rode**, *pp* **ridden**) *vi* (*as sport*) montar; (*go somewhere*: *on horse*, *bicycle*) dar un paseo, pasearse; (*journey*: *on bicycle, motor cycle, bus*) viajar // *vt* (*a horse*) montar a; (*distance*) viajar; **to** ~ **a bicycle** ir en bicicleta; **to** ~ **at anchor** (NAUT) estar al ancla; **to take sb for a** ~ (*fig*) engañar a uno; **rider** *n* (*on horse*) jinete *m*; (*on bicycle*) ciclista *m/f*; (*on motorcycle*) motociclista *m/f*.
ridge [rɪdʒ] *n* (*of hill*) cresta; (*of roof*) caballete *m*; (*wrinkle*) arruga.
ridicule ['rɪdɪkju:l] *n* irrisión *f*, mofa // *vt* poner en ridículo, mofarse de; **ridiculous** [-'dɪkjuləs] *a* ridículo.
riding ['raɪdɪŋ] *n* montar *m* a caballo; ~ **school** *n* escuela de equitación.
rife [raɪf] *a*: **to be** ~ ser muy común; **to be** ~ **with** abundar en.
riffraff ['rɪfræf] *n* gentuza.
rifle ['raɪfl] *n* rifle *m*, fusil *m* // *vt* saquear; ~ **range** *n* campo de tiro; (*at fair*) tiro al blanco.
rift [rɪft] *n* (*fig*: *disagreement*: *between friends*) desavenencia; (: *in party*) escisión *f*.
rig [rɪg] *n* (*also*: **oil** ~) torre *f* de perforación // *vt* (*election etc*) falsificar los resultados de; **to** ~ **out** *vt* ataviar de;

to ~ **up** *vt* armar; ~**ging** *n* (NAUT) aparejo.
right [raɪt] *a* (*true, correct*) correcto, exacto; (*suitable*) indicado, debido; (*proper*) apropiado, propio; (*just*) justo; (*morally good*) bueno; (*not left*) derecho // *n* (*titie, claim*) derecho; (*not left*) derecha // *ad* (*correctly*) bien, correctamente; (*straight*) derecho, directamente; (*not on the left*) a la derecha; (*to the* ~) hacia la derecha // *vt* enderezar // *excl* ¡bueno!, ¡está bien!; **to be** ~ (*person*) tener razón; **all** ~! ¡está bien!; (*enough*) ¡basta!; ~ **now** ahora mismo; ~ **in the middle** justo en medio, en pleno centro; ~ **away** en seguida; **by** ~**s** en justicia; **on the** ~ a la derecha; ~ **angle** *n* ángulo recto; ~**eous** ['raɪtʃəs] *a* justado, honrado; (*anger*) justificado; ~**eousness** ['raɪtʃəsnɪs] *n* justicia; ~**ful** *a* (*heir*) legítimo; ~**-hand** *a* por la derecha; ~**-handed** *a* (*person*) que usa la mano derecha; ~**ly** *ad* correctamente, debidamente; (*with reason*) con razón; ~**-wing** *a* (POL) derechista.
rigid ['rɪdʒɪd] *a* rígido; (*principle*) inflexible; ~**ity** [rɪ'dʒɪdɪtɪ] *n* rigidez *f*, inflexibilidad *f*.
rigmarole ['rɪgmərəul] *n* galimatías *m*.
rigorous ['rɪgərəs] *a* riguroso.
rigour, rigor (US) ['rɪgə*] *n* rigor *m*, severidad *f*.
rig-out ['rɪgaut] *n* (*col*) atuendo.
rile [raɪl] *vt* irritar.
rim [rɪm] *n* borde *m*; (*of spectacles*) aro; (*of wheel*) aro, llanta.
rind [raɪnd] *n* (*of bacon*) piel *f*; (*of lemon etc*) cáscara; (*of cheese*) costra.
ring [rɪŋ] *n* (*of metal*) aro; (*on finger*) anillo; (*of people, objects*) círculo, grupo; (*of spies*) camarilla; (*for boxing*) cuadrilátero; (*of circus*) pista; (*bull*~) ruedo, plaza; (*sound of bell*) toque *m*; (*telephone call*) llamada // (*vb*: *pt* **rang**, *pp* **rung**) *vi* (*on telephone*) llamar por teléfono; (*large bell*) repicar; (*also*: ~ **out**: *voice, words*) sonar; (*ears*) zumbar // *vt* (TEL: *also*: ~ **up**) llamar; (*bell etc*) hacer sonar; (*doorbell*) tocar; **to** ~ **back** *vt, vi* (TEL) devolver la llamada; **to** ~ **off** *vi* (TEL) colgar, cortar la comunicación; ~**ing** *n* (*of large bell*) repique *m*; (*in ears*) zumbido; ~**leader** *n* (*of gang*) cabecilla *m/f*.
ringlets ['rɪŋlɪts] *npl* rizos *mpl*, tirabuzones *mpl*.
ring road *n* carretera periférica o de circunvalación.
rink [rɪŋk] *n* (*also*: **ice** ~) pista.
rinse [rɪns] *n* (*of dishes*) enjuague *m*; (*of hair*) reflejo // *vt* enjuagar; dar reflejos a.
riot ['raɪət] *n* motín *m*, disturbio // *vi* amotinarse; **to run** ~ desmandarse; ~**er** *n* amotinado/a; ~**ous** *a* (*gen*) alborotado; (*party*) bullicioso; (*uncontrolled*) desenfrenado.
rip [rɪp] *n* rasgón *m*, rasgadura // *vt*

rasgar, desgarrar // vi correr; ~**cord** n cabo de desgarre.

ripe ['raɪp] a (fruit) maduro; (ready) listo; ~**n** vt madurar // vi madurarse; ~**ness** n madurez f.

ripple ['rɪpl] n onda, rizo; (sound) murmullo // vi rizarse // vt rizar.

rise [raɪz] n (slope) cuesta, pendiente m; (hill) altura; (increase: in wages) aumento m (: in prices, temperature) subida, alza; (fig: to power etc) ascenso // vi, pt rose, pp risen ['rɪzn] (gen) elevarse; (prices) subir; (waters) crecer; (river) nacer; (sun) salir; (person: from bed etc) levantarse; (also: ~ up: rebel) sublevarse; (in rank) ascender; to give ~ to dar lugar o origen a; to ~ to the occasion ponerse a la altura de las circunstancias.

risk [rɪsk] n riesgo, peligro // vt (gen) arriesgar; (dare) atreverse a; to take or run the ~ of doing correr el riesgo de hacer; at ~ en peligro; at one's own ~ bajo su propia responsabilidad; ~**y** a arriesgado, peligroso.

risqué ['riːskeɪ] a (joke) subido de color.

rissole ['rɪsəul] n croqueta.

rite [raɪt] n rito; **funeral** ~**s** exequias fpl.

ritual ['rɪtjuəl] a ritual // n ritual m, rito.

rival ['raɪvl] n rival m/f; (in business) competidor/a m/f // a rival, opuesto // vt competir con; ~**ry** n rivalidad f, competencia.

river ['rɪvə*] n río; **up/down** ~ río arriba/abajo; ~**bank** n orilla (del río); ~**bed** n lecho, cauce m; ~**side** n ribera, orilla // cpd (port, traffic) de río, del río.

rivet ['rɪvɪt] n roblón m, remache m // vt remachar; (fig) clavar.

Riviera [rɪvɪ'eərə] n: **the (French)** ~ la Costa Azul (Francesa).

road [rəud] n (gen) camino; (motorway etc) carretera; (in town) calle f; ~**block** n barricada; ~**hog** n loco del volante; ~**map** n mapa m de carreteras; ~**side** n borde m (del camino) // cpd al lado de la carretera; ~**sign** n señal f (de carretera o calle); ~ **user** n usuario de la vía pública; ~**way** n calzada; ~**worthy** a (car) listo para conducir.

roam [rəum] vi vagar // vt vagar por.

roar [rɔ:*] n (of animal) rugido, bramido; (of crowd) rugido; (of vehicle, storm) estruendo; (of laughter) carcajada // vi rugir, bramar; hacer estruendo; to ~ with laughter reírse a carcajadas; to do a ~ing trade hacer buen negocio.

roast [rəust] n carne f asada, asado // vt (meat) asar; (coffee) tostar.

rob [rɔb] vt robar; to ~ sb of sth robar algo a uno; (fig: deprive) quitarle algo a uno; ~**ber** n ladrón/ona m/f; ~**bery** n robo.

robe [rəub] n (for ceremony etc) toga; (also: bath ~) bata.

robin ['rɔbɪn] n petirrojo.

robot ['rəubɔt] n robot m.

robust [rəu'bʌst] a robusto, fuerte.

rock [rɔk] n (gen) roca; (boulder) peña, peñasco; (sweet) pirulí // vt (swing gently: cradle) balancear, mecer; (: child) arrullar; (shake) sacudir // vi mecerse, balancearse; sacudirse; **on the** ~**s** (drink) sobre las rocas; (marriage etc) en ruinas; **to** ~ **the boat** (fig) causar perturbaciones; ~ **and roll** n rocanrol m; ~-**bottom** a (fig) por los suelos; ~**ery** n cuadro alpino.

rocket ['rɔkɪt] n cohete m.

rocking ['rɔkɪŋ]: ~ **chair** n mecedora; ~ **horse** n caballo de balancín.

rocky ['rɔkɪ] a (gen) rocoso; (unsteady: table) débil.

rod [rɔd] n vara, varilla; (TECH) barra; (also: **fishing** ~) caña.

rode [rəud] pt of **ride.**

rodent ['rəudnt] n roedor m.

rodeo ['rəudɪəu] n rodeo.

roe [rəu] n (species: also: ~ **deer**) corzo; (of fish): **hard/soft** ~ hueva/lecha.

rogue [rəug] n pícaro, pillo; **roguish** a pícaro.

role [rəul] n papel m, rol m.

roll [rəul] n rollo; (of banknotes) fajo; (also: **bread** ~) panecillo, bollo; (register) lista, nómina; (sound: of drums etc) redoble m; (movement: of ship) balanceo // vt hacer rodar; (also: ~ **up**: string) enrollar; (: sleeves) arremangar; (cigarettes) liar; (also: ~ **out**: pastry) aplanar // vi (gen) rodar; (drum) redoblar; (in walking) bambolearse; (ship) balancearse; **to** ~ **by** vi (time) pasar; **to** ~ **in** vi (mail, cash) entrar a raudales; **to** ~ **over** vi dar una vuelta; **to** ~ **up** vi (col: arrive) presentarse, aparecer // vt (carpet) arrollar; ~ **call** n acto de pasar lista; ~**er** n rodillo; (wheel) rueda; ~**er skates** npl patines mpl de rueda.

rollicking ['rɔlɪkɪŋ] a alegre, divertido.

rolling ['rəulɪŋ] a (landscape) ondulado; ~ **pin** n rodillo (de cocina); ~ **stock** n (RAIL) material m rodante.

Roman ['rəumən] a, n romano/a; ~ **Catholic** a, n católico (romano).

romance [rə'mæns] n (love affair) amoríos mpl, aventura sentimental; (charm) lo romántico.

Romanesque [rəumə'nɛsk] a románico.

Romania [rəu'meɪnɪə] n = **Rumania.**

romantic [rə'mæntɪk] a romántico; **romanticism** [-tɪsɪzəm] n romanticismo.

romp [rɔmp] n retozo, juego // vi (also: ~ **about**) jugar, brincar.

rompers ['rɔmpəz] npl pelele m.

roof [ru:f] pl ~**s** n (gen) techo; (of house) techo, tejado; (of car) baca // vt techar, poner techo a; **the** ~ **of the mouth** el paladar, el cielo de la boca; ~**ing** n techumbre f; ~ **rack** n (AUT) baca, portaequipajes m inv.

rook [ruk] n (bird) graja; (CHESS) torre f.

room [ru:m] n (in house) cuarto, habitación f, pieza; (also: **bed**~) dormitorio; (in school etc) sala; (space) sitio, cabida; ~**s**

npl (*lodging*) alojamiento *sg*; '~s **to let'** 'se alquilan pisos *o* cuartos'; **single/double** ~ habitación individual/doble *o* para dos personas; ~**mate** *n* compañero/a de cuarto; ~ **service** *n* servicio de habitaciones; ~**y** *a* espacioso.
roost [ru:st] *n* percha // *vi* pasar la noche.
rooster ['ru:stə*] *n* gallo.
root [ru:t] *n* (*BOT, MATH*) raíz *f* // *vi* (*plant, belief*) arriesgarse; **to** ~ **about** *vi* (*fig*) andar buscando; **to** ~ **for** *vt fus* apoyar a; **to** ~ **out** *vt* desarraigar.
rope [rəup] *n* cuerda; (*NAUT*) cable *m* // *vt* (*box*) atar *o* amarrar con (una) cuerda; (*climbers: also:* ~ **together**) encordarse; **to** ~ **sb in** (*fig*) persuadir a uno a tomar parte; **to know the** ~**s** (*fig*) conocer un negocio a fondo; ~ **ladder** *n* escala de cuerda.
rosary ['rəuzəri] *n* rosario.
rose [rəuz] *pt of* **rise** // *n* rosa; (*also:* ~**bush**) rosal *m*; (*on watering can*) roseta // *a* color de rosa.
rosé ['rəuzei] *n* vino rosado, clarete *m.*
rose: ~**bed** *n* rosaleda; ~**bud** *n* capullo de rosa; ~**bush** *n* rosal *m.*
rosemary ['rəuzməri] *n* romero.
rosette [rəu'zɛt] *n* rosetón *m.*
roster ['rɔstə*] *n*: **duty** ~ lista de deberes.
rostrum ['rɔstrəm] *n* tribuna.
rosy ['rəuzi] *a* rosado, sonrosado; **a** ~ **future** un futuro prometedor.
rot [rɔt] *n* (*decay*) putrefacción *f,* podredumbre *f;* (*fig: pej*) decadencia // *vt, vi* pudrirse, corromperse.
rota ['rəutə] *n* lista (de tandas).
rotary ['rəutəri] *a* rotativo.
rotate [rəu'teit] *vt* (*revolve*) hacer girar, dar vueltas a; (*change round: crops*) cultivar en rotación; (: *jobs*) alternar // *vi* (*revolve*) girar, dar vueltas; **rotating** *a* (*movement*) rotativo; **rotation** [-'teiʃən] *n* rotación *f;* **in rotation** por turno.
rotor ['rəutə*] *n* rotor *m.*
rotten ['rɔtn] *a* (*decayed*) podrido; (: *wood*) carcomido; (*fig*) corrompido; (*col: bad*) vil, miserable; **to feel** ~ (*ill*) sentirse muy mal.
rotting ['rɔtiŋ] *a* podrido.
rotund [rəu'tʌnd] *a* rotundo.
rouble, ruble (*US*) ['ru:bl] *n* rublo.
rouge [ru:ʒ] *n* colorete *m.*
rough [rʌf] *a* (*skin, surface*) áspero; (*terrain*) quebrado; (*road*) desigual; (*voice*) bronco; (*person, manner: coarse*) tosco, grosero; (*weather*) borrascoso; (*treatment*) brutal; (*sea*) bravo; (*cloth*) basto; (*plan*) preliminar; (*guess*) aproximado; (*violent*) violento // *n* (*person*) matón *m;* (*GOLF*): **in the** ~ en las hierbas altas; **to** ~ **it** vivir sin comodidades; **to sleep** ~ pasar la noche al raso; ~-**and-ready** *a* improvisado; ~**en** *vt* (*a surface*) poner áspero; ~**ly** *ad* (*handle*) torpemente; (*make*) toscamente; (*approximately*)

aproximadamente; ~**ness** *n* aspereza; tosquedad *f;* brutalidad *f.*
roulette [ru:'lɛt] *n* ruleta.
Roumania [ru:'meiniə] *n* = **Rumania.**
round [raund] *a* redondo // *n* círculo; (*of toast*) rodaja; (*of policeman*) ronda; (*of milkman*) recorrido; (*of doctor*) visitas *fpl;* (*game: of cards, in competition*) partida; (*of ammunition*) cartucho; (*BOXING*) asalto; (*of talks*) ronda // *vt* (*corner*) doblar // *prep* alrededor de // *ad:* **all** ~ por todos lados; **the long way** ~ el camino menos directo; **all the year** ~ durante todo el año; **it's just** ~ **the corner** (*fig*) está a la vuelta de la esquina; **to go** ~ **to sb's** (*house*) ir a casa de uno; **to go** ~ **the back** pasar por atrás; **to go** ~ **a house** visitar una casa; **to go the** ~**s** (*story*) divulgarse; **to** ~ **off** *vt* (*speech etc*) acabar, poner término a; **to** ~ **up** *vt* (*cattle*) acorralar; (*people*) reunir; (*prices*) redondear; ~**about** *n* (*AUT*) glorieta, redondel *m;* (*at fair*) tiovivo // *a* (*route, means*) indirecto; **a** ~ **of applause** una salva de aplausos; **a** ~ **of drinks** una ronda de bebidas; ~**ed** *a* redondeado; (*style*) expresivo; ~**ly** *ad* (*fig*) rotundamente; ~- **shouldered** *a* cargado de espaldas; ~ **trip** *n* viaje *m* de ida y vuelta; ~**up** *n* rodeo; (*of criminals*) redada.
rouse [rauz] *vt* (*wake up*) despertar; (*stir up*) suscitar; **rousing** *a* emocionado, entusiasta.
rout [raut] *n* (*MIL*) derrota; (*flight*) fuga // *vt* derrotar.
route [ru:t] *n* ruta, camino; (*of bus*) recorrido; (*of shipping*) rumba, derrota; ~ **map** *n* (*for journey*) mapa *m* de carreteras.
routine [ru:'ti:n] *a* (*work*) rutinario // *n* rutina; (*THEATRE*) número.
roving ['rəuviŋ] *a* (*wandering*) errante; (*salesman*) ambulante.
row [rəu] *n* (*line*) fila, hilera; (*KNITTING*) pasada // [rau] (*noise*) estrépito, estruendo; (*racket*) escándalo; (*dispute*) bronca, pelea; (*fuss*) jaleo, follón *m;* (*scolding*) regaño // *vi* (*in boat*) remar // *vi* [rau] reñir(se) // *vt* (*boat*) conducir remando.
rowdy ['raudi] *a* (*person: noisy*) ruidoso; (: *quarrelsome*) pendenciero; (*occasion*) alborotado // *n* pendenciero.
rowing ['rəuiŋ] *n* remo; ~ **boat** *n* bote *m* de remos.
royal ['rɔiəl] *a* real; ~**ist** *a, n* monárquico/a; ~**ty** *n* (~ *persons*) familia real; (*payment to author*) derechos *mpl* de autor.
R.S.V.P. *abbr of* **répondez s'il vous plaît** SRC (Se Ruega Contestación).
rub [rʌb] *vt* (*gen*) frotar; (*hard*) restregar; (*polish*) sacar brillo a // *n* (*gen*) frotamiento; (*touch*) roce *m;* **to** ~ **sb up the wrong way** coger a uno a contrapelo;

to ~ off *vi* borrarse; to ~ off on influir en; to ~ out *vt* borrar.

rubber ['rʌbə*] *n* caucho, goma; (*Brit: eraser*) goma de borrar; ~ **band** *n* goma, gomita; ~ **plant** *n* árbol *m* del caucho, gomero; ~**y** *a* elástico.

rubbish ['rʌbɪʃ] *n* (*from household*) basura; (*waste*) desperdicios *mpl*; (*fig: pej*) tonterías *fpl*; (*trash*) pacotilla; ~ **bin** *n* cubo de la basura; ~ **dump** *n* (*in town*) vertedero, basurero.

rubble ['rʌbl] *n* escombros *mpl*.

ruby ['ruːbɪ] *n* rubí *m*.

rucksack ['rʌksæk] *n* mochila.

ructions ['rʌkʃənz] *npl* lío *sg*. jaleo *sg*.

rudder ['rʌdə*] *n* timón *m*.

ruddy ['rʌdɪ] *a* (*face*) rubicundo, frescote; (*col: damned*) condenado.

rude [ruːd] *a* (*impolite: person*) grosero; (: *word, manners*) rudo, grosero; (*sudden*) repentino; (*shocking*) verde, indecente; ~**ly** *ad* groseramente, toscamente; repentinamente; ~**ness** *n* grosería, tosquedad *f*.

rudiment ['ruːdɪmənt] *n* rudimento; ~**ary** [-'mentərɪ] *a* rudimentario.

rue [ruː] *vt* arrepentirse de; ~**ful** *a* arrepentido.

ruffian ['rʌfɪən] *n* matón *m*, criminal *m*.

ruffle ['rʌfl] *vt* (*hair*) despeinar; (*clothes*) arrugar; (*fig: person*) agitar.

rug [rʌg] *n* alfombra; (*for knees*) manta.

rugby ['rʌgbɪ] *n* (*also*: ~ **football**) rugby *m*.

rugged ['rʌgɪd] *a* (*landscape*) accidentado; (*features, character*) fuerte.

rugger ['rʌgə*] *n* (*col*) rugby *m*.

ruin ['ruːɪn] *n* ruina // *vt* arruinar; (*spoil*) estropear; ~**s** *npl* ruinas *fpl*, restos *mpl*; ~**ous** *a* ruinoso.

rule [ruːl] *n* (*norm*) norma, costumbre *f*; (*regulation*) regla; (*government*) dominio; (*ruler*) metro // *vt* (*country, person*) gobernar; (*decide*) disponer; (*draw: lines*) trazar // *vi* regir; (*LAW*) fallar; to ~ **out** excluir; as a ~ por regla general; ~**d** *a* (*paper*) rayado; **ruler** *n* (*sovereign*) soberano; (*for measuring*) regla; **ruling** *a* (*party*) gobernante; (*class*) dirigente // *n* (*LAW*) fallo, decisión *f*.

rum [rʌm] *n* ron *m*.

Rumania [ruː'meɪnɪə] *n* Rumanía; ~**n** *a*, *n* rumano/a.

rumble ['rʌmbl] *n* retumbo, ruido sordo; (*of thunder*) redoble *m* // *vi* retumbar, hacer un ruido sordo; (*stomach, pipe*) sonar.

rummage ['rʌmɪdʒ] *vi* revolverlo todo.

rumour, rumor (*US*) ['ruːmə*] *n* rumor *m* // *vt*: **it is** ~**ed that...** se rumorea que... .

rump [rʌmp] *n* (*of animal*) ancas *fpl*, grupa; ~**steak** *n* filete *m* de lomo.

rumpus ['rʌmpəs] *n* (*col*) lío, jaleo; (*quarrel*) pelea, riña.

run [rʌn] *n* carrera; (*outing*) paseo, excursión *f*; (*distance travelled*) trayecto; (*series*) serie *f*; (*THEATRE*) temporada; (*SKI*) pista // (*vb: pt* **ran**, *pp* **run**) *vt*

(*operate: business*) dirigir; (: *competition, course*) organizar; (: *hotel, house*) administrar, llevar; (*to pass: hand*) pasar; (*water, bath*) abrir el grifo (del baño) // *vi* (*gen*) correr; (*work: machine*) funcionar, marchar; (*bus, train: operate*) circular, ir; (: *travel*) ir; (*continue: play*) seguir; (: *contract*) ser válido; (*flow: river, bath*) fluir; (*colours, washing*) desteñirse; (*in election*) ser candidato; **there was a** ~ **on** (*meat, tickets*) hubo mucha demanda de; **in the long** ~ a la larga, a largo plazo; **on the** ~ en fuga; **I'll** ~ **you to the station** te llevaré a la estación en coche; to ~ **a risk** correr un riesgo; to ~ **about** *vi* (*children*) correr por todos lados; to ~ **across** *vt fus* (*find*) dar con, toparse con; to ~ **away** *vi* huir; to ~ **down** *vi* (*clock*) parar // *vt* (*AUT*) atropellar; (*criticize*) criticar; **to be** ~ **down** estar debilitado; to ~ **off** *vt* (*water*) dejar correr // *vi* huir corriendo; to ~ **out** *vi* (*person*) salir corriendo; (*liquid*) irse; (*lease*) caducar, vencer; (*money*) acabarse; to ~ **out of** *vt fus* quedar sin; to ~ **over** *vt sep* (*AUT*) atropellar // *vt fus* (*revise*) repasar; to ~ **through** *vt fus* (*instructions*) repasar; to ~ **up** *vt* (*debt*) incurrir en; to ~ **up against** (*difficulties*) tropezar con; ~**away** *a* (*horse*) desbocado; (*truck*) sin frenos; (*person*) fugitivo.

rung [rʌŋ] *pp of* **ring** // *n* (*of ladder*) escalón *m*, peldaño.

runner ['rʌnə*] *n* (*in race: person*) corredor/a *m/f*; (: *horse*) caballo; (*on sledge*) patín *m*; (*on curtain*) anillo; (*wheel*) ruedecilla; ~ **bean** *n* (*BOT*) judía escarlata; ~-**up** *n* subcampeón/ona *m/f*.

running ['rʌnɪŋ] *n* (*sport*) atletismo; (*race*) carrera // *a* (*water*) corriente; (*commentary*) continuo; **6 days** ~ 6 días seguidos; ~ **board** *n* estribo.

runny ['rʌnɪ] *a* derretido.

run-of-the-mill ['rʌnəvðə'mɪl] *a* común y corriente.

runt [rʌnt] *n* (*also: pej*) redrojo, enano.

runway ['rʌnweɪ] *n* (*AVIAT*) pista de aterrizaje.

rupee [ruː'piː] *n* rupia.

rupture ['rʌptʃə*] *n* (*MED*) hernia // *vt*: **to** ~ **o.s.** causarse una hernia, quebrarse.

rural ['ruərl] *a* rural.

ruse [ruːz] *n* ardid *m*.

rush [rʌʃ] *n* ímpetu *m*; (*hurry*) prisa; (*COMM*) demanda repentina; (*BOT*) junco; (*current*) corriente *f* fuerte, ráfaga // *vt* apresurar; (*work*) hacer de prisa; (*attack: town etc*) asaltar // *vi* correr, precipitarse; ~ **hour** *n* horas *fpl* punta.

rusk [rʌsk] *n* bizcocho tostado.

Russia ['rʌʃə] *n* Rusia; ~**n** *a*, *n* ruso/a.

rust [rʌst] *n* herrumbre *f*, moho // *vi* oxidarse.

rustic ['rʌstɪk] *a* rústico.

rustle ['rʌsl] *vi* susurrar // *vt* (*paper*) hacer crujir; (*US: cattle*) hurtar, robar.

rustproof ['rʌstpru:f] *a* inoxidable, a prueba de herrumbre.

rusty ['rʌstɪ] *a* oxidado, mohoso.

rut [rʌt] *n* rodera, carril *m*; (*ZOOL*) celo; **to be in a** ~ ir encarrilado.

ruthless ['ru:θlɪs] *a* despiadado; ~**ness** *n* crueldad *f*, implacabilidad *f*.

rye [raɪ] *n* centeno; ~ **bread** *n* pan de centeno.

S

sabbath ['sæbəθ] *n* domingo; (*Jewish*) sábado.

sabbatical [sə'bætɪkl] *a*: ~ **year** año de licencia.

sabotage ['sæbətɑ:3] *n* sabotaje *m* // *vt* sabotear.

saccharin(e) ['sækərɪn] *n* sacarina.

sack [sæk] *n* (*bag*) saco, costal *m* // *vt* (*dismiss*) despedir; (*plunder*) saquear; **to get the** ~ ser despedido; ~**ing** *n* (*material*) harpillera.

sacrament ['sækrəmənt] *n* sacramento.

sacred ['seɪkrɪd] *a* sagrado, santo.

sacrifice ['sækrɪfaɪs] *n* sacrificio // *vt* sacrificar.

sacrilege ['sækrɪlɪdʒ] *n* sacrilegio.

sacrosanct ['sækrəusæŋkt] *a* sacrosanto.

sad [sæd] *a* (*unhappy*) triste; (*deplorable*) lamentable; ~**den** *vt* entristecer.

saddle ['sædl] *n* silla (de montar); (*of cycle*) sillín *m* // *vt* (*horse*) ensillar; **to be ~d with sth** (*col*) quedar cargado con algo; ~**bag** *n* alforja.

sadism ['seɪdɪzm] *n* sadismo; **sadist** *n* sadista *m/f*; **sadistic** [sə'dɪstɪk] *a* sádico.

sadly ['sædlɪ] *ad* tristemente; ~ **lacking (in)** muy deficiente (en).

sadness ['sædnɪs] *n* tristeza.

safari [sə'fɑ:rɪ] *n* safari *m*.

safe [seɪf] *a* (*out of danger*) fuera de peligro; (*not dangerous, sure*) seguro; (*unharmed*) a salvo, ileso; (*trustworthy*) digno de confianza // *n* caja de caudales, caja fuerte; ~ **and sound** sano y salvo; **(just) to be on the** ~ **side** por mayor seguridad; ~**guard** *n* protección *f*, garantía // *vt* proteger, defender; ~**keeping** *n* custodia; ~**ly** *ad* seguramente, con seguridad; (*without mishap*) sin peligro.

safety ['seɪftɪ] *n* seguridad *f* // *a* de seguridad; ~ **first!** ¡precaución!; ~ **belt** *n* cinturón *m* (de seguridad); ~ **pin** *n* imperdible *m*.

saffron ['sæfrən] *n* azafrán *m*.

sag [sæg] *vi* aflojarse.

sage [seɪdʒ] *n* (*herb*) salvia; (*man*) sabio.

Sagittarius [sædʒɪ'tɛərɪəs] *n* Sagitario.

sago ['seɪgəu] *n* sagú *m*.

said [sɛd] *pt, pp of* **say.**

sail [seɪl] *n* (*on boat*) vela; (*trip*): **to go for a** ~ tomar un paseo en barco // *vt* (*boat*) gobernar // *vi* (*travel: ship*) navegar; (: *passenger*) pasear en barco; (*set off*)

zarpar; **they** ~**ed into Copenhagen** llegaron a Copenhague; **to** ~ **through** *vi, vt fus* (*fig*) hacer con facilidad; ~**boat** *n* (*US*) velero, barco de vela; ~**ing** *n* (*SPORT*) balandrismo; **to go** ~**ing** salir en balandro; ~**ing ship** *n* barco de vela; ~**or** *n* marinero, marino.

saint [seɪnt] *n* santo; **S**~ **John** San Juan; ~**ly** *a* santo.

sake [seɪk] *n*: **for the** ~ **of** por (motivo de).

salad ['sæləd] *n* ensalada; ~ **bowl** *n* ensaladera; ~ **cream** *n* mayonesa; ~ **dressing** *n* aliño; ~ **oil** *n* aceite *m* para ensaladas.

salami [sə'lɑ:mɪ] *n* salami *m*.

salary ['sælərɪ] *n* sueldo.

sale [seɪl] *n* venta; (*at reduced prices*) liquidación *f*, saldo; "**grand** ~" grandes rebajas; "**for** ~" "se vende"; **on** ~ en venta; ~**room** *n* sala de subastas; **salesman/woman** *n* vendedor/a *m/f*; (*in shop*) dependiente/a *m/f*; (*representative*) viajante *m/f*; **salesmanship** *n* arte *m* de vender.

saliva [sə'laɪvə] *n* saliva.

sallow ['sæləu] *a* cetrino.

salmon ['sæmən] *n, pl inv* salmón *m*.

saloon [sə'lu:n] *n* (*US*) bar *m*, taberna; (*AUT*) (coche *m* de) turismo; (*ship's lounge*) cámara, salón *m*.

salt [sɔlt] *n* sal *f* // *vt* salar; (*put* ~ *on*) poner sal en; ~ **cellar** *n* salero; ~**water** *a* de agua salada; ~**y** *a* salado.

salutary ['sæljutərɪ] *a* saludable.

salute [sə'lu:t] *n* saludo; (*of guns*) salva // *vt* saludar.

salvage ['sælvɪdʒ] *n* (*saving*) salvamento, recuperación *f*; (*things saved*) objetos *mpl* salvados // *vt* salvar.

salvation [sæl'veɪʃən] *n* salvación *f*; **S**~ **Army** *n* Ejército de Salvación.

salve [sælv] *n* (*cream etc*) ungüento, bálsamo.

salver ['sælvə*] *n* bandeja.

same [seɪm] *a* mismo // *ad* de la misma forma, igual // *pron*: **the** ~ el mismo/la misma; **the** ~ **book as** el mismo libro que; **all** *or* **just the** ~ sin embargo, aun así; **to do the** ~ **(as sb)** hacer lo mismo (que otro); **the** ~ **to you!** ¡igualmente!

sample ['sɑ:mpl] *n* muestra // *vt* (*food, wine*) probar.

sanatorium [sænə'tɔ:rɪəm], *pl* -**ria** [-rɪə] *n* sanatorio.

sanctify ['sæŋktɪfaɪ] *vt* santificar.

sanctimonious [sæŋktɪ'məunɪəs] *a* santurrón(ona).

sanction ['sæŋkʃən] *n* sanción *f* // *vt* sancionar.

sanctity ['sæŋktɪtɪ] *n* (*gen*) santidad *f*; (*inviolability*) inviolabilidad *f*.

sanctuary ['sæŋktjuərɪ] *n* (*gen*) santuario; (*refuge*) asilo, refugio.

sand [sænd] *n* arena; (*beach*) playa // *vt* enarenar.

sandal ['sændl] *n* sandalia; (*wood*) sándalo.

sand: ~**bag** *n* saco de arena; ~**bank** *n* banco de arena; ~**castle** *n* castillo de arena; ~ **dune** *n* duna; ~**paper** *n* papel *m* de lija; ~**pit** *n* (*for children*) cajón *m* de arena; ~**stone** *n* piedra arenisca.

sandwich ['sændwɪtʃ] *n* bocadillo, sándwich *m* // *vt* (*also:* ~ **in**) intercalar; ~**ed between** apretujado entre; **cheese/ham** ~ sándwich de queso/jamón; ~ **board** *n* cartelón *m*; ~ **course** *n* curso de medio tiempo.

sandy ['sændɪ] *a* arenoso; (*colour*) rojizo.

sane [seɪn] *a* cuerdo, sensato; (*sensible*) prudente.

sang [sæŋ] *pt of* **sing.**

sanitarium [sænɪ'tɛərɪəm] (*US*) = **sanatorium.**

sanitary ['sænɪtərɪ] *a* (*system, arrangements*) sanitario; (*clean*) higiénico; ~ **towel**, ~ **napkin** (*US*) *n* paño higiénico, compresa higiénica.

sanitation [sænɪ'teɪʃən] *n* (*in house*) saneamiento; (*in town*) sanidad *f*, higiene *f*.

sanity ['sænɪtɪ] *n* cordura; (*common sense*) juicio, sentido común.

sank [sæŋk] *pt of* **sink.**

Santa Claus [sæntə'klɔːz] *n* San Nicolás, Papá Noel.

sap [sæp] *n* (*of plants*) savia // *vt* (*strength*) minar, agotar.

sapling ['sæplɪŋ] *n* árbol nuevo *o* joven.

sapphire ['sæfaɪə*] *n* zafiro.

sarcasm ['sɑːkæzm] *n* sarcasmo; **sarcastic** [-'kæstɪk] *a* sarcástico.

sardine [sɑː'diːn] *n* sardina.

Sardinia [sɑː'dɪnɪə] *n* Cerdeña.

sari ['sɑːrɪ] *n* sari *m*.

sash [sæʃ] *n* faja.

sat [sæt] *pt, pp of* **sit.**

Satan ['seɪtn] *n* Satanás *m*.

satchel ['sætʃl] *n* bolsa; (*child's*) cartera.

satellite ['sætəlaɪt] *n* satélite *m*.

satin ['sætɪn] *n* raso // *a* de raso.

satire ['sætaɪə*] *n* sátira; **satirical** [sə'tɪrɪkl] *a* satírico; **satirize** ['sætɪraɪz] *vt* satirizar.

satisfaction [sætɪs'fækʃən] *n* satisfacción *f*; (*of debt*) liquidación *f*; **satisfactory** [-'fæktərɪ] *a* satisfactorio.

satisfy ['sætɪsfaɪ] *vt* satisfacer; (*pay*) liquidar; (*convince*) convencer; ~**ing** *a* satisfactorio.

saturate ['sætʃəreɪt] *vt*: **to** ~ (**with**) empapar *o* saturar (de); **saturation** [-'reɪʃən] *n* saturación *f*.

Saturday ['sætədɪ] *n* sábado.

sauce [sɔːs] *n* salsa; (*sweet*) crema; (*fig: cheek*) frescura; ~ **pan** *n* perola.

saucer ['sɔːsə*] *n* platillo.

saucy ['sɔːsɪ] *a* fresco, descarado; (*flirtatious*) coqueta.

sauna ['sɔːnə] *n* sauna.

saunter ['sɔːntə*] *vi* deambular.

sausage ['sɔsɪdʒ] *n* salchicha; (*cold meat*) embutido; ~ **roll** *n* empanadita.

sauté ['səuteɪ] *a* salteado.

savage ['sævɪdʒ] *a* (*cruel, fierce*) feroz, furioso; (*primitive*) salvaje // *n* salvaje *m/f* // *vt* (*attack*) embestir; ~**ry** *n* ferocidad *f*; salvajismo.

save [seɪv] *vt* (*rescue*) salvar, rescatar; (*money, time*) ahorrar; (*put by*) guardar; (*avoid: trouble*) evitar // *vi* (*also:* ~ **up**) ahorrar // *n* (SPORT) parada // *prep* salvo, excepto.

saving ['seɪvɪŋ] *n* (*on price etc*) economía // *a*: **the** ~ **grace of** el único mérito de; ~**s** *npl* ahorros *mpl*; ~**s bank** *n* caja de ahorros.

saviour ['seɪvjə*] *n* salvador/a *m/f*.

savour, savor (*US*) ['seɪvə*] *n* sabor *m*, gusto // *vt* saborear; ~**y** *a* sabroso; (*dish: not sweet*) no dulce; (: *salted*) salado.

saw [sɔː] *pt of* **see** // *n* (*tool*) sierra // *vt, pt* **sawed**, *pp* **sawed** *or* **sawn** serrar; ~**dust** *n* (a)serrín *m*; ~**mill** *n* aserradero.

saxophone ['sæksəfəun] *n* saxófono.

say [seɪ] *n*: **to have one's** ~ expresar su opinión; **to have a** *or* **some** ~ **in sth** tener voz *o* tener que ver en algo // *vt, pt, pp* **said** decir; **to** ~ **yes/no** decir que sí/no; **that is to** ~ es decir; **that goes without** ~**ing** eso va sin decir; ~**ing** *n* dicho, refrán *m*.

scab [skæb] *n* costra; (*pej*) esquirol/a *m/f*; ~**by** *a* costroso, lleno de costras.

scaffold ['skæfəuld] *n* (*for execution*) cadalso, patíbulo; ~**ing** *n* andamios *mpl*, andamiaje *m*.

scald [skɔːld] *n* escaldadura // *vt* escaldar; ~**ing** *a* (*hot*) hirviendo.

scale [skeɪl] *n* (*gen*, MUS) escala; (*of fish*) escama; (*of salaries, fees etc*) escalafón *m*; (*of map, also size, extent*) escala // *vt* (*mountain*) escalar; (*tree*) trepar; ~**s** *npl* (*small*) balanza *sg*; (*large*) báscula *sg*; **on a large** ~ a gran escala; ~ **of charges** tarifa, lista de precios; **social** ~ escala social; ~ **drawing** *n* dibujo a escala; ~ **model** *n* modelo a escala.

scallop ['skɔləp] *n* (ZOOL) venera; (SEWING) festón *m*.

scalp [skælp] *n* cabellera // *vt* escalpar.

scalpel ['skælpl] *n* escalpelo.

scamp [skæmp] *n* diablillo, travieso.

scamper ['skæmpə*] *vi*: **to** ~ **away**, ~ **off** irse corriendo.

scan [skæn] *vt* (*examine*) escudriñar; (*glance at quickly*) dar un vistazo a; (TV, RADAR) explorar, registrar.

scandal ['skændl] *n* escándalo; (*gossip*) chismes *mpl*; ~**ize** *vt* escandalizar; ~**ous** *a* escandaloso; (*libellous*) calumnioso.

Scandinavia [skændɪ'neɪvɪə] *n* Escandinavia; ~**n** *a* escandinavo.

scant [skænt] *a* escaso; ~**y** *a* escaso.

scapegoat ['skeɪpgəut] *n* cabeza de turco, chivo expiatorio.

scar [skɑː] *n* cicatriz *f* // *vt* marcar con una cicatriz // *vi* cicatrizarse.

scarce [skɛəs] *a* escaso; ~**ly** *ad* apenas; **scarcity** *n* escasez *f*; (*shortage*) carestía.

scare [skɛə*] *n* susto, sobresalto; (*panic*)

pánico // vt asustar, espantar; to ~ sb
stiff dejar muerto de miedo a uno; bomb
~ amenaza de bomba; ~crow n
espantapájaros m inv; ~d a: to be ~d
asustarse, estar asustado.
scarf [skɑ:f], pl scarves n (long) bufanda;
(square) pañuelo.
scarlet ['skɑ:lɪt] a escarlata; ~ fever n
escarlatina.
scarves [skɑ:vz] pl of scarf.
scary ['skɛərɪ] a (col) de miedo.
scathing ['skeɪðɪŋ] a mordaz.
scatter ['skætə*] vt (spread) esparcir,
desparramar; (put to flight) dispersar // vi
desparramarse; dispersarse; ~brained a
ligero de cascos; (forgetful) olvidadizo.
scavenger ['skævəndʒə*] n (refuse
collector) basurero; (ZOOL) animal m/ave f
que se alimenta de la carroña.
scene [si:n] n (THEATRE, fig etc) escena; (of
crime, accident) escenario; (sight, view)
vista, perspectiva; (fuss) escándalo; ~ry
n (THEATRE) decorado; (landscape) paisaje
m; scenic a (picturesque) pintoresco.
scent [sɛnt] n perfume m, olor m; (fig:
track) rastro, pista; (sense of smell) olfato
// vt perfumar; (smell) oler; (sniff out)
husmear; (suspect) sospechar.
sceptic, skeptic (US) ['skɛptɪk] n
escéptico/a; ~al a escéptico; ~ism
['skɛptɪsɪzm] n escepticismo.
sceptre, scepter (US) ['sɛptə*] n cetro.
schedule ['ʃɛdju:l] n (of trains) horario; (of
events) programa m; (plan) plan m; (list)
lista // vt (timetable) establecer el horario
de; (list) catalogar; (visit) fijar la hora de;
on ~ a la hora, sin retraso; to be ahead
of/behind ~ estar adelantado/en
retraso.
scheme [ski:m] n (plan) plan m, proyecto;
(method) esquema m; (plot) intriga; (trick)
ardid m; (arrangement) disposición f // vt
proyectar // vi (plan) hacer proyectos;
(intrigue) intrigar; scheming a intrigante.
schism ['skɪzəm] n cisma m.
schizophrenia [skɪtsəu'fri:nɪə] n
esquizofrenia; schizophrenic [-sə'frɛnɪk]
a esquizofrénico.
scholar ['skɔlə*] n (pupil) alumno/a,
estudiante m/f; (learned person) sabio,
erudito; ~ly a erudito; ~ship n erudición
f; (grant) beca.
school [sku:l] n (gen) escuela, colegio; (in
university) facultad f // vt (animal)
amaestrar; ~ age n edad f escolar;
~book n libro de texto; ~boy n alumno;
~days npl años mpl del colegio; ~girl n
alumna; ~ing n enseñanza;
~master/mistress n (primary)
maestro/a; (secondary) profesor/a m/f;
~room n clase f; ~teacher n
maestro/a.
schooner ['sku:nə*] n (ship) goleta; (glass)
jarra.
sciatica [saɪ'ætɪkə] n ciática.
science ['saɪəns] n ciencia; ~ fiction n
ciencia-ficción f; scientific [-'tɪfɪk] a

científico; scientist n científico.
scimitar ['sɪmɪtə*] n cimitarra.
scintillating ['sɪntɪleɪtɪŋ] a brillante,
ingenioso.
scissors ['sɪzəz] npl tijeras fpl; a pair of
~ unas tijeras.
scoff [skɔf] vt (col: eat) engullir // vi: to ~
(at) (mock) mofarse (de).
scold [skəuld] vt regañar.
scone [skɔn] n panecillo.
scoop [sku:p] n cucharón m; (for flour etc)
pala; (PRESS) exclusiva; to ~ out vt
excavar; to ~ up vt recoger.
scooter ['sku:tə*] n (motor cycle) moto f;
(toy) patinete m.
scope [skəup] n (of plan, undertaking)
ámbito; (reach) alcance m; (of person)
competencia; (opportunity) campo (de
acción).
scorch [skɔ:tʃ] vt (clothes) chamuscar;
(earth, grass) quemar, secar; ~er n (col:
hot day) día m abrasador; ~ing a
abrasador(a).
score [skɔ:*] n (points etc) puntuación f;
(MUS) partitura; (reckoning) cuenta;
(twenty) veinte m, veintena // vt (goal,
point) ganar; (mark) rayar // vi marcar un
tanto; (FOOTBALL) marcar (un) gol; (keep
score) llevar el tanteo; on that ~ en lo
que se refiere a eso; to ~ 6 out of 10
obtener una puntuación de 6 sobre 10;
~board n marcador m; ~card n (SPORT)
tanteador m; scorer n marcador m; (keeping score) tanteador m.
scorn [skɔ:n] n desprecio // vt despreciar;
~ful a desdeñoso, despreciativo.
Scorpio ['skɔ:pɪəu] n Escorpión m.
scorpion ['skɔ:pɪən] n escorpión m.
Scot [skɔt] n escocés/esa m/f.
scotch [skɔtʃ] vt (rumour) desmentir;
(plan) abandonar; S~ n whisky m
escocés.
Scotland ['skɔtlənd] n Escocia.
Scots [skɔts] a escocés(esa);
~man/woman n escocés/esa m/f;
Scottish ['skɔtɪʃ] a escocés(esa).
scoundrel ['skaundrl] n canalla m/f,
sinvergüenza m/f.
scour ['skauə*] vt (clean) fregar, estregar;
(search) recorrer, registrar; ~er n
estropajo.
scourge [skə:dʒ] n azote m.
scout [skaut] n (MIL, also: boy ~)
explorador m; to ~ around reconocer el
terreno.
scowl [skaul] vi fruncir el ceño; to ~ at
sb mirar con ceño a uno.
scraggy ['skrægɪ] a flaco, descarnado.
scram [skræm] vi (col) largarse.
scramble ['skræmbl] n (climb) subida
(difícil); (struggle) pelea // vi: to ~
out/through salir/abrirse paso con
dificultad; to ~ for pelear por; ~d eggs
npl huevos mpl revueltos.
scrap [skræp] n (bit) pedacito; (fig) pizca;
(fight) riña, bronca; (also: ~ iron)
chatarra, hierro viejo // vt reducir a

chatarra; (*discard*) desechar, descartar // *vi* reñir, armar (una) bronca; ~s *npl* (*waste*) sobras *fpl*. desperdicios *mpl*; ~book *n* álbum *m* de recortes.

scrape [skreɪp] *n* (*fig*) lío, apuro // *vt* raspar; (*skin etc*) rasguñar; (~ *against*) rozar // *vi*: **to** ~ **through** pasar con dificultad; **scraper** *n* raspador *m*.

scrap: ~ **heap** *n* (*fig*): **on the** ~ **heap** desperdiciado; ~ **merchant** *n* chatarrero; ~ **paper** *n* pedazos *mpl* de papel; ~**py** *a* (*poor*) pobre; (*speech*) inconexo; (*bitty*) fragmentario.

scratch [skrætʃ] *n* rasguño; (*from claw*) arañazo // *a*: ~ **team** equipo improvisado // *vt* (*record*) rayar; (*with claw, nail*) rasguñar, arañar // *vi* rascarse; **to start from** ~ partir de cero, empezar desde el principio; **to be up to** ~ estar a la altura (de las circunstancias).

scrawl [skrɔːl] *n* garabatos *mpl* // *vi* hacer garabatos.

scream [skriːm] *n* chillido // *vi* chillar.

screech [skriːtʃ] *vi* chirriar.

screen [skriːn] *n* (*CINEMA, TV*) pantalla; (*movable*) biombo; (*wall*) tabique *m*; (*also*: **wind**~) parabrisas *m inv*; (*fig*) cortina // *vt* (*conceal*) tapar; (*from the wind etc*) proteger; (*film*) proyectar; (*candidates etc*) investigar a; ~**ing** *n* (*MED*) investigación *f* médica; ~ **test** *n* prueba de pantalla.

screw [skruː] *n* tornillo; (*propeller*) hélice *f* // *vt* atornillar; (*also*: ~ **in**) apretar; ~**driver** *n* destornillador *m*; ~**y** *a* (*col*) chiflado.

scribble ['skrɪbl] *n* garabatos *mpl* // *vt* escribir con prisa.

script [skrɪpt] *n* (*CINEMA etc*) guión *m*; (*writing*) escritura, letra.

Scripture ['skrɪptʃə*] *n* Sagrada Escritura.

scriptwriter ['skrɪptraɪtə*] *n* guionista *m/f*.

scroll [skrəʊl] *n* rollo.

scrounge [skraundʒ] *vt* (*col*): **to** ~ **sth off** *or* **from sb** obtener algo de otro por gorronería // *vi*: **to** ~ **on sb** vivir a costa de uno; **scrounger** *n* gorrón/ona *m/f*.

scrub [skrʌb] *n* (*clean*) fregado; (*land*) maleza // *vt* fregar, restregar; (*reject*) cancelar, anular.

scruff [skrʌf] *n*: **by the** ~ **of the neck** por el pescuezo.

scruffy ['skrʌfɪ] *a* desaliñado, piojoso.

scruple ['skruːpl] *n* escrúpulo; **scrupulous** *a* escrupuloso.

scrutinize ['skruːtɪnaɪz] *vt* escudriñar; (*votes*) escrutar; **scrutiny** [-nɪ] *n* escrutinio, examen *m*.

scuff [skʌf] *vt* desgastar, restregar.

scuffle ['skʌfl] *n* refriega.

scullery ['skʌlərɪ] *n* fregadero, trascocina.

sculptor ['skʌlptə*] *n* escultor *m*; **sculpture** [-tʃə*] *n* escultura.

scum [skʌm] *n* (*on liquid*) nata; (*pej: people*) canalla; (*fig*) heces *fpl*.

scurry ['skʌrɪ] *vi*: **to** ~ **off** escabullirse.

scurvy ['skəːvɪ] *n* escorbuto.

scuttle ['skʌtl] *n* (*also*: **coal** ~) cubo, carbonera // *vt* (*ship*) barrenar // *vi* (*scamper*): **to** ~ **away**, ~ **off** escabullirse.

scythe [saɪð] *n* guadaña.

sea [siː] *n* mar *m* or *f*; **on the** ~ (*boat*) en el mar; (*town*) junto al mar; **to be all at** ~ (*fig*) estar despistado; **out to** *or* **at** ~ en alta mar; ~ **bird** *n* ave *f* marina; ~**board** *n* litoral *m*; ~ **breeze** *n* brisa de mar; ~**farer** *n* marinero; ~**food** *n* mariscos *mpl*; ~ **front** *n* (*beach*) playa; (*prom*) paseo marítimo; ~**going** *a* (*ship*) de alta mar; ~**gull** *n* gaviota.

seal [siːl] *n* (*animal*) foca; (*stamp*) sello // *vt* (*close*) cerrar; (: *with* ~) sellar; **to** ~ **off** obturar; **it** ~**ed his fate** decidió su destino.

sea level ['siːlɛvl] *n* nivel *m* del mar.

sealing wax ['siːlɪŋwæks] *n* lacre *m*.

sea lion ['siːlaɪən] *n* león *m* marino.

seam [siːm] *n* costura; (*of metal*) juntura; (*of coal*) veta, filón *m*.

seaman ['siːmən] *n* marinero.

seamless ['siːmlɪs] *a* sin costura.

seamstress ['sɛmstrɪs] *n* costurera.

seance ['seɪɔns] *n* sesión *f* de espiritismo.

sea: ~**plane** *n* hidroavión *m*; ~**port** *n* puerto de mar.

search [səːtʃ] *n* (*for person, thing*) busca, búsqueda; (*of drawer, pockets*) registro; (*inspection*) reconocimiento // *vt* (*look in*) buscar en; (*examine*) examinar; (*person, place*) registrar // *vi*: **to** ~ **for** buscar; **to** ~ **through** *vt fus* registrar; **in** ~ **of** en busca de; ~**ing** *a* penetrante; ~**light** *n* reflector *m*; ~ **party** *n* pelotón *m* de salvamento; ~ **warrant** *n* mandamiento (judicial).

sea: ~**shore** *n* playa, orilla del mar; ~**sick** *a* mareado; ~**side** *n* playa, orilla del mar; ~**side resort** *n* playa.

season ['siːzn] *n* (*of year*) estación *f*; (*sporting etc*) temporada; (*gen*) época, período // *vt* (*food*) sazonar; ~**al** *a* estacional; ~**ing** *n* condimento, aderezo; ~ **ticket** *n* billete *m* de abono.

seat [siːt] *n* (*in bus, train: place*) asiento; (*chair*) silla; (*PARLIAMENT*) escaño; (*buttocks*) culo, trasero; (*of government*) sede *f* // *vt* sentar; (*have room for*) tener asientos para; **to be** ~**ed** sentarse; ~ **belt** *n* cinturón *m* de seguridad.

sea: ~ **water** *n* agua *m* del mar; ~**weed** *n* alga marina; ~**worthy** *a* marinero, en condiciones de navegar.

sec. *abbr of* **second(s)**.

secede [sɪˈsiːd] *vi* separarse.

secluded [sɪˈkluːdɪd] *a* retirado; **seclusion** [-ˈkluːʒən] *n* retiro.

second ['sɛkənd] *a* segundo // *ad* (*in race etc*) en segundo lugar // *n* (*gen*) segundo; (*AUT. also*: ~ **gear**) segunda; (*COMM*) artículo con algún desperfecto // *vt* (*motion*) apoyar; ~**ary** *a* secundario; ~**ary school** *n* escuela secundaria; ~**·class** *a* de segunda clase; ~**hand** *a* de segunda

mano, usado; ~ **hand** n (on clock) segundero; ~**ly** ad en segundo lugar; ~**ment** [sɪ'kɔndmənt] n traslado temporal; ~-**rate** a de segunda categoría.
secrecy ['si:krəsɪ] n secreto; **secret** [-krɪt] a, n secreto.
secretarial [sɛkrɪ'tɛərɪəl] a de secretario/a.
secretariat [sɛkrɪ'tɛərɪət] n secretaría.
secretary ['sɛkrətərɪ] n secretario/a; **S**~ **of State** (Brit: POL) Ministro (con cartera).
secretive ['si:krətɪv] a reservado, sigiloso.
sect [sɛkt] n secta; ~**arian** [-'tɛərɪən] a sectario.
section ['sɛkʃən] n sección f; (part) parte f; (of document) artículo; (of opinion) sector m; ~**al** a (drawing) en corte.
sector ['sɛktə*] n sector m.
secular ['sɛkjulə*] a secular, seglar.
secure [sɪ'kjuə*] a (free from anxiety) seguro; (firmly fixed) firme, fijo // vt (fix) asegurar, afianzar; (get) conseguir.
security [sɪ'kjurɪtɪ] n seguridad f; (for loan) fianza; (: object) prenda.
sedate [sɪ'deɪt] a (calm) tranquilo; (formal) serio, formal // vt tratar con calmantes.
sedation [sɪ'deɪʃən] n (MED) sedación f; **sedative** ['sɛdɪtɪv] n sedante m, sedativo.
sedentary ['sɛdntrɪ] a sedentario.
sediment ['sɛdɪmənt] n sedimento.
seduce [sɪ'dju:s] vt (gen) seducir; **seduction** [-'dʌkʃən] n seducción f; **seductive** [-'dʌktɪv] a seductor(a).
see [si:], pt **saw**, pp **seen** vt (gen) ver; (accompany): **to** ~ **sb to the door** acompañar a uno a la puerta; (understand) ver, comprender; (look at) mirar // vi ver // n sede f; **to** ~ **that** (ensure) asegurar que; **to** ~ **about** vi atender a, encargarse de; **to** ~ **off** vt despedirse de; **to** ~ **through** vt penetrar (con la vista) // vt fus llevar a cabo; **to** ~ **to** vt fus atender a, encargarse de.
seed [si:d] n semilla; (in fruit) pepita; (sperm) semen m, simiente f; (fig) germen m; (TENNIS) preseleccionado/a; ~**ling** n planta de semillero; ~**y** a (shabby) desaseado, raído.
seeing ['si:ɪŋ] conj: ~ **(that)** visto que, en vista de que.
seek [si:k], pt, pp **sought** vt (gen) buscar; (post) solicitar.
seem [si:m] vi parecer; ~**ingly** ad aparentemente, según parece.
seen [si:n] pp of **see**.
seep [si:p] vi filtrarse.
seesaw ['si:sɔ:] n balancín m, columpio.
seethe [si:ð] vi hervir; **to** ~ **with anger** enfurecerse.
segment ['sɛgmənt] n segmento.
segregate ['sɛgrɪgeɪt] vt segregar; **segregation** [-'geɪʃən] n segregación f.
seismic ['saɪzmɪk] a sísmico.
seize [si:z] vt (grasp) agarrar, asir; (take possession of) secuestrar; (: territory) apoderarse de; (opportunity) aprovecharse

de; **to** ~ **(up)on** vt fus valerse de; **to** ~ **up** vi (TECH) agarrotarse.
seizure ['si:ʒə*] n (MED) ataque m; (LAW) incautación f.
seldom ['sɛldəm] ad rara vez.
select [sɪ'lɛkt] a selecto, escogido // vt escoger, elegir; (SPORT) seleccionar; ~**ion** [-'lɛkʃən] n selección f, elección f; (COMM) surtido; ~**ive** a selectivo; ~**or** n (person) seleccionador/a m/f.
self [sɛlf] pron se; (after prep) sí mismo // n, pl **selves** uno mismo; **him**~/**her**~ él mismo/ella misma; **the** ~ el yo.
self... pref auto...; ~-**appointed** a autonombrado; ~-**assured** a seguro de sí mismo; ~-**catering** a sin pensión; ~-**centred** a egocéntrico; ~-**coloured** a de color natural; (of one colour) de un color; ~-**confidence** n confianza en sí mismo; ~-**conscious** a cohibido; ~-**contained** a (gen) independiente; (flat) con entrada particular; ~-**control** n autodominio; ~-**defence** n defensa propia; ~-**discipline** n autodisciplina; ~-**employed** a que trabaja por cuenta propia; ~-**evident** a patente; ~-**governing** a autónomo; ~-**important** a presumido; ~-**indulgent** a inmoderado; ~-**interest** n egoísmo; ~**ish** a egoísta; ~**ishness** n egoísmo; ~**lessly** ad desinteresadamente; ~-**pity** n autocompasión f; ~-**portrait** n autorretrato; ~-**possessed** a sereno, dueño de sí mismo; ~-**preservation** n propia conservación f; ~-**reliant** a independiente, seguro de sí mismo; ~-**respect** n amor m propio; ~-**righteous** a santurrón(ona); ~-**sacrifice** n abnegación f; ~-**satisfied** a satisfecho de sí mismo; ~-**service** a de autoservicio; ~-**sufficient** a autosuficiente; ~-**taught** a autodidacta.
sell [sɛl], pt, pp **sold** vt vender // vi venderse; **to** ~ **at** or **for £10** vender a 10 libros; **to** ~ **off** vt liquidar; **to** ~ **out** vi transigir, transar (AM); ~**er** n vendedor/a m/f; ~**ing price** n precio de venta.
sellotape ['sɛləuteɪp] n celo.
sellout ['sɛlaut] n traición f; (of tickets): **it was a** ~ fue un éxito de taquilla.
selves [sɛlvz] pl of **self**.
semaphore ['sɛməfɔ:*] n semáforo.
semen ['si:mən] n semen m.
semi... [sɛmɪ] pref semi..., medio...; ~**circle** n semicírculo; ~**colon** n punto y coma; ~**conscious** a semiconsciente; ~**detached (house)** n (casa) semiseparada; ~-**final** n semi-final m.
seminar ['sɛmɪnɑ:*] n seminario.
semitone ['sɛmɪtəun] n (MUS) semitono.
semolina [sɛmə'li:nə] n sémola.
senate ['sɛnɪt] n senado; **senator** n senador/a m/f.
send [sɛnd], pt, pp **sent** vt mandar, enviar; (dispatch) despachar; (telegram) poner; **to** ~ **away** vt (letter, goods) despachar; **to** ~ **away for** vt fus despachar por; **to** ~

back vt devolver; **to** ~ **for** vt fus mandar traer; **to** ~ **off** vt (goods) despachar; (SPORT: player) expulsar; **to** ~ **out** vt (invitation) mandar; (signal) emitir; **to** ~ **up** vt (person, price) hacer subir; (parody) parodiar; ~**er** n remitente m/f; ~**-off** n: **a good** ~**-off** una buena despedida.
senile ['si:naɪl] a senil; **senility** [sɪ'nɪlɪtɪ] n senilidad f.
senior ['si:nɪə*] a (older) mayor, más viejo; (: on staff) más antiguo; (of higher rank) superior // n mayor m; (in service) miembro más antiguo; ~**ity** [-'ɔrɪtɪ] n antigüedad f.
sensation [sɛn'seɪʃən] n sensación f; ~**al** a sensacional; ~**alism** n sensacionalismo.
sense [sɛns] n sentido; (feeling) sensación f; (good ~) sentido común, juicio; (sentiment) opinión f // vt sentir, percibir; **it makes** ~ tiene sentido; ~**less** a estúpido, insensato; (unconscious) sin sentido.
sensibility [sɛnsɪ'bɪlɪtɪ] n sensibilidad f; **sensibilities** npl delicadeza sg.
sensible ['sɛnsɪbl] a sensato, juicio; (cautious) prudente; (reasonable) razonable, lógico; (perceptible) apreciable.
sensitive ['sɛnsɪtɪv] a sensible; (touchy) susceptible; **sensitivity** [-'tɪvɪtɪ] n sensibilidad f; susceptibilidad f.
sensual ['sɛnsjuəl] a sensual.
sensuous ['sɛnsjuəs] a sensual.
sent [sɛnt] pt, pp of **send**.
sentence ['sɛntns] n (LING) frase f, oración f; (LAW) sentencia, fallo // vt: **to** ~ **sb to death/to 5 years** condenar a uno a muerte/a 5 años de cárcel.
sentiment ['sɛntɪmənt] n sentimiento; (opinion) opinión f; ~**al** [-'mɛntl] a sentimental; ~**ality** [-'tælɪtɪ] n sentimentalismo.
sentry ['sɛntrɪ] n centinela m.
separate ['sɛprɪt] a separado; (distinct) distinto // (vb: ['sɛpəreɪt]) vt separar; (part) dividir // vi separarse; ~**ly** ad por separado; ~**s** npl (clothes) coordinados mpl; **separation** [-'reɪʃən] n separación f.
September [sɛp'tɛmbə*] n se(p)tiembre m.
septic ['sɛptɪk] a séptico.
sequel ['si:kwl] n consecuencia, resultado; (of story) continuación f.
sequence ['si:kwəns] n sucesión f, serie f; (CINEMA) secuencia.
sequin ['si:kwɪn] n lentejuela.
serenade [sɛrə'neɪd] n serenata // vt dar serenata a.
serene [sɪ'ri:n] a sereno, tranquilo; **serenity** [sə'rɛnɪtɪ] n serenidad f, tranquilidad f.
sergeant ['sɑ:dʒənt] n sargento.
serial ['sɪərɪəl] n novela por entregas; ~**ize** vt publicar por entregas; ~ **number** n número de serie.
series ['sɪəri:s] n serie f.
serious ['sɪərɪəs] a serio; (grave) grave;

~**ly** ad en serio; gravemente; ~**ness** n seriedad f; gravedad f.
sermon ['sɔ:mən] n sermón m.
serrated [sɪ'reɪtɪd] a serrado, dentellado.
serum ['sɪərəm] n suero.
servant ['sɔ:vənt] n (gen) servidor/a m/f; (house ~) criado/a; **civil** ~ funcionario.
serve [sɔ:v] vt (gen) servir; (in shop: goods) servir, despachar; (: customer) atender; (subj: train) pasar por; (treat) tratar; (apprenticeship) hacer; (prison term) cumplir // vi (also TENNIS) sacar; (be useful): **to** ~ **as/for/to do** servir de/para/para hacer // n (TENNIS) saque m; **to** ~ **out**, ~ **up** vt (food) servir.
service ['sɔ:vɪs] n (gen) servicio; (REL) misa; (AUT) mantenimiento; (of dishes) vajilla, juego // vt (car, washing machine) mantener; (: repair) reparar; **the S**~**s** las fuerzas armadas; **to be of** ~ **to sb** ser útil a uno; ~**able** a servible, utilizable; ~ **area** n (on motorway) servicios mpl; ~**man** n militar m; ~ **station** n estación f de servicio.
serviette [sɔ:vɪ'ɛt] n servilleta.
servile ['sɔ:vaɪl] a servil.
session ['sɛʃən] n (sitting) sesión f; **to be in** ~ estar celebrando sesión.
set [sɛt] n juego; (RADIO) aparato; (TV) televisor m; (of utensils) batería; (of cutlery) cubierto; (of books) colección f; (TENNIS) set m; (group of people) grupo; (CINEMA) plató m; (THEATRE) decorado; (HAIRDRESSING) marcado // a (fixed) fijo; (ready) listo; (resolved) resuelto, decidido // (vb: pt, pp set) vt (place) poner, colocar; (fix) fijar; (: a time) señalar; (adjust) ajustar, arreglar; (decide: rules etc) establecer, decidir // vi (sun) ponerse; (jam, jelly) cuajarse; (concrete) fraguar; **to be** ~ **on doing sth** estar empeñado en hacer algo; **to** ~ **to music** poner música a; **to** ~ **on fire** incendiar, poner fuego a; **to** ~ **free** poner en libertad; **to** ~ **sth going** poner algo en marcha; **to** ~ **sail** zarpar, hacerse a la vela; **to** ~ **about** vt fus (task) ponerse a; **to** ~ **aside** vt poner aparte, dejar de lado; **to** ~ **back** vt (in time): **to** ~ **back (by)** retrasar (por); **to** ~ **off** vi partir // vt (bomb) hacer estallar; (cause to start) poner en marcha; (show up well) hacer resaltar; **to** ~ **out** vi: **to** ~ **out to do sth** ponerse a hacer algo // vt (arrange) disponer; (state) exponer; **to** ~ **up** vt (organization, record) establecer; **to** ~ **up shop** (fig) establecerse; ~**back** n (hitch) revés m, contratiempo.
settee [sɛ'ti:] n sofá m.
setting ['sɛtɪŋ] n (frame) marco; (placing) colocación f; (of sun) puesta; (of jewel) engaste m, montadura.
settle ['sɛtl] vt (argument, matter) componer; (accounts) ajustar, liquidar; (land) colonizar; (MED: calm) calmar, sosegar // vi (dust etc) depositarse; (weather) serenarse; (also: ~ **down**)

instalarse, establecerse; **to** ~ **for sth** convenir en aceptar algo; **to** ~ **in** vi instalarse; ~ **on sth** quedar en algo; **to** ~ **up with sb** ajustar cuentas con uno; ~**ment** n (payment) liquidación f; (agreement) acuerdo, convenio; (village etc) pueblo; **settler** n colono/a, colonizador/a m/f.

setup ['sɛtʌp] n (arrangement) plan m; (situation) situación f.

seven ['sɛvn] num siete; ~**teen** num diez y siete, diecisiete; ~**th** a séptimo; ~**ty** num setenta.

sever ['sɛvə*] vt cortar; (relations) romper.

several ['sɛvərl] a, pron varios mpl, algunos mpl; ~ **of us** varios de nosotros.

severance ['sɛvərəns] n (of relations) ruptura; ~ **pay** n pago de despedida.

severe [sɪ'vɪə*] a severo; (serious) grave; (hard) duro; (pain) intenso; **severity** [sɪ'vɛrɪtɪ] n severidad f; gravedad f; intensidad f.

sew [səu], pt **sewed,** pp **sewn** vt, vi coser; **to** ~ **up** vt coser, zurcir.

sewage ['su:ɪdʒ] n (effluence) aguas fpl residuales; (system) alcantarillado.

sewer ['su:ə*] n alcantarilla, cloaca.

sewing ['səuɪŋ] n costura; ~ **machine** n máquina de coser.

sewn [səun] pp of **sew.**

sex [sɛks] n sexo; **to have** ~ **with sb** tener sexo con alguien; ~ **act** n acto sexual.

sextet [sɛks'tɛt] n sexteto.

sexual ['sɛksjuəl] a sexual.

sexy ['sɛksɪ] a sexy.

shabby ['ʃæbɪ] a (person) desharrapado; (clothes) raído, gastado.

shack [ʃæk] n choza, chabola.

shackles ['ʃæklz] npl grilios mpl, grilletes mpl.

shade [ʃeɪd] n sombra; (for lamp) pantalla; (for eyes) visera; (of colour) matiz m, tonalidad f // vt dar sombra a; **in the** ~ en la sombra

shadow ['ʃædəu] n sombra // vt (follow) seguir y vigilar; ~ **cabinet** n (POL) gabinete paralelo formado por el partido de oposición; ~**y** a oscuro; (dim) indistinto.

shady ['ʃeɪdɪ] a sombreado; (fig: dishonest) sospechoso; (: deal) turbio.

shaft [ʃɑ:ft] n (of arrow, spear) astil m; (AUT, TECH) eje m, árbol m; (of mine) pozo; (of lift) hueco, caja; (of light) rayo.

shaggy ['ʃægɪ] a peludo.

shake [ʃeɪk], pt **shook,** pp **shaken** vt sacudir; (building) hacer temblar; (perturb) inquietar, perturbar; (weaken) debilitar; (surprise) sorprender, pasmar // vi estremecerse; (tremble) temblar // n (movement) sacudida; **to** ~ **hands with** sb estrechar la mano con uno; **to** ~ **off** vt sacudirse; (fig) deshacerse de; **to** ~ **up** vt agitar; **shaky** a (hand, voice) trémulo; (building) inestable.

shall [ʃæl] auxiliary vb: **I** ~ **go** iré.

shallot [ʃə'lɔt] n chalote m.

shallow ['ʃæləu] a poco profundo; (fig) superficial.

sham [ʃæm] n fraude m, engaño // a falso, fingido // vt fingir, simular.

shambles ['ʃæmblz] n confusión f.

shame [ʃeɪm] n vergüenza; (pity) lástima // vt avergonzar; **it is a** ~ **that/to do es** una lástima que/hacer; **what a** ~! ¡qué lástima!; ~**faced** a avergonzado; ~**ful** a vergonzoso; ~**less** a descarado; (immodest) impúdico.

shampoo [ʃæm'pu:] n champú m // vt lavar el pelo (con champú).

shamrock ['ʃæmrɔk] n trébol m.

shandy ['ʃændɪ] n mezcla de cerveza con gaseosa.

shan't [ʃɑ:nt] = **shall not.**

shanty town ['ʃæntɪ-] n barrio de chabolas.

shape [ʃeɪp] n forma // vt formar, dar forma a; (sb's ideas) formar; (sb's life) determinar // vi (also: ~ **up**) (events) desarrollarse; (person) formarse; **to take** ~ tomar forma; **-shaped** suff: **heart-shaped** en forma de corazón; ~**ly** a bien informe, sin forma definida; ~**ly** a bien formado o proporcionado.

share [ʃɛə*] n (part) parte f, porción f; (contribution) cuota; (COMM) acción f // vt dividir; (have in common) compartir; **to** ~ **out (among** or **between)** repartir (entre); ~**holder** n accionista m/f.

shark [ʃɑ:k] n tiburón m.

sharp [ʃɑ:p] a (razor, knife) afilado; (point) puntiagudo; (outline) definido; (pain) intenso; (MUS) desafinado; (contrast) marcado; (voice) agudo; (person: quickwitted) astuto; (dishonest) poco escrupuloso // n (MUS) sostenido // ad: **at 2 o'clock** ~ a las 2 en punto; ~**en** vt afilar; (pencil) sacar punta a; (fig) agudizar; ~**ener** n (also: **pencil** ~**ener**) afilador m; ~-**eyed** a de vista aguda; ~-**witted** a listo, perspicaz.

shatter ['ʃætə*] vt hacer añicos o pedazos; (fig: ruin) destruir, acabar con // vi hacerse añicos.

shave [ʃeɪv] vt afeitar, rasurar // vi afeitarse // n: **to have a** ~ afeitarse; **shaver** n (also: **electric shaver**) máquina de afeitar (eléctrica).

shaving ['ʃeɪvɪŋ] n (action) el afeitarse, rasurado; ~**s** npl (of wood etc) virutas fpl; ~ **brush** n brocha (de afeitar); ~ **cream** n crema (de afeitar).

shawl [ʃɔ:l] n chal m.

she [ʃi:] pron ella; ~-**cat** n gata; NB: for ships, countries follow the gender of your translation.

sheaf [ʃi:f], pl **sheaves** n (of corn) gavilla; (of arrows) haz m; (of papers) fajo.

shear [ʃɪə*], pt **sheared,** pp **sheared** or **shorn** vt (sheep) esquilar, trasquilar; **to** ~ **off** vt cercenar; ~**s** npl (for hedge) tijeras fpl de jardín.

sheath [ʃi:θ] n vaina; (contraceptive) preservativo.

sheaves [ʃi:vz] pl of **sheaf.**
shed [ʃɛd] n cobertizo // vt, pt, pp **shed** (gen) desprenderse de; (skin) mudar; (tears) derramar.
she'd [ʃi:d] = **she had; she would.**
sheep [ʃi:p] n, pl inv oveja; ~**dog** n perro pastor; ~**ish** a tímido, vergonzoso; ~**skin** n piel f de carnero.
sheer [ʃɪə*] a (utter) puro, completo; (steep) escarpado; (almost transparent) diáfano // ad verticalmente.
sheet [ʃi:t] n (on bed) sábana; (of paper) hoja; (of glass, metal) lámina.
sheik(h) [ʃeɪk] n jeque m.
shelf [ʃelf], pl **shelves** n estante m.
shell [ʃɛl] n (on beach) concha; (of egg, nut etc) cáscara; (explosive) proyectil m, obús m; (of building) armazón m // vt (peas) desenvainar; (MIL) bombardear.
she'll [ʃi:l] = **she will; she shall.**
shellfish ['ʃelfɪʃ] n, pl inv crustáceo; (pl: as food) mariscos mpl.
shelter ['ʃeltə*] n abrigo, refugio // vt (aid) amparar, proteger; (give lodging to) abrigar; (hide) esconder // vi abrigarse, refugiarse; ~**ed** a (life) protegido; (spot) abrigado.
shelve [ʃelv] vt (fig) aplazar; ~**s** pl of **shelf.**
shepherd ['ʃepəd] n pastor m // vt (guide) guiar, conducir; ~**ess** n pastora f; ~**'s pie** n pastel m de carne y patatas.
sheriff ['ʃerɪf] n sheriff m.
sherry ['ʃerɪ] n jerez m.
she's [ʃi:z] = **she is; she has.**
shield [ʃi:ld] n escudo; (TECH) blindaje m // vt: **to** ~ **(from)** proteger (contra).
shift [ʃɪft] n (change) cambio; (of place) traslado; (of workers) turno // vt trasladar; (remove) quitar // vi moverse; (change place) cambiar de sitio; ~ **work** n trabajo por turno; ~**y** a tramposo; (eyes) furtivo.
shilling ['ʃɪlɪŋ] n chelín m.
shimmer ['ʃɪmə*] n reflejo trémulo // vi relucir.
shin [ʃɪn] n espinilla.
shine [ʃaɪn] n brillo, lustre m // (vb: pt, pp **shone**) vi brillar, relucir // vt (shoes) lustrar, sacar brillo a; **to** ~ **a torch on sth** dirigir una linterna hacia algo.
shingle ['ʃɪŋgl] n (on beach) guijarras fpl; ~**s** n (MED) herpes mpl or fpl.
shiny ['ʃaɪnɪ] a brillante, lustroso.
ship [ʃɪp] n buque m, barco // vt (goods) embarcar; (oars) desarmar; (send) transportar o enviar (por vía marítima); ~**building** n construcción f de barcos; ~**ment** n (act) embarque m; (goods) envío; ~**per** n exportador/a m/f; ~**ping** n (act) embarque m; (traffic) buques mpl; ~**shape** a en regla; ~**wreck** n naufragio; ~**yard** n astillero.
shire ['ʃaɪə*] n condado.
shirk [ʃɔ:k] vt eludir, esquivar; (obligations) faltar a.
shirt [ʃɔ:t] n camisa; **in** ~ **sleeves** en mangas de camisa.

shiver ['ʃɪvə*] n temblor m, estremecimiento // vi temblar, estremecerse.
shoal [ʃəul] n (of fish) banco.
shock [ʃɔk] n (impact) choque m; (ELEC) descarga (eléctrica); (emotional) conmoción f; (start) sobresalto, susto; (MED) postración f nerviosa // vt dar un susto a; (offend) escandalizar; ~ **absorber** n amortiguador m; ~**ing a** (awful) espantoso; (improper) escandaloso; ~**proof** a a prueba de choques.
shod [ʃɔd] pt, pp of **shoe** // a calzado.
shoddy ['ʃɔdɪ] a de pacotilla, de bajísima calidad.
shoe [ʃu:] n zapato; (for horse) herradura; (brake ~) zapata // vt, pt, pp **shod** (horse) herrar; ~**brush** n cepillo para zapatos; ~**horn** n calzador m; ~**lace** n cordón m; ~**maker** n zapatero; ~ **polish** n betún m; ~**shop** n zapatería.
shone [ʃɔn] pt, pp of **shine.**
shook [ʃuk] pt of **shake.**
shoot [ʃu:t] n (on branch, seedling) retoño, vástago // (vb: pt, pp **shot**) vt disparar; (kill) matar (con arma de fuego); (wound) herir (con arma de fuego); (execute) fusilar; (film) rodear, filmar // vi (with gun, bow): **to** ~ **(at)** tirar (a); (FOOTBALL) chutar; **to** ~ **down** vt (plane) derribar; **to** ~ **in/out** vi entrar corriendo/salir disparado; **to** ~ **up** vi (fig) subir (vertiginosamente); ~**ing** n (shots) tiros mpl; (HUNTING) caza con escopeta; ~**ing star** n estrella fugaz.
shop [ʃɔp] n tienda; (workshop) taller m // vi (also: **go** ~**ping**) ir de compras; ~ **assistant** n dependiente/a m/f; ~ **floor** a (fig) de la base; ~**keeper** n tendero/a; ~**lifter** n mechero/a; ~**lifting** n mechería; ~**per** n comprador/a m/f; ~**ping** n (goods) compras fpl; ~**ping bag** n bolsa (de compras); ~**ping centre,** ~**ping center** (US) n zona comercial o de tiendas; ~-**soiled** a usado; ~ **steward** n (INDUSTRY) enlace m/f; ~ **window** n escaparate m.
shore [ʃɔ:*] n (of sea, lake) orilla // vt: **to** ~ **(up)** reforzar.
shorn [ʃɔ:n] pp of **shear.**
short [ʃɔ:t] a (not long) corto; (in time) breve, de corta duración; (person) bajo; (curt) brusco, seco; (insufficient) insuficiente // vi (ELEC) ponerse en cortocircuito // n (also: ~ **film**) cortometraje m; (**a pair of**) ~**s** (unos) pantalones mpl cortos; **to be** ~ **of sth** estar falto de algo; **in** ~ en pocas palabras; **it is** ~ **for** es la forma abreviada de; **to cut** ~ (speech, visit) interrumpir, terminar inesperadamente; **to fall** ~ **of** resultar (ser) insuficiente; **to stop** ~ parar en seco; **to stop** ~ **of** detenerse antes de; ~**age** n escasez f, falta; ~**bread** n torta seca y quebradiza; ~-**circuit** n cortocircuito // vt poner en cortocircuito // vi ponerse en

cortocircuito; ~**coming** n defecto, deficiencia; ~**(crust) pastry** n pasta quebradiza; ~**cut** n atajo; ~**en** vt acortar; (visit) interrumpir; ~**hand** n taquigrafía; ~**hand typist** n taquimecanógrafo/a; ~ **list** n (for job) lista de candidatos escogidos; ~**-lived** a efímero; ~**ly** ad en breve, dentro de poco; ~ **ness** n (of distance) cortedad f; (of time) brevedad f; (manner) brusquedad f; ~**-sighted** a corto de vista, miope; (fig) imprudente; ~ **story** n cuento; ~**-tempered** a enojadizo; ~**-term** a (effect) a corto plazo; ~**wave** n (RADIO) onda corta.

shot [ʃɔt] pt, pp of **shoot** // n (sound) tiro, disparo; (person) tirador/a m/f; (try) tentativa; (injection) inyección f; (PHOT) toma, fotografía; ~**gun** n escopeta.

should [ʃud] auxiliary vb: **I ~ go now** debo irme ahora; **he ~ be there now** debe de haber llegado (ya); **I ~ go if I were you** yo en tu lugar me iría; **I ~ like to me** gustaría.

shoulder ['ʃəuldə*] n hombro, (of road): **hard ~** andén m // vt (fig) cargar con; ~ **blade** n omóplato.

shouldn't ['ʃudnt] = **should not**.

shout [ʃaut] n grito // vt gritar // vi gritar, dar voces; **to ~ down** vt hundir a gritos; ~**ing** n gritería.

shove [ʃʌv] n empujón m // vt empujar; (col: put): **to ~ sth in** meter algo; **to ~ off** vi (NAUT) alejarse del muelle; (fig: col) largarse.

shovel ['ʃʌvl] n pala; (mechanical) excavadora // vt mover con pala.

show [ʃəu] n (of emotion) demostración f; (semblance) apariencia; (exhibition) exposición f; (THEATRE) función f, espectáculo // (vb: pt **showed**, pp **shown**) vt mostrar, enseñar; (courage etc) mostrar, manifestar; (exhibit) exponer; (film) proyectar // vi mostrarse; (appear) aparecer; **to ~ sb in** hacer pasar a uno; **to ~ off** vi (pej) presumir // vt (display) lucir; (pej) hacer gala de; **to ~ sb out** acompañar a uno a la puerta; **to ~ up** vi (stand out) destacar; (col: turn up) presentarse // vt descubrir; (unmask) desenmascarar; ~ **business** n el mundo del espectáculo; ~**down** n crisis f, momento decisivo.

shower ['ʃauə*] n (rain) chaparrón m, chubasco; (of stones etc) lluvia; (also: ~**bath**) ducha // vi llover // vt: **to ~ sb with sth** colmar a uno de algo; ~**proof** a impermeable; ~**y** a (weather) lluvioso.

showing ['ʃəuiŋ] n (of film) proyección f.

show jumping ['ʃəudʒʌmpiŋ] n hipismo.

shown [ʃəun] pp of **show**.

show: ~**-off** n (col: person) presumido; ~**piece** n (of exhibition etc) obra más importante o central; ~**room** n sala de muestras.

shrank [ʃræŋk] pt of **shrink**.

shrapnel ['ʃræpnl] n metralla.

shred [ʃrɛd] n (gen pl) triza, jirón m // vt hacer trizas; (CULIN) desmenuzar.

shrewd [ʃru:d] a astuto; ~**ness** n astucia.

shriek [ʃri:k] n chillido // vt, vi chillar.

shrill [ʃrɪl] a agudo, estridente.

shrimp [ʃrɪmp] n camarón m.

shrine [ʃraɪn] n santuario, sepulcro.

shrink [ʃrɪŋk], pt **shrank**, pp **shrunk** vi encogerse; (be reduced) reducirse // vt encoger; **to ~ from doing sth** no atreverse a hacer algo; ~**age** n encogimiento; reducción f.

shrivel ['ʃrɪvl] (also: ~ **up**) vt (dry) secar; (crease) arrugar // vi secarse; arrugarse.

shroud [ʃraud] n sudario // vt: ~**ed in mystery** envuelto en el misterio.

Shrove Tuesday ['ʃrəuv'tju:zdɪ] n martes m de carnaval.

shrub [ʃrʌb] n arbusto; ~**bery** n arbustos mpl.

shrug [ʃrʌg] n encogimiento de hombros // vt, vi: **to ~ (one's shoulders)** encogerse de hombros; **to ~ off** vt negar importancia a.

shrunk [ʃrʌŋk] pp of **shrink**.

shudder ['ʃʌdə*] n estremecimiento, escalofrío // vi estremecerse.

shuffle ['ʃʌfl] vt (cards) barajar; **to ~ (one's feet)** arrastrar los pies.

shun [ʃʌn] vt rehuir, esquivar.

shunt [ʃʌnt] vt (RAIL) maniobrar // vi: **to ~ to and fro** mandar de aquí para allá.

shut [ʃʌt], pt, pp **shut** vt cerrar // vi cerrarse; **to ~ down** vt, vi cerrarse, parar; **to ~ off** vt (supply etc) interrumpir, cortar; **to ~ up** vi (col: keep quiet) callarse // vt (close) cerrar; (silence) callar; ~**ter** n contraventana; (PHOT) obturador m.

shuttle ['ʃʌtl] n lanzadera; (also: ~ **service**) servicio de transporte entre dos estaciones.

shuttlecock ['ʃʌtlkɔk] n volante m.

shy [ʃaɪ] a tímido; (reserved) reservado, cohibido; (unsociable) huraño; ~**ness** n timidez f; reserva; lo huraño.

Siamese [saɪə'mi:z] a: ~ **cat** gato siamés.

Sicily ['sɪsɪlɪ] n Sicilia.

sick [sɪk] a (ill) enfermo; (nauseated) mareado; (humour) negro; (vomiting): **to be ~** vomitar; **to feel ~** estar mareado; **to be ~ of** (fig) estar harto de; ~ **bay** n enfermería; ~**en** vt dar asco a // vi enfermar; ~**ening** a (fig) asqueroso.

sickle ['sɪkl] n hoz f.

sick: ~ **leave** n baja por enfermedad; ~**ly** a enfermizo; (causing nausea) nauseabundo; ~**ness** n enfermedad f, mal m; (vomiting) náuseas fpl; ~ **pay** n subsidio de enfermedad.

side [saɪd] n (gen) lado; (of body) costado; (of lake) orilla; (aspect) aspecto; (team) equipo; (of hill) ladera // a (door, entrance) accesorio // vi: **to ~ with sb** tomar el partido de uno; **by the ~ of** al lado de; ~ **by ~** juntos(as), lado a lado; **from all ~s** de todos lados; **to take ~s (with)**

tomar partido (con); ~**board** n aparador m; ~**boards**, ~**burns** npl patillas fpl; ~ **effect** n efecto secundario; ~**light** n (AUT) luz f lateral; ~**line** n (SPORT) línea lateral; (fig) empleo suplementario; ~**long** a de soslayo; ~ **road** n calle f lateral; ~**saddle** ad a mujeriegas, a la inglesa; ~ **show** n (stall) caseta; (fig) atracción f secundaria; ~**step** vt (fig) esquivar; ~**track** vt (fig) desviar (de su propósito); ~**walk** n (US) acera; ~**ways** ad de lado.

siding ['saɪdɪŋ] n (RAIL) apartadero, vía muerta.

sidle ['saɪdl] vi: **to** ~ **up (to)** acercarse furtivamente (a).

siege [siːdʒ] n cerco, sitio.

sieve [sɪv] n coladera // vt cribar.

sift [sɪft] vt cribar; (fig: information) escudriñar.

sigh [saɪ] n suspiro // vi suspirar.

sight [saɪt] n (faculty) vista, visión f; (spectacle) espectáculo; (on gun) mira, alza // vt ver, divisar; **in** ~ a la vista; **out of** ~ fuera de (la) vista; ~**seeing** n excursionismo, turismo; **to go** ~**seeing** visitar monumentos.

sign [saɪn] n (with hand) señal f, seña; (indication) indicio; (trace) huella, rastro; (notice) letrero; (written) signo // vt firmar; **to** ~ **sth over to sb** firmar el traspaso de algo a uno; **to** ~ **up** vi (MIL) alistarse // vt (contract) contratar.

signal ['sɪgnl] n señal f // vi (AUT) señalizar // vt (person) hacer señas a uno; (message) transmitir.

signature ['sɪgnətʃə*] n firma.

signet ring ['sɪgnətrɪŋ] n anillo de sello.

significance [sɪg'nɪfɪkəns] n significado; (importance) trascendencia; **significant** [-ənt] a significativo; trascendente.

signify ['sɪgnɪfaɪ] vt significar.

sign: ~ **language** n la mímica, lenguaje m por señas o de señas; ~**post** n indicador m.

silence ['saɪlns] n silencio // vt hacer callar; (guns) reducir al silencio; **silencer** n (on gun, AUT) silenciador m.

silent ['saɪlnt] a (gen) silencioso; (not speaking) callado; (film) mudo; **to remain** ~ guardar silencio.

silhouette [sɪluːˈet] n silueta; ~**d against** destacado sobre o contra.

silicon chip ['sɪlɪkənˈtʃɪp] n plata de silicio, astilla de silicona.

silk [sɪlk] n seda // a de seda; ~**y** a sedoso.

silly ['sɪlɪ] a (person) tonto; (idea) absurdo.

silt [sɪlt] n sedimento.

silver ['sɪlvə*] n plata; (money) moneda suelta // a de plata, plateado; ~ **paper** n papel m de plata; ~**-plated** a plateado; ~**smith** n platero; ~**y** a plateado.

similar ['sɪmɪlə*] a: ~ **to** parecido o semejante a; ~**ity** [-'lærɪtɪ] n parecido, semejanza; ~**ly** ad del mismo modo.

simmer ['sɪmə*] vi hervir a fuego lento.

simpering ['sɪmpərɪŋ] a afectado; (foolish) bobo.

simple ['sɪmpl] a (easy) sencillo; (foolish, COMM) simple; ~**ton** n inocentón/ona m/f; **simplicity** [-'plɪsɪtɪ] n sencillez f; (foolishness) ingenuidad f; **simplify** ['sɪmplɪfaɪ] vt simplificar.

simulate ['sɪmjuleɪt] vt simular; **simulation** [-'leɪʃən] n simulación f.

simultaneous [sɪməl'teɪnɪəs] a simultáneo; ~**ly** ad simultáneamente.

sin [sɪn] n pecado // vi pecar.

since [sɪns] ad desde entonces, después // prep desde // conj (time) desde que; (because) ya que, puesto que; ~ **then** desde entonces.

sincere [sɪn'sɪə*] a sincero; **yours** ~**ly** le saluda (afectuosamente); **sincerity** [-'serɪtɪ] n sinceridad f.

sinful ['sɪnful] a (thought) pecaminoso; (person) pecador(a).

sing [sɪŋ], pt **sang**, pp **sung** vt cantar // vi (gen) cantar; (bird) trinar; (ears) zumbar.

singe [sɪndʒ] vt chamuscar.

singer ['sɪŋə*] n cantante m/f.

singing ['sɪŋɪŋ] n (gen) canto; (songs) canciones fpl; (in the ears) zumbido.

single ['sɪŋgl] a único, solo; (unmarried) soltero; (not double) simple, sencillo; (bed, room) individual // n (also: ~ **ticket**) billete m sencillo; (record) single m; ~**s** npl (TENNIS) individual m; **to** ~ **out** vt (choose) escoger; (point out) singularizar; ~ **bed** n cama individual; **in** ~ **file** en fila de uno; ~**-handed** ad sin ayuda; ~**-minded** a resuelto, firme; ~ **room** n cuarto individual.

singular ['sɪŋgjulə*] a (odd) raro, extraño; (LING) singular // n (LING) singular m.

sinister ['sɪnɪstə*] a siniestro.

sink [sɪŋk] n fregadero // (vb: pt **sank**, pp **sunk**) vt (ship) hundir, echar a pique; (foundations) excavar; (piles etc): **to** ~ **sth** fijar algo bajo tierra // vi (gen) hundirse; **to** ~ **in** vi (fig) penetrar, calar; **a** ~**ing feeling** un sentimiento de que toda se acaba.

sinner ['sɪnə*] n pecador/a m/f.

sinus ['saɪnəs] n (ANAT) seno.

sip [sɪp] n sorbo // vt sorber, beber a sorbitos.

siphon ['saɪfən] n sifón m; **to** ~ **off** vt quitar poco a poco.

sir [sə*] n señor m; S~ **John Smith** el Señor John Smith; **yes** ~ sí, señor.

siren ['saɪərn] n sirena.

sirloin ['səːlɔɪn] n solomillo.

sister ['sɪstə*] n hermana; (nurse) enfermera jefe; ~**-in-law** n cuñada.

sit [sɪt], pt, pp **sat** vi sentarse; (be sitting) estar sentado; (assembly) reunirse // vt (exam) presentarse a; **to** ~ **down** vi sentarse; **to** ~ **in on** asistir a; **to** ~ **up** vi incorporarse; (not go to bed) velar.

site [saɪt] n sitio; (also: **building** ~) solar m // vt situar.

sit-in ['sɪtɪn] n (demonstration)

manifestación *f* de brazos caídos.
sitting ['sıtıŋ] *n* (*of assembly etc*) sesión *f*; (*in canteen*) turno; ~ **room** *n* sala de estar.
situated ['sıtjueıtıd] *a* situado.
situation [sıtju'eıʃən] *n* situación *f*.
six [sıks] *num* seis; ~**teen** *num* diez y seis, dieciséis; ~**th** *a* sexto; ~**ty** *num* sesenta.
size [saız] *n* (*gen*) tamaño; (*extent*) extensión *f*; (*of clothing*) talla; (*of shoes*) número; (*glue*) cola, apresto; **to** ~ **up** *vt* formarse una idea de; ~**able** *a* importante, considerable.
sizzle ['sızl] *vi* crepitar.
skate [skeıt] *n* patín *m*; (*fish: pl inv*) raya // *vi* patinar; ~**board** *n* skateboard *m*; **skater** *n* patinador/a *m/f*; **skating** *n* patinaje *m*; **skating rink** *n* pista de patinaje.
skeleton ['skɛlıtn] *n* esqueleto; (*TECH*) armazón *m*; (*outline*) esquema *m*; ~ **key** *n* llave *f* maestra; ~ **staff** *n* personal *m* reducido.
sketch [skɛtʃ] *n* (*drawing*) dibujo; (*outline*) esbozo, bosquejo; (*THEATRE*) pieza corta // *vt* dibujar; esbozar; ~ **book** *n* libro de dibujos; ~ **pad** *n* bloc *m* de dibujo; ~**y** *a* incompleto.
skewer ['skju:ə*] *n* broqueta.
ski [ski:] *n* esquí *m* // *vi* esquiar; ~ **boot** *n* bota de esquí.
skid [skıd] *n* patinazo // *vi* patinar; ~ **mark** *n* huella de patinazo.
ski: ~**er** *n* esquiador/a *m/f*; ~**ing** *n* esquí *m*; ~ **jump** *n* pista para salto de esquí.
skilful ['skılful] *a* diestro, experto.
ski lift *n* telesilla.
skill [skıl] *n* destreza, pericia; ~**ed** *a* hábil, diestro; (*worker*) cualificado.
skim [skım] *vt* (*milk*) desnatar; (*glide over*) rozar, rasar // *vi*: **to** ~ **through** (*book*) hojear.
skimp [skımp] *vt* (*work*) chapucear; (*cloth etc*) escatimar; ~**y** *a* (*meagre*) escaso; (*skirt*) muy corto.
skin [skın] *n* (*gen*) piel *f*; (*complexion*) cutis *m* // *vt* (*fruit etc*) pelar; (*animal*) despellejar; ~-**deep** *a* superficial; ~ **diving** *n* natación *f* submarina; ~**ny** *a* flaco, magro; ~**tight** *a* (*dress etc*) muy ajustado.
skip [skıp] *n* brinco, salto; (*container*) cuba // *vi* brincar; (*with rope*) saltar a la comba // *vt* (*pass over*) omitir, saltar.
ski pants *npl* pantalones *mpl* de esquí.
skipper ['skıpə*] *n* (*NAUT, SPORT*) capitán *m*.
skipping rope ['skıpıŋ-] *n* cuerda (de saltar).
skirmish ['skɔ:mıʃ] *n* escaramuza.
skirt [skɔ:t] *n* falda // *vt* (*surround*) ceñir, rodear; (*go round*) ladear; ~**ing board** *n* rodapié *m*.
skit [skıt] *n* sátira, parodia.
skittle ['skıtl] *n* bolo; ~**s** *n* (*game*) boliche *m*.
skive [skaıv] *vi* (*Brit: col*) gandulear.

skull [skʌl] *n* calavera; (*ANAT*) cráneo.
skunk [skʌŋk] *n* mofeta; (*fig: person*) canalla *m/f*.
sky [skaı] *n* cielo; ~-**blue** *a* azul celeste; ~**light** *n* tragaluz *m*, claraboya; ~**scraper** *n* rascacielos *m inv*.
slab [slæb] *n* (*stone*) bloque *m*; (*flat*) losa; (*of cake*) porción *f* gruesa.
slack [slæk] *a* (*loose*) flojo; (*slow*) de poca actividad; (*careless*) descuidado; ~**s** *npl* pantalones *mpl*; ~**en** (*also*: ~**en off**) *vi* aflojarse // *vt* aflojar; (*speed*) disminuir.
slag [slæg] *n* escoria, escombros *mpl*; ~ **heap** *n* escorial *m*, escombrera.
slalom ['slɑːləm] *n* slalom *m*.
slam [slæm] *vt* (*door*) cerrar de golpe; (*throw*) arrojar (violentamente); (*criticize*) hablar mal de // *vi* cerrarse de golpe.
slander ['slɑːndə*] *n* calumnia, difamación *f* // *vt* calumniar, difamar; ~**ous** *a* calumnioso, difamatorio.
slang [slæŋ] *n* argot *m*; (*jargon*) jerga; (*private language*) caló.
slant [slɑːnt] *n* sesgo, inclinación *f*; (*fig*) punto de vista; ~**ed**, ~**ing** *a* inclinado.
slap [slæp] *n* palmada; (*in face*) bofetada; (*fig*) palmetazo // *vt* dar una palmada/bofetada a // *ad* (*directly*) exactamente, directamente; ~**dash** *a* descuidado; ~**stick** *n* (*comedy*) payasadas *fpl*.
slash [slæʃ] *vt* acuchillar; (*fig: prices*) quemar.
slate [sleıt] *n* pizarra // *vt* (*fig: criticize*) criticar duramente.
slaughter ['slɔːtə*] *n* (*of animals*) matanza; (*of people*) carnicería // *vt* matar; ~**house** *n* matadero.
Slav [slɑːv] *a* eslavo.
slave [sleıv] *n* esclavo // *vi* (*also*: ~ **away**) sudar tinta; ~**ry** *n* esclavitud *f*; **slavish** *a* servil.
Slavonic [slə'vɔnık] *a* eslavo.
slay [sleı] *vt* matar.
sleazy ['sli:zı] *a* (*fig: place*) de mala fama.
sledge [slɛdʒ] *n* trineo; ~**hammer** *n* mazo.
sleek [sli:k] *a* (*gen*) lustroso; (*neat*) pulcro.
sleep [sli:p] *n* sueño // *vi, pt, pp* **slept** dormir; **to go to** ~ dormirse; **to** ~ **in** *vi* (*oversleep*) dormir tarde; ~**er** *n* (*person*) durmiente *m/f*; (*RAIL: on track*) traviesa; (: *train*) coche-cama *m*; ~**ily** *ad* soñolientamente; ~**ing bag** *n* saco de dormir; ~**ing car** *n* coche-cama *m*; ~**ing pill** *n* somnífero; ~**lessness** *n* insomnio; ~**walker** *n* sonámbulo/a; ~**y** *a* soñoliento.
sleet [sli:t] *n* nevisca.
sleeve [sli:v] *n* manga; (*TECH*) manguito; ~**less** *a* (*garment*) sin mangas.
sleigh [sleı] *n* trineo.
sleight [slaıt] *n*: ~ **of hand** escamoteo.
slender ['slɛndə*] *a* delgado; (*means*) escaso.
slept [slɛpt] *pt, pp of* **sleep.**
slice [slaıs] *n* (*of meat*) tajada; (*of bread*)

rebanada; (*of lemon*) rodaja; (*utensil*) pala // *vt* cortar, tajar; rebanar.

slick [slɪk] *a* (*skilful*) hábil, diestro; (*quick*) rápido; (*astute*) astuto // *n* (*also:* **oil** ~) masa flotante.

slid [slɪd] *pt, pp of* **slide.**

slide [slaɪd] *n* (*in playground*) tobogán *m*; (PHOT) diapositiva; (*also:* **hair** ~) pasador *m* // (*vb: pt, pp* **slid**) *vt* correr, deslizar // *vi* (*slip*) resbalarse; (*glide*) deslizarse; **sliding** *a* (*door*) corredizo.

slight [slaɪt] *a* (*slim*) delgado; (*frail*) delicado; (*pain etc*) leve; (*trifling*) sin importancia; (*small*) pequeño // *n* desaire *m* // *vt* (*offend*) ofender, desairar; **not in the** ~**est** (ni) en lo más mínimo, en absoluto; ~**ly** *ad* ligeramente, un poco.

slim [slɪm] *a* delgado, esbelto // *vi* adelgazar.

slime [slaɪm] *n* limo, cieno; **slimy** *a* limoso.

slimming [ˈslɪmɪŋ] *n* adelgazamiento; **a** ~ **diet** un régimen.

sling [slɪŋ] *n* (MED) cabestrillo; (*weapon*) honda // *vt, pt, pp* **slung** tirar, arrojar.

slip [slɪp] *n* (*slide*) resbalón *m*; (*fall*) tropezón *m*; (*mistake*) descuido; (*underskirt*) combinación *f*; (*of paper*) trozo // *vt* (*slide*) deslizar // *vi* (*slide*) deslizarse; (*stumble*) resbalar(se); (*decline*) decaer; **to give sb the** ~ eludir *o* escaparse de uno; **to** ~ **away** *vi* escabullirse; **to** ~ **in** *vt* meter // *vi* meterse; **to** ~ **out** *vi* (*go out*) salir (un momento).

slipper [ˈslɪpə*] *n* zapatilla.

slippery [ˈslɪpərɪ] *a* resbaladizo.

slip: ~ **road** *n* carretera de acceso; ~**shod** *a* descuidado; ~**-up** *n* (*error*) equivocación *f*; (*by neglect*) descuido; ~**way** *n* grada, gradas *fpl*.

slit [slɪt] *n* raja; (*cut*) corte *m* // *vt, pt, pp* **slit** rajar, cortar.

slither [ˈslɪðə*] *vi* deslizarse.

slob [slɔb] *n* (*col*) patán *m*.

slog [slɔg] *vi* sudar tinta; **it was a** ~ costó trabajo (hacerlo).

slogan [ˈsləʊgən] *n* slogan *m*, lema *m*.

slop [slɔp] *vi* (*also:* ~ **over**) derramarse, desbordarse // *vt* derramar, verter.

slope [sləʊp] *n* (*up*) cuesta, pendiente *m*; (*down*) declive *m*; (*side of mountain*) falda, vertiente *m* // *vi*: **to** ~ **down** estar en declive; **to** ~ **up** inclinarse; **sloping** *a* en pendiente; en declive.

sloppy [ˈslɔpɪ] *a* (*work*) descuidado; (*appearance*) desaliñado.

slot [slɔt] *n* ranura // *vt*: **to** ~ **into** encajar en; ~ **machine** *n* máquina tragaperras.

slouch [slautʃ] *vi*: **to** ~ **about** (*laze*) gandulear.

slovenly [ˈslʌvənlɪ] *a* (*dirty*) desaliñado, desaseado; (*careless*) descuidado.

slow [sləʊ] *a* lento; (*watch*): **to be** ~ atrasarse // *ad* lentamente, despacio // *vt, vi* (*also:* ~ **down,** ~ **up**) retardar; '~' (*road sign*) 'disminuir velocidad'; ~**ly** *ad* lentamente, despacio; **in** ~ **motion** a cámara lenta; ~**ness** *n* lentitud *f*.

sludge [slʌdʒ] *n* lodo, fango.

slug [slʌg] *n* babosa; (*bullet*) posta; ~**gish** *a* (*slow*) lento; (*lazy*) perezoso.

sluice [sluːs] *n* (*gate*) esclusa; (*channel*) canal *m*.

slum [slʌm] *n* (*area*) tugurios *mpl*; (*house*) casucha.

slumber [ˈslʌmbə*] *n* sueño.

slump [slʌmp] *n* (*economic*) depresión *f* // *vi* hundirse.

slung [slʌŋ] *pt, pp of* **sling.**

slur [sləː*] *n* calumnia // *vt* calumniar, difamar; (*word*) pronunciar indistintamente.

slush [slʌʃ] *n* nieve *f* a medio derretir; ~**y** *a* (*snow*) a medio derretir; (*street*) fangoso; (*fig*) sentimental, sensiblero.

slut [slʌt] *n* marrana.

sly [slaɪ] *a* (*clever*) astuto; (*nasty*) malicioso.

smack [smæk] *n* (*slap*) manotada; (*blow*) golpe *m* // *vt* dar una manotada a, golpear con la mano // *vi*: **to** ~ **of** saber a, oler a.

small [smɔːl] *a* pequeño; ~**holder** *n* granjero, parcelero; ~**ish** *a* más bien pequeño; ~**pox** *n* viruela; ~ **talk** *n* cháchara.

smart [smɑːt] *a* elegante; (*clever*) listo, inteligente; (*quick*) rápido, vivo // *vi* escocer, picar; **to** ~**en up** *vi* arreglarse // *vt* arreglar.

smash [smæʃ] *n* (*also:* ~**-up**) choque *m* // *vt* (*break*) hacer pedazos; (*car etc*) estrellar; (SPORT: *record*) romper // *vi* (*collide*) chocar; (*against wall etc*) estrellarse; ~**ing** *a* (*col*) cojonudo.

smattering [ˈsmætərɪŋ] *n*: **a** ~ **of** ligeros conocimientos *mpl* de.

smear [smɪə*] *n* mancha; (MED) citología // *vt* untar; (*fig*) calumniar, difamar.

smell [smɛl] *n* olor *m*; (*sense*) olfato // (*vb: pt, pp* **smelt** *or* **smelled**) *vt, vi* oler; **it** ~**s good/of garlic** huele bien/a ajo; ~**y** *a* que huele mal.

smile [smaɪl] *n* sonrisa // *vi* sonreír; **smiling** *a* sonriente.

smirk [smɜːk] *n* sonrisa falsa *o* afectada.

smith [smɪθ] *n* herrero; ~**y** [ˈsmɪðɪ] *n* herrería.

smock [smɔk] *n* blusa; (*children's*) delantal *m*.

smoke [sməʊk] *n* humo // *vi* fumar; (*chimney*) echar humo // *vt* (*cigarettes*) fumar; ~**d** *a* (*bacon, glass*) ahumado; **smoker** *n* (*person*) fumador/a *m/f*; (RAIL) coche *m* fumador; ~ **screen** *n* cortina de humo; **smoking** *n*: **'no smoking'** (*sign*) 'prohibido fumar'; **smoky** *a* (*gen*) humeante; (*room*) lleno de humo.

smooth [smuːð] *a* (*gen*) liso; (*sea*) tranquilo; (*flat*) llano; (*flavour, movement*) suave; (*person*) culto, refinado; (: *pej*) meloso // *vt* alisar; (*also:* ~ **out**) (*creases, difficulties*) allanar.

smother ['smʌðə*] vt sofocar; (repress) ahogar.

smoulder ['smɔuldə*] vi arder sin llama.

smudge [smʌdʒ] n mancha // vt manchar.

smug [smʌg] a presumido.

smuggle ['smʌgl] vt pasar de contrabando; **smuggler** n contrabandista m/f; **smuggling** n contrabando.

smutty ['smʌtı] a (fig) verde, obsceno.

snack [snæk] n bocado; ~ **bar** n cafetería.

snag [snæg] n dificultad f, pero.

snail [sneıl] n caracol m.

snake [sneık] n (gen) serpiente f; (harmless) culebra; (poisonous) víbora.

snap [snæp] n (sound) castañetazo; (of whip) chasquido; (click) golpe m seco; (photograph) foto f // a repentino // vt (fingers etc) castañetear; (whip) chasquear; (break) quebrar; (photograph) tomar una foto de // vi (break) quebrarse; (fig: person) contestar bruscamente; (sound) hacer un ruido seco; to ~ **shut** cerrarse de golpe; **to ~ at** vt fus (subj: dog) intentar morder; **to ~ off** vi (break) romperse (y separarse); **to ~ up** vt aprovecharse de, agarrar, agarrar; ~**shot** n foto f (instantánea).

snare [snɛə*] n trampa // vt cazar con trampa; (fig) engañar.

snarl [snɑːl] n gruñido // vi gruñir.

snatch [snætʃ] n (fig) robo; (small amount): ~**es of** trocitos mpl de // vt (~ away) arrebatar; (grasp) coger, agarrar.

sneak [sniːk] vi: **to ~ in/out** entrar/salir a hurtadillas // n (fam) soplón/ona m/f; ~**y** a furtivo.

sneer [snıə*] n sonrisa de desprecio // vi sonreír con desprecio; (mock) mofarse.

sneeze [sniːz] n estornudo // vi estornudar.

sniff [snıf] n (of dog) husmeo; (of person) sorbo (por las narices) // vi sorber (por la nariz) // vt husmear, oler.

snigger ['snıgə*] n risa disimulada // vi reírse con disimulo.

snip [snıp] n tijeretazo, (piece) recorte m; (bargain) ganga // vt tijeretear.

sniper ['snaıpə*] n francotirador/a m/f.

snippet ['snıpıt] n retazo.

snivelling ['snıvlıŋ] a (whimpering) llorón(ona).

snob [snɔb] n snob m/f; ~**bery** n snobismo; ~**bish** a snob.

snooker ['snuːkə*] n especie de billar.

snoop [snuːp] vi: **to ~ about** fisgonear; ~**er** n fisgón/ona m/f.

snooty ['snuːtı] a presumido.

snooze [snuːz] n siesta // vi echar una siesta.

snore [snɔː*] vi roncar // n ronquido.

snorkel ['snɔːkl] n tubo snorkel.

snort [snɔːt] n bufido // vi bufar.

snout [snaut] n hocico, morro.

snow [snəu] n nieve f // vi nevar; ~**ball** n bola de nieve // vi acumularse; ~**bound** a bloqueado por la nieve; ~**drift** n ventisquero; ~**drop** n campanilla; ~**fall**

n nevada; ~**flake** n copo de nieve; ~**man** n figura de nieve; ~**plough**, ~**plow** (US) n quitanieves m inv; ~**storm** n nevada, nevasca; **S**~ **White** n Blanca Nieves.

snub [snʌb] vt rechazar con desdén // n desaire m, repulsa.

snuff [snʌf] n rapé m.

snug [snʌg] a (sheltered) abrigado; (fitted) ajustado.

snuggle ['snʌgl] vi: **to ~ up to sb** arrimarse a uno.

so [səu] ad (degree) tan; (manner: thus) así, de este modo // conj así que, por tanto; ~ **that** (purpose) para que, a fin de que; (result) de modo que; ~ **do I** yo también; **if** ~ de ser así, si es así; **I hope** ~ espero que sí; **10 or** ~ 10 más o menos; ~ **far** hasta aquí; ~ **long!** ¡hasta luego!; ~ **many** tantos(as); ~ **much** ad, det tanto; ~ **and** ~ n Fulano.

soak [səuk] vt (drench) empapar; (put in water) remojar // vi remojarse, estar a remojo; **to ~ in** vi penetrar; **to ~ up** vt absorber.

soap [səup] n jabón m; ~**flakes** npl escamas fpl de jabón; ~ **powder** n jabón en polvo; ~**y** a jabonoso.

soar [sɔː*] vi (on wings) remontarse; (building etc) elevarse.

sob [sɔb] n sollozo // vi sollozar.

sober ['səubə*] a (serious) serio; (sensible) sensato; (moderate) moderado; (not drunk) sobrio; (colour, style) discreto; **to ~ up** vi pasársele a uno la borrachera.

Soc. abbr of **society.**

so-called ['səu'kɔːld] a llamado.

soccer ['sɔkə*] n fútbol m.

sociable ['səuʃəbl] a sociable.

social ['səuʃl] a (gen) social; (sociable) sociable // n velada, fiesta; ~ **climber** n arribista m/f; ~ **club** n club m; ~**ism** n socialismo; ~**ist** a, n socialista m/f; ~**ly** ad socialmente; ~ **science** n ciencias fpl sociales; ~ **security** n seguridad f social; ~ **work** n asistencia social; ~ **worker** n asistente/a m/f social.

society [sə'saıətı] n sociedad f; (club) asociación f; (also: **high** ~) buena sociedad.

sociologist [səusı'ɔlədʒıst] n sociólogo; **sociology** [-dʒı] n sociología.

sock [sɔk] n calcetín m.

socket ['sɔkıt] n (ELEC) enchufe m.

sod [sɔd] n (of earth) césped m; (col!) cabrón/ona m/f.

soda ['səudə] n (CHEM) sosa; (also: ~ **water**) sifón m.

sodden ['sɔdn] a empapado.

sodium ['səudıəm] n sodio.

sofa ['səufə] n sofá m.

soft [sɔft] a (gen) blando; (gentle, not loud) suave; (kind) tierno, compasivo; (weak) débil; (stupid) tonto; ~ **drink** n bebida no alcohólica; ~**en** ['sɔfn] vt ablandar; suavizar; debilitar // vi ablandarse; suavizarse; debilitarse; ~**-hearted** a

compasivo, bondadoso; ~ly *ad*
suavemente; (*gently*) delicadamente, con
delicadeza; ~ness *n* blandura; suavidad *f*;
(*sweetness*) dulzura; (*tenderness*) ternura.
soggy ['sɔgɪ] *a* empapado.
soil [sɔɪl] *n* (*earth*) tierra, suelo // *vt*
ensuciar; ~ed *a* sucio.
solace ['sɔlɪs] *n* consuelo.
solar ['sɔuləʳ] *a* solar.
sold [sɔuld] *pt, pp of* **sell;** ~ **out** (*COMM*)
agotado.
solder ['sɔuldəʳ] *vt* soldar // *n* soldadura.
soldier ['sɔuldʒəʳ] *n* (*gen*) soldado; (*army
man*) militar *m*.
sole [sɔul] *n* (*of foot*) planta; (*of shoe*) suela;
(*fish: pl inv*) lenguado // *a* único; ~ly *ad*
únicamente, sólo, solamente.
solemn ['sɔləm] *a* solemne.
solicitor [sə'lɪsɪtəʳ] *n* (*for wills etc*)
notario; (*in court*) abogado.
solid ['sɔlɪd] *a* (*not hollow*) sólido; (*gold etc*)
macizo; (*person*) serio // *n* sólido.
solidarity [sɔlɪ'dærɪtɪ] *n* solidaridad *f*.
solidify [sə'lɪdɪfaɪ] *vi* solidificarse.
solitaire [sɔlɪ'tɛəʳ] *n* (*game, gem*)
solitario.
solitary ['sɔlɪtərɪ] *a* solitario, solo;
(*isolated*) apartado, aislado; (*only*) único;
~ **confinement** *n* incomunicación *f*.
solitude ['sɔlɪtjuːd] *n* soledad *f*.
solo ['sɔuləu] *n* solo; ~ist *n* solista *m/f*.
soluble ['sɔljubl] *a* soluble.
solution [sə'luːʃən] *n* solución *f*.
solve [sɔlv] *vt* resolver, solucionar.
solvent ['sɔlvənt] *a* (*COMM*) solvente // *n*
(*CHEM*) solvente *m*.
sombre, somber (*US*) ['sɔmbəʳ] *a*
sombrío.
some [sʌm] *det* (*a few*) algunos(as);
(*certain*) algún/una; (*a certain number or
amount*) *see phrases below*; (*unspecified*)
algo de // *pron* algunos/as; (*a bit*) algo //
ad: ~ **10 people** unas 10 personas; ~
children came vinieron algunos niños;
have ~ **tea** tome té; **there's** ~ **milk in
the fridge** hay leche en la refrigeradora; ~
was left quedaba algo; **I've got** ~
(*books etc*) tengo algos; (*milk, money
etc*) tengo algo; ~**body** *pron* alguien; ~
day *ad* algún día; ~**how** *ad* de alguna
manera; (*for some reason*) por una u otra
razón; ~**one** *pron* = ~**body**.
somersault ['sʌməsɔːlt] *n* (*deliberate*)
salto mortal; (*accidental*) vuelco // *vi* dar
un salto mortal; dar vuelcos.
something ['sʌmθɪŋ] *pron* algo.
sometime ['sʌmtaɪm] *ad* (*in future*) algún
día, en algún momento; (*in past*): ~ **last
month** durante el mes pasado.
sometimes ['sʌmtaɪmz] *ad* a veces.
somewhat ['sʌmwɔt] *ad* algo.
somewhere ['sʌmwɛəʳ] *ad* (*be*) en alguna
parte; (*go*) a alguna parte; ~ **else** (*be*) en
otra parte; (*go*) a otra parte.
son [sʌn] *n* hijo.
song [sɔŋ] *n* canción *f*; ~**writer** *n*

compositor/a *m/f* de canciones.
sonic ['sɔnɪk] *a* (*boom*) sónico.
son-in-law ['sʌnɪnlɔː] *n* yerno.
sonnet ['sɔnɪt] *n* soneto.
soon [suːn] *ad* pronto, dentro de poco;
(*early*) temprano; ~ **afterwards** poco
después; *see also* **as;** ~**er** *ad* (*time*) antes,
más temprano; (*preference*): **I would**
~**er do that** preferiría hacer eso; ~**er
or later** tarde o temprano.
soot [sut] *n* hollín *m*.
soothe [suːð] *vt* tranquilizar; (*pain*) aliviar.
sophisticated [sə'fɪstɪkeɪtɪd] *a* sofisticado.
soporific [sɔpə'rɪfɪk] *a* soporífero.
sopping ['sɔpɪŋ] *a*: ~ **wet** totalmente
empapado.
soppy ['sɔpɪ] *a* (*pej*) bobo, tonto.
soprano [sə'prɑːnəu] *n* soprano *f*.
sorcerer ['sɔːsərəʳ] *n* hechicero.
sordid ['sɔːdɪd] *a* (*dirty*) sucio, asqueroso;
(*wretched*) miserable.
sore [sɔːʳ] *a* (*painful*) doloroso, que duele;
(*offended*) resentido // *n* llaga; ~**ly** *ad*: **I
am** ~**ly tempted** casi estoy por.
sorrow ['sɔrəu] *n* pena, dolor *m*; ~**ful** *a*
afligido, triste.
sorry ['sɔrɪ] *a* (*regretful*) arrepentido;
(*condition, excuse*) lastimoso; ~**!** ¡lo
siento!, ¡perdón!, ¡perdone!; **to feel** ~ **for
sb** sentir lástima por uno; **I feel** ~ **for
him** me da lástima.
sort [sɔːt] *n* clase *f*, género, tipo // *vt* (*also:*
~ **out:** *papers*) clasificar; (: *problems*)
arreglar, solucionar; ~**ing office** *n*
oficina de distribución de correos.
SOS *n abbr of* **save our souls.**
so-so ['sɔusɔu] *ad* regular, así-así.
soufflé ['suːfleɪ] *n* suflé *m*.
sought [sɔːt] *pt, pp of* **seek.**
soul [sɔul] *n* alma *m*; ~-**destroying** *a*
embrutecedor(a); ~**ful** *a* lleno de
sentimiento; ~**less** *a* desalmado.
sound [saund] *a* (*healthy*) sano; (*safe, not
damaged*) firme, sólido; (*secure*) seguro;
(*reliable, not superficial*) formal, digno de
confianza; (*sensible*) sensato, razonable //
ad: ~ **asleep** profundamente dormido //
n (*noise*) sonido, ruido; (*GEO*) estrecho //
vt (*alarm*) sonar; (*also:* ~ **out:** *opinions*)
consultar, sondear // *vi* sonar, resonar;
(*fig: seem*) parecer; **to** ~ **like** sonar a; ~
barrier *n* barrera del sonido; ~ **effects**
npl efectos *mpl* sonoros; ~**ing** *n* (*NAUT etc*)
sondeo; ~**ly** *ad* (*sleep*) profundamente;
(*beat*) completamente; ~**proof** *a* a
prueba de sonidos; ~**track** *n* (*of film*)
banda sonora.
soup [suːp] *n* (*thick*) sopa; (*thin*) caldo; **in
the** ~ (*fig*) en apuros; ~**spoon** *n* cuchara
sopera.
sour [sauəʳ] *a* agrio; (*milk*) cortado; (*fig*)
desabrido, acre.
source [sɔːs] *n* fuente *f*.
south [sauθ] *n* sur *m* // *a* del sur // *ad* al
sur, hacia el sur; **S**~ **Africa** *n* África del
Sur; **S**~ **African** *a, n* sudafricano/a; **S**~
America *n* América (del Sur); **S**~

American a, n sudamericano/a; ~-**east** n sudeste m; ~**erly** ['sʌðəli] a sur; (from the ~) del sur; ~**ern** ['sʌðən] a del sur, meridional; **S**~ **Pole** n Polo Sur; ~**ward(s)** ad hacia el sur; ~-**west** n suroeste m.
souvenir [su:və'niə*] n recuerdo.
sovereign ['sɔvrin] a, n soberano; ~**ty** n soberanía.
soviet ['səuviət] a soviético; **the S**~ **Union** la Unión Soviética.
sow [sau] n cerda, puerca // vt [səu], pt **sowed**, pp **sown** [səun] (gen) sembrar; (spread) esparcir.
soy [sɔi] n: ~ **sauce** salsa de soja.
soya bean ['sɔiəbi:n] n semilla de soja.
spa [spɑ:] n (spring) baños mpl térmicos; (town) balneario.
space [speis] n (gen) espacio; (room) sitio // vt (also: ~ **out**) espaciar; ~**craft** n nave f espacial; ~**man/woman** n astronauta m/f, cosmonauta m/f; **spacing** n espaciamiento.
spacious ['speiʃəs] a amplio.
spade [speid] n (tool) pala, laya; ~**s** npl (CARDS: British) picos mpl; (: Spanish) espadas fpl.
spaghetti [spə'geti] n espaguetis mpl, fideos mpl.
Spain [spein] n España.
span [spæn] n (of bird, plane) envergadura; (of hand) palmo; (of arch) luz f; (in time) lapso // vt extenderse sobre, cruzar; (fig) abarcar.
Spaniard ['spænjəd] n español/a m/f.
spaniel ['spænjəl] n perro de aguas.
Spanish ['spæniʃ] a español(a) // n (LING) español m, castellano.
spank [spæŋk] vt zurrar.
spanner ['spænə*] n llave f (inglesa).
spar [spɑ:*] n palo, verga // vi (BOXING) entrenarse.
spare [spɛə*] a (free) desocupado; (surplus) sobrante, de más; (available) disponible // n (part) pieza de repuesto // vt (do without) pasarse sin; (afford to give) tener de sobra; (refrain from hurting) perdonar; (be grudging with) escatimar; ~ **part** n pieza de repuesto; ~ **time** n ratos mpl de ocio, tiempo libre.
sparing ['spɛəriŋ] a: **to be** ~ **with** ser parco en; ~**ly** ad escasamente.
spark [spɑ:k] n chispa; (fig) chispazo; ~(**ing**) **plug** n bujía.
sparkle ['spɑ:kl] n centelleo, destello // vi centellear; (shine) relucir, brillar; **sparkling** a centelleante; (wine) espumoso.
sparrow ['spærəu] n gorrión m.
sparse [spɑ:s] a esparcido, escaso.
spasm ['spæzəm] n (MED) espasmo; (fig) arranque m, acceso; ~**odic** [-'mɔdik] a espasmódico.
spastic ['spæstik] n espástico/a.
spat [spæt] pt, pp of **spit**.
spate [speit] n (fig): ~ **of** torrente m de; **in** ~ (river) crecido.

spatter ['spætə*] vt salpicar, rociar.
spatula ['spætjulə] n espátula.
spawn [spɔ:n] vi desovar, frezar // n huevas fpl.
speak [spi:k], pt **spoke,** pp **spoken** vt (language) hablar; (truth) decir // vi hablar; (make a speech) intervenir; **to** ~ **to sb/of** or **about sth** hablar con uno/de o sobre algo; ~ **up!** ¡habla fuerte!; ~**er** n (in public) orador/a m/f; (also: **loud**~**er**) altavoz m, parlante m; (POL): **the S**~**er** el Presidente del Congreso.
spear [spiə*] n lanza; (for fishing) arpón m // vt alancear; arponear; ~**head** n punta de lanza.
special ['spɛʃl] a especial; (edition etc) extraordinario; (delivery) urgente; **take** ~ **care** ponga un cuidado especial; ~**ist** n especialista m/f; ~**ity** [spɛʃi'æliti] n especialidad f; ~**ize** vi: **to** ~**ize (in)** especializarse en; ~**ly** ad sobre todo, en particular.
species ['spi:ʃi:z] n especie f.
specific [spə'sifik] a específico; ~**ally** ad específicamente.
specification [spɛsifi'keiʃən] n especificación f; ~**s** npl presupuesto; **specify** ['spɛsifai] vt, vi especificar, precisar.
specimen ['spɛsimən] n ejemplar m, espécimen m.
speck [spɛk] n grano, mota.
speckled ['spɛkld] a moteado.
specs [spɛks] npl (col) gafas fpl.
spectacle ['spɛktəkl] n espectáculo; ~**s** npl gafas fpl, anteojos mpl; **spectacular** [-'tækjulə*] a espectacular; (success) impresionante.
spectator [spɛk'teitə*] n espectador/a m/f.
spectre, specter (US) ['spɛktə*] n espectro, fantasma m.
spectrum ['spɛktrəm], pl -**tra** [-trə] n espectro.
speculate ['spɛkjuleit] vi especular; (try to guess): **to** ~ **about** especular sobre; **speculation** ['lɛiʃən] n especulación f.
speech [spi:tʃ] n (faculty) habla, palabra; (formal talk) discurso; (talk) palabras fpl; (language) idioma m, lenguaje m; ~ **less** a mudo, estupefacto.
speed [spi:d] n velocidad f, rapidez f; (haste) prisa; (promptness) prontitud f; **at full** or **top** ~ a máxima velocidad; **to** ~ **up** vi acelerarse // vt acelerar; ~**boat** n lancha motora; ~**ily** ad rápido, rápidamente; ~**ing** n (AUT) exceso de velocidad; ~ **limit** n límite m de velocidad, velocidad f máxima; ~**ometer** [spi'dɔmitə*] n velocímetro; ~-**way** n (SPORT) carreras fpl de moto; ~**y** a (fast) veloz, rápido; (prompt) pronto.
spell [spɛl] n (also: **magic** ~) encanto, hechizo; (period of time) rato, período; (turn) turno // vt, pt, pp **spelt** or **spelled** (also: ~ **out**) deletrear; (fig) anunciar, presagiar; **to cast a** ~ **on sb** hechizar a

uno; **he can't** ~ no sabe escribir bien, sabe poco de ortografía; ~**bound** a embelesado, hechizado; ~**ing** n ortografía.

spend [spɛnd], pt, pp **spent** [spɛnt] vt (money) gastar; (time) pasar; (life) dedicar; ~**thrift** n derrochador/a m/f, pródigo/a.

sperm [spɔːm] n esperma; ~ **whale** n cachalote m.

spew [spju:] vt vomitar, arrojar.

sphere [sfɪə*] n esfera; **spherical** ['sfɛrɪkl] a esférico.

sphinx [sfɪŋks] n esfinge f.

spice [spaɪs] n especia // vt especiar; **spicy** a especiado; (fig) picante.

spider ['spaɪdə*] n araña.

spike [spaɪk] n (point) punta; (zool) pincho, púa; (bot) espiga.

spill [spɪl], pt, pp **spilt** or **spilled** vt derramar, verter // vi derramarse; **to** ~ **over** desbordarse.

spin [spɪn] n (revolution of wheel) vuelta, revolución f; (aviat) barrena; (trip in car) paseo (en coche) // (vb: pt, pp **spun**) vt (wool etc) hilar; (wheel) girar // vi girar, dar vueltas; **to** ~ **out** vt alargar, prolongar.

spinach ['spɪnɪtʃ] n espinaca; (as food) espinacas fpl.

spinal ['spaɪnl] a espinal; ~ **cord** n columna vertebral.

spindly ['spɪndlɪ] a zanquivano.

spin-drier [spɪn'draɪə*] n secador m centrífugo.

spine [spaɪn] n espinazo, columna vertebral; (thorn) espina; ~**less** a (fig) débil, flojo.

spinning ['spɪnɪŋ] n (of thread) hilado; (art) hilandería; ~ **top** n peonza; ~ **wheel** n rueca, torno de hilar.

spinster ['spɪnstə*] n soltera; (pej) solterona.

spiral ['spaɪərl] n espiral m // a en espiral; ~ **staircase** n escalera de caracol.

spire ['spaɪə*] n aguja, chapitel m.

spirit ['spɪrɪt] n (gen) espíritu m; (soul) alma m; (ghost) fantasma m; (humour) humor m; (courage) valor m, ánimo; ~**s** npl (drink) alcohol m, bebidas fpl alcohólicas; **in good** ~**s** alegre, de buen ánimo; ~**ed** a enérgico, vigoroso; ~ **level** n nivel m de aire.

spiritual ['spɪrɪtjuəl] a espiritual // n (also: **Negro** ~) canción f religiosa, espiritual m; ~**ism** n espiritualismo.

spit [spɪt] n (for roasting) asador m, espetón m // vi, pt, pp **spat** escupir; (sound) chisporrotear.

spite [spaɪt] n rencor m, ojeriza // vt causar pena a, mortificar; **in** ~ **of** a pesar de, pese a; ~**ful** a rencoroso, malévolo.

spittle ['spɪtl] n saliva, baba.

splash [splæʃ] n (sound) chapoteo; (of colour) mancha // vt salpicar de // vi (also: ~ **about**) chapotear.

spleen [spli:n] n (anat) bazo.

splendid ['splɛndɪd] a espléndido; **splendour, splendor** (us) [-də*] n esplendor m; (of achievement) brillo, gloria.

splint [splɪnt] n tablilla.

splinter ['splɪntə*] n (of wood) astilla; (in finger) espigón m // vi astillarse, hacer astillas.

split [splɪt] n hendedura, raja; (fig) división f; (pol) escisión f // (vb: pt, pp **split**) vt partir, rajar; (party) dividir; (work, profits) repartir // vi (divide) dividirse, escindirse; **to** ~ **up** vi (couple) separarse; (meeting) acabarse.

splutter ['splʌtə*] vi chisporrotear; (person) balbucear.

spoil [spɔɪl], pt, pp **spoilt** or **spoiled** vt (damage) dañar; (mar) estropear, echar a perder; (child) mimar, consentir; ~**s** npl despojo sg, botín m; ~**sport** n aguafiestas m inv.

spoke [spəuk] pt of **speak** // n rayo, radio.

spoken ['spəukn] pp of **speak**.

spokesman ['spəuksmən] n vocero, portavoz m.

sponge [spʌndʒ] n esponja; (cake) pastel m // vt (wash) lavar con esponja // vi: **to** ~ **on sb** vivir a costa de uno; ~ **bag** n esponjera; ~ **cake** n bizcocho, pastel m; **spongy** a esponjoso.

sponsor ['spɔnsə*] n (radio, tv) patrocinador/a m/f; (for membership) padrino; (comm) fiador/a m/f // vt patrocinar; apadrinar; (idea etc) presentar, promover; ~**ship** n patrocinio.

spontaneous [spɔn'teɪnɪəs] a espontáneo.

spool [spu:l] n carrete m; (of sewing machine) canilla.

spoon [spu:n] n cuchara; ~**-feed** vt dar de comer con cuchara; (fig) tratar como un niño; ~**ful** n cucharada.

sporadic [spə'rædɪk] a esporádico.

sport [spɔːt] n deporte m; (person) buen perdedor m; ~**ing** a deportivo; ~**s car** n coche m sport; ~**s jacket** n chaqueta sport; **sportsman** n deportista m; **sportsmanship** n deportividad f; **sportswear** n trajes mpl de deporte o sport; **sportswoman** n deportista f; ~**y** a deportivo.

spot [spɔt] n sitio, lugar m; (dot: on pattern) punto, mancha; (pimple) grano; (freckle) peca; (small amount): **a** ~ **of** un poquito de // vt (notice) notar, observar; **on the** ~ en el acto, acto seguido; (in difficulty) en un aprieto; ~ **check** n reconocimiento rápido; ~**less** a nítido, perfectamente limpio; ~**light** n foco, reflector m; ~**ted** a (pattern) de puntos; ~**ty** a (face) con granos.

spouse [spauz] n cónyuge m/f.

spout [spaut] n (of jug) pico; (pipe) caño // vi chorrear.

sprain [spreɪn] n torcedura // vt: **to** ~ **one's ankle** torcerse el tobillo.

sprang [spræŋ] pt of **spring**.

sprawl [sprɔːl] vi tumbarse.
spray [spreɪ] n rociada; (of sea) espuma; (container) atomizador m; (of paint) pistola rociadora; (of flowers) ramita // vt rociar; (crops) regar.
spread [sprɛd] n extensión f; (distribution) diseminación f, propagación f; (col: food) comilona // (vb: pt, pp **spread**) vt extender; diseminar; (butter) untar; (wings, sails) desplegar; (scatter) esparcir // vi extenderse; diseminarse; untarse; desplegarse; esparcirse.
spree [spriː] n: **to go on a** ~ ir de juerga.
sprightly ['spraɪtlɪ] a vivo, enérgico.
spring [sprɪŋ] n (leap) salto, brinco; (coiled metal) resorte m; (season) primavera; (of water) fuente f, manantial f // vi, pt **sprang**, pp **sprung** (arise) brotar, nacer; (leap) saltar, brincar; **to** ~ **up** vi nacer de repente, aparecer repentinamente; ~-**board** n trampolín m; ~-**clean** n (also: ~-**cleaning**) limpieza general; ~**time** n primavera; ~**y** a elástico; (grass) muelle.
sprinkle ['sprɪŋkl] vt (pour) rociar; **to** ~ **water on,** ~ **with water** rociar o salpicar de agua; ~**d with** (fig) sembrado o salpicado de.
sprint [sprɪnt] n sprint m // vi (gen) correr a toda velocidad; (SPORT) sprintar; ~**er** n sprinter m/f, corredor/a m/f.
sprite [spraɪt] n duende m.
sprout [spraut] vi brotar, retoñar; (**Brussels**) ~**s** npl colecillos mpl de Bruselas.
spruce [spruːs] n (BOT) pícea // a aseado, pulcro.
sprung [sprʌŋ] pp of **spring.**
spry [spraɪ] a ágil, activo.
spun [spʌn] pt, pp of **spin.**
spur [spɔː*] n espuela; (fig) estímulo, aguijón m // vt (also: ~ **on**) estimular, incitar; **on the** ~ **of the moment** de improviso.
spurn [spəːn] vt desdeñar, rechazar.
spurt [spəːt] n esfuerzo supremo; (of energy) arrebato // vi hacer un esfuerzo supremo.
spy [spaɪ] n espía m/f // vi: **to** ~ **on** espiar a // vt (see) divisar, lograr ver; ~**ing** n espionaje m.
sq. abbr of **square.**
squabble ['skwɔbl] n riña, pelea // vi reñir, pelear.
squad [skwɔd] n (MIL, POLICE) pelotón m, escuadra.
squadron ['skwɔdrn] n (MIL) escuadrón m; (AVIAT, NAUT) escuadra.
squalid ['skwɔlɪd] a vil, miserable, escuálido.
squall [skwɔːl] n (storm) chubasco; (wind) ráfaga.
squalor ['skwɔlə*] n miseria.
squander ['skwɔndə*] vt (money) derrochar, despilfarrar; (chances) desperdiciar.
square [skwɛə*] n cuadro; (in town) plaza // a cuadrado; (col: ideas, tastes) pasota //

vt (arrange) arreglar; (MATH) cuadrar; **all** ~ igual(es); **a** ~ **meal** una comida abundante; **2 metres** ~ 2 metros en cuadro; **1** ~ **metre** un metro cuadrado; ~**ly** ad en cuadro; (fully) de lleno.
squash [skwɔʃ] n (drink): **lemon/orange** ~ zumo de limón/naranja; (SPORT) squash m, frontenis m // vt aplastar; **to** ~ **together** apiñar.
squat [skwɔt] a achaparrado // vi agacharse, sentarse en cuclillas; ~**ter** n persona que ocupa ilegalmente una casa.
squawk [skwɔːk] vi graznar.
squeak [skwiːk] n chirrido, rechinamiento; (of shoe) crujido; (of mouse) chillido // vi chirriar, rechinar; crujir; chillar.
squeal [skwiːl] vi chillar, dar gritos agudos.
squeamish ['skwiːmɪʃ] a delicado, remilgado.
squeeze [skwiːz] n (gen) estrujón m; (of hand) apretón m; (in bus etc) apiñamiento // vt estrujar, apretar; (hand, arm) apretar; **to** ~ **out** vt exprimir; (fig) excluir; **to** ~ **through** abrirse paso con esfuerzos.
squelch [skwɛltʃ] vi aplastar, despachurrar.
squid [skwɪd] n calamar m.
squint [skwɪnt] vi bizquear, ser bizco // n (MED) estrabismo; **to** ~ **at sth** mirar algo de soslayo.
squirm [skwəːm] vi retorcerse, revolverse.
squirrel ['skwɪrəl] n ardilla.
squirt [skwəːt] vi salir a chorros.
Sr abbr of **senior.**
St abbr of **saint; street.**
stab [stæb] n (with knife etc) puñalada; (of pain) pinchazo; (col: try): **to have a** ~ **at (doing) sth** intentar (hacer) algo // vt apuñalar.
stability [stə'bɪlɪtɪ] n estabilidad f;
stabilize ['steɪbəlaɪz] vt estabilizar // vi estabilizarse; **stable** ['steɪbl] a estable // n cuadra, caballeriza.
stack [stæk] n montón m, pila // vt amontonar, apilar.
stadium ['steɪdɪəm] n estadio.
staff [stɑːf] n (work force) personal m, plantilla; (stick) bastón m // vt proveer de personal.
stag [stæg] n ciervo, venado.
stage [steɪdʒ] n escena; (profession): **the** ~ el escenario, el teatro; (point) etapa; (platform) plataforma // vt (play) poner en escena, representar; (demonstration) montar, organizar; (fig: perform: recovery etc) llevar a cabo; ~**coach** n diligencia; ~ **door** n entrada de artistas; ~ **manager** n director/a m/f de escena.
stagger ['stægə*] vi tambalear // vt (amaze) asombrar; (hours, holidays) escalonar; ~**ing** a (amazing) asombroso, pasmoso.
stagnant ['stægnənt] a estancado;
stagnate [-'neɪt] vi estancarse.
stag party n fiesta de solteros.

staid [steɪd] a serio, formal.
stain [steɪn] n mancha; (colouring) tintura // vt manchar; (wood) teñir; ~ed glass window n vidriera de colores; ~less a (steel) inoxidable.
stair [steə*] n (step) peldaño, escalón m; ~s npl escaleras fpl; ~case, ~way n escalera.
stake [steɪk] n estaca, poste m; (BETTING) apuesta // vt apostar; to be at ~ estar en juego.
stalactite ['stælɔktaɪt] n estalactita.
stalagmite ['stælɔgmaɪt] n estalagmita.
stale [steɪl] a (bread) duro; (food) no fresco, pasado.
stalemate ['steɪlmeɪt] n tablas fpl (por ahogado); (fig) estancamiento.
stalk [stɔːk] n tallo, caña // vt acechar, cazar al acecho; to ~ off irse con paso airado.
stall [stɔːl] n (in market) puesto; (in stable) casilla (de establo) // vt (AUT) parar // vi (AUT) pararse; (fig) buscar evasivas; ~s npl (in cinema, theatre) butacas fpl.
stallion ['stælɪən] n caballo padre, semental m.
stalwart ['stɔːlwɔt] n (in build) fornido; (in spirit) valiente.
stamina ['stæmɪnə] n resistencia.
stammer ['stæmə*] n tartamudeo, balbuceo // vi tartamudear, balbucir.
stamp [stæmp] n sello, estampilla; (mark, also fig) marca, huella; (on document) timbre m // vi patear // vt patear, golpear con el pie; (in dance) zapatear; (letter) poner sellos en; (with rubber ~) marcar con estampilla; ~ album n álbum m para sellos; ~ collecting n filatelia.
stampede [stæm'piːd] n estampida.
stance [stæns] n postura.
stand [stænd] n (position) posición f, postura; (for taxis) parada; (hall ~) perchero; (music ~) atril m; (SPORT) tribuna; (news ~) quiosco // (vb: pt, pp stood) vi (be) estar, encontrarse; (be on foot) estar de pie; (rise) levantarse; (remain) quedar en pie // vt (place) poner, colocar; (tolerate, withstand) aguantar, soportar; (cost) pagar; (invite) invitar; to make a ~ resistir; (fig) aferrarse a un principio; to ~ for parliament presentarse como candidato al parlamento; to ~ by vi (be ready) estar listo // vt fus (opinion) aferrarse a; to ~ for vt fus (defend) apoyar; (signify) significar; (tolerate) aguantar, permitir; to ~ in for vt fus suplir a; to ~ out vi (be prominent) destacarse; to ~ up vi (rise) levantarse, ponerse de pie; to ~ up for vt fus defender; to ~ up to vt fus hacer frente a.
standard ['stændəd] n patrón m, norma; (flag) estandarte m; (degree) grado // a (size etc) normal, corriente, stándard; ~s npl (morals) valores mpl morales; ~ize vt estandarizar; ~ lamp n lámpara de pie; ~ of living n nivel m de vida.

stand-by ['stændbaɪ] n (alert) alerta, aviso; to be on ~ estar sobre aviso; ~ ticket n (AVIAT) billete m standby.
stand-in ['stændɪn] n suplente m/f; (CINEMA) doble m/f.
standing ['stændɪŋ] a (upright) derecho; (on foot) de pie, en pie // n reputación f; of many years' ~ que lleva muchos años; ~ order n (at bank) giro bancario; ~ orders npl (MIL) reglamento sg general; ~ room n sitio para estar de pie.
stand: ~-offish a reservado, poco afable; ~point n punto de vista; ~still n: at a ~still paralizado, en paro; to come to a ~still pararse, quedar paralizado.
stank [stæŋk] pt of stink.
staple ['steɪpl] n (for papers) grapa // a (food etc) corriente // vt unir con grapa, engrapar; **stapler** n grapadora.
star [stɑː*] n estrella; (celebrity) estrella, astro // vi: to ~ in ser la estrella o el astro de.
starboard ['stɑːbəd] n estribor m.
starch [stɑːtʃ] n almidón m; ~ed a (collar) almidonado; ~y a feculento.
stardom ['stɑːdəm] n estrellato, calidad f de estrella.
stare [steə*] n mirada fija // vt: to ~ at mirar fijo.
starfish ['stɑːfɪʃ] n estrella de mar.
stark [stɑːk] a (bleak) severo, escueto // ad: ~ naked en cueros, en pelota.
starlight ['stɑːlaɪt] n: by ~ a la luz de las estrellas.
starling ['stɑːlɪŋ] n estornino.
starry ['stɑːrɪ] a estrellado; ~-eyed a (innocent) inocentón(ona), ingenuo.
start [stɑːt] n (beginning) principio, comienzo; (departure) salida; (sudden movement) salto, sobresalto; (advantage) ventaja // vt empezar, comenzar; (cause) causar; (found) fundar; (engine) poner en marcha // vi (begin) comenzar, empezar; (with fright) asustarse, sobresaltarse; (train etc) salir; to ~ off vi empezar, comenzar; (leave) salir, ponerse en camino; to ~ up vi comenzar; (car) ponerse en marcha // vt comenzar; (car) poner en marcha; ~er n (AUT) botón m de arranque; (SPORT. official) juez m/f de salida; (: runner) corredor/a m/f; (CULIN) entrada; ~ing point n punto de partida.
startle ['stɑːtl] vt asustar, sobrecoger; **startling** a alarmante.
starvation [stɑː'veɪʃən] n hambre f; (MED) inanición f; **starve** vi pasar hambre; (to death) morir de hambre // vt hacer pasar hambre; (fig) privar; I'm starving estoy muerto de hambre.
state [steɪt] n estado // vt (say, declare) afirmar; (a case) presentar, exponer; the S~s los Estados Unidos; to be in a ~ estar agitado; ~ly a majestuoso, imponente; ~ment n afirmación f; (LAW) declaración f; **statesman** n estadista m.
static ['stætɪk] n (RADIO) parásitos mpl // a estático; ~ electricity n estática.

station ['steɪʃən] *n* (*gen*) estación *f*; (*place*) puesto, sitio; (*RADIO*) emisora; (*rank*) posición *f* social // *vt* colocar, situar; (*MIL*) apostar.
stationary ['steɪʃnərɪ] *a* estacionario, fijo.
stationer's (shop) ['steɪʃənəz] *n* papelería; **stationery** [-nərɪ] *n* papel *m* de escribir.
station master *n* (*RAIL*) jefe *m* de estación.
station wagon *n* (*US*) break *m*.
statistic [stə'tɪstɪk] *n* estadística; ~s *npl* (*science*) estadística *sg*; ~al *a* estadístico.
statue ['stætjuː] *n* estatua.
stature ['stætʃə*] *n* estatura; (*fig*) talla.
status ['steɪtəs] *n* condición *f*, estado; (*reputation*) reputación *f*, státus *m*; **the ~ quo** el statu quo; **~ symbol** *n* símbolo de prestigio.
statute ['stætjuːt] *n* estatuto, ley *f*; **statutory** *a* estatutario.
staunch [stɔːntʃ] *a* firme, incondicional.
stave [steɪv] *vt*: **to ~ off** (*attack*) rechazar; (*threat*) evitar.
stay [steɪ] *n* (*period of time*) estancia // *vi* (*remain*) quedar, quedarse; (*as guest*) hospedarse; (*spend some time*) pasar (un) tiempo; **to ~ put** seguir en el mismo sitio; **to ~ the night** pasar la noche; **to ~ behind** *vi* quedar atrás; **to ~ in** *vi* (*at home*) quedarse en casa; **to ~ on** *vi* quedarse; **to ~ out** *vi* (*of house*) no volver a casa; **to ~ up** *vi* (*at night*) velar, no acostarse; **~ing power** *n* resistencia.
steadfast ['stɛdfɑːst] *a* firme, resuelto.
steadily ['stɛdɪlɪ] *ad* (*firmly*) firmemente; (*unceasingly*) sin parar; (*fixedly*) fijamente; (*walk*) normalmente; (*drive*) a velocidad constante.
steady ['stɛdɪ] *a* (*constant*) constante, fijo; (*unswerving*) firme; (*regular*) regular; (*person, character*) sensato, juicioso; (*diligent*) trabajador; (*calm*) sereno // *vt* (*hold*) mantener firme; (*stabilize*) estabilizar; (*nerves*) calmar; **to ~ o.s. on** *or* **against** sth afirmarse en algo.
steak [steɪk] *n* (*gen*) filete *m*; (*beef*) bistec *m*.
steal [stiːl], *pt* **stole**, *pp* **stolen** *vt*, *vi* robar.
stealth [stɛlθ] *n*: **by ~** a escondidas, sigilosamente; **~y** *a* cauteloso, sigiloso.
steam [stiːm] *n* vapor *m*; (*mist*) vaho, humo // *vt* empañar; (*CULIN*) cocer al vapor // *vi* echar vapor; (*ship*): **to ~ along** avanzar, ir avanzando; **~ engine** *n* máquina de vapor; **~er** *n* vapor *m*; **~roller** *n* apisonadora; **~y** *a* vaporoso; (*room*) lleno de vapor; (*window*) empañado.
steel [stiːl] *n* acero // *a* de acero; **~works** *n* (fábrica) siderúrgica.
steep [stiːp] *a* escarpado, abrupto; (*stair*) empinado; (*price*) exorbitante, excesivo // *vt* empañar, remojar.
steeple ['stiːpl] *n* aguja, campanario; **~chase** *n* carrera de obstáculos; **~jack**

n reparador *m* de chimeneas.
steer [stɪə*] *vt* conducir, dirigir // *vi* conducir; **~ing** *n* (*AUT*) dirección *f*; **~ing wheel** *n* volante *m*.
stellar ['stɛlə*] *a* estelar.
stem [stɛm] *n* (*of plant*) tallo; (*of glass*) pie *m*; (*of pipe*) cañón *m* // *vt* detener; (*blood*) restañar; **to ~ from** *vt fus* proceder de.
stench [stɛntʃ] *n* hedor *m*.
stencil ['stɛnsl] *n* (*typed*) cliché *m*, clisé *m*; (*lettering*) plantilla // *vt* hacer un cliché de.
step [stɛp] *n* paso; (*sound*) paso, pisada; (*stair*) peldaño, escalón *m* // *vi*: **to ~ forward** dar un paso adelante; **~s** *npl* = **~ladder**; **to ~ down** *vi* (*fig*) retirarse; **to ~ off** *vt fus* bajar de; **to ~ on** *vt fus* pisar; **to ~ over** *vt fus* pasar por encima de; **to ~ up** *vt* (*increase*) aumentar; **~brother** *n* hermanastro; **~daughter** *n* hijastra; **~father** *n* padrastro; **~ladder** *n* escalera de tijera o doble; **~mother** *n* madrastra; **~ping stone** *n* pasadera; **~sister** *n* hermanastra; **~son** *n* hijastro.
stereo ['stɛrɪəu] *n* estereo // *a* (*also*: **~phonic**) estereo(fónico).
stereotype ['stɪərɪətaɪp] *n* estereotipo // *vt* estereotipar.
sterile ['stɛraɪl] *a* estéril; **sterility** [-'rɪlɪtɪ] *n* esterilidad *f*; **sterilization** [-'zeɪʃən] *n* esterilización *f*; **sterilize** ['stɛrɪlaɪz] *vt* esterilizar.
sterling ['stɔːlɪŋ] *a* esterlina; (*silver*) de ley; (*fig*) auténtico.
stern [stɔːn] *a* severo, austero // *n* (*NAUT*) popa.
stethoscope ['stɛθəskəup] *n* estetoscopio.
stew [stjuː] *n* cocido, estofado; (*fig*: *mess*) apuro // *vt*, *vi* estofar, guisar; (*fruit*) cocer.
steward ['stjuːəd] *n* (*gen*) camarero; **~ess** *n* azafata.
stick [stɪk] *n* palo; (*as weapon*) porra; (*walking ~*) bastón *m* // (*vb*: *pt*, *pp* **stuck**) *vt* (*glue*) pegar; (*thrust*): **to ~ sth into** clavar o hincar algo en; (*col*: *put*) meter; (*col*: *tolerate*) aguantar, soportar // *vi* pegar, pegarse; (*come to a stop*) quedarse parado; (*in mind etc*) atascarse; (*pin etc*) clavarse; **to ~ out, to ~ up** *vi* sobresalir; **to ~ up for** *vt fus* defender; **~er** *n* etiqueta engomada.
stickler ['stɪklə*] *n*: **to be a ~ for** dar mucha importancia a.
stick-up ['stɪkʌp] *n* asalto, atraco.
sticky ['stɪkɪ] *a* pegajoso; (*label*) engomado; (*fig*) difícil.
stiff [stɪf] *a* rígido, tieso; (*hard*) duro; (*difficult*) difícil; (*person*) inflexible; (*price*) exorbitante; **~en** *vt* hacer más rígido; (*limb*) entumecer // *vi* endurecerse; (*grow stronger*) fortalecerse; **~ness** *n* rigidez *f*, tiesura; dificultad *f*; (*character*) frialdad *f*.
stifle ['staɪfl] *vt* ahogar, sofocar; **stifling** *a* (*heat*) sofocante, bochornoso.
stigma ['stɪgmə], *pl* (*BOT*, *MED*, *REL*) **~ta** [-tə], (*fig*) **~s** *n* estigma *m*.

stile [staɪl] *n* escalera para pasar una cerca.

stiletto [stɪ'lɛtəu] *n* (*also*: ~ **heel**) tacón *m* de aguja.

still [stɪl] *a* inmóvil, quieto // *ad* (*up to this time*) todavía; (*even*) aún; (*nonetheless*) sin embargo, aun así; ~**born** *a* nacido muerto; ~ **life** *n* naturaleza muerta.

stilt [stɪlt] *n* zanco; (*pile*) pilar *m*, soporte *m*.

stilted ['stɪltɪd] *a* afectado.

stimulant ['stɪmjulənt] *n* estimulante *m*.

stimulate ['stɪmjuleɪt] *vt* estimular; **stimulating** *a* estimulante; **stimulation** [-'leɪʃən] *n* estímulo.

stimulus ['stɪmjuləs], *pl* -**li** [-laɪ] *n* estímulo, incentivo.

sting [stɪŋ] *n* (*wound*) picadura; (*pain*) escozor *m*, picazón *m*; (*organ*) aguijón *m* // (*vb*: *pt*, *pp* **stung**) *vt* picar // *vi* picar, escocer.

stingy ['stɪndʒɪ] *a* tacaño.

stink [stɪŋk] *n* hedor *m*, tufo // *vi*, *pt* **stank**, *pp* **stunk** heder, apestar; ~**ing** *a* hediondo, fétido.

stint [stɪnt] *n* tarea, destajo; **to do one's** ~ hacer su parte // *vi*: **to** ~ **on** escatimar.

stipend ['staɪpend] *n* (*of vicar etc*) estipendio, sueldo.

stipulate ['stɪpjuleɪt] *vt* estipular, poner como condición; **stipulation** [-'leɪʃən] *n* estipulación *f*, condición *f*.

stir [stə:*] *n* (*fig*: *agitation*) conmoción *f* // *vt* (*tea etc*) remover; (*fire*) atizar; (*move*) mover; (*fig*: *emotions*) conmover // *vi* moverse, menearse; **to** ~ **up** *vt* excitar; (*trouble*) fomentar; ~**ring** *a* conmovedor(a).

stirrup ['stɪrəp] *n* estribo.

stitch [stɪtʃ] *n* (*SEWING*) puntada; (*KNITTING*) punto; (*MED*) punto (de sutura); (*pain*) punzada // *vt* coser; (*MED*) suturar.

stoat [stəut] *n* armiño.

stock [stɔk] *n* (*COMM. reserves*) existencias *fpl*, stock *m*; (: *selection*) surtido; (*AGR*) ganado, ganadería; (*CULIN*) caldo; (*fig*: *lineage*) estirpe *f*; (*FINANCE*) capital *m*; (: *shares*) acciones *fpl* // *a* (*fig*: *reply etc*) clásico, acostumbrado // *vt* (*have in* ~) tener (en existencia o almacén); (*supply*) proveer, abastecer; **to take** ~ **of** (*fig*) asesorar, examinar; **to** ~ **up with** *vt* abastecerse de; ~**s** *npl* cepo *sg*; ~**s and shares** acciones y valores.

stockade [stɔ'keɪd] *n* estacada.

stockbroker ['stɔkbrəukə*] *n* agente *m/f* o corredor/a *m/f* de bolsa.

stock exchange *n* bolsa.

stocking ['stɔkɪŋ] *n* media.

stock market *n* bolsa (de valores).

stockpile ['stɔkpaɪl] *n* reserva // *vt* acumular, almacenar.

stocktaking ['stɔkteɪkɪŋ] *n* (*COMM*) inventario, balance *m*.

stocky ['stɔkɪ] *a* (*strong*) robusto; (*short*) achaparrado.

stodgy ['stɔdʒɪ] *a* indigesto, pesado.

stoical ['stəuɪkəl] *a* estoico.

stoke [stəuk] *vt* cargar, cebar.

stole [stəul] *pt of* **steal** // *n* estola.

stolen ['stəuln] *pp of* **steal.**

stomach ['stʌmək] *n* (*ANAT*) estómago; (*belly*) vientre *m*; (*appetite*) apetito // *vt* tragar, aguantar; ~ **ache** *n* dolor *m* de estómago.

stone [stəun] *n* piedra; (*in fruit*) hueso; (*weight*) medida de peso (6.348kg) // *a* de piedra // *vt* apedrear; ~-**cold** *a* helado; ~-**deaf** *a* totalmente sordo; ~**work** *n* (*art*) cantería; (*stones*) piedras *fpl*; **stony** *a* pedregoso; (*glance*) glacial.

stood [stud] *pt*, *pp of* **stand.**

stool [stu:l] *n* taburete *m*.

stoop [stu:p] *vi* (*also*: **have a** ~) ser cargado de espaldas; (*bend*) inclinarse, encorvarse.

stop [stɔp] *n* parada, alto; (*in punctuation*) punto // *vt* parar, detener; (*break off*) suspender; (*block*) tapar, cerrar; (*also*: **put a** ~ **to**) terminar, poner término a // *vi* pararse, detenerse; (*end*) acabarse; **to** ~ **doing sth** dejar de hacer algo; **to** ~ **dead** *vi* pararse en seco; **to** ~ **off** *vi* interrumpir el viaje; **to** ~ **up** *vt* (*hole*) tapar; ~**gap** *n* recurso (temporal); ~**lights** *npl* (*AUT*) luces *fpl* de detención; ~**over** *n* parada intermedia.

stoppage ['stɔpɪdʒ] *n* (*strike*) paro; (*temporary stop*) interrupción *f*; (*of pay*) suspensión *f*; (*blockage*) obstrucción *f*.

stopper ['stɔpə*] *n* tapón *m*.

stopwatch ['stɔpwɔtʃ] *n* cronómetro.

storage ['stɔ:rɪdʒ] *n* almacenaje *m*.

store [stɔ:*] *n* (*stock*) provisión *f*; (*depot*, *large shop*) almacén *m*; (*reserve*) reserva, repuesto; ~**s** *npl* víveres *mpl* // *vt* almacenar; (*keep*) guardar; **to** ~ **up** *vt* acumular; ~**room** *n* despensa.

storey, story (*US*) ['stɔ:rɪ] *n* piso.

stork [stɔ:k] *n* cigüeña.

storm [stɔ:m] *n* tormenta; (*wind*) vendaval *m*; (*fig*) tempestad *f* // *vi* (*fig*) rabiar // *vt* tomar por asalto, asaltar; ~ **cloud** *n* nubarrón *m*; ~**y** a tempestuoso.

story ['stɔ:rɪ] *n* historia, relato; (*joke*) cuento, chiste *m*; (*plot*) argumento; (*lie*) cuento, embuste *m*; (*US*) = **storey;** ~**book** *n* libro de cuentos; ~**teller** *n* cuentista *m/f*.

stout [staut] *a* (*strong*) sólido, macizo; (*fat*) gordo, corpulento // *n* cerveza negra.

stove [stəuv] *n* (*for cooking*) cocina; (*for heating*) estufa.

stow [stəu] *vt* meter, poner; (*NAUT*) estibar; ~**away** *n* polizón/ona *m/f*.

straddle ['strædl] *vt* montar a horcajadas.

straggle ['strægl] *vi* (*wander*) vagar en desorden; (*lag behind*) rezagarse; **straggler** *n* rezagado; **straggling**, **straggly** *a* (*hair*) desordenado.

straight [streɪt] *a* recto, derecho; (*honest*) honrado; (*frank*) franco, directo; (*simple*) sencillo; (*in order*) en orden // *ad* derecho, directamente; (*drink*) sin mezcla; **to put**

or **get sth** ~ dejar algo en claro; ~ **away,** ~ **off** (*at once*) en seguida; ~ **en** *vt* (*also:* ~ **en out**) enderezar, poner derecho; ~ **-faced** *a* solemne, sin expresión; ~ **forward** *a* (*simple*) sencillo; (*honest*) honrado, franco.

strain [streɪn] *n* (*gen*) tensión *f*; (*TECH*) esfuerzo; (*MED*) torcedura; (*breed*) raza // *vt* (*back etc*) torcerse; (*tire*) cansar; (*stretch*) estirar; (*filter*) filtrar // *vi* esforzarse; ~ **s** *npl* (*MUS*) son *m*; ~ **ed** *a* (*muscle*) torcido; (*laugh*) forzado; (*relations*) tenso; ~ **er** *n* colador *m*.

strait [streɪt] *n* (*GEO*) estrecho; ~ **-jacket** *n* camisa de fuerza; ~ **-laced** *a* mojigato, gazmoño.

strand [strænd] *n* (*of thread*) hebra; (*of hair*) trenza; (*of rope*) ramal *m*; ~ **ed** *a* abandonado (sin recursos), desamparado.

strange [streɪndʒ] *a* (*not known*) desconocido; (*odd*) extraño, raro; **stranger** *n* desconocido/a; (*from another area*) forastero/a.

strangle ['stræŋgl] *vt* estrangular; (*sobs etc*) ahogar; ~ **hold** *n* (*fig*) dominio completo; **strangulation** [-'leɪʃən] *n* estrangulación *f*.

strap [stræp] *n* correa; (*of slip, dress*) tirante *m* // *vt* atar con correa; (*punish*) azotar.

strapping ['stræpɪŋ] *a* robusto, fornido.

strata ['strɑːtə] *pl of* **stratum.**

stratagem ['strætɪdʒəm] *n* estratagema.

strategic [strə'tiːdʒɪk] *a* estratégico.

strategy ['strætɪdʒɪ] *n* estrategia.

stratum ['strɑːtəm], *pl* **-ta** *n* estrato.

straw [strɔː] *n* paja; (*drinking* ~) caña, pajita.

strawberry ['strɔːbərɪ] *n* fresa.

stray [streɪ] *a* (*animal*) extraviado; (*bullet*) perdido; (*scattered*) disperso // *vi* extraviarse, perderse.

streak [striːk] *n* raya; (*fig: of madness etc*) vena // *vt* rayar // *vi:* **to** ~ **past** pasar como un rayo; ~ **y** *a* rayado.

stream [striːm] *n* riachuelo, arroyo; (*jet*) chorro; (*current*) corriente *f*; (*of people*) oleada // *vt* (*SCOL*) dividir en grupos por habilidad // *vi* correr, fluir; **to** ~ **in/out** (*people*) entrar/salir en tropel.

streamer ['striːmə*] *n* serpentina.

streamlined ['striːmlaɪnd] *a* aerodinámico.

street [striːt] *n* calle *f* // *a* callejero; ~ **car** *n* (*US*) tranvía; ~ **lamp** *n* farol *m*.

strength [streŋθ] *n* fuerza; (*of girder, knot etc*) resistencia; ~ **en** *vt* fortalecer, reforzar.

strenuous ['strɛnjuəs] *a* (*tough*) arduo; (*energetic*) enérgico; (*determined*) tenaz.

stress [strɛs] *n* (*force, pressure*) presión *f*; (*mental strain*) tensión *f*; (*accent*) énfasis *m*, acento; (*TECH*) tensión *f*, carga // *vt* subrayar, recalcar.

stretch [strɛtʃ] *n* (*of sand etc*) trecho, tramo // *vi* estirarse; (*extend*): **to** ~ **to** *or* **as far as** extenderse hasta // *vt* extender,

estirar; (*make demands of*) exigir el máximo esfuerzo a; **to** ~ **out** *vi* tenderse // *vt* (*arm etc*) extender; (*spread*) estirar.

stretcher ['strɛtʃə*] *n* camilla.

strewn [struːn] *a:* ~ **with** cubierto *o* sembrado de.

stricken ['strɪkən] *a* (*wounded*) herido; (*ill*) enfermo.

strict [strɪkt] *a* (*person*) severo, riguroso; (*precise*) estricto, exacto; ~ **ly** *ad* (*exactly*) estrictamente; (*totally*) terminantemente; (*severely*) rigurosamente; ~ **ness** *n* exactitud *f*; rigor *m*, severidad *f*.

stride [straɪd] *n* zancada, tranco // *vi*, *pt* **strode,** *pp* **stridden** ['strɪdn] dar zancadas, andar a trancos.

strident ['straɪdnt] *a* estridente; (*colour*) chillón(ona).

strife [straɪf] *n* lucha.

strike [straɪk] *n* huelga; (*of oil etc*) descubrimiento; (*attack*) ataque *m*; (*SPORT*) golpe *m* // (*vb: pt, pp* **struck**) *vt* golpear, pegar; (*oil etc*) descubrir; (*obstacle*) topar con // *vi* declarar la huelga; (*attack*) atacar; (*clock*) dar la hora; **to** ~ **a match** encender un fósforo; **to** ~ **down** *vt* derribar; **to** ~ **out** *vt* borrar, tachar; **to** ~ **up** *vt* (*MUS*) empezar a tocar; (*conversation*) entablar; (*friendship*) trabar; ~ **breaker** *n* rompehuelgas *m/f inv*; **striker** *n* huelguista *m/f*; (*SPORT*) delantero; **striking** *a* impresionante; (*nasty*) chocante; (*colour*) llamativo.

string [strɪŋ] *n* (*gen*) cuerda; (*row*) hilera // *vt, pt, pp* **strung**: **to** ~ **together** ensartar // *vi:* **to** ~ **out** extenderse; **the** ~ **s** *npl* (*MUS*) los instrumentos de cuerda; **to pull** ~ **s** (*fig*) mover palancas; ~ **bean** *n* judía verde, habichuela; ~ **(ed) instrument** *n* (*MUS*) instrumento de cuerda.

stringent ['strɪndʒənt] *a* riguroso, severo.

strip [strɪp] *n* tira; (*of land*) franja; (*of metal*) cinta, lámina // *vt* desnudar; (*also:* ~ **down**: *machine*) desmontar // *vi* desnudarse; ~ **cartoon** *n* tira cómica.

stripe [straɪp] *n* raya; (*MIL*) galón *m*; ~ **d** *a* a rayas, rayado.

stripper ['strɪpə*] *n* artista de striptease.

striptease ['strɪptiːz] *n* striptease *m*.

strive [straɪv], *pt* **strove,** *pp* **striven** ['strɪvn] *vi:* **to** ~ **to do sth** esforzarse *o* luchar por hacer algo.

strode [strəud] *pt of* **stride.**

stroke [strəuk] *n* (*blow*) golpe *m*; (*MED*) ataque *m* fulminante; (*caress*) caricia; (*of pen*) trazo // *vt* acariciar, frotar suavemente; **at a** ~ de golpe.

stroll [strəul] *n* paseo, vuelta // *vi* dar un paseo *o* una vuelta.

strong [strɔŋ] *a* fuerte; **they are 50** ~ son 50; ~ **box** *n* caja fuerte; ~ **hold** *n* fortaleza; (*fig*) baluarte *m*; ~ **ly** *ad* fuertemente, con fuerza; (*believe*)

firmemente; ~**room** n cámara acorazada.
strove [strəuv] pt of **strive.**
struck [strʌk] pt, pp of **strike.**
structural ['strʌktʃərəl] a estructural; **structure** n estructura; (building) construcción f.
struggle ['strʌgl] n lucha // vi luchar.
strum [strʌm] vt (guitar) rasguear.
strung [strʌŋ] pt, pp of **string.**
strut [strʌt] n puntal m // vi pavonearse.
stub [stʌb] n (of ticket etc) talón m; (of cigarette) colilla; **to** ~ **out** vt apagar; **to** ~ **one's toe** dar con el dedo contra algo.
stubble ['stʌbl] n rastrojo; (on chin) barba (de pocos días).
stubborn ['stʌbən] a terco, testarudo.
stuck [stʌk] pt, pp of **stick** // a (jammed) atascado; ~**-up** a engreído, presumido.
stud [stʌd] n (shirt ~) botón m; (of boot) taco; (of horses) caballeriza; (also: ~ **horse**) caballo padre o semental // vt (fig): ~**ded with** sembrado de.
student ['stju:dənt] n estudiante m/f // a estudiantil.
studio ['stju:diəu] n estudio; (sculptor's) taller m.
studious ['stju:diəs] a aplicado; (studied) calculado; ~**ly** ad (carefully) con esmero.
study ['stʌdi] n (gen) estudio // vt estudiar; (examine) examinar, escudriñar // vi estudiar.
stuff [stʌf] n materia; (cloth) tela; (substance) material m, sustancia // vt llenar; (CULIN) rellenar; (animals) disecar; ~**ing** n relleno; ~**y** a (room) mal ventilado; (person) de miras estrechas.
stumble ['stʌmbl] vi tropezar, dar un traspié; **to** ~ **across** (fig) tropezar con; **stumbling block** n tropiezo, obstáculo.
stump [stʌmp] n (of tree) tocón m; (of limb) muñón m // vt: **to be** ~**ed** quedar perplejo.
stun [stʌn] vt dejar sin sentido.
stung [stʌŋ] pt, pp of **sting.**
stunk [stʌŋk] pp of **stink.**
stunning ['stʌnɪŋ] a (fig) pasmoso.
stunt [stʌnt] n proeza excepcional; (AVIAT) vuelo acrobático; (publicity ~) truco publicitario; ~**ed** a enano, achaparrado; ~**man** n doble m.
stupefy ['stju:pɪfaɪ] vt dejar estupefacto.
stupendous [stju:'pɛndəs] a estupendo, asombroso.
stupid ['stju:pɪd] a estúpido, tonto; ~**ity** [-'pɪdɪti] n estupidez f; ~**ly** ad estúpidamente.
stupor ['stju:pə*] n estupor m.
sturdy ['stɜːdi] a robusto, fuerte.
stutter ['stʌtə*] n tartamudeo // vi tartamudear.
sty [staɪ] n (for pigs) pocilga.
stye [staɪ] n (MED) orzuelo.
style [staɪl] n estilo; **stylish** a elegante, a la moda.
stylus ['staɪləs] n (of record player) aguja.

suave [swɑːv] a cortés, fino.
sub... [sʌb] pref sub...; ~**conscious** a subconsciente // n subconsciente m; ~**divide** vt subdividir; ~**division** n subdivisión f.
subdue [səb'dju:] vt sojuzgar; (passions) dominar; ~**d** a (light) tenue; (person) sumiso, manso.
subject ['sʌbdʒɪkt] n súbdito; (SCOL) tema m, materia // vt [səb'dʒɛkt]: **to** ~ **sb to** sth someter a uno a algo; **to be** ~ **to** (law) estar sujeto a; ~**ion** [-'dʒɛkʃən] n sometimiento, sujeción f; ~**ive** a subjetivo; ~ **matter** n materia; (content) contenido.
subjugate ['sʌbdʒugeɪt] vt subyugar.
sublet [sʌb'lɛt] vt subarrendar.
sublime [sə'blaɪm] a sublime.
submachine gun ['sʌbmə'ʃiːn-] n metralleta.
submarine [sʌbmə'riːn] n submarino.
submerge [səb'mɜːdʒ] vt sumergir; (flood) inundar // vi sumergirse.
submission [səb'mɪʃən] n sumisión f; **submissive** [-'mɪsɪv] a sumiso.
submit [səb'mɪt] vt someter // vi someterse.
subnormal [sʌb'nɔːməl] a anormal; (backward) retrasado.
subordinate [sə'bɔːdɪnət] a, n subordinado.
subpoena [səb'piːnə] (LAW) n comparendo, citación f // vt mandar comparecer.
subscribe [səb'skraɪb] vi suscribir; **to** ~ **to** (opinion, fund) suscribir, aprobar; (newspaper) suscribirse a; **subscriber** n (to periodical, telephone) abonado/a.
subscription [səb'skrɪpʃən] n abono, suscripción f.
subsequent ['sʌbsɪkwənt] a subsiguiente, posterior; ~**ly** ad después, más tarde.
subside [səb'saɪd] vi hundirse; (flood) bajar; (wind) amainar; **subsidence** [-'saɪdns] n hundimiento; (in road) socavón m.
subsidiary [səb'sɪdɪəri] n sucursal f, filial f.
subsidize ['sʌbsɪdaɪz] vt subvencionar; **subsidy** [-di] n subvención f.
subsistence [səb'sɪstəns] n subsistencia; (allowance) dietas fpl.
substance ['sʌbstəns] n sustancia; (fig) esencia.
substandard [sʌb'stændəd] a inferior.
substantial [səb'stænʃl] a sustancial, sustancioso; (fig) importante; ~**ly** ad sustancialmente.
substantiate [səb'stænʃɪeɪt] vt comprobar.
substitute ['sʌbstɪtjuːt] n (person) suplente m/f; (thing) sustituto // vt: **to** ~ **A for B** sustituir B por A, reemplazar A por B; **substitution** [-'tjuːʃən] n sustitución f, reemplazo.
subterfuge ['sʌbtəfjuːdʒ] n subterfugio.
subterranean [sʌbtə'reɪnɪən] a subterráneo.

subtitle ['sʌbtaɪtl] n subtítulo.
subtle ['sʌtl] a sutil; ~ty n sutileza.
subtract [sǝb'trækt] vt sustraer, restar; ~ion [-'trækʃǝn] n sustracción f, resta.
suburb ['sʌbǝːb] n arrabal m, suburbio; ~an [sǝ'bǝːbǝn] a suburbano; (train etc) de cercanías.
subversive [sǝb'vǝːsɪv] a subversivo.
subway ['sʌbweɪ] n (Brit) paso subterráneo o inferior; (US) metro.
succeed [sǝk'siːd] vi (person) tener éxito; (plan) salir bien // vt suceder a; to ~ in doing lograr hacer; ~ing a (following) sucesivo, seguido.
success [sǝk'sɛs] n éxito; (gain) triunfo; ~ful a (venture) de éxito; to be ~ful (in doing) lograr (hacer); ~fully ad con éxito.
succession [sǝk'sɛʃǝn] n (series) sucesión f, serie f; (descendants) descendencia; **successive** [-'sɛsɪv] a sucesivo, consecutivo; **successor** [-'sɛsǝ*] n sucesor/a m/f.
succinct [sǝk'sɪŋkt] a sucinto.
succulent ['sʌkjulǝnt] a suculento.
succumb [sǝ'kʌm] vi sucumbir.
such [sʌtʃ] a, det tal, semejante; (of that kind): ~ a book un libro parecido; ~ books tales libros; (so much): ~ courage tanto valor; ~ a long trip un viaje tan largo; ~ a lot of tanto; ~ as (like) tal como; a noise ~ as to un ruido tal que; as ~ ad como tal // pron los/las que; ~-and-~ det tal o cual; until ~ time as hasta que.
suck [sʌk] vt chupar; (bottle) sorber; (breast) mamar; ~er n (zool) ventosa; (col) bobo, primo.
suckle ['sʌkl] vt amamantar.
suction ['sʌkʃǝn] n succión f.
sudden ['sʌdn] a (rapid) repentino, súbito; (unexpected) imprevisto; all of a ~, ~ly ad de repente; (unexpectedly) inesperadamente.
suds [sʌdz] npl jabonaduras fpl.
sue [suː] vt demandar.
suede [sweɪd] n ante m.
suet ['suɪt] n sebo.
suffer ['sʌfǝ*] vt sufrir, padecer; (bear) aguantar; (allow) permitir, tolerar // vi sufrir, padecer; ~er n víctima m/f; (MED) enfermo; ~ing n sufrimiento, padecimiento; (pain) dolor m.
suffice [sǝ'faɪs] vi bastar, ser suficiente.
sufficient [sǝ'fɪʃǝnt] a suficiente, bastante.
suffix ['sʌfɪks] n sufijo.
suffocate ['sʌfǝkeɪt] vi ahogarse, asfixiarse; **suffocation** [-'keɪʃǝn] n sofocación f, asfixia.
suffrage ['sʌfrɪdʒ] n sufragio; (vote) derecho de votar.
sugar ['ʃugǝ*] n azúcar m // vt echar azúcar a; ~ beet n remolacha; ~ cane n caña de azúcar; ~y a azucarado.
suggest [sǝ'dʒɛst] vt sugerir; (advise) aconsejar; ~ion [-'dʒɛstʃǝn] n sugerencia;

(hypnotic) sugestión f; ~ive a sugestivo; (pej) indecente.
suicidal [suɪ'saɪdl] a suicida; **suicide** ['suɪsaɪd] n suicidio; (person) suicida m/f.
suit [suːt] n (man's) traje m; (woman's) conjunto; (LAW) litigio, pleito; (CARDS) palo // vt (gen) convenir; (clothes) sentar a, ir bien a; (adapt): to ~ sth to adaptar o ajustar algo a; ~able a conveniente; (apt) indicado; ~ably ad convenientemente, en forma debida.
suitcase ['suːtkeɪs] n maleta.
suite [swiːt] n (of rooms) grupo de habitaciones; (MUS) suite f; (furniture): bedroom/dining room ~ (juego de) dormitorio/comedor m.
suitor ['suːtǝ*] n pretendiente m.
sulk [sʌlk] vi tener mohino; ~y a con mohino.
sullen ['sʌlǝn] a hosco, malhumorado.
sulphur, sulfur (US) ['sʌlfǝ*] n azufre m.
sultan ['sʌltǝn] n sultán m.
sultana [sʌl'taːnǝ] n (fruit) pasa de Esmirna.
sultry ['sʌltrɪ] a (weather) bochornoso; (seductive) seductor(a).
sum [sʌm] n (gen) suma; (total) total m; to ~ up vt recapitular // vi hacer un resumen.
summarize ['sʌmǝraɪz] vt resumir.
summary ['sʌmǝrɪ] n resumen m // a (justice) sumario.
summer ['sʌmǝ*] n verano // a de verano; ~house n (in garden) cenador m, glorieta; ~time n (season) verano; ~ time n (by clock) hora de verano.
summit ['sʌmɪt] n cima, cumbre f; ~ (conference) n conferencia cumbre.
summon ['sʌmǝn] vt (person) llamar; (meeting) convocar; (LAW) citar; to ~ up vt cobrar; ~s n llamamiento, llamada // vt citar, emplazar.
sump [sʌmp] n (AUT) cárter m.
sumptuous ['sʌmptjuǝs] a suntuoso.
sun [sʌn] n sol m; ~bathe vi tomar el sol; ~burn n (painful) quemadura; (tan) bronceado; ~burnt a (tanned) bronceado; (painfully) quemado por el sol.
Sunday ['sʌndɪ] n domingo.
sundial ['sʌndaɪǝl] n reloj m de sol.
sundry ['sʌndrɪ] a varios, diversos; all and ~ todos y cada uno; **sundries** npl géneros mpl diversos.
sunflower ['sʌnflauǝ*] n girasol m.
sung [sʌŋ] pp of sing.
sunglasses ['sʌnglaːsɪz] npl gafas fpl de sol.
sunk [sʌŋk] pp of sink.
sun: ~light n luz f del sol; ~lit a iluminado por el sol; ~ny a soleado; (day) de sol; (fig) alegre; ~rise n salida del sol; ~set n puesta del sol; ~shade n (over table) sombrilla; ~shine n sol m; ~spot n mancha solar; ~stroke n insolación f; ~tan n bronceado; ~tan oil n bronceador m, crema bronceadora.
super ['suːpǝ*] a (col) bárbaro.

superannuation [su:pərænju'eiʃən] *n* jubilación *f*.
superb [su:'pə:b] *a* magnífico, espléndido.
supercilious [su:pə'sılıəs] *a* (*disdainful*) desdeñoso; (*haughty*) altanero.
superficial [su:pə'fıʃəl] *a* superficial.
superfluous [su'pə:fluəs] *a* superfluo, de sobra.
superhuman [su:pə'hju:mən] *a* sobrehumano.
superimpose ['su:pərım'pəuz] *vt* sobreponer.
superintendent [su:pərın'tɛndənt] *n* superintendente *m/f*; (*POLICE*) subjefe *m*.
superior [su'pıərıə*] *a* superior; (*smug*) desdeñoso // *n* superior *m*; ~ity [-'ɔrıtı] *n* superioridad *f*; desdén *m*.
superlative [su'pə:lətıv] *a*, *n* superlativo.
superman ['su:pəmæn] *n* superhombre *m*.
supermarket ['su:pəmɑ:kıt] *n* supermercado.
supernatural [su:pə'nætʃərəl] *a* sobrenatural.
superpower ['su:pəpauə*] *n* (*POL*) superpotencia.
supersede [su:pə'si:d] *vt* suplantar.
supersonic ['su:pə'sɔnık] *a* supersónico.
superstition [su:pə'stıʃən] *n* superstición *f*; **superstitious** [-ʃəs] *a* supersticioso.
supertanker ['su:pətæŋkə*] *n* superpetrolero.
supervise ['su:pəvaız] *vt* supervisar; **supervision** [-'vıʒən] *n* supervisión *f*; **supervisor** *n* supervisor/a *m/f*.
supper ['sʌpə*] *n* cena; **to have** ~ cenar.
supple ['sʌpl] *a* flexible.
supplement ['sʌplımənt] *n* suplemento // *vt* [sʌplı'mɛnt] suplir; ~ary [-'mɛntərı] *a* suplementario).
supplier [sə'plaıə*] *n* suministrador/a *m/f*; (*COMM*) distribuidor/a *m/f*.
supply [sə'plaı] *vt* (*provide*) suministrar, facilitar; (*equip*): **to** ~ (**with**) abastecer (de) // *n* suministro, provisión *f*; (*supplying*) abastecimiento // *a* (*teacher etc*) suplente; **supplies** *npl* (*food*) víveres *mpl*; (*MIL*) pertrechos *mpl*; ~ **and demand** la oferta y la demanda.
support [sə'pɔ:t] *n* (*moral, financial etc*) apoyo; (*TECH*) soporte *m* // *vt* apoyar; (*financially*) mantener; (*uphold*) sostener; ~**er** *n* (*POL etc*) partidario; (*SPORT*) aficionado.
suppose [sə'pəuz] *vt*, *vi* (*gen*) suponer; (*imagine*) imaginarse; **to be** ~**d to do sth** deber hacer algo; ~**dly** [sə'pəuzıdlı] *ad* que se supone, según cabe suponer; **supposing** *conj* en caso de que; **supposition** [sʌpə'zıʃən] *n* suposición *f*.
suppository [sə'pɔzıtərı] *n* supositorio.
suppress [sə'prɛs] *vt* suprimir; (*yawn*) ahogar; ~**ion** [sə'prɛʃən] *n* represión *f*.
supremacy [su'prɛməsı] *n* supremacía *f*; **supreme** [-'pri:m] *a* supremo.
surcharge ['sə:tʃɑ:dʒ] *n* sobrecarga; (*extra tax*) recargo.

sure [ʃuə*] *a* (*gen*) seguro; (*definite, convinced*) cierto; (*aim*) certero; ~! (*of course*) ¡claro!, ¡por supuesto!; ~**-footed** *a* de pie firme; ~**ly** *ad* (*certainly*) seguramente.
surety ['ʃuərətı] *n* garantía, fianza; (*person*) fiador/a *m/f*.
surf [sə:f] *n* olas *fpl*.
surface ['sə:fıs] *n* superficie *f* // *vt* (*road*) revestir // *vi* salir a la superficie.
surfboard ['sə:fbɔ:d] *n* plancha (de surfing), acuaplano.
surfeit ['sə:fıt] *n*: **a** ~ **of** exceso de.
surfing ['sə:fıŋ] *n* surfing *m*.
surge [sə:dʒ] *n* oleada, oleaje *m* // *vi* avanzar a tropel.
surgeon ['sə:dʒən] *n* cirujano; **dental** ~ odontólogo.
surgery ['sə:dʒərı] *n* cirugía; (*room*) consultorio; **to undergo** ~ operarse; ~ **hours** *npl* horas *fpl* de consulta.
surgical ['sə:dʒıkl] *a* quirúrgico; ~ **spirit** *n* alcohol *m*.
surly ['sə:lı] *a* hosco, malhumorado.
surmount [sə:'maunt] *vt* superar, sobreponerse a.
surname ['sə:neım] *n* apellido.
surpass [sə:'pɑ:s] *vt* superar, exceder.
surplus ['sə:pləs] *n* (*gen*) excedente *m*; (*COMM*) superávit *m* // *a* excedente, sobrante.
surprise [sə'praız] *n* (*gen*) sorpresa; (*astonishment*) asombro // *vt* sorprender; asombrar; **surprising** *a* sorprendente; asombroso.
surrealist [sə'rıəlıst] *a* surrealista.
surrender [sə'rɛndə*] *n* rendición *f*, entrega // *vi* rendirse, entregarse.
surreptitious [sʌrəp'tıʃəs] *a* subrepticio.
surround [sə'raund] *vt* rodear, circundar; (*MIL etc*) cercar; ~**ing** *a* circundante; ~**ings** *npl* alrededores *mpl*, cercanías *fpl*.
surveillance [sə:'veıləns] *n* vigilancia.
survey ['sə:veı] *n* inspección *f*, examen *m*; (*inquiry*) encuesta // *vt* [sə:'veı] (*gen*) examinar, inspeccionar; (*look at*) mirar, contemplar; (*make inquiries about*) hacer una encuesta sobre; ~**or** *n* agrimensor *m*.
survival [sə'vaıvl] *n* supervivencia; **survive** *vi* sobrevivir; (*custom etc*) perdurar // *vt* sobrevivir a; **survivor** *n* superviviente *m/f*.
susceptible [sə'sɛptəbl] *a*: ~ (**to**) susceptible *o* sensible (a).
suspect ['sʌspɛkt] *a*, *n* sospechoso // *vt* [səs'pɛkt] sospechar.
suspend [səs'pɛnd] *vt* suspender; ~**er belt** *n* portaligas *m inv*; ~**ers** *npl* ligas *fpl*; (*US*) tirantes *mpl*.
suspense [səs'pɛns] *n* incertidumbre *f*, duda; (*in film etc*) suspense *m*.
suspension [səs'pɛnʃən] *n* (*gen, AUT*) suspensión *f*; (*of driving licence*) privación *f*; ~ **bridge** *n* puente *m* colgante.
suspicion [səs'pıʃən] *n* (*gen*) sospecha; (*distrust*) recelo; (*trace*) traza; **suspicious**

[-ʃɔs] a (suspecting) receloso; (causing ~) sospechoso.
sustain [sɔs'teɪn] vt sostener, apoyar; (suffer) sufrir, padecer; ~ed a (effort) sostenido.
sustenance ['sʌstɪnəns] n sustento.
swab [swɔb] n (MED) algodón m, torunda.
swagger ['swægə*] vi pavonearse.
swallow ['swɔləu] n (bird) golondrina; (of food etc) trago // vt tragar; **to ~ up** vt (savings etc) consumir.
swam [swæm] pt of **swim.**
swamp [swɔmp] n pantano, ciénaga // vt abrumar, agobiar; ~y a pantanoso.
swan [swɔn] n cisne m.
swap [swɔp] n canje m, intercambio // vt: **to ~ (for)** canjear (por).
swarm [swɔ:m] n (of bees) enjambre m; (gen) multitud f // vi hormiguear, pulular.
swarthy ['swɔ:ðɪ] a moreno.
swastika ['swɔstɪkə] n suástika, cruz f gamada.
swat [swɔt] vt aplastar.
sway [sweɪ] vi mecerse, balancearse // vt (influence) mover, influir en.
swear [swɛə*], pt **swore,** pp **sworn** vi jurar; **to ~ to sth** declarar algo bajo juramento; ~**word** n taco, palabrota.
sweat [swɛt] n sudor m // vi sudar.
sweater ['swɛtə*] n suéter m.
sweaty ['swɛtɪ] a sudoroso.
swede [swi:d] n nabo.
Swede [swi:d] n sueco/a; **Sweden** n Suecia; **Swedish** a, n (LING) sueco.
sweep [swi:p] n (act) barredura; (of arm) golpe m; (range) extensión f, alcance m; (also: **chimney ~**) deshollinador m // (vb: pt, pp **swept**) vt barrer; (mines) rastrear // vi barrer; **to ~ away** vt barrer; (rub out) borrar; **to ~ past** vi pasar rápidamente; (brush by) rozar; **to ~ up** vi recoger la basura; ~**ing** a (gesture) dramático; (generalized) generalizado.
sweet [swi:t] n (candy) dulce m, caramelo; (pudding) postre m // a dulce; (sugary) azucarado; (fresh) fresco, nuevo; (fig) dulce, amable; ~**corn** n maíz m; ~**en** vt endulzar; (add sugar to) poner azúcar a; ~**heart** n novio/a; (in speech) amor; ~**ly** ad dulcemente; (gently) suavemente; ~**ness** n (gen) dulzura; (amount of sugar) lo dulce, lo azucarado; ~ **pea** n guisante m de olor.
swell [swɛl] n (of sea) marejada, oleaje m // a (col: excellent) estupendo, excelente // (vb: pt **swelled,** pp **swollen** or **swelled**) vt hinchar, inflar // vi hincharse, inflarse; ~**ing** n (MED) hinchazón m.
sweltering ['swɛltərɪŋ] a sofocante, de mucho calor.
swept [swɛpt] pt, pp of **sweep.**
swerve [swɔ:v] vi desviarse bruscamente.
swift [swɪft] n (bird) vencejo // a rápido, veloz; ~**ness** n rapidez f, velocidad f.
swig [swɪg] n (col: drink) trago.
swill [swɪl] n bazofia // vt (also: ~ **out, ~**

down) lavar, limpiar con agua.
swim [swɪm] n: **to go for a ~** ir a nadar // (vb: pt **swam,** pp **swum**) vi nadar; (head, room) dar vueltas // vt pasar a nado; ~**mer** n nadador/a m/f; ~**ming** n natación f; ~**ming baths** npl piscina sg; ~**ming cap** n gorro de baño; ~**ming costume** n bañador m, traje m de baño; ~**ming pool** n piscina; ~**suit** n bañador m, traje m de baño.
swindle ['swɪndl] n estafa // vt estafar; **swindler** n estafador/a m/f.
swine [swaɪn] n, pl inv cerdos mpl, puercos mpi, (col!) canalla sg.
swing [swɪŋ] n (in playground) columpio; (movement) balanceo, vaivén m; (change of direction) viraje m; (rhythm) ritmo // (vb: pt, pp **swung**) vt balancear; (on a ~) columpiar; (also: ~ **round**) voltear bruscamente // vi balancearse, columpiarse; (also: ~ **round**) volver bruscamente; **to be in full ~** estar en plena marcha; ~ **bridge** n puente m giratorio; ~ **door** n puerta giratoria.
swipe [swaɪp] n golpe m fuerte // vt (hit) golpear fuerte; (col: steal) guindar.
swirl [swɔ:l] vi arremolinarse.
Swiss [swɪs] a, n, pl inv suizo/a.
switch [swɪtʃ] n (for light, radio etc) interruptor m; (change) cambio; (of hair) trenza postiza // vt (change) cambiar de; **to ~ off** vt apagar; (engine) parar; **to ~ on** vt encender, prender; (engine, machine) arrancar; ~**board** n (TEL) central f de teléfonos.
Switzerland ['swɪtsələnd] n Suiza.
swivel ['swɪvl] vi (also: ~ **round**) girar.
swollen ['swəulən] pp of **swell.**
swoon [swu:n] vi desmayarse, desvanecerse.
swoop [swu:p] n (by police etc) redada // vi (also: ~ **down**) calarse, precipitarse.
swop [swɔp] = **swap.**
sword [sɔ:d] n espada; ~**fish** n pez m espada.
swore [swɔ:*] pt of **swear.**
sworn [swɔ:n] pp of **swear.**
swot [swɔt] vt, vi empollar.
swum [swʌm] pp of **swim.**
swung [swʌŋ] pt, pp of **swing.**
sycamore ['sɪkəmɔ:*] n sicomoro.
syllable ['sɪləbl] n sílaba.
syllabus ['sɪləbəs] n programa m de estudios.
symbol ['sɪmbl] n símbolo; ~**ic(al)** [-'bɔlɪk(l)] a simbólico; ~**ism** n simbolismo; ~**ize** vt simbolizar.
symmetrical [sɪ'mɛtrɪkl] a simétrico; **symmetry** ['sɪmɪtrɪ] n simetría.
sympathetic [sɪmpə'θɛtɪk] a compasivo; (pleasant) simpático; ~**ally** ad con compasión.
sympathize ['sɪmpəθaɪz] vi: **to ~ with** sb compadecerse de uno; **sympathizer** n (POL) simpatizante m/f.
sympathy ['sɪmpəθɪ] n (pity) compasión f; (liking) simpatía; **with our deepest ~**

nuestro más sentido pésame; ~ **strike** n huelga por solidaridad.

symphony ['sımfənı] n sinfonía; ~ **orchestra** n orquesta sinfónica.

symposium [sım'pəuzıəm] n simposio.

symptom ['sımptəm] n síntoma m, indicio; ~**atic** [-'mætık] a sintomático.

synagogue ['sınəgɔg] n sinagoga.

synchronize ['sıŋkrənaız] vt sincronizar // vi: **to** ~ **with** sincronizarse con.

syndicate ['sındıkıt] n (gen) sindicato; (of newspapers) cadena.

syndrome ['sındrəum] n síndrome m.

synonym ['sınənım] n sinónimo; ~**ous** [sı'nɔnıməs] a: ~**ous** (**with**) sinónimo (con).

synopsis [sı'nɔpsıs], pl -**ses** [-si:z] n sinopsis f inv.

syntax ['sıntæks] n sintáxis f.

synthesis ['sınθəsıs], pl -**ses** [-si:z] n síntesis f inv.

synthetic [sın'θetık] a sintético.

syphilis ['sıfılıs] n sífilis f.

syphon ['saıfən] = **siphon.**

Syria ['sırıə] n Siria; ~**n** a, n sirio/a.

syringe [sı'rındʒ] n jeringa.

syrup ['sırəp] n jarabe m, almíbar m.

system ['sıstəm] n (gen) sistema; (method) método; (ANAT) organismo; ~**atic** [-'mætık] a sistemático; metódico; ~**s analyst** n analista m/f de sistemas.

T

ta [tɑ:] excl (Brit: col) gracias.

tab [tæb] n (gen) lengüeta; (label) etiqueta; **to keep** ~**s on** (fig) vigilar.

tabby ['tæbı] n (also: ~ **cat**) gato atigrado.

table ['teıbl] n mesa; (of statistics etc) cuadro, tabla // vt (motion etc) presentar; **to lay** or **set the** ~ poner la mesa; ~**cloth** n mantel m; ~ **d'hôte** [tɑ:bl'dəut] n menú m; ~**mat** n mantel m individual; ~**spoon** n cuchara grande; (also: ~**spoonful**: as measurement) cucharada.

tablet ['tæblıt] n (MED) tableta, pastilla; (for writing) bloc m; (of stone) lápida.

table: ~ **tennis** n ping-pong m, tenis m de mesa; ~ **wine** n vino de mesa.

taboo [tə'bu:] n tabú m // a tabú.

tacit ['tæsıt] a tácito.

taciturn ['tæsıtə:n] a taciturno.

tack [tæk] n (nail) tachuela, chincheta; (stitch) hilván m; (NAUT) bordada // vt (nail) clavar con chinchetas; (stitch) hilvanar // vi virar.

tackle ['tækl] n (gear) equipo; (also: **fishing** ~) aparejo; (for lifting) polea; (RUGBY) atajo // vt (difficulty) enfrentar; (grapple with) agarrar; (RUGBY) atajar.

tacky ['tækı] a pegajoso.

tact [tækt] n tacto, discreción f; ~**ful** a discreto, diplomático; ~**fully** ad discretamente.

tactical ['tæktıkl] a táctico; **tactics** [-tıks] n, npl táctica sg.

tactless ['tæktlıs] a indiscreto, falto de tacto; ~**ly** ad indiscretamente.

tadpole ['tædpəul] n renacuajo.

tag [tæg] n (label) etiqueta; (loose end) cabo; **to** ~ **along with sb** acompañar a uno.

tail [teıl] n (gen) cola; (ZOOL) rabo; (of shirt, coat) faldón m // vt (follow) seguir los talones a; **to** ~ **away**, ~ **off** (in size, quality etc) ir disminuyendo; ~ **coat** n frac m; ~ **end** n cola, parte f final; ~**gate** n puerta trasera.

tailor ['teılə*] n sastre m; ~**ing** n (cut) corte m; (craft) sastrería; ~-**made** a hecho a la medida; (fig) especial.

tailwind ['teılwınd] n viento de cola.

tainted ['teıntıd] a (food) pasado; (water, air) contaminado; (fig) manchado.

take [teık] pt **took**, pp **taken** vt (gen) tomar; (grab) coger; (gain: prize) ganar; (require: effort, courage) exigir, hacer falta; (tolerate) aguantar; (hold: passengers etc) tener cabida para; (accompany, bring, carry) llevar; (exam) presentarse a; **to** ~ **sth from** (drawer etc) sacar algo de; (person) coger algo a; **I** ~ **it that...** supongo que...; **to** ~ **after** vt fus parecerse a; **to** ~ **apart** vt desmontar; **to** ~ **away** vt (remove) quitar; (carry off) llevar; **to** ~ **back** vt (return) devolver; (one's words) retractar; **to** ~ **down** vt (building) demoler; (letter etc) poner por escrito; **to** ~ **in** vt (deceive) engañar; (understand) entender; (include) abarcar; (lodger) acoger, recibir; **to** ~ **off** vi (AVIAT) despegar // vt (remove) quitar; (imitate) imitar; **to** ~ **on** vt (work) emprender; (employee) contratar; (opponent) desafiar; **to** ~ **out** vt sacar; (remove) quitar; **to** ~ **over** vt (business) tomar posesión de // vi: **to** ~ **over from sb** relevar a uno; **to** ~ **to** vt fus (person) coger simpatía a; (activity) aficionarse a; **to** ~ **up** vt (a dress) acortar; (occupy: time, space) ocupar; (engage in: hobby etc) dedicarse a; ~**away** a (food) para llevar; ~-**home pay** n salario neto; ~**off** n (AVIAT) despegue m; ~**over** n (COMM) absorción f; ~**over bid** n oferta de compra.

takings ['teıkıŋz] npl (COMM) ingresos mpl.

talc [tælk] n (also: ~**um powder**) talco.

tale [teıl] n (story) cuento; (account) relación f; **to tell** ~**s** (fig: lie) chismear.

talent ['tælnt] n talento; ~**ed** a talentoso, de talento.

talk [tɔ:k] n (gen) charla; (gossip) habladurías fpl, chismes mpl; (conversation) conversación f // vi (speak) hablar; (chatter) charlar; **to** ~ **about** hablar de; **to** ~ **sb into doing sth** convencer a uno de que debe hacer algo; **to** ~ **sb out of doing sth** disuadir a uno de algo; **to** ~ **shop** hablar de asuntos

profesionales; **to** ~ **over** vt hablar de;
~**ative** a hablador(a).
tall [tɔːl] a (gen) alto; (tree) grande; **to be
6 feet** ~ medir 6 pies, tener 6 pies de
alto; ~**boy** n cómoda alta; ~**ness** n
altura; ~ **story** n historia inverosímil.
tally ['tælɪ] n cuenta // vi: **to** ~ **(with)**
corresponder (con).
talon ['tælən] n garra.
tambourine [tæmbə'riːn] n pandereta.
tame [teɪm] a (mild) manso; (tamed)
domesticado; (fig: story, style) soso.
tamper ['tæmpə*] vi: **to** ~ **with**
entrometerse en.
tampon ['tæmpɔn] n tampón m.
tan [tæn] n (also: **sun**~) bronceado // vt
broncear // vi ponerse moreno // a
(colour) marrón.
tandem ['tændəm] n tándem m.
tang [tæŋ] n sabor m fuerte.
tangerine [tændʒə'riːn] n mandarina.
tangible ['tændʒəbl] a tangible.
tangle ['tæŋgl] n enredo; **to get in(to) a**
~ enredarse.
tango ['tæŋgəu] n tango.
tank [tæŋk] n (water ~) depósito, tanque
m; (for fish) acuario; (MIL) tanque m.
tanker ['tæŋkə*] n (ship) petrolero; (truck)
camión m cisterna o tanque.
tanned [tænd] a (skin) moreno, bronceado.
tantalizing ['tæntəlaɪzɪŋ] a tentador(a).
tantamount ['tæntəmaunt] a: ~ **to**
equivalente a.
tantrum ['tæntrəm] n rabieta.
tap [tæp] n (on sink etc) grifo; (gentle blow)
golpecito; (gas ~) llave f // vt dar
golpecitos; (resources) utilizar, explotar;
~**-dancing** n zapateado.
tape [teɪp] n cinta; (also: **magnetic** ~)
cinta magnética; (sticky ~) cinta
adhesiva // vt (record) grabar (en cinta);
~ **measure** n cinta métrica, metro.
taper ['teɪpə*] n cirio // vi afilarse.
tape recorder ['teɪprɪkɔːdə*] n
grabadora.
tapered ['teɪpəd], **tapering** ['teɪpərɪŋ] a
afilado.
tapestry ['tæpɪstrɪ] n (object) tapiz m;
(art) tapicería.
tapioca [tæpɪ'əukə] n tapioca.
tar [tɑː] n alquitrán m, brea.
tarantula [tə'ræntjulə] n tarántula.
target ['tɑːgɪt] n (gen) blanco; ~
practice tiro al blanco.
tariff ['tærɪf] n tarifa.
tarmac ['tɑːmæk] n (on road)
alquitranado; (AVIAT) pista de aterrizaje.
tarnish ['tɑːnɪʃ] vt quitar el brillo a.
tarpaulin [tɑː'pɔːlɪn] n alquitranado.
tarragon ['tærəgɔn] n estragón m.
tart [tɑːt] n (CULIN) tarta; (col: pej: woman)
fulana // a (flavour) agrio, ácido.
tartan ['tɑːtn] n tartán m, escocés m // a
de tartán.
tartar ['tɑːtə*] n (on teeth) sarro; ~**(e)
sauce** n salsa tártara.

task [tɑːsk] n tarea; **to take to** ~
reprender; ~ **force** n (MIL, POLICE)
destacamento especial.
tassel ['tæsl] n borla.
taste [teɪst] n sabor m, gusto; (also:
after~) dejo; (sip) sorbo; (fig: glimpse,
idea) muestra, idea // vt probar // vi: **to**
~ **of** or **like** (fish etc) saber a; **you can** ~
the garlic (in it) se nota el sabor a ajo;
can I have a ~ **of this wine?** ¿puedo
probar el vino?; **to have a** ~ **for sth** ser
aficionado a algo; **in good/bad** ~ de
buen/mal gusto; ~**ful** a de buen gusto;
~**fully** ad con buen gusto; ~**less** a (food)
insípido; (remark) de mal gusto; **tasty** a
sabroso, rico.
tattered ['tætəd] a see **tatters.**
tatters ['tætəz] npl: **in** ~ (also: **tattered**)
hecho jirones.
tattoo [tə'tuː] n tatuaje m; (spectacle)
espectáculo militar // vt tatuar.
tatty ['tætɪ] a (col) raído.
taught [tɔːt] pt, pp of **teach.**
taunt [tɔːnt] n burla // vt burlarse de.
Taurus ['tɔːrəs] n Tauro.
taut [tɔːt] a tirante, tenso.
tawdry ['tɔːdrɪ] a cursi, de mal gusto.
tawny ['tɔːnɪ] a leonado.
tax [tæks] n impuesto // vt gravar (con un
impuesto); (fig: test) abrumar; (: patience)
agotar; **direct** ~ contribución directa;
~**ation** [-'seɪʃən] n impuestos mpl; ~
collector n recaudador/a m/f; ~**-free** a
libre de impuestos.
taxi ['tæksɪ] n taxi m // vi (AVIAT) rodar de
suelo.
taxidermist ['tæksɪdɜːmɪst] n
taxidermista m/f.
taxi: ~ **driver** n taxista m/f; ~ **rank,** ~
stand n parada de taxis.
tax: ~ **payer** n contribuyente m/f; ~
return n declaración f de ingresos.
TB abbr of **tuberculosis.**
tea [tiː] n té m; (snack) merienda; **high** ~
merienda-cena; ~ **bag** n bolsa de té; ~
break n descanso para el té; ~ **cake** n
bollo.
teach [tiːtʃ], pt, pp **taught** vt: **to** ~ **sb sth,**
~ **sth to sb** enseñar algo a uno // vi
enseñar; (be a teacher) ser profesor/a;
~**er** n (in secondary school) profesor/a
m/f; (in primary school) maestro/a; ~**ing**
n enseñanza.
tea: ~ **cosy** n cubretetera; ~**cup** n taza
para té.
teak [tiːk] n (madera de) teca.
tea leaves npl hojas fpl de té.
team [tiːm] n equipo; (of animals) pareja;
~**work** n trabajo de equipo.
teapot ['tiːpɔt] n tetera.
tear [tɛə*] n rasgón m, desgarrón m // n
[tɪə*] lágrima // (vb: pt **tore,** pp **torn**) vt
romper, rasgar // vi rasgarse; **in** ~**s**
llorando; **to burst into** ~**s** deshacerse en
lágrimas; **to** ~ **along** vi (rush)
precipitarse; ~**ful** a lloroso; ~ **gas** n gas
m lacrimógeno.

tearoom ['tiːruːm] n salón m de té, cafetería.

tease [tiːz] n bromista m/f // vt bromear, tomar el pelo a.

tea: ~ **set** n juego de té; ~**spoon** n cucharilla; (also: ~**spoonful:** as measurement) cucharadita.

teat [tiːt] n (of bottle) tetina.

tea: ~ **time** n hora del té; ~ **towel** n trapo de cocina.

technical ['tɛknɪkl] a técnico; ~**ity** [-'kælɪtɪ] n detalle m técnico; ~**ly** ad técnicamente.

technician [tɛk'nɪʃn] n técnico.

technique [tɛk'niːk] n técnica.

technological [tɛknə'lɔdʒɪkl] a tecnológico; **technology** [-'nɔlədʒɪ] n tecnología.

teddy (bear) ['tɛdɪ] n osito de felpa.

tedious ['tiːdɪəs] a pesado, aburrido.

tee [tiː] n (GOLF) tee m.

teem [tiːm] vi abundar, pulular; **to** ~ **with** rebosar de; **it is** ~**ing (with rain)** llueve a mares.

teenage ['tiːneɪdʒ] a (fashions etc) de o para los jóvenes; **teenager** n joven m/f (de 13 a 19 años).

teens [tiːnz] npl: **to be in one's** ~ ser un adolescente, no haber cumplido los 20.

tee-shirt ['tiːʃɔːt] n = **T-shirt.**

teeter ['tiːtə*] vi balancearse.

teeth [tiːθ] pl of **tooth.**

teethe [tiːð] vi echar los dientes.

teething ['tiːðɪŋ]: ~ **ring** n mordedor m; ~ **troubles** npl (fig) dificultades fpl iniciales.

teetotal ['tiː'təutl] a (person) abstemio.

telecommunications ['tɛlɪkəmjuːnɪ-'keɪʃənz] n telecomunicaciones fpl.

telegram ['tɛlɪgræm] n telegrama m.

telegraph ['tɛlɪgrɑːf] n telégrafo; ~**ic** [-'græfɪk] a telegráfico; ~ **pole** n poste m de telégrafos.

telepathic [tɛlɪ'pæθɪk] a telepático; **telepathy** [tə'lɛpəθɪ] n telepatía.

telephone ['tɛlɪfəun] n teléfono // vt (person) llamar por teléfono; (message) telefonear; ~ **booth,** ~ **box** n cabina telefónica; ~ **call** n llamada (telefónica); ~ **directory** n guía (telefónica); ~ **exchange** n central f telefónica; ~ **number** n número de teléfono; **telephonist** [tə'lɛfənɪst] n telefonista m/f.

telephoto ['tɛlɪ'fəutəu] a: ~ **lens** teleobjetivo.

teleprinter ['tɛlɪprɪntə*] n teletipo.

telescope ['tɛlɪskəup] n telescopio; **telescopic** [-'skɔpɪk] a telescópico.

televise ['tɛlɪvaɪz] vt televisar.

television ['tɛlɪvɪʒən] n televisión f; ~ **set** n televisor m.

telex ['tɛlɛks] n telex m.

tell [tɛl], pt, pp **told** vt decir; (relate: story) contar; (distinguish): **to** ~ **sth from** distinguir algo de // vi (have effect) tener efecto; **to** ~ **sb to do sth** mandar a uno que haga algo; **to** ~ **sb off** reñir o regañar a uno; ~**er** n (in bank) cajero; ~**ing** a (remark, detail) revelador(a); ~ **tale** a (sign) indicador(a).

telly ['tɛlɪ] n (col) abbr of **television.**

temerity [tə'mɛrɪtɪ] n temeridad f.

temper ['tɛmpə*] n (nature) carácter m; (mood) humor m; (bad ~) genio, mal genio; (fit of anger) cólera; (of child) rabieta // vt (moderate) moderar; **to be in a** ~ estar de mal humor; **to lose one's** ~ perder la paciencia.

temperament ['tɛmprəmənt] n (nature) temperamento; ~**al** [-'mɛntl] a temperamental.

temperance ['tɛmpərns] n moderación f; (in drinking) sobriedad f.

temperate ['tɛmprət] a moderado; (climate) templado.

temperature ['tɛmprətʃə*] n temperatura; **to have** or **run a** ~ tener fiebre.

tempered ['tɛmpəd] a (steel) templado.

tempest ['tɛmpɪst] n tempestad f.

temple ['tɛmpl] n (building) templo; (ANAT) sien f.

tempo ['tɛmpəu], pl ~**s** or **tempi** [-piː] n tempo; (fig: of life etc) ritmo.

temporal ['tɛmpərl] a temporal.

temporarily ['tɛmpərərɪlɪ] ad temporalmente.

temporary ['tɛmpərərɪ] a provisional, temporal; (passing) transitorio; (worker) temporero.

tempt [tɛmpt] vt tentar; **to** ~ **sb into doing sth** tentar o inducir a uno a hacer algo; ~**ation** [-'teɪʃən] n tentación f; ~**ing** a tentador(a).

ten [tɛn] num diez.

tenable ['tɛnəbl] a sostenible.

tenacious [tə'neɪʃəs] a tenaz; **tenacity** [-'næsɪtɪ] n tenacidad f.

tenancy ['tɛnənsɪ] n alquiler m; (of house) inquilinato; **tenant** n (rent-payer) inquilino; (occupant) habitante m/f.

tend [tɛnd] vt cuidar // vi: **to** ~ **to do sth** tener tendencia a hacer algo.

tendency ['tɛndənsɪ] n tendencia.

tender ['tɛndə*] a tierno, blando; (delicate) delicado; (sore) sensible, dolorido; (affectionate) tierno, cariñoso // n (COMM: offer) oferta; (money): **legal** ~ moneda de curso legal // vt ofrecer; ~**ize** vt (CULIN) ablandar; ~**ness** n ternura; (of meat) blandura.

tendon ['tɛndən] n tendón m.

tenement ['tɛnəmənt] n casa de pisos.

tennis ['tɛnɪs] n tenis m; ~ **ball** n pelota de tenis; ~ **court** n pista de tenis; ~ **racket** n raqueta de tenis.

tenor ['tɛnə*] n (MUS) tenor m.

tenpin bowling ['tɛnpɪn-] n los bolos mpl.

tense [tɛns] a tenso; (stretched) tirante; (stiff) rígido, tieso // n (LING) tiempo; ~**ness** n tensión f.

tension ['tɛnʃən] n tensión f.

tent [tɛnt] *n* tienda (de campaña).
tentacle ['tɛntəkl] *n* tentáculo.
tentative ['tɛntətɪv] *a* experimental; (*conclusion*) provisional.
tenterhooks ['tɛntəhuks] *npl*: **on** ~ sobre ascuas.
tenth [tɛnθ] *a* décimo.
tent: ~ **peg** *n* clavija, estaquilla; ~ **pole** *n* mástil *m*.
tenuous ['tɛnjuəs] *a* tenue.
tenure ['tɛnjuə*] *n* posesión *f*, tenencia.
tepid ['tɛpɪd] *a* tibio.
term [tə:m] *n* (*limit*) límite *m*; (*COMM*) plazo; (*word*) término; (*period*) período; (*SCOL*) trimestre *m* // *vt* llamar; ~**s** *npl* (*conditions*) condiciones *fpl*; (*COMM*) precio, tarifa; **in the short/long** ~ a corto/largo plazo; **to be on good** ~**s with sb** llevarse bien con uno; **to come to** ~**s with** (*person*) llegar a un acuerdo con; (*problem*) adaptarse a.
terminal ['tə:mɪnl] *a* terminal; (*disease*) mortal // *n* (*ELEC*) borne *m*; (*also*: **air** ~) terminal *f*; (*also*: **coach** ~) estación *f* terminal.
terminate ['tə:mɪneɪt] *vt* terminar // *vi*: **to** ~ **in** acabar por; **termination** [-'neɪʃən] *n* terminación *f*; (*of contract*) conclusión *f*.
terminology [tə:mɪ'nɔlədʒɪ] *n* terminología.
terminus ['tə:mɪnəs], *pl* **-mini** [-mɪnaɪ] *n* término, estación *f* terminal.
termite ['tə:maɪt] *n* termita.
terrace ['tɛrəs] *n* terraza; (*row of houses*) hilera de casas adosadas; **the** ~**s** (*SPORT*) gradas *fpl*; ~**ed** *a* (*garden*) escalonado; (*house*) adosado.
terrain [tɛ'reɪn] *n* terreno.
terrible ['tɛrɪbl] *a* terrible, horrible; (*fam*) malísimo; **terribly** *ad* terriblemente; (*very badly*) malísimamente.
terrier ['tɛrɪə*] *n* terrier *m*.
terrific [tə'rɪfɪk] *a* fantástico, fenomenal; (*wonderful*) maravilloso.
terrify ['tɛrɪfaɪ] *vt* aterrorizar.
territorial [tɛrɪ'tɔ:rɪəl] *a* territorial.
territory ['tɛrɪtərɪ] *n* territorio.
terror ['tɛrə*] *n* terror *m*; ~**ism** *n* terrorismo; ~**ist** *n* terrorista *m/f*; ~**ize** *vt* aterrorizar.
terse [tə:s] *a* (*style*) conciso; (*reply*) brusco.
test [tɛst] *n* (*trial, check*) prueba, ensayo; (: *of goods in factory*) control *m*; (*of courage etc, CHEM*) prueba; (*MED*) examen *m*; (*exam*) examen *m*, test *m*; (*also*: **driving** ~) examen *m* de conducir // *vt* probar, poner a prueba.
testament ['tɛstəmənt] *n* testamento; **the Old/New** **T**~ el Antiguo/Nuevo Testamento.
testicle ['tɛstɪkl] *n* testículo.
testify ['tɛstɪfaɪ] *vi* (*LAW*) prestar declaración; **to** ~ **to sth** atestiguar algo.
testimonial [tɛstɪ'məunɪəl] *n* (*reference*) recomendación *f*; (*gift*) obsequio.

testimony ['tɛstɪmənɪ] *n* (*LAW*) testimonio, declaración *f*.
test: ~ **match** *n* (*CRICKET, RUGBY*) partido internacional; ~ **pilot** *n* piloto de pruebas; ~ **tube** *n* probeta.
testy ['tɛstɪ] *a* irritable.
tetanus ['tɛtənəs] *n* tétano.
tether ['tɛðə*] *vt* atar (con una cuerda) // *n*: **at the end of one's** ~ a punto de perder la paciencia.
text [tɛkst] *n* texto; ~**book** *n* libro de texto.
textiles ['tɛkstaɪlz] *npl* textiles *mpl*, tejidos *mpl*.
texture ['tɛkstʃə*] *n* textura.
Thai [taɪ] *a, n* tailandés/esa *m/f*; ~**land** *n* Tailandia.
Thames [tɛmz] *n*: **the** ~ el (río) Támesis.
than [ðæn, ðən] *conj* que; (*with numerals*): **more** ~ **10/once** más de 10/una vez; **I have more/less** ~ **you** tengo más/menos que tú.
thank [θæŋk] *vt* dar las gracias a, agradecer; ~ **you (very much)** muchas gracias; ~**s** *npl* gracias *fpl*; ~**s to** *prep* gracias a; ~**ful** *a*: ~**ful (for)** agradecido por; ~**less** *a* ingrato; **Thanksgiving (Day)** *n* día *m* de acción de gracias.
that [ðæt, ðət] *conj* que // *det* ese/esa; (*more remote*) aquel/ aquella // *pron* ése/ésa; aquél/ aquélla; (*neuter*) eso; aquello; (*relative: subject*) que; (: *object*) que, el cual/la cual *etc*; (*with time*): **on the day** ~ **he came** el día que vino // *ad*: **high** tan alto, así de alto; **it's about** ~ **high** es más o menos así de alto; ~ **one** ése/ésa; aquél/aquélla; **what's** ~? ¿qué es eso?; **who's** ~? ¿quién es?; **is** ~ **you?** ¿eres tú?; (*formal*) ¿es Usted?; ~**'s what he said** eso es lo que dijo; **all** ~ todo eso; **I can't work** ~ **much** no puedo trabajar tanto.
thatched [θætʃt] *a* (*roof*) de paja; ~ **cottage** casita con tejado de paja.
thaw [θɔ:] *n* deshielo // *vi* (*ice*) derretirse; (*food*) descongelarse // *vt* (*food*) descongelar.
the [ði:, ðə] *def art* el/la; (*pl*) los/las; (*neuter*) lo; ~ **sooner** ~ **better** cuanto antes mejor.
theatre, theater (*US*) ['θɪətə*] *n* teatro; ~**-goer** *n* aficionado al teatro.
theatrical [θɪ'ætrɪkl] *a* teatral.
theft [θɛft] *n* robo.
their [ðɛə*] *a* su; ~**s** *pron* (el) suyo/(la) suya *etc*; **a friend of** ~**s** un amigo suyo.
them [ðɛm, ðəm] *pron* (*direct*) los/las; (*indirect*) les; (*stressed, after prep*) ellos/ellas; **I see** ~ los veo; **give** ~ **the book** dales el libro.
theme [θi:m] *n* tema *m*; ~ **song** tema (musical).
themselves [ðəm'sɛlvz] *pl pron* (*subject*) ellos mismos/ellas mismas; (*complement*) se; (*after prep*) sí (mismos/as).
then [ðɛn] *ad* (*at that time*) entonces; (*next*) pues; (*later*) luego, después; (*and also*)

además // *conj* (*therefore*) en ese caso, entonces // *a*: **the** ~ **president** el entonces presidente; **from** ~ **on** desde entonces.
theological [θɪə'lɔdʒɪkl] *a* teológico; **theology** [θɪ'ɔlədʒɪ] *n* teología.
theorem ['θɪərəm] *n* teorema *m*.
theoretical [θɪə'rɛtɪkl] *a* teórico; **theorize** ['θɪəraɪz] *vi* elaborar una teoría; **theory** ['θɪərɪ] *n* teoría.
therapeutic(al) [θɛrə'pju:tɪk(l)] *a* terapéutico.
therapist ['θɛrəpɪst] *n* terapeuta *m/f*; **therapy** *n* terapia.
there [ðɛə*] *ad* allí, allá, ahí; ~, ~! ¡cálmate!; **it's** ~ está ahí; ~ **is**, ~ **are** hay; ~ **he is** ahí está; **on/in** ~ allí encima/dentro; ~**abouts** *ad* por ahí; ~**after** *ad* después; ~**fore** *ad* por lo tanto; ~**'s** = ~ **is**; ~ **has**.
thermal ['θə:ml] *a* termal.
thermometer [θə'mɔmɪtə*] *n* termómetro.
Thermos ['θə:mɔs] *n* termo.
thermostat ['θə:məustæt] *n* termostato.
thesaurus [θɪ'sɔ:rəs] *n* tesoro.
these [ði:z] *pl det* estos/as // *pl pron* éstos/as.
thesis ['θi:sɪs], *pl* **-ses** [-si:z] *n* tesis *f*.
they [ðeɪ] *pl pron* ellos/ellas; (*stressed*) ellos (mismos)/ellas (mismas); ~ **say that...** (*it is said that*) se dice que...; ~**'d** = **they had; they would**; ~**'ll** = **they shall, they will**; ~**'re** = **they are**; ~**'ve** = **they have**.
thick [θɪk] *a* espeso; (*fat*) grueso; (*dense*) denso, espeso; (*stupid*) torpe // *n*: **in the** ~ **of the battle** en plena batalla; **it's 20 cm** ~ tiene 20 cm de espesor; ~**en** *vi* espesarse // *vt* (*sauce etc*) espesar; ~**ness** *n* espesor *m*, grueso; ~**set** *a* rechoncho; ~**skinned** *a* (*fig*) insensible.
thief [θi:f], *pl* **thieves** [θi:vz] *n* ladrón/ona *m/f*.
thieving ['θi:vɪŋ] *n* robo.
thigh [θaɪ] *n* muslo.
thimble ['θɪmbl] *n* dedal *m*.
thin [θɪn] *a* (*gen*) delgado; (*watery*) aguado; (*light*) tenue; (*hair, crowd*) escaso; (*fog*) poco denso // *vt*: **to** ~ **(down)** (*sauce, paint*) diluir.
thing [θɪŋ] *n* (*gen*) cosa; (*object*) objeto, artículo; (*matter*) asunto; (*mania*) manía; ~**s** *npl* (*belongings*) efectos *mpl* (personales); **the best** ~ **would be to...** lo mejor sería...; **how are** ~**s?** ¿qué tal?
think [θɪŋk], *pt, pp* **thought** *vi* pensar // *vt* pensar, creer; (*imagine*) imaginar; **what did you** ~ **of them?** ¿qué te parecieron?; **to** ~ **about sth/sb** pensar en algo/alguien; **I'll** ~ **about it** lo pensaré; **to** ~ **of doing sth** pensar en hacer algo; **I** ~ **so/not** creo que sí/no; **to** ~ **well of sb** tener buen concepto de alguien; **to** ~ **over** *vt* reflexionar sobre, meditar; **to** ~ **up** *vt* imaginar; ~**ing** *a* pensante.

thinly ['θɪnlɪ] *ad* (*cut*) en lonchas finas; (*spread*) con una capa fina.
thinness ['θɪnnɪs] *n* delgadez *f*.
third [θə:d] *a* tercer(a) // *n* tercero; (*fraction*) tercio; (*SCOL: degree*) de tercera clase; ~**ly** *ad* en tercer lugar; ~ **party insurance** *n* seguro contra terceras personas; ~-**rate** *a* (de calidad) mediocre; **the T**~ **World** *n* el Tercer Mundo.
thirst [θə:st] *n* sed *f*; ~**y** *a* (*person*) sediento; **to be** ~**y** tener sed.
thirteen ['θə:'ti:n] *num* trece.
thirty ['θə:tɪ] *num* treinta.
this [ðɪs] *det* este/esta // *pron* éste/ésta; (*neuter*) esto; ~ **is what he said** esto es lo que dijo; ~ **high** así de alto.
thistle ['θɪsl] *n* cardo.
thong [θɔŋ] *n* correa.
thorn [θɔ:n] *n* espina; ~**y** *a* espinoso.
thorough ['θʌrə] *a* (*search*) minucioso; (*knowledge, research*) profundo; ~**bred** *a* (*horse*) de pura sangre; ~**fare** *n* calle *f*; **'no** ~**fare'** "prohibido el paso"; ~**ly** *ad* minuciosamente; profundamente, a fondo.
those [ðəuz] *pl pron* esos/esas; (*more remote*) aquellos/as // *pl det* ésos/ésas; aquéllos/as.
though [ðəu] *conj* aunque // *ad* sin embargo.
thought [θɔ:t] *pt, pp of* **think** // *n* pensamiento; (*opinion*) opinión *f*; (*intention*) intención *f*; ~**ful** *a* pensativo; (*considerate*) considerado; ~**less** *a* desconsiderado.
thousand ['θauzənd] *num* mil; **two** ~ dos mil; ~**s of** miles de; ~**th** *a* milésimo.
thrash [θræʃ] *vt* apalear; (*defeat*) derrotar; **to** ~ **about** *vi* revolcarse; **to** ~ **out** *vt* discutir largamente.
thread [θrɛd] *n* hilo; (*of screw*) rosca // *vt* (*needle*) enhebrar; ~**bare** *a* raído.
threat [θrɛt] *n* amenaza; ~**en** *vi* amenazar // *vt*: **to** ~**en sb with sth/to do** amenazar a uno con algo/ con hacer.
three [θri:] *num* tres; ~-**dimensional** *a* tridimensional; ~**fold** *ad*: **to increase** ~**fold** triplicar; ~-**piece suit** *n* traje *m* de tres piezas; ~-**piece suite** *n* tresillo; ~-**ply** *a* (*wool*) triple; ~-**wheeler** *n* (*car*) coche *m* de tres ruedas.
thresh [θrɛʃ] *vt* (*AGR*) trillar.
threshold ['θrɛʃhəuld] *n* umbral *m*.
threw [θru:] *pt of* **throw**.
thrift [θrɪft] *n* economía; ~**y** *a* económico.
thrill [θrɪl] *n* (*excitement*) emoción *f*; (*shudder*) estremecimiento // *vt* emocionar; estremecer; **to be** ~**ed** (*with gift etc*) estar encantado; ~**er** *n* película/novela de suspense.
thrive [θraɪv], *pt* **thrived** *or* **throve** [θrəuv], *pp* **thrived** *or* **thriven** ['θrɪvn] *vi* (*grow*) crecer; (*do well*) prosperar; **thriving** *a* próspero.
throat [θrəut] *n* garganta; **to have a sore** ~ tener dolor de garganta.
throb [θrɔb] *n* (*of heart*) latido; (*of engine*)

vibración f // vi latir; vibrar; (pain) dar punzadas.

throes [θrəuz] npl: **in the ~ of** en medio de.

thrombosis [θrɔm'bəusɪs] n trombosis f.

throne [θrəun] n trono.

throttle ['θrɒtl] n (AUT) acelerador m // vt ahogar.

through [θruː] prep por, a través de; (time) durante; (by means of) por medio de, mediante; (owing to) gracias a // a (ticket, train) directo // ad completamente, de parte a parte; **to put sb ~ to sb** (TEL) poner a alguien (en comunicación) con alguien; **to be ~** (TEL) tener comunicación; (have finished) haber terminado; **"no ~ way"** "calle sin salida"; **~out** prep (place) por todas partes de, por todo; (time) durante todo, en todo // ad por o en todas partes.

throw [θrəu] n tirada, tiro; (SPORT) lanzamiento // vt, pt **threw**, pp **thrown** tirar, echar; (SPORT) lanzar; (rider) derribar; (fig) desconcertar; **to ~ a party** dar una fiesta; **to ~ away** vt tirar; **to ~ off** vt deshacerse de; **to ~ out** vt tirar; **to ~ up** vi vomitar; **~away** a para tirar, desechable; **~-in** n (SPORT) saque m.

thru [θruː] (US) = **through**.

thrush [θrʌʃ] n zorzal m, tordo.

thrust [θrʌst] n (TECH) empuje m // vt, pt, pp **thrust** empujar; (push in) introducir.

thud [θʌd] n golpe m sordo.

thug [θʌg] n (criminal) criminal m/f; (pej) bruto.

thumb [θʌm] n (ANAT) pulgar m, dedo gordo (col) // vt (book) hojear; **to ~ a lift** hacer dedo o autostop; **~tack** n (US) chinche m.

thump [θʌmp] n golpe m; (sound) porrazo // vt, vi golpear.

thunder ['θʌndə*] n (gen) trueno; (sudden noise) tronido; (of applause etc) estruendo // vi tronar; (train etc): **to ~ past** pasar como un trueno; **~bolt** n rayo; **~clap** n trueno; **~storm** n tormenta; **~struck** a pasmado; **~y** a tormentoso.

Thursday ['θəːzdɪ] n jueves m.

thus [ðʌs] ad así, de este modo.

thwart [θwɔːt] vt frustrar.

thyme [taɪm] n tomillo.

thyroid ['θaɪrɔɪd] n tiroides m.

tiara [tɪ'ɑːrə] n tiara, diadema.

tic [tɪk] n tic m.

tick [tɪk] n (sound: of clock) tictac m; (mark) palomita; (ZOOL) garrapata; (col): **in a ~** en un instante // vi hacer tictac // vt marcar; **to ~ off** vt marcar; (person) poner como un trapo.

ticket ['tɪkɪt] n billete m, tíquet m; (for cinema) entrada; (in shop: on goods) etiqueta; (for library) tarjeta; **~ collector** n revisor m; **~ office** n taquilla.

tickle ['tɪkl] n cosquillas fpl // vt hacer cosquillas a; **ticklish** a que tiene cosquillas.

tidal ['taɪdl] a de marea; **~ wave** n maremoto.

tiddlywinks ['tɪdlɪwɪŋks] n juego de la pulga.

tide [taɪd] n marea; (fig: of events) curso, marcha.

tidiness ['taɪdɪnɪs] n (good order) buen orden m; (neatness) limpieza, aseo.

tidy ['taɪdɪ] a (room) ordenado; (dress, work) limpio; (person) (bien) arreglado // vt (also: ~ up) poner en orden.

tie [taɪ] n (string etc) atadura; (also: neck~) corbata; (fig: link) vínculo, lazo; (SPORT: draw) empate m // vt (gen) atar // vi (SPORT) empatar; **to ~ in a bow** hacer un lazo; **to ~ a knot in sth** hacer un nudo a algo; **to ~ down** vt atar; (fig): **to ~ sb down** to obligar a uno a; **to ~ up** vt (parcel) envolver; (dog) atar; (boat) amarrar; (arrangements) concluir, despachar; **to be ~d up** (busy) estar ocupado.

tier [tɪə*] n grada; (of cake) piso.

tiger ['taɪgə*] n tigre m/f.

tight [taɪt] a (rope) tirante; (money) escaso; (clothes) ajustado; (budget, programme) apretado; (col: drunk) borracho // ad (squeeze) muy fuerte; (shut) herméticamente; **~s** npl pantimedias fpl; (for gym) malla sg; **~en** vt (rope) estirar; (screw) apretar // vi apretarse, estirarse; **~-fisted** a tacaño; **~ly** ad (grasp) muy fuerte; **~-rope** n cuerda floja.

tile [taɪl] n (on roof) teja; (on floor) baldosa; (on wall) azulejo, baldosín m; **~d** a embaldosado.

till [tɪl] n caja (registradora) // vt (land) cultivar // prep, conj = **until**.

tiller ['tɪlə*] n (NAUT) caña del timón.

tilt [tɪlt] vt inclinar // vi inclinarse.

timber ['tɪmbə*] n (material) madera; (trees) árboles mpl.

time [taɪm] n tiempo; (epoch: often pl) época; (by clock) hora; (moment) momento; (occasion) vez f; (MUS) compás m // vt (gen) calcular o medir el tiempo de; (race) cronometrar; (remark etc) elegir el momento para; **a long ~** mucho tiempo; **for the ~ being** de momento, por ahora; **from ~ to ~** de vez en cuando; **in ~** (soon enough) a tiempo; (after some time) con el tiempo; (MUS) al compás; **in a week's ~** dentro de una semana; **on ~** a la hora; **5 ~s 5** 5 por 5; **what ~ is it?** ¿qué hora es?; **to have a good ~** pasarlo bien, divertirse; **~ bomb** n bomba de efecto retardado; **~keeper** n (SPORT) cronómetro; **~less** a eterno; **~ limit** n (gen) limitación f de tiempo; (COMM) plazo; **~ly** a oportuno; **~ off** n tiempo libre; **timer** n (in kitchen) reloj m programador; **~ switch** n interruptor m; **~table** n horario; **~ zone** n huso horario.

timid ['tɪmɪd] a tímido.

timing ['taɪmɪŋ] n (SPORT) cronometraje

m; (*gen*) elección *f* del momento; **the ~ of his resignation** el momento que eligió para dimitir.

timpani ['tɪmpənɪ] *npl* tímpanos *mpl*.

tin [tɪn] *n* estaño; (*also*: **~ plate**) hojalata; (*can*) lata; **~ foil** *n* papel *m* de estaño.

tinge [tɪndʒ] *n* matiz *m* // *vt*: **~d with** teñido de.

tingle ['tɪŋgl] *n* picotazo // *vi* sentir picazón.

tinker ['tɪŋkə*] *n* calderero; (*gipsy*) gitano; **to ~ with** *vt* manosear.

tinkle ['tɪŋkl] *vi* tintinear // *n* (*col*): **to give sb a ~** dar un telefonazo a alguien.

tinned [tɪnd] *a* (*food*) en lata, en conserva.

tin opener ['tɪnəupnə*] *n* abrelatas *m inv*.

tinsel ['tɪnsl] *n* oropel *m*.

tint [tɪnt] *n* matiz *m*; (*for hair*) tinte *m*.

tiny ['taɪnɪ] *a* minúsculo, pequeñito.

tip [tɪp] *n* (*end*) punta; (*gratuity*) propina; (*for rubbish*) basurero; (*advice*) aviso // *vt* (*waiter*) dar una propina a; (*tilt*) inclinar; (*overturn*: *also*: **~ over**) dar la vuelta a, volcar; (*empty*: *also*: **~ out**) vaciar, echar; **~-off** *n* (*hint*) aviso, advertencia; **~ped** *a* (*cigarette*) con filtro.

tipsy ['tɪpsɪ] *a* algo borracho, mareado.

tiptoe ['tɪptəu] *n*: **on ~** de puntillas.

tiptop ['tɪp'tɔp] *a*: **in ~ condition** en perfectas condiciones.

tire ['taɪə*] *n* (*US*) = **tyre** // *vt* cansar // *vi* (*gen*) cansarse; (*become bored*) aburrirse; **~d** *a* cansado; **to be ~d of sth** estar cansado *o* harto de algo; **tiredness** *n* cansancio; **~less** *a* incansable; **~some** *a* aburrido; **tiring** *a* cansado.

tissue ['tɪʃuː] *n* tejido; (*paper handkerchief*) pañuelo de papel, kleenex *m*; **~ paper** *n* papel *m* de seda.

tit [tɪt] *n* (*bird*) herrerillo común; **to give ~ for tat** dar ojo por ojo.

titbit ['tɪtbɪt] *n* (*food*) golosina; (*news*) suceso.

titillate ['tɪtɪleɪt] *vt* estimular, excitar.

titivate ['tɪtɪveɪt] *vt* emperejillar.

title ['taɪtl] *n* título; **~ deed** *n* (*LAW*) título de propiedad; **~ role** *n* papel *m* principal.

titter ['tɪtə*] *vi* reírse entre dientes.

titular ['tɪtjulə*] *a* (*in name only*) nominal.

to [tuː, tə] *prep* a; (*towards*) hacia; (*of time*) a, hasta; (*of*) de; **give it ~ me** dámelo; **the key ~ the front door** la llave de la puerta; **the main thing is ~...** lo importante es...; **to go ~ France/school** ir a Francia/al colegio; **a quarter ~ 5** las 5 menos cuarto; **pull/push the door ~** tirar/empujar la puerta; **to go ~ and fro** ir y venir.

toad [təud] *n* sapo; **~stool** *n* hongo venenoso.

toast [təust] *n* (*CULIN*: *also*: **piece of ~**) tostada; (*drink, speech*) brindis *m* // *vt* (*CULIN*) tostar; (*drink to*) brindar; **~er** *n* tostador *m*.

tobacco [tə'bækəu] *n* tabaco; **~nist** *n* estanquero; **~nist's (shop)** *n* estanco.

toboggan [tə'bɔgən] *n* tobogán *m*.

today [tə'deɪ] *ad*, *n* (*also fig*) hoy *m*.

toddler ['tɔdlə*] *n* niño que empieza a andar.

toddy ['tɔdɪ] *n* ponche *m*.

toe [təu] *n* dedo (del pie); (*of shoe*) punta; **to ~ the line** (*fig*) obedecer, conformarse; **~nail** *n* uña del pie.

toffee ['tɔfɪ] *n* caramelo; **~ apple** *n* pirulí *m*.

toga ['təugə] *n* toga.

together [tə'geðə*] *ad* juntos; (*at same time*) al mismo tiempo, a la vez; **~ with** *prep* junto con; **~ness** *n* compañerismo.

toil [tɔɪl] *n* trabajo duro, labor *f* // *vi* esforzarse.

toilet ['tɔɪlət] *n* (*lavatory*) servicios *mpl*, wáter *m* // *cpd* (*bag, soap etc*) de aseo; **~ bowl** *n* palangana; **~ paper** *n* papel *m* higiénico; **~ries** *npl* artículos *mpl* de aseo; (*make-up etc*) artículos *mpl* de tocador; **~ roll** *n* rollo de papel higiénico; **~ water** *n* agua de tocador.

token ['təukən] *n* (*sign*) señal *f*, muestra; (*souvenir*) recuerdo; (*voucher*) cupón *m*; **book/record ~** vale *m* para comprar libros/discos.

told [təuld] *pt*, *pp of* **tell.**

tolerable ['tɔlərəbl] *a* (*bearable*) soportable; (*fairly good*) pasable.

tolerance ['tɔlərns] *n* (*also*: *TECH*) tolerancia; **tolerant** *a*: **tolerant of** tolerante con.

tolerate ['tɔləreɪt] *vt* tolerar; **toleration** [-'reɪʃən] *n* tolerancia.

toll [təul] *n* (*of casualties*) número de víctimas; (*tax, charge*) peaje *m* // *vi* (*bell*) doblar; **~bridge** *n* puente *m* de peaje.

tomato [tə'mɑːtəu], *pl* **~es** *n* tomate *m*.

tomb [tuːm] *n* tumba.

tombola [tɔm'bəulə] *n* tómbola.

tomboy ['tɔmbɔɪ] *n* marimacho.

tombstone ['tuːmstəun] *n* lápida.

tomcat ['tɔmkæt] *n* gato.

tomorrow [tə'mɔrəu] *ad*, *n* (*also fig*) mañana; **the day after ~** pasado mañana; **~ morning** mañana por la mañana.

ton [tʌn] *n* tonelada; **~s of** (*col*) montones *mpl* de.

tone [təun] *n* tono // *vi* armonizar; **to ~ down** *vt* (*colour, criticism*) suavizar; (*sound*) bajar; (*MUS*) entonar; **to ~ up** *vt* (*muscles*) tonificar; **~-deaf** *a* que no tiene oído.

tongs [tɔŋz] *npl* (*for coal*) tenazas *fpl*; (*for hair*) tenacillas *fpl*.

tongue [tʌŋ] *n* lengua; **~ in cheek** *ad* irónicamente; **~-tied** *a* (*fig*) mudo; **~-twister** *n* trabalenguas *m inv*.

tonic ['tɔnɪk] *n* (*MED*) tónico; (*MUS*) tónica; (*also*: **~ water**) (agua) tónica.

tonight [tə'naɪt] *ad*, *n* esta noche.

tonnage ['tʌnɪdʒ] *n* (*NAUT*) tonelaje *m*.

tonsil ['tɔnsl] *n* amígdala, anginas *fpl* (*col*); **~litis** [-'laɪtɪs] *n* amigdalitis *f*, (inflamación *f* de las) anginas.

too [tu:] ad (excessively) demasiado; (very) muy; (also) también; ~ **much** ad demasiado; ~ **many** det demasiados/as.

took [tuk] pt of **take.**

tool [tu:l] n herramienta; ~ **box** n caja de herramientas.

toot [tu:t] n (of horn) bocinazo; (of whistle) silbido // vi (with car-horn) tocar la bocina.

tooth [tu:θ], pl **teeth** n (ANAT, TECH) diente m; (molar) muela; ~**ache** n dolor m de muelas; ~**brush** n cepillo de dientes; ~**paste** n pasta de dientes; ~**pick** n palillo.

top [tɔp] n (of mountain) cumbre f, cima; (of head) coronilla; (of ladder) lo alto; (of cupboard, table) superficie f; (lid: of box, jar) tapa, tapadera; (: of bottle) tapón m; (of list etc) cabeza; (toy) peonza // a más alto; (in rank) principal, primero; (best) mejor // vt (exceed) exceder; (be first in) ir a la cabeza de; **on** ~ **of** sobre, encima de; **from** ~ **to toe** de pies a cabeza; **to** ~ **up** vt llenar; ~**coat** n sobretodo; ~ **hat** n sombrero de copa; ~-**heavy** a (object) desequilibrado.

topic ['tɔpɪk] n tema m, tópico; ~**al** a actual.

top: ~**less** a (bather etc) con el pecho al descubierto, topless; ~-**level** a (talks) al más alto nivel; ~**most** a más alto.

topple ['tɔpl] vt volcar, derribar // vi caerse.

topsy-turvy ['tɔpsi'tɔːvi] a, ad patas arriba.

torch [tɔːtʃ] n antorcha; (electric) linterna.

tore [tɔː*] pt of **tear.**

torment ['tɔːmɛnt] n tormento // vt [tɔː'mɛnt] atormentar; (fig: annoy) fastidiar.

torn [tɔːn] pp of **tear.**

tornado [tɔː'neɪdəu], pl ~**es** n tornado.

torpedo [tɔː'piːdəu], pl ~**es** n torpedo.

torrent ['tɔrnt] n torrente m; ~**ial** [-'rɛnʃl] a torrencial.

torso ['tɔːsəu] n torso.

tortoise ['tɔːtəs] n tortuga; ~**shell** ['tɔːtəʃɛl] a de carey.

tortuous ['tɔːtjuəs] a tortuoso.

torture ['tɔːtʃə*] n tortura // vt torturar; (fig) atormentar.

Tory ['tɔːrɪ] a, n conservador/a m/f.

toss [tɔs] vt tirar, echar; (head) sacudir (la cabeza); **to** ~ **a coin** echar a cara o cruz; **to** ~ **up for sth** jugar a cara o cruz algo; **to** ~ **and turn in bed** dar vueltas en la cama.

tot [tɔt] n (drink) copita; (child) nene/a m/f.

total ['təutl] a total, entero // n total m, suma // vt (add up) sumar; (amount to) ascender a.

totalitarian [təutælɪ'tɛərɪən] a totalitario.

totem pole ['təutəm-] n poste m totémico.

totter ['tɔtə*] vi tambalearse.

touch [tʌtʃ] n (gen) tacto; (contact) contacto; (FOOTBALL) fuera de juego // vt (gen) tocar; (emotionally) conmover; **a** ~ **of** (fig) una pizca o un poquito de; **to get**

in ~ **with sb** ponerse en contacto con uno; **to lose** ~ (friends) perder contacto; **to** ~ **on** vt fus (topic) aludir (brevemente) a; **to** ~ **up** vt (paint) retocar; ~-**and-go** a arriesgado; ~**down** n aterrizaje m; (on sea) amerizaje m; ~**ed** a conmovido; (col) chiflado; ~**ing** a conmovedor(a); ~**line** n (SPORT) línea de banda; ~**y** a (person) susceptible.

tough [tʌf] a (gen) duro; (difficult) difícil; (resistant) resistente; (person) fuerte; (: pej) bruto // n (gangster etc) gorila m; ~**en** vt endurecer; ~**ness** n dureza; dificultad f; resistencia; fuerza.

toupee ['tuːpeɪ] n peluca.

tour ['tuə*] n viaje m, vuelta; (also: package ~) viaje m organizado; (of town, museum) visita // vt viajar por; ~**ing** n viajes mpl turísticos, turismo.

tourism ['tuərɪzm] n turismo.

tourist ['tuərɪst] n turista m/f // cpd turístico; ~ **office** n oficina de turismo.

tournament ['tuənəmənt] n torneo.

tousled ['tauzld] a (hair) despeinado.

tout [taut] vi: **to** ~ **for** solicitar clientes para // n: **ticket** ~ revendedor/a m/f.

tow [təu] vt remolcar; **'on** ~**'** (AUT) "a remolque".

toward(s) [tə'wɔːd(z)] prep hacia; (of attitude) respecto a, con; (of purpose) para.

towel ['tauəl] n toalla; ~**ling** n (fabric) felpa; ~ **rail** n toallero.

tower ['tauə*] n torre f; ~ **block** n rascacielos m inv; ~**ing** a muy alto, imponente.

town [taun] n ciudad f; **to go to** ~ ir a la ciudad; (fig) hacer con entusiasmo; ~ **clerk** n secretario del Ayuntamiento; ~ **council** n consejo municipal; ~ **hall** n ayuntamiento; ~ **planning** n urbanismo.

towrope ['təurəup] n cable m de remolque.

toxic ['tɔksɪk] a tóxico.

toy [tɔɪ] n juguete m; **to** ~ **with** vt fus jugar con; (idea) acariciar; ~**shop** n juguetería.

trace [treɪs] n rastro // vt (draw) trazar, delinear; (follow) seguir la pista de; (locate) encontrar.

track [træk] n (mark) huella, pista; (path: gen) camino, senda; (: of bullet etc) trayectoria; (: of suspect, animal) pista, rastro; (RAIL) vía; (on tape, SPORT) pista // vt seguir la pista de; **to keep** ~ **of** mantenerse al tanto de, seguir; **to** ~ **down** vt (prey) averiguar el paradero de; (sth lost) buscar y encontrar; ~ **suit** n chandal m.

tract [trækt] n (GEO) región f; (pamphlet) folleto.

tractor ['træktə*] n tractor m.

trade [treɪd] n comercio, negocio; (skill, job) oficio, empleo // vi negociar, comerciar; **to** ~ **in** vt (old car etc) ofrecer como parte del pago; ~-**in price** n valor m de un objeto usado que se descuenta del precio de otro nuevo; ~**mark** n marca de fábrica; ~ **name** n marca registrada;

trader n comerciante m/f; **tradesman** n (shopkeeper) tendero; ~ **union** n sindicato; ~ **unionism** n sindicalismo; **trading** n comercio; **trading estate** n zona comercial.

tradition [trə'dɪʃən] n tradición f; ~al a tradicional.

traffic ['træfɪk] n (gen, AUT) tráfico, circulación f; (air ~ etc) tránsito // vi: to ~ in (pej: liquor, drugs) traficar en; ~ **circle** n (US) cruce m giratorio; ~ **jam** n embotellamiento; ~ **lights** npl semáforo sg; ~ **warden** n guardia m/f de tráfico.

tragedy ['trædʒədɪ] n tragedia.

tragic ['trædʒɪk] a trágico.

trail [treɪl] n (tracks) rastro, pista; (path) camino, sendero; (wake) estela // vt (drag) arrastrar; (follow) seguir la pista de; (follow closely) vigilar // vi arrastrarse; to ~ **behind** vi quedar a la zaga; ~**er** n (AUT) remolque m; (US) caravana; (CINEMA) trailer m, avance m.

train [treɪn] n tren m; (of dress) cola; (series) serie f; (followers) séquito // vt (educate) formar; (teach skills to) adiestrar; (sportsman) entrenar; (dog) amaestrar; (point: gun etc): to ~ **on** apuntar a // vi (SPORT) entrenarse; (be educated) recibir una formación; ~**ed** a (worker) cualificado, adiestrado; (teacher) diplomado; (animal) amaestrado; ~**ee** [treɪ'niː] n persona que está aprendiendo; (in trade) aprendiz/a m/f; ~**er** n (SPORT) entrenador/a m/f; (of animals) domador/a m/f; ~**ing** n formación f; adiestramiento; entrenamiento; **in** ~**ing** (SPORT) en forma; ~**ing college** n (for teachers) escuela normal; (gen) colegio de formación profesional.

traipse [treɪps] vi andar con desgana.

trait [treɪt] n rasgo.

traitor ['treɪtə*] n traidor/a m/f.

tram [træm] n (also: ~car) tranvía m.

tramp [træmp] n (person) vagabundo // vi andar con pasos pesados.

trample ['træmpl] vt: to ~ (underfoot) pisotear.

trampoline ['træmpəliːn] n trampolín m.

trance [trɑːns] n trance m; (MED) catalepsia.

tranquil ['træŋkwɪl] a tranquilo; ~**lity** n tranquilidad f; ~**lizer** n (MED) tranquilizante m.

transact [træn'zækt] vt (business) tramitar; ~**ion** [-'zækʃən] n transacción f, negocio.

transatlantic [trænzət'læntɪk] a transatlántico.

transcend [træn'sɛnd] vt trascender.

transcript ['trænskrɪpt] n copia; ~**ion** [-'skrɪpʃən] n transcripción f.

transept ['trænsɛpt] n crucero.

transfer ['trænsfə*] n (gen) transferencia; (SPORT) traspaso; (picture, design) calcomanía // vt [træns'fəː*] trasladar, pasar; to ~ **the charges** (TEL) llamar a cobro revertido; ~**able** [-'fɔːrəbl] a trans-

ferible; '**not** ~**able**' "intransferible".

transform [træns'fɔːm] vt transformar; ~**ation** [-'meɪʃən] n transformación f; ~**er** n (ELEC) transformador m.

transfusion [træns'fjuːʒən] n transfusión f.

transient ['trænzɪənt] a transitorio.

transistor [træn'zɪstə*] n (ELEC) transistor m; ~ **radio** n radio f a transistores.

transit ['trænzɪt] n: **in** ~ de tránsito, de paso.

transition [træn'zɪʃən] n transición f; ~**al** a transitorio.

transitive ['trænzɪtɪv] a (LING) transitivo.

transitory ['trænzɪtərɪ] a transitorio.

translate [trænz'leɪt] vt traducir; **translation** [-'leɪʃən] n traducción f; **translator** n traductor/a m/f.

transmission [trænz'mɪʃən] n transmisión f.

transmit [trænz'mɪt] vt transmitir; ~**ter** n transmisor m; (station) emisora.

transparency [træns'pɛərnsɪ] n (PHOT) diapositiva.

transparent [træns'pærnt] a transparente.

transplant [træns'plɑːnt] vt transplantar // n ['trænsplɑːnt] (MED) transplante m.

transport ['trænspɔːt] n (gen) transporte m; (also: **road/rail** ~) transportes mpl // vt [-'pɔːt] transportar; (carry) acarrear; ~**ation** [-'teɪʃən] n transporte m; ~ **café** n cafetería de carretera.

transverse ['trænzvɔːs] a transversal.

transvestite [trænz'vɛstaɪt] n travesti m/f.

trap [træp] n (snare, trick) trampa; (carriage) cabriolé m // vt coger en una trampa; (immobilize) bloquear; (jam) atascar; ~ **door** n escotilla.

trapeze [trə'piːz] n trapecio.

trappings ['træpɪŋz] npl adornos mpl.

trash [træʃ] n (pej: goods) pacotilla; (: nonsense) basura; ~ **can** n (US) cubo de la basura.

trauma ['trɔːmə] n trauma m; ~**tic** [-'mætɪk] a traumático.

travel ['trævl] n viaje m // vi viajar // vt (distance) recorrer; ~ **agency** n agencia de viajes; ~**ler**, ~**er** (US) n viajero/a; ~**ler's cheque** n cheque m de viajero; ~**ling**, ~**ing** (US) n los viajes mpl, el viajar; ~ **sickness** n mareo.

traverse ['trævəs] vt atravesar, cruzar.

travesty ['trævəstɪ] n parodia.

trawler ['trɔːlə*] n barco rastreador o de rastra.

tray [treɪ] n (for carrying) bandeja; (on desk) cajón m.

treacherous ['trɛtʃərəs] a traidor(a); **treachery** n traición f.

treacle ['triːkl] n melaza.

tread [trɛd] n (step) paso, pisada; (sound) ruido de pasos; (of tyre) banda de rodadura // vi, pt **trod**, pp **trodden** pisar; to ~ **on** vt fus pisar sobre.

treason ['triːzn] n traición f.

treasure ['trɛʒə*] n tesoro // vt (value) apreciar, valorar; ~ **hunt** n caza del tesoro.

treasurer ['trɛʒərə*] n tesorero.

treasury ['trɛʒərɪ] n: **the T**~ (POL) el Ministerio de Hacienda.

treat [tri:t] n (present) regalo; (pleasure) placer m // vt tratar; **to** ~ **sb to sth** invitar a uno a algo.

treatise ['tri:tɪz] n tratado.

treatment ['tri:tmənt] n tratamiento.

treaty ['tri:tɪ] n tratado.

treble ['trɛbl] a triple // n (MUS) triple m // vt triplicar // vi triplicarse.

tree [tri:] n árbol m; ~ **trunk** n tronco de árbol.

trek [trɛk] n (long journey) viaje m largo y peligroso; (tiring walk) caminata; (as holiday) excursión f.

trellis ['trɛlɪs] n enrejado.

tremble ['trɛmbl] vi temblar; **trembling** n temblor m // a tembloroso.

tremendous [trɪ'mɛndəs] a tremendo; (enormous) enorme; (excellent) estupendo.

tremor ['trɛmə*] n temblor m; (also: **earth** ~) temblor m de tierra.

trench [trɛntʃ] n trinchera.

trend [trɛnd] n (tendency) tendencia; (of events) curso; (fashion) moda; ~**y** a (idea) según las tendencias actuales; (clothes) a la última moda.

trepidation [trɛpɪ'deɪʃən] n agitación f; (fear) ansia.

trespass ['trɛspəs] vi: **to** ~ **on** entrar sin permiso en; **"no** ~**ing"** "prohibido el paso".

tress [trɛs] n trenza.

trestle ['trɛsl] n caballete m; ~ **table** n mesa de caballete.

trial ['traɪəl] n (LAW) juicio, proceso; (test: of machine etc) prueba; (hardship) desgracia; **by** ~ **and error** por tanteo.

triangle ['traɪæŋgl] n (MATH, MUS) triángulo; **triangular** [-'æŋgjulə*] a triangular.

tribal ['traɪbəl] a tribal.

tribe [traɪb] n tribu f; **tribesman** n miembro de una tribu.

tribulation [trɪbju'leɪʃən] n tribulación f, sufrimiento.

tribunal [traɪ'bju:nl] n tribunal m.

tributary ['trɪbju:tərɪ] n (river) afluente m.

tribute ['trɪbju:t] n homenaje m; (payment) tributo; **to pay** ~ **to** rendir homenaje a.

trice [traɪs] n: **in a** ~ en un santiamén.

trick [trɪk] n trampa; (deceit) truco; (joke) broma; (CARDS) baza // vt engañar; **to play a** ~ **on sb** gastar una broma a uno; ~**ery** n astucia.

trickle ['trɪkl] n (of water etc) hililo // vi gotear.

tricky ['trɪkɪ] a difícil, delicado.

tricycle ['traɪsɪkl] n triciclo.

trifle ['traɪfl] n bagatela; (CULIN) dulce m de bizcocho, fruta y natillas // ad: **a** ~ **long** un poquito largo; **trifling** a insignificante.

trigger ['trɪgə*] n (of gun) gatillo; **to** ~ **off** vt desencadenar.

trigonometry [trɪgə'nɔmətrɪ] n trigonometría.

trill [trɪl] n (of bird) trino.

trim [trɪm] a (elegant) aseado; (house, garden) en buen estado; (figure) con buen tipo // n (haircut etc) recorte m; (on car) tapicería // vt arreglar; (cut) recortar; (decorate) adornar; (NAUT. a sail) orientar; ~**mings** npl decoraciones fpl; (cuttings) recortes mpl.

Trinity ['trɪnɪtɪ] n: **the** ~ la Trinidad.

trinket ['trɪŋkɪt] n chuchería; (piece of jewellery) baratija.

trio ['tri:əu] n trío.

trip [trɪp] n viaje m; (excursion) excursión f; (stumble) traspié m // vi (also: ~ **up**) tropezar; (go lightly) andar a paso ligero // vt poner la zancadilla a.

tripe [traɪp] n (CULIN) callos mpl; (pej: rubbish) bobadas fpl.

triple ['trɪpl] a triple.

triplets ['trɪplɪts] npl trillizos/as m/fpl.

triplicate ['trɪplɪkət] n: **in** ~ por triplicado.

tripod ['traɪpɔd] n trípode m.

trite [traɪt] a gastado, trillado.

triumph ['traɪʌmf] n triunfo // vi: **to** ~ **(over)** vencer; ~**ant** [-'ʌmfənt] a triunfante.

trivia ['trɪvɪə] npl trivialidades fpl.

trivial ['trɪvɪəl] a insignificante; (commonplace) trivial; ~**ity** [-'ælɪtɪ] n trivialidad f.

trod [trɔd], **trodden** ['trɔdn] pt, pp of **tread**.

trolley ['trɔlɪ] n carrito; ~ **bus** n trolebús m.

trombone [trɔm'bəun] n trombón m.

troop [tru:p] n grupo, banda; ~**s** npl (MIL) tropas fpl; **to** ~ **in/out** vi entrar/salir en grupo; ~**er** n (MIL) soldado de caballería.

trophy ['trəufɪ] n trofeo.

tropic ['trɔpɪk] n trópico; ~**al** a tropical.

trot [trɔt] n trote m // vi trotar; **on the** ~ (fig: col) de corrido.

trouble ['trʌbl] n problema m, dificultad f; (worry) preocupación f; (bother, effort) molestia, esfuerzo; (unrest) inquietud f; (MED): **stomach** ~ problemas mpl gástricos // vt molestar; (worry) preocupar, inquietar // vi: **to** ~ **to do sth** molestarse en hacer algo; ~**s** npl (POL etc) conflictos mpl; **to be in** ~ estar en un apuro; **to go to the** ~ **of doing sth** tomarse la molestia de hacer algo; **what's the** ~**?** ¿qué pasa?; ~**d** a (person) preocupado; (epoch, life) agitado; ~**maker** n elemento perturbador; (child) niño alborotado; ~**shooter** n (in conflict) conciliador m; ~**some** a molesto, inoportuno.

trough [trɔf] n (also: **drinking** ~)

abrevadero; (*also*: **feeding** ~) comedero; (*channel*) canal *m*.
troupe [tru:p] *n* grupo.
trousers ['trauzəz] *npl* pantalones *mpl*.
trousseau ['tru:səu]. *pl* ~x *or* ~s [-z] *n* ajuar *m*.
trout [traut] *n*, *pl inv* trucha.
trowel ['trauəl] *n* paleta.
truant ['truənt] *n*: **to play** ~ hacer novillos.
truce [tru:s] *n* tregua.
truck [trʌk] *n* camión *m*; (*RAIL*) vagón *m*; ~ **driver** *n* camionero; ~ **farm** *n* (*US*) huerto de hortalizas.
truculent ['trʌkjulənt] *a* agresivo.
trudge [trʌdʒ] *vi* andar con dificultad *o* pesadamente.
true [tru:] *a* verdadero; (*accurate*) exacto; (*genuine*) auténtico; (*faithful*) fiel.
truffle ['trʌfl] *n* trufa.
truly ['tru:lı] *ad* auténticamente; (*truthfully*) verdaderamente; (*faithfully*) fielmente; **yours** ~ (*in letter*) (le saluda) atentamente.
trump [trʌmp] *n* triunfo; ~**ed-up** *a* inventado.
trumpet ['trʌmpıt] *n* trompeta.
truncheon ['trʌntʃən] *n* porra.
trundle ['trʌndl] *vt, vi*: **to** ~ **along** rodar haciendo ruido.
trunk [trʌŋk] *n* (*of tree, person*) tronco; (*of elephant*) trompa; (*case*) baúl *m*; ~**s** *npl* (*also*: **swimming** ~s) bañador *m*; ~ **call** *n* (*TEL*) llamada interurbana.
truss [trʌs] *n* (*MED*) braguero; **to** ~ (**up**) *vt* atar.
trust [trʌst] *n* confianza; (*COMM*) trust *m*, cartel *m*; (*obligation*) responsabilidad *f*; (*LAW*) fideicomiso // *vt* (*rely on*) tener confianza en; (*entrust*): **to** ~ **sth to sb** confiar algo a uno; ~**ed** *a* de confianza; ~**ee** [trʌs'ti:] *n* (*LAW*) depositario, fideicomisario; (*of school etc*) administrador/a *m/f*; ~**ful**, ~**ing** *a* confiado; ~**worthy** *a* digno de confianza; ~**y** *a* fiel.
truth [tru:θ], *pl* ~s [tru:ðz] *n* verdad *f*; ~**ful** *a* (*person*) que dice la verdad; ~**fully** *ad* sinceramente; ~**fulness** *n* veracidad *f*.
try [traı] *n* tentativa, intento; (*RUGBY*) ensayo // *vt* (*LAW*) juzgar, procesar; (*test*: *sth new*) probar, someter a prueba; (*attempt*) intentar; (*strain*) hacer sufrir // *vi* probar; **to** ~ **to do sth** intentar hacer algo; **to** ~ **on** *vt* (*clothes*) probarse; **to** ~ **out** *vt* probar, poner a prueba; ~**ing** *a* penoso, cansado.
tsar [zɑ:*] *n* zar *m*.
T-shirt ['ti:ʃə:t] *n* camiseta.
tub [tʌb] *n* cubo; (*bath*) tina, bañera.
tuba ['tju:bə] *n* tuba.
tubby ['tʌbı] *a* regordete.
tube [tju:b] *n* tubo; (*underground*) metro; (*for tyre*) cámara de aire; ~**less** *a* sin cámara.

tuberculosis [tjubə:kju'ləusıs] *n* tuberculosis *f*.
tube station *n* estación *f* de metro.
tubing ['tju:bıŋ] *n* tubería; **a piece of** ~ un trozo de tubo.
tubular ['tju:bjulə*] *a* tubular; (*furniture*) de tubo.
TUC *n abbr of* **Trades Union Congress**.
tuck [tʌk] *n* (*SEWING*) pliegue *m* // *vt* (*put*) poner; **to** ~ **away** *vt* esconder; **to** ~ **in** *vt* meter; (*child*) arropar // *vi* (*eat*) comer con mucho apetito; **to** ~ **up** *vt* (*child*) arropar; ~ **shop** *n* tienda de golosinas.
Tuesday ['tju:zdı] *n* martes *m*.
tuft [tʌft] *n* mechón *m*; (*of grass etc*) manojo.
tug [tʌg] *n* (*ship*) remolcador *m* // *vt* remolcar; ~**-of-war** *n* lucha de la cuerda.
tuition [tju:'ıʃən] *n* enseñanza; (*private* ~) clases *fpl* particulares.
tulip ['tju:lıp] *n* tulipán *m*.
tumble ['tʌmbl] *n* (*fall*) caída // *vi* caerse, tropezar // *vt* tirar; ~**down** *a* destartalado; ~ **dryer** *n* secador *m* de ropa automático.
tumbler ['tʌmblə*] *n* vaso.
tummy ['tʌmı] *n* (*col*: *belly*) barriga; (: *stomach*) vientre *m*.
tumour ['tju:mə*] *n* tumor *m*.
tumult ['tju:mʌlt] *n* tumulto; ~**uous** [-'mʌltjuəs] *a* tumultuoso.
tuna ['tju:nə] *n*, *pl inv* (*also*: ~ **fish**) atún *m*.
tune [tju:n] *n* (*melody*) melodía // *vt* (*MUS*) afinar; (*RADIO, TV, AUT*) sintonizar; **to be in/out of** ~ (*instrument*) estar afinado/desafinado; (*singer*) cantar bien/ mal; **to be in/out of** ~ **with** (*fig*) armonizar/desentonar con; **to** ~ **up** *vi* (*musician*) afinar (su instrumento); ~**ful** *a* melodioso; **tuner** *n* (*radio set*) sintonizador *m*; **piano tuner** afinador *m* de pianos.
tunic ['tju:nık] *n* túnica.
tuning ['tju:nıŋ] *n* sintonización *f*; (*MUS*) afinación *f*; ~ **fork** *n* diapasón *m*.
Tunisia [tju:'nızıə] *n* Tunez *m*.
tunnel ['tʌnl] *n* túnel *m*; (*in mine*) galería // *vi* construir un túnel/una galería.
tunny ['tʌnı] *n* atún *m*.
turban ['tə:bən] *n* turbante *m*.
turbine ['tə:baın] *n* turbina.
turbulence ['tə:bjuləns] *n* (*AVIAT*) turbulencia; **turbulent** *a* turbulento.
tureen [tə'ri:n] *n* sopera.
turf [tə:f] *n* turba; (*clod*) césped *m* // *vt* poner césped; **to** ~ **out** *vt* (*col*) echar a la calle.
turgid ['tə:dʒıd] *a* (*speech*) pesado.
Turk [tə:k] *n* turco/a.
turkey ['tə:kı] *n* pavo.
Turkey ['tə:kı] *n* Turquía; **Turkish** *a, n* turco; **Turkish bath** *n* baño turco.
turmoil ['tə:mɔıl] *n* desorden *m*, alboroto.
turn [tə:n] *n* turno; (*in road*) curva; (*tendency*: *of mind, events*) disposición *f*,

propensión f; (THEATRE) número; (MED) desmayo // vt girar, volver; (collar, steak) dar la vuelta a; (change): to ~ sth into convertir algo en // vi volver; (person: look back) volverse; (reverse direction) dar la vuelta; (milk) cortarse; (change) cambiar; (become) convertirse en; a good ~ un favor; it gave me quite a ~ me dio un susto (bastante grande); 'no left ~' (AUT) 'prohibido girar a la izquierda'; it's your ~ te toca a ti; in ~ por turnos; to take ~s turnarse; to ~ about vi dar una vuelta completa; to ~ away vi volver la cabeza; to ~ back vi volverse atrás; to ~ down vt (refuse) rechazar; (reduce) bajar; (fold) doblar (hacia abajo); to ~ in vi (col: go to bed) acostarse // vt (fold) doblar hacia dentro; to ~ off vi (from road) desviarse // vt (light, radio etc) apagar; (engine) parar; to ~ on vt (light, radio etc) encender; (engine) poner en marcha; to ~ out vt (light, gas) apagar // vi: to ~ out to be... resultar ser...; to ~ up vi (person) llegar, presentarse; (lost object) aparecer // vt (gen) subir; ~ing n (in road) vuelta; ~ing point n (fig) momento decisivo.

turnip ['tə:nɪp] n nabo.

turnout ['tə:naut] n asistencia, número de asistentes.

turnover ['tə:nəuvə*] n (COMM: amount of money) cifra de negocios; (: of goods) movimiento.

turnpike ['tə:npaɪk] n (US) autopista de peaje.

turnstile ['tə:nstaɪl] n torniquete m.

turntable ['tə:nteɪbl] n (on record player) plato.

turn-up ['tə:nʌp] n (on trousers) vuelta.

turpentine ['tə:pəntaɪn] n (also: turps) trementina.

turquoise ['tə:kwɔɪz] n (stone) turquesa // a color turquesa.

turret ['tʌrɪt] n torrecilla.

turtle ['tə:tl] n tortuga marina.

tusk [tʌsk] n colmillo.

tussle ['tʌsl] n (fight) lucha; (scuffle) pelea.

tutor ['tju:tə*] n (gen) profesor/a m/f; ~ial [-'tɔ:rɪəl] n (SCOL) seminario.

T.V. [ti:'vi:] n abbr of television.

twaddle ['twɔdl] n tonterías fpl, bobadas fpl.

twang [twæŋ] n (of instrument) punteado; (of voice) timbre m nasal // vi vibrar // vt (guitar) puntear.

tweed [twi:d] n tweed m.

tweezers ['twi:zəz] npl pinzas fpl de depilar.

twelfth [twelfθ] a duodécimo; T ~ Night n Día de Reyes.

twelve [twelv] num doce.

twentieth ['twentɪɪθ] a vigésimo.

twenty ['twentɪ] num veinte.

twerp [twə:p] n (col) imbécil m/f.

twice [twaɪs] ad dos veces; ~ as much dos veces más.

twig [twɪg] n ramita // vi (col) caer en la cuenta.

twilight ['twaɪlaɪt] n crepúsculo, ocaso.

twin [twɪn] a, n gemelo/a // vt tener como gemelo.

twine [twaɪn] n bramante m // vi (plant) enroscarse.

twinge [twɪndʒ] n (of pain) punzada; (of conscience) remordimiento.

twinkle ['twɪŋkl] n centelleo // vi centellear; (eyes) parpadear.

twirl [twə:l] n giro // vt dar vueltas a // vi girar rápidamente.

twist [twɪst] n (action) torsión f; (in road, coil) vuelta; (in wire, flex) enroscadura; (in story) cambio imprevisto // vt torcer, retorcer; (weave) entrelazar; (roll around) enrollar; (fig) deformar // vi serpentear.

twit [twɪt] n (col) tonto.

twitch [twɪtʃ] n sacudida; (nervous) tic m nervioso // vi moverse nerviosamente.

two [tu:] num dos; to put ~ and ~ together (fig) atar cabos; ~-door a (AUT) de dos puertas; ~-faced a (pej: person) falso; ~fold ad: to increase ~fold duplicar; ~-piece (suit) n traje m de dos piezas; ~-piece (swimsuit) n dos piezas m inv, bikini m; ~-seater n (plane) avión m biplaza; (car) coche m de dos plazas; ~some n (people) pareja; ~-way a: ~-way traffic circulación f en ambas direcciones.

tycoon [taɪ'ku:n] n: (business) ~ magnate m.

type [taɪp] n (category) tipo, género; (model) modelo; (TYP) tipo, letra // vt (letter etc) escribir a máquina; ~-cast a (actor) encasillado; ~script n texto mecanografiado; ~writer n máquina de escribir; ~written a mecanografiado.

typhoid ['taɪfɔɪd] n tifoidea.

typhoon [taɪ'fu:n] n tifón m.

typhus ['taɪfəs] n tifus m.

typical ['tɪpɪkl] a típico; typify [-faɪ] vt ser típico de.

typing ['taɪpɪŋ] n mecanografía; typist n mecanógrafa.

tyranny ['tɪrənɪ] n tiranía.

tyrant ['taɪərnt] n tirano/a.

tyre, tire (US) ['taɪə*] n neumático, llanta.

tzar [za:*] n = **tsar.**

U

U-bend ['ju:'bend] n (in pipe) recodo.

ubiquitous [ju:'bɪkwɪtəs] a ubicuo, omnipresente.

udder ['ʌdə*] n ubre f.

UFO ['ju:fəu] n abbr of unidentified flying object O.V.N.I. m (objeto volante no identificado).

ugliness ['ʌglɪnɪs] n fealdad f; ugly a feo; (dangerous) peligroso.

U.K. n abbr of United Kingdom.

ulcer ['ʌlsə*] n úlcera.

Ulster ['ʌlstə*] *n* Úlster *m*, Irlanda del Norte.

ulterior [ʌl'tɪərɪə*] *a* ulterior; ~ **motive** motivo oculto.

ultimate ['ʌltɪmət] *a* último, final; (*authority*) supremo; ~**ly** *ad* (*in the end*) por último, al final; (*fundamentally*) en el fondo.

ultimatum [ʌltɪ'meɪtəm] *n* ultimátum *m*.

ultraviolet ['ʌltrə'vaɪəlɪt] *a* ultravioleta.

umbilical cord [ʌmbɪ'laɪkl-] *n* cordón *m* umbilical.

umbrella [ʌm'brelə] *n* paraguas *m inv*.

umpire ['ʌmpaɪə*] *n* árbitro // *vt* arbitrar.

umpteen [ʌmp'tiːn] *a* tantísimos; **for the** ~ **th time** por enésima vez.

UN, UNO *abbr of* **United Nations (Organization).**

unable [ʌn'eɪbl] *a*: **to be** ~ **to do sth** ser incapaz *o* no poder hacer algo.

unabridged [ʌnə'brɪdʒd] *a* íntegro.

unaccompanied [ʌnə'kʌmpənɪd] *a* no acompañado.

unaccountably [ʌnə'kauntəblɪ] *ad* inexplicablemente.

unaccustomed [ʌnə'kʌstəmd] *a*: **to be** ~ **to** no tener costumbre de.

unaided [ʌn'eɪdɪd] *a* sin ayuda, por sí solo.

unanimous [juː'nænɪməs] *a* unánime; ~**ly** *ad* unánimemente.

unarmed [ʌn'ɑːmd] *a* (*without a weapon*) desarmado; (*defenceless*) inerme.

unassuming [ʌnə'sjuːmɪŋ] *a* modesto, sin pretensiones.

unattached [ʌnə'tætʃt] *a* (*person*) libre; (*part etc*) suelto, separable.

unattended [ʌnə'tɛndɪd] *a* (*car, luggage*) sin vigilancia.

unattractive [ʌnə'træktɪv] *a* poco atractivo.

unauthorized [ʌn'ɔːθəraɪzd] *a* desautorizado.

unavoidable [ʌnə'vɔɪdəbl] *a* inevitable.

unaware [ʌnə'wɛə*] *a*: **to be** ~ **of** ignorar, no darse cuenta de; ~**s** *ad* de improviso.

unbalanced [ʌn'bælənst] *a* desequilibrado; (*mentally*) trastornado.

unbearable [ʌn'bɛərəbl] *a* insoportable.

unbeatable [ʌn'biːtəbl] *a* (*team*) imbatible; (*price*) inmejorable.

unbeaten [ʌn'biːtn] *a* imbatido.

unbeknown(st) [ʌnbɪ'nəun(st)] *ad*: ~ **to me** sin saberlo (yo).

unbelievable [ʌnbɪ'liːvəbl] *a* increíble.

unbend [ʌn'bɛnd] (*irg: like* **bend**) *vi* suavizarse // *vt* (*wire*) enderezar.

unblock [ʌn'blɔk] *vt* (*pipe*) desatascar.

unborn [ʌn'bɔːn] *a* sin nacer.

unbounded [ʌn'baundɪd] *a* ilimitado, sin límite.

unbreakable [ʌn'breɪkəbl] *a* irrompible.

unbridled [ʌn'braɪdld] *a* (*fig*) desenfrenado.

unbroken [ʌn'brəukən] *a* (*seal*) intacto;

(*series*) continuo; (*record*) imbatido; (*spirit*) indómito.

unburden [ʌn'bɔːdn] *vr*: **to** ~ **o.s.** desahogarse.

unbutton [ʌn'bʌtn] *vt* desabrochar.

uncalled-for [ʌn'kɔːldfɔ:*] *a* gratuito, inmerecido.

uncanny [ʌn'kænɪ] *a* extraño, extraordinario.

unceasing [ʌn'siːsɪŋ] *a* incesante.

uncertain [ʌn'sɔːtn] *a* incierto; (*character*) indeciso; ~**ty** *n* incertidumbre *f*.

unchanged [ʌn'tʃeɪndʒd] *a* sin cambiar *o* alterar.

uncharitable [ʌn'tʃærɪtəbl] *a* poco caritativo.

uncharted [ʌn'tʃɑːtɪd] *a* inexplorado.

unchecked [ʌn'tʃɛkt] *a* desenfrenado.

uncivil [ʌn'sɪvɪl] *a* grosero.

uncle ['ʌŋkl] *n* tío.

uncomfortable [ʌn'kʌmfətəbl] *a* incómodo; (*uneasy*) molesto.

uncommon [ʌn'kɔmən] *a* poco común, raro.

unconcerned [ʌnkən'sɔːnd] *a* indiferente, despreocupado.

unconditional [ʌnkən'dɪʃənl] *a* incondicional.

unconscious [ʌn'kɔnʃəs] *a* sin sentido; (*unaware*) inconsciente // *n*: **the** ~ **el** inconsciente; ~**ly** *ad* inconscientemente.

uncontrollable [ʌnkən'trəuləbl] *a* (*temper*) ingobernable; (*laughter*) incontenible.

uncouth [ʌn'kuːθ] *a* grosero, inculto.

uncover [ʌn'kʌvə*] *vt* (*gen*) descubrir; (*take lid off*) destapar.

undecided [ʌndɪ'saɪdɪd] *a* (*character*) indeciso; (*question*) no resuelto, pendiente.

undeniable [ʌndɪ'naɪəbl] *a* innegable.

under ['ʌndə*] *prep* debajo de; (*less than*) menos de; (*according to*) según, de acuerdo con // *ad* debajo, abajo; ~ **there** allí abajo; ~ **repair** en reparación.

under... [ʌndə*] *pref* sub; ~**-age** a menor de edad; ~**carriage** *n* tren *m* de aterrizaje; ~**clothes** *npl* ropa *sg* interior; ~**coat** *n* (*paint*) primera mano; ~**cover** *a* clandestino; ~**current** *n* corriente *f* submarina; (*fig*) tendencia oculta; ~**cut** *vt irg* rebajar los precios para competir con; ~**developed** *a* subdesarrollado; ~**dog** *n* desvalido; ~**done** *a* (*CULIN*) poco hecho; ~**estimate** *vt* subestimar; ~**exposed** *a* (*PHOT*) subexpuesto; ~**fed** *a* subalimentado; ~**foot** *ad* bajo los pies; ~**go** *vt irg* sufrir; (*treatment*) recibir; ~**graduate** *n* estudiante *m/f*; ~**ground** *n* (*railway*) metro; (*POL*) movimiento clandestino // *a* subterráneo; ~**growth** *n* maleza; ~**hand(ed)** *a* (*fig*) turbio; ~**lie** *vt irg* estar debajo de; (*fig*) ser la razón fundamental de; ~**line** *vt* subrayar; ~**ling** ['ʌndəlɪŋ] *n* (*pej*) subalterno; ~**mine** *vt* socavar, minar; ~**neath** [ʌndə'niːθ] *ad* debajo // *prep* debajo de, bajo; ~**paid** *a* mal pagado; ~**pants** *npl*

(*Brit*) calzoncillos *mpl*; ~**pass** *n* paso subterráneo; ~**price** *vt* vender demasiado barato; ~**privileged** *a* desamparado; ~**rate** *vt* menospreciar, subestimar; ~**side** *n* parte *f* inferior, revés *m*; ~**skirt** *n* enaguas *fpl*.

understand [ʌndə'stænd] (*irg: like* stand) *vt, vi* entender, comprender; (*assume*) sobreentender; ~**able** *a* comprensible; ~**ing** *a* comprensivo // *n* comprensión *f*, entendimiento; (*agreement*) acuerdo.

understatement [ʌndə'steɪtmənt] *n* descripción *f* insuficiente; (*quality*) modestia (excesiva).

understood [ʌndə'stud] *pt, pp of* **understand** // *a* entendido; (*implied*) sobreentendido.

understudy ['ʌndəstʌdɪ] *n* suplente *m/f*.

undertake [ʌndə'teɪk] (*irg: like* take) *vt* acometer; **to** ~ **to do sth** comprometerse a hacer algo.

undertaker ['ʌndəteɪkə*] *n* director *m* de pompas fúnebres, sepulturero.

undertaking [ʌndə'teɪkɪŋ] *n* empresa; (*promise*) promesa.

underwater [ʌndə'wɔːtə*] *ad* bajo el agua // *a* submarino.

underwear ['ʌndəwɛə*] *n* ropa interior.

underweight [ʌndə'weɪt] *a* de peso insuficiente; (*person*) demasiado delgado.

underworld ['ʌndəwəːld] *n* (*of crime*) hampa, inframundo.

underwriter ['ʌndəraɪtə*] *n* (*INSURANCE*) (re)asegurador/a *m/f*.

undesirable [ʌndɪ'zaɪərəbl] *a* indeseable.

undies ['ʌndɪz] *npl* (*col*) paños *mpl* menores.

undignified [ʌn'dɪɡnɪfaɪd] *a* indecoroso.

undisputed [ʌndɪ'spjuːtɪd] *a* incontestable.

undo [ʌn'duː] (*irg: like* do) *vt* deshacer; ~**ing** *n* ruina, perdición *f*.

undoubted [ʌn'dautɪd] *a* indudable; ~**ly** *ad* indudablemente, sin duda.

undress [ʌn'drɛs] *vi* desnudarse.

undue [ʌn'djuː] *a* indebido, excesivo.

undulating ['ʌndjuleɪtɪŋ] *a* ondulante.

unduly [ʌn'djuːlɪ] *ad* excesivamente, demasiado.

unearth [ʌn'əːθ] *vt* desenterrar.

unearthly [ʌn'əːθlɪ] *a* (*hour*) inverosímil.

uneasy [ʌn'iːzɪ] *a* intranquilo; (*worried*) preocupado.

uneconomic(al) ['ʌniːkə'nɔmɪk(l)] *a* antieconómico.

uneducated [ʌn'ɛdjukeɪtɪd] *a* sin educación, inculto.

unemployed [ʌnɪm'plɔɪd] *a* parado, sin trabajo // *n*: **the** ~ los parados; **unemployment** [-'plɔɪmənt] *n* paro, desempleo.

unending [ʌn'ɛndɪŋ] *a* interminable.

unenthusiastic [ʌnɪnθuːzɪ'æstɪk] *a* poco entusiasta.

unerring [ʌn'əːrɪŋ] *a* infalible.

uneven [ʌn'iːvn] *a* desigual; (*road etc*) quebrado, accidentado.

unexpected [ʌnɪk'spɛktɪd] *a* inesperado.

unfair [ʌn'fɛə*] *a*: ~ (**to**) injusto (con); ~**ly** *ad* injustamente.

unfaithful [ʌn'feɪθful] *a* infiel.

unfamiliar [ʌnfə'mɪlɪə*] *a* nuevo, desconocido.

unfashionable [ʌn'fæʃnəbl] *a* pasado *o* fuera de moda.

unfasten [ʌn'fɑːsn] *vt* desatar.

unfavourable, unfavorable (*US*) [ʌn'feɪvərəbl] *a* desfavorable.

unfeeling [ʌn'fiːlɪŋ] *a* insensible.

unfinished [ʌn'fɪnɪʃt] *a* incompleto, sin terminar.

unfit [ʌn'fɪt] *a* con mala salud, enfermo; (*incompetent*) incompetente, incapaz; ~ **for work** no apto para trabajar.

unflagging [ʌn'flæɡɪŋ] *a* incansable.

unfold [ʌn'fəuld] *vt* desdoblar; (*fig*) revelar // *vi* abrirse; revelarse.

unforeseen ['ʌnfɔː'siːn] *a* imprevisto.

unforgettable [ʌnfə'ɡɛtəbl] *a* inolvidable.

unforgivable [ʌnfə'ɡɪvəbl] *a* imperdonable.

unfortunate [ʌn'fɔːtʃnət] *a* desgraciado; (*event, remark*) inoportuno; ~**ly** *ad* desgraciadamente.

unfounded [ʌn'faundɪd] *a* infundado.

unfriendly [ʌn'frɛndlɪ] *a* antipático.

unfurnished [ʌn'fəːnɪʃt] *a* desamueblado.

ungainly [ʌn'ɡeɪnlɪ] *a* desgarbado.

unhappiness [ʌn'hæpɪnɪs] *n* tristeza; **unhappy** *a* (*sad*) triste; (*unfortunate*) desgraciado; (*childhood*) infeliz; **unhappy with** (*arrangements etc*) poco contento con, descontento de.

unharmed [ʌn'hɑːmd] *a* ileso; (*col*) sano y salvo.

unhealthy [ʌn'hɛlθɪ] *a* (*gen*) malsano; (*person*) enfermizo, con poca salud.

unheard-of [ʌn'həːdɔv] *a* inaudito, sin precedente.

unhook [ʌn'huk] *vt* desenganchar; (*from wall*) descolgar; (*dress*) desabrochar.

unhurt [ʌn'həːt] *a* ileso.

unidentified [ʌnaɪ'dɛntɪfaɪd] *a* no identificado.

uniform ['juːnɪfɔːm] *n* uniforme *m* // *a* uniforme; ~**ity** [-'fɔːmɪtɪ] *n* uniformidad *f*.

unify ['juːnɪfaɪ] *vt* unificar, unir.

unilateral [juːnɪ'lætərəl] *a* unilateral.

unintentional [ʌnɪn'tɛnʃənəl] *a* involuntario.

union ['juːnjən] *n* unión *f*; (*also:* **trade** ~) sindicato // *a* sindical; **U**~ **Jack** *n* bandera del Reino Unido.

unique [juː'niːk] *a* único.

unison ['juːnɪsn] *n*: **in** ~ en armonía.

unit ['juːnɪt] *n* unidad *f*; (*team, squad*) grupo; **kitchen** ~ mueble *m* de cocina.

unite [juː'naɪt] *vt* unir // *vi* unirse; ~**d** *a* unido; **U**~**d Kingdom (U.K.)** *n* Reino Unido; **U**~**d Nations (Organization) (UN, UNO)** *n* (Las) Naciones Unidas *fpl* (O.N.U.); **U**~**d States (of America)**

(US, USA) *n* (Los) Estados Unidos *mpl* (EE.UU.).

unity ['ju:nɪtɪ] *n* unidad *f*.

universal [juːnɪ'vɜːsl] *a* universal.

universe ['juːnɪvɜːs] *n* universo.

university [juːnɪ'vɜːsɪtɪ] *n* universidad *f*.

unjust [ʌn'dʒʌst] *a* injusto.

unkempt [ʌn'kɛmpt] *a* descuidado; (*hair*) despeinado.

unkind [ʌn'kaɪnd] *a* poco amable; (*comment etc*) cruel.

unknown [ʌn'nəun] *a* desconocido.

unladen [ʌn'leɪdn] *a* (*ship, weight*) vacío.

unleash [ʌn'liːʃ] *vt* soltar; (*fig*) desencadenar.

unless [ʌn'lɛs] *conj* a menos que, a no ser que; ~ **he comes** a menos que venga; ~ **otherwise stated** salvo indicación contraria.

unlike [ʌn'laɪk] *a* distinto // *prep* a diferencia de.

unlikely [ʌn'laɪklɪ] *a* improbable.

unlimited [ʌn'lɪmɪtɪd] *a* ilimitado.

unload [ʌn'ləud] *vt* descargar.

unlock [ʌn'lɔk] *vt* abrir (con llave).

unlucky [ʌn'lʌkɪ] *a* desgraciado; (*object, number*) que da mala suerte; **to be** ~ tener mala suerte.

unmarried [ʌn'mærɪd] *a* soltero.

unmask [ʌn'mɑːsk] *vt* desenmascarar.

unmistakable [ʌnmɪs'teɪkəbl] *a* inconfundible.

unmitigated [ʌn'mɪtɪgeɪtɪd] *a* no mitigado, absoluto.

unnatural [ʌn'nætʃrəl] *a* (*gen*) antinatural; (*manner*) afectado; (*habit*) perverso.

unnecessary [ʌn'nɛsəsərɪ] *a* innecesario, inútil.

unnoticed [ʌn'nəutɪst] *a*: **to go** ~ pasar desapercibido.

unobtainable [ʌnəb'teɪnəbl] *a* inconseguible.

unoccupied [ʌn'ɔkjupaɪd] *a* (*seat etc*) libre.

unofficial [ʌnə'fɪʃl] *a* no oficial; (*strike*) espontáneo, sin la aprobación de la central.

unorthodox [ʌn'ɔːθədɔks] *a* poco ortodoxo.

unpack [ʌn'pæk] *vi* deshacer las maletas.

unpalatable [ʌn'pælətəbl] *a* (*truth*) desagradable.

unparalleled [ʌn'pærəlɛld] *a* (*unequalled*) sin par; (*unique*) sin precedentes.

unpleasant [ʌn'plɛznt] *a* (*disagreeable*) desagradable; (*person, manner*) antipático.

unplug [ʌn'plʌg] *vt* desenchufar, desconectar.

unpopular [ʌn'pɔpjulə*] *a* poco popular.

unprecedented [ʌn'prɛsɪdəntɪd] *a* sin precedentes.

unpredictable [ʌnprɪ'dɪktəbl] *a* imprevisible.

unproductive [ʌnprə'dʌktɪv] *a* improductivo.

unqualified [ʌn'kwɔlɪfaɪd] *a* (*teacher*) sin título, no cualificado; (*success*) total, incondicional.

unravel [ʌn'rævl] *vt* desenmarañar.

unreal [ʌn'rɪəl] *a* irreal.

unrealistic [ʌnrɪə'lɪstɪk] *a* poco realista.

unreasonable [ʌn'riːznəbl] *a* poco razonable; (*demand*) excesivo.

unrelated [ʌnrɪ'leɪtɪd] *a* sin relación; (*family*) sin parentesco.

unrelenting [ʌnrɪ'lɛntɪŋ] *a* implacable.

unreliable [ʌnrɪ'laɪəbl] *a* (*person*) informal; (*machine*) de poca confianza.

unrelieved [ʌnrɪ'liːvd] *a* (*monotony*) monótono.

unrepeatable [ʌnrɪ'piːtəbl] *a* (*offer*) irrepetible.

unrepresentative [ʌnrɛprɪ'zɛntətɪv] *a* poco representativo *o* característico.

unrest [ʌn'rest] *n* inquietud *f*, malestar *m*; (*POL*) disturbios *mpl*.

unroll [ʌn'rəul] *vt* desenrollar.

unruly [ʌn'ruːlɪ] *a* indisciplinado.

unsafe [ʌn'seɪf] *a* (*journey*) peligroso; (*car etc*) inseguro.

unsaid [ʌn'sɛd] *a*: **to leave sth** ~ dejar algo sin decir.

unsatisfactory ['ʌnsætɪs'fæktərɪ] *a* insatisfactorio.

unsavoury, unsavory (*US*) [ʌn'seɪvərɪ] *a* (*fig*) repugnante.

unscathed [ʌn'skeɪðd] *a* ileso.

unscrew [ʌn'skruː] *vt* destornillar.

unscrupulous [ʌn'skruːpjuləs] *a* sin escrúpulos.

unsettled [ʌn'sɛtld] *a* inquieto, inestable; (*weather*) variable.

unshaven [ʌn'ʃeɪvn] *a* sin afeitar.

unsightly [ʌn'saɪtlɪ] *a* feo.

unskilled [ʌn'skɪld] *a*: ~ **worker** obrero no cualificado.

unspeakable [ʌn'spiːkəbl] *a* indecible; (*bad*) horrible.

unsteady [ʌn'stɛdɪ] *a* inestable.

unstuck [ʌn'stʌk] *a*: **to come** ~ despegarse; (*fig*) fracasar.

unsuccessful [ʌnsək'sɛsful] *a* (*attempt*) infructuoso; (*writer, proposal*) sin éxito; **to be** ~ (*in attempting sth*) no tener éxito, fracasar; ~ **ly** *ad* en vano, sin éxito.

unsuitable [ʌn'suːtəbl] *a* inconveniente, inapropiado.

unsure [ʌn'ʃuə*] *a* inseguro, poco seguro.

unsuspecting [ʌnsə'spɛktɪŋ] *a* confiado.

unswerving [ʌn'swɜːvɪŋ] *a* inquebrantable.

untangle [ʌn'tæŋgl] *vt* desenredar.

untapped [ʌn'tæpt] *a* (*resources*) sin explotar.

unthinkable [ʌn'θɪŋkəbl] *a* inconcebible, impensable.

untidy [ʌn'taɪdɪ] *a* (*room*) desordenado, en desorden; (*appearance*) descuidado.

untie [ʌn'taɪ] *vt* desatar.

until [ən'tɪl] *prep* hasta // *conj* hasta que; ~ **he comes** hasta que venga; ~ **then** hasta entonces.

untimely [ʌn'taɪmlɪ] *a* inoportuno; *(death)* prematuro.
untold [ʌn'təuld] *a* *(story)* inédito; *(suffering)* indecible; *(wealth)* incalculable.
untoward [ʌntə'wɔːd] *a* desfavorable.
unused [ʌn'juːzd] *a* sin usar, nuevo.
unusual [ʌn'juːʒuəl] *a* insólito, poco común.
unveil [ʌn'veɪl] *vt* *(statue)* descubrir.
unwavering [ʌn'weɪvərɪŋ] *a* inquebrantable.
unwelcome [ʌn'wɛlkəm] *a* *(at a bad time)* inoportuno; *(unpleasant)* desagradable.
unwell [ʌn'wɛl] *a*: **to feel** ~ estar indispuesto; **to be** ~ estar enfermo.
unwieldy [ʌn'wiːldɪ] *a* difícil de manejar.
unwilling [ʌn'wɪlɪŋ] *a*: **to be** ~ **to do sth** estar poco dispuesto a hacer algo; ~**ly** *ad* de mala gana.
unwind [ʌn'waɪnd] *(irg: like* **wind**) *vt* desenvolver // *vi* *(relax)* relajarse.
unwitting [ʌn'wɪtɪŋ] *a* inconsciente.
unworthy [ʌn'wɔːðɪ] *a* indigno.
unwrap [ʌn'ræp] *vt* desenvolver.
up [ʌp] *prep*: **to go/be** ~ **sth** subir/estar encima de algo // *ad* hacia arriba, arriba; ~ **there** allí arriba; ~ **above** encima, allí arriba; **to be** ~ *(out of bed)* estar levantado; **it is** ~ **to you** Ud. decide/tú decides; **what is he** ~ **to?** ¿qué es lo que quiere?, ¿qué está tramando?; **he is not** ~ **to it** no es capaz de hacerlo; ~-**and-coming** *a* prometedor(a); ~**s and downs** *npl (fig)* altibajos *mpl*.
upbringing ['ʌpbrɪŋɪŋ] *n* educación *f*.
update [ʌp'deɪt] *vt* poner al día, modernizar; *(contract etc)* actualizar.
upgrade [ʌp'greɪd] *vt* ascender; *(job)* revalorizar.
upheaval [ʌp'hiːvl] *n* trastorno, conmoción *f*.
uphill [ʌp'hɪl] *a* cuesta arriba; *(fig: task)* penoso, difícil // *ad*: **to go** ~ ir cuesta arriba.
uphold [ʌp'həuld] *(irg: like* **hold**) *vt* sostener.
upholstery [ʌp'həulstərɪ] *n* tapicería.
upkeep ['ʌpkiːp] *n* mantenimiento.
upon [ə'pɒn] *prep* sobre.
upper ['ʌpə*] *a* superior, de arriba // *n (of shoe)* pala; ~-**class** *a* de clase alta; ~**most** *a* el más alto; **what was** ~**most in my mind** lo que me preocupaba más.
upright ['ʌpraɪt] *a* vertical; *(fig)* honrado.
uprising ['ʌpraɪzɪŋ] *n* sublevación *f*.
uproar ['ʌprɔː*] *n* tumulto, escándalo.
uproot [ʌp'ruːt] *vt* desarraigar.
upset ['ʌpsɛt] *n (to plan etc)* revés *m*, contratiempo; *(MED)* trastorno // *vt* [ʌp'sɛt] *(irg: like* **set**) *(glass etc)* volcar; *(spill)* derramar; *(plan)* alterar; *(person)* molestar, perturbar // *a* [ʌp'sɛt] preocupado, perturbado; *(stomach)* trastornado.
upshot ['ʌpʃɒt] *n* resultado.
upside-down ['ʌpsaɪddaun] *ad* al revés.

upstairs [ʌp'stɛəz] *ad* arriba // *a (room)* de arriba // *n* el piso superior.
upstart ['ʌpstɑːt] *n* advenedizo.
upstream [ʌp'striːm] *ad* río arriba.
uptake ['ʌpteɪk] *n*: **he is quick/slow on the** ~ es muy listo/ algo torpe.
up-to-date ['ʌptə'deɪt] *a* moderno, actual.
upturn ['ʌptəːn] *n (in luck)* mejora.
upward ['ʌpwəd] *a* ascendente; ~**(s)** *ad* hacia arriba.
uranium [juə'reɪnɪəm] *n* uranio.
urban ['əːbən] *a* urbano.
urbane [əː'beɪn] *a* cortés.
urchin ['əːtʃɪn] *n* pilluelo, golfillo.
urge [əːdʒ] *n (force)* impulso; *(desire)* deseo // *vt*: **to** ~ **sb to do sth** incitar a uno a hacer algo.
urgency ['əːdʒənsɪ] *n* urgencia; *(of tone)* insistencia; **urgent** *a* urgente.
urinal ['juərɪnl] *n* urinario.
urinate ['juərɪneɪt] *vi* orinar; **urine** *n* orina, orines *mpl*.
urn [əːn] *n* urna; *(also:* **tea** ~) tetera.
us [ʌs] *pron* nos; *(after prep)* nosotros/as.
US, USA *n abbr of* **United States (of America)**.
usage ['juːzɪdʒ] *n* uso, costumbre *f*.
use [juːs] *n* uso, empleo; *(usefulness)* utilidad *f* // *vt* [juːz] usar, emplear; **she** ~**d to do it** (ella) solía hacerlo; **in** ~ en uso; **out of** ~ anticuado, que ya no se usa; **to be of** ~ servir; **it's no** ~ *(pointless)* es inútil; *(not useful)* no sirve; **to be** ~**d to** estar acostumbrado a; **to** ~ **up** *vt* agotar, consumir; ~**d** *a (car)* usado; ~**ful** *a* útil; **to be** ~**ful** servir; ~**less** *a* inútil; **user** *n* usuario/a.
usher ['ʌʃə*] *n* ujier *m*, portero; ~**ette** [-'rɛt] *n (in cinema)* acomodadora.
USSR *n*: **the** ~ la U.R.S.S.
usual ['juːʒuəl] *a* normal, corriente; ~**ly** *ad* normalmente.
usurp [juː'zəːp] *vt* usurpar.
utensil [juː'tɛnsl] *n* utensilio; **kitchen** ~**s** batería *sg* de cocina.
uterus ['juːtərəs] *n* útero.
utilitarian [juːtɪlɪ'tɛərɪən] *a* utilitario.
utility [juː'tɪlɪtɪ] *n* utilidad *f*; ~ **room** *n* trascocina.
utilize ['juːtɪlaɪz] *vt* utilizar.
utmost ['ʌtməust] *a* mayor // *n*: **to do one's** ~ hacer todo lo posible.
utter ['ʌtə*] *a* total, completo // *vt* pronunciar, proferir; ~**ance** *n* palabras *fpl*, declaración *f*; ~**ly** *ad* completamente, totalmente.
U-turn ['juː'təːn] *n* viraje *m* en U.

V

v. *abbr of* **verse; versus; volt; vide** véase.
vacancy ['veɪkənsɪ] *n (job)* vacante *f*; *(room)* cuarto libre; **vacant** *a* desocupado, libre; *(expression)* distraído; **vacate**

[və'keɪt] vt (house) desocupar; (job) salir de; (throne) renunciar a.
vacation [və'keɪʃən] n vacaciones fpl.
vaccinate ['væksɪneɪt] vt vacunar; **vaccination** [-'neɪʃən] n vacunación f.
vaccine ['væksiːn] n vacuna.
vacuum ['vækjum] n vacío; ~ **cleaner** n aspiradora; ~ **flask** n termo.
vagabond ['vægəbɔnd] n vagabundo.
vagina [və'dʒaɪnə] n vagina.
vagrant ['veɪgrnt] n vagabundo.
vague [veɪg] a vago; (blurred: memory) borroso; (uncertain) incierto, impreciso; (person) distraído; ~**ly** ad vagamente.
vain [veɪn] a (conceited) vanidoso; (useless) vano, inútil; **in** ~ en vano.
vale [veɪl] n valle m.
valentine ['væləntaɪn] n: **V**~**'s Day** Día m de los Enamorados.
valid ['vælɪd] a válido; (ticket) valedero; (law) vigente; ~**ity** [-'lɪdɪtɪ] n validez f; vigencia.
valley ['vælɪ] n valle m.
valour, valor (US) ['vælə*] n valor m, valentía.
valuable ['væljuəbl] a (jewel) de valor; (time) valioso; ~**s** npl objetos mpl de valor.
valuation [vælju'eɪʃən] n tasación f, valuación f.
value ['væljuː] n valor m; (importance) importancia // vt (fix price of) tasar, valorar; (esteem) apreciar; (cherish) tener en mucho; ~ **added tax (VAT)** n valor añadido o agregado; ~**d** a (appreciated) apreciado.
valve [vælv] n (gen) válvula; (MED) valva.
vampire ['væmpaɪə*] n vampiro/vampiresa.
van [væn] n (AUT) furgoneta; (RAIL) furgón m (de equipajes).
vandal ['vændl] n vándalo; ~**ism** n vandalismo; ~**ize** vt dañar, destruir.
vanilla [və'nɪlə] n vainilla.
vanish ['vænɪʃ] vi desvanecerse, esfumarse.
vanity ['vænɪtɪ] n vanidad f; ~ **case** n neceser m.
vantage point ['vɑːntɪdʒ-] n posición f ventajosa.
vapour, vapor (US) ['veɪpə*] n vapor m; (steam) vaho.
variable ['veərɪəbl] a variable.
variance ['veərɪəns] n: **to be at** ~ **(with)** desentonar (con), estar en desacuerdo (con).
variation [veərɪ'eɪʃən] n variedad f; (in opinion) variación f.
varicose ['værɪkəus] a: ~ **veins** varices fpl.
varied ['veərɪd] a variado.
variety [və'raɪətɪ] n variedad f, diversidad f; (quantity) surtido; ~ **show** n variedades fpl.
various ['veərɪəs] a varios(as), diversos(as).

varnish ['vɑːnɪʃ] n (gen) barniz m; (nail ~) esmalte m // vt (gen) barnizar; (nails) pintar (con esmalte).
vary ['veərɪ] vt variar; (change) cambiar // vi variar; (disagree) discrepar; (deviate) desviarse; ~**ing** a diversos(as).
vase [vɑːz] n florero.
vaseline ['væsɪliːn] n vaselina.
vast [vɑːst] a enorme; (success) abrumador(a); ~**ness** n inmensidad f.
vat [væt] n tina, tinaja.
VAT [væt] n abbr of **Value Added Tax.**
Vatican ['vætɪkən] n: **the** ~ el Vaticano.
vault [vɔːlt] n (of roof) bóveda; (tomb) tumba; (in bank) sótano // vt (also: ~ over) saltar (por encima de).
veal [viːl] n ternera.
veer [vɪə*] vi virar.
vegetable ['vedʒtəbl] n (BOT) vegetal m; (edible plant) legumbre f, hortaliza; ~**s** npl (cooked) verduras fpl // a vegetal; ~ **garden** n huerto.
vegetarian [vedʒɪ'teərɪən] a, n vegetariano/a.
vegetate ['vedʒɪteɪt] vi vegetar.
vegetation [vedʒɪ'teɪʃən] n vegetación f.
vehement ['viːɪmənt] a vehemente; (impassioned) apasionado.
vehicle ['viːɪkl] n vehículo.
veil [veɪl] n velo // vt velar.
vein [veɪn] n vena; (of ore etc) veta.
velocity [vɪ'lɔsɪtɪ] n velocidad f.
velvet ['velvɪt] n terciopelo // a aterciopelado.
vendetta [ven'detə] n vendetta.
vending machine ['vendɪŋ-] n distribuidor m automático.
vendor ['vendə*] n vendedor/a m/f.
veneer [və'nɪə*] n chapa, enchapado; (fig) barniz m, apariencia.
venereal [vɪ'nɪərɪəl] a: ~ **disease (VD)** enfermedad f venérea.
Venetian blind [vɪ'niːʃən-] n persiana.
Venezuela [vene'zweɪlə] n Venezuela; ~**n** a, n venezolano/a.
vengeance ['vendʒəns] n venganza; **with a** ~ (fig) con creces.
venison ['venɪsn] n carne f de venado.
venom ['venəm] n veneno; ~**ous** a venenoso.
vent [vent] n (opening) abertura; (air-hole) respiradero; (in wall) rejilla (de ventilación) // vt (fig: feelings) desahogar.
ventilate ['ventɪleɪt] vt ventilar; **ventilation** [-'leɪʃən] n ventilación f; **ventilator** n ventilador m.
ventriloquist [ven'trɪləkwɪst] n ventrílocuo.
venture ['ventʃə*] n empresa // vt aventurar; (opinion) ofrecer // vi arriesgarse, lanzarse.
venue ['venjuː] n lugar m; (meeting place) lugar m de reunión.
veranda(h) [və'rændə] n terraza; (with glass) galería.
verb [vəːb] n verbo; ~**al** a verbal.

verbatim [vɔ:'beɪtɪm] a, ad palabra por palabra.

verbose [vɔ:'bɔus] a prolijo.

verdict ['vɔ:dɪkt] n veredicto, fallo; (fig) opinión f, juicio.

verge [vɔ:dʒ] n borde m, margen m; **to be on the ~ of doing sth** estar a punto de hacer algo; **to ~ on** vt fus rayar en.

verify ['vɛrɪfaɪ] vt comprobar, verificar.

vermin ['vɔ:mɪn] npl (animals) bichos mpl; (insects, fig) sabandijas fpl.

vermouth ['vɔ:mɔθ] n vermut m.

vernacular [vɔ'nækjulɔ*] n vernáculo.

versatile ['vɔ:sɔtaɪl] a (person) de talentos variados; (machine, tool etc) que tiene muchos usos; (mind) ágil, flexible.

verse [vɔ:s] n versos mpl, poesía; (stanza) estrofa; (in bible) versículo.

versed [vɔ:st] a: **(well-)~ in** versado en, conocedor de.

version ['vɔ:ʃɔn] n versión f.

versus ['vɔ:sɔs] prep contra.

vertebra ['vɔ:tɪbrɔ], pl **~e** [-bri:] n vértebra; **vertebrate** [-brɪt] n vertebrado.

vertical ['vɔ:tɪkl] a vertical.

vertigo ['vɔ:tɪgɔu] n vértigo.

very ['vɛrɪ] ad muy // a: **the ~ book which** el mismo libro que; **the ~ last** el último (de todos); **at the ~ least** al menos; **~ much** muchísimo.

vespers ['vɛspɔz] npl vísperas fpl.

vessel ['vɛsl] n (ANAT, NAUT) vaso; (container) vasija.

vest [vɛst] n camiseta; (US: waistcoat) chaleco; **~ed interests** npl (COMM) intereses mpl creados.

vestibule ['vɛstɪbju:l] n vestíbulo.

vestige ['vɛstɪdʒ] n vestigio, rastro.

vestry ['vɛstrɪ] n sacristía.

vet [vɛt] n abbr of **veterinary surgeon** // vt repasar, revisar.

veteran ['vɛtɔrn] n veterano; **~ car** n coche m antiguo.

veterinary ['vɛtrɪnɔrɪ] a veterinario; **~ surgeon** n veterinario.

veto ['vi:tɔu], pl **~es** n veto // vt vetar, vedar.

vex [vɛks] vt (irritate) fastidiar; (make impatient) impacientar; **~ed** a (question) batallón(ona), controvertido.

via ['vaɪɔ] prep por, por vía de.

viable ['vaɪɔbl] a viable.

viaduct ['vaɪɔdʌkt] n viaducto.

vibrate [vaɪ'breɪt] vi vibrar; **vibration** [-'breɪʃɔn] n vibración f.

vicar ['vɪkɔ*] n párroco; **~age** n parroquia.

vice [vaɪs] n (evil) vicio; (TECH) torno de banco.

vice- [vaɪs] pref vice; **~chairman** n vicepresidente m.

vice versa ['vaɪsɪ'vɔ:sɔ] ad viceversa.

vicinity [vɪ'sɪnɪtɪ] n (area) vecindad f; (nearness) proximidad f.

vicious ['vɪʃɔs] a (violent) violento; (depraved) depravado; (cruel) cruel;

(bitter) rencoroso; **~ness** n violencia; depravación f; crueldad f; rencor m.

victim ['vɪktɪm] n víctima m/f; **~ization** [-'zeɪʃɔn] n (gen) persecución f; (in strike) represalias fpl; **~ize** vt (strikers etc) tomar represalias contra.

victor ['vɪktɔ*] n vencedor/a m/f.

Victorian [vɪk'tɔ:rɪɔn] a victoriano.

victorious [vɪk'tɔ:rɪɔs] a vencedor(a).

victory ['vɪktɔrɪ] n victoria.

video ['vɪdɪɔu] cpd video; **~(-tape) recorder** n video-grabadora.

vie [vaɪ] vi: **to ~ with** competir con.

Vienna [vɪ'ɛnɔ] n Viena.

view [vju:] n vista, perspectiva; (landscape) paisaje m; (opinion) opinión f, criterio // vt (look at) mirar; (examine) examinar; **on ~** (in museum etc) expuesto; **in full ~ (of)** en plena vista (de); **in ~ of the fact that** en vista del hecho de que; **~er** n (small projector) visionadora; (TV) televidente m/f; **~finder** n visor m de imagen; **~point** n punto de vista.

vigil ['vɪdʒɪl] n vigilia; **to keep ~** velar; **~ance** n vigilancia; **~ant** a vigilante.

vigorous ['vɪgɔrɔs] a enérgico, vigoroso; **vigour, vigor** (US) n energía, vigor m.

vile [vaɪl] a (action) vil, infame; (smell) asqueroso.

vilify ['vɪlɪfaɪ] vt vilipendiar.

villa ['vɪlɔ] n (country house) casa de campo; (suburban house) chalet m.

village ['vɪlɪdʒ] n aldea; **villager** n aldeano/a.

villain ['vɪlɔn] n (scoundrel) malvado; (criminal) maleante m/f.

vindicate ['vɪndɪkeɪt] vt vindicar, justificar.

vindictive [vɪn'dɪktɪv] a vengativo.

vine [vaɪn] n vid f.

vinegar ['vɪnɪgɔ*] n vinagre m.

vineyard ['vɪnjɑ:d] n viña, viñedo.

vintage ['vɪntɪdʒ] n (year) vendimia, cosecha; **~ wine** n vino añejo.

vinyl ['vaɪnl] n vinilo.

violate ['vaɪɔleɪt] vt violar; **violation** [-'leɪʃɔn] n violación f.

violence ['vaɪɔlɔns] n violencia; **violent** a (gen) violento; (intense) intenso.

violet ['vaɪɔlɔt] a violado, violeta // n (plant) violeta.

violin [vaɪɔ'lɪn] n violín m; **~ist** n violinista m/f.

VIP n abbr of **very important person.**

viper ['vaɪpɔ*] n víbora.

virgin ['vɔ:dʒɪn] n virgen m/f // a virgen; **the Blessed V~** la Santísima Virgen; **~ity** [-'dʒɪnɪtɪ] n virginidad f.

Virgo ['vɔ:gɔu] n Virgo.

virile ['vɪraɪl] a viril; **virility** [vɪ'rɪlɪtɪ] n virilidad f; (fig) machismo.

virtually ['vɔ:tjuɔlɪ] ad (almost) virtualmente.

virtue ['vɔ:tju:] n virtud f; **by ~ of** en virtud de.

virtuoso [vɔ:tju'ɔuzɔu] n virtuoso.

virtuous ['vəːtjuəs] *a* virtuoso.
virulent ['vɪrulənt] *a* virulento.
virus ['vaɪərəs] *n* virus *m*.
visa ['viːzə] *n* visado, visa (*AM*).
vis-à-vis [viːzəˈviː] *prep* respecto de.
visibility [vɪzɪˈbɪlɪtɪ] *n* visibilidad *f*.
visible ['vɪzəbl] *a* visible; **visibly** *ad* visiblemente.
vision ['vɪʒən] *n* (*sight*) vista; (*foresight, in dream*) visión *f*; ~**ary** *n* visionario.
visit ['vɪzɪt] *n* visita // *vt* (*person*) visitar, hacer una visita a; (*place*) ir a, (ir a) conocer; ~**or** *n* (*gen*) visitante *m/f*; (*to one's house*) visita; (*tourist*) turista *m/f*; (*tripper*) excursionista *m/f*; ~**ors' book** *n* libro de visitas.
visor ['vaɪzə*] *n* visera.
vista ['vɪstə] *n* vista, panorama.
visual ['vɪzjuəl] *a* visual; ~**ize** *vt* imaginarse; (*foresee*) prever.
vital ['vaɪtl] *a* (*essential*) esencial, imprescindible; (*important*) de suma importancia; (*crucial*) crítico; (*person*) enérgico, vivo; (*of life*) vital; ~**ity** [-'tælɪtɪ] *n* energía, vitalidad *f*; ~**ly** *ad*: ~**ly important** de primera importancia.
vitamin ['vɪtəmɪn] *n* vitamina.
vivacious [vɪˈveɪʃəs] *a* vivaz, alegre.
vivid ['vɪvɪd] *a* (*account*) gráfico; (*light*) intenso; (*imagination*) vivo.
vivisection [vɪvɪˈsɛkʃən] *n* vivisección *f*.
V-neck ['viːnɛk] *n* cuello de pico.
vocabulary [vəuˈkæbjulərɪ] *n* vocabulario.
vocal ['vəukl] *a* vocal; (*noisy*) ruidoso; ~ **chords** *npl* cuerdas *fpl* vocales; ~**ist** *n* cantante *m/f*.
vocation [vəuˈkeɪʃən] *n* vocación *f*; ~**al** *a* vocacional.
vociferous [vəˈsɪfərəs] *a* vocinglero.
vodka ['vɔdkə] *n* vodka.
vogue [vəug] *n* boga, moda.
voice [vɔɪs] *n* voz *f* // *vt* (*opinion*) expresar.
void [vɔɪd] *n* vacío; (*hole*) hueco // *a* (*gen*) vacío; (*vacant*) vacante; (*null*) nulo, inválido.
volatile ['vɔlətaɪl] *a* volátil.
volcanic [vɔlˈkænɪk] *a* volcánico; **volcano** [-ˈkeɪnəu], *pl* ~**es** *n* volcán *m*.
volley ['vɔlɪ] *n* (*of gunfire*) descarga; (*of stones etc*) lluvia; (*TENNIS etc*) voleo; ~**ball** *n* balonvolea, vol(e)ibol *m* (*AM*).
volt [vəult] *n* voltio; ~**age** *n* voltaje *m*.
voluble ['vɔljubl] *a* locuaz, hablador(a).
volume ['vɔljuːm] *n* (*gen*) volumen *m*; (*book*) tomo.
voluntarily ['vɔləntrɪlɪ] *ad* libremente, de su propia voluntad.
voluntary ['vɔləntərɪ] *a* voluntario, espontáneo; (*unpaid*) (a título) gratuito.
volunteer [vɔlənˈtɪə*] *n* voluntario // *vi* ofrecerse (de voluntario).
voluptuous [vəˈlʌptjuəs] *a* voluptuoso.
vomit ['vɔmɪt] *n* vómito // *vt, vi* vomitar.
vote [vəut] *n* voto; (*votes cast*) votación *f*; (*right to* ~) derecho de votar; (*franchise*) sufragio // *vt* (*chairman*) elegir // *vi* votar,

ir a votar; **voter** *n* votante *m/f*; **voting** *n* votación *f*.
vouch [vautʃ]: **to** ~ **for** *vt* garantizar, responder de.
voucher ['vautʃə*] *n* (*for meal, petrol*) vale *m*.
vow [vau] *n* voto // *vi* hacer voto.
vowel ['vauəl] *n* vocal *f*.
voyage ['vɔɪdʒ] *n* (*journey*) viaje *m*; (*crossing*) travesía.
vulgar ['vʌlgə*] *a* (*rude*) ordinario, grosero; (*in bad taste*) de mal gusto; ~**ity** [-ˈgærɪtɪ] *n* grosería; mal gusto.
vulnerable ['vʌlnərəbl] *a* vulnerable.
vulture ['vʌltʃə*] *n* buitre *m*.

W

wad [wɔd] *n* (*of cotton wool, paper*) bolita; (*of banknotes etc*) fajo.
waddle ['wɔdl] *vi* anadear.
wade [weɪd] *vi*: **to** ~ **through** caminar por el agua; (*fig: a book*) leer con dificultad.
wafer ['weɪfə*] *n* (*biscuit*) galleta, barquillo; (*REL*) oblea.
waffle ['wɔfl] *n* (*CULIN*) buñuelo, panqueque *m* // *vi* meter paja.
waft [wɔft] *vt* hacer flotar // *vi* flotar.
wag [wæg] *vt* menear, agitar // *vi* moverse, menearse.
wage [weɪdʒ] *n* (*also*: ~**s**) sueldo, salario // *vt*: **to** ~ **war** hacer la guerra; ~ **claim** *n* demanda de aumento de sueldo; ~ **earner** *n* asalariado/a; ~ **freeze** *n* congelación *f* de salarios.
wager ['weɪdʒə*] *n* apuesta // *vt* apostar.
waggle ['wægl] *vt* menear, mover.
wag(g)on ['wægən] *n* (*horse-drawn*) carro; (*truck*) camión *m*; (*RAIL*) vagón *m*.
wail [weɪl] *n* gemido // *vi* gemir.
waist [weɪst] *n* cintura, talle *m*; ~**coat** *n* chaleco; ~**line** *n* talle *m*.
wait [weɪt] *n* espera; (*interval*) pausa // *vi* esperar; **to lie in** ~ **for** acechar a; **I can't** ~ **to** (*fig*) estoy deseando; **to** ~ **for** esperar (a); **to** ~ **on** *vt fus* servir a; **'no** ~**ing'** (*AUT*) 'prohibido aparcar'; ~**er** *n* camarero; ~**ing list** *n* lista de espera; ~**ing room** *n* sala de espera; ~**ress** *n* camarera.
waive [weɪv] *vt* renunciar a.
wake [weɪk], *pt* **woke** *or* **waked,** *pp* **woken** *or* **waked** *vt* (*also*: ~ **up**) despertar // *vi* (*also*: ~ **up**) despertarse // *n* (*for dead person*) vela, velatorio; (*NAUT*) estela; **waken** *vt, vi* = **wake**.
Wales [weɪlz] *n* País *m* de Gales.
walk [wɔːk] *n* paseo; (*hike*) excursión *f* a pie, caminata; (*gait*) paso, andar *m*; (*in park etc*) paseo, alameda // *vi* andar; (*for pleasure, exercise*) pasearse // *vt* (*distance*) recorrer a pie, andar; (*dog*) sacar de paseo, pasear; **10 minutes'** ~ **from here** desde aquí hay 10 minutos a pie; **people from all** ~**s of life** gente de todas las esferas; ~**er** *n* (*person*)

paseante m/f, caminante m/f; ~ie-talkie ['wɔːkɪ'tɔːkɪ] n walkie-talkie m, transmisor-receptor m (portátil); ~ing n el andar; ~ing shoes npl zapatos mpl para andar; ~ing stick n bastón m; ~out n (of workers) huelga sorpresa; ~over n (col) triunfo fácil; ~way n paseo.

wall [wɔːl] n pared f; (exterior) muro; (city ~ etc) muralla; ~ed a (city) amurallado; (garden) con tapia.

wallet ['wɔlɪt] n cartera.

wallflower ['wɔːlflauə*] n alhelí m; to be a ~ (fig) comer pavo.

wallop ['wɔləp] vt (col) zurrar.

wallow ['wɔləu] vi revolcarse.

wallpaper ['wɔːlpeɪpə*] n papel m pintado.

walnut ['wɔːlnʌt] n nuez f; (tree) nogal m.

walrus ['wɔːlrəs], pl ~ or ~es n morsa.

waltz [wɔːlts] n vals m // vi bailar el vals.

wand [wɔnd] n (also: magic ~) varita (mágica).

wander ['wɔndə*] vi (person) vagar, deambular; (thoughts) divagar; (get lost) extraviarse // vt recorrer, vagar por; ~er n vagabundo; ~ing a errante; (thoughts) distraído.

wane [weɪn] vi menguar.

wangle ['wæŋgl] vt (col): to ~ sth agenciarse algo.

want [wɔnt] vt (wish for) querer, desear; (demand) exigir; (need) necesitar; (lack) carecer de // n: for ~ of por falta de; ~s npl (needs) necesidades fpl; to ~ to do querer hacer; to ~ sb to do sth querer que uno haga algo; ~ing a falto, deficiente; to be found ~ing no estar a la altura de las circunstancias.

wanton ['wɔntn] a (playful) juguetón(ona); (licentious) lascivo.

war [wɔː*] n guerra; to make ~ hacer la guerra.

ward [wɔːd] n (in hospital) sala; (POL) distrito electoral; (LAW: child) pupilo; to ~ off vt desviar, parar; (attack) rechazar.

warden ['wɔːdn] n (of institution) director m; (of park, game reserve) guardián m; (also: traffic ~) guardia m/f.

warder ['wɔːdə*] n guardián m, carcelero.

wardrobe ['wɔːdrəub] n (cupboard) armario; (clothes) guardarropa.

warehouse ['wɛəhaus] n almacén m, depósito.

wares [wɛəz] npl mercancías fpl.

war: ~fare n guerra; ~head n cabeza armada.

warily ['wɛərɪlɪ] ad con cautela, cautelosamente.

warlike ['wɔːlaɪk] a guerrero.

warm [wɔːm] a caliente; (thanks) efusivo; (clothes etc) cálido; (welcome, day) caluroso; it's ~ hace calor; I'm ~ tengo calor; to ~ up vi (person, room) calentarse; (athlete) hacer ejercicios de calentamiento; (discussion) acalorarse // vt calentar; ~-hearted a afectuoso; ~ly ad afectuosamente; ~th n calor m.

warn [wɔːn] vt avisar, prevenir; ~ing n aviso, advertencia; ~ing light n luz f de advertencia.

warp [wɔːp] vi diformarse.

warrant ['wɔrnt] n (guarantee) garantía; (LAW) mandato judicial.

warranty ['wɔrəntɪ] n garantía.

warren ['wɔrən] n (of rabbits) madriguera; (house) conejera.

warrior ['wɔrɪə*] n guerrero.

warship ['wɔːʃɪp] n buque m o barco de guerra.

wart [wɔːt] n verruga.

wartime ['wɔːtaɪm] n: in ~ en tiempos de guerra, en la guerra.

wary ['wɛərɪ] a cauteloso, cauto.

was [wɔz] pt of be.

wash [wɔʃ] vt lavar // vi lavarse // n (clothes etc) lavado; (bath) baño; (of ship) estela; to have a ~ lavarse; to ~ away vt (stain) quitar lavando; (subj: river etc) llevarse; (fig) regar; to ~ off vt quitar lavando; to ~ up vi fregar los platos; ~able a lavable; ~basin n lavabo; ~er n (TECH) arandela; ~ing n (dirty) ropa sucia; (clean) colada; ~ing machine n lavadora; ~ing powder n jabón m en polvo; ~ing-up n fregado, platos mpl (para fregar); ~-out n (col) fracaso; ~room n servicios mpl.

wasn't ['wɔznt] = was not.

wasp [wɔsp] n avispa.

wastage ['weɪstɪdʒ] n desgaste m; (loss) pérdida; natural ~ desgaste natural.

waste [weɪst] n derroche m, despilfarro; (wastage) desgaste m; (of time) pérdida; (food) sobras fpl; (rubbish) basura, desperdicios mpl // a (material) de desecho; (left over) sobrante; (land) baldío // vt (squander) malgastar, derrochar; (time) perder; (opportunity) desperdiciar; (use up) consumir; to ~ away vi consumirse; ~bin n cubo de la basura; ~ disposal unit n triturador m de basura; ~ful a derrochador(a); (process) antieconómico; ~ ground n terreno baldío; ~paper basket n papelera; ~ pipe n tubo de desagüe.

watch [wɔtʃ] n reloj m; (act of watching) vigilia; (vigilance) vigilancia; (guard: MIL) centinela m; (NAUT: spell of duty) guardia // vt (look at) mirar, observar; (: match, programme) ver; (spy on, guard) vigilar; (be careful of) cuidarse de, tener cuidado de // vi ver, mirar; (keep guard) montar guardia; to ~ out vi cuidarse, tener cuidado; ~dog n perro guardián; ~ful a vigilante, observador(a); ~maker n relojero; ~man n guardián m; (also: night ~man) sereno; (in factory) vigilante m nocturno; ~ strap n pulsera (de reloj); ~word n lema m.

water ['wɔːtə*] n agua // vt (plant) regar; to ~ down vt (milk) aguar; ~ closet n wáter m; ~colour n acuarela; ~cress n berro; ~fall n cascada, salto de agua; ~ hole n charco; ~ing can n regadera; ~

level *n* nivel *m* del agua; ~ **lily** *n* nenúfar *m*; ~**line** *n* (NAUT) línea de flotación; ~**logged** *a* empapado; ~ **main** *n* cañería del agua; ~**mark** *n* (*on paper*) filigrana; ~**melon** *n* sandía; ~ **polo** *n* polo acuático; ~**proof** *a* impermeable; ~**shed** *n* (GEO) cuenca; (*fig*) momento crítico; ~**-skiing** *n* esquí *m* acuático; ~ **tank** *n* depósito de agua; ~**tight** *a* hermético; ~**works** *npl* central *f* depuradora; ~**y** *a* (*colour*) desvaído; (*coffee*) aguado; (*eyes*) lloroso.

watt [wɔt] *n* vatio.

wave [weɪv] *n* ola; (*of hand*) ademán *m*, señal *f*; (RADIO) onda; (*in hair*) ondulación *f*; (*fig*) oleada // *vi* agitar la mano; (*flag*) ondear // *vt* (*handkerchief*) agitar; (*weapon*) blandir; (*hair*) ondular; ~**length** *n* longitud *f* de onda.

waver ['weɪvɔ*] *vi* oscilar; (*person*) vacilar.

wavy ['weɪvɪ] *a* ondulado.

wax [wæks] *n* cera // *vt* encerar // *vi* (*moon*) crecer; ~**works** *npl* museo *sg* de cera.

way [weɪ] *n* (*gen*) camino; (*distance*) trayecto, recorrido; (*direction*) dirección *f*, sentido; (*manner*) modo, manera; (*habit*) costumbre *f*; (*condition*) estado; **which** ~? ¿por dónde?, ¿en qué dirección?; **to be on one's** ~ estar en camino; **to be in the** ~ bloquear el camino; **to go out of one's** ~ **to do sth** desvivirse por hacer algo; **to lose one's** ~ extraviarse; **in a** ~ en cierto modo *o* sentido; **by the** ~ a propósito; '~ **out**' 'salida'; **the** ~ **back** el camino de vuelta; '**give** ~' (AUT) 'ceda el paso'.

waylay [weɪ'leɪ] (*irg: like* lay) *vt* acechar.

wayward ['weɪwɔd] *a* (*wilful*) voluntarioso; (*capricious*) caprichoso; (*naughty*) travieso.

W.C. ['dʌblju'si:] *n* wáter *m*.

we [wi:] *pl pron* nosotros/as.

weak [wi:k] *a* (*gen*) débil, flojo; (*tea*) claro; ~**en** *vi* debilitarse; (*give way*) ceder // *vt* debilitar; (*lessen*) disminuir; ~**ling** *n* persona débil *o* delicada; ~**ness** *n* debilidad *f*; (*fault*) punto débil.

wealth [wɛlθ] *n* (*money, resources*) riqueza; (*of details*) abundancia; ~**y** *a* rico.

wean [wi:n] *vt* destetar.

weapon ['wɛpən] *n* arma.

wear [wɛə*] *n* (*use*) uso; (*deterioration through use*) desgaste *m*; (*clothing*): **sports/baby**~ ropa de deportes/para niños // (*vb: pt* **wore**, *pp* **worn**) *vt* (*clothes*) llevar; (*shoes*) calzar; (*put on*) ponerse; (*damage: through use*) gastar, usar // *vi* (*last*) durar; (*rub through etc*) desgastarse; ~ **and tear** *n* desgaste *m*; **to** ~ **away** *vt* gastar // *vi* desgastarse; **to** ~ **down** *vt* gastar; (*strength*) agotar; **to** ~ **off** *vi* (*pain etc*) pasar, desaparecer; **to** ~ **out** *vt* desgastar; (*person, strength*) agotar.

weariness ['wɪərɪnɪs] *n* cansancio; (*boredom*) aburrimiento, hastío.

weary ['wɪərɪ] *a* (*tired*) cansado; (*dispirited*) abatido // *vt* cansar // *vi:* **to** ~ **of** cansarse de, aburrirse de.

weasel ['wi:zl] *n* (ZOOL) comadreja.

weather ['wɛðə*] *n* tiempo // *vt* (*storm, crisis*) hacer frente a; ~**-beaten** *a* curtido; ~ **cock** *n* veleta; ~ **forecast** *n* boletín *m* meteorológico; ~ **vane** *n* = ~ **cock.**

weave [wi:v] *pt* **wove**, *pp* **woven** *vt* (*cloth*) tejer; (*fig*) entretejer; **weaver** *n* tejedor/a *m/f*; **weaving** *n* tejeduría.

web [wɛb] *n* (*of spider*) telaraña; (*on foot*) membrana; (*network*) red *f*; ~**bed** *a* (*foot*) palmeado; ~**bing** *n* (*on chair*) cinchas *fpl*.

wed [wɛd], *pt, pp* **wedded** *vt* casar // *vi* casarse // *n:* **the newly-**~**s** los recién casados.

we'd [wi:d] = **we had; we would.**

wedded ['wɛdɪd] *pt, pp of* **wed.**

wedding ['wɛdɪŋ] *n* boda, casamiento; **silver/golden** ~ bodas *fpl* de plata/de oro; ~ **day** *n* día *m* de la boda; ~ **dress** *n* traje *m* de novia; ~ **present** *n* regalo de boda; ~ **ring** *n* anillo de boda.

wedge [wɛdʒ] *n* (*of wood etc*) cuña; (*of cake*) porción *f* // *vt* acuñar; (*pack tightly*) apretar.

wedlock ['wɛdlɔk] *n* matrimonio.

Wednesday ['wɛdnzdɪ] *n* miércoles *m*.

wee [wi:] *a* (*Scottish*) pequeñito.

weed [wi:d] *n* mala hierba, maleza // *vt* escardar, desherbar; ~**-killer** *n* herbicida *m*.

week [wi:k] *n* semana; ~**day** *n* día *m* laborable; ~**end** *n* fin *m* de semana; ~**ly** *ad* semanalmente, cada semana // *a* semanal // *n* semanario.

weep [wi:p], *pt, pp* **wept** *vi, vt* llorar; ~**ing willow** *n* sauce *m* llorón.

weigh [weɪ] *vt, vi* pesar; **to** ~ **down** *vt* sobrecargar; (*fig: with worry*) agobiar; **to** ~ **up** *vt* pesar; ~**bridge** *n* báscula-puente *f*.

weight [weɪt] *n* peso; (*on scale*) pesa; **to lose/put on** ~ adelgazarse/engordarse; ~**lessness** *n* ingravidez *f*; ~ **lifter** *n* levantador *m* de pesos; ~**y** *a* pesado.

weir [wɪə*] *n* presa.

weird [wɪəd] *a* raro, extraño.

welcome ['wɛlkəm] *a* bienvenido // *n* bienvenida // *vt* dar la bienvenida a; (*be glad of*) alegrarse de; **welcoming** *a* acogedor(a); (*speech*) de bienvenida.

weld [wɛld] *n* soldadura // *vt* soldar; ~**er** *n* (*person*) soldador *m*; ~**ing** *n* soldadura.

welfare ['wɛlfɛə*] *n* bienestar *m*; (*social aid*) asistencia social; ~ **state** *n* estado de bienestar.

well [wɛl] *n* fuente *f*, pozo // *ad* bien // *a:* **to be** ~ estar bien (de salud) // *excl* ¡vaya!, ¡bueno!; **as** ~ también; **as** ~ **as** igual que; ~ **done!** ¡bien hecho!; **get** ~ **soon!** ¡que te mejores pronto!; **to do** ~ ir *o* salir bien; **to** ~ **up** *vi* brotar.

we'll [wi:l] = **we will, we shall.**

well: ~-**behaved** a bien educado, formal; ~-**being** n bienestar m; ~-**built** a (person) fornido; ~-**deserved** a merecido; ~-**developed** a bien desarrollado; ~-**dressed** a bien vestido; ~-**heeled** a (col: wealthy) rico; ~-**informed** a enterado.

wellingtons ['wɛlɪŋtənz] n (also: **wellington boots**) botas fpl de goma.

well: ~-**known** a (person) conocido; ~-**mannered** a educado; ~-**meaning** a bienintencionado; ~-**off** a pudiente, con dinero; ~-**read** a culto; ~-**to-do** a acomodado; ~-**wisher** n admirador/a m/f, amigo.

Welsh [wɛlʃ] a galés(esa) // n (LING) galés m; ~ **man/woman** n galés/esa m/f.

went [wɛnt] pt of **go**.

wept [wɛpt] pt, pp of **weep**.

were [wɔː*] pt of **be**.

we're [wɪə*] = **we are**.

weren't [wɔːnt] = **were not**.

west [wɛst] n oeste m // a occidental, del oeste // ad hacia el o al oeste; **the W** ~ n el Oeste, el Occidente; **the W** ~ **Country** n el suroeste de Inglaterra; ~ **erly** a (situation) oeste; (wind) del oeste; ~ **ern** a occidental // n (CINEMA) película del oeste; **W** ~ **Germany** n Alemania Occidental; **W** ~ **Indies** npl Antillas fpl; ~ **ward(s)** ad hacia el oeste.

wet [wɛt] a (damp) húmedo; (~ through) mojado; (rainy) lluvioso; **to get** ~ mojarse; '~ **paint**' 'recién pintado'; **to be a** ~ **blanket** (fig) ser un/una aguafiestas; ~ **ness** n humedad f; ~ **suit** n traje m de buzo.

we've [wiːv] = **we have**.

whack [wæk] vt dar un buen golpe a; ~ **ed** a (col: tired) reventado.

whale [weɪl] n (ZOOL) ballena.

wharf [wɔːf], pl **wharves** [wɔːvz] n muelle m.

what [wɔt] excl ¡qué!, ¡cómo! // det que // pron (interrogative) ¿qué?, ¿cómo?; (relative, indirect: object) lo que; (: subject) el/la que; ~ **are you doing?** ¿qué haces?; **I saw** ~ **you did** he visto lo que hiciste; ~ **a mess!** ¡que lío!; ~ **is it called?** ¿cómo se llama?; ~ **about me?** ¿y yo?; ~ **ever** det: ~ **ever book you choose** cualquier libro que elijas // pron: **do** ~ **ever is necessary** haga lo que sea necesario; **no reason** ~ **ever** or ~ **soever** ninguna razón sea la que sea; **nothing** ~ **ever** nada en absoluto.

wheat [wiːt] n trigo.

wheel [wiːl] n rueda; (AUT: also: **steering** ~) volante m; (NAUT) timón m // vt (pram etc) empujar // vi (also: ~ **round**) dar la vuelta, girar; ~ **barrow** n carretilla; ~ **chair** n silla de ruedas; ~ **house** n timonera.

wheeze [wiːz] n respiración f ruidosa // vi resollar.

when [wɛn] ad cuándo // conj cuando; (whereas) mientras; **on the day** ~ **I met him** el día que le conocí; ~ **ever** conj cuando, todas las veces que; (every time that) siempre que.

where [wɛə*] ad dónde // conj donde; **this is** ~ aquí es donde; ~ **abouts** ad ¿dónde? // n: **nobody knows his** ~ **abouts** nadie conoce su paradero; ~ **as** conj visto que, mientras; **wherever** [-'ɛvə*] ad dondequiera que; (interrogative) ¿dónde?; ~ **withal** n recursos mpl.

whet [wɛt] vt estimular.

whether ['wɛðə*] conj si; **I don't know** ~ **to accept or not** no sé si aceptar o no; ~ **you go or not** vayas o no vayas.

which [wɪtʃ] det (interrogative) ¿qué?, ¿cuál?; ~ **one of you?** ¿cuál de vosotros?; ~ **picture do you want?** ¿qué cuadro quieres? // pron (interrogative) ¿cuál?; (relative: subject) que, lo que; (: object) el que etc, el cual etc, lo cual; **I don't mind** ~ no me importa cuál; **the apple** ~ **is on the table** la manzana que está sobre la mesa; **the chair on** ~ **you are sitting** la silla sobre la que estás sentado; **he said he knew,** ~ **is true** él dijo que sabía, lo cual es cierto; **in** ~ **case** en cuyo caso; ~ **ever** det: **take** ~ **ever book you prefer** coja el libro que prefiera; ~ **ever book you take** cualquier libro que coja.

whiff [wɪf] n bocanada.

while [waɪl] n rato, momento // conj durante; (as long as) mientras; (although) aunque; **for a** ~ durante algún tiempo.

whim [wɪm] n capricho.

whimper ['wɪmpə*] n (weeping) lloriqueo; (moan) quejido // vi lloriquear; quejarse.

whimsical ['wɪmzɪkl] a (person) caprichoso; (look) extraño.

whine [waɪn] n (of pain) gemido; (of engine) zumbido // vi gemir; zumbar.

whip [wɪp] n látigo; (for riding) fusta; (Brit: POL) oficial disciplinario del partido // vt azotar; (snatch) arrebatar; ~ **ped cream** n crema batida; ~ **round** n colecta.

whirl [wɔːl] n remolino // vt hacer girar, dar vueltas a // vi girar, dar vueltas; (leaves, water etc) arremolinarse; ~ **pool** n remolino; ~ **wind** n torbellino.

whirr [wɔː*] vi rechinar, zumbar.

whisk [wɪsk] n (CULIN) batidor m // vt batir; **to** ~ **sth away from sb** arrebatarle algo a uno; **to** ~ **sb away** or **off** llevar rápidamente a uno.

whisker [wɪskə*] n: ~ **s** (of animal) bigotes mpl; (of man) patillas fpl.

whisk(e)y ['wɪskɪ] n whisky m.

whisper ['wɪspə*] n cuchicheo; (rumour) rumor m; (fig) susurro, murmullo // vi cuchichear, hablar bajo; (fig) susurrar.

whist [wɪst] n whist m.

whistle ['wɪsl] n (sound) silbido; (object) silbato // vi silbar.

white [waɪt] a blanco; (pale) pálido // n blanco; (of egg) clara; ~ **collar worker** n oficinista m/f; ~ **elephant** n (fig) maula; ~ **lie** n mentira piadosa; ~ **ness** n blancura; ~ **paper** *n* (*POL*) libro rojo; ~**wash** *n* (*paint*) jalbegue *m*, cal *f* // *vt* enjalbegar; (*fig*) encubrir.

whiting ['waɪtɪŋ] *n*, *pl inv* (*fish*) pescadilla.

Whitsun ['wɪtsn] *n* pentecostés *m*.

whittle ['wɪtl] *vt*: **to ~ away, ~ down** reducir poco a poco.

whizz [wɪz] *vi*: **to ~ past** *or* **by** pasar a toda velocidad; ~ **kid** *n* (*col*) prodigio, portento.

who [hu:] *pron* (*relative*) que, el que *etc*, quien; (*interrogative*) ¿quién?; (*pl*) ¿quiénes?; ~**ever** *pron*: ~**ever finds it** cualquiera *o* quienquiera que lo encuentre; **ask** ~**ever you like** pregunta a quien quieras; ~**ever be marries** no importa con quién se case.

whole [həul] *a* (*complete*) todo, entero; (*not broken*) intacto // *n* (*total*) total *m*; (*sum*) conjunto; **the ~ of the town** toda la ciudad, la ciudad entera; **on the ~, as a ~** en general; ~**hearted** *a* sincero, cordial; ~**sale** *n* venta al por mayor // *a* al por mayor; (*destruction*) sistemático; ~**saler** *n* mayorista *m/f*; ~**some** *a* sano; **wholly** *ad* totalmente, enteramente.

whom [hu:m] *pron* que, a quien; (*interrogative*) ¿a quién?

whooping cough ['hu:pɪŋkɒf] *n* tos *f* ferina.

whopper ['wɒpə*] *n* cosa muy grande; (*lie*) bola; **whopping** *a* (*col*: *big*) enorme.

whore [hɔ:*] *n* (*col*: *pej*) puta.

whose [hu:z] *det*: ~ **book is this?** ¿de quién es este libro?; **the man ~ son you rescued** el hombre cuyo hijo salvaste; **the girl ~ sister you were speaking to** la chica con cuya hermana estabas hablando // *pron*: ~ **is this?** ¿de quién es esto?; **I know ~ it is** yo sé de quien es.

why [waɪ] *ad* por qué; (*interrogative*) ¿por qué?, ¿para qué? // *excl* ¡toma!, ¡cómo!; **tell me ~** dime por qué, dime la razón; ~**ever** *ad* por qué.

wick [wɪk] *n* mecha.

wicked ['wɪkɪd] *a* malvado, cruel.

wicker ['wɪkə*] *n* (*also*: ~**work**) artículos *mpl* de mimbre.

wicket ['wɪkɪt] *n* (*CRICKET*) palos *mpl*.

wide [waɪd] *a* ancho; (*region, knowledge*) vasto, grande; (*choice*) grande // *ad*: **to open ~** abrir de par en par; **to shoot ~** errar el tiro; ~**-awake** *a* bien despierto; (*fig*) despabilado; ~**ly** *ad* (*different*) muy; **it is ~ly believed that...** hay una convicción general de que...; **widen** *vt* ensanchar; ~**ness** *n* anchura; ~ **open** *a* abierto de par en par; ~**spread** *a* (*belief etc*) extendido, general.

widow ['wɪdəu] *n* viuda; ~**ed** *a* viudo; ~**er** *n* viudo.

width [wɪdθ] *n* anchura; (*of cloth*) ancho.

wield [wi:ld] *vt* (*sword*) manejar; (*power*) ejercer.

wife [waɪf], *pl* **wives** [waɪvz] *n* mujer *f*, esposa.

wig [wɪg] *n* peluca.

wiggle ['wɪgl] *vt* menear (rápidamente) // *vi* menearse.

wild [waɪld] *a* (*animal*) salvaje; (*plant*) silvestre; (*rough*) furioso, violento; (*idea*) disparatado, descabellado; (*person*) loco; ~**s** *npl* regiones *fpl* salvajes, tierras *fpl* vírgenes; ~**erness** ['wɪldənɪs] *n* desierto; ~**life** *n* fauna; ~**ly** *ad* (*roughly*) violentamente; (*foolishly*) locamente; (*rashly*) descabelladamente.

wilful ['wɪlful] *a* (*person*) voluntarioso; (*action*) deliberado; (*obstinate*) testarudo; (*child*) voluntario.

will [wɪl] *auxiliary vb*: **he ~ come** vendrá // *vt*, *pt*, *pp* **willed**: **to ~ sb to do sth** desear que alguien haga algo; **he ~ed himself to go on** con gran fuerza de voluntad, continuó // *n* voluntad *f*; (*testament*) testamento; ~**ing** *a* (*with goodwill*) de buena voluntad; (*submissive*) complaciente; ~**ingly** *ad* con mucho gusto; ~**ingness** *n* buena voluntad.

willow ['wɪləu] *n* sauce *m*.

will power *n* fuerza de voluntad.

wilt [wɪlt] *vi* marchitarse.

wily ['waɪlɪ] *a* astuto.

win [wɪn] *n* (*in sports etc*) victoria, triunfo // (*vb*: *pt*, *pp* **won**) *vt* ganar; (*obtain*) conseguir, lograr // *vi* ganar, tener éxito; **to ~ over, ~ round** *vt* atraerse.

wince [wɪns] *vi* estremecerse.

winch [wɪntʃ] *n* torno.

wind [wɪnd] *n* viento; (*MED*) flatulencia; (*breath*) aliento // (*vb*: [waɪnd], *pt*, *pp* **wound**) *vt* enrollar; (*wrap*) envolver; (*clock, toy*) dar cuerda a // *vi* (*road, river*) serpentear // *vt* [waɪnd] (*take breath away from*) dejar sin aliento a; **to ~ up** *vt* (*clock*) dar cuerda a; (*debate*) concluir, terminar; ~**break** *n* abrigada; ~**fall** *n* golpe *m* de suerte; ~**ing** *a* (*road*) tortuoso; ~ **instrument** *n* (*MUS*) instrumento de viento; ~**mill** *n* molino de viento.

window ['wɪndəu] *n* ventana; (*in car, train*) ventanilla; (*in shop etc*) escaparate *m*; ~ **box** *n* jardinera (de ventana); ~ **cleaner** *n* (*person*) limpiacristales *m inv*; ~ **ledge** *n* alféizar *m*; ~ **pane** *n* cristal *m*; ~**sill** *n* alféizar *m*.

windpipe ['wɪndpaɪp] *n* tráquea.

windscreen ['wɪndskri:n], **windshield** ['wɪndʃi:ld] (*US*) *n* parabrisas *m inv*; ~ **washer** *n* lavaparabrisas *m inv*; ~ **wiper** *n* limpiaparabrisas *m inv*.

windswept ['wɪndswɛpt] *a* azotado por el viento.

windy ['wɪndɪ] *a* de mucho viento; **it's ~** hace viento.

wine [waɪn] *n* vino; ~ **cellar** *n* bodega; ~ **glass** *n* copa (para vino); ~ **list** *n* lista de vinos; ~ **merchant** *n* vinatero; ~ **tasting** *n* degustación *f* de vinos.

wing [wɪŋ] *n* (*gen*) ala; (*AUT*) aleta, guardabarros *m inv*; ~**s** *npl* (*THEATRE*) bastidores *mpl*; ~**er** *n* (*SPORT*) extremo.

wink [wɪŋk] *n* guiño, pestañeo // *vi* guiñar,

pestañear; (*light etc*) parpadear.
winner ['wɪnə*] *n* ganador/a *m/f.*
winning ['wɪnɪŋ] *a* (*team*) ganador(a); (*goal*) decisivo; ~**s** *npl* ganancias *fpl*; ~ **post** *n* meta.
winter ['wɪntə*] *n* invierno // *vi* invernar; ~ **sports** *npl* deportes *mpl* de invierno.
wintry ['wɪntrɪ] *a* invernal.
wipe [waɪp] *n*: **to give sth a** ~ pasar un trapo sobre algo // *vt* limpiar; **to** ~ **off** *vt* limpiar con un trapo; **to** ~ **out** *vt* (*debt*) liquidar; (*memory*) borrar; (*destroy*) destruir.
wire ['waɪə*] *n* alambre *m*; (ELEC) cable *m* (eléctrico); (TEL) telegrama *m* // *vt* (*house*) instalar el alambrado de; (*also*: ~ **up**) conectar // *vi* poner un telegrama.
wireless ['waɪəlɪs] *n* radio *f.*
wiring ['waɪərɪŋ] *n* instalación *f* eléctrica, alambrado.
wiry ['waɪərɪ] *a* nervioso, nervudo.
wisdom ['wɪzdəm] *n* sabiduría, saber *m*; (*good sense*) cordura; (*care*) prudencia; ~ **tooth** *n* muela del juicio.
wise [waɪz] *a* sabio; (*sensible*) cuerdo; (*careful*) prudente.
...wise [waɪz] *suff*: **time**~ en cuanto a *o* respecto al tiempo.
wisecrack ['waɪzkræk] *n* broma.
wish [wɪʃ] *n* (*desire*) deseo // *vt* desear; (*want*) querer; **best** ~**es** (*on birthday etc*) felicidades *fpl*; **with best** ~**es** (*in letter*) saludos *mpl*, recuerdos *mpl*; **to** ~ **sb goodbye** despedirse de uno; **he** ~**ed me well** me deseó mucha suerte; **to** ~ **to do/sb to do sth** querer hacer/que alguien haga algo; **to** ~ **for** desear; **it's** ~**ful thinking** es un espejismo.
wisp [wɪsp] *n* mechón *m*; (*of smoke*) voluta.
wistful ['wɪstful] *a* pensativo.
wit [wɪt] *n* (*wittiness*) ingenio, gracia; (*intelligence*) entendimiento; (*person*) chistoso/a.
witch [wɪtʃ] *n* bruja; ~**craft** *n* brujería.
with [wɪð, wɪθ] *prep* con; **red** ~ **anger** rojo de cólera; **the man** -- **the grey hat** el hombre del sombrero gris; **to be** ~ **it** (*fig*) estar al tanto *o* a la moda; **I am** ~ **you** (*I understand*) te entiendo.
withdraw [wɪθ'drɔ:] (*irg*: *like* **draw**) *vt* retirar, sacar // *vi* retirarse; (*go back on promise*) retractarse; **to** ~ **money (from the bank)** retirar fondos (del banco); ~ **al** *n* retirada; ~**n** *a* (*person*) reservado, introvertido.
wither ['wɪðə*] *vi* marchitarse; ~**ed** *a* marchito.
withhold [wɪθ'həuld] (*irg*: *like* **hold**) *vt* (*money*) retener; (*decision*) aplazar; (*permission*) negar; (*information*) ocultar.
within [wɪð'ɪn] *prep* dentro de // *ad* dentro; ~ **reach** al alcance de la mano; ~ **sight of** a la vista de; ~ **the week** antes de acabar la semana.
without [wɪð'aut] *prep* sin.
withstand [wɪθ'stænd] (*irg*: *like* **stand**) *vt* resistir a.

witness ['wɪtnɪs] *n* (*person*) testigo; (*evidence*) testimonio // (*event*) presenciar; (*document*) atestiguar la veracidad de; ~ **box**, ~ **stand** (*US*) *n* tribuna de los testigos.
witticism ['wɪtɪsɪzm] *n* dicho ingenioso.
witty ['wɪtɪ] *a* ingenioso, salado.
wives [waɪvz] *pl of* **wife.**
wizard ['wɪzəd] *n* hechicero.
wk *abbr of* **week.**
wobble ['wɔbl] *vi* tambalearse; (*chair*) ser poco firme.
woe [wəu] *n* desgracia.
woke [wəuk], **woken** ['wəukən] *pt, pp of* **wake.**
wolf [wulf], *pl* **wolves** [wulvz] *n* lobo.
woman ['wumən], *pl* **women** *n* mujer *f*; ~**ly** *a* femenino.
womb [wu:m] *n* (ANAT) matriz *f*, útero.
women ['wɪmɪn] *pl of* **woman.**
won [wʌn] *pt, pp of* **win.**
wonder ['wʌndə*] *n* maravilla, prodigio; (*feeling*) asombro // *vi*: **to** ~ **whether** preguntarse si; **to** ~ **at** asombrarse de; **to** ~ **about** pensar sobre *o* en; **it's no** ~ **that** no es de extrañarse que; ~**ful** *a* maravilloso; ~**fully** *ad* maravillosamente, estupendamente.
won't [wəunt] = **will not.**
woo [wu:] *vt* (*woman*) cortejar.
wood [wud] *n* (*timber*) madera; (*forest*) bosque *m*; ~ **carving** *n* escultura de madera; ~**ed** *a* arbolado; ~**en** *a* de madera; (*fig*) inexpresivo; ~**pecker** *n* pájaro carpintero; ~**wind** *n* (MUS) instrumentos *mpl* de viento de madera; ~**work** *n* carpintería; ~**worm** *n* carcoma.
wool [wul] *n* lana; **to pull the** ~ **over sb's eyes** (*fig*) dar a uno gato por liebre; ~**len**, ~**en** (*US*) *a* de lana; ~**lens** *npl* géneros *mpl* de lana; ~**ly**, ~**y** (*US*) *a* lanudo, de lana; (*fig*: *ideas*) confuso.
word [wɔ:d] *n* palabra; (*news*) noticia; (*message*) aviso // *vt* redactar; **in other** ~**s** en otras palabras; **to break/keep one's** ~ faltar a la palabra/cumplir la promesa; ~**ing** *n* redacción *f.*
wore [wɔ:*] *pt of* **wear.**
work [wɔ:k] *n* (*gen*) trabajo; (*job*) empleo, trabajo; (ART, LITERATURE) obra // *vi* trabajar; (*mechanism*) funcionar, marchar; (*medicine*) ser eficaz, surtir efecto // *vt* (*clay, wood etc*) tallar; (*mine etc*) explotar; (*machine*) manejar, hacer funcionar; (*cause*) producir; **to be out of** ~ estar parado, no tener trabajo; ~**s** *n* (*factory*) fábrica // *npl* (*of clock, machine*) mecanismo *sg*; **to** ~ **loose** *vi* (*part*) desprenderse; (*knot*) aflojarse; **to** ~ **on** *vt fus* trabajar en, dedicarse a; (*principle*) basarse en; **to** ~ **out** *vi* (*plans etc*) salir bien, funcionar // *vt* (*problem*) resolver; (*plan*) elaborar; **does it** ~ **out?** ¿da resultado?; **it** ~**s out at £100** suma 100 libras; **to get** ~**ed up** exaltarse; ~**able** *a* (*solution*) práctico, factible; ~**er** *n* trabajador/a, obrero; ~**ing class** *n* clase

f obrera; ~**ing-class** *a* de clase obrera; **in** ~**ing order** en funcionamiento; ~**man** *n* obrero; ~**manship** *n* (*art*) hechura, arte *m*; (*skill*) habilidad *f*, trabajo; ~**shop** *n* taller *m*; ~**-to-rule** *n* huelga de celo.
world [wɔːld] *n* mundo // *cpd* (*champion*) del mundo; (*power, war*) mundial; **to think the** ~ **of sb** (*fig*) tener un concepto muy alto de uno; ~**ly** *a* mundano; ~**-wide** *a* mundial, universal.
worm [wɔːm] *n* gusano; (*earth*~) lombriz *f*.
worn [wɔːn] *pp of* **wear** // *a* usado; ~**-out** *a* (*object*) gastado; (*person*) rendido, agotado.
worried ['wʌrɪd] *a* preocupado.
worry ['wʌrɪ] *n* preocupación *f* // *vt* preocupar, inquietar // *vi* preocuparse; ~**ing** *a* inquietante.
worse [wɔːs] *a, ad* peor, inferior // *n* el peor, lo peor; **a change for the** ~ un empeoramiento; **worsen** *vt, vi* empeorar; ~ **off** *a* (*fig*): **you'll be** ~ **off this way** de esta forma estarás peor que nunca.
worship ['wɔːʃɪp] *n* culto; (*act*) adoración *f* // *vt* adorar; **Your W**~ (*to mayor*) señor alcalde; (*to judge*) señor juez; ~**per** *n* devoto/a.
worst [wɔːst] *a* (el/la) peor // *ad* peor // *n* lo peor; **at** ~ en lo peor de los casos.
worth [wɔːθ] *n* valor *m* // *a*: **to be** ~ valer; **it's** ~ **it** vale *o* merece la pena; ~**less** *a* sin valor; (*useless*) inútil; ~**while** *a* (*activity*) que merece la pena; (*cause*) loable.
worthy [wɔːðɪ] *a* (*person*) respetable; (*motive*) honesto; ~ **of** digno de.
would [wud] *auxiliary vb*: **she** ~ **come** ella vendría; **he** ~ **have come** él hubiera venido; ~ **you like a biscuit?** ¿quieres una galleta?; **he** ~ **go on Mondays** solía ir los lunes; ~**-be** *a* (*pej*) presunto, aspirante.
wound [waund] *pt, pp of* **wind** // *n* [wuːnd] herida // *vt* [wuːnd] herir.
wove [wəuv], **woven** ['wəuvən] *pt, pp of* **weave**.
wrangle ['ræŋgl] *n* riña // *vi* reñir.
wrap [ræp] *n* (*stole*) chal *m*; (*cape*) capa // *vt* (*also*: ~ **up**) envolver; ~**per** *n* (*of book*) cubierta, tapa; ~**ping paper** *n* papel *m* de envolver.
wrath [rɔθ] *n* cólera.
wreath [riːθ] *pl* ~**s** [riːðz] *n* (*funeral* ~) corona; (*of flowers*) guirnalda.
wreathe [riːð] *vt* ceñir.
wreck [rɛk] *n* naufragio; (*ship*) restos *mpl* del barco; (*pej: person*) ruina // *vt* destruir, hundir; (*fig*) arruinar; ~**age** *n* restos *mpl*; (*of building*) escombros *mpl*.
wren [rɛn] *n* (*zool*) reyezuelo.
wrench [rɛntʃ] *n* (*tech*) llave *f* inglesa; (*tug*) tirón *m* // *vt* arrancar; **to** ~ **sth from sb** arrebatar algo violentamente a uno.
wrestle ['rɛsl] *vi*: **to** ~ (**with sb**) luchar (con *o* contra uno); **wrestler** *n* luchador *m*

(de lucha libre); **wrestling** *n* lucha libre; **wrestling match** *n* partido de lucha libre.
wretched ['rɛtʃɪd] *a* miserable.
wriggle ['rɪgl] *n* (*gen*) culebreo // *vi* (*gen*) serpentear.
wring [rɪŋ], *pt, pp* **wrung** *vt* torcer, retorcer; (*wet clothes*) escurrir; (*fig*): **to** ~ **sth out of sb** sacar algo por la fuerza a uno.
wrinkle ['rɪŋkl] *n* arruga // *vt* arrugar // *vi* arrugarse.
wrist [rɪst] *n* muñeca; ~ **watch** *n* reloj *m* de pulsera.
writ [rɪt] *n* mandato judicial; **to issue a** ~ **against sb** demandar a uno (en juicio).
write [raɪt], *pt* **wrote**, *pp* **written** *vt, vi* escribir; **to** ~ **down** *vt* escribir; (*note*) apuntar; **to** ~ **off** *vt* (*debt*) borrar (como incobrable); (*depreciate*) depreciar; **to** ~ **out** *vt* escribir; **to** ~ **up** *vt* redactar; ~**-off** *n* pérdida total; **the car is a** ~**-off** el coche es pura chatarra; **writer** *n* escritor/a *m/f*.
writhe [raɪð] *vi* retorcerse.
writing ['raɪtɪŋ] *n* escritura; (*hand*~) letra; (*of author*) obra; **in** ~ por escrito; ~ **paper** *n* papel *m* de escribir.
written ['rɪtn] *pp of* **write**.
wrong [rɔŋ] *a* (*bad*) malo; (*unfair*) injusto; (*incorrect*) equivocado, incorrecto; (*not suitable*) inoportuno, inconveniente // *ad* mal; equivocadamente // *n* mal *m*; (*injustice*) injusticia // *vt* ser injusto con; (*hurt*) agraviar; **you are** ~ **to do it** estás equivocado en hacerlo, cometes un error al hacerlo; **you are** ~ **about that, you've got it** ~ en eso, estás equivocado; **to be in the** ~ no tener razón, tener la culpa; **what's** ~**?** ¿qué pasa?; **to go** ~ (*person*) equivocarse; (*plan*) salir mal; (*machine*) tener una avería; ~**ful** *a* injusto; ~**ly** *ad* injustamente.
wrote [rəut] *pt of* **write**.
wrought [rɔːt] *a*: ~ **iron** hierro forjado.
wrung [rʌŋ] *pt, pp of* **wring**.
wry [raɪ] *a* irónico.
wt. *abbr of* **weight**.

X

Xmas ['ɛksməs] *n abbr of* **Christmas**.
X-ray [ɛks'reɪ] *n* radiografía; ~**s** *npl* rayos *mpl* X // *vt* hacer una radiografía a.
xylophone ['zaɪləfəun] *n* xilófono.

Y

yacht [jɔt] *n* yate *m*; ~**ing** *n* (*sport*) balandrismo; **yachtsman** *n* balandrista *m*.
Yank [jæŋk] *n* (*pej*) yanqui *m/f*.
yap [jæp] *vi* (*dog*) aullar.
yard [jɑːd] *n* patio; (*measure*) yarda; ~**stick** *n* (*fig*) criterio, norma.
yarn [jɑːn] *n* hilo; (*tale*) cuento, historia.
yawn [jɔːn] *n* bostezo // *vi* bostezar.

yd. *abbr of* **yard(s).**

year [jɪə*] *n* año; **to be 8 ~s old** tener 8 años; **~ly** *a* anual // *ad* anualmente, cada año.

yearn [jɔːn] *vi*: **to ~ for sth** añorar *o* suspirar por algo; **~ing** *n* ansia, añoranza.

yeast [jiːst] *n* levadura.

yell [jɛl] *n* grito, alarido // *vi* gritar.

yellow ['jɛləu] *a, n* amarillo.

yelp [jɛlp] *n* aullido // *vi* aullar.

yeoman ['jəumən] *n*: **Y ~ of the Guard** alabardero de la Casa Real.

yes [jɛs] *ad, n* sí *m*.

yesterday ['jɛstədɪ] *ad, n* ayer *m*.

yet [jɛt] *ad* todavía // *conj* sin embargo, a pesar de todo; **it is not finished ~** todavía no está acabado; **the best ~** el mejor hasta ahora; **as ~** hasta ahora, todavía.

yew [juː] *n* tejo.

Yiddish ['jɪdɪʃ] *n* judío.

yield [jiːld] *n* producción *f*; (AGR) cosecha; (COMM) rendimiento // *vt* (*gen*) producir; (*profit*) rendir // *vi* rendirse, ceder.

yoga ['jəugə] *n* yoga.

yog(h)ourt, yog(h)urt ['jəugət] *n* yogur *m*.

yoke [jəuk] *n* (*of oxen*) yunta; (*on shoulders*) balancín *m*; (*fig*) yugo // *vt* acoplar.

yolk [jəuk] *n* yema (de huevo).

yonder ['jɔndə*] *ad* allá (a lo lejos).

you [juː] *pron* tú; (*pl*) vosotros; (*polite form*) usted; (: *pl*) ustedes; (*complement*) te; (: *pl*) os; (*after prep*) tí; (: *pl*) vosotros; (: *formal*) le/la; (: *pl*) les; (*after prep*) usted; (: *pl*) ustedes; (*one*): **~ never know** uno nunca sabe; (*impersonal*): **~ can't do that** eso no se hace.

you'd [juːd] = **you had; you would.**

you'll [juːl] = **you will, you shall.**

young [jʌŋ] *a* joven // *npl* (*of animal*) la cría *sg*; (*people*): **the ~** los jóvenes, la juventud *sg*; **~er** *a* (*brother etc*) menor; **~ish** *a* bastante joven; **~ster** *n* joven *m/f*.

your [jɔː*] *a* tu; (*pl*) vuestro; (*formal*) su.

you're [juə*] = **you are.**

yours [jɔːz] *pron* tuyo; (: *pl*) vuestro; (*formal*) suyo; **is it ~?** ¿es tuyo *etc*?; **~ sincerely** *or* **faithfully** le saluda atentamente.

yourself [jɔːˈsɛlf] *pron* (*reflexive*) tú mismo; (*complement*) te; (*after prep*) tí (mismo); (*formal*) usted mismo; (: *complement*) se; (: *after prep*) sí (mismo); **yourselves** *pl pron* vosotros mismos; (*after prep*) vosotros (mismos); (*formal*) ustedes (mismos); (: *complement*) se; (: *after prep*) sí mismos.

youth [juːθ] *n* juventud *f*; (*young man*: *pl* **~s** [juːðz]) joven *m*; **~ful** *a* juvenil; **~ hostel** *n* albergue *m* de juventud.

you've [juːv] = **you have.**

Yugoslav ['juːgəuˈslɑːv] *a, n* yugoeslavo/a; **~ia** *n* Yugoeslavia.

Yuletide ['juːltaɪd] *n* Navidad *f*.

Z

zany ['zeɪnɪ] *a* tonto.

zeal [ziːl] *n* celo, entusiasmo; **~ous** ['zɛləs] *a* celoso, entusiasta.

zebra ['ziːbrə] *n* cebra; **~ crossing** *n* paso de peatones.

zenith ['zɛnɪθ] *n* cénit *m*.

zero ['zɪərəu] *n* cero.

zest [zɛst] *n* ánimo, vivacidad *f*.

zigzag ['zɪgzæg] *n* zigzag *m* // *vi* zigzaguear.

zinc [zɪŋk] *n* cinc *m*, zinc *m*.

Zionism ['zaɪənɪzm] *n* sionismo; **Zionist** *n* sionista *m/f*.

zip [zip] *n* (*also*: **~ fastener, ~per**) cremallera // *vt* (*also*: **~ up**) cerrar la cremallera de.

zodiac ['zəudɪæk] *n* zodiaco.

zombie ['zɔmbɪ] *n* (*fig*): **like a ~** como un sonámbulo.

zone [zəun] *n* zona.

zoo [zuː] *n* (jardín *m*) zoológico.

zoological [zuəˈlɔdʒɪkl] *a* zoológico.

zoologist [zuˈɔlədʒɪst] *n* zoólogo.

zoology [zuːˈɔlədʒɪ] *n* zoología.

zoom [zuːm] *vi*: **to ~ past** pasar zumbando; **~ lens** *n* zoom *m*.

SPANISH VERB TABLES

1 Gerund. *2* Imperative. *3* Present. *4* Preterite. *5* Future. *6* Present subjunctive. *7* Imperfect subjunctive. *8* Past participle. *9* Imperfect.
Etc indicates that the irregular root is used for all persons of the tense, e.g. **oír**: *6* oiga, oigas, oigamos, oigáis, oigan.

acertar *2* acierta *3* acierto, aciertas, acierta, aciertan *6* acierte, aciertes, acierte, acierten

acordar *2* acuerda *3* acuerdo, acuerdas, acuerda, acuerdan *6* acuerde, acuerdes, acuerde, acuerden

advertir *1* advirtiendo *2* advierte *3* advierto, adviertes, advierte, advierten *4* advirtió, advirtieron *6* advierta, adviertas, advierta, advirtamos, advirtáis, adviertan *7* advirtiera *etc*

agradecer *3* agradezco *6* agradezca *etc*

aparecer *3* aparezco *6* aparezca *etc*

aprobar *2* aprueba *3* apruebo, apruebas, aprueba, aprueban *6* apruebe, apruebes, apruebe, aprueben

atravesar *2* atraviesa *3* atravieso, atraviesas, atraviesa, atraviesan *6* atraviese, atravieses, atraviese, atraviesen

caber *3* quepo *4* cupe, cupiste, cupo, cupimos, cupisteis, cupieron *5* cabré *etc* *6* quepa *etc* *7* cupiera *etc*

caer *1* cayendo *3* caigo *4* cayó, cayeron *6* caiga *etc* *7* cayera *etc*

calentar *2* calienta *3* caliento, calientas, calienta, calientan *6* caliente, calientes, caliente, calienten

cerrar *2* cierra *3* cierro, cierras, cierra, cierran *6* cierre, cierres, cierre, cierren

COMER *1* comiendo *2* come, comed *3* como, comes, come, comemos, coméis, comen *4* comí, comiste, comió, comimos, comisteis, comieron *5* comeré, comerás, comerá, comeremos, comeréis, comerán *6* coma, comas, coma, comamos, comáis, coman *7* comiera, comieras, comiera, comiéramos, comierais, comieran *8*

comido *9* comía, comías, comía, comíamos comíais, comían

conocer *3* conozco *6* conozca *etc*

contar *2* cuenta *3* cuento, cuentas, cuenta, cuentan *6* cuente, cuentes, cuente, cuenten

costar *2* cuesta *3* cuesto, cuestas, cuesta, cuestan *6* cueste, cuestes, cueste, cuesten

dar *3* doy *4* di, diste, dio, dimos, disteis, dieron *7* diera *etc*

decir *2* di *3* digo *4* dije, dijiste, dijo, dijimos, dijisteis, dijeron *5* diré *etc* *6* diga *etc* *7* dijera *etc* *8* dicho

despertar *2* despierta *3* despierto, despiertas, despierta, despiertan *6* despierte, despiertes, despierte, despierten

divertir *1* divirtiendo *2* divierte *3* divierto, diviertes, divierte, divierten *4* divirtió, divirtieron *6* divierta, diviertas, divierta, divirtamos, divirtáis, diviertan *7* divirtiera *etc*

dormir *1* durmiendo *2* duerme *3* duermo, duermes, duerme, duermen *4* durmió, durmieron *6* duerma, duermas, duerma, durmamos, durmáis, duerman *7* durmiera *etc*

empezar *2* empieza *3* empiezo, empiezas, empieza, empiezan *4* empecé *6* empiece, empieces, empiece, empecemos, empecéis, empiecen

entender *2* entiende *3* entiendo, entiendes, entiende, entienden *6* entienda, entiendas, entienda, entiendan

ESTAR *2* está *3* estoy, estás, está, están *4* estuve, estuviste, estuvo, estuvimos, estuvisteis, estuvieron *6* esté, estés, esté, estén *7* estuviera *etc*

HABER *3* he, has, ha, hemos, han *4* hube, hubiste, hubo, hubimos, hubisteis, hubieron *5* habré *etc 6* haya *etc 7* hubiera *etc*

HABLAR *1* hablando *2* habla, hablad *3* hablo, hablas, habla, hablamos, habláis, hablan *4* hablé hablaste, habló, hablamos, hablasteis, hablaron *5* hablaré, hablarás, hablará, hablaremos, hablaréis, hablarán *6* hable, hables, hable, hablemos, habléis, hablen *7* hablara, hablaras, hablara, habláramos, hablarais, hablaran *8* hablado *9* hablaba, hablabas, hablaba, hablábamos, hablabais, hablaban

hacer *2* haz *3* hago *4* hice, hiciste, hizo, hicimos, hicisteis, hicieron *5* haré *etc 6* haga *etc 7* hiciera *etc 8* hecho

instruir *1* instruyendo *2* instruye *3* instruyo, instruyes, instruye, instruyen *4* instruyó, instruyeron *6* instruya *etc 7* instruyera *etc*

ir *1* yendo *2* ve *3* voy, vas, va, vamos, vais, van *4* fui, fuiste, fue, fuimos, fuisteis, fueron *6* vaya, vayas, vaya, vayamos, vayáis, vayan *7* fuera *etc 8* iba, ibas, iba, íbamos, ibais, iban

jugar *2* juega *3* juego, juegas, juega, juegan *4* jugué *6* juegue *etc*

leer *1* leyendo *4* leyó, leyeron *7* leyera *etc*

morir *1* muriendo *2* muere *3* muero, mueres, muere, mueren *4* murió, murieron *6* muera, mueras, muera, muramos, muráis, mueran *7* muriera *etc 8* muerto

mostrar *2* muestra *3* muestro, muestras, muestra, muestran *6* muestre, muestres, muestre, muestren

mover *2* mueve *3* muevo, mueves, mueve, mueven *6* mueva, muevas, mueva, muevan

negar *2* niega *3* niego, niegas, niega, niegan *4* negué *6* niegue, niegues, niegue, neguemos, neguéis, nieguen

ofrecer *3* ofrezco *6* ofrezca *etc*

oír *1* oyendo *2* oye *3* oigo, oyes, oye, oyen *4* oyó, oyeron *6* oiga *etc 7* oyera *etc*

oler *2* huele *3* huelo, hueles, huele, huelen *6* huela, huelas, huela, huelan

parecer *3* parezco *6* parezca *etc*

pedir *1* pidiendo *2* pide *3* pido, pides, pide, piden *4* pidió, pidieron *6* pida *etc 7* pidiera *etc*

pensar *2* piensa *3* pienso, piensas, piensa, piensan *6* piense, pienses, piense, piensen

perder *2* pierde *3* pierdo, pierdes, pierde, pierden *6* pierda, pierdas, pierda, pierdan

poder *1* pudiendo *2* puede *3* puedo, puedes, puede, pueden *4* pude, pudiste, pudo, pudimos, pudisteis, pudieron *5* podré *etc 6* pueda, puedas, pueda, puedan *7* pudiera *etc*

poner *2* pon *3* pongo *4* puse, pusiste, puso, pusimos, pusisteis, pusieron *5* pondré *etc 6* ponga *etc 7* pusiera *etc 8* puesto

preferir *1* prefiriendo *2* prefiere *3* prefiero, prefieres, prefiere, prefieren *4* prefirió, prefirieron *6* prefiera, prefieras, prefiera, prefiramos, prefiráis, prefieran *7* prefiriera *etc*

querer *2* quiere *3* quiero, quieres, quiere, quieren *4* quise, quisiste, quiso, quisimos, quisisteis, quisieron *5* querré *etc 6* quiera, quieras, quiera, quieran *7* quisiera *etc*

reír *2* ríe *3* río, ríes, ríe, ríen *4* rio, rieron *6* ría, rías, ría, riamos, riáis, rían *7* riera *etc*

repetir *1* repitiendo *2* repite *3* repito, repites, repite, repiten *4* repitió, repitieron *6* repita *etc 7* repitiera *etc*

rogar *2* ruega *3* ruego, ruegas, ruega, ruegan *4* rogué *6* ruegue, ruegues, ruegue, roguemos, roguéis, rueguen

saber *3* sé *4* supe, supiste, supo, supimos, supisteis, supieron *5* sabré *etc 6* sepa *etc 7* supiera *etc*

salir *2* sal *3* salgo *5* saldré *etc 6* salga *etc*

seguir *1* siguiendo *2* sigue *3* sigo, sigues, sigue, siguen *4* siguió, siguieron *6* siga *etc 7* siguiera *etc*

sentar *2* sienta *3* siento, sientas,

sienta, sientan *6* siente, sientes, siente, sienten

sentir *1* sintiendo *2* siente *3* siento, sientes, siente, sienten *4* sintió, sintieron *6* sienta, sientas, sienta, sintamos, sintáis, sientan *7* sintiera *etc*

SER *2* sé *3* soy, eres, es, somos, sois, son *4* fui, fuiste, fue, fuimos, fuisteis, fueron *6* sea *etc* *7* fuera *etc* *9* era, eras, era, éramos, erais, eran

servir *1* sirviendo *2* sirve *3* sirvo, sirves, sirve, sirven *4* sirvió, sirvieron *6* sirva *etc* *7* sirviera *etc*

soñar *2* sueña *3* sueño, sueñas, sueña, sueñan *6* sueñe, sueñes, sueñe, sueñen

tener *2* ten *3* tengo, tienes, tiene, tienen *4* tuve, tuviste, tuvo, tuvimos, tuvisteis, tuvieron *5* tendré *etc* *6* tenga *etc* *7* tuviera *etc*

traer *1* trayendo *3* traigo *4* traje, trajiste, trajo, trajimos, trajisteis, trajeron *6* traiga *etc* *7* trajera *etc*

valer *2* val *3* valgo *5* valdré *etc* *6* valga *etc*

venir *2* ven *3* vengo, vienes, viene, vienen *4* vine, viniste, vino, vinimos, vinisteis, vinieron *5* vendré *etc* *6* venga *etc* *7* viniera *etc*

ver *3* veo *6* vea *etc* *8* visto *9* veía *etc*

vestir *1* vistiendo *2* viste *3* visto, vistes, viste, visten *4* vistió, vistieron *6* vista *etc* *7* vistiera *etc*

VIVIR *1* viviendo *2* vive, vivid *3* vivo, vives, vive, vivimos, vivís, viven *4* viví, viviste, vivió, vivimos, vivisteis, vivieron *5* viviré, vivirás, vivirá, viviremos, viviréis, vivirán *6* viva, vivas, viva, vivamos, viváis, vivan *7* viviera, vivieras, viviera, viviéramos, vivierais, vivieran *8* vivido *9* vivía, vivías, vivía, vivíamos, vivíais, vivían

volver *2* vuelve *3* vuelvo, vuelves, vuelve, vuelven *6* vuelva, vuelvas, vuela, vuelvan *8* vuelto.

VERBOS IRREGULARES EN INGLÉS

present	pt	pp	present	pt	pp
arise	arose	arisen	eat	ate	eaten
awake	awoke	awaked	fall	fell	fallen
be (am,	was,	been	feed	fed	fed
is, are;	were		feel	felt	felt
being)			fight	fought	fought
bear	bore	born(e)	find	found	found
beat	beat	beaten	flee	fled	fled
become	became	become	fling	flung	flung
befall	befell	befallen	fly	flew	flown
begin	began	begun	forbid	forbade	forbidden
behold	beheld	beheld	forecast	forecast	forecast
bend	bent	bent	forget	forgot	forgotten
beset	beset	beset	forgive	forgave	forgiven
bet	bet,	bet,	forsake	forsook	forsaken
	betted	betted	freeze	froze	frozen
bid	bid	bid	get	got	got, (US)
bind	bound	bound			gotten
bite	bit	bitten	give	gave	given
bleed	bled	bled	go	went	gone
blow	blew	blown	(goes)		
break	broke	broken	grind	ground	ground
breed	bred	bred	grow	grew	grown
bring	brought	brought	hang	hung,	hung,
build	built	built		hanged	hanged
burn	burnt,	burnt,	have	had	had
	burned	burned	hear	heard	heard
burst	burst	burst	hide	hid	hidden
buy	bought	bought	hit	hit	hit
can	could	(been able)	hold	held	held
cast	cast	cast	hurt	hurt	hurt
catch	caught	caught	keep	kept	kept
choose	chose	chosen	kneel	knelt,	knelt,
cling	clung	clung		kneeled	kneeled
come	came	come	know	knew	known
cost	cost	cost	lay	laid	laid
creep	crept	crept	lead	led	led
cut	cut	cut	lean	leant,	leant,
deal	dealt	dealt		leaned	leaned
dig	dug	dug	leap	leapt,	leapt,
do (3rd	did	done		leaped	leaped
person;			learn	learnt,	learnt,
he/she/				learned	learned
it/does)			leave	left	left
draw	drew	drawn	lend	lent	lent
dream	dreamed,	dreamed,	let	let	let
	dreamt	dreamt	lie	lay	lain
drink	drank	drunk	(lying)		
drive	drove	driven	light	lit,	lit,
dwell	dwelt	dwelt		lighted	lighted

present	pt	pp	present	pt	pp
lose	lost	lost	speed	sped,	sped,
make	made	made		speeded	speeded
may	might	—	spell	spelt,	spelt,
mean	meant	meant		spelled	spelled
meet	met	met	spend	spent	spent
mistake	mistook	mistaken	spill	spilt,	spilt,
mow	mowed	mown,		spilled	spilled
		mowed	spin	spun	spun
must	(had to)	(had to)	spit	spat	spat
pay	paid	paid	split	split	split
put	put	put	spoil	spoiled,	spoiled,
quit	quit,	quit,		spoilt	spoilt
	quitted	quitted	spread	spread	spread
read	read	read	spring	sprang	sprung
rend	rent	rent	stand	stood	stood
rid	rid	rid	steal	stole	stolen
ride	rode	ridden	stick	stuck	stuck
ring	rang	rung	sting	stung	stung
rise	rose	risen	stink	stank	stunk
run	ran	run	stride	strode	strode
saw	sawed	sawn	strike	struck	struck,
say	said	said			stricken
see	saw	seen	strive	strove	striven
seek	sought	sought	swear	swore	sworn
sell	sold	sold	sweep	swept	swept
send	sent	sent	swell	swelled	swollen,
set	set	set			swelled
shake	shook	shaken	swim	swam	swum
shall	should	—	swing	swung	swung
shear	sheared	shorn,	take	took	taken
		sheared	teach	taught	taught
shed	shed	shed			
shine	shone	shone	tear	tore	torn
shoot	shot	shot	tell	told	told
show	showed	shown	think	thought	thought
shrink	shrank	shrunk	throw	threw	thrown
shut	shut	shut	thrust	thrust	thrust
sing	sang	sung	tread	trod	trodden
sink	sank	sunk	wake	woke,	woken,
sit	sat	sat		waked	waked
slay	slew	slain	wear	wore	worn
sleep	slept	slept	weave	wove,	woven,
slide	slid	slid		weaved	weaved
sling	slung	slung	wed	wedded,	wedded,
slit	slit	slit		wed	wed
smell	smelt,	smelt,	weep	wept	wept
	smelled	smelled	win	won	won
sow	sowed	sown,	wind	wound	wound
		sowed	wring	wrung	wrung
speak	spoke	spoken	write	wrote	written

NOTES TO THE USER OF THIS DICTIONARY

I Using the dictionary

II Notes on Spanish grammar

III Spanish verb conjugations

IV The sounds of Spanish

V The time, dates and numbers

I. Using the dictionary

In using this book, you will either want to check the meaning of a Spanish word you don't know, or find the Spanish for an English word. These two operations are quite different, and so are the problems you may face when using one side of the dictionary or the other. In order to help you, we have tried to explain below the main features of this book.

The 'wordlist' is the alphabetical list of all the items in large bold type, i.e. all the 'headwords'. Each 'entry', or article, is introduced by a headword, and may contain additional 'references' in smaller bold type, such as phrases, derivatives, and compound words. Section 1. below deals with the way references are listed.

The typography distinguishes between three broad categories of text within the dictionary. All items in bold type, large or small, are 'source language' references, for which an equivalent in the other language is provided. All items in standard type are translations. Items in italics are information about the words being translated, i.e. either labels, or 'signposts' pinpointing the appropriate translation, or explanations.

1. *Where to look for a word*

1.1 Derivatives

In order to save space, a number of derivatives have been listed within entries, provided this does not break alphabetical order. Thus, **laborar, laborioso,** and **laborista** are listed under the entry for **labor,** and **caller** and **calling** under **call.** You must remember this when looking for a word you don't find listed as a headword. These derivatives are always listed last within an entry (see also I.2 on entry layout).

1.2 Homographs

Homographs are words which are spelt in exactly the same way, like **pago** (payment) and **pago** (district), or **hacha** (axe) and **hacha** (torch). As a rule, in order to save space, such words have been treated under one headword only. In the very few cases where this was not possible, the presence of a feminine form helps distinguish between two consecutive homograph entries (e.g. **rapaz** and **rapaz, -a**).

1.3 Phrases

Because of the constraints of space, there can be only a limited number of idiomatic phrases in a pocket dictionary like this one. Particular emphasis is given to verbal phrases like **sacar a luz, dar a luz, dar una vuelta, dar vueltas, estar de vuelta**, etc, and also to basic constructions (see the entries for **apply, agree, ponerse, deber, dar**). Verbal phrases with the ten or so basic verbs (ser, estar, poner etc.) are listed under the noun. Other phrases and idioms are listed under the first key word, for instance **de antemano** under **antemano, no obstante** under **obstante**.

1.4 Abbreviations and proper names

For easier reference, abbreviations, acronyms and proper names have been listed alphabetically in the wordlist, as opposed to being relegated to the appendices. **M.O.T.** is used in every way like **certificate** or **permit, OVNI** like **objeto**, and these words are treated like other nouns.

1.5 Compounds

Housewife, smoke screen, caja fuerte and **lámpara de pie** are all compounds. One-word compounds like 'housewife' are not a problem when consulting the dictionary, since they can appear only in one place and in strict alphabetical order. When it comes to other compounds, however – hyphenated compounds and compounds made up of separate words – each language presents its own peculiar problems.

1.5.1 Spanish compounds

There are many compounds made up of two or more 'words'. When checking a Spanish compound, you might not be aware that you are dealing with a compound and not a string of autonomous words, and there may inevitably be some toing and froing between entries.

As spelling is regular in Spanish, we have listed Spanish compounds under the first word, and grouped them alphabetically within that entry. For instance, **cama de matrimonio** is within the entry for **cama** and comes before the headword **camada. Tos ferina** comes before the headword **tosco**, in the entry for **tos**. Remember that the meaning of a phrase or of a compound can be quite different from that of its elements taken separately, so be prepared to check through an entry thoroughly before giving up.

1.5.2 English compounds

Here there is a problem of where to find a compound because of less predictable spelling than is the case with Spanish: is it **airgun, air-gun** or **air gun**? This is why we choose to list them according to strict alphabetical order. Thus **coal field** and **coalman** are separated by **coalition**. The entries between **tax** and **technical** will provide a good illustration of the system of listing. It has drawbacks, for instance in that **tax-free** and **tax-payer** are separated by **taxi, taxidermist** and three 'taxi' compounds. However, in a short dictionary used by beginners, it has the merit of simplicity and consistency.

1.5.3 English 'phrasal verbs'

'Phrasal verbs' are verbs like **go off, blow up, cut down** etc. Here you have the advantage of knowing that these words belong together, whereas it will take the foreign user some time before he can identify these verbs immediately. They have been listed under the entry for the basic verb (e.g. **go, blow, cut**), grouped alphabetically before any other derivative or compound — for instance, **pull up** comes before **pulley**. (See also **to back out, to look up** (a word), **to look out**.)

1.6 Irregular forms

When looking up a Spanish word, you may not immediately find the form you are looking for, although the word in question has been duly entered in the dictionary. This is possibly because you are looking up an irregular noun or verb form, and these are not always given as entries in their own right.

We have assumed that you know basic Spanish grammar. Thus you will be expected to know that 'cantan' is a form of the verb **cantar,** 'luces' the plural of **luz** and so on. However, in order to help you, we have included the main irregular forms as entries in their own right, with a cross-reference to the basic form. Thus, if you come across the word 'fui' and attempt to look up a verb 'fuir', you won't find it, but what you will find between **fuga** and **fulano,** is the entry **fui** *vb ver* **ser, ir.** Similarly **hizo, hecho** etc.

With past participles, it sometimes happens that in addition to the purely verbal form there is an adjectival or noun use, for instance **herido** or **bendito.** These usages are translated as autonomous words, but they are also cross-referred to the verb whenever appropriate (see for instance entries for **abierto** or **muerto**).

2. *Entry layout*

All entries, however long or complex, are arranged systematically. But it may be a little difficult at first to find one's way through an entry like Spanish **parte**, or English **back, round** or **run** because homographs are grouped under the same entry (see 1.2) and the text is run on without any breakdown into paragraphs, in order to save space. Ease of reference comes with practice, but the guidelines below will make it easier for you.

2.1 'Signposting'

If you look up a Spanish word and find a string of quite different English translations, you are unlikely to have much trouble finding out which is the relevant one for the context, because you know what the English words mean, and the context will almost automatically rule out unsuitable translations. It is quite a different matter when you want to find the Spanish for, say, **lock**, in the context 'we got to the lock around lunchtime', and are faced with an entry that reads 'lock: cerradura; esclusa; mechón *m*.' You can of course go to the other side and check what each translation means. But this is time-consuming, and it doesn't always work. This is why we have provided the user with signposts which pinpoint the relevant translation. For instance with **lock**, the entry reads: ... (*of door, box*) cerradura; (*of canal*) esclusa; (*of hair*) mechón *m* ... For the context suggested above, it is now clear that 'esclusa' is the right word.

2.2 Grammatical categories and meaning categories

Complex entries are first broken down into grammatical categories, e.g.: **lock** *m // vt // vi*. Be prepared to go through entries like **run** or **back** carefully, and you will find how useful all these 'signposts' are. Each grammatical category is then split where appropriate into the various meanings, e.g.:

> **lock** *n* (*of door, box*) cerradura; (*of canal*) esclusa; (*of hair*) mechón *m* // *vt* (*with key*) cerrar con llave; (*immobilize*) inmovilizar // *vi* (*door etc*) cerrarse con llave; (*wheels*) bloquearse, trabarse.

3. *Using the translations*

3.1 Gender

Feminine endings for Spanish adjectives ending in -o have not been given on the English-Spanish side, but endings for other adjectives are shown: 'charming *a* encantador(a)'; 'Danish *a* danés(esa)'; 'German *a* alemán(ana)'. This may appear to duplicate information given in the Spanish-English side of the dictionary, but we feel it is a useful reminder where and when it matters. The feminine form is also given for words like **teacher, researcher** etc.

3.2 Plurals

Information on the formation of plurals in Spanish, including the plural of compounds is given in section II. Most plural forms in Spanish are regular and are not shown, but where a problem could arise, the plural is shown beside the headword on the Spanish side, e.g. **carácter,** *pl* **caracteres.** We have shown when the translation of a word used in the singular is plural; see for instance **hair, jealousy, offal.**

3.3 Verb forms

Irregular Spanish verbs appearing as translations have not been marked as such, and the user should refer to the Spanish verb tables when in doubt (pp. 400–402).

3.4 Colloquial language

You should as a rule proceed with great caution when handling foreign language which has a degree of informality. When an English word or phrase has been labelled *(col)*, i.e. colloquial, you must assume that the translation belongs to a similar level of informality. If the translation is followed by (!) you should use it with extreme care, or better still avoid it unless you are with close friends!

3.5 'Grammatical words'

It is exceedingly difficult to give adequate treatment for words like **for, away, whose, which, out, off** etc. in a short dictionary such as this one. We have tried to go some way towards providing as much relevant information as possible about the most frequent uses of these words. However, for further information use a good monolingual dictionary of Spanish, and a good modern Spanish grammar.

3.6 'Approximate' translations and cultural equivalents

It is not always possible to give a genuine translation, when for instance an English word denotes a thing or institution which either doesn't exist in Spain, or is quite different. Therefore, only an approximate equivalent

411

can be given, or else an explanation. See for instance **whip, shadow cabinet**, and on the Spanish-English side **gazpacho, doña.**

3.7 Alternative translations

As a rule, translations separated by commas can be regarded as broadly interchangeable for the meaning indicated. Translations separated by a semi-colon are not interchangeable and when in doubt you should consult either a larger bilingual dictionary such as the Collins Spanish Dictionary, or a good monolingual Spanish dictionary. You will find however that there are very few cases of translations separated by a semi-colon without an intervening 'signpost'.

II. Notes on Spanish grammar

Although a relatively easy language to learn, Spanish may seem very different from English when you first meet it in school or hear a Spanish speaker talk. Certainly the order of words and the way a Spaniard says certain things will be strange (in fact a general feeling might be that everything is the wrong way round), but if you were to compare it to languages like Arabic, Swahili or Chinese, you would soon recognize that the basic structure and pattern of Spanish is quite close to English.

We have tried here to show some of these differences, especially with the beginner and the dictionary user in mind, without dwelling on subtleties or the aspects of Spanish which are broadly similar to English. Among the greatest obstacles for the beginner are gender, verb forms and tenses, the position of adjectives, the uses of prepositions and of course, in a few cases, the sounds of Spanish (although once you have mastered each sound it is arguably one of the easiest languages to speak and understand). There are of course many more differences, some of which take us into the realm of style etc., but this is beyond the scope of this introduction.

1. *Nouns and 'satellite' words (i.e. articles, adjectives etc.)*

1.1   Gender

Note the basic difference: 'the table and the knife', but '*la* mesa y *el* cuchillo'. Gender can usually be determined by the ending of the word: 'mesa' ends in *a* and is feminine; 'cuchillo' ends in *o* and is masculine. Certain endings are always one gender, e.g. -ción is always feminine and -tor masculine. Otherwise you just have to learn the genders in each case. What *is* important, however, is that you get the article right and also the agreement of adjectives and past participles: '*un* hombre alto con *la* nariz torcida'. See also 1.4 (possessive adjectives).

413

1.2   Articles: *'el, la, lo; un; del'* etc.

Apart from the problem of gender, there is the question of whether the article is used or not, and Spanish does not always follow the English pattern. For instance, you say 'I like wine', but the Spanish say 'me gusta el vino'. Conversely, 'my father is a mechanic', but 'mi padre es mecánico'.

1.2.1   *'el, la, lo; los, las'*

(a)   In almost all cases where 'the' is not used in English, the article must be used in Spanish. For instance:

apples are good for you   las manzanas son buenas para la salud
salmon is expensive   el salmón es caro

patience is a virtue   la paciencia es una virtud
I don't like fighting   no me gustan las peleas

N.B.   With names of countries, Spanish is gradually losing the habit of using the article, but you may still find a few cases where it persists:

e.g.   el Canadá, el Japón, la China.

(b)   Use of 'el/la' with parts of the body

Where the possessive is used in English, 'el/la' tends to be used in Spanish (often in conjunction with a pronoun):

I've twisted my ankle   me he torcido el tobillo
Put up your hand   levante la mano
My nose is bleeding   me está sangrando la nariz

(c)   'a + el; de + el'

Remember the contracted forms (shown in the dictionary under a and de):
voy al cine; vengo del huerto

(d)   'lo'

Spanish also has a neuter gender: 'lo' is often used with an adjective to express general or abstract ideas, e.g. 'eso es lo bueno' (that's the good thing about it)

1.2.2 'un, una, uno; unos, unas'

(a) In structures like 'my father is a postman' (i.e. expressing occupation, nationality or rank), Spanish does not use the indefinite article:

my brother is a mechanic   mi hermano es mecánico
he's a Frenchman   es francés

(b) After negatives, the article 'un/una' is not used with unspecified nouns:

I don't have a car   no tengo coche
she went out without saying a word   ella salió sin decir palabra

(c) The form 'uno' is used either to express the number 'one' when a masculine noun is understood, or to express the neuter idea of 'one' (i.e. we, people)

how many cats have you? **One**   ¿cuántos gatos tiene? **Uno**
(whereas: he has only **one cat**   tiene sólo **un gato**)

when **one** thinks about it   cuando **uno** lo piensa

(d) 'unos/unas'

Remember to use the plural of the article, even though there may be no article in English:

friends from Madrid have arrived   **unos** amigos de Madrid han llegado

1.2.3 'some/any'

Unless 'some/any' expresses something specific, it is normally not translated in Spanish, especially after a negative:

me quedan **unas** pesetas   I have **some** pesetas left

BUT: ¿quiere usted patatas?   do you want *some/any* potatoes?
quiero pan   I want *some* bread
no tengo cigarillos   I haven't *any* cigarettes

1.3 Adjectives

Apart from the question of gender, the main difficulty is the position of adjectives. As a general rule, they follow the noun (las leyes físicas, una comida sabrosísima, unos guantes rojos). Some adjectives or types of adjectives will *always* go after the noun, especially if their meaning can only be literal (una casa desmoronada, las leyes físicas, un vestido rojo). Others can also go before the noun in a figurative sense or for stylistic effect (una sabrosísima comida).

Adjectives, however, which 'limit' rather than 'describe' (mucho, poco, demasiado, tanto, primero, último) always come in front of the noun.

Finally, many common adjectives like 'bueno, malo; grande, pequeño; viejo, joven; nuevo, antiguo; pobre, rico' and others like 'mismo, cierto' will be found before or after, but with different meanings: before the meaning is usually figurative, after it is literal (the dictionary makes these differences clear).

1.3.1 Remember that certain adjectives have a shortened masculine form before nouns: bueno, BUT: un buen hombre

1.4 Possessives:

1.4.1 'su/sus'

Since this form can be ambiguous (his, hers, its; yours, theirs), Spanish often substitutes 'el ... de él, de ella; de usted, de ellos':

e.g. their father   su padre: **el** padre **de ellos**

1.4.2 'el mío/la mía; los míos/las mías' etc.

The possessive pronouns vary according to the gender of the noun they qualify as well as the number:

¿de quién es este **coche**?   es mío   whose is this car?   it's mine.
aquí están las entradas; las tuyas costaron más   here are the tickets; yours cost more

1.5 Demonstratives: 'este, ese, aquel; esta, esa, aquella; esto' etc.

1.5.1

Demonstrative adjectives agree in gender and number with the noun they qualify. Spanish also has a neuter form for the pronouns 'this' and 'that'.

¿qué es **eso**? what's that? ¿qué es **esto**? what's this?

The main problem, however, is choosing between the three forms of demonstrative: the 'este' forms are straightforward and mean 'this'; the 'ese' forms mean 'that' in the sense of 'that nearby or near you'; the 'aquel' forms mean 'that yonder':

este libro **this** book
¿qué es **eso** que tienes en la mano? what is **that** you have (*there*) in your hand?
¿cómo se llaman **aquellas** montañas? what are **those** mountains called (*yonder*)?

1.6 Comparative and superlative: '*más ... que*' etc.

1.6.1

Generally you use '*más*' + *adjective* or *adverb* to form the comparative; the superlative is slightly more complicated because you use the definite article with the '*más*' and the article must agree in gender and number with the adjective. The superlative adverb is formed with '**lo**' + '*más*' + *adverb*.

más bonito/más frecuentemente   prettier/more frequently
esa cas*a* es l*a más* bonit*a*   that is the pretti*est house*
l*o más* frecuentemente   the *most* frequent*ly*

2. *Verbs*

This is one of the main areas of difficulty for English-speaking learners. There are four major problems. First, the variety of endings (hablo, hablamos etc.) and the number of irregular or 'semi-irregular' forms. Second, the difference in the formation of negative or interrogative phrases (no equivalent of 'do', 'did' etc., as in 'I didn't go; did you?'). Third, the difference in the use of tenses (e.g. two past tenses, imperfect and preterite). Fourth, the use of two verbs meaning 'to be' (ser, estar).

2.1 Verb forms

The verb tables on pp. 424 and 425 will give you the patterns for the main verb groups; irregular verb forms are shown on page 400. There is no substitute for practice on this, but try not to look upon these forms as a vast array of separate items to be learnt: there are two basic combining patterns, one relating to the person doing the action ('*I* speak vs *you* speak: habl*o*/habl*as*) and one relating to the tense (I *speak*/I *spoke*:

417

hablo/hablé). The present, perfect, imperfect, future and conditional will cater for most of your needs at first.

2.2   Negatives and questions

Although the simple negative 'no' is the same as English, most other negative words also need a 'no' in front when they follow the verb, but their meaning is not a 'double' negative:

no lo sé   I do *not* know
nunca lo sé   I *never* know
BUT: **no** lo sabía **nunca**   I *never* knew
ALSO: **no** lo sabe **nunca nadie**   *nobody ever* knows

The way Spanish forms questions is really a matter of the tone of voice in which the sentence is said and presents no real problem because we often use the same tone in English. When Spanish questions are written therefore, they need a special question mark at the beginning to warn you that it is a question:

es loco   he is mad
¿es loco?   is he mad?

2.3   Tenses

2.3.1

The Spanish equivalent to our continuous '-ing' form is just the same but you must remember to use the 'estar' verb 'to be' and not 'ser':

estoy ley*endo*   I am read*ing*
estaré ley*endo*   I shall be read*ing*

2.3.2

The perfect tense in English (I have done it) corresponds fairly closely to the Spanish (lo he hecho); but what seems to be a preterite in English (I did it) can in certain circumstances be translated by any of the three past tenses in Spanish (lo hice, lo he hecho, lo hacía). Basically it is a question of 'when' and 'how often'.

2.3.2.1   The imperfect

The 'imperfect' describes an action done repeatedly in the past or which went on for some time (often being a replacement for the continuous tense), e.g. lo hacían means 'they *used to* do it' or 'they *were* doing it', which is what the English preterite implies in a sentence such as 'they *did* it *all the time*'.

2.3.2.2.   The perfect

The perfect in Spanish describes an action which has been carried out recently, usually that day. Because it expresses recent time, it can therefore translate English 'preterites': such as 'they *did* it this morning' lo *han hecho* esta mañana.

2.3.2.3   The preterite

The preterite denotes completed actions in the more distant past and is more a tense of written Spanish, e.g. 'he *did* it yesterday/the day before lo *hizo* ayer/el día anterior.

2.3.3

Don't be surprised to see Spanish use a present tense instead of the future in phrases like 'I *shall go* tomorrow': me *voy* mañana.

2.3.4   The subjunctive: 'quiero que lo haga' *vs* 'sé que lo hace' etc.

Good command of both the present and imperfect subjunctive is necessary in order to speak good Spanish, but you can probably cover a lot of situations with just the present. Even without the subjunctive you would probably be understood, except that is with verbs like 'decir' where misunderstandings might arise, e.g. dígale que **venga** means 'tell him *to come*', but dígale que **viene** means 'tell him he *is coming*'.

It is not possible to give you all the rules governing the use of the subjunctive but here are a few basic ideas explaining its use:

(a)   The subjunctive is used to express a command when the polite form 'usted' is implied:
hágalo usted   you do it
lea esto   read this

(b)   The subjunctive is used in subordinate clauses when doubt, hypothesis and denial are expressed (i.e. it is not a fact):

dudo que lo tenga   I doubt if he has it
no creo que lo tenga   I don't believe he has it

(c) The best guide perhaps is to see whether the subjects of the clauses
change: if they do, then there will probably be a subjunctive.

I want *him* to do it   quiero que lo **haga** él
it is good for *him* to do it   es bueno que él lo **haga**

(d) It is also used for actions which are not yet facts.
until he comes   hasta que *venga*.

2.4   Spanish has two verbs 'to be': ser, estar.

2.4.1   *ser*

Ser means 'to exist' but it also covers the meanings of 'to be' which
express qualities or permanent states: 'es bueno'   he is good (always);
'es profesor'   he is a teacher. It is also used to form the passive tense:
'fui herido'   I was wounded.

2.4.2   *estar*

Estar means 'to be situated' or 'to be in a state of ...': ' ¿dónde está el
banco?'   where is the bank (situated)?; 'estaba herido'   I was (in a)
wounded (state); 'está sentado'   he is (in a) sitting down (state); 'está
bueno'   he is well.

3. *Prepositions*

Most prepositions present no problems. The main confusion will be
about when to use 'por' and when to use 'para' when translating English
'for'. Essentially, 'por' expresses *cause* or *reason* and 'para' expresses
purpose:

lo hizo *por* mí   he did it *for* me (because of me, for my sake)
¿*para* qué lo quieres?   what do you want it *for*?

'por' also expresses exchange: ¿cuánto me da *por* esto?   how much
will you give me *for* this?

3.1   Don't forget that many verbs in English are followed by
prepositions but they are usually contained in the Spanish verb: to go
up   'subir'; to sit *down*   'sentarse' etc.

420

4. Adverbs

Adverbs can be formed from most adjectives by taking the feminine form and adding '-mente': quick-ly rápida-mente; easi-ly fácil-mente. Spanish often uses idiomatic constructions, such as 'por lo general' (generally).

5. Pronouns: yo, te, le, sí etc.

5.1 Subject pronouns are not normally used in Spanish except for emphasis since the verb form tells you who is doing the action: hablo *I* speak; *él* lo tiene, *yo* no *he* has it, not *me*.

5.2 Pronoun table

	SUBJECT	REFLEX.	INDIRECT OBJECT	OBJECT	PREPOSITIONAL
I	yo	me	me	me	para mí/conmigo
you	tu	te	te	te	para ti/contigo
he	él	se	le (se)	le, lo	para él
she	ella	se	le (se)	le, la	para ella
it	(ello)	se		lo, la	para (ello)
you	usted	se	le (se)	le	para usted
we	nosotros/as	nos	nos	nos	para nosotros/as
you	vosotros/as	os	os	os	para vosotros/as
they	ellos	se	les (se)	les, los	para ellos
they	ellas	se	les (se)	les, las	para ellas

III. Spanish verb conjugations

1. The table of irregular verbs on p. 400 is self-explanatory. Unless stated otherwise, if one form only is given it is the first person singular; if two forms are given, they are the third person singular and plural; if four forms are shown, they are the first, second and third person singular plus the third person plural. Any forms not shown are regular and can be found by consulting the model verb tables below: table A for an infinitive ending in '-ar' and table B for infinitives ending in '-er' or '-ir'.

2. Do not forget to use the appropriate pronoun with reflexive verbs: *me* lavo, *te* lavaste, *se* había cortado.

3. 'Semi-irregular' verbs.
Some verbs appear to be irregular but they are in fact predictable with reference to the following guidelines:

   3.1   Because a 'c' or a 'g' in Spanish is pronounced differently depending on the vowel which follows, these letters will change in certain cases in order to maintain the original root sound:
   Roots ending in 'c': sac-ar, saqu-é; venc-er, venz-o; zurc-ir, zurz-o
   Roots ending in 'g': pag-ar, pagu-é; proteg-er, protej-o; fing-ir, finj-o
   Roots ending in 'qu' and 'gu': delinquir, delinco; averiguar, averigüé; distinguir, distingo
   Roots ending in 'z': cazar, cacé

   3.2   A root ending in 'i' or 'u' has to be strengthened by an accent when it takes the stress:
   'i' – confiar: confío, confías, confía, confiamos, confiais, confían
   'u' – situar: sitúo, sitúas, sitúa, situamos, situais, sitúan
   (N.B. there are exceptions, e.g. cambiar: cambio, cambias, cambia, etc.)

3.3.1   When a root ends in 'ñ', 'll' and 'ch' it will 'absorb' any unstressed 'i' which follows: thus 'gru*ñ* + *i*endo' becomes 'gru*ñ*endo', 'gru*ñ* + *i*ó' 'gru*ñ*ó'.

3.3.2   The opposite happens when the root is a vowel itself: when an unstressed 'i' follows, it is strengthened into a 'y', e.g. '*o* + *i*endo' becomes '*o*yendo', 'arg*ü* + *i*endo' 'arg*u*yendo'.

3.4   Spanish also has what are called 'root-changing' verbs, where the vowel within the root becomes a diphthong when stressed: e>ie; o>ue. The common verbs like 'acertar' and 'acordar' are already in the verb tables, but be prepared for other verbs to follow this model, e.g. fregar *friego*; doler *duele*.

4. The 'compound tenses' are formed as follows:
Indicative:
(a)   'perfect': *present* of 'haber' + *past participle* (he hablado/comido)
(b)   'pluperfect': *imperfect* of 'haber' + *past participle* (había hablado/comido)
(c)   'future perfect': *future* of 'haber' + *past participle* (habré hablado/comido)
(d)   'conditional perfect': *conditional* of 'haber' + *past participle* (habría hablado/comido)

Subjunctive:
(a)   'perfect': *present subjunctive* of 'haber' + *past participle* (haya hablado/comido)
(b)   'pluperfect': *imperfect subjunctive* of 'haber' + *past participle* (hubiera/hubiese hablado)

5. The passive is formed by using the verb 'ser' + *past participle*. The past participle agrees in number and gender with the subject: la televisión *fue* inventad*a* en el año... television was invented in... (Note that Spanish often avoids the passive by using a reflexive construction: la televisión *se inventó* en el año...)

6. Irregular past participles not appearing in the verb tables are formed as follows:
abrir *abierto*; cubrir *cubierto*; escribir *escrito*; imprimir *impreso*; freír *frito*; romper *roto*.

7. Imperative forms:
The familiar imperative forms are found in the verb tables (tú, vosotros). The formal imperative (usted, ustedes) adopts the form of the subjunctive: habl*e* (usted); habl*en* (ustedes).

A. A regular '-ar' verb: 'hablar'

PRESENT: Indicative		Subjunctive	
habl	o as a amos áis an	habl	e es e emos éis en

IMPERFECT: Indicative		Subjunctive	
habl	aba abas aba ábamos ábais aban	habl	ara/ase aras/ases ara/ase áramos/ásemos arais/aseis aran/asen

PRETERITE	
habl	é aste ó amos asteis aron

FUTURE		CONDITIONAL	
hablar	é ás á emos éis án	hablar	ía ías ía íamos íais ían

IMPERATIVE: habla, hablad

PAST PARTICIPLE: hablado

GERUND: hablando

B. Regular '-er' and '-ir' verbs: 'com*er*' and 'part*ir*'

PRESENT: Indicative		Subjunctive	
com/part	o es e emos/imos éis/ís en	com/part	a as a amos áis an

IMPERFECT: Indicative		Subjunctive	
com/part	ía ías ía íamos íais ían	com/part	iera/iese ieras/ieses iera/iese iéramos/iésemos ierais/ieseis ieran/iesen

PRETERITE			
com/part	í iste ió imos isteis ieron		

FUTURE		CONDITIONAL	
comer/partir	é ás á emos éis án	comer/partir	ía ías ía íamos íais ían

IMPERATIVE: come/parte, comed/partid

PAST PARTICIPLE: comido/partido

GERUND: comiendo/partiendo

425

IV. The sounds of Spanish

Learning to pronounce Spanish well is, as with all foreign languages, largely a matter of adopting different 'speech habits' from those used in speaking English.

A 'foreign accent' results from using the sounds of one's own language to approximate the sounds of the foreign language. This is particularly tempting when the same letter or letters represent similar sounds in each language. For instance the letter 'i' is used in both Spanish and English, but to represent slightly different sounds in each, and many Spanish speakers are unable to pronounce it in the English manner. It is possible that many do not even realise that the English speaker uses a different sound from the Spanish — hence the typical Spanish pronunciation of 'it is' which to the English speaker sounds as if it were written 'eet eess'.

These are the main ways in which Spanish 'speech habits' differ from the English:

1. *Activity of the lips, tongue etc.*

When you first hear (or even just see) a Spaniard talking, your immediate impression will probably be one of great activity and speed. However the truth is that he/she is not necessarily talking any quicker, but merely using all the 'instruments' of speech (lips, tongue, cheeks, jaw, throat, etc.) to their fullest extent.

English-speakers, on the other hand, tend to be 'lazy' in the use of these instruments — lip position, especially, is fairly unimportant and as a result vowel sounds tend to merge together, whereas in Spanish the activity of the lips etc. means that every vowel sound is clearly distinct from every other.

2. *Fewer diphthongs*

A diphthong is a glide between two vowel sounds in the same syllable. In English there are few 'pure' vowel sounds and a great many diphthongs

427

instead. Although speakers of English may think they produce one vowel sound in the word 'day', in fact they use a diphthong, which in this instance is a glide between the vowels [e] and [ɪ] : [deɪ]. In Spanish the tension maintained in the lips, tongue and the mouth in general prevents diphthongs occurring, as the vowel sound is kept constant throughout. Hence the Spanish word corresponding to the above example, 'de', is pronounced with no final [ɪ] sound, but is phonetically represented thus: [de]. Spanish does have diphthongs, of course, but they are always a combination of two 'pure' vowel sounds.

3. Consonants

Consonants in Spanish are always given their full value (except in regional dialects). In English, consonants are often pronounced with a degree of laxness that can result in their becoming 'muted' but not entirely silent. In a relaxed pronunciation of a word such as 'hat', the 't' is often scarcely heard, or may even be replaced by a 'glottal stop' (a sort of 'stutter' in the throat, as in Cockney: bottle = bo'le). Hence a Spaniard sounds unmistakeably foreign to an English speaker if he 'over'-pronounces the 't' and 'l' in 'bottle' as if it were Spanish.

4. Stress

In English, each word has its own particular stress pattern – for instance, the two different stress patterns for the word 'escort' produces two different words, one a noun and one a verb (*an escort bureau; may I escort you*). This does not happen in Spanish because each word can only be stressed in one way, the rules for which are as follows:

(a) When a word ends in a *vowel* or in 'n' or 's', the *next to last* syllable is stressed: pat*a*ta, pat*a*tas, com*e*dia, c*o*me, c*o*men.

(b) When a word ends in a consonant *other* than 'n' or 's', the stress falls on the last syllable: par*e*d, habl*a*r, aud*a*z.

(c) Whenever these rules (a,b) are not applied, then an acute accent appears over the stressed vowel: hablar*á*, comi*ó*, geograf*í*a.

(d) Normally the same syllable is stressed in the plural as in the singular, so that accents may appear or disappear accordingly: c*a*rmen, c*á*rmenes; ingl*é*s, ingl*e*ses. There are two exceptions to this rule: car*á*cter, caract*e*res; r*é*gimen, reg*í*menes.

Pronunciation of the sounds of Spanish

I. Vowel

symbol	as in	hints on pronunciation
[a]	*a*mo	not as long as 'a' in English f*a*r
[æ]	am*a*nte	in a closed syllable (ending in a consonant) the 'a' is short, as in English 'b*a*t'
[e]	c*e*lo	like 'e' in the 'th*e*y' (or even 'a' in 'p*a*y') but without the 'y' sound
[ɛ]	g*e*nte	in a closed syllable the 'e' is short, as in English 'p*e*t'
[i]	m*i*na	as in English 'm*ea*n', 'mach*i*ne', but without slight 'y' sound
[o]	l*o*c*o*	as in English 'l*o*cal', but without slight 'w' sound
[ɔ]	c*o*ntr*o*l	in a closed syllable the 'o' is short as in English 'c*o*t'
[u]	m*u*la	as in English 'r*u*le', 'r*u*e', but without slight 'w' sound. It is silent after 'q' and in the groups 'gue', 'gui' unless marked with a diaeresis (argüir, averigüe).

II. Diphthongs

[ai]	ba*i*le, car*ay*	like the 'i' in English 'r*i*de'
[au]	fra*u*de	like the 'ou' in English 'sh*ou*t'
[eɪ]	p*ei*ne, r*ey*	like the 'ey' in English 'gr*ey*'
[eu]	d*eu*da	like 'ay' as in 'b*ay*' plus 'oo' as in 't*oo*', in rapid succession
[oɪ]	*oi*go, h*oy*	like the 'oy' in English 't*oy*'

III. Semiconsonants

[j]	b*i*en, *y*ugo	both '*i*' and '*y*' can stand for the sound 'y' in English 'yacht'
[w]	ag*u*a, f*u*era	the Spanish 'u' can also convey the 'w' sound of English

IV. Consonants

[b]	*v*oy, en*v*iar, *b*ola	'*b*' and '*v*' are pronounced the same in Spanish. Here at the beginning of a phrase, or after 'm' or 'n', they are pronounced like English 'b' in '*b*oy', em*b*er'
[ß]	hu*b*o, de *v*eras	in any other position they are pronounced like an English 'v' but with *both lips* and not lip and teeth together
[k]	*c*o*c*o, *c*al*c*ulo	'c' before 'a', 'o' or 'u' is pronounced as in English '*c*at'
[θ]	*c*ero, *c*inco	before 'e' or 'i' it is pronounced like 'th' in English '*th*ink'
[d]	*d*oy, bal*d*e	at the beginning of a phrase, or after 'l' or 'n', 'd' is pronounced as in English
[ð]	mo*d*o, Madri(*d*)	in any other position it is pronounced something like the 'th' in English '*th*e'; at the end of words it almost disappears
[g]	*g*ano, pon*g*o	'g' before 'a', 'o' or 'u' is pronounced as in English 'gap' if at the beginning of a phrase or after 'n'
[ɣ]	ha*g*a	'g' before 'a', 'o', 'u' but in median position and not after 'n' is pronounced more softly
[x]	*g*iro, *g*ente	before 'e' or 'i' it is pronounced as the Spanish 'j' below
[x]	*j*oven	'j' (and 'ge', 'gi') is similar to the 'ch' sound of Scottish 'lo*ch*' or Welsh 'ba*ch*'

[ʎ]	ca*ll*e, *ll*uvia	'll' is like the 'lli' in English 'mi*lli*on', but is being pronounced more and more like 'y' in '*ye*t'
[n]-[m]	e*n*viar	when followed by a 'v', an 'n' changes to 'm'
[ñ]	ca*ñ*a	something like the 'ni' in English 'o*ni*on
[k]	*qu*ien, *qu*ince	'q' is always followed by a silent 'u' and pronounced as 'k' in English '*k*ing'
[ʀ]	*r*ápido, co*rr*e	('r' is *always* pronounced in Spanish, unlike the often silent 'r' in English 'dance*r*'); after 'l', 'n' or 's', at the beginning of a phrase or when the 'r' is doubled, it is trilled something like a Scottish or Welsh 'r'
[s]	pa*s*a, ca*s*tillo	's' is usually pronounced as in English 'pa*ss*'
[z]	mi*s*mo, de*s*de	before 'b', 'd', 'g', 'l', 'm' or 'n' it sounds like the 's' in English 'ro*s*e'
[ks]	pró*x*imo	as in English 'pro*x*y'
[gs]	e*x*amen	like the 'gs' in 'pi*gs*kin
[s]	se*x*ta	before a consonant (and even in the other cases above) the 'x' is more and more being pronounced as an English 's' as in 'pe*s*t'
[i]	y	by itself the 'y' is pronounced as the Spanish 'i'
[θ]	*z*ona, lu*z*	like the 'th' in English '*th*ink' (but in many regions it will be pronounced as an 's')

Note that the 'h' is always silent in Spanish: 'haya' [ˈaja], 'ahora' [aˈɔra]

From Spelling to Sounds

1. Spanish is an *almost* 'phonetic' language, by which we mean that every vowel and consonant has a fixed sound value. As you will have seen from the previous list, this value changes for only a few letters, and even

431

then in only one alternative position: pon*go*; *ca*cé etc. Some letters also duplicate the same sound (i/y; b/v) or are not even pronounced (h).

If you look at the language in this manner, you will soon appreciate how simple it is to pronounce. There are only two important factors, therefore, which hinder this: first, the temptation (as with any foreign language) to see the language as if it were written in English, e.g. Spanish 'lee' [lee] might be seen as English 'lee' [li:]; and secondly, the related problem of knowing when two or more vowels *do* form a diphthong or are pronounced separately.

1.2.1   The solution to the first is always to look upon Spanish vowels as clearly distinct, individual sounds which are *always* pronounced.

1.2.2   The second is solved according to the following rules:

(a)   to start with, vowels are either *weak* or *strong*: 'i' and 'u' are weak, whereas 'a', 'e' and 'o' are strong.
(b)   a *weak* and *strong* combination forms a diphthong in which the stress falls on the *strong* vowel: b*a*ile, vu*e*stro, si*e*rra, p*e*ine, p*a*usa.
(c)   a *weak* and *weak* combination forms a diphthong and the stress falls on the *second* vowel: fu*i*, ru*i*do, vi*u*da.
(d)   a *strong* and *strong* combination remains as two separate vowels, and stress follows the normal rules (4a,b): ca-*e*r; cre-*e*r; cre-*e*; c*a*-os.
(e)   any word which is to be pronounced otherwise will carry an accent on the stressed vowel: ca*í*do, r*í*o, cre*í*, ba*ú*l.

2. The letters of the Spanish alphabet

When a Spaniard wishes to spell out a word he pronounces the letters like this:

a [a]	b [be]	c [θe]	ch [tʃe]	d [de]	e [e]
f [efe]	g [xe]	h [atʃe]	i [i]	j [xota]	k [ka]
l [ele]	ll [eʎe]	m [eme]	n [ene]	o [o]	p [pe]
q [ku]	r [ere]	rr [erre]	s [ese]	t [te]	u [u]
v [uße]	x [ekis]	y [iɣrjeɣa]	z [θeta]		

The letters are feminine and you therefore talk of 'una a' or 'la a'. 'Miguel se escribe con una *m* mayúscula'.

3. It is virtually impossible for a Spaniard to pronounce an 's' at the beginning of a word without an 'e' in front: this explains why English loan-words which are established in the language already are spelled with an 'e' (*e*snob), or why you will hear new additions *pronounced* with an 'e' though not written with one (slip = 'eslip').

V. The time

what is the time? ¿qué hora es?

it's... es... (*midnight, noon, 1 o'clock*), son... (*other times*)

00.00	*es* medianoche; *son* las doce (de la noche)
01.00	*es* la una (de la noche)
01.10	la una y diez
01.15	la una y cuarto
	la una y quince
01.30	la una y media
01.45	*son* las dos menos quarto
01.50	las dos menos diez
	la una cincuenta
02.00	*son* las dos
12.00	mediodía
	las doce (de la tarde)
13.00	la una
	las trece (horas)
18.00	las seis
	las dieciocho
22.30	las diez y media
	las veintidós horas y media

at what time? ¿a qué hora?

at one a la una

at 2.15 a las dos y cuarto

just after 3.00 a las tres y pico

about 4.30 hacia las cuatro y media

from 6.00 to 8.00 de seis a ocho

it's nearly 9.00 son casi las nueve

at 4.00 sharp a las cuatro en punto

Dates and numbers

1. The date

what is the date today? ¿qué día es hoy?

the first of May	el primero de mayo
the 2nd of March	el dos de marzo (*cardinals are used from 2nd to 31st*)
today is the 14th	hoy es catorce; estamos a catorce
on the 10th of June	el diez de junio
on Tuesday	el martes
on Tuesdays	los martes

from the 1st to the 3rd desde el día uno hasta el día tres

Letter headings: dates on Spanish letters are usually written thus:

22nd October, 1949   22 de octubre de 1949

Years:
1981	mil novecientos ochenta y uno
2000 B.C.	2000 a. de J.C. (= antes de Jesucristo)
70 A.D.	70 d. de J.C. (= después de Jesucristo)
in the 12th century	en el siglo doce
in the 1940s	durante los años cuarenta

2. Notes on numbers

Cardinals

(a) 'uno' (+ 'veintiuno' etc.) agrees in gender (but not number) with its noun: treinta y un*a* person*as*; the masculine form is shortened to 'un' unless it stands alone: veinti*ún* caballos, veinti*uno*

(b) 'cien' is the commonest form; 'ciento' is mainly used for the compound numbers (except when it multiplies: 'cien mil')

434

(c)   large numbers are divided by a full stop in Spanish:
3.461.203 = English 3,461,203

Ordinals

(a)   they are adjectives and therefore agree in number and gender.

(b)   'primero' and 'tercero' lose the final 'o' in front of masculine nouns: 'el primer año', 'en tercer lugar'.

(c)   they are not commonly used above 21, except for 100th and 1,000th.

(d)   in the case of centuries and titles, the ordinals are only used up to 9th, and from then on the cardinals are used: 'en el siglo *quinto*' BUT 'en el siglo *diecinueve*'; 'Alfonso *primero*' BUT 'Alfonso *doce*'.

(e)   the ordinals are also used for fractions:
a third   un tercio
a quarter of a kilo   un cuarto de kilo

(f)   Spanish abbreviations for 1st, 2nd, 3rd etc. depend on gender and are written thus:
1st   1°(masculine), 1ª(feminine)
4th   4°, 4ª etc.

Decimals
Where English uses a point, Spanish uses a comma:

101.7   101,7 (ciento uno coma siete)
0.031   0,031 (cero coma cero tres uno)

Calculations
4 + 7 = 11   cuatro *más* siete *son* once
12 − 3 = 9   doce *menos* tres *resta* nueve
3 × 7 = 21   tres *por* siete *son* veintiuno
16 ÷ 4 = 4   dieciséis *divido por* cuatro *es* cuatro

Telephone numbers
Spaniards normally read telephone numbers by dividing them into two-figure numbers:

019567   01-95-67 (cero uno, noventa y cinco, sesenta y siete)

Numbers

1	uno(un, una)*	1st	primero(primer, primera)*
2	dos	2nd	segundo(a)
3	tres	3rd	tercero(tercer, tercera)*
4	cuatro	4th	cuarto(a)
5	cinco	5th	quinto(a)
6	seis	6th	sexto(a)
7	siete	7th	séptimo(a)
8	ocho	8th	octavo(a)
9	nueve	9th	noveno(a); nono(a)
10	diez	10th	décimo(a)
11	once	11th	undécimo(a)
12	doce	12th	duodécimo(a)
13	trece	13th	decimotercero(a)***
14	catorce	14th	decimocuarto(a)
15	quince	15th	decimoquinto(a)
16	dieciséis	16th	decimosexto(a)
17	diecisiete	17th	decimoséptimo(a)
18	dieciocho	18th	decimoctavo(a)
19	diecinueve	19th	decimonono(a)
20	veinte	20th	vigésimo(a)
21	veintiuno(-ún, -una)*	21st	vigésimo primero(a)**
22	veintidós	22nd	vigésimo segundo(a)
30	treinta	30th	trigésimo(a)
31	treinta y uno(un, una)*	31st	trigésimo primero(a)**
32	treinta y dos	32nd	trigésimo segundo(a)
40	cuarenta	40th	cuadragésimo(a)
50	cincuenta	50th	quincuagésimo(a)
60	sesenta	60th	sexagésimo(a)
70	setenta	70th	septuagésimo(a)
80	ochenta	80th	octogésimo(a)
90	noventa	90th	nonogésimo(a)
100	cien(ciento)*	100th	centésimo(a)
101	ciento uno(un, una)*		
102	ciento dos	5 1/2	cinco y medio
156	ciento cincuenta y seis	0.31	cero coma tres uno (0,31)
200	doscientos(as)	10%	diez por ciento
500	quinientos(as)		
1,000	mil	1000th	milésimo(a)
1,003	mil tres		
2,000	dos mil	2^2	dos al cuadrado
1,000,000	un millón	2^4	dos a la cuarta potencia

*, **, ***: *see notes on pages 434, 435*